"Value-packed, accurate, and comprehensive..."

—Los Angeles Times

"Unbeatable..."

—The Washington Post

Let's Go
MEXICO

is the best book for anyone traveling on a budget. Here's why:

■ No other guidebook has as many budget listings.

Take Mexico City, for example. We found 11 places to stay for under $15 a night. We tell you how to get there the cheapest way, whether by bus, plane, or bike, and where to get an inexpensive and satisfying meal once you've arrived. We give hundreds of money-saving tips that anyone can use, plus invaluable advice on discounts and deals for students, children, families, and senior travelers.

■ Let's Go researchers have to make it on their own.

Our Harvard-Radcliffe researcher-writers travel on budgets as tight as your own—no expense accounts, no free hotel rooms.

■ Let's Go is completely revised each year.

We don't just update the prices, we go back to the place. If a charming café has become an overpriced tourist trap, we'll replace the listing with a new and better one.

■ No other guidebook includes all this:

Honest, engaging coverage of both the cities and the countryside; up-to-the-minute prices, directions, addresses, phone numbers, and opening hours; in-depth essays on local culture, history, and politics; comprehensive listings on transportation between and within regions and cities; straight advice on work and study, budget accommodations, sights, nightlife, and food; detailed city and regional maps; and much more.

■ Let's Go is for anyone who wants to see Mexico, Belize, Guatemala, Costa Rica, and Nicaragua on a budget.

Books by Let's Go, Inc.

EUROPE

Let's Go: Europe

Let's Go: Austria

Let's Go: Britain & Ireland

Let's Go: France

Let's Go: Germany & Switzerland

Let's Go: Greece & Turkey

Let's Go: Ireland

Let's Go: Italy

Let's Go: London

Let's Go: Paris

Let's Go: Rome

Let's Go: Spain & Portugal

NORTH & CENTRAL AMERICA

Let's Go: USA & Canada

Let's Go: Alaska & The Pacific Northwest

Let's Go: California & Hawaii

Let's Go: New York City

Let's Go: Washington, D.C.

Let's Go: Mexico

MIDDLE EAST & ASIA

Let's Go: Israel & Egypt

Let's Go: Thailand

Let's Go

The Budget Guide to

MEXICO

1994

Michael Kai Ng
Editor

Sarthak Das
Assistant Editor

Written by
Let's Go, Inc.
A subsidiary of
Harvard Student Agencies, Inc.

M
Macmillan Reference

HELPING LET'S GO

If you have suggestions or corrections, or just want to share your discoveries, drop us a line. We read every piece of correspondence, whether a 10-page letter, a velveteen Elvis postcard, or, as in one case, a collage. All suggestions are passed along to our researcher-writers. Please note that mail received after May 5, 1994 will probably be too late for the 1995 book, but will be retained for the following edition. Address mail to:

Let's Go: Mexico
Let's Go, Inc.
I Story Street
Cambridge, MA 02138
USA

In addition to the invaluable travel advice our readers share with us, many are kind enough to offer their services as researchers or editors. Unfortunately, the charter of Let's Go, Inc. and Harvard Student Agencies, Inc. enables us to employ only currently enrolled Harvard students.

Published in Great Britain 1994 by Pan Macmillan Ltd., Cavaye Place, London SW10 9PG.

10 9 8 7 6 5 4 3 2 1

Maps by David Lindroth, copyright © 1994, 1993, 1992, 1991, 1990, 1989 by St. Martin's Press, Inc.

Published in the United States of America by St. Martin's Press, Inc.

ISBN: 0333-61158-6

Let's Go: **Mexico** is written by the Publishing Division of Let's Go, Inc., 1 Story Street, Cambridge, MA 02138.

Acknowledgments

An entire summer of shifting fonts and, as one of our researchers wrote, "adjusting the price of pork tortas in Tijuana," has left just enough creative juices puddled at the bottom of our crania to eke out this final and wholly inadequate note of gratitude to all those who have helped us in our endeavor. First and foremost, thanks goes to the researcher-writers, underappreciated and underpaid. This book is theirs. Fortunately for us, **Gabriela Carrión** stuck out in the interviewing process. Her sensual descriptions of Costa Rica and cultural insights in southern Mexico have been invaluable contributions to this book. **Sarah Dry** weathered the commercialism of Cancún, waded through the flooded streets of Mérida, and peeked under every Mayan stone on the entire Yucatán Peninsula. After suffering the almost-unbearable heat for weeks, she rewarded herself with a Red Stripe or two on the Belizian Cayes, and rewarded us with action-packed copybatches. **Nadia Herman** turned in a solid performance in the Guadalajara region, surviving a hurricane and Puerto Vallarta.

    Allen Hutcheson wrote in Chihuahua (¡Ay!), "I have great respect for anyone who can write anything besides the straight facts on the road." The man should then have a tremendous amount of self-respect—his perfectly deadpan humor kept us rolling at every turn of the page. **Plamen Russev** sent back volumes, undaunted by Mexico City and its environs. His detailed research set the standard for thoroughness for the entire series. Weeks into his original itinerary, **David Shafer** volunteered to venture down to Nicaragua, new territory uncharted by *Let's Go*. With minimal preparation and only a few supplies, David produced an incredibly complete and complex section. Only the Corn Islands eluded him, casting doubt on their existence.

    The eleventh *avatar* of Vishnu and our mentor, Jonathan Taylor, cannot be thanked enough for his tireless efforts. His late nights, intelligent commentary, and seamless coordination have won our unending respect. Ed's patience with our computer ineptitude ran as deep as the *Barrancas del Cobre*. Thanks, too, to the JT group's toleration of our music, humor, and early deadline. The work of many others around the office and around the world are contained in these pages: Sue Krause, Sidney Chen, Anna More and roommates, World Teach, Ileana Ricci, Leda Nemor, sales group, and the residents of San Blas.

I would like to thank Sarthak Das for keeping my mind healthy while erasing ",000" over and over again. You have an amazing gift of insight that I know will never be wasted. I would also like to thank my entire family, Andy, Vania, Min Ji, Chris, Kevin, Charlie, Tasha, Bunchai, Min Yung, Mary, Barry, Mom, and Dad; my summer roomates (esp. Ashley for the daily report); Kochi, Stipe, Mikane, the Krush, WCSR, and Garen; and Marina for extending the reaches of understanding. Finally, thanks to the whole *Let's Go* crew for a thoroughly entertaining spring and summer.

    — MKN

Before anyone else, I would first like to thank Mike Ng for tolerating my ignorance about Mexico, my trip to Cancún, and my distracting chatter. Your great candor and openness has produced not only a great book but also a friendship. and your love for others and desire to give have earned my deep respect. I would also like to thank my school-year roommates. Thank you Maitri for your ability to listen. Thanks Sujatha for understanding me for two summers now—I know you'll succeed in the Bay area and beyond, besides you'll have baba and a ghanoush. Thanks also to my sister Sarba and dog PeeWee. Finally, I thank most of all my parents for instilling me with my love of travel, supporting me, and allowing me the opportunity to see so much already. This book is dedicated to you Ma and Baba, I love you both very much indeed!

    — SD

Contents

List of Maps xii
How To Use This Book xiv

ESSENTIALS 1
Planning Your Trip 1
Getting There 37
Traveling In Mexico 40
Life and Times 48

MÉXICO CITY 58
Orientation 59
Safety 70
Practical Information 70
Accommodations 73
Food 77
Sights 82
Entertainment 104
Near Mexico City 109

BAJA CALIFORNIA   112
Getting Around 112

Baja California Norte 113
Tijuana 113
Rosarito 118
Mexicali 119
San Felipe 120
Ensenada 122

Baja California Sur 124
Guerrero Negro 124
San Ignacio 125
Mulegé 126
Mulegé to Loreto 128
Loreto 129
La Paz 130
Todos Santos 133

Los Cabos 134
San José del Cabo 134
Cabo San Lucas 136

NORTHWEST MÉXICO 138
Sonora 138
Nogales 138

Puerto Peñasco 139
Hermosillo 140
Guaymas 142

Chihuahua 143
Ciudad Juárez and
El Paso, Texas 143
Casas Grandes and
Nuevo Casas Grandes 147
Chihuahua 149
Creel 152
Barrancas del Cobre 155

Sinaloa 156
Los Mochis 156
Mazatlán 157

Durango 163
Durango 163

Zacatecas 166
Zacatecas 166

NORTHEAST MÉXICO 170
Coahuila 170
Saltillo 170

Nuevo León 173
Monterrey 173

Tamaulipas 177
Matamoros and
Brownsville, Texas 177
Tampico 183

CENTRAL MÉXICO ..185
Nayarit 185
Tepic 185

Jalisco 187
Guadalajara 187
Puerto Vallarta 199
Jalisco Coast 205
Bahía de Navidad 206
Melaque 206
Barra de Navidad 208

Colima 210
  Manzanillo 210
  Colima 213

Aguascalientes 217
  Aguascalientes 217

San Luis Potosí 218
  San Luis Potosí 218

EL BAJÍO 224

Guanajuato 224
  Guanajuato 224
  Dolores Hidalgo 230
  San Miguel de Allende 232

Querétaro 237
  Querétaro 237

Michoacán de Ocampo ...241
  Morelia 242
  Pátzcuaro 246
  Uruapan 252
  Playa Azul 254

Hidalgo 255
  Tula 255

Northern Veracruz 257
  Tuxpan (Tuxpam), Veracruz .257
  Papantla, Veracruz 260
  Jalapa (Xalapa) 264
  Veracruz 267

Southern Veracruz 274
  Catemaco 274
  San Andrés Tuxtla 276
  Santiago Tuxtla and
    Tres Zapotes Ruins 279

SOUTHERN MÉXICO 281

Puebla 281
  Puebla 281
  Cholula 291

Morelos 295
  Cuernavaca 295

México 304
  Malinalco 304

Guerrero 305
  Taxco 307
  Zihuatanejo and Ixtapa 311

Costa Grande: Zihuatanejo/
  Ixtapa to Acapulco 316
  Acapulco 318

Oaxaca 327
  Oaxaca de Juárez 327
  Monte Albán 336
  Oaxaca to Mitla 338
  Mitla 339
  Oaxaca to Puerto Angel 341
  Puerto Angel 341
  Puerto Escondido 344

Tabasco 348
  Villahermosa 348
  Teapa 354
  La Venta Archaeological Site .356

Chiapas 356
  Tuxtla Gutiérrez 358
  Chiapa de Corzo 363
  San Cristóbal de las Casas 365
  Comitán and Parque Nacional
    Lagunas de Montebello 376
  Ocosingo 377
  The Lacandón Rainforest 380
  Palenque 381
  Tonalá 386
  Tapachula 389

YUCATÁN
PENINSULA............ 392

Campeche 394
  Escárcega 394
  Campeche 394
  Campeche to Mérida
    (Long Route) 401
  Grutas de Loltún 405
  Kabah 405
  Uxmal 406
  Ticul, Yucatán 408

Yucatán 410
  Mérida 410
  Progreso 422
  Mérida to Chichén Itzá 424
  Chichén Itzá 424
  Valladolid 431
  Río Lagartos 437

Quintana Roo **439**
Cancún 439
Isla Mujeres 447
Playa del Carmen 451
Isla Cozumel 454
Tulum 458
Cobá 464
Chetumal 465
Chetumal to Escárcega 468

BELIZE **470**
Planning Your Trip 471
Once There 473
The Cayes 478
Caye Caulker 478
Ambergris Caye and
  San Pedro 482
Western Belize 484
The Belize Zoo 485
San Ignacio 485
Belize/Guatemala Border 488
Dangriga 488
Placencia 490
Punta Gorda 492

GUATEMALA **495**
Planning Your Trip 496
Getting There 498
Once There 499
Guatemala City 500
Antigua 508
Panajachel 513
Iximché 517
Santa Cruz del Quiché 517
Quetzaltenango/Xela 519
Tecún Umán 521
Cobán 523
Quiriguá 525
Lago Izabal 526
Mariscos 526
El Estor 526
Río Dulce 527
Castillo San Felipe 527
Livingston 528
Puerto Barrios 530
Poptún 530
Santa Elena and Flores 532

Tikal 533

COSTA RICA **537**
Planning Your Trip 540
Getting There 544
Once There 545
San José 546
Volcán Arenal and Laguna de
  Arenal 551
Fortuna 552
Arenal 553
Tilarán 554
Liberia, Guanacaste 555
Península Nicoya 556
Playa del Coco 557
Playa Hermosa 557
Puntarenas 558
Montezuma 561

NICARAGUA **564**
Planning Your Trip 564
Getting There 568
Once There 569
Life and Times 570
Managua 572
León 581
Estelí 585
Matagalpa 587
Masaya 588
Granada 590
Rivas 592
San Juan del Sur 592
El Castillo 593
San Juan del Norte 593
Isla de Ometepe 594
San Carlos 596
Rama 598
Bluefields 598

APPENDICES **601**
Glossary 601
Notes About Language 603
Useful Phrases 603

INDEX **605**

Maps

Mexico 2-3
Mexico Transportation Map 42-43
Metropolitan Mexico City 60
Central Mexico City 66
Guadalajara 188
Michoacán de Ocampo... 242
Puebla 282
Cuernavaca 296
Guerrero 306
Acapulco 320
Oaxaca 328
Chiapas 357
San Cristóbal de las Casas 366
Yucatán Peninsula 393
Mérida 411
Cancún 440
Belize and Guatemala 472
Guatemala City 502
Costa Rica 538-539
Nicaragua 565
Managua 573

About Let's Go

Back in 1960, a few students at Harvard got together to produce a 20-page pamphlet offering a collection of tips on budget travel in Europe. For three years, Harvard Student Agencies, a student-run nonprofit corporation, had been doing a brisk business booking charter flights to Europe; this modest, mimeographed packet was offered to passengers as an extra. The following year, students traveling to Europe researched the first full-fledged edition of *Let's Go: Europe*, a pocket-sized book featuring advice on shoestring travel, irreverent write-ups of sights, and a decidedly youthful slant.

Throughout the 60s, the guides reflected the times: one section of the 1968 *Let's Go: Europe* talked about "Street Singing in Europe on No Dollars a Day." During the 70s, *Let's Go* gradually became a large-scale operation, adding regional European guides and expanding coverage into North Africa and Asia. The 80s saw the arrival of *Let's Go: USA & Canada* and *Let's Go: Mexico*, as well as regional North American guides; in the 90s we introduced five in-depth city guides to Paris, London, Rome, New York, and Washington, DC.

This year we're proud to announce three new guides: *Let's Go: Austria* (including Prague and Budapest), *Let's Go: Ireland*, and *Let's Go: Thailand* (including Honolulu, Tokyo, and Singapore), bringing our total number of titles up to twenty.

We've seen a lot in thirty-four years. *Let's Go: Europe* is now the world's #1 best selling international guide, translated into seven languages. And our guides are still researched, written, and produced entirely by students who know firsthand how to see the world on the cheap.

Every spring, we recruit nearly 100 researchers and an editorial team of 50 to write our books anew. Come summertime, after several months of training, researchers hit the road for seven weeks of exploration, from Bangkok to Budapest, Anchorage to Ankara. With pen and notebook in hand, a few changes of underwear stuffed in our backpacks, and a budget as tight as yours, we visit every *pensione, palapa*, pizzeria, café, club, campground, or castle we can find to make sure you'll get the most out of *your* trip.

We've put the best of our discoveries into the book you're now holding. A brand-new edition of each guide hits the shelves every year, only months after it was researched, so you know you're getting the most reliable, up-to-date, and comprehensive information available. And even as you read this, work on next year's editions is well underway.

At *Let's Go*, we think of budget travel not only as a means of cutting down on costs, but as a way of breaking down a few walls as well. Living cheap and simple on the road brings you closer to the real people and places you've been saving up to visit. This book will ease your anxieties and answer your questions about the basics—to help *you* get off the beaten track and explore. We encourage you to put *Let's Go* away now and then and strike out on your own. As any seasoned traveler will tell you, the best discoveries are often those you make yourself. If you find something worth sharing, drop us a line and let us know. We're at Let's Go, Inc., 1 Story Street, Cambridge, MA, 02138, USA.

Happy travels!

■ How To Use This Book

The purpose of this book is not to hold your hand, but rather to facilitate your independent exploration of Mexico, Belize, Costa Rica, Guatemala, and Nicaragua. In place of planned itineraries, you will find the nitty-gritty information you need to develop your own. Our researchers have been crawling over every inch of the region for over a decade, discovering the best bargains and improving the listings contained here so that you, the budget traveler, can experience these countries from your own perspective, and hopefully refine that perspective.

The first pages of this book are dedicated to the **Essentials** section. This section contains sections on **Planning Your Trip, Getting There, Traveling in Mexico,** and **Life and Times.** The Essentials section gives information on general information which pertains to travel in the entire region covered by this book, not just a specific area. "Planning Your Trip" includes sections on **Climate, Useful Organizations, Documents and Formalities** (including information on visas and passports), **Customs, Money, Packing, Safety and Security, Health, Insurance, Alternatives to Tourism, Keeping in Touch** and subsections regarding **Women and Travel, Older Travelers, Travelers with Disabilities,** and **Bisexual, Gay, and Lesbian Travelers.** "Getting There" covers various modes of transportation to Mexico with listings of discount ticket agents. "Traveling in Mexico" is an overview of Mexico **By Plane, By Train, By Bus, By Car** and **By Thumb,** and a preview of coming attractions in **Accommodations,** including **Hotels, Hostels,** and **Camping.** "Life and Times" takes a brief look at Mexico's history and culture. Belize, Costa Rica, Guatemala and Nicaragua each have a similar introductory section with information specific to that country; for more general travel information refer back to the Mexico Essentials section.

This Mexico section of this book is organized geographically, beginning with Mexico City and then moving southeast from Baja California, through Northwest Mexico, Northeast Mexico, Central Mexico, El Bajío, Southern Mexico, to the Yucatán Peninsula. Coverage of Belize, Guatemala, Costa Rica, and Nicaragua follows in that order. This book also contains a glossary and an appendix on language.

Each city or town is further divided. The introduction, meant to convey a sense of the city, its culture, and its history, is followed by **Orientation,** which describes the geography and layout of the city. Orientation is often integrated into **Practical Information,** which also lists essential schedules, offices, addresses, and phone numbers. **Accommodations, Food, Sights,** and **Entertainment** are, or should be, self-explanatory. The listings we feel are the best bargains, that is, the most for the money, are given first. Food listings are weighted towards restaurants which are difficult to locate or unusual, like vegetarian restaurants, since no one in Mexico needs a guidebook to find a cheap *típico* taco stand.

A NOTE TO OUR READERS

The information for this book is gathered by *Let's Go*'s researchers during the late spring and summer months. Each listing is derived from the assigned researcher's opinion based upon his or her visit at a particular time. The opinions are expressed in a candid and forthright manner. Other travelers might disagree. Those traveling at a different time may have different experiences since prices, dates, hours, and conditions are always subject to change. You are urged to check beforehand to avoid inconvenience and surprises. Travel always involves a certain degree of risk, especially in low-cost areas. When traveling, especially on a budget, you should always take particular care to ensure your safety.

■ Essentials

PLANNING YOUR TRIP

■■■ CLIMATE

The Tropic of Cancer bisects Mexico into a temperate north and tropical south, but the climate varies considerably even within these belts. For each of the geographic divisions used in this book, very general climate conditions hold true. **Northwest Mexico,** including Baja California, is the driest area of the country, but still offers a unique array of desert flora and fauna, while the **Northeast** is a bit more temperate. Pleasant beaches are scattered on the **Gulf Coast** although they do not compare with the beauty of those elsewhere in Mexico. The central region north of Mexico City, known as the **Bajío,** and **South Central Mexico** both experience the cooler climates of the highlands as well as coastal warmth. Natural beauty extends from world-famous beaches to inland forests. Lush, green jungles obscure ruins of the ancient civilizations of the **Yucatán Peninsula.**

The rainy season lasts from May until October (with a hurricane season in the south Aug.-Oct.). The southern half of the country averages over 100 in. per year (75% of that during the rainy season), so a summer vacation is likely to be on the damp side. Exhaustive statistics on climate are available in a chart compiled by the International Association for Medical Assistance to Travelers (IAMAT) (see Health below).

■■■ USEFUL ORGANIZATIONS

■ Government Agencies

Embassy of Mexico, 1911 Pennsylvania Ave. NW, Washington, DC 20006 (tel. (202) 728-1600); in the **U.K.,** 42 Hertford St., Mayfair, London W1 (tel. 071 499-85-86, fax 071 495-40-35); in **Canada,** 130 Albert St. #1800, Ottawa, Ont. K1P 5G4 (tel. (613) 233-8988); in **Australia,** 14 Perth Ave., Yarralumla, 2600 Canberra (tel. (+61 6) 273-3905 or 273-3947, fax 273-1190).

Consulate of Mexico, 1019 19th St. NW, #810, Washington, DC 20036 (tel. (202) 736-1000); in **Canada,** 60 Bloor St. W #203, Toronto, Ont. M4W 3B8 (tel. (416) 922-2718); in the **U.K.,** 8 Halkin St., London SW1 X7DW (tel. (+44 71) 235-63-93); in **Australia,** 135-153 New South Head Rd., Edgecliff, Sydney 2027 NSW (tel. (+61 2 326-1311 or 326-1292, fax +61 2 327-1110).

Mexican Government Tourism Office (Secretaría de Turismo or SECTUR): In the **U.S.,** 405 Park Ave. #1402, New York, NY 10022 (tel. (212) 838-2949 or 755-4756; fax 753-2874; 24-hr. information tel. (800) 262-8900); 10100 Santa Monica Blvd. #224, Los Angeles, CA 90067 (tel. (310) 203-8191, fax 203-8316); 128 Aragon Ave., Coral Gable, FL 33134 (tel. (305) 443-9160, fax 443-1186); 70 E. Lake St. #1413, Chicago, Illinois 60601-5977 (tel. (312) 606-9015, fax 606-9012); 2707 N. Loop W. #450, Houston, TX 77008 (tel. (713) 880-5153, fax 880-1833); 1911 Pennsylvania Ave., Washington, DC 20036 (tel. (202) 728-1750, fax 728-1758); in **Canada,** 2 Floor St. W #1801, Toronto, Ont. M4W 3E2 (tel. (416) 925-0704, fax 925-6061) or 1 Place Ville Marie, #2409, Montreal, Qc. H3B 3M9 (tel. (514) 871-1052, fax 871-3825), 1610-999 West Hastings Ave., Vanvcouver, B.C. V6C 2W2; in **Germany,** Wiessenhuttenplatz 26, D 6000 Frankfurt Am Main 1 (tel. (4969) 25-3413, 25-3541, fax 25-3755); in **Japan,** 2-15-1 Nagata-Cho., Chiyoda-Ku, Tokyo 100 (tel. (813) 580-2962, fax 581-5539); in the **U.K.,** 60/61 Trafal-

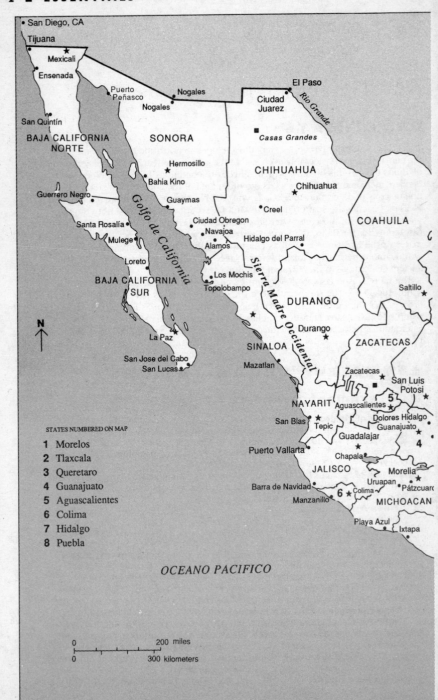

San Diego, CA
Tijuana
Mexicali
Ensenada
Puerto Peñasco
Nogales
Nogales
El Paso
Ciudad Juarez
Rio Grande
San Quintín
BAJA CALIFORNIA NORTE
SONORA
Casas Grandes
CHIHUAHUA
Hermosillo
Bahia Kino
Chihuahua
Guerrero Negro
Guaymas
Creel
Golfo de California
Ciudad Obregon
Navajoa
Hidalgo del Parral
COAHUILA
Santa Rosalía
Alamos
Mulege
Los Mochis
Topolobampo
Saltillo
Loreto
BAJA CALIFORNIA SUR
Sierra Madre Occidental
DURANGO
N
Durango
ZACATECAS
La Paz
SINALOA
San Jose del Cabo
San Lucas
Mazatlan
Zacatecas
San Luis Potosi
NAYARIT
Aguascalientes
San Blas
Dolores Hidalgo
Guanajuato
Tepic
Guadalajar
STATES NUMBERED ON MAP
Puerto Vallarta
Chapala
Morelia

1 Morelos
2 Tlaxcala
3 Queretaro
4 Guanajuato
5 Aguascalientes
6 Colima
7 Hidalgo
8 Puebla

JALISCO
Uruapan
Barra de Navidad
Colima
Pátzcuaro
Manzanillo
MICHOACAN
Playa Azul
Ixtapa

OCEANO PACIFICO

0   200 miles
0   300 kilometers

gar Sq., London WC2N 5DS (tel. (+44 71) 839 3177). Provides maps, information and tourist cards. Check your phone book for local offices. Also operates a 24-hr. hotline out of Mexico City (tel. (5) 250-01-23) for complaints, emergencies and less urgent information.

■ Travel Organizations

Council on International Educational Exchange (CIEE), 205 E. 42nd St., New York, NY 10017 (tel. (212) 661-1414; for charter flights (800) 223-7402, in New York (212) 661-1450). CIEE offers information on budget travel as well as educational, volunteer, and work opportunities around the world. CIEE also offers dicount fares on major airlines and issues ISICs (International Student Identity Cards) and International Youth Cards (for non-students under the age of 26). They publish *Work, Study, and Travel Abroad: The Whole World Handbook* ($10.95, postage $1) and *Volunteer! The Comprehensive Guide to Voluntary Service in the U.S. and Abroad* ($6.95, postage $1). Students should pick up the annual *Student Travel Catalog* for free at any CIEE office or send for one ($1 for postage and handling). Operates 56 **Council Travel** offices throughout the U.S., including those listed below and branches in Providence, RI; Amherst and Cambridge, MA; Berkeley, La Jolla, and Long Beach, CA. **Boston,** 729 Boylston St. #201, MA 02116 (617-266-1926). **Chicago,** 1153 N. Dearborn St., IL 60610 (312-951-0585). **Dallas,** 6923 Snider Plaza, B, TX 75205 (214-363-9941). **Los Angeles,** 1093 Broxton Ave. #220, CA 90024 (310-208-3551). **Portland,** 715 S.W. Morrison #600, OR 97205 (503-228-1900). **San Diego,** 953 Garnet Ave., CA 94108 (619-270-6401). **San Francisco,** 919 Irving St. #102, CA 94122 (415-566-6222). **Seattle,** 1314 N.E. 43rd St. #210, WA 98105 (206-632-2448).

STA Travel: In U.S., 17 E. 45th St., New York, NY 10017 (tel. (800) 777-0112 or (212) 986-9470). Operates 10 offices in the U.S. and over 100 worldwide. Offers discount airfares for travelers under 26 and full-time students under 32; sells ISICs, HI memberships, and Eurail passes. **Boston,** 273 Newbury St., MA 02116 (617-266-6014). **Los Angeles,** 7202 Melrose Ave., CA 90046 (213-934-8722). **New York,** 48 E. 11th St., NY 10003 (212-477-7166). **Philadelphia,** University City Travel, 3730 Walnut St., PA 19104 (215-382-2928). **San Francisco,** 51 Grant Ave., CA 94108 (415-391-8407). In **Great Britain,** 86 Old Brompton Rd., London SW7 3LQ and 117 Euston Rd., London NW1 2SX England (tel. (071) 937 9921 for European travel; (071) 937 9971 for North American; (071) 937 9962 for long haul travel; (071) 937 1733 for round the world travel). **In Australia,** 220 Faraday St., Melbourne, Victoria 3053 (tel. (03) 347 69 11). In **New Zealand,** 10 High St., Auckland (tel. (09) 309 9995).

Travel CUTS (Canadian Universities Travel Service), 187 College St., Toronto, Ont. M5T 1P7 (tel. (416) 979-2406). 35 offices throughout Canada. In Britain, 295-A Regent St., London W1R 7Y4 (tel. (071) 637-3161). Offers discounted flights with special student fares. Sells the ISIC, FIYTO, and HI hostel cards, and discount travel passes. The *Student Traveler* is available at all offices and campuses across Canada.

International Student Exchange Flights (ISE Flights), 5010 E. Shea Blvd., #A104, Scottsdale, AZ 85254 (tel. (602) 951-1177). Budget student flights, travelers' checks, and travel guides.

Campus Travel, 52 Grosvenor Gardens, London SW1W 0AG (tel. (071) 730 8832, fax (071) 730 5739). Offers special student and youth fares on travel by plane, train, boat and bus, as well as flexible airline tickets; discount and ID cards for youths; special insurance for students and those under 35; and maps and guides.

London Student Travel, 52 Grosvenor Gardens, London WC1 (tel. (071) 730 3402).

USIT Ltd., Aston Quay, O'Connell Bridge, Dublin 2 (tel. (01) 679 8833, fax (01) 677 8843).

Laughing Heart Adventures, P.O. Box 669, Willow Creek, CA 95573 (tel. (800) 541-1256 or (916) 629-3516). Offers 7-21 day packages in Baja, Barrancas del Cobre, and Belize. Trips range from backpacking and canoeing to whale-watching

to barrier reef snorkeling off Belize. Fees run US$80-150 per day and include meals, transportation, gear and accommodations.

Servicio Educativo de Turismo de los Estudiantes y la Juventud de México (SETEJ), Hamburgo 301, Col. Juárez, 06600 México D.F. (tel. (5) 211-07-43 or 211-66-36). Sells ISIC and FIYTO cards. Arranges group tours with Mexican students. Has information about hostels and budget hotels. Offers language courses and helps with domestic and international flights. See Accommodations below for hostel information.

■Transportation Services

American Automobile Association (AAA), 1000 AAA Dr., Box 75, Heathrow, FL 32746-5063 (tel. (407) 444-7000). Sells road maps and travel guides. American Express traveler's checks commission-free for members. Issues Mexican auto insurance (see Getting There: By Car below). No routing service for Mexico.

Asociación Mexicana Automovilística, A.C. (AMA), Av. Orizaba 7, México, D.F. 06700 (tel. (5) 511-62-85). Write for up-to-date road maps and information about car travel in Mexico.

Asociación Nacional Automovilística (ANA), Oficinas ANA, José María Iglesias 59, México, D.F. 06470 (tel. (5) 705-05-01 or 705-10-01); emergency services Lerdo 361, Entre San Timor y Manuel González, México, D.F. 06470 (tel. (5) 597-42-83 or 597-19-62).

Canadian Automobile Association, 60 Commerce Valley Dr. E, Markham, Ont L3T 7P9 (tel. (416) 771-3170). Maps of Mexico for members. Will highlight routes directly on the maps.

Ferrocarriles Nacionales de México (National Railways of Mexico), Buenavista Gran Central Estación, Departamento de Tráfico de Pasajeros, México, D.F. 06358 (tel. (5) 547-89-72).

■ Publications

Adventures in Mexico (AIM), Apdo. 31-70, Guadalajara, Jalisco, 45050 México. Newsletter on retirement and travel in Mexico. Endearing approach to the country's quirks. Annual subscription (6 issues) costs US$16 or CDN$19. Personal checks accepted. Back issues, most of which are devoted to a single city or region, available for US$2 each.

Animal and Plant Health Inspection Service, 6505 Belcrest Rd., #G110, Hyattsville, MD 20782 (tel. (301) 436-8413). Gives information on the U.S. agriculture quarantine on certain food, plant and animal products. Write for free *Traveler's Tips* pamphlet.

Forsyth Travel Library, P.O. Box 2975, Shawnee Mission, KS 66201 (tel. (800) 367-7984). Mail-order maps and travel guides for Mexico. Write for a free newsletter and catalogue.

Wide World Books and Maps, 1911 N. 45th St., Seattle, WA 98103 (tel. (206) 634-3453). Open Mon.-Fri. 10am-7pm, Sat. 10am-6pm, Sun. noon-5pm. Wide selection of books about Mexico as well as hard to find maps of the country.

Hippocrene Books, Inc., 171 Madison Ave., New York, NY 10016 (tel. (212) 685-4371; orders (718) 454-2360, fax (718) 454-1391). Publishes travel reference books, travel guides, maps, and foreign language dictionaries. Free catalog.

Gateway Books, 13 Bedford Cove, San Rafael, CA 94901 (tel. (415) 454-5215, fax 454-1901). Publishes comprehensive *RV Travel in Mexico* (US$9.95) as well as guides to seasonal and retirement living in Latin America, like *Choose Mexico: Retire on $600 a Month* (US$10.95).

Hunter Publishing, 300 Raritan Center Parkway, Edison, NJ 08818 (tel. (908) 225-1900, fax 417-0482). Sells the exhaustive *Bicycling Mexico* (US$16.95 plus $2.50 shipping).

John Muir Publications, P.O. Box 613, Santa Fe, NM 87504 (tel. (800) 888-7504 or (505) 982-4078, fax 988-1680). Publishes the *Shopper's Guide to Mexico* (US$9.95) on the subject of folk art, the *People's Guide to Mexico* (US$17.95), which includes Belize and Guatemala, and the *People's Guide to RV Camping in Mexico* (US$13.95). Add US$3.75 shipping for one book, 50¢ for each additional book.

México Desconocido, Monte Pelvoux 110-104, Lomas de Chapultepec, México, D.F. 11000 (tel. (5) 202-65-85 or 259-09-39, fax 540-17-71). Monthly travel magazine in Spanish and English describing little-known areas and customs of Mexico. Write for information.

Superintendent of Documents, Washington, DC 20402 (tel. (202) 783-3238). Publishes *Your Trip Abroad* (US$1), *Safe Trip Abroad* (US$1), *Health Information for International Travel* (US$5), *Tips for Travelers to Mexico* (US$1) and *Tips for Travelers to Central and South America* (US$1). To order the latter two, call the Citizens Emergency Hotline at (202) 647-5225.

Travelling Books, P.O. Box 77114, Seattle, WA 98177 (tel. (206) 367-5848). Wide selection of handbooks and maps for Mexico, Guatemala, Belize and Costa Rica.

Wide World Books and Maps, 1911 N. 45th St., Seattle, WA 98103 (tel. (206) 634-3453). Wide selection of books about Mexico and hard-to-find maps of the country.

■■■ DOCUMENTS AND FORMALITIES

■ Tourist Cards

All foreigners in Mexico must carry a **tourist card** (**FMT,** Spanish for *folleto de migración turística*). Although cards are available at Mexican embassies, consulates and tourist offices (see Useful Addresses), most people pick them up when they cross the border or when they check in at the airline ticket counter for their flight into Mexico. On the FMT, you must indicate your intended destination and expected length of stay. If your financial condition looks suspect, you will be asked to prove that you have a return ticket. Finally, proof of citizenship is a necessity. Travelers from outside North America must present a passport. U.S. and Canadian citizens can obtain a tourist card with an original birth certificate or naturalization papers, plus some type of photo ID. But be forewarned: traveling in Mexico without a passport is asking for trouble. A passport carries much more authority with local officials than does a birth certificate. U.S. and Canadian citizens spending no more than three days in Mexico, if they remain in the duty-free border towns or ports, do not need tourist cards but still must carry proof of citizenship.

Tourist cards are valid for 90 or 180 days. Try to get a card that will be valid longer than your projected stay. It is easier to obtain a 180-day tourist card at the border than to extend a 90-day card or validate an expired card (which requires that you leave the country temporarily). If you do need an extension, visit a local office of the Delegación de Servicios Migratorios several weeks before your card expires. (They also take care of lost cards.) You must get a new FMT every time you re-enter the country even if your old one has not expired.

While in Mexico, you are required by law to carry your tourist card at all times. Make a photocopy and keep it in a separate place. Although it won't replace a lost or stolen tourist card, a copy should facilitate replacement. If you do lose your card, expect at least two hours of delay and bureaucratic inconvenience while immigration verifies your record of entrance.

■ Passports

As a precaution in case your passport is lost or stolen, be sure *before you leave* to photocopy the page of your passport that contains your photograph and identifying information. Especially important is your passport number. Carry this photocopy in a safe place apart from your passport, perhaps with a traveling companion, and leave another copy at home. Better yet, carry a photocopy of all the pages of the passport, including all visa stamps, apart from your actual passport, and leave a duplicate copy with a relative or friend. These measures will help prove your citizenship and facilitate the issuing of a new passport. Consulates also recommend that you carry an expired passport or an *official* copy of your birth certificate in a part of your baggage separate from other documents. You can request a duplicate birth certificate from the Bureau of Vital Records and Statistics in your state or province of birth.

Losing your passport can be a nightmare. It may take weeks to process a replacement, and your new passport may be valid only for a limited time. In addition, any visas stamped in your old passport will be irretrievably lost. If it is lost or stolen, however, immediately notify the local police and the nearest embassy or consulate of your home government. To expedite the replacement of your passport, you will need to know *all the information that you had previously recorded and photocopied* and to show identification and proof of citizenship. Some consulates can issue new passports within two days if you give them proof of citizenship. In an emergency, ask for immediate temporary traveling papers that will permit you to return to your home country.

Remember that your passport is a public document that belongs to your nation's government. You may have to surrender your passport to a foreign government official; if you don't get it back in a reasonable time, inform the nearest mission of your home country.

Applying for a passport is complicated, so make sure your questions are answered in advance; you don't want to wait two hours in a passport office just to be told you'll have to return tomorrow because your application is insufficient.

U.S. citizens may apply for a passport, valid for 10 years (5 yrs. if under 18) at any one of several thousand federal or state **courthouses** or **post offices** authorized to accept passport applications, or at any of the 13 **U.S. Passport Agencies.** Parents must apply in person for children under age 13. You must apply in person if this is your first passport, if you are under age 18, or if your current passport is more than 12 years old or was issued before your 18th birthday.

For a U.S. passport, you must submit the following along with a completed application form: (1) proof of U.S. Citizenship (either a certified birth certificate, naturalization papers, or a previous passport); (2) identification bearing your signature and either your photo or a personal description and (3) two identical, recent passport-size (2 in. by 2 in.) photographs with a white or off-white background taken within the past six months. Bring these items and $65 (under 18 $40) in check or money order. Passport Agencies accept cash in the exact amount. Write your date of birth on the check, and photocopy the data page for your personal records. You can **renew** your passport by mail (or in person) for $55.

Processing usually takes three to four weeks, perhaps fewer from a Passport Agency, more in spring and summer. Passports are processed according to the departure date indicated on the application form. *File your application as early as possible.* If you fail to indicate a departure date, the agency will assume you are not planning any immediate travel. Your passport will be mailed to you. You may pay for express mail return of your passport. Passport agencies offer **rush service:** if you have proof that you are departing within five working days (e.g. an airplane ticket), a Passport Agency will issue a passport while you wait.

Abroad, a U.S. embassy or consulate can usually issue new passports, given proof of citizenship. For more information, contact the U.S. Passport Information's helpful 24-hour recorded message (tel. (202) 647-0518) or call the recorded message of the passport agency nearest you.

Canadian application forms in English and French are available at all passport offices, post offices, and most travel agencies. Along with the application form, a citizen must provide: (1) citizenship documentation (as an old passport does *not* suffice as proof); (2) two identical passport-size photographs less than one year old that indicate the photographer, the studio address, and the date the photos were taken; and (3) a $35 fee. Both photographs must be signed by the applicant, and the application form and one of the photographs must be certified by a guarantor (someone who has known the applicant for two years and whose profession falls into one of the categories listed in the application form). Citizens may apply in person at any one of 29 regional Passport Offices across Canada. Citizens who reside in the U.S. can contact a Canadian diplomatic mission; those outside Canada and the U.S. should contact the nearest embassy or consulate. You can apply by mail by sending a completed application form with appropriate documentation and the $35 fee to Passport Office, External Affairs, Ottawa, Ontario, K1A OG3.

The processing time is approximately five business days for in-person applications and three weeks for mailed ones. Applicants over age 16 should file form A. Citizens under 16 who travel with a parent should use Form B and may be included on the parent's passport. Keep in mind that some countries require that a child carry his or her own passport whether traveling with a parent or not. A passport is valid for 5 years and is not renewable. If a passport is lost abroad, Canadians must be able to prove citizenship with another document.

For additional **information,** call the 24-hour number (tel. (800) 567-6868, in Metro Toronto 973-3251, Montreal, 283-2152). Refer to the booklet *Bon Voyage, But...* for further help and a list of Canadian embassies and consulates abroad. It is available free of charge from any passport office or from: Info-Export (BPTE), External Affairs, Ottawa, ON, K1A OG2, Canada.

British citizens can obtain either a full passport or a more restricted Visitor's Passport. For a **full passport** valid for 10 years (5 yrs. if under 16), apply in person or by mail to the London Passport Office or by mail to a passport office located in Liverpool, Newport, Peterborough, Glasgow, and Belfast. Along with a completed application, you must submit: 1) a birth certificate and marriage certificate (if applicable); 2) two identical, recent photos signed by a guarantor (a professional who is not a relative who has known you for two years); and 3) the £18 fee. Children under 16 may be included on a parent's passport. Processing usually takes four to six weeks. The London office offers same-day walk-in rush service; arrive early.

Irish citizens can apply for a passport by mail to one of the following two passport offices: Department of Foreign Affairs, Passport Office, Setanta Centre, Molesworth St., Dublin 2 (tel. (01) 6711633), or Passport Office, 1A South Mall, Cork (tel. (021) 272 525). You can obtain an application form at a local Garda station or request one from a passport office. First-time applicants should send their long-form birth certificate and two identical photographs. To renew, citizens should send the old passport (after photocopying it) and two photos. Passports cost £45 and are valid for 10 years. Citizens younger than 18 and older than 65 can request a 3 year passport that costs £10.

Australian citizens must apply for a passport in person at a local post office, a passport office, or an Australian diplomatic mission overseas. An appointment may be necessary at all three. A parent may file an application for a child who is under 18 and unmarried. Along with your application, you must submit: 1) proof of citizenship (such as an expired passport, a birth certificate, or a citizen's certificate from the Immigration service); 2) proof of your present name; 3) two identical, signed photographs (45mm by 35mm) less than six months old; 4) other forms of ID (such as a driver's license, credit card, rate notice, etc.) Application fees are adjusted every three months; call the toll-free information service for current details (tel. 13 12 32).

A **visa** is an endorsement or stamp placed in your passport. Visas are not necessary for U.S., Canadian, or British citizens unless they will be in Mexico for more than six months. Holders of European Community passports need only their **permanent resident cards ("green cards").** Australians and New Zealanders, however, do need visas, regardless of the length of stay. Businesspeople, missionaries and students who expect to earn a diploma in Mexico also must obtain a visa. Applications require a valid passport, six frontal photos and five profile photos. Consulates claim to have 24-hr. visa service if you apply in person; by mail, however, they may take weeks.

■ Student and Youth Identification

It's hardly worth your while to buy a student ID card to use in Mexico; foreign students are only rarely entitled to special discounts on accommodations, long-distance bus and train fares, and admission to archaeological sites, theatrical performances and museums. Where a student rate is advertised, a current university ID card is generally sufficient proof of student status.

Still, you might consider spending your hard-earned money on an **International Student Identity Card (ISIC),** available at many student travel offices (see Useful Addresses: Travel Organizations, above). It provides access to CIEE student airfares and includes repatriation insurance of US$3000, US$3000 of accident-related coverage, and US$100 per day for up to 60 days of in-hospital illness (if issued in the U.S., this insurance covers only foreign travel). To get an ISIC, you must supply dated proof of student status and a 1½ by 2 in. photo with your name printed on the back. The card costs US$15 and is valid for 16 months, from September 1 of one year until the end of the following year. You cannot purchase a new card in January unless you were in school during the fall semester.

If you are ineligible for the ISIC but are under 26, you can take advantage of the **International Youth Card,** issued by the **Federation of International Youth Travel Organizations (FIYTO),** which entitles you to some price reductions in Mexico. To get the card, you must submit proof of birthdate, a passport-sized photo with your name printed on the back, and US$10 (with insurance $15). The card is offered by most of the travel organizations listed above.

Once in Mexico, those under 26 may purchase a **SETEJ card,** which provides discounts in hostels, hotels, restaurants and museums. (See Useful Addresses: Travel Organizations and Mexico City: Practical Information for addresses.) Even if you don't have student identification, never hesitate to ask about youth discounts, and carry proof of age with you.

■ Driver's License and Vehicle Permits

An international driver's license is not necessary for driving in Mexico; any valid driver's license is acceptable. You will, however, need a Mexican **vehicle permit,** issued as you cross the border. Requirements for these permits have changed rapidly in the past year and become progressively stricter; contact a Mexican consulate or tourist office for the most up-to-date information. As of April 1993 you had to be able to prove ownership of your vehicle. Bring the title with you or, if the car is rented or not fully paid for, a notarized letter from the bank or other owner authorizing you to take the vehicle into Mexico. Having a credit card (AmEx, MC, or Visa) makes the process easiest—you can charge the US$10 fee. You will have to sign an affidavit stating you won't sell the car or let someone else drive it and then leave a photocopy of your proof of ownership, driver's license and credit card. You will receive a multiple-entry permit good for a maximum of six months. Without a credit card, you must post a bond based on the value of the vehicle as determined by the Mexican government. Fees and requirements vary at different border crossings, but the bond could be for as much as 50% of the Blue Book value of the vehicle, and non-refundable processing charges average 1-2% of the bond value with an $80 minimum. Regulations change frequently; the Mexican government has a hotline for info at tel. (800) 446-8277. To extend a vehicle permit beyond its original expiration date, contact the temporary importation department of Mexican customs. Permits are not required within the **Free Zone** (see Getting There: By Car below).

Resist the temptation to abandon, sell or give away your car in Mexico. Once you enter the country with a car, your tourist card will be marked such that you will not be allowed to collect the bond or to leave without the vehicle. Even if your car disintegrates somewhere in Mexico, you must get permission to leave without it; permission can be obtained (for a fee) at either the federal registry of automobiles in Mexico City or a local office of the treasury department. If you have received permission to leave your broken-down car behind in Mexico, you have up to 45 days after the expiration of your vehicle permit to reclaim the car before the Mexican government disposes of it.

A vehicle permit is valid only for the person to whom it was issued unless another driver is approved by the federal registry. Violation of this law can result in confiscation of the vehicle or heavy fines. Furthermore, only legitimate drivers may purchase car-ferry tickets.

■ Fishing Licenses

If you plan to fish in Mexico, you will need a license. The fee is US$7.50 per week, US$10 per month, or US$20 per year. Licenses are available in port cities at any Mexican **Oficina de Pesca.**

■■■ CUSTOMS

■ Entering Mexico

A clean, neat appearance will help upon your arrival. Don't pass out *mordidas* (bribes; literally, "little bites"). These days they are often inappropriate and may do more harm than good. *Do not* attempt to bring drugs into Mexico.

Entering Mexico overland, you'll first see the border guards. They will direct travelers to the immigration office, where a new batch of officials will issue a tourist card to those who don't have one already and a car permit to auto drivers. Customs officials will then inspect luggage and stamp papers. If there is anything amiss when you arrive at the immigration checkpoint 22km into the interior, you'll have to turn back.

Entering Mexico by air is somewhat easier. Agents process forms and examine luggage right in the airport. Because air passengers are rarely penniless, immigration officials are less strict than at the border. If your papers are out of order at any official location, however, count on a long wait. Keep some form of picture ID with you at all times, since customs officials stop buses all over Mexico, not just at the border.

Each visitor may enter with up to 110 pounds of luggage (140 lb. on Mexicana Airlines). Adults may carry 50 cigars, 200 cigarettes and 250 grams of tobacco with them. One camera and one 8mm motion picture camera, with 12 rolls of film for each, are also allowed. To use flashes or a tripod at archaeological sites, you must get permits (for personal use, flashes and tripods not permitted; for videos, 25 peso permit required, other permits available) from the Instituto Nacional de Antropología e Historia, Director de Asuntos Jurídicos, Cordoba No. 45, 2o piso, Col. Roma, México, D.F. 06700 (tel. (5) 511-08-44).

A dog or cat may accompany you into the country if the little critter has proof of vaccination for rabies, hepatitis, pip and leptospirosis, and a health certificate issued by a veterinarian less than 72 hours before entry and stamped by a local office of the U.S. Department of Agriculture and a Mexican consulate. The consulate pet visa fee is US$20. Keep in mind that animals will be unwelcome at most hotels.

■ Leaving Mexico

Crossing the border can take five minutes or five hours; the better your paperwork, the shorter your ordeal with customs should be. When reentering your home country, you must declare all articles acquired abroad and pay a duty on those which exceed your country's customs allowance. To establish value when you return home, keep receipts for items purchased abroad. Since you pay no duty on goods brought from home, record the serial numbers of any expensive items (cameras, computers, radios, etc.) you are taking on vacation before you leave. Check with your country's customs office to see if it has a special form for registering these valuables and turn in your list to the airport customs office before you depart.

Most countries object to the importation of firearms, explosives, ammunition, obscene literature and films, fireworks and lottery tickets. Do not try to take drugs out of Mexico. To avoid problems when carrying prescription drugs, label bottles clearly and have the prescription or a doctor's certificate ready to show the customs officer.

Crossing the border (on your return) with live animals is usually prohibited. For information on wildlife and wildlife products, contact TRAFFIC USA, World Wildlife Fund, 1250 24th St. NW, Washington, DC 20037 (tel. (202) 293-4800), or the Animal and Plant Health Inspection Service (see Useful Addresses: Publications).

United States citizens returning home may bring $400 worth of accompanying goods duty-free and must pay a 10% tax on the next $1000. You must declare all purchases, so remember to have sales slips ready. Goods are considered duty-free if they are for personal or household use (this includes gifts) and cannot include more than 100 cigars, 200 cigarettes (1 carton), and one liter of wine or liquor. You must be over 21 to bring liquor into the U.S. To be eligible for the duty-free allowance, you must have remained abroad for at least 48 hours and cannot have used this exemption or any part of it within the preceding 30 days.

You can mail unsolicited gifts duty-free if they are worth less than $50, though you may not mail liquor, tobacco, or perfume. Officials occasionally spot check parcels, so mark the price and nature of the gift and the words "Unsolicited Gift" on the package. If you send back a non-gift parcel or a gift worth more than $50, the Postal Service will collect a duty for its value plus a handling charge to deliver it. If you mail home personal goods of U.S. origin, you can avoid duty charges by marking the package "American goods returned." For more information, consult the brochure

Know Before You Go, available from R. Woods, Consumer Information Center, Pueblo, CO 81009 (item 477Y). You can direct other questions to the U.S. Customs Service, P.O. Box 7407, Washington, DC 20004 (tel. (202) 927-6724). Foreign nationals living in the U.S. are subject to different regulations; refer the leaflet *Customs Hints for Visitors (Nonresidents).*

Canadian citizens who remain abroad for at least one week may bring back up to CDN$300 worth of goods duty-free once every calendar year; goods that exceed the allowance will be taxed at 20%. You are permitted to ship goods home under this exemption as long as you declare them when you arrive. Citizens over the legal age (which varies by province) may import in-person (not through the mail) up to 200 cigarettes, 50 cigars, 400g loose tobacco, 1.14L wine or alcohol, and 355ml beer; the value of these products is included in the CDN$300 allowance. For more information, contact External Affairs, Communications Branch, Mackenzie Ave., Ottawa, Ontario, K1A 0l5 (tel. (613) 957 0275).

British citizens are allowed an exemption of up to £36 of goods purchased outside the EC, including not more than 200 cigarettes, 100 cigarillos, 50 cigars, or 250g of tobacco; and no more than 2L of still table wine plus 1L of alcohol over 22% volume. You must be over 17 to import liquor or tobacco. For more information about U.K. customs, contact Her Majesty's Customs and Excise, Custom House, Heathrow Airport North, Hounslow, Middlesex, TW6 2LA (tel. (081) 750-1603, fax 081 750 1549). HM Customs & Excise Notice 1 explains the allowances for people traveling to the U.K. both from within and without the European Community.

Australian citizens may import AUS$400 (under 18 AUS$200) of goods duty-free, including 250 cigarettes, 250g tobacco, and 1L alcohol. You must be over 18 to import either. For information, contact the nearest Australian consulate.

■■■ MONEY

The prices given in the book were accurate in the summer of 1993, when the book was researched.

As of January 1993 new currency was introduced by the Mexican Treasury Department in an effort to stabilize the currency. The new bills are worth 1000 times the old peso. In some areas, prices may be listed in the old peso or both old and new peso as the old peso is gradually removed from circulation. Travelers should be particularly careful to know which currency to purchase, carry, and spend to avoid the potential for confusion. *All prices in this book are listed in new pesos; simply multiply by 1000 to derive the price in old pesos.* If you find that *Let's Go* prcies are consistently high or low by a certain amount, use that figure to anticipate other recent changes.

US$1 = 3.115 pesos	**1 peso = US$0.32**
CDN$1 = 2.41 pesos	**1 peso= CDN$0.41**
UK£1 = 4.638 pesos	**1 peso = UK£0.21**
AUS$1 = 2.116 pesos	**1 peso = AUS$0.47**
NZ$1 = 1.705 pesos	**1 peso = NZ$0.58**

■ Currency and Exchange

Be sure to buy approximately US$50 worth of pesos before leaving home, especially if you will arrive in the afternoon or on a weekend, including the equivalent of US$1 in change. This will save you time at the airport and help you avoid the predicament of having no cash after bank hours. The symbol for pesos is the same as for U.S. dollars (although an "S" with *two* bars is always a dollar-sign). The common abbreviation **"M.N."** (*Moneda Nacional*) also stands for the peso.

Changing money in Mexico can be inconvenient. Some banks won't exchange until noon, when the daily peso quotes come out, and then stay open only until

Don't forget to write.

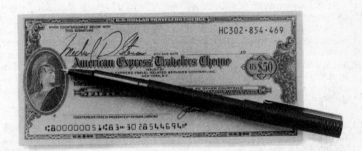

Now that you've said, "Let's go," it's time to say "Let's get American Express® Travelers Cheques." If they are lost or stolen, you can get a fast and full refund virtually anywhere you travel. So before you leave be sure and write.

1:30pm. You can switch U.S. dollars for pesos anywhere, but some banks refuse to deal with other foreign currencies. **Banks** use the official exchange rates, but they sometimes extract a flat commission as well. Therefore, the more money you change at one time, the less you will lose in the transaction. The lineup of national banks in Mexico includes **Bánamex, Bancomer, Comermex** and **Serfin.**

Casas de cambio (currency exchange booths) may offer better exchange rates than banks and are usually open as long as the stores near which they do business. In most towns, the exchange rates at restaurants and hotels are extremely unfavorable; avoid them unless it's an emergency.

■ Traveler's Checks

If money makes your world go round, then a pickpocket could bring the world to a screeching halt. Traveler's checks will take the sting out of theft, but there are places (especially in northern Mexico) accustomed to the real, green dollar that will not accept any substitute. To avoid problems when cashing your checks, always have your passport with you (not just the number); it often means the difference between apologetic refusal and grudging acceptance. Carry traveler's checks in busy towns and cities, but stick to cash, risky though it may be, when traveling through the less touristed spots.

Many banks and companies sell traveler's checks, usually for the face value of the checks plus a 1-2% commission. Bank of America WorldMoney traveler's checks are sold commission-free in California, and AAA supplies American Express traveler's checks to its members *sans* commission. Even if you don't have a card, holding AmEx Cheques allows you to use their offices to receive mail.

The following toll-free numbers provide information about purchasing traveler's checks and obtaining refunds:

American Express: In the **U.S.** and **Canada,** tel. (800) 221-7282; in the **U.K.,** tel. (0800) 52-13-13; in **Australia,** tel. (008) 25-1902; in **Australia, New Zealand** and **South Pacific,** tel. (02) 886-0689; from elsewhere, call U.S. collect tel. (801) 964-6665 for referral to offices in individual countries. AmEx traveler's cheques are the most widely recoginzed worldwide and easiest to replace if lost or stolen—just call the information number or the AmEx Travel office nearest you. AmEx offices cash their own cheques commission-free (except where prohibited by national government) and sell cheques which can be signed by either of two people traveling together ("Cheque for Two"). Cheques available in seven currencies. American Automobile Association memebers can obtain AmEx traveler's cheques commission-free at AAA offices.

Barclays Bank: In the **U.S.** or **Canada,** tel. (800) 221-2426; in the **U.K.,** tel. (202) 67-12-12; from elsewhere, call New York collect tel. (212) 858-8500. Associated with Visa. Checks available in four currencies. Commission 1%. Representative banks in many locations throughout Mexico.

Citicorp: In the **U.S.** and **Canada,** tel. (800) 645-6556; from elsewhere; in London (071) 982-4040; from abroad call collect (813) 623-1709. Commission 1-1½%, four currencies available. Checkholders are automatically enrolled in Travel Assist Hotline (tel. (800) 523-1199) for 45 days after purchase.

MasterCard: In the **U.S.** and **Canada,** tel. (800) 223-9920; elsewhere, call New York collect (609) 987-7300. Checks available in 11 currencies. MasterCard itself charges no commission, but depending on the bank where you purchase the checks, you may have to pay 1-2%.

Thomas Cook: Thomas Cook and Mastercard have formed a partership whereby Thomas Cook distributes checks with both logos in US dollars and ten other currencies. Call (800) 223-7373 for refunds in the U.S., (800) 223-4030 for orders. From elsewhere call collect (212) 974-5696. Some Thomas Cook Currency Services offices (located in major cities around the globe) do not charge any fee for purchase of checks while some charge a 1-2% commission.

Visa: In **U.S.** and **Canada,** tel. (800) 227-6811; from the **U.K.,** call collect tel. (+44 71) 937 8091; elsewhere, call New York collect tel. (212) 858-8500. Checks in 13 currencies. No commission through Visa but individual banks might charge 1%.

Each agency refunds lost or stolen traveler's checks, but expect hassles if you lose track of them. When buying checks, get a list of refund centers. To expedite the refund process, separate your check receipts and keep them in a safe place. Record check numbers as you cash them to help identify exactly which checks might be missing. As an additional precaution, leave a list of the numbers with someone at home. Even with the check numbers in hand, you will probably find that getting a refund involves hours of waiting and spools of red tape.

It's best to buy most of your checks in small denominations (US$20) to minimize your losses at times when you need cash fast and can't avoid a bad exchange rate. Don't keep all your money in the same place: split it up among pockets and bags, or better yet, use a money belt. If possible, purchase checks in U.S. dollars, since many *casas de cambio* refuse to change other currencies.

■ Credit Cards and Cash Cards

Most of the banks that cash traveler's checks will make cash advances on a credit card as well. Be prepared to flash your passport. Major credit cards—**Visa, Master-Card,** and **American Express**—can prove invaluable in a financial emergency. Not only are they accepted by many Mexican businesses, especially in tourist areas, but they can also work in some **automated teller machines (ATMs).** And if you lose your airline ticket, you can charge a new one.

All major credit card companies have some form of worldwide lost card protection service, and most offer a variety of additional travel services to cardholders—make sure to inquire before you leave home. Students and other travelers who may have difficulty procuring a credit card should know that family members can sometimes obtain a joint-account card. American Express will issue an extra green card for US$30 per year or an extra gold card for US$35 (bills go to the main cardholder). Visa also issues extra cards on accounts, but the fee varies. For more information contact your local bank. They can also give you ATM locations throughout the U.S. and Mexico; also call tel. (800) 4-CIRRUS (424-7787) for current ATM availability information. Foreign ATM machines often have keypads with numbers only. If you remember your ATM password by letters only, be sure to jot down its numeric equivalent before leaving the U.S.

Some Mexican ATM machines have been known to withdraw money from an account without issuing any money. If you attempt to withdraw money and are turned down, be sure to keep any record of the transaction and write down the time, location and amount of the transaction, and check this against bank statements.

■ Sending Money

Sending money to Mexico requires a somewhat existential leap of faith. The cheapest way to receive emergency money is to have it sent through a large commercial bank that has associated banks within Mexico. The sender must either have an account with the bank or bring in cash or a money order, and some banks cable money only for regular customers. The sender can specify whether the money is to be disbursed in pesos or U.S. dollars. The service costs US$25-80, depending on the amount sent. Cabled money should arrive in one to three days if the sender can furnish exact information (i.e. recipient's passport number and the Mexican bank's name and address); otherwise, there will be significant delays. To pick up money, you must show some form of positive identification, such as a passport. The sender will receive no confirmation that the money has reached you.

Western Union (tel. (800) 325-6000) offers a convenient service for cabling money. Visa or MasterCard holders can call (800) 225-5227, recite their card number, and send any amount of money that the sender's credit limit can sustain. If the sender has no credit card, he or she must go in person to one of Western Union's offices with cash—no money orders accepted, and cashier's checks are not always accepted. The money will arrive at the central telegram office or post office of the designated city, where the recipient can obtain it upon presentation of suitable identification. If you are in a major Mexican city, the money should arrive within 24 hrs. In a smaller city, it could take 48 hrs., and if you are out on a donkey trail somewhere, the time frame is indefinite. The money will arrive in pesos and will be held for 30 days. If no one picks it up, it will be returned to the sender minus the transaction cost. Cabling costs run up to US$48 for sending as much as US$1000.

Sending money through **American Express** (in U.S., tel. (800) 543-4080; in Canada, tel. (800) 933-3278) costs about as much as using a bank, and the sender need not have an American Express card. Money will arrive immediately at any of the 41 international offices in Mexico, or in three to five days at other designated offices, where it will be held until further notice. Money is disbursed in traveler's checks (U.S. dollars) to the international offices and in peso form to other locations. It costs between US$15 and $35 to send to one of the international offices. When sending money to Mexico with a credit card, you are limited to US$1000 per day.

Finally, if you are a U.S. citizen and suddenly find yourself in an extreme emergency, you can have money sent via the State Department's Citizen Emergency Center (tel. (202) 647-5225, open Mon.-Fri. 8:15am-10pm, Sat. 9am-3pm; after hours call tel. (202) 647-4000). The center will need to know the sender's name and address, the recipient's name, and the reason for sending the money. The quickest way to get the money (preferably less than US$500) to the State Department is to cable it through Western Union or else to drop off cash, certified check, bank draft, or money order at the center itself. It takes longer to send the money through your own bank. Once they receive it, the State Department will cable the money, for a fee of US$15, to the nearest embassy or consulate, which will then release the cash according to the sender's instructions. The money should arrive within 24 hrs. If you want to, you can send a short telegraphic message along with the money. The center's address is: Bureau of Consular Affairs, CA/PA #5807, U.S. Dept. of State, Washington, DC 20520.

■■■ PACKING

Pack light. That means you.

Set out everything you'll need, and then take half of that plus more money. One *New York Times* correspondent recommends that you "take no more than you can carry for half a mile at a dead run." This advice may be extreme (unless you expect to be pursued by *federales*), but the gist is clear.

Decide whether a light suitcase, shoulder bag, backpack or shoebox is best for the kind of traveling you'll be doing. A **convertible pack** could spare you this difficult decision. If you will be staying in one city or town for a while, a light suitcase ought to suffice. Those striving for the more casual, unobtrusive look should take a large **shoulder bag** that closes securely. If you will be riding a lot of buses or covering a lot of ground by foot, a **backpack** may be the best choice. An internal-frame model is less bulky and can't be broken as easily by baggage handlers. For hiking, an external frame lifts weight off the back and distributes it more evenly, allows for some ventilation, and is more pleasant to carry over uneven terrain; internal frames mold to the back better, keep a lower center of gravity, and are more comfortable for long-distance hiking on the level. If you're taking a sleeping bag, keep in mind that you can strap it onto the outside of an **external frame,** while you usually must allow room for bedding inside an internal frame pack. A pack that loads from the front rather than the top saves you from having to grope at the bottom for hidden items, but the greater stress on a larger zipper area makes this a weaker design. Packs with several compartments are convenient, but outside zippers and flaps make easy targets for pickpockets. When choosing a backpack, consider how much more cumbersome it will be with 50 pounds of gear stuffed inside. Decent packs start at about US$120.

In addition to your main bag, bring a smaller day-pack for sightseeing or carry-on; it is a good idea to keep some of your valuables with you. A small **purse, neck pouch,** or **moneybelt** helps guard your money, passport and other important articles. Moneybelts are available at most camping supply stores and through the Forsyth Travel Library (see Useful Organizations: Publications).

Shorts, on either sex, are appropriate only at the beach and in the more cosmopolitan parts of Mexico.

Many Mexican cities have no public places to do **laundry.** One solution is to give your clothes to the hotel cleaning person, who is often more-than-eager to earn some extra money and will do a much better job than a washing machine would. Make sure that whomever you approach is a permanent employee of the hotel and establish a price in advance. Another possibility is to carry a mild laundry soap and do laundry by hand in hotel sinks. A soft squash ball will magically serve as a plug where there are usually none.

Footwear is not the place to cut costs. Comfortable walking shoes or a good pair of running shoes is essential. Save your sandals and other non-utilitarian shoes for short walks and evenings out. If you plan to hike or climb over pyramids and ruins, bring a pair of sturdy hiking shoes. Most toiletries such as aspirin and razor blades are available in Mexican pharmacies, but some items—tampons, prescription drugs and contraceptives—are best brought from home. Even when these items are available over the counter, their ingredients may differ from the same-named product in the U.S. Cities sometimes carry U.S. brands of saline solution for contact lens wearers, but no stores stock comparable cleaners. Toilet paper is often elusive; always carry some for those out-of-the way places and cheap hotels.

If your Spanish is not fluent, buy a good Spanish-English dictionary before you leave, because language dictionaries are scarce and expensive in Mexico. A compass may actually come in handy for orienting yourself in new places and for following the directions in *Let's Go* listings. You should also bring film and batteries from home, since the quality and variety of such goods are poorer in Mexico.

■ ■ ■ SAFETY AND SECURITY

Contrary to what you've probably heard about *bandidos*, squalor and other perils, Mexico is relatively safe, although large cities (especially Mexico City) demand extra caution. After dark, keep away from bus and train stations, subways and public parks. Shun empty train compartments; many travelers avoid the theft-ridden Mexican train system altogether. When on foot, stay out of trouble by sticking to busy, well-lit streets, and conducting yourself as the local people do. Act as if you know exactly where you are going: an obviously bewildered bodybuilder is more likely to be harassed than a stern and confident 98-lb. weakling. Ask the manager of your hotel or hostel for advice on specific areas. In small, cheap and dark accommodations, check to make sure your door locks to guard against unwanted visitors and thieves. Rural areas may seem blissfully free of the dangers of the city, but make sure that in your quest for isolation you do not stray too far from help.

To protect belongings, buy small luggage locks and keep your bags locked when storing them in your hotel room or in a bus or train station. When traveling, it's best never to let possessions out of your sight; even checking baggage on trains and buses poses a risk. Keep your money and valuables near you at all times: under the pillow at night and in the bathroom while you shower. A **money belt** is probably the best idea. A **neck pouch**, although less accessible, is equally safe. In city crowds and especially on public transportation, pickpockets are amazingly deft at their craft. Hold your bags tightly. *Ladrones* have been known to surgically remove valuables by slitting the underside of bags as unsuspecting travelers hold on to them. Fanny packs worn loosely outside clothing scream "steal me!" to thieves. If you must keep money in a pocket, place it in the front pocket with your hand over it. Make two photocopies of all important documents; keep one copy with you (separated from the original) and leave one with someone at home.

■ Drinking and Drugs

Drinking in Mexico is not for amateurs; bars and *cantinas* are strongholds of Mexican *machismo*. When someone calls you *amigo* and orders you a beer, bow out quickly unless you want to match him glass for glass in a challenge that could last several days.

You are also likely to be offered marijuana, which is potent and inexpensive in Mexico. Note that a minimum 10-year jail sentence awaits anyone found guilty of possessing more than a token amount of any drug, and that Mexican law does not distinguish between marijuana and other narcotics. Even if you aren't convicted, arrest and trial might just ruin your day. Derived from Roman and Napoleonic law, the Mexican judicial process does *not* assume that you are innocent until proven guilty, and it is not uncommon to be detained for a year before a verdict is even reached. Foreigners and suspected drug traffickers are not released on bail. Furthermore, there is little your consulate can do to help you out (except inform your relatives and bring care packages to you in jail), even if it wants to. Bearing all this in mind, many opt for the less risky alternative: they drink themselves under the table in thousands of Mexican bars and the only sentence they face will be tomorrow morning's *cruda*.

Finally, don't even think about bringing drugs back into the U.S. Customs agents and their perceptive K-9s are not to be taken lightly. Every few weeks they auction off the cars they've confiscated from unsuccessful smugglers. On the northern highways, especially along the Pacific coast, expect to be stopped repeatedly by burly, humorless troopers looking for contraband. That innocent-looking hitchhiker you were kind enough to pick up may be a drug peddler with a stash of illegal substances. If the police catch it in your car, the drug possession charges will extend to you, and your car may be confiscated. For the free pamphlet *Travel Warning on Drugs Abroad*, send a self-addressed, stamped envelope to the Bureau of Consular Affairs, Public Affairs #5807, Dept. of State, Washington, DC 20520 (tel. (202) 647-1488).

■■■ HEALTH

Before you can say "pass the *jalapeños*," a long-anticipated vacation can turn into an unpleasant study of the wonders of the Mexican health care system. Keep your body and, more importantly, everything you put into it, clean; don't cut out nutritious food in favor of junk just to save money. Stop short of physical overexertion, drink lots of replenishing fluids like juice and purified water, and stay away from too many dehydrating caffeinated sodas.

Take a look at your **immunization records** before you go. **Typhoid** inoculations are good for three years, tetanus for 10. Although visitors to Mexico (unless from an area infected with yellow fever) do not need to carry vaccination certificates, gamma globulin shots that protect against **hepatitis** are recommended for back-country travel in Chiapas and the Yucatán. **Malaria** still exists in some rural parts of southern Mexico and is most prevalent on the southwest coast. Doctors frequently prescribe a chloroquine regimen and mosquito repellent with DEET. Ask your doctor or check the malaria chart published by IAMAT to find out if you will be traveling in a high-risk area (see below for address). **Dengue** has also been reported in Mexico and is just one more reason to arm yourself against dive-bombing mosqui-

HEALTH

toes. *Health Information for International Travel* (US$5) is available from the Superintendent of Documents (see Useful Addresses: Publications, above).

Anyone with a chronic condition requiring medication on a regular basis should see a doctor before leaving. People with allergies should find out if their conditions are likely to be aggravated in the regions they plan to visit. Obtain a full supply of any necessary medication before your trip, since matching your prescription to a foreign equivalent is not always easy, safe or possible. Always carry up-to-date, legible prescriptions and/or a statement from your doctor, especially if you use insulin, a syringe, or any narcotic drug. Distribute medicines among your bags to minimize potential loss. You may also want to write out a brief medical record (half a page or so) and keep it with your passport in case you need a doctor and are unable to communicate.

Those with medical conditions that cannot be immediately recognized (e.g. diabetes, allergies to antibiotics, epilepsy, heart conditions) should obtain a steel **Medic Alert identification tag** (US$35), which identifies the disease and gives a toll-free number to call for more information. Contact Medic Alert Foundation International, P.O. Box 1009, Turlock, CA 95381 (tel. (800) 432-5378).

One of the greatest health threats to travelers in Mexico is the water. The Mexican government now advises its own citizens to boil their water before drinking it. **Traveler's diarrhea,** known in Mexico as *turista*, is the dastardly consequence of ignoring this advice. *Turista* often lasts two or three days; symptoms include cramps, nausea, vomiting, chills and a fever as high as 103°F (39°C). Consult a doctor if symptoms persist. To avoid *turista,* never drink unbottled water. Do not brush your teeth with or even rinse the brush in running water. During showers or baths, keep your mouth closed. Do not eat uncooked vegetables, including lettuce. If you go to a bar, avoid the clever disguise of impure water—the ice-cube. Beware of food from markets or street vendors that may have been washed in dirty water or fried in rancid cooking oil. Peel all fruits and vegetables before eating them, and beware of watermelon, which is often injected with impure water. Don't forget mother's advice; always wash your hands before eating. Watch out for open bottles of hot sauce sitting on tables in restaurants. Also beware of ice or frozen treats that may have been made with bad water. A golden rule in Mexico: boil it, peel it, cook it, or forget it.

Be sure to drink plenty of liquids—much more than you're accustomed to drinking. Heat and high altitudes will dehydrate you more swiftly than you expect, and you can avoid many health problems if you drink enough fluid to keep your urine clear. Buy bottled water, boil tap water, use water purification tablets (available in U.S. drugstores), or obtain a small water filter. Many restaurants and hotels offer *agua purificada*. Alcoholic beverages are dehydrating, as are coffee, strong tea and caffeinated sodas.

When you absolutely must eat questionable food, many douse it with lime juice and wash it down with a beer to kill bacteria. Lots of garlic may do the trick and keep away vampires to boot.

Since *turista* is such a common problem, many travelers bring along over-the-counter remedies (like Pepto-Bismol). Another possible tactic is to flush out your system by drinking lots of fruit juice and pure water. Rest and let the heinous disease run its course. Locals try 8 oz. of fruit juice, ½ tsp. of honey or sugar and a pinch of salt in one glass, and 8 oz. of water with ¼ tsp. of baking soda in another glass. They then alternate sips from each glass, downing several per day.

In addition, don't eat mangos, chiles or anything greasy while you're sick. Do eat bananas, toast, rice and especially papaya. Heavy doses of *té de manzanilla* (chamomile tea), *caldo de pollo* (chicken soup) and ginger ale could improve the outlook for a diarrhea-free future.

The sun seems to shine more forcefully on Mexico than on the rest of the world, especially in the high altitudes of the interior. Take sunscreen and a wide-brimmed hat; use them even on overcast days. Common sense goes a long way in preventing

H
E
A
L
T
H

heat prostration and **sunstroke:** relax in hot weather, and drink lots of fluids. Symptoms of heat prostration include pallor, chills, clamminess, dizziness, blurred vision and a lowered pulse rate. In general, if you're out in the midday sun and start feeling awful, get inside, drink something non-alcoholic and lie down. Sunstroke (which can occur without direct exposure to the sun) is much more serious. The victim will be flushed and feverish, won't be sweating, and must be cooled off with wet towels and taken to a doctor as soon as possible.

Contact lens wearers should bring an adequate supply of cleaning solutions and lubricating drops from home. Mexican equivalents will be hard to find and could irritate your eyes. If you disinfect with a heat system, pack voltage and outlet adapters or switch to cold sterilization. Also bring an extra pair of glasses or a copy of the prescription, or leave either with a friend who can send it along in an emergency.

Local pharmacists can give shots and dispense other remedies for mild illnesses. A sterile, disposable needle is crucial. In every town, at least one *farmacia*, called the *farmacia de la guardia*, remains on duty 24 hrs. Wherever possible, *Let's Go* lists a pharmacy open for extended hours if not 24 hrs. If not listed, you can ask a policeman or cab driver where the pharmacy is. If the door is locked, knock loudly; someone is probably sleeping inside.

All travelers should be concerned about **Acquired Immune Deficiency Syndrome (AIDS),** transmitted through the exchange of body fluids with an infected individual (HIV-positive). Remember that there is no assurance that someone is not infected: HIV tests only show antibodies after a six-month lapse. Do not have sex without using a condom or share intravenous needles with anyone. Those travelers who are HIV-positive or have AIDS should thoroughly check on possible immigration restrictions in the country which they wish to visit. The Center for Disease Control's **AIDS Hotline** provides information on AIDS in the U.S. and can refer you to other organizations with information on Mexico (tel. (800) 342-2437; Spanish (800) 344-7432; TTD (800) 243-7889). Call the **U.S. State Department** for country-specific restrictions for HIV-positive travelers (tel. (202) 647-1488, fax (202) 637-3000; modem-users may consult the electronic bulletin board at (202) 647-9225; or write the Bureau of Consular Affairs, Rm. 5807, Dept. of State, Washington D.C. 20520). The **World Health Organization** provides written material on AIDS internationally (tel. (202) 862-3200).

Reliable **contraception** may be difficult to come by when traveling. Women on the pill should bring enough to allow for possible loss or extended stays. Although **condoms** are increasingly available and used throughout the world to prevent AIDS and unwanted pregnancies, you might want to stock up up on your favorite national brand before you go as quality varies in other countries.

Abortion is illegal in Mexico and permitted only in cases when the mother's life is in danger. The **National Abortion Federation's hotline** (tel. (800) 772-9100, Mon.-Fri. 9:30am-5:30pm) refers its callers to U.S. clinics that perform abortions. Its personnel can direct you to organizations which provide information on abortion in other countries.

For additional information before you go, you may wish to contact the **International Association for Medical Assistance to Travelers (IAMAT).** IAMAT provides several brochures on health for travelers, an ID card, a chart detailing advisable immunizations for 200 countries, and a worldwide directory of English-speaking physicians who have had medical training in Europe or North America. Membership to the organization is free (although donations are welcome) and doctors are on call 24 hrs. a day for IAMAT members. Contact chapters in the U.S., 417 Center St., Lewiston, NY, 14092, (tel. (716) 754-4883); in **Canada**, 40 Regal Rd., Guelph, Ontario, N1K 1B5 (tel. (519) 836-0102), and 1287 St. Clair Ave. West, Toronto, M6E 1B8 (tel. (416) 652-0137); in **New Zealand**, P.O. Box 5049, 438 Pananui Rd., Christchurch 5 (tel. (03) 352-9053, fax (03) 352-4360).

Complete health information travelers is available from a variety of published sources. Consult your local bookstore for books on staying healthy at home or on the road or write the **Superintendent of Documents,** U.S. Government Printing Office, Washington D.C. 20402 (tel. (202) 783-3238). $5 will get you their publication *Health Information for International Travel* detailing immunization requirements and other health precuations for travelers.

■■■ INSURANCE

Beware of unnecessary coverage—your current policies might well extend to many travel-related accidents. **Medical insurance** (especially university policies) often cover costs incurred abroad. **Medicare's** foreign travel coverage is limited and is valid only in Canada and Mexico. Canadians are protected by their home province's health insurance plan: check with the provincial Ministry of Health or Health Plan Headquarters. Your **homeowners' insurance** (or your family's coverage) often covers theft during travel.

Buying an **ISIC,** International Teacher ID or Student Card in the U.S. provides some insurance (see Documents and Formalities below). **CIEE** offers the inexpensive Trip-Safe plan with options covering medical treatment and hospitalization, accidents, baggage loss, and even charter flights missed due to illness; **STA** offers a more expensive, more comprehensive plan. American Express cardholders receive automatic car-rental and flight insurance on purchases made with the card. (For addresses for CIEE and STA, see Useful Organizations—Budget Travel Services.)

Remember that insurance companies usually require a copy of the police report for thefts, or evidence of having paid medical expenses (doctor's statements, receipts) before they will honor a claim and may have time limits on filing for reimbursement. Have all documents written in English to avoid possible translating fees. Always carry policy numbers and proof of insurance. Note that some of the plans listed below offer cash advances or guaranteed bills. Check with each insurance carrier for specific restrictions. If your coverage doesn't include on-the-spot payments or cash transferrals, budget for emergencies.

Access America, Inc., 6600 West Broad St., P.O. Box 11188, Richmond, VA, 23230 (tel. (800) 284-8300). Covers trip cancellation/interruption, on-the-spot hospital admittance costs, emergency medical evacuation. 24-hr. hotline.

ARM Coverage, Inc./Carefree Travel Insurance, P.O. Box 310, Mineola, NY, 11501 (tel. (800) 323-3149 or (516) 294-0220). Offers two comprehensive packages including coverage for trip delay, accident and sickness, medical, baggage loss, bag delay, accidental death and dismemberment, travel supplier insolvency. Trip cancellation/interruption may be purchased separately at a rate of $5.50 per $100 of coverage. 24-hr. hotline.

Globalcare Travel Insurance, 220 Broadway, Lynnfield, MA, 01940 (tel. (800) 821-2488, fax (617) 592-7720). Complete medical, legal, emergency, and travel-related services. On-the-spot payments and special student programs.

Travelers Aid International, 918 16th St., NW, Washington C 20006 (tel. (202) 659-9468, fax (202) 659-2910). Provides help for theft, car failure, illness, and other "mobility-related problems." No fee, but you are expected to reimburse the organization for expenses.

Travel Assistance International, 1133 15th St., NW, Washington DC 20005 (tel. (202) 821-2828, fax (202) 331-1609). Provides on-the-spot medical coverage ranging from US$15,000 to US$90,000 and unlimited medical evacuation insurance, 24-hr. emergency multilingual assistance hotline and worldwide local presence. Optional coverages such as trip cancellation/interruption, baggage and accidental death and dismemberment insurance are also offered. Short-term and long-term plans available.

■■■ ALTERNATIVES TO TOURISM

■ Work

Despite recent immigration legislation imposing heavy penalties on employers of illegal aliens, Mexican workers continue to pour over the border into the U.S., where most live in poverty. This should give you a sense of the job market in Mexico. Just as the U.S. spends billions of dollars every year to safeguard jobs for its own citizens, the Mexican government isn't about to give up precious jobs to traveling *gringos* when many of its own people are unemployed. It used to be that only 10% of the employees of foreign firms located in Mexico could have non-Mexican citizenship; now, as "development" has become a priority, the limit depends on the sector. Hotels, for instance, are often eager to hire English-speaking personnel for prestige and the convenience of their patrons, and are allowed as many legal work permits as they wish. It is no longer the case that to get a job you must have some specialized skill that cannot be found in Mexico; but attitudes are in flux, and you might still be unwelcome even as an English teacher. If you manage to secure a position with a Mexican business, your employer must get you a work permit. It is possible, but illegal, to work without a permit. You risk deportation if caught.

CIEE (see Useful Addresses, Travel Organizations) publishes *Work, Study, Travel Abroad: The Whole World Handbook* (US$12.95 plus $1.50 shipping), *Volunteer! The Comprehensive Guide to Voluntary Service in the U.S. and Abroad* (US$8.95 plus $1.50 shipping) and *Going Places: The High School Student's Guide to Study, Travel, and Adventure Abroad* (US$13.95 plus $1.50 shipping). **Peterson's**, P.O. Box 2123, Princeton, NJ 08543 (tel. (800) 338-3282), publishes the *Directory of Overseas Summer Jobs* (US$14.95, $4.75 shipping) with 50,000 openings worldwide, volunteer and paid. **Vacation Work Publications**, 9 Park End St., Oxford, England OX1 1HJ (tel. (+44 865) 24-19- 78) publishes *The International Directory of Voluntary Work* (£8.95) and *The Directory of Work and Study in Developing Countries* (£7 plus £2 shipping, £1 if within England).

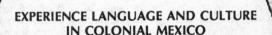

EXPERIENCE LANGUAGE AND CULTURE IN COLONIAL MEXICO

The Baden-Powell Institute invites you to come and study Spanish in the intimate setting of our school in Morelia, one of the most beautiful cities in colonial Mexico.

With us, you may form your own study plan, which may start any Monday year-round, with the option of flexible schedules and various subjects. We offer ONE-ON-ONE Lessons or group classes (3 to 5 students).

At Baden-Powell you can enjoy Mexican culture your way. On which we can help you in different forms, for example with the choice of living with a local family while studying.

We feel confident that our experience and qualified faculty will be a valuable asset to profit from.

If you'd like to receive further information about our program and the way we could fulfill your needs of studying Spanish, give us an idea about them.

... live the Mexico experience!!!

Eugenio Cortes, Director
Baden-Powell Institute
Antonio Alzate 565
Morelia, Michoacan
Mexico 58000
Phone (451) 240 70

Mr. or Mrs. Muzquiz
7337 Amherst Avenue
St. Louis, MO 63130 USA
Phone (314) 726-5409

If you have your heart set on extended work in Mexico, contact:

American Friends Service Committee, 1501 Cherry St., Philadelphia, PA 19102 (tel. (215) 241-7295). Runs volunteer work camps in Mexican villages for 18- to 26-year-olds. Work has included construction, gardening, reforestation, health and nutrition, and education. Programs run each summer from late June to early August (participation fee US$700). Fluency in Spanish required. Limited financial aid available. Address inquiries to the Personnel Dept.

Archaeological Institute of America, 675 Commonwealth Ave., Boston, MA 02215 (tel. (617) 353-9361, fax 353-6550). Lists field projects in the *Archaeological Fieldwork Opportunities Bulletin* which is available in Jan. for the following summer (US$10.50, $8.50 for members, plus $3.00 shipping). Sometimes nothing, sometimes one or two sites in Mexico. *Bulletin* also available directly from Kendall/Hunt Publishing Co. (tel. (800) 338-5578).

■ Study

Studying in Mexico is one of the best ways to learn Spanish while broadening your knowledge of Hispanic culture. The *Teenager's Guide to Study, Travel, and Adventure Abroad* (US$9.95 plus $1 postage) is available from CIEE (see Useful Addresses, Travel Organizations) or bookstores, as are the work/study guides listed above. **UNIPUB,** 4611-F Assembly Dr., Lanham, MD 20706-4391 (in U.S., tel. (800) 274-4888; in Canada, (800) 233-0504) distributes UNESCO's unwieldy but fascinating book *Study Abroad* (US$24 plus $2.50 shipping). Programs which take place in Mexico are described in Spanish. The **Institute of International Education (IIE),** 809 United Nations Pl., New York, NY 10017-3580 (tel. (212) 984-5412 for info only; also 883-8200; fax for orders 984-5452) publishes *Academic Year Abroad* (US$39.95 plus $3 shipping) and *Vacation Study Abroad* (US$31.95 plus $3 shipping), which have information on courses, costs and accommodations for programs in Mexico. Together with CIEE and the National Association for Foreign Student Affairs, IIE publishes *Basic Facts on Study Abroad* (free). IIE also operates the **Inter-**

national Education Information Center at the UN Plaza address (open Mon.-Fri. 10am-4pm), but can't provide assistance by phone or letter.

If you're already proficient in Spanish, consider enrolling in the regular programs of a Mexican university—but don't expect to receive credit at your home institution. The **Universidad de las Américas,** Apdo. 100, Santa Catarina Martír, Cholula, Puebla 72820 (tel. (22) 47-00-00, ext. 1108) is the only Mexican university accredited in the U.S.

For general information on studying at Mexican universities, contact the Secretaría de Relaciones Exteriores, Homero 213, 3r piso, México, D.F.

Many U.S. universities offer students the opportunity to study in Mexico for a semester or a year, and some Mexican universities organize programs specifically designed for foreign students. The **Universidad Nacional Autónoma de México (UNAM)** has a school in Mexico City for foreign students that operates semester, intensive and summer programs in Spanish, as well as in art, history, literature and Chicano studies. The program is open to both undergraduates and graduates. The school also has a campus in Taxco, a colonial mining town located on the road between Mexico City and Acapulco. Write to: UNAM, Centro de Enseñanza para Extranjeros, Apdo. 70-391, Ciudad Universitaria, Delegación Coyoacán, México, D.F. 04510 (tel. (5) 550-51-72, fax 548-99-39).

Less intensive programs are offered in Guadalajara and San Miguel de Allende; for more information, see Academic Institutions under those cities. Cuernavaca is the home of a number of language schools. Enrollment is often by the week, and students are usually housed with families in the area. For more information, see a copy of IIE's *Vacation Study Abroad*.

Finally, the Experiment in International Living's **School for International Training (SIT),** College Semester Abroad Admissions, Kipling Rd., P.O. Box 676, Brattleboro, VT 05302 (tel. (800) 451-4465 or (802) 257-7751) runs summer and semester programs in Mexico that include cross-cultural orientation, intensive language, homestay and field study. Summer programs cost US$1600-5200, semester US$6600-10,500, but the Pell Grant, Stafford Loan and PLUS/SLS Loan can apply to

SIT tuition. Some home institutions will provide additional aid and often accept SIT transfer credits. If you are over 14, speak Spanish fluently and have lived in Mexico, you can apply to lead programs for the **Experiment in International Living,** which pays leaders' expenses as well as an honorarium.

■■■ KEEPING IN TOUCH

The modes of communication in Mexico vary greatly in efficiency. The most reliable way to send a message—or money—is by wire; the least reliable is by surface mail.

■ Mail

Mexican mail service can be slow, but it is fairly dependable. Airmail often reaches the U.S. in as few as six days, but can just as easily take a month or more. It takes even longer (at least two weeks) to Europe and other destinations, since it is usually routed through U.S. surface mail. Official estimates average 40 days by boat, but in reality may take months. The set-rate postage for all light mail including postcards, letters and parcels weighing between 20 and 100g is about 1.50 pesos to North American countries, more to other locations. Printed matter receives a cheaper rate than regular mail if it is open for inspection and secured, if necessary, only by string or cord. Anything important should be sent registered mail for an additional charge of several hundred pesos, or else duplicates should be sent. Never deposit anything important in the black holes Mexicans call mailboxes. *La estampilla* or *el timbre* is "stamp" in Spanish, and *la carta* is "letter."

You can have letters sent to you in Mexico through **Lista de Correos,** a letter-holding service similar to General Delivery in the U.S. When picking up mail sent to you via *Lista de Correos,* look for a list posted in the post office. Check it carefully for any possible misspellings or confusions. If there is no list posted, ask the attendant *¿Está la lista de hoy?* (Is today's list here?). If it is, give your name. Letters and packages will be held no more than 15 days and sometimes fewer. If you

What can you do with a Bachelor's Degree?

Travel to a foreign country and teach someone to speak English. WorldTeach offers you the opportunity to share your skills and knowledge with those in need, while they share their unique culture with you.

WorldTeach is a non-profit organization that matches dedicated volunteers with schools in developing countries. Our volunteers spend a year teaching English in Thailand, Namibia, South Africa, Costa Rica, Ecuador, Russia, or Poland. Programs for undergraduates include spending a semester coaching sports in South Africa or teaching English for a summer in China.

For a program fee ranging from $3300 to $4000, volunteers receive housing and board or a living allowance from their school or community as well as airfare, health insurance, training, placement, and field support. Many volunteers find private sponsors in their own community to help pay the fee, and student loans can be deferred while you teach. WorldTeach also offers a minimal amount of financial aid for outstanding applicants.

You can do something with your Bachelor's degree, something that will make a difference in the lives of others and your own. To apply you need a Bachelor's Degree in any subject area and a desire to share. For an application and more information, call us at (617) 495-5527, or write WorldTeach, Harvard Institute for International Development, One Eliot St., Cambridge, MA. 02138-5705.

WORLDTEACH

have friends or family in Mexico, using their address may be preferable. Hotels where you have reserved a room will usually hold mail for you. **American Express offices** will also hold mail for 30 days before returning it; just write "Client's Mail" on the envelope. Call American Express customer service at (800) 528-4800 for more information and ask for the free *Directory of Traveler Service Offices*.

Mail sent to *Lista de Correos* should be addressed to a first and last name only, capitalizing and underlining the name under which the item should be filed alphabetically. Keep names as simple as possible. Because Mexican *apellidos* (paternal last names) fall in the middle of the written name, confusion arises for foreigners with more than a simple first and last name, or in the case of mail addressed to more than one person. A letter could be filed under any misspelled permutation of the recipient's names. If possible, go through the *Lista de Correos* yourself. If not, watch the person who does and ask for the mail under both your first and your last name, just to make sure. Address letters as follows:

Plamen RUSSEV
a/c Lista de Correos
Tampico [city], Veracruz [state]
12345 [postal code, if you know it], MEXICO

The letter should also be marked *Favor de retener hasta la llegada* ("Please hold until arrival").

To send letters from Mexico, it is wise to use the Spanish abbreviations or names for countries (EEUU or EUA for the U.S.). Write *Por Avión* on all postcards and letters not otherwise marked, unless you don't mind it arriving sometime in the next millennium.

Regulations for mailing parcels are confusing and vary from state to state. While it is often possible to send packages from smaller towns, post offices in large cities (especially ports or trade centers such as Mérida and Acapulco) provide more reliable service. Mailing a package involves locating a box, tape, string, wrapping paper and the correct forms to be stamped and signed by the appropriate officials. Before attempting to send anything, go to the post office and carefully note the size and weight limitations, necessary documentation, addresses and hours of the customs and trade offices in the city, and whether the box should be brought open or sealed. There is a fairly standard size limitation for boxes of 40cm by 60cm. After the contents have been inspected at the post office and at customs, you can wrap your package (usually on the post office floor). All packages are reopened and inspected by customs at the border, so closing the box with string rather than tape is recommended.

In some cases, customs and the post office are under the same roof. In others, the two lie at opposite ends of town and have conflicting schedules. In general, in order to send packages you must provide the following: tourist card data (number, duration of validity, date of issue, place of issue), list of contents including estimated value and nature of the package ("Gift" works best), address and return address. It is customary for those mailing parcels to use their home address, or at least some address in the same country as the parcel's destination, as a return address to ensure eventual delivery.

In a trade office, you may need to show receipts for each item purchased in Mexico. Postal officials usually record the information from the customs form on the front of the package as well. Should it prove impossible or too frustrating to send items by regular mail, look into the alternatives. From the larger cities, airlines will take parcels to the U.S. for enormous fees. Well-established *artesanía* stores often provide a mailing service for their customers. You can sometimes persuade them to include in the package items not bought in the store. Not only will the package be wrapped and addressed professionally, but connections with the post office can often ease processing and delivery. Finally, if you are following a fairly rigid itinerary, use trains, buses and domestic airlines to send packages to points within Mexico (for example, to the airport from which you plan to leave the country). Always double check the requirements of each method and have packages held at the other end long enough to guarantee that parcel and owner meet again.

KEEPING IN TOUCH

■ Telephones

When trying to reach Mexico from another country, patience is the key to success. If you are calling Mexican information, don't be surprised if the phone is not answered right away. To reach Mexico from the U.S., dial 011-52, then the city code (5 for Mexico City), and then the phone number.

Patience is also crucial when you're placing a call within Mexico. Half of the public phones are out of service, and the other half take rare low-denomination coins or LADATEL phone cards.

Getting lines to foreign countries is very difficult. Many public phones don't have access to international lines. If you speak Spanish fluently and can't reach the international operator, call the national operator, who will connect you (sometimes even a local operator can help). The term for a collect call is a *llamada por cobrar* or *llamada con cobro revertido*. Calling from hotels is usually faster.

Calling abroad from Mexico is extremely expensive thanks to taxes and surcharges. Long-distance charges vary from city to city, but calls to the U.S. usually set you back about 8 pesos per minute. Call collect if you can; not only is it cheaper (about half the price of direct), but you will avoid the enormous surcharges that hotel switchboards impose if you call direct. Remember, however, that there can be a fee of 1-5 pesos for collect calls that are not accepted, depending on where you place the call. Using a U.S. operator to call collect or with a calling card will let you pay U.S. rates (around $5-6 per min. depending on distance between cities).

LADATEL phones, increasingly prevalent, take coins or LADATEL phone cards. International calls using these phones are cheaper (2 pesos for 1 min. to Cambridge, MA) and involve less waiting than any of the alternatives. LADATEL **phone cards,** available at Teléfonos Mexicanos offices and various stores, eliminate the need for coins. Without them, the challenge is to find enough coins of large denominations, because these phones take no more than 10 coins at a time and some calls require a minimum initial deposit. When dialing, use the station-to-station prefixes. The blue

push-button phones do direct dial while the orange old-fashioned ones do not. Dial 95-800-462-4240 from most phones to reach the **AT&T USADirect operator**.

To reach the English-speaking international operator on a plain old phone, dial 09 and wait until the operator answers (sometimes immediately, but be prepared to wait 30min. or more). For direct calls, dial 01; national operator 02; local assistance 04; for bilingual (Spanish and English) emergency operators 06. To make long-distance phone calls within Mexico, dial 91 plus the telephone code and number (station to station), or 92 plus the telephone code and number (person to person). The prefixes for calling the U.S. or Canada are 95 for station to station and 96 for person to person; for all other countries the prefixes are 98 and 99, respectively. For international phone information, call tel. (800) 874-4000 in the U.S.

■■■ SPECIFIC CONCERNS

■ Women And Travel

"She is an undifferentiated manifestation of life, a channel for the universal appetite," wrote Octavio Paz, Mexican literary great, describing the Mexican view of woman. Women traveling in Mexico and Central America will find that attitudes like that described by Paz can profoundly influence their travel experience. Female *Let's Go* researchers report that as solo travelers they develop an entirely different mindset and perspective because of the daily confrontation with this ethos.

If you look like an *extranjera* (foreigner), you will find it difficult to remain alone except when locked in your hotel room. Persistent men will insist on joining you; walking down the street, you will hear whistles and propositions (called *piropos* in Mexico). If you're fair-skinned, "*güera, güera, güera*" will follow you everywhere. The best response to this is no response and no eye contact, because any kind of answer could be interpreted as a come-on. An obnoxious reply might only prolong the encounter. Should a situation become threatening, however, do not hesitate to lash out. In real emergencies, scream for help. Don't consider yourself safe just because people in uniform are around.

Awareness of Mexican social standards can also prevent unpleasant and dangerous confrontations. Women wearing shorts (opt for a light skirt even in big resort towns), halter tops, or not wearing bras, will most likely attract unwanted attention. *Cantinas* are all-male institutions; the only women who ever enter are working, either as servers or as prostitutes.

Northern Mexico is less congenial to women travelers than anywhere else in Mexico; Oaxaca, Chiapas, and the Yucatán are the most congenial. If you are traveling with a male friend, it may help to pose as a couple. This will assuage any misgivings hotel proprietors have about letting you share rooms and may serve to chill the blood of your Mexican admirer.

Remember, too, that as often as foreign women are stereotyped by Mexican men, Mexican men are stereotyped by foreigners. A man who offers to give you a lift or show you the sights may be acting innocently, but if you feel uncomfortable, politely refuse.

A series of recent travelogues by women outline their sojourns; check a good library or bookstore for these and other books: *Wander Women,* a travel and adventure networking organization for women over 40, publishes a quarterly newsletter. For a sample copy send US$1 to Wander Women, 136 Grand Ave. #237, West Covina, CA 91791; *Nothing to Declare: Memoirs of a Woman Traveling Alone* (Penguin Books; US$9) and *Wall to Wall: From Beijing to Berlin by Rail* (Penguin Books; US$10) by Mary Morris; *Women Going Places* (Inland; US$14); *One Dry Season* (Knopf) by Caroline Alexander; *Tracks* (Pantheon) by Robin Davidson; *The Road Through Miyama* (Random House/Vintage) by Leila Philips, and anything by Isak Dinesen, especially *Out of Africa* (Random House). For additional tips and suggestions, consult *The Handbook for Women Travelers* (£7.99) by Maggie and

Gemma Moss, published by Piatkus Books, 5 Windmill St., London W1P 1HF England (tel. +44 (071) 6310710).

■ Older Travelers And Senior Citizens

The need or wish to travel inexpensively knows no age limits. Older travelers can often travel on a shoestring budget by taking advantage of the numerous discounts available to them. Many youth hostels welcome seniors, and transportation costs and entrance fees to tourist attractions are often lower. National chapters of HI/IYHF (see Useful Addresses: Travel Organizations) sell HI/IYHF cards to those over 54 for US$15. Although a card isn't required in Mexican hostels, it does lower the rates.

Senior travelers should bring a medical record that includes an update on conditions and prescriptions; the name, phone number and address of a regular doctor; and a summary of their recent medical history. Find out if you have insurance that will cover costs you may incur in Mexico.

Travel Tips for Older Americans (US$1) provides information on passports, health and currency for those traveling abroad. Write to the Superintendent of Documents (see Useful Addresses above). The *International Health Guide for Senior Travelers* (US$5.95 plus US$1 postage) is available from Pilot Books, 103 Cooper St., Babylon, NY 11702 (tel. (516) 422-2225).

For more information, write to a Mexican Government Tourism Office (see Useful Addresses: Government Organizations). The following organizations and publications can also be helpful:

American Association of Retired Persons (AARP), Special Services Dept., 601 E St. NW, Washington, DC 20049 (tel. (800) 927-0111 or (202) 434-2277). US$8 annual membership fee. People over 49 receive benefits including group travel programs, discounts on lodging, car and RV rental, and sight-seeing.

Elderhostel, 75 Federal St., 3rd floor, Boston, MA 02110 (tel. (617) 426-7788). Educational workshops at over 1500 locations internationally for those over 59 and those over 49 who have a spouse or companion over 59. U.S. university-sponsored programs in Mexico. Options include Mexican history, folk art and archaeology. US$1500-5000 covers room, board, tuition and extracurricular activities for 1-4 weeks. Registration is an ongoing process, and no membership dues are required. Scholarships available. Free catalogue upon written request.

National Council of Senior Citizens, 1331 F St. NW, Washington, DC 20004 (tel. (202) 347-8800). Membership is open to all ages and costs US$12 per year or US$150 for a lifetime. Hotel and auto rental discounts, newsletter, discount travel agency and supplemental Medicare insurance for those over 64.

Gateway Books, P.O. Box 10244, San Rafael, CA 94912. Publishes Gene and Adele Malott's *Get Up and Go: A Guide for the Mature Traveler* (US$10.95, postage US$1.90). Offers recommendations and general hints for the budget-concious senior. Call (800) 669-0773 for orders.

■ Traveling With Children

Children under 18 need consent from both parents to enter Mexico. One parent must have a decree of sole custody or notarized, written permission from the other parent to bring the fruit of their union into the country. Check with the nearest Mexican consulate for more information.

If a child accompanies you to Mexico, special circumstances may arise. The new atmosphere, climate and diet may be unsettling at first, but most children adapt more quickly than their parents do. If you bring a baby, make sure to carry a piece of mosquito netting large enough to cover a cradle or stroller.

For general information concerning children on the road, consult *Travel with Children* (US$10.95 plus $1.50 postage), chock-full of user-friendly tips and international anecdotes, from Lonely Planet Publications, 155 Filbert St., Oakland, CA 94607-2538 (tel. (800) 275-0122 or (510) 893-8555, fax (510) 893-8563) or P.O. Box 617, Hawthorn, Victoria 3122, Australia; *Sharing Nature with Children* (US$7.95) from Wilderness Press, 2440 Bancroft Way, Berkeley, CA 94704 (tel. (800) 443-7227 or (510) 843-8080); and/or *Backpacking with Babies and Small Children* (US$8.95), also from Wilderness Press.

■ Travelers With Disabilities

Mexico is becoming increasingly accessible to travelers with disabilities, especially in popular resorts such as Acapulco and Cancún. Money talks—the more you are willing to spend, the less difficult it is to find accessible facilities. Most public and long-distance modes of transportation and most of the non-luxury hotels don't accommodate wheelchairs. Public bathrooms are almost all inaccessible, as are many historic buildings and museums. Still, with some advance planning, an affordable Mexican vacation is not impossible.

Air travel in general is gradually becoming less restrictive. Give prior notice of your needs to the airline, which may require a traveling companion or doctor's letter allowing you to fly. Cruises are a costly alternative to flying. When you choose a cruise line, ask about ramps, doorways and special services. Most ships also require a doctor's permission.

If you intend to bring a seeing-eye dog to Mexico, you must have a veterinarian's certificate of health stamped at a Mexican consulate (see Customs—Entering Mexico for pet fee).

The following organizations provide useful information and can help plan your vacation:

American Foundation for the Blind, 15 W. 16th St., New York, NY 10011 (tel. (212) 620-2147). ID cards (US$10); write for an application, or call the Product Center at (800) 829-0500. Also call this number to order AFB catalogs in braile, print, or on cassette or disk.

Disability Press, Ltd., Applemarket House, 17 Union St., Kingston-upon-Thames, Surrey KT1 1RP, England (tel.+44 (081) 549 6399). Publishes the *Disabled Traveler's International Phrasebook,* including French, German, Italian, Spanish, Portuguese, Swedish, and Dutch phrases (£1.75). Supplements in Norwegian, Hungarian and Serbo-Croatian (60p each).

The Guided Tour, Inc. Elkins park house, Suite 114B, 7900 Old York Road, Elkins Park, PA 19117-2348. (tel. (215) 782-1370 or (800) 738-5843) Year-round travel programs for persons with developmental and physical challenges as well as those geared to the needs of persons requiring renal dialysis. Trips and vacations planned both domestically and internationally. Call or write for a free brochure.

Mobility International, USA (MIUSA), P.O. Box 3551, Eugene, OR 97403 (tel. (503) 343-1284 voice and TDD). International headquarters in Britain, 228 Borough High St., London SE1 1JX (tel. +44 (071) 403 5688). Contacts in 30 countries. Information on travel programs, international work camps, accommodations, access guides, and organized tours. Membership costs US$20 per year, newsletter US$10. Sells updated and expanded *A World of Options: A Guide to International Educational Exchange, Community Service, and Travel for Persons with Disabilities* (US$14 for members, US$16 for non-members, postpaid).

Twin Peaks Press, P.O. Box 129, Vancouver, WA 98666 (tel. (800) 637-2256) publishes three books for disabled travelers: *Wheelchair Vagabond* (US$14.95), *Directory for Travel Agencies for the Disabled* (US$19.95), and *Travel for the Disabled* (US$19.95). Add US$2 shipping for the first book, $1 each additional book.

Further sources of information are *The Disabled Traveler's International Phrasebook* (£1.75), which includes Spanish, from Disability Press, Ltd., Applemarket

House, 17 Union St., Kingston-upon-Thames, Surrey, KT1 1RP England (tel. (+44 81) 549-63-99) and *Access to the World* (US$16.95) from Facts on File, Inc., 460 Park Ave. S, New York, NY 10016-7382 (tel. (800) 322-8755 or (212) 683-2244, fax (212) 213-4578).

■ Bisexual, Gay, And Lesbian Travelers

In Mexico, the legal age for consensual homosexual intercourse is 18. Police often ignore the legal status of homosexual activity and Mexicans generally disapprove of public displays of gay affection, but there is a gay rights movement in Mexico and discreet homosexuality is tolerated in most areas.

Giovanni's Room, 345 S. 12th St., Philadelphia, PA 19107 (tel. (215) 923-2960) is an international feminist, lesbian, and gay bookstore and mail-order house with resources and information for tourists.

Ferrari Publications, P.O. Box 37887, Phoenix, AZ 85069 (tel. (602) 863-2408). Publishes *Ferrari's Places of Interest* (US$14.95), *Ferrari's Places for Men* (US$13.95), *Ferrari's Places for Women* (US$12), and *Inn Places: USA and Worldwide Gay Accommodations* (US$14.95). Also available from Giovanni's Room (see below).

Spartacus International Gay Guide, (US$29.95). Order from 100 East Biddle St., Baltimore, MD 21202 (tel. (410) 727-5677) or c/o Bruno Lützowstraße, P.O. Box 301345, D-1000 Berlin 30, Germany (tel. +49 (30) 25 49 82 00); also available from Giovanni's Room (see above) and from Renaissance House, P.O. Box 292, Village Station, New York, NY 10014 (tel. (212) 674-0120). Extensive list of gay bars, restaurants, hotels, bookstores and hotlines throughout the world. Very specifically for men.

Women Going Places, a new women's travel and resource guide emphasizing women-owned enterprises. Geared towards lesbians, but offers advice appropriate for all women. US$14. Available from Inland Book Company, P.O. Box 120261, East Haven, CT 06512 (tel. (203) 467-4257).

Wherever possible, *Let's Go* lists gay and lesbian information lines, centers, bookstores and nightclubs in specific towns and cities.

■ Travelers On Special Diets

Keeping **kosher** in Mexico is a breeze with the *Jewish Travel Guide* (US$10.75 plus $1.50 postage) from **Jewish Chronicle Publications,** 25 Furnival St., London EC4A 1JT, England (tel. (+44 1) 405-92-52). In the U.S., write or call **Sepher-Hermon Press,** 1265 46th St., Brooklyn, NY 11219 (tel. (718) 972-9010).

Vegetarians can obtain information and possibly the slightly out of date *Vegetarian Travel Guide* (US$16 plus $3 shipping) from the **North American Vegetarian Society,** P.O. Box 72, Dolgeville, NY 13329 (tel. (518) 568-7970) or from the **Vegetarian Society of the U.K.,** Parkdale, Dunham Rd., Altrincham, Cheshire WA14 4QG, England (tel. (+44 61) 928-07-03).

For diabetic concerns, see Health.

GETTING THERE

■ By Plane

About 450 flights leave for Mexico from the U.S. each week. A little research can pay off with discounts or cheaper flights. A travel agent is often a good source of information on scheduled flights and fares, and student travel organizations provide leads on airfare discounts (see Useful Addresses, Travel Organizations). If you're coming from Europe, it's cheapest to fly first to a U.S. city, then connect to Mexico City or some other Mexican airport.

Round-trip airfares to Mexico City, in particular those from the U.S., have remained relatively low: in the summer of 1993, round-trip for students from New York cost about US$368. Getting to less central areas from the U.S. often entails flying to Mexico City and transferring. A travel agent can arrange routings within Mexico in advance. The following cities serve as good bases for travel to outlying areas if you are flying into Mexico City: Mérida for the Yucatán, Puerto Vallarta or Guadalajara for Jalisco and Colima, Tuxtla Gutiérrez for Chiapas.

Mexicana (tel. (800) 531-7921) and **Aeroméxico** (tel. (800) 237-6639) are the two major national airlines, covering most of Mexico; regional airlines also provide service in many areas. Though more expensive than land travel, flying in Mexico is very inexpensive compared to air-travel costs in the U.S. and other countries. Mexicana gives occasional discounts that make flying even more attractive. If the alternative is an interminable bus ride through completely rustic territory, a flight may be worth the extra pesos.

Confirm reservations 72 hours in advance for your flight and be aware of the **departure tax** levied at Mexican international airports (US$11.50). Bring pesos with you to the airport in order to avoid losing money in a last-minute currency exchange. Regardless of the airline, expect delays of a few hours.

Many airlines sell package deals that include accommodations and car rental. These deals sacrifice flexibility and may end up including too many expensive extras for the budget traveler; it is advisable to use them only if you are planning a one- to two-week vacation during peak tourist season (around Christmas or during Spring Break), when especially cheap packages are available. You usually have to book well in advance and may receive no refund should you cancel.

The availability of standby flights is declining on many airlines, but if you can find them, their advantage is flexibility. The disadvantage is that during peak season, flying standby can randomize your vacation more than you would like—the number of available seats is established only minutes before departure. Call individual carriers for availability and prices. Tickets are usually sold at the airport on the day of departure. Some travel agents can issue standby tickets, but may hesitate to do so.

More expensive than standby, **Advanced Purchase Excursion (APEX)** fares provide confirmed reservations and permit arrival and departure from different cities. Reservations must be made 21 days in advance, and stays are limited from one week to three months. Changing APEX reservations results in a penalty of US$50-$100, depending on the airline and the type of change.

Couriers are sometimes needed; in return for surrendering luggage space, travelers who agree to serve as couriers receive a considerable discount (50-80%) on the airfare. **Now Voyager,** 74 Varick St. #307, New York, NY 10013 (tel. (212) 432-1616) and **Halbart Express,** 147-05 176th St., Jamaica, NY 11434 (tel. (718) 656-8189), among other firms, mediate such transactions. The *Courier Air Travel Handbook* (US$10.70) explains step-by-step how to work with courier companies. For a copy, contact **Thunderbird Press,** 5930-10 W. Greenway Blvd., #112H, Glendale, AZ 85306 (tel. (800) 345-0096 or (602) 843-6716, fax (602) 978-7836). **Travel Unlimited,** P.O. Box 1058, Allston, MA 02134-1058, publishes comprehensive, monthly newsletters detailing all possible options for international travel on air couriers. Couriers do not advertise, so this is an invaluable resource (1-year subscription US$25, US$35 outside U.S.).

Discount clearing houses also offer savings on charter flights, commercial flights, tour packages, and cruises. These clubs make unsold tickets available from three weeks up to a few days before departure. Annual dues run US$30-50, but the fares offered can be extremely cheap, often less than US$160 each way. Places to investigate include:

Last Minute Travel Club, 1249 Boylston St., Boston, MA 02215 (tel. (800) 527-8646 or (617) 267-9800). No membership fee. Hotline for customers.

Last Minute Travel Connection, 601 Skokie Blvd. #224, Northbrook, IL 60062 (tel. (708) 498-9216, fax 498-5856). Provides information about bargains on air fares, hotels, package tours, cruises and condominiums. Services include registration service, plus bargain listings subscriptions ($40 per month, $200 per week) and 900 number for current travel bargains: tel. (900) 446-8292, $1 per minute (demonstration at tel. (708) 498-3883). Booklet *How to Save Money on Last Minute Travel* available.

Sunline Express, 607 Market St., San Francisco, CA 94105 (tel. (800) SUN-LINE (786-5463) or (415) 541-7800). Specializes in flights to Mexico and South America.

Travel Avenue, 180 N Desplaines St., Chicago, IL 60606 (tel. (800) 333-3335). Discount of 5-16% on international flights, with a US$25 surcharge.

Travelers' Advantage, 49 Music Sq. W, Nashville, TN 37203 (tel. (800) 548-1116). Primarily for U.S. travelers flying round-trip from the U.S.

■ By Bus or Train

Greyhound serves El Paso, Laredo and Brownsville, TX, and Calexico and San Diego, CA. Smaller lines serve these cities plus Eagle Pass, TX, and Nogales, AZ. Buses tend not to cross the border, but at each of these stops you can pick up Mexican bus lines on the other side. Tres Estrellas de Oro, Estrella Blanca, and Transportes Del Norte provide service from the border.

By train, you can take Amtrak to El Paso (US$279 round-trip from New York), walk across the border to Ciudad Juárez and from there use Mexican National Railways trains—or other forms of transportation—to reach points within Mexico. Amtrak also serves San Diego (US$339 round-trip from New York). The San Diego Trolley (information recording tel. (619) 231-8549) marked "San Ysidro" will take you down to the Mexican border for US$1.50. Once in Tijuana you must take a bus to Mexico City, since there is no train service (although trains do serve Mexicali). It is also possible to travel by Amtrak to San Antonio (US$279 round-trip from New York) and take a bus from there to the border towns.

■ By Car

Entrance by car into Mexico is not complicated as long as you keep your vehicle within the *Zona Libre* (Free Zone). The *Zona Libre* extends from the U.S. border 22km into Mexico; it also includes all of Baja California. You will encounter checkpoints as soon as you reach the end of the *Zona Libre* (see Planning Your Trip: Documents and Formalities: Driver's License and Vehicle Permits for details on bringing your car farther into Mexico).

There are 16 entry cities along the U.S.-Mexico border, in California, Arizona, New Mexico and Texas. AAA endorses only three (Laredo, Reynosa, and Matamoros). The main highways into Mexico are Route 1, which leads from Tijuana to the southern tip of Baja California Sur (1680km); Route 15, from Nogales, AZ, to Mexico City (2320km); Route 49, from El Paso, TX, to Mexico City (1800km); Route 57, from Eagle Pass, TX, to Mexico City (1264km); and Route 85 from Laredo or Brownsville, TX, to Mexico City (1176km).

On the U.S. side of the border, several **auto clubs** provide routing services and protection against breakdowns. Find out if your auto club is affiliated with Mexican auto clubs through international motoring agreements; if so, you may receive limited travel services and information from the **Asociación Mexicana Automovilística (AMA)** and the **Asociación Nacional Automovilística (ANA)** (see Useful Addresses: Transportation Services). Both the AMA and the ANA sell road maps. The Mexican consulate or nearest tourist office provides free road maps. **Guía Roji** publishes excellent maps; write them at Governador José Moran 31, Delegación M.

Hidalgo, San Miguel, Chapultepec, 11850 México, D.F. (tel. (5) 515-03-84 or 515-79-63, fax 277-23-07).

If you choose to drive to a border town and then continue by plane, train, or bus, consider storing your car in one of several garages along the U.S. side of the border to avoid permit and insurance hassles.

All non-Mexican **car insurance** is invalid in Mexico, no matter what your policy says. Make sure you arrange to have your car insured in Mexico if you plan to drive it there. **Sanborn's,** Home Office, P.O. Box 310, McAllen, TX 78502 (tel. (512) 686-3601, fax 686-0732) offers insurance with all the trimmings, including road maps, newsletters, a ride board and "Mexico Mike" in Dept. N at the McAllen address (write him for up-to-date, priceless information on driving in Mexico). Remember that if you are in an accident, the police might hold you in jail until everything is sorted out and all claims are settled. If you can prove your ability to pay or can get an adjuster to come out, they will release you.

TRAVELING IN MEXICO

■■■ USEFUL ORGANIZATIONS

Embassies and **consulates** provide a variety of services for citizens away from home. They can refer you to an English-speaking doctor or lawyer, help you replace a lost tourist card, and wire family or friends if you need money and have no other means of obtaining it. They cannot, however, cash checks, act as a postal service, get you out of trouble, supply counsel, or interfere in any way with the legal process in Mexico. Once in jail, you're on your own. (For a list of embassies, see Mexico City Practical Information below.)

Mexico does not want for tourist offices. Branches of the **Mexican Government Tourism Office (Secretaría de Turismo** or **SECTUR)** are located in the capital city of each state and wherever else tourists gather. The address in Mexico City is Av. Presidente Mazaryk 172, Col. Polanco, México, D.F. 11570 (tel. (5) 250-85-55).

■■■ GETTING AROUND

■ By Plane

Flying within Mexico is more expensive than taking a bus or train, but it is considerably cheaper than comparable flights between U.S. cities. In the summer of 1993, you could fly from Huatulco to Oaxaca for US$53.80, from Guadalajara to Manzanillo for $48.50, or from La Paz to Mexico City for US$208.90. Check with Mexican airlines for special rates (see telephone numbers in Getting There: By Plane).
Always double-check ticket prices and departure times listed in *Let's Go,* as they were accurate at the time the book was researched in the summer of 1993.

■ By Train

The 15,000 miles of railroad in Mexico are all government-owned, with most lines operating under the name of **Ferrocarriles Nacionales de Mexico** (National Railways of Mexico). Trains run from the border at Nogales, Piedras Negras, Nuevo Laredo, Matamoros, Mexicali and Juárez. The train system is not as extensive nor as punctual as the bus system. Even when they are on time, trains can take twice as long as buses to reach their destination. Riding the rails is best for leisurely travel in very picturesque areas. (The 12-hr. sleeper from Guadalajara to Mexico City is reputed to be pure joy.)

Train fares are generally less expensive than buses, but there is a great risk of theft (of either money or suitcases); the small amount you might save over bus travel could rapidly become a major loss. Pickpockets make their living by boarding first class or other trains at major stops (those which last more than 10min.) and brushing past unwary foreigners. Make sure your luggage is locked and your valuables are with you and inaccessible to prying hands.

There are several train options: *rápido* trains, which cost more than *locales*, cut travel time in half by chugging past smaller towns without stopping. *Rápido* trains are almost always cleaner and more comfortable. *Primera clase* (first class) or, better yet, *primera clase especial* (comparable to "business" or "ambassador" class), cost significantly more than *segunda clase* (second class), but you get cleanliness and comfort for your money. *Segunda clase* may be the cheapest form of transportation in the world (about US$3 for the ride from Guadalajara to Mexico City, as compared to US$7 for a first-class ticket), and according to some travelers it's the only way to see the "real" Mexico. But the "real" Mexico respects only the most intrepid and experienced of budget travelers: those who can stand for 20 hours in a hot, dirty, crowded car, with pickpockets and animals for company, and a hole cut in the floor for a toilet.

Mexico by Rail, P.O. Box 3508, Laredo, TX 78044 (tel. (800) 228-3225 or (512) 727-3814) can reserve first-class railway tickets for travelers. Make arrangements two to three weeks in advance, and the company will mail the tickets to your home.

Another option for arranging train reservations is to write or call the appropriate railroad officer in Mexico. Expect this to take about 30 days, and do so only when you plan to travel on the major routes. Less-traveled stations may misplace such advance orders and may not even sell tickets at all.

■ By Bus

If you have any qualms about being without your own set of wheels in Mexico, the extensive, astoundingly cheap bus service should lay them to rest. A first-class ticket from Tijuana all the way to Mexico City costs US$55. First-class buses are relatively comfortable and efficient; they occasionally even have bathrooms and functioning air-conditioners (ask at the ticket window). Second- and third-class buses, which are only slightly cheaper than first class, are often overcrowded, hot, and uncomfortable. However, they are full of life (human and chicken alike), run more frequently and have food service—at the numerous stops, vendors jump on the bus to sell snacks.

When you buy your ticket the agent will ask where you want to sit. At night, the right side of the bus won't face the constant glare of oncoming headlights. During the day, the shady side of the bus will be a lot cooler (the left when going south, the right when heading north). Mexicans usually refuse to open the windows when the bus is moving.

Buses are either *de local* or *de paso*. *De local* originate at the station from which you leave. Buy your ticket a day (or at least a few hours) in advance because only a few *de locales* leave per day. Once you get on the bus, guard your ticket stub as you may be asked to show it at a later stop.

De paso buses originate elsewhere and pass through your station. First-class *de pasos* sell only as many tickets as there are available seats—when the bus arrives, the driver disembarks to give this information to the ticket seller. When these tickets go on sale, forget civility, chivalry and any ism which might possibly stand between you and a ticket, or plan to spend the greater portion of your vacation in bus stations. Second-class *de paso* buses sell tickets based on the number of people with assigned seats who have gotten off the bus. This system does not, unfortunately, take into account the people and packages jammed into the aisle. You may find someone (or something) already in your assigned seat when you reach it; in this case, enlist the bus driver's help. Hold your ground and try to keep calm. It is proper to offer to hold someone's heavy equipment (such as children or chickens), but if

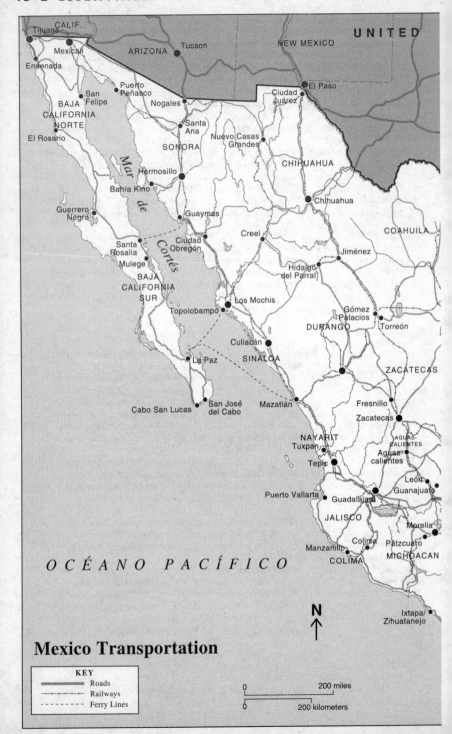

Mexico Transportation

KEY

——— Roads

+—+—+—+ Railways

- - - - Ferry Lines

0   200 miles

0   200 kilometers

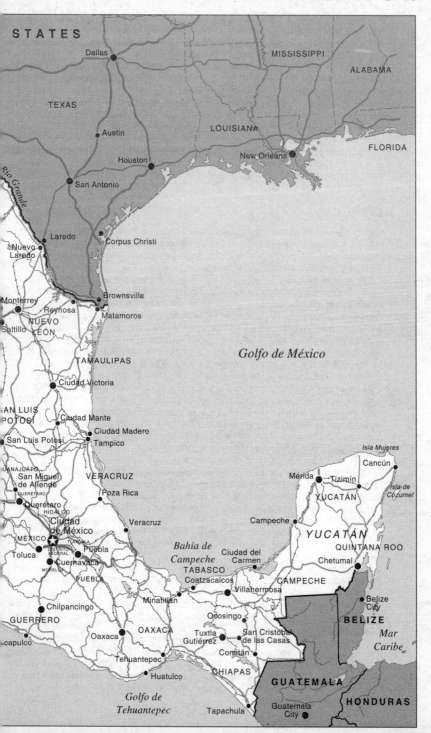

you feel the urge to give up your seat to someone who looks more in need of a rest than you, just envision how much you'll need it in ten hours.

Though prices are now reasonably stable, the schedules fluctuate constantly; check at the station before making travel plans.

Offering an alternative to traditional bus travel, **Green Tortoise (G.T.)** maintains a fleet of old diesel coaches with foam mattresses, sofa seats, and dinettes, and their self-proclaimed mission is to go where no bus has gone before. G.T. trips roam all over the Mexican mainland, the Baja, and Belize for two to five weeks at a time. Prices average about US$250 per week and include use of the bus at night for sleeping as well as tours of the pertinent regions. Travelers pitch in about US$5.50 a day for communal meals. If a tour isn't full, passengers can abort the program at any point and only pay for the portion they have traveled. During summer months, tours may fill up four to six weeks in advance, so book ahead. Call or write Green Tortoise, P.O. Box 24459, San Francisco, CA 94124 (tel. (800) 227-4766, in CA (415) 821-0803).

■ By Car

Mexican roads vary from smooth turnpikes (with tolls that cost more than gas) to rutted, mountain roads used by trucks for bombing runs. Mexican drivers are just as disparate: some believe that driving over 40km per hour constitutes dangerous folly, while others employ folly as their navigational credo.

The maximum speed on Mexican highways is 100km per hour (62mph) unless otherwise posted. Speed limits can be frustratingly low. In most small towns, you'll come across speed bumps. Usually one slows traffic on each side of town, and another perches right in the middle. Roadwork is continually in progress across Mexico; you will regularly drive by construction workers making utterly incomprehensible but codified signals, at which point you should slow down until you figure out what is going on. One particularly confusing signal looks like a plea for you to back up. In fact, it is a request to move forward. In general, take it easy until you master the sign language of Mexican roads.

Be especially careful driving during the rainy season (May-Oct.), when roads are often in poor condition and landslides are common. At night, pedestrians and livestock pop up on the roadway at the darndest times. This doesn't seem to bother the locals, many of whom drive without headlights. If you can help it, don't drive at night. (And whatever you do, never spend the night on the side of the road.) When approaching a one-lane bridge, labeled *puente angosto* or *solo carril*, the first driver to flash headlights has the right of way.

Exercise particular caution when driving along: Highway 15 in the state of Sinaloa; Highway 2 in the vicinity of Carborca, Sonora; Highway 57 between Matehuala and San Luis Potosí; the highway between Palomares and Tuxtepec, Oaxaca; and Highway 40. A number of assaults have occurred on these stretches of pavement. Check with local authorities or the nearest U.S. consulate to update the situation and to identify other areas of potential danger. When driving on roads near the capital, watch out for fog. A sign warning *Maneje despacio* (Drive slow) should be taken seriously.

To help reduce the heinous pollution in Mexico City, tourist traffic in the metropolis is restricted (see Mexico City: Transportation Within Mexico City for details.)

In Baja California, if you want to leave your car and go somewhere by public transportation for a few days, you must pay to park in an authorized lot; otherwise, the car will be towed or confiscated. The Motor Vehicle Office will tell you where to leave your car legally.

When parking in the rest of the country, someone may help you pull into a space. A rhythmic tap-tap, tap-tap on your back bumper means that you still have room to back up. A sharp, sudden tap means stop. When you return to your car and someone informs you that they have been watching it while you were gone, hand them some change. If a group of kids approaches, pay only one of them.

When asking for directions, don't take your high school Spanish for granted. The word you probably learned for "road"—*camino*—means "path" away from the cities. You'll want to stick to *carreteras* (highways).

PEMEX (Petroleos Mexicanos) sells two types of gas: Nova (regular) and Extra (unleaded). Nova (*no va* in Spanish means "doesn't go") is appropriately named, and one whiff of a Nova-burning car will make you realize why emissions controls are so important. Unless your car is old, rugged, and satisfied with low-quality leaded gas, driving it through Mexico is not the brightest idea. Unleaded gas, no longer as hard to get as in years past, is making its presence felt in Mexico. You will find it throughout the Baja as well as in Guadalajara, Monterrey, Mexico City, most border towns, and all major metropolitan areas. But beware: even if you do find a silver Extra pump, it may be filled with Nova gasoline. The Mexican government has introduced two new types of gas, Nova Plus and Extra Plus, but the gasoline situation remains unpredictable. Mechanically inclined drivers might want to order a "test" pipe from a specialty parts house to replace the catalytic converter so the car can process Nova upon its arrival in Mexico.

Both Nova and Extra are extremely cheap by all but Saudi Arabian standards. Don't get overcharged: know how much gas you'll need before you pull in and make sure the register is rung back to zero before pumping begins. PEMEX accepts cash only. When you pull into a PEMEX station to check the tires, remember that pumps in Mexico are calibrated in kilograms (1kg = 2.2 lb.).

The heat, bumpy roads, and fair-to-middling gas may well take a toll on your car. Mexican mechanics are good and charge very reasonable rates, but if they've never seen your model, reconcile yourself to a lengthy stay. Oil is scarce, and parts are available only for those models that Mexicans drive; all the various VWs are in plentiful supply, especially the Beetle (known as the *Vochito*), as are Datsun/Nissans and 1970s Detroit boat-cars. No matter what kind of car you sport, bring spare oil, spark plugs, fan belts and air and fuel filters—these should take care of all but the biggest problems.

If you break down on one of the major highways sometime between dawn and sunset, pull off the road, raise the hood, and wait for an *Angel Verde* (Green Angel) to come to the rescue. **Green Angels** are the Mexican Government Tourism Office's innovation—emergency trucks dispatched by radio, staffed by English-speaking mechanics and equipped for common repair jobs and minor medical problems (radio communications office at tel. (5) 250-48-17). Your green saviors may take a while to show up, but the service (except for parts, gas and oil) is free. They go everywhere but the Distrito Federal.

If you get into a car accident realize that as soon as the police arrive, they will detain everybody until they have figured out what happened, no matter who's to blame, an immense, and unnecessary legal mess. An insurance policy, which demonstrates your ability to pay, will spring you from jail. You may also become liable by coming to the aid of someone hurt in an accident. Leave the area before the police arrive or risk paying a heavy price for your good Samaritanism.

■ By Thumb

> *Let's Go* urges you to use common sense if you decide to hitch, and to seriously consider all possible risks before you make that decision. The information listed below and throughout the book is not intended to recommend hithchiking; *Let's Go* does not recommend hitchhiking as a means of transportation.

You'll see plenty of Mexicans and *gringos* standing by the side of the road with thumbs pointed skyward. Accepting rides from strangers is potentially dangerous, and caution and knowledge can go a long way. If your Spanish or tolerance for local customs is weak, the ordeal may take more out of you than would the extra pesos for a bus.

ACCOMMODATIONS

The Mexicans who pick up tourists are often friendly, often offering meals, tours, or other extras, but equally often suspicion is warranted. Those who hitch find out where the driver is going before they get in, and think twice if he or she opens the door quickly and offers to drive anywhere. Do not accept a ride if any cause for concern arises; make an excuse and wait for another car to come along. Women should not hitchhike alone. Never accept a ride without sizing up the driver. On many highways (the Mexico City-Acapulco road, for example), *bandidos* are common.

Before getting in, make sure the passenger window or door opens from inside. If there are several people in the car, do not sit in the middle. Assume a quick-exit position, which rules out the back seat of a two-door car. Keep backpacks and other baggage where they are easily accessible—don't let the driver store them in the trunk. If you have trouble getting out for any reason, affecting the pose of someone about to vomit works wonders.

Every city and every road has a best and worst spot for hitchhiking. Hitchers reccomend stretches near a major intersection where many cars converge or PEMEX stations. They also reccomend that hitchers should be cautious when standing on the shoulders of highways, since they are not considered off-limits to drivers, and that they should bring along something to drink and some sort of protection from the sun and rain. Furthermore, it is said that those who appear neat and travel light, have a better chance of getting a ride.

Some drivers may ask for payment for the ride, especially in areas where no alternative form of public transportation exists, or when riding in a pickup truck. Truck drivers often earn extra revenue by taking on passengers. As with a taxi, riders should always ask what a ride in a truck will cost before getting in; it may seem expensive, it is usually based on expenses. Those in the know say that cargo trucks are easy to hitch with, but women are often prohibited from riding in trucks by many companies who feel that a nearby female presence would distract the driver.

■■■ ACCOMMODATIONS

■ Hotels

Though hotels in Mexico include some of the world's most overpriced, the majority are shockingly affordable. All hotels, ranging from luxury resorts in Cancún to dumps in Monterrey, are controlled by the government's **Secretaría de Turismo (SecTur)**. SecTur ensures that hotels of similar quality charge similar prices and requires that all hotels display the official tariff sheet. You should always ask to see this sheet if you doubt the quoted price; make sure it is up-to-date. Although hotel prices are regulated, proprietors are not prohibited from charging *less* than the official rate. If the hotel looks like it hasn't seen a customer in several days, a little bargaining may work wonders, especially if you offer to stay a number of days. For a room with one bed, request *un cuarto con una cama*. If bedding down with a fellow way-farer, ask for one *con dos camas* (with two beds).

Usually located within a block or two of the *zócalo* (central plaza), the cheapest hotels (US$4-7) rarely provide private bathrooms or other amenities. Slightly higher-priced hotels (US$9-15) usually reside in the same district but are much better equipped, including rooms with private bathrooms. Before accepting any room, ask to see it—the proprietor should comply gladly. Always ask if the price, no matter how low it seems, includes any meals. Tourists often are so surprised at low hotel prices that unwittingly they forgo meals for which they have paid.

If the hotels listed in *Let's Go* are full or don't appeal to you, ask cab drivers or vendors in the market for a good recommendation. Also, hotel people in one town are often a good source for hotel leads in the next town on your itinerary. For the bare-bones budget traveler, the hammock is the way to go. If you plan to travel on a shoe-string, buy one. Most towns in Mexico are dotted with *palapas*. For a small fee, these open-air restaurants double as places to hang your hat and hammock when the sun goes down. In small *yucateco* towns, locals often let travelers use hammock hooks for a pittance.

Hotels in Mexico often lock their doors at night, and small-town establishments may do so surprisingly early. A locked door doesn't necessarily mean "closed for the night," as someone usually is on duty. By arriving early in small towns or calling ahead if you can't avoid arriving late, and by checking with the hotel desk before going out for a late night on the town, you'll help dispel the Mexican myth of the obnoxious foreigner. If, however, you must choose between angering the hotel guard and sharing the gutter with the drunks and the rats, knock to raise the dead.

Reservations are not absolutely necessary (except during Christmas, Semana Santa, and other festivals), but if you're exhausted upon arrival, they make life much easier. You can just about always find a bed somewhere, but without reservations you may waste money and time.

■ Hostels

Mexican hostels are often run-down, far from town, and no cheaper than local hotels (US$2-10 per night, with meals an additional US$8 per day). The only people who should consider hostelling are younger travelers who want the security and discipline of an orderly establishment with regular meals and nighttime supervision. Their ban on alcohol, smoking restrictions, and limited hours (most are open from 7-9am and 5-10pm) also deter many budget travelers.

Most Mexican hostels will give you a bed even if you don't have a hostel card. They may, however, charge you more for it. If you plan to stay in hostels regularly, get a Hostelling International (HI, formerly International Youth Hostel Federation, IYHF) card (see Useful Addresses: Travel Organizations). For more information, write the Agencia Nacional de Turismo Juvenil, Glorieta del Metro Insurgentes, Local CC-11, Col. Juárez, 06600 México, D.F. (tel. (5) 525-26-99, 525-29-16, 533-12-91, or 525-29-74) for information.

The two Mexican hostel chains, **Consejo Nacional de Recursos para la Atención de la Juventud (CREA)** and **Servicio Educativo de Turismo de los Estudiantes y la Juventud de México (SETEJ)** have their own hostel cards. CREA is the HI-affiliated, government-subsidized hostel chain. SETEJ is internationally subsidized and, in general, the more run-down of the two, though there are exceptions (notably, Acapulco).

For **youth hostel brochures,** write: Asociación Mexicana de Albergues de la Juventud, AC, Av. Francisco 1 Madero No. 6, Despachos 314 y 315, Delegación Cuauhtémoc, 06000 México, D.F., or Red Nacional de Albergues Turísticos, Oxtopulco N. 40, Col. Oxtopulco Universidad, 04310 México, D.F.

For information about the **YMCA** in Mexico, call or write Y's Way International, 224 E. 47th St., New York, NY 10017 (tel. (212) 308-2899).

■ Camping

For the budget travel experience par excellence, try camping in Mexico—it eliminates hotel costs, and if you bring fishing gear to the beach, it can also save you money on food. Campers accustomed to prim and proper campgrounds will be taken aback, however. Mexican national parks often exist only in theory; many are indistinguishable from the surrounding cities. Trails, campgrounds and rangers are strictly *norteamericano* concepts.

Privately owned **trailer parks** are relatively common on major highways—look for signs with a picture of a trailer, or the words *Parque de Trailer, Campamento,* or *Remolques*). These places may or may not allow campers to pitch tents. Don't set up camp next to a well-traveled road, or screeching brakes and the shattering glass of your car may shake you from that peaceful slumber.

The best guide for campers is *The People's Guide to RV Camping in Mexico,* which is an expanded version of the camping section in *The People's Guide to Mexico* (both from John Muir; see Useful Addresses: Publications). The **Sierra Club Bookstore,** 730 Polk St., San Francisco, CA 94109 (tel. (415) 776-2211) offers *Adventuring Along the Gulf of Mexico* (US$10.95 plus $3 shipping, 10% discount for members). For adventure narratives or *Mexico's Volcanoes, A Climbing Guide* (US$12.95), which contains maps, photos, and a bilingual mountaineering glossary, write or call **Mountaineers Books,** 1011 SW Klickitat Way, #107, Seattle, WA 98134 (tel. (800) 553-4453, fax (206) 223-6306). **Wilderness Press,** (see address in Planning Your Trip: Additional Concerns: Traveling With Children) disseminates general backpacking information and publishes outdoor guides such as the *Baja Adventure Book* (US$19.95) and *Adventure Travel in Latin America* (US$12.95), which includes Mexico.

For information on hostel-affiliated campgrounds, write to Agencia Nacional de Turismo Juvenil (see Hostels).

LIFE AND TIMES

■ History

Indigenous Civilizations

Human history in Mexico began 30,000-40,000 years ago, with the migration from Asia of the people a disoriented Columbus would later call "Indians." During the first epoch of *indígena* history, known as the Archaic Period (5000-1500 BC), nomads began to shift their means of subsistence. As animal populations thinned out, roaming hunters turned to a more sedentary, agricultural existence. Their main crop, *maíz* (corn), remains a staple of the Mexican diet.

The **Olmecs** formed what is believed to be Mexico's first settled society around 1200BC, in the lowlands of today's Veracruz and Tabasco. The dominant culture during the Pre-Classical Period (1500BC-300 AD), the Olmecs built the cities now known as La Venta, San Lorenzo and Tres Zapotes. Their original inhabitants revered the jaguar, wrote in hieroglyphics and sculpted giant stone figures. San Lorenzo was violently destroyed around 900 BC, and La Venta suffered a similar fate before another four centuries had elapsed. While the Olmecs perished, many of their cultural achievements were transmitted to other Mesoamerican peoples, notably the **Maya.**

The genius of the Maya stands in the remains of their ancient cities: Palenque, Chichén Itzá, Uxmal, Tulum, Bonampak. During the first 300 years of the Mexican Classic Period (300-900 AD), the Maya came to rival and often better contemporary Europe in engineering, mathematics, astronomy, and calendrical calculations. Their architecture and artwork are similarly fabulous.

Around 900 AD, however, the Mayan empire mysteriously collapsed; widespread peasant revolts are one proposed culprit. A Mayan renaissance occurred in the northern Yucatán after 1200 AD, but with a new influence from the west—Teotihuacán culture, as elaborated by the **Toltecs**. Parallel Maya/Toltec legends tell how Quetzalcóatl (The Feathered Serpent), a great Toltec king, broke away from the Toltec empire and made his way to the Yucatán with his people; the myths predict his eventual return.

The Toltec empire dominated most of central Mexico during the Post-Classic Period (900-1540 AD). Its warlike subjects practiced human sacrifice and, like the Olmecs, placed the jaguar at the center of their iconography. The cultural hegemony of the Toltecs was such that their decline in the 12th century AD has been compared, in catastrophic significance, to the fall of the Roman Empire. The Aztecs, also known as the Tenochca or the Mexica, came into contact with the Toltecs from their mythical homeland in northwestern Mexico; the perished Toltec culture would provide the framework for the Aztec civilization, next to forge an empire. Their dominance would crumble only with the Spanish Conquest. After the fall of the Toltecs, they wandered hither and thither from the end of the 12th century until 1325, when at the southwestern border of Lake Texcoco they beheld an eagle with a serpent in its talons. This would be the site of their legendary floating city **Tenochtitlán.**

The Aztecs practiced a religion derived from their Toltec predecessors; they worshipped a supreme being, the aggregate force of numerous deities. The chief Aztec deity was the war-like Huitzilopochtli, the personification of the sun. According to legend, he perished red and sated every evening only to be reborn anemic the following dawn, craving the blood of human victims. In contrast to this solar vampire, Quetzalcóatl, the god of the air, instructed the natives in the use of metals, in agriculture, and in the art of government. He was thought to have been light-skinned with dark hair and a long flowing beard. When Cortés arrived, he was mistaken for this beloved Aztec deity by an insecure and mystical emperor Moctezuma II—an error which would prove costly.

The Aztecs practiced human sacrifice on a large scale. In the yearly offering to Tezcatlipoca, the god of honor, the most attractive youth in the land was selected to live like a king for eleven months and then, stripped of his lavish accoutrements, to part with his heart at the hands of the head-priest and master of ceremonies.

The Aztecs built Mexico's largest *indígena* empire; their penchant for sanguinary expansion helped secure a dominion stretching from the Atlantic to the Pacific and all the way to Guatemala and Nicaragua. The beauty and architectural sophistication of the island city Tenochtitlán, connected to the mainland by a network of canals and causeways, led Western chroniclers to compare it to the fabulous cities of their chivalric romance tales and to dub it the Venice of the New World. *Chinampas*, or "floating gardens," enabled the Aztecs to cultivate the swamp efficiently. Tenochtitlán developed into one of the world's largest cities.

Conquest and Colonization

In 1519, the Spanish arrived on the east coast of Mexico, in what is now the state of Tabasco, prepared to carry out a campaign that would become the tragic foundation of the Mexican nation. Where Cortés passed, history ended and began over again.

His men disembarked from what natives saw as "floating castles" and were carrying "fire-breathing" weapons. They were lavished with gold and other gifts by awed local chieftains. Mexican natives may have believed Cortés to be the returning Quetzalcóatl, who had departed from his devotees after mysteriously incurring the wrath of the gods. Dressed in his snakeskin wizard suit, Quetzalcóatl had embarked on an ocean voyage declaring that he and his descendants would one day return. This myth of a future return would ultimately accelerate the Spanish victory. Moctezuma II felt bound to receive the explorers as gods. He presented them with the ancient treasures of the errant deity.

Pushing on toward Tenochtitlán, the *conquistadores* capitalized on the Aztec empire's lack of cohesion. Defeated inhabitants of a domain held together by sheer force, conquered tribes hated their Aztec overlords. With the help of an Aztec mistress and interpreter known to the Spanish as Doña Marina (or Malinche), Cortés recruited armies of disaffected *indígenas*. By November, the Spanish had reached Tenochtitlán. An initial period of peaceful, if tense, relations quickly soured, and Cortés was driven from the city in a rout. An incredible string of coincidences and luck let Cortés regroup quickly, and two years later, on August 13, 1521, the Aztec capital fell for good. The Spanish erected a cathedral atop the rubble of the temple to the Aztec war-god, ironically dedicating it to their own patron of war, Santiago. Modern-day Mexico City sprawls over the ruins of Tenochtitlán.

Cortés became the first governor-general of the vanquished Aztec empire, renaming it *Nueva España*. As the conquistadors searched for gold to mine and missionaries searched for *indígenas* to convert, the colony expanded northward and southward, but power remained concentrated. The ruling class of New Spain—a few bureaucrats, landowners, and religious officials—lived comfortably while the *encomienda* system made virtual slaves out of the native population who worked the estates and mines. Two-thirds of the *indígena* population died of European diseases.

Meanwhile, the Catholic church was amassing real estate and capital. Religious and economic exploitation were the girders of Spanish-dominated Mexico. Economic disparity gave birth to political tension, and the 18th century saw the decline of Spanish colonial rule. As the peasants struggled under the brunt of imperialism, absentee rule heated the revolutionary kettle. *Criollos*—those of Spanish blood born in the New World—particularly resented the privileges of the displaced Spanish aristocracy, or *peninsulares*. Approximately 300 years after Hernán Cortés won the Aztec empire for the monarch of Spain, Mexico began to reconsider its allegiance to the mother country.

Sporadic rebellion took place during the first few years of the 19th century. Mexico celebrates its independence on September 16 to commemorate the 1810 uprising known as *El Grito de Dolores* (The Cry of Dolores), when **Padre Miguel Hidalgo y Costilla** roused the villagers of Dolores with a cry for racial equality, land reform and—in a bid for moderate support—an end to the rule of those Spanish who had acquiesced to the conqueror Napoleon. The revolt gained in violence and momentum as it approached Mexico City but subsided before reaching the capital. Hidalgo ordered a retreat but was captured and shot in July of 1811.

The cause was then taken up by **José María Morelos y Pavón**, a parish priest committed less to social justice and more to outright independence than Hidalgo had been. Rebellion swept through southern Mexico but lost much of its effectiveness after Morelos was executed in December of 1815. Only scattered bands of insurgents remained.

Mexican independence finally came about by default. Ferdinand had regained the Spanish crown but in 1820 was pressured into approving the Constitution of Cádiz, a document too liberal to suit the rich *criollos* and *peninsulares* of Mexico. **Agustín de Iturbide,** the general who had led the Spanish against Hidalgo and Morelos, suddenly joined forces with the rebels in hopes of maintaining the precarious status quo. Their combined Army of Three Guarantees declared the fight for independence, union, and Roman Catholicism; shortly thereafter the viceroy of New Spain signed the Treaty of Córdoba. By August 24, 1821, Mexico was officially a nation.

Independence

Iturbide reigned as Emperor Agustín of Mexico for about a year, until discontented military groups persuaded him to abdicate. A constitutional convention proclaimed the Republic of Mexico in 1823. For the next 50 years, the landed gentry, the military, and the church pursued contradictory interests in the public domain. Mexico had no experience with self-government, and a capricious economy contributed to the political instability. The national debt grew enormous. If military salaries were not paid in full, officers would simply seize control of the state and negotiate new international loans at ever-higher interest. Mexico was independent, but socio-economic conditions did not reflect the change. The *criollo* elite took over right where their predecessors had left off, while most *indígenas* and mestizos continued to live in abject poverty.

Political power swung back and forth between conservative and liberal factions for decades after the establishment of the Republic, but the spotlight singled out one man. Of the 50 governments that cluttered the first 30 years of Mexico's independence, fully 11 were headed by **General Antonio López de Santa Ana.** Corruption, greed, and a touch of the bizarre marked Santa Ana's tenure.

Santa Ana is best known, however, for having presided over the dismemberment of the new nation. The Mexican-American War began in 1836 as a border dispute between Mexico and the Republic of Texas, but when the U.S. annexed Texas in 1845, Mexico found itself up against a more formidable adversary. Despite the protests of Abraham Lincoln and other pacifist politicians, President James K. Polk claimed everything north of the Río Grande for the U.S. In pursuit of Santa Ana, Generals Zachary Taylor and Winfield Scott closed in on Mexico City from the north and east. Young cadets, the *Niños Héroes* (Boy Heroes), valiantly fought off U.S. troops from their military school in Chapultepec Castle, then, wrapped in the Mexican flag, dashed themselves to their deaths when all hope was lost. The war ended in 1847 when the capital fell. Under the terms of the Treaty of Guadalupe-Hidalgo, the U.S. paid US$15 million for Texas, New Mexico and California. Five years later, Santa Ana sold off Arizona as well. Mexico lost half of its territory and most of its pride in the war, and the U.S. inherited states rich with Mexican culture.

Reform

The uniquely "Mexican" self-consciousness that had evolved since independence was shaken by the ease of the U.S. victory. Reforms had to be instituted for Mexico to remain autonomous. **Benito Juárez,** an expatriate *indígena* lawyer, wrote the Constitution of 1857 in New Orleans. He and his fellow liberals called for a clean break with colonialism and for the separation of church and state. In 1860, after a short civil war between the liberals (supported by U.S. President James Buchanan) and the ruling conservatives, Juárez became president of Mexico. Ironically, Mexico's first *indígena* president would exhibit little concern for the native population, which was actually worse off than it had been under the paternalism of the Spanish crown.

Three years later, the country was once again in foreign hands. Under the pretext of enforcing debt payment, the French invaded and conquered Mexico, which was an integral part of the "Latin League" envisioned by Napoleon III. Austrian **Duke Maximilian von Habsburg** became the new emperor of Mexico but did not prove equal to the job. The second empire collapsed when the French withdrew their support in order to counter a Prussian threat across the ocean. Maximilian was executed in 1867, and Juárez resumed office until a heart attack in 1872.

Mexico began to modernize under Juárez, but it was **General Porfirio Díaz** who truly ushered Mexico into the industrial age. Díaz took power through a military coup in 1876, and his dictatorship (known as the *Porfiriato*) lasted until 1911. A scientific positivist, Díaz demanded order and progress at the cost of liberty. His administrative method was simply stated: *pan o palo* (bread or the stick). The press was censored, the congress stultified, elections rigged, and resistance crushed. The economy stabilized, but the country's resources were controlled entirely by a handful of wealthy Mexicans and foreign investors. None of the material prosperity trickled down to workers, peasants, or *indígenas*. Díaz retained control of Mexico for so long possibly because his reign brought peace and progress (of a sort) to a country which had known little of either since independence. Though Díaz did not actually abolish the reforms instituted by Juárez, by the early 1900s, a majority of Mexicans opposed the oppressive *Porfiriato*.

Revolution

Díaz's announcement in 1908 that he would not run for office in the next "election" touched off a frenzy of political activity as the *anti-reeleccionistas* campaigned for their candidate **Francisco Madero,** a wealthy landowner. A sham election returned Díaz to the presidency, and in June of 1910, Madero was arrested. Although he escaped in October, imprisonment turned out to be a step on the road to Madero's martyrdom. Opposition to the *Porfiriato* coalesced around him. From exile in San Antonio, Madero declared November 20 to be the day that Mexicans would rise in arms. Begun as a contest for executive power, the revolution ballooned into an economic and social struggle over who would mold the face of modern Mexico.

Díaz did not fare well over the next year. He resigned in 1911 and Madero was elected president. The notorious leaders of the revolution—**Emiliano Zapata, Pancho Villa,** and **Venustiano Carranza**—bickered and plotted as Madero pursued a moderate course. Rebellions plagued Madero's administration until the day he was murdered. His successor, **Victoriano Huerta,** came from the ranks of his own army.

The years that followed were characterized by political chaos and infighting among former revolutionary allies. When the dust cleared, the moderate Carranza, who had been endorsed by the U.S., governed Mexico under a somewhat radical constitution that he was disinclined to enforce. This Constitution of 1917 nominally guaranteed free secular education, restored land to peasants, limited property accumulation, instituted a 48-hour work week and a minimum wage, and established equal rights for women and workers. The Constitution derived its anti-clericalism from Juárez's 1857 document. It prevented the church from owning land, including temples of worship, and banned priests from wearing cassocks in public. Religious publications were prohibited from commenting on political matters. This civil attack on the church stemmed from the dominance of religion in earlier Mexican politics.

One out of every eight Mexicans was killed during the revolution, and very few were left unaffected by the violence. Zapata and many other Mexicans were dissatisfied with the sluggish progress of reform under Carranza and continued to fight, but by 1920 they had all been bought off or murdered. A brief series of dictators carried Mexico to new dimensions of repression.

Post-Revolutionary Mexico

Champions of radical reform came into power once again when **Lázaro Cárdenas** was elected president in 1934. His government started to fulfill some of the promises of the Constitution of 1917, seizing 49 million acres of land from private owners and distributing it among *ejidos* (communal cooperative farms). He strengthened the labor movement and nationalized the oil companies that had been controlled by foreign countries since the *Porfiriato*, in a crucial step toward economic independence that was widely protested by U.S. oil interests.

The modern feminist movement in Mexico took off during Cárdenas's administration. The United Front for Women's Rights, organized in 1935, had 50,000 members by 1940. Mexican women finally won the right to vote in 1955.

The administrations following that of Cárdenas were conservative and business-oriented. The economy boomed, but most urban and rural workers still suffered from low wages and underemployment. Wary of uprisings, the government began to buy off both workers and landowners with subsidies on everything from tortillas to gasoline. As population growth began to accelerate, the economy weakened and Mexico had to turn to foreign nations for loans again.

In the early 1960s, President **Adolfo López Mateos** further damaged the budget by spending billions of pesos setting up various social welfare programs and redistributing land. Mexico's one-party system received increasing criticism, but the **Institutional Revolutionary Party (PRI)** retained tight control over Mexican politics. Student unrest and worker dissatisfaction in these years culminated in 1968 at Mexico City's Tlatelolco Plaza, where police killed an estimated 300 to 400 peaceful demonstrators just 10 days before the Olympic Games were to open.

Protest subsided in the following years, but other problems have marred more recent administrations, among them large budget deficits, high unemployment, burgeoning population, lagging agricultural production, high inflation, rapid devaluation of the peso, and persistent corruption. Enormous economic disparity has persisted, despite the influx of petrodollars from oil exports.

Under President **Miguel de la Madrid Hurtado,** elected in 1982, the economy rebounded slightly, but, under pressure from the International Monetary Fund, the administration initiated an austerity program to curtail the country's 150% inflation and US$104 billion foreign debt. Between January and October of 1988, the rate of inflation fell drastically, but the economy's growth rate remained at zero during de la Madrid's six-year term.

Current Politics

"The era of one-party rule in Mexico is over," declared PRI presidential candidate **Carlos Salinas de Gortari** during the tense week following the 1988 presidential elections. Salinas officially (and conveniently) received 50.4% of the vote when the final contested results were announced, but many interpreted his remarks and the election itself as a fresh start for Mexican politics.

From 1929 to 1988, Mexico's ruling party did not lose a single presidential, senatorial, or gubernatorial race. In the few local elections that it did lose, the PRI often installed its own candidates anyway. Through a combination of patronage, fraud and ineffectual opposition, the party ran Mexico like a political machine. But in the 1982 election, the murmurs of dissent were heard, and the right-of-center **National Action Party (PAN)** won 14% of the vote, most of it in the northern states. In 1983, the PRI experimented with fraud-free elections, and the PAN picked up three mayorships in the state of Chihuahua alone.

In October of 1989, PRI and PAN voted together for the first time in favor of electoral reform, and the government launched investigations into other kinds of political corruption. The PAN finally broke the PRI stranglehold on national office in the same year, when the first non-PRI state governor was elected in Baja California Norte. Chihuahua followed suit in 1992, electing a PAN governor by a large (and officially acknowledged) margin, even amid charges of pro-PRI fraud.

When Salinas, a Harvard graduate, began his six-year term as president on December 1, 1988, he had to confront high unemployment, a US$105 billion foreign debt, the domestic production and transport of drugs, and a skeptical nation. Salinas instituted wage and price controls to keep inflation down, then boosted his popularity with several prominent arrests of a union boss, a fraudulent businessman, and a drug trafficker.

On February 4, 1990, representatives of the Mexican government and its 450 foreign commercial creditors signed a debt reduction agreement designed to ease the U.S. banking crisis and deflect outlandishly high interest payments. This reprieve, along with Salinas's austerity program, has led to growing foreign investment and steady growth (3% a year) in Mexico's gross domestic product. Inflation has stuck at 16-22%, however, and unemployment remains near 20%. Reduced or not, foreign debt has continued to suck capital out of the country, and a blossoming trade deficit is squeezing out small and medium businesses as foreign franchises move in.

The fate of these smaller firms was at the center of the controversial North American Free Trade Agreement (NAFTA), concluded August 12, 1992. When approved by the legislatures of the U.S., Canada and Mexico, the treaty will eliminate the tariffs, quotas, and subsidies that have protected Mexican industry and agriculture since the 1940s. It will also open up Mexican banking, insurance and securities industries to U.S. and Canadian competition by the year 2000. U.S. unions oppose the pact because they fear the loss of factories and jobs to low-wage competition in Mexico, where workers earn one-tenth as much as U.S. union labor. *Maquiladora* plants, the North American-owned assembly and automotive-sector factories, have already begun to both squeeze Mexican-owned smaller businesses and wreak havoc on the environment and health conditions in the towns which surround them.

In 1991, PRI technocrats dismantled the *ejido* system, which ostensibly guaranteed communal land rights for rural *campesinos*. With this constitutional reform and other changes, including rapid privitization, an agrarian culture thousands of years old is being phased out to pave the way for industrialism. Traditional support systems are lost in urbanization while government safety nets are eliminated, all part of an economic streamlining backed by the U.S. and international lenders. The costs of this structural adjustment program (centered around NAFTA) have yet to be determined, but fall heavily on the lower classes in the meantime, while the benefits loom on the long-term horizon.

■ The Arts

Literature

The literary tradition in Mexico begins with the *indígenas*, but little of their literature escaped the fervor of early Spanish missionaries' bonfires. The oral tradition has bequeathed upon the modern student many examples of Aztec poetry, however, which sound surprisingly contemporary and exhibit considerable artistic self-consciousness. Miguel León Portilla's *Visión de los vencidos* (The Vision of the Conquered, translated in *The Broken Spears*) is a fascinating collection of the *indígena* prose and poetry that did survive to show the other side of the Conquest. The best European account of contact is the remarkable prose work *Verdadera historia de la conquista de Nueva España* (The True History of the Conquest of New Spain) by Bernal Díaz de Castillo, a soldier under Cortés who took pride in the American experience without glorifying it excessively.

Colonial Mexico produced more poetry than prose, leading one 16th-century dramatist to observe that there were "more poets than dung" in New Spain. Most merely imitated the latest European styles. One notable exception came on the scene in the 17th century; **Sor Juana Inés de la Cruz,** an early feminist who became a nun in order to make time for intellectual pursuits, wrote such poems as "Hombres Necios" (Silly Men) and "Primero Sueño" (First Dream). "Primero Sueño," a mystical visionary poem, is considered a masterpiece of the Golden Age on both sides of the Atlantic.

During the 18th century, the Inquisition vied with the French Enlightenment to distract Mexican writers from anything that could be described as innovative. In 1816, **José Fernández de Lizardi,** a prominent Mexican journalist, wrote the first Latin American novel: *El Periquillo Sarmiento* (The Itching Parrot). With the

Spanish-American Modernists of the later 19th century, poetry reached an affective level it had not even approached since Sor Juana.

As discontent spread in the early 20th century, the group called **Anteneo de la Juventud** dissolved genres in the name of socio-political revolution. For the most part, however, intellectuals kept their distance from the revolutionary arena. After the fact, many witnesses took up their pens. **Mariano Azuela's** Los de abajo (The Lowly Ones) conveys extreme disillusionment in a rural dialect. Other novels of this period include El águila y la serpiente (The Eagle and the Serpent) by **Martín Luis Guzmán** and El resplandor (Sunburst) by **Mauricio Magdaleno.** Juan Rulfo's Pedro Páramo, set in rural Jalisco, blurs the line between life and death and between past and present in relating one man's allegoric search for his father and is seen as the beginning of magical realistic boom which would later hit the continent.

Mexican literature in the post-revolutionary era is marked by a frustrated desire to forge a national tradition from the vestiges of pre-colonial culture. **Octavio Paz,** in such works as El laberinto de la soledad (The Labyrinth of Solitude), draws on Marxism, Romanticism and post-Modernism to explore the making and unmaking of a national archetype. Paz, like his more famous successor **Carlos Fuentes,** concerns himself with stuff of myth and legend in an effort to come to terms with Spanish cultural dominance. Fuentes, Mexico's most celebrated author and one-time Harvard professor, published his first novel, La región más transparente, in 1958. His latest novel, Cristóbal nonato (Christopher Unborn), chronicles the lengthy search for a god-head who will accurately and unproblematically personify the true spirit of the Mexican people.

Since the "boom," Mexican literature has become even more pluralistic and serves an ever-growing pool of readers. Western prototypes retain their fascination for writers and readers alike, as is evidenced by the wildly popular work of **Gustavo Sainz** and **José Agustín,** the instigators of literatura de la onda ("hip" literature). On the other hand, **Luis Spota,** one of Mexico's most widely read authors, restricts himself to Mexican themes and boasts, as a result, international anonymity.

Art and Architecture

Early indígena art, like Western art, was devoted to the sacred. The colonial period favored stilted European imitation, but the revolution instilled a sense of nationalism and resuscitated native styles, now informed by modern themes.

Fortunately, this revival is well-supplied with indígena prototypes. The Olmecs carved altars and monumental heads out of stone. In western Mexico, the Tarascan people embellished funereal accessories with motifs from daily life. Mayan sculptors excelled at well-proportioned nudes, and the Aztecs imbued enormous figures with both strength and grace.

Much of Mexico's pictorial tradition, however, is attached to buildings. Mayan architecture was richly ornamented in relief, but the Aztecs were the greatest in this field. The monuments and pyramids at **Teotihuacán** put Egypt's stolid emphasis on engineering to shame. Architecture became the province of the church once the Spaniards arrived, and some native flourishes on the portals and altars notwithstanding, Old World structures were essentially transplanted onto Mexican soil. Ever since, Mexican architecture has struggled to keep up with European styles and thus has neglected to forge its own character. The closest thing to a Mexican architectural movement, though technically imported from Spain, was the **Churriguer-esque**—baroque carried to an extreme.

During the Porfiriato, the **National Academy of San Carlos,** established in 1785, dominated the artistic community. Most Mexican artists rejected the Spanish influence of the 17th and 18th centuries by producing down-to-earth portrayals of indígena life. Among these artists was **Dr. Atl** (Gerardo Murillo), whose pseudonym is the Nahuatl word for water.

As the Revolution reduced their land to shambles, Mexican painters developed an unapologetic national style. This success was made possible by José Vasconcelos's

Ministry of Education program, which commissioned murals for public buildings and sent artists into the countryside to teach and participate in rural life.

The Mexican **mural,** unequivocally nationalistic in its current form, ironically dates back to the early days of the conquest when Catholic evangelists, fighting the language barrier, used allegorical murals to impart the rudiments of Christian iconography. Among the famous muralists to have worked in the formative years of the revolution, **Diego Rivera** has achieved the most renown. His murals at the Detroit Institute of Arts and the Rockefeller Center in New York City exposed his political themes—land reform and Marxism—to a wide audience and embroiled him in international controversy. The two other prominent muralists of the 1920s and 1930s, **David Alfaro Siqueiros** and **José Clemente Orozco**, also had disciples outside Mexico. The formally innovative Siqueiros could not resist a curved surface. Orozco focused on the violence and brutality of the Revolution, but was less explicitly political than his colleagues. In his work, the mythic dimension of human history and existence prevails.

The therapeutic role of art receives its most eloquent testimony, however, in the life and work of **Frida Kahlo** (1907-54). Partially paralyzed in a traumatic bus accident at the age of 18, Kahlo married Diego Rivera and was welcomed by Andre Breton into the Surrealist fold of the 1930s. Her paintings and self-portraits are icons of pain: red smudges on the frame of *A Few Small Nips* project the bed-ridden, writhing body from the canvas out into the world. The Museo Frida Kahlo is in her childhood home, Coyoacán, a part of Mexico City.

Film

Mexican film-making began in 1917 and reached its peak in the 1940s. Ex-actor Emilio Fernández won the *Palme D'Or* at the 1943 Cannes Film Festival for his *María Candelaria* and two years later directed *La Perla*, an adaptation of John Steinbeck's novel. Together with legendary cinematographer Gabriel Figueroa, who had studied in Hollywood, Fernández forged the classic image of Mexico: polychrome skies, ornate architecture, and interiors geometricized by beams of light. Thereafter the Mexican film industry went into decline. Poorly financed film-makers suffered in competition with the U.S. and fell back on low-budget pop formulas. Most recently, the magical realism of *Como Agua para Chocolate* ("Like Water for Chocolate") by Esquível Laura, provides a surreal and beautiful portrait through its fantastical romance set in northern Mexico.

Music

Experts know that music played an important role in pre-Conquest *indígena* daily life—but little more. Dancing was a central religious ritual. High-pitched, thin voices were cultivated for their associations with metallic gold and the roar of the jaguar.

The Spanish introduced their own instruments, lyrics and rhythms to Mexico. Music contributed to the conversion of the native population to Christianity and thus contributed materially to the Conquest. The arrival of African slaves and contact with the Caribbean added another musical strain, especially in the Gulf region. In this fertile atmosphere, percussion and syncopation formed the basis for *marimba* music.

Just as music had been used to subdue them, Mexicans used music to regain their autonomy. The *jarabe* exhibition dance was frequently banned during Mexico's last years as a colony and rallied would-be dancers behind the cause. The *corrido*, a narrative ballad, played a similar role during the Revolution, when insurgents sang news to each other to boost morale.

Apart from José Cuervo and the sombrero, the most persistent emblems of Mexico are the *mariachis*, who started out as ragtag groups of farmers singing at country gatherings in Guadalajara. Along with the hat dance—another Guadalajara product—the *mariachi* craze swept across the country. By the 1920s, many were touring Mexico, and as radio became a greater social force in Mexico, *mariachi* music adapted to the times.

■ Food and Drink

Mexicans wait until between 2 and 4pm for the *comida*, the largest meal of the day, often an elaborate banquet of several courses. *Comida corrida* or *corriente*, served at most Mexican restaurants, is a multi-course *à la carte* meal. *Cena* (dinner) is a light meal served after 8pm.

Mexican cuisine is the product of an *indígena* heritage enriched by Spanish and, to a lesser degree, French practices. The enormous variety of Mexican dishes is due in part to the wide range of herbs and spices native to Mexico—including over 60 types of chile peppers. Contrary to stereotype, not all Mexican food is hot. Often *salsas picantes* (hot sauces) are served on the side, so whether to scorch your palate or not is your decision.

Corn is the staple of Mexican existence, and it appears most frequently in tortilla form. An Aztec creation, the **tortilla** is a soft, thin patty, served at nearly every meal. Wrap anything on your plate—meat, cheese, beans—in a tortilla to make a **burrito. Enchiladas** are tortillas dipped in sauce, filled and fried. **Tostadas** are fried tortillas topped with vegetables, meat, and cheese. **Tamales,** made out of a ground-corn dough, are fried in corn husks and have the consistency of thick dumplings. Beans will appear on your table almost as often as tortillas. **Frijoles fritos** (refried beans) are a popular variety.

Avoid overdosing on tacos and try some other Mexican dishes. Pork dishes include **chuletas** (pork chops), **carnitas** (bits of pig meat), and **chicharrones** (fried pig skins). **Barbacoa** is lamb that has been covered with *maguey* leaves and buried beneath a fire. **Pollo** (chicken) is also common; don't miss out on **pollo con mole. Mole,** one of Mexico's most interesting culinary creations, is a sauce combining over 30 ingredients, including chiles and chocolate (which, along with vanilla, was introduced to the rest of the world by Mexico).

At restaurants, always find out the price of a meal before you order. Many of the smaller eateries don't have a list of prices and might overcharge if you do not ask in advance. Tips run 15% or so.

Strict vegetarians and those keeping kosher may have difficulty outside of Guadalajara and Mexico City. Many Mexican foods, including tamales, some tortillas and many bean dishes, contain lard. (See Specific Concerns: Travelers on Special Diets in Essentials.)

You can sample a tremendous variety of **aguas frescas** (fruit drinks) in Mexico. Beware of *aguas* made with unpurified water. **Licuados** (made with fruit and milk) are less likely to be contaminated. **Mezcal** is distilled from the *maguey* plant: tequila is a famous *mezcal* from Tequila, Jalisco. If you get a chance to sample *pulque*, the fermented juice of the *maguey*, don't hesitate—it was the sacred drink of the Aztec nobility.

México City

"City" is not the word for it: the 522 square miles of urban settlement that line the Valley of Mexico make up far more than one city. The high-efficiency bustle of the executive areas on *Reforma*, the impoverished neighborhoods on the northern outskirts, the commercial coagulation of the *Centro*, and the wealthy southern ultra-suburbs of Coyoacán and San Ángel cohabitate in the omnipresent smog. Shantytowns sprawl out bereft of public support, themselves as large as cities; a sleek slab of bars and boutiques rises up above the city in the tallest tower in the Republic. Mexico City is a breeding ground for staggering statistics: 2000 new residents and 700 million gallons of water go in every day; 12,000 tons of air pollution come out.

With the simultaneous rising and falling of *indígena* and colonial civilizations, this phoenix-like metropolis contains a plurality of cities, and no one can decide upon a single significance for any single structure. The massive Templo Mayor is simultaneously a paean to the magnificent Aztec empire of which it was once the capital, and a memorial of the carnal sacrifices the Aztecs staged for the sake of their hungry god Huitzilopochtli. The awe and faith inspired by the grand Catedral Metropolitana struggle eternally with bitter resentment at the economic and cultural imperialism of those who forced the indigenous peoples to build it. A few blocks away stands the Palacio de Bellas Artes, a glorious symbol of modern Mexico built by the Porfiriato dictatorship that also sapped the money of a direly struggling nation. Less than a mile to the west, the Monument to the Revolution, originally intended by Díaz as the spectacular seat of his regime's legislature, reaffirms the democratic freedom of a "new" Mexico, transmogrified by ten long years of bloody battle.

Mexicans call this oxymoronic conglomeration **el D.F.**, short for *Distrito Federal* (Federal District), or simply *México*. It's the second largest population center in the world with more than 20 million people in over 220 *colonias* (neighborhoods). Virtually the entire federal bureaucracy inhabits the Distrito Federal, including the Ministry of the Navy (2240m above sea level). The principal national collections of art, ethnography, and archaeology are also found here; the gargantuan Museo Nacional de Antropología is reason enough for a visit. The Aztec Templo Mayor, prostrated though it is on the altar of the majestic Catedral Metropolitana, still inspires awe. Spectacular mosaics and murals by Rivera, Orozco, Siqueiros, and Tamayo twist and shout on the walls of the city.

While more people are arriving (to live in the narrowest apartment building in the world and to pray in the smallest church), Mexico City's denizens are uncomfortably aware of bad tidings to come. The 1985 quake cast citizens as extras in a geological nightmare that is not necessarily over. As water shortages become increasingly serious, citizens curse the topography of their metropolis: landlocked and ringed by mountains, it lets neither water in nor sewage out. Mexico City's infamous demographic crisis becomes daily more difficult to ignore. Within a decade Mexico City will merge with Puebla, Cuernavaca, Tlaxcala, Pachuca, and Querétaro to form a sprawling megalopolis of 35 million. As formerly food-producing rural migrants flock to the shantytowns on the city's edge and the city expands to engulf their abandoned plots, the prospect of feeding everyone becomes decreasingly realistic.

One-quarter of Mexico's population lives in the D.F., and one-quarter of those are employed as *comerciantes*, the independent vendors which crowd the streets. Both the commerce and life of the city are unabashedly displayed as such—Mexico City has neither the space nor the desire to hide its history, culture, and manic vitality. Even art takes on this massive and external character in the immense and awesome murals which celebrate Mexican life. Here, no one buries the ruined triumphs and fiascoes of the past, nor apologizes for the excesses of the present.

ORIENTATION

■■■ GETTING THERE

Don't worry—all roads really do lead to Mexico City. The many temples of transport include the Benito Juárez International Airport, four main bus stations, a train station, and a network of freeways. Airports and stations in Mexico City nearly always have tourist information booths equipped with free or cheap maps and some sort of referral service to lead you into the *Centro*.

■ By Air

Flying into Mexico City from abroad entails the usual customs and immigration procedures. Tourist cards are distributed on the plane and stamped at the airport. If you fly out of the the D.F. always have about 12-15 pesos or the equivalent in dollars for the airport tax.

The **Benito Juárez International Airport** lies 6.5km east of the *zócalo*, the formal center of the city. Blvd. Capitán Juan Sarabío heads northeast to the airport from Blvd. Puerto Aéreo, one of the major roads circling the city. Airport facilities include: **INFOTUR,** *Sala* A (tel. 571-16-63 or 762-67-73) and *Sala* E (tel. 784-85-53 or 784-89-69), open daily 9am-9pm daily, with information and free maps of the city and the metro; a booth operated by the **Instituto Nacional de Antropología y Historia,** which distributes information about archaeological sites and museums throughout the country (*Sala* A, open Mon.-Sat. 8am-10pm, Sun. 8am-3pm); a **map-and-book store** with novels in Spanish and English (*Sala* C, open Mon.-Sat. 7am-9:30pm, Sun. 8am-8pm); a **pharmacy** (*Sala* C, open daily 6am-10pm); **Banamex, Banco Internaciona,** and **Bancomer** with branches in different *salas* for international currency and traveler's check exchange; **ATMs** in *Salas* A and B; *casas de cambio* (*Salas* B, D, and E), open 6am-10pm; **lockers** (10 pesos per 24 hrs.; 15-44 pesos for larger bags), next to the snack bar in *Sala* A; **post office** (*Sala* A, open for full service Mon.-Fri. 8am-7pm, Sat.-Sun. 9am-5pm); **telegram office** (*Sala* A; open Mon.-Fri. 9am-8pm, Sat.-Sun. 9am-noon). Some magazine booths sell phonecards for the **LADATELs** around the airport; some phones take international credit cards. **Restaurants** and **cafeterias** are open 24 hrs. **Car rental** desks are in *Sala* E (see Getting Around below).

¡Bienvenidos a México! Transportation into the city is uncomplicated. The *venta de boletos* desks in *Sala* A or E will sell you, at an authorized going rate, a ticket presentable to any white and yellow taxi labeled *transporte terrestre* waiting outside. The price is set by which zone of the city you're traveling to (35 pesos to the center, more after hours). Ask to see the map. *Don't* pay cash for a ride from the airport, unless you're willing to pay heavily for the convenience. Call 784-48-11 or 571-36-00 (24 hrs.) to get a taxi back to the airport from the city.

The airport subway station, **Terminal Aérea** (Line 5), located at the junction of Capitán Juan Sarabío and Blvd. Puerto Aéreo, is only a five-minute walk from *Sala* A. The subway is dirt cheap (.40 pesos) but prohibitively inconvenient; no luggage larger than a small suitcase is allowed. If you choose to sneak through the turnstile with your pack, it may be impossible to maneuver through the swarming crowds in the station. Guarding your bags and dealing with fellow passengers irritated by your ungainliness may prove difficult on the crowded trains. Still, the Metro is by far the most convenient and fastest transportation; just avoid the rush hours (see Getting Around below). If returning to the airport by Metro, remember that the airport stop is Terminal Aérea, *not* Aeropuerto.

Travelers driving to *el Centro* should take Blvd. Puerto Aéreo north to Eje 2 Nte. (see Circuito Interior and Ejes Viales under Getting Around below), then Eje 2 Nte.

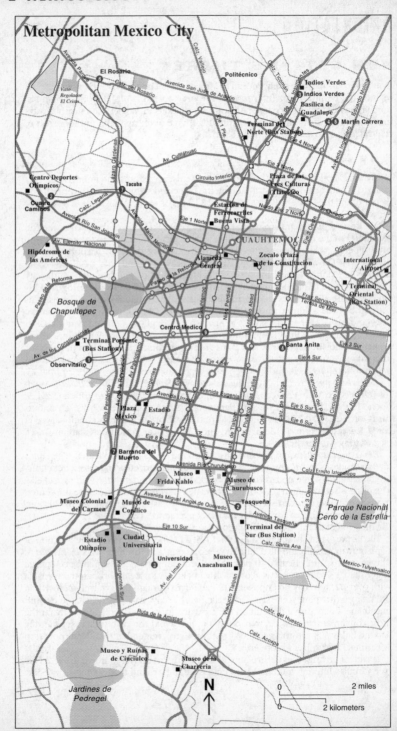

Metropolitan Mexico City

El Rosario

Politécnico

Avenida San Juan de Aragón

Indios Verdes
Indios Verdes
Basílica de
Guadalupe
Martín Carrera

Terminal del
Norte (Bus Station)

Vaso
Regulador
El Cristo

Calz. del Rosario

Centro Deportes
Olímpicos

Tacuba

Av. Cuitláhuac

Circuito Interior

Eje 3 Norte

Plaza de las
Tres Culturas
Tlatelolco

Cuatro
Caminos

Calz. Legaria

Avenida Río San Joaquín

Avenida Marina Nacional

Estación de
Ferrocarriles
Buena Vista

Eje 1 Norte

Eje 2 Norte

CUAUHTEMOC

Av. Ejército Nacional

Hipódromo de
las Américas

Paseo de la Reforma

Alameda
Central

Zócalo (Plaza
de la Constitución)

International
Airport

Oceanía

Bosque de
Chapultepec

Terminal
Oriental
(Bus Station)

Fray Servando
Teresa de Mier

Centro Médico

Av. de los Constituyentes

Terminal Poniente
(Bus Station)

Observatorio

Eje 4 Sur

Santa Anita

Eje 3 Sur

Av. de las Constituyentes

Insurgentes

Avenida Urbina

Avenida Eugenia

Eje 5 Sur

Calz. de la Viga

Francisco del Paso

Circuito Interior

Av. Río Churubusco

Plaza
México

Estadio

Eje 7 Sur

Eje 8 Sur

Eje 6 Sur

Av. Cinco

Barranca
del Muerto

Avenida Río Churubusco

Museo
Frida Kahlo

Museo de
Churubusco

Av. División del Norte

Calz. Ermita Iztapalapa

Eje 3 Oeste

Parque Nacional
Cerro de la Estrella

Museo Colonial
del Carmen

Museo de
Coplico

Avenida Miguel Angel de Quevedo

Tasqueña

Eje 10 Sur

Terminal del
Sur (Bus Station)

Calz. Santa Ana

Estadio
Olímpico

Ciudad
Universitaria

Universidad

Museo
Anacahualli

Mexico-Tulyehualco

Av. del Imán

Insurgentes Sur

Ruta de la Amistad

Calz. del Huesco

Calz. Acoxpa

Museo y Ruinas
de Cuicuilco

Museo de la
Charrería

Jardines de
Pedregal

N

0   2 miles

0   2 kilometers

west to Paseo de la Reforma. A left turn here leads southwest to Juárez or, farther down, to Insurgentes.

Benito Juárez International Airport: Tel. 571-36-00 or 571-34-69, for information on domestic flights dial ext. 2303 or 2258, international ext. 2288.

Domestic Flights: Flight schedules and prices change frequently and seasonally. Prices are roughly the same from airline to airline. There are usually no discounts for students, but always ask about *tarifas promocionales* (some of which may be available to students only) that can save you up to 50% on flights. **Aeroméxico,** Paseo de la Reforma 445 (tel. 207-82-33 for reservations, 762-40-22 for information), close to Mississippi. Also at Reforma 80 (566-1078). Open Mon.-Fri. 9am-6:15pm, Sat. 9am-6pm. At the airport (*Sala* A, tel. 571-18-55), open daily 5am-10pm. Flight information: 762-40-22. Reservations: 228-99-10. (Both daily 6am-10pm.) The following information is incomplete and changes frequently. Prices given are one-way coach fare; round-trip is approximately double. To: Acapulco (9 per day, 254 pesos), Aguascalientes (4 per day, 245 pesos), Cancún (4 per day, 567 pesos), Chihuahua (4 per day, 574 pesos), Guadalajara (13 per day, 229 pesos), Ixtapa-Zihuatanejo (2 per day, 352 pesos), La Paz (3 per day, 807 pesos), Los Mochis (8:30am, 663 pesos), Durango (3 per day, 390 pesos), Hermosillo (6 per day, 655 pesos), Hualtco (1:36pm, 373 pesos), Ciudad Obrégon (2 per day, 735 pesos), Manzanillo (4 per day, 370 pesos), Mazatlán (4 per day, 428 pesos), Mérida (4 per day, 547 pesos), Oaxaca (2 per day, 229 pesos), Puerto Vallarta (4 per day, 437 pesos), Tapachula (2 per day, 388 pesos), Villahermosa (2 per day, 527 pesos). **Mexicana,** Amberes and Reforma 312 (tel. 511-04-24), in the Zona Rosa ; Also Reforma 51 (tel. 592-17-71). Open Mon.-Fri. 9am-6pm. At airport (*Sala* B, tel. 227-22-61) and for reservations 325-09-90. Open daily 6am-10:30pm. Again, prices given are one-way coach. To: Acapulco (5 per day, 217 pesos), Cancún (5 per day, 516 pesos), Cozumel (2 per day, 516 pesos), Guadalajara (11 per day, 241 pesos), Hermosillo (7:35am, 196 pesos), Ixtapa/Zihuatanejo (2 per day, 299 pesos), Los Cabos (10:55am, 559 pesos), Manzanillo (7:50am, 336 pesos), Mazatlán (7:45am or 2:20pm, 439 pesos), Mérida (3 per day, 496 pesos), Monterrey (5 per day, 301 pesos), Puerto Vallarta (3 per day, 396 pesos), Tijuana (5 per day, 683 pesos), Villahermosa (3 per day, 447 pesos), Zacatecas (6:15pm, 241 pesos).

International Flights: Air Canada, Hamburgo 108, 5th floor (tel. 511-20-94); **Air France,** Reforma 404, 15th floor (tel. 627-60-60, 566-00-66), at airport (tel. 571-54-43); **American,** Reforma 300, 1st floor (tel. 399-92-22 or 533-54-46), at airport (tel. 571-34-71); **British Airways,** Escobedo 752, 3rd floor (tel. 525-91-33); **Canadian,** Reforma 390-1402 (tel. 208-16-54); **Continental,** Andrés Bello 45 (tel. 208-34-34), at airport (tel. 571-36-65); **United,** Hamburgo 213, ground floor (tel. 627-02-22); **Delta,** Reforma 381 (tel. 202-16-08), at airport (tel. 571-32-37); **KLM,** Reforma 735, 7th floor (tel. 202-44-44), and at airport (tel. 571-32-46); **Lufthansa,** Reforma 239 (tel. 202-88-66), at airport (tel. 571-27-13); **Swissair,** Hamburgo 213, ground floor (tel. 533-63-63).

■ By Train

The train station **Estación Buenavista** (tel. 547-10-97, open daily 6am-10pm), north of the *Alameda* at the corner of Insurgentes and Mosqueta, inconveniently far from the nearest Metro station, Revolución (Line 2). Taxis leave from the parking lot on the Mosqueta side of the Guerrero station. Be sure to check the meter and the official fare chart in the cab before you pay, as abuses are par for the course.

An **information booth** (tel. 547-10-97 or 547-10-84) in the middle of the train station's main lobby provides schedule and price information. (Open daily 6am-9:30pm.) The station also has a 24-hr. restaurant and a *paquetería* (storage room) for luggage (open daily 6:30am-9pm, 4 pesos per item per day). There are four classes: *primera especial* (reserved, without bed), *dormitorio camarin* (reserved with two separate beds per compartment), *alcoba* (reserved, with bunk bed), *primera general* (unreserved). Though you can buy tickets for first class one month in advance, tickets for anytime other than Semana Santa are usually available up to 1hr. before departure. All trains, regardless of the class, tend to be excruciatingly slow, except for those to Guadalajara, Veracruz, Monterrey (without 2nd class service), and Piedras Negras. Other immensely popular routes from the D.F. to Oaxaca, Yucatán, Ciudad, Juárez, and Nuevo Laredo. Get train information in English from the **Gerencia de Trafico de Pasajeros** in the main station lobby (tel. 547-86-55, fax 547-89-72), open Mon.-Fri. 9am-3pm.

Deluxe 1st-class reserved service: Service daily to: Guadalajara (8:30pm, 12hrs., 71 pesos), Veracruz (9:15pm, 10hrs., 47 pesos), San Luis Potosí (9pm, 8hrs., or 6am, 6hrs.; both 47 pesos), Saltillo (9am, 5hrs., or 6pm, 12hrs.; both 88 pesos), Monterrey (6pm, 14hrs., 100 pesos), Querétaro (7am, 9am, and 8pm, 3½hrs., 27 pesos), Aguascalientes (8pm, 10½hrs., 66 pesos), San Miguel de Allende (9am, 5½hrs., 35 pesos), Oaxaca (7pm, 14hrs., 68 pesos).

2nd-class service: Service daily to: Guadalajara (8:30pm, 12hrs., 18.30 pesos), Oaxaca (7pm, 14hrs., 17.35 pesos), Veracruz (7:45am, 11hrs., or 9:15pm, 10hrs.; both 13 pesos), Querétaro (9am, 4hrs., or 8pm, 3½hrs.; both 7.35 pesos), Aguascalientes (8pm, 10hrs., 17.50 pesos), Zacatecas (8pm, 13½hrs., 20.95 pesos), Chihuahua (8pm, 29½hrs., 48.20 pesos), Ciudad Juárez (8pm, 35 hrs., 58.90 pesos), San Miguel Allende (9am, 5½hrs., 9.65 pesos), San Luis Potosí (9am, 8hrs., 15.05 pesos), Monterrey (9am, 17hrs., 30 pesos), Nuevo Laredo (9am, 22½hrs., 37.95 pesos).

■ By Bus

Mexico City's four main bus stations correspond to the points of the compass. **Central de Autobuses del Norte** (North Station) serves the Bajío, northern Veracruz, Jalisco, and most of northern Mexico; **Central de Autobuses del Poniente** (South Station) launches buses to the states of Morelos and Guerrero; **Terminal de Autobuses de Pasajeros de Oriente (TAPO)** (East Station) runs to Puebla, southern Veracruz, Oaxaca, Chiapas and the Yucatán Peninsula; and the **Terminal Central de Autobuses del Sur** (West Station) serves the states of México and Michoacán.

All stations are served by the Metro and offer an official 24-hr. taxi service that charges fixed rates for a ride to any point in the city (rates set by zones) or adjacent parts of Mexico state. Buy your ticket inside to avoid a ripoff, but be wary of being charged for an extra zone—consult the often nonexistent zone map. *Peseros* (a.k.a. *colectivos*) also serve the four stations. The following listings are by no means comprehensive; given the extensive network, it is possible to go almost anywhere at any time. All ticket sales are final and all seats reserved.

Central de Autobuses del Norte

On Cien Metros (tel. 587-15-52), Metro station Autobuses del Norte (Line 5). 24-hr. restaurant, post office, telegrams office, *casa de cambio,* luggage storage room (small 8 pesos, big 16 pesos per 24 hrs.). More companies than those listed below operate out of this terminal/zoo. They appear in the order they appear from waiting room 1 to 8.

Estrella Blanca (tel. 587-12-19). 1st class to: León (13 per day, 44 pesos), Guanajajuato (14 per day, 45 pesos), Guadalajara (36 per day, 69-82 pesos), Aguascalientes (34 per day, 57-67 pesos), San Luis Potosí (24 daily, 46 pesos), Ciudad Juárez (6 per day, 160 pesos), Poza Rica (24 per day, 33 pesos), Chihuahua (6 per day, 127 pesos), Durango (5 per day, 98 pesos).

Primera Plus (tel. 587-52-22). 1st class to: Gudalajara (34 per day, 77 pesos,; Aguascalientes (12 per day, 62 pesos), León (38 per day, 50 pesos), Irapuato (16 per day, 43 pesos), Manzanillo (13 per day, 35 pesos).

ETN (tel. 368-11-88). 1st class to: Moreila (5 per day, 55 pesos), Querétaro (36 per day, 40 pesos, San Luis Potosí (18 per day, 70 pesos).

Transportes del Norte (tel. 587-54-80). 1st class to: Nuevo Laredo (14 per day, 128 pesos), Monterrey (every 1hr., 100 pesos), Saltillo (9 per day, 92 pesos); Matamoros (6 per day, 112 pesos), San Luis Potosí (11 per day, 46 pesos), Ciudad Juárez (11 per day, 197 pesos), Chihuahua (11 per day, 157 pesos).

Autobuses Blancos (tel. 587-53-23). To: Tijuana (4 per day, 292 pesos), Mexicali (4 per day, 294 pesos), Hermosillo, (4 per day, 220 pesos), Culiacán (4 per day, 146 pesos), Los Mochis (4 per day, 167 pesos), Tampico (7 per day, 69 pesos).

Autobuses del Oriente (ADO) (tel. 567-62-47). To: Tampico (6 per day, 65 pesos), Tuxpan (12 per day, 38 pesos), Tulancingo (12 per day, 17 pesos), and many more.

Tres Estrellas de Oro (tel. 587-57-77). 1st class to: Mazatlán (9 per day, 114 pesos), Los Mochis (10 per day, 167 pesos), Tepic (8 per day, 87 pesos), Tijuana (8 per day, 287 pesos), Mexicali (8 per day, 289 pesos).

Transportes México-Pachuca (tel. 577-74-39). To Pachuca every 5min., 5:45am-11pm, less frequent after 9pm (10 pesos).

Flecha Amarilla, primarily 2nd-class service to Querétaro, Guanajuato, and Jalisco.

Terminal de Autobuses de Pasajeros de Oriente (TAPO)

General Ignacio Zaragoza 200 (tel. 762-59-77), Metro station San Lázaro (Line 1). The finest of bus stations. TAPO services include a 24-hr. restaurant and pharmacy, a branch of the federal tourist office, and lockers (10 pesos). Taxi ticket stand and tourist information booth near the entrance to the Metro station.

ADO (tel. 542-71-92). 1st class to: Puebla (every 15min., 2hrs., 16-20 pesos), Oaxaca (23 per day, 15hrs., 60 pesos), Cancún (3 per day, 27hrs., 194 pesos), Jalapa (9 per day, 5hrs., 39 pesos), Mérida (5 per day, 24hrs., 175 pesos), Palenque (2 per day, 14hrs., 111 pesos), Veracruz (14 per day, 7hrs., 52 pesos), San Andrés Tuxtla (5 per day, 15hrs., 64 pesos), Villahermosa (20 per day, 12hrs., 106 pesos), Campeche (6 per day, 22hrs., 156 pesos), Poza Rica (3 per day, 4½hrs., 32 pesos), Tampico (10pm, 15hrs., 67 pesos), Tuxtla Gutiérrez (2 per day, 13 hrs., 128 pesos), Tuxtepec (5 per day, 11hrs., 59 pesos).

Autobuses Unidos (AU) (tel. 542-42-10). To: Cordoba (37 per day, 35 pesos), Jalapa (32 per day, 32 pesos), Oaxaca (13 per day, 50 pesos), Orizaba (39 per day, 32 pesos), San Andrés Tuxtla (4 per day, 57 pesos), Tuxtepec (9 per day, 48 pesos), Villahermosa (3 per day, 85 pesos), Veracruz (37 per day, 41 pesos).

Autobuses Cristóbal Colón (tel. 542-72-63). 1st class to: San Cristóbal de las Casas (4 per day, 17hrs., 125 pesos), Tuxtla Gutiérrez (6 per day, 116 pesos), Tonalá (3 per day, 105 pesos), Tapachula (6 per day, 116 pesos), Oaxaca (8 per day, 56 pesos).

Estrella Roja (tel. 522-72-00), to Puebla every 5min. between 6am and 9:30pm, daily (2hrs., 18 pesos).

Autotransportes Mexico-Texcoco (tel. 542-20-09). To Tlaxcala (2hrs., 17 pesos), plus many others.

Terminal de Autobuses de Poniente

Av. Sur 122 (tel. 271-00-38), Metro station Observatorio (Line 1). Take a left as you exit the metro station, a market-covered bridge leads to the terminal. Operates mainly second-class routes, mostly slow indirect service. 24-hr. station services include: restaurant, long distance *caseta*, luggage storage (5 pesos for 24 hrs.). Pharmacy (open daily 7am-10pm); post and telegram offices (Mon.-Fri. 8am-5pm, Sat. 8am-1pm). Foodstands, shops, and newpaper stands.

Turismos México-Toluca (tel. 271-14-33). To Toluca (every 5min. 6am-10:30pm, 1½hrs., 9 pesos). Altacomulco (every 15min., 6am-8pm, 2hrs., 14 pesos), El Oro (every 30min., 6:10am-8:10pm, 2hrs., 15 pesos).

Herradura de Plata (tel. 271-03-35). To Morelia (16 per day, 4hrs., 31 pesos), Patzuacaro (11 per day, 5½hrs., 40 pesos).

Autobuses de Occidente (tel. 231-01-00), To: Zamora (13 per day, 40 pesos), Moreila (every 20min., 29 pesos), Patzuacuaro (every 20min, 16 pesos).

Terminal de Autobuses del Sur (Taxqueña)

Taxqueña 1320 (tel. 549-02-57), Metro station Taxqueña (Line 2). Telegrams office (Mon.-Fri. 9am-8pm, Sat. 9am-noon), long-distance *caseta* (daily 7am-9:30pm). LADATELs, tourist agency for hotel reservations in Mexico City, Acapulco, and Mazatlan (daily 7am-9:30pm). 24-hr. cafeteria and pharamacy. Lockers (small 12 pesos, 24 hrs., big 16 pesos, 24 hrs.).

Pullman de Morelos (tel. 549-35-05). 1st class to Cuernavaca (every 5min., 5:30am-10:45pm, 1¼hrs., 12-18 pesos), Topoztlán (20 per day, 1½hrs., 10 pesos).

Estrella de Oro (tel. 549-85-20). 1st class to: Taxco (5 per day, 55 pesos), Acapulco (10 per day, 7hrs., 55 pesos; 8 per day 65 pesos), Ixtapa (4 per day, 90 pesos), Zihuatanejo (7 per day, 90 pesos).

Turi-Star (tel. 689-80-00). 1st class to Iguala (9 per day, 29 pesos), Chilapaucingo (13 per day, 50 pesos), Acapulco (30 per day, 75 pesos).

Estrella Blanca (tel. 689-80-00). 1st class to Cuernavaca (32 per day, 15 pesos).

■ By Car

Several major highways lead into the Federal District from elsewhere and intersect with the Circuito Interior, the highway that rings the city, at which point they continue under assumed names. **Route 57,** from Querétaro and Tepotzotlán, becomes Manuel Ávila Camacho just outside the Circuito. **Route 15,** from Toluca, turns into Reforma as it enters the city. **Route 95,** from Cuernavaca and Acapulco, becomes Insurgentes, which plugs into the Circuito on the south side. **Route 150,** from Puebla and Texcoco, becomes Ignacio Zaragoza, which connects to the Circuito on the east side. **Route 85,** from Pachuca, Teotihuacán, and Texcoco, becomes Insurgentes in the city.

■■■ GEOGRAPHY

Circuito Interior and Ejes Viales

The **Circuito Interior** is a roughly rectangular artery made up of several smaller, connected highways. **Boulevard Puerto Aéreo** forms the upper east side of the box, running north from the airport. As it bends left at the northeast corner of the box and heads west it becomes **Avenida Río Consulado.** Río Consulado turns south and becomes **Calzada Melchor Ocampo.** Ocampo heads south until it intersects Paseo de la Reforma at Bosque de Chapultepec, after which it continues as **Avenida Vasconcelos.** From Vasconcelos, two roads run to the southwest corner of the Circuito at this point. At that point they turn into Av. Río Mixcoac, which becomes **Avenida Río Churubusco,** running east-west. Río Churubusco is the longest and sneakiest of the highways that constitute the Circuito; it continues east, turns north for a while, heads east again, then turns north once more to connect with Blvd. Puerto Aéreo south of the airport to complete the Circuito.

Aside from the large thoroughfares—Insurgentes, Reforma, and Miguel Alemán—a system of **Ejes Viales** (axis roads) conducts the majority of traffic within the Circuito. *Ejes* run one way (except for the bus lanes, which go against traffic). Running east-west, Eje 1 Nte. and Eje 2 Nte. are north of the *zócalo,* while Ejes 2 through 8 Sur run south of it. The numbers increase heading away from the *zócalo.* **Eje Central Lázaro Cárdenas** runs north-south and bisects the box formed by the Circuito. East of it and parallel lie Ejes 1 through 3 Ote., which veer off to the northwest; west of it are Ejes 1 through 3 Pte. Using the Ejes along with the Circuito you can theoretically reach any general area of the city without much delay. The Guía Roji street atlas (40 pesos), entitled *Ciudad de México,* is available at many newsstands, bookstores, and at the airport.

City Center

Huge as Mexico City is, almost everything of interest to visitors lies within the northern half of the area circumscribed by the Circuito Interior. Moreover, many attractions are within easy reach of **Paseo de la Reforma,** the broad thoroughfare that runs southwest-northeast, or **Av. Insurgentes,** the boulevard running roughly north-south through the city; these streets constitute the heart of the Federal District. The **Bosque de Chapultepec,** home to the principal museums of the city, marks the southwestern limit of most tourists' wanderings. From Chapultepec, Reforma proceeds northeast, punctuated by *glorietas* (traffic circles), each with a distinguishing monument in the center, with which one can orient oneself along Reforma's great length. Moving up Reforma from Chapultepec, the *Zona Rosa* area is followed by *Buenavista* (near the Monumento a la Revolucíon), then the *Alameda* and the *Centro* just before the *zócalo.*

The accommodations and food listings for Mexico City are divided according to the four areas which are of most interest to tourists. The area termed the **Centro** contains most of the historic sights and museums, extensive budget accommodations, and lively inexpensive restaurants. This area is bounded by Cárdenas to the west, Uruguay to the south, Correo Mayoto the east, and Rep. de Peru to the north. The area called the **Alameda** contains budget accommodations and many restaurants, and is bounded by Bucareli to the west, Arcos de Belén to the south, Cárdenas to the east and Violeta to the north. The **Monumento a la Revolución Buenavista** area, like the *Alameda*, contains many inexpensive hotels and eateries. It's bounded by Insurgentes Norte to the west, Reforma to the south and east, and Mosqueta to the north. The **Zona Rosa** (Pink Zone) is the capital's most affluent commercial district. It's the neighborhood contained within Reforma to the north and west, Av. Chapultepec to the south, and Insurgentes to the east.

Unlike the streets themselves, names in Mexico City are systematic. **Streets** in a given area generally carry names that are generically related. For example, streets in the *Zona Rosa* are all named after European cities, while the streets directly across Reforma are named after large rivers of the world. North of Chapultepec, streets are named after famous people. One point to remember when looking for street numbers is that they start from zero at the end of the street nearest the main post office (on *Parque Alameda*'s northeast corner) and continue to the border of the next *colonia* (neighborhood), where the street name changes and the addresses start at zero again. Note that different neighborhoods can use the same street name; the 300 Benito Juárez streets in the Mexico City area attest to this tradition of redundancy.

Outlying Districts

Mexico City reaches outward from the *Centro* roughly 20km to the south, 10km to the north, 10km to the west, and 8km to the east. Year after year, the city's boundaries extend hungrily into neighboring cities. Because of the central location of most sights, few travelers venture past the Bosque de Chapultepec on the west, Tlatelolco on the north, the *zócalo* on the east side of the *Centro*, or south past San Ángel and the university. The major southern thoroughfare is Insurgentes Sur, which extends to the southern limit of the city. Metro Line 3 parallels Insurgentes on Cuauhtémoc and then Universidad, ending at Ciudad Universitaria, well before the city's edge. Most sights to the south, including San Ángel, Coyoacán, Ciudad Universitaria and the Pyramid of Cuicuilco, lie near or along Insurgentes. Metro Line 2 runs east of Line 3 and is closer to Xochimilco, one of the few southern sights not along Insurgentes.

Also beyond reach by Metro are the ruins at Teotihuacán, Tenayuca, Acatitlán and the small town of Tepotzlán, all north of the Distrito Federal boundary. These are best reached by bus from the northern station.

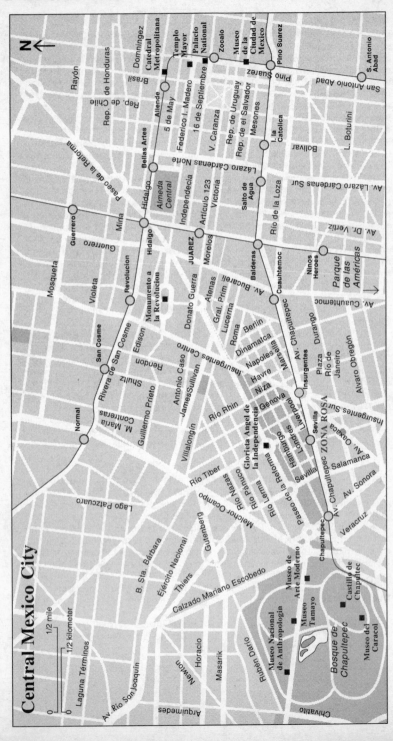

Central Mexico City

■■■ TRANSPORTATION WITHIN MEXICO CITY

The main obstacle to spatial shifts in Mexico City is congestion. Walking sometimes proves as fast as the various other means of surface transportation, which include the municipal gray with green and blue buses (.40 pesos), the thousands of mini-buses (white and green) known as *peseros, colectivos, or camiones* (.50–1.50 pesos), and the considerably more expensive but omnipresent taxis. The **Metro** is usually the fastest and most efficient but also inhumanly crowded at peak commuting hours. Most transportation depots in Mexico City are large, clean, well-lit, well-policed, and well-marked. Public transportation—whether by bus, Metro, or *pesero*—is easy to use and economical.

Travelers who plan to make frequent use of the Metro and bus systems should purchase an *abono de ahorro de transporte* (13.30 pesos) at a subway ticket window. *Abonos* (each is a pair of cards), available at all subway stations, Lotería Nacional stands, and Conasupo markets, entitles the bearer to unlimited use of the Metro (the blue card) and public city buses (the purple card) for 15 days following the purchase date. *Abonos* are sold at the beginning and in the middle of every month.

■ By Metro

The Metro always amazes—trains come quickly and regularly, the fare is insanely cheap, the crowds enormous and bizarre, the ride smooth, the service extensive, and the stations immaculate and marmoreal. Built in the late 1960s, the Metro transports 5 million people daily. Its tracks and stations are in continual pursuit of Mexico City's ever-expanding perimeter.

The .40-peso fare includes transfers. Gates operate by inserting a magnetically coded ticket, which must be bought at the booths marked *taquilla*. Transfer gates are marked *correspondencia* and exits are marked *salida*; passing through the turnstiles leaves you outside the station, and you must pay again to re-enter. If you have an *abono*, be sure to enter only through the blue turnstiles. If you use a white turnstile your ticket will be swallowed. Color-coded subway guides are available at the tourist office or at a Metro information booths.

Metro tickets are sold in booths at every station. For lines 1, 2, and 3, the first train runs Monday through Friday at 5am, Saturday at 6am, and Sunday at 7am. For lines 4-9, the first train runs Monday through Friday at 6am, Sunday at 7am. For all lines the last train runs at 12:30am from Sunday through Friday, and on Saturday as late as 1:30am. Try to avoid using the Metro from 7:30 to 9am and 7 to 9pm on weekdays, as well as the lunch break from 2-4pm; huge crowds during these hours attract pickpockets. Cars at either end of the train tend to be slightly less crowded, *ergo* safer and less uncomfortable.

Directions are stated in terms of the station at the end of a given line. Each of the two *andenes* (platforms) has signs indicating the terminus toward which trains are heading. (For example, if you are on Line 3 between Indios Verdes and Universidad, you can go "Dirección Indios Verdes" or "Dirección Universidad.")

Theft occurs frequently on the Metro when it's crowded (and it almost invariably is). Carry bags in front of you or on your lap; simply closing the bag does little good, because thieves have used razors to slit the bag open from the bottom. Subway thieves often work in pairs—one will distract you while the other pulls your wallet. Rear pockets are easy to pick; front pockets are safer, empty pockets are best. If you ride with a backpack on your back, the small pocket will invariably be violated. Non-Mexicans run a higher risk of being robbed, so it is always wise to avoid the outer trappings of tourist status while on the Metro.

Women riding the Metro often have the horrible experience of being groped in a crowd. Do not be afraid to call attention to the offender. During rush hours, many lines have cars reserved for women and children. Use them. They are usually located at the front of the train; often you will see women and children gathering on a separate part of the platform reserved for their car. The safest place in a crowded car is with your back against the wall keeping your backpack (if you have one) in front of you. Don't, however, feel rude when you must push, shove, and trample to exit the car. It is not unheard of to miss stops due to inability to get to the door.

Because of overcrowding, large bags, parcels, or suitcases are not allowed on the Metro. People slip bags past the gate, but you may regret it if you try. On a crowded train, your luggage will make fellow passengers uncomfortable and make you an immobile duck for thieves.

Some Metro stops serve as their own sights. Pino Suárez has a small Aztec building inside the stop, and La Raza houses the science tunnel with space pictures and a huge glow-in-the-dark star map.

For Metro and bus information, contact **COVITUR (Comisión de Vialidad y Transporte Urbano del D.F.),** Public Relations, Universidad 800 on the 14th floor, at the corner of Félix Cuervas just outside the Zapata Metro station (tel. 688-89-55 or 211-90-09), or ask at any information booth. For complaints about the Metro dial 709-11-33, ext. 5009 or 5010. If you lose something on the Metro, call the **Oficina de Objetos Extraviados** (tel. 709-11-33, ext. 3365), located in the Fray Servando station (Line 4). Keep hope alive, but keep expectations modest.

Overall, the Metro is by far the cleanest, fastest, and safest means of transportation in Mexico City. Almost all the restaurants, clubs, and museums of interest to the budget traveler can be reached most easily on the Metro.

■ By Bus

The public bus system extends much farther than the Metro; however, there is no published information about routes and schedules available to the tourist, so unless you stick to the major thoroughfares you might find it difficult to navigate the city by bus. Also, although you do get to see the city above ground, buses are usually slower than the Metro, particularly in the morning and evening rush hours. Buses are tastefully brown and yellow or blue and gray and cost .40 pesos; have change ready when you board. They run daily from 5am to midnight, but are scarce after 10pm. They pass bus stops every 20-30 minutes.

Buses are required to stop only at the bus stops along Ejes Viales and the following major streets: Reforma, Insurgentes, Calzada de Tlalpan, and Viaducto Miguel Alemán. Anywhere, flag the driver by holding out your arm and pointing at the street in front of you. To get off the bus, press the button above the exit door at the rear of the bus. If you don't hear a buzz, bang once on the wall or bark *¡Bajo!* to let the driver know you want out.

In an effort to meet the growing demand for efficient transportation, the city is slowly incorporating "Express" buses into the system. These swift steeds stop only on major avenues such as Insurgentes, Reforma, and Mazaryk. Like the Metro, buses are crowded and seats are hot items. The popular buses along Paseo de la Reforma are notorious for robbery and are plagued by organized gangs of businesslike thieves. Leave your valuables at the hotel; don't keep money in your pockets; carry your bag in front of you; or best yet, avoid this route altogether.

■ By Pesero (Minibus)

Peseros, a.k.a. *colectivos, combis,* or *micros,* are white and green minibuses, often with a "Magna Sin" gasoline logo on the side. Priced economically between cabs and buses, they cruise the streets on set routes. Though, like buses, no printed information is available, the destinations are either painted on or posted on the front window. To hail a *pesero,* wave your hand or hold out as many fingers as there are people in your group. Drivers will honk (horns are often rigged to play an annoying melody) at virtually every pedestrian to signal availability.

The fare varies according to distance, averaging .80-1 peso for cross-city routes, 1.50 for over 17km. Pay when you get on and tell the driver your destination, which often prevents a missed stop. Some *peseros* run only until midnight, but the major routes—on Reforma, between Chapultepec and San Ángel, and along Insurgentes—run 24 hrs. The fare is 20% higher between 10pm and 6am. Central City routes are indicated by Metro stops, while suburban *peseros* may also have numbers.

Other well-traveled *pesero* routes include: Metro Hidalgo to Ciudad Universitaria (via Reforma, Bucareli, and Av. Cuauhtémoc); La Villa to Chapultepec (via Reforma); Reforma to Auditorio (via Reforma and Juárez); *zócalo* to Chapultepec (via 5 de Mayo and Reforma); San Ángel to Izazaga (via 5 de Mayo and Reforma); Bolívar to Ciudad Universitaria/Coyoacán (via Bolívar in the *Centro*); and San Ángel to Metro Insurgentes (via Av. de la Paz and Insurgentes Sur). Many depart from Chapultepec Metro station to San Ángel, La Merced, and the airport. Be sure you know exactly where you're going when boarding the *pesero* and clearly state your destination to the driver.

■ By Taxi

Cabs constantly cruise the major avenues, offering a quick, private alternative to the public systems. Meters don't show prices but a reference number for the driver's price conversion table. Ask to see it before you pay, to insure that the price you're given matches the meter number. Hotel cabs and *turismo* taxis have no meters and charge up to three times more than regular taxis; green VW bugs are the cheapest but must be hailed; larger, orange taxis have digital meters that require no conversion. At night, all meters tend to be *descompuesto* (broken). Make sure the taxi meter is in clear view so that you can see the numbers turn as you travel. *Insist* on setting the price beforehand so you aren't at the driver's mercy when you reach your destination. Tips are unnecessary unless the cabdriver grants you a special service (helps carry your luggage, gives you a previously agreed-to tour, etc.).

At the airport and at all bus terminals, purchase a taxi ticket for a set fee (according to destination) at a registered booth. In the rare instance that no taxi is in sight, call **Servi-taxi** (tel. 516-60-20) or **Taxi Radio Mexicana** (tel. 574-45-96). VW bug taxis should display the driver's photo, credentials, and license over the glove compartment. Taxis commonly prey on the easy tourist victim. At the airport or bus terminals, try to consult a zone map before buying your ticket and always count your change. On the street, ask a local what the fare should be and insist on paying that and no more, there'll always be a driver who will accept.

■ By Car

Be forewarned that driving is the craziest and least economical way to get around the Federal District. Central Mexico City is encircled by a number of connected highways that together make up the **Circuito Interior.** This system allows motorists to get as close as possible to their destination before hitting the gridlocked streets of the center. Unfortunately, the Circuito itself is frequently jammed, especially during rush hour (Mon.-Fri. 7-9am and 6-9pm).

Mexico City's drivers are notoriously evil; they became so partly because highway engineers did not design the roads with drivers in mind. Highway dividers are often absent, stop signs are planted midstream, and red lights are routinely defied. The fast, efficient and cost-free *Ángeles Verdes* do *not* serve the Distrito Federal, where even angels fear to tread. If your car should break down within city boundaries, call **Asociación Automovilística Mexicana** (tel. 519-34-36) and request assistance. Wait for them beside your car, with the hood raised. If you leave your car alone, kiss it goodbye before you go.

Parking within the city is seldom a problem: parking lots are everywhere (approx. 1-8 pesos per hr., depending on the location and condition of the lot). Street parking in Mexico City is rare, and vandalism is extremely common. Never leave anything valuable inside the car. Police will remove your license plate if you park illegally; should this happen, wait near your car with some cash in your pocket until they return. If anything else was missing and you suspect the police were tampering with your car, report it to LOCATEL (tel. 658-11-11).

SAFETY

All vehicles, even those of non-Mexican registration, must follow Mexico City's anti-smog regulations. Depending on the last digit of the license plate, cars are forbidden from driving one day a week, according to this schedule Monday final digits 5 or 6; Tuesday: 7 or 8; Wednesday: 3 or 4; Thursday: 1 or 2; Friday: 9 or 0. Restrictions apply from 5am-10pm, and penalties for violations are stiff. (No limitations on weekends and between 10pm and 5am daily.)

Car rental rates are exorbitant, driving a hassle and the entire process draining. Requirements to rent vary, but all require the renter to be at least 21 yrs. old but some require the renter to be 26, have a major credit card and show a passport or tourist card,) Any driver's license is valid in Mexico. Prices for rentals tend to be similar; try the *Zona Rosa* or *Sala* E in the airport. **Auto Renta Facil** Río Lerma 157 (tel. 511-76-41), near Río Tiber, rents VW sedans for 71 pesos per day, plus .55 pesos per km, plus 22 pesos insurance; or 186 pesos per day with free mileage. Renter must be 26 yrs. old. (Open Mon.-Sat. 9am-8pm.) **Dollar** Av. Chapultepec 322 (tel. 207-38-38), in the Col. Roma, has similar rates. Renter must be 25. (Open daily 7am-8pm.) **Budget** Hamburgo 71 (tel. 533-04-50), in the *Zona Rosa*, charges 95 pesos, plus .75 pesos per km. (Open Mon.-Fri. 7am-9pm, Sat. 8am-6pm.)

SAFETY

Like all large cities, Mexico City presents safety problems to the traveler. Misconceptions about the magnitude of these problems can easily prevent an enjoyable visit, however. In general, the downtown area, where most sights and accommodations are located, tends to be safer, although the backstreets near Buenavista and the *Alameda* are significantly less so. Try to avoid carrying large amounts of cash and use a money belt or similar security device. Ignore strangers who seem even slightly suspicious, no matter how friendly their chatter or smile may seem. Never follow a vendor or shoeshiner out of the public view.

Women are, unfortunately, at higher risk of attack. Avoid being alone, especially at night or in a lonely area. Light hair and North American-style shorts will attract undesirable stares and propositions. A loud clear *¡Déjame!* (DEH-ha-meh) will make your intentions clear.

Transportation presents its own safety concerns (see Getting Around for more info). Mexico City's drivers are notoriously aggressive and often ignore traffic signals. Insist on seeing a taxi driver's photo license. Locals warn of late-night (1am on) attacks by *bandidos* posing as policemen.

Sidewalk vendors hawk scrumptious-looking food at enticing prices, but a cheap taco may force frequent trips to the *baño* down the road. Remember, too, what everyone back home said and don't drink the water. The city's notoriously smoggy air may cause problems for contact lens wearers and people with allergies. *The News* publishes a detailed smog report daily.

Overall, common sense rules. A rewarding trip can be easily stifled by hyper-caution and worry. Be careful, but don't spend your time in one of the world's greatest cities under a blanket locked in your hotel room.

PRACTICAL INFORMATION

Federal Tourist Office: Infotur Amberes 54 (tel. 525-93-80 through -84), at Londres in the *Zona Rosa*. Most employees speak some English and are well-informed. Metro and city maps available. Standardized price list of mid-range tourist hotels in major Mexican cities. Solves all riddles in person or by phone. Open daily 9am-9pm. During the same hours, the office operates information booths in *Salas* A (tel. 571-16-63 or 762-67-73) and E (tel. 784-85-53 or 784-89-69) at the airport, and at the TAPO bus station.

Ministry of Tourism: Presidente Masaryk 172 (tel. 250-85-55), at Hegel in Col. Polanco. From line 7, 1 block down Arqímeded and left onto Masaryk. The huge selection of maps and brochures on every place in Mexico may run low. All sorts of tourist information but a somewhat bewildered staff. Best for hotel reservations throughout the Republic. Open Mon.-Fri. 8am-8pm (24-hr. phone lines).

Department of Tourist Security: Presidente Masaryk 172 (tel. 250-01-51 or 250-04-93), in Col. Polanco. Calls answered by employees of the Ministry of Tourism, who will respond to complaints, suspected abuses, emergencies, and questions. Report all problems with tourist establishments here. Some English. A very good place to start after a mishap. Open 24 hrs. for phone calls; staffed 8am-8pm.

Legal Advice: Supervisión General de Servicios a la Comunidad, Florencia 20 (tel. 625-87-61), in the *Zona Rosa*, nearest the Metro Insurgentes (line 1). 24-hr. **hotline** (tel. 625-86-68). If you are the victim of a robbery or accident and need legal advice. Some employees speak English.

Tourist Card Information: Secretaría de Gobernación, Dirección General de Servicios Migratorios, Av. Chapultepec 284, 5th floor; Col. Juárez, Line 1, Insurgentes (tel. 626-72-00 or 206-05-06). Open Mon.-Fri. 8am-2pm.

Accommodations Service: Hoteles Asociados, Airport *Sala* E (tel. 571-59-02 or 571-63-82). Up-to-date information on prices and locations of Mexico City hotels. Give 'em a price range and an area, they'll get you a reservation, free of charge. If you want budget lodgings, be sure to ask for rock-bottom prices. English spoken.

Embassies: Will replace lost passports, issue visas, and provide legal assistance and sympathy. Visa processing can take up to 24 hrs.; bring plenty of ID. **Australia,** Jaime Balmes 11 (tel. 395-99-88), between Ejército Nacional and Homero. Open Mon.-Fri. 8am-2pm. **Belize,** Thiers 152-B (tel. 203-56-42). Open Mon.-Fri. 9am-1pm. **Canada,** Schiller 529 (tel. 724-79-00), behind the Museum of Anthro. Open Mon.-Fri. 8:30am-2pm. **Costa Rica,** Río Po 113 (tel. 525-77-66), between Río Lerma and Río Pánnco, behind the U.S. embassy. Open Mon.-Fri. 9:30am-4:30pm. **Denmark,** Tres Picos 52 (tel. 255-34-05), between Hegel and Lamartines. Open Mon.-Thurs. 8:30am-3:30pm, Fri. 8:30am-12:30pm. **France,** Havre 15 (tel. 533-13-60), between Hamburgo and Reforma. Open Mon.-Fri. 8:30am-1:30pm. For visas, consulate at Alejandro Dumas 16 (tel. 281-04-47), close to the corner of Campos Eliseos. Open Mon.-Fri. 9am-noon. **Germany,** Byron 737 (tel. 545-66-55). Open Mon.-Fri. 9am-12:30pm. **Guatemala,** 1025 Av. Explanada (tel. 545-75-20). Open Mon.-Fri. 9am-12:30pm. **Honduras,** Alfonso Reyes 220 (tel. 211-57-47), between Saltillo and Ometusco. Open Mon.-Fri. 10am-2pm. **Japan,** Paseo de la Reforma 395, 2nd floor (tel. 211-00-28). Open Mon.-Fri. 9:30am-1:30pm and 3:30-6pm. **Netherlands,** Montes Urales Sur 635; 2nd floor (tel. 202-82-67), before Petroleos Mexicanos. Open Mon.-Fri. 9am-2pm. **New Zealand,** Homero 229 (tel. 250-59-99), on the 8th floor. Open Mon.-Thurs. 8:30am-1:30pm and 3-5pm, Fri. 8:30am-2pm only. **Nicaragua,** Payo de Rivera 120 (tel. 520-24-49), between Virreyes and Monte Atos. Open Mon.-Fri. 10am-2pm. **Norway,** Av. Virreyes 1460 (tel. 540-34-86), between Apalachis and Montes Auberne. Open Mon.-Fri. 9am-2pm. **Panama,** Campos Eliseos 111 (tel. 250-42-29), between Hegel and Lope de Vega. Open Mon.-Fri. 8:30am-2:30pm. **Sweden,** Avila Camacho 1 (tel. 540-63-93), at Plaza Comermex. Open Mon.-Fri.10am-noon. **U.K.,** Río Lerma 71 (tel. 207-20-89), at Cuauhtémoc. Consulate open Mon.-Fri. 8:30am-3:30pm. Visa office open Mon.-Fri. 9am-2pm. **U.S.,** Reforma 305 (tel. 211-00-42), at Glorieta Ángel de la Independencia. Open Mon.-Fri. 8:30am-12:45pm for passports and visas, Mon.-Fri. 8:30am-5:30pm for general business. Call after hours and on weekends for emergencies only.

Currency Exchange: All banks offer the same exchange rate and usually charge commissions. Exchange hours for all 9am-1:30pm, but the wait may be considerable. The nation-wide **ATM** network, **Red Cajeros Compartidos** takes MC and Visa for cash advances, any many work with other U.S. system cards. Scores of ATMs are located along Reforma, in the Zona Rosa and Polanco, and in the Centro. Lost or stolen cards can be reported 24 hrs. to 227-27-77. **Citibank,** Reforma 390 (tel. 211-30-30; 24 hrs.), and **Bank of America,** Reforma 116, 10th-12th floors (tel. 591-00-11), can also help in an emergency. *Casas de cambio* keep longer hours than banks, give better exchange rates, and most are open on Saturday . They are concentrated along Reforma and in the *Zona Rosa*. Most in the *Zona Rosa* can change a number of non-U.S. currencies. The downtown area, where most sights, restaurants, and accommodations are located, has *casas de cambio* within a short distance of everything. Call the **Asociación Mexicana de Casas de Cambio** (tel. 264-08-84 or 264-08-41) to locate an exchange bureau near you. In the *Centro*: **Casa de Cambio Euromex,** Venustiano Carranza 64, 3rd floor (tel. 518-41-99); **Casa de Cambio Velasco Sucesores,** Gante 12, local B (tel. 521-50-28). Near the *Alameda*: **Casa de Cambio Plus,** Juárez 38 (tel. 510-22-88), on the southeast corner of the *Alameda Central*. Open Mon.-Fri. 9am-4pm, Sat. 10am-2pm. *Reforma,* closer to Buenavista and Revolución: **Casa de Cambio Catorce,** Reforma 51 (tel. 705-14-94).

American Express: Reforma 234 (tel. 207-72-82), at Havre in the *Zona Rosa*. Will cash personal checks and accept mail for customers only. Money can be wired here. Report lost credit cards to the branch at Patriotismo 635 (tel. 326-26-66), lost traveler's checks to either branch. Open Mon.-Fri. 9am-6pm, Sat. 9am-1pm. In case of a lost **Visa** card, call 625-21-88.

Central Post Office: Lázaro Cárdenas (tel. 521-73-94), at Tacuba across from Bellas Artes. Open for stamps, regular mail, and *Lista de Correos* Mon.-Fri. 8am-11pm, Sat. 9am-1pm, for registered mail Mon.-Fri. 9am-5pm, Sat. 9am-1pm. Postal museum upstairs. **Postal code:** 06002.

Telephones: For direct long-distance calls, long-distance *casetas* at: Airport *Sala* D (open daily 6am-8:30pm); Buenavista train station (open Mon.-Fri. 9am-9pm, Sat.-Sun. 9am-2pm); or Central Camionera del Norte (open daily 8am-9pm). Also, look for **LADATEL** phones at the airport, bus stations, Metro stations, VIPs Restaurant and on the street in the *Zona Rosa* or *centro* district to make collect calls to the U.S. (See Mexico Essentials: Keeping in Touch: Telephones.) Special phones in the airport take major credit cards. **Telephone code:** 5.

Telegrams: Tacuba 8 (tel. 510-03-94), at the Museo Nacional de Arte in the right wing of the building, behind the central post office. Domestic and international service. From the U.S., send through Western Union to **México Central Telégrafos.** Open Mon.-Fri. 8am-mdnight, Sat. 9am-12:45pm. To send telegrams by phone call 709-8500 national, 709-8625 international.

Courier Services: Estafeta Mensajería y Paquetería, Praga 31 (tel. 208-50-47, 24-hr. service at 325-91-00), at Hamburgo in the *Zona Rosa*. International parcel delivery. Open Mon.-Fri. 9am-5:30pm. **DHL,** Reforma 30 (tel. 562-57-00, 24-hr. service at 227-02-99), also at Insurgentes Sur 859 (tel. 592-60-11), in Col. Nápoles. **Federal Express,** Estocolmo 4 (tel. 228-99-04). Send before 3:30pm for overnight service. Also at Leibnitz and Víctor Hugo (tel. 251-41-40) in the Col. Anzures. Open Mon.-Fri. 8am-7pm.

English Bookstores: American Bookstore, Madero 25 (tel. 512-72-84), in the *Centro* with an extensive selection of fiction, guides and a matchless Latin American history and politics section. Also a branch at Revolución 1570 (tel. 661-1916) in San Ángel. Both branches open Mon.-Sat. 10am-7pm. **Portico de la Ciudad de Mexico,** Central 124 (tel. 510-96-83), at Carranza. Sells English and Spanish Mexican history books and guides to archaeological sites. Open Mon.-Sat. 10am-7pm. For magazines and newspapers in Spanish, English, French, and German try **La Casa de la Prensa Internacional,** Florencia 57 in the *Zona Rosa*. Open Mon.-Sat. 8am-9pm. The **Museo Nacional de Antropología** has a wide selection of archaeological guides in English (see Sights). The English-language newspaper, *The News,* is sold at most newsstands.

Ben Franklin Library: Londres 16 (tel. 211-00-42), at Berlin, 2 blocks southeast of the Cuauhtémoc monument. 75% of the books are in English, including a large variety of newspapers and periodicals. Open Tues.-Thurs. 10am-3pm, Mon. and Fri. 3-7:30pm.

Cultural and Arts Information: Palacio Nacional de Bellas Artes, Juárez and Eje Central (tel. 709-31-11 or 512-36-33), for information and reservations for all Bellas Artes events.

Laundromats: Near the monument to the Revolución: **Lavandería Automática,** Edison 91. Wash 9 pesos per 5 lb., dry 9 pesos. Full service 9 pesos extra. Soap 3 pesos. Open Mon.-Fri. 10am-7pm, Sat. 10am-6pm. In the *Zona Rosa*: **Lavanderet,** Chapultepec 463 (tel. 514-01-06), at Toledo. 9 pesos to wash, 9 pesos to dry. Full service 20 pesos. Open Mon.-Sat. 9am-7pm. Most hotels have laundry service or can tell you where to find the nearest facility.

Supermarket: Most supermarkets are away from the city center at residential Metro stops. **Bodega,** Serapio Rendón 117, just south of Antonio Caso. Open Mon.-Sat. 8am-9pm, Sun. 9am-8pm. **Aurrera,** 5 blocks north of Puente de Alvaro on Insurgentes. Open daily 9am-9pm. **Commercial Mexicana,** at Corregidora and Correo Mayor, on the coutheast side of the Palacio Nacional in the *centro*. Open daily 8am-8pm.

Rape Crisis: Hospital de Traumatología de Balbuena, Cecilio Robelo 103 (tel. 552-16-02 or 764-03-39), near Calle Sur, east of *Alameda*. **Hospital de la Mujer,** (tel. 541-46-61). Also call 06 or LOCATEL.

Gay, Lesbian, and Bisexual Information: Colectivo Sol. Address inquiries care of Apdo. 13-320 Av. México 13, D.F. 03500. A mainly political group that offers information on upcoming political and social events.

Sexually Transmitted Disease Information: Secretaría de Salud (tel. 277-63-11), open Mon.-Fri. 8am-2pm and 3:30-7pm, Sat. 9am-1pm.

AIDS Hotline: TELSIDA/CONASIDA, Florencia 8 (tel. 207-41-43 or 207-40-83), Col. Roma, Metro Cuauhtémoc. Information and help center

LOCATEL: (tel. 658-11-11.) City's official lost-and-found hotline. Call if your car (or friend) is missing. Also information and directions in cases of medical emergencies and information about sports events, etc.

Red Cross: Ejército Nacional 1032 (tel. 557-57-58 or 557-57-57), in the Col. Polanco. Open 24 hrs. Fastest and most efficient ambulance service.

Pharmacies: VYR, San Jerónimo 630 (tel. 595-59-83 or 595-59-98), near Periférico Sur shopping center. Open 24 hrs. More convenient during the day might be **Farmacia El Fénix,** Isabel La Católica 15 (tel. 585-04-55), at 5 de Mayo. Open Mon.-Sat. 9am-10pm. Well-stocked, but will take Spanish prescriptions only. All big markets have well-stocked pharmacy counters.

Medical Care: The **U.S. Embassy** (see above) has a list of doctors in the city, with their specialties, addresses, telephone numbers and languages spoken. **Dirección General de Servicios Médicos** (tel. 518-51-00) has information on all city hospitals, (Open Mon.-Fri. 9am-6pm.) Free emergency medical assistance is available at **Procuraduría General de Justicia del D.F.** Florencia 20 (tel. 625-87-61), in the *Zona Rosa*. For tourists, the **American British Cowdray (ABC) Hospital,** Calle Sur 136 (tel. 227-50-00) at Observatorio, Col. Las Américas. No U.S. health plans valid, but all major credit cards accepted. 24 hrs. **Torre Medica,** José Maria Iglesias 21 (tel. 546-24-80); Metro Revolución. Near Monumento de la Revolución.

Emergency Shelter: Casa de Protección Social (tel. 530-47-62 or 530-85-36).

Police: Secretaría General de Protección y Vialidad (tel. 768-80-44). Dial 08 for the Policía Judicial to report assaults, robberies, crashes, abandoned vehicles, or other emergencies.

ACCOMMODATIONS

Rooms abound in the *Centro* (between *Alameda* and the *zócalo*) and the *Alameda Central*, and are sprinkled throughout the area surrounding the Monumento a la Revolución on the Pl. de la República. Mexico City offers high-quality budget accommodations relative to other large cities in the country. Rooms costing 40-50 pesos and up for one bed and 60-70 pesos and up for two beds should be clean, have carpeting, a TV, and a telephone (with free local calls), or you're getting the high, hard one. Most budget hotels charge according to the number of beds needed and not per person; beds tend to be large enough for two people. If you can deal, this is a potential source of substantial savings.

Avoid the filthier sections of the *Alameda*, and any area which makes you feel uncomfortable—there's plenty more from which to choose. Don't be put off by the mid- to high-priced hotels around Insurgentes Sur and Reforma, just northeast of the *Zona Rosa* tourist belt; they are still inexpensive by U.S. standards. Also stay away anyplace where the hotel, not the parking lot, is marked "Hotel Garage." These rooms are frequented by businessfolk "working late at the office;" the hourly charge is sky-high. Always ask to look at a room before you accept it; they are most likely to be free after check-out time (between noon and 2pm). Hotels whose prices are above 55 pesos per single and 70 pesos per double usually accept MC and Visa. AmEx is less common.

For hostel information, call Villa Deportiva Juvenil (tel. 525-26-99), which operates the city's lone hostel on the Plaza de la Independencia, near the *Zona Rosa* (18 per night). They can't guarantee you a spot and often fill up with visiting sports teams competing in the city.

■ Centro

Situated between the *zócalo* and *Alameda Central*, this *colonia* is the historic colonial heart of Mexico City. Its hotels are reasonably priced and feel fairly safe, though the throngs disappear as they head home for the night, leaving the streets relatively empty. Nonetheless, the *Centro* remains the most exciting place to stay and the best base from which to explore the traditional core of one of the world's largest cities. Along with the action, however, comes noise and congestion. If you are in town for a lengthy stay, consider moving west to the *Buenavista* or *Alameda* areas to escape the roar of the stampede.

Many of the hotels listed are north of Madero and 5 de Mayo, the parallel east-west streets that connect the *Alameda* with the *zócalo*, and east of Lázaro Cárdenas, the north-south Eje Central that runs one block east of *Alameda*. Metro stations Bellas Artes and Allende (both Line 2) serve these hotels. The hotels on 5 de Mayo, Isabel la Católica, and Uruguay are better served by the *zócalo* and Isabel la Católica stations. All the listings in this area except Hotel Rioja accept MasterCard and Visa.

Hotel Antillas, Belisario Domínguez 34 (tel. 526-56-74), near Allende. A wonderfully restored and maintained colonial building. Half of the lobby is dedicated to a small restaurant, which shares the polished wooden beams and iron chandeliers which give the foyer a historic feel. Comfortable rooms with good bathrooms come with TV, phone, drinking wate,r and carpet—ask to see the room beforehand. Singles 60 pesos. Doubles 75 pesos.

Hotel La Marina, Allende 30 (tel. 518-24-45), B. Dominguez. Mid-sized rooms try to match orange and brown furniture with inadequately azure-blue seascapes. Phone, color TV, central radio, and nice bathrooms. An even better deal than Antillas. Singles 45 pesos. Doubles 70 pesos.

Hotel Congreso, Allende 18 (tel. 510-44-46), between Républica de Cuba and Donceles. A darkish hotel, surprisingly quiet for the area, but all amenities are right (TV, phone, radio, carpet). Smallish rooms seductively combine orange and crimson colors. Singles 45 pesos. Doubles 60 pesos.

Hotel Atlanta, Domníquez Belisario 31 (tel. 518-12-00), across from Hotel Antillas. Rooms are a bit more worn than those in the above 3 hotels, but offer TV, phone, radio, and good bathrooms. Heavy curtains let in little light but also keep noise out. Singles 45 pesos. 1-bed doubles 50 pesos, 2 beds 70 pesos.

Hotel Florida, Belisario Domínguez 57 (tel. 521-77-64). Nice but small, dark rooms with hideously mismatched brown rugs and red bedcovers make you feel like you really are in Florida. All rooms have TV, radio, and phone. Immaculate bathrooms. 5 floors of smallish rooms overlook a clean, marbled courtyard. Free bottled water at main desk. A good value. Singles 40 pesos. Doubles 65 pesos.

Hotel Monte Carlo, Uruguay 69. Metro Isabel la Católica, Metro Allende: equally far away. Very spacious courtyard, beautifully tiled in brown. The outstanding collection of world currencies at reception desk once paid for solid rooms with radio, phone, and *agua purificada*. Good bathrooms. Singles 50 pesos. Doubles 55 pesos for 1 bed, 70 pesos for 2 beds.

Hotel Principal, Bolivar 29 (tel. 521-13-33), Metro Allende, between Madero and 16 de Septiembre. Spacious rooms dominated by almost equally sized wardrobes. TV, phones, meager lighting, and decent bathrooms. Singles 50 pesos. Doubles 60 pesos.

Hotel Isabel, Isabel la Católica 63 (tel. 518-12-13), between El Salvador and Uruguay across from the old Biblioteca Nacional. A sprawling old-fashioned hotel that is a refreshing alternative to its boring modern counterparts. Step into the vast, wood-panelled lobby (complete with coat of arms) through the huge wooden doors with carved lion's heads. The hotel's character continues in the darkish worn rooms with contain shiny brass beds, dark wood dressers and great bathrooms. Singles 60 pesos. Doubles 75 pesos.

Hotel Rioja, 5 de Mayo 45 (tel. 521-83-33). Not particularly comfortable, but a good location and the rooms are as close to free as you'll find. Noisy—room doors open onto inner patio, designed to magnify every stray street sound. Bare lightbulbs illuminate clean mid-sized rooms. Singles 35 pesos. Doubles 40 pesos. Top floor rooms have no private bathrooms (singles 26 pesos, doubles 30 pesos) but offer a somewhat romantic view of the surrounding rooftops.

■ Alameda Central

The long-expected construction of Metro line 8 should have finished by the fall of 1993 thus ending the constant noise and omnipresent dust in the area and a two-year suppression of prices. Prices will probably increase more rapidly in this area than in others. The *Alameda* is probably the least safe of the three areas listed; women in particular will feel more secure in the *Centro, Buenavista,* and *Zona Rosa* areas.

Hotel Hidalgo, Santa Veracruz 37 (tel. 521-87-71), at the 2 de Abril walkway, behind Bellas Artes Metro station. The stalwart exterior, one of the few to survive the 1985 earthquakes, is a paragon of the concrete jungle, a cinder-block stalwart amidst new construction. Fortunately, the interior is better: a modern lively lobby, flawless wood trim, new-looking furniture and decently-lit rooms that afford city views. Restaurant in the lobby. Parking available. Singles 70 pesos. Doubles 85 pesos. Triples 100 pesos.

Hotel Manolo, Luis Moya 111 (tel. 521-77-09), just north of Arcos de Belén; an arrow across the street points the way. Big rooms require a map; landmarks include the enormous bed, color TV, radio and phone. The 4 wild patterns on the carpet, bedspread, curtains, and wallpaper may give you vertigo. Tiled bathrooms with out-of-place bidet. Dire thirsts slaked in the lobby, which is amply stocked with soda and bottled water. Singles and doubles 70 pesos.

Hotel Conde, Pescaditos 15 (tel. 521-10-84), at Revillagigedo. Exit the Metro at Juárez, follow Artículo 123 to Revillagigedo, then take a right and walk 3 blocks. A big white building with a sterilized central lobby. Phone, TV, and blue-tiled bathrooms fit for nobility. Priced lower than its rivals in the area. Lots of parking space in back. Singles 60 pesos. 1 bed doubles 75 pesos, with 2 beds 85 pesos.

Hotel Cosmos, Lázaro Cárdenas 12 (tel. 512-26-31), just south of Madero. Shabby lobby, and the good-sized rooms with TV and phone are worth the meager asking price. An old-fashioned elevator with exposed shaft. Singles and 1-bed doubles 45 pesos. 2-bed doubles 75 pesos. 3-bed triples 100 pesos.

■ Near the Monumento a la Revolución/ Buenavista

Accommodations in the Monumento a la Revolución area offer more peace and quiet than do those in the *Centro* or the *Alameda,* for two main reasons: there are few historical sites here of interest to tourists, and not many people have moved back since the area was heavily damaged in the 1985 quake. These older and less centrally located hotels charge less than their counterparts in the *Alameda* and *Centro*. As a result, budget travelers tend to congregate here, particularly in the hotels on Mariscal and Edison. Metro Revolución and Metro Hidalgo serve those hotels south of Puente de Alvarado/Hidalgo; while Metro Guerrero serves those to the north near the train station.

Hotel Royalty, Jesus Terán 21 (tel. 566-92-55), just block towards the Monumento a la Revolución along Av. de la Républica, to the left. The tiger-design of the carpet makes the rooms darkish, but they're all clean, comfortable, have ancient phones, TVs, and excellent bathrooms. Exceptional for the price. Singles and doubles 40 pesos.

Hotel Londres, Pl. Buenavista 5 (tel. 705-09-10), off Buenavista, 3 blocks south of the train station, 2 blocks north of Puente de Alvarado. Step out of the smoggy exterior and into a cool courtyard with chilly blue tile, a splashing fountain, and lush greenery. Nothing fancy in the rooms, but clean with bright bedspreads. A deal and a half at 40 pesos for singles and doubles.

Hotel Atoyac, Guerreo 161 (tel. 526-9917), between Degollado Mosqueto, 2 blocks to your left as you exit the train station onto Mosqueto. Excellent conditions for the low asking price. Reasonably large rooms with TVs, wall-to-wall carpeting, and clean, bright bathrooms. Often full; try to get a room after 3pm. Singles and doubles 35 pesos.

Hotel Estaciones, Berual Díaz 17 (tel. 566-68-55), off Puente de Alvarado, 1½ blocks west from Metro Revolucíon. not to be confused with the bland white building next door with same conditions but higher prices. Exceedingly colorful bedcovers are the only bright spot in the dark rooms with TVs. Paint peeling in the area's biggest bathrooms, but still avery good value at 40 pesos for singles or doubles.

Casa de Los Amigos, Ignacio Mariscal 132 (tel. 705-05-21 or 705-06-46), across from Gran Hotel Texas. Originally home to José Clemente Orozco, the House of Friends (Quakers) is a cultural and refugee center and temporary boardinghouse for people working for peace and international justice in Central America. Beds are given to casual travelers on a space-available basis. Not a hostel but a place with its own character, international atmosphere, and reasonable requirements. The staff will give you an information sheet when you arrive so that you understand the purpose of the *casa* and agree to respect their cooperative atmosphere. Friendly, helpful, English-speaking proprietors. Kitchen facilities. Meditation room was once Orozco's art studio. Will hold mail. 2-day minimum stay, 15-day max. stay. Be in by 10pm or pay a 10-peso deposit for a key. Storage fee .80 pesos. Breakfast of yogurt and granola 6 pesos. Dorm room 24 pesos. Private room (when available) 28-60 pesos.

Hotel Oxford, Ignacio Mariscal 67 (tel. 566-05-00), at Alcázar, next to the small park. Fresh flowers in the entry welcome you to this stellar budget option. An elegant winding staircase leads to carpeted rooms blessed by round wood tables, large color TV with several English channels. Drinking water. The only slight drawback: a newspaper distribution center on the street below that cranks up noisily at the crack of dawn. Singles 50-55 pesos. Doubles 75 pesos.

Hotel Carlton, Ignacio Mariscal 32 (tel. 566-29-11), between Alcázar and Arizpe, across from the park. Notoriously good value has attracted budget travelers from afar. A bit more worn than more expensive options, but the friendly management, location, and mid-sized carpeted rooms with TV outweigh this small indiscretion. Restaurant and lively bar attached. Singles 50 pesos. Doubles 60 pesos.

Hotel Yale, Mosqueta 200 (tel. 591-14-88), between Zaragoza and Guerrero, to the left of the train station (if you exit). The rooms in this unfortunately-named hotel are well-maintained and have the works (TV, radio, thick carpet, and *agua purificada*), yet continue to be rated second-best by *U.S. News and World Report*. Those that face the inner courtyard are darker but have the calming whisper of the small water fountain. 50 pesos for both singles and doubles.

Hotel Detroit, Zaragoza 55 (tel. 566-07-55), at Mina in Col. Guerrero. Guerrero runs parallel to Zaragoza. The lobby and halls are run down, with peeling plaster, linoleum floors, and only religious paraphernalia to add luster. Rooms have fake wood floors that are kept clean, curtains with molecular orbit patterns, spotless sheets and tightly made beds. The dimly lit neighborhood is not a place to hang out for an extended period of time. Singles 35 pesos. Doubles 70 pesos.

Hotel Parador Washington, Dinamara 42 (tel. 566-8648), at the corner with Londres, on Plaza Jirge Washington, close to the *Zona Rosa:* Upscale locale without the impossible prices. Winding hallways lend to classy sitting rooms. Bright bedrooms with large beds. Color scheme attempts to reconcile orange and green. Prices very acceptable for the area. Singles 70 pesos. Doubles 80 pesos.

FOOD

The teeming masses which inhabit Mexico City demand an unparalleled quantity and diversity of edibles, a demand readily met by the apparently equal number of stores, stands, restaurants, and vendors. The wide range of choices is matched only by the disparity in cleanliness; as always, no matter how delicious that beef tongue in vinegar dressing looks, inspect it as carefully as possible before popping it into your mouth.

The food in Mexico City is often cheaper than in many other parts of the country, and there are some definite local favorites: *huevos* (eggs) and *pan dulce* (sweet bread) for breakfast, *quesadillas* (fried tortillas with cheese) or *tortas de pierna* (pork sandwiches) for lunch, and *pollo con mole poblano* (chicken with *mole* sauce) or enchiladas for dinner. There are many natural products stores throughout the city, and a surprisingly high representation of vegetarian restaurants (see listings below).

Creativity is the key to enjoying Mexico City's edible diversity. *Panaderías* make mounds of bread daily and sell it at ridiculously low prices. A bag full of breakfast often costs only a few pesos. Overcome aversions and be sure to at least sample the street fare. The options fall into five basic categories: fast and inexpensive *taquerías*, slightly more formal *cafeterías*, more pricy and decorous Mexican restaurants, locally popular and inflated North-Americanized diners, and expensive international fare. In addition, U.S. fast-food chains mass-produce predictable fare for the timid palate. **VIP's** offers 60 commercialized Denny's-like eateries throughout the D.F. If you're preparing your own food, **Conasupos** supermarkets throughout the city stock almost anything you could need; if you can't find what you want there, head to **La Merced** (the market).

Soda is sold at every corner. *Agua mineral* means mineral water; *sidral* is a great carbonated apple drink; and *refrescos* are your standard soda pops. Cans and bottles are customarily recycled here, and patrons pay extra for the privilege of keeping them. Avoid a deposit, however, by imitating the locals and taking your drink in a plastic bag *(bolsa)* with straw *(popote),* to go.

■ Centro

This area offers the most variety and lowest prices around. Bustling *cafeterías* dish out three meals a day. Portions are usually large, and many small counters offer fruit plates and drinks. *Comidas corridas,* even the vegetarian variety, are in copious supply. Cheap eats can be picked up from the many small *taquerías* or street vendors.

Café Tacuba, Tacuba 28 (tel. 518-49-50), at Allende Metro stop. Authentic Mexican cuisine in a colorful setting. Elaborately painted arches, tiled floors and murals depicting dated scenes of the colonial aristocracy. A bastion of serenity in the heart of downtown since 1912. Beef tongue with vinegar dressing 25 pesos. *Pollo tacuba* 25 pesos. MC, Visa accepted. Open daily 8:30am-11:30pm.

Restaurante El Vegetariano, Filomeno Mata 13 (tel. 510-01-13), between 5 de Mayo and Madero. Crammed with happy and healthy people all walking the meatless path. Nutritious *comida corrida* includes choices of fruit or vegetable salad, soup, entree, and fruit-based dessert (20 pesos). Try the *croquetas de elote* with papaya sauce. All kinds of whole-wheat pastries sold at the register. MC, Visa accepted. Other locations include Matriz Madero 56 altos and San Javier Sorondo 367 y 369. Open Mon.-Sat. 8am-8pm.

Restaurant Danubio, Uruguay 3, just east of Lázaro Cárdenas. Classy, old-fashioned, and popular seafood place with its own coat-of-arms; curtained windows shelter the diners inside. Famous artsy types have left their scribbling on the walls framed. Pricey entrees big enough to feed 2—stick to the 5-course *comida corrida* 30 pesos, Sun. 35 pesos. Open daily 1-10pm for a la carte.

Café La Blanca, 5 de Mayo 40 (tel. 510-03-99). A popular, conveniently located cafeteria with snappy service and fair-sized portions. A high ceiling over 2 circular counters and numerous tables. The bilingual menu offers an immense selection and the staff is warm and friendly towards foreigners as they hustle to serve delicious, although predictable, dishes. Green, red, or sweet corn tamales 7-9 pesos for an order of 2. Inexpensive *antojito* entrees run 10 pesos. The menu offers daily suggestions ranging in price from 14-20 pesos. Open daily 7am-11:30pm.

Super Frutas-La Casa de Ensaladas, Uruguay 52, just west of Isabel la Católica. Simple, open-air fruit shop daubed in bright orange, yellow, and green. Specializes in tasty old and new takes on fruit drinks, desserts, and more. Papaya, melon, banana, alfalfa, celery, carrot, and other *licuados, aguas,* juices, single flavor or combined (3-7 pesos). Self-serve bins of fruits and veggies. Salads (7 pesos) and *tortas* (3-6 pesos) are also served. Open Mon.-Sat. 7:30am-7:30pm.

Café París, 5 de Mayo 10 (tel. 521-54-56), at Filomeno Mata. Eurocentrism meets the diner. Clean and comfortable with A/C. A mile-long counter faces a mirrored wall—great for spying on activity behind you. Soft music to set the mood while you dine in a private booth. Great homemade hot biscuits in the morning (1 peso). Breakfast 10 pesos. Daily menu 4 dishes and coffee 16 pesos. Open daily 8am-midnight.

Pastelería La Ideal, 16 de Septiembre 14, just east of Cárdenas. Mexico City does everything on a large scale, and this bakery is no exception. ¼-block-long baking factory, composed of 4 huge sections with a fountain in the center. One section is for plain bread, one for cakes and pies, one with hundreds of pastries, and a 2nd level full of elaborate wedding cakes weighing as much as 70kg. Crowds battle in the afternoon over the steaming bread brought straight out of the oven on baking racks. Open daily 7am-10pm.

■ Zona Rosa

The myth: only moneyed tourists eat in the *Zona Rosa*. The fact: many area eateries cater chiefly to clerks from the scores of surrounding office buildings. However, the city's most expensive restaurants, from all types of international cuisine to traditional Mexican cooking, are located in the *Zona Rosa*. Check out the open-air ambience and consult the prominently displayed menus before choosing a restaurant. Prices vary widely, and it's almost always possible to find a cheap meal, though the street vendors which are crammed into every other inch of Mexican sidewalk are sparse. If you're more interested in the *Zona Rosa's* slick party atmosphere than in filling your stomach, skip dinner and settle for a drawn-out evening appetizer. But hey, this is Mexico, and a very good meal won't run you more than 35 pesos in all.

La Luna, Oslo 11, in the tiny walkway between Niza and Copenhagne. Peaceful and relaxed atmosphere in a bustling zone. Bright and clean small restaurant with whitewashed walls decorated with a tasteful but stylistically chaotic selection of graphics, lithographs, photos, etc. Fresh flowers on the tables and friendly family service. Very popular among experienced *Zona Rosa* inhabitants, who come here for the tasty 4-course daily menu for 10 pesos. Open daily 7am-3am, with plenty of beer flowing after 10pm.

La Bonne Cuisine, Lourdes after Insurgentes. Despite the pretentious name, an inexpensive and very popular lunch spot. The bread is the only French here. Walls plastered with posters of Marilyn Monroe. Daily 15-peso special, 9-12-peso entrees. Pay at the cashier. Open Mon.-Sat. 1-6pm.

Fonda Don Lucas, Lourdes 178-C (tel. 511-20-67), after the crossing with Florencia. A *jovenes-ejecutivos* filled restaurant, with mirrored walls adding to the checkered ambience. Come early for more space and faster service. The *economica* menu costs 12 pesos and the *especial* 14 pesos. Both include 3 dishes, free water, and dessert. Beer 3.50 pesos. *Refresco* 1.50 pesos. Open Mon.-Fri. 1-5pm.

Restaurant Jacarandas, Genova 44 (tel. 514-18-13), in a plaza off the east side of the street. In the heart of the *Zona Rosa*, a respite from the pricey international cuisine in a cozy nook off the main street. Join the crowd of locals that jams the inside and outside tables at this popular lunch spot. 5-course daily menu 15 pesos. MC, Visa accepted. Open Mon.-Fri. noon-6pm.

La Oficina, Hamburgo 45, near Insurgentes. Small family-run place like millions around the Republic, but an oddity in the *Zona Rosa*. Breakfasts of coffee, eggs and ham for 8 pesos, *comida corrida* 8 pesos.

Tacos el Caminero, Río Lerma 138 (tel. 514-56-15), between Tíber and Danubio across Reforma from the *Zona Rosa*. Not far from the U.S. consulate. An authentic taco restaurant, with grill-style specialties for meat-lovers. The small windowless restaurant has only counter eating space and an immense corner grill, but is popular at all hours featuring 13 types of tacos. Steak, sausage and pork chop tacos with delicious hot sauces. 6 tacos 16 pesos, 9 tacos 18 pesos. MC, Visa accepted. Open Mon.-Thurs. noon-midnight, Fri.-Sat. noon-1am, Sun. noon-11pm. An identical *taquería* at Iganacio Ramirez 17.

Parri, Hamburgo 154 (tel. 207-93-19), between Florencia and Amberes. The lack of originality in the plain yet typical decor is compensated for by the grilling process. House-recipe chicken is beheaded then barbecued on massive grill as hungry crowds watch. Eat in or take out. ¼-chicken with burrito, guacamole, and black beans 15 pesos. MC, Visa accepted. Open Mon.-Thurs. 8am-3am, Fri.-Sat. 8am-3pm, Sun. 8am-midnight.

■ Alameda Central

In spite of the inevitable construction work (or perhaps because of the construction workers' hearty appetites), you'll find plenty of good, cheap food in the *Alameda*.

Café La Habana, Bucareli and Morelos (tel. 535-26-20), south of the monument to the revolution. A sign proclaims it home to the best coffee in Mexico City. No need to buy a cup to sample—the whole place is permeated with the delicious aroma. Relaxed atmosphere with couples and groups chatting into the evening makes a great place to sip java and chow down. Fun-to-watch old-fashioned coffee bean roaster/grinder in the front window. Coffee sells by the kg. *Asada Habana* 33 pesos. *Quesadillas sincronizadas* 15 pesos. Open Mon.-Sat. 8am-11pm.

Fonda Santa Anita, Humboldt 48 (tel. 518-46-09), near Juárez. Pan-chromatic restaurant serving Mexican food only. The walls and ceilings fetishize Mexican village life. Flying birds and pigs spiral up the columns. World record for friendly service. Claims to have served its food at 5 World's Fairs. AmEx, MC, Visa accepted. Soups 6.50 pesos. Enchiladas 11 pesos. Meat dishes 25 pesos. Open Mon.-Fri. noon-10pm, Sat.-Sun. 1:30-9pm.

Humboldt 34, Humboldt 34 (tel. 521-22-93), near Juárez. Eclectic but bland mixture of old and new. Wood paneling and leather chairs face off with Aztec and electric guitars. Courteous service. Local families and executives dig the chicken entrees. Bottled music always playing, and late afternoons and evenings may find a small band groovin' in the corner. Full bar. 3 daily menus 13-17 pesos. MC, Visa accepted. Open Mon.-Sat. noon-3am.

Taquería Tlaquepaque, Independencia 4 (tel. 521-30-82), just west of Cárdenas. A popular *taquería* with more sit-down space than the average street *comedor*. Grab tacos to go from the outside grill or a sit a spell and watch the cooks do their thing. All orders of meaty taco delights 3 for 5.50 pesos. Open daily 9am-3am.

Grand Chose, Luis Moya 62 (tel. 521-05-53). Lacks the polish and size of some more expensive restaurants, but a true budget find. Solid *comida corrida* a deal at 9.50 pesos. Breakfasts for 6-9 pesos. Open 7am-6pm.

■ Near the Monumento a la Revolución

Though they lack the variety and innovation of the *Alameda*, *Centro*, or *Zona Rosa*, restaurants in this area serve hefty portions for low prices. Few will tease the taste buds, but almost all will fill your stomach.

Restaurant Mansión, Antonio Caso 31 (tel. 566-61-16), toward Colón from Revolución, just west of Vallarta. Surround yourself with the trappings of luxury—elaborately carved ceilings, huge chandeliers, red velvet curtains, and replicas of Greek masterpieces—while you enjoy a well-cooked afternoon meal, all for scandalously low prices. *Comida corrida* 8-12 pesos. Open Mon.-Fri. 1-6:30pm.

La Taberna, Arriaga at Ignacio Mariscal, next to Hotel Pennsylvania. Below street level, this small, always-packed pizzeria also serves Mexican food. Wood walls, low ceiling, and minimal space make for a cozy, quiet atmosphere. For the best value, order your pizza as part of the *comidas corrida* (soup, starter, pizza and dessert 12.50-23 pesos). MC, Visa accepted. Open Mon.-Sat. 1-10pm.

Xin Guang Zhou, Insurgentes Centro 62-B. Pretentious-looking small restaurants with dark mirrors on two of the walls and a trivially colorful photo-wall paper of a forest. The daily menu (8 pesos) is, unfortunately, either entirely Mexican or Chinese, thus limiting the possibility of exotic combinations. An occasional English-subtitled Taiwanese movie. Open daily 8am-11pm.

Restaurant Samy's, Ignacio Mariscal 42 (tel. 591-11-00). A cool hideaway restaurant with orange seats and flower pots livening up the walls. A modest selection of wines is proudly displayed on a wooden shelf around a central column. A good sized 5-item daily menu 13 pesos. Open Mon.-Fri. 8am-6pm.

Restaurant Regis, Edison 57-B (tel. 592-01-78). Decoratively bankrupt. Convenient if you are staying near Mariscal or Edison. The service can be slow. Good-sized *comida corrida* 13 pesos. *Bistek a la plancha* 15 pesos. MC, Visa accepted. Open daily 7am-11pm.

Café Gran Premio, Antonio Caso 72 (tel. 535-09-34), between Insurgentes Norte and Serapio Rendón, under the big coffee cup sign. A great place for connoisseurs to come for coffee and a pastry. Javarama. *Americanos* 4 pesos. *Café con leche* or cappuccino 3.80 pesos, hot chocolate 4 pesos. Open Mon.-Sat. 8am-8pm.

■ Near Chapultepec

In Mexico City's western corner, south of Chapultepec and west of Chapultepec Park, great food greets you in restaurants that provide their own scenery. One is built around a greenhouse, another with maniacal roving *mariachis*, and yet another that is devoutly macrobiotic, reserving half of its dining room to floor seating (remember to sit lotus-style). This area is a fun place to eat, a getaway from the more standardized central eateries. All restaurants are within walking distance of the Sevilla Metro station (Cozumel is right around the corner from the Sevilla exit) and from the museums in Chapultepec park.

Las Palomas Fonda, Cozumel 37 (tel. 553-79-72), in Col. Roma just north of Durango. As if the *mariachis* and vocalists were not entertaining enough, the food is delicious and the prices are reasonable. The exterior dining room is built into a greenhouse, with exotic plants and flowers draped over the tables and hand-painted chairs. Try the *carne asada* (broiled steak) with salad and potatoes (24 pesos). Open Mon.-Fri. 1:30-11pm, Sat.-Sun. 1:30-5pm.

Centro Macrobiótico Tao, Cozumel 76 (tel. 211-46-41), in Col. Roma south of Colima on the east side of the street. No steak and potatoes here. A display case holds stacks of holistic diet books. The dining room features music, bamboo screens, and floor seating at miniature tables with miniature placemats. The front room is an adjoining store that sells miso, lentils, ginger, oats, eastern spices, tofu and honey. Vegetarian *comida corrida* of soup, whole wheat bread, spiced rice, various vegetables, and chef's specialty (19 pesos), served to the mystic rhythm of the funky background music. Open daily 1:30-4:30pm. Store open 10am-6pm.

El Mesón de la Mancha, Puebla 326 (tel. 286-87-64), at Cozumel. Great food and service at a virtuous price. Popular on weekday afternoons with the dapper business crowd, but a haven for solitude for the weekend museum visitor. Occasional live *mariachis*, non-stop Mexican pop, and a big-screen TV to entertain. Complete meals 12-18 pesos; breakfast specials 7 pesos. AmEx, MC, Visa accepted. Open Mon.-Fri. 8am-10pm, Sat. 8am-6pm.

Casa de Nutrición and Cafetería Yug, Puebla 326-6 (tel. 553-38-72), at Cozumel in Col. Roma next door to El Mesón de la Mancha. A multi-faceted store and wholesome restaurant filled with granola, soy products, incense, vitamins, health manuals, and healing crystals. Books on alternative medicine, martial arts, astrology, magic, and discovering your inner self. The place to go if your vitamin supply has dwindled. Reasonably priced lunches or afternoon snacks. Veggie burgers 9 pesos. MC, Visa accepted. Open Mon.-Sat. 10am-8pm.

■ Coyoacán

The southern suburb of Coyoacán attracts students, young couples, and literati to its complement of elegant restaurants. Coyoacán is the birthplace of many Mexican politicians and presidents, and its restaurants play to that upper-level clientele. Outdoor cafés and ice-cream shops fill the colonial buildings which line the cobbled streets. You will find lots of menu items you don't usually see in downtown Mexico City: if you crave brie, cheesecake, or pesto, spend the afternoon in these 'burbs.

Café El Parnaso, Carrillo Puerto 2, at Jardín Centenario across from the cathedral. A beautiful outdoor café, book and record store, and art gallery. Come and brush elbows with Coyoacán's budding intelligentsia. Great for a cup of coffee and a view of the Pl. Hidalgo gardens. Inhale mocha cake, cheesecake with strawberries, or carrot cake 6 pesos. All kinds of pies 6 pesos, coffees 3-6 pesos, and a few sandwiches and salads (8-10 pesos). Open daily 9am-9:30pm.

Restaurante los Balcones, Allende 15-A (tel. 554-79-61), on the northeast corner of the park, above the Farmacia Coyoacán. Great pizza served in a classy dark wood interior decorated with lush greenery. 3 balconies overlook the Pl. Hidalgo for people watching. The pizza is priced to move at 14-16 pesos—try the Hawaiian (16 pesos). Open 8am-11pm.

El Murral, Allende 2 (tel. 554-02-98), across the street from Los Balcones. A surprisingly large restaurant with a glass roof with a tree growing through an opening for a more quaint ambience. Very nicely tiled and creatively decorated. Fresh hot tortillas prepared on the spot. Daily menu 34 pesos. Open 7:30am-8:30pm.

Restaurant El Guarache, Jardín Centenario 14, the green awning next to El Parnaso. The outdoor setting of El Parnaso for the hungry traveler. Mexican food at typically rising Mexican prices. *Pollo a la mexicana* 17.50 pesos. *Guarache verde o rojo* 15.50 pesos. Open daily 9am-10pm.

La Casa de los Tacos, Carrillo Puerto 23, 1 block south of Parque Hidalgo. This *taquería's* no converted garage operation. Upscale decor and a long list of tacos (2.50-15 pesos per order). A superstitious bunch runs this thriving taco business: garlic, horseshoes, and old knives and daggers dot the walls. Open daily 9am-midnight.

■ San Ángel

Especially on Saturdays, when crowds are drawn to the decidedly upscale Bazaar Sábado, both the chic restaurants and *típico* taco stands of San Ángel manage to pack 'em in. If snazzy dining is your thing, then the restaurants on the Plaza San Jacinto won't disappoint, but your wallet will feel plenty lighter afterwards.

Restaurante Hasti Bhawan, Pl. San Jacinto 9. Hindustani atmosphere inside a beautiful colonial building with impressive elephant-shaped planters. Featuring *pakora* and *samosa* appetizers and *lassi*, a thick Indian yogurt drink (5 pesos). Curry dishes and other entrees run 20-40 pesos. Sit at the exquisitely tiled green booth shaded by straw umbrellas. Live jazz Fridays and Saturdays 9pm-midnight. Open Tues.-Thurs. noon-11pm, Fri.-Sat. 1pm-midnight, Sun. noon-6pm.

El Rincón de La Lechuza, Miguel Angel de Quevedo 34 (tel. 661-59-11), to your left as you walk from Metro M.A. Quevedo to the Parque de la Bombilla. Joyfully crowded and very popular. Clay owls dot the walls surrounded by a bright yellow interior. Tacos 5.50-12.50 pesos. *Especiales* casseroles prepared with imported meat from New Zealand 18-26 pesos. Open Mon.-Thurs. 1pm-1am, Fri.-Sat. 1pm-2am, Sun. 1pm-midnight.

SIGHTS

It would be impossible to see everything in Mexico City in a month. You'll need a week to come away with anything resembling a well-rounded picture of the city. If you desire a chaperone, **Promoción Social del Centro Historic,** Chile 8 (tel. 510-25-41, ext. 1499), sponsors free walking tours in English, a different one each Sunday. Call for this week's destination and meeting spot. The **Sindicato Nacional de Guías Turísticos** (tel. 535-77-87), Virginia Fabregas, in Col. San Rafael dispatches licensed guides who cover special sights by foot or by car.

■■■ CENTRO

The heart of Mexico City, the **Centro,** could easily take weeks to explore. From the grand **Palacio Nacional** and the enormous **Catedral Metropolitana** to the **Monte Nacional de Piedad** (National Pawn Shop) and **Museo de la Ciudad de México,** the area is the cradle of much of the nation's culture. Like all of Mexico, the Centro contains history dating back thousands of years. A sometimes uneasy truce has been struck, allowing the ruins of Aztec pyramids to lie peaceably beside the cathedral which usurped its glory and the Palacio Nacional from which the modern state of Mexico is run.

The sights described in this section are divided into those east, north and south of the *zócalo*. To get there by Metro, take Line 2 to the Zócalo station. The station's entrance sits on the east side of the square, in front of the Palacio Nacional. The Catedral Metropolitana lies to the north, the Federal District offices to the south and the Suprema Corte de Justicia to the southeast. For an intelligently annotated checklist of every sight in the *Centro*, get a copy of the *Historic Center of the City of Mexico* from the map's publisher, SAC BE, Apdo. 22-315, 14000 México, D.F. *The Official Guide to Mexico City's Historic Center,* available in the shops of the Museum of Anthropology, Palacio de Bellas Artes, and major Spanish-English language bookstores (35-45 pesos) is another excellent and detailed source of information.

The Zócalo

The principal square of Mexico City, officially named the **Plaza de la Constitución,** is more widely known by its adopted title, the *zócalo*. Now surrounded by imposing colonial monuments, the square was originally the nucleus of the Aztec capital **Tenochtitlán.** The conquistadors razed Tenochtitlán, then built the seat of New Spain on top of the ruins, using stones from the destroyed city to construct Spanish churches and government buildings. To the southwest of the Templo Mayor (the Aztecs' principal place of worship, which they called Teocalli) was the Aztec marketplace and major square. Cortés paved this expanse with stones from the main pyramid, calling it *Plaza de Armas* or *Plaza Real*. He also assigned the plaza its perimeter (the dimensions of 240m on each side persist to this day), but it has since gone through many transformations. In 1692 it went up in flames, and in 1790 it was leveled and reorganized after a Moorish design, with many fountains because the Moors held water sacred. In the re-building process, two very important archaeological objects were unearthed: the statue of Coatlicue (deity of life and death) and "Piedra del Sol ("Stone of the Sun", the Aztec calendar). This second stone spent nearly a century leaning quietly against the cathedral's west side before the old Museo Nacional claimed it in 1885.

The square became the Plaza de la Constitución in 1812 when the representative assembly of the viceroyalty adopted the liberal Constitución de Cádiz here to protest Napoleon Bonaparte's occupation of Spain. This act of rebellion gave direction to the turmoil that eventually led to Mexico's independence. In 1843, the dictator Santa Ana destroyed the Mercado del Parián and ordered that a monument to independence be constructed in the center of the square. Only the *zócalo* (pedestal) was in place when the project was abandoned. The citizens of Mexico began to refer to the square as *el zócalo*, which has become the generic name for the central plazas in nearly all of the Republic's cities and towns. In 1952, Mexico City's *zócalo* was flattened into its present form.

Today, devoid of both merchants and fountains, the *zócalo* is instead filled with protesting groups, *artesanías*, street artists, indigeneous dancers and gaping tourists. Above this esoteric mix of life, the Mexican flag looms large. The flag is lowered daily at 6pm with militaristic and somewhat adolescent pomp, a hollow attempt to match the grandeur of the surrounding *zócalo's* 700 year history.

East of the Zócalo

Palacio Nacional

During his reign, Moctezuma II built a new palace, called the "New Houses," just south of the Teocalli. The Spaniards obliterated the palace, and in 1529 the King of Spain granted the land to Hernán Cortés, who proceeded to erect a new house of his own there. Architects Rodrigo de Pontecillas and Juan Rodríguez designed the building and *indígena* slave laborers built it using the stones from Moctezuma's palace. In 1562, the King of Spain bought back this house and the property from Don Martín Cortés (son of the conquistador) and made it the palace of the king's viceroys. The palace was destroyed during the Riot of 1692 and rebuilt a year later with stones from the original building. Subsequent modifications have given the building a Baroque character, although vestiges of earlier styles remain. The first two stories of the present palace date from the 1692 riot. In 1927, President Plutarco Calles ordered the construction of a third story to beautify the remains of the old palace. On the eastern patio are traces of the botanical gardens once cultivated by Emperor Maximilian's wife. The central patio hosted the first Mexican bullfight, in honor of Cortés's famous return from present day Honduras to resume leadership of the capital. For a time bullfights were staged here every Friday afternoon to entertain viceroys of the palace.

Now called the **Palacio Nacional de México** (tel. 512-20-60), the building occupies the entire east side of the *zócalo*, bounded on the north and south, respectively, by Moneda and Corregidora. Chief executive center of the Republic, the Palacio houses the federal treasury boys and g-men, as well as monumental murals, historical rooms and a museum in honor of Benito Juárez. Connected to the palace is the Museo de Las Culturas (see next section), once Emperor Maximilian's national mint.

It took Diego Rivera from 1929 to 1951 to sketch and paint the **frescoes** on the Palacio's western and northern walls. *Mexico Through the Centuries*, one of his most famous works, is on the west wall of the Palacio at the top of the grand staircase. The mural is divided into five smaller scenes, each depicting an event in the social evolution of Mexico. To the left and right of this grand central mural are two other of Rivera's most famous works. Covering the southern portion of the palace's western wall, *La Lucha de las Clases* (The Class Struggle). The mural depicts Mexican *campesinos* next to workers from around the world. Opposite it on the north-ern wall is a work entitled *La Leyenda de Quetzalcóatl*, which illustrates the life of the legendary Toltec priest-king who fled from his kingdom, conquered the Mayan people and ruled over the Yucatán Peninsula. The murals on the second floor of the palace on the north and east wall delve even further into Mexico's ancient history. On the east wall, *El Desembarco en Veracruz* graphically depicts the injustices of the slave trade. Three murals relate the achievements of the great Tarascan, Zapotec and Totonac civilizations, and three others show the evolution of corn, the harvest-ing of cacao, and the all-important *maguey* (a plant used in making tequila) indus-try. *La Gran Tenochtitlán* is dominated by the Mercado de Tlatelolco and filled out with the Temple of Tlatelolco, the center of Tenochtitlán, and the volcanoes Popoc-atépetl (Smoking Mountain) and Iztaccíhuatl (Sleeping Woman). Guides and post-cards of the murals are sold at the base of the central staircase (10 pesos), but are sometimes unavailable.

The Palacio also contains the **Bell of Dolores,** which was brought to the capital in 1896 from Dolores Hidalgo in Guanajuato state. It can be seen from outside the Palacio, at the top of the baroque façade. Padre Miguel Hidalgo de Dolores rang this bell on September 16, 1810, calling the people of Mexico to fight for their indepen-dence. Every year on that date it rings in memory of the occasion, and the Mexican President repeats the words once shouted by the father of independence. (Palacio open daily 8am-6pm. Guided tours Mon.-Fri. 10am-4pm. Free.)

The museum dedicated to Mexico's most revered President, Benito Juárez, is in the room in which he died on the Palacio's second floor. At the entrance to the **Museo Recinto Homenaje a Benito Juárez** (tel. 522-56-46), on the first floor, is a statue of Juárez that is supposedly cast from the bronze of enemy ammunition used in the War of Reform. The museum contains furniture from Juárez's house, some personal belongings and, best of all, a death mask cast before his body had even cooled. In the back room is Juárez's personal library, which houses more than 3000 documents from the reform years. To reach the museum, enter through the north-ern door of the palace, or walk north through the palace's central court. (Open Tues.-Fri. 9am-7:30pm. Free.)

Other Sights

La Merced, Circunvalación at Anaya east of the *zócalo*, or at Metro Merced on Line 2 (turn left out of the subway's eastern exit), is the largest food market of its kind in the world. Farmers from all over Mexico sell their goods here. The fruit section alone covers a large fraction of the 600 square blocks. Here you'll find fruits of every sort imaginable—papayas, home-grown lichee nuts, *mameyes* from Tabasco, man-gos, nine different kinds of *plátanos,* hot tamales and two full blocks of assorted chiles. Exotic indigenous foods such as fried turtles, steamed chicken intestines, *charales*—corn husks stuffed with shiners—and steamed crayfish abound. Die of happiness among infamous displays of *dulces* (candies) that stretch for five blocks; each vendor's stall displays over 300 kinds. The market is well worth a visit if only to get an idea of the diversity of Mexican food. The crowds picking through the pile of scraps and throwaways in the back, however, testify to the economic challenges Mexico still faces.

Near the beehive-like market blocks, on the corner of Manzanares and Circunva-lación, sits the faintly bizarre smallest church in the world, **El Señor de la Humil-idad,** measuring a mere six yards by nine yards and seating a maximum of 20. (Open daily 9am-8pm.) On the corner of Calle de la Santísima and Zapata is an elaborate Rococo church, the exquisite **Templo de la Santísima,** finished in 1783, one of the most important examples in the city of the ornamental Churrigueresque style. Fig-ures on the façade were intended to appear as if constructed of ivory, wood and cloth. The interior is unimpressive as the original decorations are long gone. Don't come here after dusk; the temple is lit but not well-patrolled. (Open daily 7am-1pm and 5-8pm.)

North of the Zócalo

Catedral Metropolitana

The conquest of Aztec religion by the forces of Christianity is perhaps more astonishing than Cortés's military triumph over Moctezuma's warriors. Mexico, once a land devoted to Quetzalcóatl, Tlaloc and Huitzilopochtli, became a New World stronghold of Christianity. In 1524, Cortés had Mexico's first cathedral built on the northwest corner of the *zócalo*, recycling stones from the temples of Tenochtitlán. Until 1552, this was the main church in Mexico and apparently the one the Franciscans used before building their own convent and church near the present site of the Torre Latinoamericana. In 1530, another cathedral went up on the site of the Templo Mayor and remained there until 1624. In 1544, the Spanish began construction of the **Catedral Metropolitana** (tel. 521-76-37), the massive structure on the north side of the *zócalo*. The 109m-long and 54m-wide cruciform cathedral encompasses the architectural styles of three centuries. Between 1544 and 1573, architect Claudio Arciniega directed the construction of the cathedral, modeling it after the one in Sevilla, Spain (Arciniega also designed America's first true cathedral in Santo Domingo). Dedicated in the middle of the 17th century, the Catedral Metropolitana wasn't finished until 1813. In that year, Manuel Tolsá completed the great central dome, the façade and the statues of Faith, Hope and Charity which crown the clock tower. There is an office on the far east side of the cathedral which can answer your questions (open Mon.-Fri. 9am-6:30pm, Sat. 9am-2pm. Cathedral open daily 8:30am-8pm; the schedule for mass is posted on the door furthest west).

The cathedral has several attached **annexes**. The main annex, with its door to the left of the cathedral, holds the **Altar de Perdón** (Forgiveness), a replica of a Churrigueresque altarpiece built by Jerónimo de Balbás between 1731 and 1736 and destroyed by fire in 1967. The cedar interior of the choir gallery, constructed in 1695 by Juan de Rojas, is decorated with an elegant grille of gold, silver and bronze. Juan Correa's murals of the coronation of the Virgin, St. Michael's slaying of the dragon and the triumphant entrance of Jesus into Jerusalem cover the sacristy's walls. Cristóbal de Villalpando painted the two other grand murals in this section, *La Immaculada Concepción* and *El Triunfo de la Iglesia*. Of the cathedral's many altars, one of the most magnificent is Balbás's Churrigueresque **Altar de los Reyes** (Kings), dedicated to those kings who were also saints.

The Spanish introduced the Aztecs to what Roman Catholics refer to as the communion of saints. In the annex holding the Altar de Perdón, there are 14 *capillas* (chapels) dedicated to those saints. Two chapels near the entrance honor Mexico's patron, the Virgin of Guadalupe. Legend holds that she appeared on a mountain before a poor peasant named Diego, entreating him to have a church built in her honor at that site. In order to convince the Mexican bishop of his vision, Diego laid a sheet full of fresh roses cut during the cold of December in front of the bishop. Both in awe, they watched the Virgin's portrait emerge on the sheet. The church was built, and today's paintings depict that first impression on the sheet.

The eastern annex holds the **Sagrario Metropolitano** (sanctuary). The Sagrario holds six chapels, with one main and two lateral altars. The Sagrario Metropolitano, designed by the great Churrigueresque architect Lorenzo Rodríguez, was built between 1749 and 1768 and its façades have since been copied in thousands of Mexican churches. Left of center are statues of the 12 apostles; to the right, the 12 prophets. In the center, above the door, are two statues, St. John and, above him, St. Joseph. Elaborate reliefs decorate the whole façade, and the Virtues crown the structure.

Unfortunately, the splendor of the cathedral is occluded by the green support structures constucted to stem the sinking of the temple into the ground.

Templo Mayor (Teocalli)

North of the *zócalo*'s northeast corner, a pool of water laps at a brass model of the Aztec capital, Tenochtitlán. At the center of this city was a great religious square surrounded by walls, each side 0.5km long. After wandering for hundreds of years, driven by the hummingbird god Huitzilopochtli, this was the first place that the Aztecs could call home. Legend has it that the high priest Tenoch saw an eagle perched on a cactus, which he took as a sign that the people from Aztlán had found their home. The Templo Mayor, or Teocalli, was built on the spot where Tenoch saw the eagle, now the corner of Seminario and República de Guatemala, a few meters north of the brass model. Teocalli is the major excavated archaeological site in Mexico City.

On February 28, 1978, workers digging east of the cathedral struck an immovable rock. They eventually unearthed an eight-ton Aztec stone on which had been carved the dismembered figure of the moon goddess Coyolxauqui, sister of Huitzilopochtli. The stone identified the area as the site of Teocalli, earlier believed to be buried under the Catedral Metropolitana to the southwest.

According to Aztec legend, Coatlicue, the terrible goddess of earth and death (whose monolithic statue now sits in the Museo Nacional de Antropología), became pregnant while sweeping out the temple. Her daughter Coyolxauqui grew jealous of her and plotted with her 400 brothers to kill their mother. When they reached her, however, they discovered that Huitzilopochtli had already been born, full-grown. He beheaded his sister; his brothers he turned into the planets and stars. The stone that the diggers found served in ancient times as part of the base of a great pyramid. At the pyramid's summit were two temples, one dedicated to the war god Huitzilopochtli and one dedicated to the rain god Tlaloc. Moctezuma I, who ruled the Aztec kingdom from 1440-1468, and his ruthless bloodthirsty half-brother Tlacaelel popularized the practice of ritual human sacrifice to the almighty Huitzilopochtli. Having become the head god, the hummingbird god Huitzilopochtli constantly demanded warm, beating human hearts. As sacrifice and a more than a touch of cannibalism rose to the rate of 10,000-20,000 victims per year, the supply of local victims ran low and Moctezuma I and Tlacaelel brilliantly devised the "Flower Wars." These practices were ceremonial battles where the Aztecs coerced their rival neighbors into giving them sacrificial victims in order to avoid a full-scale Aztec attack. (See Essentials: Life and Times for the broader picture.)

When the conquistadors arrived, Teocalli measured 103m by 79.5m at the base and was 61m high. Moctezuma II led Cortés on the grand tour of the temple, proudly pointing out the caked walls and sacrificial stones. Unfortunately the Castillian wasn't as impressed as Moctezuma had originally hoped. Instead of singing praises for the bloody empire, Cortés requested that Moctezuma clear a small place in the temple for an altar to the Virgin Mary. Moctezuma's violent refusal marked the pair's first major disagreement and paved the way for the Aztec's road to destruction.

Today the ruins lie gaping just east of the cathedral and north of the Palacio Nacional. That the huge site appears at first to be no more than the foundation of a demolished modern complex adds to the feeling of ancient grandeur once you are inside exploring the ruins. The excavated ruins reveal five layers of pyramids, built one on top of the other as the Aztec empire grew. Signs along the paths help explain which layer belongs to which temple. Over 7000 artifacts, including sculpture, jewelry and pottery, have been found amidst the ruins. Many of the pieces have been traced to distant societies dominated by the long arm of the Aztec empire. The extraordinary **Museo del Templo Mayor,** now part of the archaeological complex, houses this unique collection. This museum is a requisite for visitors even on a whirlwind tour of Mexico City. The exhibit is divided into eight *salas* (halls): antecedents and the settling of the Aztecs at the site of Tenochtitlán, war and sacrifice, tribute and commerce, Huitzilopochtli, Tlaloc, *faunas*, religion and the fall of Tenochtitlán. The museum was designed to imitate the layout of the original temple, and is constructed so that the artifacts found in the excavation are accompanied by excerpts from the ancient Aztec texts which describe them. Highlights of this exhibit are a scale model of Tenochtitlán at the height of its power, along with the stone of Coyolxauqui and the *Tzompantli* (skull rack), a platform where the freshly picked skulls of sacrificial victims were proudly displayed to the public and the gods above. Along with the silent and decapitated ruins adjacent to it, the museum bears witness to the glories of México-Tenochtitlán and makes the arrogant pride of their *cantares mexicanos* more understandable: "Oh giver of life! Bear it in mind, oh princes. Forget it not. Who can siege Tenochtitlán? Who can disturb the foundations of the sky? With our arrows, with our shields, the city exists. México-Tenochtitlán persists! Proud of herself rises the city of México-Tenochtitlán. No one fears death in combat here. This is our glory. This is your mandate."

(Museums and ruins open Tues.-Sun. 9am-5pm. Guided tours in Spanish free, in English 10 pesos per person. Admission 13 pesos. Sun. Free.)

Iglesia de Santo Domingo

The Iglesia de Santo Domingo, on the corner of Brasil and Venezuela, four blocks north of the *zócalo's* northwest corner, was founded by 12 Dominicans who arrived in 1526, three years after the first 12 Franciscans came from Spain. Within a year, five of the Dominicans had died and the other seven had fallen very ill. In 1527 all but three of the remaining friars returned to Spain. Among the three who stayed behind was Domingo de Bentanzos who founded the Convento de Santo Domingo in Mexico City as well as many more in the provinces of Guatemala. The first church, completed in 1590, was destroyed in a flood; by 1736 the present church was completed. The baroque edifice, considered one of the most beautiful in Mexico City, was built at a cost of 200,000 pesos, an enormous sum at the time. Its highlight, the façade, features the intertwined arms of Santo Domingo and St. Francis, as well as statues of the two saints. Also depicted is Diego holding up the impression of the Virgin of Guadalupe, with the Mexican bishop looking on in awe. There is an exegetical office to the left of the altar. (Office open Mon.-Fri. 10am-2pm and 4-6pm. Church open daily 7:30am-8pm.)

South of the Zócalo

In 1691, a heavy rainfall destroyed the wheat crop, causing a famine among the working classes the following year. The viceroy, Count de Gálvez, initiated rationing, but when rumors of nearly exhausted grain supplies spread, a group of *indígenas* was sent to investigate. De Gálvez turned them away, bringing on the Riot of 1692, the most violent Mexico has ever seen. Several buildings were burned, including part of the palace and much of the Casas del Cabildo, which had sheltered the city government offices and archives. These are now located in the two buildings that compose the offices of the **Departamento del Distrito Federal** (tel. 518-11-00). The older one, on the southwest end of the *zócalo*, was built according to the same plan as the pre-riot structure; on the exterior of this building are tiled mosaic shields that chronicle scenes from the history of Mexico. The newer building, on the southeast end of the *zócalo*, was built between 1940 and 1948, 400 years after its twin. Fortunately, Don Carlos de Sigüenza y Góngora saved the building's archives, currently located in the Archivo Nacional. Now most of the buildings are administrative.

Suprema Corte de Justicia

The Suprema Corte de Justicia, built in 1929, stands on the corner of Pino Suárez and Corregidora, on the spot where the southern half of Moctezuma's royal palace once stood. After the palace was leveled, Spanish colonists turned the area into a garbage dump. Cortés claimed the property, had it cleared and designated it the site of city festivities, including a maypole dance, in which men suspended by ropes swung in circles from a pole. Four rather ferocious Orozco murals cover the second-floor walls of the present day Supreme Court. On the west wall hangs *Riquezas Nacionales*, in which a giant tiger, representing the national conscience, defends the mineral riches of the Republic. The mural on the east wall, *El Trabajo* (Work), symbolizes Article 123 of the Mexican Constitution, which guarantees workers' rights. The two remaining murals are called *La Justicia*. The one on the north wall shows a bolt of fire taking human form; the apparition wields a huge axe, with which it threatens a group of masked evil-doers. On the south wall, Justice sleeps on a pedestal, holding a sword and the law. (Open Mon.-Fri. 9am-2pm.)

Museo de la Ciudad de México

The Museo de la Ciudad de México, Pino Suárez 30 (tel. 542-04-87), at República de El Salvador, three blocks south of the *zócalo's* southeast corner, is dedicated to the founders of Mexico City, and houses maps, photographs, lithographs and murals charting their lives and achievements. The exhibits start on the ground floor and progress chronologically, illustrating the progression of pre-Conquest development in the Valley of Mexico as you move counter-clockwise around the central court-yard. The first showcases depict the geological formation of the Valley of Mexico and Lake Texcoco. Other rooms detail the rise of the Aztec empire in the 15th and 16th centuries, with models of Tenochtitlán and diagrams of its social structure. The upstairs exhibit again progresses counterclockwise, this time chronicling the evolution of "New Spain" from the 16th century to the usurpations, betrayals and victories of the Revolution of 1910. The final exhibit of the museum is the south wing of the second story which portrays contemporary Mexico City, featuring the construction of the Metro and a gigantic model of the Torre Latinoamericana. A photo of the modern city center fills an entire wall, successfully communicating the immensity of this metropolis. Though the dark building is somewhat gloomy, it contributes to the historical feel of the museum, an appropriate place to display the city's artifacts.

In contrast to the Templo Mayor Museum and its archaeological view of Aztec culture, the Museo de la Ciudad offers an historical account of Mexican culture and provides a broad background for most of your other sight-seeing, making it an ideal first stop in your quest to understand the significance of the city's treasures. (Open Tues.-Sun. 10am-6pm. Free.)

Other Sights

Across the street from the cathedral's west side on Calle Monte de Piedad is the **Monte Nacional de Piedad** (tel. 521-19-46), or the National Pawn Shop. This building holds a state-controlled flea market at which dealers sell mostly high-quality jewelry at reasonable prices. (Market open Mon.-Fri. 10am-5pm, Sat. 10am-3pm.)

Calle Corregidora, the street between the Suprema Corte and Palacio Nacional, skirts part of an **ancient canal system** that once connected the Aztec capital to the *pueblos* around Xochimilco. The construction of this intricate and efficient transport system was key in the Aztec's rise to power in the valley. After the conquest of Tenochtitlán, Cortés ordered that the remains of the buildings be dumped into the canals. The Spanish, who had animals for transport, had no use for the canal system. Today, both sides of the ancient canal system are paved as a pedestrian thoroughfare and the canal itself is covered by shrubs and small flower bushes.

Founded in 1603, the **Templo de Porta Coeli** (tel. 542-02-25), across Calle Carranza from the Suprema Corte's southern end, was among the first institutions to inculcate Catholicism to young Spaniards and *indígena* Mexicans. The temple houses a replica of the original **Cristo Negro** (Black Christ), now at the Catedral Metropolitana. (Open Mon.-Sat. 9am-6pm, Sun. 9am-1pm.) **Calle Carranza,** was known for a long time after the Conquest as *Celada* (trap or ambush): during the fighting that led to the conquest of the city, the Aztecs killed many Spaniards by setting ingenious snares in this area.

Southwest of the *zócalo*, at the corner of 5 de Febrero and 16 de Septiembre, is the famous **Gran Hotel de la Ciudad de México.** Visit at midday to see the light shine through the Tiffany stained-glass ceiling with three flower-shaped central domes. Every detail is pure art nouveau; even the parakeets live in elaborate brass cages with stained glass ceilings. Directly above Restaurante El Malecón, Carranza 9, is the skinniest apartment building in the world. Its four stories measure 11m high and only 3m wide.

■■■ ALAMEDA

A large park in the middle of downtown Mexico City, *Alameda Central* is a symbol of the city's glory seen in the light of its history of bloody conquest. Many of the city's historical landmarks are located in the surrounding area, known simply as *Alameda*. Because many bus and Metro routes criss-cross the area, *Alameda* is a superb base for budget travelers.

There are two Metro stations near the park: the Hidalgo station (Lines 2 and 3) is at the intersection of Hidalgo and Paseo de la Reforma, just one block west of the park's northwest corner, and the Bellas Artes station (Line 2) is one block east of the park's northeast corner, between the park and Bellas Artes itself. Maps of the area are available at the tourist office (see Practical Information).

At the corner of Arranza and Puente del Alvarado, three blocks north of the Monumento a la Revolución, the **Museo San Carlos** houses an old art school and an impressive collection of 16th through 19th-century paintings from the European schools. (Open Tues.-Sun. 10am-5pm. Admission 10 pesos, free Sun.)

Alameda Central

Although *Parque Alameda* has existed for hundreds of years, it is only in this century that it became open to the public. It is an icon of the city, as Diego Rivera recognized in his mural of the *Alameda* (see below). All elements of society congregate around it.

While the expansive *zócalo* may serve as the city's centerpiece and the Bosque de Chapultepec as its cultural center-playground, the *Alameda* serves as a microcosm of life in Mexico City. Under the shadow of the grand Palacio de Bellas Artes (see below), rock groups jam and vendors perform skits to hawk their wares. Mime groups, all too willing to poke fun at anyone showing signs of *gringo* background, draw victims from the crowds which relax in the grassy patches that were once the exclusive domain of the rich and powerful. Protesters camping out in makeshift huts mix amiably with the hordes of young couples seeking a quiet moment alone.

Palacio de Bellas Artes

This palace, located at Juárez and Eje Central, at the northeast corner of *Alameda Central* (tel. 709-31-11 ext. 133), is but one result of the progressive "capitalization" plan established during the *Porfiriato*, Porfirio Díaz's dictatorship (1876-1911). Apart from its role as a repository of great works by 20th-century Mexican artists, the Palacio de Bellas Artes, facing the eastern end of *Alameda*, is a fascinating artifact of Díaz's time and the subsequent revolution. Construction began in 1904 under the Italian architect Boari, who promised a fantastically innovative building. The Italian extravaganza was intended to serve as a symbol of national progress and as a theater for Mexico's upper class. Soon after construction began, however, the theater started to sink into the city's soft ground. (It has sunk 5m to date; the sinking is not widely held to be part of the symbolism.) By the time activity was resumed in 1932, Boari was dead and the new government decided to open the Palacio de Bellas Artes instead of a theater. The job was finished in 1934, and the museum finally opened in 1946. In completing the building, the second architect, Federico Mariscal, respected Boari's exterior design but dramatically altered the interior.

Mariscal's art deco interior strikingly contrasts with the conservative exterior. This style, made popular in Paris at the 1925 decorative arts exposition, is characterized by sharp angles, geometric forms and imaginative lighting. The majority of the museum's collection is 19th-century Mexican art, featuring José María Velasco, Eugenio Langesio, Julio Ruelasa and Joaquín Clausell. Most people, however, come to the palace to see the walls of the second and third floors, painted by the most celebrated Mexican muralists of the 20th century. That the murals' aggressive imagery clashes with the industrial decor is tribute to the vitality the artists' talents lend to the building's grandeur.

ALAMEDA

The Palacio displays a collection of the frescoes of David Alfaro Siqueiros (1896-1974), the 20th-century Mexican muralist, Stalinist, nationalist, and the would-be assassin of Leon Trotsky. Siqueiros experimented with lighting, colors and surfaces, but he is best known as a *típico* muralist. Look for his work on the third floor of the Palacio. Like his contemporary Diego Rivera, Siqueiros's favorite themes were class struggle and social injustice, and he flaunted, like his contemporary, a cavalier disregard for topical subtlety. Two examples of the latter are his *Caín en los Estados Unidos*, an attack on racism in the U.S., and *Nacimiento del Fascismo*. Many of his paintings are layered with masonite, lending them a three-dimensional effect. A good example of this technique is *Explosión en la Ciudad*, in which the smoke from an explosion seems to stream toward the viewer. On the east wall hang of the third floor murals by José Clemente Orozco depicting the tension between natural human characteristics and industrialization.

If you have time for only one mural, see the one by Diego Rivera on the west wall of the third floor. Intended for a North American audience, the original was to be painted in New York City's Rockefeller Center with Rockefeller's chosen theme: "Man at Crossroads Looking with Hope and High Vision to the Choosing of a New and Better Future." Rivera was prohibited from finishing the mural, however, when Rockefeller noticed Lenin in the foreground. When an angry Rivera petitioned the Mexican government to allow him to duplicate the work, he was given this space in the Palacio. This second, more vehement rendering includes an unflattering portrayal of John D. Rockefeller, Sr. (Open daily 10am-8pm.)

On the fourth floor of the palace is the **Museo Nacional de Arquitectura** (National Museum of Architecture). The exhibit is of early sketches and blueprints for the most architecturally complex and distinctive buildings in Mexico City, including the *Teatro Nacional*, the monument to the Revolution, and the Hotel Del Prado. There is a bookstore on the first floor of the museum that sells numerous books about the history of art and Mexican artists, as well as guides to museums in Mexico City. (Palacio de Bellas Artes open Tues.-Sun 10am-6pm. Free, though some traveling exhibits charge 5 pesos admission, free for students and teachers with ID.) The **Ballet Folklórico de México** performs regional and historical dances in the **Palacio de Bellas Artes** and the **Teatro Ferrocarrilero** (Revolución Metro stop). Their two companies, one resident and one traveling, are known the world over for their choreographic and theatrical skill. (Performances Wed. at 9pm, Sun. at 9:30am and 9pm. Tickets 80-110 pesos, sold 3 or 4 days in advance at Bellas Artes but usually available, Mon.-Sat. 11am-3pm and 5-7pm, Sun. 10:30am-1pm and 4-7pm. Tel. 529-17-01.) Travel agencies snatch up lots of tickets during Christmas, *Semana Santa*, and summer; check first at Bellas Artes, then try along Reforma or in the *Zona Rosa*. These performances are the only way to see the wonderful crystal curtain designed by Gerardo Murelli, one of Mexico's greatest painters. It consists of almost one million pieces of multi-colored crystal which, when illuminated from behind, represent the Valley of Mexico in twilight.

Museo Nacional de Arte

The Museo Nacional de Arte, Tacuba 8 (tel. 512-32-24 or 512-16-84), half a block east of the Palacio's north side, is even more representative of the Díaz era than is the Palacio de Bellas Artes. It was intended to house the Secretary of Communications, the brainchild of Porfirio Díaz. The architect, Silvio Conti, designed its pre-Cambrian façade and paid particular attention to the central staircase: its beautifully sculpted baroque handrails and lampposts and ornate blue and gold ceilings were crafted by artists in Florence and shipped to Mexico. The design leaves the museum with an empty feel, and footsteps echo through the lonely galleries.

Unlike the Palacio de Bellas Artes, this museum contains works from the stylistic and ideological schools of every era in Mexican history. The galleries are divided by style and era. The works of the second floor include some by Doctor Atl ("water" in Nahuatl), the great precursor of Mexican muralism. He is best known for his volcano paintings, but *La Nube* (the cloud) is unique among his works in its use of sprightlier blues, yellows and greens. Other works on the second floor include paintings by Orozco, Ramón, Cano Manilla (renowned for his use of color to celebrate *indígena* life) and José María Velasco, whose paintings include several panoramic landscapes of the Valley of Mexico. The upper floors exhibit art from New Spain, religious art, and cartoon and newspaper art. Special temporary exhibits occupy the rear of the ground floor. (Museo Nacional de Arte open Tues.-Sun. 10am-5:30pm. Admission 10 pesos, free Sunday.)

In front of the building is a brilliant bronze equestrian statue, *El Caballito*. At the close of the 18th century, the viceroy of Mexico commissioned Neoclassical sculptor Don Manuel Tolsá to cast this monument in honor of Carlos IV de Borbón, King of Spain. Between 1824 and 1852, the monument had to be hidden at the University of Mexico because of strong anti-Spanish sentiment.

At Tacuba 5, across the street from the Museo Nacional, stands the original **Palacio de Minería** (Palace of Mining, tel. 521-40-20), also built by Tolsá in the late 18th century. It is thought to be one of the best examples of Neoclassical architecture in the country. In 1867 it became the **Escuela Nacional de Ingeniería,** probably the first technical school in the Americas. (Open daily 7am-8pm. Free.)

Near Alameda Central

José Martí was a poet-intellectual and leader of the Cuban independence movement in the late 19th century. He dreamt of a united and free Latin America with Mexico a leader in the region, and repeatedly warned of the dangers of North American imperialism. A poem Martí wrote for Mexico is inscribed on the wall of the **Centro Cultural José Martí,** Dr. Mora 2 (tel. 521-21-15), at Hidalgo on *Alameda's* west end. The center contains books by Martí and other anti-interventionists, and sponsors a program of musical performances, poetry readings and art exhibits. The major visual attraction at the center is an immense mural covering two walls with Martí as the centerpiece and the people of Latin America behind. A tally sheet in the corner of the mural records the Spanish, British, French and U.S. foreign interventions into Latin American countries from 1800 to 1969. (Mexico has the most—with a grand total of 284). The program is posted just outside the center and advertised in *Tiempo Libre*, which can be found at any newsstand. McCarthyites may find the blaring (and largely ignored) Communist propaganda outside annoyingly proletarian but therapeutic. (Open Mon.-Fri. 9am-9pm, Sat. 9am-2pm. Free, of course)

The **Pinacoteca Virreinal de San Diego,** Dr. Mora 7 (tel. 510-27-93), next door to Centro Cultural José Martí, was once a large monastery inhabited by the order of San Diego. The building was originally constructed in the Baroque style, but Neoclassical elements were added in the 19th century. Now the monastery's large rooms with high, decorated ceilings and wooden floors contain an extensive collection of baroque and Mannerist paintings, generally of religious themes. (Open Tues.-Sun. 9am-5pm. Admission 5 pesos.)

The **Museo de la Alameda,** (tel. 521-10-16) on Calzada Colón and Balderas, facing the small park at the west end of the *Alameda*, holds Diego Rivera's *Sueño de un Tarde Dominical en la Alameda Central* (Dream of a Sunday afternoon at the *Alameda Central*), the only item in the museum's permanent collection. Originally commissioned by the Hotel del Prado in 1946, the painting depicts the dreams of different (but in some way fundamentally equal) classes of people parading about the *Alameda* on a Sunday afternoon at the turn of the century. Rivera finished the masterpiece in 1948, but when the Hotel Del Prado proudly hung the just-finished work, a national controversy ensued over the figure of Ignacio Ramírez, who is shown holding up a pad of paper that reads "God does not exist," an excerpt from a speech he gave in 1836. The archbishop of Mexico refused to bless the hotel, and on June 4th at dawn, more than 100 pro-God students broke into the hotel, erased the "does not exist" fragment from the original phrase and damaged the face of the young Diego Rivera in the center of the mural. Newspapers ran headlines about the incident for days, and Rivera later "chose" to change the slogan. On the wall of the museum is a 15-page letter from Frida Kahlo to President Miguel Alemán expressing her outrage at the defacement of her husband's work.

The Hotel del Prado partially collapsed during the 1985 quake, and the mural was moved to the museum, constructed solely to hold this piece. An entire wall chronicles the engineering feat involved in moving a national treasure. The key in front of the mural points out the portrayal of historical figures woven into the crowd: Frida Kahlo, José Martí and a chubby young Rivera, among others. (Museum open daily 10am-2pm and 3-5pm. 3 pesos. Free Sundays and for students and teachers.)

The **Torre Latinoamericana** (Latin American Tower), 181m and 42 stories high, touches the sky over the corner of Lázaro Cárdenas and Madero (the continuation of Juárez), one block east of *Alameda Central's* southeast corner. From the top of the tallest building in Mexico, you can often see the entire city and the mountains surrounding it. (Top-floor observatory open daily 10am-11pm. Admission 10 pesos.) If you are interested in seeing the natural order inverted, visit the 38th floor of the tower which holds "the highest **aquarium** in the world," probably the most fish you will ever see at 2358m above sea level for a mere 8 pesos. (Open daily 10am-11pm.) On the 41st floor, the Miralto bar, separate from the observatory and aquarium, charges prices almost as high as the tower itself for food and drinks—try stalling here for a free view only one story from the top.

La Iglesia de San Francisco (built in 1716) rests in the shadow of the Torre Latinoamericana just to the east on Madero. It was once a vast Franciscan complex that included several churches, a school and a hospital. Two fragments of the original cloisters can be seen at Gante 5, on the east side of the church, and Lázaro Cárdenas 8, behind a vacant lot. The Franciscans were the first order to arrive in Mexico; among the 12 initial monks were some of the greatest linguists, ethnographers and chroniclers of indigenous custom and belief in the annals of Mexican history. The church is open daily 7am to 8:45pm, but avoid visiting Saturday morning and afternoon and all day Sunday during mass hours. Questions are answered in the office in the central nave (open Mon.-Fri. 9am-1pm and 5-7pm, Sat 9am-1pm).

Across the street from San Francisco shimmers the **Casa de Azulejos,** an early 17th-century building covered with *azulejos* (blue and white tiles) from Puebla, now a property of Sanborn's. To be able to afford even a token few of these tiles was a mark of considerable status. This mansion was festooned by an insulted son who set out to prove his worth to his father. There is an Orozco mural on the staircase wall, but you have to pass through Sanborn's restaurant to view it (open daily 7:30am-10pm).

Palacio Iturbide, at Madero 17 between Bolívar and Gante (tel. 521-57-97), one-and-a-half blocks east of Lázaro Cárdenas and near the Iglesia de San Francisco, is a grand 18th-century palace with an impressive colonnaded courtyard. The Count of San Mateo Valparaíso lived here, but in 1821 Emperor Agustín de Iturbide took over the residence. Bánamex took over the building from the Emperor, but there is a gallery on the ground floor with exhibits that change every three months. (Open daily 9am-2pm and 4-6pm.)

Just north of the *Alameda* is the new **Museo Franz Mayer,** Hidalgo 45 (tel. 518-22-65), at Pl. de Santa Veracruz. Formerly the Hospital de San Juan de Dios, the building has been expertly restored and now houses an extensive collection of colonial furniture and other applied arts. (Open Tues.-Sun. 10am-5pm. Admission 5 pesos, 1 peso for students with ID. Free Sun. Spanish tours for 3 pesos, and English or Spanish brochures for .40 pesos.)

Next door to the Franz Mayer museum in the pink building at Hidalgo 39 (tel. 521-22-24), is the **Museo Nacional de la Estampa.** This museum holds the National Institute of Fine Arts's graphic arts and engraving collection, tracing the art of printmaking from pre-Hispanic seals to contemporary engravers, and also displays an extensive exhibit on the method of printmaking, the techniques and tools used to create the intricate and colorful prints. The highlight of the museum is the work of the acclaimed José Guadalupe Posada: skeletons dancing, singing and generally carousing. (Open Tues.-Sun. 10am-6pm. Admission 8 pesos, free Sun.)

The **Mercado de Artesanías de la Ciudadela** is a huge, tourist-patronized crafts market spreading southwest from the corner of Balderas and Ayuntamiento. Even further west, at the Plaza de la República under the **Monumento a la Revolución,** is the **Museo Nacional de la Revolución** (tel. 546-21-15). Díaz originally planned the site as the seat of Congress, but as the revolutionary fighting entered the city streets, progress was halted, and the dome was left only half-way completed. It wasn't until the 1930s that the monument and space below were finally dedicated to the memory of the revolution. Today flag poles of each of the 32 Mexican states line the pathway to this marmoreal dome. The hardest job in the city may be that of the workers who must keep the copper dome polished, a virtually perpetual task.

A star-shaped opening in the ground below the monument provides a preview to the subterranean museum. Just inside the main door, a quote endeavors to capture the revolutionary spirit. From there the exhibit powers into a chronological history of the revolutionary movement, from Porfirio Díaz's dictatorship to the creation of Mexico's current constitution in 1917. The exhibits are mostly 3-D dioramas of scenes and events from this period, created with props, video and life-size cut-outs of important figures. The best scene is probably the revolutionary camp, with clothing, bags and supplies slung up against a photo backdrop of a revolutionary base hidden deep in the hills. (Museum open Tues.-Sun. 9am-5pm. Free.)

■■■ BOSQUE DE CHAPULTEPEC

Literally "Forest of Grasshoppers," this is the area where the Aztecs, new and unwelcome arrivals to the Valley of Mexico, first settled, ending their centuries of wandering by becoming a vassal state to the then all-powerful Tepanecas. Lying on the western side of the city's center, this area is now an enormous park. With its manifold museums, hiking paths and modern sports facilities, it could easily consume several days of your stay. Mexico's most famous museum, the **Museo Nacional de Antropología,** sits among the hills of the park.

All the museums listed are in Old Chapultepec, the eastern half of the park, which fans out to the east of the *Zona Rosa*. Take the Metro to Auditorio (Line 7) or to Chapultepec (Line 1) to reach the park. The Auditorio stop is closer to the zoo; the Chapultepec stop is directly in front of the **Niños Héroes** monument, closer to most of the museums and much more convenient.

Visit the Bosque on Sunday, when families flock here for cheap entertainment. Musical spectacles enliven the park, and voices fill the air promoting foods and trinkets. Best of all, most of the museums in the area and the zoo are free on Sundays. (Open daily 5am-5pm.)

Museo Nacional de Antropología

Some journey to Mexico just to consult this massive mega-museum, located at Paseo de la Reforma and Gandhi (tel. 553-62-66). It is 4km of Mexico's finest archaeological and ethnographic treasures and the yardstick by which all other Mexican museums are measured.

Constructed of volcanic rock, wood and marble, the museum opened in 1964. Pedro Ramírez Vásquez and his team of 42 engineers and 52 architects designed and built the structure in 18 months; meanwhile, archaeologists, buyers and 20 teams of ethnographers scrambled to enlarge the museum's collection. After the huge stone image of the rain-god Tlaloc greets you outside, 23 exhibition halls await on two floors surrounding a spacious central courtyard. Poetry from ancient texts and epics graces the entrances from the main courtyard. In the center of the courtyard, a stout column covered with symbolic sculptures supports a vast, water-spouting aluminum pavilion.

You'll need about three days to do homage to the entire museum. Though after a few hours even the most hardy of visitors may suffer from pottery overload, there is more than enough to fascinate anyone from the dilettante to the Ph.D. candidate. Archaeological *salas* (halls), each devoted to a specific culture or region, occupy the ground floor. On the northern side of the ground floor, galleries display chronologically ordered artifacts of cultures that have dominated the Valley of Mexico. The Oaxacan, Mayan, Gulf Coast, Northern and Western displays are on the southern side. Upper-level rooms contain modern ethnographic displays and lie directly above the rooms devoted to the corresponding ancient culture. All the ethnographic halls of the museum have more or less the same agenda: displaying the cultural accoutrements of the peoples now living in Mexico. Large shelters were built by indigenous people commissioned to duplicate their buildings in the museum.

The museum also contains a **restaurant** (open Tues.-Sun. 9am-6pm) and a large **bookshop** that sells English guides to archaeological sites around the country as well as histories and ethnographies of Mexico's indigenous populations (some of these guides are not available at the sites themselves, so plan ahead). (Museum open Tues.-Sat. 9am-7pm, Sun. 9am-6pm. Admission 13 pesos, free Sun.) To reach the museum, take bus #55 or #76 southwest on Reforma and signal the driver to let you off at the second stop after entering the park. On the Metro, take Line 1 to the Auditorio station; the museum is just down Reforma. For a more scenic route, take Line 1 to Chapultepec station. Outside stands the **Monumento a los Niños Héroes,** six black monoliths dedicated to the young cadets of the 19th-century military academy (then at Castillo de Chapultepec). In 1847, during the last major battle of the war with the U.S., the *Niños Héroes* fought the invading army of General Winfield Scott. Refusing to surrender, the last six boys wrapped themselves in the Mexican flag and threw themselves from the castle wall. Behind the monument, Avenida Gran cuts through the park. Walk west on this street and take the second right on Gandhi. A five-minute stroll north takes you to Reforma and the museum.

Museo Tamayo and Museo de Arte Moderno

Just to the east of the Museo Nacional de Antropología is the **Museo Tamayo de Arte Contemporáneo Internacional** (tel. 286-65-19), on the corner of Reforma and Gandhi. The Mexican government created the nine halls of the museum after Rufino and Olga Tamayo donated their international collection to the Mexican people. Rufino Tamayo, born in 1889 in the city of Oaxaca, was considered un-Mexican during the nationalist era following the Revolution of 1910. Only recently has he been included in the distinguished group of Rivera, Siqueiros and Orozco, rounding out the "Big Four" of modern Mexican art. The museum, opened in 1981, has important works by Max Ernst, de Kooning and the Surrealists Joan Miró and Masson. Other highlights include a few paintings by Pablo Picasso, Torres García, Mathías Goeritz and mainly Tamayo himself. Architects Gonzalo de León and Abraham Zabludovsky designed the building with non-converging lines and planes; the idea was to create a feeling of openness. (Open Tues.-Sun. 10am-5:45pm. Admission 10 pesos. Free Sun and for students and teachers with ID. Call to arrange guided tours.)

The **Museo de Arte Moderno,** at Reforma and Gandhi (tel. 553-62-11), north of the Monumento a los Niños Héroes, houses an impressive collection of contemporary paintings by Mexican artists such as Siqueiros, José Luis Cuevas, Rivera and Velasco. The museum is linked to the smaller circular Galería Fernando Camboa by an outdoor sculpture garden. (Enter the museum on Reforma. Open Tues.-Sun. 10am-6pm. Admission 10 pesos, free Sun.)

Museo Nacional de Historia

Inside the Castillo de Chapultepec, on top of the hill behind the Monumento a los Niños Héroes waits the Museo Nacional de Historia (tel. 553-72-02). This hill has seen its share of action, beginning in 1521 when after the Conquest Hernán Cortés claimed the hill and built a fortress here. Later the King of Spain snapped it up as a wildlife preserve. It then became the official viceroy's residence, then the last bastion against U.S. invaders, and then, redecorated, the palace of Emperor Maximilian and his successors as Mexican head of state. By 1940 the hill had had enough and became the Museo Nacional de Historia.

The intention of the museum is to pick up where the anthropology museum left off, starting at the lower floor of the building where artifacts, murals and documents narrate the history of Mexico from before the time of the Conquest. The galleries contain displays on Mexican economic and social structure during the war for independence, the *Porfiriato* and the Revolution. The upper level exhibits Mexican art, dress and culture from the viceroyalty until the 20th century. The section of the museum termed the *Alcázar* models the offices, homes and belongings of the presidents who lived in the castle. The rooms entered from outside the castle exhibit carriages used by Maximilian (the elaborate ones) and Juárez (the basic black ones). *Sala* 5 contains a Juan O'Gorman mural depicting the revolution, from the cruelties of the aristocracy to the triumph of the constitution as the background moves from night into day. *Sala* 13's walls are completely covered by Siqueiros's *Del Porfirismo a la Revolución*. The skyscrapers abutting the museum afford a view surpassed only by the Torre Latinoamericana. (Open Tues.-Sun. 9am-5pm, tickets sold until 4pm. Admission 13 pesos. Free Sun., but all 2nd-floor *salas* are closed. Video 10 pesos. Camera 5 pesos.)

Museo del Caracol

The **Museo Galería de la Lucha del Pueblo Mexicano por su Libertad** (the Museum of the Struggle of the Mexican People for Liberty, tel. 553-62-85), on the southern side of Chapultepec hill, can be reached by way of the road leading to the castle/museum, to the right as the path turns straight to meet the castle. Designed by Pedro Vásquez, this museum is often listed as **Galería de Historia** or even more commonly as **Museo del Caracol** (Conch) because of its spiral design. The gallery consists of 12 halls dedicated to the greatest hits of Mexican history from the early 19th to the early 20th century. From the start of your downward spiral, the gist of the museum's message is clear: foreign intervention has made Mexico's fight for its liberty an uphill battle. Documented events in the exhibit include the execution of Javier Mina, the compassion of Nicolás Bravo, the executions of Hidalgo and Morelos, the flight of Benito Juárez, the execution of Maximilian, the railroad-building of the dictator Díaz, the strike and massacre at Cananea and the battles of Villa, Zapata and Obregón. The museum's exhibits consist of fading dioramas and non-riveting historical artifacts. Visitors unfamiliar with the major events in Mexican history will be bewildered by the Spanish-only explanations. The staircase leads to a beautiful round skylit hall, the sides of which form the inner wall of the spiral you have been ascending. Also inside is a copy of the Constitution of 1917 in Venustiano Carranza's hand. (Open Tues.-Sat. 9am-5pm, Sun. 10am-4pm. Admission 7 pesos, free Sun.)

Elsewhere in Chapultepec

Twenty-five days before his death in January of 1974, the handy David Alfaro Siqueiros donated his house and studio to the people of Mexico. In compliance with his will, the government created the **Museo Sala de Arte Público David Alfaro Siqueiros,** Tres Picos 29 (tel. 531-33-94), at Hegel just outside the park. Walk north from the Museo Nacional de Antropología to Rubén Darío; west about one block until you come to Hegel; and north on Hegel for one block—the museum is on your left. Fifteen thousand murals, lithographs, photographs, drawings and documents of Siqueiros's life and thoughts fill the galleries. Before his death in 1974, Siqueiros cleared out the garage and garden of his house to make room for *Maternity*, the monstrous work that now covers the walls and parts of the ceiling and floor of the main room. Even if you are not a die-hard Siqueiros fan, come to see the products of a lifetime of prolific work together in the place it was created. Call before visiting to arrange a guided tour in English or Spanish. (Open Mon.-Fri. 10am-2pm and 5-7pm, Sat. 10am-2pm. Admission 3 pesos, students with ID 1.50 pesos. Free Sun.)

West of the Siqueiros museum along Rubén Darío, at the intersection with Reforma, lies the **Jardín Escultórico,** a park containing realist and symbolist statues. To the south and east of the sculpture garden, at Reforma and Av. Heróico Colegio Militar, flourishes the **Jardín Botánico,** a botanical garden whose lake contains a variety of fish. (Open daily 9am-5pm. Free.) Those tired of murals'n'churches make a swim for **Parque Zoológico de Chapultepec,** just east of the Jardín Botánico. The first zoos in the Americas were established in this region. The emperor of Texcoco, Netzahualcóyotl, kept animals; Cortés founded bird sanctuaries and aquariums in Ixtapalpa; and Moctezuma II had a zoo that the Spaniards rudely destroyed to build the Iglesia de San Francisco. Today, the zoo's most noteworthy residents are the rare panda bears, a gift from the People's Republic of China in 1975. Also worth seeing are the *Xoloitzcuintles*, bald Mexican dogs of pre-Conquest origin. The name means "dogs of Xolotl," and they were said to guide people in their passage to Xolotl, the god of death. Though the zoo's collection is quite impressive, animal lovers may shed a tear for the proud beasts restricted to humble habitats, and subjected to the D.F. smog. (Zoo open Wed.-Sun. 9am-4:45pm. Free.)

■■■ TLATELOLCO

Recent archaeological digs have proven that the pre-Hispanic city Tlatelolco ("Mound of Sand" in Nahuatl) existed much earlier than the great Aztec capital of Tenochtitlán. The first king of Tlatelolco, Teutlehuac, began his rule in 1375. He and his warriors distinguished themselves in battle, conquering enemy territory near Tepeyac on the outskirts of Tenochtitlán. The Aztecs, living on an island in the central part of Lake Texcoco, realized by the middle of the 15th century that the rulers of Tlatelolco, built on the northern part of the same lake, were threatening their political and military power.

By 1463, the Tlatelolco king, Moquihuix, had built his city into a busy trading center coveted by the Aztec ruler, Axayacatl. Tension mounted over territorial and fishing boundaries, and soon Moquihuix learned that the Aztecs were preparing to attack his city. Even forewarned, Moquihuix couldn't handle the Aztec war machine, and Tlatelolco was absorbed into the huge empire. Ironically, it was here that the Aztec nation made its own last stand against Cortés, and here that it lived in poverty soon after.

Today, a state low-income housing project surrounds the early 17th-century church that stands on the grounds of Tlatelolco's ancient temple. Three cultures— ancient Aztec, colonial Spanish and modern mestizo—have left their mark on this square, giving rise to the name **Plaza de las Tres Culturas,** at the corner of Lázaro Cárdenas and Ricardo Flores Magón, 13 blocks north of the Palacio de Bellas Artes. This plaza has had an extremely bloody history, starting with its defense by Cuauhtémoc in August of 1521. A plaque in the southwest corner of the plaza states philosophically: "On August 13, 1521, although heroically defended by Cuauhtémoc, Tlatelolco fell to Hernán Cortés. It wasn't a triumph or a defeat, but the birth of the mestizo city that is the México of today."

More than 400 years later, this plaza was the site of the famous Tlatelolco Massacre of October 2, 1968. An innocent rivalry between two secondary schools that led to fighting in the streets. With the 1968 summer Olympic games in Mexico City just a few short months away, the government thought it necessary to quell any disturbance violently. Protests followed, tying into the more general dissatisfaction of workers and students with Mateos and the PRI's economic policies, until government soldiers occupied the city universities in September. On October 2, after a cancelled protest march, students and families gathered in the Plaza de Las Tres Culturas for a peaceful protest rally. Towards the end of the rally, government troops descended on the plaza ruthlessly, shooting and killing hundreds of protesters.

In the plaza, parts of the **Pyramid of Tlatelolco** and its ceremonial square remain. Enter from the southwest corner, in front of the Iglesia de Santiago, and walk alongside the ruins, down a steel and concrete path which overlooks the eight building stages of the main pyramid. By the time of the Conquest, the base of the pyramid extended from what is now Insurgentes to the current site of Iglesia de Santiago. The pyramid was second in importance to the great Teocalli of the Aztec capital, and its summit reached nearly as high as the modern skyscraper just to the south (the **Relaciones Exteriores** building). During the Spanish blockade of Tenochtitlán, the Aztecs heaved the freshly sacrificed bodies of Cortés's forces down the temple steps, within sight of the conquistadors camped to the west at Tacuba. Aztec priests would collect the leftover body parts at the foot of the steps; food was scarce during the siege and all meat was valuable. Today the walls are reconstructed and are surrounded by a well-tended lawn. Though the massive glory of the site has dwindled into the past, the well-kept remnants provide a striking foreground for the colonial church and modern buildings which complete the promised three cultures.

On the east side of the plaza stands the **Iglesia de Santiago,** an enormous, fortress-like church named after the patron saint of Spain, without whose help the Spaniards believed the Conquest could not have succeeded. The church was built in 1609 to replace an earlier structure of 1543. Before this, only a small altar and a cemetery were used to administer the sacraments to converted *indígenas*. Continue past the church for two blocks to get to the **Museo de Siqueiros,** the white building housing a lone three-dimensional mural. (Open Tues.-Sun. 9am-5pm. Free.)

To get to Tlatelolco take the Metro to the Tlatelolco station and exit through the González *salida*. From the exit turn right on González, walk three long blocks east until you reach Cárdenas, turn right and walk one block south until you see the plaza on your left. Be careful as traffic along Cárdenas is insane and buses run against the general flow.

■■■ LA BASÍLICA DE GUADALUPE

In 1531, the Virgin Mary appeared to Juan Diego, an early convert, on the hill where Aztecs worshiped the mother of their gods. The Virgin asked him to petition Fray Zumárraga to build a church on the spot. The petition was granted when, during an audience with the bishop, an image of the Virgin appeared on Diego's mantle. Our Lady of Guadalupe has since been the patron of Mexico, an icon of the religious culture of the nation. The image is found everywhere, from roadside shrines to the windshields of buses. Today the mantle can be seen in **La Basílica de Guadalupe** north of the city center in Col. Gustavo A. Madero. The new Basílica is an immense, aggressively modern structure, yet another city monument built by the venerated Pedro Ramírez Vásquez in the 1970s. The Basílica draws crowds of thousands daily to the Virgin's miraculous likeness and people flock around the central altar and impressive organ to catch a glimpse of Diego's holy cloak. (Basílica open daily 5am-9pm.)

Next to the new Basílica is the old Basílica, built at the end of the 17th century. Today the old Basílica houses the **Museo de la Basílica de Guadalupe,** Pl. Hidalgo 1 (tel. 577-60-22), in the Villa de Guadalupe. The colonial paintings dedicated to the virgin pale beside the intensely emotional collection of *retablos* or *exvotos*, small paintings made by citizens to express their faith in the Virgin of Guadalupe. (Museum open Tues.-Sun. 10am-6pm. Admission .50 pesos.)

Behind the Basílica, winding steps lead up the side of a small hill, past lush gardens, crowds of the faithful and cascading waterfalls. A small chapel dedicated to the Virgin of Guadalupe surmounts the hill. The bronze and polished wood interior of the chapel depicts the apparitions witnessed by Juan Diego. Descending the

COYOACÁN

other side of the hill, and past the spouting gargoyles bearing a surprising resemblance to Quetzalcóatl, statues of Juan Diego and of other *indígena* faithful kneel before a gleaming Virgin white-doused with the spray from a rushing waterfall. On the other side of the hill, another waterfall drenches a bed of flowers. At the foot of the waterfall, a superhuman statue of Juan Diego kneels before the Virgin offering her gifts.

Authorized and unauthorized vendors both inside and outside of the Basílica grounds hawk enough religious paraphernalia to satiate even the most devout. You'd be wise, however, to heed the signs and ignore those inside selling stamps and other allegedly consecrated doo-dads.

To get to the Villa de Guadalupe, take the Metro to La Villa (Line 6), walk two blocks north on Calzada de Guadalupe and two blocks west on Zumarroga. Alternatively, take the Metro to Basílica (Line 3) and walk about 0.5km east straight down Montier to the plaza.

■■■ COYOACÁN

The Toltecs founded Coyoacán ("Place of the Coyotes" in Nahuatl) between the 10th and 12th centuries. Hernán Cortés later established the seat of the colonial government here, until he decided that Tenochtitlán would be more appropriate. After the fall of Tlatelolco, Cortés had Cuauhtémoc tortured here, in the hope that he would reveal the hiding place of the legendary Aztec treasure. This community of conquistadors and their heirs holed up in *haciendas* and remained independent of the metropolis to the north for quite some time.

South-southwest of the center, Coyoacán is Mexico City's most pleasant and attractive suburb, worth visiting for its astonishing museums or simply for a walk through peaceful **Plaza Hidalgo** or **Placita de la Conchita.** If you come to Coyoacán for a visit from downtown Mexico City, your racing pulse will be soothed by the difference in atmosphere. Life in this suburb, especially on the weekends, progresses at a much slower pace. Many people spend the afternoon just chilling with the sculpted hedges of the **Jardín Centenario** or Pl. Hidalgo. Because of the close proximity of the **Universidad Nacional Autónoma de México (UNAM)** to the west, the suburb makes an ideal student residence and social center. Coyoacán is centered on the Pl. Hidalgo, which is just east of the Jardín Centenario. The two parks are split by Calle Cabrillo Puerto which runs north-south just west of the church.

Near the plaza's northeast corner is a bronze statue of Don Miguel Hidalgo, the first spokesperson for Mexican independence. The **Casa de Cortés** (tel. 544-78-22), the one-story, reddish structure at the north end of the plaza, which is now the Palacio Municipal of Coyoacán, was once the administrative building of the conquistador himself in the early colonial period. On the porch sits the coat of arms given to Coyoacán by the King of Spain, and inside are murals by local hero Diego Rivera showing scenes from the Conquest. Public access to the building is sporadic. (Opén Mon.-Fri. 9am-9pm.)

South of the plaza, beyond the Hidalgo statue, is the 16th-century **Parroquia de San Juan Bautista,** bordered by Pl. Hidalgo on the north and Jardín Centenario on the west. The church interior is elaborately decorated with gold and bronze. Enter south of the church's main door. (Open Tues.-Sat. 5:30am-8:30pm, Mon. 5:30am-7:30pm.) A few blocks southeast of Pl. Hidalgo, facing the Placita de la Conchita and marked by the gardened plaza at the end of Higuera, is the famous **Casa Colorada,** Higuera 57, which Cortés built for La Malinche, his Aztec lover. When Cortés's wife arrived from Spain, she stayed here briefly with her husband, but soon disappeared without a trace. It is believed that Cortés murdered his spouse because of his passion for La Malinche, although he later gave her away as loot to one of his conquistador cronies. The **Museo Nacional de Culturas Populares,** Hidalgo 289 (tel. 658-12-65), has temporary exhibits on the history of popular culture in Mexico. (Museum open Tues.-Sat. 10am-6pm, Sun. 10am-5pm. Free.)

After Leon Trotsky was expelled from the Soviet Union by Stalin in 1927, he wandered in exile until Mexico's President Lázaro Cárdenas granted him political asylum at the suggestion of Diego Rivera, a friend of the Russian revolutionary. Trotsky arrived in Mexico in 1937 with his wife Natalia Sedova and settled into the house that is now the **Museo y Casa de Leon Trotsky** (tel. 658-87-32), Viena 45, 7 blocks north of Pl. Hidalgo's northeast corner up Allende, then three blocks east on Viena to the corner of Morelos. The entrance is around back at Río Churubusco 410.

The house was heavily fortified; bullet holes riddle many parts of the house from an attack on Trotsky's life led by the brilliant muralist David Alfaro Siqueiros on May 24, 1940. Trotsky and Sedova survived the attack, but Siqueiros's group abducted Trotsky's secretary, Robert Sheldon Harte, whose body was found a few days later on the road to Toluca. A marble plaque just inside the entrance to the house is dedicated to Harte. A monument in the center of the garden holds Trotsky's and Sedova's ashes. Trotsky died on August 20, 1940, stabbed through the skull with an ice pick by Ramón Mercader, a Stalinist agent.

Everything in the house has been left as it was when Trotsky lived. The rooms are very simple, almost stark, decorated only by Mexican rugs. Notice that the library is filled with books in Spanish, English and Russian, and that a book about Stalin is open on Trotsky's desk, in the study where he was assassinated. The rooms display many of the couple's belongings, including a turn-of-the-century Russian dictionary and the complete works of Lenin, Marx and Engels. In the guardhouse outside is a detailed chronology of Trotsky's life, along with a photo exhibit illustrating his childhood and youth in Russia and his old age walking, fishing and gardening in Mexico. There is also a touching letter from Natalia Sedov-Trotsky (his wife) to President Cárdenas, dated a month after Trotsky's death, thanking him for his kindness in allowing them to enter Mexico. (Museum open Tues.-Sun. 10am-5pm. Admission 10 pesos, students with ID 5 pesos. Free Sun.)

One of Coyoacán's truly affecting sights is the **Museo Frida Kahlo,** Londres 247 (tel. 554-59-99), at Allende five blocks north of Pl. Hidalgo's northeast corner, in the blue and brown building. The museum is the dark blue house at the northeast corner of the intersection. Works by Rivera, Orozco, Duchamp and Klee hang in this well-restored colonial house, the birthplace and home of one of Mexico's most artistically talented citizens, Frida Kahlo (1907-1954). Having suffered a debilitating accident as a young woman, Kahlo was confined to a wheelchair and bed for most of her life. While married to Diego Rivera, she began painting and became a celebrated artist. Her chronic health problems, together with a devotion to an adulterous husband, inspired the fantastic and shocking subject matter of her works. During Rivera's absences she became emotionally attached to Leon Trotsky, but after a personal and political break between Rivera and Trotsky, a bust of Stalin replaced the pictures of Trotsky that she once hung in her home. Her wheelchair, crutches and the cast that covered her entire upper torso are still in the house. The cast is covered with patterns and figures painted by Kahlo and her husband. Display cases also show the couple's personal possessions and a death mask of Kahlo along with her ashes wrapped up in the clothes she died in. As testament to Kahlo's ardent support for *indígena* culture, the rooms contain pottery, ceramics, cookware and other provincial decorations. She died at the age of 42, in the upper-story studio that Rivera built for her. (Open Tues.-Sun. 10am-6pm. Admission 10 pesos, students 5 pesos.)

To the northeast of the Pl. Hidalgo once stood a pyramid dedicated to the Aztec war god Huitzilopochtli. Over time, the name degenerated from *Ocholopocho* to *Ochorobusco* to *Churubusco*, and the convent there got called the **Convento de Nuestra Señora de Los Ángeles de Churubusco,** at 20 de Agosto and General Anaya. Built in 1524 over the ruins of the Aztec pyramid, it was originally a Franciscan convent, dedicated to Santa María de los Ángeles. The Franciscans soon abandoned it, and in 1580 the Diegans moved in. The present church was built in 1668. On August 20, 1847, General Manuel Rincón, Pedro Anaya and 800 Mexicans halted 8000 advancing U.S. soldiers here. When the U.S. General Twiggs asked General Anaya to turn over the remaining munitions, Anaya responded, "If we had munitions you would not be here."

Still guarding the convent's main entrance are two of the original seven cannon that defended the convent during the 1847 invasion. Two more cannon and a monument to Anaya flank the western side of the structure. Inside, a beautiful old garden grows, with indecipherable inscriptions and dedications on some of its walls. (Convent open Mon.-Fri. 7am-10pm, Sat. noon-2pm and 6-8:30pm, Sun. 8am-2pm and 5:30-8pm.)

Mexico has been invaded more than 100 times, most often by the U.S. Inside the Convento de Churubusco is a museum dedicated to the history of the invasions, the **Museo Nacional de Las Intervenciones** (tel. 604-06-99). The museum's halls cover four eras, from the late 18th century to 1917. There are also a few halls dedicated to exhibits on North American expansionism and cruelty to *indígenas*, U.S. slavery and its significance for Mexico, and European imperialism. The walls of the museum are decorated with religious paintings from the convent and lists of the interventions and the related historical circumstances. Displays in the halls recount the social, economic and political circumstances that encouraged other nations to intrude. (Museum open Tues.-Sun. 9am-6pm. Admission 10 pesos.)

To get to the convent and museum from Coyoacán, walk four blocks down Hidalgo and then follow Anaya as it branches left, four blocks farther to the convent grounds. If you are coming straight from the Metro, it is far easier to get off at the General Anaya stop (Line 2) and walk two blocks west on 20 de Agosto.

Atop a hill, the **Museo Anahuacalli,** Calle Museo (tel. 677-29-84), is an ominous moated palace. Designed by the ubiquitous Diego Rivera with Aztec, Mayan and Riveran architectural styles in mind, Museo Anahuacalli houses the artist's huge collection of pre-Conquest art. Anahuacalli commands one of the best views in Mexico, comparable to those of the Torre Latinoamericana and Castillo de Chapultepec. (Open Tues.-Sun. 10am-2pm and 3-6pm.) To reach the museum from Pl. Hidalgo or Churubusco, go by *pesero* 5km south on Av. División del Nte. to Calle Museo.

To reach Coyoacán from downtown, take the Metro directly to the Coyoacán station (Line 3). *Pesero* "Coyoacán" at the station stops within two blocks of Pl. Hidalgo. One can also walk; it's a pleasant route. You might want to ask the driver to point out the stop as it is not visible immediately. Turn right onto Museo and soon you'll reach the place.

■■■ SAN ÁNGEL

South of Mexico City is the wealthy, thoroughly suburban community of San Ángel, dotted with exquisite colonial homes and churches whose layouts lend themselves to strolling. To reach the area, 10km south of the *Centro* along Insurgentes, take the Metro to the M.A. Quevedo station (Line 3). Turn left out of the Metro station and left at the intersection, then head west on Quevedo for three blocks to the lush **Parque de la Bombilla,** at the intersection of Insurgentes and Miguel Angel de Quevedo. The centerpiece of this lovely park is the two-tiered circular concrete **Monumento al General Alvaro Obregón,** at Insurgentes Sur, between Arenal and Abasolo. Obregón was one of the four leaders of the revolution united against Huerta, the usurper who seized power and executed Madero in 1913. Obregón became allied with Venustiano Carranza and helped to construct the 1917 constitution. With Carranza's death in 1920, Obregón became the first president of the post-revolutionary era. Reliefs at the entrance to the monument represent peace, agriculture, industry and the people in arms. The inscription on the far wall of the chamber reads, "I die blessing the revolution." In the main hall of the monument is a statue of the one-armed Obregón and a plaque that reads "in place of your sacrifice." (Open daily 7am-3pm. Free.)

For a quiet walking tour of San Angel's quaint residential backstreets, return east on MiguelAngel de Quevedo and then south on Chimalistac. On the east side of the park, you will come to the lovely 16th-century **Plaza** and **Iglesia de San Sebastián Chimalistac,** between the streets of Abasolo and Federico Gamboa. Continuing east along Gamboa, you will come to Paseo del Río (which becomes Río Magdalena further south), a winding road running north-south along an old riverbed. South on Río Magdalena, you'll see the bridges that still span the dry bed. At the third bridge, make a right and walk along the cobblestoned Calle Carmen for a clear view of some of the nicer colonial homes; many of the streets are shaded with trees and decorated with running fountains. Carmen leads directly back to the Insurgentes Sur, on the other side of Parque de la Bombilla.

Walking two blocks along La Paz, the street that runs through *Parque de la Bombilla*'s southwest corner and crosses Insurgentes, you'll come to an intersection. To the south are the three tiled domes of **Iglesia del Carmen,** Revolución at La Paz. Designed and built between 1615 and 1617 by Fray Andrés de San Miguel of the Carmelite order, the church and adjacent ex-convent are decorated with tiles and paintings. An outstanding statue of *Christ the Nazarene* is located in the Capilla del Señor Contreras. (Open daily 7am-1pm and 4:30-9pm.) The ex-convent, now the **Museo del Carmen** (tel. 616-11-77), displays colonial art. The main tourist attraction is the mummy collection. Descend into the coffin's crypt to see these grotesque cadavers, which have more shock value than actual historical significance. Monastic and aristocratic mummies headline. (Museum open Tues.-Sun. 10am-5pm. Admission 7 pesos. Free for students with ID.)

The Pl. del Carmen is across the street and west of the church. One block up Madero is the Pl. de San Jacinto, at San Francisco, Benito Juárez and Frontera. Every Saturday, the plaza fills up with ritzy shoppers scoping pricey arts and crafts at the **Bazaar Sábado.** Although most pieces are beyond the budget travelers' economic grasp, there are plenty of bargains and shady places to relax. The plaza also contains the **Casa de Risco,** and is one block east of the **Iglesia de San Jacinto.** The Casa de Risco, Plaza San Jacinto 15 (tel. 548-23-29), is a well-preserved 17th-century house donated by Isidro Fabela which holds his collection of 14th-18th-century European art. The whitewashed inner courtyard contains an exquisitely tiled fountain made out of pieces of bowls and plates (called *riscos*) that were collected from around the world. If you continue from the plaza one block west on Juárez, you'll reach the **Iglesia de San Jacinto.** Sit in the tranquil garden of this 16th-century church after a walk around the cobblestone streets of the area and take in its ancient orange façade and beautifully carved wooden doors. This neighborhood, the oldest in San Angel, contains many swanky modern mansions as well. (Church open daily 8am-8pm.)

Three blocks north on Revolución from the intersection of La Paz and Madero resides the **Museo Carrillo Gil,** Revolución 1608 (tel. 548-74-67), a modern building housing the contemporary art collection of the late Mr. Carrillo Gil. The museum/gallery contains paintings by Rivera, Siqueiros, Carrillo Gil and a whole floor of Orozcos. Some of the early Riveras on the first floor are interesting contrasts to his later work. (Open Tues.-Sun. 10am-6pm. Admission 3 pesos. Sun. Free.)

Shopping is one of the most popular activities in San ángel. An decent **FONART** (government-run Mexican crafts store) is at La Paz 37. (Open Mon.-Sat. 10am-7pm.) The much richer **Caretta,** another crafts store, is just a few shops down the street at Insurgentes Sur 2105 on the corner of La Paz. (Open Mon.-Sat. 10am-7pm.)

■■■ CIUDAD UNIVERSITARIA

The **Universidad Nacional Autónoma de México** (National Autonomous University—UNAM) is Mexico's largest public university, boasting an enrollment that has now far surpassed the 300,000 mark. Immediately after the new colonial regime was established, the religious orders that arrived in Mexico built elementary and secondary schools to indoctrinate the new converts and Spanish youth. After petitions were made to the king of Spain, the first university was established in 1553 in the building at the corner of the present streets Moneda and Seminario, just off the *zócalo*. As the university grew, classes were moved to the building that now houses the Monte de Piedad, on the west side of the *zócalo*, and then to a building at the east end of the Pl. del Volador, where the Suprema Corte now stands. Today's ultra-modern buildings belie its status as one of the three oldest universities in the Americas, older than Harvard, even, and way, way older than UC Berkeley.

The university now fulfills Mexico's constitutional guarantee of universal education. The sacred power of this right was evidenced by the student strikes which shut down the school in the summer of 1992, in response to proposals to raise tuition from a virtually non-existent 200 pesos to 2,000 pesos (20 pesos new money) per anum.

The **Estadio Olímpico 1968** is located on the west side of Insurgentes Sur, just past the entrance into Ciudad Universitaria. The stadium was built in the 1950s, designed to resemble a volcano with a huge crater—an appropriate motif since lava coats the ground on which it is built. Several small volcanoes lurk in the surrounding area. The stadium is one of the most beautiful monuments in the city. The impressive mosaic that covers it was made by the indefatigable Rivera using large colored rocks, and it depicts a man and a woman holding high two torches, symbolic of the 1968 Olympics held in the stadium.

Although the university's architecture is impressive, most visitors come to see the various murals which meditate upon subjects appropriate to their venue. From Insurgentes, head east from the stadium; west of the Jardín Central's southern half, the university's administrative building is distinguished by a 3-D Siqueiros mosaic on the south wall, which shows students studying at desks supported by society. One of the world's largest mosaics, the work of Juan O'Gorman, wraps around the university library, a windowless box next to the rectory tower. A pre-Hispanic eagle and Aztec warriors peer out from the side facing the philosophy department. The side facing the esplanade shows the arrival of the Spanish and their first encounter with the natives; the opposite side depicts a huge atom and its whirling components, a symbol of scientific and academic progress in modern Mexico.

Facing the Siqueiros mural is the **Museo Universidad de Ciencias y Arte,** central esplanade of the Ciudad Universitaria (tel. 548-99-53). This museum hosts temporary exhibits on contemporary issues and art. It is staffed by the students of the university. (Open Tues.-Fri. 10am-2pm and 4-7pm, Sat.-Sun. 11am-6pm. Admission 5 pesos, 2.50 pesos for students with ID.)

South of the university on Insurgentes is a sculpture park known as the **Espacio Escultórico,** just west of the Biblioteca y Hemeroteca Nacional. Out of a huge lava bed and surrounding cave formations rises a pan-chromatic collection of Herculean sculptures constructed in the early 1980s of metal, cement and wood. The artists wanted to revive through modern techniques the traditions of monumental architecture in pre-Conquest ceremonial centers and plazas. The Espacio Escultórico is optimally visited during the day, since it is located on the outskirts of the campus in a secluded area. From the center of the university, take bus #17 or #130 ("San Fernando") from the stadium and get off at the first designated stop (at the yellow pedestrian overpass).

To get to Ciudad Universitaria, take the C.U. Metro (Line 3) to Universidad. Free shuttle service, though limited timewise and irregular after classes end, is available to all campus areas. From Metro Universitaria, take line #1 to both the stadium and esplanade/museum areas. Alternatively, take the Metro to Copilco (Line 3) and follow the collegiate crowd the short distance to campus. Take the first left as you exit the station and walk two blocks, crossing Av. Copilco. Turn right at the dead end and then left to reach the edge of campus, the Paseo de las Facultades. A right on this main street will lead eventually to the junction with Insurgentes near the Estadio Olímpico.

Near the end of the pre-Classic Period, the tiny volcano **Xitle** erupted, leaving an eight-square-km area covered with several meters of lava rock, inadvertently preserving one of the first pyramids constructed in the Valley of Mexico and forming the **Cuicuilco Archaeological Zone** (tel. 553-22-63) on the southeast corner of the intersection of Insurgentes Sur and Anillo Periférico. Take bus #130 ("San Fernando Huipulco") to the entrance on the west side of Insurgentes Sur, south of the Periférico. The **Pyramid of Cuicuilco,** which means "Place of the Many-Colored Jasper," was built between 600 and 200 BC, when ceremonial centers began to spring up in Mesoamerica and priests gained extraordinary powers. Measuring 125m across at its base and 20m in height, Cuicuilco consists of five layers, with an altar to the god of fire at the summit. The lava rock around the base has been removed, allowing visitors to walk along it and up to the altar, from where, on less smoggy days, you can see Xitle to the south and Popocatépetl to the east. (Zone open daily 9am-4pm. Free.) Next to the pyramid is a small museum with exhibits on volcanology, the geology and ecology of the area, and the eruption of Xitle, as well as pieces of pottery and ceramics found near the pyramid and in the mounds surrounding it. The museum focuses on the general characteristics of the pre-Classic period, tracing the origin and development of ceremonial centers and the increases in pyramid-size. Other exhibits show the lifestyle, adornments, technology and burial practices of the inhabitants of Cuicuilco before the eruption. The three-room museum takes about 15 minutes to meander through. (Open Tues.-Sun. 9am-4pm. Free.)

Pick up a copy of the leaflet **Cartelera,** listing all scheduled events for the month (some of also appear in Tiempo Libre) during your visit at the Centro Cultural Universitario, a bus stop further south along Insurgentes Sur, at another yellow pedestrian crossing. This pleasant, modern complex houses the **Teatro Juan Ruíz de Alacón** (tel. 662-71-66), a few concert halls—biggest is **Nizahualcóyotl** (tel. 622-70-21) and movie theaters—**Salas José Revueltas** and **Julío Braucho** (tel. 665-28-50). many of the performances and movies are excellent and you can get a 50% discount with a student ID.

■■■ XOCHIMILCO

Centuries ago, the Aztecs cultivated floating gardens to feed the inhabitants of Tenochtitlán, a tradition which is celebrated daily in a vastly different form in the southern district of Xochimilco. The multi-colored *chalupa* boats which crowd the maze of canals ferry passengers past a floating market offering food, flowers and music, celebrating Mexico City's aquatic past. Especially on Sunday, the busiest day, hordes of city dwellers and tourists relax in the hand-poled *chalupas*, listening to the water-borne *mariachis* and munching tacos from floating taco bars, which tie up pirate-style to the passenger boats.

The keyword for almost anything you do in Xochimilco is bargaining. From the markets to the boats, this is the only way to get around in this overly-popular tourist spot. Be aware that if you come earlier, you'll find a much emptier (thus much less fun) Xochimilco, with far less boats and ridiculously higher prices. In the summer of 1993 a private boat with a capacity of 6 people should have charged 30 pesos per hour and 20 people 50 pesos per hour according to the offical diagram which also sets the price for almost everything else. The boat owners, however, will try to blow these prices up to 200 pesos per hour. Merely wait for more people to arrive and begin bargaining. The *colectivo* boats cost only 2 pesos per person and are much more colorful and authentic. They run on weekends only starting around noon.

The posted standardized rates also price *mariachis* per song at 25 pesos. To get to Xochimilco, take the Metro to Taxqueña (Line 2) and then *pesero* #26 , #36, or any bus marked "Xochimilco" that leaves from platform "L" outside the Metro station (45min., .80 pesos). Tour guides often wait near the fruit market to escort foreign travelers to the boats. To reach the docks, walk down Nuevo León, past the tremendous **Iglesia de San Bernandino de Cera,** then turn right on Violeta and left on Embarcadero, the next block.

If you wish to stay in this area, a clean and new hotel, **Hotel Xochimilco,** Netzahualcoyotl 7 (tel. 676-08-00) at the corner of Morelos, is one block south of the central market. The rooms are clean and carpeted, with TVs. (Singles and 1 bed doubles 50 pesos, 2 bed doubles 90 pesos.) For more information, call the Director of Tourism at 676-08-10. (Open Mon.-Fri. 9am-9pm, Sat.-Sun. 10am-5pm.)

ENTERTAINMENT

Wearied of the disco neon-scape that swings into view nightly in burgs all over the Republic? Fear no more. The chameleon that is Mexico City entertainment can turn all shades of the spectrum. Be it the Ballet Folklórico at Bellas Artes, an old film by Emilio Fernández at an art cinema, a bullfight in the Pl. México, or blues in a smoke-filled bar, the city has something for everyone and more than enough for anyone.

For current listings of performances and show times, pick up a copy of *The News*, an English-language daily, or look for the weekly issue of *Tiempo Libre* (Free Time), each for 3 pesos at most corner newsstands and is published every Thursday. *The News* has film and theater listings; *Tiempo Libre* also covers galleries, restaurants, dances, museums and most cultural events. *La Jornada* (1.50 pesos), one of the best national newspapers, lists art films showing in less well-known locations such as the university. *Macho Tips*, available at newstands along Reforma, publishes information on gay events in the city. The *Mexico City Daily Bulletin*, a potpourri of news and information on tourist sights, with a helpful map of Mexico City, is available free at the City Tourism Office and all over the *Zona Rosa*.

■■■ BARS AND CLUBS

Bars with dimly lit interiors, no windows, or swinging doors are called *cantinas*; women are not welcome in these bastions of *machismo*. At large nightclubs that make some attempt at respectability, dates of the opposite sex are sometimes prerequisites for admission. Cover charges range from 5 to 50 pesos, but women are sometimes admitted free. Those places without a cover often have minimum consumption requirements and high drink prices. Be aware that Mexican-made drinks, from Kahlúa to *sangría*, are considerably cheaper than imported ones. Watch out for ice-cubes—avoid at all costs these secret agents of *turista*.

The *Zona Rosa* offers the most variety for your entertainment peso. Tourists and Mexicans alike flood the streets in the evenings, often dressed to the hilt and set to have a good time. Bars and discos clog the streets, each attempting to outdo the others in flashiness and decibel output. Although the *Alameda* and other areas also have some places to dance, discos in more run-down parts of town can get seedy. Women venturing out alone should be aware that they will most likely be approached by a gaggle of men offering drinks, dances, dates and their first-born.

For safety, the *Zona Rosa* offers the best lighting and least lonely streets, which are a problem in other areas. Taxis run all night, as do *peseros* on the major routes (see Getting Around above). Try to avoid going out at night alone, however, and the bigger the group, the safer.

■ Zona Rosa—Bars

There is a drinking establishment everywhere you look in the *Zona Rosa*. Taverns here are generally expensive and high-class, but the expense may include live performers and tasty *botanas* (appetizers). *Zona Rosa* bars cater to all ages and tastes, from teeny-bopper to elderly intellectual. Many feature live music or beamed-in video entertainment. The variety of style here may make up for the dominance of male-only cantinas in the rest of the country. Women will probably feel safe at this area's establishments, though the pick-up scene never ceases.

Yarda's Bar, Niza 39 (tel. 514-57-22), not to be confused with Yarda's restaurant on the corner. Big screen entertainment and happening party atmosphere maintain a touch of class with starched white tablecloths, black leather furniture and absence of tacky neon. Half-pitcher of beer 20 pesos. Mixed drinks 15 pesos. Cover Fri.-Sat. 25 pesos. Open Mon.-Sat. 5pm-midnight.

Keops, Hamburgo 146 (tel. 528-57-51). Restaurant by day, intimate bar with live performers playing classic rock by night. Responsive sit-down crowd in dark but social atmosphere. Cocktails 9 pesos. Cover 25 pesos. Restaurant service daily 1-7pm. Nightclub action Tues.-Sat. 8pm-3am.

Liverpool Pub, Hamburgo 111 (tel. 207-23-36). 3 generations of British royalty smile from the entrance while an enormous Union Jack billows down from the ceiling. Beatlemaniacal interior. Live bands rock nightly, mostly to '50s and '60s U.S. favorites but with a sprinkling of Spanish tunes. More sedate, mostly late-20s crowd, but all ages represented. Drinks average 15 pesos. Cover 30 pesos. Open Tues.-Sat. 6:30pm-3am.

Harry's Bar and Grill, Liverpool 155 (tel. 208-63-55), enter on Amberes. Near-beer signs and framed menus from famous bars and *cantinas* all over Mexico. A packrat's paradise; collections of cigarette packs, beer bottles, liquor bottles, business cards and old trumpets line the walls. An extremely lively and popular establishment both for eating and swigging beers. International clientele kicks back and watches the game o' the day on central TV sets. Mini *batanas* 13-26 pesos. Open Mon.-Sat. 1pm-1am.

El Chato, Londres 117. A 3-in-1 bonanza. This elegant and quiet restaurant wines and dines until late in the evening. Mingle with quaint antique typewriters and old-fashioned rifles. Many a loner stares despondently into many a drink. Don't miss the informal jazz-piano bar with Sinatra sound-alikes an arm's reach away. Frequented by famous Mexican actors, politicians, and businessfolk. No glitz, no booming beat, but the almost-thirtysomething clientele likes it that way. A great place to wind down and to imbibe quality beer out of steins (8 pesos). Cocktails 13 pesos, imports 16 pesos. Open Mon.-Sat. 1pm-1am.

El Taller, Florencia 37-A (tel. 533-49-70), in the basement. You might miss the small entrance to this underground bar. Well known, classic hangout for blue-collar gay men. Private, conservative barroom attracts an older, quieter crowd. Drinks, snacks and small paperback bookstand available in the afternoon; dancing during the evening. Male revue Wed. at midnight. Tues. lectures are well-attended. Cover 20 pesos with 1 drink, Fri.-Sat. 35 pesos. Open Tues.-Sun. 9pm-4am.

Salón de Té Auseba, Hamburgo 159-B (tel. 511-37-69), near Florencia. Comfortable tea-room pushes calories on a quiet, older, upper-class clientele. A glass case in front shows off the delicious pastries, cakes, pies, tarts and scones. An alternative for the teetotaler. Teas 5.50 pesos. Try the *manzana en chemise*, an apple tart (8 pesos). Open Mon.-Sat. 9am-10pm, Sun. 11am-10:30pm.

Bar Orsis, Niza 22 (tel. 208-49-54). A younger crowd tosses back beer (12 pesos) while sitting on high barstools and rocking with the live *super grupos*. Cover 20 pesos Thurs.-Sat., free Sun.-Wed. Open daily 7pm-3am.

■ Zona Rosa—Discos

The *Zona Rosa* can claim some of the nation's best discos and highest cover charges. Without a doubt, *the* place to party on a weekend night. High covers and long lines are sure signs of a disco phenom, but the same crowds overflow into less crowded and cheaper clubs. The sidewalk recruiters will try to lure in groups, especially those with high female to male ratios, and may even cut you a deal.

Rock Stock Bar & Disco, Reforma 258, at Niza. Chic disco, very popular with young Mexicans. Often packed; non-famous single men will have difficulty getting in. After a brief examination by the metal detector, enter through rotating air-lock style doors and follow street signs upstairs. You enter into a huge open attic room with fluorescently painted railings, scaffolding and metal cages. A black light shines on the painted floors and walls decorated with handprints, footprints and graffiti art. Free barrels of chips and popcorn. Central band hammers out rock tunes as the young, hip crowd mingles freely. Drinks 12 pesos. Cover 85 pesos. Women get in free on Thurs. Open Thurs. 8pm-1am, Fri.-Sat. 8am-3am.

Boots Bar and Disco, Niza 45 (tel. 514-46-08). Mirrors, a disco ball, black light bulbs and a large-screen TV provide more sensory input, as if the lights, dancing and music weren't enough. Casual crowd both dancing and hanging out at tables. Drinks 15-20 pesos. The best part: no cover Tues.-Thurs. On Fri.-Sat., cover is 20 pesos. Open Tues.-Sun. 8pm-2am.

Celebration, Florencia 56. A busy disco rigged up with speakers heard 'round the world, cranking out the modern rock dance tunes. Stylish set models the latest fashions sold in the *Zona Rosa*'s designer outlets. Admission includes *barra nacional* (open bar, national brands). Cover 80 pesos. Open daily 7pm-3am.

Melódica, Florencia 56 (tel. 523-22-42), just south of Londres. "A new concept in Mexican bars." Probably the first karaoke in Mexico: a TV screen flashes song lyrics while you sing over the bar's sound system, which leaks out into the street within earshot of unfortunate passers by. Neon pink and purple trim. Drinks 10-30 pesos. Cover 20 pesos. Open Mon.-Sat. 7pm-2am.

■ Alameda Central—Bars And Discos

Nightspots here lack the luster and glitter of those in the *Zona Rosa*; fortunately the prices reflect it. An evening here may well be worthwhile, but the surrounding neighborhoods may be dangerous. Caution is advised, especially late at night when streets are deserted. Be sure to check out nearby **Garibaldi Plaza** (see below). Taxis are somewhat sparse in this area.

Zotano's, 20 Revillagigedo (tel. 518-40-37), at Independencia. Quaint subterranean dance club with peppy performers playing *salsa*, *mambo* and rock. The red-lights-and-tinfoil decor suggests the inside of a broiler. *Refrescos* 3 pesos, cocktails 8 pesos. Cover a mere 5 pesos. Open Mon.-Sat. 8pm-4am.

El Miralto, Torre Latinoamericana, Madero at Lázaro Cárdenas. Atop the tallest building in Mexico. Mixed drink prices steep (over 10 pesos), but worth the expense for the best view in the city, especially at night. You'll need an extra drink when you see what you've been breathing all day. Open Mon.-Sat. 1pm-1am, Sun. 2-10pm.

Hostería del Bohemico, Hidalgo 107 (tel. 512-83-28), just west of Reforma. A romantic coffee haven with music, singing and poetry. Seating is on the outdoor terraces of both levels and all 4 sides of a lush 2-tiered courtyard with a central burbling fountain. The slice-of-a-tree tables and chairs lit by old-fashioned lanterns make for intimate conversations above the guitar-accompanied *canciones* in the background. No cover, but coffees, cakes and ice creams run high at 11.50 pesos each. Open daily 5-11pm.

■ Centro—Bars

A few of the bars here are popular among the adult, administrative set, and some have as long and distinguished a history as the buildings that stand over them. Explore, but bear in mind that by midnight the *Centro* streets are completely deserted and potentially dangerous. The following bars spill over into the *Alameda* area, but are distinguished by their clientele and atmosphere.

La Opera, 5 de Mayo 10, just west of Filomeno Mata. A real class-act. Restaurant service daily, but evenings are crowded by couples and groups chatting and downing cocktails. Baroque gold-wrought ceiling, mirrored walls, a grandfather clock, and carved dark wood booths. Suit-and-tie crowd sips martinis, but a significant tourist minority tones down the formality. Drinks 10.50-13 pesos. Open daily 1pm-midnight.

Bar de los Azulejos, Casa de los Azulejos on Madero 14 (tel. 518-66-76), 2nd floor. Small bar tucked away in a corner of Sanborn's. Spiral staircase, leather chairs, dimmed lights and red-coated waiters lend a touch of class appropriate for the historic building. Food available from the downstairs restaurant. Mixed drinks, including frozen margaritas, 10-16 pesos. 50% off domestic wines and liquors from 2-3pm and 6-7pm. Open daily 7am-11pm.

Humboldt 34, Humboldt 34 (tel. 521-22-93), near Juárez. Intimate club with wood paneling and leather chairs. Polished brass Aztec calendar prominent on wall, but the electric guitars on center stage keep the place looking modern. Live performances nightly. Open Mon.-Sat. 9pm-3am.

■ Garibaldi Plaza

Garibaldi Plaza hosts some of Mexico City's gaudiest and seediest nightlife. On weekend nights, roving *mariachi* bands compete for pesos along with other regional *ranchera* groups, and will play your favorite tune for 20-50 pesos. Tourists, locals, prostitutes, pickpockets, musicians, food vendors and other flavors of humanity mingle, a significant portion reeling from the liquor sold by the plastic cupful. Big nightclubs, each with their own *mariachi*, do their best to lure the crowds. Though they advertise no cover and no minimum charge, the per-drink price is jaw-droppingly high.

Beware of the many pickpockets and purse-snatchers who target tourists here. The plaza is at the intersection of Lázaro Cárdenas and República de Honduras, north of Reforma. Walk 7 blocks north of the Bellas Artes Metro station. The best time to visit Garibaldi is between 8pm and 2am on weekends, but it's also the least safe then. Prostitutes turn tricks here, and the neighboring streets and small *cantinas* can be dangerous at night. Women and lone travelers should take particular caution.

■■■ SHOPPING

Whereas most Mexican cities have one central market, Mexico City has one central market for every retail good. Rumor has it that *La Merced* moves as much money every day as the entire city of Monterrey. These markets are relatively cheap, since the city usually pays the overhead. Every *colonia* has its own market, but all the major marketplaces are in the center of town. The following are the more important market areas.

La Merced, Circunvalación at Anaya, east of the *zócalo*. Merced Metro stop (Line 2). Primarily food, shipped from all over the country. Huge selection of fresh produce at rock bottom prices. Open daily 8am-7pm. (See Sights: *Centro*.)

Sonora, Teresa de Mier and Cabaña, 2 blocks south of Merced. If you want to turn your significant other into a toad, head for Sonora. Specializes in witchcraft, medicinal teas and spices, ceramic pottery, figurines and ceremonial figures. *The* place to replenish your supply of: lucky cow's feet, shrunken heads, eagle claws, aphrodisiacs, black salt (for nosey neighbors), talismans to ward off evil eye, poison antidotes, powdered skull (for the domination of one's enemies), amber, patchouli incense, energy pills, courage powder, lucky bath oil (for success in business), black candle figurines and dead butterflies, among other things. Tell them your problem, they'll give you a panacea for it. Outside the market are cage-fulls of birds, spiders, dogs, ducks and turtles. Rare species sometimes appear. All for sale, but remember that Mexican pets are turned away at the U.S. border. A great place to pick up a cheap and distinctive souvenir of your Mexican travels. Open daily 8am-7pm.

Tepito, between Metro stops Revolución and San Cosme, accessible by a *pesero* called "Tepito" along Reforma. Blocks of outdoor clothing stalls and indoor shoe racks—you've never seen more shoes in one place. Tepito is the national clearing-house for gray-market imports from the U.S. and South Asia, everything from counterfeit watches to refrigerators. Neat-o police raids occur daily. Watch your wallet. Open daily 9am-9pm.

San Juan, Pl. El Buen Tono, 4 blocks south of *Alameda Central*, 2 blocks west of Lázaro Cárdenas. Bounded by Ayuntamiento, Aranda, Pugibet and Dolores. The painted footprints will lead you in. Targets the tourist money. An incredible variety of baskets, furniture, blankets, traditional clothing, keychains, t-shirts, dolls, sombreros, wall hangings and fake parrots. Open Mon.-Sat. 9am-7pm, Sun. 9am-4pm.

La Lagunilla, Comonfort at Rayón, east of the intersection of Lázaro Cárdenas and Reforma. 2 large yellow buildings on either side of the street. Although famous for its historic Sunday market specializing in antiques and old books, the market has metamorphosed into a daily vending site for practical goods. Open daily 8am-7pm.

Buenavista, Aldana 187, at Degollado in Col. Guerrero. Giant blue and pink crafts warehouse. Like San Juan, it is geared almost exclusively to the tourist. Flyers advertise over 90,000 typical Mexican articles under one roof. Merchandise ranges from stuffed bulls' heads to "genuine" obsidian blades, to videos about traditional Mexico. If you're lucky the man at the door will give you a mini-*sarape* good for a free *refresco* inside. Open Mon.-Sat. 9am-6pm, Sun. 9am-2pm.

Bazaar Sábado, Pl. San Jacinto 11, in San Ángel. Sat. only, as the name suggests, and a good excuse to voyage out to San Ángel. Highest quality folk crafts: dolls, paintings, rugs, papier-mâché, jewelry and much more. A great place to browse—but bring lots of cash if you plan to buy. Slightly cheaper bazaar in the plaza just outside. Open Sat. 10am-7pm.

FONART, one of the government crafts stores selling regional crafts from all over Mexico. No bargaining allowed, but deals are good anyway. Giant tapestries, Oaxacan rugs, silver jewelry, ponchos, glassware, pottery, masks, colorful embroidery, papier-mâché dolls and folk art. There's a FONART near you: Patriotismo 691; Juárez 89; Insurgentes 1630 Sur; Londres 6 at the Museo de Cera; Londres 136, in San Ángel at Av. de La Paz 37; and Ciudad Satélite on Manuel Izaguirre 10. Open Mon.-Sat. 10am-7pm.

Museo Nacional de Artes del Instituto Nacional Indigenista, Juárez 44, across from the *Alameda*. A shop as well as a museum. A map on the wall shows the typical regional crafts from all areas of Mexico. The store stocks most of those crafts and a lot of jewelry. The museum part is a gallery with contemporary artists' work. Open Mon.-Fri. 9am-6pm, Sat.-Sun. 10am-6pm.

■■■ SPORTS

Whether consumed by bullfighting, soccer, jai alai or horse racing, Mexican fans consider their *deportes* to be art forms and are less fans than connoisseurs—albeit rowdy ones.

Plaza México, Insurgentes Sur (tel. 563-39-59). Accessible by the Metro station San Antonio (Line 7). Mexico's principal bullring. Bullfights begin Sun. at 4pm. Professionals fight only Dec.-April; *novilladas* (novices) replace *matadores* in off-season. Stadium capacity: 50,000 fans. Tickets are 10-60 pesos, depending on proximity to the ring and shady or sunny side. Bring sunglasses and a hat. Binoculars come in handy.

Aztec Stadium, SA-Tlalpan 3465 (tel. 677-71-98). Take shuttle train or *pesero* directly from the Tasqueña Metro station (Line 2). The Azteca is the greatest of the many large stadiums where professional soccer—the national sport—is played. Read the sports pages of any newspaper for information on games. The season runs Oct.-July.

Frontón México (tel. 546-14-69), Pl. de la República, 3 blocks south of the Revolución Metro station (Line 2). Watch and bet on jai alai, a rapid-action game played with a little ball and curious curved wicker *cestas*. A dressy occasion; men wear coats and ties, women dresses or skirts. Games usually take place Tues.-Thurs. and Sat.-Sun. Box office opens at 6:30pm. Admission 20 pesos. Betting (not required) starts at 1 peso.

Hipódromo de las Américas, Av. ávila Camacho. Take a *pesero* labeled "Hipódromo" west along Reforma, or bus #17 from Metro Tacuba—the beautiful horsetrack is on the outskirts of the city. Races Thurs. and Sat.-Sun. at 2:15pm. Admission free unless you sit in the upper level, where purchase of food and drink is obligatory.

NEAR MEXICO CITY

■■■ TEOTIHUACÁN

While Europeans lived in caves eating nuts and berries and the group that would one day found Tenochtitlán wandered haplessly, a great civilization flourished in the Valley of Mexico. Little is known about the people who founded Teotihuacán around 200BC; their consummately organized, theocratic society lasted nearly 1000 years and then vanished as mysteriously as it had appeared. Today we speculate that the city's boundaries grew to exceed its capacity to function. Teotihuacán had no means of moving supplies in from outside the valley, and its inhabitants hadn't yet invented the wheel. There is evidence of severe malnutrition and conflagrations in the wreckage of the city. In 850 AD, when the Toltecs founded Tula, not a single citizen walked the paths of that once enormous urban complex. When the Aztecs founded Tenochtitlán in 1325, Teotihuacán, 50km northeast of their capital, lay in ruins. The Aztecs adopted the area as ceremonial grounds and attributed its huge structures to giants who inhabited the world during the era of the first sun. Believing that the lords buried in this hallowed place had become gods, the Aztecs called the area Teotihuacán, meaning "Place of the Gods."

The ruined city's latest incarnation is the most-visited archaeological site in the Republic. The archaeological zone, more commonly referred to as *Las Pirámides*, covers a vast area. The ceremonial center, a 13-square-km expanse, was built along a 2km stretch now called **Calle de los Muertos** (Road of the Dead) after the countless human skeletons that were discovered alongside it. The road leads from the Pyramid of the Moon to the Temple of Quetzalcóatl. Since the Teotihuacanos planned their community around the four cardinal points, Calle de los Muertos runs nearly north-south. The main structure, the Pyramid of the Sun, is on the east side and is squared with the point on the horizon where the sun sets at summer solstice. On the north end of Calle de los Muertos are the Plaza and Pyramid of the Moon. The Palace and Temple of Quetzalcóatl stand on the east side of the southern end.

The best way to wander the ruins is on a general south-to-north vector. Start your visit on the west side of the southern end of the Calle de los Muertos, where a small museum struggles to explicate this civilization. Displays compare the size of the ancient city with various present-day cities, illustrate the architecture and technology of the pyramids, describe the social, religious and economic organization of the society, and exhibit *indígena* art. Although all the pieces you see are replicas (the originals are at the Museo Nacional de Antropología in Mexico City), the museum is a good introduction to the zone. Much of what is known about the area was learned through records kept by the contemporary civilizations in Cholula, Oaxaca, the Yucatán and northern Mexico, all of which traded with Teotihuacán.

As you exit the museum, directly across the Calle de los Muertos is the **Temple of Quetzalcóatl**, once a giant walled-in stadium sheltering a group of ancient temples. Its four flanking platforms served as grounds for priestly ceremonies and dances. The central plaza houses an altar upon which the centennial sacrifice of the "New Fire" was celebrated. Although the temple has lately suffered tremendous erosion from the gods of rain and wind, on the east side of the pyramid you can still make out fierce serpent heads of Quetzalcóatl and traces of the red paint that originally decorated it.

Continuing north along the Calle de los Muertos, you will cross what was once the San Juan river. On the west side of the street are the remains of two temples that were built in two phases, 200-400AD and 400-750AD. Further to the north and east is the **Pyramid of the Sun,** the single most tremendous structure in the ceremonial area. Second in size only to the pyramid at Cholula in Puebla, its base measures 222m by 225m—dimensions comparable to those of Cheops in Egypt. The pyramid rises 63m today, but the grand temple that once crowned its summit is missing. The miniature temple that now stands atop the pyramid once served Tonacatecutli, the god of sun and spiritual warmth. The grueling climb to the top of the pyramid (don't worry, the platforms of the multi-tiered pyramid make convenient rest stops) pays off with a view of the entire site and surrounding valley.

Between the Pyramid of the Sun and the Pyramid of the Moon on the west side of the street is the **Palace of Quetzalpaploti** (the *quetzal* butterfly). This columned structure was the residence of the elites who staked out the area next to the ceremonial space and far from the residential complexes of the common folk. There are bird motifs and geometric patterns carved into the columns. Behind the palace of Quetzalpaploti is the **Palacio de los Jaguars.** Although the palace is entirely restored, complete with fluorescent lights and plastic handrails, some of the original frescoes remain, with red, green, yellow and white symbols that represent birds, maize and water.

At the northern end of the Calle de los Muertos is the stunning **Pyramid of the Moon.** Although it appears to equal the height of the Pyramid of the Sun, it is in fact much shorter, but built on higher ground. The view from the summit down the Calle de los Muertos hints at the magnitude of Teotihuacán.

If you still have the energy, there are two other areas, signless and unmarked, to visit off the Calle de los Muertos on the outskirts of the excavated site. On the northeast side of the Pyramid of the Sun near entrance #4 is the **Tepantitla Palace,** which has some of the best-preserved frescoes on the site. You can still make out priests with elaborate headdresses and representations of Tlaloc, the god of rain. On the southeast border of the site are the palaces of **Atetelco, Zacuala** and **Tetitla,** mostly mazes of what once were elaborate palaces, but now contain only the vestiges of eagle and jaguar frescoes.

Be sure to bring plenty of water, a hat and sunglasses on your jaunt. Vendors do sell water if you run out. You may want to buy a written guide here at the site (25 pesos) or at the Museo de Antropología in Mexico City. Expect to spend about an hour at the museum and another three to four hours walking as many miles exploring the ruins. (Site open daily 8am-5pm. Admission 13 pesos. Free parking.)

An unusual place for a meal is **La Gruta** (The Cave), which is east of the Pyramid of the Sun, near Tepantitla Palace. As the name suggests, the restaurant is in an immense cave, with delicate rainbow-painted tables and chairs. The setting provides a respite from the arid heat; strains of Vivaldi surround the patrons. (Hamburgers 15 pesos, full meals 25 pesos. Open daily 11am-6pm.)

To contact the Teotihuacán offices, dial 601-88 or 600-52 (from Mexico City add the prefix 91-595). Direct **bus service** from Mexico City to the pyramids is available from Autobuses Teotihuacán (every 15 min. 5am-6pm, 1hr., 6 pesos) located in the Terminal de Autobuses del Norte at *Sala* 8. The same bus line runs from Tepexpan should you come from Texcoco or Chiconcuac. The last bus back from the pyramids to Mexico City leaves the main entrance at 6pm. A few miles before reaching

Teotihuacán, the bus passes just to the right of the town of Acolmán, founded shortly after the Conquest by the Franciscans. The majestic lines of the ex-monastery of Acolmán rise to the sky, breaking the monotony of the corn fields. Even at a distance, the architectural solemnity of this early religious settlement is evident. If you want to stop at the ex-monastery on your way back to Mexico City, take the Indios Verdes bus from the main entrance and get off at Acolmán.

■■■ TEPOTZOTLÁN

On the highway from Mexico City to Tula and Querétaro, the town of Tepotzotlán is a feasible and enjoyable daytrip from Mexico City. The Monastery and Church of Tepotzotlán contain inspirational religious art in the Museo del Virreinato (viceroyalty), attached to the church. For those itching to escape the city, Tepotzotlán offers a view of small-town life and atmosphere. Its proximity to the city makes it popular with tourists, a fact reflected in the steep prices in the town's restaurants and market.

In 16th-century Tepotzotlán the Jesuits established a convent for ambitious indígenas to study language, art, theology and mathematics. An *indígena* convert, Martín Maldonado, donated the land to the missionaries in 1582. Construction of the buildings continued until the end of the following century, and the huge bell in the tower was added in 1762. To the rear of the **Iglesia de San Francisco Javier** is the **Capilla de la Virgen de Loreto.** Behind it, the ridiculously ornate **Camarín de la Virgen** (altar room) is fitted with a mirror so that visitors can see the decorations on the dome that crowns it.

After the expulsion of the Jesuits in 1767, the church and buildings became a reform school for priests. Early in this century, they were returned to the Jesuits, and in 1964, the whole complex went secular as the **Museo del Virreinato** (tel. 207-91-37). Although the actual collection, illustrating the history of the Conquest and formation of New Spain, is somewhat sparse, the exhibit contains many valuable treasures from the colonial period. Jesuit imagery predominates in the monastery's halls. St. Ignatius stares at you from every other altar, and St. Francis Xavier is only slightly less ubiquitous. The **Iglesia de San Francisco Xavier** is a Churrigueresque masterpiece. Paintings hang between the arches of the ex-convent, and other galleries contain sculptures, exhibits of locks from the glorious viceregal era and other artifacts. Be sure not to miss the concealed entrance to the upper floor near the exit. The hall contains mostly paintings of unhappy-looking priests and nuns, but also has a map of Mexico City from 1793 and a balcony with a great view of the surrounding area. The monastery's orchard, acres of greenery, is soothing, particularly for those coming from Mexico City. (Open Tues.-Sun. 11am-5:45pm. Admission 13 pesos, free Sun.)

The plaza outside the church is packed with immaculate eateries alongside a few hotels. Tepotzotlán's best lodgings are in the **Posada Familiar** (tel. 876-05-20), at the center of the *zócalo*. Although the rooms are smallish, they contain sturdy wood furniture, tiled floors and handsome wood beamed ceilings. (Singles 40 pesos. Doubles 60 pesos.) The **Hostería del Convento de Tepotzotlán** (tel. 525-02-43), next to the museum, serves Mexican food atop cheery pink and yellow tables in a flower-filled side courtyard of the monastery. (Soups 9.50 pesos. Entrees 20 pesos. Open daily 1-6pm.) Adjoined to the Posada is the **Restaurant/Bar Pepe** which serves delicious *antojitos* in a music-filled outdoor setting. (*Comida corrida* 21 pesos.) *Mariachis* wander the plaza and will play for a hefty sum while you eat.

To get to Tepotzotlán, take the Metro to Cuatro Caminos (Line 2), then the yellow bus from *salida* H. Buses run from 6am-10:30pm, leaving approximately every 20 min. (2.30 pesos). To get back, catch a bus on Juárez up the street from the church to any of a number of Metro stations.

Baja California

Peeled away from the mainland geological ages ago by earthquakes, Baja California is a 40,000 square mile desert peninsula between the Sea of Cortés on the east and the Pacific Ocean on the west. Spurred by advances in oceanic transportation and economic developments at home, Menán Cortés, and later the Spanish Jesuit missionaries, came to conquer, control, and convert the cave-dwelling indigenous people of Baja in the late 16th and 17th centuries. Many of the missions, like San Felipe and San Jose del Cabo, still lend names and churches to Baja towns.

Nowadays, Californians from Burbank to Berkeley form the solid stream of tourists flowing into Baja to surf, fish, and drink to their hearts' content. The lower prices and lower drinking age, as well as the warm climate, fine beaches, and productive fisheries, are more accessible than ever due to the construction of the Transpeninsular Highway, institution of ferry service, and improvement of toll roads in the north.

Large, usually pink, resort hotels and condominium complexes are sprouting to house human torrents, but they have a ways to go before filling Baja California. A secluded beach is never far away, especially if you have a car, and the central mountains in particualar are far from being overpopulated.

■■■ GETTING AROUND

BY LAND

The completion of the Transpeninsular Highway has made it quicker to travel the peninsula by **car,** but driving through Baja is still far from easy. The road was not designed for high-speed driving; often you'll be safely cruising along at 60mph and suddenly careen into a hidden, poorly banked, rutted curve that can only be taken at 30mph.

The *Angeles Verdes* (Green Angels) pass along Route 1 twice per day (for details see Mexico Essentials: Once There: Transportation: By Car). Remember that extra gas (unleaded) may be in short supply along this highway, so don't pass a PEMEX station without filling your tank. All of Baja is in the *Zona Libre* (Free Zone), so strict vehicle permits are not required. If you will be driving in Baja for more than 72 hours, you merely need to get a free permit by showing vehicle title and proof of registration.

All major towns in Baja are served by **bus.** The gruelling 25-hour bus trip from Tijuana to La Paz costs 168 pesos, whence you may zip directly to the mainland by **ferry** for as little as 51 pesos. If you plan to navigate the peninsula by bus, be forewarned that almost all *camiones* between Ensenada and La Paz are *de paso*. This means you have to leave at inconvenient times, fight to procure a ticket and then probably stand the whole way. A much better idea is to buy a reserved seat in Tijuana, Ensenada, La Paz, or the Cabos, and traverse the peninsula in one shot while seated. Unfortunately you'll miss the fantastic Mulegé-Loreto beaches.

Anyway you cut it, Baja beaches and other points of interest off the main highway are often inaccessible on public transportation; buses don't stop at coastal spots between Tijuana and San Quintín. Near Mulegé, Loreto, La Paz and the Cabos (capes) on Baja's southern tip, travelers tied to the bus system can make a short walk from the main road to some of the beaches. Many find that the best way to see Baja is to hitchhike. Baja has but one well-traveled main-drag. Some tourists may not stop for thumbers, but many oblige if caught at a pit stop—PEMEX stations are thick with rides. Mexicans, however, are much more amenable to thumbers. Getting a lift still largely relies upon old-fashioned luck and appearance. Remember, hitchhiking is unpredictable and potentially hazardous; use common sense and don't hesitate to turn down a ride if something doesn't feel right. *Let's Go* does not recommend hitching.

BY SEA

Ferry service was instituted in the mid-'60s as a means of supplying Baja with food and supplies, not as a means of tourist transportation. Boats have come to serve *via-jeros*, and passenger vehicles may take up any space left over after the top-priority commercial vehicles. For those who plan to take a car, the best advice is to make reservations one month in advance, either through a travel agent or with the ferry office directly. (See La Paz: Practical Information for details.)

There are three different ferry routes: Santa Rosalía to Guaymas (7hrs.), La Paz to Topolobampo/Los Mochis (9hrs.) and La Paz to Mazatlán (16hrs.). The La Paz to Topolobampo/Los Mochis route provides direct access to the train from Los Mochis through the Barrancas del Cobre (Copper Canyon).

Ferry tickets are generally expensive, even for *turista* class berths—two to a cabin with a sink (bathrooms and showers down the hall). It's extremely difficult to find tickets for *turista* (75 pesos) and *cabina* class (113 pesos, bathroom in the room), and snagging an *especial* berth (a real hotel room, 138 pesos) is as likely as stumbling upon a snowball in the central Baja desert; there are only two such suites on each ferry. This leaves the bottom-of-the-line *salón* ticket (38 pesos), which entitles you to a bus-style seat. If, as is likely, you find yourself traveling *salón* at night, ditch the seats and stake out a spot on the floor early on—just spread out your sleeping bag and snooze. As always, take appropriate security measures. For prices, check the transportation listings for each of the towns. For further ferry information call the State Tourist Department (tel. 2-11-99, 2-79-75, fax 2-77-22).

Always bring food on ferry trips; boat restaurants are prohibitively expensive.

BY AIR

Air travel can save you time, but it is not cheap. A flight from La Paz to Los Mochis takes 20 minutes (223 pesos); the flight between Tijuana and La Paz takes one and a half hours (558 pesos). **Aeroméxico, Mexicana,** and **Aerocalifornia** all have regular daily service from Tijuana to Los Mochis, Guadalajara, La Paz, the Cabos, and Mexico City.

BAJA CALIFORNIA NORTE

■■■ TIJUANA

Like it or not, Tijuana *is* Mexico and (as many *norteamericanos* and other guide books are reluctant to admit) it is *also* the United States in its rawest, most bleakly industrial sense. It's hard to know which of the two largest industries which created this Mexican border city the U.S. should feel prouder of—the tons of day-glo tourist garbage that adorns hundreds of market stalls along Av. Revolución or the thousands of stinking pools of day-glo factory waste that adorn the streets and backyards of the over 2 million people (and 500,000 stray dogs) who call Tijuana home. Sound appealing? Prepare yourself. It's hard to say whether it's the city's certain raunchy charm, its cheap beer, or a perverse celebration of *yanqui imperialismo* which attracts tourists like flies. No matter what the reason, however, no one can leave the same as they came—especially if they take an educational detour from the well-worn tourist paths and into the labyrinthine streets of the *colonia* shantytowns which spread out from the city's center.

Banners boldly proclaim Avenida Revolución the "Most Visited Street in the World," and when you see the crowds, you'll find that boast easy to swallow. If shopping for that which is small and purely ornamental is your passion, Tijuana is your long-lost homeland. There are enough black-velvet portraits of Jesus and Elvis for sale here to start your own gallery back home. Don't despair, however, authenticity (or near authenticity) can be found, but it is often slightly pricier than the flourescent striped sarapes—check the smaller stalls on the side streets off Av. Revolución. As for nightlife, what you see is what you get: every weekend, swarms of Berkeley types join U.S. Marines stationed in San Diego and abandon themselves to the pulsating waves of music at the numerous flashy discos, drowning their PC woes and military consciences in drink and dancing till dawn.

If you feel that Tijuana is good at what it's famous for, there's a reason—it's been the United States' number one cheap vacation and party-zone (rivalling, significantly enough, Havanna for that title) every since prohibition in the 1920s. First settled by the Cochimie, Tijuana made it onto the map in 1829, when Don Santiago Argüello received the title to the Rancho de Tía Juana (Aunt Jane's Ranch). After the 1848 Mexican-American War, the ranch became the new border, and its name was amalgamated. Since World War II, industry has changed the desert horizon, attracting over 1 million people in the past ten years—whole towns from Southern Mexico and still more hopefuls from D.F.'s own destitute slums. Other Mexicans come here to study at the Ibero-American University, one of the finest in northern Mexico or to buy discounted foreign goods.

Despite the common North American perception that Tijuana is simply a springboard for undocumented emigration to the States, many Mexicans have no desire to risk being shot by border patrol or xenophobic right-wing San Diegans and have come simply to work. Still, you may see a poetic irony and a metaphor for economic and political power relations in the two crowds that line up to cross the border every evening at dusk. North American partiers cross confidently, smugly assured of their right, documentation in hand. Stand at the border, off the highway, at this time and you will see the other crossing. Except for the few Mexicans with enough in the bank to assure the U.S. that they will return, most run as *pollitos* (in the absence of a river, Tijuana's name for *mojados*—the wetbacks of El Paso/Juárez), sometimes paying *coyotes* hundreds to safely carry them across.

Warnings: as at all border towns, crime is rampant and can surface in surprising ways. Above all, do not attempt to carry drugs across the border as the German shepherds will not be amused. Indeed, don't even think of buying or using in Mexico—although notoriously cheaper and more lax than the U.S., Mexico also loves a rich American bribe against the threat of a night in the Tijuana jail. If you are a resident alien of the United States or simply have a Latino surname you may receive a lot of hassling from immigration upon your return. This is a deplorable result of racism and you must make up your own mind as to how to react. The most pragmatic manner is to answer as straighforwardly as possible any questions the border patrol might ask (they have been known to ask things such as "who won the Civil War" and other "prove-it" puzzles).

ORIENTATION AND PRACTICAL INFORMATION

Getting to Tijuana from San Diego is easy: take the **San Diego Trolley** marked "San Ysidro" from downtown (US$1.75), or park and join it anywhere along its south-bound route. It lets you off right at the border. Long customs inspection lines when returning can be a hassle on busy days. Bring proper ID for readmission to the U.S. Kindly leave any fruits, vegetables and firearms behind. Driving across the border may seem appealing at first, but the hassles of obtaining Mexican insurance, not to mention parking, make this a bad idea for a day trip. You must buy insurance—or face the possibility of having your car confiscated in the event of an accident. It's a much better idea to leave your car in a parking lot on the U.S. side and join the throngs of people walking across. Parking rates start at US$3 per day and increase closer to the international line.

If you arrive at the central **bus station,** avoid the cab drivers' high rates and head for the public bus (1.10 pesos). When you exit the terminal, just turn to your left, walk to the end of the building and hop a bus marked "Centro Linea." After a half-hour ride, it will let you off on **Calle 3** and any of the central Avenidas, most notably **Revolución**. *Calles* run east-west in sequential numerical order; *avenidas* run north-south.

Tourist Office: Av. Revolución y Calle 1 (tel. 88-05-55). English-speaking staff can help you find any store or bar you desire. Open Sun.-Thurs. 9am-7pm, Fri.-Sat. 9am-9pm.

State Attorney for the Protection of the Tourist: Jesús Montañez Roman and staff take seriously any problems tourists may encounter. Don't hesitate. Same address as tourist office (above). Answering machine operates after hours.

Customs Office: At the international border (tel. 83-13-90).

Consulates: U.S., Tapachula Sur 96 (tel. 81-74-00), in Col. Hipódromo, adjacent to the Agua Caliente racetrack southeast of town. Open Mon.-Fri. 8am-4:30pm. **Canada,** German Gedovius 5-202 (tel. 84-04-61), Zona del Río.

Currency Exchange: Banks along Constitución change at the same rate. **Bánamex,** at Calle 4 open Mon.-Fri. 9am-5pm. *Casas de cambio* abound and offer better rates.

Post Office: Negrete at Calle 11 (tel. 84-79-50). *Lista de Correos.* Open Mon.-Fri. 8am-7pm, Sat.-Sun. 9am-1pm. **Postal code:** 22000.

Telephones: Farmacia Mayo, Calle 1 and Mutualismo (tel. 85-97-07). No collect calls. Local calls .50 pesos. Open daily 8am-midnight. Street pay phones are unreliable and operators are few and far between. Long distance is cheaper from the U.S. **Telephone code:** 66.

Telegrams: To the right of the post office. Open Mon.-Fri. 8am-5:30pm, Sat.-Sun. 8am-1pm.

Bus Station: (Tel. 26-11-46). Tijuana is a major transportation hub so buses leave frequently from huge terminal. Served by **Transportes Norte de Sonora** with buses to: Mexico City (271 pesos), Guadalajara (218 pesos), Mazatlán (173 pesos) and all points in between. **Auto Transportes de Baja California** specializes in Baja routes. To: Ensenada (15 pesos), Guerrero Negro (82 pesos), and La Paz (168 pesos). Other carriers include **Transportes del Pacífico, Tres Estrellas de Oro** and **Greyhound** (to San Diego US$4 and points as far as Yakima, WA US$195). Greyhound also leaves San Ysidro from the station one block past the end of the trolley line (LA US$12). **Mini-buses** to Rosarito (3 pesos) leave from Madero and Calle 1 in front of Farmacia Long's TJ.

Car Insurance: If you'll be driving in Mexico, spend US$5 per day in San Ysidro to get insurance. There are several drive-through insurance vendors just before the border at Sycamore and Primero who distribute a free booklet with maps and travel tips. (For more details, see Baja California: Getting Around: By Land.)

Red Cross: In an emergency dial 132.

Pharmacy: Farmacia Mayo, Calle 1 at Mutualismo (tel. 85-09-22). Open daily 8am-midnight.

Hospital: Hospital General, Av. Padre Kino, *Zona Río* (tel. 84-09-22).

Police: Constitución at Calle 8. In case of emergency dial 134. For other matters, dial 89-05-15. There's always a bilingual officer at the station.

ACCOMMODATIONS

Tijuana's budget hotels are trapped in the vortex of the town, off Revolución and Calle 1. Prices are monstrous by Mexican standards, and hotels offer little in the luxury department. There's no escaping the blaring music and blaring drinkers since most places are near or above the local *cantinas*. Hotels fill up quickly on weekends, so make reservations and expect to dish out extra *dinero*.

Hotel El Jalisciense, Calle 1 #1715 (tel. 85-34-91), between Niños Héroes and Martínez. Has all the necessities for a romantic evening: soft couches in the hall, large wood paddles on the keys, and *agua purificada* for after a workout. Bedrooms with private bath drenched in pink. Single 50 pesos. Doubles 60 pesos.

Hotel La Posada, Calle 1 #1956 (tel. 85-54-33), across from the tourist office. Cave-like entrance on the street leads back to numerous rooms. Tiny rooms have comfortable beds and hot water, but bed time could be a struggle since the hotel is flanked by two *cantinas*. Singles 45 pesos. Doubles 60 pesos.

Hotel Perla de Occidente, Mutualismo 528 (tel. 85-13-58), between Calles 1 and 2. The healthy hike from the center of "action" makes this a haven from bounding noise. Friendly staff will allow you to see a number of comfortable rooms with a variety of different features. Immaculate private baths. Singles 50 pesos. Triples 70 pesos.

Hotel Las Palmas, Calle 1 #1637, between Mutualismo and Martínez. The cheapest spot around serves up about what you pay out. Freshly made beds and clean towels included. Communal bathrooms located around the central jungle/garden. Singles and doubles 30 pesos.

Motel Díaz, Revolución 375 (tel. 85-71-48), next to Hotel Plaza de Oro. Welcome to CandyLand—a playful pastel color scheme and fresh mint-green doors. Impressive matching bedspreads and curtains. Singles 75 pesos. Doubles 110 pesos.

FOOD

The less expensive *típico* restaurants line Constitución and streets leading from glitzy Revolución to Constitución. Taco vendors set up their carts and stands along Calle 1. Tasty tacos (3 for US$1) can be scarfed while standing in the midday sun. Deep fried *churros*, a heart-stopping snack, cost 1.50 pesos. As always, use your head when choosing what to eat; some vendors are not scrupulous about how long they hold on to stock. If you'd rather not gamble with your health on the street, bar munchies are cheap, filling and generally fresh. Almost all of the *gringo* franchise eateries, including Jack-in-the-Box and Denny's, are conspicuously located on Revolución. Big-name joints serve the same *antojitos* as the small guys at inflated prices.

Los Panchos Taco Shop, Revolución at Calle 3 (tel. 85-72-77). Orange plastic booths are packed with hungry locals chowing on cheap Mexican favorites. Tortillas freshly rolled on the premises. Breakfast served too. *Quesadillas* US$1.50, *tortas* US$2.85 and 2 eggs with ham US$2.50. Open daily 8am-midnight.

Restaurant Nelson, Revolución and Calle 1 (tel. 85-67-50), under Hotel Nelson. Smack in the center of action with enough windows to get a view of it all. Filling meals served up on country-heart place mats. Burger with fries 6.50 pesos, beef *tostadas* 10 pesos, hot cakes with ham 7.50 pesos. Open daily 7am-11pm.

Chico Pollo, Niños Héroes and Calle 1. May seem like another club by a blaring Mexican disco, but in fact it's an open-air restaurant. As the name implies, they specialize in roasted chicken. Whole bird with rice, beans, salad and tortillas 16 pesos. ¼ chicken with all the above 5 pesos. Open daily 9am-9pm.

El Pipirin Antojitos, Constitución between Calles 2 and 3 (tel. 88-16-02). Load up your tacos with a counterful of condiments. Seating under the orange arches and easy street service too. *Flautas gigantes* 7 pesos, *super quesadilla* 12 pesos. Open daily 9am-9pm.

Tía Juana Tilly's, at Revolución and Calle 7, buttressing the Jai Alai Palace. The original and vaguely legendary; black and white photos on the walls tell the story how the bar—now with the restaurant, dance floor and outside patio—has been generating high-action, high-price atmosphere since 1947. All national drinks US$3, beer US$1.75. Bring a healthy appetite for all-you-can-eat tacos (US$5) Fri.-Sun. 11am-4pm. Bar entices Fri.-Sun. 6pm-close with national drinks US$1. Dancing starts around 9pm.

ENTERTAINMENT

Fun in TJ revolves around clubs or money and its concomitant vices—shopping, drinking and gambling. For mild, inexpensive diversion, try snacking and people-watching while strolling down **Revolución.** When your feet get tired, relax in **Teniente Guerrero Park,** Avenidas F and G, off Díaz Mirón. It's one of the more pleasant parts of Tijuana and only a few blocks from Revolución. Tijuana is also a great place to get your car re-upholstered—really. Animal lovers should avert their eyes from the donkeys painted as zebras, adorned with gaudy sombreros and used as picture backdrops.

The cultish game of **jai-alai** is played every night at 8pm in the **Frontón Palacio,** Revolución at Calle 7, a building decorated more like a palace than a sports center. Two two-player teams use arm-baskets to catch and throw a Brazilian ball of rubber and yarn encased in goatskin at speeds reaching 180 mph. All employees are bilingual, and the gambling is carried out in greenbacks. Seating costs from US$3-15, depending on view. Games every night but Wednesday, 8pm-1:30am.

More betting can be done at **Agua Caliente Racetrack** (tel. 81-78-11), also called the **Hipódromo**. Enormous crowds pack the stands for both greyhound and horse racing. (Races daily 7:45pm and 11pm, plus Mon., Wed., Fri.-Sun. 2pm and 5pm.) The track's enclosed **Turf Club** (tel. 86-39-48) has comfortable seating and a restaurant; grandstand admission (nearly 11,000 seats) is free.

Tijuana has two bullrings, **El Toreo de Tijuana,** downtown, and **Plaza Monumental,** 3km east on Agua Caliente. The former presents *corridas* (bullfights) on chosen Sundays at 4pm from early May to late September; the latter is more modern, employs famous *matadores* and hosts fights from early August to mid-September. Tickets are sometimes sold at a booth on Revolución, between Calles 3 and 4 (tel. 85-22-10), but always at the gate. Admission ranges from US$5-22, depending on the seat.

When you finally get tired of all these sports, the **Tijuana Centro Cultural,** on Paseo de los Héroes at Mina (tel. 84-11-11), awaits as "your window to all of Mexico." The architecture alone is reason enough to visit. The center includes the **Space Theater,** a 180-degree giant screen auditorium that shows a film on Mexican culture and history, *People of the Sun,* daily at 2pm (US$4.50). The museum continues the education in Mexican tradition with an impressive chronological and geographical exhibition of Mexico. (Open daily 11am-7pm. Admission US$1, free with movie admission.) A performance center (**Sala de Espectáculos**) and open-air theater (**Caracol al Aire Libre**) host visiting cultural attractions, including the **Ballet Folklórico,** *mariachis,* and various drama performances.

All of this is fine and dandy but if you're here to party, a brief stroll down Revolución at dusk will get you bombarded by thumping music and abrasive club promoters all hawking basically the same thing (2-for-1 margaritas, starting from an inflated price). Although a few sleazy strip joints stud the strand, most clubs scream out for old-fashioned boozin' and *bailando,* and they get it. All Tijuana clubs check IDs (18 plus), with varying criteria for what's acceptable.

Freeday, Revolución 605 (tel. 80-27-05) at Calle 2. With a small dance floor and rock music, this club stands mostly as a place for drinking. From Sun.-Thurs. beer (US$0.99) and 2-for-1 national drinks (US$2.50). No cover. Open Sun.-Thurs. noon-2am, Fri.-Sat. noon-4am. Credit cards accepted.

Tequila Sunrise, Revolución 918 (tel. 88-37-13). An enormous 2-story monster, with terrace and sand-filled volleyball court. Plenty of disco strutting. No promotions. US$2 cover Fri.-Sun. Beer US$1.55. Open Mon.-Thurs. 5pm-2am, Fri.-Sun. 11am-2am.

Tilly's 5th Avenue, Revolución and Calle 5 (tel. 85-72-45). Wooden dance floor in the center resembles a boxing ring, and C&C Music Factory and Marky Mark pump from the speakers. Beer US$1.75, margaritas US$3. Cover Fri.-Sat. US$5. Open Mon.-Thurs. 11am-2am, Fri.-Sun. 11am-4am.

Scandal, Revolución at Calle 6 (tel. 85-82-15). Slamming music in a completely metallic room that resembles the trash compactor from *Star Wars.* Tropical drinks (US$2.50) come 2-for-1. Open Sun.-Thurs. 1:30pm-midnight, Fri.-Sat. 1:30pm-3am.

Margarita's Village, Revolución at Calle 3 (tel. 85-73-62). Forget dancing—drinking is the favorite pastime here. All mixed drinks 2-for-1 and never a cover. Open Sun.-Thurs. 10am-2am, Fri.-Sat. 10am-3am.

ROSARITO

■■■ ROSARITO

This town is a string of hotels, restaurants and shops that line the toll-free Route 1 about 27km south of Tijuana. Now growing into a happening time-share spot, Rosarito evolved from ranches owned by the well-endowed Machaca family. It can be a quiet, laid-back place to relax during the weekdays, but it's close enough to the border that come Friday, the Californians descend with the sole intention of escaping to drunken revelry. Sand beaches and cool sea breezes welcome those escaping from the concrete mayhem of the noisy northern neighbor.

Practical Information Everything in Rosarito is on the main street, **Boulevard Juárez,** which is a section of the generally north-south highway. Street numbers are non-sequential; almost everything listed is near the purple Ortega's Restaurant in Oceana Plaza.

To get to Rosarito from Tijuana, board a **mini-bus** (3 pesos) in front of Farmacia Long's TJ at Calle 1 and Negrete, two blocks toward the border from the tourist office. Yellow *taxis de ruta* (3 pesos per person, extra for baggage) leave from Madero between Calles 5 and 6; they guarantee snug seating and make the trip 15 minutes faster than the buses. To return back to Tijuana, once again the surest way is a *taxi de ruta*, which can be flagged down along Juárez or taken from the starting point in front of the Rosarito Beach Hotel. Getting to Ensenada is more of an adventure, because you're at the mercy of buses passing by the Rosarito toll booth (*caseta de cobro*) on Route 1. To get there, take a regular taxi to the *caseta de cobro* (1.50 pesos). Buses pass by frequently (about every ½hr.) but with standing room only (15 pesos).

The **tourist office,** on Juárez at Acacias (tel. 2-02-00), has all the brochures you'll need and lawyers for the protection of tourists. (Open Mon.-Sat. 9am-7pm, Sun. 10am-6pm.) **Bánamex,** Juárez at Cipres (tel. 2-15-56), exchanges currency Mon.-Fri. from 9am-1pm. On weekends, you'll have to go to a *casa de cambio*, which charges a commission. The **post office** is on Acacias (tel. 2-13-55) directly behind the tourist office. (Open Mon.-Fri. 9am-1pm and 3-6pm, Sat. 9am-1pm.) The **postal code** is 22710. **Farmacia Hidalgo,** on Juárez at Acacias (tel. 2-05-57), offers long distance service (no collect calls) daily from 10am-10pm. The **telephone code** is 661. One door down on Juárez, **Lavamática Moderna** (wash 4 pesos, dry 1 peso) is open Mon.-Sat. 8am-8pm and Sun. 9am-6pm. **Calimax Supermarket,** at the north end of Juárez next to Quinta del Mar Resort (tel. 2-15-69) is open daily 7am-10pm. For the **Red Cross,** dial 132. The **police** are located next to the tourist office (tel. 2-11-21); in an **emergency,** dial 134.

Accommodations and Food Nice, cheap accommodations don't exist in Rosarito; even the budget spots sap the wallet. **Rosarito Beach Rental Cabins,** on Lázaro Cárdenas, provide the cheapest beds in the area though the management may be hard to find. Small cabins house cubicle rooms with bunk beds and half baths. Its location, the dirt road on the corner behind Calimax, two blocks from the ocean, is easily identified by the Disney castle spires. (Singles without bath US$5, with shower US$10. Doubles without bath US$8, with shower US$12; US$38 per week.) Three blocks inland from Juárez on the same street is the **Hotel Palmas Quintero** (tel. 2-13-59). Family couch in the clean, large rooms can sleep an extra person. (Singles and doubles US$20.) **Hotel Villanueva,** on Juárez 97 (tel. 2-00-54) across from the tourist office, offers less quality but an excellent location close to the beaches and bar. (Singles and doubles US$17.)

Food is one of Rosarito's strengths, with fresh produce from the fields just south and seafood caught in the bountiful seas. For an economical seafood dinner, go to **Vince's Restaurant,** on Juárez (tel. 2-12-53) next to Hotel Villanueva. Toast the succulent lobster (25 pesos) and shrimp cocktail (15 pesos) with a good stiff drink. The casual atmosphere is enhanced by sturdy plastic plates and vacationers in swimwear. (Open daily 8am-10pm.) Fresh Mexican tacos and the like are served up with spicy salsa in the midday heat at **Tacos Sonora,** on Juárez 306. Fish tacos or *quesadillas* 3 pesos. (Open Mon.-Fri. 7am-10pm, Sat.-Sun. 7am-noon.) Sit down to a staggeringly cheap breakfast (Mon.-Fri. 7am-noon) at **Ortega's Ocean Plaza,** Juárez 1001 in an offensive purple building. A variety of dishes, including cactus omelette (US$1.99) and an all-you-can-eat Mexican buffet (Sat.-Sun. 8am-1pm, US$3.95). Restaurant open Sun.-Thurs. 7am-10pm, Fri.-Sat. 7am-11pm.

Entertainment People don't come to Rosarito to change the world. They come to dance and drink. They live the dream at **Papas and Beer** (tel. 2-04-44), one block north of the Rosarito Beach Hotel and two blocks toward the sea on Calle de Nogal. Open-air dance floor, bar and sand volleyball court are packed and writhing on weekends. Beer is 7 pesos and mixed drinks 9-15 pesos. Cover charge US$4 on Saturday and Sunday. If you're going to drink, the trick is to buy a 40oz. Corona at a liquor store (US$1) and drink it beforehand. (Open daily noon-3am.) Even the most gray-haired will be carded for the 18-year age requirement.

For those who have somehow misplanned their trip and are stuck in Rosarito beyond the weekend, the Rosarito Beach Hotel hosts, unintentionally, great *gringo*-watching. They also have a large-screen cable TV in their lobby. For cheap curios and Guatemalan backpacks, avoid street shops and bargain at the open air market behind Tacos Sonora. Plenty of selection at flexible prices.

■ ■ ■ MEXICALI

A couple clubs, a couple restaurants, and the train south. Border town Mexicali is a bulky industrial brute, disinclined to welcome tourists. Unless you have a definite reason to come here, stay away. Mexicali supports a few good restaurants and some active nightspots, but chances are you'll be bored out of your gourd within a few hours. For one brief annual moment in mid-October, during Mexicali's **Fiesta del Sol,** bands, skits, a parade and countless street vendors entertain the crowds.

Practical Information Far from the ordinary route between the U.S. and Mexico, Mexicali can still serve as a jumping-off point for travelers heading south; a train runs via Mazatlán to Guadalajara and Mexico City. The city lies on the California border 189km inland from Tijuana, with Calexico and the Imperial Valley immediately to the north. Because of its valley location, it suffers extreme temperatures; the winter months are chilly, and *normal* summer temperatures are 38-43°C (100-110°F).

Both the bus and train stations are near the intersection of **Mateos,** the main boulevard leading away from the border, and **Independencia,** about 4km south of the border. **Autotransportes de Baja California** buses flee to Tijuana (every hr., 24 pesos) and Ensenada (40 pesos). **Transportes Norte de Sonora** covers routes on the mainland south to Mexico City (265 pesos), Hermosillo (68 pesos) and Mazatlán (163 pesos). **Tres Estrellas de Oro** goes the same places with slightly higher rates. **Golden State** has four buses per day directly to Los Angeles (US$27). To get to the border, take the urban bus marked "Centro" (1.10 pesos) outside the bus terminal, just across the foot bridge. Ride past the mammoth new mall to downtown, then walk down Mateos until the border crossing. **Tourist cards** are readily available at the Federal Immigration office *en la línea* (at the border).

Two **trains** leave daily—the *estrella* (fast) is air-conditioned, serves food and, theoretically, goes twice as fast as the grubby *burro* (slow). *Estrella* leaves daily and promptly sometime in the morning (10-ish) and goes as far as Guadalajara, stopping at major cities; tickets are on sale only from 9am-noon. The *estrella* is often booked far in advance. The *burro*, on the other hand, only sells tickets on the day of departure (5:30-9pm), so tickets are usually available. It departs in the late evening and tools along at 50km/hr. The only difference between the first and the second class on the *burro* is that the first-class tickets have assigned seats. To get to the **train station**, turn off Mateos opposite Denny's onto Ferrocarrilero. Take the first right and it's on the right. To Guadalajara US$75 *estrella*, US$17 *burro*.

Tourist information is available at **El Comité de Turismo y Convenciones** (tel. 57-23-76), at Mateos and Compresora 3km from the border. (Open Mon.-Fri. 8:30am-6pm.) **Currency** can be exchanged in any of the banks along Madero. (Open Mon.-Fri. 9am-1:30pm). The **post office**, at Madero 491, is open Mon.-Fri. 8am-6pm, Sat. 8am-3pm and posts a Lista de Correos daily. The **postal code** is 21101. **Telegrams** are in the same building. (Open Mon.-Fri. 8am-4pm, Sat. 8am-1pm.) **LATADEL** magic international telephones are dispersed throughout the city; one is in the post office and one is in front of Hotel Imperial. The **telephone code** is 65. **Farmacia Patty,** México and Obregón (tel. 57-75-38), is open 24 hrs. In a medical emergency, dial the **Red Cross** (tel. 132), and for other problems contact the **police** (tel. 134).

Accommodations and Food A night in Mexicali will cost you dearly. Alternatively, for about US$25 you can find excellent budget accommodations on the Calexico side of the border. Deep wooden panelling and dim chandelier give the eerie feeling that Elvis *does* live south of the border and here at **Hotel Plaza,** Madero 366 (tel. 52-97-57). Everything is kept tidy, but the TVs can be fuzzy. Range of rooms starting at 55 pesos for a single. Doubles 80 pesos. 24-hr. restaurant downstairs. **Hotel México,** Av. Lerdo 476 (tel. 54-06-69) boasts nondescript rooms in the middle of the *cantina* scene that supply cranking A/C and TV diversion. Sinks are conveniently placed in the middle of the bedrooms. Singles 60 pesos. Doubles 80 pesos. Think of your eventual destinations while at **Hotel Imperial,** Madero 222 (tel. 53-67-33). Don't worry about the unnaturally off-green towels and sink wobbling on 1 leg; just sit on the brown bed and blast the color TV. Noon check-out. Singles 75 pesos. Doubles 95 pesos. 5 peso key deposit.

With Mexicali's large Chinese population, you can count on every restaurant in the *centro*, including those with Mexican surnames, to offer big plates of chow mein and the like. **Café Yin Tun,** Morelos 379 (tel. 52-88-86), has good A/C and Christmas colors all year long. The *comida corrida* and pork chop suey each go for 12 pesos. (Open daily 9pm-midnight.) **Restaurant Buendía,** Altamirano 263 (tel. 52-69-25), specializes in Chinese cuisine, but chefs are happy to whip up authentic *antojitos* anytime. (8-vegetable stir-fry 14.50 pesos. Beef tacos or pork chops 9.50 pesos. Open daily 7am-9pm.) For a fast-food joint with quick service and plastic booths, try **Tortas de Charo,** on Mateos three blocks from the border. *Tortas*, any style, are 5 pesos. (Open daily 8am-9pm.)

You will notice there is no **entertainment** section.

■■■ SAN FELIPE

San Felipe's position on the map would seem to place it too far away from the action on the Pacific coast to be bothered with. The number of *gringo* RV parks lining the desert beaches (200 and counting) definitely shatters that myth. The town was christened San Felipe de Jesús in 1721 but was largely ignored due to its isolation from the western populace. One hundred years later, a U.S. firm began harvesting tons of seafood from the deserted shores of Bahía San Felipe. Finally, in the 1950s northern snowbirds claimed the desert resort as a regular hangout, bringing handfuls of greenbacks and a new industry—tourism—to the area. These sandy beaches have satisfied many a romantic evening.

The **malecón** follows the municipal beach in the center of town. It tends to be crowded and a bit untidy, but its location close to the markets and bars is key in the sweltering 100°F temperature. The *malecón* is also home to the local fishermen, who gladly take vacationers on fishing excursions near Isla San Felipe and the recently planted artificial reefs. Wooden motor-powered boats launch at about 7am for a half-day of angling and seal-watching near the rocks of the *isla* (US$25 per person). **Playa Punta Estrella,** 3km south of town, and **Playa Norte,** several blocks north of the center, offer some relief from the beach congestion and plenty of yellow sand. Take some time to visit the **Shrine of the Virgin Guadalupe** at the top of the *cerritos* near the lighthouse. After a scorching hike, you'll be rewarded with a spectacular view of San Felipe and the blue bay.

Practical Information Located 198km south of Mexicali, San Felipe is a lone town at the end of sizzling-hot Route 5. **Los arcos** are immediately recognizable when entering the village; **Chetumal** is the street continuing straight from the arches toward the sea. All tourist concerns, including hotels, restaurants, banks, etc., cluster on **Mar de Cortés,** one block form the beach. The new **bus terminal** is off on Mar Caribe, a 15-minute walk from the center of action. To get to the main drag from there, walk north on Mar Caribe to the first street, Manzanillo, then hang a right toward the blue water. The extremely helpful English-speaking staff at the **tourist office,** Mar de Cortés at Manzanillo (tel. 7-11-55), knows tons about the town and surrounding areas, and is a **tourist protection center.** (Open Mon.-Fri. 8am-7pm, Sat. 9am-3pm, Sun. 10am-2pm.) **Bancomer,** Mar de Cortés Nte. near Rockodile Bar (tel. 7-10-90) **exchanges currency** from 9am-11pm. The **post office** is on Mar Blanco between Chetumal and Ensenada (tel. 7-13-30), 4 blocks inland from Cortés. (Open Mon.-Fri. 9am-3pm, Sat. 9am-1pm. **Postal code:** 21850.) **Telegrams** can be sent from the office on Mar Bermejo between Peurto Peñasco and Zihunatejo (tel. 7-11-12) in a yellow building. (Open Mon.-Fri. 8am-2pm.) The **Farmacia San Angelín,** Chetumal at Mar de Cortés (tel. 7-10-43), has *casetas* for **long distance calls.** (Open daily 9am-9:30pm. **Telephone code:** 657.) The **bus station** on Mar Caribe Sur (tel. 7-15-16) is served by **Autotransportes Baja California** and **Transportes Norte de Sonora,** which run daily buses to Ensenada (2 per day, 28 pesos) and Mexicali (4 per day, 22 pesos). Gas up at **PEMEX,** Mar Caribe Sur, next to the new bus terminal. Help available with the **Red Cross,** (tel. 7-15-44). In an emergency dial 132. **Farmacia San Angelín,** Mar de Cortés at Chetumal (tel. 7-10-43), is open daily 9am-9:30pm.For **medical services,** go to the **Clínica de S.S.A** on Mar Bermejo Sur (tel. 7-15-21), behind the **police station,** which is on Mar Blanco Sur (tel. 7-13-50), just south of Chetumal.

Accommodations There are two types of accommodations in San Felipe: those with walls and A/C, and those without. Travelers who prefer the former will end up paying *mucho dinero* for mediocre rooms. A number of independently-owned hotels fill San Felipe, the cheapest among them being **Motel El Pescador,** Mar de Cortés at Chetumal. This motor lodging crammed in between the curio shops has icy A/C and private bathrooms. (Singles 80 pesos. Doubles 100 pesos.) The other cheap option is to rent a room in a private residence. **Casa Morada,** on Manzanillo one block behind the tourist office, is easily located by its purple facade. Cluttered with garage-sale-type furniture, the house offers complete use of kitchen and dining room. Inquire within for Jose. (1 bed with A/C US$20, 2 beds with A/C and bath US$30.)

As any Californian with an RV can tell you, San Felipe is well-known for its trailer parks. The most famous and least seasonal is **Ruben's,** out toward the end of Av. Golfo de California in Playa Norte (tel. 7-14-42). Individual parking spaces are topped with two-story open-air bungalows. Spots easily accommodate a simple car-load of folks with sleeping bags or RVs that need full hook-ups. (US$15 per vehicle, up to two people, US$20 beachfront, US$2 for every extra person.) Smack in the middle of town on Mar de Cortés, **Campo San Felipe** (tel. 7-10-12) lures campers with the fabulous beachfront location and groomed, desert garden entrance. Thatched-roof overhangs shelter each fully-loaded trailer slip. (Spaces go for US$11-16.)

Food and Entertainment Mar de Cortés is crammed with a variety of restaurants advertising air-conditioned relief from the blistering heat. Just one block over along the *malecón*, *ostionerías* and fish *taquerías* serve up fresh seafood, hot sauces and crackers for fewer clams. **Restaurant Ruben's**, at Ruben's campground (tel. 7-14-42), is a natural prodigy of its parent's success. The sheer turnover of *norteamericanos* guarantees hot, fresh meals anytime of the day. Shrimp and steak kabob 16 pesos, *antojitos* 13 pesos. (Open daily 7am-11pm.) A less touristed eatery in the center on Mar de Cortés at Acapulco is **Restaurant Petunia.** Vinyl booths and slick plastic placemats add to the homey decor. Scrumptious burritos 12 pesos. Roast beef with guacamole 18 pesos, a whole fried fish 12.50 pesos. (Open daily 7:30am-10pm.)

Restaurant/bars for the weekend warriors in San Felipe abound up and down the main drag. The seasoned veterans nurse drinks all day long at **Bar Miramar,** Mar de Cortés 315 (tel. 7-11-92). The place looks like a *cantina* from the 60s, but the patrons come for company, not glitz. (Beer US$1.25, margaritas US$2. Open daily 10am-2am.) Younger folks usually head a few doors down to **Rockodile**, on the *malecón* at Acapulco (tel. 7-12-19). The new kid on the block tries to imitate the phenomenon of its sister restaurants/bars/discos on the west coast with fluorescent paint, a weirdo name and plenty of t-shirts and caps. (Happy hour daily 10am-4pm and all day Wed. Otherwise beer US$2, jumbo piña colada US$2.75. Open daily 10am-2am. Closed Mon.-Thurs. in winter.)

■■■ ENSENADA

The secret is out—beachless Ensenada is fast becoming the top weekend hot spot south of the border. The masses of Californians that arrive every Friday night have *gringo*-ized the town to an extreme degree; everyone speaks English, down to salespeople pitching tacos, and the store clerks need calculators if you try to buy something with pesos. Still, Ensenada is less brash than its insatiable cousin to the north, and becomes quite pleasant Monday morning when the *gringos* go home and the cool sea breeze kicks in.

The drive from Tijuana to Ensenada is beautiful if you take the Ensenada Cuota (toll road), which costs 7 pesos. The *libre* (free road) is atrocious, poorly maintained, dangerous and about as scenic as a municipal garbage dump. Along the toll road you'll enjoy sparkling ocean vistas, large sand dunes, stark cliffs, and broad mesas. Drive in the right lane only; the left is strictly for passing and the law is enforced. Also, drive only in daytime as there are no streetlights.

Orientation and Practical Information Ensenada is 108km south of Tijuana on Route 1. **Buses** from Tijuana arrive at the main terminal, at Calle 11 and Riveroll, every half hour 7am-10pm and every hour 11pm-1am. Turn right as you come out the door of the bus station (tel. 8-67-70) and 10 blocks will take you to **Mateos** (also called First), the main tourist drag. Five blocks to the left along Mateos you'll find inexpensive motels. **Juárez** (Calle 5) runs parallel to Mateos, while **Espinoza** is perpendicular. The **tourist office,** at Blvd. Castero and Gatelum (tel. 8-24-11) dispenses brochures from expensive hotels, some town maps, and Baja travel material. (Open Mon.-Fri. 9am-7pm, Sat.-Sun. 9am-2pm.) The **Chamber of Commerce,** Mateos 693 (tel. 8-37-70), at Macheros, is closer to the center of town, with brochures, city maps and more helpful English-speaking staff. (Open Mon.-Fri. 8:30am-2pm and 4-6:30pm.) The **customs office** is on Reyersow 1 block up from Uribe (tel. 4-08-97). (Open Mon.-Fri. 8am-3pm.) Banks clump along Av. Juárez, for **currency exchange,** but few will exchange traveler's checks. **Bancomer,** on Juárez at Ruíz (tel. 8-11-08), is the best choice. All open Mon.-Fri. 9am-1:30pm. **Casas de cambio** all over but charge hefty commission and are closed Sun. The **post office** is on Mateos at Floresta (tel. 6-10-88), 1 block past the *arroyo*. (*Lista de Correos*. Open Mon.-Fri. 8am-7pm, Sat.-Sun. 9am-1pm. **Postal code:** 22800.) 2 types of **phones** line Juárez and Mateos. Orange are touchtone and have operator assistance (collect calls 09). Gray phones only accept pesos or credit cards, allowing direct international calling. **Telephone code:** 617. **Blanca,** Cortés at Reforma (tel. 6-26-48) is a frighteningly large laundromat. Hike out Mateos 8 blocks past the *arroyo* to Soto, then turn left, and go a few more blocks to the Limón shopping center. For medical care, contact the **Red Cross,** on Blvd. de Jesús Clark at Flores (tel. 4-45-85). In an **emergency,** dial 132. **Farmacia Del Sol,** Cortés at Reforma (tel. 6-37-75), in the Limón shopping center, is open 24 hrs. **Hospital General,** Carretera Transpeninsular km111 (tel. 6-78-00), is also open 24 hrs. **Police** are available at Calle 9 at Espinoza (tel. 6-24-25).

Accommodations

The rooms in Ensenada are expensive when compared to points farther south, but they include ample features that the cheaper spots lack. Leftover motor hotels from the '60s boast the works in each room (kitchens, couches, etc.). Economical hotels line Mateos between Espinoza and Riveroll, while luxury lodgings are on the water closer to the center of town. Most rooms lie about a 20-minute hike from the beaches and a good 10 minutes from the club scene. Although most owners quote prices in greenbacks, they also accept the national currency. **Motel Coronado,** Mateos at the *arroyo* (tel. 6-14-16). Homely yellow facade welcomes guests to humongous rooms that reach back to the good ol' days when value equalled size. (Singles 50 pesos. Doubles 70 pesos.) **Motel Pancho,** Alvarado at Calle 2 (tel. 8-23-44), 1 block off Mateos, has big rooms with yellow walls and beds with ultra-thin white sheets. Huge, clean bathrooms. Closest location to the bar scene. Wooden bed stands are marked by all of those who spent a cheap night before you. Clean, large bathrooms. (Singles US$17. Doubles US$25.) **Hotel Rosita,** Gastelum between Calles 3 and 4 (tel. 8-16-25) is also close to the bars. The rooms are dark and have holes in the floor, but what is important is that the beds hold people and the toilet flushes. (Single (for 1 or 2 people) 20 pesos with communal bath, 30 pesos with private bath. Doubles 35 pesos with bath and 2 or 3 people.)

Food

The cheapest restaurants are along Juárez and Espinoza; those on Mateos and near the water jazz up the surroundings and prices for *los turistas.* At **Asadero Chispa,** on Mateos, at Guadalupe, fresh condiments crowding the counter top the tastiest grilled tacos in Baja California. Seats are rarely found at lunchtime. Scrumptious burritos made with whole beans and beef strips on one-ft.-wide tortillas, 9 pesos. Tacos 3.50 pesos. (Open Tues.-Sun.11am-11pm.) **Cafetería Monique Colonial,** Calle 9 and Espinoza (tel. 6-40-41), is popular with locals for its cheap, middle-of-the-line food. Fish filet 16 pesos, steak 17 pesos, yogurt with granola 9 pesos. (Open Mon.-Sat. 6am-10pm, Sun. 6am-3pm.) Add to the hundreds of business cards that fill the walls of **Restaurant Corralito,** Mateos 627 (tel. 8-23-70). White wrought-iron pushcart in center overflows with salad and sauces. Variety of *tortas* 6 pesos, create-your-own Mexican combo 15 pesos, *licuados* 7 pesos. (Open 24 hrs.) Chefs at **Las Parrillas,** Espinoza at Calle 6 (tel. 6-17-28), grill up fresh meat cutlets on the flaming pit as locals watch in anticipation. Squeeze onto a counter stool and prepare yourself for *super antojitos.* Tacos or tostadas 3 pesos and juicy double burger 10 pesos. (Open daily 8am-11:45pm.)

Sights and Entertainment

Seeing Ensenada requires more than a quick cruise down Mateos. Climb the **Chapultepec Hills** for a view of the entire city. The steep road leading to the top of the hill begins at the foot of Calle 2. Any number of dirt paths also wind over the nearby hills, which afford a pleasant ocean view. Watch out for broken glass and pack sunscreen and refreshments.

The English-language *Baja Times* is full of bureaucratic propaganda and upcoming event announcements. Enormous quantities of curios are for sale along **Mateos** and **Blvd. Costero;** people spend days in these stores. Also on Costero, known to the locals simply as Boulevard, shuffle through piles of fresh fish and buckets of shellfish, and dine at one of the fish taco stands.

The mild, dry climate of Northern Baja's Pacific coast has made it Mexico's prime grape-growing area. **Bodegas de Santo Tomás,** Miramar 66 (tel. 67-82-509) has produced wine since 1888. Today, they distill over 500,000 cases of wine every year, including rosé and champagne. Tours (US$2) are conducted thrice daily, complete with complimentary wine tasting and an assortment of breads and cheeses.

Most of the popular hangouts along Mateos are members of that common hybrid species, the restaurant/bar/disco. In most, food and drink are served only until 8pm or so, when they turn into full-fledged dance clubs. On the weekends, almost every place has a good number of *norteamericanos* and locals in the festive mood, but during the week only the most popular thrive.

Better known than Ensenada itself is **Hussong's Cantina,** on Ruíz between Mateos and Calle 2 (tel. 8-32-10). It strives to offer all the authentic features of the traditional Mexican watering-hole. (Beer 5 pesos, tequila 10 pesos.) When you tire of the pencil drawings and continuous stream of *mariachi* musicians, cross the street to **Papas and Beer** (tel. 4-01-45). This high-tech music emporium is more popular with the twentysomething crowd, who swill huge margaritas (10 pesos) and spend corresponding amounts of cash. Every Thursday night has a theme with plenty of dancing after 10pm. Cover is US$5 Thursday through Saturday if you arrive after 9pm. (Open daily noon-3am.)

■ Near Ensenada

Since the town's beaches suffer from their proximity to a major fishing port, visitors to Ensenada concentrate on shopping, eating and partying. About 11km north lies **Playa San Miguel.** About 8km to the south are **Playas Santa María** and **Estero.** All are sandy and clean, but the seething crowds might drive you over the edge. Farther south you'll find passable beaches; try **San Quintín,** two hours south of town by car. Locals make their way to the Bahía San Quintín for three reasons: the cool climate, the lack of tourists and the large clam population close to the **Molino Viejo,** near El Presidente 6km south of the city of San Quintín. **Rosario,** another modest beach town, lies 58km south of San Quintín on the Transpeninsular Highway.

La Bufadora, the largest geyser on the Pacific coast, is 30km south of Ensenada. On a good day, the "Blowhole" shoots water 40m into the air. Share the spectacle with the local sea lions. **Agua Caliente** hot springs are 35km east on Route 3. **San Carlos** hot springs, accessed by a dirt road 16km south of town, are not especially clean; both are hot.

BAJA CALIFORNIA SUR

■■■ GUERRERO NEGRO

Twenty degrees cooler than the bleak Desierto de Vizcaíno to the southeast, Guerrero Negro (Black Warrior) will earn a soft spot in the hearts of heat-weary northbound travelers who don't mind wind and lots of gray. Situated about halfway between Tijuana and La Paz, Guerrero Negro is the place to spend a cool night if you'd like to break up the killer 25 hour trans-Baja bus trip. If you're heading south, stock up on cold drinks; several hundred miles of sweltering terrain await you.

Guerrero Negro was founded about 40 years ago, when a North American company began a salt export business. Some excitement is generated between December and early March, when thousands of gray whales make the annual 6000-mile swim from the Bering Sea to the lagoons here to reproduce.

Commune with the whales in the **Parque Natural de las Ballenas Grises,** on the **Laguna Ojo de Liebre,** formerly a deep-water port facility of the salt company.

In the early morning, whales swim right up to the docks, and during the rest of the day you can ascend a tall observation tower to view the 100-odd whales. No public transportation is available to the park. To get there head south on Rte. 1 toward Santa Rosalía for 8 to 15km. A sign points out the 30km dirt road to the *laguna*. Mario Rueda, the administrator of the park, sometimes leads whale-watching tours in early January and February.

For tours of about 10 people, get in touch with **Agencia de Viajes** on Carretera Transpeninsular near the Pemex (tel. 7-10-56, fax 7-07-88). Tours run US$30 per person, including transportation, snacks, a bilingual guide, and beers. (Open Mon.-Fri. 9am-1pm and 3-7pm, Sat. 9am-1pm.)

Unfortunately, when the whales leave for the summer, the pace in Guerrero Negro flatlines once again. Five motor lodges line the access road for those travelers in need of a bed in the middle of the long transpeninsular haul. Nothing special— rooms go for expensive rates, and no one accepts credit cards. The cheapest place in town, **Motel Las Dunas** (tel. 7-00-57), Carretera Transpeninsular below the water tank, has immaculate rooms comparable to more expensive spots. Warm, courteous staff helps in every way possible, but they can't shut down the noisy factory churning right outside your window. (Key deposit10 pesos . Singles 35 pesos, doubles 42 pesos.) To pay the price for color TV, move on to **Motel San Ignacio,** Carretera Transpeninsular, 200m north of the bus station; second floor rooms afford a view of the salt flats across the highway. (Singles 66 pesos, doubles 77 pesos.)

Many aspects of Guerrero Negro are difficult to swallow; its food is no exception. **Restaurant Bar Lupita,** on Carretera Transpeninsular (tel. 7-02-05), near the Union 76 ball and Motel Brisa Salina, is Guerrero Negro's attempt at elegance; miniature wooden tables and chairs with full place settings clump in a small dining area. Chicken enchiladas 13 pesos. *Quesadillas* 13 pesos. (Open daily 7am-11pm.) Across the road, **Cocina Económica Letty** occupies a new building with big new furniture and TV provides entertainment. Fish 12 pesos, enchiladas and the like 10 pesos. (Open Mon.-Sat. 6:30am-10pm.)

Guerrero Negro is for the traveler, scattered along 3km of the **Carretera Transpeninsular.** The highway runs from the bus station at the south end to the riverbed and salt plant, where it turns. The road that continues into Guerrreo Negro is Avenida Baja California, which jogs to the left at the park and church. Change money at **Bánamex,** Av. Baja California (tel. 7-05-55), just across the small bridge in front of the salt plant. (Open Mon.-Fri. 9am-4pm.) The **post office** (tel. 7-03-44) is off Baja California across from the Lion's Club, two blocks past the church. (Open Mon.-Fri. 9am-1pm and 3-6pm.) The **postal code** is 23940. **Telephones** are in **Farmacia San Martín,** on Carretera Transpeninsular (tel. 7-01-11), 100m north of the clinic. (Open Mon.-Sat. 8am-10pm, Sun. 9am-4pm.) An **IMSS Clinic** is on Carretera Transpeninsular ½km north of the water tower (tel. 7-04-33). The **police** are in the Delegación Municipal on Carretera Transpeninsular, just before the salt plant (tel. 7-02-22).

Buses leave from one of the first buildings from the highway on the access road (tel. 7-06-11). *De paso* service goes north and south six to seven times daily. *De local* buses go to Tijuana at 7:30pm (82 pesos), La Paz at 4pm (86 pesos), San Quintín (52 pesos), Santa Rosalía (26 pesos), and Mexicali (100 pesos).

■■■ SAN IGNACIO

More than any other stop on the arid Baja Peninsula, San Ignacio, between Guerrero Negro and Santa Rosalía on the Transpeninsular Highway, is a veritable tropical oasis. The sight of forest green, of leafy date palms, and of flowering bushes in the middle of the blistering desert seems to be only a cruel illusion, the mind playing games after miles of dry sand. But in fact, inhabitants have dammed up an underground water source to form a murky lake used for everything from local orchards to swimming. The locals pioneer a fishing industry on the Pacific coast, some 70km from home.

The colonial colossus towering over the wild vegetation looks like it was built there by accident. Nonetheless, Mexican Jesuits founded the **Mission of San Ignacio** in 1728 and decorated the temple with gold ornaments and original paintings. A visit here and a relaxing nap under the cool, shady palms are the only things to do in town. A winding road canopied by sweet date palms leads from the Transpeninsular Highway to the *zócalo*. Abundant **trailer parks** and **camping** spots line this 2km stretch of road. The town is smaller than you would believe; hence, it lacks services and activities for tourists. A **market, Bancomer,** and the **post office** all surround the plaza, as does the mission.

■■■ MULEGÉ

Veteran beachcombers claim that heaven on earth is the 48km arc of rocky outcrops and shimmering beaches in Southern Baja known as the Bahía de la Concepción, which neighbors Mulegé. Millions of shells in the area will keep you busy for days and vastly expand your collection. Grown sport fishers weep at the variety and sheer size of the specimens caught here, and divers fall under the spell of Mulegé's underwater sights. Located 136km north of Loreto on Rte. 1, Mulegé proper is just a base, to be abandoned during the day for the marvelous beaches to the south.

Practical Information Shortly after leaving the highway, the road into Mulegé forks. To the left is Moctezuma, to the right Martinez which merges into Morelos after the plaza. Zaragoza crosses both and leads to the plaza one block from Martinez. The Hotel Las Casitas, Madero 50 (tel. 3-00-19) serves as the unofficial **tourist office**, with plenty of information regarding beaches, camping, and fishing. Ask for Javier to get to the real nitty-gritty. The **post office** is on the north side of the plaza. (Open Mon.-Fri. 8am-3pm, Sat. 8am-noon. **Postal code:** 23900.) Minisuper Padilla, on Zaragoza at General San Martín, 1 block north of plaza has **phones** for international calls. (Open Mon.-Sat. 9am-1pm and 3-8pm, Sun. 9am-1pm.) A public phone is located in the plaza. (**Telephone code:** 685.) The **bus station** is but a sheltered blue bench at the turnoff to Mulegé from Rte. 1. All buses are *de paso*, roughly translatable as "inevitably arrives late and full." Southbound and northbound buses depart 4 times per day. Buses trail to La Paz and Loreto down under and north to Santa Rosalía, Guerrero Negro, and Tijuana. Southbound buses generally pass in the morning, northbound in the evening, after 4pm. A lucky few catch rides here. **Lavamática Claudia** (tel. 3-00-57), on Moctezuma beside Hotel Terraza is the town laundromat. (Wash 6 pesos, dry 2.50 pesos, soap 1.50 pesos. Open Mon.-Sat. 8am-6pm.) **Farmacia Mulegé** (tel. 3-00-23), is on Zaragoza near General San Martín. (Open daily 8am-9pm.) **Centro de Salud B,** Madero 28 (tel. 3-02-98), also referred to as the ISSTE clinic or the Puesto Periférico, serves medical emergencies. (Open 24 hrs.) **Police,** or **Delegación Municipal de Seguridad y Tránsito,** Madero 30 (tel. 3-02-48), are next to the hospital.

Accommodations and Food A number of economical hotels pile up in the center of town, but they are quite a distance from the beaches. Many find that the best deal for those with a sleeping bag is on the shore. Bargaining might be helpful at any of the several *casas de huéspedes* in town. On hot nights, rooms at **Casa De Huéspedes Mañuelita,** on Moctezuma around the corner from Zaragoza (tel. 3-01-75), relieve the traveler with table fans and private showers if the fans don't quite do the trick. All rooms look onto a cluttered courtyard with thriving grapevines. Campers who just need to use the bathroom and shower pay 6 pesos. (Singles 25 pesos. Doubles 35 pesos.) Suites at **Hotel Rosita,** Madero 2 (tel. 3-02-70), just east of the plaza, are so enormous you could invite the in-laws and still have fun.

Two bedrooms, bath, sitting room, kitchen, all furnished with A/C. Bring your own utensils. (Singles 60 pesos. Quads 80 pesos.) **Hotel Terazas,** on Zaragoza 2 blocks north of the plaza (tel. 3-00-09), is a pleasant establishment with every modern convenience except the boob tube. Restaurant and bar inside lobby. (All rooms without A/C cost 60 pesos, rooms with A/C 75 pesos. AAA membership discounts.) **Casa de Huéspedes Nachita** is on Moctezuma 50m down the left branch of the fork as you enter Mulegé (tel. 3-01-40). Spartan rooms include free fans on request. Bathrooms and shower centrally located in the dirt courtyard. (Singles 30 pesos. Triples 45 pesos.)

Grocery stores equipped to feed nomadic beach bums are plentiful (one is on the plaza), and a few unremarkable restaurants cluster near the bus station. **El Candil Restaurant,** north of the plaza on Zaragoza, serves guests Mon.-Sat. from 7am to 11pm. Dine on sizzling steak for 20 pesos, chicken *a la mexicana* for 15 pesos, or shrimp on the stone floor patio under flowering vines and bushes. For the best seafood in town, try **La Almeja** (tel. 3-01-84), at the end of Morelos near the lighthouse. The floor is the beach, and should you find a bone in your garlic fish (16 pesos) you can spit it into the Sea of Cortés. (Open daily 8am-10pm.) The hike down whets the appetite and rides can usually be begged for the trip back to town. **Restaurant Bar Los Equipales,** on Moctezuma next to Casa Mañuelita's (tel. 3-03-30), boasts a second-story terrace with wicker furniture. Almost all breakfast items for 10.50 pesos, barbecue chicken 20 pesos, shrimp cocktail 20 pesos. (Open daily 8am-10pm.)

At night, most *norteamericanos* in the area meet at the bar of the **Hotel Las Casitas** for drinking and dancing with no cover. The last watering hole to close each night is the bar at the **Hotel Vieja Hacienda,** on the plaza.

Sights Pre-Colombian cave paintings are located four hours by car from Mulegé, in the **Cuevas de San Borjita.** Unfortunately, the caves are located on a private estate called San Bartasar Ranchero (tel. 3-03-56), so you must pay the owner to catch a view. Narciso Villavisecio organizes trips to the caves and will provide explanations (in Spanish) of what you see. If you have transportation to the ranch, then a group tour costs US$25, but if you need a ride from Mulegé, the price soars to US$100. For more information, inquire at the unofficial tourist office at the Hotel La Casita. They have pictures of the cave paintings on view free of charge—a cheaper alternative.

In town, Mulegé's **mission** sits on a hill to the west, down a lane shaded by bananas and palms and past the bridge south of the *zócalo*. The mission is not a museum; services are still held every Sunday. And for those who can't make it to Bahía de la Concepción, two beaches lie only 2km from the center of town. **El Faro** is at the very end of Madero long after it becomes a dirt road; reach the public beach by following the Mulegé River to its finish at the Sea of Cortés. Neither spot, with well-trodden black sand and light waves, can compare to the beaches 18 km south. Watch out for jellyfish, especially in early summer.

■ Near Mulegé: Santa Rosalía

The wooden houses, general stores, and saloons along Santa Rosalía's streets recall the town's previous incarnation as the base for a 19th century French copper operation that mined the surrounding hills. The spectacular prefabricated cast-iron **Iglesia Santa Bárbara,** at Obregón and Calle 1, truly makes the town shine. Designed by Gustave Eiffel (of Tower fame) and installed in the 1890s, this church was one of four destined for missions in Africa before the company that commissioned them forgot to pick up their order. French mining *concessionaires* spotted the iron church at the 1889 *Exhibition Universal de Paris* and decided Santa Rosalía couldn't do without it.

The town's only other draw is as the home to the northernmost **ferry** connecting Baja to the mainland. The boat leaves Santa Rosalía only two times per week, on

Wednesday and Sunday at 8am from the **Sematur** terminal on Rte. 1 (tel. 2-00-13), just south of town. Tickets go on sale the day before the departure date, and those with cars must purchase their spot a day in advance. (Office open Tues., Wed., Fri., and Sun. 9am-5pm. *Salón* 38 pesos, *turista* 76 pesos.) Statistics concerning departure days and times, prices and office hours are in constant flux, so be sure to call the office or talk to a travel agent to confirm the schedule. The ferry dock is across the street about 200m from the bus station. To get from the ferry to Obregón, Santa Rosalía's main strip, turn right as you leave the ferry compound; Obregón is your second left.

Those travelers looking for fun in the sun and abundant water sports would do better to make tracks out of this port down to the heavenly beaches further south.

■■■ MULEGÉ TO LORETO

There's nothing like a swim in the bath-warm waters of the Sea of Cortés followed by a bask in the soft sand or under a *palapa*, and maybe a beer provided by the friendly *norteamericano* RVer up the beach. Forget the northern beaches—the Bahía de la Concepción shines the brightest in Baja. Cactus-studded hills drop straight to white sand beaches and warm transluscent waters. Lying 16km south of Mulegé, the beaches of Bahía de la Concepción are studded with campers and RVs that enjoy the surrounding area as if it were a personal paradise. Many nomadic travelers hitch from Mulegé to the beaches: RVs shuttle to and from the coast frequently, and local produce trucks often carry more than fresh fruits; they shuttle beachseekers down the Transpeninsular Highway towards the bay.

Here's the lineup. **Playa Punta Arena,** 16km south of Mulegé, is one of the most attractive beaches in the area. Connected to the highway by a 2km rutted dirt road barely passable by car, this stretch of sand is distant enough from the traffic that the roar of the waves drowns out the noise from muffler-less trucks. A dozen palm-frond *palapas* line the beach (hammock hookups US$4 per night), with sand-flush toilets behind them. The Paleolithic people who once inhabited the caves on the hillside south of the beach left behind millions of discarded shells; the biggest cave is of some interest to sightseers for its collection of stones worn smooth from grinding.

The next beach down is **Playa Santispac,** whose tranquil shores are overrun with RVs. Tent-pitching is also permitted; a man comes around once per day to collect the US$3-4 camping fee. Yachts and sailboats bob in the harbor at Santispac, making it the liveliest of the beaches on the bay. Santispac is directly on the highway; those hitching will find it more convenient than Punta Arena. **Playas Burro, Los Cocos,** and **Escondido** cling to the neighboring southern coast and also have *palapas*. Batting cleanup is **Playa El Coyote,** perhaps the most dazzling beach, with *palapas* and a restaurant across the street called **Estrella del Mar.** Part of this beach has been privatized by RV settlers; the better beach and *palapas* are down on the southern end.

Fifteen km farther down the road, at primitive **Playa Resquesón,** a beautiful spit of sand broadens into a wide beach. The next beach south, small and undeveloped except for a lone toilet, is the last beach before the highway climbs into the mountains separating Mulegé from Loreto.

All of these main beaches are marked from the main highway. Those with cars, dune buggies, motorized tricycles, or other similar blessings can undoubtedly find more remote options. Divers rave about this area; it teems with underwater life, including gigantic sea turtles. **Mulegé Divers,** Madero 45 (tel. 3-01-34), down the street from Hotel Las Casitas, rents scuba equipment and conducts boat excursions. The day-long scuba-diving trip, including guide and equipment, costs US$50 per person; the snorkeling trip costs US$25 per person including mask, fins, and snorkel. Make reservations one day in advance.

■■■ LORETO

Founded by Jesuit missionaries in 1697, Loreto became the first capital of the Californias and the first link in a chain of missions along the west coast. Not more than 130 years later, a dastardly combination of hurricanes and earthquakes wiped out the town and its mission in 1829. Recent construction has beautifully restored **Our Lady of Loreto Mission,** but the town still pines for its former glory. From the hills just south of town, you can see a maze of roads and sidewalks, palm trees, sprinklers and street lights, but no buildings. Years ago, the Mexican government began to lay the foundations for a major resort, but funds were diverted to other projects. Loreto thus remains a simple town, despite its three luxury hotels. Most of the foreigners in town are middle-aged *norteamericanos* who come to fish the spectacular waters off Loreto's coast. **Tourist information** is in the travel agency on Hidalgo one block from shore. (Open Mon.-Sat. 9am-1pm and 3-7pm.)

The new sidewalk with benches along the water is a popular place for an evening stroll. The **Museo de las Misiones,** which recounts the complete history of the European arrival in and subsequent conquest of Baja California in pictures, artifacts and words, is located next to the reconstructed Mission Loreto, one block west of the plaza. Here you can also receive information on the various other missions scattered throughout the peninsula. (Open Mon.-Fri. 9am-5pm. Admission 5 pesos.)

Budget accommodations in Loreto perished with the missions. The most economical hotel in town is **Hotel San Martín,** two blocks north of the *zócalo,* on Juárez (tel. 5-04-42). The rooms seem to be filled with whatever random furniture there happened to be around the day the place was built. (Singles and doubles 36 pesos. Bargaining may work) A number of pricey restaurant-bars have popped up around the docks, proving supply meets demand. **Café Olé,** north of the *zócalo* on Madero (tel. 5-04-96), offers cheap, quick meals for those travelers passing through. Dine on *chile relleno* (13 pesos) and a banana split (13 pesos). (Open Mon.-Sat. 7am-10pm, Sun. 7am-2pm.)

The principle street in Loreto is **Salvatierra,** which connects *Carretera Transpeninsular* to the Gulf. Hidalgo forks off when Salvatierra becomes a walking only zone, and Francisco Madero crosses Salvatierra two blocks up from the waters and passes directly in front of the *zócalo.* The **bus terminal** (tel. 5-07-67) is on Salvatierra just off the highway, about 2km from Madero. *De paso* buses run north to Loreto and Santa Rosalía and south to La Paz a few times daily. PEMEX **gas stations** stare at the terminal across the street.

You can exchange currency at **Bancomer,** on Madero across from the *zócalo* (tel. 3-03-15, open Mon.-Fri. 8:30am-1pm). International collect **calls** (6 pesos) can be made at the *caseta* on the *zócalo* (open Mon.-Sat. 8am-1pm and 5pm-9pm, Sun 10am-2pm and 5pm-9pm). Loreto's **telephone code** is 683. The **post office** (tel. 5-06-47), off Salvatierra near the bus station, behind the Red Cross, is open Mon.-Fri. 9am-1pm and 3-6pm, Sat. 9am-1pm. The **postal code** is 23880. Stock up for the day at **Supermarket El Pescador,** on Salvatierra and Independencia (tel. 5-00-60, open daily 7am-10pm). The **Centro de Salud,** on Salvatierra 1km from the bus terminal (tel. 5-00-39), is open 24 hrs. Finally, in an emergency, the **police** (tel. 5-00-35) are on the plaza in the building with the sign proclaiming "Capital Histórica de las Californias."

North of Loreto, the road passes the gorgeous **Bahía de la Concepción** on its way to Mulegé. South of Loreto, the road winds away from the coast into rugged mountains and the **Planicie Magdalena,** an intensively irrigated and cultivated plain. The striking white stripes on the first hillside beyond town consist of millions of shells, the refuse left by the region's Paleolithic inhabitants. This whole area is strewn with clam, conch, oyster, and scallop shells. Some caves on the hillside, inhabited as recently as 300 years ago, contain shells and polished stone.

■■■ LA PAZ

For most of the 454 years since Hernán Cortés founded it, La Paz has been a quiet fishing village beloved for its extraordinary off-shore pearls. Cut off from the rest of the world and accessible only by sea, La Paz's iridescent treasure became a frequent target for pirate raids. John Steinbeck set *The Pearl* in La Paz, depicting it as a tiny, unworldly fishing village glittering with small semi-precious orbs. In the 1940s, La Paz's oysters mysteriously sickened and died, wiping out the pearl industry. With the institution of the Baja ferries and the completion of the Transpeninsular Highway in the '60s, however, tourists and new industries discovered La Paz. As night approaches, locals and *viajeros* alike flock to the beach to cruise the strip and watch exquisite sunsets.

ORIENTATION

La Paz overlooks the **Bahía de la Paz,** on the Baja's east coast, 222km north of Cabo San Lucas and 1496km southeast of Tijuana, on the Transpeninsular Highway (Rte. 1). Ferry is by far the cheapest way to get from La Paz to the mainland, but for those with a car procuring a ticket is nearly impossible; ferries carry mostly commercial trucks and the few slots for other vehicles sell out far in advance.

    Sematur Company (tel. 5-46-66), 5 de Mayo and Prieto, operates the ferry from La Paz to Topolobampo and Mazatlán (open daily 7am-1pm). In order to secure a place to the mainland, be sure to get there early to get a prime spot in line. Acquiring a *salón* ticket should be no problem on the day of departure, but for other classes, call ahead to make reservations. In all cases, tickets may only be bought on the day of departure (for more about ferries see Baja California: Getting Around). The ferry dock is a 17km hike from the center of town in Pichilingue; don't fret, **buses** run down Obregón hourly from 8am to 6pm, except 3pm, for 3 pesos. To the dock, catch the bus at the downtown terminal on Obregón between Independencia and 5 de Mayo.

    During holidays, ferry demand is great. In order to get a vehicle on the ferry you will need—at a minimum—proof of Mexican insurance, car registration and a tourist card; oh, and two photocopies of each. Travelers themselves will at least need a tourist card. Try to procure all of this paper work at the border when entering Mexico (see Planning Your Trip: Documents and Formalities: Driver's License and Vehicle Permits for details on bringing your car farther into Mexico). If not, **Servicios Migratorios** can set you up in La Paz, on Obregón between Allende and Juárez (tel. 2-04-29; open Mon.-Fri. 8am-3pm.) The tricky part is that all of the paper work must be in place before you purchase the ticket; otherwise Sematur will deny you a spot, reservations or not.

    Maps of La Paz depict perfect rectilinear blocks around a tiny enclave of disorder on the waterfront. The main streets for travelers are **Obregón,** which follows the waterfront, and **16 de Septiembre,** which runs south (they intersect at the tourist office). On some maps, the stretch of Obregón near the tourist office is called **Malecón.** La Paz can be confusing: on a peninsula, the waterfront faces the bay to the northwest, and street names are very similar.

    The municipal bus system in La Paz serves the city sporadically. In general, city buses run daily from 6am to 10pm every half hour (1 peso). Flag them down anywhere, or wait by the stop at Degollado (which runs parallel to 16 de Septiembre and Revolución), next to the market.

PRACTICAL INFORMATION

    Tourist Office: Obregón at 16 de Septiembre (tel. 2-59-39), in a pavilion on the water. Excellent city maps and information about Baja Sur, especially Los Cabos. English-speaking staff. Open Mon.-Fri. 8am-8pm.

    Currency Exchange: Bancomer, 16 de Septiembre, ½ block from the waterfront. Other banks scattered in small downtown area. All open Mon.-Fri. 8:30am-1pm.

Immigration Office: Servicios Migratorios (tel. 2-04-29), on 2140 Obregón between Allende and Juárez. You must stop here for a tourist card and a stamp on your car permit if you entered Mexico via Baja and are mainland-bound. Open Mon.-Fri. 8am-3pm. After hours, you can go to their outpost in the airport outside of town (tel. 2-18-29; open 7am-7pm).

Post Office: Revolución at Constitución (tel. 2-03-88). Open Mon.-Fri. 8am-7pm, Sat.-Sun. 9am-12:30pm. **Postal code:** 23000.

American Express: Obregón 1570 (tel. 2-83-00), in the Hotel Perla. Open Mon.-Fri. 9am-2pm and 4-6pm, Sat. 9am-2pm. La Paz and Esquerro (tel. 2-83-00, fax 5-52-72), behind the Hotel Perla. Open Mon.-Fri. 9am-2pm and 4-6pm. Sat 9am-2pm.

Telephones: *Caseta* located on Obregón between Muelle and Degollado (tel. 2-12-33). International collect calls 6 pesos. Open daily 8am-10pm. Otherwise, touch-tone public phones on streets and in post office. **Telephone code:** 112.

Telegrams: Upstairs from post office (tel. 2-03-22). Fax service also. Mon.-Fri. 8am-7pm, Sat. 8-11am.

Airport: West of La Paz. Accessible only by 30 peso taxis. Served by **Aeroméxico,** (tel. 2-00-91), **Aerocalifornia** and **Lineas del Noroeste.** Flights to: Los Mochis (223 pesos), Tijuana (558 pesos), Mexico City (874 pesos), and Los Angeles (US$190).

Bus Station: Independencia at Jalisco, about 25 blocks south of downtown. Municipal bus "Central Camionera" (1 peso) runs between the terminal and the public market at Degollado and Revolución, but these are infrequent (every hr. 6am-8pm),and the hike is long, so consider taking a taxi (8 pesos). **Tres Estrellas de Oro, Autotransportes Águila**, and **Norte de Sonora** operate out of the terminal. Buses leave several times daily from La Paz to Tijuana (150 pesos). To: Loreto (40 pesos), Mulegé (50 pesos), and Cabo San Lucas (28 pesos). Also, **mini-bus station** at Obregón and Independencia runs buses to Pichilingue and surrounding beaches (3 pesos) and to Cabo San Lucas (28 pesos).

Ferries: Sematur Company, at 5 de Mayo and Prieto (tel. 5-46-66). To Mazatlán (Sun.-Fri. at 3pm, 16hrs., *salón* 57 pesos, *turista* 76 pesos, cars up to 5m long 417 pesos, motorcycles 95 pesos) and Topolobampo (daily at 8pm except for unfixed "cargo only" days—call for precise info—8hrs., *salón* 38 pesos, *turista* 76 pesos, *cabina* 114 pesos). Open Mon.-Fri. 7am-1pm, Sat.-Sun. 8am-1pm for ticket sales, Mon.-Fri. 4-6pm for reservations. Boats leave Sun.-Fri. at 3pm.

Bookstores/Libraries: Biblioteca de las Californias, at 5 de Mayo and Madero. Books about Baja. **Librería Contempo,** Arreola 2B just off the waterfront, has a section of English-language books, magazines and newspapers. Open daily 9am-9pm.

Laundromat: Lavamática, 5 de Mayo at Rubio (tel. 2-10-01), across the street from the stadium. Wash 4 pesos, 5-min. dry .40 pesos. Open Mon.-Sat. 7am-9pm, Sun. 8am-3pm.

Red Cross: (tel. 2-11-11), 1901 Reforma between Isabel la Católica and Félix Ortega.

Pharmacy: Farmacia Baja California, Independencia at Madero (tel. 2-02-40), facing the plaza. 24 hr.

Hospital: Salvatierra, Bravo at Verdad (tel. 2-14-96).

Police: Colima at México (tel. 2-20-20). Open 24 hrs. In **emergency**, dial 06.

ACCOMMODATIONS

Hotels in La Paz seem to be competing with each other for the cluttered artistic look; a student of Mexican folk art could skip the Museo Antrolpologico and tour the lobbies of these hotels instead. There is a **CREA** youth hostel (tel. 2-46-15) in the youth center of Forjatero near the Technical University, but its distance from the *centro* makes rooms in the hotels a safer, more convenient, and perhaps even cheaper option, considering the La Paz bus and taxi system.

Pensión California Casa de Huéspedes, Degollado at Madero (tel. 2-28-96). Bungalows rooms with concrete floors and beds on concrete slabs. Pleasant sitting area in courtyard, especially if you like small children. Bring your own blanket. Singles 25 pesos. Doubles 38 pesos.

Hostería del Convento, Madero 85 (tel. 2-35-08), almost at Degollado. Eerily similar to the Pensíon around the corner. Rooms are arranged in an open-air maze that is lined with old maps of Baja and Mexico, but alas, no map of the hotel. Light blue rooms and ceiling fans provide comfort from the sticky heat. Private baths. Singles 25 pesos. Doubles 38 pesos.

Hotel Posada San Miguel, B. Domínguez 151 (tel. 2-18-02), just off 16 de Septiembre. Lodgings with fountained courtyards, tiled arches, and wrought-iron scroll work on windows and railings. Cubical rooms with sinks next to large comfortable beds. Singles 30 pesos. Doubles 40 pesos.

Hotel Yeneka, Madero 1520 (tel. 5-46-88). Motel doubles as a museum with a host of eccentric items: a 1916 model T-Ford and a pet hawk. All Tarzan-hut rooms remodeled in matching twig furniture. Singles 48 pesos. Doubles 58 pesos. No to credit cards, yes to traveler's checks.

Hotel San Carlos, 16 de Septiembre at Revolución (tel. 2-04-44). Wide white corridors glowing with fluorescent lighting give the air of an asylum. Bedrooms with grubby pink walls, tile floor, and a fan. Singles and doubles 33 pesos.

FOOD

On the waterfront you'll find decor, menus and prices geared toward peso-spewing tourists. Move inland a few blocks and food prices begin to drop zeros at the end. The **public market,** at Degollado and Revolución, offers a selection of fruits, veggies and fresh fish.

Restaurant El Mexicano, 16 de Septiembre at Serdán (tel. 2-89-65). Bright, striped *mexicano* blankets on the tables accompany good service. Authentic *antojitos* cooked to order. Loaded tostadas 7.50 pesos, fried fish 10 pesos. Open daily (except every other Mon.) 9am-9pm.

Restaurante El Quinto Sol, B. Domínguez at Independencia (tel. 2-16-92). Stands proud as one of the few vegetarian joints in western Mexico. Menu includes sausage *á la soybean,* as well as esoteric and relaxant juices. Half of the eatery doubles as a health food store with plenty of dried fruits and vitamins. Avocado and cheese sandwich 8 pesos. Yogurt smoothie with fruits 18 pesos. Open Mon.-Sat. 7am-10pm.

Rosticería California, Serdán between Degollado and Ocampo (tel. 2-51-18). Everybody and their *hermano* comes here for finger-licking roasted cluckers. Plenty of seating with attentive waiters, or take it to go. Don't miss the exotic live peacocks in the back. Whole chicken including fries 27 pesos, ½ chicken 15 pesos. Open Sun.-Fri. 8am-6pm.

Antojitos de Sinaloa, on 16 de Septiembre between Revolución and Serdán. Enjoy cheap Mexican favorites from the English-Spanish menu scrawled on the wall. Scrumptious tostadas and *gorditas* 10 pesos. Eggs 7 pesos. Open daily 7am-10pm.

Café Olimpia, on 16 de Septiembre, across from Antojitos de Sinaloa. Customers hop on loud orange stools to devour a quickly fried up meal and slurp on frosty *licuados* (3.50 pesos). *Flautas* 9 pesos. Gigantic Mexican-style Egg McMuffin 7 pesos. Open daily 7:30am-11pm.

SIGHTS AND ENTERTAINMENT

Beaches in La Paz and much of eastern Baja are not your usual long, curving expanses of wave-washed sand. Instead, they snuggle into small coves sandwiched between cactus-studded hills and calm, transparent water; this is a prime windsurfing zone.

The best beach near La Paz is **Playa Tecolote** (Owl Beach), 25km northeast of town. A quiet extension of the Sea of Cortés laps against this gorgeous stretch of gleaming white sand, backed up by tall, craggy mountains. Even though there are no bathrooms, Tecolote is terrific for **camping**. You may need to drive here; buses run only during peak seasons—spring break, July, and August. Plenty of other beaches are easily accessible by taking the "Pichilingue" **bus** up the coast (station on Obregón and Independencia, 3 pesos). Be forewarned that the bus only runs back to La Paz until 6pm, so don't be caught stranded. The bus goes as far as the ferry dock, at which point you need to walk 2km further on the dirt road to **Playa de Pichilingue.** This beach is a favorite among the teen set, who dig its eatery and public bathrooms. Along the same bus route lies **Playa El Coronel** near La Concha Hotel. Because of its proximity to downtown, visitors and locals alike flock to its shores on weekends. These are all a hefty hike or a short ride away. Closer to town, there's fine swimming in the placid waters near the tourist office with plenty of eateries and hotels nearby in case the mean sun wears you out. But the farther you venture from La Paz, the better and more secluded it gets.

The fun in La Paz doesn't stop at the beach for those who want to venture out onto the water. Nautilius, on Martinez at Obregón, rents snorkelling equipment for US$25 per day. (Open Mon.-Fri. 9am-2:30pm, 4:30-9pm, Sat.-Sun. 9am-3pm.) **Baja Diving and Service,** Independencia 107-B (tel. 2-18-26), just north of B. Domínguez, organizes daily scuba and snorkeling trips to nearby reefs, wrecks, and islands, where you can mingle with hammer heads, manta rays, giant turtles, and other exotica. (Scuba adventure US$70 per day, snorkeling trips US$40 per day, including equipment and lunch.)

If you tire of the ocean and wish to escape the blistering sun, take a break at the **Museo Antropológico,** 5 de Mayo and Altamirano (tel. 2-01-62), which displays local art and reproductions of pre-Conquest cave paintings, as well as exhibits on the Baja's pre-Conquest past. (Open Mon.-Fri. 11am-6pm. Free.)

On the south side of Constitución Square (the main plaza) soars the **Misión de Nuestra Señora de la Paz** (Our Lady of La Paz Mission), on Revolución between Independencia and 5 de Mayo. This cathedral was founded by Jesuit missionaries in 1720.

Every Sunday evening, La Paz denizens attend concerts under the enormous kiosk on the plaza east of the tourist office. Called "Sunday in the Park with Tecate," these weekly parties are popular with both Mexicans and *gringos*. If you decide to stroll down the pier to stargaze afterward, keep an eye out for missing floorboards.

■■■ TODOS SANTOS

For now, Todos Santos is one of the few towns on the southern Baja coast which is easily accessible by bus, offers budget accomodations, and is for the most part unmutilated by the hand of *norteamericano* resort development. Yet another in the string of towns founded by Jesuit missionaries in the 17th century, Todos Santos was more recently a major producer and exporter of sugar cane. The ruins of old sugar mills are reminders of that boom period, which ended with a decrease in the water level. But another boom is on the horizon in Todos Santos. A large resort hotel, complete with yacht basin and water park, is being planned for the land near Playa Los Lobos. Until its completion, however, the cool Pacific breezes and excellent surf make Todos Santos a welcome relief from the desert heat and tourist excess.

Practical Information Todos Santos's two main streets, **Colegio Militar** (part of the Carretera Transpeninsular) and **Juárez**, which passes beside the church, run parallel to each other. León crosses these at the church and plaza, and three blocks down the highway, Degollado marks the end of the downtown.

The **bus station** is Pilar's taco stand, at the corner of Zaragoza and Colegio Militar, one block from the spotlight. *De paso* buses run south to the Cabos (15 pesos) and north to La Paz (12 pesos) several times daily. Change dollars and traveler's checks at the other end of town at the **Bancomer** on Juárez one block past Topete (open Mon.-Fri. 8:30am-1pm). **Long distance calls** can be made from the *caseta* at the bus station (9am-7pm) or the public phone at the Pememex on Degollado. The **tele-**

phone code is 114. The *Lista de Correos* is posted at the **post office,** on Colegio Militar, on the northbound side of León. (**Postal code:** 23300; open Mon.-Fri. 8am-1pm and 3-5pm.) **Isstotiendas,** the market on Juárez between Morelos and Zaragoza, is open daily 8am-8pm. Next door, **Farmacia Todos Santos** (tel. 5-00-30) offers 24-hr. emergency service. The **police** are at tel. 4-101-22.

Accommodations and Food The **Hotel California** (tel. 4-00-02) at Juárez and Morelos, has a swimming pool, gift shop, view of the church, and good-sized, clean rooms with ceiling fans, all for only 35 pesos for a single, 42 pesos for a double. Visa and MC accepted. If the Hotel California is full, or if you want to prove your mettle on some of the most uncomfortable furniture in the world, go across the street to **Departamentos Gabi,** where the sign just reads "Motel." Rooms come with fan, TV, and furniture. (Singles 50 pesos, doubles 60 pesos.) **El Molino** trailer park, off Degollado at the Pemex corner, offers tired RVers and Airstreamers a 10 peso full hook-up, a book shelf, and coin-operated washing machines.

Food is not hard to find. Several *loncherías* line Colegio Militar near the bus station, offering triple tacos and the like for 9 pesos. Restaurant-bar **Los Fuentes** (tel. 4-02-57), at the stoplight corner, has pleasant fountains and good food: fried fish with rice and salad 20 pesos, breakfast about 12 pesos. English spoken and clean public bathrooms, too. (Open daily 7am-9pm.)

Sights Action in Todos Santos revolves around the **farm** and the **beach.** Most tourists will probably prefer the beach, though the farms are more accessible. The closest beach to town (2km) is **La Posa.** To get there, go up Juárez and turn left on Topete. Follow that as it winds around and across the valley, and comes to a white building that says "Do not pass." Pass that, and you're on the beach. The more popular **Playa Los Lobos** is 3 or 4 km down the dirt road by El Molino trailer park. Turn left at the stadium. **Los Cerritos,** known far and wide for its surf, is 10km south of town on the highway, then a couple more on a dirt road. Rock climbers, hikers, and hunters enjoy **La Laguna de la Sierra,** a beautiful lake on top of a mountain, accessible by dirt road (2hrs. by car) from the other side of town.

LOS CABOS

The towns of **Cabo San Lucas** and **San José del Cabo** comprise the southwestern part of the governmental district of Los Cabos, which includes a significant portion of the coast on the southeastern tip of Baja California. The *vía larga* section of Route 1 passes through this area, but winds through the mountains rather than along the coast. Bus service (Frailes del Sur line) is expanding in this region, but many roads still need improvement. To get to Cabo Pulmo and some of the best diving and snorkelling in the hemisphere, for instance, it is necessary to drive or hitchike 40 or 50km from Las Cuevas or Santa Ribera.

The real tourist draws to the Cabos are the towns of Cabo San Lucas and San José del Cabo. Here luxury hotels intercede between the desert and the ocean, and (sport-fishing, sunbathing, sightseeing, gift-buying, jetskiing) *norteamericanos* congregate by the thousands.

■■■ SAN JOSÉ DEL CABO

This is much more of a town and less of a resort than Cabo San Lucas, but the tourists are taking over. Golf courses and huge hotels separate San José del Cabo from the beach, and institutions like the post office and police station are being pushed out of their traditional locations in the *centro* by tourist information centers and gift shops.

In some ways, this budding resort atmosphere can be kind to budget travelers. Promoters for new hotels and time-shares will snap up anyone who looks like they may have a credit card and offer free boat trips, transportation, even free lunch. Just be sure no strings are attached.

Practical Information The **Transpeninsular Highway** on the west and **Avenida Mijares** on the east connect the town with San José's broad sweep of beautiful beach 2km away. The town is not hard to figure out; the cathedral and the *zócalo* are conspicuous landmarks on Zaragoza. One street over runs **Doblado.** Maps are free at the tourist information center on Zaragoza at Mijares.

Change all your money for new pesos at **Banca Serfín** on Zaragoza between 9:30am and noon. The **tourist information center** is next to the *zócalo* on Zaragoza; many important establishments have flyers there. International collect calls cost 3 pesos at the **caseta** outside the front entrance of the cathedral. (Open Mon.-Fri. 8am-2pm.) The new telephone area code is 114. The **post office** is on Mijar toward the beach. Mail letters or check the *Lista de Correos.* (Open Mon.-Fri. 8am-6pm, Sat. 9am-1pm.) The **postal code** is 23400.

San José del Cabo is such a whirring, buzzing metropolis that it needs two **bus stations**. The **Aguila terminal** launches buses to La Paz (3hrs., 28 pesos) and Cabo San Lucas (40min., 5 pesos). To get to town, walk all the way down González to Mijares to Zaragoza. The **Frailes terminal** (tel. 2-19-06) operates buses to Cabo San Lucas (5 pesos) from 6am-8pm, and has some service up the *vía larga* to La Ribera. The Frailes terminal is just outside the *centro* on Doblado, about a 10-min. walk from Mijares.

Buy groceries at the **Almacen** on Mijares at Zaragoza (tel. 2-09-12). (Open Mon.-Fri. 8am-8pm, Sat.-Sun. 8am-12:30pm.) **Farmacía Profesor Aurora** (tel. 226-11) is up on Green at Dobaldo, across from the Jardín de Niños. (Open daily 9am-2pm and 3-9pm.) The **Red Cross** is always ready at 2-08-84 and the **police** respond to 2-03-61.

Accommodations and Food As prices rise with the approach of the monster resorts, spots on the beach look more and more appealing. Many random rooms are for rent for about 30 pesos a day; look for signs, especially on Obregón. **Hotel Ceci,** Zaragoza 22 (tel. 2-00-5), 1½ blocks up from Mijares, offers comfortable beds with bright, white sheets and standing fans, and is the only real budget hotel in town. (Singles 44 pesos, doubles 50 pesos.) **Hotel San José Inn,** Obregón at Guerrero (tel. 0-11-52), outclasses the Ceci by offering newer, cleaner rooms with ceiling fans, some with a balcony. (Singles 60 pesos, doubles 75 pesos. Additional children 15 pesos.) **Trailer Park Brisa del Mar,** just off the highway to San Lucas when it reaches the coast, provides beach campers, communal bathrooms, and a bar with TV. (Full hook-up US$2 plus tax, US$5 for tent.)

Budget restaurants in San José del Cabo are being pushed out by real estate offices and fancy tourist eateries, leaving few options in between taco stands and filet mignon. **Cafetería Rosy,** on Zaragoza past Banca Serfín, cooks up delicious Mexican seafood dishes and serves them with a smile. Garlic fish 19 pesos. *Quesadillas* 10 pesos. (Open Mon.-Sat. 8am-10pm.) **Cafetería Arco Iris,** Morelos at Zaragoza (tel. 2-17-60), has small orange stools at a little counter. Tacos and *sincronizadas* 10 pesos each. (Open daily 8am-9:30pm.) **Panadería Princesa,** on Zaragoza past Green, sells rolls and muffins for a quick breakfast.

Sights and Entertainment The most popular beach in town is **Costa Azul,** on Palmilla Pt. 1km south of the Brisa del Mar trailer park. It has three- to five-foot waves and four different breaks of great interest to veteran surfers. Many hitch or persuade the bus driver to let them off there; those who do should ask first in order to avoid being driven all the way to Cabo San Lucas. A 15-minute walk down Mijares will lead you to perfectly good beaches much closer to town. The newest luxury

CABO SAN LUCAS

hotels line the sand at some spots, but there's plenty of natural, clean coast line in between the artificial structures.

The **Killer Hook Surf Shop,** on Hidalgo between Doblado and Zaragoza (tel. 2-24-30), rents anything you need for a good time around here (snorkel gear US$8, fishing pole US$10, surf board US$15, bike US$11 for 24 hrs.). They also repair surfboard and dispense tips. (Open Mon.-Sat. 9am-1pm and 4-8pm.)

At night, the **Eclipse** on Mijares (tel. 2-16-94), one block down from Dobaldo jams rock music beneath flashing lights and a disco ball. (Never a cover. Margaritas 10 pesos, free Thurs.10-11pm. Happy hour Tues.-Wed. 7-9pm. Open Tues.-Sun. 7pm-3am.) The newest disco, **Bones,** next to the Hotel Presidente, offers a heavily strobe-lit dance floor to sweat out the beer calories. (Open Tues.-Sun. 7pm-2am.)

■■■ CABO SAN LUCAS

Cabo San Lucas is the first of the two Cabos on the *vía corta* bus route from La Paz. Until recently a peaceful fishing village, Cabo San Lucas is fast becoming one of the largest resorts in all of Mexico. For now, the town is haunted more by the skeletons of future pleasure domes than by hotels already completed. Due to the small size of the native population (about 3000), investors import young souls from the mainland to power the service economy. If you had planned to practice your rusty high school Spanish here, think again; waiters at the popular restaurants and bars receive daily English classes in addition to their weekly paychecks. Despite all of this fervor, Cabo San Lucas has yet to develop extensive facilities for the budget traveler. Prices at most eating establishments are high, even by US standards.

Budget travelers would do best to visit Cabo San Lucas only for the day or to camp out on the beach and treat the town solely as one big supermarket; buy your Neutrogena and make tracks for San José del Cabo.

Practical Information The bus station, served by **Tres Estrellas de Oro** and **Aguila,** is located on the corner of Zaragoza and 16 de Septiembre. Buses run daily until 9pm to San José (5 pesos) and La Paz (28 pesos), with one per day to Tijuana (165 pesos). To get to the center of action, take Zaragoza down toward the water 2 blocks to Cárdenas. City maps are handed out in bushels at one of the trillion info booths through the town. **Banca Serfín,** at Cárdenas and Zaragoza, and **Bánamex,** at Cárdenas and Hidalgo, exchange cash and traveler's checks Mon.-Fri. 8:30am-1pm. Most hotels and restaurants will gladly exchange dollars at lower rates. The **long-distance caseta** at Cárdenas and Hidalgo charges 3 pesos for international collect calls (Mon.-Sun. 8am-10pm). The **telephone code** is 114. The local supermarket, **Almacenes Grupo Castro,** at Morelos at Revolucíon (tel. 3-05-66), is open daily 9am-11pm. Finally, in case of an emergency, dial the **police** (tel. 3-02-96) or the **Red Cross** (tel. 3-11-14).

Accommodations and Food Multi-million dollar resorts with every service imaginable dominate San Lucas's coast line; for that same reason, simple, cheap beds are seriously lacking. In any case, make reservations early for the winter vacation period and be prepared to shell out more *dinero* than you would during the slower summer months. **CREA Youth Hostel (HI)** (tel. 3-01-48), is a 10-min. walk down Morelos from Cárdenas to Av. de la Juventud, then turn right and 5 min. to the large Instituto Sur Californiano building. Excitement over the cheapest beds in town is certainly dampened by the inconvenient location and hot hike to the beach. (Dorm bunk with communal bath 16 pesos, singles with private bath 25 pesos, doubles with bath 34 pesos.) **Hotel Dos Mares** is on Zapata between Hidalgo and Guerrero (tel. 3-03-30). Prime location near the docks and popular bars are the most attractive aspects of this joint; otherwise, aggressively average rooms. Not a single guest dares to venture into the questionable poolette. (Singles 66 pesos, doubles 76 pesos. Group rates and long-term discounts.)

Like their fellow shops and hotels, the restaurants in San Lucas have been forced into submission by prevailing *gringo* tastes. Restaurant-bars gang up on tourists along the water, all competing for the prized U.S. dollar. But the cheap spots line Morelos, a safe distance from the million-dollar yachts. **Taquería del Cheef,** Morelos at 20 de Noviembre, a small taco stand, boasts a baseball cap collection of 700 and counting (with no duplicates). Stop by, add a hat to the group and try one of eight varieties of burritos (6 pesos) or a juicy half-pound burger (13 pesos). (Open daily 7:30am-1am.) **The Broken Surfboards,** Hidalgo at Zapata, is an old and repectable taco joint with character. *Quesadillas* 3 pesos, but their pride and joy is breakfast for US$2. (Open daily 6:30am-9pm.) **Mariscos Mocambo,** Morelos at 20 de Noviembre (tel. 3-21-22), across from Taquería del Cheef, is a thatched -roof establishment which offers a refreshing break from the "tourist zone" three blocks away. *Puro* seafood served up fresh daily. Shrimp cocktail 18 pesos, fish and shrimp *empanada* 20 pesos. (Open Mon.-Sat. 9am-9pm.)

Sights and Entertainment All major activity in Cabo San Lucas revolves around the pristine waters surrounding the coast. One of the best beaches in the area, **Playa de Médano,** stretches east on the bay around the corner from the marina. Escape from the blazing sun in one of the beach's restaurants or many *palapas*, which serve up beverages and snacks for parched sun-seekers. The waters of the Playa del Médano are alive with buzzing jet-skis, parasailers, and motorboats full of lobster-red, beer-guzzling vacationers. **Cabo Acuadeportes,** in front of the **Hotel Hacienda** (tel. 3-01-17), offers every watersport desirable, at a price. Explore the busy underwater life with complete snorkeling gear (US$10 per day) or stay above the foamy waves on a catamaran (US$25 per hr.). (Open daily 9am-5pm. Last rental at 3:30pm.) The famous **Arch Rock** of Cabo San Lucas rises only a short boat ride from the marina. To get there, walk through the Plaza Las Glorias hotel, or the big Mexican crafts mart further down Paseo Marina, to the docks, where eager boat captains will be waiting to transport you (US$5 per person). On the same excursion, you'll have the opportunity to disembark and lounge on **La Playa del Amor,** the only beach with access to both the rough, deep blue Pacific and the tranquil Sea of Cortés. Among the many actvities for sale to land-lubbers are horse rentals with guided tours.

The beaches on the Pacific side are farther away than those by the marina, and the ferocious tide makes them unsuitable for swimming. Seclusion-seekers, however, may find them to be just the right thing. To get there, walk out on Marina (or hop a yellow school bus for 1.50 pesos) and turn right across from the Mexican crafts mart. Slip out to the beach between massive condominium complexes right after you pass the Terra Sol Hotel.

The 5-peso bus to San José del Cabo provides access to more beaches. These streches of white sand and glowing blue water are the reason that the Cabos are exploding with tourists, but if you pick the right one you may be able to escape the crowds, even during high season. **El Chileno,** closer to Cabo San Lucas, offers water sports like snorkelling, but **Tulé** boasts nicer surf. Just ask around to find names and descriptions of others, and ask the driver to leave you at the beach of your choice. Buses run to Cabo San Lucas until 8pm, to San Jose until 9pm.

At night, you too can join in the nightly ritual of alcohol-induced gastrointestinal reversal. **El Squid Roe,** Cárdenas and Zaragoza (tel. 3-06-55) serves clients in their singular drive towards inebriation. (Dancing (on any surface) from 11pm-3am. Well drinks 8 pesos. Open daily noon-3am.) A louder, middle-aged crowd at **The Giggling Marlin,** Marina at Matamoros, enjoys a full mug and hanging upside-down like the big catch. (Piña coladas 10 pesos. Happy hour(s) 2-6pm. Open daily 10am-1am.)

■ Northwest México

SONORA

■■■ NOGALES

Nogales has many of the same charms as Tijuana (ease of border crossing, cheap-o curio shops, off-track betting, and cheesy bars), yet fewer Tucsonans visit Nogales than San Diegans do Tijuana. The shorter distance between the San Diego and Tijuana and the maturity level of southern Californians contribute to this disparity. Nogales retains a distinct Mexican flavor and serves as a fine beginning point for those who want to feel like they're in Mexico the instant they cross the border. Its twin city is the smaller and less interesting **Nogales, Arizona.**

Practical Information The **bus terminal** (tel. 3-17-00) and **train station** (tel. 2-00-24) sit directly across from each other on Carretera Internacional, 4.5km from town. **Transportes Norte de Sonora** runs buses to Hermosillo (28 pesos), Tijuana (1 per day, 85 pesos), and Los Mochis (77 pesos). **Tres Estrellas de Oro** has daily departures to the same points, including Mexico City (246 pesos) and Chihuahua (88 pesos). Reserved seating can be purchased one hour before departure. **Greyhound** buses leave for Tucson (US$6.50). The bus station is ½ block from the main border, accessible from the Nogales on the U.S. side of the border every two hours from 6am to 8pm.

Two southbound trains depart daily to Mazatlán and Guadalajara; the *burro* (slow) leaves at 7am and the *estrella* (fast) leaves at 3:30pm. Tickets go on sale one hour before the time of departure, and reservations for the *estrella* can be made at from 8 to 11am. To reach the border and center of town, catch a white school bus market "Centro" (.50 pesos).

Nogales is small enough to navigate on your own. If you usually feel lost without a map, pray that the **tourist office** (tel. 2-64-46) at the border has one in stock. The office is open Mon.-Fri. 8am-5pm, and the staff is friendly but sometimes only Spanish-speaking. In emergencies, call the **Red Cross** (tel. 2-08-10) or **police** (tel. 2-01-04).

It's possible to walk across the border into Mexico without ever talking to a border official. However, if you plan to venture beyond Nogales, obtain a tourist card at the frontier. It's much simpler and cheaper to get the card there than farther south. A grand new border-crossing station *a la* Tijuana is still under construction here, so the immigration and tourism office is not as easy to find as it was once and will be. It's in the other side of the long white buildings that are on the left as you come into Mexico through the temporary crossing.

Most of the curio and craft shops line Obregón, and, just as in Tijuana, you *may* get good deals if you bargain and know something about product quality. Potential turquoise jewelry buyers should ask the vendor to put the rock to "the lighter test." Plastic or synthetic material will quickly melt under a lighter flame. Likewise, when buying silver make sure you see a ".925" stamp on the piece; if it's not there, the goods are bad.

Accommodations and Food A string of budget hotels is situated one block behind the tourist office on Av. Juárez and Obregón. As in most of northern Mexico, rates are steep. **Hotel Imperial,** Obregón 19 (tel. 2-70-62), is a long building with a central spiral staircase and cafeteria on the second floor. Small neat rooms with fan but few windows. (Singles and doubles 60 pesos.) For a bit of class, try **San Carlos Hotel,** Juárez 22 (tel. 2-13-46). Comfy lazy-boys fill the lobby and large rooms with TV and A/C charm the guests. (Singles 72 pesos, doubles 94 pesos.)

There are a fair number of **restaurants** packed in the center of Nogales, and most are overpriced. **La Posada Restaurant,** on Pierson 116 (tel. 2-04-39) off Obregón, jazzes up its walls and ceilings with painted tiles and curious objects. The town's bourgeoisie enjoy fresh foods served on colorful dishes. (*Chimichanga* 6 pesos, steak milanesa 18 pesos, *huevos rancheros* 11 pesos. Open daily 7:30am-10pm.) On Juárez, only half a block from the border, **Restaurant Olga** (tel. 2-16-41) has a TV and dysfunctional counter. (*Comidas corridas* 13 pesos, *chorizo* with eggs US$3. Open daily 6:30am-2am.)

■■■ PUERTO PEÑASCO

Puerto Peñasco partakes of the current of North Americans drifting down toward the prime sun-basking points of mainland Mexico's western coast.

The metaphysical maelstrom of the 20th century has failed to suck in Puerto Peñasco. The business here is sun and fun. Just 65 miles from the border and about three hrs. from Tucson, Arizona, Puerto Peñasco, like northern Baja, attracts hordes of weekenders (albeit with different license plates). It even has an English sobriquet: Rocky Point. If heavily peopled beaches and big hotel discos aren't your thing, 30 mi. north on the road to Sonoita is the **El Pinacate** volcanic area, pockmarked by over 600 craters. Otherwise, the detour off the main road isn't worth it—the beaches farther south are better.

Practical Information The main road, **Blvd. Juárez,** runs into town parallel to the train tracks. From the bus station take a left past the Pemex, and follow Juárez. An orange walking bridge, **Calle Armada Nacional,** goes to the right acros the train tracks to Playa Hermosa. A few blocks farther down Juárez, at the plaza, **Calle Fremont** goes off to the left. Juárez continues through the *centro* to the point.

Puerto Peñasco's **tourist office** (tel. 3-41-29) is in the Jim Bur shopping center on Juárez, next to **Bancomer.** (Open Mon.-Fri. 9am-2pm and 4-7pm, Sat. 9am-2pm.) **Bancomer,** on Juárez and Estrella (tel. 3-24-30), next to the plaza, exchanges currency and traveler's checks Mon.-Fri. 9am-noon. **Chiapas,** 2 blocks east of Juárez on Fremont (tel. 3-23-50), holds the **post office.** (Open Mon.-Fri. 8am-7pm, Sat. 8am-11am. **Postal code:** 83550.) **Buses** depart from Juárez and Calle 24 (tel. 3-35-55). **Transportes Norte de Sonora** has limited service to Mexicali (two per day, 38 pesos) and to Sonoita (daily, 10.50 pesos). Connections south to Hermosillo and Mazatlán can be made on *de paso* buses from Sonoita. The **train station** lies off Constitución, two blocks north of the oblique intersection with Juárez (tel. 3-26-10). Southbound *estrella* (fast) arrives at 1pm (tickets on sale 10am-noon) and the *burro* (slow) at 2am (tickets sold 1-2am). Northbound *estrella* at 5:30pm (tickets 1hr. before) and the *burro* at 3am (tickets 1hr. before). The *estrellas* are often full arriving from both directions, but the *burro's* times are inconvenient. **Lavamática Peñasco,** on Constitución at Morua (tel. 3-22-63), across from Hotel Paraíso del Desierto, will wash or dry clothes for 4 pesos. (Open Mon.-Sat. 9am-7pm.) The **Red Cross,** Fremont at Chiapas (tel. 3-22-66), is open 24 hrs. **Farmacia Don Antonio,** Juárez 89 (tel. 3-21-70) is open Mon.-Sat. 9am-9pm, Sun. 9am-2pm and has a long distance *caseta.* **Hospital Municipal,** Morua and Barrera (tel. 3-33-10), is one block east of Juárez. **Police** wait at Fremont and Juárez (tel. 3-26-26).

Accommodations and Food Budget rooms in Puerto Peñasco are as rare as deserted beaches. Those with proper equipment or a car would do best to stake out a camping spot on the sand. The hotels seemed to have agreed on a US$20 minimum. **Motel El Faro,** Pino Suárez and Armada de Mexico (tel. 3-32-01), is the closest budget hotel to the beach (two blocks). It boasts freshly remodeled rooms covered in piglet pink. Tidy rooms and matching bedspreads charm those Mexican travelers unaccustomed to such coordination. (Singles US$20, doubles US$25. Add US$5 for weekend rates.) **Hotel Villa Granada,** Madero 47 at León de la Barra (tel. 3-27-75), near Las Irresistibles has clay tile roofs hanging over the leafy central courtyard and outdoor restaurant. Screen doors and colored-glass windows give an unusual charm to clean rooms with all the standard features. All-you-can-eat Mexican buffet Sat. US$5. (Singles US$30, each extra person US$5.)

As always, *taquerías* are best for budget grub. The beachside restaurants cater to the North American masses. For typical *gringo* grub, try **Las Irrestibles,** on Constitución (tel. 3-53-47), in front of Hotel Cisar, which is locally famous for its scrumptious donuts and sticky cinnamon buns. Three piece fried chicken US$4, tuna melt US$2.45, pancakes and eggs and bacon US$2. Donuts US$6 per dozen. (Open daily 7am-11pm.) From the minute you sit down at **Asadero Sonora,** on Constitución, in front of the train station, service begins with rows of fresh condiments and ice-cold drinks. Handmade tortillas make the difference here. *Quesadillas* dripping with cheese 2.50 pesos, grilled steak tacos 2.75 pesos. Open daily noon-4am. **Cenaduría Brocheta Crazy,** Juárez and Constitución, is a triangular dining room which barely fits 6 tables and waiters in the stifling heat, but benches outside afford a fresh breeze. Cheap *antojitos* rule. *Sincronizada* 4 pesos, *flautas* with fries 8 pesos.

■■■ HERMOSILLO

If you get an early start and the buses run on time, you can breeze from Tucson to the beaches of Guaymas or Mazatlán in a single day, skipping the lonelier parts of Sonora entirely. But the habitual tardiness of Mexican buses may force you to spend a night in Hermosillo, the Sonoran state capital. Hermosillo is a wealthy, modern city in the heart of a productive agricultural and mining region. Wheat, corn, cotton, pecans, oranges, and grapes all grow in the surrounding countryside, nourished by extensive irrigation and the desert sun.

For the tourist, the most interesting things about Hermosillo are associated with the University of Sonora. The **Museo Regional de Historia** at the university contains many *indígena* artifacts and exhibits on pre-Hispanic and colonial history. It's on Encinas at Rosales on the ground floor of the tall University building. (Open Mon.-Fri. 9am-1pm and 4-6pm., Sat. 9am-1pm.) The tourist office (see Practical Information) has all the information on current exhibits here and at other museums.

Practical Information 277km south of the border, Hermosillo lies on Route 15, the main north-south highway connecting the western U.S. and central Mexico. **Buses** depart from the main terminal on Blvd. Encinas, 2km east of the city center. North and southbound buses depart every hour and with even greater frequency during the afternoon. All service out of Hermosillo is *de paso*; during holidays and weekends you've got to lace up your boxing gloves to win a seat. To get from the bus station to the center of town, cross the street and catch a bus (.80 pesos) marked "Ranchito" or "Mariachi." Taxis will ask 20 pesos for a trip to *el centro*. Pay no more than half this and don't jump in until you agree on a price.

One of the city's most recognizable landmarks is the Hermosillo Flash, a tall structure that flashes the time, temperature, news and brief advertisements day and night. At the junction of Boulevards Luis Encinas (also known as Transversal) and Rosales, the Flash helps the mapless (and those planning to hitch out of town) to orient themselves. The **University of Sonora** is located at this intersection. South on Rosales are the **cathedral** and the **government buildings,** as well as the road to Guaymas. Most of the activity lies inside the square area bordered by Rosales, Juárez, Serdán, and Blvd. Encinas.

The **tourist office** is on Tehuantepec and Comonfort (tel. 17-29-64), 2 blocks west of Rosales on the bottom floor of the Palacio Administrativo. (Open Mon.-Fri.

8am-3pm and 6-9pm, Sat. 9am-1pm.) For **currency exchange,** banks line Encinas and Serdán. **Bancomer,** Serdán and Yáñez (tel. 17-36-81) and all others are open 8:30am-1pm. **Hermex Travel,** Rosales at Monterrey (tel. 17-17-18) serves as the **American Express** office. (Open Mon.-Fri. 8:30am-1pm and 3-6pm, Sat. 9am-1pm.) The **post office,** Serdán and Rosales (tel. 12-00-11) has a *Lista de Correos*. (Open Mon.-Fri. 8am-7pm, Sat. 9am-noon. **Postal code:** 83000.) **Farmacia Margarita,** Morelia and Guerrero (tel. 13-17-73), has *casetas* upstairs in the back for long distance phone calls. Collect calls 3.50 pesos. Open 24 hrs. (**Telephone code:** 62.) Hermosillo even has an **airport,** 10km from town on Transversal toward Kino, served by **Noroeste, Aeroméxico** and **Mexicana** with daily flights to the major cities including Mexico City (544 pesos), and Los Angeles (US$165). **Trains** leave from Estación Pitíc (tel. 17-17-11), north of the city on Rte. 15. Northbound *estrella* (fast) to Nogales and Mexicali leave at 8:50am, and the *burro* (slow) at 4:45pm. Southbound *estrella* to Los Mochis and Guadalajara at 7:50pm, and the *burro* at 12:20pm. Travelers should make reservations for the *estrella* in advance; otherwise, tickets on sale 1hr. before departure at the station or at the **Agencia de Fletes y Pasaje** at Blvd. Transversal and Manuel Gonzaléz. Times subject to change. Take the bus marked "Anapolas" to get to the train station. **Tres Estrellas de Oro** (tel. 13-24-16) dispatches frequent **buses** to: Tijuana, Mexicali, Nogales, Mexico City, and Mazatlán. Buses to Tijuana and Mexico City fill early, so buy tickets at least a day in advance. Buses run to Kino (10 pesos) from the **Transportes de la Costa** bus terminal on Sonora between García and González (tel. 12-05-74). **Lavandería Automatica de Hermosillo,** Yañez and Sonora (tel. 17-55-01), washes or dries clothes for 7 pesos. (Open Mon.-Sat. 8am-8pm, Sun. 8am-2pm.) Medical needs are attended to by the **Red Cross,** Encinas at 14 de Abril (tel. 14-07-69), **Farmacia Margarita,** Morelia at Guerrero (tel. 13-17-73, open 24 hrs.), and **Hospital General del Estado de Sonora,** Transversal at Reyes (tel. 13-25-56). The **police** wait on Periférico Nte. and Noroeste (tel. 18-55-64).

Accommodations and Food Hermosillo offers many budget shelters, but few establishments fall into that comfortable middle bracket. Air conditioning is costly but indispensable, especially in the blistering summer heat. For the truly indigent, five *casas de huéspedes* line Sonora, two blocks west of the park; two more are on Guerrero near Sonora. Prices here are rock-bottom, but the area, which also includes nicer hotels like the Montecarlo, is a red-light district, especially unsafe for lone female travelers. **Hotel Niza,** Elías Calles 66 (tel. 17-20-28), a grandiose hotel of yesteryear, screams art deco with a gigantic colorful globe hanging in the pink atrium. Rooms branching off this marvelous centerpiece have cable TV, A/C and comfortable beds. (Singles 70 pesos, doubles 85 pesos. Traveler's checks accepted.) **Hotel Monte Carlo,** Juárez at Sonora (tel. 12-13-54), features a lobby with ever-blasting TV, and rooms with tile floors and brown furniture. Unfortunate failure of icy A/C downstairs and quiet upstairs to coincide. (Singles 68 pesos. Doubles 74 pesos.) **Hotel Washington,** Dr. Noriega 68 Pte. (tel. 13-11-83), between Matamoros and Guerrero has friendly managment who welcome guests to good-sized rooms with no A/C. (Singles 50 pesos, each additional person 5 pesos.)

A cheap, quick feed can be had at the counters that line the entrances to the public market at Elías calles and Matamoros, and taco and *torta* places cluster around Serdán and Guerrero, serving *taquitos* and *quesadillas* for 3-4 pesos. **Restaurant Jung,** Niños Héroes 75 (tel. 13-28-81), at Encinas, is a vegetarian restaurant dedicated to "health and long life"; every aspect is all-natural, except for the fake silk plants. Connected to a natural products store with funky books. Soybean burgers 10.50 pesos, guacamole 8 pesos, and a big cup of yummy fro-yo 6 pesos. (Open Mon.-Sat. 8am-8pm.) **My Friend,** Elías Calles 105 (tel. 13-10-44), at Yáñez, an air-conditioned fast food joint, whips up the standards: burger with fries and Coke 12 pesos, *torta milanesa* 9 pesos, eggs and ham 10 pesos. (Open Mon.-Sat. 8am-6pm.)

■■■ GUAYMAS

The principal port in Sonora state, and proud home of an extensive shrimping fleet, Guaymas was originally inhabited by the Guaymas and Yaqui tribes. In 1701, Father Kino built the mission of San José 10km north of town. In 1769 the first Spanish settlement was founded. Today, suntanned *norteamericanos* drop by to take a break from the resort life of nearby San Carlos.

Lacking convenient beaches, Guaymas deserves no lengthy stay, but it's the nicest place to break up the trip south to the more alluring resorts at Mazatlán, San Blas, and Puerto Vallarta: its cool ocean breezes give it an advantage over Hermosillo.

The area's beaches are to the north in **Miramar** and **San Carlos.** Yachts hover off San Carlos, but the beaches accessible to the budget crowd are dull and pebbly. In San Carlos the beach gets better past the end of the bus route near Club Med and Howard Johnson's. In Miramar it's better, but small, back along the bus route in front of the big fancy houses.

Nightlife in Guaymas consists of a couple of fairly standard discos. **Casanova,** in the Hotel Armida at the junction of Serdán and the highway (tel. 2-30-50), charges 10 pesos cover and US$2 for a drink (open Wed.-Sun. 9pm-2am); at **Xanadu,** Malecón Malpíca (Av. 11) between 23 and 24 (tel. 2-83-33), the cover is the same and drinks start at 7 pesos,open daily 9pm-2am).

Practical Information Guaymas is six hours south of Nogales by bus and five hours north from Los Mochis. **Buses** and **trains** service inland Mexico, and the **ferry** steams to Santa Rosalía in Baja California. Municipal buses (.60 pesos) run up and down Guaymas's main strip, Avenida Serdán. Buses marked "Miramar" (1 peso) and "San Carlos" (1.50 pesos) reach those beaches north of the city from various points along Serdán. Some travelers at the junction of Serdán and the highway also try thumbing as they wait for bus. Almost everything in Guaymas takes place on Serdán, with the crossing streets running numerically up to the harbor. Women should not walk alone more than two blocks south of Serdán after dark.

Northbound vehicles, including buses, are often stopped by narcotics police. Avoid spending the rest of your vacation in a Mexican prison cell by having your identification ready. Let them search whatever they want: it's better not to assert the right to privacy when dealing with humorless armed *federales* .

The **Tourist Office,** at Serdán at Calle 12 (tel. 2-56-67) on the 2nd floor of the building, is staffed sporadically Mon.-Fri. 9am-2pm and 4-6pm. Banks are located along Serdán for **currency exchange. Bánamex,** Serdán and Calle 20 (tel. 2-00-72), exchanges traveler's checks and greenbacks. (Open Mon.-Fri. 8:30am-midnight.) The **post office,** at Av. 10 between Calle 19 and 20 (tel. 2-07-57), is open Mon.-Fri. 8am-7pm, Sat.-Sun. 8am-noon. **Postal code:** 85400. **Farmacia Santa Martha,** Serdán and Calle 19, has 3 booths for long distance collect calls (5 pesos). (Open Mon.-Sat. 8am-9pm, Sun. 9am-2pm. **Telephone code:** 622.) **Aeroméxico** serves Guaymas with daily **airplane flights** to La Paz (326 pesos), Mexico City (650 pesos), and Tucson (US$103). The Aeroméxico office is located at Serdán and Calle 15. To get to the airport, take the bus marked "San Jose." The **Bus Station,** served by **Tres Estrellas de Oro** and **Transportes Norte de Sonora,** Calle 14 at Rodríguez (tel. 2-12-71), 2 blocks south of Serdán. If you're planning on a northern trip, catch the earliest bus, because the later ones are jammed with chickens and people. Buy tickets 1hr. in advance. Buses leave every hr. to: Hermosillo (15 pesos), Tijuana (120 pesos), Mazatlán (94 pesos), Mexico City (190 pesos), Guadalajara (120 pesos)., and Nogales (8 per day, 49 pesos). Across the street is the **Pacífico** terminal (tel. 2-30-19), which runs to the same destinations at slightly lower prices (Nogales 40 pesos). The old **train** station and current office is located on Serdán at Calle 30 (tel. 2-49-80). Office open Mon.-Fri. 8am-noon and 2-5pm for information or reservations. Trains actually arrive and depart from **Empalme,** 10km south on the International Highway. Buy tickets at Empalme station 1hr. before the train arrives. From

Serdán take the municipal bus marked "Empalme" to the end of the route, then transfer to the other bus marked "Estación." Fast *estrella* train goes south at 9:40pm, north at 6am. To: Hermosillo (15 pesos), Nogales (40 pesos), Mazatlán (75 pesos) and Guadalajara (161 pesos). The slow *burro* train leaves north at 1pm and south at 2:30pm. First class to: Hermosillo (5 pesos), Nogales (13 pesos), Mazatlán (22pesos), and Guadalajara (40 pesos).

The **ferry** ferminal is on Serdán about 1km past. Electricidad (tel. 2-23-24). Boat steams to Santa Rosalía Tues. and Fri. at 8am; tickets are only sold 1 day in advance 8am-2:30pm (*salón* 38 pesos, *turista* 76 pesos). For more detail, see Baja California: Getting Around: By Sea. To get to the ferry terminal, hop an outbound bus and get off at the "Transbordador" sign.

The **Red Cross,** (tel. 4-08-76), is at the northern limit of Guaymas. **Farmacia Sonora,** Serdán at Calle 15 (tel. 4-24-04), is open 24 hrs. **Hospital Municipal:** tel. 2-01-22. **Police** are in Palacio Municipal on Serdán at Calle 22 (tel. 4-01-04).

Accommodations and Food **Casa de Huéspedes Lupita,** Calle 15 #125, (tel. 2-84-09), 2 blocks south of Serdán, is a mammoth "house" with 30 rooms and 12 communal baths, every corner glowingly clean. Iron gates on bedroom doors and 2 fans in every room allow for much-needed ventilation. (Noon check-out. Towel deposit 5 pesos. Singles 23 pesos, with bath 35 pesos. Doubles 33 pesos, with bath 45 pesos.) Look for the "HO EL" sign at **Hotel Rubi,** Serdán at Calle 29 (tel. 2-04-95). Friendly management shows guests to average fare with TV and A/C, and also helps with local questions. Convenient location for those who want work on a shrimp trawler. (Singles 50 pesos. Doubles 60 pesos.) **Hotel Impala,** Calle 21 #40 (tel. 4-09-22), 1 block south of Serdán, displays its antiquity in the black-and-white pictures of Guaymas's past hanging on the walls. Rooms are renovated to present-day glory with matching polyester bedspreads and curtains, A/C and TV. (Key deposit 5 pesos. Singles 70 pesos. Doubles 90 pesos. Triples 120 pesos. Credit cards accepted.)

Seafood is the Guaymas specialty. Local favorites include frog legs, turtle steaks and oysters in a garlic/chile sauce. The **Mercado Municipal,** on Calle 20, one block from Serdán, sells fresh produce as well as clothes, flowers, toys and carved goods. Hot dog vendors line Serdán. **Las 1000 Tortas,** Serdán 188 (tel. 4-30-61), between Calles 17 and 18, has no menu, but the name of this family-run eatery reveals the item of choice: *torta* (6 pesos). Three types of delicious *comidas corridas* (15 pesos) are prepared daily and served noon-4pm. Enchiladas and *gorditas* 12 pesos. (Open daily 8am-11pm.) Red painted picnic tables and funky mirrored walls accompany the weirdo spelling of **Jax Snax,** Serdán at Calle 14 (tel. 2-38-65). Cheap, delicious breakfasts and oven-fresh pizzas are choice. French toast with fresh fruit 8 pesos, yogurt and fruit 8 pesos, mini-pizza 15 pesos. (Open Tues.-Sun. 8am-11pm.)

CHIHUAHUA

■■■ CIUDAD JUÁREZ AND EL PASO, TEXAS

El Paso del Norte was the least difficult way for people, horses, and automobiles to cross the Occidental del Norte and the Sierra Madre into and out of Mexico, and so it nurtured the twin cities of Ciudad Juárez and El Paso. The strategic site, once part of an important *indígena* trading route, was one of the first occupied. Where they merge at the border, El Paso and Juárez are remarkably similar; in fact, if it weren't for the murky Río Grande, it would be impossible to tell the cities apart. Juárez has better wild and seedy border town activity, and while it seems relatively safe during the day, as darkness increases, so does the ratio of the drunk to the sober people wandering the streets. Women should not walk alone or in dark places; everyone should avoid the area more than two blocks west of Juárez's mains street, Juárez.

ORIENTATION

Where to cross the border into Juárez depends on your goal. From downtown El Paso, the **Stanton Bridge** (on Stanton St.) and **Santa Fe Bridge** (on El Paso St.) lead into the heart of **Old Juárez,** also called *el centro*, where markets, restaurants, and bars thrive. Santa Fe Bridge actually becomes **Av. Juárez,** the main drag, while Stanton Bridge turns into **Av. Lerdo.** Two miles east, U.S. 54 crosses the border at the Puente Córdova and becomes **Av. Lincoln:** this road leads to the ProNaf shopping mall and studio complex with resident craftspeople and predictably high prices. The Stanton St. Bridge is restricted to traffic and pedestrians entering Juárez, the Santa Fe to departing vehicles. The **Córdova Bridge** allows two-way traffic. Pedestrians can come and go on the Córdova and Santa Fe bridges.

To cross the border on foot, simply pay the border guard US$.25 per person the way in, US$1.50 on the way out. Cars to Mexico pay US$1, to El Paso US$1.95. To venture farther into Mexico, you must obtain a **tourist card** at the immigration office. You won't need it until you reach the immigration checkpoint 22km into the interior, but if you don't have it then, they'll send you back (see Mexico General Introduction: Documents and Formalities above for more information). The immigration office (Departamento de Población) is located immediately to the right as you cross the Stanton St. Bridge. (Immigration open 24 hrs.) From El Paso airport avoid expensive cabs (US$20) and catch the bus (US$.75) to San Jacinto Park. Walk two blocks up Main St.until you run into the **Tourist Information Center.**

Most of Old Juárez can be covered on foot. Street numbers start in the 600s near the two border bridges and descend to zero at 16 de Septiembre, where Av. Juárez ends. Both Lerdo and Francisco Villa run parallel to Juárez. The ProNaf center can be reached by hopping on the public bus "Ruta 8-A" (.70 pesos) on Malecón between the Departamento de Población and Secretaría de Turismo across the street from bus shelter. Taxis are always available in any part of downtown, but they usually overcharge. Negotiate the price before getting in.

■ El Paso, Texas

Practical Information The **tourist office,** 1 Civic Center Plaza (tel. 544-0062), opposite Greyhound Bus Station at the Santa Fe St. and San Francisco St. intersection, is friendly and well-stocked with brochures, and also sells **El Paso-Juárez Trolley Co.** tickets for day-long tours across the border (Mon.-Fri. US$8, Sat.-Sun. US$10). Open daily 8:30am-5pm; trolleys run daily on the hour, 10am-5pm. **Exchange currency** at **Valuta** (tel. 544-1152), corner of Mesa and Paisano, which has all exchange services, plus a fax. (Open 24 hrs.) The **Greyhound bus station,** 111 San Francisco St. (tel. 532-2365), is sandwiched between Santa Fe St. and El Paso St., in the heart of downtown. Daily service to and from Dallas, Phoenix, New York, Los Angeles, and numerous other U.S. cities. (Storage lockers for US$1. Open 24 hrs.)

Accommodations and Food Staying in El Paso is a better option than facing the dearth of appealing hotels in Juárez. The **Gardner Hotel/Hostel (AYH/HI),** 311 E. Franklin (tel. 532-3661), is 2 blocks up Mesa St. from San Jacinto Park. A friendly group staffs this 75-year-old establishment, which features quiet, clean rooms in the heart of downtown. Weary travelers obtain money-saving advice and maps for both El Paso and Juárez. Reception open 24 hrs. Lockers US$.75 per day, long term, US$.50 per day. Washing machines (US$1.50) and dryers (US$.50). (**Hotel:** TV. Check-out 1pm. Singles US$23, with bath US$35. Doubles US$30, with bath US$40. Add about US$5 to all these prices for tax. **Hostel:** Members only. Spotless kitchen and common room with pool table. Check-out 10am. Bed in 4-person dorm room with sink US$12.) The **Gateway Hotel,** 104 S. Stanton St. (tel. 532-2611), at the corner of S. Stanton St. and San Antonio, features a diner downstairs, clean rooms with bathrooms, and A/C upstairs. A favorite stop for middle-class Mexicans; speak Spanish to get respect and a room. Check-out 4pm. Parking $2 per 24 hrs. (Singles US$21 and up. Doubles US$27 and up.)

El Paso is an American city, and few restaurants other than McDonalds and business-lunch hot dog mills are in the downtown business district. Look for the flashing lights of the **Tap and Bar Restaurant** (tel. 548-9049), at Stanton St. and San Antonio, where the US$3 huevos rancheros or Mexican plate are popular with the locals. Mini-dance floor and disco ball for nighttime use. (Open daily 9am-2am.) **Big Bun** (tel. 533-3926) at 500 N. Stanton serves tacos and burritos as well as big burgers (US$1.10) with salsa on the side. (Open Mon.-Sat. 8am-8pm, Sun. 10am-3pm.)

■ Ciudad Juárez

PRACTICAL INFORMATION

Tourist Office: Secretaría de Turismo, Malecón and Francisco Villa (tel. 14-08-37), in the basement of gray Unidad Administrativa Municipal bldg. on the left of the Santa Fe Bridge. Plenty of brochures, easier if you know Spanish. (Open Mon.-Fri. 8am-8pm, Sat.-Sun. 7am-3pm.)

U.S. Consulate: López Mateos Nte. 924 (tel. 13-40-48). For emergencies dial (915) 525-6060.

Currency Exchange: In Juárez, banks congregate near the bus station and along 16 de Septiembre. Most open Mon.-Fri. 9am-1:30pm. Virtually no *casa de cambio* or bank will accept traveler's checks (a problem throughout northern Mexico, where real greenbacks are the weapon of choice). If you find a place that will take your checks, unload them *pronto.* It is easier and cheaper to exchange in El Paso banks along Stanton, Main, and Mills.

Post Office: Lerdo at Ignacio Peña (tel. 12-02-44). Open Mon.-Fri. 8am-7pm, Sat.-Sun. 9am-1pm. **Postal Code:** 32000.

Telephone: Secrefax, Av. Juárez (tel. 15-15-10), 1 block from Santa Fe Bridge. For an El Paso operator, dial 08; US$1 per minute. Local call 2 pesos for 3 minutes. International calls, fax, and UPS. Open 24 hrs. **Telephone Code:** 16.

Abraham González Airport: (tel. 19-07-57) about 17km out Rte. 45 (Carretera Panorámica). Primary carrier is **Aeroméxico** with flights to Mexico City, Monterrey, and Chihuahua. Catch the crowded school bus marked "Aeropuerto" (.70 pesos).

Train Station: Francisco Villa at Insurgentes (tel. 14-97-17), 12 blocks down Francisco Villa from the Santa Fe Bridge with service to Chihuahua and Mexico City.

Bus Station: Blvd. Oscar Flores 4010 (tel. 13-20-83), just north of the ProNaf center and next to the Río Grande mall; way too far for walking. Take Chihuahuenses from the El Paso terminal to Juárez (US$5) or cram into the school bus "Ruta 1A" at Av. Insurgentes and Francisco Villa. Open 24 hrs. **Chihuahuenses** (tel. 13-06-57) and **Omnibus** offer numerous departures to Mexico City, Monterrey, Guadalajara, and Nuevo Casas Grandes.

Laundromat: Lavasolas, Tlaxcala and 5 de Mayo (tel. 12-54-61).

Red Cross: Henry Durnant in ProNaf center (tel. 16-58-06).

Pharmacy: Farmacia Vibar, 16 de Septiembre (te. 15-61-32), across from the church. Turn right from Juárez. (Open 8am-midnight.)

Hospitals: Hospital Latinoamericano: 250 N. Lopez Mateos (tel. 16-14-67). Supposedly caters to *gringos.* Open 24 hrs.

Emergency: tel. 06.

Police: Oro and 16 de Septiembre (tel. 15-51-51).

FOOD AND ACCOMMODATIONS

In Juárez, hotels that meet only minimal standards are nonetheless some of the most expensive budget accommodations in all of Mexico. The **Hotel Santa Fe,** Lerdo Nte. 673 at Tlaxcala (tel. 14-02-70, fax 12-56-27) houses a helpful, English-speaking staff who are justifiablly proud of their modern conveniences and safety features. Freshly renovated and clean rooms have A/C and TVs with satellite hook-up. (Singles US$29. Doubles US$33. MC, Visa.) Less than a mile from the Santa Fe bridge, the **Hotel San Carlos,** Av. Juárez Nte. 126, (tel. 15-04-19) offers a convenient location for those who want to drink the night away on Av. Juárez. Expect to speak Spanish to obtain a sagging, worn mattress, and baño. (Singles 67 pesos. Doubles 80 pesos. MC, Visa.)

Eateries vary from clean, air-conditioned restaurants catering to tourists to road-side shacks with picnic tables and TV in Spanish. Take your pick; prices vary according to the atmosphere. **Restaurant La Sevillana,** (tel. 12-63-12), ½ block from corner of Juárez and Abraham González, is a relaxed diner with bilingual menus and A/C. Generous servings of filet mignon (28 pesos) and shrimp sautéed in garlic sauce (17 pesos). Serves breakfast, too (9-10 pesos). (Open daily 8am-8pm.) Waiters with bright white shirts and bow ties service **Hotel Santa Fe Restaurant,** Lerdo Nte. 673 (tel. 14-02-70), at Tlaxcala across from the Hotel Impala. This quiet, back street place offers *enchiladas de pollo* (10 pesos) and club sandwiches (10 pesos) served with tortilla chips and salsa. (Open 24 hrs.) **Nuevo Restaurante Martino,** Juárez 643 (tel. 12-33-70), two blocks from the Santa Fe Bridge, is Juárez's attempt at elegance. It boasts more than 100 dishes of all kinds of cuisines and higher than average prices. On weekends, Mexican businessmen give way to tourist families. (Open daily noon to midnight.) Paleteria Michoacanas are everywhere, but the newest, with the widest selection of American thirst quenchers as well as Mexican fruit drinks, is at the corner of M.A. Martinez and Juárez, about halfway from the bridge to the end of the street. Ice cream 2 pesos or US $0.75. (Open daily 10am-5pm.)

SIGHTS

The deforested **Parque Chamizal,** near the Córdova Bridge, is a good place to escape the noise of the city, if not the heat. The **Museo Arqueológico,** Av. Pellicer 1 in mid-park, displays little of interest: one room features plastic facsimiles of pre-Conquest sculptures, and the other wows the crowds with trilobite fossils, rocks, and bones. (Open Mon.-Sat. 9am-2pm, Sun. 1-8pm. Free.) In *el centro* visit the **Aduana Frontensa** where Juárez and 16 de Septiembre cross. Built in 1889 as a trading outpost, it hosts an exhibit of the region's history during the Mexican Revolution. (Open Tues.-Sun. 10am-6pm. Free.) The ProNaf center, distant from the park at Lincoln and 16 de Septiembre, contains the **Museo de Arte** (tel. 13-17-08) with exhibits of Mexican art, past and present. (Open Tues.-Sun. 11am-7pm. Admission 1 peso, students free.) Also at the ProNaf center, the **Centro Artesanal** sells handmade goods at maximum prices; haggle here. The "Ruta 8" bus will take you from *el centro* to ProNaf for .70 pesos; a taxi charges 25 times as much.

ENTERTAINMENT

The *toro* and the *matador* battle in traditional bullfights on occasional evenings during the summer at the **Plaza Monumental de Toros**, República and Huerta (tel. 13-16-56). Seats in the shade cost US$11. Call for dates and times. The **Lienzo de Charro,** on Av. Charro off República, also conducts bullfights and *charreada* (rodeo) on Sunday afternoons during the summer; get the specifics at the tourist office. At the western edge of town, the **Juárez Racetrack** (tel. 17-03-11) rises from Vicente Guerrero. Dogs run Wed.-Sun. at 7:30pm. Sunday matinees during the summer at 2:30pm. Horse racing can be seen only on closed-circuit TV.

Juárez has so many bars that simply counting them can make you dizzy even before you carouse. Many establishments are unsavory, and even some of the savory ones can become dangerous; stick to the glutted strip along Av. Juárez. On weekends, North Americans swarm to Juárez to join their Mexican friends in a 48-hour quest for fun, fights, fiestas, and inexpensive dental work. **Kentucky Club,** Juárez 629 (tel. 14-99-90), was voted Best Bar 1991 by an El Paso paper. Sidle up to the long mahogany bar, backed by intricate woodwork and embossed mirrors so the middle-aged clientele can see and be seen. Must be 21 to be served. (Open 11am-midnight.) **Mr. Fog Bar,** Juárez Nte. 140 (tel. 14-29-48), is also popular. This dimly lit saloon with soft love songs becomes a *romántico* escape from the crazy city. Beer US$1.75. Margaritas US$2.50. (Open Sun.-Thurs. 11am-midnight, Fri.-Sat. 11am-2am.)

■■■ CASAS GRANDES AND NUEVO CASAS GRANDES

Even though the 3½-hour journey south from Juárez through the scenic Chihuahuan Desert is extraordinarily peaceful, arriving at the foothills of the Sierra Madres in the valley of Nuevo Casas Grandes is a cool relief. The valley's claim to fame is the ruins of **Paquimé** (pah-kee-MEH) in Casas Grandes, the most important city in pre-Conquest northern Mexico. Nuevo Casas Grandes may remind you of cities in the North American West. Cowboy hats and enormous brass belt buckles adorn many inhabitants. The absence of tourists lends this slow-paced town an authenticity rare in the North.

ORIENTATION

Nuevo Casas Grandes lies to the southwest of Cd. Juárez and northwest of Chihuahua. The only way to get there is by road. **Omnibus de México** provides the most reliable service with buses to both Cd. Juárez (30 pesos) and Chihuahua (6 per day, 5am-5pm, 36 pesos). The **bus station** is located on Obregón, a half block from 16 de Septiembre.

All of the town's streets are laid out in a nice grid, with the center of town situated between Constitución and Juárez (Obregón runs parallel to these streets) and Minerva and 16 de Septiembre. Go right from the bus terminal two blocks until 5 de Mayo then turn left, go one block, cross the tracks and you are on the main drag **Constitución.**

PRACTICAL INFORMATION

Everything important is within the 10-block downtown area. Exchange currency at the **Casa de Cambio California,** Constitución 207 (open Mon.-Sat. 9am-7pm), or **Banamex,** on 5 de Mayo between Juárez and Constitución (open Mon.-Fri. 9am-2pm and 4-6pm). **Bancomer** at 16 de Septiembre on Constitución has an **ATM** which takes Visa, with 24 hr. access. The **post office,** at 16 de Septiembre and Madero, one block from Obregón, has Lista de Correos (Open Mon.-Fri. 9am-1pm and 3-6pm, Sat. 9am-1pm). The **postal code** is 31700. The **Supermarket: Hiperama,** is located at Juárez and Minerva and is open daily 9am-9pm. **Laundromat, Lavasolas Paquimé** (tel. 4-13-20), stands right behind the Hotel Paquimé on Jesus Urueto. (Open Mon.-Sat. 7:30am-7pm.) **Farmacia Benavides,** at Obregón and 5 de Mayo (tel. 4-55-55) is open daily 8am-10pm. The **police** are on the outskirts of town on Madero. In an **emergency,** dial 4-09-73.

ACCOMMODATIONS

Stock up on water before you hit town because none of these hotels offer *agua purificada*, only *agua potable*. Also, the price of quality hotels has drastically risen here. Check-out time for all listed below is 2pm.

Hotel California, Constitución 209 (tel. 4-08-34), between 5 de Mayo and Minerva. Located on the noisy, central street. The large rooms with tiled floors and wicker furniture are complemented with spotless bathrooms. Rooms in back may be quieter. Old black and white TVs with cable. Mirrors on the ceiling, pink champagne on ice. Check-out: anytime. Singles 80 pesos. Doubles 75 pesos. MC, Visa.

Hotel Juárez, Obregón 110 (tel. 4-02-33), a block from the bus stations. Much English spoken here by the affable owner, Mario, who offers a small dark room with bed and shower to the less affluent traveler. Singles 25 pesos, 39 pesos with two people. Doubles 49 pesos.

Motel Piñón, Juárez Nte. 605 (tel. 4-06-55), 2 blocks down from Minerva. This refurbished motel wrapped around a courtyard boasts a museum with pieces from Paquimé, and free guides to the ruins for groups of five or more. Clean rooms with new carpet and colorful bathrooms also offer cable TV diversion. Singles 85 pesos. Doubles 95 pesos. MC, Visa.

FOOD

The lack of tourists makes dining out with the locals (and the local flies) cheap. The low gringo count, however, means that nightlife is soporific, and the few bars in town do not welcome women.

Restaurante Constantino, Juárez at Minerva (tel. 4-10-05). Convenient to every big hotel. Bilingual menu, but speak Spanish to avoid pointing. *Quesadilla* 12 pesos, big lunch special 17.60 pesos. Bright, clean, large windows give a view of the plaza. Open daily 7am-midnight.

Dinno's Pizza, Minerva and Constitución (tel. 4-02-40). This clean and icily air-conditioned joint features rare English-speaking staff and all-you-can-eat Sunday buffet (20 pesos) including fresh fruit, orange juice and eggs. There's always pizza (small 22 pesos, medium 27 pesos). Open daily 11am-midnight. MC, Visa.

Café de La Esquina, 5 de Mayo at Obregón (tel 4-39-59). Sit down in this simple, worn spot and enjoy a Coke in a frosted mug while the cook prepares fresh tacos (9 pesos) or enchiladas (14 pesos). A/C and breakfast too. Open daily 7am-9pm.

Restaurant Playa Ayul, 16 de Septiembre at Obregon (tel. 4-24-72). Specializing in seafood. A nice, air-conditioned eatery, where you can enjoy a cheap breakfast (5-15 pesos) if you don't mind the smell of fish. Open daily 7am-10pm.

■ Casas Grandes (Paquimé)

Eight km southwest of Nuevo Casas Grandes, the pre-Conquest city of Paquimé lay hidden underground for 600 years. Its architecture suggests that **Casas Grandes** (so named upon excavation) grew out of two different cultures: its many-storied *pueblos* resemble those in the southwestern U.S., but its step pyramids are similar to those in central and southern Mexico. Among the ruins lie a partially-excavated **central market** area as well as a **ball court.** Between 1000 and 1200 AD, Paquimé was the most important agricultural and trading center in northern Mexico. The inhabitants kept parrots and turkeys in adobe pens and built indoor aqueducts and hidden cisterns to supply the *pueblos* in times of siege. Around 1340, Aztec invaders burned the already-abandoned buildings. First exhumed in the early 1970s, Paquimé is now an archaeological zone administered by the Mexican government. Unfortunately, once it had been exposed to the satisfaction of both archaeologists and tourists, its high mud walls began to crumble. Visitors should avoid eroding the thin walls. A plaque commemorates archaeologist Eduardo Contreras, "El Señor de Paquimé," who died in 1986. Restoration efforts continue today.

Paquimé is hidden in the tranquil mountains of Casas Grandes. On summer afternoons, the dry and shadeless ruins can become a blazing inferno with temperatures near 100°F. Be sure to bring sun protection, a broad-brimmed hat (cheap sombreros are available in town) and, most importantly, a gigantic bottle of water to quench your thirst. When traveling from Chihuahua or Juárez, pick up information on the dig ahead of time, because none exists at the site.

To reach Paquimé, take the **yellow municipal bus** at the corner of Constitución and 16 de Septiembre to the central park in Casas Grandes (hourly, 1 peso). Get off the bus at the main plaza, walk toward the back of the bus and continue down that dirt road for about 10 minutes. You will pass through two large dips, turn to the right and then to the left. (Admission to the site Mon.-Sat. 8 pesos, Sun. free. Open daily 10am-5pm.) Some information may be obtained at the tourist center and pottery store at the opposite end of the square, or at the Motel Piñon back in Nuevo Casas Grandes.

■■■ CHIHUAHUA

The capital of Mexico's largest state of the same name was founded in 1709 and quickly grew into a major trading and administrative center, supporting mining operations in the resource-rich western range and cattle enterprises in the surrounding valleys. Today, the lumber industry of the Sierra Madre yields most of the city's income.

Exposed to the sandstorms of Mexico's vast northern desert, Chihuahua may seem little more than an inconveniently located outpost of the civilization to the south. This seclusion convinced Pancho Villa to establish his revolutionary *División del Norte* headquarters here. During the conflict, his eclectic band of cowboys, bandits and vagabonds staged flamboyant attacks against the Porfiriato, streaming down from Chihuahua and assaulting social inequities. The man is a legendary figure to most *Chihuahuenses*, and Quinta Luz, Villa's sprawling colonial home, shines as the city's major attraction.

The peoples who converge on Chihuahua and the surrounding area are as diverse as the land itself. Mennonites came here in flocks from the Pennsylvania Dutch country in the 1920s, attracted by the bountiful pastures. Today they maintain their seclusion and purity in the nearby town of Cuauhtémoc and in other agricultural communities around Chihuahua. Known country wide for their delicious fresh cheese, the Mennonites prosper from beef and dairy cattle ranching. Equally secluded but radically different, the *indígena* Tarahumara people live isolated in the nearby Sierra Madres. They arrive at the city market in the early morning to sell handmade crafts, the men dressed in cowboy attire or baggy shorts and shirts, the women in sandals, shawls and bright skirts.

Chihuahua can become almost charming on a still and sunny day, but beware—the winds that whip across the surrounding desert do not stop for mere budget-traveling mortals. When the gales slice through town—summoning dirt, garbage and rain—the city becomes a river of sorrow.

ORIENTATION

¡Ay! Chihuahua sprawls in every direction, reaching onto the surrounding mountains. Skewered by Route 45 (the Pan American Hwy.), it serves as an important transportation hub for northern Mexico. Trains arrive from the north and south at the **Estación Central de los FFNN,** just north of downtown. Trains to Los Mochis and Creel via the Barrancas del Cobre leave from a different station, south of the city center off Ocampo, three blocks from 20 de Noviembre. To shorten the 20-minute walk to *el centro*, hop on a public bus running up and down Ocampo to Libertad. Pay about 8 pesos for a cab, and set the price before you step in.

Buses arrive at the **Camionera Central** on Blvd. Juan Pablo, far from *el centro*. Go out the other side of the station and across the parking lot to catch a bus to the Cathedral (.90 pesos). Get off when the Cathedral comes into view and walk to the left from Av. Juárez to reach Libertad, which is a pedestrians-only shopping arcade between Independencia and Guerrero. Two other main streets, Victoriá and Juárez, run parallel to Libertad, and Av. Ocampo crosses Juarez one block past the Cathedral. For a good map, get off the bus at Av. Carranza and walk two blocks to the left of the tourist office in the Palacio de Gobierno.

Energetic travelers can easily reach Quinta Luz on foot. Budget hotels and restaurants cluster on the streets behind the cathedral (the boot district). **Avenida Independencia,** which runs in front of the *zócalo*, marks the dividing line for the streets or *calles*. Even-numbered *calles* lie on the south side of Independencia, and those with odd numbers rest on the north side. *Avenidas* running north-south are named.

CHIHUAHUA

PRACTICAL INFORMATION

Tourist Office: By 1994 the tourist office will probably have moved from Libertad and Calle 13 to the Palacio de Gobierno (tel. 16-17-42). Friendly information in English and indispensable maps. Open Mon.-Fri. 9am-3pm. **Información y Documentación Turística:** Tecnológica and Padre Infante. Convenient only for motorists arriving in Chihuahua from the highway.

Currency Exchange: Banpaís on Victoira is the first block away from the front of the Cathedral (tel. 16-16-59). Go to the dolares desk. Traveler's checks changed free. Open Mon.-Fri. 9am-1:30pm. For 24-hr. dollar exchange, go across the street to **Hotel San Francisco** (tel. 16-75-50). **ATM: Cajeros Automaticos,** are located near the lobbies of all the tall banks downtown. **Banamex** at Doblado and Carranza accepts the most card types.

American Express: Vincente Guerrero 1207 (tel. 15-58-58), past Allende, right wher Guerrero curves to become Paeo Bolívar. Open Mon.-Fri. 9am-6pm, Sat. 9am-noon.

Post Office: On Libertad, between Vincente Guerrero and Carranza, 1 block from the arcade. Lista de Correos. Open Mon.-Fri. 8am-7pm, Sat. 9am-1pm. **Postal Code:** 31000.

Telephones: In better hotels and scattered among the various parks and plazas. Long distance service available in the plaza in front of the *catedral*. **Telephone Code:** 14.

Telegrams: At the post office with the same hours.

Airport: Blvd. Juan Pablo II (tel. 20-06-16), 14km from town. Served by **Aeroméxico** (tel. 15-63-03) and **Aero Leo López.** To Monterrey, Ciudad Juárez, Mexico City, and El Paso. Ground transportation to town available from a booth to your right as you exit the baggage area.

Trains: FFCC Chihuahua al Pacífico, the southern station near Quinta Luz. Walk south on Ocampo and turn right at 20 de Noviembre. Walk to Calle 24 and take a left; you will hit the station after 2 blocks. *Primera* and *segunda* trains through Barrancas del Cobre to Creel (2 per day, about 42 pesos) and Los Mochis (2 per day, about 90 pesos). You must have a ticket to board *primera* trains, and there's a 25% charge to buy a *segunda* ticket on board. Children 5-11 years old are ½ price. *Primera* ticket includes breakfast. Tickets sold Sun.-Fri. 6am-7:30pm, Sat. 6-9am and 3-6pm. (For an explanation of *primera* and *segunda*, see Barrancas del Cobre.) **FFCC Nacionales de México,** the northern station on Av. Tecnologico, has service to and from the north and south.

Bus Station: Huge new structure with restaurants and money changing facilties. Daily service to Acapulco, Mazatlán, Guadalajara, Mexico City, and Creel.

Supermarket: El Fénix, Libertad 505 (tel. 10-26-21), in the shopping arcade. Open daily 9am-9pm.

Laundromat: Lavafácil, Universidad 3500 (tel. 13-82-85).

Red Cross: Calle 24 and Revolución (tel. 11-22-11).

24-hr. Pharmacy: Farmacia Nocturno, Calle Aldama 1510 at Calle 19 (tel. 16-44-14).

Hospital: Hospital Central, Calle 33 and Rosales (tel. 15-90-00), at the end of Colón.

Emergency: Dial 06.

Police: Calle 4 and Ochoa (tel. 10-02-38).

ACCOMMODATIONS

Hotels in Chihuahua are like the city itself—charm is visible through the grit. Half a dozen economical hotels lie between Victoria and Juárez in the area behind the *catedral*.

Nuevo Hotel Reforma, Victoria 809 (tel. 16-24-55). Hotel created from a 2-story Spanish colonial mansion with a central courtyard. Rooms with thin walls can at least boast clean bathrooms and ceiling fans. Check-out 2pm. *Agua purificada.* Singles 30 pesos. Doubles 40 pesos.

Hotel Apolo, Juárez 907 (tel. 16-11-00), across from the post office in the noisy center of town, 1 block from the shopping arcade. Clean rooms, comfortable beds and A/C make for a pleasant stay. Check-out 2pm. Singles 80 pesos. Doubles 85 pesos. Credit cards accepted.

Hotel Santa Regina, Calle 3 and Manuel Doblado (tel. 15-38-89, fax 10-1411) Pristine lobby, but small brown rooms with cable TV and central A/C. Check-out 2pm. Singles 87.50 pesos. Doubles 100 pesos. AmEx, MC, Visa. Copies .50 pesos.

Casa de Huespedes Bolívar, Bolívar 309 (tel. 10-09-45), 7 small blocks from Aldama on Calle 5, then look right. Old painted brick house around a sunny little coutyard. Basic bed and bath. Singles 20 pesos. Doubles 40 pesos.

FOOD

Eateries in Chihuahua are not geared toward tourists. Some of the best meals can be found in small *cantinas* with bands (and many drunk, rowdy men).

Mi Café, Victoria at Calle 10 (tel. 10-12-38), across from Hotel San Juan. Put on your sunglasses for this bright, 1950s-style diner with melon-colored vinyl booths, and orange and white checkered ceiling. A 15-peso order of chicken comes as a huge meal, with bread, soup, rice, and poatoes, and dessert. Open daily 7:30am-11pm. Yes to credit cards.

La Parrilla, Victoria 420 (tel. 15-58-56), just south of the *catedral*. Chefs sizzle up fresh meat dishes right before your eyes. Choose the appropriate red wine to accompany your steak and it could be the perfect romantic evening. Juicy T-bone steak 28 pesos. *Quesito con Chorizo*, 13.50 pesos. Open daily noon-midnight. Credit cards accepted.

Dino's Pizza, Manuel Doblado 301 (tel. 16-57-07), across from the Santa Regina. Bakes hot, cheesy pizzas in a comfortable, cool atmosphere. It's a welcome escape from tacos and burritos. Medium pizza with ham 20 pesos, spaghetti 15 pesos. Open daily 8am-midnight. Credit cards: *sí*.

SIGHTS AND ENTERTAINMENT

Heading southwest of the *zócalo* offers an excellent retreat from the grime of downtown. At **Quinta Luz** (the Pancho Villa museum, tel. 16-29-58), visitors can immerse themselves in the turbulence of the revolution through the collection of documents and photographs, paintings of Sr. Villa, his household furnishings, his vast collection of rifles and machine guns (still enough to outfit a small army) and the bullet-ridden Dodge in which he was assassinated. To reach Quinta Luz, head 1.5km south on Ocampo. On the left you will pass a statue of Simón Bolívar, the lively Parque Lerdo, and a monument dedicated to patriot Manuel Ojinaga. A few more blocks down Ocampo bring you to an intersection with a large stone church. This is 20 de Noviembre; turn left and go two blocks to Calle 10, then turn right. Villa's house is two blocks down on the right. (Open daily 9am-1pm and 3-7pm. Admission 1.50 pesos.)

Back in *el centro*, the basement of the *catedral* hides the **Sacred Art Museum,** Libertad and Calle 2 (tel. 10-37-77). Pastoral religious paintings from the 18th century mingle with photos and portraits from the Pope's most recent visit to Chihuahua. (Open Mon.-Fri. 10am-2pm and 4-6pm. Admission 2 pesos adults, 1 peso for children.) For those craving more artistic pleasure, the **Centro Cultural Universitario,** Bolívar and Calle 4 (tel. 16-66-84), hosts a larger exposition of *arte nuevo* from the turn of the century, including the work of many French painters.

Occasional bullfights in the **Plaza de Toros,** Cuauhtémoc and Canal. The **Lienzo Charro,** on Av. Américas west of town, hosts weekend rodeos. Inquire at the tourist office for dates, times and prices. Downtown, Av. Libertad is closed to traffic east of the cathedral and becomes a large, open-air shopping mall on weekends.

Various *cantinas* house themselves in hotel lobbies, offering cheap beer, drunk locals and lively *mariachi*s in traditional costumes (women usually not welcome). Relax tired feet at **Bar Los Primos** in the Hotel San Francisco. At the corner of Calle 4 and Paseo Bolívar is the architectural gem **Museo Regional de Chihuahua,** Bolívar 401 (tel. 16-64-84), which houses a collection of elaborate furniture from the early 20th century. There are also exhibits on the Mennonites and the ruins of Paquimé. (Open Tues.-Sun. 10am-2pm and 4-7pm. Admission 3 pesos.)

On Juárez between Guerrero and Carranza, a golden eagle bearing the inscription "Libertad" points to the door of the **prison cell** where Padre Miguel Hidalgo, leader of an early bid for Mexican independence, was held for two months prior to his execution in 1811. Most interesting to Mexican history buffs, the small room displays some of Hidalgo's belongings and letters from early participants in the uprising. (Open Tues.-Fri. 10am-2pm and 4-7pm. Sat.-Sun. 10am-2pm. Admission 1.50 pesos.) Another eagle points to the **Templo de San Francisco** on Libertad and Calle 17, which contains Hidalgo's decaptitated body.

■■■ CREEL

High amid the peaks of the Sierra Madres, the small village of Creel welcomes travelers with a natural beauty and warmth unmatched in northern Mexico. The inhospitable Chihuahuan desert gives way here to spectacular gorges and looming peaks, the land of the Tarahumara people. Easy-going Creel, with its cool mountain climate, is a refreshing oasis from the rest of Chihuahua.

Be forewarned, this mountain retreat is developing rapidly. In the past few years, tourists have journeyed to Creel in increasing numbers, and most hotels have retaliated by expanding and renovating existing structures. The Chihuahuan state government has recently remodeled the *zócalo* and all main streets, planting numerous pine trees throughout town and expanding pavement.

Many Tarahumara come to Creel to sell crafts to curio shops and to pick up supplies. Of Mexico's many *indígena* groups, the Tarahumara have best warded off modern Mexican culture, by still living in isolated caves and wooden houses and resisting all efforts to settle them in villages. The Tarahumara are famous for their non-stop long-distance footraces, which last up to 72 hours. Tarahumara pine-needle baskets, blankets, figurines, ribbons and violins are sold throughout town.

The Tarahumara greatly value their seclusion and tend to shy away from contact with tourists. If you pass Tarahumara cave dwellings, look at the caves from the road, but don't take their obvious accessibility as an invitation to approach more closely or to walk in and have a look-see. Refrain from photographing the Tarahumara at will. If you ask to photograph them, they may agree only out of graciousness and not because they really don't mind. Fortunately, Artesanías Misión (see Practical Information below) sells excellent color prints of the Tarahumara. These photos were taken by the local Jesuit priest, who knows the Tarahumara well enough to do so without offending.

ORIENTATION AND PRACTICAL INFORMATION

The **train station** is located just southwest of the *zócalo*. To reach the *zócalo*, walk 1 block along the tracks in the direction of Los Mochis and turn left. Main street **Mateos** runs parallel to the trains on the opposite side of the *zócalo*.

Tarahumara Information: Artesanías Misión (tel. 6-01-50), on the north side of the *zócalo*. Although not an official tourist office, it is the best source of information on Creel and the surrounding area. Sells books about the Tarahumara, crafts and a map of the region. The mission supports the Tarahumara's cultural development, and the local hospital receives store profits. English-speaking staff. Open Mon.-Sat. 9:30am-1pm and 3-6pm, Sun. 9:30am-1pm. Credit cards and traveler's checks accepted.

Currency Exchange: Banca Serfín (tel. 6-02-50), next door to the Misión. Dollars exchanged 10:30-11:45am. 5% commision for changing traveler's checks. Open Mon.-Fri. 9am-1:30pm.

Post Office: (tel. 6-02-58), on the 1st floor of the Presidencia Municipal bldg. on south side of the *zócalo*. Lista de Correos. Open Mon.-Fri. 9am-1pm and 3-6pm. **Postal Code:** 33200.

Telephones: Long-distance service available at *caseta de larga distancia* in the **Papelería de Todo** on Mateos. Collect calls 2 pesos. Fax. Open daily 9am-8pm. **Telephone Code:** 145.

Train Station: On Av. Tarahumara. Trains leave daily for Chihuahua at 3:15pm (*primera* 43 pesos) and 5:10pm (*segunda* 9 pesos), and for Los Mochis at 12:25pm (*primera*, 51 pesos) and 2pm (*segunda,* 11 pesos). Trains usually run close to schedule. Tickets go on sale at 11:30am for the *primera* to Los Mochis and a half hour before departure time for other trains. Be forewarned that some trains might be "full". In that case, scramble on quickly and aggressively when the train arrives and purchase a ticket on board.

Bus Station: Estrella Blanca (tel. 6-00-73), across the tracks from the *zócalo*. To Chihuahua (8 per day, 26.40 pesos) via Cuauhtémoc (17 pesos).

Market: La Barata de Creel, on Mateos next to Cabañas Bertis. Open daily 9am-8pm.

Laundromat: Lavandería Santa María (tel. 6-00-71), at the Pension Creel on Mateos. Admire the water purification equipment while your clothes spin. Open Mon.-Fri. 9am-2pm and 3-6pm, Sat. 9am-2pm. **Pharmacy: Farmacia Rodríguez,** Mateos 39 (tel. 6-00-52). Open Mon.-Sat. 9am-2pm and 3-8pm, Sun. 9am-1pm.

Police: (tel. 6-00-81), in the Presidencia Municipal bldg. on south side of the *zócalo*.

ACCOMMODATIONS

As Creel flourishes, hotels multiply and prices grow, and the competition for tourist dollars becomes more intense.

Margaritas Casa de Huespedes: Mateos 11 (tel. 16-00-45) is one of the liveliest and cheapest places to stay in all of Mexico. You'll have no trouble finding it—an emissary meets every train to lead you to the house, where you mingle with Margarita's family, friends, and guests. All rooms are freshly renovated, with floor tiles, pine furniture, and heating. Rooms with two single beds and a private bath cost 70 pesos, shared dormitories go for 15-20 pesos per head. To top it off, all prices include two home cooked meals (breakfast at 8am, dinner at 7pm, vegetarians accomodated) and bathroom use. Maragarita's popularity increases with her hectic turnover of guests, but none slip by without some Spanish lessons from the owner herself. Reservations accepted.

Pensión Creel (tel. 6-00-71, fax 6-02-00), at Mateos 61. Bunk or double beds in newly renovated cabins that have well equipped bathrooms and kitchens with microwave. Or opt for the larger hacienda farther from downtown and closer to trails and woods, with shared bathrooms, a fully-equipped kitchen, and a large common room featuring a roaring fireplace and a magazine shelf. Prices range from US$3 if you have your own sleeping bag, through several gradations up to US$10 per person for all features, including breakfast. Group rates. Pesos and credit cards accepted. French and English spoken by those in charge.

Cabañas Bertis, López Mateos 31 (tel. 6-01-08). Log cabin feel with panelled walls, thick wool blankets, and fireplace or wood stove in each abode (wood supplied free). Small private bath included. Rooms with kitchens 150 pesos. Singles 42 pesos. Doubles 65 pesos.

Hotel Korachi (tel. 6-22-07), across the tracks from the train station. A wanna-be hunting lodge where dead animal skins stretch across log-lined walls. Small rooms come without any heat or private bath. Singles 40 pesos. Doubles 60 pesos. Dusty *cabañas* sit under shady trees and include private bath and wood supply. Singles 60 pesos. Doubles 80 pesos.

CREEL

A campsite can be had for 10 pesos among the boulders and pines around **Lake Arrareco,** 8km down the road where only an occasional port-a-john intrudes upon the scenic views.

FOOD

Creel has yet to spawn gourmet restaurants that cater to the jet set tourists who pass through. The best and cheapest way to dine in Creel is to relish a picnic lunch of fruit and bread on the quiet hillsides outside town. Otherwise, many options exist along Mateos, the main drag. **Restaurant Tío Molcas** attracts many a passerby with fresh pine furniture and woven place mats. Mountain-size serving of steak and fries for 15 pesos, cheese enchiladas for 9 pesos. (Open daily 7am-10:30pm.) **Restaurante Veronica** is a simple joint, popular with the locals, that has unfinished wood floors and mix and match dinner chairs. Sit down to homemade eggs and sausage (8 pesos) and shredded beef *tortas* (7.50 pesos). (Open daily 7am-11pm.)

SIGHTS AND ENTERTAINMENT

The least expensive way to explore the gorges and rivers is to camp or backpack through the region. No extensive supply shop exists in the area for camping needs, but **Pensión Creel** has various gadgets for the outdoors.

Some of the popular sites lie far from the center of Creel. Sympathetic locals gladly offer rides to weary travelers, but the cars in secluded mountain areas may be few and far between (sometimes 1 car per hour), stretching an otherwise reasonable trip into an all-day affair (see Mexico General Introduction: Once There: By Thumb above for more information). *Let's Go* does not recommend hitchhiking. Barrancas del Cobre requires at least a three-hour ride and then quite a hike.

Several outfits in Creel offer **group tours** for those averse to roughing it. **Margarita's** offers some of the cheapest tours in town. A full-day tour runs only US$14 per person, featuring a one hour downhill hike and a warm bath in a winding green stream. Bring plenty of water and food, adequate footwear (no sandals) and a sun hat. Another all-day tour (75 pesos) takes you to **Basaseachic Falls,** a spectacular cascade that plunges 806 ft. into a cool lake. A shorter and cheaper tour (½ day, about US$14) takes you 22km out to the smaller **Cusárare Falls** and the village and mission nearby. Tours require a minimum of four to six people. With the number of visitors at Margarita's, it isn't hard to muster enough takers to venture to Barrancas del Cobre or Cusárare Falls, but assembling a tour to Basaseachic Falls can be a bit tricky. You needn't be staying at Margarita's to take any of these tours.

Pensión Creel, Hotel Nuevo, and Cabañas Bertis all run similar tours to popular sites. **Motel Parador** (tel. 6-00-75) tours include a bag lunch, and are a little more expensive.

If you really want to experience the Barrancas, consider a trip to **Batopilas,** 140km south of Creel. This involves a 10-hour bus trip over some of the most terrifying roads in existence, and meteorological conditions that can range from suffocating heat to blinding snow in the course of a single voyage. You can jump on the bus in front of the Farmacia Rodríguez on Mateos on Tuesdays, Thursdays and Saturdays at 7am. It returns Mondays, Wednesdays and Fridays at 4am. Remember to take your passport and tourist card; you could be stopped by uptight and heavily armed soldiers. Weary survivors of the voyage can spend the evening at **Casa Bustillos,** across the basketball court as you get off the bus. Fix the room price beforehand to avoid being overcharged. From Batopilas, short daytrips to local villages are easily arranged.

Sticking close to Creel offers many natural delights too. Just ask your hostess to point you in an interesting direction and start walking. The **Valley of Mushroom Rocks** and the **San Ignacio Mission** can be combined into a daytrip, though the government now charges 10 pesos for each site (more if you want to take home photos). To reach the valley and mission, walk down Mateos past the Motel Parador. When the road forks, take the smaller branch to the left, beside the cemetery. A kilometer or so out of town you will pass through the gates of the Tarahumara's *ejidos* (communal lands) containing the caves in which they live. After the cultivated fields, the valley is to the right and the mission at the bottom of the hill. The large **Lake Ararreco** is a cost-free attraction that lies 8km (a half-hour walk) down the highway from Creel. Lazier people hop a ride with one of the passing trucks, but *Let's Go* does not recommend hitching.

At night, the **Motel Parador** and the **Restaurante Tío Molcas** have bars (though officially alcohol may not be served after 8pm). A beer at the more sedate Molcas costs 3 pesos. The Parador rocks late into the night with live guitar and song and many all-too-willing dance partners; it is the job of the *animador* to get women up and dancing with the male patrons.

■■■ BARRANCAS DEL COBRE (COPPER CANYON)

The train daringly careens along canyon walls, plunges into 96 tunnels, and passes briefly along the rim of Barrancas del Cobre, a gorge even deeper than the Grand Canyon. The Barrancas explode with color during the rainy season (July-Sept.) when the plants are in full bloom; they lie sublimely under drifts of snow during the winter months. Any time of year, Copper Canyon is one of Mexico's greatest natural wonders. The **Chihuahua-Pacífico railroad** stretches its tracks from Chihuahua to Los Mochis through the Sierra Madre Occidental and across the Continental Divide. During the 80 years it took to complete, the trans-territorial link was derided by many *gringo* engineers as an impossible task.

Two types of trains make the daily journey. The *primera* is for tourists. Cleaner and equipped with bathrooms and air conditioning, trains run close to schedule. The large, comfortable seats provide amazing leg room. The *segunda* trains carry livestock as well as passengers and have none of the virtues of the *primeras* except that they cost one-third as much and screech along the same tracks. They do, however, have windows that open and an occasional amateur musician.

From the Los Mochis station, the *primera* departs at 6am and the *segunda* at 7am. From Chihuahua, the *primera* leaves at 7am, the *segunda* at 8am. A *primera* ticket from Los Mochis to Chihuahua costs 94 pesos; the *segunda* runs about 20 pesos (see Creel Practical Information above for applicable prices there). The Chihuahua to Creel leg takes six hours by *primera*, while the Creel to Los Mochis track is an eight-hour journey. The *segunda* makes twice as many stops as the *primera*, adding about four hours to any *primera* travel time.

The serious mountain scenery lies between Creel and Río Fuerte, so if you take the *segunda*, you'll zoom by some great views in the dark. For more expansive natural spectacles and less mountain wall out your window, grab seating on the left side of the train traveling towards Los Mochis, and the right side if going toward Chihuahua. Bring food for the trip or you will be forced to rely on either the enchilada saleschildren who run through the train during stops in small towns, or the burrito and *gordita* salespeople at Divisadero. Even worse, you may find yourself at the mercy of the bland, expensive train entrees.

The train ride itself is a spectacular tour of the Sierra Madre mountains, but it can't compare to spending a few days in the region for personal exploration. Between Creel and Chihuahua, the only noteworthy stop is Cuauhtémoc, the center of a community of Mennonites who arrived in the 1920s and are the primary agricultural producers of the region. They maintain the customs and traditions of their Germanic ancestors as well as the language.

At the **Divisadero station,** the jagged mountain edges overlap to create a maze of gorges and rocks at the rim of the Barrancas del Cobre. Seven hours out of Los Mochis on the *primera*, the train stops for 15 minutes of sight-seeing. Everyone on board scrambles out, sprints to the brink, gapes, and sprints back. On the *segunda*, it's more informal. Ask the conductor when the train is going to leave, and be back early. Resist the urge to buy anything from the Tarahumaras, strategically positioned between the train and the canyon, because better examples of their craft are available in Creel at lower prices.

Besides providing a great view, Divisadero is a good point to begin your canyon adventure; guides lounge around outside the expensive hotel. Make no mistake: abundant water, appropriate footwear and a first-aid kit are necessities for even the shortest day trips.

SINALOA

■■■ LOS MOCHIS

The sad truth is that being in Los Mochis is like having to pay to count hunks of dirt. The town is the commercial center of a prosperous agricultural district which exports sugar, cotton, rice, and wheat. Tourists stop here only to catch the train through the Barrancas del Cobre to Creel and Chihuahua, or to catch the ferry to La Paz. The citizens of Los Mochis know that their town is not what you came to Mexico to see; their constant question is, "Where are you going?" But this awareness seems to provoke an eager-to-please attitude in an effort to ease your short stay in their hot and mildly uninteresting city. Though it is possible to disembark the ferry at 6am and catch the second class train that departs an hour later, the prospect of another long ride could keep you in Los Mochis for the day. It's very difficult to get a seat on a northbound bus; you'll have to wait at the station from the crack of dawn to have a fighting chance of boarding. The unlucky souls unable to buy tickets will find themselves stranded in Los Mochis an extra night.

Orientation and Practical Information The ferry to La Paz, Baja California Sur leaves at 9am every day except Sunday from **Topolobampo,** a small fishing hamlet 24km south of Los Mochis. (*Salón*-class tickets only between Topoplobampo and La Paz, 38 pesos). Cars and motorcycles can be brought on the ferry for an additional fee; space is limited. Check prices and times and buy tickets at the Sematur office on Rendón 519 (tel. 5-82-62), open Mon.-Fri. 8am-1pm and 3-7pm, Sun. 9am-1pm. To get to the office, walk nine small blocks out from Juárez on Flores, then turn left on Rendón. You must buy tickets one day in advance before 11am at this office or on the same day on the ferry at Topolobampo.

A **bus** runs to Topolobampo every half hour in the morning starting at 6am (13 pesos); it leaves from a small side street down from the Hotel Santa Anita, between Hidalgo and Obregón. The bus can also be flagged down at Castro and Zaragoza.

When the **Barrancas del Cobre train** stops at Los Mochis, its passengers still have not quite finished the journey to their hotels. The taxis have you captive—they know if you had any other choice you wouldn't be there. In an intriguing phenomenon, bargaining can drive the prices up. All the drivers report in to a price-fixer, dubbed the Godfather by one frustrated backpacker. This situation tempts unscrupulous travelers to bluff their way onto the free bus to the Santa Anita Hotel.

It is hard to find a map of Los Mochis, and the small faded street signs on corner buildings can be hard to read. If you are averse to asking directions from the very friendly *los mochisinos*, it still should not take too long to figure out the simple grid.

Set office hours are the butt of town jokes. The lines at the ever-popular **Bancomer,** (tel. 5-80-81) Leyva and Juárez, may be 30min. long. (Open Mon.-Fri. 8:30am-1pm. Dollars exchanged 9-11am only.) The **post office,** a den of philatelical debauchery, lies at Ordoñez 226 (tel. 2-08-23), lies 2 blocks off Castro, away from Obregon (turn right); 1 block off Prieto. (Open Mon.-Fri. 8am-7pm, Sat. 9am-1pm. **Postal code:** 81200.) **Farmacia Karla,** Obregón at Degollado (tel. 2-81-80), charges 4 pesos to charge other people for international **collect calls.** (Open 24 hrs.) Cheap but noisy collect calls can be placed on public telephones scattered throughout downtown. (**Telephone Code:** 681.) **Tres Estrellas de Oro buses** leave from the station on Obregón just east of Allende (tel. 2-17-57). *De paso* buses run every ½hr., north through Guaymas, Hermosillo and Mexicali to Tijuana and south to Mazatlán. They are often chock-full when they reach Los Mochis; you must wait and see when the bus arrives. Secure seats are easier to obtain on the slower *de local* buses to Guadalajara (2 per day, 102 pesos), to Tijuana (3 per day, 146 pesos) and to Mazatlán (2 per day, 47 pesos). All others are *de paso*, so be on your toes (see Mexico Essentials: Traveling in Mexico). **Norte de Sonora** and **Transportes del Pacífico,** side by side on Morelos between Leyva and Zaragoza, have scrungier buses to the same places for less. Buses to El Fuerte leave from the corner of Independencia and Degollado. For **taxis,** call 2-02-83. For fresh fish, fruit, and vegetables, check the **market** on Obregon between Leyva and Zaragoza, especially on weekends. Los Mochis' hippest threads get washed at **Lavamatic,** Allende 218 just before Juárez, for only 5 pesos, then dry out for 7 more. (Open Mon.-Sat. 7am-7pm, Sun. 7am-1pm.) **Red Cross,** diligent at Tenochtitlán and Prieto (tel. 2-02-92), 1 block off Castro, has ambulance service that never calls it a night. **Farmacia Karla,** Obregon at Degollado (tel. 5-70-07), is open 24 hrs. Hit the **Hospital Fátima,** Blvd. Jiquilpan Pte. 639 (tel. 12-33-12) to check out the local medical scene. **Police** life revolves around Degollado at Cuauhtémoc in the Presidencia Municipal (tel. 2-00-33).

Accommodations and Food Don't waste all night looking for the cozy bed of your childhood dreams. **Hotel Lorena,** Obregón Pte. 186 (tel. 2-02-39), one block from the bus station, is the only place nearly worth its price. Hard-blowing A/C, color cable TV, and comfortable bed provide an oasis of cool in the mid-day sweltering heat. Cafeteria on third floor open 7-11am, 7-11pm for tired early-morning or late-night arrivees. (Singles 75 pesos. Doubles 110 pesos. Traveler's checks and credit cards accepted.) **Hotel Montecarlo,** Flores 322 Sur (tel. 2-18-18), blue building at corner of Independencia. Sizeable, clean, new rooms in well-kept old building with a quiet courtyard; the only old and pretty hotel in Los Mochis. Central A/C. (Singles 75 pesos, with two people 90 pesos. Doubles 110 pesos.) **Hotel Hidalgo,** Hidalgo 260 Pte. (tel. 2-34-56), has deep blue furniture and baby blue walls to cool down rooms with ceiling fan. Open lobby with balcony can become a local hangout if a big game is on TV. (Singles 40 pesos, with A/C 50 pesos. Doubles 50 pesos, with A/C 60 pesos.)

   The best and cheapest food is sold in the **public market** between Prieto and Leyva along Castro. One of Los Mochis' few virtues is that the produce for sale is grown nearby, meaning prices are low and quality is high. The *taquerías* and *loncherías* in the market dish out cheap, home-brewed mysteries, many of which pack an excellent punch. The restaurants below are pricier but cleaner than the questionable street-side eateries. Except for the *cantinas* (which women should avoid) and the corner *taquerías,* just about everything in town shuts down at 8pm and alcohol evaporates at 11pm. After that, enter **The Closet,** the bar in the Santa Anita Hotel (on Leyva, between Hidalgo and Obregón), which is as dark and as cramped as its name implies. **El Taquito** is on Leyva between Hidalgo and Independencia (tel. 2-81-19). Sit comfortably in the vinyl booths and bask in cold A/C. Waiters in red jackets serve up fried chicken (10 pesos) and breaded shrimp (30 pesos). Open 24 hrs., **El Terome** at Flores and Independencía under the Hotel Montecarlo (tel. 2-18-18) features high quality seafood , A/C, and TV in a more formal setting. Filet of garlic fish 23 pesos. (Open daily 7am-7pm. Credit cards accepted.)

■■■ MAZATLÁN

Mazatlán means "place of the deer" in Nahuatl. A less appropriate name can hardly be imagined, since there is nothing even remotely pastoral or ruminant about this city. The only wildlife present—genus *Bronzus*, species *norteamericanus*—roams the beaches in large herds.

For centuries Mazatlán has been the youth hostel of history. In 1531, Mazatlán's harbor was chosen as the launching pad for Spanish galleons loaded with gold mined in the Sierra Madres. Three centuries later, the town suffered a U.S. blockade (1847) and then a French bombardment (1864). Mazatlán was also the temporary stomping ground for a group of Confederate Civil War veterans out to preserve their Southern ideals on Mexican soil, and during the Revolution of 1914 the city became only the second in the world to be shelled from the air. A substantial Chinese population once lived here but was summarily expelled 50 years ago.

Despite its eventful past, Mazatlán presents nothing of historical or cultural interest to the traveler. Like other great resorts, the most attractive aspects of Mazatlán are gifts of nature—beautiful sunsets, a glittering ocean and wide golden beaches. Unlike other Mexican resorts which maintain at least a facade of cute *mexicanidad* and cultivate an exotic sheen, Mazatlán couldn't care less. Its tourist zone, spread along a highway, matches its Floridian prototypes gift-shop-for-gift-shop but boasts lower prices and nicer beaches.

ORIENTATION

Mazatlán is a raging cornucopia of transportation, but bus is still the most economical and versatile way to get in and out of the city. The **bus station** lies three blocks behind the **Sands Hotel,** about 2km north of Old Mazatlán. The area around the bus station, with several reasonably priced hotels and restaurants, along with a good beach and the vital "Sábalo" bus line only three blocks away, makes a convenient home base. You can catch the downtown-bound "Insurgentes" bus at the stand one block off the beach across from the chicken barbecuer.

On the far eastern edge of Mazatlán, the **Ferrocarriles del Pacífico** train station opens an hour before departures and closes soon after arrivals. Make your way to a better part of town: the yellow "Insurgentes" bus or the green, beat-up "Cerritos-Juárez" will take you to and from downtown. **Sematur** (tel. 81-70-20) operates ferries Sun.-Fri. to and from La Paz, on Baja California. Their office and dock sit on the southern end of Carnaval, which runs south from Ángel Flores. Meeting the ferry requires a hot 20-min. walk from *el centro*; the "Playa Sur" bus (.70 pesos) makes the trip, and for 10 pesos so will a taxi. Sematur accepts reservations for all classes up to a month in advance during the high season (Dec., July, and Aug.), and recommends that you make them at least two weeks ahead of your scheduled date of departure. In any case, tickets are only sold the day of departure; be sure to reach the office early to procure a spot. (Open daily 8:30am-3pm.)

The Mazatlán **airport** is 30km south of the city. Bus "Atamsa" brings arrivals to their hotels, but no bus returns to the airport; resign yourself to a cab (a whopping 35-40 pesos).

Built on a rocky spur jutting southwest into the Pacific, Old Mazatlán's downtown area surrounds and spills north of the *zócalo*. **Angel Flores,** the southern boundary of the *zócalo*, runs west to **Olas Altas,** a quiet waterfront area that remained Mazatlán's most fashionable district until the tourist onslaught arrived. Both **Juárez,** the eastern boundary of the *zócalo*, and **Serdán,** one block farther east, run north (toward the back of the cathedral) to the cheap hotel district and the area's beach, **Playa del Norte.** From Playa del Norte, the coast arcs to the northeast; the main road tracing the *malecón* starts off as **Olas Altas** south of downtown then becomes **Paseo Clausen** until the tall fisherman's statue where it turns into **Avenida del Mar;** finally it changes once more into **Sábalo** past Valentino's disco emporium. Glitz feeds upon itself through the **Golden Zone,** a colony of exclusive time-share condos, high-rise hotels, overpriced gift shops, and day-glo 7km north of Old Mazatlán, before reaching its apotheosis in the **El Cid Resort,** a world unto itself.

Mazatlán's efficient **bus system** makes getting around the city a breeze. At some point, all the ramshackle municipal buses pass the public market on Juárez, three

MAZATLÁN

blocks north of the *zócalo*; if you get lost, you'll eventually return to familiar territory. The most useful bus line is the "Sábalo-Centro," serviced by smaller air-conditioned express buses (1 peso) that run from the downtown market to Olas Altas as well as up to Playa Sábalo. The "Cerritos-Juárez" bus (.80 pesos) continues up to Playa Bruja at Puerta Carritos. "Insurgentes" services the bus and train stations, and "Playa Sur" goes to the ferry dock, the lighthouse, and the *Olas Altas* neighborhood. Fare is .60-.80 pesos; buses run every 15min. from 5am-10pm. Feel free to wave down a bus at any point on its route since no set bus stops exist. For late-night disco hopping, you'll have to take a cab or a *pulmonía*, an open vehicle resembling a golf-cart that putters along at 60mph blasting raucous music. Always set the price before you commit yourself to the ride.

Since many of Mazatlán's streets are numbered twice-over, tracking down a particular address can prove difficult.

PRACTICAL INFORMATION

Tourist Office: Olas Altas 1300 (tel. 85-12-20). Walk down Angel Flores past the *zócalo* until you reach the beach, turn left—it's in the tall Bank of Mexico complex. Hands out popular poster ad-maps of the town. Open Mon.-Fri. 8am-3pm.

Consulates: Canada, Loaiza at Bugamblia (tel. 83-73-20), in the Hotel Mazatlán.

Currency Exchange: Banks throughout town exchange Mon.-Fri. 8:30am-11am.

American Express: In the Balboa Plaza Centro Comercial on Camarón Sábalo just before Balboa Towers (tel. 83-06-00). Open Mon.-Fri. 9am-5pm, Sat. 9am-noon.

Post Office: Juárez at Ángel Flores (tel. 81-21-21), across from the *zócalo*. *Lista de Correos* posted. Open Mon.-Fri. 9am-6pm, Sat. 9am-1pm. **Postal code:** 82000.

Telephones: *Caseta* at Serdán 1510. International collect calls 3 pesos for first 3 minutes. Open Mon.-Sat. 7am-8:30pm, Sun. 8am-1pm. Public touch-tone phones are scattered throughout downtown and hotel lobbies. **Telephone Code:** 91.

Telegrams: In the same building as the post office (tel. 81-36-62). Open Mon.-Fri. 8am-8pm, Sat. 8am-12pm.

Airport: 18km south of the city. **Aeroméxico,** Sábalo 310-A (tel. 14-11-11). To Mexico City (5 per day, 580 pesos) and Tijuana (2 per day, 800 pesos). **Mexicana,** Clausen 101-B (tel. 82-77-22). To Guadalajara and Los Angeles.

Train Station: In Col. Esperanza on the east edge of town (tel. 84-67-10). To Guadalajara (*primera* 61 pesos at 11am., *segunda* 18 pesos at 5am) and Mexicali (*primera* 162 pesos at 7am, *segunda* at 11:30pm).

Bus Station: Tres Estrellas de Oro, Transportes del Norte, Estrella Blanca and **Transportes del Pacífico** all serve Mazatlán. Tres Estrellas de Oro has express service to Tijuana (196 pesos) and Los Mochis (44 pesos); regular rides to Nogales (134 pesos) and Guadalajara (50 pesos). Transportes del Norte to Durango (34 pesos), Monterrey, and beyond.

Ferry: Sematur (tel. 81-70-20), port and office located at end of Carnaval, south of *el centro*. To La Paz (at 3pm, 16hrs., *salón* 57 pesos, *turista* 114 pesos, and *cabina* 170 pesos). See "Baja California: Getting Around By Sea" for an explanation of the classes of ferries.

Car Rental: National, Sábalo 7000 (tel. 83-60-00). 85 pesos per day, plus 676 pesos per km. Doesn't include insurance and A/C. Must be 24 years old. **Scooters** available along Malecón for US$15 per day.

Laundromat: Lavafácil, across from the bus station in the same pink building as the Hotel Fiesta. Wash 2 pesos, 10-min. dry 2 pesos. Open Mon.-Sat. 8am-10pm, Sun 9am-2pm.

Red Cross: Obregón 73 (tel. 81-36-90).

24-hr. Pharmacy: Farmacia Parque Zaragoza, Nelson and Morales (tel. 82-83-78). In the pink building at the corner of the park.

Hospital: IMSS, Av. Ejército Mexicano (tel. 83-27-00).

Police: Rafael in Col. Juárez (tel. 81-39-19). **Emergency:** tel. 06.

ACCOMMODATIONS

In the good ol' days, budget hotels in Mazatlán ran about the same as those in other Mexican cities. Of late many seem to have used Mexico's extreme inflation as an excuse to jack up their prices to resort levels. Nonetheless, fine cheap rooms do exist—except on the waterfront, where rates are exorbitant at even the shabbiest places. Budget hotels concentrate around the bus station and in Old Mazatlán along the three avenues east of the main square: Juárez, Serdán, and Azueta. Cheap beds can even be found on Sábalo, near the beaches, for larger groups. Check around.

The busiest seasons in Mazatlán are Christmas and the month following Semana Santa (Easter week). At these times of year, check in early. At other times, prices are negotiable, especially for extended stays. Summer nights in Mazatlán can be very hot and humid; always inspect the cooling system or ventilation in your room before paying. Don't forget: The value of a car rises in direct proportion to its decibel output. If you are looking at a room on the street, keep looking.

Old Mazatlán

This is the noisier part of town and the hotels here are farther from the beach—in Mazatlán that means you can't spit in the ocean from your window—so the rooms are a little cheaper. But if the discos are your scene, cabs will cost more from here than from the hotels west of the bus station. The **Hotel Vialta,** on Azueta (tel. 81-60-27), 3 blocks north of 21 de Marzo, offers a friendly refuge in the leafy courtyard and rooms with a fan and a big shower. (Singles 35 pesos. Doubles 50 pesos.) **Hotel Santa Barbara,** Juárez at 16 de Septiembre (tel. 82-21-20), one block from shore. Has a new pink paint job that makes it stand out like a sore concrete block. Cage yourself in tiny rooms with glowing green showers. (Singles 30 pesos. Doubles 45 pesos. 10 pesos extra for A/C.) No to credit cards, yes to dollars.

Near the Bus Station

Because of greater proximity to sandy beaches and the Golden Zone, hotels in this area put more strain on the wallet. But better rooms can have views of the ocean.

- **Hotel Club Playa Mar,** Av. de Mar 139 (tel. 82-08-33), on the *malecón*. Sip piña coladas while lounging in the tropical landscaped alcove complete with large swimming pool. All rooms offer A/C, TV, private bath, and bar-like area. Parking too. Singles and doubles 66 pesos. Credit cards accepted.
- **Hotel Emperador,** Río Panuco (tel. 82-67-24), across from the bus terminal. 4-story (not 4-star) hotel offers firm beds on concrete slabs and clean bathrooms. Rooms with cable TV and A/C 60 pesos for 1-2 persons; without the luxuries 40 pesos for 1-2 persons, 50 for 3-4 guests. Credit cards accepted.
- **Hotel Fiesta,** Espinoza Ferrusquilla 306 (tel. 81-38-88), also next to the bus terminal. Beds come complete with safety belts so the ceiling fan doesn't blow you away to the land of Oz. Singles and doubles 50 pesos, with A/C 60. Black and white TV costs 5 pesos extra.
- **Hotel Cabínas,** Av. del Mar 123 (tel. 81-57-52), also on the *malecón*. Run down rooms host paintings of Mexican dancers with 11 different signatures. Apartment suites for up to 7 guests with kitchen and ocean view rented on weekly basis (130 pesos per night). Otherwise singles 40 pesos, doubles 50 pesos.

South to Olas Altas

A welcome oasis from the grime and noise of downtown or the frosted hair of the Golden Zone, *Olas Altas* offers tranquility and beauty. Colonial architecture overlooks the beach and crashing sea from which the area took its name.

Back in the 1950s, long before wily developers began constructing multi-million-dollar pleasure palaces along the north shore, Mazatlán's fledgling resort scene clung to *Olas Altas*, a winding 1km road hugging the shore south of town. Today, these old regal hot spots still grace the old strip, but the majority of Mazatlán's tourists bypass their aging displays, choosing instead the flashy young hotels from the north. The majesty and opulence of **Hotel Belmar,** Olas Altas 106 (tel. 85-11-11), is hidden in the hazy marble floors and colorful tiles lining the arches, reminiscent of a resort of yester-year. Monstrous guest rooms with dark wood paneling and bathrooms bigger than some budget bedrooms. Swimming pool, deck and barber shop. Singles with A/C and TV 42 pesos, with ocean view (no A/C) 55 pesos. Doubles with A/C and TV 55 pesos, with ocean view (no A/C) 66 pesos. Credit cards accepted. White-washed building with tropical green trim houses **Hotel La Siesta,** Olas Altas 11 (tel. 81-23-34), with a jungly central courtyard that spills over in the rooms. In case you get bored in Mazatlán, you can play with the A/C, TV, or phone, or just lounge on the balcony overlooking the sea. Singles 60 pesos. Doubles 75 pesos with ocean view. Credit cards accepted.

FOOD

Mazatlán offers a wide variety of culinary tastes from standard *comida corrida* meals to charbroiled T-bone steak, a tourist favorite. Of course, all menus are filled with all-time "Mexican" classics: spicy guacamole, crisp nachos dripping with cheese, and *jalapeño* peppers. All restaurants have adopted the colorful tablecloth as their crowning trademark. What's more, Mazatlán's restaurants are relatively cheap, although, like everything else, food prices escalate as you get sucked north toward the Golden Zone.

Old Mazatlán

The busy **public market,** between Juárez and Serdán, three blocks north of the *zócalo,* serves the cheapest meals in the area. And if you need a headless pig, this is the place. Ample snacking opportunities exist outside in the *fruterías, loncherías,* and taco stands.

Restaurant Ostioneria Avenida, Av. Alemán 808 (tel. 82-63-98), south of downtown on the way to the cruise ports. Quite a hike from downtown, but the delectable seafood is well worth it. Mixed platter offers every conceivable item of seafood and more. Tequila and barbecued shrimp 28 pesos, breaded oysters 21 pesos and octopus in garlic sauce 16 pesos. Open daily 8am-8pm.

La Casa de Ana, Consitución 515 (tel. 85-28-39). *Comida vegetariana* on the peaceful Plaza Machado; where the elite meet in Mazatlán. Salads, yogurt, and soyburgers for 4-8 pesos, Sunday buffet 15 pesos. Also beer and breakfast. Open Mon.-Sat. 10am-10pm, Sun. 11am-7pm.

Doney, Escabedo 610 (tel. 81-26-51), right at 5 de Mayo. With a single short name, you know that this place is a few notches up in class—and price. The dark oak doors and huge brick arches lend an ambience that the tourists dig. English menu, naturally. All dishes served with a big basket of nachos. Chicken tacos 9 pesos. *Sincronizadas* 15 pesos. Open daily 11am-10:30pm. Credit cards accepted.

Restaurant Joncol's, Flores 608 Pte. (tel. 81-21-87). Relieve yourself from the midday heat in this air-conditioned restaurant with yellow table cloths and various local awards on the wall. Menu ranges from tostadas (10 pesos) to shrimp in garlic sauce (30 pesos) or fruit salad (10 pesos). Open daily 7am-11pm. Credit cards accepted.

Restaurant Fonda Santa Clara, Olas Altas 106 (tel. 81-64-51). Plastic Corona patio furniture cling together under a shady awning to form a surf-side café. *Quesadillas* 11 pesos, shrimp salad 17 pesos, small nachos 10 pesos. Full bar service.

Restaurant Playa Norte, Paseo Clausen (tel. 85-13-29), next to the fisherman's statue on the beach. Small stone waterfall trickles near the bar as thirsty beach bathers enjoy a tropical drink and *vista del mar* in the shade. Great breakfast special with 2 eggs, beans, potatoes, tortillas and coffee 7.50 pesos. Also fish in garlic butter 22 pesos. Open daily 8am-pm.

North to the Golden Zone

As you move north, prices soar and *norteamericano* culinary influence becomes more pronounced. Look no further if you feel the need for U.S. music, tourists, and Caesar salads.

El Mambo Lonchería, Espinoza Ferrusquilla 204 (tel. 85-04-73), across from the bus station. Mexican pottery, hanging seashells, eclectic art, a macaw, and tasty, large, cheap meals. Beware of the howling buses passing by the entrance. Shrimp in several different styles 16 pesos. *Huevos rancheros* 6.50 pesos. Open daily 7am-7pm.

Restaurant Roca Mar, Av. del Mar at Isla de Los Lobos (tel. 81-00-23). Like most other places along the beach, this offers full bar and an open-air view of the crashing waves, past the rushing traffic. Prices tainted by tourism. Shrimp cocktail 16 pesos. Filet mignon 34 pesos. Grilled fish 25 pesos. Open daily 10am-1am.

SIGHTS AND ACTIVITIES

The alcohol-free **Yate Fiesta** harbor cruises depart daily at 11am for a three-hour tour of Mazatlán by sea. Tickets (35 pesos) are sold at the yacht office (tel. 81-77-00); to get there, take the "Playa Sur" bus to the end of the first dock, past various sport fishing boats near the foot of the lighthouse.

For a 360° "aerial" view of Mazatlán, the sea and the surrounding hills, climb to the top of *el faro* (lighthouse). Once off the Playa Sur bus, walk/hike up the twisting dirt road to the lighthouse at the peak. The walk (about ½hr.) is scorching in the summer sun and the road narrows to a rocky path. Rumor has it that the Mazatlán tower divers practice here.

Mazatlán's tower divers don't quite match the exploits of the cliff divers in Acapulco, but their acrobatic plunges are so extraordinarily dangerous that the discrepancy won't bother you much. Performances take place daily from 10-11am and 4:30-5:30pm, weather permitting. The best viewing angles are just south of the towers; on days when the water is too rough for diving, you can climb the tower to watch the waves break below. Walk to the waterfront on Zaragoza and head south to get to the towers. Though it may seem like it at first, the spectacle is not free—tips are expected.

The **Acuario Mazatlán** (tel. 81-78-15), on Av. de los Deportes, keeps piranhas and 249 other feisty breeds in a slew of cloudy tanks and also has displays on fishing and performing sea lions and birds. The pet pigeons in the aviary are less interesting than the hooded orioles, bar-vented wren, and social flycatchers in the surrounding trees. The Acuario is one block back from the beach and north of the Sands Hotel; the turn-off is marked by a shimmering blue sign. (Open daily 9:30am-7pm. Admission 12 pesos, ages 6-18 6 pesos.)

Mazatlán's greatest asset is its 16km of beach. Just north of Old Mazatlán along Av. del Mar sprawls **Playa Norte,** a decent stretch of sand if you don't mind small waves and the stares of the local *machos* who hang out on the waterfront. Solo women in particular should consider swimming farther north. As you hone in on the Golden Zone, the beach gets cleaner, the waves larger, and the name becomes **Playa Las Gaviotas.** Just past Punta Sábalo, in the lee of the islands, basks **Playa Sábalo** with great waves and manicured golden sand co-opted by crowds of *norteamericanos* and assorted peddlers. Air-conditioned "Sábalo-Centro" buses access all of these beaches.

As Playa Sábalo recedes to the north, crowds thin rapidly and you can frolic on the glorious beaches and in the dramatic surf all by yourself. If you take the yellow "Sábalo bus" (among others) to the last stop and walk left to the beach, you'll be at nearly deserted **Playa Bruja,** with tons of beautiful sand and four- to six-foot waves. Because of its seclusion, it's also the only beach on which you can camp.

William Blake saw the universe in a grain of sand and eternity in an hour. You too may get bored at the beach. Should this befall you, don't abandon Mazatlán. You may simply be in need of a brief change of locale. Hop on one of the boats to the **Isla de la Piedra,** where locals go to escape the crowds. Boats leave from the wharf on Av. del Puerto at Gutierrez Najera. To walk there, go out 21 de Marzo from the Cathedral past Serdan to the water, then turn left on Av. del Puerta. (3 pesos round trip.) Boats leave for **Islas Venados,** an island with fine diving and without those annoying fellow-travelers, from **El Cid Resort** in the Golden Zone (5 per day, 15 pesos). Finally, waterpark mania has hit south of the border with the new **Mazagua.** Go crazy in the wave pool or shoot down slippery slides. Located north of the Golden Zone near Puerta Cerritos. (Open daily 10am-6pm. 35 pesos).

ENTERTAINMENT

Hordes of north-of-the-border high schoolers ditch the prom and hit Mazatlán for a reason. Discos and bars clamor for the Golden Zone bucks and the hike (about ½hr. from the bus station) is actually worth it if drunken fiestas are your scene. If not, the thrice-balconied **Teatro Angela Peralta** in the square at Constitución and Carnaval has (sometimes free) plays. As for the clubs:

Bora-Bora, on Sábalo at the southern end of the Golden Zone. You can't miss it— it's in a white stucco version of the haunted Disney mansion on a rocky point. Jammed with touring teenagers clad in neon and dancing on the bars. Cover of 15 pesos includes 2 beers. Open daily 9pm-4am.

Bali Hai, also in Disney mansion. The restaurant-bar offers a small dance floor for those who want to make an exhibition. Popular with the local teens who jam to the Mexican disco/rock. No cover. Open daily noon-4am.

El Caracol, a.k.a. the $6 million disco in the El Cid complex (tel. 83-33-33). The flashing lights, video screens, and fake smoke are almost demolished by the music: New Kids On the Block, C&C Music Factory, and Vanilla Ice, to name just a few. Cover 16 pesos includes 2 drinks. Open 9pm-4am.

Frankie-Oh's, Av. del Mar 1003 (tel. 82-58-00), next to Señor Frog's. Popular with the younger set and often features live Mexican bands with Los Lobos sound. Cover 15 pesos. Open 9pm-4am.

DURANGO

■■■ DURANGO

Durango, a Basque word that means "meadow bathed by a river and surrounded by high mountains beyond the river," was founded in 1563 by Francisco de Ibarra, the man who seems to have colonized half of northern Mexico. Although it lacks the grand colonial architecture of its southern neighbors, the city has a kind of rugged beauty all its own. Buildings adorned with a combination of stone scrollwork, wrought-iron grilles, and glistening blue paint fill the side streets. On top of this, the amazing friendliness of Durango's citizens makes most visits to the city a pleasure; people here pause on the street to give the inquisitive traveler detailed advice and directions and may even deliver visitors to their destinations. Very few residents speak English, but most good-naturedly attempt to understand broken Spanish and crazy gesticulations. Despite the lack of English-speakers, Durango rocks the house with U.S. rap; car stereos and shops pump up the bass and boom. These modern trappings contrast the beautiful mesas on the city's edge that give some idea of the origins of that pithy Basque name and accentuate the town's rough-hewn, frontier feel.

ORIENTATION AND PRACTICAL INFORMATION

The central **bus station** is 3km east of the city center. Getting to the center of town is easy. When you exit the bus terminal, cross the parking lot to the covered benches and take the municipal bus (.50 pesos) marked "Centro" to the **Plaza de Armas** across from the **Catedral**. To return, catch the "Central Camionera" bus from the plaza (.50 pesos). Buses run daily 7am-11pm. If you arrive by **train,** walk a dozen short blocks down Martínez until you reach Durango's main street, **20 de Noviembre.** Turn left and walk a block to the plaza. 20 de Noviembre runs east-west through the plaza with Serdán parallel; Constitución and Zaragoza cross 20 de Noviembre heading north-south. Streets are numbered north and south of Serdán; the *catedral* is on the north side of the Plaza de Armas.

Tourist Office: Hidalgo Sur 408 (tel. 1-21-39), 3 blocks west of the plaza on 20 de Noviembre and left (south) 2 blocks. Good starting point with helpful city maps and advice. Historical literature about Durango on request. Open Mon.-Sat. 10am-3pm and 6-9pm, Sun. 10am-1pm.

Currency Exchange: Bancomer, 20 de Noviembre at Constitución, across from the plaza (tel. 3-20-22). Changes traveler's checks as well as currency. Open Mon.-Fri. 9am-1:30pm. The alternative, **Casa de Cambio** at 20 de Noviembre under the Hotel Roma, stays open Mon.-Fri. 9am-6pm.

American Express: Av. 20 de Noviembre 810 Ote. (tel. 7-00-23, fax 7-01-43).

Post Office: 20 de Noviembre at Laureano Roncal, more than ten blocks east of the *catedral.* Open Mon.-Fri. 8am-5pm, Sat. 8am-1pm. *Lista de Correos* posted around 11:30am. **Postal Code:** 34000.

Telephones: *Caseta* at Martínez Sur 206. Collect calls 4 pesos. Open Mon.-Sat. 8am-9:30pm. Touch-tone public phones found throughout Durango's squares. **Telephone Code:** 181.

Bus Station: On Blvd. Francisco Villa. **Transportes del Norte** (tel. 8-30-81), **Transportes Chihuahuenses** (tel. 8-37-81), **Omnibus de México** (tel. 8-33-61) and **Estrella Blanca** go to most major cities. Prices vary among them, but Estrella Blanca is usually the cheapest. Some destinations: Aguascalientes (29 pesos), Mexico City (66 pesos), Mazatlán (28 pesos), Torreón (17 pesos).

Train Station: Felipe Pescador, at Martínez (tel. 3-34-22). Daily departures north only to Torreón. Connections can be made there. Call for more information.

Red Cross: 5 de Febrero at Libertad (tel. 7-34-44).

24-hr. Pharmacy: Farmacia Pensiones, Constitución at Coronado (tel. 2-99-92).

Hospital: Hospital General, 5 de Febrero at Fuentes (tel. 1-91-15).

Police: Reforma at 5 de Febrero (tel. 754-06).

Emergency: dial 06.

ACCOMMODATIONS

The various old streets in downtown Durango hold plenty of hotels. Many of the cheaper accommodations are centuries-old renovated mansions, complete with courtyard and colonial arches; almost all claim to have housed or hid Pancho Villa for at least a night. Beware the first two weeks of July during the popular Feria Nacional. If you're in town then, grab the first bed you see or prepare to sleep in the bus station.

Hotel Posada Durán, 20 de Noviembre Pte. 506 (tel. 1-24-12), across from the *catedral.* Mahogany-finished French doors open up to a spacious bedroom with desks, four poster beds, and balcony. The interior red-tiled courtyard with trickling fountains comforts the weary traveler with its former colonial grandeur. Singles with bath 44 pesos. Doubles 55 pesos. Reservations, credit cards, and traveler's checks accepted.

Hotel Posada San Jorge, Constitución 102 Sur (tel. 3-32-57). Similar ancient *hacienda* establishment with balcony and courtyard that lacks the refurbishment and charm of the Durán. Large rooms come with mix-and-match '70s furniture and bath. Singles 52 pesos. Doubles 66 pesos. Credit cards accepted.

Hotel Roma, 20 de Noviembre 705 Pte. (tel. 2-01-22). Large hotel tries to supply many of the comforts from home: wall-to-wall carpeting, TV, telephone, bath, even elevator. Small circular windows peep out over random palm trees in the halls. Singles 61 pesos. Doubles 72 pesos. Accepts traveler's checks and credit cards.

FOOD

Durango has slews of little restaurants offering pretty much the same *comida corrida* (7-9 pesos) and *carne asada*. Many cluster along 20 de Noviembre, with some more upscale joints on Constitución Nte.

Al Grano, Negrete 804 at Zaragoza. This small eatery packed with square wooden tables and bright pictures of fruit is popular with the local *vegetarianos*. Breakfast 7 peso or 4-course meal including fruit salad, soup, dish of the day and dessert for 12 pesos. Whole-grain breads and pastries to go. Open Mon.-Sat. 8am-8pm.

Corleone Pizza, Constitución Nte. 114 (tel. 3-31-38). A wide variety of lamps, old movies posters, and fancy drinks make this the ideal setting for a romantic evening. Pizza in flaky pie crusts. Small pizza 11 pesos, spaghetti 6 pesos. Open daily 11:30am-11:30pm.

Far West Steak House Bar and Grill, Florida 1106, at the western end of 20 de Noviembre. The 2-story restaurant has the get-up of an old-West saloon complete with swinging-door entrance, hitching post and gentle piano. This tourist spot lists all the Western films ever shot in Durango and boasts the autographs of celebrities as recent as Kevin Costner. Steak Buffalo Bill 34 pesos. Big Jake Plate 17 pesos. Credit cards accepted. Open daily 1-11pm.

SIGHTS AND ENTERTAINMENT

Few standard tourist attractions in Durango deserve your undivided attention. The **Plaza de Armas,** surrounded by upscale stores, is the city's center of activity and its most interesting sight. Every Thursday and Sunday the state band livens up the area with a wide range of music from the central kiosk. Directly across from the north end of the plaza stands the grandiose 300-year-old **Catedral.** Its construction initiated a period of baroque popularity in the city. The **Palacio del Gobierno,** on 5 de Febrero at Martínez, surrounds a central courtyard with colorful murals depicting the heroic strides toward Mexican independence and democracy. (Open Mon.-Fri. 8am-3pm.)

During the last week of June and first two weeks of July, Durango holds its **Feria Nacional,** which features Mexican singers and bands, cultural demonstrations, bullfights and industrial and agricultural displays. Ask for details at the tourist office (see Practical Information).

A 10km drive north on Route 45 toward Parral will take you to **Villa del Oeste** and **Chupaderos.** These two towns were given makeovers for the filming of westerns, among them John Wayne's *Chisum* and *Big Jake*. While Villa del Oeste is still occasionally used, Chupaderos is a ghost town inhabited by people who act as if it were an ordinary Mexican village. Talk to the tourism office for details and for group bus trips to these and to Los Alamos motion picture village.

Nightlife isn't hopping in Durango. Catch a Mexican flick at **Cinema El Dorado 70,** at 20 de Noviembre and Progreso (6 pesos), or tune in to one of the many radio stations and catch the blend of Mexican, U.S., and even French *música*.

ZACATECAS

■■■ ZACATECAS

The second-to-last thing a traveler expects to find in the prickly desert of Central Mexico is a charming city, yet out of nowhere rises Zacatecas. The arid surroundings augment the colonial beauty of this town, perched between, on, and over mineral-laden hills.

The lifeblood of Zacatecas, like that of Guanajuato, once flowed through veins of silver. A silver trinket, given to early Spanish colonists by an indigenous Cascane in the mid-16th century, triggered the mining bonanza that gave birth to the city. In the 200 years after the Conquest, the hills surrounding Zacatecas were stripped of over US$1 billion worth of silver and other precious metals. Among mining towns, Zacatecas was unusually fortunate: the arts flourished under the patronage of affluent silver barons, and the rows of grand colonial mansions lining the downtown streets speak of generations that displayed their wealth lavishly. In the early 19th century, one devout mine owner paved a walkway from his home to the cathedral with solid silver bars.

The tumultuous history of modern Mexico has left its thumbprint on Zacatecas; in 1914 Francisco "Pancho" Villa's revolutionary forces proved victorious here over Carranza's troops. As revolution atrophied into institution and the mines ran dry, Zacatecas emerged as a hub of sophistication laden with architectural, artistic and natural treasures.

ORIENTATION AND PRACTICAL INFORMATION

At the junction of several major highways, Zacatecas is easily accessible from many cities, including Guadalajara (318km south), Aguascalientes (129km south), and Chihuahua (832km north). All buses arrive and depart from the **central bus terminal** on the outskirts of town. City buses (.30 pesos) await outside: to get to *el centro*, take "Ruta 7"; to return to the bus station, take the "Camionera Central" or "Ruta 8" bus from the east end of Juárez (see below).

Unlike most Mexican cities, Zacatecas has no identifiable center of town. Instead, activity revolves around two main streets: **Juárez,** running roughly northwest, and **Hidalgo,** renamed González Ortega southwest of Juárez. Use the intersection of the two, one block northwest of **Plaza Independencia,** as your point of orientation. Many of the city's colonial monuments lie on or near Hidalgo; if you keep its location vaguely in mind as you try to navigate the twisting, cobblestone streets, you may spend less time bothering people for directions.

Tourist Office: Oficina de Turismo, Hidalgo 61 (tel. 4-05-52), at Callejón del Santero across from the cathedral. The staff is eager to help, and the map is helpful. Open daily 8am-8pm. The Café Acropolis across the street sells more extensive maps for 5 pesos.

Guided Tours: Cantera Tours, Centro Comercial, El Mercado Local A-21 (tel. 2-90-65). Guided 5-hr. tour of the city 60 pesos (children 30 pesos) includes transportation and admission to museums. Office open daily 9am-8pm.

Currency Exchange: Bánamex, Hidalgo 132. Open Mon.-Fri. 9am-5pm. **Bancomer,** Hidalgo at Allende. Open Mon.-Fri. 9am-12:30pm.

Post Office: Allende 111 (tel. 2-01-96), off Hidalgo. *Lista de Correos.* Open Mon.-Fri. 8am-7pm, Sat. 9am-1pm. **Postal code:** 980001.

Telephones: Callejón de Cuevas 111, at the corner of Café Zas, above the bookstore. Collect international calls in the morning only, 5 pesos. Open Mon.-Fri. 8:30am-9:20pm, Sat. 9am-2pm and 4-8pm. Also at Independencia 88-A, across from the Jardín Independencia inside a small mall. International collect calls in the morning only, 2 pesos. Open daily 8am-8:30pm. **Telephone code:** 492.

Telegrams: Hidalgo at Juárez (tel. 2-00-70). Open Mon.-Fri. 9am-8pm, Sat. 9am-noon.

Airport: Accessible by *combi* (every hr., 3 pesos) from the **Mexicana office,** Hidalgo 406. Open Mon.-Fri. 9am-6:30pm, Sat. 9am-5:30pm. They provide the airport's only service to Los Angeles (daily, US$140), Mexico City (daily, 232 pesos), and Tijuana (daily, 425 pesos).

Train Station: Estación de Ferrocarriles (tel. 2-12-04), on González Ortega southeast of *el centro.* A walkable distance from downtown, but all bus routes also pass the station. Southward to: Mexico City (at 8pm, 55 pesos) via Querétaro (36 pesos). Northward toward Ciudad Juárez (at 9:30am, 35 pesos) via Torreón (12 pesos).

Bus Station: Central de Autobuses, Lomas de la Isabélica at Tránsito Pesado (tel. 2-11-12). **Autobuses III Blancos, El Aguila, Autobús de Mexico, Transportes Zacatecas,** and **Camiones Rojos de los Altos** all exist here, but **Estrella Blanca** has the most destinations by far: Monterrey (every hr., 38 pesos); Aguascalientes (every ½hr., 11 pesos); Mexico City (20 per day, 57 pesos); San Luis Potosí (7 per day, 16 pesos) and Guadalajara (hourly, 36 pesos) are among them.

Car Rental: Budget, Mateos 104 (tel. 2-94-58). 2-door Subaru 101 pesos per day, .70 pesos per km.

Laundromat: Rosa Blanca, López Mateos 129, ½ block downhill past the Hotel Colón. 16 pesos for 3kg. Open Mon.-Fri. 8am-7pm, Sat. 8am-5pm.

Red Cross: (tel. 2-30-05) on Héroes de Chapultepec.

Pharmacy: Las Perlas Hidalgo 131, (tel. 2-14-09). Open daily 9am-9:30pm.

Hospital: Hospital General, García Salinas 707 (tel. 3-30-04).

Emergency: tel. 06.

Police: (tel. 2-05-07), on 5 Señores.

ACCOMMODATIONS

Unfortunately, the less expensive hotels in Zacatecas tend to be dingier than budget hotels elsewhere in Mexico. Unless you are able to spend approximately 60 pesos for a single, the youth hostel is the cleanest and least depressing option.

CREA Youth Hostel (HI), Lago La Encantada (tel. 2-11-51), southwest of the city. You'll never find it on foot; fortunately, yellow "Ruta 8" buses run from the Pl. Independencia and from the bus station. Ask drivers for the *Albergues CREA* or get off at the sign for La Encantada. On the city's public land equipped with soccer field, swimming pool and courts for basketball, volleyball and racquetball, the hostel is surrounded by rose bushes and kids. The small, sterile rooms sleep 4 people. Single-sex floors. Clean communal bathroom. 11 pesos per person. Breakfast 9 pesos, lunch and dinner 11.50 pesos each. Open daily 7am-11pm.

Hotel Candesa, Juárez 102 across the street from Pl. Independencia. 3 floors of clean, comfortable modern views. Rooms overlooking Juárez are particularly nice, though almost all have windows. Singles 60 pesos. Doubles 75 pesos.

Hotel El Parque, Gonzalez Ortega 302, near the aqueduct. A longish haul with packs in a quiet area next to a nice park. The rooms are depressingly dark in this modern building, though clean, in a shabby way. Singles 40 pesos. Doubles 50 pesos.

Hotel Zamora, Juárez at Pl. Independencia (tel. 2-12-00). Central location a definite plus. Dirty yellow courtyard leads into somewhat less dirty rooms with less than comfortable beds. Singles 30 pesos. Doubles 40 pesos.

FOOD

Café Acrópolis, on Hidalgo near the cathedral (tel. 2-12-84). Prime location with prices to suit. The brown vinyl booths are filled with middle-aged women and the odd bunch of teenagers gossiping over coffee. Breakfasts 15 pesos. *Quesadillas* on pita bread 13 pesos. Open daily 8am-10:30pm.

La Terraza, in mall right next to cathedral. Although the menu is limited, the atmosphere is pleasant with tables outside on a terrace overlooking the city. Hamburgers 3.50 pesos. Ice cream 3 pesos. Coffee 2.50 pesos. Open daily 10am-9pm.

El Tragadero, Juárez 132. Decorated with New England treescapes, a suit of armor and tasteful hanging lamps. Delicious aromas waft tableward. *Lomito Zacatecas* 7.50 pesos, onion soup 4 pesos. Open daily 8am-10pm.

Café Zas, Hidalgo 201. Lots of couples fill the brown-vinyl booths, eating dessert and listening to the radio. *enchiladas* 6 pesos. Chicken 14 pesos. Coffee 3 pesos. Open daily 8am-10pm.

Los Faroles, Tacuba 129, 2 blocks from the cathedral. Yellow and brown dominate. Tacos in a rainbow of flavors 2 pesos each. Beer 2.50 pesos. Open daily 1pm-midnight.

SIGHTS

Zacatecas's steep winding streets are anointed with colonial churches, monasteries, and plazas. Keep the map in your pocket and you may round a corner and find yourself face-to-face with a soaring red *cantera* stone cathedral, a crumbling convent, or a bustling market.

The towering 18th-century **cathedral,** on Hidalgo four blocks northeast of Juárez, combines three architectural styles. The northern façade is Churrigueresque, the southern is European baroque, while the western facade, a richly carved celebration of the Eucharist, is rumored to be the country's most lavish example of Mexican baroque. St. Gregory's cowboy hat is said to be the signature of the cathedral's unknown Spanish architect. (Open daily 8am-noon and 5-8:30pm.)

The **Palacio de Gobierno,** now the state capitol, stands next to the cathedral. Its centerpiece is the arresting mural which surrounds the interior stairwell. Executed in 1970 by the prominent artist Antonio Pintor Rodríguez, the work traces the history of Zacatecas from the heyday of the Cascanes *indígenas* to today's industrial sophistication. (Open Mon.-Fri. 8am-8pm.)

Across Hidalgo and up the steep Callejón de Veyna, is the **Templo de Santo Domingo.** Built by the Jesuits in 1746, the church contains eight impressive baroque altars of gilded wood and an elaborate 18th-century German pipe organ. (Open daily 10am-2pm and 4-7pm.) Next door, in a building whose past incarnations include a monastery and a jail, is the **Museo de Pedro Coronel,** named after the Zacatecan artist (1922-1985) and containing his tomb, sculptures, and paintings, and one of the best modern art collections in Latin America. Works by Picasso, Braque, Chagall, and Miró jostle for space amidst extensive exhibits of Hogarth's tragicomic drawings and Daumier's caricatures. Mesoamerican and African masks, as well as Japanese, Chinese, Tibetan, Greek, and Roman pieces break the Eurocentric spell. (Open Fri.-Wed. 10am-2pm and 4-7pm, Sun. 10am-5pm. Admission 8 pesos.)

The **Museo Rafael Coronel** is housed amidst the dramatic ruins and plentiful sculpted gardens of the **Ex-Convento de San Francisco.** To get there from the cathedral, follow Hidalgo. At the first fork, bear left; at the second, bear right. The museum's reputation rests on its fabulous collection of masks from around the world, gathered by Rafael Coronel (incidentally the grandson of muralist Diego Rivera). Subsequent galleries boast local "primitive" figurines and Mesoamerican pottery. The final chambers are dedicated to a playful collection of marionettes depicting scenes ranging from hell to a military parade to a village wedding. (Museum open Thurs.-Sat. 10am-2pm and 4-7pm. Admission 5 pesos. Ex-Convent open daily 10am-10pm. Free.)

Southeast of downtown, 39 rose-colored arches mark the end of Zacatecas's famous colonial aqueduct, **El Cubo.** Beside the aqueduct, the verdant **Parque Estrada** borders the former governor's mansion, now the **Museo de Francisco Goitia.** The museum contains a permanent exhibit of the work of Goitia and four other renowned 20th-century Zacatecan artists, including Pedro Coronel and his younger brother Rafael. (Open Tues.-Sun. 10am-2pm and 5-7pm. Admission 5 pesos, student groups free. Sun. free.)

The **Cerro de la Bufa,** named for its resemblance to a Spanish wine-stone, peers down from the city's highest crag. The adjacent **Museo de la Toma de Zacatecas,** erected to commemorate Pancho Villa's decisive victory over Victoriano Huerta's federal troops in the summer of 1914, lays claim to a fascinating array of photographs, cannon, small arms, and other revolutionary memorabilia. (Open Tues.-Sun. 10am-5pm. Admission 5 pesos. Sun. free.) The museum is flanked by a monument to the revolution installed in 1989 to mark the 75th anniversary of the Battle of Zacatecas, and by the early 18th-century **Capilla del Patrocinio,** whose gracefully sculpted *cantera* facade and cloistered courtyards are carved from deep red Zacatecan stone. A short but steep assault on the peak of the hill leads to the **Mausoleo de los Hombres Ilustres de Zacatecas.** The ornate, Moorish structure is worth the hike if only for the view of the city. An even better vista is available from the **Meteorological Observatory,** behind the museum. Also in the vicinity of the museum are a few shops selling arts and crafts, and lodes of geodes for rock jocks. Just below the shops, several small stands serve snacks. Unfortunately, public buses run to La Bufa only on religious holidays, and taxis suck up 5 pesos. The most appealing way to make the trip is by **teleférico** (cable car), which runs between the peak of El Grillo hill and La Bufa every 10 minutes. The imported Swiss cars carry passengers on a seven-and-a-half-minute journey high above Zacatecas. (Open daily 12:30-7:30pm. 8 pesos round-trip. Cable cars run in fine weather only.) Follow Calle Garcia Rojas to its end to the cable car stop.

The **Mina de Edén** (tel. 2-30-02) was one of the region's most productive silver mines during the 19th and early 20th centuries. To get to the mine entrance, follow Juárez northwest (along the *Alameda*, an oblong park lined by some of Zacatecas's grandest colonial mansions), continue along Torreón until it ends, and then turn right—the mine is on that street. About 30 years ago, continual flooding from underground springs made mineral extraction uneconomical. Today a mini-locomotive whisks tourists into the mountain, where they are treated to a guided tour (in Spanish) of the cool subterranean tunnels. A pricy **souvenir shop** down below sells chunks of silver. A **restaurant** and **disco** have crept into one of the mine's larger caverns; on weekends the same locomotive carts partiers who dance to the latest U.S. top-40 hits and buy expensive drinks. (Mine open daily noon-7:30pm. Admission 10 pesos. Disco open Thurs.-Sun. 9pm-3am. Cover 30 pesos.)

Trips to La Bufa and Mina de Edén can easily be combined. At the end of the mine tour, you can either go back the way you came or take an elevator up to El Grillo, where you can catch the *teleférico* to La Bufa. The entire excursion takes about two hours.

■ Near Zacatecas: Guadalupe

The **Museo de Virreinal** (open Tues.-Sun. 10am-5pm; admission 10 pesos) is in the beautiful tiny village of Guadalupe, 7km east of Zacatecas on the highway to Mexico City. A Franciscan convent built in 1707, the museum contains the finest collection of colonial art in the republic. Highlights include a mural by the 18th-century painter Miguel Cabrera, two 16th-century mosaics of St. Peter and St. Francis comprised solely of bird feathers and a 1621 Gutenberg volume on mining. The exhibit is superb. Ask to be shown the choir room where the 30 resident Franciscan monks gather every afternoon for prayer and hymnody. Two people standing in opposite corners of the room can carry on a conversation by whispering into the walls. (Open Tues.-Sun. 10am-4:30pm. Admission 10 pesos, students free.) The collection of antique wagons, carriages, and cars housed next door in the fledgling **Museo Regional** (tel. 3-20-89) is worth a quick peek. (Open Tues.-Sun. 10am-5pm. Free.) "Ruta 13" buses to Guadalupe (.60 pesos) leave from the *Centro Comercial* carpark at the corner of Salazar and López Mateos every 15 minutes.

■ Northeast México

The cities of northeastern Mexico are often regarded as portals into the country or as pollution-spewing industrial centers; most travelers pass through without appreciating their surroundings. While the area is by no stretch of the imagination the most scenic in the Republic, it is not altogether devoid of charm. Matamoros introduces the traveler to the country's history and to border-town commercialism. Monterrey's wealth has brought a misplaced modicum of cultural sophistication to the city, while Saltillo effortlessly retains a certain unspoiled grace.

COAHUILA

■■■ SALTILLO

Unlike its booming neighbor, Saltillo retains the relaxing small-town feel which Monterrey has forsaken in its quest for economic prosperity. Though the population of this state capital of Coahuila has swelled to over 700,000, Saltillo offers a pace of life that is refreshingly slow. Few structures tower more than a few stories, and the scattered government buildings blend easily into the surroundings. The buses slow down and actually stop for pedestrians crossing the street. Saltillo's homey charm, lack of egotistical ambition, and dry climate make it a prime choice for those en route to Mexico City or other more frequented tourist havens.

Saltillo prides itself on its citizens and history. The first inhabitants of the mountainous region were 400 Tlaxcalteca families. These families were craftsmen and weavers by profession and began weaving the brightly colored *sarapes* that are a symbol of Saltillo today. Saltillo's other claim to fame is that it is the birthplace of Venustiano Carranza, the "father of the Mexican Constitution," a general of the Revolution, and Francisco Madero, the first man to seize power from Díaz in 1911. A good time to visit is during the **Feria de Saltillo,** a series of artistic and cultural events from July 18 to August 3.

ORIENTATION

Nestled in a valley surrounded by the jagged Sierra Madre mountains, Saltillo lies 87km southwest of Monterrey, along the desolate Highway 40, which roffers great views of the mountains. Frequent buses plod to and from Monterrey, Guadalajara, San Luis Potosí and Mexico City. Trains are less frequent but chug by en route from Nuevo Laredo to Mexico City and Monterrey to San Luis Potosí.

The **Central de Autobuses** is located about 3km southwest of city center on Blvd. Echeverría Sur. Transport to and from the city center is cheap and easy. After you exit the bus terminal, cross the pedestrian overpass and catch minibus #10 from the small street perpendicular to the boulevard, on the side of Restaurant Jaslo. All buses cost .80 pesos and run daily 6:30am-11pm. Catch a return bus at the corner of **Aldama** and **Hidalgo,** a block down the street from the Cathedral, in front of the entry to the big furniture store.

The train station is much closer to the city center (about 1km) but still a hike if you are laden with baggage. Exit onto Emilio Carranza, turn left, and walk about 400m to **R. Arizpe.** Turn right up to the Alameda. Alternatively, minibus #1B along E. Carranza will take you directly to the center; taxis should charge about 10 pesos.

Although great accommodations can be found near the bus station, most hotels, restaurants, and sights of interest for the budget traveler are located in the center of Saltillo, in or around the two main plazas. The center's streets form a slightly distorted grid not quite aligned with the four cardinal directions. The quiet **Plaza de Armas,** formerly the city's main plaza, contains the cathedral and is bordered by Victoria to the south and Hidalgo to the east. To get to the **Plaza Acuña,** the more commercial of the two, continue past the cathedral down Hidalgo for a block, turn left on Aldama and walk one more block. Plaza Acuña will be on your right.

PRACTICAL INFORMATION

Tourist Office: Acuña and Blvd. Francisco Coss (tel. 12-40-50), about 1.5km north of the center, in the old, red railway station building. Accessible by the same #1B bus from the center and train station. Excellent maps of Saltillo. Open daily 9am-5pm.

Currency Exchange: Unlike many other cities, banks in Saltillo offer the best exchange rates, however, they change dollars only. Most are on Victoria which begins behind the Palacio de Gobierno, across from the cathedral at Plaza de Armas. There are only four *casas de cambio* in the whole city, all offering poor rates—exchange pesos before coming to Saltillo. Closest to the city center is **Casa de Cambio Coin,** Acuña 167 (tel. 14-12-96), across the street from Hotel San Jorge, which changes traveler's checks at miserable rates. Open Mon.-Fri. 9am-1:30pm and 3:30-6pm, Sat. 9am-1pm. **Banamex,** at Allende and Ocampo, behind the Palacio de Gobierno, has a 24-hr. ATM that takes almost anything; AmEx, MC, Visa, Cirrus, and Plus.

Post Office: Victoria 453 (tel. 12-20-90), after Urdiñola. Open for stamps and *Lista de Correos* Mon.-Fri. 9am-5pm, Sat. 9am-1pm. Other branches in the bus station and by the tourist office. Both Mon.-Fri. 8am-3pm. **Postal code:** 25000.

Telephones: Collect calls and direct dial can be made from the pay phones in the post office. Long distance calls paid for directly can be made from Café Victoria, Padre Flores 221. Long distance lines in the bus station as well. **Telephone code:** 84.

Telegrams: Directly next door to the post office on Victoria. Open Mon.-Fri. 9am-5pm, Sat. 9am-noon.

Airport: Aeropuerto Plan de Guadalupe, 20min. northeast of city center off Hwy. 40. The **Saltill-Ramos Arizpe** bus from the bus station or along Acuña in the center can let you off 200m from the airport if you signal the driver on time (until 10:30pm, 1 peso). Taxis in Pl. Acuña charge about 3 pesos to the airport. **Taesa** flies to Mexico City (7am, 260 pesos). Tickets can be purchased at the travel agency in the Hotel San Jorge (tel. 14-95-84). Make reservations 1-2 days in advance.

Trains: E. Carranza, past the Alameda (tel. 14-95-84). The 2 major lines are from Nuevo Laredo to Mexico City and to Piedras Negras. Daily to: Mexico City 1st class (10:15pm, 12hrs., 88 pesos), 2nd class (3am, 20 hrs., 27 pesos), Piedras Negras (8:15am, 12-14hrs., 15 pesos).

Bus Station: Central de Autobuses, Echeverría Sur and Garza, reachable by mini-bus #10. **Transportes del Norte** (17-07-08), to: Mexico City (8 per day, 92 pesos), Durango (8 per day, 58 pesos), San Luis Potosí (6 per day, 43 pesos), Tampico (6:45, 48 pesos). **Omnibus de México** (tel. 17-03-15) to: Reynosa (12 per day, 32 pesos), Matamoros (9 per day, 42 pesos), Aguascalientes (6 per day, 51 pesos), Mexico City (9 per day, 91 pesos). **Tranportes Frontera** to: Guadalajara (8 per day, 65 pesos), Zacatecas (every hour, 24hrs., 31 pesos), Torreon (every 15mins., 24 hrs., 24 pesos). **Autobuses Blancos** (tel. 17-01-83) to: Tijuana (10pm, 382 pesos), Hermosillo (10pm, 310 pesos), Celaya (7pm, 86 pesos), Moreila (7pm, 102 pesos), Uruapan (7pm, 115 pesos).

Market: De las Fuentes, Treviño 328, between Allende and Acuña also at the bus station, across Blvd. Echverña Sur. Open Mon.-Fri. 9am-8pm, Sat. 9am-9pm, Sun. 9am-3pm. **Soriana,** at Blvd. Francisco Coss. Open Mon.-Sat. 9am-8pm, Sun. 9am-3pm.

Laundry: Laundrymatic, Mutualismo Pte. 310, at Allende, near the tourist office. Self-service 6 pesos to wash and dry. For full service, leave 3 pesos per kg. Open Mon.-Fri. 9am-1pm and 3-8pm.

Red Cross: Cárdenas and Rayón (tel. 14-33-33), northeast of the city center. 24 hrs.

SALTILLO

Hospital: Hospital Universitario, Madero 1291 (tel. 12-30-00). 24 hrs.
Police: Treviño and Echeverría Ote. (tel. 15-55-61 and 15-51-62). 24-hr. **emergency phone:** 06.

ACCOMMODATIONS

A few inexpensive and comfortable hotels lie just across the street from the bus station, and there are plenty to be found within a few blocks. Because Saltillo sees relatively few tourists, the few budget accommodations near the center tend not to fill up and offer better conditions for fewer pesos.

Near the center

Hotel Saade, Aldama Pte. 397 (tel. 12-91-20 or 12-91-21), is 1 block west of Pl. Acuña. Professional and well-kept but slightly worn, with bright, airy hallways and clean rooms. (Singles 65 pesos, with TV 75 pesos, doubles 75 pesos, with TV 85 pesos.) **Hotel De Avila,** Padre Flores 211 (tel. 12-59-16). Don't let the huge "Hotel Jardín" sign above fool you. Primo location at the corner of Mercado Juárez, but rooms and floors could use a dusting. Light yellow and baby blue decor will either lull you to sleep or give you inland sea-sickness. An occassional TV. (Singles 40 pesos, doubles 50 pesos.) **Hotel Premier,** at the corner of Allende and Múzquiz (tel. 12-10-50), about 2 blocks down from Pl. Acuña along Allende Similar to Saad, but with even cleaner and fresher room. Phone, TV, and choice bottled water in each. (Singles 75 pesos, doubles 90-100 pesos.)

Across from the bus station

Hotel Central, Echeverría 231 (tel. 17-00-04 or 17-09-03), sits next door to the Hotel Saltillo (below). Lacks the extra touch, but easily compensates with comfort and low price. (Singles 30 pesos, doubles 40 pesos.) **Hotel Saltillo,** Echeverría 249 (tel. 17-22-00), is located directly across from the bus station. Entrepreneurial manager might talk your ear off, but it's worth hearing him out. Spanking new hotel. Untainted rooms have color TV and telephone. Adjoining 24-hr. seafood restaurant. (Singles 75 pesos., doubles with 2 beds 100 pesos.) **Hotel Siesta,** (tel. 17-07-24), to the left of Saltillo. Is almost identical with Central, but has higher prices and stuffier rooms. (Singles 35 pesos, with TV 55 pesos; doubles 50 pesos, with TV 75 pesos.)

FOOD

Saltillo hasn't yet been pegged by the multinational fast-food chains or the mod *cafeterías* that plague Monterrey. Although most eateries are simple family-run cafeterias, there are a few larger restaurants with more varied and distinctive menus.

Boca del Río, Acuña 533 Nte. (tel. 12-41-05), 2 blocks north of Pl. Acuña. Immense restaurant serves only massive portions of sea critters. Anchors and tillers crowd the walls and a giant iron swordfish guards the grill. Octopus in its ink 26 pesos. Fish filet prepared as you like 15-20 pesos. Open daily 9am-10pm.
Taquería Alanís, Padre Flores 231 (tel. 14-09-29). Slightly upscale *taquería* with flower baskets hanging from the ceiling. Sit at the long taco bar to order individual tacos to your belly's content (all kinds only 1.20 pesos a piece).
Café Victoria, Padre Flores 221 (tel. 12-91-31). Clean and efficient cafeteria is well-occupied at all hours. Large *cafés con leche* and baskets of sweet bread popular in the morning. Entrees 6-18 pesos. Open daily 7am-10:30pm.
Restaurant Jalso, Echeverría and Ramón Ruiz (tel. 17-09-75), across the pedestrian overpass from the bus station. Great for a quick breakfast or lunch en route to the city. *Comida corrida* 15 pesos, breakfasts for 12 pesos, entrees 5-19 pesos. Open daily 7am-midnight.
Restaurant El Principal, Allende 702 (tel. 14-33-84), at the corner with Alessio Robles, 4 blocks down Allende from Pl. Acuña. The inevitable window display of freshly roasted baby-goats. Happily orange tablecloths provide nice colorful accents in the stylish brown interior with intimate booths, a small atrium, and

hundreds of pictures on the walls. Standard Mexican fare 4-15 pesos. *Cabrito* in a cardboard box for those on the go. Open daily 7am-midnight.

SIGHTS

Although you won't tire from running sight to sight in Saltillo, the few worthy points make for sedate yet satisfying enjoyment. The city offers more beautiful and better-preserved architecture than other northern cities and plenty of pleasant spots to sit outside and enjoy the festive atmosphere. The **Plaza de Armas,** Saltillo's main plaza, differs slightly from the crowded and noisy *zócalos* found in other large Mexican cities. This paved plaza contains neither trees nor benches, but a central fountain gives it a slightly southern European feel. On the east side of the plaza, 200 years of holiness have left the Churrigueresque **Cathedral** in good condition. Try to come in the evening when the bells ring, as families cluster around the fountain and the setting sun highlights the cathedral against the dark mountains behind. On the south side of the plaza is the **Cavie Museum,** which houses exhibits of regional literature, art and culture that change every two to three months. (Open Tues.-Sun. 9am-7pm. Free.) Knock on the door of the adjoining IEBA (Instiuto Estatal de Bellas Artes) if the museum is closed during normal hours.

   Plaza Acuña, two blocks northwest of the Plaza de Armas, bustles. Vendors spill out of the **Mercado Juárez,** in the northwest corner of the plaza, while xylophonists hammer away and guitar-players and accordionists rove through the crowds. A typical northern market, it sells mostly souvenir items including hats, rugs, ukeleles and colorful *sarapes.* (Open daily 8:30am-8pm.)

   Once you've relaxed in the Pl. de Armas, try relaxing in the **Alameda,** just west of the city center (follow Victoria west from Pl. de Armas), or in the **Church and Park San Francisco,** south of Pl. de Armas. The Alameda is larger and more shaded than others in the north, filled with winding paths frequented by herds of joggers in the wee hours. San Francisco Park is at the corner of Juárez and Cepeda. Plaza Mexico or **El Mirador** (aptly named by the locals), on a hill above the city, offers an astonishing panoramic view of the whole area and the unconquerable mountains around. Take Miguel Hidalgo uphill for a kilometer, turn left on General Cepeda and follow it for another 20-50m, turning onto the winding Gustavo Espinoza to the small plaza with benches and nice old street lamps.

NUEVO LEÓN

■■■ MONTERREY

Unbeknown to most travelers, Monterrey prospers as the base of Mexico's largest industrial complex, a testimonial to the painful potential of development. The downtown *Zona Rosa's* gaudy overexertion cannot sustain itself for more than a few miles from the gleaming epicenter. Although Monterrey lacks baroque churches and ancient ruins, it offers a breath-altering skyline with skyscrapers set against the untouched (if sometimes smoggy) Sierra Madres.

ORIENTATION

As the largest city in northern Mexico, Monterrey is an important transportation hub. All **buses** in and out of the city pass through Monterrey's gargantuan **Central Camionera** at Av. Colón and Villagrán. To reach the center from the bus station, simply take any bus heading south on Pino Suárez. No. 18 stops at Pino Suárez and Colón and will let you off at the southern end of the central Gran Plaza. All local buses run from 6am-11pm. Easier still, hail a **taxi;** you can probably finagle a fare of 20 pesos to the *Zona Rosa.*

The **train station** is at Calzada Victoria, six blocks west of the bus station. To get to the bus station, walk straight ahead on Victoria for two blocks, turn right on Bernardo Reyes, then left on Colón. Bus and train stations are in the northern end of the city, 3km north of the *centro*.

Downtown, **Avenida Constitución** runs west and east along the Río Catarina, a dry 10km-long riverbed that has been converted into athletic fields. From west to east, the largest streets running north-south across Constitución are Gonzalitos, Pino Suárez, Cuauhtémoc, Benito Juárez, Zaragoza and Zua Zua. From north to south, streets running east-west parallel to Constitución are Ocampo, Hidalgo, Padre Mier, Matamoros, 15 de Mayo and Washington. Around Morelos sprawls the *Zona Rosa*, bounded by Padre Mier, Zaragoza, Ocampo and Juárez.

PRACTICAL INFORMATION

Tourist Office: Oficina de Turismo, Zaragoza at Matamoros (tel. 345-08-70 or 345-09-02, also toll free from the U.S. (800) 235-2438 and from Nuevo León 91 800 83-222), in the gray complex of modern buildings on the lower level of the west side of the main plaza. Follow the blue "INFOTUR" signs for English assistance and maps. Open daily 10am-5pm.

Consulates: U.S., Constitución Pte. 411 (tel. 345-21-20), downtown. **U.K.,** PRIV Tamazunchale 104 (tel. 356-91-14). Both are open Mon.-Fri. 8am-5pm.

Currency Exchange: Banks flood the *Zona Rosa* and line Padre Mier in particular, but they don't cash traveler's checks. Most open Mon.-Fri. 9am-1:30pm. **Casa de Cambio Trebol,** Padre Mier Pte. (tel. 42-21-40), across from the Banco Internacional, changes traveler's checks. Open Mon.-Fri. 9am-6pm, Sat. 9am-1pm. Traveler's checks 9am-2pm only, but they may run out of pesos. The best bet for exchanging AmEx checks is at the American Express office (see below).

American Express: Padre Mier Pte. 1424 (tel. 43-09-10), about 1.5km west of the *centro*. Take #4 bus on Padre Mier from the *Zona Rosa*. Open Mon.-Fri. 9am-1pm and 3-6pm, Sat. 9am-1pm.

Post Office: Zaragoza at Washington (tel. 42-40-03), inside the Palacio Federal. Open for stamps Mon.-Fri. 8am-7pm, Sat. 9am-1pm; for registered mail Mon.-Fri. 8am-5pm. **Postal Code:** 64000.

Telephones: Long-distance phones in the pharmacy at the bus station. Long-distance office on 5 de Mayo between Carranza and Galeana. No change for collect calls. Open daily 9am-8pm. Most hotels also offer international services for nominal fees. **Telephone Code:** 83.

Telegrams: Above the post office. Open Mon.-Fri. 9am-8pm, Sat. 9am-1pm.

Airport: 4km northeast of the city center. Taxis charge 27 pesos for the trip, *colectivos* only 11 pesos.

Airlines: Aeroméxico, Cuauhtémoc 818 Sur at Padre Mier (tel. 344-00-87; reservations: 343-55-60), to Mexico City (13 per day, 1½hrs., 454 pesos); Guadalajara (6 per day, 431 pesos); Villahermosa (3 per day, 901 pesos); Hermosillo (2 per day, 654 pesos). **Mexicana,** Hidalgo 922 Pte. (tel. 340-55-11); to Mexico City (6 per day, 500 pesos); Guadalajara (6 daily, 828 pesos); Hermosillo (2 per day, 1347 pesos). **Aerolitoral** (tel. 343-55-60), to Villahermosa (683 pesos); **American Airlines,** Zaragoza 1300 Sur (tel. 340-30-31). **Continental,** Insurgentes 2500 (tel. 33-26-82). All offices open Mon.-Fri. 9am-7pm, Sat. 9am-1pm. Make reservations at least 2-3 days in advance, more for weekend travel.

Train Station: Región Noreste, Calzada Victoria (tel. 375-46-04). The daily train to Mexico City (87 pesos) via Saltillo (10 pesos) is slower and more expensive than the buses.

Bus Station: Colón at Villagrán to Amado Nervo. Center of a bus route universe. **Transportes del Norte,** (tel. 375-42-81) to: Mexico City (14 per day, 12hrs., 100 pesos); Guadalajara (8 per day, 10hrs., 90 pesos); Querétaro (5 per day, 8hrs., 76 pesos); Chihuahua (6 per day, 85 pesos); Aguascalientes (5 per day, 59 pesos); Durango (6 per day, 67 pesos); Mazatlán (4 per day, 100 pesos); Tampico (5 per day, 6hrs., 55 pesos); San Luis (10 per day, 54 pesos); Matamoros (5 per day, 32 pesos); Reynosa (6 per day, 23 pesos); and an hourly service which runs 24hrs. a day to Laredo (28 pesos) and Torreon (38 pesos). **Transportes Frontera,** (tel.

375-09-87) to: Tampico (5 per day, 8hrs., 44 pesos); Tuxpan (4 per day, 10 hrs., 66 pesos); Salamanca (3 per day, 67 pesos); Mexico City (6 per day, 12hrs., 83 pesos). **Autobuses Anahuac,** (tel. 375-64-80) to Morelos (7 per day, 38 pesos). **Estrella Blanca,** (tel. 375-09-87) to Zacatecas (14 per day, 38 pesos). **Rojo de Los Altos,** (tel. 374-72-73) next to Frontiera, by Sala 4 to: Saltillo, every 15min., 24hrs. a day (7.50 pesos). **Futura** and **Turistar** have fewer, more luxurious buses (20-50 pesos more than above prices). The bus station has a 24-hr. pharamacy, an emergency medical help unit in the basement, long distance phone service, and 24-hr. luggage storage in Sala 4 (.80 pesos an hour).

English Bookstore: Sanborn's Department Store, Escombedo just south of Morelos. Open daily 7:30am-11pm. **VIP's,** Hidalgo and Emilio Carranza. Open daily 8am-11pm. **Iztlacihuatl,** Morelos, between Escobedo and Emilio Carranza. Open Mon.-Sat. 10am-8pm.

Market: Gigante, just over the pedestrian overpass from the bus station. Open daily 9am-9pm. **Mercado del Norte,** also known as La Pulga, this huge street market starts about two blocks to your left as you exit the bus station. Anything from cologne to car tires sold daily 7am-10pm.

Medical Emergencies and Assitance: Red Cross, at Alfonso Reyes and Henry (tel. 342-12-12 or 375-12-12), 24hrs. **Cruz Verde,** at Ciudad Madero and Ciudad Victorio (tel. 371-50-50 or 371-52-59), 24hrs.

24-hr. Pharmacy: In the bus station or **Benavides,** at Pino Suárez and 15 de Mayo.

Emergency: Tel. 06.

Police: at Venustanio Carranza and Roberto Matínez, to report theft or loss.

ACCOMMODATIONS

Hotels in Monterrey tend to be overpriced. The unpleasant area around the bus station is home to most of the city's budget hotels, including all those listed below. Many rooms are full by early afternoon. If you are staying in this area alone, take precautions when walking at night, since the streets become deserted around 10pm.

Hotel Conde, Reforma Pte. 427 (tel. 375-71-59 and 372-18-79), off the labryinthine market on your right after heading left (east) down Colón from the bus station. This spotless, modern hotel outshines the others in the area. Sterile rooms have fans, TVs, and phones. Singles or doubles 66 pesos, with A/C 77 pesos.

Hotel Nuevo León, Amado Nervo 1007 (tel. 374-19-00). The best pick of its neighbors on Amado Nervo. Clean and quiet lobby and hallways. Rooms lack spots and some furniture. Hallway phone available. Singles 55 pesos.

Hotel Virreyes, Amado Nervo 902 (tel. 74-66-10). Stalactite-adorned ceilings. The grandmotherly *dueña* may show more concern for you than is necessary. Large rooms a bargain for a big group. Phones. Singles or doubles 50 pesos, with A/C 70 pesos. Room for four with noisy A/C 90 pesos.

Hotel Posada, Amado Nervo 1138 (tel.3 72-39-08). Closest to the bus station means a few pesos more. Small clean rooms with TVs and phones. Adjoining restaurant open 24 hrs. Singles and doubles 66 pesos.

FOOD

Barbecued meats, especially *cabrito* (goat kid), are a specialty of northern Mexico. Charcoal-broiled specimens in restaurant windows lure hungry passersby. Popular dishes include *agujas* (collar bone), *frijoles a la charra* or *borrachos* (beans cooked with pork skin, coriander, tomato, peppers and onions), *machacado con huevos* (scrambled eggs mixed with dried, shredded beef), hot tamales and, for dessert, *piloncillo con nuez* (hardened brown sugar candy with nuts) or *glorias* (candy balls of goat's milk and nuts). Downtown Monterrey is littered with fast-food joints, while the bus station area is filled with cheap, but possibly unhealthy restaurants.

Cafetería y Mariscos Flores, Colón 876, across the street from the bus station. Casual and cheerful. Colorful tablecloths and *piñatas* hanging from the ceiling.

MONTERREY

True to its claim, "Always the attention you deserve." Entrees 8-15 pesos. *Comida corrida* 9 pesos, breakfast 5 pesos.

Restaurant Cuatro Milpas, Madero at Julián Villagran (tel. 374-36-03), near the bus station. Ranch-style BBQ smell and atmosphere. The log cabin/ranch house decor takes you away from the concrete jungle. *Machacado* 15 pesos. *Cabrito* filet 35 pesos. Open 24 hrs.

La Puntada, Hidalgo Ote. 123 (tel. 340-69-85), near Juárez in the *Zona Rosa*. Efficient service allows quick turnover of much-coveted tables. Varied menu features piping hot homemade flour tortillas, juices and milkshake-type drinks—pineapple, papaya or melon. Most entrees 6-12 pesos. Open daily 7am-10pm.

Los Pilares, Hidalgo 485 Ote. and Escobedo (tel. 345-36-01), at the Zona Rosa's mini-plaza with the cool fountain. A refrigerated happily pink and green interior offers a peaceful refuge from the bustling heat of the city. All-you-can-eat Mexican and regional fare for 20 pesos daily noon-4pm. All-you-can-eat breakfast for 15 pesos daily 7-11:30am. Entrees range 8-30 pesos. Open daily 7am-midnight.

SIGHTS

Monterrey's disproportionately huge and loud Gran Plaza, also known to many locals as "la Macro" shows the style-less hypocrisy of *nouveau riche* arrogance. La Macro replaced hundreds of old townhouses, as if trying to reject the painful realities of poverty and misery just a few kilometers away. The plaza is bounded by Washington on the north, Constitución on the south, Zaragoza on the west and Zua Zua on the east. The stylish colonial Palacio de Gobierno, which houses the cabinet of the governor of Nuevo Leon state, loiters at its very northern extreme. In front of its southern facade, fountains, waterfalls, and statues of illustrious Mexicans punctuate the **Esplanada de los Héros.** Miguel Hidalgo stands at the northwest corner, Benito Juárez at the northeast, Morelos at the southwest, and Carranza at the southeast. South of the Esplanada is **Parque Hundido** (Sunken Park), a cool and verdant garden gateway for the city's young couples, surrounded by an overlooking complex of tastelessly dark-grey concrete buildings: **Congreso del Estado, Palacio Legislativo,** and **Teatro de La Ciudad.** Further along the Gran Plaza sits **Fuente de La Vida** (Fountain of Life) which douses an immense statue of Neptune with cavorting nymphs and naiads, across the street from the **Monumento al Obrero.** The ultimate addition to the stylistic disjointedness of the whole plaza, however, is the painfully orange needle-like 30m high structure called **Faro del Comercio** (Lighthouse of Business), across Blvd. Zua Zua. from the humble-yet-stately **Catedral.** La Macro's south end is marked by the metal and concrete cube of the **Palacio Municipal**—yet another bow to bureaucracy. The most balanced and tasteful modern buiding in the Plaza is the fascinating **MARCO** (Museo de Arte Contemporaro), Monterrrey's museum of contemporary art, just across the small street from the cathedral. MARCO displays modern Mexican art and major travelling exhibits. (Open Tues. and Thurs.-Sat. 11am-7pm, Wed. and Sun. 11am-9pm. Admission 10 pesos. Students with ID 5 pesos. Free on Wed.)

The **Obispado,** former palace of the bishop of Monterrey, is now a state museum. Constructed in the late 18th century on the side of a hill overlooking the city (ostensibly to employ drought-ravaged *indígenas*), the palace served in the 1860s as a fortress for both the French and Mexican armies. In 1915, Pancho Villa's revolutionary forces stormed the palace and drove the loyalists of Porfirio Díaz out of Monterrey. The museum displays murals, paintings, historic pictures and old weapons, but the view of the city from the site and the decayed exterior are more of a draw than the museum itself. (Open Tues.-Sat. 10am-6pm, Sun. 10am-5pm. Admission 10 pesos.) Take bus #4 from Washington or Juárez crosspoint of Pare Mier and Degollado. Ask the driver to point out the stop.

The Cuauhtémoc Company, for over a century the major producer of beer in Monterrey, has graciously converted one of its old factories into the **Jardines Cuauhtémoc,** two blocks west on Colón and about four blocks north on Universidad from the bus terminal. The "gardens" are a few cement patios surrounded by grass, where visitors sit and drink beer in the shade after visiting the three museums and the **Hall of Fame** (a collection of photographs and documents commemorating Mexico's baseball heroes) located in the old factory.

The **Museo Deportivo,** part of the Hall of Fame, celebrates *charriadas* (rodeos), boxing, soccer and bullfighting. Not surprisingly, the complex also contains a museum devoted to beer—located just to the north of the gate that leads into the gardens, the **Museo de la Cervecería** (tel. 375-22-00) foams over with elegant beer mugs from various countries and other beer culture artifacts. Another gallery, the **Museo de Monterrey,** displays a pedestrian permanent collection of art as well as traveling exhibits; past exhibitions have included work by Robert Mapplethorpe. (Museos Deportivo and Monterrey open Tues.-Sat. 9:30am-9pm, Sun. 9am-5pm. Free.) An appointment must be made to see the Museo de la Cervecería or brewery; check at the other museums for more info. Even without the intellectual and nostalgic stimulation of the museums, the trip is worthwhile if only for the icy bottles of Carta Blanca given away a the stand on the edge of the *museo*. Like nothing else in Monterrey, free beer soothes the weary soul.

Also worth a visit are the **Grutas de García,** 45km northwest of the city. Accesesible by car or bus. Once there, avoid the hard climb of more than 700m by taking the cable railway car (included in the 180 pesos admission). (Open daily 9:30am-5:30pm.) The Grutas are a system of natural chambers; the dozens of sedimentary layers in their walls reveal that 50 or 60 million years ago the caves lay on the ocean floor. Take a **Transportes Monterrey-Saltillo** bus from the terminal; buses only go to the Grutas de García on Sundays, hourly after 9am. The most convenient way to see them is on one of the organized tours by the tourist office every Saturday, beginning at 1:30pm (end 5:30pm back in Monterrey), 25 pesos per person.

TAMAULIPAS

■■■ MATAMOROS AND BROWNSVILLE, TEXAS

In the early 19th century, the recently settled Congregación de Nuestra Señora del Refugio was re-named Villa de Matamoros after a priest slain during Mexico's war for independence. In 1846 Matamoros fell to U.S. general (and later president) Zachary Taylor, who divided the city in two, designating the Río Bravo as the international border.

The unscenic, muddy trickle separating the U.S. and Mexico, mislabeled by Mexicans as the Río Bravo and by *norteamericanos* as the Río Grande, divides two communities which reflect the nations that claim them. Though geographically insignificant, the river marks the transition between two cultures and ways of life.

■ Matamoros

Matamoros offers the inevitably North-Americanized first taste of borderline Mexico, yet due to its distinictive past, remains more authentic than other border cities. The small and chaotically crowded center belies the city's population of 350,000. Locals patiently exploit their proximity to the U.S. and have gladly converted most of the downtown area into a big marketplace. Street vendors can always pull out "something special" that you must need and numerous stands sell tacos, *aguas de frutas* (fruit juices), and *elotes* (corn on the cob; try it with chili and lime). On Sunday evenings residents file into the plaza for their weekly *paseo* (promenade).

ORIENTATION

Matamoros lies 38km west of the Gulf Coast on the Río Bravo. Route 2, which follows the course of the river northwest to Reynosa (100km) and Nuevo Laredo (350km), also passes through the center of Matamoros. Local buses (1.50 pesos) run from the airport to the city center every hour from 5:30am to 8:30pm, dropping off passengers at the corner of Abasolo and Calle 12, 6 blocks northwest of the plaza. Taxis charge 40 pesos for the journey into town. Until 7pm, downtown-bound buses depart regularly from the train station for .80 pesos.

In the center of town, streets form a grid pattern: numbered *calles* run north-south, named *calles* run east-west. The pedestrian mall, where vendors hawk their wares, lies between Calles 6 and 7 on Abasolo. The main plaza lies two blocks east, down Gonzalez. The International Bridge, the only (legal) border crossing, and its immediate area lie in a crook of the Río Grande. Calle Obregón twists from the bridge towards the crossing with Calles 5 and higher, which lead to the market. After crossing the International Bridge, located at the northernmost part of the city, you will pass the customs and tourist offices. To reach the border area from the center of town, take one of the buses or *colectivos* labeled "Puente" (.80 pesos), which let you off in the parking lot of the customs building and tourist office. Taxi drivers in the market area will try to charge exorbitant prices to the border, but the persistent should be able to whittle them down to 5 pesos.

CROSSING THE BORDER

Due to prohibitive increases in insurance rates, few buses and taxis have crossed the border since 1989. Currently, the two best options are by foot or by private car whose entire documentation is with you (see Mexico General Introduction: Planning Your Trip: Vehicle Permits).

A 100m-long bridge joins Matamoros and Brownsville. Pedestrians pay 25¢ or .80 pesos to leave either country. Crossing by foot is as easy as inserting a quarter and passing through a turnstile. Autos pay US$1 or 32 pesos, but be sure you have checked your insurance before you cross—most U.S. insurance is null and void in Mexico.

To get a six-month permit (the only kind available) at the border, you must have your Social Security number, documentation showing ownership of the car and license plate identification and registration. The fee is determined on the spot according to the value of the car (you may unexpectedly find that you are driving a treasure chest), and can be paid in cash or with any major credit card. If you're going to Matamoros just for the day, it may may be a much better idea to park on the U.S. side and walk.

U.S. citizens need to obtain a tourist card (FMT) for travel beyond Matamoros. An FMT can be obtained in the immigration office to the right directly after the International bridge or in the Matamoros bus station. The immigration desk is the first one immediately to your left as you enter the door closest to the to the International Bridge, and is supposedly open 24 hrs. Look for the green uniformed officers; there are no signs. If the officer marks only 30 days on your card, ask for more, now rather than later. There are checkpoints at all roads leading out of Matamoros into Mexico, considerably further from the U.S. border.

Finding transportation on either side of the border is no problem; taxis and *peseras* (public buses, all cost .80 pesos) circle the area in buzzard-like search of prospective passengers.

PRACTICAL INFORMATION

Because of U.S. daylight savings time, Matamoros clocks run one hour behind of those in Brownsville from April to October.

Tourist Offices: Delegación Turismo. Get your Matamoros maps in Brownsville at the Brownsville Chamber of Commerce, only two blocks from the border.

About 50m beond the border, the proudly amanteurish "Tourist Information an Guides" service is run by local English-speaking taxi drivers. Open roughly between 8am and 10pm daily. **Informacíon Turism,** in a small building across the street from the **Gran Hotel Residencial,** where Obreón turns into Hidalgo. Photocopied maps and touristy hotel and restaurant listings (tel. 3-82-41; open Mon.-Fri. 9am-2pm and 3-7pm). Try upscale hotels for English information.

U.S. Consulate: 232 Calle 1 (tel. 6-72-70 or 6-72-72), at Azaleas. Open Mon.-Fri. 8am-10am and 1-4pm.

Currency Exchange: Banks line Calle 6 and the new central Plaza Hidalgo. Open for exchange 9am-1:30pm. Both **Bancomer** at Matamoros and Calle 6, across from **Hotel Colonial** and **Serfín,** on Plaza Hidalgo, at Calle 6 and Gonzalez, have 24-hr. ATMs for advances on Visa and Diner's Club, while **Multibanco Comermex,** 2 blocks into the center of Matamoros from the **Gran Hotel Residencial,** along Obregón, offers a 24-hr. Cirrus ATM. Better rates at the *casas de cambio* near the plaza, on Calle 6, and on Abasolo (the pedestrian mall). Open (approx.) Mon.-Fri. 9am-6pm, Sat. 10am-1pm.

Post Office: In the bus station. Open Mon.-Fri. 8am-5pm. **Postal Code:** 87300.

Telephones: Try the small, nondescript *casa de larga distancia* at Morelos and Calle 8. Open daily 8am-1pm and 3-6pm. **Telephone Code:** 891.

Airport: Servando Canales Aeropuerto, on Rte. 101, the highway to Ciudad Victoria, 5km south of town. **Aeroméxico,** Obregón 21 (tel. 3-07-02), has service to Mexico City (6pm, 555 pesos). Open Mon.-Sat. 10am-5pm.

Train Station: Ferrocarriles Nacionales de México (tel. 6-67-06), on Hidalgo between Calles 9 and 10. Slow daily service to Reynosa (18 pesos) and Monterrey (38 pesos) beginning at 9:20am. Buy a ticket ahead of time and arrive early for boarding. Crowds of vendors hop on at every stop to sell everything from tacos to ten-pound slabs of freshly butchered raw meat.

Bus Station: Central de Autobuses, Canales at Aguiles. Take any bus or *pesera* (minibus) marked "Central"; taxis line up outside. Like a supermarket—pick your favorite brand of bus line: first or second class. Luggage lockers available in the 24-hr. restaurant for 6 pesos per day or 3 pesos for 2 hr. **Omnibus de México** (tel. 3-76-93) to Monterrey (5 per day, 5 hr., 33 pesos), Laredo, and Durango. **ADO** (tel. 2-01-81), to Veracruz via Tampico and Tuxpan (3 per day, 45 pesos). **Monterrey Codereyta Reynosa Transporte** (tel. 3-57-68) offers the cheapest and most frequent buses to Monterrey (15 per day, 28.50 pesos). Buy a *directo* ticket to avoid endless local stops. **Autobuses de Norte** (tel. 2-27-77) to Monterrey (videobus, 5 per day, 5 hr.,33 pesos), to Mexico City (2 per day, *ejecutivo* with a snack bar, 205 pesos, 4 per day; *primera* and video, 150 pesos).

Market: Gigante, directly across from the bus station, with a big red "G." Supermarket, general store, pharmacy, and cafeteria. Open daily 9am-9pm .

Laundromat: 313 Calle 1, 3 doors north of Ocampo. Exit the bus station and go right immediately; 1 short block down Canales, at Calle 1, go right 2½ blocks. On your left as you head toward city center. Self-service wash and dry 3 pesos each. Open daily 8:30am-9pm.

Red Cross: Caballero at García (tel. 2-00-44). 24 hrs. For emergency medical aid also try the **clinica** along Canales, 3 blocks from the Central towards the center of the city along Calles 4 and 5. Open 24 hrs.

24-hr. Pharmacy: Farmacia Aristos del Golfo. On Calle 1 between Gonzalez and Morelos. Joined to the hospital—large beige building with blue writing on the sides. Many pharmacies in market area are open during the day.

Police: Tel. 2-03-22 or 2-00-08. Friendly and helpful, but little English spoken. Open 24 hrs.

ACCOMMODATIONS

Budget travelers will be able to find plenty of low-cost accommodations in the market area. Though less comfortable and grubbier, these hotels cost at least half as much as those in Brownsville.

Hotel Majestic, Abasolo 89 (tel. 3-36-80), between Calles 8 and 9 on the pedestrian mall. Feels homiest of all, with colorful curtains and bedspreads in the darkish rooms; some even have TVs. Excellent location outweighs lack of toilet seats and peeling paint. Singles 30 pesos. Doubles 35 pesos.

Hotel México, Abasolo 87 (tel. 2-08-56), next door to the Majestic. Yellow-and-red-tiled decor. Shabby but clean rooms, toilets without seats, but a great location. Some rooms have balconies over the pedestrian mall. Singles 30 pesos. Doubles 40 pesos.

Hotel Colonial, Matamoros 601 (tel. 6-64-18), at Matamoros and Calle 6, 3 blocks east of the market. Large white building with brown trim, across from Bancomer. Lobby lies below three floors of clean red-tiled rooms with fans. Bathrooms lack toilet seats, showers lack curtains. Suspicious-looking drinking water available. Adjoining cafeteria. Singles 30 pesos. Doubles 35 pesos.

Hotel Araujo, Abasolo 401 (tel. 2-22-66), between Calles 4 and 5. Similar room conditions but less convenient than the hotels farther up on Abasolo. Two stories of rooms open onto a small, dingy central courtyard. Attentive family keeps rooms and sheets clean (though both have seen better days) and the noisy, sporadic A/C running. Singles and doubles 32 pesos.

FOOD

Select from family-run cafeterias or predictably-inflated tourist joints.

Café y Restaurant Frontera, Calle 6 between N. Bravo and Matamoros (tel. 3-24-40). Yellow building with red heart hanging outside. A popular weekend hangout for drinking and winding down. Two floors of booths and a jukebox. A wide range of seafood, steaks, and salads, all under 12 pesos. Open daily 7am-10pm.

Cafetería 1916, 191 Calle 6, (tel. 3-07-27), between Matamoros and Abasolo. A cool and quiet refuge from the bustle. Try *sincronizadas 1916* (flour tortilla with ham, chicken and avocado) for 9.50 pesos, or other Mexican specialties for 7.50-9.50 pesos. Open daily 10am-10pm.

Café de Mexico, on Gonzalez between Calle 6 and Calle 7. Huge central TV allows you to keep up with the soaps while you eat. Everything 12 pesos or less. *Fajitas con frijoles* or *chiles rellenos* 11 pesos. Open daily 7:30am-11pm.

Krystá l, Matamoros between Calle 6 and Calle 7 acros the unavoidable Hotel Ritz (big neon R); (tel. 2-11-90 will connect you to the Ritz, ask for a transfer to Krystál). Modern and hip eatery by Matamoros standards. Green booths are surrounded by mirrored walls. *Plato de frutas* 7 pesos, *quesadillas* with french fries and guacamole 9 pesos. All entrees 8.50-12.50 pesos. Open daily 7am-11pm.

SIGHTS AND ENTERTAINMENT

Matamoros's indoor market spreads for several blocks and spills out into the street. It is divided into the old market, or **Pasaje Juárez,** and the new market, **Mercado Juárez.** Entrances to Pasaje Juárez are on both Matamoros and Bravo between Calles 8 and 9 under a sign that says "Old Market." The new market's entrance is on Abasolo between Calles 9 and 10. Both markets cater largely to "spring-breakers" and the tourist trade, selling such souvenirs as jewelry, hammocks, hats, T-shirts, and hard liquor (each person of age can carry 1 quart back to the U.S.). Shop proprietors will flog their wares with gusto, but consider making major purchases farther south, where souvenirs like piñatas and blankets are cheaper. (Markets open daily : "Old" 7am-7pm, "New" 7am-8pm).

The city's central plaza, the **Plaza Hidalgo,** is a shady, pleasant place to sit, a fact well-known to young *matamorense* couples who relax there in the afternoon shade. Statues of Miguel Hidalgo and Benito Juárez stand on the west side along Calle 6. **City Hall** is the large white building with murals on its facade, also on Calle 6. Across the plaza lies the cathedral.

Mexican history buffs should visit the **Casa Mata Museum,** at the corner of Guatemala and Santos Degollados. Here you can look at revolutionary photographs, artifacts, and picayunes, as well as figurines and pottery from southern *indígena* groups. From the bus station, take the first right out the entrance and walk seven blocks on Guatemala or take the *pesera* to the hospital and walk down Calle 1 to Santos Degollados and turn left. (Open Tues.-Sun. 9:30am-5:30pm. Free.)

For a refreshing break from souvenir-hunting, join hordes of bar-hoppers and sink into the the ventilated out-of-this-dirty-hot-world atmosphere of **Las dos Republicás** on Calle 9, between Matamoros and Abasolo (tel. 2-97-50; open daily 8am-8pm). Huge 18-oz. frozen Maragritas (US$6) are served in glasses that could almost hold a basketball, and *piña de la casa* is served in a real pineapple. You keep the pineapple, they keep US$7. For something more authentically Mexican, try the **Bar Los Toros,** two doors down from Las Dos Repúblicas, where rowdy groups of men swig Coronas (3 pesos). Although permitted inside, females may not feel at ease.

■ Brownsville, Texas

At first, Brownsville may seem to be just another Mexican town which happens to lie within U.S. borders. However, a trip across the bridge reveals that, despite a common language and historical ties, Matamoros' crowded markets and packed *colectivos* (with their destinations shoe-polished on the windows) have a vastly different flavor and feel. Brownsville residents enjoy a more peaceful pace of life in surroundings where public hygiene still has meaning. Brownsville provides travelers from either direction with a wide range of services and a relatively uncrowded border crossing. While both directions remain fast and easy on foot, automobile crossing can become congested. The influence of Mexican language and culture fades away as the miles from the border increase.

ORIENTATION

Brownsville's streets are laid out in a grid, by a large bend in the Río Grande near the International Bridge. Texas Rte.4 from the northeast (International Blvd.) and Texas Rte.415 from the northwest (Elizabeth St.) converge at the tip of this bend. North-south Highways 83 and 77 cut through the middle of the city. Boca Chica (Hwy. 281 and 48) swoops from the mid-west to Brownsville and South Padre international airport at the eastern extreme of the city. Elizabeth St., lined mostly with clothing and shoe stores, is Brownsville's main commercial district and a good point of reference.

Local buses, which can be confusing, run 6am-7pm (fare US$.75). Buses to all areas of the city leave from city hall, which is on E. Washington St. between E. 11th and E. 12th. Pick up schedules at the desk inside the building or call 548-6050 for route and schedule information.

PRACTICAL INFORMATION

Chamber of Commerce: 1600 E. Elizabeth (tel. 542-4341). Brimming over with maps and brochures but not a great source of tourist information. Open Mon.-Fri. 8am-5pm.

Brownsville Information Center: Farm Rd. 802 (tel. (800) 626-2639 or 541-8455), at Central Blvd. adjacent to Motel 6. Friendly and knowledgeable staff. Maps and brochures like there's no tomorrow. Get your Matamoros maps here. From City Hall, take the "Jefferson Central" or *Los Ebanos* bus. Get off right before the highway at the pyramid-shaped tan building. The stop is after the Sunrise mall. Open Mon.-Sat. 8am-5pm, Sun. 9am-4pm.

Currency Exchange: *Casas de cambio* litter International Blvd. **Interex Money Exchange,** 801 International Blvd. (tel. 548-0303), exchanges traveler's checks. Open daily 10am-6pm.

Telephone area code: 210

Telegrams: Western Union, 2814 International Blvd. (tel. 542-8695). Send or receive telegrams, messages and money orders. Open daily 7:30am-8pm. Two other locally reputable companies provide the same services. **Valley Check Cashiers** at 1401 E. Washington St. (tel. 546-6634) and 2921 Boca Chica Blvd.

(541-7700) as well as H.E. Butt Grocery 2250 Boca Chica Blvd. (541-1251) and 1628 Central Blvd. (541-4816).

Airport: The most convenient airport is **Valley International Airport** (tel. 430-8600), in Harlingen, Texas, 25mi. (42km) northwest of Brownsville. From Brownsville, a taxi to the airport costs US$40-45. The bus charges US$24 for the lonesome cowpoke plus $12 a head for company. Some get free rides from the airport to Brownsville on one of the vans to the expensive hotels. **Brownsville and South Padre International Airport,** at 700 S. Minnesota (tel. 542-4373) currently offers four flights a day to Houston. They are all served by Continental (tel. (800) 231-0856).

Bus Stations: Greyhound, 1134 E. Charles St. (tel. 546-7171). Luggage locker US$1 per day. Service to McAllen (8 per day, US$7.50), and Laredo (2 per day, US$32). Also serves Houston, Dallas, and San Antonio (4 per day). Schedule changes frequently; call to confirm. Reservations can be made up to 1 day in advance. **Valley Transit Company,** 1305 E. Adams (tel. 546-2264), at 13th St. Lockers available for 75¢ per day. To: Laredo (at 8:15am and 2:15pm, US$32); McAllen (at 6:45am, 7:00am, 10:30am, 2:45pm, 4:30pm, 10pm, US $7.50); Del Río (2 per day, US$55).

Market: H.E.B. #1 food and drug stores. Across the street from the post office on Elizabeth. Open Mon.-Sat. 7am-9pm. and Sun. 8am-9pm.

Laundromat: Holiday Laundry, Elizabeth and West 6th. About ½ mi. (1km) NW from the International Bridge. Self service wash US$.75 per load, US$.25 per dry.

Emergency: Tel. 911, 24 hrs.

Police: 600 E. Jackson (tel. 911 or 548-7000), 24 hrs.

ACCOMMODATIONS

Brownsville hotels look and feel like the Ritz for those coming from Mexico, but the prices can't compare to Mexican bargains. The downtown area near the International Bridge offers the best bargains and convenience, but is less safe at night than the distant area along the North Expressway.

Hotel Colonial, 1147 E. Levee St. (tel. 541-9176). Refrigerated *hacienda*-style lobby leads to ample, clean rooms with phone and TV. US$40 for singles or doubles, $5 for each additional person over 16 years old. Turn on the A/C yourself and endure the heat for 1hr.

Cameron Motor Hotel, 912 E. Washington (tel. 542-3551). Unblemished lobby/lounge with an affable staff. Sparkling rooms with fan, A/C, TV and phone. Singles US$23, with bath $34. Doubles with bath $40.

Motel 6, 2255 North Expressway (tel. 546-4699), off Hwys. 77 and 802. Large, clean rooms with the works (TV with movies, A/C, phone), but miles from the city center. Take the "Jefferson Central" or *Los Ebanos* bus (last bus leaves at 7pm). US$30.50, additional adults $7, kids under 18 free in parents' room.

FOOD

Brownsville restaurants serve a border blend of Mexican and U.S. cuisine in casual cafés. The downtown area (near the International Bridge) hosts a plethora of affordable restaurants.

Texas Café, in Market Square, adjoining City Hall (tel. 542-5772). Murals of Brownsville circa 1890 give it a historical feel, and the location makes it perfect for a quick bite while waiting for the bus. Simple grill food for about US$3, dine in or take out. Open 24 hrs.

Lucio's Café, 1041 E.Washington (tel. 542-0907). Bright café packed with regulars at all hours for good reason. Multiple ceiling fans and colorful Mexican fabrics cloak the walls, making the atmosphere cool, pleasant, and relaxed. Jukebox in the corner plays Spanish soft-rock favorites. Monstrous portions at low prices. Try the roast pork with rice or French fries, beans, and salad (US$4.50). Open 24 hrs.

Mr. Amigo Café, 1141 E. Levee, off 12th St. Small and simple (tel. 541-1231). Decor must have been a low priority. Great for breakfast—huge stack of pancakes (US$2) and homemade hot biscuits with jelly ($.50). Open Mon.-Sat. 7am-4pm.

Oasis Café, 1417 E. Adams, 1 block down from the Valley Transit bus station. Crowded with locals eating full meals even early in the morning. *Carne guisada* goes for US$3.25. Lengthy list of burgers. Open Mon.-Sat. 6am-5pm.

■■■ TAMPICO

If you've ever seen John Huston's *The Treasure of the Sierra Madre*, you might remember Tampico as the hot, dirty, unfriendly oil town that every foreigner was itching to skip. Tampico may be more friendly today, but otherwise Huston's portrayal holds true: a kidney stone of a city. Ironic geographic fate has made Tampico a necessary transport pit stop in the race south to more beautiful locales. Enough amenities have cropped up here to make a brief stay tolerable, but hold your breath and remember that the shorter your stay, the happier you will be. A relaxing nearby beach, **Playa Miramar,** is accessible on bus "Playa" or "Escollera". (1 peso from the corner of López de Lara and Madero).

Orientation and Practical Information To get the the city center from the bus stop, take the yellow taxis (10-12 pesos), the minibuses (1 peso), or the *colectivos* (shared taxis, .70 pesos, 1.40 with luggage). Like most routes, these stop on López de Lara at the intersection with Madero. The town is centered around the nearby **Plaza de Armas** and the **Plaza de la Libertad.**

The **tourist office,** Olmos Sur 101 (tel. 12-00-07), on the 2nd floor, in the orange and white building on the northeast corner of Pl. de Armas, dispenses photocopied city maps and useless brochures. (Open Mon.-Fri. 9am-2pm and 3-7pm.) The **U.S. Consulate agency** is located at Ejército Mexicano 503, Suite 203, in the northern colonia Guadalupe (tel. 13-22-17). (Open Mon.-Fri. 10am-1pm.) Exchange currency or AmEx traveler's cheques at **Banorte** (tel. 12-47-91) at the Pl. de Armas, corner of Oolmos and Mirón. (Open: Mon.-Fri. 10am-1pm). **Post Office:** Madero 309 OTE at Juárez (tel. 12-19-27), on Pl. de la Libertad. (Open for *Lista de Correos,* stamps, and registered mail Mon.-Fri. 8am-7pm, Sat. 9am-1pm.) Another branch is in 2nd-class bus terminal. (Open Mon.-Fri. 9am-3pm.) **Postal Code:** 89000. Collect calls can be placed at pay **phones** in both plazas and the 24-hr. long-distance *caseta* at the bus station. **Phone code:** 12.

Trains leave from the small station located in small park at corner of Héroes de Nacozári and Aduana (tel. 12-11-79), 3 blocks south of Pl. de Armas. Trains to Monterrey (7:45am, 16 pesos) and San Luis Potosí (8am, 13.50 pesos). Tickets available daily 5:30-8am. The **bus station,** on Zapotal, north of the city, has adjoining 1st- and 2nd-class terminals. Carriers **ADO** (tel. 13-41-82), **Omnibus Oriente** (tel. 13-37-18), and **Blancos** (tel. 13-48-67) run almost continuously to Poza Rica (25-30 pesos), Mexico City (75-90 pesos) and Veracruz (80 pesos), with fairly frequent service to Tuxpan, Reynosa, Villahermosa, Pachuca, San Luis Potosí, and Matamoros. For other destinations, investigate other carriers.

In an emergency, dial 06. The **Red Cross** (15-03-38 or 16-50-79; 15-40-47 in Ciudad Madero) has 24-hr. ambulance service. Some doctors speak English at the **Hospital General de Tampico** (tel. 15-22-20, 15-30-30, 13-09-32, or 13-20-35), Ejército Nacional 1403 near the bus station. The **police** (tel. 12-11-57 or 12-10-32; 15-03-22 in Ciudad Madero) are located on Tamulipas at Sor Juana de la Cruz.

Accommodations and Food Clean and secure budget accommodations are rare in Tampico. In the city center, near the plaza, try the **Hotel Capri,** Juárez 202 Nte. (tel. 12-26-80). Spartan rooms, bare walls, clean sheets, fans and nicely tiled baths and floors are an excellent deal at 35 pesos for both singles and doubles. Close to the bus station, **Hotel Allende,** Allende 122 (tel. 13-82-57), the newish-looking gray building, has simple, almost clean rooms with noisy and wobbly fans. To get there, exit the bus station to the right, take the first right, and walk ½ block. (Singles and doubles 33 pesos.) **Hotel La Central,** Bustamante 224 (tel. 17-09-18), is directly across from the bus station. Cool fish logo and funky swan chairs, but the hotel itself is really nothing special. Slightly more worn-out than the Allende. Fans in rooms, which are survivable for a short stay. (Singles 33 pesos, doubles 39 pesos.)

For its size, Tampico does not have an especially wide variety of restaurants. It does, however, support countless replicas of standard seafood cafeterias. **Café Mundo,** López de Lara y Díaz Mirón (tel. 14-18-31) is a good value and nice atmosphere relative to the other options; sit at the mile-long counter under the massive clock. All menus (15-17 pesos) come with beans, fresh bread and coffee. (Open 24 hrs.) The 25 tables of the **Cafetería Emir,** Olmos Sur 107 (tel. 12-51-39) are always filled with people drinking coffee, eating fresh bread from the adjoining bakery and people watching in a relaxed atmosphere. Their old-fashioned coffee machine makes delicious *café con leche*, and chicken *tamales* (2.60 pesos) are a specialty. (Open daily 6am-midnight.)

■ Central México

NAYARIT

■■■ TEPIC

The border between the states of Sinaloa and Nayarit is a geographical as well as a political watershed—volcanic highlands and a tropical coastline erupt where the northern desert comes to an end. Home of the Cora and Huichol peoples, Nayarit entered the world's consciousness via Carlos Castaneda's book *Journey to Ixtlán*, which was inspired by the hallucinogens of a small town halfway between Tepic and Guadalajara. Nayarit, the greatest exporter of fruit among the Mexican states, reputedly produces the lion's share of the nation's marijuana crop. Tepic, the capital of Nayarit, is an important crossroads because of its proximity to San Blas (70km northwest), Puerto Vallarta (169km south), Mazatlán (278km north), and Guadalajara (240km southeast).

Located just a holler away from the intersection of Routes 15 (running from Mexico City through Guadalajara to Nogales) and 200 (which runs from Guatemala along the Pacific coast), Tepic is something of a transport hub, and not much more. The **bus station** is served by **Norte de Sonora, Tres Estrellas de Oro, Omnibus de México, Transportes del Pacífico, Estrella Blanca,** and **Transportes Frontera.** Norte de Sonora runs the most buses, with service to every major destination save Puerto Vallarta, including Mexico City (4 per day, 12hrs., 74 pesos), Guadalajara (13 per day, 4hrs., 22 pesos); Nogales (also through Mazatlán, 2 per day, 24hrs., 140 pesos) and San Blas (7 per day, 1¾hrs., 65 pesos). Transportes del Pacífico has the most frequent service to Puerto Vallarta (27 per day, 3½hrs., 17.50 pesos), but the last bus leaves at 8pm. Activity at the station is so frenetic that turn-around time need not exceed one hour unless a bus is canceled or completely full.

As you leave the **bus station,** *el centro* is down the highway to the left; cross the street and catch one of the orange buses (.25 pesos) at the *parada.* The **train station,** on Allende at Juárez has a train daily to Guadalajara, at noon (8 pesos). To get there, hop on a "Ferrocarril" bus at the bus station or downtown at the corner of México Sur and Hidalgo.

If, for whatever reason, you should wind up spending a night in Tepic, two hotels corner the market on cheap and easy layovers. The **Hotel Tepic,** Martínez 438 (tel. 3-13-77), has halls that summon up visions of cheap, shabby hospitals. Painters ran out of blue before getting to the rooms, which are bare but for a thin-mattressed bed and a warped desk. (Singles 30 pesos. Doubles 35 pesos for one bed, 47 pesos for 2 beds.) Next door at Martínez 430, the **Hotel Nayar** (tel. 3-23-22), has slightly larger rooms and bathrooms and makes some effort at decoration in the form of fluorescent plastic flower arrangements. (Singles 25 pesos. Doubles 32 pesos for 1 bed, 40 pesos for 2 beds.) In both hotels, rooms looking away from the bus station are much quieter, although you'll pass up the charming view of the dark satanic sugar mill. To find these budget waystations, take a left leaving the bus station, another left on the first street, and they'll be on your right after a block. If you want to stay downtown, **Hotel Serita** has clean rooms with large windows and a pleasant lobby. (Singles 35 pesos. Doubles 45 pesos.)

Economical food can be found at **Altamirano,** México Sur 109, which serves a scrumptious plate of *enchiladas con pollo y crema* for 10 pesos (open daily 7am-11pm) and **Parroquia,** Amado Nervo 18, 2nd floor, overlooking the main plaza.

TEPIC

Three monstrous *quesadillas* go for 7 pesos, a generous orange juice for 3.50 pesos. (Open daily 9am-9pm.)

The **regional tourist office,** México Sur 34, files its brochures under a thick layer of dust for that hip-yet-elusive casual look. Nonetheless the staff is friendly and helpful, but has no maps. (Open Mon.-Fri. 9am-7pm.) Bundles of **banks** and *casas de cambio* along México Sur make this the best area to change money. The former operate Monday through Friday, 9am-noon. The latter have variable hours, but Monday through Saturday 9am-7pm is a common schedule.

The bus station holds a **post office** and a **telegram office** (both open Mon.-Fri. 9am-1pm). The bus station has **LADATEL** phones and **telephone service** every day from 6am to 10pm. Credit card calls can be made from the public telephone on the east side of the station. The desperate can surrender a mean 6 pesos to the *Larga Distancia* on México Nte. 286, across from the cathedral. Tepic's **telephone code** is 321.

If you are in need of a hospital try **Hospital General de Tepic** (tel. 3-41-27), on Pasco de la Loma. To make the 20-minute walk from the bus station, take a left as you leave the building and another left at the intersection with Arenide México. After three blocks, take the right-hand fork at the rotary, and two blocks later the hospital is on your left. A cab is 4.50 pesos. The **police station** (tel. 2-01-63) is at the intersection of Avenidas Mina and Oaxaca, but it's too far to walk from the center, and no buses go there; take a cab for 5 pesos.

Avenida México, running north-south, is downtown Tepic's main drag. At its northern terminus, the fountainous **Plaza Principal** is incessantly active, dominated on one end by the cathedral and on the other by the **Palacio Municipal.** South of the plaza lie the **Museo Regional de Nayarit** (open Mon.-Fri. 10am-3pm; free), at México Nte. 91, and the **state capitol,** a gracefully domed structure dating from the 1870s, at México and Abasolo. At Av. México's southern end, turn west (uphill) on Insurgentes and you'll come to the huge and enchanting park known as **La Loma.** A miniature train encircles the park, running Tues.-Sat. 10am-4pm (1.50 pesos).

■ Near Tepic: Beaches and Ixtlán

Puerto Vallarta and San Blas are the most compelling lures for beach-o-philes passing through Tepic, but southern Nayarit has a number of little-known beaches which sacrifice social life for the greater goal of unpopulated sand. Chief among these is the beautiful, undeveloped **Chacala,** which lies on a dirt road out of **Las Varas;** also **Rincón de Guayabitos,** 16km farther south, with limited accommodations, and **Punta de Mita,** close enough to Puerto Vallarta for nightlife and far enough away for peaceful sleep.

Fifty km south of Tepic spreads the deep and clear **Laguna de Santa María del Oro,** a lovely 3km-wide lagoon which reaches into the depths of an extinct volcano. A second-class **México y Victoria** bus departs every hour from the Tepic bus terminal for the town of Santa María. From there you can hitch the remaining 8km to the lagoon. The lake's banana tree-lined rim is riddled with scenic camping sites, though facilities are sparse and the water features the usual gang of amoebas.

Another 50km south toward Guadalajara is the town of **Ixtlán,** of Carlos Castaneda fame. Only the **Toltec ruins** 1km south of town make Ixtlán worth mentioning. Though inferior in size and importance to sites farther south and east, they may be your only taste of Mexico's pre-Conquest days if you're not going beyond Guadalajara. Of particular interest is the **Temple of Quetzalcóatl,** the largest structure on the site, replete with sacrificial altars.

JALISCO

■■■ GUADALAJARA

The state of Jalisco revolves around the dipole of Puerto Vallarta, a vacuous seaside resort, and Guadalajara, a metropolis of considerable sophistication. *Tapatíos*, as Guadalajarans call themselves, have parlayed their geographically marginal position into a tremendous expansive force. When violent revolutionary unrest shook the streets of Mexico City during the early 19th century, many Spanish colonists were forced to flee northwest to then-remote Guadalajara. Here, the frontier of civilization gave birth to the cultural icons of the fledgling republic: tequila, *mariachi*, and the hat dance.

Alas, history has given way to urbanization and devleopment; Guadalajaran cultural innovations have slipped into stereotype. Still, the four large central plazas, stately Spanish architecture, and numerous museums and theatres of the city's downtown guard the vestiges of Guadalajara's past. Appreciation of the city requires more effort than appreciation of the gorgeous coast to the east and the postcard-perfect cities of the Bajío. Summer heat waves and the infinity of unspectacular one-story houses away from the central plazas occlude the *Tapatío* charm.

ORIENTATION

Guadalajara lies 650km west-northwest of Mexico City. Hourly buses in all directions, several trains per day and daily planes to all points in Mexico and many U.S. cities ensure that Guadalajara remains readily accessible.

Buses run from Guadalajara's **airport,** Aeropuerto International Miguel Hidalgo, every hour to the *antigua* **bus station** in the south of town (1.50 pesos). From there any "Centro" bus will take you into the center of town. A *combi* will drop you anywhere downtown for 7-20 pesos, depending upon how full it is, but beware—some drivers have commission arrangements with downtown hotels. *Combis* run from town to the airport from the Mexicana office (Díaz de Leon 951, via minibus #625 along Avenida Juárez) every hour. A taxi costs up to 45 pesos, depending on the time of day; be sure to settle the fare before getting taken for a ride.

A new bus station, the well-organized, clean and efficient **Nueva Central Camionera,** has arisen in the town of **Tlaquepaque,** southeast of Guadalajara on the highway to Mexico City. Each of seven terminals has been conveniently outfitted with a hotel and tourist information booth near the exit. The people who staff these kiosks are startlingly well-informed. If you tell them the name of a hotel, even a dirt cheap one, they'll tell you how much it costs, which bus to catch and how to get there from the bus stop. Buses (.70 pesos), *combis* (.70-1 peso), and taxis (18 pesos) all head downtown from directly in front of any terminal. To reach the station from downtown, catch a bus on Av. Revolución, or Av. de Septiembre across from the cathedral. Both the red bus #275 (or 275A) and a green bus marked "Nueva Central" will take you there. In a taxi, be sure to specify the *new* bus station, since some drivers may zip you to the old station and then make you pay extra to go to Tlaquepaque.

The **train station** lies at the foot of Independencia Sur. To get from the station to the heart of Guadalajara, at the intersection of **Independencia** and **Juárez,** take a taxi (12 pesos) or bus #60 or #62. You can also walk to Independencia, only a block from the station, and take bus #45 north to the intersection with Juárez.

A plethora of street signs makes Guadalajara easy to navigate. Intersections in the compact downtown district are clearly marked, and only a few streets run at rebellious angles. Finding your way around outside the *centro* is more difficult because the streets change names at the borders between Guadalajara's four sectors. Guadalajara's **shopping district** centers around the intersection of Av. Juárez and Avenida Alcalde/16 de Septiembre.

GUADALAJARA

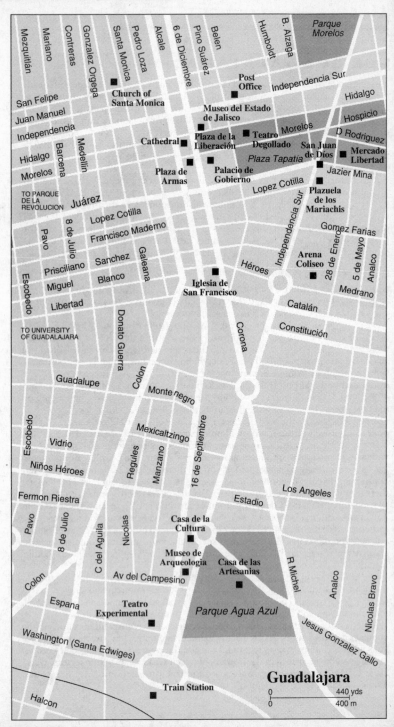

Parque Morelos

Church of Santa Monica

Post Office

Independencia Sur

Hidalgo

Hospicio

Museo del Estado de Jalisco

D Rodriguez

Cathedral

Plaza de la Liberación

Teatro Degollado

Morelos

San Juan de Dios

Mercado Libertad

Plaza Tapatia

Plaza de Armas

Palacio de Gobierno

Jazier Mina

Lopez Cotilla

TO PARQUE DE LA REVOLUCION

Juárez

Plazuela de los Mariachis

Lopez Cotilla

Francisco Maderno

Gomez Farias

Sanchez

Héroes

Arena Coliseo

Miguel

Blanco

Priciliano

Libertad

Medrano

Iglesia de San Francisco

Catalán

TO UNIVERSITY OF GUADALAJARA

Constitución

Donato Guerra

Guadalupe

Monte negro

Vidrio

Mexicaltzingo

Niños Héroes

Fermon Riestra

Los Angeles

Estadio

Casa de la Cultura

Museo de Arqueologia

Casa de las Artesanias

Av del Campesino

Teatro Experimental

Parque Agua Azul

Washington (Santa Edwiges)

Jesus Gonzalez Gallo

Guadalajara

Train Station

| 0 | 440 yds |
| 0 | 400 m |

Halcon

The **Plaza Tapatía** is an oblong area which contains the **cathedral**, the **Teatro Degollado,** many churches and museums, broad open spaces, and countless stores. With many of the most expensive hotels and restaurants, as well as the university and the U.S. Consulate, the area west of Pl. Tapatía is the most prosperous part of town.

The poorer *colonias* (suburbs) could be dangerous at any time of day. Check with the tourist office before exploring. Throughout Guadalajara, it is wise to stick to lit streets after dark and to take taxis after 11pm. Solo women travelers should avoid Av. Independencia after this hour as well. Independencia has a magnetic field which attracts raucous, drunken men. A massive sewage explosion in 1992 has also brought a resurgence of cholera to the city, though mainly confined to poorer districts. Visitors should be vaccinated against the infection.

The city's extensive **bus system** runs far, wide and often. Though somewhat rough around the edges (usually crowded, always noisy, and sometimes uncomfortable), buses (.70 pesos to any destination) are an excellent way to get just about anywhere in the city. Buses #60 and #62 run the length of Calzada Independencia, from the train station to the *Parque Mirador*. The "Par Vial" bus used to run down Javier Mina and Juárez, but due to subway construction on those roads it now goes down Independencia, then turns onto Vallarta and travels west, turning just short of López Mateos. Coming back eastward it cruises Hidalgo, three blocks north of Juárez. Bus #258 from San Felipe, three blocks north of Hidalgo, runs from near the Pl. Tapatía down López Mateos to the **Plaza del Sol,** the grand central station of nightlife, surrounded by *discotecas* and more expensive nightspots and shopping centers. Bus #24 goes the length of López Mateos, from Zapopan to beyond the Pl. del Sol, in both directions. Buses run between 6am and 10:30pm. Guadalajara recently opened the first part of its subway system. Of little use to travelers, the lone route lies beneath the pavement of Av. Federalismo, a north-south city bisector. Your cards rightly played, a taxi anywhere within the city limits should not cost more than 25 pesos. Haggle 'til it hurts.

PRACTICAL INFORMATION

Tourist Offices: State Office, Morelos 102 (tel. 658-22-22), in the Pl. de la Liberación, next to the Pl. Tapatía. A native English speaker, others who are more or less fluent, and a cornucopia of helpful information. They hand out *"centro"* maps (a better city map in the free tourist paper, *Guadalajara Weekly*). The magazine *Very Oir* lists cultural events for the month. Also complete listing of hotels, restaurants, and emergency hotlines. Open Mon.-Fri. 9am-8pm, Sat.-Sun. 9am-1pm. **Federal Tourist Office,** Degollado 50 (tel. 614-83-71), around the corner from the state tourist office. Sketchy material on Guadalajara, but they have free information on every Mexican state. Open Mon.-Fri. 8am-3pm.

Tours: Panoramex, Federalismo 948-305 (tel. 610-51-09). A wide range of trips, including to Ajijic, Chapala, Tlaquepaque, and Tonalá, for budgets of all sizes, beginning at 50 pesos for a city tour, plus Tlaquepaque, lasting 4 hrs. Open Mon.-Fri. 9am-2:30pm and 4:30-7pm, Sat. 9am-1pm. More information available at the state tourist office (above).

Consulates: U.S., Progreso 175 (tel. 625-27-00; emergencies 626-55-53). Open Mon.-Fri. 8am-2pm. **U.K.,** Paulino Navarro 1165 (tel. 611-16-78). Open Mon.-Fri. 9am-2pm and 4-7pm. **Canada,** Fiesta Americana Hotel, Local 30 on the Minerva traffic circle (tel. 15-86-65, ext. 3005). Open Mon.-Fri. 10am-1pm. For other countries, try the **Oficina de la Asociación Consular** (tel. 15-55-55), or the state tourist office (above) which has complete listings.

Currency Exchange: Banks have higher rates for traveler's checks, but *casas de cambio* offer better rates for cash. **Bancomer,** Corona 140, between Juárez and López Cotilla, open Mon.-Fri. 9am-1:30pm. **Bánamex,** Juárez at Corona, same hours. **Casa de Cambio Escobedo,** López Cotilla 221, offers a particularly good rate on dollars, a few pesos above other exchange houses. Open Mon.-Fri. 9am-6pm, Sat. 9am-2pm.

American Express: Vallarta 2440 (tel. 630-02-00), at Plaza los Arcos. Take the "Par Vial" bus and look for the office on your right after about 15 blocks. Full financial services and travel agency. Open Mon.-Fri. 9am-2:30pm and 4-5pm, Sat. 9am-noon.

Post Office: On Carranza, between Juan Manuel and Calle de Independencia (not Independencia Sur), 1 block north of the Teatro Degollado. Open Mon.-Fri. 8am-7pm, Sat.-Sun. 9am-1pm. City mailboxes rumored to be unreliable. **Postal code:** 44100 or 44101 for surrounding area.

Telephones: Long distance office, Donato Guerra 72, between Moreno and Juárez. No charge for collect calls. Open daily 7am-8:30pm. Orange public phones are for local calls and take 50- or 100-peso coins. Blue phones are for long distance and take 1000-peso coins. **Telephone code:** 36.

Telegrams: Palacio Federal, Alcalde and Juan Álvarez (tel. 613-99-16); and at the airport. Open Mon.-Sat. 9am-3pm.

Airport: 17km south of town on the road to Chapala. Don't pay more than 40 pesos for a cab. Served by: **Aeroméxico** (tel. 689-02-57), **Mexicana** (tel. 649-22-22), **American** (tel. 689-03-04), and **Delta** (tel. 630-35-30).

Train Station: At the foot of Independencia Sur, just before the tunnel, south of the *centro* (tel. 650-08-26, 650-04-44 for a Spanish recording). Prices vary widely depending on train and class of ticket. Southbound to: Mexico City (7:30pm, 12hrs., 11-61 pesos) via Querétaro (10 pesos); Manzanillo (8hrs., 18 pesos); and Colima (5hrs., 20 pesos). Northbound to: Mazatlán (17 pesos), Mexicali (200pesos), and Los Mochis (43-83 pesos). Buy tickets at least a week in advance. In the station, desk to the left as you enter is far more helpful than the recalcitrant ticket-window staff. Open for ticket sales daily 8am-8:30pm. (See Orientation for info on bus and taxi rides to and from station.)

Bus Station: In Tlaquepaque (see Orientation above). 30-odd carriers insure easy access to the northern half of the Republic. **Terminal 1: Servicios Coordinados** is the most frequent to Mexico City (22 per day, 8hrs., 44 pesos). **Autobuses la Piedad** to Celaya (transport hub of the Bajío, every ½hr., 6hrs., 30 pesos). **Terminal 2: Autobuses del Occidente** to Lázaro Cárdenas (5 per day, 11hrs., 45 pesos). **Terminal 3: Transportes del Pacífico** to Tijuana (16 per day, 36hrs., 190 pesos). **Tres Estrellas de Oro** to Puerto Vallarta (14 per day, 6hrs., 38 pesos) and Mazatlán (3 per day, 8hrs., 35 pesos; some Tijuana-bound buses also stop in Mazatlán). **Terminal 4: Autocamiones del Pacífico** to Manzanillo (15 per day, 8hrs., 30 pesos). **Terminal 6: Estrella Blanca** to Zacatecas (17 per day, 6½hrs., 35 pesos) and Fresnillo (12 per day, 7hrs., 38 pesos). **Terminal 7: Omnibus de México** to Tepic (8 per day, 4 hrs., 23 pesos) and Laredo (2 per day, 15hrs., 94 pesos).

Car Rental: Most places are on Niños Héroes or at the airport. **Budget,** Niños Héroes 934 (tel. 613-00-27); **Avis,** Niños Héroes 9 (tel. 613-90-11); **National,** Niños Héroes 961c (tel. 614-71-75), or **Hertz** (tel. 614-61-39). U.S. citizens need U.S. driver's license, major credit card, and 21 years under their belt. Prices around 75 pesos per day plus .60 pesos per km and 35 pesos per day insurance.

English Bookstores: Sandi Bookstore, Tepeyac 718 (tel. 621-08-63), in Colonia Chapalita. Take bus #50 from Garibaldi. Extensive selection of new books and North American newspapers. Open Mon.-Fri. 9:30am-2:30pm and 3:30-7pm, Sat. 9:30am-2pm. The Hyatt carries day-old copies of the *New York Times*, while the Sanborn department store at Juárez and Corona carries a mind-boggling range of magazines.

Cultural and Arts Information: Departamento de Bellas Artes (tel. 614-16-14), Jesus Garcia 720. Publishes a seasonal calendar of events. Open Mon.-Fri. 8am-3pm, Sat. 8am-1pm.

Laundromat: Lavandería San Antonio, López Cotilla 1234. Wash and dry 8 pesos; soap 1.50 pesos. Open Mon.-Sat. 8:30am-7:30pm, Sun. 8:30am-1:30pm.

Red Cross: Accqui and Juan Manuel (tel. 614-27-07), near the Pl. Morelos.

Green Cross Hospital: Tel. 614-52-52.

Pharmacies: Farmacia de Descuento, Pedro Moreno 518, open 8am-10pm; **Farmacia Guadalajara,** Javier Mina 221 (tel. 617-85-55). Open 24 hrs.

GUADALAJARA

Hospitals: Hospital del Carmen, Tarascos 3435 (tel. 647-48-82). **Nuevo Hospital Civil,** Salvador Quevedo y Zubieta 750 (tel. 618-93-62). If your *turista* shackles you to the toilet, most hotel managers know a doctor who speaks English. **Police:** Independencia Nte. 840 (tel. 617-60-60 or 618-02-60).

ACCOMMODATIONS

Although Guadalajara is a major city with numerous five-star hotels, there are some good finds available for the budget traveler as well, many of which offer special rates for stays of one week.

A good alternative to budget hotels is the *posada*. *Posadas* are small, family-run establishments that, for a few extra pesos, provide large and better-furnished rooms, better security, and frequently include meals as well. The drawbacks are less privacy and less freedom to stay out late. Check at the tourist office for a list.

Outside of the *posadas*, reservations are only necessary in February, when the city plays host to a large cultural festival.

Near the Plaza Tapatía

With room prices more or less consistent (and prices often based as much on haggling ability as quality), bedding down in the convenient *centro* isn't a bad idea. It's probably safer, though noisier, than other options, and convenience is a definite plus.

Posada San Pablo, Madero 218 (tel. 613-33-12). Not only the nicest, but also the cheapest place in town. Large clean rooms with ceilings over 15ft. high, some with balconies. Lovely green tinted covered courtyards and canaries in this gracious family's house. Singles 35 pesos. Doubles 45 pesos.
Hotel Las Américas, Hidalgo 76 (tel. 613-96-22). Unimaginative but comfortable. Wall-to-wall carpets, curtains and gleaming hallways. *Agua* galore. Traffic noise is the sole drawback to this hotel's great location: right down the street from Pl. Tapatía. Singles 50 pesos. Doubles with 1 bed 55 pesos, with 2 beds 60 pesos.
Hotel Sevilla, Sánchez 413 (tel. 614-90-37). Modern and basic, but clean. Phones and TVs. Singles 40 pesos. Doubles with 1 bed 60 pesos, with 2 beds 70 pesos.
Posada Regis, Corona 171 (tel. 613-30-26). Large clean rooms with very tall ceilings off of large, dark courtyard with an ancient movie projector that shows movies each day. Deals for multi-night stays. Singles 80 pesos. Doubles 100 pesos.
Hotel Universo, López Cotilla 161 (tel. 613-28-15). A bargain which offers a lot for the dough. TVs and phones in every room. Suites available for extra *dinero*. Singles 88 pesos. Doubles 99 pesos.
Hotel Hamilton, Madero 381 (tel. 614-67-26). This hotel is dark for a number of reasons: its dark side-street location, the scarcity of lightbulbs, the dark maroon bedspreads, and the dust. But the dark can be almost cozy in a away, and its not too expensive. Singles 35 pesos. Doubles with 1 bed 40 pesos, with 2 beds 45 pesos.
Hotel Maya, López Cotilla 39 (tel. 614-54-54). Walls, showers, bedspreads, restaurant are all basic, all concrete, all dizzying sky blue—the rooms feel like large, underwater prison cells. Singles 40 pesos. Doubles 50 pesos.

East on Javier Mina

Nicer hotels are closer to Plaza Tapatia, where the neighborhood is not only more central, but also safer. Javier Mina and especially the dark side streets off of it can become dangerous at night. If the cheaper options above don't work out (or if you just want to be closer to Plaza de los Mariachis) these hotels are basic, modern, and clean.

Hotel Ana Isabel, Javier Mina 164 (tel. 617-79-20). Like a cruise ship (not that any budget traveler would know) with a thin narrow hall, small rooms with small windows, tiny TVs, and tiny sinks with rings (to hold onto or hang a towel). Also clean. Singles 45 pesos. Doubles 55 pesos.

Hotel Imperio, Javier Mina 180 (tel. 617-50-42). A yellow color scheme and remarkably polite staff brighten the central courtyard. The bathrooms show their age but continue to function. The traffic below might as well be routed through the rooms. Singles 40 pesos. Doubles 45 pesos.

Hotel Azteca, Javier Mina 311 (tel. 617-74-66). Lobby a bit snazzier than the others in the neighborhood; an elevator whisks you upward. Plenty of furniture, fans and linoleum-esque floors. Pistachio-green bathrooms want to be loved. Singles 40 pesos. Doubles 45 pesos.

Hotel México 70, Javier Mina 230 (tel. 617-99-78). Clean large rooms with blue walls and blue bathrooms. Rooms overlooking the street have balconies. Singles 35 pesos. Doubles 45 pesos.

West to University

Strange as it may seem, the university campus located eight long blocks west of Pl. Tapatía is considerably more peaceful than the rest of the *centro*. Because most university-related action ends by nightfall you gain nothing but tranquility by staying in this area. **Posada de la Plata,** López Cotilla 619 (tel. 614-91-46). A large clean rooms around a comfortable courtyard with red tile and a large lazy dog. The place remains popular with travelers. (Singles 35 pesos. Doubles 55 pesos.) **Hotel La Paz,** La Paz 1091 (tel. 614-29-10), near Donato Guerra. Clean, basic and in the boonies, but the rooms do have TVs. (Singles 40 pesos. Doubles 50 pesos.)

South to Train Station

Before opting to bed down in this industrial wasteland, it would be wise to remember that there is nothing to do in this area except sleep. Better hotels await you in Guadalajara's lively *centro*. **Hotel Estación,** Independencia Sur 1297 (tel. 619-00-51), is—unfortunately—just to the left as you leave the station. Rooms have as much charm as a baggage compartment, though the lobby and bathrooms appear uncontaminated by dirt. (Singles 39 pesos. Doubles 49 pesos.) Six long blocks from the station is **Hotel Flamingos,** Independencia Sur 725 (tel. 619-99-21). Catch the #60 bus and get off at Los Angeles if you have bags. It is small, noisy, and dark, but very cheap with a pleasant cafeteria in lobby. (Singles 25 pesos. Doubles with 1 bed 30 pesos.)

FOOD

There is a Guadalajaran restaurant for almost any budget. Those to whom money is no object will find that Guadalajara is packed with high-class French, Italian and Japanese restaurants.

All sorts of bacteria cavort in the food and water in Guadalajara; even locals have to reckon with the microscopic creatures. A program has been launched by the state of Jalisco to improve the hygiene in food establishments, and many insist that the food quality has improved. Restaurants and cafeterias should be relatively safe, but avoid sidewalk stalls and the food in *Mercado Libertad*, and drink only when you can see the cooler whence the fluid came.

Near Plaza Tapatía

Hidalgo 112, at Hidalgo 112. A glorified juice bar with pine tables and traditional blue glass. Read the paper and chat with the locals after the lunchtime rush. Fantastically cheap. Large good fruit yogurt with granola served in a huge martini glass (3 pesos), as well as juices and sandwiches (from 3 pesos). Open daily 8am-9pm.

Restaurante La Alemana, on Blanco at 16 de Septiembre. Live Germanesque music nightly, great cheap food and free-flowing beers from the huge wooden bar. Huge plate of *enchiladas con pollo* 6 pesos, ½ chicken 16 pesos. Open daily noon-1am.

El Farol, Moreno 466, 2nd floor. Decent food at low prices. 2 prized tables overlook the street in this tiled restaurant with vinyl chairs. Friendly owner. Complementary *buñuelos*, dripping with sugary syrup, for dessert. Entrees 10-16 pesos. Plate of enchiladas 12 pesos. Open daily 10am-2am.

La Chata, Corona 126 (tel. 613-05-88). Colorful checked tablecloths and dark wooden chairs. Unfortunately, the open kitchen makes this restaurant hot Entrees around 20 pesos. *Huevos* 10 pesos. Open daily 9am-10:30pm.

Restaurant Aquarius, Sánchez 416, across from Hotel Sevilla. New Age Mexi-style. Wear your finest peasant shirt and brandish your cosmic conscious-ness. Freshly squeezed orange juice 3 pesos. Vegetarian *comida corriente* 18.40 pesos.

Café Madrid, Juárez 262 (tel. 614-95-04). Looks like a small-town bus depot lunch spot in front, the men watching TV et al. In back more formal tables and a large mural on the wall. Steak 18 pesos. *Commida corrida* 18 pesos. Open daily 8am-10pm.

Las Yardas Bar, Juárez 37. A fun, music-filled bar with a few simple dishes. Eclec-tic decor. During happy hour (Mon.-Thurs. 7-9pm) enjoy the 2-for-1 beer (45 pesos) special. Open daily noon-11pm.

Sandy's Restaurant, Alcalde 130. Gray carpeting, booths, and balconies overlook-ing Pl. de los Mártires. Suit-clad men and elegant women hit this place during power lunch breaks. Breakfasts 10 pesos. Mexican dishes 16-22 pesos. Open daily 7am-8pm.

East to Javier Mina

Restaurants near Javier Mina will fill your stomach, but not in any particularly refined way. **Restaurant del Pacífico,** Pl. de los Mariachis (tel. 621-91-88). Surpris-ingly, the *carne asada* (12 pesos) here beats that of many more expensive places, and it'll fill you up with no trouble. Lots of beer drinking transpires here till the cows come home. Brew 3.50 pesos. (Open daily 8am-1am.) **Restaurant Flam-boyen,** Independencia Sur 164 (tel. 613-00-76), in the Hotel de los Reyes. Denny's just might be able to win a copyright infringement suit, except this place gets sur-real around midnight, when other places close. A serious late-night hang out, the bar stocks all sorts of crazy drinks. *Huevos a la mexicana* 10 pesos. Beer 5.60 pesos. (Open 24 hrs.) **Restaurant Nuevo Faro,** López Cotilla 24. Quick and filling. Good breakfast dishes: *omeleta mexicana* 7.50 pesos. Entrees 7-12 pesos. *Comida corri-ente* 11 pesos. (Open daily 8am-10pm.)

West from Chapultepec to López Mateos

Here, a few extra pesos buy superior quality and elegant atmosphere. Most places below cluster near the intersection of Vallarta and Chapultepec, on the "Par Vial" bus route. It's worth the trip.

Los Itacates Fonda, Chapultepec Nte. 110 (tel. 625-11-06). Fancy *típico* restaurant with an extensive menu of many Mexican delicacies. Blessed by better and cheaper food than most other restaurants in any district. Full of middle- and upper-class Mexican families. Mexican ceramic plates and crafts on the stucco walls and large blue painted wooden chairs. Great breakfast buffet 15 pesos. *Pollo molle* 15 pesos. Tacos 5 pesos. Open Mon.-Sat 8am-11pm, Sun. 8am-6:30pm.

Café Don Luis, Chapultepec 209 at Libertad (tel. 625-65-99). Coffees and desserts. A great place to revive your sleepy bones after a *siesta*; the Angel's Kiss (Kahlúa, coffee and eggnog) will add some zip for 5 pesos. Open daily 10am-2pm and 5-10pm.

Recco, Libertad 1973 (tel. 625-07-24), just off Chapultepec. White tablecloths, metal plates, and old block and white photos on the walls. Those in T-shirts or shorts will feel underdressed. *Fettucine alfredo* 17 pesos. The friendly owner speaks almost fluent English. Filet mignon 35 pesos. Mon.-Sat. 1pm-midnight, Sun. 1-10pm.

La Trattoria, Niños Héroes 305 (tel. 622-18-17), 1 block east of López Mateos. Call for reservations or face the prospect of a long wait. Italian food in a large, sterile room. Fettucini alfredo 17 pesos. Most meat dishes 27 pesos. Large portions. Open Mon.-Sat. 1pm-midnight, Sun. 1-8pm.

Las Margaritas, López Cotilla 1477 (tel. 16-89-06), just west of Chapultepec. Inventive (and expensive) vegetarian food. Yellow and green middle-eastern motif and tunes by the Mamas and the Papas. Menu in English and Spanish. Open Mon.-Sat. 8:30am-9pm, Sun. 8:30am-6pm.

La Hacienda de Jazo, Justo Sierra 2022, just off Chapultepec Nte. In a courtyard so quiet you'll forget you're in a city. Live piano daily 3-6pm; at all other times, Lionel Richie, et al. are piped in. Meat and fish entrees 12-18 pesos. Open Mon.-Sat. 1-8pm.

SIGHTS

Guadalajara's museums are the best introduction to Mexican culture and history outside Mexico City.

Downtown

The four plazas in downtown Guadalajara provide a wide-open refuge from the otherwise packed streets. Most corners are punctuated by horse-drawn carriages that offer hour-long tours for about 35 pesos. The spacious **Plaza de la Liberàción,** with its large, bubbling fountain, is surrounded by the **cathedral, Museo Regional, Palacio de Gobierno** and **Teatro Degollado.** A modern sculpture depicts Hidalgo breaking the chains of slavery in commemoration of his 1810 decree, signed in Guadalajara, to abolish the trade.

The **Palacio de Gobierno,** built in 1774 on the plaza's south side, is a Churrigueresque and neoclassical building graced by yet another mural by Orozco; the sight of Hidalgo's feverish eyes looking down from the wall strikes fear in the heart of many an unsuspecting visitor. A second Orozco mural covers the ceiling in the **Sala de Congreso.** This one depicts *indígenas* in slavery and the heroic Miguel Hidalgo and Benito Juárez. (Open Mon.-Sat. 9am-3pm and 6-9pm; *Sala de Congreso* open 9am-6pm when the legislature is not in session.)

The imposing **cathedral** faces the Teatro Degollado across Pl. de la Liberación. Begun in 1558 and completed 60 years later, this edifice is a whirl of architectural styles. An 1848 earthquake destroyed the original towers, and ambitious architects replaced them with much taller ones. Fernando VII of Spain donated the 11 richly ornamented altars in appreciation of Guadalajara's help during the Napoleonic Wars. One of the remaining original altars is dedicated to Our Lady of the Roses; it is this altar, and not the botanical beauties, that gave Guadalajara its nickname, "City of Roses."

The doors to the sacristy are usually shut, but one of the attendants may let you in. Required proper dress is a show of respect. Inside the sacristy rests the *Assumption of the Virgin*, by famed 17th-century painter Bertolemé Murillo. The towers, known as the *cornucopias*, can be climbed with the permission of the cathedral's administrators, who hole up in the rear of the building to the right of the altar. Enter the cathedral from the back. The 60m jaunt affords the best view in town. (Church open Mon.-Sat. 8am-8pm; tourists unwelcome on Sunday.) On the cathedral's west side lies the arboreal **Plaza de los Laureles;** on the north, the **Plaza de los Mártires** commemorates *tapatíos* who died in various wars.

A building constructed in 1696 on the north side of the Pl. de la Liberación houses the **Museo Regional de Guadalajara.** Also known as the Museo del Estado de Jalisco, Liceo e Hidalgo, this museum chronicles the history of western Mexico, beginning with the Big Bang. The first floor is devoted to the country's pre-Hispanic development and includes meteorites, woolly mammoth bones, metalwork, jewels, and some Aztec art lamenting the Spanish Conquest. Maps of human migratory routes and patterns of settlement and disquisitions on various indigenous peoples give an excellent sense of the continuity of the country's development before the arrival of the Spanish. Collections of colonial art, modern paintings, and an exhibit on the history of the revolution occupy the second floor. (Open Tues.-Sun.

9am-3:45pm. Admission 10 pesos, students free. Free to all on Sundays. Movies, plays and lectures in the museum auditorium. Call tel. 614-99-57 for information.)

Attend the Ballet Folklórico at 10am on Sunday mornings to get a good look at the **Teatro Degollado,** a neoclassical structure on the Pl. de la Liberación's east end. The interior features gold-and-red balconies, a sculpted allegory of the seven muses on the pediment, and Gerardo Suárez's depiction of Dante's *Divine Comedy* on the ceiling. You can visit any time when there is no performance scheduled (tel. 613-11-15). Tickets available at the theater box office (see Entertainment below).

The **Plazuela de los Mariachis** lies on the south side of San Juan de Dios, the church with the blue neon cross at Independencia and Javier Mina. The *plazuela* is really a glorified alley, lined with bars and budget restaurants where flashy *maria-chis* hustle soused *gringos*. Immediately after sitting down, roving musicians will att-mempt to separate you and your pesos at the rate of 8 pesos a song, post-haggling. The daily festivities peak at lunch time, again at dinner and continue late into the night.

From the Pl. Tapatía, you can see the dome of the 190-year-old **Hospicio Cabañas** at the corner of Hospicio and Cabañas, 3 blocks east of Independencia. It was here that Padre Hidalgo signed his proclamation against slavery in 1811; the building has since served as an orphanage and an art school. In the main chapel, Orozco painted a series of murals in 1938-39, which some regard as his best work; the dome holds Orozco's nightmarish rendition of the Four Riders of the Apocalypse. *Espejos* (mir-rors) are available free for those who don't want to strain their necks, or you can lie down on one of the many benches set up for reclined viewing. The *hospicio* also houses a collection of Orozco drawings and lithographs recently moved from his home in west Guadalajara, as well as other rotating exhibits. (Open Tues.-Sat. 10:15am-6pm. Admission 5 pesos, 3 pesos with student ID.)

If you've heard the promotional hoopla for the **Mercado Libertad,** at Javier Mina and Independencia, reality may disappoint. Mexico's largest daily market offers three floors of schlock and cheap food. The prices here are much lower and the shopkeepers less frenzied, however, making it possible to browse in relative tran-quility. Most of the food has been sitting out all day and may not be clean. (Open daily 9am-8pm, but some merchants do not open on Sun.) A more authentic and fas-cinating market is **El Baratillo** on Javier Mina, approximately 15 blocks east of *Mer-cado Libertad*. El Baratillo lasts all day Sunday and sometimes stretches for 30 or 40 blocks. Everything imaginable is peddled here, from hot tamales to houses. From *Mercado Libertad*, walk two blocks to Gigantes and catch bus #37 or #38 heading east.

South

Almost everything inside the **Casa de las Artesanías de Jalisco** on González Gallo (the street which bisects *Parque Agua Azul*) is for sale. Pottery, jewelry, furniture, and clothing, all of it from Tlaquepaque and Tonalá (see Near Guadalajara below), cost more here than they do in those two villages, but the quality is extraordinary. For those who don't have the time and the energy to do the legwork involved in trips from the city, the *casa* will show you the best of what you're missing. (Open Mon.-Fri. 10am-7pm, Sat. 10am-4pm, Sun. 10am-2pm.)

A large, fenced-in tract of woods and gardens with numerous fountains and stat-ues, **Parque Agua Azul** provides a haven for those tired of the noise of south Guad-alajara. (Open daily 10am-6pm. Admission 3 pesos.)

West

Guadalajara's **Zona Rosa,** the upper-class shopping district, centers on Chapulte-pec, west of the university. Cultural activity in the city's wealthier areas focuses on the **Plaza del Arte,** one block south on Chapultepec from its intersection with Niños Héroes. Local artists bare their souls on a rotating basis in the plaza's **Centro de Arte Moderno.** (Open daily 8am-2pm and 4-7pm.) The **Galería Municipal,** on the Pl. del Arte, also showcases local painters. Stand-up comedy and performance art periodically enliven the premises. Watch for notices on the blackboard at the Departamento de Bellas Artes, at García 720 (tel. 614-16-14).

The **Tequila Sauza Bottling Plant,** Vallarta 3273 (tel. 647-66-74), on the outskirts of Guadalajara, is a shrine for serious tequila fans. Pay homage here to the golden elixir of life. (Free tours Mon.-Fri. 10am-noon.) Take the "Par Vial" bus west to the end of the line then catch *combi* #130 in front of the Hotel Fiesta Americana. The plant is just before the overpass. Bus #45 will take you back into town.

ENTERTAINMENT

Although there is no lack of things to do at night in Guadalajara, the streets usually become deserted at night fall and are often dangerous.

The **Ballet Folklórico** has toured the world, entertaining audiences with stage antics and the famed Mexican hat dance. There are two troupes in Guadalajara, one affiliated with the University of Guadalajara and the other with the state of Jalisco. The former, reputedly better, performs in the Teatro Degollado on Sunday at 10am (followed by the **State Philharmonic Orchestra** at noon). Tickets (10-50 pesos) are sold the day before the show at the Teatro Degollado ticket office (open daily 9:30am-5:30pm). Spend the extra pesos for a front seat and arrive a half-hour before the show because seats are not reserved within sections, and performances nearly always sell out. The state troupe performs Wednesdays at 8:30pm in the theater of the Hospicio Cabañas (tickets 15 pesos). Call tel. 617-44-40, ext. 22, for more information.

University facilities, scattered throughout the city, have created a market for high culture on a low budget. The **Departamento de Bellas Artes** coordinates activities at a large number of stages, auditoriums, and movie screens across the city. The best source of information on cultural events is the blackboard in their lobby at García 720 (see Sights above) which lists each day's attractions. The two principal dramatic stages are the **Teatro de Guadalajara** (tel. 619-58-23) and the **Teatro Experimental** (tel. 619-37-70), across the street from each other at Pl. Juárez, on the west side of *Parque Agua Azul*. While the works at the Experimental are recommended only for those proficient in Spanish, the program at the Teatro de Guadalajara includes more easily understood comic and popular works.

The **Instituto Cultural Cabañas** presents live music on an open-air stage in the Hospicio Cabañas at least once a week (tickets 15 pesos, students 12 pesos). Drop by the Hospicio Cabañas ticket counter (see Sights above), or look for flyers with the Cabañas insignia (a building with pillars) for current schedules. Each October, Guadalajara hosts a month-long festival of cultural and sporting events with fireworks and special displays representing each state in the republic.

For Luis Buñuel retrospectives and other vintage screenings, head to the cinema at Bellas Artes. The **Cine Cinematógrafo,** at Vallarta 1102 (tel. 25-05-14), just west of the university, is a repertory film house that changes its show weekly (tickets 3 pesos).

For live jazz, try the **Copenhagen,** at Américas and López Mateos near the statue of Columbus, or **La Hosta,** at México and Rubén Darío. Nightlife in this hopping town centers on the Pl. del Sol, near the southern end of López Mateos. **Osiris** (20 pesos), at Jardines de los Arcos on Lázaro Cárdenas, receives rave reviews from locals. It's private, but if you convince the bouncers of your foreign origin (it shouldn't be hard), they'll let you in. **Ciros,** on the Pl. del Sol, is another popular disco. Again, members only, but foreigners accepted. They may even let you in wearing sneakers, but don't count on it (cover 25 pesos). **Oz,** next door, is the ultimate in glam. Far away from Kansas. Couples only, preferably with expensive clothing. Non-Mexican non-members admitted, but the bouncers have fun making people wait. (Cover 30 pesos per couple.) A younger, hipper crowd (guys with long hair) inhabits the kinder, gentler **Iceburg** (tel. 622-77-78) in the Hyatt Hotel complex on López Mateos, two blocks from the Pl. del Sol. People here are actually friendly, and if you rap with the bouncer long enough, he may give you free passes. Otherwise, cover 25 pesos. (All of the above places are open Thurs.-Sun. 10pm-2 or 3am.) **Terraza del Oasis,** Hidalgo 436, occasionally has live bands.

Gay clubs support more nightlife here than in any other city outside the Federal District. The upscale *Zona Rosa* along Chapultepec is a favorite gathering place. The best-known gay disco is **Unicornio,** López Mateos. Other hangouts include **S.O.S.,** La Paz 1413 at Escoza (closed Sun.), which has incredibly vibrant drag shows, and **Monica's,** Alvaro Obregón 1713, popular with the young crowd. (Open Wed.-Sun. 11pm-4am.) The **Jesse James,** Ramos Millán 955, is a honky tonk complete with country-and-western music. A mixed gay and straight crowd also frequents **Chivas López Cotilla** and **Degollado.**

Sports

Bullfights take place in the Pl. de Toros, at Nuevo Progreso on the northern end of Independencia, almost every Sunday from October to April. Posters throughout the city broadcast each contest. Take bus #62 north. The ticket and information office is at Morelos 229 (tel. 613-55-58). Guadalajara also features *charreadas* (rodeos), held in Parque Agua Azul every Sunday.

Soccer games draw the biggest crowds in this city. The *Chivas,* the local professional team, is the crowd's favorite and a powerful contender for the national championship each season. Don't even think about uttering the name of the team's arch-rival from Mexico City, the *Pumas.* Matches are held from September through May in **Jalisco Stadium,** at the University of Guadalajara and at the Universidad Autónoma. The ticket office (tel. 642-18-40) is on Colomos Pte. 2339 at López Mateos. Tickets can also be purchased at the stadium box office on the day of the game.

Ice-skating, of all things, is possible year-round at the Hyatt Regency on Pl. del Sol (tel. 622-59-32). You can rent skates for around 12 pesos. (Open Mon.-Thurs. 5-7pm and 7:30-9pm, Fri.-Sun. 4:15-6:15pm and 8:15-9:45pm.)

Public **swimming pools** in Guadalajara are filthy. If you've got to get wet, try one of the private sports clubs (at least 10 pesos), but many no longer permit non-members. People have been known to sneak into the Hyatt's pool. The easiest option may be an extended shower at your hotel.

■ Near Guadalajara

Excursions from Guadalajara are prime opportunities for souvenir-hunting. East of the city, **Tlaquepaque** and **Tonalá** peddle high-priced artisanry; to the north **Zapopan** craft work sells at the Casa de Artesanías de los Huichol; on the shores of Laguna Chapala, 40km to the south, the villages of Chapala, Ajijic, and Jopotlán welcome tourist excursions and an ever-expanding population of North American retirees.

Northwest of the city is the town of **Zapopan,** site of the **Basílica de la Virgen de Zapopan,** a giant edifice erected in the 16th century to commemorate a peasant's vision. The walls of the church are hung with many decades' worth of *ex-votos,* small paintings on sheet metal honoring the Virgin's aid in diseases and accidents. Pope John Paul II visited the shrine in 1979, and a statue of him holding hands with a beaming *campesino* boy now stands in the courtyard in front of the church. The **Casa de Artesanías de los Huichol,** a museum and crafts market for Huichol handwork, remains Zapopan's chief point of interest. Clothing, *ojos de dios* (eyes of god) and *makrames,* colorful designs of yarn on wood, are sold at bargain prices. To get there, catch the #275 bus northbound on the Av. 16 de Septiembre and de-bus at the big church. (Open Mon.-Fri. 10am-1:30pm and 3:30-6pm. Free.)

The "village" of **Tlaquepaque,** on the #275 (or 275A) bus route a few stops before the Nueva Central, is a pleasant tourist trap. High class shops set in old colonial mansions line Independencia, the main drag, selling silver, handicrafts, leather and ceramics. Cheaper goods of lesser quality can be found in the *mercado* just off the main square. The **Museo Regional de las Cerámicas y los Artes Populares de Jalisco** has an interesting collection of antique regional crafts, as well as newer pieces for sale. Another fun if touristy spot is **La Roja de Cristal,** Independencia 232, where artisans blow glass by hand Mon.-Fri. 9:30am-2:30pm, Sat. 9:30am-12:30pm. Their goods are then sold Mon.-Sat. from 10am to 7pm. Just don't visit on a Sunday when virtually all the shops are closed.

It is best to go to Tlaquepaque on a daytrip from Guadalajara. There are only two hotels in the town. The clean, dark, mildew-smelling rooms at **Posada en el Parián,** Independencia 74 (tel. 35-21-89) go for 40 pesos for singles and 55 pesos for doubles. Reserve in advance or arrive early. The **Hotel Tlaquepaque,** Juárez 36 (tel. 35-00-87) features very turquoise and not-so-clean rooms. (Singles 35 pesos, Doubles 40 pesos.) The central block of restaurants, along Independencia, boasts a number of more or less identical establishments. Of these restaurants, **Paco's** seems to avail itself of slightly better people-watching potential. *Mole poblano* (at the neighboring places too) 15 pesos, *quesadillas* 10 pesos. If Paco's doesn't suit you, try **Salón Imperial, Monterrey,** or **Beto's.** *Mariachi* groups strut their stuff there, too. Bands will perform at your table for a hefty 25 pesos. When you want to return downtown, hop on a #275 bus at the corner of Niños and Independencia.

Had it with shopping? Head to **Parque Mirador,** at the northern end of Independencia. The park's main attraction is its proximity to the 670m gorge of the Río Santiago, where waterfalls cascade over the cliffs during the rainy season. (Open daily 9am-7:30pm. Admission .60 pesos. Take bus #60 north along Independencia.) Also on Independencia is the modern, lush **Guadalajara Zoo.** There's nary a cage to be seen inside, and the place has more of the feel of a theme park with train rides, dolphin shows, fun fair, and hordes of awe-struck children. (Open daily 10am-6pm. Admission 10 pesos, children 8-16 5 pesos.)

Tonalá is a scaled-down version of Tlaquepaque, mainly because it's harder to reach. Visit Tonalá on Thursday or Sunday, when the town briefly awakens from its near-perpetual *siesta*. Tonalá specializes in inexpensive, conservatively decorated ceramics. While Tlaquepaque offers greater variety, Tonalá has made fewer concessions to the tourist industry and retains more of its natural charm. You can still find women weaving beautiful, multi-colored rugs and sewing dolls. Patient ceramics merchants paint personalized messages onto their products. In Tonalá, you get the soft sell as people take the time to converse with you without making you feel obligated to purchase something.

Tonalá has the added benefit of letting you visit a near-rural village with the safety of a long *combi* lifeline back to the more comfortably urban Guadalajara. Buses #103 and #104, which run through downtown Guadalajara along Moreno, are the best way to reach Tonalá (.50 pesos).

Forty km south of Guadalajara lies **Lago de Chapala,** Mexico's second largest lake. The towns of **Chapala, Ajijic,** and **Jocotepec** along the northern shore of the lake present a peaceable mix of Mexican tourists, North American retirees, artists, and would-be artists from around the world. While living in Ajijic in the 1940s, before the plague of industrial development rendered swimming in the lake impossible, D.H. Lawrence wrote *The Plumed Serpent*. Stark mountains still haunt the lake's opposite shore, keeping the setting beautiful. English-speakers will feel at home in Chapala and Ajijic: there are so many expatriates here that half of the signs are in English and the other half are bilingual.

You can get to Chapala from the *antigua* bus station (every ½hr., 45min., 4.50 pesos). There are two acceptable options for anyone wishing to stay near the lake. A haunt for Mexico's wealthy, staying near the lake can be expensive, though you do get a lot for your pesos. In Chapala, the **Hotel Nino,** Madero 202 (tel. 5-21-16) once played host to dictator Díaz's weekend soirées. Now considerably more sedate, the airy hotel has clean, simple rooms with floral stencils set around a pretty courtyard with restaurant and pool. (Singles 40 pesos, doubles 60 pesos. *Menú del día* 24 pesos, breakfasts 8-12 pesos.)

Just down the road lies the prettier village of **Ajijic** (catch the bus—1.20 pesos—from the corner of Madero and de Velasco in Chapala). The **Posada Las Calandrias,** on the Carretera Chapala (tel. 5-28-19), has clean singles for 50 pesos and doubles for 75 pesos, set around a gleaming pool popular with local wedding parties. Next door, Brady Bunch-style bungalows go for 80 pesos with all the amenities, including kitchens. Have the area to yourself during the week; the crowds from Guadalajara hit Chapala mostly on the weekends. Tours are also available; call Panoramex (tel. 10-51-09).

For food try **Beto's**, right next to the Hotel Nino. The food is generally decent, and the pace relaxed: entrees 8-14 pesos. Beer is by far the most popular item on the menu, but the chilly margaritas go down easy. For a great lunch in Ajijic, try **Danny's,** located just off the highway. Gorgeous burgers, lunches and sandwiches run 4-7 pesos. (Open Mon.-Sat. 8am-5pm, Sun. 8am-1pm.) For those who feel like a splurge, try the lunchtime buffet in **Hotel Nueva Posada**, Donato Guerra 9 (tel. 5-33-95). Sumptuous Italianate interior and sculpted gardens leading down to the lake just might make the feast worth 34 pesos.

■■■ PUERTO VALLARTA

In 1956 tabloid headlines were touting Puerto Vallarta as an unspoiled paradise. Richard Burton and Elizabeth Taylor's torrid affair while on location shooting *Night of the Iguana* helped paint Puerto Vallarta as the world headquarters of sensuality. Back then, neither highway nor telephone wire hitched it to the outside world; since that time, Puerto Vallarta has undergone a radical facelift. Thirty-five years and millions of dollars later, Puerto Vallarta is a world-class resort with stunningly groomed beaches, luxurious hotels and gorgeous mansions. What brought people here in the first place—the clear water and beautiful beaches—though more crowded now, still remain beautiful.

While all of Puerto Vallarta revolves around tourism, the form it takes varies greatly; the city naturally divides itself into different areas. In the south end of town, where the best swimming beach is and where the more reasonable hotels are located, there is a certain, if somewhat artificial charm: white stucco buildings, red-tiled roofs, and cobbled streets. On the north side of the river, larger nightclubs, and more expensive clothing stores find a home, while still further north international resorts line the highway.

ORIENTATION

Running west to the shore, the **Río Cuale** bisects Puerto Vallarta before emptying into the ocean. The southern half of town maintains a more authentic Mexican identity and contains virtually all the cheap hotels, best beaches, budget restaurants, and frantic dance clubs. The glitzy area north of the river could be mistaken for a stateside beach resort and it houses nearly all of the city's tourist services.

The main streets in the southern half are **Insurgentes** and **Vallarta,** which run north-south two blocks apart, and **Lázaro Cárdenas,** which runs east-west. A park two blocks south of the western end of Lázaro Cárdenas serves as a **bus** and **combi terminal;** you'll find it at the northern end of Olas Altas and Playa de los Muertos, the waterfront area. Route 200 from Manzanillo runs into town south of the river, becoming Insurgentes. It and Vallarta run north from Lázaro Cárdenas to the two bridges that link the south and north sections.

The main streets in the north are **Morelos,** the continuation of Vallarta, and **Juárez,** one block east. Four blocks north of the Vallarta bridge is the **Plaza Mayor,** whose cathedral, with its crown of open metalwork, serves as a landmark. The ritzy waterfront between Pl. Mayor and 31 de Octubre, called the **Malecón,** contains overpriced restaurants and cheesy t-shirt shops. North of the Malecón, Morelos becomes **Perú** and runs through a working-class neighborhood before joining the coastal highway. North along the highway lie the **airport,** the **marina,** and the **ferry terminal.**

Taxis charge about 10 pesos to travel between the **Playa de los Muertos** and the entrance to the highway. The municipal **buses,** which operate daily from 6am to 10:30pm, cost only .80-1.20 pesos (*combis* .80-1.50 pesos). All northbound buses and *combis* originate at the park on Olas Altas and run up Lázaro Cárdenas to Insurgentes, across the Insurgentes Bridge, west on Libertad a few blocks, north on Juárez, and onto the highway. In the opposite direction, buses enter the city on México, which turns into Díaz Ordaz and then runs into Morelos, crossing the Vallarta bridge before heading back to the party.

PRACTICAL INFORMATION

Tourist Office: In the Presidencia Municipal (tel. 2-02-42), on the northern side of the Pl. Mayor; enter on Juárez. Centrally located and loaded with maps and other information. Excellent English spoken. Open Mon.-Fri. 9am-9pm, Sat. 9am-1pm.

U.S. Consulate: Miramar at Libertad (tel. 2-00-69), just north of the Río Cuale. Open Mon.-Fri. 9am-9pm.

Currency Exchange: Several large banks around the Pl. Mayor change currency, but many only 9am-1pm. **Banca Promex,** Juárez 386, changes money Mon.-Fri. 9:30am-12:30pm. *Casas de cambio* have lower rates and are open longer, typically Mon.-Sat. 9am-2pm and 4-8pm.

American Express: Centro Comercial Villa Vallarta (tel. 2-68-77), a few blocks north of the Sheraton via buses marked "Pitillal," "Juntas," or "Ixtapa." English is spoken. Open Mon.-Fri. 9am-2:30pm and 4-6pm, Sat. 9am-1pm.

Post Office: Morelos 444 (tel. 2-37-02), at Mina, 2 blocks north of the Pl. Mayor. *Lista de Correos.* Open Mon.-Fri. 8am-7pm, Sat.-Sun. 9am-1pm. **Postal code:** 48300.

Telephones: LADATEL phones can be found on every corner. **Telephone code:** 322.

Airport: 8km north of town via the coastal highway. Buses labeled "Ixtapa" or "Juntas" pass the airport; you can catch them on Lázaro Cárdenas or Insurgentes. If you're coming from the airport, there is a bus stop on the same side of the highway, 30m to your right as you leave the airport area. Buses run 5am-11pm and cost .90 pesos. *Combis* to and from the airport cost 17 pesos per person to and from south of the river, 5 pesos per person to and from north of the river. Taxi fare is 16 pesos to the Plaza Mayor. **Aeroméxico,** at the airport (tel. 1-18-97), **Mexicana,** Juárez 152 (tel. 2-50-00), and other airlines have frequent flights to: Guadalajara (190 pesos one-way), Mexico City (320 pesos one-way), Los Angeles (US$229 one-way) and New York (US$426 one-way).

Bus Station: No central bus station. Each bus line operates its own office-*cum*-depot in the south side of the city. Destinations, frequency of service, and prices all vary by company. **Tres Estrellas de Oro,** Carranza 322 (tel. 2-62-82), has the most frequent service to Guadalajara (6hrs., 45 pesos), and Tijuana (1 per day, 190 pesos); **Transportes Cihuatlan,** at Madero and Constitución, operates more buses south to Manzanillo (6hrs., 30 pesos); **Transportes del Pacífico,** Insurgentes 282 (tel. 2-10-15), sends buses to Tepic (every ½hr., 18 pesos); **Transportes Norte de Sonora,** Madero 343 (tel. 2-16-50), serves Guadalajara (6hrs., 42 pesos), Mexico City (16hrs., 98 pesos), and Tepic (3hrs., 17 pesos).

Ferry: Terminal Marítima (tel. 2-04-76), 4½km north of town off the coastal highway.

Car Rental: There's a slew of options at the airport, or try **Hertz** in the Hotel Camino Real on Carranza (tel. 3-01-23 ext. 310), **Budget** in the Sheraton (tel. 2-67-66) or **Del Alba,** Centro Matamoros 179 (tel. 2-29-59). Most firms require drivers be 25 yrs. of age and have a valid credit card.

English Bookstore: Super Mercado Gutiérrez Rizo (known as "GR"), at Constitución and Serdán, has a selection analogous to that of U.S. supermarkets—trashy romances and adventure novels. No James Joyce. Books 20-30 pesos. Open daily

6:30am-10pm. **A Page in the Sun,** Olas Altas at Rodriguez. Sells used English books. Open daily 9am-10pm.
Laundromats: Lavandería Automática, Madero 407. Wash for 10 pesos per 3kg. Open daily 3am-8pm.
Pharmacy: Farmacia CMQ, Basilio Badillo 367, ½ block inland from Insurgentes (tel. 2-29-41). Open 24 hrs.
Hospital: CMQ Hospital, Basilio Badillo 365 (tel. 3-00-11 or 3-19-19). English spoken. Open 24 hrs.
Police: Iturbide at Morelos (tel. 3-25-00).

ACCOMMODATIONS AND CAMPING

Puerto Vallarta's sleeping options conveniently queue up in ascending socio-economic order, from the beach south of town (free) to the Sheraton in the north. The best cheap hotels are south of the Río Cuale, on or near Madero. Make sure the fan works before whipping out your wallet.

In general, hotels do not accept unpaid reservations. Go room-hunting as early as possible; 1pm is a common check-out time, but most hotels know what's available before then and fill up early in the day. Larger hotels don't mind storing even the grungiest of backpacks for the day, usually free of charge, and most of the cheaper places will do the same if they're full when you show up. The first price listed applies for June, the least expensive month of the year. December tends to be the most expensive. Prices vary in other months.

Officially, Puerto Vallarta frowns on shiftless beach bums, but most travelers encounter no problems. Even many of the local dogs are friendly. Some beachfront clubs have night guards who may keep an eye on those who request their permission before bedding down. Many people dig into the sand behind the Hotel Los Arcos or the Castle Pelícanos, which is government property, or into the open space between the John Newcombe tennis courts and the Sheraton.

Hotel Yasmin, Basilio Badillo 168 (tel. 2-00-87), 1 block from the beach. By far the nicest place for the money. A verdant courtyard with tables and chairs leads to clean, airy rooms with fans, floral stencils, desks, and spotless bathrooms. Singles 45 pesos. Doubles 50 pesos.

Hotel La Misión, Lázaro Cárdenas 207 (tel. 2-05-52). Dwarfed by its ritzier neighbors and just 1½ blocks from the beach. Small rooms have fans, clean bathrooms and a view of the pool. Singles 45 pesos. Doubles 60 pesos. Dec. singles 50 pesos. Doubles 70 pesos.

Hotel Villa del Mar, Madero 440 (tel. 2-07-85), 2 blocks east of Insurgentes. Best of the rest with tacky sea-faring motif. Clean but dark rooms cooled by strong fans and bathrooms in this large brick building. Singles 34 pesos. Doubles 42 pesos.

Hotel Azetca, Madero 473 (tel. 2-27-50). Clean, if small, rooms off of a motel-like brick courtyard. Singles 26 pesos. Doubles 32 pesos. December singles 31 pesos. Doubles 37 pesos.

Hospedaje Hortencia, Madero 339 (tel. 2-24-84). Basic, somewhat tattererd rooms, off a dilapidated open-air courtyard. Singles 35 pesos. Doubles 40 pesos.

Posada El Real, Madero 285 (tel. 2-05-87). Narrow peach concrete courtyard and small basic rooms. Friendly owner. Singles 30 pesos. Doubles 40 pesos.

Hotel Bernal, Madero 423 (tel. 2-36-05).Peewee sized rooms with basic amenities off of a closed courtyard. Singles 26 pesos. Doubles 32 pesos.

FOOD

Puerto Vallarta's Malecón specializes in tourist traps with North American cuisine. Cheaper, down-home places are numerous on the south side, especially on Madero near Insurgentes, and in the market on the north side, where Insurgentes crosses Río Cuale. The **market** is open Monday through Saturday from 8am to 8pm. **Super Mercado Gutiérrez Rico (GR),** at Constitución and Serdán, provides a huge array of foodstuffs (open daily 6:30am-10pm). Many taco and *quesadilla* stands prosper south of the river, near the cheap hotels.

South

Cafe de Olla, Basillo Badillo 168, next to Hotel Yasmin. Good Mexican and American fare in a friendly atmosphere. Great smelling grilled food and iced tea (with purified ice!). Grilled chicken 20 pesos. Lime-meringue pie 5 pesos.

La Fonda China Poblana, 222 Insurgentes (tel. 2-04-49). A pleasant surprise. Plain dark ground floor gives way to an airy 2nd floor, devoid of decor, with a balcony. Stuff yourself for 20 pesos, drinks included. Tasty and enormous order of enchiladas 13 pesos. Guacamole to match, 8 pesos. Open 24 hrs.

El Galieto-The Corner Bar, Vallarta 264, serves tiny tacos with gourmet ingredients, or normal-sized steamed tacos (6 pesos). *Quesadillas?* Choose from chicken, beef, eggplant and mushroom (12 pesos). 8 sauces to choose from, but unfortunately a bar atmosphere and a lot of *gringos.* Open daily noon-1am.

Restaurant Gilmar, Madero 418. Red chairs under red and white arches. A local favorite for the breakfast special (7 pesos), which includes juice, coffee, and 2 eggs any style with beans and tortillas. Complete dinner 15 pesos. Open Mon.-Sat. 7:30am-11pm.

North

Me Gusta, Domínguez 128, just east of Díaz Ordaz (tel. 2-41-31). A generally nifty if expensive, open-air spot. Beer (4 pesos) comes in enormous ceramic mugs and the burgers are juicy ½-pounders. Bacon burger 20 pesos. Order of 3 enchiladas 38 pesos. Sweeping view of the pelicans swooping over the ocean. Open daily 3-11pm.

Frutilandia, Díaz Ordaz 520, on the waterfront, but look hard—it's dwarfed by chintzier places. Giant plastic bananas and mangoes hang from the ceiling. Epic mango shakes 5 pesos, fruit salad with yogurt and granola 8 pesos. Open daily 8am-10pm.

El Pollo Vagabundo, México 1295, a few blocks south of the Sheraton (tel. 2-43-99). In a more Mexican neighborhood, a real Mexican restaurant—small, unpretentious with maps of Puerto Vallarta on the walls; breakfast special 11 pesos. Roasted ½-chicken 13 pesos. Open daily 8am-10pm.

SIGHTS

To get the most out of Puerto Vallarta, cultivate a taste for its 40km coastline. Some of the least crowded and most gorgeous beachfronts stretch along the coast south of town on the road to **Mismaloya** (see Near Puerto Vallarta). The best beach in Puerto Vallarta itself, **Playa de los Muertos,** extends south from Muelle de los Muertos in the southern part of town near the budget hotels. Named for the victims of a conflict between pirates and *indígenas,* the beach has withstood attempts to dub it the cheerier *Playa del Sol.* To get there, walk all the way west on Lázaro Cárdenas and then south along the poorly-named **Playa de Olas Altas** (Big Waves Beach). If you spend much time here, watch out or you may buy something—hawkers of everything imaginable prowl about aggressively, preying on tourists.

Various water sports generate a lot of activity during the morning hours but trickle off by mid-afternoon. **Parasailing** (US$20-$30 a shot) is particularly popular; parachutes are scattered on the beach across from the square where the *combis* leave, and their owners will descend upon you if you look even remotely interested. **Aquamarina,** Rodríguez 125, charges 17 pesos per day for snorkel, mask and fins. (Open Mon.-Sat. 11am-3pm.)

On the northern beach, around the Sheraton, the currency of choice is the U.S. dollar—in bulk. Parasailing is even more popular in this area (US$30 per ride), and **waterskiing** is also possible (US$20 per hr.). The patio of the Sheraton bar is only a few steps from the pool.

Municipal efforts to render the **Río Cuale** a cosmopolitan waterway meet with mixed success for about ¼mi. inland and fail completely thereafter. Walk inland along the riverbank to get an idea of the town's layout. Anyone alone (particularly and predictably women) should be careful when walking this stretch of the river and should avoid doing so altogether after dark. **Isla Río Cuale,** between the two bridges, supports small stores selling simple baubles, bangles, and *botanas*. The **Museo del Cuale,** at the seaward end of the island, divides its single room between contemporary works by local artists and a small collection of pre-Aztec figurines from Jalisco and Nayant. (Open daily 9am-3pm. Donation requested.)

The river can also be reached from the north via Zaragoza, which merits a casual meander. Stairs lead up the mini-mountain beginning behind the Church of Guadalupe, breaking out amid bougainvillea and hibiscus into the wealthy **Zaragoza** neighborhood, known locally as **Gringo Gulch.** The prominent bridge spanning the apex of the street connects Elizabeth Taylor's humble *pied-à-terre* with Richard Burton's. Other ritzy cliff dwellings accompany Zaragoza on its descent to the river.

In the square from which *combis* leave, three-hour **horse rentals** go for 55 pesos; bargaining may work here.

ENTERTAINMENT

Puerto Vallarta proffers something for everyone, whether it's a cocktail in the moonlight or a dance across a crowded room. Most of the upscale action is along Díaz Ordaz on the northern waterfront, where clubs and restaurants cater to suntanned professionals holding pricey rum drinks and bopping to "American Top-40" dance tracks. Down south, and at **Carlos O'Brian's,** the crowds of young teeny-boppers are aware of the latest New Kids hit but not much else. Discos cater to those who can spring a 20- to 30-peso cover charge in high season and pay 6 pesos per beer. Puerto Vallarta is home to a thriving, if small, gay scene, and gay men are generally accepted here. Lesbians, however—as in most of Mexico—meet with a less understanding reception. Two bars in Vallarta are frequented primarily by gay men: **Los Balcones** and the **Piano Bar.** Save a small fortune by obtaining free passes (which may not be honored during peak tourist season) from the condo hawkers who lurk around the Malecón. Most discos aren't worth visiting until 11pm or midnight; the time is well-spent drinking in cheaper bars.

Los Balcones, Juárez 182 at Libertad (tel. 2-46-71). The best club in town. International crowd lazes on the many balconies overlooking Juárez and Libertad and gets busy on the dance floor to house music and older dance faves. Many gay couples and a few lesbian couples hang out here. Beer and soda 6 pesos, mixed drinks 8 pesos, margaritas and piña coladas 9 pesos. Starts hopping at 11:30pm. Open daily noon-3am.

Carlos O'Brian's Bar & Grill & Pawnshop, Díaz Ordaz at Pipila (tel. 2-14-44). Pawning is not the main event. O'Brian's attempts successfully to be the biggest party in town—block-long lines wrap around the building all night, waiting to enter the 3 bars, 2 dining rooms, and 1 large dance floor. There's nothing Mexican about this place except the Corona served up in buckets; by the 8-oz. bottle it costs 4.50 pesos. Cover 20 pesos, includes 2 drinks. Open noon-1:30am.

Andale, Olas Altas 425 (tel. 2-15-04). Video bar caters to a teeming crowd of *norteamericanos* and Mexicans of all ages who down shots to collective shouts of *¡ándale!* Margaritas 6 pesos, beer 3 pesos. Open daily 10am-3am; most crowded 7pm-2am.

Franzi, on Isla Río Cuale, at the foot of the Vallarta Bridge. Find a table on the shady patio, order a margarita and listen to the jazz. Entertainment gets no mellower than this. Promotes itself as a "twilight" spot. Frequented by a professional Mexican crowd and lots of *nuevo-wavo gringo* couples. Entrees 20-45 pesos, mixed drinks 8 pesos. Live music Wed. and Fri.-Sun. 8-11pm. Open daily 6pm-1am.

■ Near Puerto Vallarta

Puerto Vallarta's best beaches start a few km south of town. The first two or three you come across are monopolized by resorts and condos, and though they're nicer and quieter than the ones back in town access to them is usually only through the hotels. Farther down the coast lies **Los Arcos,** a group of pretty rock islands hollowed out in places by pounding waves. Similar rocks litter much of Mexico's

Pacific coast, but the waves of Bahía de Banderas render these formations most impressive. The coastline here lacks sand, but it still serves as a platform from which to start the 150m swim to the islands. Bring a mask or goggles or risk missing the tropical fish that flit through the underwater reefscape. Flippers avail against the heavy currents, and be careful where you step as the coral is sharp enough to draw blood. To get there take the bus to Mismaloya and ask the driver to stop at Los Arcos or Hotel de los Arcos. It's not only cheaper to go by yourself (and not on the cruises that are advertised everywhere) you also get to spend more time enjoying the fish.

The beautiful crescent beach of **Mismaloya** lies just around the bend to the south. Best known as the setting of *Night of the Iguana* and Schwarzenegger's *Predator*, Mismaloya has recently been encircled by large hotels and is only slightly less crowded than the beaches in town. The area still harbors both sets; the former is now a series of crumbling castle-like houses, overlooking the southern end of the beach. All that remains of the latter, 40 minutes by foot down the dirt road through town, is a burned out helicopter hull displayed proudly by the locals.

The road veers away from the coast just beyond the **Boca de Tomatlán.** This narrow cove contains only a small beach but offers a breather from the touristy hubbub of the northern coastline. A couple of small **restaurants** cater to the *gringos* who pass through. Don't come here trying to find cheaper passage to beaches farther south—boats from the Boca are more expensive than the cheapest cruises from Vallarta, unless you have a party of eight.

The last place to check out on the southern road is **Chico's Paradise,** 5km inland from the Boca de Tomatlán. Take in a gorgeous view of the **Tomatlán Falls** while having a drink at Chico's huge and airy *palapas*. You'll have to take a **taxi** (25 pesos from Mismaloya) or a long-distance Transportes de Cihuatlan bus (see Practical Information) to get there unless you have your own vehicle.

Further south along the coast lie the beaches of **Las Ánimas, Quimixto,** and **Yelapa,** all of which are accessible only from the ocean. Las Ánimas and Quimixto are twins—long stretches of unoccupied sand backed by small villages and a few *palapas* offering seafood to tourists. Quimixto also proffers a small waterfall to those who tire of the beach. The trip can be made in an hour by foot from the beach, or in a half hour by rented mule.

The popular boat ride to **Yelapa** is, in a way, a bit of a fake. Yelapa is supposed to be a secluded peasant fishing village but its seemingly simple *palapa* huts were designed by a *norteamericano* architect whose definition of rustic included interior plumbing and hot water. Many of these are occupied for only part of the year, and short- and long-term rentals can be arranged easily for widely varying and sometimes surprisingly low prices. Many travelers opt to slough off their packs for a time and join the sizeable expatriate community that exists here. The beach fills with hawkers and parasailers during the day, but the town, a 15-minute walk from the beach, remains *tranquilo*—with waterfalls and nude bathing upstream and poetry readings downstream, nobody's ready to leave. Don't miss the secluded swimming hole at the top of the stream that runs through town; follow the path uphill along the stream, and just before the restaurant, duck under the water pipes to the right of the trail and head up the track. About 50 ft. before it rejoins the stream bed, an inconspicuous trail leads off to the left to a deep pool which overlooks the bay.

The cheapest way to get to the boats-only beaches is via the **Autobús Acuático** water shuttle. It leaves twice a day (10am and 1pm) from the Muelle de los Muertos and stops at Mismaloya, Las Ánimas, and Yelapa. It's cheaper to take bus #2 or an **Autotransportes del Pacífico Camioneta** from the municipal bus station by Muelle de los Muertos to Mismaloya or La Boca and catch the water shuttle from there. It cruises by about 20 minutes after it leaves Los Muertos. Passage from Mismaloya to Yelapa costs 15 pesos. Boats return at noon and 4pm, but don't miss the last one or you will be stranded.

If you prefer something more organized, **cruises** to points south of Vallarta leave the marina every day from 8am on. The cheapest cruise to Yelapa is 40 pesos, but most are more of a splurge. Tops is 130 pesos, including food and drink. Information about the dazzling variety of tours available can be found in the tourist office, at any large hotel, or in the marina. If you are over 25 (in some cases 23), gainfully employed, and have a major credit card, you can save money on all of the activities listed above, or on a 24 hr. jeep rental (US$5-15). Lots of new developments, condos and resort facilities offer freebies to potential buyers; the most common deal is an invitation to eat a free breakfast or lunch at the resort, spend a few hours enjoying its facilities and then buy tickets (usually at half-price) to any or all of a list of popular tours and cruises. The catch is that you have to listen to their ultra-high-pressure sales pitch which can verge on coercion. Don't under any circumstances relinquish your credit card. Remember, you are under no obligation to do anything whatsoever. If by some fluke the salespeople overlook you, you can find them in booths on the *Malecón*. While you're at it, try to scrounge a few free disco passes off these rather unsavory characters.

■■■ JALISCO COAST

North of the Bahía de Navidad, the highway swings toward the sea to reach the **Bahía Tenacatita,** fringed with idyllic beaches. The sparse settlements are the kinds of villages where the locals stop sipping their early morning sodas to stare as you get off the bus (they are just curious and usually incredibly helpful). The larger villages of **Tenacatita** and **La Manzanilla** offer a stray hotel or two, but most visitors prefer camping on the beach. Even farther north, on the **Costa Careyes,** budget travelers are as rare a species as the *careyes* (turtles) for which the area is named. Steep cliffs and rocky shoals render most of the "Turtle Coast" inaccessible, and what little isn't might as well be. The infamous Club Med in one secluded cove and a newly spawned hotel-and-condo complex in the next are both prohibitively expensive. If you wish to exercise (discreetly) your right to public beach, share the sand in front of the **Hotel Careyes** with its well-to-do Mexican clientele. A tame pelican and a beautiful pool should satisfy even the fussiest of moochers. Buses travel all along this coast—just tell the driver where you want to hop off, then cross your fingers and ask lots of directions to catch the bus out.

The beaches here are some of the coast's finest. Gradually sloping white sand meets waves whose irregular patterns result from the offshore islands. Flying fish taunt cruising pelicans, and the diving birds provide entertainment until the sunset takes over that role. Well-marked access roads lead from the highway to the local favorites **Playa Pérula, Playa La Fortuna,** and **Playa Chamela.**

The **Bahía Chamela** has been completely overlooked by the tourist circuit. The village itself is more a cartographical expression than a true community. A few ramshackle stores and a couple of restaurants cluster on the inland side of the highway near San Mateo in the middle of Chamela. The lack of development is no fluke; ruthless resort magnates have met their match in the Mexican armed forces, who control most of the beach and have squelched almost all plans for development in the area. Many, however, are still not deterred. The beaches of the Bahía are largely deserted, and many find them a perfect place to pitch your tent and soak up the sun. Large, forbidding signs label army property "off-limits," and travelers should certainly get permission from local soldiers before pounding any stakes. The number of army personnel on the beaches swells in February, March, May and June, so you may want to give this adventure a miss.

Three villages in the area offer the visitor rudimentary supplies and services. **Pérula** is the largest of these, sporting two hotels and a number of restaurants, most of which fill up in the afternoon but close down for dinner. The cheapest accommodation besides the beach goes for 65 pesos for two, but rumor has it that a cheaper place will soon be hosting visitors. In addition, haggling may well work, especially in low season. Pérula can be reached from the highway via a 2.5km stretch of dirt road, which begins immediately south of the road to **Ejido La Fortuna,** directly across from where the bus stops.

Under no circumstances should a single traveler attempt to get to the beaches. Several local people have disappeared from this area; women should go in groups of no less than three.

San Mateo is on the highway, but don't blink or you'll miss it. There's one **hotel** in town run by Señor Pío Nogales, known locally as Don Pío. The rooms aren't exactly luxurious, but they do have their own dusty bathrooms and the view of the bay is stunning. Don Pío's house is two blocks up the dirt road from the bus station on the inland side of the highway; look on the left for the gray, breeze-block domicile. (Singles 20 pesos, 2-bed rooms 30 pesos, 3-bed rooms 35 pesos.) Chances of a vacancy are pretty good, but the house has no phone so a trip to San Mateo should hold some suspense.

Restaurant Los Pelícanos serves good food but has no fixed menu or prices (haggling is feasible). Alternatively, head north down the road 2km to **Villa Polenesia** for reliable chow at good prices. They also have official camping spaces and room for a handful of RVs, should you so require.

Many find hitching conditions along the highway to be excellent during the day, but hitching is not a recommended practice. Those hitching to a specific beach travel with the flow of people (beachward at dawn, homeward at dusk). Otherwise the beaches lie about one hour by **bus** from Melaque (7 pesos) and four-and-a-half hours from Puerta Vallarta (28 pesos). Buses pass about every half hour, connecting the villages (2 pesos).

■■■ BAHÍA DE NAVIDAD

Completing Jalisco's "Tourist Trangle," this placid haven juxtaposes the *gringo*-trodden Guadalajara and Puerto Vallarta. Poised on the north and east banks of the Bahía de Navidad, a sheltered cove of talcum sand and shimmering water, the towns of **Melaque** and **Barra de Navidad** are only are a few kilometers apart. Both towns remain largely unmarred by tourist activity. Barra retains the authenticity of a charming small Mexican town—so small, in fact, that it has neither bank nor *panadería*—while at the same time it has sufficient facilitites to absorb substantial numbers of tourists. Melaque is larger, busier, and less charming than Barra. Made up almost exclusively of one-story concrete buildings, its streets are wider and dirtier than Barra's narrow the tree-lined ones, its restaurants less homey, its beachfront more developed, and its waves less exciting. Nevertheless, both beaches are spectacular, their picturesque sunsets framed between the two spits of the cove.

Melaque and Barra de Navidad are 55km northwest of Manzanillo on Rte. 200, or 240km southwest of Guadalajara on Rte. 54. The towns themselves lie a few km apart: two if by sea, five if by highway. Northbound buses hit Barra first and southbound ones do the reverse.

Municipal buses or **combis** (1.50 pesos) connect the two towns every 15 minutes or so. But it is faster to take one of the larger buses heading to Manzanillo that leave on the hour from both towns' bus stations. These cost the same, but are faster and more comfortable. Of course, the 30- to 40-minute walk along the beach between the towns is the true hard-core budget option; don't go alone and take a cab after dark (15 pesos); as some women have been harassed along this stretch,.

■■■ MELAQUE

Practical Information Melaque's new bus station sits at the intersection of **Carranza Gómez Farías,** the main drag, which runs parallel to the beach. From the bus station, turn left on Gómez Farías and walk two blocks to reach **López Mateos.** Another left turn takes you to the town plaza, a few blocks inland. López

Mateos and **Hidalgo,** one block beyond it and parallel to it, are the main cross streets towards the ocean.

Despite its size and swank bus station, Melaque has no bank; nor does Barra de Navidad. A **casa de cambio** across from the bus station changes dollars at a poor rate. (Open Mon.-Fri. 9am-1pm and 3-6pm.) The **post office,** Morelos 44 (tel. 7-02-30), on the plaza at López Mateos, has *Lista de Correos.* (Open Mon.-Fri. 9am-1pm and 3pm-6pm, Sat. 9am-1pm. **Postal code:** 48980.) The **phone office,** on Morelos 52 (tel. 7-00-23), charges 5 pesos for collect calls. (Open Mon.-Sat. 7am-2pm and 4-9pm, Sun. 8am-2pm and 5-9pm.) LADATELs are by the bus station. **Telephone code:** 333. **Buses** leave from the bus station (see above) to Puerto Vallarta (5hrs., 25 pesos), Guadalajara (6½hrs., 34 pesos), and Manzanillo (1½hrs., 8 pesos). **Red Cross,** (tel. 8-23-00), is 15km away in Cihuatlán. **Farmacia Plaza,** López Mateos 43 on the Plaza (tel. 7-00-67), is south of the plaza. (Open Mon.-Sat. 8am-2pm and 4-9:30pm, Sun. 8am-2pm and 6-8pm.) The **hospital,** or **Centro de Salud,** Cordiano Guzmán, between Corona and Gómez Farías,)on the right going toward the beach), is open 24 hrs. The **police,** (tel. 7-00-80), on López Mateos, north of the plaza, are available 9am-3pm.

Accommodations and Camping Melaque is larger than Barra de Navidad and has more hotels, but some are beyond the budget range. **Bungalows Villamar,** Hidalgo 1 (tel. 7-00-05), just off the beach, merit staying in Melaque on their own. Large, well-scrubbed beachside bungalows with two bedrooms, each with two double beds and a large living-dining room area with fully equipped kitchen. Well-kept flowery grounds and a deck with spectacular view of the ocean. (2 people 65 pesos. 4 people 95 pesos. 8 people 140 pesos. 5 bungalows. Call in advance to reserve.) **Hotel Hidalgo,** Hidalgo 7 (tel. 7-00-45), halfway between the plaza and the beach, is a family affair, with an especially friendly English-speaking proprietor. 14 clean and small rooms (with chests of drawers and spotless but microscopic bathrooms) surround the schizophrenic courtyard, living room, and kitchen (which also serves as the family's laundry room). Ask the management to turn on the fan, since there are no switches in the room. (Singles 35 pesos. Doubles 45 pesos. Winter singles 58 pesos. Doubles 74 pesos.) Pleasant **Hotel San Nicolás,** Gómez Farías (tel. 7-00-66), ½ block west of López Mateos, has somewhat decrepit rooms, some with small balconies above the street, bay views, and sliding glass doors bathrooms that could be in better shape. (Singles 40 pesos. Doubles 50 pesos. More expensive in winter.) **Playa Trailer Park,** marring the beach at Gómez Farías and López Mateos (tel. 7-00-65). 45 lots with electricity, water, sewer hook-ups and access to bathrooms (.50 pesos) and showers (2 pesos). Two-person trailer or camping site 35 pesos. Each additional person 5 pesos. Six-person bungalows 120 pesos.

Many people park trailers or pitch tents at the far western end of Melaque, between the sandy beach and rock formations. The site is flat but strewn with litter and rocks, not to mention vehicles and tents. If you only need room for one tent, a far better spot lies along the shore past this rentable parking lot, just before the rocky beach. Otherwise, hunt for more creative sites between the two towns. A small, land-locked lagoon separates the beach and jungle; people pitch tents on the oceanside or crash among the crabs between Melaque and the lagoon. But look before you sleep; at least one landowner has posted a "no camping" sign. As always, clean up after yourself.

Food During the summer, restaurants ship in shrimp from the north, but in high season local fishing boats catch everything that is served on the waterfront. Lobster here is trapped illegally, so help the persecuted crustacean's cause by ordering oysters instead. Beachfront restaurants exude tropical ambience, with an appropriate price tag attached. More authentic (and less expensive) Mexican places lie around the central plaza. Cheaper still are the nameless, dirt-floored eateries in the *mercado* and near the bus station or the sidewalk food stands that materialize after the sun sets and the plaza awakes from its heat-induced slumber. Watch out for the amoebas that hang out in *mercados*.

Los Pelícanos, lies in the row of *palapas* on the beach 50m beyond Hotel Melaque. The proprietor, New Yorker Philomena "Phil" García, considers herself the fairy godmother of the wayworn *gringo* and is a fixture of the local expatriate scene. Breakfast (around 8 pesos) and great seafood (19 pesos) will cure most cases of homesickness. (Open daily 8am-11pm, off-season daily 11am-7pm.) **El Buen Gusto,** Lopes Mateos 18, is a family run restaurant located in a shed with a metal roof. Eat on card tables with white tablecloths and enjoy the tasty inexpensive food. *Huevos* 6 pesos. (Open daily 8am-11pm.) **Restaurante Bar el Dorado,** a *palapa* connected to the Hotel Club Náutico at the western end of Gómez Farías, sets the mood with pink tablecloths and napkins and a full bar that's even open for breakfast. *Huevos rancheros* 9 pesos, pancakes 9 pesos, shrimp 32 pesos. (Open daily 8am-10:30pm.)

Sights and Entertainment In Melaque the beach gets more crowded towards its western end, and the waves get smaller. Restaurants and aqua-activities, such as **jet-ski rental** (US$30 per hr.) also increase in density towards this end of the beach.

Melaque's most famous attraction is its **Fiesta de San Patricio** (March 8-17), which has achieved a near-mythic stature in the surrounding area for its raucous intensity. After filling yourself with Jalisco's finest tequila, dancing to *salsa* until your legs feel like *mermelada*, and watching fireworks while riding the bucking bronco, try not to pass out until after you've attended the blessing of the fleet and the all-day procession. Philomena García's bash the night before, rumor has it, keeps the residents across the bay awake with its commotion. Drop by her restaurant, **Los Pelícanos** (see Food), to get in on it.

Although probably very few people actually come to Melaque for the nightlife there, few refuse it when it's thrust upon them. **Disco Tango,** where Gómez Farías runs into Vallarta, monopolizes the chic action and is home after hours to Melaque's under-30 tourist crowd. (Cover 10-15 pesos, beer 5 pesos.) Melaque's other dance floors are comparatively modest and relatively interchangeable: **Discotheque Albatros** is a half-block inland from the *zócalo*; **Discotheque Hollywood,** on Ramón Corona, lies two blocks east of Hidalgo. (Cover 5-15 pesos.)

■■■ BARRA DE NAVIDAD

Practical Information Barra de Navidad's bus stop is at Veracruz 226, on the corner of Nayarit. Veracruz runs roughly parallel to **Legazpi,** the main street that hugs the beach. Turn left on Veracruz from the bus station to get to *el centro*. Depending on who is working at the **tourist office,** Sonora 15 (tel. 7-02-37), English may or may not be spoken, and their information is better for other places than for Barra itself. (Open Mon.-Fri. 9am-7pm, Sat. 9am-1pm.) **Agencia de Viajes Viacosta,** Veracruz 204 (tel. 7-06-65), arranges plane tickets only. (Open Mon.-Fri. 9am-8pm, Sat. 9am-6pm, Sun. 10am-noon.) Barra has neither bank nor *casa de cambio;* the closest *casa de cambio* is in Melaque (see above), or try the small general store on **Legazpi,** a block from the police station. The **post office,** Guanajuato 100, is 1½ blocks inland from Veracruz on the south side of the maritime monument, near the bus station. *Lista de Correos* is posted around 10:30am. (Open Mon.-Fri. 8am-3pm. **Postal code:** 48987.) The **telegram office** is at Veracruz 69, on the corner by the plaza. (Open Mon.-Fri. 9am-3pm.) **Farmacia Zurich,** Legazpi 156 (tel. 7-07-31), is open daily 8am-10pm. For medical attention, the **Centro de Salud,** on Puerto Navidad (no phone), is down Veracruz out of town, make a right just after the signs for El Marquez, and just before Veracruz becomes a highway. The Centro is the second building on the right. **Police** wait at Veracruz 179 (tel. 7-03-99).

Accommodations and Food Barra has a deceptive dearth of budget accommodations. The best spot to camp or park your trailer is the extreme south end of town, on the sandbar near the breakwater. Use the toilet (.50 pesos) and the shower (2 pesos) in one of the nearby sand-floored eateries; look for the hand-lettered signs that read "Sanitario/Regadera." **Posada Pacífico,** Mazatlán 160 (tel. 7-03-59), features comfortable, white rooms, a pleasant courtyard, clean, shower curtains and killer fans. The friendly *dueña* lets guests park in the driveway if there's room. (Singles 40 pesos. Doubles 50 pesos. In winter singles 60 pesos. Doubles 80 pesos.) Immaculate rooms with large bathrooms at **Hotel Delfín,** Morelos 23 (tel. 7-00-68), have access to a dreamy terrace overlooking the leafy courtyard, pool and lagoon. Worth the extra pesos. (Singles 65 pesos. Doubles 75 pesos. In winter singles 90 pesos, double 100 pesos.) **Bungalows Karelia,** on Legazpi (tel. 7-01-87), at the beach next to the Hotel Bogavante, are a good deal for 3 or more. Airy suites house refrigerator, table, chairs, stove and fan but lack the crucial screens and kitchen utensils. (Doubles 75 pesos. Each additional person 15 pesos.)

Restaurants line the south end of the beach with beautiful views, and on Veracruz, many families open their living rooms as informal restaurants. For basic Mexican food in a pleasant atmosphere—checkered tablecloths and wooden chairs—try **Restaurant Paty,** on the north corner of Veracruz and Jalisco, across from restaurant Chela. It is popular with locals for its delicious, inexpensive food. Grilled *pollo* 10 pesos. Three *quesadillas* 6 pesos. (Open daily 8:30am-11pm.) The beachside tables at **Restaurant Pacífico,** Legazpi 206, offer great sunset viewing and a stirring vista which inspires the 2-for-1 happy hour (4-7pm). Breakfast special is a bargain at 8 pesos. Fish 16 pesos. (Open daily 8am-10:30pm.) **Crepes y Café,** Veracruz 101, is 50% vegetarian. The French proprietor whips up delicious sweet and non-sweet crepes. Healthy alternatives include *pan integral* and yogurt. Their boast of "best coffee in town" may be true. Complete breakfast with crepe, yogurt, and fruit 17 pesos. Unfortunately, dinner tends to be on the expensive side. Basic ham and cheese crepe 16 pesos. (Open Fri.-Wed. 8am-noon and 5-10pm.) **Restaurant Eloy,** Yucatán 47, jutting out into the lagoon, is small and cheesy with colorful flowers and pleasant owners. Fish 15 pesos. *Huevos* 8 pesos. (Open daily 8am-9:30pm.) Dine outdoors on the tree-lined sidewalk or indoors amidst potted plants at **Restaurant y Cenaduría Chela,** Veracruz 102. Very popular locally at dinnertime. Order of four tacos, 6 pesos. Fish fillet 12 pesos. (Open daily 8am-midnight.)

Sights and Entertainment The slightly larger waves of Barra de Navidad are seldom big enough for surfing, but the crowd here tries admirably. During the rainy season, however, the waves between Barra and Melanque are sometimes close to perfect. **Mariner,** Legazpi 154, across the street from the church, rents surfboards, boogie boards and skindiving equipment (each 5 pesos per hr. plus deposit of passport or credit card), as well as **bicycles** (16 pesos per day; open daily 9am-10pm).

While the short trip across the lagoon to the village of **Colimilla** makes a pleasant diversion, the steep price for small groups is considerably less than pleasant. For 30 pesos round-trip, a *lancha* will deposit up to eight passengers amid Colimilla's palms, pigs, cows, and open-air restaurants, or at the far end of the lagoon. A 1km stroll from here is the deserted **Playa de los Cocos,** which has larger breakers than those in Barra. If you don't want to swim back, remember to fix a time to be picked up. For 50 pesos per hour, zoom off in the same *lancha* full of equipment for tuna, sailfish, or marlin fishing. Big catches are most common June through December; operators have formed a cooperative, so the prices are fixed. Their office and docks lie at the very end of Veracruz.

A source of sinful pride for Barra is the **Iglesia de San Antonio,** on the corner of Jalisco and Veracruz, four blocks south of the bus station. The church, a modern structure, holds a different attraction for visitors than the stately colonial architecture prevalent in Mexico's touristed places of worship. Inside hangs *El Cristo del Ciclón* (Christ of the Hurricane). Its arms, instead of being extended to form the tra-

MANZANILLO

ditional crucifix, are bent and, still attached to the body, droop earthward as if in a shrug. Legend has it that when Hurricane Lilly furiously struck the bay at dawn on September 10, 1971, a young girl burst into the church begging the icon for help, causing Christ's arms to detach from the crucifix in order to hold the hurricane back and save the town from destruction. (Church open daily 7am-8pm.)

The only game down the strand in Barra de Navidad is **El Gaeón/Aladino's** (cover 10 pesos). The all-age clientele throbs as one, as everyone out past midnight is here. (Beer 3.50 pesos, mixed drinks 6 pesos.) A number of 2-1 happy hours along Legazpi make the giddy trip towards inebriation that much cheaper.

COLIMA

■■■ MANZANILLO

Residents of Colima state proudly point to Manzanillo as the home of its finest beaches and the brightest hope of its economic future. In their delirious efforts to transform Manzanillo into the next Cancún, however, these worshippers of the tourist god have overlooked the undeniable fact that a working port can never become a world-class resort. The workhorse of Mexico's Pacific coast, Manzanillo attracts ships from as far away as Russia. A navy repair station faces the city's main plaza, and *el centro* is a sweaty, workaday place unappealing to the beachgoing tourist.

Most tourists, therefore, avoid central Manzanillo altogether, and stay at glossy resorts on Manzanillo's two bays of golden-brown sand to the north and west of town. Life in these areas is good thanks to the fortuitous combination of currents and latitude, keeping Manzanillo cooler in summer than Acapulco and Puerto Vallarta. The reasonably priced hotels of Manzanillo, however, all lie in the midst of the loud and brazen port action. A 20-minute bus trip (1 peso) or a 12-peso taxi ride separates *el centro* from the beaches. If all you seek is sand and surf, you'd do better to repair to some secluded village, such as Cuyutlán or Barra de Navidad, where there is no metropolis between your hotel and the Pacific. Even the smaller town outside of Manzanillo proper tends to be grimier than most Mexican beach towns; the resorts themselves bad imitations of Club Meds that look out onto the highway, the beaches black from the nearby volcanoes, with litter occasionally strewn about.

Practical Information Manzanillo lies 96km west of Colima and 355km south of Guadalajara. The main **bus station** lies on the outskirts of town between Laguna Cuyutlán and the ocean. The local bus labeled "Centro" runs from the station to the corner of 21 de Marzo and Hidalgo (.50 pesos). From there, a right turn onto Allende and another one onto México will lead you to the *zócalo*. A **taxi** (tel. 3-23-20) from the bus station to the center of town costs 4 pesos.

The **Jardín Obregón**, Manzanillo's plaza, is the most useful orientation point in town. The plaza faces north onto the harbor, but boxcars often obstruct the glorious view of PEMEX tankers. **Morelos** runs along the north (waterfront) edge of the plaza, **Juárez** along the south. **Avenida México**, Manzanillo's main street, runs south from the plaza. Most hotels and services are nearby. The **tourist office** has basic information in the Palacio Municipal on the *Jardín*. (Open Mon.-Fri. 9am-11pm.) **Bancomer**, México 220 (tel. 2-26-90), exchanges currency Mon.-Fri. 8:30am-noon. Many banks line México. The **post office** is on 5 de Mayo between Juárez and Morelos (tel. 2-00-32), 1 block east of the *Jardín*. (Open Mon.-Fri. 8am-7pm, Sat. 9am-1pm.) **Computel**, Madero 72, ½ block off the *zócalo*, charges 5 pesos for collect calls. (Open daily 6:45am-10pm.) **LADATELs** lie two blocks from the *Jardín* on México and on the *Jardín* itself. Manzanillo's **airport** is actually in Playa de Oro, on the highway between Manzanillo and Barra de Navidad, about one hour from Manzanillo. **Combis** (tel. 3-21-80) to the airport (20 pesos) leave every hr. from the hotel Fiesta Mexicana (tel. 3-21-80), on the Miramar bus route 2.5km out of the city on the left. **Mexicana,** Mexico 382 (tel. 2-17-01), is open Mon.-Fri. 9am-2pm and 2:45-6pm, and **Aeroméxico,** (tel. 2-17-11) in the Centro Comercial, Carrillo Puerto 107 (tel. 2-12-67), is open Mon.-Sat. 9am-7pm. Flights to: Mexico City (350 pesos), Guadalajara (200 pesos), and Los Angeles (US$300). More importantly, the **bus station,** on Hidalgo, about 1km east of downtown, features **Soc. Coop. de Autotransportes** (tel. 2-04-32), with buses every 15min. to Armería (2.50 pesos), Tecomán (3 pesos), and Colima (5 pesos). **Autobuses de la Costa** (tel. 2-10-03) serves Puerto Vallarta (4½-6½ hrs., 20 pesos), and Guadalajara (17 per day, 8hrs., 45 pesos). **Tres Estrellas de Oro** (tel. 2-01-35) serves Mexico City (15hrs., 121 pesos). The **train station,** on Niños Héroes, near Morelos east of the plaza, has one second-class train per day at 6am, to Colima (1½hrs., 4 pesos), Guzmán (6hrs., 7 pesos), Guadalajara (9hrs., 15 pesos), and 49 other stops en route. Tickets can only be purchased the same day, starting at 5am. The **Red Cross** (tel. 2-00-96) is 10 de Mayo and Bocanegra. **Farmacia Manzanillo,** Juárez 10, faces the plaza. (Open daily 9am-10pm.) **Hospital Civil,** is on the San Pedrito circle (tel. 2-10-03 or 2-09-03). **Police** are in the Presidencia Municipal (tel. 2-10-04).

Accommodations and Food It's slim pickings; Manzanillo does not cater to the tourist of any stripe. Hotels in the center of town are better than those near the bus station, a rough nighborhood that is dangerous at night. **Camping** on Playa Miramar is also feasible, and restaurants may allow you do it. Many of the houses on the beach are deserted for part of the year. As far as safety is concerned, it's generally a good idea to situate yourself near an occupied house, hotel or restaurant, unless you are traveling with a large body of retainers.

Hotel Flamingo, Madero 72 (tel. 2-10-37), is one block south of the *zócalo*. No flamingos here, but still the best bet for your money. Clean, basic rooms, if a bit musty. Bathrooms clean with shower curtains. (Singles 40 pesos. Doubles 50 pesos. Reservations recommended.) **Hotel Emperador,** Dávalos 69 (tel. 2-23-74), one block west of the plaza's southwest corner, is above a restaurant whose aromas make the mouth water; this may be its only virtue. No hot water but clean bathrooms. The barren rooms, some without windows, are a claustrophobe's nightmare. (Singles 40 pesos. Doubles 45 pesos.) Psychedelic staircases lead to large rooms at **Hotel Miramar,** Juárez 122 (tel. 2-10-08), probably untouched since the birth of rock-and-roll. You could fit a small roller rink on any of the vast, checkered balconies. (Singles 40 pesos. Doubles 45 pesos. Reservations recommended.) The cell-like rooms at **Casa de Huéspedes Petrita,** Allende 20 (tel. 2-01-87), feature odd bar/screens over the windows and a clunky, functional communal bathroom. (Singles 25 pesos. Doubles 30 pesos.)

Manzanillo is sprinkled with a few good restaurants, but because tourists mostly put up closer to the beach, the market is strictly local and the food downtown comes with few frills. **Restaurante Chantilly,** on the plaza at Juárez and Moreno, provides the usual Mexican staples to crowds of newspaper-reading professionals. Though the food is nothing to write home about, the view of the *zócalo* makes it a good spot for people-watching. (Waffles 7 pesos. Shrimp 19 pesos. Open Sun.-Fri. 7am-10pm.) Below the hotel of the same name, **Restaurant Emperador,** Dávalos 69 (tel. 2-23-74), has blank walls and fluorescent lights that aren't nearly as pleasing as the food. (Enchiladas 5 pesos. Open daily 9am-10:30pm.) Look hard for **Los Narangos,** México 366; there's not even a sign outside. If there's a table available here at lunchtime, however, you're lucky: it's an institution with locals. Breakfast is not quite so popular. (*Huevos a la mexicana* 6 pesos. *Caldo de pollo* 7 pesos. Generous juices 3.50 pesos.)

Sights Two nearby, bays, **Bahía Manzanillo** and **Bahía Santiago,** serve Manzanillo's beach needs. The former has more expensive hotels and cleaner golden sand

MANZANILLO

than its neighbor's, but its beach slopes more steeply, creating a strong undertow. The beaches at Bahía Santiago, though twice as far from *el centro*, are more popular among *aficionados*, though the noisy highway lies just behind them.

The closest good beach on Bahía Manzanillo, **Playa Las Brisas,** has a few secluded spots, but parts of the beach are crowded with luxurious hotels and bungalows. To get to Las Brisas from downtown Manzanillo, take a **taxi** (12 pesos) or the "Las Brisas" **bus** (1 peso). Catch the bus on México or on the highway going toward the airport and Barra de Navidad. Alternatively, catch the "Miramar" bus and ask the driver to let you off at the *crucero*. From the crossroads, turn left toward populated shores or stake out a private section of beach right at the junction.

The "Miramar" bus continues west of Peninsula Santiago, gear-grinding toward other excellent beaches on Bahía Santiago. The bay here is not used for shipping, and thus the water is cleaner than at Las Brisas. The "Miramar" buses (1.40 pesos to the Bahía) leave every 15 minutes from the train station, three blocks east of the plaza on Niños Héroes. The best place to get off is where everyone else does—at **Miramar Beach,** where a footbridge crosses the highway. This is the most crowded section of the beach, but it has the best beachfront restaurants where you can rent boogie boards and surfboards (5 pesos per hr.). Crowds disappear 20m east or west of the beach club that owns this stretch of sand. The waves are adequate for boogie boarding and bodysurfing, but if you can figure out a way to use a surfboard here, you should move to Waikiki and give lessons. For tranquility, head for **La Avedencía,** a calm cove on the west side of the peninsula, or get the bus to stop just before it turns away from the coast after the footbridge.

■ Near Manzanillo: Paraíso and Cuyutlán

Paraíso may soon be destroyed by the gods for its hubris, but while it exists it outclasses its unsightly brother city, nearby **Armería.** A well-paved road connects the two towns, cutting through 7km of banana and coconut plantations before it dead-ends into the black sands that surround Paraíso's thatched, beachfront restaurants. A few weathered fishing boats litter the tranquil shoreline, holding back the emerald green surf.

Just before the main road becomes the beach, you'll see Paraíso's only other street, the lushly named **Calle Adán y Eva,** which runs along the back of the beachfront restaurants. A left turn here will take you to the village's only hotel, the **Hotel Paraíso** (tel. 2-47-87), with big well-maintained rooms, spotless showers and a pool. (Singles and doubles 60 pesos.) The extensive beach makes perfect terrain for bootleg campers, and owners of some of the *enramadas* may let you shack up under their thatched roofs if you're worried about rain. The Hotel Paraíso offers showers (2 pesos) and bathrooms (.50 pesos) to anyone who should care to use them. In high season (especially Dec. and April) there may be rooms available in private Paraíso houses, so ask around.

Restaurants run the slim gamut from rustic *enramadas* to dirt-floored *comedores*. Predictably, locally caught seafood dominates menus, which barely differ from place to place in either offerings or prices. **Restaurant Paraíso,** in the Hotel Paraíso (see above), is reliable and has snazzy service. The tasty *shrimp a la diable* even come without their shells for 19 pesos. (Open daily 8am-6pm.)

Buses (1.50 pesos) run to and from the vestibule in Armería, a last resort place to pass the night, every 45 minutes from 6am to 7:30pm. There is also a **long distance telephone** in the *tienda rural* across the street from the bus stop (tel. 4-29-10). They charge using the "give me whatever you think is appropriate" scale. (Open Mon.-Sat. 9am-9pm, Sun. 9am-6pm.)

If you're a budding Thoreauvian hungry for peace and silence, then **Cuyutlán** is a wonderful place to visit (pop. sub-1000), especially in the off season when shut-up buildings and empty streets give it a ghost-town feel. Local residents of this sleepy town choose not to perform concerts, instead they leave entertainment to the natural attractions. In fact, the *zócalo* is usually as deserted as the beaches, where, after a quick stroll away from deserted umbrellas, you have the sand all to yourself. However, within the high season (Dec.-May), lifeguards and a well-planned *malecón* make the dark-brown sands even more attractive for the domestic tourists who come in droves. During the summer months, the wild blue waves pound the shore's dark sand without an audience.

Cuyutlán's most unusual distinction is the renowned **green wave,** a phenomenon that occurs regularly in April or May. Quirky currents and phosphorescent marine life combine to produce 10m swells that glow an unearthly green.

The road from Armería, 15km to the northeast, becomes **Yavaros,** running east to west, parallel to the coastline, as it enters town. It intersects **Hidalgo,** which runs north-south, along the east side of the town square, and a left at this intersection takes you to the beach. Buses coming from Armería (2 pesos) make a right here onto Hidalgo, off Yavaros and away from the beach before they stop at the *parada* (bus stop) which serves as a bus station on Hidalgo. **Veracruz,** Cuyutlán's other mighty boulevard, is parallel to Yavaros, one block off the beach and three blocks from Yavaros.

Most of Cuyutlán's municipal services are within one block of the *zócalo.* The owner of the Hotel Morelos will **change money** if they have the cash. **Telephones** are at Hidalgo 47 (tel. 4-18-10), one block north of the *zócalo.* (Collect calls 2 pesos. Open Mon.-Sat. 9am-1pm and 4-8pm, Sun. 9am-1pm.) **Farmacia del Carmen** is at Hidalgo 121. (Open Mon.-Fri. 4-8pm, Sat.-Sun. 9am-2pm and 4-8pm.) A **Centro de Salud** is one block west of the *zócalo* on Yavaros at Madero. The **police** reside at Hidalgo 143 (tel. 1-00-13), one block south of the *zócalo.* **Buses** leave from the *parada* for Armería every 40 minutes from 6:30am to 7:30pm (2 pesos). There is no public transportation to Paraíso from Cuyultlán, or vice versa.

Waves, green or regular, lap at the doorsteps of most of the budget hotels. The **Hotel Morelos,** Hidalgo 185 (tel. 17), at Veracruz, sports incredibly plush, spacious rooms with fans and hot water, not to mention the privilege of dwelling amongst all the flowers in Cuyutlán. All this can be yours for 30 pesos per person. In the **Hotel Fénix,** Hidalgo 201 (tel. 147), at Veracruz, the rooms may be taller than they are wide, but there's a fan in each one, and the bathrooms are tidy enough to use. (20 pesos per person.) If you arrive in Cuyutlán during a crunch period (e.g. Christmas or *Semana Santa*) you may have to try one of the inland hotels, such as **Posada San Antonio,** Hidalgo 139, one block seaward from the plaza. It is only open during Mexican vacations. If you'd rather **camp,** a trek 200m to the right of Cuyutlán's hotels will lead to a private patch of black sand. Or string up a hammock in one of the *palapas* to the left of the hotels—most of them are vacant in summer. Campers and daytrippers can use the toilets (1 peso) and showers (1.50 pesos) at Hotel Morelos.

Even if you do like seafood, you may get sick of it—the lack of variety boggles the mind. Below the hotel, the **Restaurant Fénix,** Hidalgo 201, grows decorative flowers. Somehow, the Fénix also stays pretty well-stocked—you might be able to get *tostadas.* (Shrimp any style 22 pesos. Orange juice 3 pesos. Open daily 8am-10pm.)

■■■ COLIMA

The capital of Colima state is hardly a tiny village (pop. 100,000), but nonetheless manages to maintain a certain small-town benevolence—men and women sit around and chat all afternoon on the benches of the *zócalo,* and locals smile as they give directions to tourists. The central plazas are as picturesque now as they were when the city was founded in 1523, but modern civilization has not left Colima unmarked; serenades in the *zócalo* on Sunday afternoons must now contend with cruising automobiles blaring Vanilla Ice's greatest hits. This under-visited city rewards those few who stray from the well-trodden coastal route. Visitors are welcomed with a gratifying change of scenery and a good place to shake the sand from the shoes, and visit its great little museums and theaters.

COLIMA

ORIENTATION

A string of plazas runs east to west across downtown Colima. The arcaded **Plaza Principal,** flanked by the cathedral and the Palacio de Gobierno, is the business center of town. On the other side of the cathedral and *palacio* is the smaller, quieter **Jardín Quintero.** Three blocks farther east on Madero is the large, lush **Jardín Núñez,** the other significant reference point in town. Many tourist services are on **Hidalgo,** which parallels **Madero** one block to the south.

The main **bus station** is 2km out of town, but mini-buses zip by incessantly. Buses #4 and 5 pass through the center a few blocks from the *zócalo.* Buses run by **Soc. Coop. Colima Manzanillo** (from Tecomán and Manzanillo) have their own depot, just north of the suburban stop and downhill from the *centro* on Degollado.

PRACTICAL INFORMATION

Tourist Office: Hidalgo 75 (tel. 2-40-60), 1 block west of Pl. Principal. Staffed by young'uns who try to be helpful. Maps that won't quit. English spoken. Open Mon.-Fri. 9am-3pm and 5-9pm, Sat. 9am-1pm.

Currency Exchange: Bánamex, on Hidalgo 188, 1 block east of Pl. Principal. No commission and a good rate, but hell might freeze over as you wait in line. Money exchange in the basement. Open Mon.-Fri. 9am-noon. **Casa de Cambio** on the corner of Morelos and Juárez on Park Nuñez. Open Mon.-Fri. 9am-2pm and 4:30-6:30pm, Sat. 9am-2pm.

Post Office: Madero 247 at Revolución, on the northeast corner of the *Jardín Núñez. Lista de Correos.* Open Mon.-Fri. 8am-6pm, Sat. 8am-noon.

Telephones: Computel, Morelos 234 on the south side of the *Jardín Núñez.* Collect calls 5 pesos. Open daily 7am-10pm. Also **Farmacia Colima** (see below). Collect calls 2 pesos for 3min. Open daily 7am-10pm. There is also a multitude of blue international phones. **LADATELs** on both plazas. **Telephone code:** 331.

Telegrams: Madero 243, at the post office. Open Mon.-Sat. 9am-8pm.

Bus Stations: Colima has 3. The well-mopped and airport-like **Central de Autobuses,** is 2km out of town on bus #4 or #5 (.50 pesos). **La Linea** operates the most buses to Guadalajara (3hrs., 20.50 pesos) and also serves Uruapan (1 per day at 10:30pm, 6hrs., 30 pesos). **Tres Estrellas de Oro** has 1st class service to Tijuana via the coast (1 per day, 220 pesos) and Mexico City direct (70 pesos), plus other northern points. **Omnibús de México,** your best bet to the east, goes to Monterrey (1 per day, 14hrs., 110 pesos) and Aguascalientes (1 per day, 6hrs., 37 pesos). Until the station on Nicolás Bravo reopens, **Soc. Coop. Colima** operates from a makeshift station 3 blocks south on Degaldo from Pl. Principal. They have buses to Manzanillo (1¼hrs., 7 pesos) that also stop in Tecomán (4.50 pesos). Suburban buses, with destinations like San Antonio (see near Colima), Agua Caliente, Comala and La Becerrera come and go irregularly from a parking lot 2 blocks further south on Degaldo, next to the *Parque Regional.*

Train Station: At the southern edge of town (tel. 2-92-50). Taxi fare 4 pesos. To Guadalajara (1st class 9 pesos, 2nd 5 pesos) at 3pm, and Manzanillo (1st class 3 pesos, 2nd 2 pesos) at 1:30pm. Offices open daily noon-3pm.

Laundromat: Lavandería Automática Jando, Juárez 70. 3 pesos per kg. Open Mon.-Sat. 9am-9pm.

Red Cross: Aldama at Obregón (tel. 2-14-51).

Pharmacy: Farmacia Colima, Madero 1, at the northeast corner of the Pl. Principal (tel. 2-00-31). Open Mon.-Sat. 9am-9pm.

Hospitals: Hospital Civil, San Fernando at Ignacio Zandoval (tel. 2-02-27). **Centro de Salud,** Juárez at 20 de Noviembre (tel. 2-00-64 or 2-32-38).

Police: Juárez at 20 de Noviembre (tel. 2-18-01 or 2-64-00).

ACCOMMODATIONS

Hotel San Lorenzo, Calle Cuauhtemoc 149, from Pl. Principal go west 2 blocks to Calle Cuauhtemoc and walk left 3 blocks. Basic, large, clean rooms for a good price with professional service. Singles 35 pesos. Doubles 45 pesos.

Hotel Ceballos, Portal Medellín 12 (tel. 2-44-49), on the north side of the Pl. Principal with large French doors. Elegant columned halls with high ceilings sweep towards your spacious room some with desks and A/C. One of the nicest hotels you will find for this amount of money. Singles 65 pesos. Doubles 71 pesos.

Casa de Huéspedes, Morelos 265 (tel. 2-34-67), just off the southeast corner of *Jardín Núñez*. Somewhat decrepit rooms in a very friendly family's house with flowery entrance-way and chickens filling the courtyard. Singles 20 pesos, with bath 25 pesos. Doubles 30 pesos, with bath 35 pesos.

Hotel Flamingos, Rey Colimán 18 (tel. 2-25-25), 1 block south of Park Nuñez. Cool, clean, 70's-style rooms, some with balconies. Modern building without much personal charm. Singles 50 pesos. Doubles 60 pesos.

FOOD

Most of Colima's pleasant restaurants and cafes cluster around the Pl. Principal.

Samadhi, on Mequina, near Guerrero opposite the church. Delicious vegetarian food served in a leafy courtyard with pink portals and comfortable chairs. Free newspapers and classical music promise to extend lunch until twilight. Yogurt with fruit 4 pesos. *Quesadillas* with mushrooms 5.50 pesos. Open Fri.-Wed. 8am-10pm, Thurs. 8am-5pm.

Los Naranjos, Barreda 34. *Periódico*-perusing *señores* sip coffee between mellow lilac and beige walls. Eggs start at 6.50 pesos, *filet mignon au champiñones* 32 pesos. Open daily 8am-11pm.

Restaurant Típico Los Portales, Serdán 15, in Comala, on the south side of the *zócalo*. Basic Mexican fare on a terrace overlooking the Plaza. Very popular with locals for food and drinks. Coronas 3 pesos. Chicken 17 pesos. Open daily 9am-1am.

La Arábica, Guerrero 162. A treat for caffeine fiends. Fed up with instant Nescafé? Take a seat in the verdant courtyard among poetry-reading types and enjoy your cappuccino (4.50 pesos) and homemade grenadine (4 pesos). Mostly drinks. Open daily 8am-11pm.

SIGHTS

In Colima's well-maintained **Plaza Principal,** white park benches surround a gazebo and several decorative fountains. The double arcade around the plaza encompasses the **Museo de Historia,** the Hotel Ceballos and a handful of stores and sandwich shops. The commercial establishments continue along the pedestrian malls, which radiate from the plaza's corners.

On the east side of the plaza, much of the state government is housed in the **Palacio de Gobierno.** An inviting building with breezy courtyards, the *palacio* also contains a four-wall **mural,** completed in 1954 by Jorge Chávez Carrillo in honor of the bicentennial of Hidalgo's birth. The intricate mural, covering the walls of the staircase closest to the Pl. Principal, moves counterclockwise through Mexico's tumultuous history. The staff the **information booth** at the foot of the stairs doesn't speak much English, but the free lecture on the mural (about 15min.) is thorough and interesting. Anglophones get an abbreviated version (booth staffed Mon.-Fri. 9am-3pm).

Adjoining Colima's municipal complex is the renovated colonial **Santa Iglesia Cathedral.** The Spanish first built a church on this spot in 1527, but an earthquake destroyed the original structure of wood and palm, and fire consumed its replacement. They had the gall to build another one. To this day the paintings of the evangelists bear scars from the earthquakes and volcanic eruptions of 1900, 1932, and 1941. The cathedral is still the most striking building in Colima, and the fading paint of its dome and towers does little to decrease its grandeur. The Neoclassical interior glitters with gilt paint, chandeliers and polished marble. In the pulpit designed by Othón Bustos rests a statue of San Felipe de Jesús, the city's patron saint. (Open daily 8am-9pm. Avoid visiting during services.)

COLIMA

Colima's **Museo de Las Culturas de Occidente** (tel. 2-31-55), is an excellent museum devoted to pre-Columbian art from the area. Rarely seen outside the state, the Colima ceramic figurines are among the most playful and captivating artifacts in Mexico. To get there take the bus towards University of Colima from Av. Rey Colimán. Open Tues.-Sun. 7am-9pm.

Colima's newest museum, the **Museo de Historia,** is at 16 de Septiembre and Reforma on the south side of the Pl. Principal, and houses a small collection of pre-Columbian ceramics, in addition to a gallery devoted to contemporary works by local artists. (Open Mon.-Sat. 10am-2pm and 4-8pm, Sun. 5-8pm. Free.) Colima's **Museo Universitario de Culturas Populares,** at Manuel Gallardo and 27 de Septiembre, has a very small informal museum and gift shop with handmade reproductions of local ceramics. (Open Mon.-Sat. 9am-2pm and 4-7pm.) A far more extensive collection of pre-Columbian artifacts from the region are displayed at the **Museo de Cultura y Arte Popular,** part of the Universidad de Bellas Artes (tel. 2-29-90) at 27 de Septiembre and Gallard Azmoro. The collection is dominated by figurines recovered from nearby tombs, and, if you can read Spanish and dig archaeology, the descriptions of the pre-Aztec western coast serves as a useful complement to the pieces. (Open daily 9am-7:30pm. Free.) Catch the "Nte." bus (.60 pesos) from the Gran Flamingo and get off on the corner of 27 de Septiembre and San Fernando. Mural fanatics also may wish to investigate two other wall pieces at the University of Colima's **Rectoría.** The first is at the Rectoría bus stop (route "Sur" or "Norte," .50 pesos), completed in 1989 entirely with naturally colored pebbles. The second is inside the Rectoría itself.

The church of **San Francisco** (on bus #5 route), with its brick, circular nave and simple interior, sits amidst the ruins of the first church erected in Colima by the Spanish and a host of *primavera* trees that bloom a vibrant yellow in March. (Open daily 10-11:30am and 5-8pm.) Also of note are the churches of **San José,** on Quintero just a short walk up Madero from the Pl. Principal, which is the focus of a scenic well-to-do colonial neighborhood; and **El Sagrado Corazón,** on the corner of 27 de Septiembre and Aldama, known for its beautiful interior and stained glass. (Open 9am-2pm and 4-8pm.)

Beyond the city to the southeast (also visible from the top of the cathedral) rises **Colina La Cumbre.** The chapel on its summit is open to "the entire brotherhood of man" (women included)—but only on the eighth day of each month. The chapel and its grounds are a popular site for picnics. Seek access to the hill via any bus to Pihuamo or Tepames from the suburban bus stop (1 peso; see Orientation); just ask for La Cumbre. Remember to bring your own drinking water.

■ Near Colima

In Nahuatl, Colima means "place where the old god is dominant." The old god is **El Volcán de Fuego** (3820m). Recorded eruptions date back to the pre-Conquest era, and today El Fuego emits frequent puffs of smoke and steam to assert its status as the only active volcano in Mexico. **El Nevado de Colima** (4240m), stands taller than its neighbor but is dormant and not much fun at parties. Guadalajara-bound *locales* (from the new bus station) pass through the town of **Atenquique,** 57km away. From here a 27km unimproved dirt road runs to the summit of El Fuego. The trip is only recommended for four-wheel-drive vehicles, though logging trucks based at the factory in Atenquique make trips up this road to spots near the summit. Almost at the top of El Fuego is the **Joya Cabin,** which lacks all amenities except a roof. Because of the frequency of volcanic activity, the park is only open sporadically; if you're planning a trip to the top, call the **police** ahead of time (tel. 2-18-01 or 2-64-00). The twin peak, **El Nevado,** can also be climbed. Buses from **Guzmán** (83km away) limp up to **Joya,** whence you can make your epic assault on the summit.

If you don't mind a few insects and just have to get away from it all, think about going to **Laguna Carrizalillo,** 12km north of Comala. Visitors come to sit in the pervading peace. **Bungalows** with kitchens and fire-places are available (quads 7 pesos). **Laguna La María** is larger, closer to the volcanoes and more visited, so options for accommodations are diverse. (*Cabañas* for 6 with a full kitchen 96 pesos; no kitchen, 21 pesos.) **Buses** (2.50 pesos) marked "La Becerrera" for La María leave Colima's suburban bus station daily at 7am, 1pm and 5pm, but the schedule is not strictly adhered to, especially returning to Colima (official times 7:30am, 2pm and 4:30pm). To make accommodations reservations at Carrizalillo or La María, ask at the Colima **tourist office** (tel. 2-40-60).

If your hotel rooms lack hot water, find some at **El Hervidero,** 35km to the east. The thermal waters there (77°F) are said to have medicinal properties. Closer to town, the spring at **Agua Caliente** (17km east) bubbles away, but the swimming doesn't rival El Hervidero's. To get to either pool, catch the "Pihuamo" bus from the suburban station (4 per day, returning 2hrs. later). At the *crucero* of Agua Caliente (2.50 pesos from town), a dirt road leads through 2km of ranch land before reaching the yellow waters. Follow it straight ahead (there are a number of forks and intersections) despite your best instincts (ignore the cows). El Hervidero is 6km from **Puerto de Anzar,** the closest point to the spring on the bus route (4 pesos to this hamlet). From there a nice hike separates you from soothing heat. It is best, at any time of year, to ask a local whether it is possible to reach these springs before setting off.

A small colony of *indígena* artisans thrives 9km north of Colima in **Comala** where the *tianguis* (*indígena* market) sells bamboo baskets, clocks and wooden furniture on Mondays from 8am to 3pm. The town's **church,** at Degollado and Madero on the *zócalo,* supports a thriving population of bats who have free run of the nave. There is a row of popular restaurants on the south side of the *zócalo;* a nice place to enjoy the afternoons. Buses to Comala leave Colima's suburban bus station (every 15min. 6am-10pm, 1.20 pesos).

AGUASCALIENTES

■■■ AGUASCALIENTES

The capital city of Aguascalientes lies in the center of the state of the same name. Rich soil and abundant spring water (much of which is naturally hot, giving the area its composite name, meaning "hot waters") make this area ideal for agriculture. Little has disrupted Aguascalientes over its 400-year history. The signing of the Convention of Aguascalientes, which united Villa and Zapata in their ill-fated alliance against Carranza during the revolution, was the city's cameo in the drama of history. Today, Aguascalientes is a huge, sleepy industrial and agricultural town, relatively uninteresting to the casual visitor.

The most worthwhile stop in town is the **Museo de Guadalupe Posada.** Its namesake, an engraver and cartoonist, helped turn public opinion against Porfirio Díaz at the end of the dictator's reign. The museum, which exhibits Posada's engravings and caricatures of Díaz, sits on León next to the Templo del Encino, 4 blocks south of López Mateos. (Open Tues.-Sun. 10am-2pm and 4-8pm. Free.) The charming **Basílica de la Asunción de las Aguascalientes** (open daily 6am-9pm) and the **Palacio de Gobierno** (open Mon.-Fri. 8am-9pm), on the Pl. de la Patria, will satisfy desperate colonial history buffs wandering up from the Bajío. Inside the Palacio courtyard is a mural painted in 1961 by Osvaido Barra Cunighan, part of which portrays the atrocious condition of *indígena* miners at La Mina de Edén. From March 10 to April 15, visitors pour into Aguascalientes to witness the annual **Feria de San Marcos.** Make hotel reservations at least a month in advance.

Though Aguascalientes has the full range of hotels, **accommodations** are inexplicably expensive near the bus station, especially since there is nothing there but *torta* stands and concrete. An exception to this rule is the **Hotel Continental** (tel. 15-55-48) on Brasil (the side street on the left directly as you leave the station) at the corner with Guatemala. The simple rooms have TVs and closets, and the bathrooms gush hot water. The restaurant dishes up huge quantities of burritos for a mere 5 pesos. (Singles 38 pesos. Doubles 45 pesos.) Closer to the *centro* there are a few affordable options. **Hotel Senioral,** Colon 104 (tel. 15-16-30) has clean pleasant rooms, those overlooking the Plaza de Patria with door-size windows. (Singles 40 pesos. Doubles 52 pesos.) On the other side of the plaza, across the street from cathedral, is **Hotel Rosales,** Guadalupe Victoria 108 (tel. 15-21-65). The plants in the old, dark courtyard areas are as dusty as the rooms and the bathrooms could be cleaner. (Singles 40 pesos. Doubles 50 pesos.)

Aguascalientes does not offer great variety in the way of **food**. Small stands line the pedestrian walkways —especially Juárez— and fresh produce can be bought of at the **mercado** on 5 de Mayo. For the hungry, the **Pizza Palace,** López Mateos 207, has an all-you-can-scarf buffet of pizza, spaghetti, burgers, and salad daily noon-5pm (13 pesos). Pizzas start at 9 pesos. (Open daily 11am-1am.) Near the plaza, at Madero 220, is **Mitla.** Management encompasses three generations of the same family. Wood paneling and waiters in white jackets. *Huevo* for 7.50 pesos, enchiladas at 13 pesos.

Shake it all night long with the locals at **Disco El Cabus,** Blvd. Zacateca at Campestre (tel. 8-28-80), in the Hotel Las Trojes. (Beer 6 pesos. Cover 35 pesos. Open Thurs.-Sun. 9pm-2am.) Check out the raucous laser light at **Fantasy,** Ayuntamiento 117-201 (tel. 6-82-02). Mixed drinks will set you back about 8 pesos. (Cover about 20 pesos. Open Thurs.-Sat. 9pm-2am.) Both spots are 18 and over, and men must wear pants.

Aguascalientes is 168km west of San Luis Potosí, 128km south of Zacatecas and 252km northeast of Guadalajara. **Avenida Circunvalación** encircles the city; **Avenida López Mateos** cuts through town on an east-west slant. The **bus station** is a few blocks west on Av. Circunvalación from the north-south Av. José María Chávez. "Centro" buses (.70 pesos) run from outside the bus station to the Mercado Morelos, two blocks north (on Morelos) of the central **Plaza de Patria.** To get back, "Central Camionera" buses traverse the length of Rivero y Gutiérrez (parallel to and 1 block north of Madero). Taxis cost about 5 pesos to the center.

The **tourist office** is located at Pl. Patria 141 (tel. 15-11-55), in the first floor of the *zócalo* de Gobierno. Comprehensive maps of the city and English brochures covering just about every state. Open Mon.-Fri. 8am-3pm and 5-8pm, Sat. 10am-1pm. **Currency Exchange:** Bánamex, 5 de Mayo, at the Pl. de la Patria. Open Mon.-Fri. 9am-1:30pm. The **post office** is at Hospitalidad 108 (tel. 5-21-18), 1 block east of the plaza on Madero, then left on Morelos and right on Hospitalidad. Open for stamps and *Lista de Correos* Mon.-Fri. 8am-5pm, Sat.-Sun. 9am-1pm. **Police**: López Mateos at Héroes de Nacozari (tel. 15-41-75), or tel. 06 for emergencies.

SAN LUIS POTOSÍ

■■■ SAN LUIS POTOSÍ

A sprawling, urban capital of 80,000 people, San Luis Potosí advertises itself as "The City of Plazas" and indeed it does have three splendid central plazas. Unfortunately, the charm and colonial architecture of these quiet plazas is not reflected in the rest of city. Elsewhere the streets are lined with modern buildings, bargain department stores, and street vendors selling mostly plastic goods.

Founded in 1592, San Luis Potosí was named to honor Louis, King of France. After the Spaniards learned from the Huachichiles of the rich mines in the region, the word "Potosí" was appended because the city's mineral wealth was comparable to that of Potosí in Bolivia. Gold and silver helped make San Luis Potosí one of the three most important cities in Mexico during the 17th century, when it had jurisdiction over most of northern Mexico, including Texas and Louisiana.

ORIENTATION AND PRACTICAL INFORMATION

San Luis Potosí is at the approximate center of a triangle of Mexico's largest cities—Monterrey, Guadalajara and Mexico City. Five main highways (Rtes. 57, 85, 70, 49, and 80) lead into San Luis Potosí.

To get downtown from the bus station catch an "Alameda" or "Centro" **bus** (.50 pesos) and get off at **Parque Alameda**, the first big stretch of green after the railway tracks. Always confirm the destination because drivers are sometimes fail to change their windshield signs and your bus could be headed for Timbuktu even if it says "Centro." **Taxis** to *el centro* cost 7 pesos.

San Luis' main drag is **Avenida Carranza,** which runs east-west and passes the north side of the **Plaza de Armas,** the city's historic center, east of which it answers to **Los Bravos. Madero,** parallel to Carranza/Los Bravos and one block south, is another important thoroughfare. It touches the Plaza de Armas's south side, east of which it goes by **Othón.** Two blocks east of the plaza on this street lies the **Plaza del Carmen.** One block further east lies the *Alameda*, where the bus from the station leaves visitors. The train station is on Othón opposite the *Alameda*.

Tourist Office: Carranza 325 (tel. 12-30-68), to the right of the Hotel Panorama. Just about the swankiest tourist office in Mexico. Helpful staff abound with excellent maps and info. Open Mon.-Sat. 8am-9pm.

U.S. Consulate: Carranza 1430 (tel. 12-15-28), via the "Morelos" bus. Open Mon.-Fri. 9am-noon, but can be reached in the afternoons as well. The police (see below) and the tourist office have consulate employees' home numbers in case of emergency.

Currency Exchange: Many banks around the Pl. de Armas open Mon.-Fri. 9am-noon, including **Banco Mexicano Somex,** Allende at Arista, 2 blocks north of the plaza's northwest corner. **Bancomer,** at Allende and Los Reyes, 3 blocks north of the plaza, open 9am-1:30pm. The *casa de cambio* at Obregón 407 is open Mon.-Fri. 9am-2pm and 4-8pm, Sat. 9am-2pm.

Post Office: Morelos 235 (tel. 2-27-40), between Salazar and Insurgentes, 1 block east and 4 blocks north of Pl. de Armas. *Lista de Correos* posted Mon.-Fri. 8am-2pm. Open Mon.-Fri. 9am-7pm, Sat. 9am-noon. **Postal code:** 78000.

Telephones: Computel, Carranza 360, opposite the Hotel Panorama. International collect calls 2 pesos. Open Mon.-Sat. 7am-10pm. Also try at Los Bravo 423, ½ block west of Constitución. International collect calls 5 pesos per 5 min. Open Mon.-Sat. 9am-8pm. **Telephone code:** 48.

Telegrams: Escobedo 200 (tel. 12-33-18), at the south end of Pl. del Carmen. Open Mon.-Fri. 9am-8pm, Sat. 9am-noon.

Airport: (tel. 2-00-95), Served by **Mexicana,** Madero at Uresti. Flights to: Mexico City, Monterrey, Chicago. Office open Mon.-Fri. 9am-6pm.

Train Station: On Othón near the middle of the north side of the *Alameda*. To: Mexico City (5:30pm and 10:30am, 6hrs., 45 pesos); Monterrey (5:35am and midnight, 8hrs., 43 pesos); Aguascalientes (noon, 6hrs., 7 pesos).

Bus Station: Central Camionera Plan de San Luis (tel. 12-74-11), 2 blocks south of the Glorieta Benito Juárez, several kms east of the city center along Av. Universidad. 12-odd different bus companies, each serving 15-40 cities. From here you can easily get anywhere in the northern half of the republic. **Transportes Vecedor** goes to Tampico (6 per day, 54 pesos). **ETN** sends first-class buses to Mexico City (about every hr., 70 pesos) and Guadalajara (8 per day, 55 pesos). **Flecha Amarilla** provides second-class service to: Mexico City (8 per day, 36 pesos), Dolores Hidalgo (11 per day, 12.50 pesos), Guanajuato (7 per day, 19 pesos), San Miguel de Allende (5 per day, 16 pesos), and Gogorrón (every 15min., 4.50 pesos). **Estrella Blanca** to Zacatecas (7 per day, 11.50 pesos),

Monterrey (hourly, 45 pesos), and Matamoros (3 per day, 79 pesos). **Autobuses Rojos** head for Santa María del Río (every hr., 6:30am-11:30pm, 3.80 pesos).
Taxis: tel. 12-21-22.
Car Rental: Budget, Carranza 885A (tel. 14-50-59).
Car Trouble: Ángeles Verdes Auxilio Turístico, Jardín Guerrero 14 (tel. 14-09-06).
Laundromat: Lavandería La Burbuja, Nicolás Zapata 535. 4kg load costs 14 pesos and takes 2hrs. Open Mon.-Sat. 9am-7pm.
Red Cross: Juárez at Díaz Gutiérrez (tel. 15-33-22 or 15-36-35).
Pharmacy: Farmacia Impina, Carranza 326 (tel.12-77-75). Open daily 8am-10pm.
Hospital: Hospital Central, Carranza 2395 (tel. 13-03-43 or 13-43-95), several km west of *el centro* along Carranza, on the west side of the city.
Police: Palacio Municipal (tel. 12-28-04 or 12-54-76).

ACCOMMODATIONS

Try to avoid all lodgings near the bus station: the neighborhood is sleazy and you'll get better deals closer to the center of the city. But if proximity to the bus station is a priority, stay at **CREA Youth Hostel (HI)** (tel. 12-66-03 or 2-11-51), on Diagonal Sur in front of Glorieta Benito Juárez, 2 blocks straight ahead as you exit the bus station. Tiny 4-person rooms with uncomfortable beds and unbearable mosquitoes, but everything is clean, including the communal bathrooms. Separate women's and men's areas. Access to sports complex with basketball courts, soccer fields, swimming pool, and track. (11pm curfew. 11 pesos per person, 1 peso discount with CREA, HI, or AYH card. Blankets, sheets, pillowcase, towel and locker included. Breakfast an additional 9 pesos, lunch and dinner 11.50 pesos.)

Hotel de Gante, 5 de Mayo 140 (tel. 12-14-93). By far the nicest hotel for the money. Impeccable rooms with phones, TVs and the occasional bathtub or view of the plaza. Singles 54 pesos. Doubles 64 pesos.
Hotel Plaza, Jardín Hidalgo (tel. 12-46-31), on the south side of the Pl. de Armas, next to Sears. Respectful and helpful older staff. Rooms have a certain faded charm. Rooms with plaza views a clear cut above the rest. Singles 45 pesos. Doubles 55 pesos.
Hotel Principal, Juan Sarabía 145 (tel. 12-07-84), ½ block from Pl. San Juan. Near Juan Sarabía and Plaza del Carmen. Don't be put off by the uninviting exterior. The rooms are clean and basic, management elderly and poetic. Singles 30 pesos. Doubles 40 pesos.

FOOD

For some reason all the restaurants in this town look like they belong in airports or bus depots, with prices to match. There are several dishes that are particular to San Luis Potosí. *Taquitos dorados* are thin slices of chicken or beef rolled in corn tortillas and deep-fried; *tacos potosinos* are stuffed with cheese and vegetables. *Enchiladas potosinas* are filled with cheese, red chiles and onions, sometimes smothered in more cheese. Delicious *nopalitos* are tiny pieces of cactus cooked in a tomato, oregano and onion sauce. *Cabuches* are small, yellow cactus fruit, served in a *ranchero* sauce. As unusual as it sounds, *chongos coronados* (curdled milk in sweet maple water) is a popular dessert.

La Conicute, Carranza 700 (tel. 12-93-04). High ceilings, heavy wooden tables, Mexican tiles, hanging plants, and colored ceramic plates. Great Mexican and *potosino* dishes for around 28 pesos. *Comida corriente* 15 pesos. Open daily 8am-midnight.
Restaurante Posada del Virrey-Cafetería, Jardín Hidalgo 3 (tel. 12-70-55), on the north side of Pl. de Armas. This popular restaurant in the plaza is housed in a building that was once the home of Mexico's only female viceroy. 7 kinds of beer in huge, frosty mugs 3.50 pesos each. Breakfasts 15-20 pesos. Spanish chicken 17 pesos. Open daily 8am-11pm.

Mac's (tel. 14-18-63), across the street from the Cathedral. Mock wooden tables but real wood chairs with leather seats, orange stucco partitions, and waitresses in pink diner outfits. Buffet breakfast of coffee and 4 different *platillos* 13 pesos, banana split 9 pesos. Open daily 8am-10:30pm.

Tortería Nueva, Allende 220 (tel. 12-77-80). Your basic sandwich plate but bigger, always crowded, and slightly classier. *Tortas* 5 pesos. Enchiladas 9 pesos. Makes deliveries. Open Mon.-Sat. 8am-9pm. For slightly longer hours and Sunday service try the somewhat more expensive Las Tortas on the corner.

Rendez Vous, Carranza 315 (tel. 12-17-77). This square, airport-style restaurant (two walls filled with pictures of Paris) attracts an older professional crowd discussing the nuances of life in San Luis. Somewhat less expensive than many of its look-alikes. *Menú del día* 16 pesos, breakfast 7-15 pesos, cappuccino 2.50 pesos. Open daily 7am-10:30pm.

Restaurante La Parroquia, Carranza 301 (tel. 12-66-81), on the south side of Pl. de los Fundadores. An interior reminiscent of a bus terminal cafeteria—the lunchtime traffic is about as heavy. Booths have great people-watching potential. Breakfasts 10-20 pesos, *tacos de pollo* 12 pesos. Open daily 8:30am-10pm.

SIGHTS AND ENTERTAINMENT

Often called the "City of Plazas," San Luis Potosí has three main plazas, the most central of which is the **Plaza de Armas** (also known as **Jardín Hidalgo**). At the beginning of the 17th century, residents watched bullfights in the dusty plaza from the balconies of the surrounding buildings. Now you can watch a red sandstone gazebo, completed in 1848, that bears the names of famous Mexican musicians.

From the **Palacio de Gobierno,** on the west side of the Pl. de Armas, Benito Juárez dispatched assassins to murder Emperor Maximilian. Maximilian, Miramón, and Mejí were eventually executed on June 19, 1867, near Querétaro, the imperial stronghold established after General Bazaine abandoned the country. On the second floor, in the **Sala Juárez,** is a diorama of the dramatic meeting between Juárez and Princess Salm Salm, who begged Juárez for Maximilian's life on the night before the execution. Plastic figures of the unmoved Juárez and the beautiful princess are positioned in front of the table at which Juárez signed Maximilian's sentence. The *sala* also contains a mask and a portrait of the President. As you enter the palace, go upstairs and turn left at the top of the staircase—the Sala Juárez is the first room on your left. (No fixed hours, but usually open Mon.-Fri. 9:30am-3pm.)

Opposite the Palacio de Gobierno stands the **cathedral,** its two towers crowned at night by blue neon crosses. The cathedral was completed in 1710, but in 1855, when San Luis became a diocese, the building was "upgraded." Miners are said to have donated gold and silver to beautify the interior, and marble statues of the apostles (small copies of those at the Basilica of San Juan de Letrán in Rome) were placed in the niches between the Solomonic columns of the baroque facade. The northern gray sandstone tower was built at the beginning of this century to commemorate the centennial of Mexico's independence. (Open daily 8am-7pm. The religious community of San Luis is particularly concerned that tourists not visit on Sundays or during mass.)

The **Palacio Municipal,** on the northeast corner of the plaza, was rebuilt after local citizens torched the original structure to protest Carlos III's expulsion of the Jesuits from the Americas. It boasts a traditional red stone courtyard with painted stairwell and simple mosaic steps. One block west of the southwest corner of the Pl. de Armas is the **Antigua Real Caja** (Old Royal Treasury), the city's only existing secular baroque building. With its truncated corner facade, the building belongs now to the Universidad Autónoma de San Luis Potosí.

East of the Pl. de Armas on Othón is the modest **Casa Othón,** home of the illustrious *poeta potosino* Manuel José Othón (1858-1906). The house has been restored to its original state and contains a collection of original works, photographs and documents relating to the poet. (Open Tues.-Fri. 8am-2pm and 4-6pm, Sat.-Sun.

10am-2pm. Free.) One block further east on Othón is the **Plaza de Carmen,** with its elaborate fountain supported by bronze fish.

Nicolás Fernando de Torres, a rich *Sevillano* of the early 18th century, made his fortune in San Luis Potosí. After his death, his estate was used to found a church and convent of the ascetic Carmelite order. The complex encompassed a large area, but today only the **Iglesia del Carmen** remains on the northwest corner of the plaza of the same name. In the opinion of many *potosinos*, the church is the most beautiful religious building in the city. Affixed to the facade are statues of San Eliseo, San Elías and, at the very top, the Madonna. The main altar was reconstructed with sandstone by architect Tresguerras after the original was destroyed in 1827. (Open daily 7:30am-1:30pm and 4-9pm. Again, avoid visiting during religious ceremonies.)

The colorful **Museo Nacional de la Máscara,** Villerías 2 (tel. 230-25), is in the Palacio Federal, ½ block south of the Pl. del Carmen along Villerías. This beautiful building of pink sandstone contains hundreds of masks from every Mexican region. An eloquent diatribe against cultural Eurocentrism opens this remarkable exhibit. (Open Tues.-Fri. 10am-2pm and 4-6pm, Sat.-Sun. 10am-2pm. Free.)

Two blocks south and one block west from the Pl. de Armas's southwest corner is the **Plaza de San Francisco,** with its own bronze fountain, quaint cobblestone street and red sandstone buildings. Eight years after the city's founding, construction began on the **Iglesia de San Francisco,** on the west side of the plaza. Less ornate than its local counterparts, the orange stucco facade boasts a Sevillian clock (1785) and statues of St. Francis. Inside, the doorway to the Salón de Profundis depicts St. Frailón washing the sacred cuts of St. Francis. A wonderful Churrigueresque fountain dominates this room where Franciscans are said to have chanted the *De Profundis* each morning. (Open daily 8am-7pm.) The **Plaza de Aranzazu** (or western Pl. de San Francisco) is a simple plaza that sits at the end of cobbled Universidad.

The **Museo Regional Potosino,** Galeana 450 (tel. 12-51-85), along the street on San Francisco's southern side, occupies the former Franciscan convent grounds. The government seized the land in 1950 and converted part of it into the museum. Inside on the museum's first floor is the marvelous **Capilla a la Virgen de Aranzazu.** *Aranzazu* means "from within the thorns"—a shepherd found the altar's image of the Virgin in a prickly thicket. The *ex-votos* along the walls are a tradition among Mexico's faithful; each depicts a miracle that a parishioner has experienced. They are often painted anonymously and hung in the church near an image of the Virgin Mary. A huge 18th-century hymnal stands to the right of the altar and next to the bishop's sedan chair. (Museum open Tues.-Fri. 8am-2pm and 4-6pm, Sat.-Sun. 10am-2pm.)

Archaeological exhibits on the first floor consist of artifacts from different parts of the country: two *yogos*, large stone rings placed around people's heads for burial; the dress of modern *indígenas*; and artifacts from San Luis Potosí's colonial past–boxes, locks, irons, spears, branding irons, daggers and 12th-century chain mail. (Museum open Tues.-Sat. 10am-6pm, Sun. 10am-2pm. Free.) Three blocks east along Manuel Othón from the Pl. de Armas is the expansive **Alameda Juan Sarabia** with its trees, benches, statues, and artificial ponds, but beware: the area is dangerous at night. A San Luis Potosí anomaly erupts on park's south side. The **Centro de Difusión Cultural** of the Instituto Potosino de Bellas Artes, Av. Universidad and Negrete (tel. 2-43-33), is not a graceful colonial edifice but a modern structure of bold curves and concrete. The museum devotes four large halls to contemporary artists, while caretakers provide New Age music to complete the mood. (Open Tues.-Sat. 10am-2pm and 5-8pm, Sun 10am-2pm and 6-8pm.)

The **Parque Tangamanga** has it all: three lakes for paddle-boating and fishing; a baseball field; motor-cross, auto-cross, and bike-cross grounds; a running path; and a playground complete with electric cars. Other park facilities include a planetarium, an observatory, and the open-air **Teatro de la Ciudad,** which hosts frequent cultural and artistic events (information at tourist office). To get to the park, catch a yellow and blue Perimetral bus (.80 pesos) on Constitución across the *Alameda*. Get off at the Monumento a la Revolución. (Open daily 9am-6pm. Free.)

Chic *potosinos* insist that **Arushal,** Muñoz 195 (tel. 17-42-30), is the best club in town. The decor almost matches its namesake, a city in Tanzania. A gigantic elephant's head (fake), some stuffed animals (real), and incredible lights and sound create quite a *selva* (jungle) mood. (Cover 25 pesos, drinks 7 pesos, and the usual dress required–no shorts, sandals, or sneakers. Open Thurs.-Sat. 9pm-3am.) **Oasis,** on the highway to Mexico City, is somewhat more intimate and also much beloved. (Cover 25 pesos. Open Thurs.-Sat. 8pm-2am.) Taxis after dark to either place cost 10 pesos.

The last two weeks of August mark the **Fiesta Nacional Potosina.** Concerts, cock and bullfights, fireworks, and a parade guarantee a swell time for all.

■ Near San Luis Potosí

Santa María del Río, 45 minutes south of San Luis, is the state's renowned *rebozo* (shawl) capital. The **Escuela de Artesanías** here has a wide selection, but the best of the best are made in private homes. Ask one of the instructors or administrators in the school to direct you to private craftspeople. (See San Luis Potosí: Bus Station above for transport details.)

Also south of San Luis is the state-run and reasonably priced resort of **Gogorrón.** Make reservations at the office of Centro Vacacional Gogorrón in the Edificio San Rafael, Othón and Zaragoza, 4th floor (tel. 14-66-55 or 12-36-36). Guests enjoy the waters of the hot spring, even hotter Roman baths, and swimming pools. Staying the night in this facility is an expensive but restorative way to end an extended low-budget stay in Mexico. (*Cabañas chicas* 124 pesos, 34 pesos per additional person; 3 meals and bath included.) For daytrippers, the Roman baths cost 8 pesos per hour. Use of the other facilities costs only 6 pesos per day, including access to the pool and shower. **Flecha Amarilla** buses (3 pesos) leave for Gogorrón every ½ hour from San Luis Potosí bus station. If you're driving, take the highway to Querétaro, go right at the sign that says Villa de Reyes and proceed 19km to Gogorrón. All reservations and arrangements should be made at the San Luis office.

There are also mineral springs at **Ojo Caliente,** 40km south of San Luis Potosí on Hwy. 57 to Querétaro and at Lourdes, 64km from San Luis Potosí on Hwy 57. Agua de Lourdes supposedly cures all ills, especially gastric and intestinal ones, and is sold in take-home bottles in case the baths fail to heal you on the spot. A small hotel here serves meals. (For reservations call (48) 17-14-04 from San Luis Potosí or go in person to the Lourdes office at Francisco Zarco 389.)

▓ El Bajío

A vast, bowl-shaped plateau of fertile soil, rolling farms and verdant hillsides stands slightly below central Mexico's volcanic range. However, it was the rich underground that has brought prosperity to the region since the 16th century: silver. For nearly four centuries, the mineral wealth of the Bajío has determined the course of its history. The area's richest mines—Real de Santa Fe, Real de Rayas, and Real de San Bernabé—had been discovered by the local aristocracy by 1550, but it was not until 1750, when the silver trade was rerouted to Mexico City, that Bajío's cities rose to be among the wealthiest and most influential in Mexico. As the city of Guanajuato began to supply most of the country's minting silver, it became the commercial and banking center of this thriving region, trading manufactured goods for crops from the nearby agricultural towns of Salamanca, Irapuato, León, San Miguel and Celaya.

The Bajío has long been a favorite destination for questing U.S. expatriates because of its vibrant social life and distinguished history.

GUANAJUATO

▪▪▪ GUANAJUATO

Guanajuato's history has been molded by economic success and historical tragedy. In 1558, incredible veins of silver were discovered in the area; veins which, over the next 200 years, would produce much of the world's silver supply and make Guanajuato one of Mexico's richest and most important cities.

After amassing its wealth under Spanish domination, however, Guanajuato led the way in the fight for independence. When King Carlos III raised taxes in 1765 and cut the landowners' and miners' share of silver profits, Guanajuato protested. When he banished the Jesuits from Latin America in 1767, Guanajuato, where the Jesuits had just completed their Templo de la Compañía, was outraged. During Hidalgo's stop here in 1810, sons of both the wealthy *guanajuatense* landowners and poor mine workers helped him overrun the Spaniards' stronghold at Alhóndiga de Granaditas. The loyalist Colonel Calleja then marched from Mexico City to make an example of Guanajuato. Calleja reclaimed the city from the rebels, ordered scaffolds built in all the plazas and began a gruesome "lottery of death," in which names were randomly drawn from a sombrero and citizens hanged as a lesson to those who dared to rise against the Spanish Empire.

The colonial silver barons also left behind a less political legacy—Guanajuato overflows with beautiful monuments to their ostentation. Guanajuato is also the birthplace of muralist Diego Rivera, whose earliest works are infused with impressions of the city. Today, the city supports five outstanding museums, several film clubs and four theaters. During the **Festival Internacional Cervantino**, held in October in honor of the author of *Don Quijote*, Guanajuato sponsors performances of drama, classical music, and ballet in an atmosphere of Dionysian debauchery. Guanajuato's university students and numerous musicians provide an animated and youthful social life, which keeps even older folks awake.

ORIENTATION

The city of Guanajuato is in the center of Guanajuato state, 54km southwest of Dolores Hidalgo and 44km north of Irapuato. The shortest way from Mexico City is via that wonderful burg Celaya on Rte. 57/45. León and Irapuato have become the state's main crossroads, with many bus connections to Guanajuato from either of these cities. Guanajuato's **bus station** is about 3km west of town. From the bus station catch the "El Centro" bus (.80 pesos) or take a taxi for considerably more money (8 pesos).

In Guanajuato, accurate maps are almost impossible to find, few streets are open to traffic, and still fewer follow a linear path. The best map on record can be purchased at the offices of INEGI, on the third floor in the same white building as the Agora Restaurant, on Allende near the **Jardín Unión** (though it is expensive). At the center of the city are the **Plaza de la Paz** and the imposing **basilica. Avenida Juárez** zigzags in a westerly direction from here to the market, the tourist office and the bus station; to the east of the plaza, it is called **Avenida Sopeña.** Roughly following the path of Juárez/Sopeña, the **Subterránea** is an underground avenue constructed between 1963 and 1966 beneath the former bed of the Río Guanajuato, which now flows in an adjacent concrete channel. On the surface, innumerable alleys branch off Juárez/Sopeña. When you become lost (a fact, not a possibility), remember that the avenue is always downhill from where you are. Because of the topography, only one or two streets with automobile traffic run north-south for more than a couple of blocks. Buses (.80 pesos) cross the city both on the surface and underground; service terminates at 10pm. To get to destinations that buses don't reach, taxis run for 4-8 pesos.

PRACTICAL INFORMATION

Tourist Office: Dirección General de Turismo, Juárez at Pl. de la Paz (tel. 2-00-86). A poor map and useless brochures, but some helpful verbal information. They sell better literature for 4-5 pesos. Open Mon.-Fri. 8am-7:30pm, Sat.-Sun. 10am-2pm.

Currency Exchange: Banks line Juárez and the Pl. de la Paz, but many exchange currency only Mon.-Fri. 9:30am-12:30pm. The best hours are at **Banco Mexicano Somex,** Sopeña 18, 1 block east of the Teatro Juárez. Open for exchange Mon.-Fri. 9am-1:30pm. There are no *casas de cambio,* but some restaurants and hotels change U.S. dollars.

Post Office: Ayuntamiento (tel. 2-03-85), down the street from the Universidad de Guanajuato. Open for stamps and *Lista de Correos* Mon.-Fri. 8am-8pm, Sat. 9am-1pm; for registered mail Mon.-Fri. 9am-6pm, Sat. 9-11:30am. **Postal code:** 37700.

Telephones: Lonchería y Caseta de Larga Distancia Pípila, Alonso 14 (tel. 2-09-83), down the street from Casa Kloster. International collect calls 3000 pesos. Open Mon.-Sat. 9:30am-9:30pm, Sun. no fixed hours. Another *caseta de larga distancia* on 28 de Septiembre, near the Museo de la Alhóndiga. Collect calls 5 pesos. Open 9am-9:30pm. **Telephone code:** 473.

Telegrams: Sopeña 1 (tel. 2-04-29), to the left of the Teatro Juárez. Open Mon.-Sat. 9am-8pm.

Bus Station: Central de Autobuses, west of the *centro.* **Flecha Amarilla** to San Miguel de Allende (9 per day, 6.50 pesos), Morelia (every hr. 6:30am-7:40pm, 14.50 pesos), San Luis Potosí (5 per day, 10.50 pesos), Aguascalientes (6 per day, 15 pesos), Dolores Hidalgo (every 20min., 3.50 pesos), Mexico City (3 per day, 42 pesos), and to the Monumento a Cristo Rey (5 per day, 4 pesos). **Estrella Blanca.** 1st class to Monterrey (2 per day, 60 pesos) and Guadalajara (3 per day, 23 pesos). Other carriers: **Servicios Coordinados, Tres Estrellas de Oro,** and **Omnibus de México.**

Laundromat: Lavandería Automática, Manuel Doblado 28 (tel. 2-67-18). Wash 5 pesos. Dry 5 pesos. Open 8am-8:15pm.

Red Cross: (Tel. 2-04-87), on Juárez west of the market.

Pharmacy: Farmacia La Perla de Guanajuato, Juárez 146 (tel. 2-11-75). Makes deliveries. Open daily 9am-9pm.

Hospital: Moving near bus station in summer of 1993, contact police or tourist office for number.

Police: Alhóndiga 8 (tel. 2-02-66 or 2-27-17), 1 block from Juárez.

ACCOMMODATIONS

The neighborhood around the *basílica* is the quietest and also the prettiest. If you're coming for the Festival Cervantino, it is best to make reservations in advance.

Casa Kloster, Alonso 32 (tel. 2-00-88). From the *basílica* take a right just after the tourist office, then another right on Alonso. The best deal in town. Modern, spotless, tiled communal bathrooms. Rooms surround an open courtyard filled with flowers, plants and birds. Ebullient guests. Very popular with longer-term travelers. 25 pesos per person.

Hotel Posada San Francisco, Juárez at Gavira (tel. 2-20-84), next to the market. Dark and narrow lobby, proudly sporting letters of appreciation from government officials, gives way to dark, but clean bedrooms with wood beds, some with balconies. The 2nd floor lounging area offers TV and a suit of armor for your enjoyment. Singles 50 pesos. Doubles 60 pesos.

Hotel Posada La Condesa, Pl. de la Paz 60 (tel. 2-14-62), a block from the *basílica*. The lobby is a wild and crazy mix of neon, a shrine to the Madonna, and rusty suits of armor. The rooms, in need of a paint job, smell like mildew. Singles 30 pesos. Doubles 40 pesos for 1 bed, 70 pesos for 2 beds.

Hotel Central, Juárez 103 (tel. 2-04-60), across the street, 1 block from the market. Clean but small rooms surround a narrow covered courtyard. Many without windows. Singles 50 pesos. Doubles 60 pesos.

FOOD

Although prices tend to rise near the Jardín Unión—due to the high density of *gringos* in the area—there are a number of pleasant, inexpensive restaurants in Guanajuato's numerous plazas and on the streets close to the *basílica*. For cheaper food, try the Mercado Hidalgo with its numerous fruit and taco stands.

Truco No. 7, at (hey!) Truco 7 (tel. 2-83-74), 1st left beyond the *basílica*. High ceilings, local art, fine pottery, jazz, and the long-term *gringo* crowd. Extremely reasonable *comida corrida* (9 pesos) and *huevos* (3-6 pesos), though entrees are more like 20 pesos. Cappuccino 3 pesos. Open daily 8am-11:30pm.

Cafetería y Restaurante Pinguin, *Jardín Unión* (tel. 2-14-14). Excellent central location and extremely low prices make it a great breakfast place, with espresso machine and a bulletin board advertising local cultural events. Clientele a mix of university students and *norteamericanos*. Eggs 3-4 pesos, juices 3 pesos. Open daily 8am-9:30pm.

La Flor Allegre, Pl. San Fernando (upstairs from Pl. de la Paz). This small north american-run restaurant has only a few tables outside. Inside, classical music plays, and on the bright blue walls is a wild collection of posters and a shelf with English language books. *Comida corrida* 8 pesos. Open Fri. and Mon. 2-10pm, Sat.-Sun. 10am-10pm, though somewhat erratic hours.

Café El Retiro, Sopeña 12 (tel. 2-06-22), across from Teatro Juárez. Dark, "romantic" lighting, round tables, round-backed chairs, and incongruously loud music. Primarily a bar, but also serves reasonably-priced food. Big tacos 6.5-10 pesos. *Tortas* 4.5-5.5 pesos. *Comida corrida* 14 pesos. Kitchen open daily 8am-11pm. Bar open until 2am.

La Carreta, Juárez 96 (tel. 2-43-58). Chicken rotisserie outside, wagon wheels, picnic tables, and faded black-and-whites of older Guanajuato inside. If it's too crowded, share a table with other diners. ¼ chicken 7 pesos, brew 3-5 pesos. Open daily 8am-9:30pm.

SIGHTS

Nestled deep in a ravine, Guanajuato's colonial center is a maze of narrow streets, massive stone bridges, and ex-aqueduct walkways. Columns of *cantera verde*—greenish layered stones—mark many of Guanajuato's colonial structures (including the interior of the Alhóndiga de Granaditas and the porch of the Pl. de Roque). At night, guitarists roam the streets, folk groups play in plazas, and bars resound with oldies.

Signs spread throughout the city denote self-guided walking tours. The most popular is "Ruta 2," between Pl. de los Ángeles and the Templo de San Diego. This route takes in the most famous alley in the city, the **Callejón del Beso** (Alley of the Kiss), which at some points is narrower than one meter. Tradition has it that two lovers who lived on opposite sides of the alley were kept apart by their families but could still kiss each other from their balconies.

Museums in Guanajuato explore the historical, the artistic, the monumental and the macabre. Qualifying for the last is the **Museo de las Momias,** next to the city cemetery. The minerals and salty water of Guanajuato's soil naturally mummified the 100-odd corpses now on display in the museum. Exhumation began a century ago when the state government decreed that those in city cemeteries whose relatives did not begin paying crypt rights within two years would have to be disinterred. Somebody decided to put them on exhibit, and before long a lucrative business reared its ugly head. A guide points out the purplish, inflated body of a drowning victim; a woman buried alive, frozen in her attempt to scratch her way out of the coffin; a Chinese woman; two fashionable Frenchmen; a man who died by hanging and another who was stabbed. Some buried babies still wear the colorful attire of saints—they were dressed like St. Martin and St. Joseph to ensure divine intercession on their ride to heaven. The mummies are the most popular sight in Guanajuato, drawing a larger crowd than the unghastly museums downtown. At the exit, vendors hawk morose candy figurines of the most memorable mummies. The museum is west of town; to get there, catch a "Momias" bus (.40 pesos) in front of the Cine or Mercado. (Open daily 9am-6pm. Admission 5 pesos. For those fun vacation slide shows, photo permits cost 3 pesos.)

The **Museo y Casa de Diego Rivera,** Pocitos 47 (tel. 2-11-97), chronicles the life of Guanajuato's most famous native son. While the first floor recreates the Rivera home at the time of Diego's birth, the upper floors are devoted to his paintings and sketches. Arranged chronologically, early works show the influence of Parisian friends like Picasso and Mondigliani, as Spanish landscapes give way to Cubist sketches and elongated nudes. Yet by 1920 and *Paisaje zapatista* ("Zapata Countryside"), the bright colors and simple tones of Rivera's own Mayan-influenced style are evident. Don't miss his outstanding watercolor illustrations for the *Popol Vuh* (sacred book of the Maya), in which he imitates Mayan iconography, and a sketch for a section of the mural commissioned in 1933 by New York's Rockefeller Center (it was destroyed after a portrait of Lenin was discovered in it). A second version now hangs in the Palacio de Bellas Artes in Mexico City. This sketch, which portrays a woman enslaved by a machine with the head of Adolf Hitler, was not incorporated into the final mural. (Open Tues.-Sat. 10am-1:30pm and 4-6:30pm, Sun. 10am-2:30pm. Admission 5 pesos.)

The **Museo de la Alhóndiga de Granaditas,** on Calarza at the west end of Pocitos (tel. 2-11-12), is more conventional. Constructed as a granary between 1797 and 1809, this building witnessed some of the most crucial and bloody battles in the fight for Mexican independence. In 1810, the supporters of Spanish rule locked themselves inside to defend the building against rebels led by the priest Don Miguel Hidalgo y Costilla. The rebels won the battle after an *indígena* mine worker known as Pípila (whose historic importance the giant statue above the city commemorates) strapped a huge slab of stone to his back, rendering him impervious to loyalist musket balls, and set the building's wooden door ablaze. Later that same year, the leaders of the independence movement, among them Hidalgo, Juan Aldama and Ignacio Allende, were captured and decapitated; their heads were strung up from the four corners of the Alhóndiga. Now the Alhóndiga is an ethnographic, archaeological, and historical museum. A chamber on the first floor charts the course of Mexico's nationhood. Other exhibits display *indígena* artisanry of the Bajío region: toys, masks, firecrackers, engraved machetes, tapestries, clay *indígena* deities and odd little candy dolls and sculptures of horse skeletons, to be consumed on *El Día de los Muertos* (Day of the Dead). The hall, containing huge busts of the heroes of independence is stunning, but the museum's finest exhibit—and one of the best historical accounts in any Mexican museum—traces the social history of Guanajuato from the Conquest through the Revolution with texts, illustrations, and local artifacts. Another gallery shows Romualdo García's photographs of Mexican people just before the Revolution of 1910. (Open Tues.-Sat. 10am-2pm and 4-6pm, Sun. 10am-4pm. Admission 10 pesos, free Sun. Photo permit 2 pesos.)

The **Museo del Pueblo de Guanajuato,** Pocitos 7 (tel. 2-29-90), next to the Universidad de Guanajuato, was inaugurated in 1979. It features rotating exhibits of local artwork, 18th-century religious oils, one gallery of colorful pre-Conquest ceramics, and samples of the Bajío's best pottery. Two rooms are dedicated to the work of recent local artists Olga Costa and José Chávez Morado. Chávez Morado has recently finished a new mural in what served as the baroque chapel of this ancient building. The hall, which hosts chamber music concerts, is also decorated by stained glass, murals with *indígena* motifs, and Mexican poetry. (Open Tues.-Sat. 9am-1pm and 4-6:30pm, Sun. 10am-3pm. Admission 5 pesos.)

The new, fascinating, and most single-minded museum in Guanajuato is the **Museo Iconográfico del Quijote,** Manuel Doblado 1 (tel. 2-67-21), east of the *Jardín Unión.* Housed in a gorgeous colonial mansion, its ten big galleries contain over 600 works of art inspired by Cervantes's *Don Quijote*: paintings and sculptures, stained-glass windows, candlesticks, and clocks. Artists like Dalí, Picasso, Daumier and Pedro Coronel have all interpreted Quijote; so have scores of lesser-knowns. (Open Tues.-Sat. 10am-1:30pm and 4-6:30pm, Sun. 10am-2:30pm. Free.)

The **Jardín Unión,** in the heart of the city, one block east of the basilica, is the town's social center. This triangular plaza has shops, cafés, and enough guitar-strumming locals to appease the tourist and student hordes. Looking down on the *Jardín* from the nearby hill is the **Monumento a Pípila,** which commemorates the miner who torched the Alhóndiga's front door. The angry, titanic effigy of Pípila looks most impressive at night, when it is illuminated by spotlights. The patio in front of the statue commands an outstanding view of the city. To reach the statue, follow Sopeña to the east and take the steep Callejón del Calvario to your right across the street from Lavandería El Centro (a 10-min. climb), or hop a bus marked "Pípila" from Pl. de la Paz.

The **Teatro Juárez** (tel. 2-01-83) faces one corner of *Jardín Unión.* After designing the theater to suit his tastes, Porfirio Díaz inaugurated the building in 1903 for a Verdi opera. The Romanesque facade is unabashedly gaudy, consisting of 12 columns, 10 lampposts with multiple branching lights, nine statues of muses standing loftily on the cornices, and two bronze lions. The auditorium betrays its Moorish design: half-circles, Arabesques, and endlessly weaving frescoed flowers in green, red, yellow, and brown make the interior look like a gigantic Arabian carpet. Imported materials, such as embellished metal and textiles from France and stained glass from Italy, abound in the smoking rooms, bar, and corridors. On one stairway, a rich painting depicts the old emblem of Guanajuato—a blindfolded virgin who stands for unconditional faith. The blindfold was removed by revolutionaries to signify that the Porfiriato could no longer deceive the people with illusions of fortune and progress. The Teatro Juárez still hosts plays, governmental offices, and the main events of the Festival Cervantino. (Open Tues.-Sun. 9:15am-1:45pm and 5-7:45pm. Admission 3 pesos. Camera permit 1.50 pesos.)

Another self-aggrandizing Porfirian edifice is the **Palacio Legislativo de la Paz,** the state capital, across from the Posada de la Condesa near the basilica. Christened by Díaz in 1900, the building is an adaptation of the Greek Parthenon. Italian marble, wall and floor mosaics, and a decorative zinc ceiling ornament the interior. (Open for viewing Mon.-Fri. 10am-5pm, extended and weekend hours for special events. Free.)

Outdoors, the many parks, plazas and lakes of the city provide unpretentious pleasure. Perhaps most beautiful of Guanajuato's many natural attractions is the **Ex-Hacienda de San Gabriel de Barrera** (tel. 2-06-19). Seventeen glorious gardens in different styles (Italian, Arab, English, etc.) cover about three acres of territory. Cobbled paths, well-groomed flora of all sorts, and abundant whistling birds make this place a stroller's dream. The *ex-hacienda* itself, a 16th-century structure, abuts the gardens. The rooms contain furniture, silverware, and paintings of the epoch. The most interesting chamber is the medieval-looking dining/living area, spanned by a wide, low, brick archway. Strangely violent sacred paintings suggest the return of Catholicism's repressed barbarism under the influence of the New World. To get there, take a bus from Juárez for the *Central*, and tell the driver you're headed to San Gabriel de Barrera. (Open daily 9am-7pm.)

The white Moorish towers known as **El Faro,** high in the mountains to the right of the reservoirs, make a good climb. From here you can admire the peculiar jutting stone mounds that have inspired many *guanajuatense* painters. To get to this part of town, take an eastbound "Presa" bus (.60 pesos), which stops at the underground stop by the *mercado*. (Open daily 9am-6pm. Admission 5 pesos. Camera permit 2 pesos.)

Dozens of candelabra in the lush Doric interior of the **Basílica de Nuestra Señora de Guanajuato,** looming over the Pl. de la Paz, illuminate fine ornamental frescoes, relics and three paintings of the Madonna by Miguel Cabrera. The wooden image of the city's protector, Nuestra Señora de Guanajuato, rests on a pure silver base and is believed to be the oldest piece of Christian art in Mexico. Next to the university and one block north of the basilica is the more interesting Jesuit **Templo de la Compañía.** The temple was finished in 1765, but shut down two years later when the Jesuits were expelled from Latin America. Characterized by eccentric *estípite* pilasters, the facade shows off Guanajuato's Churrigueresque architecture at its best. (Open daily 7am-8pm.)

Mercado Hidalgo, one block east of the tourist office, went up in 1910 with a monumental neoclassical arch as an entrance. Inside, both the seafood *coctelerías* and the vendors who sell musical instruments are trustworthy. Guanajuato's famed ceramic mugs have declined in quality, but the woolen items are quite cheap and the wide variety of sombreros will satisfy any head. (Most vendors open daily 9am-9pm.)

Finally, about 3km north of Guanajuato stands the Templo de San Cayetano, better known as **La Valenciana.** The church was finished in 1788 with three magnificent altars, carved from wood and covered with a sheet of 24-karat gold to inflame the covetous. To get to the church, take the "Valenciana" bus, which leaves approximately every hour from the street immediately downhill from the Alhóndiga de Granaditas. (Open daily 9am-6pm.)

ENTERTAINMENT

Each year, for two or three weeks in late October, Guanajuato stages the **Festival Internacional Cervantino,** also known by its old name, the **Entremeses Cervantinos.** The city invites repertory groups from all over the world to participate with the *estudiantinas*, strolling student minstrels of the Universidad de Guanajuato. The festival takes place mostly at local theaters. Guanajuatans put on the bulk of the always sold-out dramatic productions, while foreigners contribute films, folk dances and music ranging from classical and opera to jazz and rock. Make hotel reservations early.

From June 22 to 26, Guanajuato celebrates the **Feria de San Juan** at the Presa de la Olla with cultural events, fireworks, sports, and much more. Similar but shorter celebrations occur on **Día de la Cueva** (July 1), on May 31 and on August 9 (commemorating the arrival of the Virgin of Guanajuato to the city). The religious celebrations in December include the famous *posadas*, which re-create Mary and

Joseph's search for budget accommodations in Bethlehem without the *Let's Go: Israel and Egypt* guide.

Throughout the rest of the year, theater, dance and music are performed regularly if less frequently; check the tourist office for information, or consult the posters around town. Student groups present films almost every day of the week. Call the **Teatro Principal** (tel. 2-15-26), the **Teatro Cervantes** (tel. 2-11-69), or the **Teatro Juárez** (tel. 2-01-83) for specifics. (Tickets 5-10 pesos.)

The bars and cafés in the immediate vicinity of the *Jardín Unión* are friendly and comfortable, even for single women; **La Perla**, right on the *Jardín*, is probably the classiest of the bunch (beer 5 pesos). If things slow down on the *Jardín*, it's because they're picking up in the **Guanajuato Grill**, at Alonso 20. When school's in, the grill fills nightly with Guanajuato's friendly and thirsty students (beers 6 pesos). Couples only, but these pairs can easily be arranged spontaneously at the door—no cover. (Open nightly 8pm-2am.) As night wears on, many of them move on to **Donde** at Sopeña 19, source of some of Guanajuato's cheapest beer. Buckets of Corona (6 normal-sized bottles) go for 15 pesos, but there's no dancing (open Tues.-Sun. 8pm-2am, no cover). The trendy **Galería,** in the Hotel Parador San Javier, is the best-known spot for the seriously dance-minded. Look sharp (slacks, no sandals) or risk not getting in. (Cover 25 pesos.)

The most offbeat and entertaining club in town is **El Rincón del Beso** (a.k.a. Peña Bohemia), on Alonso east of Casa Kloster. The nightly sing-alongs and riotous poetry interpretations get going around 11pm (no cover). (Open Thurs.-Sat. 9pm-2am.)

Other popular discos include **Sancho's,** Pl. de Cata (tel. 2-19-76, cover averages 20 pesos); The plush **El Cantador,** Nejayote 17 (tel. 2-14-60), in the luxurious Hotel Real d'Minas, features live groups doing romantic Mexican numbers. **De los Santos,** on Guillermo Valle near the music school (tel. 2-07-09), impersonates the interior of a mine, with high stone walls and large wooden beams across the ceiling. The dark, romantic atmosphere and tranquil music call for candlelight.

■ Near Guanajuato

About 20km from Guanajuato, on top of a mountain 2850m above sea level, is the **Monumento a Cristo Rey,** completed in 1956. The mountain, called the **Cerro del Cubilete,** is considered the geographical center of Mexico. The dark bronze statue of Jesus is over 16m tall and weighs more than 80 tons. Although the statue is striking, you may spend more time observing the surrounding landscape; miles of wavy green and blue hills are visible from the top, and on rainy days you may be above the clouds. Take the "Cristo Rey" bus from the bus station (4 pesos, 1hr.).

■■■ DOLORES HIDALGO

The mild-mannered Don Miguel Hidalgo y Costilla, resident priest in the town of Dolores, was calmly plotting to sever Mexico's relations with the Spanish crown when he discovered that the government of New Spain had learned of his plans. He took decisive action. On Sunday, September 16, 1810, the people of Dolores were woken at 5am by the tolling of the parish church bell. In response, they gathered at the church, where they heard Hidalgo proclaim Mexico's independence from Spain. Hidalgo rallied an army to march on the capitol, but he didn't live to see the birth of the Republic.

Though Dolores witnessed these great events, not much of historical significance has happened here since. Late in 1947, the Mexican government declared Dolores Hidalgo the "Cradle of Independence." Today, the only things cradled in this sleepy town are a handful of museums and the communal memory of the glorious struggle. The best way to see Dolores is on a daytrip from San Miguel or Guanajuato.

ORIENTATION AND PRACTICAL INFORMATION

Dolores Hidalgo sits in the middle of the state of Guanajuato, about 50km northeast of the state capital and about 42km away from San Miguel de Allende. To get downtown from the **bus station** at Hidalgo and Chiapas, walk straight out the door, take a left on Hidalgo and go three blocks. This brings you to the **Jardín**, the **tourist office**, **Plaza Principal**, and the **Parroquia**. The **Río Dolores** runs east-west through the city; streets are arranged in a grid parallel and perpendicular to the river. A city map is useful since streets have different names on opposite sides of the city.

Tourist Office: Delegación de Turismo (tel. 2-08-01), on Pl. Principal in the arcade to the left of the *Parroquia*. The staff is enthusiastic when they are there. Official hours Mon.-Fri. 9am-6pm, Sat.-Sun. 10am-2pm, if door happens to be unlocked.

Currency Exchange: Banco del Centro, Guerrero and Jalisco (tel. 2-07-55), on the southeast corner of the Pl. Principal. Open for currency exchange Mon.-Fri. 9am-2pm. **Bancomer** (tel. 2-05-90), on the west side of the plaza. Open Mon.-Fri. 10am-1:30pm.

Post Office: Puebla 22 (tel. 2-08-07). Open Mon.-Fri. 8am-7pm, Sat. 8am-noon. **Postal code:** 37800.

Telephones: Restaurante Plaza (tel. 2-01-59), on the south side of the plaza. International collect calls 5 pesos. Open Mon.-Sat. 9am-2pm and 4-8pm. The **Hotel Caudillo** provides 24-hr. service for guests. International collect calls free for guests. **Telephone code:** 468.

Telegrams: Puebla 22 (tel. 2-04-63), in the post office. Open Mon.-Fri. 9am-1pm and 3-6pm, Sat. 9am-noon.

Bus Station: Hidalgo at Chiapas. **Flecha Amarilla** is the lone carrier. To: Mexico City (1 per hr., 5hrs., 30 pesos); San Luis Potosí (every ½hr. 5:40am-7pm, 12 pesos); León (about 1 per hr., 10 pesos); Guanajuato (every ½hr., 6 pesos); and San Miguel de Allende (every 15min., 7am-8pm, 3.5 pesos).

Pharmacy: Farmacia Dolores, Pl. Principal 21 (tel. 2-09-48). Open daily 9am-6pm.

Hospital: Hospital Ignacio Allende, Hidalgo 12 (tel. 2-00-13).

Police: In the Cárcel Municipal (tel. 2-00-21), on San Luis Potosí 1 block north of Pl. Principal.

ACCOMMODATIONS

Most of the lodgings in this village are posh for the sake of urban tourists visiting their national shrine. Nonetheless, they are reasonably priced, especially compared to those in San Miguel. Even so, you might wish to stay in San Miguel or Guanajuato because unless you enjoy browsing in ceramic shops, there isn't much to keep you occupied here.

Hotel Posada Cocomacán, Querétaro at Guanajuato (tel. 2-00-18), on the *Jardín*. Wood floors, tiled walls and romantic lighting in rooms off a central courtyard. Clean bathrooms. Singles 60 pesos. Doubles 70 pesos.

Hotel Caudillo, Querétaro 8 (tel. 2-01-98), across the street from the *Parroquia*. Clean rooms with TVs and that rustic motel something—unfortunately, including that smell. Local tiles everywhere, including the ceilings. Singles 45 pesos. Doubles 49 pesos.

Posada Dolores, Yucatán 8 (tel. 2-06-42), 1 block west of the Pl. Principal. Very small but clean, stark cell-like rooms. Every corner and, perhaps, closet forms a room in this friendly establishment. Passable communal bathroom. Singles 20 pesos. Doubles 25 pesos, with bath 35 pesos.

FOOD

Dolores Hidalgo offers nothing remarkable in the way of food, and one restaurant is pretty much like the rest.

Alborada Restaurante, Zacatecas 9 (tel. 2-09-51), across from the Museo Independencia. A sunny-courtyard restaurant decorated with plants, flowers, and umbrellas over each table. *Huevos al gusto* 6 pesos. *Quesadilla* 2 pesos. *Comida corrida* 16 pesos. Open daily 8am-8pm.

D'Jardín, Pl. Principal 30, on the Jardín. Tile resembles 1970s high-fashion linoleum. Colorful simulated hanging plastic plants put on the finishing touches. *Comida corrida* 15 pesos, tacos 7 pesos. Open daily 8am-7pm.

Restaurant El Delfín, Guerrero at Veracruz (tel. 2-22-09). Don't be fooled by the demure-looking bottle of picante sauce on the table, but if you do slip up, they stock 6 types of beer (3.50 pesos) to cool your tongue. Mostly seafood dishes. Shrimp 27 pesos. Meat 10 pesos. Open daily 9am-7pm.

SIGHTS AND ENTERTAINMENT

Mexico's "Cradle of Independence" is a small, minimally interesting community. In the four blocks between the bus station and Museo Independencia you've just about seen it all. That said, the beautiful **Parroquia,** where the *Grito de Dolores* was sounded, still stands. Constructed between 1712 and 1778, the church, with its large and intricately worked facade and twin towers of pink stone, dominates the Pl. Principal. Although the interior is dusty and somewhat deteriorated, the two side altars are magnificent examples of baroque art. It's not unusual for Mexico's presidents to return to the *Parroquia* on the anniversary of Hidalgo's proclamation to repeat it verbatim. (Open daily 7am-2pm and 4-7pm.)

The **Museo Casa Hidalgo,** at Morelos and Hidalgo, one block from the Pl. Principal, was Hidalgo's home from 1804 until 1810. Many of his belongings, including fine Mexican and European furniture and ceramics, are on display. Documents and works of art relating to the independence movement, as well as diverse lottery cards and a fabulous Mutepec **Tree of Life** (with Hidalgo at its center), fill rooms off a central scenic courtyard. (Open Tues.-Sat. 10am-6pm, Sun. and holidays 10am-5pm. Admission 12 pesos, free Sun. and for students with ID.)

The **Museo Independencia,** Zacatecas 6, lies less than one block northwest of the *Parroquia.* Here the exigencies of Spanish rule, the onset of independence, and the life and works of Miguel Hidalgo are presented in melodramatic murals and modern dioramas. Grisly paintings depict *conquistador* brutality in disturbing realism. (Open Mon.-Fri. 9am-2pm and 4-7pm, Sat.-Sun. 9am-3pm. Admission 2 pesos. Free for students with IDs.)

Dolores Hidalgo is heralded as Mexico's foremost **pottery** center, and ceramic shops abound. Though quality work may certainly be found, especially on smaller streets, don't hold your breath, as three-foot mass-produced frogs were the current fashion in summer 1993.

The **Cine Telocali,** on Guanajuato just off the square, shows the latest Mexican greats for 5 pesos. Otherwise, you might have to wait for the **Fiestas Patrias,** celebrated September 1-17, for official entertainment. Most of the cultural activities (folk dancing and singing), athletic tournaments (basketball, baseball, soccer), and fireworks take place during the final week.

■■■ SAN MIGUEL DE ALLENDE

Juan de San Miguel, a Franciscan friar accompanied by a group of Tarasco and Otoní *indígena* converts, founded San Miguel el Viejo in 1542. The first years of the village's existence were ill-starred; in the heart of Chichimec territory, the *pueblo* almost perished from their attacks. In 1555, however, when silver was discovered in Zacatecas, the *virrey* (viceroy) of New Spain saw the need to secure the lines of communication between his office in Mexico City and the ore. San Miguel falls on a straight line between those two points, and by the end of the 16th century the silver trade had re-christened the town San Miguel el Grande.

San Miguel's fifteen minutes of fame came in 1810. On September 16, Hidalgo arrived in the city with a rebel army. The question of San Miguel's allegiance was soon resolved by Ignacio Allende, who convinced the population of the righteousness of Hidalgo's mission. The army stayed three days in San Miguel, reorganizing and assimilating new recruits, before pushing on toward the capital. In 1826, the infant republic commemorated Allende's deeds by renaming the town after him.

Today San Miguel attracts flocks of foreign tourists (especially *gringos*) and has become a center of expatriate life. It was here that Neal Cassady, the prototype of Kerouac's hero in *On the Road*, died, hit by a train while walking the tracks to Celaya. While hip young Americans still visit or study here, many older American retirees have settled here as well and middle-aged vacationers fill the five-starred hotels. Here it is no feat to find a Reuben sandwich or Haagen Daz ice cream. Mexican life does continue amidst the American activity, especially in the *mercado,* and many of the natives are particularly friendly toward Americans, eager to practice their English or help you with your Spanish.

Renowned for its artisanry and academics, San Miguel has another resource that prospective visitors often overlook—a mild climate. The town is almost never oppressively hot, thanks to its 2000m elevation. Beware the ides of June and July, however. Cold afternoon drizzle or drenching all-day downpours can turn the streets into gushing streams.

ORIENTATION AND PRACTICAL INFORMATION

San Miguel lies midway between Guanajuato and Querétaro, 428km northwest of Mexico City. From the **bus station** to the center (known as the **Jardín** or **Plaza de Allende**), take the bus (.80 pesos) or a taxi (5 pesos). On foot, turn right (east) as you exit the station and walk 1km on Calzada de la Estación, which turns into San Francisco before coming upon the *Jardín*. The **train station** lies another km west of the bus station on the same road.

Most attractions are within walking distance of the *Jardín*. Getting lost here is no easy feat. The small size of the town and the near-grid of its streets facilitate navigation. Streets south of the *Jardín* that run east-west change their names every few blocks. A good source of current information on the town is the weekly newspaper *Atención*, available at the tourist office next to the *Jardín*.

San Miguel has a small and tolerated gay and lesbian population, mostly *gringo* expatriates. Furthermore, San Miguel has a reputation as a place for men and women to meet each other. To avoid desperate Don Juans, women should not walk alone at night. Crime, though, is virtually nonexistent.

Tourist Office: Dirección General de Turismo (tel. 2-17-47), on the Pl. de Allende next to the *Parroquia* and Restaurante La Terraza. Knowledgeable and helpful staff speaks English and distributes handy maps. Open Mon.-Fri. 10am-2:45pm and 5-7pm, Sat. 10am-1pm, Sun. 10am-noon.

U.S. Consular Representative: Macías 72 (tel. 2-23-57), opposite Bellas Artes. Office hours Mon. and Wed. 9am-1pm and 4-7pm, Tues. and Thurs. 4-7pm, or by appointment. In case of emergency dial 2-00-68 or 2-09-80.

Currency Exchange: Bánamex, on the west side of the *Jardín*, changes money 9am-noon and 4-6pm. Most other banks exchange 9am-noon. *Casas de cambio* give slightly lower rates: **Allen W. Lloyd y Asociados,** Jardín at Hidalgo (open Mon.-Fri. 9am-5pm), and **Deal,** Correos 15 (open Mon.-Fri. 9am-2pm and 4-6pm, Sat. 9am-2pm).

American Express, Hidalgo 1 (tel. 2-18-56). Full financial and travel services and cardholders' mail. Employs a few English speakers but won't exchange checks. Open daily 9am-2pm and 4-6:30pm.

Post Office: Appropriately at Correos 16 (tel. 2-00-89), 1 block east of the *Jardín*. *Lista de Correos.* Open for registered mail Mon.-Fri. 9am-6pm; for all other services Mon.-Fri. 8am-7pm, Sat. 9am-1pm.

Telephones: El Toro Lonchería, Macías 52, across from the Hotel Sautto. International collect calls 2 pesos. Open Mon.-Sat. 9am-1:30pm and 3-8pm, Sun. 10am-2pm.

SAN MIGUEL DE ALLENDE

Telegrams: (Tel. 2-00-81), adjacent to the post office. Open Mon.-Fri. 9am-1pm and 3-6pm, Sat. 9am-noon.

Train Station: Ferrocarriles Nacionales de México (tel. 2-00-07), located 2km west of town.

Bus Station: (Tel. 2-22-06), on Calzada de la Estación, 1km west of the center. **Herradura de Plata** to Mexico City (every 2hrs. 5am-7pm, 29 pesos) and Querétaro (every ½hr., 6 pesos). **Flecha Amarilla** to Guanajuato (every 2hrs., 7 pesos), Aguascalientes (3 per day, 23 pesos), San Luis Potosí (every 2hrs., last at 5:40pm, 16 pesos), and Dolores Hidalgo (every ½hr., 305 pesos). **Omnibus de México, Tres Estrellas de Oro,** and **Servicios Coordinados** also have less frequent service to and from San Miguel.

Taxis: Sitios de Taxis (tel. 2-01-92), or on the Jardín.

Car Rental: Gama Rent-a-Car, Hidalgo 3 (tel. 2-08-15). 68 pesos per day and extra per km. Special weekly rates. Open Mon.-Sat. 9am-2pm and 4-7pm.

English Bookstore: El Colibrí, Sollano 30 (tel. 2-07-57). Superb, if expensive, selection of classics, science fiction, history and current best sellers. After 25 years, staff knows just about all there is to know about San Miguel. Open Mon.-Sat. 10am-2pm and 4-7pm. Also, the public library (see below) evacuates old paperbacks by selling them for about 2 pesos each.

Public Library: Insurgentes 25 (tel. 2-02-93), next to La Española. An important feature of expatriate social life. Free language exchange. Open Mon.-Fri. 9am-2pm and 4-7pm, Sat. 10am-1pm.

Laundromat: Lavamágico, Pila Seca 5 (tel. 2-08-99). Will pick up and deliver a 4kg load for a mere 12 pesos. Open Mon.-Sat. 8am-8pm.

Red Cross: (Tel. 2-16-16), km1 on Carretera Celaya.

Pharmacy: Farmacia Allende, San Francisco 3 (tel. 2-00-74), ½ block from the *Jardín.* Open daily 9am-9pm.

Hospital: Clínica la Salud, Hidalgo 28 (tel. 2-04-30). Open 24 hrs. for emergencies. English-speaking physician.

Police: (Tel. 2-00-22), in the Presidencia Municipal.

ACCOMMODATIONS

The invisible hand of supply and demand is at work here. Plenty of room-hungry, dollar-toting *gringos* and relatively few hotels have sent prices skyward—accommodations here are dearer (and nicer) than in most other spots in Mexico. May and June you may want to make a reservation several days in advance to play it safe. If you're planning an extended stay, check for notices of rooms for rent on the bulletin board at the Instituto Allende, Ancha de San Antonio 20, southwest of the *Jardín,* and in popular *norteamericano* cafés and hotels.

The San Miguel International Hostel, Organos 34 (2-06-74), 1 block west of Jardín on Canal, right on Macias, 3 blocks to Organos, left on Organos another block and a half. This friendly American-run establishment makes you feel right at home. A sitting room equipped with English books, music and a piano, chairs arranged outside in the courtyard, kitchen use (3 pesos per day for the privilege), and optional Spanish lessons (5 pesos) in the afternoon. Clean single-sex dorms (4-10 people per room) and bathrooms. (15 pesos, continental breakfast included.) 2 private single rooms and 1 private double, as well (35 pesos each; reserve several days in advance to play it safe).

Casa de Huéspedes, Mesones 23 (tel. 2-13-78). Serene, flower-filled courtyard complete with lounge chairs and *New Yorker* magazines. Immaculate rooms, some with kitchens, and wonderfully friendly staff. Singles 40 pesos. Doubles 60 pesos. Better rates for extended stays.

Hotel Posada de Allende, Cuna de Allende (tel. 2-06-89), around the corner from the Parroquia. Large, wallpapered rooms off of a small courtyard, 1 wall of which is the Parroquia. Run by 2 elderly women who make candy on the side. Singles 40-50 pesos. Doubles 60 pesos.

Hotel Quinta Loreto, Loreto 13 (tel. 2-00-42), 3 blocks north and 1 block east of the *Jardín,* down a cobbled driveway. Popular place with *norteamericanos.*

Great large rooms with tiled bathrooms, a flower-filled garden, tennis courts, and a pool. Singles 70 pesos. Doubles 85 pesos.

Hotel Posada de las Monjas, Canal 37 (tel. 2-01-71), 3 blocks west of the *Jardín*. A good deal: elegant lobby comes complete with rug, prints, flowers, TV and goldfish. A maze of plant-filled courtyards with fountains. Dirt-free carpeted rooms with desks and stone-floored bathrooms. Restaurant and bar. Singles 70 or 150 pesos (2 sizes). Doubles 90 or 180 pesos.

FOOD

The sweet aroma of international cuisine wafts through the cobbled streets of San Miguel and fine restaurants grace almost every corner. Unfortunately, their prices are as *norteamericano* as their clientele. As a general rule, American and European fare tends to be expensive, and not quite the home cooking you miss. Taco stalls and inexpensive *loncherías* hide in and around the *mercado* on Colegio. *Elotes* and *tortas* can be found in the tiny square on Insurgentes between Macías and Hidalgo.

El Correo Restaurante, Correo 23 (tel. 2-01-51), 1 block from La Parroquia and across from, yes, the Casa de Correos. Luxurious appearance pleasantly belies reasonable prices. Loaded: stencilled walls, flowered placemats, a sophisticated crowd, and its own bird. Waffles 7 pesos. Quesadillas 6 pesos. *Spaghetti bolognese* 14 pesos. Open Thurs.-Tues. 9am-9:30pm.

Restaurant "El Infiernito," Mesones 23 (tel. 2-23-55). Ceramic bulldogs, stuffed iguanas, pictures of Jesus and psychedelic art adorn the dining area. The specialty is *pollo rostizado* (10 pesos). *Huevos al gusto* 7 pesos. *Menú del día* 13 pesos. Open daily 9am-midnight.

Mama Mía, Umarán 8 (tel. 2-20-63), west of the *Jardín*'s southwest corner. Eat your dinner to live mariachi music under paper lanterns hung from the trees overhead. It's a *norteamericano* crowd here eating this Italian food (although the cooks and waiters are native). Pasta 16-25 pesos. Meat 29-48 pesos. Open 8am-1am.

La Colima, El Reloj 21, north of the *Jardín*. A great little bakery with constantly warm sesame rolls. Cheapest breakfast in town. *Bolillos* (Mexican breads) .50 pesos. *Conches* 1 peso. Rolls .20 pesos. Open Mon. 8:30am-2pm, Tues.-Sat. 6am-2pm and 5:30-9pm, Sun. 6-9am.

SIGHTS

Magnificent churches, colonial homes, an art gallery and artisans' boutiques populate the cobbled streets around the *Jardín*. The only way to experience San Miguel is on your own two feet. The public library gives guided **home and garden tours** of the city in English most days at noon (25 pesos). Alternatively, just wander off on a random tangent from the *Jardín*; almost every street has an interesting shop, and San Miguel's small size makes it hard for even the klutziest to get lost.

La Parroquia, next to the *Jardín*, is one of the most distinctive churches in Mexico. Its facade and tower were designed and realized by the *indígena* mason Zeferino Gutiérrez, who is said to have learned the Gothic style from postcards of French cathedrals. The size and beauty of the church make it a landmark for miles around. (Open daily 8am-9pm.)

The **Museo Histórico de San Miguel de Allende,** on the corner of Canal and Cuna de Allende, just west of *La Parroquia*, resides in the home where Allende, a leader of the anti-colonial putsch, once lived. Don Ignacio's status is obvious from his magnificent, partly Baroque mansion. The eclectic museum combines tributes to Allende with unrelated exhibits on astronomy and paleobiology. (Open Tues.-Sun. 10am-4pm. Free.)

At the corner of Canal and Macías, two blocks west of the *Jardín*, stands the enormous **Iglesia de la Concepción.** Distinguished by its splendid two-story dome crowned with a representation of the Immaculate Conception, the church was finished in 1891. Pairs of Corinthian columns adorn the lower level. Inside are polychrome sculptures of St. Joseph and the Immaculate Conception, and an interesting juxtaposition of paintings and graves. (Open daily 8am-8:30pm.)

Founded in 1712, the **Templo del Oratorio de San Felipe Neri** lies at the corner of Insurgentes and Loreto, two blocks east of the library. Its engraved baroque facade shows *indígena* influence, and its interior is mainly Neoclassical, but the styles collide, as the church has been rebuilt many times. On the west side of the church, the towers and the dome belong to the **Santa Casa de Loreto,** a reproduction of the building of the same name in Italy (enter on the right side of the altar in San Felipe Neri). The floors and the lower wall friezes are covered with glazed tiles from China, Spain and Puebla. (Open daily 7-8pm.)

One block east of the *Jardín* at Juárez and San Francisco, the **Iglesia de San Francisco** includes a tall, dark red neoclassical tower attributed to the architect Tresguerras. Finished in 1799, the church's Churrigueresque facade honors many saints. Several small paintings in the interior are so elevated and enveloped in darkness that you'd have to be a bat to appreciate them. To the right as you face San Francisco is the **Iglesia del Tercer Orden,** one of the oldest and most decayed churches in San Miguel, constructed by the Franciscan order between 1606 and 1638. The main facade contains an image of St. Francis and symbols of the Franciscan order. (Both open daily 8am-8pm.)

The two contemporary cultural centers of San Miguel are the **Bellas Artes** and **Instituto Allende**. Set in a converted 18th-century convent, the Bellas Artes (a.k.a. Centro Cultural Ignacio Ramírez El Nigromante, on Macías next to the Iglesia de la Concepción, tel. 2-02-89) boasts a traditional courtyard that overflows with cappuccino-sipping artists. Shifting exhibits by both contemporary Mexican and foreign artists fill the main three halls. The upper floor sports studios for current art students and smaller galleries for local craftspeople. (Open daily 10am-1pm and 4:30-6pm.) Built as a church in 1735, the **Instituto Allende**, Ancha de San Antonio 20, in the southwestern part of the city, received its present incarnation as an art school in 1985. Affiliated with the University of Guanajuato, its two galleries show and sell the works of current students. (Open daily 9am-noon and 3-6:30pm.)

The **Parque Juárez,** three blocks south of the *Jardín* on Aldama and then Carranza, is the greenest, but unfortunately, also the smelliest (because of its stagnant stream) of San Miguel, reverberating with the calls of tropical birds. Die-hard cagers can often join a pick-up basketball game involving both *gringos* and locals. Some of the most elegant houses in San Miguel surround this park.

Tres Cruces is a hill east of town with three crosses on it. San Miguel, the surrounding valley and the faraway mountains are magnificently visible from the hill. Walk three blocks east on San Francisco from the *Jardín*, turn right (south) on Real (you'll pass a PEMEX station) and walk until you see the crosses on the right. This part of the walk takes about 15 minutes and passes through some picturesque alleys along the way. Three blocks before reaching the official *mirador* (lookout), you can turn right and ascend to the hilltop (another 15min.).

The mild climate of San Miguel rarely demands aquatic relief, but should the mercury rise to swim level, head to the *balneario* at **Taboada,** 6km down the road to Dolores Hidalgo. The facilities here include two pools, a bar/restaurant and playing fields. Before you can immerse, you must catch the bus marked "Taboada" at the municipal bus stop. To get to the stop, head east along Mesones toward the market. Turn left on Colegio and, after one block, turn right onto a small plaza. Buses (3 pesos) leave here for Taboada at 9am, 11am, 1pm and 3pm, and return to San Miguel 15 minutes after the above hours. (*Balneario* open Wed.-Mon. 7am-5pm. Admission 6 pesos.)

ENTERTAINMENT

San Miguel's cultural calendar is full. The magazine *Atención,* on sale at the public library, has details of most events. In addition, both the Bellas Artes and Instituto Allende have bulletin boards crammed with information on upcoming jazz, classical guitar, dance and folk song concerts, as well as theatrical productions and lectures by both locals and *gringos*. Concerts and theater usually cost a few pesos and are held at either site—double check there for details. The **Biblioteca Pública** (public library), Insurgentes 25, arranges informal evenings of conversation in Spanish and English (Thurs. 7-9pm, Sat. 5-7pm), providing a relaxed atmosphere in which to meet Mexican students and other travelers, as well as near-complimentary cookies. (Sometimes held at **Casa Luna,** Cuadrantes 2; check at the library or in *Atención*.)

San Miguel has a deserved reputation as a town with a real nightlife. On Wednesdays, many popular clubs dispense with the normal cover charge, and the whole town turns out. **Pancho and Lefty's,** is on Mesones between Macías and Hidalgo. At night, the mostly *gringo* crowd gets busy to live rock'n'roll. (Open Wed.-Sat. 7pm-2:30am. Fri.-Sat. cover for men 20 pesos. Wed. 2-for-1. Beer 7 pesos. Mixed drinks 11 pesos.) **Mama Mía** in front of the restaurant (see Food) has a huge TV screen in a small dark room. (Drinks 7 pesos. Open daily 7pm-3am.) **Laberintos,** Ancha de San Antonio 7, is distantly related to a wine cellar. Vintage disco and *salsa* tunes permeate the dance floor. (No cover Thurs; Fri. cover 6-10 pesos; Sat. cover 15 pesos; Sun. cover 5 pesos. Open Thurs.-Sun. 8pm-3am.) **El Ring,** Hidalgo 25, the best dance floor in town, heats up around 11:30pm when the tireless from other hot-spots come like moths to the flame.Play the latest dance tracks from the U.S. and Latin America. (Cover Thurs.-Sun. 30 pesos, drinks 7-11 pesos. No shorts or sandals allowed for males. Open Wed.-Sun., 10pm until everyone leaves, usually around 5am.)

San Miguel is reputed to have more festivals than any other town in Mexico. Most nights the gazebo in front of the cathedral plays host to some musical extravaganza. Beyond national and religious holidays, San Miguel celebrates the birthday of Ignacio Allende on January 21; the Fiesta de la Candelaria on February 2, marking the start of spring and the birthday of El Padre de Miguel; and the festival of San Miguel's guardian saint (third weekend in Sept.), when bulls run free through the center of the city in imitation of the *encierro* in Pamplona, Spain.

ACADEMIC INSTITUTIONS

Many visitors to San Miguel study at one of its schools for foreign students. Starting dates, intensity of instruction, and hiring policies vary, though many foreigners arrange classes and a homestay (approximately US$450 a month) upon arrival. The **Bellas Artes** (tel. 2-02-89) conducts a number of four-week courses throughout the year in fine arts and language at a cost of about US$70 per month. For information, write to Señora Carmen Masip de Hawkins, Macías 75. During the year the **Academia Hispano-Americana** (tel. 2-03-49) runs two-, four-, eight- and twelve-week sessions in Spanish language, literature, history, psychology, current events and Mexican folklore. Two weeks cost US$200. For information write to the Registrar, Academia Hispano-Americana, Mesones 4. **Inter Idiomas** (tel. 2-21-77) organizes language programs of two hours per day at US$45 per week or US$160 per month, plus a one-time US$15 registration fee. Address inquiries to Mesones 15.

QUERÉTARO

■■■ QUERÉTARO

On June 19, 1867, on Querétaro's Cerro de las Campanas (Hill of Bells), after handing each of the assembled soldiers a gold coin, Emperor Maximilian uttered his famous last words: "Mexicans, I am going to die for a just cause: the liberty and the independence of Mexico. May my blood be the last shed for the happiness of my new country. *¡Viva México!*" Fifty years later, at the end of a bloody revolution, the victorious leader Carranza chose this spot for the drafting of the constitution that governs the Republic to this day. Querétaro has also been the site of less noble events. It was here that the peace treaty after the Mexican-American War of 1848 was signed, in which Mexico was forced to cede much of its northern territories, the present U.S. states of California, Arizona, New Mexico, Colorado and Nevada.

Today, Querétaro has the feel of a European city: elegant 18th- and 19th-century architecture, wide brick streets, traffic jams, chic clothing stores, couples strolling on the pedestrian promenades, and flocks of pigeons—the emblem of all real cities—in its numerous fountain-centered squares.

ORIENTATION AND PRACTICAL INFORMATION

Querétaro is on two of the country's most heavily traveled highways—Rte. 120 and Rte. 57. Its streets form a grid, and nearly all important sites are within walking distance of the **Jardín Obregón,** the four streets Corregidora, Madero, Juárez, and 16 de Septiembre on each of its sides. The **bus station** is on Carretera Panamericana, across the street from the **Alameda Hidalgo,** a wild park. To reach the Jardín, turn left (west) upon leaving the station, walk one block to Corregidora, then turn right (north) and walk four blocks. The **train station** is a good distance from the Jardín, about two blocks beyond the end of Corregidora in the northernmost part of the city. To get to the train station from downtown, catch a "Ruta 13" *taxibus* (.70 pesos) and get off at the railroad tracks. Take a right on the tracks and walk two blocks.

Tourist Office: State Tourist Office, Pasteur Sur 17 (tel. 14-56-23), in the Pl. de Independencia. Friendly English-speaking staff hands out helpful maps and listings of cultural events around the city. Free city tours in Spanish daily at 10:30am. Open Mon.-Fri. 9am-2pm and 5-8pm, Sat.-Sun. 10am-1pm. **Federal Tourist Office,** Constitución 10020 (tel. 13-85-11).

Currency Exchange: Banks near the Jardín Obregón are open Mon.-Fri. 9am-12:30pm, but some exchange currency only until noon. **Casa de Cambio de Querétaro,** Madero 6, in the mall on the Jardín Obregón's south side, is open Mon.-Fri. 9am-3pm. At other times, try the jewelry stores near the Gran Hotel, but expect unfavorable rates.

Post Office: Arteaga Pte. 7 (tel. 12-01-12), 2 blocks south of the Jardín Obregón, between Juárez and Allende. Open Mon.-Fri. 8am-7pm, Sat. 9am-noon.

Telephones: Long-distance *caseta* at the bus station. No collect calls. Open 24 hrs. Efficient *caseta* at 5 de Mayo 33. International collect calls 12 pesos. Open Mon.-Sat. 9:30am-2pm and 4:30-9pm. **Telephone code:** 463.

Telegrams: Allende Nte. 4 (tel. 12-01-63), 1 block west of the Jardín Obregón. Open Mon.-Fri. 9am-8pm, Sat. 9am-1pm.

Train Station: Allende (tel. 12-17-03), in the northern part of the city. To: San Miguel de Allende (12:45pm, 10.8 pesos); Mexico City (5:30am, 26 pesos); San Luis Potosí (12:45pm, 21 pesos); Guadalajara (midnight, 11 pesos).

Bus Station: (Tel. 12-17-30), on Carretera Panamericana, 4 blocks south and 1 block east of the Jardín. Station contains a 24-hr. long-distance telephone booth, a cafeteria and a squadron of food booths and shops. Frequent service, but almost all buses are *de paso.* **Flecha Amarilla** sends the most buses to: Irapuato (from there a change of buses to Guanajuato, every 15min., 9 pesos); Aguascalientes (4 per day, 25 pesos), Guadalajara (hourly, 34 pesos), and Dolores Hidalgo (hourly, 4.5 pesos). **Tres Estrellas de Oro** sends buses to Mexico City (hourly, 22.5 pesos) and **Herradura de Plata** to San Miguel de Allende (every ½hr., 6 pesos). 10 or so other carriers also operate from Querétaro.

Taxis: (Tel. 12-36-66 or 12-31-43), but they're cheaper if flagged down.

Laundromat: Lavandería Automática La Cascada, Loc 18 Commercial Mexicana (tel. 16-56-96). 3kg for 15 pesos. Open Mon.-Fri. 9am-2pm and 4-8pm, Sat. 9am-2pm.

Red Cross: Hidalgo Pte. 93 (tel. 12-17-06).

Pharmacies: Farmacia Central, Madero 10 (tel. 2-11-29), on the Jardín's south side. Open Mon.-Sat. 9am-8pm. **Farmacia El Fénix,** Juárez Nte. 73 (tel. 2-01-79), 1½ blocks north of the Jardín Obregón. Open daily 8am-10pm.
Hospital: Hospital Civil, Reforma 21 (tel. 16-20-36).
Police: Constituyentes Pte. 20 (tel. 12-15-07).

ACCOMMODATIONS

Resist the urge to curl up at the hotels near the bus station. Cheaper and considerably more charming places abound a few blocks away, around the Jardín Obregón. Because Querétaro is such a large city, the finest hotels are outside the budget traveler's range while the cheapest lack that small-town family charm.

Hotel Hidalgo, Madero Pte. 11 (tel. 12-00-81), 1 block west of the Jardín. Pleasant colonial architecture and central location. Rooms with terraces are considerably nicer than their hot and claustrophobic counterparts without. Singles 40 pesos. Doubles 55 pesos.

Hotel San Agustín, Pino Suárez 12 (tel. 2-39-19), between Allende and Juárez. This modern building has no charm, but the rooms and bathrooms are clean and cool and the staff friendly. Rooms overlooking the street lack the cell-like ambiance of the others. Singles 45 pesos. Doubles 60 pesos.

Hotel San Francisco, Corregidora Sur 144 (tel. 2-08-58), 3 blocks south of the Jardín Obregón, near the bus station. Functional, clean rooms with bright blue walls. Most rooms have windows to the outside and are, therefore, cooler than many other Querétaro hotels. Singles 40 pesos. Doubles 50 pesos.

Hotel del Márquez, Juárez Nte. 104 (tel. 2-04-14), 3 long blocks north of the Jardín Obregón. The beautiful newly tiled bathrooms are an anomaly in this hotel. One wonders whether the bedrooms have been touched—or the windows opened—since the 1950s. Orange and brown ratty material clothes these furnace-like rooms. Singles 40 pesos. Doubles 50 pesos.

FOOD

Several inexpensive restaurants face the Jardín Obregón. Charming but expensive *loncherías* and outdoor cafés rim the nearby Pl. Corregidora, while taco, *torta,* and other fast-food stands line 5 de Mayo. Beware, most restaurants stop serving their *menú del día* at 5 or 6pm.

Restaurante de la Rosa (tel. 14-47-22), on Juárez at Peralta, across from the Teatro República. Basic Mexican food served in a friendly atmosphere by a woman who will eagerly encourage you to "practice your Spanish." Eat beneath hanging plants and lanterns in your straight-back wooden chair. Buffet breakfast, *menú del día* (until 5pm at 10-12 pesos), *carne a la carta* (usually 15 pesos). Open Mon.-Sat. 9am-9pm.

Restaurante Manolo's, Madero 6 (tel. 14-05-50), on the south side of the Jardín Obregón. Some tables sit outside the restaurant in the corridor of a quiet mall. Tranquil, relaxed restaurant with white and yellow walls and wooden chairs. The white-tiled kitchen is open to show the cooks at work. Specialty is *paella. Menú del día* 15/21 pesos. Open daily 8am-9pm.

Café del Fondo, Jardín Corregidora 12. Small coffee establishment ideal for cracking that new novel. Pink staircase, pine tables and local art enhance the tranquility. Breakfasts from 5-8 pesos. Fancy coffees 3.2-9.7 pesos. *Comida corriente* 8.4 pesos. Open daily 8am-10pm.

Ibis Natura Vegetana, Juárez Nte. 272, ½ block north of the Jardín Obregón (tel. 4-22-12). Restaurant in a health-food store set up fountain-shop style. Long narrow room with wooden counter and reflecting stainless-steel ceiling. Yogurt 4.5 pesos. Soyburger 5.5-7.5 pesos. Open Sun.-Fri. 9:30am-9:30pm.

QUERÉTARO

SIGHTS

Querétaro draws crowds with its rich historical and religious past. The city abounds not only in beautiful architecture, but also in intriguing legends and patriotic memories. Many sights are within easy walking distance of the Jardín Obregón.

Most intriguing of all is the **Convento de la Santa Cruz,** south of the Jardín. Follow Corregidora to Independencia and turn left; after walking a few blocks, you'll reach the convent on a plaza dedicated to the founders of the city. Nearly everything inside Santa Cruz is original, including the furnishings of the room in which Emperor Maximilian awaited his execution. In one courtyard, trees grow thorns in the form of crucifixes. Legend has it that the thorns began growing in this manner after one of the original friars accidently left his cane stuck in the ground near the trees. They are reportedly the only trees of their kind in the world, and attempts to plant seedlings in other locations have failed. (Guided tours daily 10am-6pm. Some donation expected and a few English guides available. Open Mon.-Fri. 9am-2pm and 4-6pm, Sat.-Sun. 11am-6pm.)

Northeast of the Alameda, along Calzada de los Arcos at the end of Independencia, rises the **Acueducto,** now an emblem of the city of Querétaro. The aqueduct, with its 74 arches of quarry stone, was constructed between 1726 and 1738 as a gift from the Marqués del Villas del Águila to a perpetually dry community.

Up 5 de Mayo to the east of the Jardín is the **Plaza de la Independencia,** a monument to Don Juán Antonio Urrutia y Aranda, that quenching *marqués.* Four stone dogs around his statue drool respectfully into a fountain. The plaza is bordered by beautiful colonial buildings, the most notable being the **Casa de la Corregidora,** home of Doña Josefa Ortíz de Domínguez, heroine of the 1810 Independence movement. The *casa* is now the seat of the state's government, so only the courtyard may be viewed. (Open Mon.-Fri. 8am-9pm, Sat. 9am-2pm.)

The colorful **Templo de la Congregación,** one block north of the Casa de la Corregidora at Pasteur and 16 de Septiembre, has two white towers and a central dome. The frescoes and stained glass are splendid and the pipe organ is one of the most elaborate in Mexico. (Open Mon.-Sun. 7:30am-9pm.)

Teatro de la República (tel. 102-58), at Ángela Peralta and Juárez. Many an historic event has transpired here: in 1867, the final decision on Emperor Maximilian's fate; in 1917, the drafting of the constitution; and in 1929, the formation of the Partido Nacional de la Revolución (PNR), the precursor of today's ruling Partido Revolucionario Institucional (PRI). (Open Mon.-Fri. 9am-8pm, Sat. 9am-1pm.)

The **Museo Regional** is located in the **Ex-Convento de San Francisco,** at Corregidora and Madero (tel. 12-20-36), to the east of the Jardín Obregón. Rebuilt in the 17th century's idea of the Renaissance style, the former convent possesses a cloister with two stories of colonnades. The museum displays many of the artifacts associated with the events that have taken place in Querétaro, and it even played a gloomy part in that history as the sentencing site of the leaders of the 1810 movement for independence. Exhibits include various artifacts culled from the dustbin of history, such as the table upon which the unjust 1848 peace treaty with the U.S. was signed. Temporary exhibits of contemporary art greet you at the entrance, and the entire upstairs area is devoted to 17th- and 18th-century religious paintings. (Open Wed.-Sat. 10am-6pm, Sun.-Tues. 10am-3:30pm. 10 pesos. Free for students with ID.)

Overshadowing the Museo Regional is the newer **Museo de Arte de Querétaro,** Allende 14 (tel. 12-23-57), across the Jardín Obregón at Pino Suárez. The original edifice, an 18th-century Augustinian monastery, was reconstructed in 1889 during the Porfiriato. Richly decorated arches and sculpted columns punctuate the patio. An exhibit on *querétana* architecture supplements an entire floor of Baroque paintings. Galleries of European painting, 19th- and 20th-century Mexican art and work of the 20th-century *queretareano* Abelarto Ávila complete the collection. (Open Tues.-Sun. 11am-7pm. Admission 5 pesos, students free.)

The **Cerro de las Campanas,** where Maximilian surrendered his sword to General Escobedo in 1867, is a half-hour walk from *el centro.* To reach the monument, walk a few blocks north of the Jardín Obregón on Corregidora and turn left onto General Escobedo. Proceed on Escobedo until the street ends at Tecnológico, then take a right, and you will come to the monument. To the left of the Cerro de las Campanas and up a low hill, Maximilian's family built a small chapel over the ground where the emperor and two of his generals were shot. Three small white memorials inside designate the places where each took his last breath. The man at the entrance to the chapel will gladly provide further historical detail. Up the stairs to the left of the chapel stands a large stone sculpture of Benito Juárez, the man responsible for Maximilian's execution. (Open Tues.-Sun. 6am-6pm. Free.)

ENTERTAINMENT

Local entertainment, like most everything else in Querétaro, revolves around the Jardín Obregón. Open-air brass band concerts are given in the gazebo Sunday evenings from 6 to 8pm, and myriads of jugglers, *mariachis,* and magicians perform there less regularly. *Mariachi* goes strong in the Jardín de los Platitos, where Juárez meets Av. Universidad north of the *zócalo*. Things start to heat up at about 11pm on Fridays and Saturdays when people head for the Jardín, request a song or two, and sing and dance along.

Call the **Academía de Bellas Artes,** Juárez Sur at Independencia (tel. 6-36-01), to find out what the students of the Universidad Autónoma de Querétaro have in store for the public (ballets, piano recitals, theatrical events and, less frequently, folk dance presentations). The annual **Feria de Querétaro** takes place during the second week of December.

The Querétaro student body spends its money at a number of discos. The classiest spot in town is **Discoteca Misiones,** on the highway to Mexico City in 5-star Hotel Ex-Hacienda Jurica. More convenient to the center of town are **JR's,** at Zaragoza and Tecnológico, and **Tiffani's,** at Zaragoza Pte. 67. The local twentysomething crowd does its thing at **JBJ,** Blvd. Zona Dorada 109 (tel. 14-32-32).. Club-goers tend to stay home during the week, so you may find establishments shut then.

MICHOACÁN DE OCAMPO

The Aztecs dubbed the lands surrounding Lake Pátzcuaro Michoacán, or "country of fishermen," because nearly all of the region's indigenous Purépeche subsisted by the rod and net. The Purépeche empire, which at one point controlled most of western Mexico, was one of the few civilizations to successfully resist Aztec expansionism. In fact, the Purépeche diverge from other Mesoamericans in more than just their fighting prowess: their language, culture, and even their terraced agricultural plots have led archaeologists to believe that they originally emigrated from what is now Peru—and are thus culturally closer to the Incas than to any of their neighbors in Mexico.

Purépeche hegemony lasted from around 800 AD, when they first settled Michoacán, until the Spanish expedition arrived in 1522. The conquistadors enslaved the Purépeches and forced their conversion to Christianity, but some cultural traditions persisted. Purépeche music, dances (such as *la danza de los viejitos)* and art were insuppressible. Their language, which you may hear spoken in Janitzio and the smaller villages around Lake Pátzcuaro, also survives intact. Locals refer to themselves as *Tarascos,* and thousands of stories exist to explain how they came to be known by this name. The most plausible claims that the last Purépeche lord, cowardly Tangaxhuán II, turned over the whole empire to ruthless and gold-hungry conquistador Nuño de Guzmán in 1530. The Purépeche lord also gave his four daughters to Nuño and the other Spanish officers. Some witty Purépeches started calling the Spaniards *tarascues* (sons-in-law), and conquistadors in turn used the term when addressing the Purépeches.

Michoacán de Ocampo

Michoacán's fierce tradition of independence has spawned three separate revolts or conspiracies, José Mariá Morelos's being the most significant. Though the state played a small role in the 1910 Revolution, its inhabitants are nonetheless proud of their history of rebeling against injustice. The state's official name, Michoacán de Ocampo, honors Melchor Ocampo, a leader in the wars for independence.

Since the colonial period, Michoacán's mild weather, fertile soil, and abundant water has made the state one of Mexico's leading agricultural centers. The surrounding forest-covered mountain ranges also attract hunters and wildlife enthusiasts. Large parts of the state still maintain their pristine natural character, untouched by modern civilization. But Michoacán is by no means simply mile after mile of *maíz* and cattle; the state also offers bustling, densely populated towns.

■■■ MORELIA

Morelia remains largely unmarred by the 20th century: rose-colored stone arcades surround the *zócalo*, government buildings with high ceilings and open courts line **Avenida Madero,** and outside the center, whitewashed houses wear parapeted roofs and windows as big as doors. Despite its charm, Morelia has escaped becoming a tourist trap. Here one can see a busy and habitable city at work. Rural life and urban sophistication coexist here with women from the surrounding countryside selling fruit to the students who crowd the theatres and discos at night.

ORIENTATION

Situated 287km west of Mexico City via Rte. 15, Morelia is the largest city on the southerly route from the capital to Guadalajara, another 312km to the northwest. The streets in Morelia form a large grid, and walking in the city is pleasant and relatively uncomplicated. Most sights are well within walking distance of the **zócalo** and the adjacent **cathedral** which are on **Avenida Madero,** Morelia's central boulevard. North-south street names change at Madero, and east-west street names change every other block; Madero never forsakes its name. Where there are two street names on a corner, the newest looking placard is usually correct.

The "Ruta Verde" *combi* (8.50 pesos) connects the **train station** to **Plaza Carrillo,** four blocks south and two blocks west of the *zócalo.* Coming from the train station, cross the street and wait at the *parada* (stop). To get downtown from the **bus station,** go left (east) as you leave the building, take your first right onto Valentín Gómez Farías, walk two blocks, and then make a left on Av. Madero—the *zócalo* is three blocks ahead. For longer trips, public transit in Morelia is adequate (see Morelia Practical Information: Public Transportation below). If you're in need of a cab, head for the bus station, where taxis are prolific 'round the clock.

PRACTICAL INFORMATION

Tourist Offices: State Tourist Office, Nigromante 79 (tel. 13-26-54), on Nigromante at Madero Pte. in the Palacio Clavijero, 2 blocks west of the *zócalo.* From the bus station, walk two blocks south on Valentín Gómez Farías to Av. Madera Pte. and turn left—it is on the far corner of that block. Very clear, though somewhat distorted, map of the center of town and more sketchy ones of the areas outside a 5-block radius are distributed by a helpful and friendly young staff. Walking tours arranged here. Open Mon.-Fri. 9am-2:30pm and 4-8pm, Sat.-Sun. 10am-8pm.

Currency Exchange: Banks are scattered throughout the center of the city and there is a particularly high concentration on Av. Madero east of the cathedral. Most are open for exchange Mon.-Fri. 9am-1pm, but will only change dollars until noon; the sole exception is **Bancomer,** which changes until closing time. Two **casas de cambio** near the *zócalo* are Ocampo 178 (tel. 2-84-48) at Zaragoza, which doesn't have great rates but is open Mon.-Fri. 9am-2pm and 4-6:30pm, Sat. 9am-2pm; and Valladolid 38, which has an English-speaking staff and is open Mon.-Fri. 9am-6pm, Sat. 9am-1pm.

American Express: On the east side of town several miles from the center. Servicentro Las Américas L-27, Artilleros Del 471520, postal code 5820 (tel. 14-19-50). Open Mon.-Fri. 9am-2pm and 4-7pm, Sat. 10am-2pm.

Post Office: Av. Madero Ote. 369 (tel. 12-05-17), 5 blocks east of the cathedral. Open for Lista de Correos and stamps Mon.-Fri. 8am-7pm, Sat.-Sun. 9am-1pm. **Postal Code:** 58000.

Telephones: 24 hr. long-distance service in the bus station. **Casas de larga distancia** dot the city (usually around 8 pesos per minute to the U.S). Fax machine on Madero opposite the *zócalo,* but no collect calls. For international collect calls, try the phones at the post office (free). **Telephone Code:** 451.

Telegrams: Av. Madero Ote. 371 (tel. 12-06-81), next to the post office. Open Mon.-Fri. 9am-8pm, Sat. 9am-1pm.

Airport: Aeropuerto Francisco J. Múgica (tel. 3-67-80), on Carretera Morelia-Cinapécuaro at km27. Has Aeroméxico and Mexicana information. Destinations include Mexico City (around 297 pesos) and Guadalajara (around 207 pesos).

Train Station: (tel. 16-16-97), on Av. del Periodismo. To Mexico City (1 per day at 10:55pm, 8hrs., sleeper 40 pesos), and Uruapan (1 per day at 5:25am, 3hrs., 10 pesos).

Bus Station: Ruíz, at V. Gómez Farías (tel. 2-56-64). **Herradura de Plata** to Mexico City (more than 1 per hr., 4½hrs., 33 pesos). **Flecha Amarilla** goes most frequently to Guadalajara (17 per day, 5hrs., 16 pesos); Guanajuato (10 per day, 4hrs., 9.10 pesos); and San Luis Potosí (via Querétaro, 4 per day, 7hrs., 28 pesos). **Ruta Praíso/Galeana** goes to Cárdenas (15 per day, 8hrs., 20.50 pesos); frequent departures to Pátzcuaro and Uruapan. **Tres Estrellas de Oro,** longer-distance to Mazatlán (1 per day, 15hrs., 51.50 pesos) and Monterrey (1 per day, 13hrs., 63 pesos).

Public Transportation: Buses (.50 pesos) and *combis* (.70 pesos) serve the city well (6am-10pm), but during rush hour they inevitably overflow with passengers and move slowly through horrendous traffic. *Rutas* 2 and 4 ply Av. Madero regularly in both directions, and are useful for getting to and from the Parque Cuauhtémoc and the aqueduct.

Laundromat: There are numerous *lavenderías* throughout the city. One is: **Lavandería Automática Ivon** (tel. 14-31-58), on the Circuito de Campestro. 7 pesos per kg. Open Mon.-Fri. 9am-8:30pm, Sat. 9am-7:30pm.

Red Cross: Ventura 27 (tel. 14-51-51), at the end of Banuet, next to the Parque Cuauhtémoc.

Pharmacy: Farmacia Moderna, Corregidora 566 (tel. 12-91-99). Open daily 9am-10pm.

Emergency: Call the police at tel. 12-22-22.

Police and Transit Police: (tel. 12-30-24), on 20 de Noviembre, 1 block northwest of the Fuente de las Tarascas at the end of the aqueduct.

ACCOMMODATIONS

Despite a multitude of budget hotels south of Av. Madero and just west of the cathedral, rooms can be hard to find during the university summer session (July-Aug.). At other times, something is sure to be available. None of the hotels are outstanding bargains, but all budgets and tastes are covered.

CREA Youth Hostel (HI), Chiapas 180 (tel.13-31-77), at Oaxaca. Take a taxi or walk west on Madero Pte. and turn left on Cuautla. Continue south on Cuautla for 7 blocks, then turn right on Oaxaca and continue 3 blocks to Chiapas. A good deal if you don't mind sacrificing a little privacy. Cleaner than most CREAs, with a ping-pong table and swimming pool to boot. Beds 11 pesos, breakfast 6 pesos, lunch and dinner 7.50 pesos.

Hotel Colonial, 20 de Noviembre (tel.12-18-97). Cozy courtyard graced by stone arches and pillars. Glows a deep yellow. High ceilings, large windows, and a friendly staff. All rooms with bath and TV. Singles 35 pesos. Doubles 50 pesos.

Hotel El Carmen, Ruíz 63 (tel. 12-17-25), 3 blocks north of Av. Madero between Juárez and Morelos. Melon-colored tiled lobby with stone pillars. Small but clean rooms, some without windows, but those with look out onto a beautiful, quiet plaza. All rooms with bath. 30 pesos single, 40 pesos double, an extra 10 pesos for a room with TV.

Posada Don Vasco, Vasco de Quiroga 232 (tel. 12-14-84), 3 blocks east and 2 blocks south of the cathedral, adjacent to La Hostería del Laurel restaurant. Open courtyard with green plants, brown walls. Dark rooms with peeling paint, but high ceilings and clean bathrooms. Singles 45 pesos. Doubles 57 pesos. *Cuartos economicos* (smaller, sparser, and darker): singles 25 pesos, doubles 30 pesos.

Hotel Mintzicuri, Vasco de Quiroga 227 (tel. 12-06-64), across from the Posada Don Vasco (above). Origin of the intriguing name is unknown, but the mural spanning the walls of the lobby may provide a clue. Small, uniform, clean rooms overlooking a courtyard with cars parked below. Sparkling clean bathrooms. Singles 52 pesos. Doubles 66 pesos.

Posada Lourdes, 340 Av. Morelos Nte. (tel. 12-56-03), across from the Casa de Cultura. True to its name's religious motif. If all you want is a clean bed for a few dollars, then disregard the narrow foreboding stairs. Singles 25 pesos. Doubles 30 pesos.

FOOD

Good inexpensive food can be found throughout the city. Almost every street has at least one family-run restaurant that opens onto the street with a few tables, makeshift chairs and *comida corrida* (usually around 7 pesos). The restaurants on the *zócalo* tend to be more expensive, but are reasonable and pleasant for breakfast.

Numerous taco and tortilla stands can be found around **Plaza Agustín** and in front of the bus station.

Cafe Lefiance, Pino Suarez 567. 1 block north of Madero. A real restaurant: uniform carved wood chairs, tablecloths, romantic lighting and all, with prices that match the smaller, more informal restaurants. *Comida corrida* 8 pesos.

La Hostería del Laurel, Quiroga 232, adjacent to Posada Don Vasco. You may have to share a table. Lively crowd, including families, chows down 'neath the arched ceiling with exposed beams. *Comida corriente* 6.50 pesos.

Restaurant-Bar La Huacana, Aldama 116 (tel. 12-53-12), at Obeso. The gargantuan oil painting behind the stage makes a nice backdrop for the large cafeteria-like dining area. Stone walls provide great acoustics for the *mariachis* who play Mon.-Sat. 3-5pm and 9-10pm. *Comida corrida* 15 pesos. Enchiladas 12-17 pesos. Open Mon.-Sat. 9am-11pm, Sun. 9am-5pm.

Pizza Real, Muñiz 158-B (tel. 13-34-89). Big, tasty pies smothered in sauce served by friendly, talkative folk. Individual pizza 14 pesos, double 18 pesos and group-sized 27 pesos. Open daily noon-11pm.

Super Pollos, Av. Madero Ote. at Silva (tel. 12-11-14), 2 blocks east of the post office. Cheap oil paintings and an even cheaper wine-bottle clock are the only things to look at here. Great *pollo placero con enchilada* 12 pesos. Breakfast from 5 pesos. Open daily 8am-9pm.

SIGHTS

On its 100th anniversary in 1986, the **Museo Michoacano,** Allende 305 (tel. 12-04-07), one block west of the *zócalo* at Abasolo, underwent a complete renovation. Museum exhibits are now divided into five categories: ecology, archaeology, the colonial period, the struggle for freedom and independent Mexico. Among the most important exhibits is a huge, anonymous painting completed in 1738, *La Procesión del Traslado de las Monjas.* Notes by Diego Rivera call the canvas a ground-breaking work of profound realism in an era when religious themes still dominated art. It depicts colonial society with encyclopedic attention to each social group and its relative importance. Oils on religious themes by Miguel Cabrera and his students are also worth a look, as are those by a trio of indigenous 19th-century artists—Manuel Ocaraza, Felix Parra and Jesús Torres. On the stairway, a powerful mural by Alfredo Zalce portrays those who have shaped Mexico's history and criticizes Mexicans' blind admiration of U.S. mass culture. (Open Tues.-Sat. 9am-7pm, Sun. 9am-2pm. Admission 17 pesos. Free for those under 13 and over 60, for students with ID, and for everyone on Sundays.)

Construction of the **cathedral** overlooking the *zócalo* continued for almost a century (1660-1745) and the drama of its construction can be traced through the different styles of the final product. The massive structure combines the neoclassical idiom with earlier baroque and *Herreriano* (named for the architect of El Escorial, outside Madrid) styles. In the 19th century, a bishop removed the elaborate baroque filigree from the altarpieces and frescoes, and renovated the church's interior in the symmetric and sober Doric neoclassical style. *Indígenas* sculpted the *Señor de la Sacristía,* the oldest treasure of the church, out of dry corn cobs and orchid nectar. In the 16th century, Felipe II of Spain donated a gold crown to top off the masterpiece. (Open 9am-8:30pm.)

Morelos's former residence now contains the **Museo de Morelos,** Morelos 232 (tel. 13-26-51), one block east and two blocks south of the cathedral. The museum displays *El Caudillo's* sable, religious vestments, military ornaments and uniform, as well as other mementos of the surge for independence. Plaques (in Spanish) describe the phases of the war and maps illustrate the campaigns and troop movements. (Open daily 9am-7pm. Admission 1 peso. Free on Sun.) More of a civic building than a museum, the **Casa Natal de Morelos** (Birthplace of Morelos) stands at Corregidora 113, one block south of the cathedral. Glass cases preserve his war cartography, communiqués, letters and additional paraphernalia. Both areas are embla-

PÁTZCUARO

zoned with murals by Alfredo Zalce. Outside there is a beautiful and, yes, shady, courtyard watched over by the martyr's stein bust. Great for an afternoon read. (Open Mon.-Fri. 9am-2pm and 4-8pm, Sat. 9am-2pm. Free.)

The **Casa de Cultura**, Morelos Nte. 485, 3½ blocks north of Madero (13-13-20), is a gathering place for artists and musicians, students and the artistic American traveler. This elegant peach colored stone building houses a bookstore, numerous art galleries, a theater, and a lovely shady cafe. Dance, voice, and silkscreen classes are also offered here as well as a complete listing of the cultural events around the city.

The **Museo de Artesanías**, at Humbolt and Juan de San Miguel, is a huge craft museum and retail store. Actual examples of the crafts are organized by the town of their origin; on display are colorful macramé *huipiles*, straw airplanes, and guitars. Other crafts include geometrically decorated pottery from workshops in Patambán, painstakingly carved white wood furniture, and clay biblical vignettes. The *museo* is impressive, but better prices await you in Pátzcuaro. (Open daily 9am-8pm. Free.) Outside, on the **Plaza Valladolid,** many similar crafts are sold in the market. This plaza marks the site of the 1541 founding of the city of Valladolid. But don't be fooled; despite its colonial appearances, the plaza was built in 1968.

The city's aqueduct, built in 1788, sides a pleasant pedestrian avenue perfect for evening strolls in the western part of the city. Nearby, the well-lit **Plaza de Morelos** is marked by an equestrian monument to José Maria Morelos commissioned by the Diaz dictatorship and ironically inaugurated by the revolutionary forces that toppled him. The **Fuente de las Tarascas** completes the city's romantic center, a copy of the original whose fate remains the subject of imaginative local lore. At night, the area is expertly illuminated to highlight its relaxing splendor.

ENTERTAINMENT

Lisitngs of events can be found at the Casa de Cultura (see Sights above). The **Casa Natal de Morelos** (see Sights above) projects excellent international art and history movies during the week at different times in the early evening (call tel. 13-26-51 for more information). The Cine-Club, sponsor of the films, alternates movies weekly and organizes Eastern European and contemporary Mexican film festivals. Admission is free so seats are rare. **Cinema Victoria,** at Madero Pte. 944-C (tel. 12-43-10), two blocks west of the Hotel San Jorge, features Hollywood's latest interspersed with slice-and-dice and Bruce Lee flicks (admission 4 pesos). For older North American movies, check out **Sala Eréndira** (tel. 12-12-87) on Santiago Tapia behind the Palacio Clavijero.

See plays at 8pm on Wednesday night in the **ISSTE Morelos theater** (tel. 12-92-36), on Av. Madero in the western part of the city. The theater's university and amateur groups perform picaresque plays, pantomime, and—hold on to your black garters!—a Spanish version of *The Rocky Horror Picture Show.*

For a wilder night out, try the **Disco Molino Rojo,** in front of the Plaza Las Américas shopping center in the far eastern reaches of town. At the **Baron Rouge,** in the Plaza Rebullones's basement, next to Parque Cuauhtémoc, the young rowdies are more interested in drinking than dancing. (Both open Thurs.-Sun. 8pm-1am, Fri.-Sat. 8pm-2am.)The college kids flock to **Club XO,** at Calzada Capistre and Acueducto. (Open Thurs.-Sun. 9pm-2am.) Also popular but a smidgen more sedate is **Bambalina's,** Escutín 225 at Lázaro Cárdenas. (Open Thurs.-Sun. 9pm-2am.) Cover about 10 pesos; domestic drink prices about 5 pesos.

Drag the kids off to the zoo in the **Parque Benito Juárez.** To get there, take the "Guenda" *combi* from the corner of Allende and Galeano. (Open daily 11am-6pm. Admission 2 pesos.)

■■■ PÁTZCUARO

Ordained priest and bishop in 1540 at the age of 75, Vasco de Quiroga established his episcopate in the former Purépeche capital, Pátzcuaro. He had been sent to supersede Núñex de Guzmán, the avowed enemy of Cortés and a man with "a reputation for cruelty and extortion, unrivalled even in the annals of the New World." Four years later, Pátzcuaro was selected as the capital of the Michoacán region. Inspired by the humanitarian ideals of Thomas More, Bishop Quiroga defended the Purépeche people from landowners and mining magnates. He taught the residents of each Purépeche village around the Lago de Pátzcuaro a different craft, thereby stimulating community trade and economic health.

Pátzcuaro, with its well-planned colonial architecture, locally crafted woolen goods, and proximity to the island of Janitzo, attracts numerous tourists; its two main squares, **Plaza Bocanegra** and **Plaza Quiroga,** are lined with hotels. Each square has its own atmosphere, reflected in its hotels. The first, near the market, is so busy as to make walking difficult at any time of day, while the second, with its central fountain and well-shaded and rosebush-lined paths, is elegant and quiet. Despite the tourists and surprisingly large population of 40,000, Pátzcuaro retains the atmosphere and authenticity of a peaceful, friendly small town.

ORIENTATION

Route 14 leads into the city of Pátzcuaro from Morelia (70km) and Mexico City, first crossing Quiroga and Tzintzuntzán to the north and nearby Tzurumútaro to the east, and then continuing on to Uruapan, 67km to the southwest.

The quickest way to reach the center from the **bus station** is by *combi* (.75 pesos) or city bus (.50 pesos). Make sure the vehicle you're using is in fact going to the center—many drivers neglect to change their signs when they change routes.

The city of Pátzcuaro encompasses two distinct areas. **Downtown** perches on a hill about 5km south of the mainly residential lakefront. To reach the **lake** from downtown, jump on a public bus labeled "Lago," "San Pedro," or "Sta. Ana," which passes by the east side of Pl. Gertrudis Bocanegra, Portal Regules and Portal Juárez about every five minutes (.50 pesos). These buses rattle down the hill along Av. de las Américas and will brake long enough to drop you off at the restaurant-lined docks, from which *lanchas* (boats) depart for the island of Janitzio and other points around the lake.

PRACTICAL INFORMATION

Tourist Office: Ibarra 1 at Mendoza (tel. 2-12-14), ironically placed in a sanatorium. Office is the 3rd door on the right in the courtyard. Helpful staff. Good map. Mon.-Sat. 9am-2pm and 4-7pm, Sun. 9am-2pm.

Currency Exchange: Banco Serfín, Portal Morelos 54 (tel. 2-15-16), on the north side of Pl. Quiroga. Open Mon.-Fri. 9am-1:30pm.

Post Office: Obregón 13 (tel. 2-01-28), ½ block north of Pl. Bocanegra. Open Mon.-Fri. 8am-7pm, Sat. 9am-1pm. **Postal code:** 61600.

Telephones: Hotel San Agustín, Portal Juárez 29, on Pl. Bocanegra. International collect calls 5 pesos. Open Mon.-Fri. 8am-10pm, Sat. 2-4pm. **Telephone code:** 454.

Telegrams: Títere 15 (tel. 2-00-10), 1 block east and 1 block south of the library. Open Mon.-Fri. 9am-6pm, Sat. 9am-noon.

Train Station: (Tel. 2-08-03), at the bottom of Av. de las Américas near the lakefront. 1st class to Mexico daily at 9:30pm, 2nd class 9am. 1st and 2nd class to Uruapan daily at 7am.

Bus Station: Off of Circunvalación, south of town. **Herradura de Plata** to Mexico City (6hrs., 40 pesos). **Flecha Amarilla** to Guadalajara (11:30pm, 5hrs., 27 pesos). **Galeana,** frequent service to Morelia (every 15min., 5.5 pesos), Uruapan (every 15min., 5.5 pesos), Quiroga (every 10min., 3.5 pesos), and Santa Clara del Cobre (every ½hr., 2 pesos).

Laundromat: Lavandería Automática, Terán 14 (tel. 2-18-22), 2 blocks west of the Pl. Quiroga. 4 pesos per kg, wash and dry. Takes 3-5 hrs. Open Mon.-Sat. 9am-2pm and 4-8pm.

Pharmacy: Principal, Portal Juárez 33 (tel. 2-06-97, after hours 2-26-50). Open daily 9am-9pm.

Hospital: Romero 10 (tel. 2-02-85). **Clínica del Centro,** Portal Hidalgo, on Pl. Quiroga (tel. 2-19-28). 24-hr. service.

Emergency: Cuerpo de Rescate, Pl. Quiroga, booth 79 (tel. 2-18-89). 24-hr. service.

Police: Hidalgo 1 (tel. 2-18-89), on the western edge of the Pl. Quiroga.

ACCOMMODATIONS

Pátzcuaro has hotels to suit all budgets, including those on the tighter budget. Hotels away from the busy Plaza Bocanegra are usually quieter.

Posada de la Salud, Serrato 9 (tel. 2-00-58), 3 blocks east of either plaza, ½ block past the basilica on its right. Beautiful courtyard, gorgeous carved furniture from Cuanajo, cloud-soft mattresses, and clean bathrooms. Hot water 24 hrs. Singles 35 pesos. Doubles 55 pesos.

Hotel Valmen, Lloreda 34 (tel. 2-11-61), 1 block east of the Pl. Bocanegra. Aztec tile and squawking birds fill the courtyards. Well-lit rooms, some with balconies, though the plumbing is a bit erratic. Singles 25 pesos. Doubles 40 pesos.

Hotel San Agustín, Portal Juárez 27 (tel. 2-04-42), on the western side of Pl. Bocanegra. Don't be turned away by the dark narrow hallway. The rooms are large, bathrooms clean, and staff friendly. Rooms on the right side of the hall are significantly nicer, their door-size windows overlooking the roof of Pátzcuaro.

Posada de la Rosa, Portal Juárez 30 (tel. 2-08-11), on the west side of Pl. Bocanegra. Red tiles and lots of sunlight. Rooms with a view onto the plaza are the nicest. Communal bathroom is functional. 20 pesos, 30 pesos with bath for singles and doubles.

FOOD

Fish from the nearby lake can be found in restaurants throughout the city. *Pescado blanco* is far and away the most plentiful and popular dish. *Charales* (smelts), served in the restaurants along Pátzcuaro's lakefront and on Janitzio, are small sardine-like fish fried in oil and eaten whole by the fistful. Their popularity is proving an environmental nightmare (they are consistently overfished), so if you can resist their attractive appearance, do so. *Caldos de pescado* (fish broth) bubble in large clay vats outside open-air restaurants, particularly on Janitzio. These spicy soups, loaded with fish and sometimes shrimp, crab, and squid, are a meal in themselves.

Most of the small restaurants by the docks close daily at 7pm. *Pescado blanco* usually goes for 25 pesos and fish soup for 10 pesos. More traditional Mexican food, as well as seafood, can be found in town. More formal restaurants with tablecloths, locally crafted furniture, and sometimes tables outside under the arcades, ring Plaza Quiroga. Less formal, and also less expensive, restaurants tend to be closer to Plaza Bocanegra and the market area where good street food is sold as well.

Restaurant El Patio, Pl. Quiroga 19 (tel. 2-04-84), on the south side of the plaza. The quality food and pleasant atmosphere explain the somewhat lofty prices. The sophisticated decor blends still-lifes, empty wine bottles and pillars of rough stone. Read your menu by the light of locally crafted hanging lamps. Complete breakfasts 10-20 pesos. *Menú del día* 18 pesos. Fish 25 pesos. Open daily 8am-10pm.

Fonda del Santuario, Codallos 44 (tel. 2-01-29), 1 block from El Santuario in the market on the left. Cheery courtyard with hanging plants and great lunchtime *menú del día* for a mere 10 pesos. Open Sun.-Fri. 9am-4pm.

Restaurant y Cafetería La Casona, Quiroga 30 (tel. 2-11-79), on the north side of Pl. Quiroga. White walls, wooden beams, and black metal chandeliers create a classy minimalist look. Complete breakfasts 7-8 pesos, fish 28 pesos. Open daily 8am-9pm.

SIGHTS

Pátzcuaro's unique handcrafts—hairy Tócuaro masks, elegant Zirahuén dinnerware, and thick wool textiles—are sold in the Pl. Bocanegra's **market** and in small shops along the passage next to Biblioteca Gertrudis Bocanegra. Bargaining is easier when you buy more than one item, but don't expect a deal on the arrestingly handsome wool articles, which include thick sweaters, brilliantly colored *saltillos* and *ruanas* (stylized ponchos), rainbow-colored *sarapes*, and dark shawls. Retailers stubbornly stick to their prices, however beseechingly you may plead. Still, these items are far from expensive. Sweaters usually sell for the equivalent of US$12-20. Naturally dyed articles generally cost more than brightly colored chemically dyed ones. The haphazard piles of woolens in the market may conceal more treasures than the boutique displays, so nosing around before buying may be productive.

When Vasco de Quiroga came to Pátzcuaro, he initiated not only social change, but bold architectural projects as well. Quiroga conceived the **Basílica de Nuestra Señora de la Salud,** at Lerín and Serrato, as a colossal structure with five naves arranged like the fingers of an extended hand. Each finger was to represent one of Michoacán's cultures and races, with the hand's palm as the central altar representing the Catholic religion. Although construction began in 1554, civil opposition to the ostentation of the building and repeated earthquakes prevented all but the first nave from being opened until 1805. Later, two more earthquakes and a fire forced the church to shut down and undergo reconstruction several times. (Open daily 7am-8pm.)

Today the basilica features a grandiose Romanesque altar. Intricate parallel stripes of frescoed arabesques cross the high, concave ceiling of the church, forming impressive vaults. An enormous glass booth with gilded Corinthian columns and a dome protects the Virgen de la Salud sculpture; when Vasco de Quiroga asked a few Tarascans to design an image of the Virgin in 1546, they complied by shaping her out of *tatzingue* paste made from corn cobs and orchid honey. On the eighth day of May and December, pilgrims from all over Mexico crawl from the plaza to the basilica on their knees to beg the Madonna to perform miracles.

Down the street from the basilica, on Lerín near Navarette, is the **Casa de Artesanías.** Originally a convent for Dominican nuns, also called the **Casa de los Once Patios,** this complex now contains non-clerical craft shops, a small gallery of modern Mexican art and a mural depicting Vasco de Quiroga's accomplishments. The Casa de Artesanías sells superb musical instruments (guitars, flutes and *güiros*) and cotton textiles. For woolens, the market is still your best bet. (Open daily 9am-2pm and 4-7pm.)

The **Museo Regional de Artes Populares,** on the corner of Lerín and Alcanterillas, one block south of the basilica, was once the Colegio de San Nicolás Obispo, a college founded by Vasco in 1540. This fantastic museum displays pottery, copperware and textiles produced in the region. Particularly appealing are the *maque* and *laca* ceramics collections. (Open Mon.-Sat. 9am-7pm, Sun. 9am-3pm. Admission 12 pesos, free Sun.)

Statues of Pátzcuaro's two most honored citizens stand vigil over the town's two principal plazas. The ceremonious, banner-bearing Vasco de Quiroga inhabits the plaza that bears his name. Vast and well-forested, the Pl. Quiroga feels more like a city park than a *zócalo*. The massive, Amazonian, bare-breasted Gertrudis Bocanegra looks out from the center of **Plaza Gertrudis Bocanegra.** A martyr for Mexican independence, Bocanegra was executed by a Spanish squadron in the Pl. Quiroga in October 1817. People say bullet holes still mark the ash tree to which she was tied. Calle Zaragoza spans the two blocks that separate the plazas.

Biblioteca Gertrudis Bocanegra, on the plaza of the same name, occupies the former site of a temple to St. Augustine. The library's multicolored mural by Juan O'Gorman illustrates the history of the Purépeche civilization from pre-Conquest times to the Revolution of 1910. (Open Mon.-Fri. 9am-7pm.) When the next-door **Teatro Caltzontzín,** once part of the Augustinian convent, became a theater in

1936, an as-yet-unfulfilled prophecy was uttered: one Holy Thursday, the theater will crumble as punishment for the sin of projecting movies in a sacred place. You can peek at it in the afternoons, Monday through Saturday. If you dare to test the prophecy, catch a flick (from Mexico and the U.S., 5 pesos); check the posted schedule.

Three km east of the city, at the end of Av. Benigno Serrato, is **El Humilladero** (Place of Humiliation), where the cowardly king Tangaxhuán II surrendered his crown, dominions and daughter to the sanguinary Cristóbal de Olid and his Spanish troops. Two peculiar features distinguish this chapel: on its altar stands a rare monolithic cross, undoubtedly older than the date inscribed on its base (1553); on the facade are images of gods which represent the sun and the moon—used to lure Purépeches to Catholicism.

ENTERTAINMENT

At night, the life shifts to the **Disco El Padian,** in the shopping center of the same name (cover 5-10 pesos; take a taxi for about 5 pesos from the square) and the bar **El Padierna,** on Av. de las Américas, between the two Glonettas, which has live music most nights for after-hours fun. But on the whole, such urban eccentricities are not tolerated here. The **Pátzcuaro Cine Club** shows films Tuesdays at 7:30pm in the Escuela Vasco de Quiroga (next to the Museo de Artes Populares). Inquire at the tourist office (see Practical Information) for details.

The town hosts several fiestas during the year. An animated post-Christmas tradition in Pátzcuaro is the pair of **pastorelas,** celebrated on January 6 to commemorate the Adoration of the Magi, and on January 17 to honor St. Anthony of Abad. On both occasions, the citizens dress their domestic animals in bizarre costumes, ribbons and floral crowns. Pátzcuaro's *Semana Santa* attracts people from all across Mexico. Particularly moving is the **Procesión del Silencio** on Good Friday, when a crowd marches around town mourning Jesus' death in silence. The biggest celebration is the **Feria Artesanal y Agrícola,** held at the beginning of December to honor the Virgen de la Salud. This festival includes craft contests, plant sales and fireworks shows. **Noche de Muertos** (Nov. 1-2) holds special importance for the Tarascan community; candle-clad fishing boats row out to Janitzio on the first night, heralding the start of a two-night vigil in the graveyard. The first night commemorates lost children; the second remembers adults.

■ Near Pátzcuaro

The tiny island of **Janitzio,** inhabited exclusively by Tarascan *indígenas* who speak the Purépeche dialect, subsists solely on its tourist trade, another example of the economic marginalization of the *indígenas* in modern Mexico. The very steep main street is lined with stores selling woolen goods, hard-carved wooden chess sets, masks, and kick-knacks. (Unfortunately, both the quality and the prices tend to be geared towards the tourist.) Between the shops are numerous restaurants that all sell the same thing: *pescado blanco* and *charales* (the restaurants towards the top of the island tend to be nicer, with views overlooking the lake). At the summit of the island towers the monumental **statue of Morelos,** the father of Mexican independence. Once inside this statue that is so big it can be seen clearly from Pátzcuaro, a mural tracing the principle events in Morelos's life and the independence struggle follows a winding staircase into the shoulder of the statue. From there, the stairs continue into the cuff of Morelos's sleeve, where openings in the statue permit a spectacular view of the lake. (Admission 1 peso.)

To get to the island, first hop on a **bus** labeled "Lago," "San Pedro," or "Sta. Ana" at the corner of Portal Regules and Portal Juárez at the Pl. Bocanegra. The bus (.60 pesos) rambles to the docks, where you'll stand in a long but fast-moving line to get a **ferry** ticket (round-trip 8 pesos). Ferries leave when they fill up (about every 30 min., 9am-5pm, ½hr.). Check the time of the last boat, since Janitzio does not accommodate the stranded. From the boats, the serene towns of Jarácuaro,

Nayízaro, Puácuaro and Ihuatzio are visible along the verdant lake shore. Before docking, the boats are inundated by Janitzio's fishing people, who paddle out in canoes and briefly demonstrate the use of their butterfly-shaped nets for picture-takers in hopes of earning a small contribution. To reach the other towns around the lake, take a second-class **Flecha Amarilla** bus. (See Practical Information.)

Santa Clara del Cobre, 16km south of Pátzcuaro, was a copper-mining town in its heyday. After the mines closed down, the village devoted itself exclusively to crafting copperware. Every single store sells copper plates, pans, bowls and bells. Prices here are only slightly better than elsewhere in Mexico, but the quality and variety are vastly superior. For a quick look at some of the more exotic pieces, step into the **Museo de Cobre,** close to the plaza. There is little to see in Santa Clara beyond *artesanías*; this side trip requires only a couple of hours. Galeana **buses** leave for Santa Clara every 30min. (2 pesos, 20min.) from the bus station in Pátzcuaro.

The lake at **Zirahuén** makes for another scenic daytrip as well as a good spot for camping. Not as large as Lago de Pátzcuaro, Zirahuén (Where Smoke Rose) is more open, unobstructed by marshes and islands and considerably cleaner (many people actually swim in it). If you want to **camp,** hike up one of the ridges that border the lake and set up in any one of the numerous spots that overlook the water; the landowner—if there is one—may ask you to pay a few pesos. Heavy afternoon rains during June and July can turn summer camping into a soggy experience.

The colonial town itself, with its woodwork shops, also merits a visit. To get there, take the **bus** from the second class station in Pátzcuaro (3 per day, 20min., 2 pesos). If you have wheels, take the road to Uruapan and look for signs to Zirahuén. From Santa Clara del Cobre you can hike about 11km along a dirt road that traverses the wooded slopes to Zirahuén, or catch a ride with people headed to Uruapan from Pátzcuaro. Hitching is not recommended, however.

Tzintzuntzán (Place of the Hummingbirds) was the last great city of the Tarascan empire. In the middle of the 15th century, the great Purépeche lord, Tariácori, on his deathbed, divided his empire among his three sons. When, some years later, Tzitzipandácuari reunited the empire, he chose Tzintzuntzán as the capital; the old capital, Pátzcuaro, became a dependency. It's former glory relegated to history, Tzintzuntzán is but a tiny town now famed for its delicate multi-colored ceramics displayed on tables along Calle Principal.

A peculiar pre-Conquest temple, the **Yácatas,** sits on a hill just outside the city. The base of each *yácata*—all that remains today—is a standard rectangular pyramid. The missing parts of the *yácatas*, however, are what made them unique; each was originally crowned with an unusual elliptical pyramid constructed of shingles and volcanic rock. The pyramids are situated along the long edge of an artificial terrace 425m long and 250m wide. Each building represents a bird. This vantage point commands a view of the **Lago de Pátzcuaro.** (Open daily 10am-5pm. Admission 10 pesos.) Also of interest is the 16th-century Franciscan **convent** closer to town. The olive shrubs that now smother the extensive, tree-filled atrium were originally planted by Vasco de Quiroga.

Tzintzuntzán perches on the northeastern edge of the Lago de Pátzcuaro, on the road to Quiroga and Morelia about 15km from Pátzcuaro. Bring a sweater; Tzintzuntzán can be chilly and damp.

Wooden toys are among the specialties of **Quiroga,** 8km north of Tzintzuntzán near the highway to Morelia. Quiroga's excellent daily **market** sells crafts from most of the region. Intricately carved and painted wooden masks are produced in **Tócuaro,** west of Pátzcuaro on the road around the lake to Erongícuaro. Masks here cost half of what they do in Morelia or Mexico City. To get to Tócuaro, walk down toward the Pátzcuaro pier, cross the railroad tracks, and follow signs to Erongícuaro to the left. You can take the **Flecha Amarilla** bus, too; watch for people waiting by the side of the street.

URUAPAN

■■■ URUAPAN

A checker on a checkerboard of ex-*encomienda* farmland, Uruapan offers a convenient base for exploring the nearby waterfall, national park and Parcutín Volcano. About 175km west of Morelia and 320km southeast of Guadalajara, Uruapan can be a stopover on the way to or from Playa Azul (260km to the south) and other Pacific coast resorts, or a side trip from Morelia or Pátzcuaro. Everything in town is within easy walking distance of the *zócalo*, a good orientation point. The statue in the center faces south, looking down **Cupatitzio, Carranza** runs into the southwest corner of the square from the west, and **Obregón** is its continuation on the eastern side of the plaza. The east and south sides of the square are lined with various **portales,** and **Ocampo** runs along its western edge. The **train station** (tel. 4-09-81) is located on Lázaro Cárdenas in the eastern part of town, accessible by the "Zapata," "Zapata Revolución," or "Foviste" buses. Trains to Mexico City (1st class 7:15pm, 12hrs., 18 pesos, sleeper 65 pesos; 2nd class 6:35am, 14 hrs., 15.30 pesos); office open daily 7:30am-7:30pm. **Buses** leave from Benito Juárez (Rte. 15 to Pátzcuaro), in the northeast corner of town. To reach the station from the zócalo, take bus "Central Camionera" or simply "Central" (8 pesos). **Galeana** serves Morelia (2hrs., 11 pesos) and Pátzcuaro (1hr., 5.50 pesos). **Flecha Amarilla** (tel. 3-18-70) has buses to: Querétaro (6hrs., 26 pesos), Mexico City (7hrs., 48 pesos), San Luis Potosí (10hrs., 44 pesos), Manzanillo (10hrs., 34 pesos) and Zamora (50min., 10 pesos). **La Linea** is a good bet for Guadalajara (5hrs., 34 pesos). To get to *el centro* from the bus station, jump a bus marked accordingly (.60 pesos). Cabs also do the trick. The 2.5km trek to the center is a bit much with luggage.

Practical Information The **tourist office,** 5 de Febrero 17 (towards the back of the shopping mall, ½ block south of the eastern end of the *zócalo*, tel. 4-06-33) is open Mon.-Fri. 9am-2pm and 4-7pm, Sat. 9am-2pm. To change money, try **Centro Cambiario,** at Portal Matamoros 19; open Mon.-Fri. 9am-2pm and 4-7pm. Sat. 9am-1pm. The **post office,** Reforma 13 (3 blocks south from *zócalo* on Copitizio and left one block, tel. 3-56-30), is open Mon.-Fri. 8am-7pm, Sat-Sun. 8am-1pm. **Long distance** services at the High Life Perfumery, 5 de Febrero, across the street from the tourist office, and open daily 9am-8pm, or the bus station (open 24 hrs.) **Telephone Code:** 452. A **laundromat** on Carranza 47 at García, 4 blocks west of the *zócalo* (tel. 3-26-69) washes 3kg for 14 pesos. (Open Mon.-Sat. 9am-2pm and 4-8pm.) **Farmacia Fénix,** Carranza 1 at Ocampo (tel. 4-16-40) is open daily 8am-9pm. For medical needs, try the **Red Cross** (tel. 4-03-00) or the **Hospital Civil** on San Miguel (tel. 3-46-60), 7 blocks west of the northern edge of the *zócalo*. The **police** can be found at Eucalyptos at Naranjo (tel. 4-06-20).

Accommodations Cultivating a taste for the "good ol' days" may help you relate better to Uruapan's hotel selection. The nicest joint in town, **Hotel Villa de Flores,** Carranza 15 (1½ blocks from the *zócalo*, tel. 4-28-00), features spotless, post-independence bathrooms, large tasteful cool rooms, a beautiful flower-filled courtyard that invites hummingbirds, and lounging in its comfortable, shady lounge areas. The hotel has its own restaurant and bar and TVs in all rooms. (Singles 55 pesos, doubles 65 pesos.) An evening of melodramatic Victorian prints, narrow stairways and an occasional view of the zócalo costs only 25 pesos for both singles and doubles at the **Hotel Moderna,** Portal S. Degollado 7 (on the eastern edge of the zócalo, tel. 4-02-12). The peeling blue and brown rooms of the **Hotel Capri,** Portal Santo Degollado 10, are tolerable because of the hotel's location (right on the zócalo) and low prices. (One bed, for 1 or 2 people, 25 pesos; 2 beds 35 pesos.)

Food Residing in an agricultural region of fruit and avocadoes, food is cheap and tasty in Uruapan. Fresh fruit abounds, and the marketplace (½ block north of the *zócalo* on Constitución) dedicated to *antojitos típicos* does a booming business.

Good food is sold by many vendors around the *zócalo*; you can even get pancakes in the morning for 1 peso. Between **Constitución** and **Patzcuaro y Quiroqa** (walk ½ block down Constitución to a small store stairway on the left and up the stairs) is an outdoor square where, for very little money (7 pesos for most dishes) you can get a great dinner, lunch, or snack. Try the **Café Tradicional de Uruapan,** Carranza 5-B, for coffee (3-5 pesos) and cake, or breakfast (7-17 pesos). Though the prices are steep, this cafe with large carved wood chairs offers a place to relax, talk, or read for a while, escaping the bustle of the city. (Open daily 8:30am-2pm and 4-10pm.) To mix with PRI *politicos,* head to the **Restaurant La Pérgola,** Portal Carrillo 4 (tel. 3-50-87). Opening onto the south side of the *zócalo*, this smoky, stately restaurant is a nice place for drinks underneath the wood arches and murals, but too pricey for dinner. (Open daily 8am-11:30pm.)

Sights A few lesser sights may fill the lingering moments in Uruapan. Crafts of Michoacán state are displayed at the **Museo Regional de Arte Popular** (tel. 4-21-38) on the *zócalo*. The building which now houses the museum was the first hospital in the Americas, and today it is home to a smattering of ceramic dining equipment and a small but interesting collection of masks. (Open Tues.-Sun. 9:30am-1:30pm and 3:30-6pm. Free.) If you haven't the time to catch the natural wonders surrounding Uruapan, the **Parque Nacional Barranca del Cupatitzio** at the western end of Independencia is a little bit of jungle on the edge of town. (Open daily 8am-6pm. Admission 1 peso.)

■ Near Uruapan

Further afield sits the town of **Angahuan**, precariously perched near the still active **Paricutín Volcano.** In 1943, the volcano erupted and gushed lava for eight straight years, consuming entire towns and leaving a 700m mountain in its wake. The surrounding land mass is pure, porous, hardened lava. In one area, the lava covered an entire village except for the church steeple, which now sticks out of a field of cold, black stone. You can rent horses and a guide to ascend the volcano (about 15-30 pesos, but haggle hard), or go down into the valley to take a closer look at the church. Both trips take about three to four hours unless you are feeling manic. There are **bungalows** on the outskirts of the village, near the track to the church, that rent big, basic six-bed rooms for 90 pesos (ask the tourist office to make reservations). **Buses** run to Paricutín and Angahuan from the bus station (every ½hr. 7am-8pm, 45min., 4 pesos).

The waterfalls at **Tzaráracua** (sah-RA-ra-kwa), 10km from Uruapan on the road to Playa Azul, cascade 20m into small pools. The first waterfall, called Tzaráracua, is about 1km from the small parking lot—you can walk or ride a horse there (round-trip 15 pesos). The path goes down a flight of cobbled stairs, and hoofing it yourself should take about five to ten minutes, but getting back uphill takes at least twice as long. Another 1.5km beyond the large pool is the **Tzarárecuita,** actually two smaller pools that are free of pollution, perfect for swimming and well worth the extra hike. For an extra 15 pesos you can get there with horses and a guide. Skinny-dipping is popular in the chill water, but watch out for peepers and keep an eye on your clothes. Buses marked "Tzaráracua" leave the south side of the *zócalo* every hour but without a precise schedule (2 pesos). Buses mainly run in the morning, so be sure to to find out what time the last bus back to Uruapan leaves, or you might be stranded at the waterfall.

If guitars are on your Mexican shopping list, go to **Paracho,** 30km north of Uruapan. Carefully crafted six-strings pack just about every store. Fantastic bargains are available; top-of-the-line guitars go for the equivalent of US$130; some are as cheap as US$15. Even if you're not buying, the trip should still prove interesting for the beauty of the scenery and the chance to watch the skillful artisans at work. In the first week of August the town holds an internationally renowned **guitar festival.** Musicians and craftspeople partake in a musical orgy that includes classical concerts in the *zócalo's* church, fireworks, dancing and guitar-making competitions. If you decide to stay over in the town, the **Hotel Oriental,** behind the market across the *zócalo*, has clean rooms with baths. (Singles 20 pesos. Doubles 25 pesos.) To get to Paracho, hop a bus bound for Zamora (3 pesos) from the Central Camionera.

■■■ PLAYA AZUL

A mere 30km from the border with Guerrero, Playa Azul maintains an easygoing and tolerant posture, attracting people from an array of geographic locations and tax brackets. A pretty (albeit slightly rocky) beach and sunset boost Playa Azul's appeal. Waves break far from shore, and at any given moment at least three lines of white water face the potential surfer or swimmer. The gap between the first and second is calmest and suitable for children; swimmers of average ability should feel comfortable between the second and third.

Practical Information To get to Playa Azul, you'll probably have to go through Lázaro Cárdenas, 24km away. Most bus lines, regardless of what their representatives tell you, stop only at the crossroads 1.5km outside Playa Azul. Buses and *combis* in Lázaro Cárdenas run from 5am to 9pm, leaving from the PEMEX station on the western end of Cárdenas and dropping you off at another PEMEX station on the western edge of Playa Azul. The trip costs 2.50 pesos and takes anywhere from 25 to 45 minutes, depending on how many stops are made along the way. Departures are very frequent at both ends of the ride.

Admirers of orderly city planning will be distressed by the breezy informality of Playa Azul. Although all streets theoretically have names, no one seems to know or care what they are. This can be a bit disconcerting if you arrive at night without a clue as to your current location. (Bring a flashlight—the lack of street lights makes it really dark.) By day, however, the town is easy to navigate. The PEMEX station, where buses stop, is on **Cárdenas,** which runs south to the sea on the western edge of town. If you walk two blocks seaward, you'll reach the stretch of tarmac called **Carranza** that serves as Playa Azul's main street, running parallel to and one block from the beach. Turn left and walk east a few blocks to reach the would-be center of town, marked by the Hotel Playa Azul and a cross street on which you'll find restaurants, taco stands and *fondas*. A dirt and/or mud road, parallel to the main street but closer to the sea, runs past most of the *enramadas* (thatched-roof restaurants) that line the beach. Two blocks inland from the main street is another paved east-west road called **Independencia,** where you'll find most of Playa Azul's pharmacies, *papelerías* and other stores.

The **post office** is more or less across the street from Hotel Pacífico, about a 20-min. walk from the PEMEX station. From the center of town, walk on Carranza with the ocean on your right and turn left when you reach the park; it's the building on your right at the first dirt road you come to. (Open Mon.-Fri. 9am-1pm and 3-6pm. **Postal code:** 60982.) **Telephones** are on Independencia, 2 blocks north of the Hotel Playa Azul; collect calls cost 4 pesos and up. (Open Mon.-Sat. 8am-9pm, Sun. 9am-1pm. **Telephone code:** 753.) **Telegrams** (tel. 6-01-06), are next door to the post office. (Open Mon.-Fri. 9am-3pm.) **Public Bathrooms and Showers** are inland of Palapa Maracaiboon Cárdenas, 2 blocks south of PEMEX station. **Farmacia Eva Carmen,** on Cárdenas next to the PEMEX station, is open daily 8am-9pm. For medical services and 24-hour emergency care, go to the **Centro de Salud,** next door to the post office. **Police** are at the east end of Carranza (no phone).

Accommodations and Food Some doze in sleeping bags directly on the sand. Others use the free hammocks slung in the *enramadas*, whose owners usually don't mind that you use the space as long as you eat there beforehand. If you plan on using a restaurant's hammock, make sure the proprietors are aware of that fact before closing; otherwise you may be discomfited when all unoccupied hammocks are taken down at night. Bear in mind that a tent or elaborate foreign equipment could tempt the otherwise harmless passerby. When camping on the beach, stay within sight of an inhabited *enramada* and inform the occupants of your presence, especially if you plan to leave your belongings in one place for an extended period of time.

If you must have the luxury of a bed, Playa Azul offers adequate albeit somewhat overpriced lodgings. **Hotel del Pacífico,** on Carranza (tel. 6-01-06), a couple of blocks east of Hotel Playa Azul, is the best buy. Rooms are large, clean and comfortable. More importantly, they're only 15 yards from the beach. (Singles 25 pesos. Doubles 45 pesos. May be negotiable.) **Bungalows de la Curva** (tel. 6-00-58), which sits one block south of the PEMEX station, is a small step up in both quality and price. The small pool is a welcome addition to the basic, clean rooms and *agua purificada*. (Singles 40 pesos. Doubles 60 pesos. Bungalow with kitchen for 1-2 people 80 pesos.) **Hotel Costa de Oro,** on Zapata (tel. 6-00-86), is four blocks east of the PEMEX station. Rooms are clean though overwhelmingly brown. Bathrooms are fitted with those ever-elusive toilet seats. (Singles 30 pesos. Doubles 40 pesos.) Prices go up in high-season (Dec.-May).

Don't worry about finding the cheapest *enramada* in Playa Azul—they all charge the same prices for meals. *Ceviche* costs 1 peso, fish entrees 15-20 pesos, eggs *al gusto* 6 pesos. Baby Coronas are 2 pesos, Modelos 3.50 pesos and all *refrescos* 1.50 pesos. Shrimp *al gusto* 25 pesos. If you can't face an *enramada* early in the morning, the best breakfasts in town emanate from the **Hotel Playa Azul.** Try the fantastic hotcakes (6 pesos) and freshly squeezed (or however it's done) papaya juice (2 pesos). Eat by the hotel's beautiful pool and after breakfast take a few laps—better yet, stay for the day and get the most out of the 10 pesos it will cost you, as a non-guest, to use the pool.

HIDALGO

Many of Hidalgo's cities are easily explored on a daytrip from Mexico City, but although the state has been economically important to Mexico since Aztec rule, few areas are of interest to the foreign visitor. Hidalgo has spent history under the influence of the mighty cities of Mexican history: El Tajín, built by the Totonacs, the mysterious Teotihuacán, and Tula, the Toltec city built by the god-king Quetzalcóatl. In latter days, the dull exigencies of production have made Hidalgo less of a prize. Hidalgan cuisine is delicious and exotic. If you do venture into Hidalgo, visit the capital city, Pachuca, and the archaeological ruins of Tula.

■■■ TULA

The signs on the road leading into Tula admonish visitors and residents alike to keep the town clean because of its historical significance. That significance, however, could be easily overlooked—the quiet *zócalo*, bustling market and plentiful taco stands do little to distinguish Tula from other Mexican towns. It doesn't even feel old. The city is in easy daytrip range from Mexico City (80km along Rte. 57 and 85) and from Pachuca (75km); it's also a nice stop for those traveling to or from the Bajío.

Once the Toltec's greatest city, ancient Tula was constructed at the foot of a hill in a region of brooding volcanic mountains. In the final years of Teotihuacán, a band of Chichimecs and Toltecs, led by Mixcoatl-Camaxtli, wandered through the Valley of Mexico before deciding to conquer the Otomí area between present-day Tula and Jilotepec. Supposedly Mixcoatl-Camaxtli then led his people to what is now the state of Morelos, where he married, had a son and subsequently lost his throne. When the son, Ce Acatl Topitzin, grew up, he is thought to have recovered the throne and moved the capital to the foot of the mountain called Xicuco, where he founded Tula.

Ce Acatl Topitzin (a.k.a Quetzalcóatl) is the most venerated king in *indígena* history and mythology. After he founded Tula, he fled (in 884 AD) to the Gulf coast because of strife with neighbors who did not agree with his peaceful ways and who rejected the god he worshiped (for whom he was named). In the years following, several kings expanded Tula into the center of the mighty Toltec empire.

The Toltecs, meaning "builders" in Nahuatl, relied on irrigation for their agricultural success and modeled their architecture after the Teotihuacán style, although the buildings at Tula are of poorer quality than those at Teotihuacán. During the 200-year-long Toltec heyday, the kingdom abandoned its once passivist stance for the violent and bloody sacrificial scene for which it is now notorious. Crop failures and droughts may have weakened the Toltec capital in 1116, and the Chichimecs saw their chance and destroyed Tula, leaving the ruins that exist today at the foot of Xicuco.

Despite its historical significance, the archaeological site at Tula–part of a **national park** (tel. 9-17-73) dedicated to preserving the plants and animals of this semi-desert–is relatively unimpressive. The first structures you see as you reach the main plaza are ballcourt #1, on the north side of the plaza, and Pyramid B, the **Temple of the Atlantes** (sculptured columns), on your left. Dangerously steep steps go up the temple's south face. The roof of this temple was held up by the four monolithic statues known as the *atlantes*. These 4.6m-high statues represent the warrior priests who led the worship of the warlike Tezcatlipoca.

The wall at Pyramid B's northern side, termed the **Coatepantli**, is a facade with reliefs of jaguars in procession, a deity in headdress and heart-devouring eagles. Reliefs of serpents feasting on live humans beautify the adjacent wall.

To the west of Pyramid B is a plaza filled with remains of many columns. This area is called the **Palacio Quemado,** or burnt palace; it is thought to have been either an administrative center in ancient Tula, or the city market. Even without its gaping mouth you can recognize a familiar Chac-Mool. On the east side of the plaza, to your left as you descend Pyramid B, is **Pyramid C.** This building, still not entirely excavated, is sometimes called the Main Building. In front of the ballcourt is a wall called the **Tzompantli,** or place of skulls, thought to have been built by the Aztecs. Early excavations found skulls and teeth on this wall.

The only other excavated structure of interest in the area is **El Corral,** 1.5km north of the main plaza. Because this building is rounded, it is thought to have been dedicated to the god of wind. A dirt path leads north to his shrine from the northern border of the main plaza. The **Museo Jorge R. Acosta,** at the entrance to the ruins, concerns itself with Toltec religion, crafts, leisure-time activity and socioeconomic hierarchy. Although the explanatory information is in Spanish, the museum is definitely worth a visit even for English-speakers.

A written guide is sold for 10 pesos. The museum complex also includes a cafeteria, bathrooms and an information desk where you can request a free guided tour and brochures. (Site open daily 9:30am-4:30pm. Admission 13 pesos. Free Sun. and holidays. Museum free with site ticket.) The town-to-ruins walk is long but manageable: from the plaza, turn left on Zaragoza (the first street toward the bus station). When you reach Ocampo, a sign points to the "Parque Nacional Tula";turn right, and head towards the highway. One street before the main highway, turn left on the road marked by the stone statue. The park lies about 1km up, off the road to the left. For those not up to the hike, **taxis** will take you to the site from town for 5 pesos. Taxis aren't available at the site itself for the return, but hailing one on the highway usually poses no problem.

Because Tula is a small town and most people book through just to see the ruins, the budget accommodation is a rare animal. A few cheap and clean hotels do exist. Not the most luxurious place in town, but probably the best deal, **Auto Hotel Cuéllar,** 5 de Mayo 23 (tel. 2-04-42), is well-furnished with a bureau and wardrobe in each room. (Singles 40 pesos, with TV 50 pesos. Doubles 50 pesos, with TV 62 pesos.) Hard to miss in the cream-colored building with red trim, bright orange lettering and the sign advertising TV and 24-hr. hot water, is **Hotel Cathedral,** Zaragoza 106 (tel. 2-08-13), right off the plaza. It has small bathrooms, but it's a centrally located and comfortable crash pad. (Singles 49 pesos. Doubles 55 pesos.) Eating establishments are sparse too. Typical *taqueterías* can be found on 5 de Mayo and Zaragoza. Though you may be lonely dining out in Tula, **Restaurant Casa Blanca,** at Hidalgo and Zaragoza, offers a slightly more refined atmosphere in which to sit alone. (5-course *comida corrida* 15 pesos, chicken entrees 15 pesos. Open 8am-10pm.) **Restaurant El Ranchito,** Zaragoza near Hidalgo, is a casual and unembellished family-run restaurant. The place looks tiny when you first enter, but don't worry, there's another room in back. No official menu, but the nice family will cook whatever you feel like eating for unbelievably low prices (5-12 pesos). (Open daily 9am-8pm.)

Downtown Tula consists of a few commercial streets surrounding a central *zócalo*. To reach the *zócalo* from the bus station, turn right down Xicotencatl and then left at Ocampo. Follow the signs to the centro, turning left down Zaragoza. There is no **tourist office,** but the town is small and friendly enough that people on the street will probably be willing and able to answer any question. **Change money** at Bánamex, Leandro Valle 21, down Juárez from the *zócalo*. (Open Mon.-Fri. 9am-noon.) The **post office** is on Av. Ferrocarril. (Open Mon.-Fri. 8am-7pm, Sat. 9am-1pm.) Make **calls** at Teléfonos de Mexico, Av. 5 de Mayo 3, near Mina. (Open Mon.-Sat. 8am-10pm, Sun. 8am-3pm.) **Telegrams** (tel. 2-00-37) are behind the market, in a construction zone. The small gray building is behind the white Loconsa building. (Open Mon.-Fri. 9am-9pm, Sat. 9am-noon.) The **IMSS Clínica Hospital,** Ocampo at Xicotencatl (tel. 2-10-46) in the large brown building, is open for emergencies 24 hrs. The **pharmacy** there is open Mon.-Fri. 24 hrs. The police are on 5 de Mayo 408 (tel. 2-01-85).

NORTHERN VERACRUZ

The northern half of Veracruz generally receives little attention from budget travelers, which is surprising, considering its indisputable attractions. Tuxpan's miles of white sand beaches and shoreside solitude are unavailable to the same extent anywhere else in Mexico. Papantla is an open-air museum dedicated to the culture of the Totonacs, while ruins of their ancient past lie nearby in El Tajín. Jalapa, the state capital, is blessed with all the graces of an inland colonial city—comfortable, cool, cultured, and cosmopolitan.

■■■ TUXPAN (TUXPAM), VERACRUZ

For those descending from the north, Tuxpan and its nearby beaches are a peaceful though provincial relief. For those traveling from the south or west, they may be a disappointment. The friendly family atmosphere, evident in the narrow streets filled with cycling kids and the shaded outdoor cafés in the *zócalo*, marks a departure from the industrial north and its grimy cities. The beach, only 12km away, fills with families every weekend as both kids and parents splash in the clear blue-green water and dig in the fine sand. The town, whose name derives from the Totonac word Tochpan meaning "Place of Wildly Hopping Rabbits" hosts the streams of shoppers and fruit vendors who flow freely along the city's riverfront, where boats incessantly load and unload fish, mangos and bananas.

Orientation And Practical Information Route 180 connects Tuxpan and Papantla and continues north to Tampico, three to five hours away depending on the route taken. Route 180 requires a ferry ride from Tampico; alternatively, Route 127 curves west from Route 180 in Potrero del Llano. Veracruz is 347km southeast, and Mexico City 328km southwest via Route 130. Tuxpan spreads along the northern bank of Río Tuxpan. Two small city gardens, ambitiously called parks, and what lies between constitute the center of town. Parque Reforma is one block inland from the river on Humboldt, west of the central commercial center. Parque Rodríguez Cano lies on the waterfront, just south of the busiest part of town. To reach these parks from the ADO bus station, turn left from the exit and head to the water. Rodríguez Cano is three blocks to your right (west). Continue three more blocks along the river to reach Parque Reforma, one block inland from the river on Humboldt. To get to the beach, take the "Playa" bus east from the riverfront road. Catch the bus at the lone tree along the boardwalk, two blocks west of the ADO station (every 10 min., 6am-8:30pm, 2 pesos).

When making local calls, it may be necessary to dial a 1 before the five-digit numbers listed here. The **tourist office,** run by the Delegación de Turismo (tel. 4-01-77), on Garizurieta 2 #302 along the western edge of Parque Rodríguez Cano (enter building under DELMAR doorway and climb to the 3rd floor), employs a youthful staff with bad maps. (Open Mon.-Sat. 8am-3pm and 4-7pm.) Currency exchange is difficult; an outbreak of counterfeiting has induced local paranoia. Try **Bancomer,** Juárez at Zapata. (Open Mon.-Fri. 9am-1:30pm. Changes currency and checks Mon.-Fri. 9:30am-noon. Rates are mediocre.) Checks may be easier to cash at **Banco Internacional,** along Juárez, about 1½ blocks west from Parque Reforma (Mon.-Fri. 10am-12:30pm), or **Banamex,** at the side street off the northern part of Parque Reforma, for a 24-hr. ATM. The **post office,** on Morelos 12 (tel. 4-00-88), 2 blocks east of Parque Reforma, is open for stamps, *Lista de Correos,* and packages Mon.-Fri. 8am-8pm, Sat. 9am-1pm; for registered mail Mon.-Fri. 8am-6:30pm, Sat. 9-11am. **Postal Code:** 92800. Make collect calls from the special long distance **phones** on the side of Parque Reforma, on the back of the Hotel Riveria. (Open Mon.-Fri. 8:30am-1:30pm.) A credit card phone in the telegram office takes MC, Visa, and AmEx. **Telegram office,** Ortega 20 (tel. 4-01-67), just beyond "Pollo Feliz" sign on left-hand side of the street, is open for telegrams Mon.-Fri. 9am-8pm, Sat. 9am-5pm; for money orders Mon.-Fri. 9am-5pm, Sat. 9am-1pm.

Tuxpan has several **bus stations. ADO** Rodríguez 1 (tel. 4-01-02), has first-class service to: Tampico (29 pesos), Mexico City (38 pesos), Poza Rica (60 pesos) (where buses leave to Papantla every 10 mins., 6am-11:30pm, 1.50 pesos), Papantla (58 pesos), Veracruz, Puebla, and Jalapa. **Blancos,** Constitución 18 (tel. 4-20-40), 2 blocks past the bridge, has second-class service to many of ADO's destinations, without the cleanliness or comfort. Many buses run off schedule; call or stop by to confirm departure times. **Omnibus de México,** (tel. 4-11-47), at the bridge and waterfront is a small first-class station with only a few destinations; to Mexico City (2 per day, 36 pesos), Guadalajara (2 per day, 91 pesos), Tampico (2 per day, 26 pesos), Queretaro (3 per day, 48 pesos), and Poza Rica (10 per day, 6 pesos).

For medical attention, contact the **Red Cross,** Galeana 40 (tel. 4-01-58), 8 blocks west of the center along the river, right on Galeana and 4 blocks north, next to the police station. They provide 24-hr. emergency and ambulance service to any medical facility. **Farmacia Independencia,** (tel. 4-03-12) Independencia 4, on the riverfront side of the market. The **Hospital Civil,** Obregón 13 (tel. 4-01-99), 1 block west of the bridge, then 1½ blocks inland and up the inclined driveway on the right, provides 24-hr. emergency service. The **police** can be found at Galeana 38 (tel. 4-02-52 or 4-37-23), 8 blocks west of the center along the river, next door to the Red Cross. (Open 24 hrs.)

Accommodations and Food Budget hotels lie between Parque Reforma and Parque Rodríguez Cano. **Hotel El Huasteco,** Morelos 41 (tel. 4-18-59), diagonally across the street from Lonchería Mérida (below) at Parque Reforma, is the best budget option despite its tiny and dark rooms. The noisy A/C is a life-saver in the unbreatheable hot and humid Tuxpan nights. (Singles 40 pesos, doubles 46 pesos.) **Hotel Parroquia,** at the sidstreet to the left of the Cathedral on Parque Rodríguez Cano (tel. 4-16-30). Light rooms with strong neon lamps, fans, almost comfortable beds, shower curtains and toilet seats. Tender white lizards will guard you in your sleep from evil mosquitoes and other bugs. The rooms up front are far breezier and noisier. (Singles 44 pesos, doubles 55 pesos.) **Hotel del Parque,** Humboldt 11 (tel. 4-08-12), on the east side of *Parque Reforma*, puts you right in the thick of things if you can deal with a little noise (the hotel is right above a gym/Tae Kwan Do studio). Uncomfortable beds and worn showers, but the rooms are large and clean. Terrace overlooks the *Parque Reforma*. (Singles and doubles 44 pesos.)

Soulless hotel cafeterias permeate Tuxpan. The majority serve mostly *antojitos mexicanos* and lots of seafood. **Barra de Mariscos del Puerto,** at Juárez and Humboldt (tel. 4-46-01), across from the southeast corner of Parque Reforma is decorated with a sea motif to set the mood. *Parrillada de Mariscos* (a veritable seafood menagerie) can feed two for 30 pesos. (Open daily 8am-11pm.) **Lonchería Mérida,** Humboldt and Morelos (tel. 5-74-24), on the northeast corner at the *Parque Reforma* serves authentic fare to locals and Tuxpan's sporadic tourist alike. *Plátanos fritos* and *tamales* for 2 pesos each, everything else 6-8 pesos. Take-out available. (Open daily 7am-2pm and 5-11:30pm.) **Cafetería El Mante,** Rodríguez 11, two doors up from ADO station (away from waterfront), is busier and livelier than any of the hotel cafés. Strictly Mexican and reasonably priced (10-15 pesos) entrees are served round the clock in an open atmosphere decorated with a poster of Seattle.

Sights and Entertainment Although Tuxpan can boast neither grand cathedrals nor museums of world renown, the city's sights are like a draft of local vintage—pleasant and soothing. Near the simple white cathedral lie several parks ideal for a good book, a quiet meal or a fine afternoon watching the world-as-movie. On the west side of the Parque Reforma lies the **Museo Regional de Antropología e Historia** (open Mon.-Sat. 10am-2pm and 4-6pm, Sun. 10am-1pm. Free), which is inside the **Casa de la Cultura** and has a smattering of Huastec pottery. The Mercado Rodríguez Cano sells mostly food, clothing and practical goods. The main entrance is at Rodríguez and the waterfront, near the ADO station.

A true find rests on the other side of the river. Accessible by blue ferry for .50 pesos (1 peso for foreigners) the **Casa de la Amistad México Cuba** (a.k.a. La Casa de Fidel Castro) chronicles Mexican-Cuban connections over the past three centuries. The helpful caretaker will make sure you appreciate the exhibits and will add personal commentary. The first part of the museum is in an old warehouse and consists mostly of photographs of Havana before and after the revolution. *Sala #1* of the second building revisits the days of piracy and Spanish imperialism in the Caribbean. *Sala #2* is the main event, containing pictures of a slim Fidel and a young Ché Guevara practicing their marksmanship. In addition, it houses Castro's uniform, a map of Castro's route from Tuxpan to Cuba in 1956 and various pictures of the young revolutionaries flexing their muscles on a beach near Tuxpan. The final building is the actual bedroom and bath Castro used for the three years he stayed in Tuxpan. Pictures like *Castro in the Mountains of Cuba* and *Castro with Mexican President Cárdenas* (who nationalized the petroleum industry in 1938) line the walls. The exhibit ends with a farewell letter from Ché to Castro and a replica of the *Granma*, the ship which carried the soon-to-be victorious revolutionary fighters to Cuba. To get to the museum, after you disembark the ferry, walk to the right along the river on the wide sidewalk and continue straight up the dirt road. It's parallel to the northern part of Tuxpan, beyond even Galeana. (Open Mon.-Sun. 7am-5pm. Free, of course.)

Tuxpan's greatest asset is its 2km of very merry riverfront. The *malecón* (pier) is a lively place, with Spanish rap tunes drifting through the squads of people walking to and from town. Palm trees and benches line the boardwalk, which parallels the water and offers views of the fishing people hauling in their catch. They sell their haul up and down the waterfront and congregate in the greatest numbers under the bridge, where piles of pineapples, bananas, shrimp, and fish can be had for a bare minimum.

Twelve km east of Tuxpan's city center, the river flows to the gulf, and the beach used to extend 20km in either direction. Near the bus stop the beach can be crowded and slightly dirty, especially in season, but the wide expanse of fine sand continues far enough for you to stake a private claim somewhere down the line. The water is relatively clean and safe for swimming, though coagulated oil from a nearby refinery sometimes washes ashore. Seafood cocktails from the quintillions of cheap seafood stands cost 8-12 pesos. Buses (2 pesos) marked "Playa" leave Tuxpan for the beach every 15 minutes from 6am to 10pm; the last bus returns at 8:30pm. Though there are a number of bars in the center, the best nightlife begins a few blocks down the river after the crowds in the *Parque Reforma* thin out. Just past Allende on Reyes Heroles, facing the river, sits **La Puesta del Sol,** which serves food, beer and mixed drinks to quiet customers enjoying the live music, tropical and salsa (tel.4-73-66). Just a block down is **Charlôt** (tel. 4-40-28; open Tue.-Sun. noon-midnight), which serves appetizers or drinks outdoors or inside its classy establishment. Turn right on Pérez to find **La Bamba,** a high-tech sunken video bar accentuated by its glowing neon entrance and large-screen musical entertainment. A professional crowd drinks cocktails and beers served by the bucket.

■■■ PAPANTLA, VERACRUZ

The Totonacs dominated the top half of what is now the state of Veracruz for hundreds of years, until Aztec conquest circa 1450. In turn, Cortés, with assistance from the Totonacs, crushed the Aztec Empire in the 16th century. Ultimately the Totonacs fared no better than any other indigenous group under the Spanish, but in Papantla (pop. 125,000) Totonac culture persists, beautifully and accessibly. The ancient ritual flight of the *voladores* is justly famous, thrilling observers with commercial regularity in the *zócalo*. Papantla is the best base to explore El Tajín, the Totonac capital city ruins and one of the most impressive archeological sites in Mexico. Crawling up the green foothills of the Sierra Madre Oriental, Papantla looks out onto the gorgeous plains of Northern Veracruz. The *zócalo* is crowded with friendly locals, while *indígenas* continue to don traditional dress: the men in wide white bloomers, the women in lacy white skirts and embroidered blouses with shawls. The city is exceptionally proud of its indigenous history; when Totonac rebels rose up in 1836, Papantla was their stronghold. Though their struggle was politically unsuccessful, in Papantla the *indígena* culture prevailed.

Orientation and Practical Information Papantla lies 250km northwest of Veracruz and 21km southeast of Poza Rica along Route 180. The ruins of El Tajín lie 12km south of the city. The *centro* is marked by the plaza (formally known as **Parque Téllez**), the cathedral to the south, Enríquez on the plaza's downhill northern edge, Juárez perpendicular to the left, and 20 de Noviembre perpendicular to the right as you face the cathedral. To get from the first-class bus station to the *centro*, turn left onto Juárez out of the station and veer left at the fork. Taxis (8 pesos to the *centro*) pass frequently along Juárez. If you arrive at the second-class bus station (on a microbus from Poza Rica, 1.50 pesos), turn left outside the station and ascend 20 de Noviembre three steep but short blocks to the northwest corner of the plaza.

The tourist office (tel. 2-01-23), in the yellow building at the base of the **Monumento al Volador,** dispenses Spanish brochures, a joke map and vanilla-scented souvenirs. (Open Mon.-Fri. 9am-1pm and 3-6pm, Sat. 9am-2pm.) Exchange currency at any of the three banks on Enríquez. **Banamex,** Enríquez 102, may be the most helpful, and has a 24-hr. ATM for MC, Visa, Cirrus, and Plus. (All banks open for exchange Mon.-Fri. 9am-1pm.) The **post office,** at Azueta 198 (tel. 2-00-73), on the second floor, is open for stamps and *Lista de Correos* Mon.-Fri. 9am-1pm and 4-7pm, Sat. 9am-noon; for registered mail Mon.-Fri. 9am-1pm and 3-5pm. (**Postal Code:** 93400.) Make international collect calls at local hotels or at the pharmacy on the eastern side of the plaza (7 pesos; open daily 9am-10pm). **Hotel Tájin,** Nuñez y Domínguez 104, charges 15 pesos for collect calls, and is open 24 hrs. (**Telephone Code:** 784.) The **telegram office** is located at Enríquez 404 (tel. 2-05-84), about 5 blocks east of the *zócalo.* (Open for telegrams Mon.-Fri. 9am-8pm, Sat. 9am-noon; for money orders Mon.-Fri. 9am-1pm and 3-5pm, Sat. 9am-noon.)

Papantla has two bus stations. The first-class **ADO** station, on Juárez 207 serves Poza Rica (10 daily, 3 pesos), Jalapa (7 daily, 30 pesos), Veracruz (daily, 39 pesos), Mexico City (4 daily, 32 pesos), Tuxpam (3 daily, 9 pesos), Puebla (8 daily, 38 pesos), and Tampico (7 daily, 33 pesos). The **second class terminal,** known better as *Transportes Papantla,* 20 de Noviembre 200, is best for its frequent service (approximately every 10-15min. 6am-11:30pm) to Poza Rica (35min., 1.50 pesos). All buses leave as they fill up, pay after you board. **Poza Rica** (21km northwest) is a much more convenient bus transfer spot. Their **ADO** terminal (tel.2-04-29 or 2-00-85) serves Mexico City (21 daily, 33 pesos), Tampico (21 daily, 33 pesos), Papantla (15 daily, 2.50 pesos), Veracruz (13 daily, 45 pesos), Villhermosa (12 daily, 88 pesos), Jalapa (11 daily, 32 pesos), Tuxpan (9 daily, 7 pesos), Puebla (5 daily, 32 pesos). The **Red Cross** on Pino Suárez, at Juárez (tel. 2-01-26), responds to emergencies and minor accidents, with ambulances or appropriate specialists. (Open 24 hrs.) **Farmacia Aparicio,** Enríquez 103, on northern border of the plaza, is open daily 7am-10pm. For **emergency medical assistance,** try the Clínica IMSS, 20 de Noviembre at Lázaro Cárdenas (tel. 2-01-94), in a big beige building. From the ADO station, take a right and walk 2 blocks to Cárdenas (no sign except "Clínica IMSS"), then turn left. IMSS is ½ block up on your right. (Open 24 hrs.) **Police** can be reached at 2-00-75 or 2-01-50, or in the Palacio Municipal 24 hrs.

Accommodations and Food Few accommodations of any variety are available in Papantla; try nearby Poza Rica, 21 km from Papantla, easily accessible by bus. **Hotel Pulido,** Enríquez 205 (tel. 2-00-36), 1½ blocks down Enríquez, has dark rooms and crusty bathrooms with fans, flowery sheets and amusing curtains. Beware of the basement "restaurant," a bar where it's often drunk amateur night on the piano until all hours. (Singles 40 pesos, doubles 60 pesos.) **Hotel Tajín,** Nuñez y Domínguez 104 (tel. 2-01-21), ½ block to the left as you face the cathedral, is a light-blue building with rounded terraces overlooking the valley. Spotless rooms with TV and phone, with A/C or fan. (Singles with fan 60 pesos, with A/C 86 pesos; doubles with fan 73 pesos, with A/C 100 pesos.) Attractive murals in the lobby and hallways belie the worn rooms in **Hotel Totanacapán,** 20 de Noviembre and Olivo (tel. 2-12-24 or 2-12-18), 4 blocks down from the plaza. TV, fans, and nice bathrooms do manage to compensate, however. (Singles with fan 52 pesos, with A/C 75 pesos; doubles with fan 75 pesos, with A/C 90 pesos.)

Papantla's few restaurants serve regional delicacies to tourists looking for the real thing. Most restaurants stick to very reasonably priced *antojitos mexicanos* ("little cravings"); try some pork tamales wrapped in banana leaves. **Restaurante Los Costales,** Obisbo de las Casas 105, lies 4-5 short blocks down Lázaro Muño, and right 1½ blocks uphill. This authentic and enchanting family-run restaurant is decorated with artifacts and *costales* (regional tough cloth bedsheets). Excellent menus *del día* all cost 8 pesos, including soup and a huge main dish. (Open Mon.-Sat. 9am-11pm.) **Restaurante Enrique,** Enríquez 103, attached to the Hotel Premier is somewhat expensive, but worth it. Great ale, bright blue tablecloths and porthole fish tanks add to the surreal effect. *Fillete relleno* is a richly-garnished filled and breaded fillet (25 pesos) while *casuela de mariscos* is just as tempting, but prepared in a clay pot (25 pesos). (Open daily 8am-7pm.) **Restaurante Terraza,** Reforma 100, on the second floor, southwest corner of the *zócalo,* isn't fancy, but a pleasant spot where you can sit outside and survey plaza activity below. All dishes, including *cecina* (dried meat), cost less than 15-20 pesos. (Open daily 7:30am-midnight.)

Sights and Entertainment Most of the sights in town are on or adjacent to the park, and relate to the city's Totonac heritage. South of the plaza but slightly farther uphill is the **Catedral Señora de la Asunción,** remarkable not so much for its interior but for the 50m-long, 5m-high stone mural carved into its northern wall. The mural, called Homenaje a la Cultura Totonaca, was created by Teodoro Cano to honor local Totonac heroes and folkloric figures. The focus is on the plumed serpent Quetzalcóatl whose image runs along the full length of the carving. At the far left of the mural is a representation of the Dios del Trueno (god of thunder), who announces the coming of the rains. From left to right, the mural follows a rough chronological outline, moving from the mythical first family to the discovery of maize, which ended the nomadic lifestyle and established Totonac agricultural civilization. The mural moves on to depict the Pyramid of the Niches, the focal point of El Tajín, flanked by characteristic male and female faces with typical round cheeks, smallish noses and smiles. Next, the ballplayers from the courts of El Tajín vie for the right to ritualistic death but deified mortality. Modern products, oil and the vanilla bean, lie to the right, and the mural ends with the head of Quetzalcóatl. Five faces belonging to local figures important in the history of Papantla are carved near the open jaw.

The cathedral's spacious courtyard on the hill commands a view of the *zócalo.* The courtyard, christened the **Plaza de los Voladores,** is the site of the ceremony in which five male *voladores* acrobatically entreat the rain god Tlaloc to water the year's crops. The performance begins with five elaborately costumed men climbing a stationary pole to a platform about 20m above the plaza. Having consumed courage-enhancing fluids, four of the hardy five start to "fly"—hanging by their feet from ropes wound around the pole. They spin through the air and slowly descend. All this to the music of the fifth man, who plays a flute and dances on the pin-head of the pole. Originally, the four fliers corresponded to the four cardinal directions, and the different positions assumed during descent were related to requests for specific weather conditions. With the rise in tourism, however, the performance has lost its meteorological significance and gone the way of much *indígena* religion, subjugated to commercial exigencies. Instead of once every 52 years , the *voladores* now fly as often as the tourist is able to pay them. If you visit during the ten-day Festival of Corpus Christi, held in mid-June, you might see the *voladores* perform as often as thrice a day. Papantla comes alive with games, typical food stands, artistic expositions, fireworks, traditional dances and cockfights.

Papantla's latest effort to enshrine its *voladores* is the **Monumento al Volador,** a gigantic flute-wielding *indígena* statue erected in 1988 atop a hill, visible from all over town. To get to the monument, where you can read explanatory plaques and see Papantla in its entirety, walk up Reforma along the right side of the cathedral; bear left and walk uphill. At night the monument is marked by a small red light, which looks oddly like the tip of a burning cigarette.

A mural decorates the inside of the *zócalo*'s centerpiece, a domed kiosk. Painted by Arturo Cano in the 1960s, the mural represents the indigenous conception of creation. The four cardinal points are personified as warriors, each representing different natural calamities that have befallen Mesoamericans. The *zócalo* is also furnished with a set of mosaic benches framing small paintings of the Totonacs, in a style typical of northern Veracruz.

The town's two markets lie next to the central plaza. Mercado Juárez, at Reforma and 16 de Septiembre, off the southwest corner of the *zócalo*, specializes in poultry and veggies but is neither particularly colorful nor low-priced. Mercado Hidalgo, on 20 de Noviembre, off the *zócalo*'s northwest corner on a small triangular block, vends many of the same items as Mercado Juárez. In addition Hidalgo offers a large collection of traditional handmade clothing amidst its supply of machine-made outfits. The men's garb consists of striking white sailor shirts and baggy white pants. Unlike *indígenas* from other regions of Mexico, the Totonacs have no qualms about women wearing clothing designed for men, and often gather in amused groups to watch fitting sessions.

■ Near Papantla: El Tajín

The Totonacs' most important city and religious center, El Tajín lies in ruins a half-hour bus ride south of Papantla. Named after the Totonac god of thunder, the site has revealed Aztec, Mixtec/Zapotec and Mayan influence, but it has otherwise shed little light on the origins of Totonac culture. The well-preserved buildings contain enough alluring carvings and artwork to require a visit. June through August *voladores* perform here daily. The rest of the year, they perform only on Saturday and Sunday. The exhibition lasts about 15 minutes, and starts when enough spectators assemble at the pole inside the entrance booth. A seated man in costume requests a donation of a few pesos.

A **museum** near the entrance shows pottery and carvings discoveries of El Tajín, but lacks explanatory plaques for most of the objects. The exhibit of local poisonous beasties should dissuade you from wandering off the clearly marked paths.

Beyond these buildings, at the entrance to the site, a detailed map stand greets visitors. From there, a path leads to the central area among four large symmetrical and well reconstructed pyramids. Due to the recent completion of their restoration, explanatory signs may not exist for every site. Those that do are written in Spanish, English, French, German, and Totananco. The next area is El Tajín's main plaza. The first temples to the left enclose the most interesting of Tajín's ballcourts. Three pairs of wall carvings, two at each end and one in the center of each wall, all in excellent condition, give tips for fans of the ubiquitous pre-conquest ball game, *pok-ta-pok*. The grassy ballcourt is in between the two long walls directly to your left. Returning to the main cluster of ruins, you will see buildings labeled #1, 3, 4 and 5 on the map. Directly in front lies building 4, to the right building 3, and diagonally to the left building 1, the famous Pyramid of the Niches.

The **Pyramid of the Niches** is a unique piece of calendrical architecture: seven levels with a total of 365 niches corresponding to the days of the year—they were once done up in red and blue paint. Some archaeologists believe that the temple guarded the Totonac llama (flame), a symbol of life and prosperity. The Totonacs marked time in 52-year epochs, during which a single flame was kept continuously burning. At the end of each epoch, the carefully nurtured flame was used to ritually torch many of the settlement's buildings. Each new epoch of rebuilding and regeneration was inaugurated by the lighting of the new flame.

Building 5, to the left of the Pyramid of the Niches, is notable for the well preserved statue of a Totonac god. Visitors may pay their respects by bowing their heads.

The **main plaza** near the Pyramid of the Niches is known simply as Tajín; the area beyond these structures, set on a series of hills and terraces, is called Tajín Chico. Archeologists hypothesize that this was the residential and administrative center of El Tajín. Some buildings here are in good condition, but most have not been excavated, reconstructed or even carefully preserved. As a result, park officials don't mind if visitors scamper up the higher buildings to get a view of the site and surrounding rolling hills.

To get to Tajín Chico, head north to a long flat building; to the right is a small, recently excavated ballcourt, with another series of wall carvings, smaller and more faded than the first set. To the left of the ballcourt is a tiny sign pointing the way to Tajín Chico. Turn left at this sign and ascend the stairs of the building all the way at the western border of the site. Turn right at the top of the stairs to see structures "B" and "C" ahead.

Nothing in Tajín Chico is clearly marked. The first building at the far end is worth visiting for its interior. This building has a Mayan-influenced primitive arch (*cor-*

beled). If you ascend the steep staircase, you can walk all the way around the square and view the surrounding hills from each direction. The building farthest to the north is the building of the columns, not much to look at itself, but offering the best view of the whole complex. It is barely reachable by a tiny winding path among rich vegetation.

The entrance to the entire El Tajín site is 300m down the access road off Route 180 beside the "Archaeological Zone" billboard. (Site open daily 9am-5pm. Admission 13 pesos, free for Mexican students—try your foreign ID anyway, Sun. and holidays free.) Be equipped with an adventurous spirit and plenty of water to battle the dry, hot sun of Tajín Chico. There is no guidebook available at the site, but one may be purchased at the **Museo Nacional de Antropología** in Mexico City.

El Tajín is accessible from the **Transportes Papantla** second-class terminal. Board any bus headed for the tiny village El Chote (6 pesos); from there, pick up the bus bound for Poza Rica (1 peso). This bus stops at the very entrance of the site. To return to Papantla, take the "San Andrés," "Coyutla," or "Coxquihui" bus to El Chote and change there for Papantla. If lucky, you might be able to catch one of the minibuses that runs directly between Papantla and El Tajín. These buses run every hour to hour and a half (schedule not dependable) and leave from the southwest corner of the park (2 pesos).

■■■ JALAPA (XALAPA)

Sitting high on a mountain slope, Jalapa (or sometimes Xalapa) will surprise visitors with its decrepit colonial beauty, cultural legitimacy, and strapping heavy atmosphere. The capital of the state of Veracruz, Jalapa is home to the University of Veracruz, a world-class museum of anthropology and a handful of beautiful parks and gardens.

Downtown Jalapa is a busy, giddy place; from there the city ripples outward. Take time to kick up and down the cobblestone streets that cling to ravines, cliffs, and even a small extinct volcano. Every avenue offers a magnificent vista of the craggy peaks surrounding the city, and most streets cut through a park at some point.

ORIENTATION

Jalapa lies 104km northwest of Veracruz along Route 140 and 308km east of Mexico City. Trains and first- and second-class buses stop in Jalapa; buses offer the most frequent service and most varied destinations. The train station is at the extreme northeastern edge of the city, a good 40-minute walk or about a 6-peso taxi ride from the center.

The first class ADO and the second class AU bus terminals are both housed at 20 de Noviembre 571, east of the city center. They share a brand-new, state-of-the-art building. Upon arrival, you'll have to fight the urge to spend a few days in the bus station. Not only is it clean and efficient, it seems a sparkling emporium, offering long-distance phone service, baggage check, and a wide selection of food and drink, as well as the requisite complement of eager taxi drivers (4 pesos to the *zócalo*). To catch a bus to the *zócalo* (1 peso), first exit the station complex by descending the long, terraced steps to street level. From there buses marked Centro or, inexplicably, Terminal head downtown.

Jalapa is initially quite confusing. Many streets follow no discernible pattern and change names every few blocks. El Parque Juárez functions as the whole *zócalo* and approximate center of the city. Enríquez, the main east-west thoroughfare, fronts the park on its north side. One block south of Enríquez, Zaragoza runs (roughly) parallel to both of them. Clavijero, at the west of the park, and Revolución, at the east end, ascends north, perpendicular to Enríquez.

Orienting yourself in the park is not difficult. Facing north, the Palacio Munipal will be directly in front of you, across Enríquez. The huge Palacio del Gobierno will be to your right. The Cathedral is just off the northeast corner of the park. Two

JALAPA (XALAPA)

blocks east of the park, Enríquez splits in two: Zamora continues east while Xalapeños veers up to the northeast.

PRACTICAL INFORMATION

State Tourist Office: Camacho 191 (tel. 8-72-02), a 20min. walk from the *zócalo*. Any yellow minibus heading west on Enríquez will get you there (1 peso). The office will be on your left. Relatively unhelpful. Good maps (5 pesos) and a slew of free brochures. No English spoken. Open Mon.-Fri. 8am-3pm and 6-9pm, Sat. 9am-1pm.

Currency Exchange: None of the banks in downtown Jalapa will exchange traveler's checks. Try the American Express office or the *casa de cambio* at Zamora 36. (Open Mon.-Thurs. 9am-1:30pm and 4-6pm, Fri. 9am-1pm and 4-6pm.)

American Express: Carrillo 28, 3 blocks east of the *zócalo* off Enríquez (tel. 7-41-14). Helpful staff will change money or traveler's checks, but only when the office has the cash. They will also hold mail for card members. (Office open Mon.-Fri. 9am-8pm. Cashier open Mon.-Fri. 9am-2pm and 4-7pm.)

Post Office: In the Palacio Federal, at Zamora and Diego Leño. Open Mon.-Fri. 8am-8pm, Sat. 9am-1pm. Open for Lista de Correos Mon.-Sat. 8am-1pm. Postal code: 91001.

Telephones: Many *casetas* hide in the cafés along Zamora, but the best bet is the southwest corner of the Parque Juárez at Guerrero 9. International collect calls 4 pesos. Open daily 8am-10pm.

Telegrams: Around the corner from the post office at Zamora 70. Open Mon.-Fri. 9am-8pm, Sat. 9am-1pm.

Buses: from CAXA (Central de Autobuses de Xalapa), first class ADO buses run to Puebla (20 pesos, 5am, 6am, 7am, 8am, 10:45am, 12:30pm, 3pm, 7pm, 8:30pm), Mexico City (38.50 pesos, 6am, 7am, 8am, 9am, 10am, 11am, 1pm, 3pm, 7pm, 9:30pm, midnight) and to Veracruz (13.50 pesos, about every 20 min.) From the same terminal, AU buses go to Puebla (17.50 pesos, every hr.), Mexico City (31 pesos, every hr.) and Veracruz (10 pesos, every ½-hr.)

English Language Bookstore: Books-R-Us, Diego Leño 30 (tel. 8-45-40), around the corner and 3 blocks south of the post office. Full selection of American comics and magazines. Also used paperbacks (5 pesos) and current bestsellers (25 pesos). Will trade books as well. Open Mon.-Sat. 10am-2pm, 4-8pm.

Library: Biblioteca de la Ciudad, Juárez 2. Open Mon.-Fri. 8am-10pm, Sat. 8am-9pm, Sun. 8am-8pm.

Market: Revolución at Altamirano, 2 blocks north of the Parque Juárez. Open daily 8am-sunset, but for the freshest, cheapest food in town come at night when the trucks unload their cargo. **Chedraui,** in the mall, Plaza Crystal, on the corner of Independencia and Lázaro Cárdenas. The biggest (and only) supermarket in town. Open daily 8am-9pm.

Laundromat: Lavandería Los Lagos, Diche 25 (tel. 7-93-38), right around the corner from Casa de Artesanías. 3.5kg washed and dried for 14.80 pesos. Open Mon.-Sat. 9am-8pm.

Red Cross: Clavijero 13 (tel. 7-81-58 or 7-34-31), 1 block north of the Parque Juárez. 24-hr. ambulance service.

Pharmacies: Farmacia del Dr. Rancón, on the corner of Saraga and Revolución (tel. 8-09-35). Open 24 hrs. Many other pharmacies nearby on Revolución.

Police: Officially at the Cuartel San José, at the corner of Arteaga and Aldama (tel. 8-18-10), but lots of heavily armed cops hang out at the at the Palacio de Gobierno, across the street from the cathedral.

ACCOMMODATIONS

Jalapa is full of comfortable, economical, and convenient accommodations. On warm nights the mosquitoes may get to you. On cool nights ask for extra blankets. Many budget hotels are conveniently grouped on Revolución, close to the *zócalo*, the parks, and the market.

Hotel Limón, Revolución 8 (tel. 7-22-07). Probably the best deal in the city. Some of the rooms are tiny, but without exception spotlessly clean. The tall courtyard is covered with pretty multicolored tiles, but the turquoise-blue paint lends the interiors an unfortunate swimming-pool feel. Singles 28 pesos. Doubles 32 pesos, with two beds 40 pesos.

Hotel Citlalli, Clavijero 43 (tel. 8-34-58). Plain concrete rooms with dark wood accents. This newly built hotel has all the amenities (TV, *agua purificada*, huge sparkling bathrooms), even if it's a bit short on character. For busy executives, the hotel has four fax lines. Singles 40 pesos. Doubles 55 pesos. Triples 67 pesos.

Hotel Continental, Zamora 4 (tel. 7-35-30). Musty rooms with ancient bathrooms, but a great location and cheap restaurant in hotel's tall inner courtyard. (*Comida corrida* 8 pesos.) Check out 5pm. Singles 30 pesos. Doubles 35 pesos.

FOOD

For those tired of beans and tortillas, Jalapa will provide happy relief; many eateries prepare excellent, imaginative meals at low cost. Particularly inexpensive cuisine can be found in the market and at the many stands around it.

La Sopa, Callejon del Diamante 3-A (tel. 7-80-69). Hip, happening, and filling, this hang-out can't be beat. When it's crowded (as it usually is), join an occupied table and make a friend. First-rate *comida corrida* for 6.50 pesos. Two block east of the *zócalo*, off Enríquez. Open daily 1-5pm, 7pm-midnight.

Restaurant Terraza Jardín, Enríquez, on the Parque Juárez (tel. 8-97-13). Inside it's just a big room with tables; relax there with a newspaper, or grab a space at one of the many outdoor tables to watch the crowds in the park go by. Crazy bronze sculpture entertains on the west wall. Full breakfast of corn flakes, toast, juice, and coffee 6 pesos. Eggs start at 5 pesos. No English. No credit cards. Open Mon.-Sat. 8am-11pm.

Café de la Parroquia, Zaragoza 18, right next door to the Beaterio. Much more casual than its neighbor, but similarly fine fare. Steak and fries 11 pesos. Lemonade with mineral water 2.10 pesos. Open daily 7:30am-10:30pm.

Casona del Beaterio, Zaragoza 20, near the Palacio de Gobierno. Among the best Jalapa has to offer, at great prices. Open courtyard features small bar. As popular for drinks and coffee as for dinner. Entrees 7-30 pesos. The Italian food can be heavy. Crepes are rich and soupy. Visa/MC accepted. Open daily 8am-10pm.

SIGHTS

Jalapa's beautiful, brand-new **Museo de Antropología** (tel. 5-09-20) displays an excellent collection approaching that of the all-encompassing Museo Nacional de Antropología in Mexico City. The museum is extremely well-organized and takes visitors through the ages of ancient civilizations in Mexico, region by region. All exhibits (including maps, timelines and photos) are in Spanish. The museum sits on a large open lawn that makes for excellent sunning on a clear day. (Open Tues.-Sun. 10am-5pm.) Admission 8 pesos. Video camera 35 pesos extra. Wheelchair-accessible and wheelchairs available on-site. To reach the museum from the *zócalo*, walk north on Revolución, turn left at the first busy intersection (Juárez) and follow to Acueducto; the museum is on the left. The walk takes approximately 45 minutes—or catch one of the yellow buses on Enríquez (1 peso), all of which pass the museum. You may choke on exhaust fumes before one of the yellow buses is empty enough to let you on; the surest method is to compromise—walk part-way to escape the *zócalo* crowds and ride the rest. Taxis cost about 4 pesos. Photography buffs will enjoy the **Centro Recreativo Xalapeño,** Xalapeño 31, which houses excellent and diverse exhibits by international artists. (Open Mon.-Sat. 11am-8pm, Sun. 11am-6pm. Free.)

Jalapa's two main public parks merit visits. The **Parque Ecológico Macuitepetl** is essentially a preserve for the flora and fauna indigenous to the Jalapa area. Neat brick paths wind up the side of an extinct volcano through thick vegetation that hides flocks of screeching birds. The summit, the highest point in the area at 1586m above sea level, affords a sublime view. (Open Tues.-Sun. 6am-5pm. Free.) To get to the park, catch one of the buses marked "Mercado/Corona" at the corner of Revolución and Altamirano. Two blocks south of the *zócalo* on Diche lies the second park, the **Paseo de los Lagos,** which consists of a large lake and beautiful lawns and gardens. The **Casa de Artesanías,** at the north end of the lake, is a state-run handicrafts store. (Open Mon.- Sat. 9am-3pm.)

The **zócalo** itself is of some interest to the sightseer. Across Enríquez from the plaza stands the **Palacio de Gobierno,** notable largely for its interesting French design. The Convento de San Francisco once stood on the site of Parque Juárez. It was built in 1534 (three years after the arrival of the *conquistadores*) and razed in 1886. Today the park is a busy spot with terrific views of Jalapa and the surrounding mountains. Also on the *zócalo*, the colonial cathedral contains a body of religious paintings and a huge bronze bell which was shipped from London in 1778.

ENTERTAINMENT

El Ágora de la Ciudad, beneath the Parque Juárez downtown (enter through the stairwell in the southwest corner of the park), serves as the city's cultural center. Its theater shows many foreign films; paintings and sculptures fill the corridors. A sophisticated crowd mills about. Fine books and musical recordings for sale. (Open daily 8:30am-9pm.) **El Teatro del Estado,** at Ignacio de la Llave and Rubén Bouchez (tel. 7-31-10), holds enticing performances—the Orquesta Sinfónica de Jalapa and the Ballet Folklórico de la Universidad Veracruzana appear regularly. The tourist office has posters for some events; contact the theater directly for schedules and ticket prices. From the *zócalo*, walk left on Enríquez and then left on Llave.

Jalapa also boasts a few moderately busy discos, including **Ya'x** at the **Plaza Crystal** (tel. 5-65-00) on the corner of Lázaro Cardenas. (Open daily from 10pm; 15 peso cover Sat. and Sun. nights only.) **Mama Mia** has live rock 'n roll, jazz, and other species of music on Wednesdays and Thursdays; look for prominently posted notices in town.

■■■ VERACRUZ

Upon reaching the east coast of New Spain in 1519, Hernán Cortés constructed a base from which he would launch one of the most effective military episodes in history. After the Spanish Conquest, his coastal headquarters grew into Veracruz, the principal city and main port in the state.

An English fleet took a Spanish beating here in 1567, but, unfortunately for the Spanish, Sir Francis Drake was among the few who escaped. Then, in 1683, 600 pirates, rowdy and French, held and looted the city. During the "Pastry War," President Santa Anna fled Veracruz but would soon return to expel the French invaders. Winfield Scott's 10,000 American troops took the city in 1847 after a week-long siege. Napoleon III had designs on all of Mexico, and used Veracruz as his toe-hold, installing Maximilian as ruler in 1864. Veracruz saw more action in the Revolution of 1910 and again in 1914, when American troops returned, this time to keep German guns from reaching Victoriano Huerta, the conservative dictator.

The crumbling fortresses along the coast bear witness to the extensive destruction, but these days their seaward-pointed cannon see no action save what the beachside revelers provide.

Music and dancing are higher priorities in Veracruz than in other Mexican cities. The number of marimba bands squeezed into the *zócalo* boggles the mind, and many restaurants and bars feature nightly music. In the evening, brassy military and civic bands blare through the plaza as the flag of the Republic is lowered. After the sun sets, the volume of the marimba bands and soulful crooners is elevated even further still.

As Mexico's major port on the Gulf Coast, Veracruz hosts sailors and merchants from around the world. A strong Caribbean accent lilts in the speech of some of the

VERACRUZ

locals, while others have a European inflection, and any number of regional Mexican accents will test the limits of your Spanish. Other cultures influence not just the city's voices but also its architecture, a graceful hybrid of the colonial and the modern. Although Veracruz offers a few standard tourist sights, the *zócalo* remains the biggest draw. Here, wandering vendors sell everything: t-shirts bearing random English slogans, mass-produced handicrafts, and even your name written on a grain of sand. Veracruz is quite popular with vacationing Mexicans; it is a busy port town, almost devoid of peace and quiet. Come here to dance and drink deep of a somewhat debauched marrow.

ORIENTATION

Veracruz lies on the southwestern shore of the Gulf of Mexico. Tampico is 421km to the north via Route 180; Jalapa, the state capital, sits 140km inland via Route 140; Puebla and Mexico City are due west on Route 150, 304km and 421km respectively; and Oaxaca is 421km to the south.

Veracruz's **Central de Autobuses** houses both the first- and second-class bus stations. First-class ADO lies directly on Díaz Mirón, the city's major cross-town street. Second-class AU opens onto La Fragua, one block to the east. About 14 blocks north of the Central de Autobuses (to the right when leaving the building) the *Parque Zamora* interrupts Mirón. Seven blocks on Independencia beyond the park, buildings give way to the *zócalo*. Buses labeled "Díaz Mirón" travel along Díaz Mirón to *Parque Zamora* and points farther downtown (.70 pesos). Taxis will take you downtown for 5 pesos.

The **train station** is at the north end of the Pl. de la República. To reach the *zócalo* from the station, turn right from the exit, walk diagonally across the plaza and turn right on Lerdo at the far end of the plaza; the *zócalo* is one block ahead. Taxis from the Central de Autobuses to the train station cost about 6 pesos. The city's **airport** is 4km south of town on Route 150. Taxis to the *zócalo* cost about 35 pesos.

Downtown Veracruz is laid out grid-style with streets either parallel or perpendicular to the coast. **Díaz Mirón** runs north-south and converges with **Avenida 20 de Noviembre** south of downtown at the **Parque Zamora**. Here, the two streets become **Independencia**, the main downtown drag.

Independencia forms the western boundary of the **zócalo**, also called the **Plaza de Armas** or **Plaza de la Constitución**. The northern boundary, **Lerdo**, runs east and becomes the southern limit of the **Plaza de la República**, home of the train station and post office, and drop-off point for many municipal bus routes. **Insurgentes**, one block south of the *zócalo* behind the cathedral, runs east into **Camacho**; the two streets serve as Veracruz's waterfront promenade.

Women may find themselves the object of more male attention in Veracruz than in smaller towns. The attention usually amounts to no more than invitations to discos and city tours from waiters, bank tellers, and random men on the street. Women may want to exercise caution when going out at night, however—a firm and polite refusal will be grudgingly accepted during the day, but at night it may well be taken as a challenge to overcome.

PRACTICAL INFORMATION

Most services are conveniently located downtown, either near the *zócalo*, on Independencia, or in the Pl. de la República.

Tourist Office: Dirección de Turismo. In the Palacio Municipal (tel. 32-19-99), on the *zócalo*. Helpful staff speaks some English and distributes reams of excellent maps and pamphlets. The photocopied map of downtown is especially useful. Open daily 9am-9pm.

U.S. Consulate: Víctimas del 25 Junio 388 (tel. 31-01-42). On the corner with Gómez Farias, several blocks south of the *zócalo*. Open Mon.-Fri. 9am-1:30pm.

The addresses and phone numbers of several other consulates in Veracruz are readily available at the tourist office.

Currency Exchange: Bancomer and **Bánamex** both have branches at the intersection of Independencia and Juárez, one block from the *zócalo*. **Bancomer** (tel. 31-07-07) is open for exchange Mon.-Fri. 9:30am-1:30pm. **Bánamex** (tel. 36-05-80) is open for exchange Mon.-Fri. 9am-1pm, and also has an automated teller that accepts Cirrus, MC, and Visa. **La Amistad Casa de Cambio,** Juárez 112 (tel. 31-24-50), just east of Independencia, offers slightly lower rates but is open Mon.-Fri. 9am-5pm. Front desks of the big hotels will change cash all hours, but it is difficult to impossible to change traveler's checks on weekends.

American Express, Camacho 222 (tel. 31-45-77), across from Villa del Mar beach. Catch the "Villa del Mar" bus from the corner of Serdán and Zaragoza; office is on the right—their blue and white sign is clearly visible. They won't cash traveler's checks, but will hold client mail. Open Mon.-Fri. 9am-1pm and 4-6pm, Sat. 9am-noon.

Post Office: Pl. de la República 213 (tel.32-20-38), several blocks north of the *zócalo*. Facing the Palacio Municipal, walk east on Lerdo for 2 blocks to Aduana, turn left and walk 2 blocks to Pl. de la República; it's the large white colonnaded building on the right. Open for stamps and *Lista de Correos* Mon.-Fri. 8am-8pm, Sat. 9am-1pm. **Postal code:** 91700.

Telephones: Long distance *caseta* at 5 de Mayo 1243, in between Molina and Serdán. Surcharge for collect calls is a whopping 20 pesos. Open Mon.-Sat. 9am-8pm, Sun. 9am-1pm. **Telephone code:** 29.

Telegrams: (tel. 32-25-08) on the Pl. de la República next to the post office. Open for telegrams Mon.-Fri. 9am-5pm, Sat. 9am-noon. For money orders Mon.-Fri. 9am-5pm, Sat 9am-noon.

Airport: (tel. 34-00-08) on the highway to Mexico City, 4km south of downtown Veracruz. Both **Aeroméxico** and **Mexicana** are represented by **Viajes Carmi,** Independencia 837 (tel. 31-27-23), north of the *zócalo*. Open Mon.-Fri. 9am-1pm and 3:30-7:30pm, Sat. 9am-1pm. **Mexicana** also has a separate office at the corner of 5 de Mayo and Serdán, north-east of the *zócalo* (tel. 32-22-42). Open Mon.-Fri. 9am-1:30pm and 3:45pm-7:30pm. Office at the airport (tel. 38-00-08). Open Mon.-Fri. 6am-11pm. 4 flights per day to Mexico City (50min., .30 pesos).

Train Station: Ferrocarriles Nacionales de México (tel. 32-25-69), on the Pl. de la República in a large, white bldg. near the water at the northern extreme of the plaza. Baggage check available. (Open 7am-noon and 6-9:30pm. 3 pesos per suitcase per day.) Slow, cheap trains leave for Mexico City and Jalapa every morning. Buy tickets the same day as the train. Ticket office opens at 6am.

Bus Station: Díaz Mirón 1698 (tel. 37-57-49), about 20 blocks south of the *zócalo*. **ADO** 1st class to: Mexico City (51.50 pesos, 1am, 6am., 4pm), to Jalapa (13.50 pesos, about every half hour), to Puebla (37 pesos 6:15am, 8:15am, 10:15am, 11:30am, 1:30pm, 3:15pm, 6pm, 11:30pm), to Santiago Tuxtla (14.50 pesos, aprox. every half hour), to José Cardel (5 pesos, about every half hour). 2nd class **AU** terminal sits behind the ADO terminal on La Fragua, 1 block east of Díaz Mirón.

Taxis: Taxis Por Teléfono de Veracruz (tel. 34-62-99) will send you a taxi at a slightly higher price than if you flag one down yourself. Veracruz is divided into zones, with set fares for taxi travel between the zones, which should be posted in the taxi. Fares outside these zones are negotiable.

Car Rentals: Fast Auto Rental, Lerdo 241 (tel. 31-83-29), between 5 de Mayo and Independencia. Open Mon.-Sat. 9am-2pm and 4-7pm, Sun. 9-11am. Small VWs for 137.50 pesos (includes insurance) plus .83 pesos per km. **Jomar,** in the Hotel Colonial (tel. 31-63-79). Small VWs for 80 pesos per day plus 35 pesos insurance and .605 pesos per km. Open Mon.-Sat. 9am-9pm, Sun. 9am-2pm.

Supermarket: Chedraui, Díaz Mirón 440 (tel. 31-42-75), 4 blocks south of *Parque Zamora* on the way to the ADO station. Open 8am-9pm.

Laundromat: Lavandería Automática Mar y Sol, Madero 572, between Arista and Serdán. 3kg washed and dried for 12 pesos for same day service, 9.70 pesos for next day pick-up. Open Mon.-Fri. 9am-2pm and 4-8pm, Sat. 9am-5pm.

VERACRUZ

Red Cross: On Díaz Mirón between Orizaba and L. Abascal (tel. 37-55-00) , 1 block south of the Central de Autobuses. No English spoken. 24-hr. emergency service and ambulance on call.

Pharmacy: Farmacias El Mercado, Independencia 1197 (tel. 32-08-83), next to the Gran Café de la Parroquia. Open daily 7am-2am.

Police: On Allende between Cortés and Canal (tel. 32-37-61 or 32-28-33). From the *zócalo*, walk (with the Palacio Municipal behind you) 7 blocks on Zamora and turn left on Allende for 5½ blocks. Little English spoken. Open 24 hrs.

ACCOMMODATIONS

Veracruz is full of hotels. You're looking for a ceiling fan or at least a big window. Many hotels offer air-conditioned rooms. If you're going to be in town anytime around the Carnaval (see Entertainment) book ahead or arrive early, as the city is jam-packed. Otherwise, reservations are unnecessary.

Downtown Area

These hotels are either on the *zócalo* or around the corner to the northeast, on Morelos.

Hotel Sevilla, Morelos 359 (tel. 32-42-46), on Pl. de la República. Just around the corner from the *zócalo*. Rooms to be happy in—high ceilings, color TV, clean bathrooms and quiet ceiling fans. Ask for a corner room to get a cross breeze (and cross-marimba). Singles 50 pesos. Doubles 60 pesos. Triples 70 pesos.

Casa de Huéspedes La Tabasqueña, Morelos 325 (no telephone) 100m north of Hotel Sevilla, this small operation rents cozy rooms, some with no windows, all with working fans and thin walls. Singles 30 pesos. Doubles 45 pesos.

Hotel Concha Dorada, Lerdo 77 (tel. 31-29-96), on the *zócalo*. Hey, Man! Groovy '70s spreads! 100% poly, right? Nice rooms. Dreary hallways. Terrifying elevator. Notable primarily for its air-conditioning and prime (read: musical revellers yards from your pillow) location. Many singles have no A.C., making them of questionable value. Singles 60 pesos. Doubles 100 pesos.

Parque Zamora and Bus Station

Hotel Avenida, Uribe 1300 (tel. 32-44-92), at Mirón, about halfway between *Parque Zamora* and the bus stations. These rooms lose their sunlight-enhanced charm at night. Clean and neat. Location fairly inconvenient, despite proximity to Díaz Mirón. Singles 30 pesos. Doubles 40 pesos. Triples 50 pesos.

Hotel Acapulco, Uribe 1327 (tel. 31-88-97), down the street from Hotel Avenida. Slightly more expensive and slightly nicer than its neighbor. Clean, functional. Singles 39 pesos. Doubles 48 pesos. Anytime the city is crowded prices rise to Singles 60 pesos. Doubles 75 pesos.

Hotel Central, Díaz Mirón 1612 (tel. 32-22-22), next to the ADO station. Large, modern building with marble lobby and leatherette easy chairs. Rooms and bathrooms likewise: modern and sanitary. Watch cars race by on Díaz Mirón from rooms with a balcony. All rooms have fans, phones; most have a TV. Singles 50 pesos. Doubles 70 pesos, with 2 beds 90 pesos.

Hotel Rosa Mar, La Fragua 1100 (tel. 37-07-47), behind the ADO station and across the street from AU station. The location is nothing to holler about unless you're just passing through Veracruz, in which case it's very convenient. Small, but spotlessly clean, swimming-pool green rooms. Communal TV in lobby. Singles 35 pesos. Doubles 55 pesos.

FOOD

It's that coastal thing—all the menus in Veracruz are stuffed with seafood. Shrimp, octopus, *dorada*, red snapper, and a host of other sea beasts are hauled in daily from the Gulf. The cheapest way to enjoy these delicacies is to head for the **fish market** on Landero y Coss between Arista and Zaragoza. A healthy portion of *ceviche*, the regional specialty, runs about 3.50 pesos. Other local favorites include

VERACRUZ

paella (whatever happens to be on hand, mixed with saffron rice) and fish served *a la veracruzano* (in an olive, onion, tomato and caper sauce). The greatest concentrations of restaurants are on and around the *zócalo* and in the area east of Zaragoza. Cheaper *antojitos* and *torta* restaurants are located further south of the *zócalo*.

Gran Café de la Parroquia, Independencia 105, on the southwest corner of the *zócalo*. Drink its famous *café con leche*, in a large open hall filled with the sound of clinking glasses (the preferred method of getting more hot milk for your coffee). *Marimba* bands serenade the patrons from the outside. Large coffee 3 pesos. Big plate of papaya 3 pesos. Open daily 6am-1am. Less crowded with consequently better and friendlier service at the 2nd location, Insurgentes at 16 de Septiembre. Open daily 8am-2am.

Cocina Veracruz, on the corner of Madero and Zamora. A pearl of a place. Escape the inflated prices of the *zócalo* and the waterfront. Great food and a fully local crowd. Soup with vegetables 2 pesos. Delicious *comida corrida* 4.50 pesos. Eggs to taste 3.50 pesos. Newsprint for napkins. Open daily 7am-11pm.

Pizzería Piro Piro Da Antonio, Arista 692 (tel. 31-61-44), between Independencia and Zaragoza. Excellent pizza with thick floury crust and hundreds of pictures of Italy all over the walls. Also pasta and beer by the yard. (Very) small cheese pizza 10 pesos. Large cheese pizza 36 pesos.Open daily 9am-1am. Buffet served 11am-5pm.

El Tiburón, Landero y Coss 167 (tel. 31-47-40), at Serdán. Lots of tables with messproof vinyl tablecloths in a big room clearly devoted to the art of eating without distractions. Filet of fish and salad 16 pesos. Most meat dishes under 23 pesos. Open daily 6am-7pm.

SIGHTS

Most of the spiritual energy in Veracruz concentrates on the *zócalo*, and the most energy you must expend here to stay entertained involves moving from café to café around the plaza. A colonial cathedral takes up the south side of the *zócalo*, and under its high-domed mosaic ceiling, the clinking of glasses at the nearby *Parroquia* is barely audible.

For one take on the city's history, visit the **Museo Histórico de la Revolución Carranza** by a small park near the waterfront, on Insurgentes between Hernández and Xicoléncatl. The museum, also called Museo Constitucionalista, is upstairs and to the left in a yellow colonial lighthouse which also houses offices of the Mexican Navy. When entering the building, do not approach the armed sailor at the door. Stay to your right, and polite Navy personnel will direct you upstairs. One room contains Carranza's bed, desk and furniture, replicating the room in which ideas for reform laws and the Constitution germinated and grew. Another room traces Carranza's life from baptism to his term as governor of Coahuila state. A third room marks his presidency and participation in writing the Constitution of 1917, three years before his death. The sailor at the museum's front desk can provide you with a written guide explaining (in English) many of the exhibits. (Open Tues.-Sun. 9am-1pm and 4-6pm. Free.) For a deeper glimpse into the past, visit the **Baluarte de Santiago,** on 16 de Septiembre between Canal and Rayón. This 17th-century bulwark protected inhabitants from swashbuckling pirates like Francis Drake. It is the last fort still standing along the old city wall. The tiny museum inside the fort displays a beautiful collection of pre-Hispanic gold ornaments. (Museum open Tues.-Sun. 10am-4:30pm.)

The **Museo Cultural de la Ciudad,** Zaragoza 397 (tel. 31-84-10) at Morales, is a funky museum set in an old orphanage. Check out the displays of Latin American and African anthropology, photos of the city, and scenes from daily life. (Open Mon.-Sat. 9am-4pm. Admission 3 pesos.)

Around the corner from the Museo Cultural de la Ciudad lurks the **Instituto Veracruzano de Cultura** (IVEC), ensconced in a huge purple building on the corner of Canal and Zaragoza (tel. 31-69-67). Temporary exhibits feature work from accomplished art students throughout Mexico. (Open Mon.-Fri. 9am-9pm, Sat. 9am-7pm, Sun. 10am-noon. Free.)

El Castillo de San Juan de Ulúa, begun in 1582, is another reminder of the city's former military importance. There isn't much to see inside the fort, but its architecture is intriguing, and the view across the harbor to the city is superb. To reach the fort, take the bus of the same name (.70 pesos) from the east side of the Pl. de la República, in front of the Aduana building. (Open Tues.-Sun. 9am-5pm (no one admitted after 4:30). Admission 13 pesos. Free Sun.)

Once upon a time, bathing was possible directly off the golden shores of the city. Today, however, the bay is a case study of the toxic impact of big oil on big cities. Locals still swim in the water, but, considering the health risk, the short trip south to **Playa Villa del Mar** is a better idea. The beach is fairly clean and reasonably uncrowded. Restaurants, juice-bars, and some expensive hotels line **Blvd. Camacho** across the street from the beach. Playa Villa del Mar is a fairly pleasant hour-long walk from the *zócalo* along the waterfront, or catch one of the frequent buses from the corner of Serdán and Zaragoza (.90 pesos for the big rickety buses, 1.20 pesos for the smaller, more modern vans; both have either "Villa del Mar" or "Boca del Mar" plainly visible on the front). Beyond **Villa del Mar, Boca del Río, Antón,** and **Linzaro** offer increasingly acceptable swimming conditions. The brand-new aquarium, billed as the largest in Latin America can be reached on the bus; ask to be let off at *El Acuario* or *Playón de Hornas.*

ENTERTAINMENT

The city's best entertainment is free in the *zócalo*, at least in December and in the summer months when musicians, dancers and clowns entertain every night except Monday. Performances begin at 8pm, but the audience begins to gather at 7pm.

Discotheque La Capilla, Independencia 1064, in the Hotel Prendes between Lerdo and Juárez, plays top-40 spiced with some local *mariachi* pieces. (Open Thurs.-Sat. 10pm-3:30am. There is no cover per se, but a 20 peso drink minimum instead.) The **Disco Morruchos,** in the Hotel Emporio at Insurgentes and Xicoléncatl on the water (tel. 31-38-20), is a bit more chic but plays the same tunes. (Open Thurs.-Sat. 11pm-4am. Cover 10 pesos.) The hippest disco is also the most expensive: **Ocean,** Ruiz Cortines y Callo 8 (tel. 37-63-27), in Playa del Mar charges a 40 peso cover. Cough up the pesos and boogy amidst elaborate fountains, pulsing lights, and lush greenery.

Bars are ubiquitous in Veracruz. The entire north side of the *zócalo* is a series of indistinguishable bars serenaded by *marimba* bands and solicited by Chiclets-pushers (beers 4 pesos). For cheaper, tuneless fare, try one of the many indoor bars located on and near Landero y Coss, east of the *zócalo.*

If a dark, cold room full of strangers suddenly appeals to you, Veracruz has several **cinemas.** For English language films, check out **Plaza Cinema,** Arista 708, next to Pizzería Piro Piro Da Antonio (tel. 31-37-87). At Díaz Mirón 941, between Iturbide and Mina, is **Cinema Gemelos Veracruz** (tel. 32-59-70). Admission for all cinemas 8 pesos.

Billares Maupome, at the intersection of Landero y Coss and Serdán, charges 8 pesos per hour for one of their ten well-maintained pool tables. If you ask nicely, they'll even tune the TV set to cable-delivered CNN (Open daily 9am-midnight.)

Veracruz's **Carnaval**—a nationally renowned, week-long festival of parades, concerts and costumes—takes place in late February or early March (during the week before Ash Wednesday). For further information on *Carnaval*, contact the offices of the organizers, in the Palacio Municipal on the *zócalo* (tel. 36-10-88, ext. 149 or 32-99-62), right next door to the tourist office. (Open Mon.-Fri. 10am-2pm and 6:30-8:30pm.) Make reservations early.

■ Near Veracruz: Zempoala Ruins and José Cardel

One of the most impressive archaeological sites in the state of Veracruz, the ruins at Zempoala (or just as often, Cempoala) lie 40 kilometers north of Veracruz, just off Route 180. Buses from Veracruz run frequently to nearby José Cardel, making the ruins an easy and edifying excursion.

Zempoala was one of the largest southern Totonac cities, part of a federation that covered much of Veracruz in pre-Hispanic times. In 1469, Zempoala was subdued by the Aztecs and reluctantly joined their federation. Thus, when Cortés arrived in 1519, the Totonacs and their chief, Chicomacatl (famous, primarily, for having been enormously fat), welcomed the Spaniard and lent him soldiers for his campaign against Moctezuma at Tenochtitlan in 1521. It was at Zempoala that Cortés defeated (and imprisoned) Panfilo de Narváez, who had been sent by Diego de Velázquez, the governor of Cuba, to teach the cocky *conquistador* some respect for his higher-ups.

To reach Zempoala from Veracruz, you must first take a bus to José Cardel; a trip of 45 minutes. From its Central on Díaz Mirón, ADO runs first-class buses to José Cardel (about every half hour, 5.50 pesos). From the second-class bus station on La Fragua, Autotransportes Teziutecos makes the same trip (every 10 minutes, 5am-9:30pm. 2.60 pesos). In José Cardel, ADO buses stop on Independencia, two blocks from the southeast corder of the *zócalo*. The second-class bus station lives on the south side of the *zócalo*.

To reach Zempoala from José Cardel, catch a *colectivo* (1 peso) one block east and one block north of the northeast corner of the *zócalo*, ask the driver to let you out at *las ruinas*. The trip takes about 10 minutes. In Zempoala, you will be dropped off at the intersection of Av. Prof. José Ruiz and Av. Fco. del Paso y Troncoso Norte. Walk 100m on Fco. del Paso y Troncoso Norte, where a small ticket booth marks the entrance to the site. If driving from Veracruz, follow Route 180 past the city of José Cardel until you come to the Zempoala city turn-off. Follow it until a half-hidden sign for the ruins appears on the right (about 1km before town; the sign has a Coca Cola insignia on top and "Sitio Arqueológico" on the bottom). A microscopic museum, to your left as you enter, displays a small collection of pottery and figurines unearthed here, and sells a much-needed English mini-guide to the ruins (3 pesos).

The large structure at the north end of the site is the Main Temple, with a wide staircase ascending its front. Just south and to the right of the Main Temple is a structure known as Las Chimeneas, wherein was found a Mayan-like clay figure. In front of the Main Temple and Las Chimeneas are two somewhat mysterious "Round Structures."

The Great Pyramid, probably a monument to the Sun God, and the smaller Temple of the Wind God are at the western boundary of the site, off to your left (beyond the museum) as you enter. (Site open daily 9am-6pm, 10 pesos. Free for students and teachers with I.D. Free Sun.) catch a *colectivo* back to José Cardel across the street from where you were dropped off. If you can't stand the heat, get out of the kitchen or catch a cab (about 20 pesos back to José Cardel). Buses run all afternoon and into the evening.

Because of Cardel's proximity to Veracruz, there is really no reason to stay the night. Should the need arise, however, **José Cardel** has all the amenities. Most services cluster either around the *zócalo* or by the first class ADO bus station. On the southeast corner of the *zócalo*, **Farmacia Santiago** (2-04-31) is open daily from 7am-10pm. Across the street is **Supermarket Mi Super** (Open Mon-Sat. 7am-8pm. Sun. 7am-2pm.) The **police** station (2-03-52) is in the Palacio Municipal, on the north side of the *zócalo*. The **Red Cross** (tel. 2-02-26. 24 hr. ambulance service) is four blocks west of the *zócalo* on Emiliano Zapata, the street leading into town from Route 180. **Bancomer,** on the south side of the *zócalo*, is open for exchange Mon.-

Fri. 9am-noon. Small **restaurants,** *refresco* stands and a movie theater round out the *zócalo*. **Hotel Plaza** (tel. 2-02-88) sits across from the ADO bus station and offers huge, frilly, pastel rooms, each with A/C and color TV. (Singles 50 pesos, doubles 70 pesos.) The restaurant in the lobby is open daily 7am-11pm.

SOUTHERN VERACRUZ

The polluted ports of Coatzacoalcos and Veracruz flank the most enticing stretch of Mexico's Gulf Coast. The verdant, rolling volcanic hills beckon to visitors in vain— the area remains virtually untouristed (and cool) even in summer. Only Laguna Catemaco draws a heavy (domestic) crowd to its shores in season. Catemaco monopolizes the area's fun-in-the-sun business because of its proximity both to fine beaches on the lake and to some of Mexico's best Gulf Coast beaches. Nearby San Andrés Tuxtla, the region's largest city and unofficial capital, offers a healthy range of hotels and restaurants and swanky Mexican cigars. San Andrés also has excellent bus connections to Catemaco, Santiago Tuxtla, the Tres Zapotes ruin site and larger cities such as Veracruz and Mexico City. Horseback riding and hiking are popular outside San Andrés. In Santiago Tuxtla, the only other town of note in the Dos Tuxtlas, life is even slower than in Catemaco. With only two hotels and a small museum, the fastest moves in town are made at the *zócalo*'s foosball tables.

Route 180 is the main artery of the Dos Tuxtlas area. From Acayucán in the south, it passes north to Catemaco, San Andrés and Santiago Tuxtla before continuing along the coast to Veracruz. All sights outside these three cities lie on secondary dirt roads served by local buses.

▪▪▪ CATEMACO

Catemaco rests beside a large lake on the green volcanic slopes of the Tuxtlas range. The town is tremendously popular with Mexican tourists during *Semana Santa,* Christmas and the summer holidays. On the first Friday in March, Catemaco hosts an annual gathering of shaman, medicine men, and witches from all over Mexico— hence the profusion of *brujos* (sorcerers) in business establishment names. For disbelievers, swimming and scenic lake-isles, bars and dance clubs, suffice to entertain.

Practical Information Although Catemaco lies along Route 180, few first class **ADO buses** stop here on journeys north or south to major cities; you usually have to change in San Andrés and catch another bus to Catemaco. Buses run frequently from Catemaco to major cities like Mexico, Veracruz and Jalapa, as well as to San Andrés Tuxtla and Santiago Tuxtla. Streets in Catemaco are poorly marked, but the basilica on the *zócalo* is usually visible. **Carranza** runs along the west side of the *zócalo*, while **Aldama** runs parallel on the east side (closer to the lake). They are both unlabeled, but between the *zócalo*, with its landmark basilica, and the road that follows the lake (called either Playa or Malecón), it's difficult to lose your way. The entire town can be covered on foot in 10 minutes, and all services crowd around the *zócalo*. The **ADO** station sits on Aldama north of the *zócalo*, one block behind the basilica. **Autotransportes Los Tuxtlas** stops two blocks south of the *zócalo*, on Cuahtemoc, which runs parallel to, and one block north of, Aldama.

Las Brisas Hotel, Carranza 3 (tel. 3-00-57), provides **tourist information.** Sr. Moreno is the official "State Tourist Coordinator" for Catemaco and the coastal areas. He speaks no English but will gladly show you a map of the region. **Multibanco Comermex** (tel. 3-01-15), on the *zócalo* exchanges traveler's checks only Mon.-Fri. 10am-noon. **Post office,** Mantilla, in between the lake and Hotel Los Arcos. (Open Mon.-Fri. 9am-1pm and 3-6pm, Sat. 9am-1pm. Usually open all afternoon, contrary to official hours. **Postal Code:** 95870.) Official **telephone** *caseta* does not allow international collect calls, but the larger hotels may let you call collect for a hefty fee. Best bet: call from elsewhere. **Telephone Code:** 294. **ADO buses** leave for Jalapa (7am, 31.50 pesos), Mexico City (9:30am, 65.50 pesos), and Veracruz (11 per day, 17 pesos). You may be better off heading first to San Andres. **Autotransportes Los Tuxtlas** makes the trip every 10 minutes for 1.30 pesos. **Farmacia Nuestra Sra. del Carmen,** at the corner of Carranza and Boettinger (tel. 3-00-91), attached to the Hotel Acuario, is open daily 7am-2pm and 3:30-9pm. **Centro de Salud,** on Carranza (tel. 3-02-47), 3 blocks south of the zócalo, on the left, provides medical services. Near the *colinita* (little hill) on the way out of town toward Coatzacoalcos, in a 1-story white bldg. with a bright blue roof (not clearly marked otherwise). (Open 24 hrs.) The **police** are in the Palacio Municipal (tel. 3-00-55), on the *zócalo*. (Open 24 hrs.)

Accommodations and Food There are plenty of hotels in Catemaco. The majority are grouped near the *zócalo* or along the lakefront. During *Semana Santa* and Christmas, hotels are fully booked and more expensive. Meanwhile, dozens of young Mexicans and members of the international beard-and-sandal brigade gather on the beach, packing guitars, harmonicas and sleeping bags. **Hotel Julita,** Playa 20 (tel. 3-00-08), on the waterfront, is probably the best deal in Catemaco. Great location and large, clean rooms around a plant and flower-filled courtyard with chairs for hanging out. Restaurant downstairs. (Singles 25 pesos. Doubles 50 pesos.) **Hotel Acuario,** Boettinger at Carranza (tel. 3-04-18), on the *zócalo* provides large, clean rooms with tiny soaps in spotless bathrooms. Bedspreads with little tulips make you feel young at heart. Dark naval prints on walls seem misplaced and may confuse. Ask for a room with a balcony; there are a few. (Singles 20 pesos. Doubles 40 pesos.)

Restaurants along the waterfront specialize in shrimp, cooked any way you like it. The restaurants differ primarily in their view of the lake rather than in the price or quality of their cuisine. The best of them is **Restaurant La Casona del Recuerdo,** Aldama 6, just off the *zócalo* (tel. 3-05-76). Stately entrance leads to a beautiful porch with a view of the lake through a wooded garden. *Comida corrida* a surprisingly reasonable 10 pesos. *Sopa de mariscos* 24.50 pesos. Open daily 8am-8pm. **El Pescador,** on Playa and Bravo, to the left coming down from the *zócalo* (tel. 3-06-25), is an airy restaurant with great lake view. Fish 15-30 pesos. Beer 2 pesos. (Open daily 9am-9pm.) The hot cakes are a 4 pesos steal at **Restaurant La Ola**, on Playa across from Hotel Julita, if you're not too put off by the alligator kept in a small, dirty cage. (Open Mon.-Sat. 8am-8:30pm, Sun. 8am-10pm.) The color theme is blue and white at **Restaurant La Suiza,** right next door to El Pescador (tel. 3-08-74). This matches the lake and the ubiquitous Corona beach chairs. Excellent shrimp any which way you like it for 16 pesos. (Open daily 8am-9pm.)

Sights and Entertainment The rocky beaches of **Laguna Catemaco** inspire no hyperbole, but the swimming is safe and pleasant. A hiking path runs along the edge of the lake—walk down from the *zócalo* to the waterfront and turn left—transporting you 1.5km to **Playa Expagoya** and to the more secluded and sandy **Playa Hermosa** 0.5km down the road.

The lake is nearly circular, about 15km across. Several small islands dot its smooth surface and dozens of small outboard *lanchas* lie in wait to take you on an hour-long trip to the best-known of the lot, **Isla de Changos.** A tribe of semi-wild, red-cheeked *changos* (mandrills, a kind of baboon), brought from Africa for a scientific experiment, have thrived on the island. Knowing that the *lancha* operators bring coconuts and tortillas, the bravest *changos* climb right into the boat to pose for camera shots and collect their reward. En route to the island, you'll pass close to a cave-shrine that stands on the spot where a woman had a vision of the Virgin Mary over a century ago. The *lanchas* leave from the docking area below the *zócalo*. Launch prices are pre-set and clearly posted. A standard tour of the lake, including the Isla de Changos and the shrine of The Virgin, costs 120 pesos for one to six passengers and 25 pesos for each additional passenger. To see only the Isla de Changos will cost 70 pesos for one to six passengers. Negotiate with the *lanchistas* for longer trips, including an exploration of the rivers that feed the lake. Many of the *lanchistas* know something about the birds that live along the lake.

Catemaco's **bars** and **discos** are the best in the area, serving just as many residents of the Tuxtlas as those of Catemaco itself. **Chanequa's,** in the Hotel Playa Azul (tel. 3-00-42 or 3-00-01), some distance outside of Catemaco, is said to be the hottest. It is possible to walk there, but somewhat difficult and, at night, dangerous. A launch will take you to the hotel for 20 pesos. The **7 Brujas** (tel. 3-01-57) on Playa behind the *zócalo*, is in a nifty wooden circular building on the lakefront. It's well-advertised and serves a many non-Catemacans. (Beers 2.5 pesos, cocktails 11 pesos. Open Tues.-Sun. 7am-10pm.) There's a disco above **Restaurant La Luna** (open Sat. and Sun. after 9pm; cover 5 pesos) and another above **El Pescador** (open Fri. and Sat. 9pm-3am; cover 10-15 pesos). Both are big with the locals.

■ Near Catemaco

Buses operated by **Autotransportes Los Dos Tuxtlas** (the line without mufflers) leave regularly for the coast between 7am and 6pm. From Catemaco, the bus rockets down through miles of picturesque green slopes before finally approaching the ocean. Soon after passing a series of small resorts, it arrives at the intersection of two dirt roads, an hour-and-a-half from Catemaco. Here a small, faded sign makes the modest announcement: "Playa Escondida, El Edén de Dios." A pretty beach but beware the fierce undertow.

Few tourists visit the small villages near the sandbar or the beaches at the lagoon's mouth. Fishing people there sometimes give stray foreigners a hard time, especially those intending to spend the night. At the La Palma intersection, the right fork leads to two lakeside settlements, **La Barra** and **El Real.** Sometimes, if you introduce yourself to locals, especially to those living or working nearby, they'll show you a modicum of hospitality; they often allow *viajeros* to set up camp near their homes.

The next intersection after La Palma leads to Dos Tuxtlas's most beautiful beaches, Playas Jicacal and Escondida. From the road where the bus drops off passengers, make the hilly but beautiful 1km walk through meadows, streams and woodland to **Playa Jicacal,** an extensive crescent of gently sloping white sand populated by a few fishing families. Campers who wish to spend the night here would do best to ingratiate themselves with the *jicacaleños*, thereby increasing the safety of their stay on the beach. After Jicacal, the access road bends left and ascends the jutting cliff that divides Jicacal from Playa Escondida.

Atop the hill, 1km beyond the beach on this road, **Hotel Playa Escondida** commands a magnificent view of Jicacal, to the right, and Escondida, to the left. The restaurant here is moderately priced and serves adequate food—a lucky break, given that the next closest eating establishment is tucked away in Sontecomopán. The neat and well-furnished rooms are also a pretty good deal. (Singles about 5 pesos. Doubles about 6 pesos.) Some rooms have views of the crescent bays. **Playa Escondida** (Hidden Beach) lives up to its name: it's a hot, 10-minute hike to the beach.

■■■ SAN ANDRÉS TUXTLA

If you were to rob a bank and escape to Mexico, you might consider retiring in San Andrés Tuxtla (usually just "San Andrés." A quiet, content little town, San Andrés offers no more or less than a cache of budget hotels, an entertaining zócalo, suprisingly friendly people, and some nearby natural attractions.

Practical Information San Andrés lies midway between Catemaco and Santiago Tuxtla on Route 180. Buses run frequently to all nearby destinations as well as to more distant points such as Oaxaca, Tampico, Mexico City, Jalapa and Veracruz. The first class **ADO bus station** lies at the edge of town, at the intersection of Route 180 and Juárez, which leads to *el centro*. When leaving the station, turn left and walk downhill toward the *zócalo*. The walk takes about 10 minutes; a taxi will charge 2.50 pesos to most points downtown. **AU** and **Cuenca** share a smaller terminal just across the street from ADO; a right turn from the terminal takes you down Juárez to *el centro*. **Autotransportes Los Tuxtlas** (usually called "Las Rojas" by the locals, owing to the color scheme of their vehicles) runs a bus to Catemaco every 10 minutes and to Santiago Tuxtla slightly less often. (Daily 6am-6pm. Both trips cost 1 peso.) Cuenca goes to Tuxtepec for 16 pesos (4:40am, 8am, 12:50pm, 6pm) and to Oaxaca for 35 pesos (6pm). ADO goes to Tampico for 87 pesos (1:10pm, 5:40pm, 8:30pm, 11pm) to Jalapa for 27.50 pesos (12.20am, 1:10am, 7:30am, 8:30am, 2pm, 2:20pm), to Mexico City for 64 pesos (1:10pm, 4pm, 9pm, 9:45pm, 10pm, 10:15pm, 11pm), and to Veracruz (about every ½hr.)

San Andrés is built on and around a volcanic range that hugs the Gulf Coast. The downtown area lies in the slightly raised center of a valley. Branching off Route 180, **Juárez**, the city's main street, descends a steep hill, crosses a small stream and gradually ascends to the cathedral, the *zócalo* at its north corner. As Route 180 swings around north of the city, it becomes Blvd. 5 de Febrero.

For tourist information, you can try **Turística Sanandrescana** (tel. 2-33-55), a friendly travel agency at Zamora 299, four blocks north of Piño Suárez, on the left. Open Mon.-Fri. 9am-2pm and 4-8pm, Sat. 9am-2pm. Exchange your money at **Banamex** (tel. 2-03-50), on the south side of the *zócalo*. (Open for exchange Mon.-Fri. 9am-1:30pm.) They also have an automatic teller that accepts Cirrus cards. The **post office** is at La Fragua and 20 de Noviembre (tel 2-01-89), 1 block from the *zócalo*. Open Mon.-Fri. 8am-8pm, Sat. 9am-1pm. **Postal code:** 95700. **Pipisoles**, Madero 6B has 3 larga distancia casetas, and charges 3.70 pesos for collect calls. (Open Mon.-Fri 8am-9pm, Sat. 8am-2pm and 5-9pm, Sun. 8am-2pm and 6-10pm.) **Lavandería Tintorería Roxy** (tel. 2-12-94), at Agosto 776, will wash and dry 3 kilos of your dirtiest for 10 pesos. (Open Mon.-Sat. 8am-8pm.) **Farmacia El Fénix**, Juárez 2 (tel. 2-27-27), across from the cathedral is open Mon.-Sat. 8am-9pm, Sun. 8am-8pm. The **Red Cross** is at Boca Negra 25 (tel. 2-05-00), north of the *zócalo*. Open 24 hrs. Ask for *servicio de ambulancia* to go directly to the hospital at the edge of town. The **police** are located on Pasaje Rascón, in the south side of the Palacio Municipal (tel. 2-02-35. Open 24 hrs.) The **State Police** are on Zamora, 3 blocks north of Piño Suárez, on the right.

Accommodations and Food

San Andrés remains almost tourist-free; budget accommodations are abundant and unfailingly available (without reservations). Three of the best hotels are within spitting distance of each other, just north of the *zócalo*, behind the cathedral. All three hotels have abundant hot water, but during warm weather, you may have to ask the management to spark it up. The bright and cheerful yellow and green rooms at **Hotel Figueroa**, Pino Suárez 10 (tel. 2-02-57), at Belisario Domínguez across from the Colonial, 1 block east and 2 north of the *zócalo*, is run by a friendly family. Unfortunately, the bugs that stream in at night seem to have carried away all the toilet seats. A pokey little dog named Cookie completes the picture. (Singles 20 pesos. Doubles 35 pesos, with two beds 40 pesos.) The rooms are clean if not well-maintained at **Hotel Colonial**, Pino Suárez 7 (tel. 2-05-52), at Belisario Domínguez. You get what you pay for; in this case, you pay for big, run-down rooms, great views, a laid-back atmosphere and even a roof suitable for sunning. A fabulous bargain for couples who like to look at each other instead of the room they're in. (Singles 15 pesos. Doubles 20 pesos, with 2 beds 25 pesos.)

Several sidewalk cafés on the *zócalo* serve breakfast and large coffees, and afford ample opportunity to watch the morning activity of San Andrean citizens. A number of good lunch spots line Madero past the more expensive hotels, while the cheapest sidewalk stands proliferate in the market and its environs. **Restaurant La Caperu-**

cita (tel 2-05-11), at Juárez 108, achieves a beach-side feel with its palapa-shaded outdoor dining area. Eggs to taste from 4 pesos. In the afternoon, a large Hawaiian pizza will run you 18 pesos. (Open daily 7am-4pm and 5pm-12 midnight.) In the evening, a chic, young crowd gathers for *cockteles* and conversation at **Restaurant del Parque,** Madero 5, in the Hotel del Parque on the *zócalo*. This is where the wealthy *políticos* make deals over coffee and spend hours attempting to look busy while they check out attractive passersby. Excellent service. Delicious chicken soup 5 pesos. *Café con leche grande* 4 pesos. (Open daily 8am-11:30pm.) Ask for whatever's cooking at **Restaurant El Pequeño Archie,** on Pino Suárez across from Cine San Andrés; it's bound to be delicious. *Comida corrida* 7.50 pesos. Open wall affords a great view of the action on the street. (Open daily 8:30am-11pm.)

Sights and Entertainment Outside the *zócalo*, San Andrés is a bit of a vacuum. Then again, there are cigars. If your sole acquaintance with the manufacture of cigars comes from one episode of *I Love Lucy,* a visit to the Santa Clara cigar factory outlet is definitely in order. From the *zócalo*, walk up to Juárez to the ADO and turn right—it's about 200m down Route 180 (here called Blvd. 5 de Febrero) on the right. The smell of tobacco may knock you over momentarily, but when you recover, the amiable and talkative staff will let you wander through the factory, where workers make cigars by hand.

Cigars sold at the factory office (in the same building) cost less than those in downtown San Andrés. Keep in mind that customs regulations in most countries limit the number of cigars that can be taken across the border, and you can't ship them. (See customs information in Mexico Essentials for more information.) *Ejecutivos* come in attractive cedar boxes with Santa Clara's name and your initials burned on the cover. Twenty-five of their best cigars will set you back 100 pesos, but the stogies start at around 30 pesos. (Open Mon.-Sat. 9am-1pm and 3-7pm.)

Nightlife is virtually nonexistent in San Andrés, but the bars and discos in Catemaco fill the gap well. **Cinema Lux** at the south end of Piño Suárez often shows North American films. Admission is 5 pesos.

■ Near San Andrés

From their station on Route 180, **Autotransportes Los Tuxtlas** runs buses to Catemaco and the Gulf Coast, Santiago Tuxtla and Tres Zapotes, and one or two other popular tourist destinations.

La Laguna Encantada is a volcanic lake 2km northeast of the city, known mainly for its queer tendency to rise during dry season and fall during the rainy season. It makes a nice walk of about an hour. To get there, walk north on Serapio Rendón (perpendicular to, and a couple of blocks north of, Piño Suárez) until you hit Blvd. 5 de Febrero (route 180). Walk east on 5 de Febrero until a sign for the lake appears on the left. Taxis will take you there for 5 pesos, but returning, it's a seller's market.

The more accessible **Salto de Eyipantla** waterfall (*cascada*) makes a beautiful trip. From a distance, an impressive volume of muddy white water pours over a cliff. Other, lesser falls create a solid wall of mist, coating everything at one end of the gorge with a fine dew. Unfortunately, the *cascadas* are not the idyllic retreat most of the 12 movies filmed there would make them out to be. *Refresco* stands and seashell jewelry vendors proliferate. Small children haunt each and every of the 246 stairs to the falls, begging for money and offering their services as guides. Much of the area directly next to the falls has been paved with concrete, to facilitate the *refresco* business. Fortunately, access both to and from the falls is extremely easy. Minibuses leave every half hour from the market at San Andrés and from the falls and charge only 1 peso for the 30-minute ride.

■ Santiago Tuxtla and Tres Zapotes Ruins

Santiago Tuxtla is a tiny, tranquil daydream of a town, an amiable, if sleepy, destination in itself or a staging point for a trip to the Tres Zapotes ruins, whence the Olmecs once reigned over a sizable area.

Olmec civilization spent a happy adolescence in the area of Northern Tabasco and Southern Veracruz and passed on important aspects of its religion, architecture and daily life to the Maya and Aztecs. Nothing but cornfields and grassy mounds remain at the actual site of Tres Zapotes, but the museums in Santiago and the small village of Tres Zapotes, near the ruins, are interesting.

The ADO bus station (tel. 7-04-28) in Santiago sits on Av. Morelos, right off Route 180. From here, ADO runs first-class buses to san Andrés Tuxtla (.50 pesos, 8:05am, 8:30am, 8:35am, 9:20am, 10:20am, 11:20am, 12:30pm, 1:30pm, 2:30pm, 3pm, 3:15pm, 4:20pm, 4:30pm, 5pm, 6pm, 10:30pm, 10:35pm, 11:50pm) and to Veracruz (16 pesos, 6:15am, 7:35am, 9:15am, 9:45am, 10:20am, 1:15pm, 2:50pm, 3:15pm, 4:45pm, 5:05pm, 6:50pm, 8:15pm). The second-class bus station, served primarily by Autotransportes Los Tuxtlas, is also on Morelos, 100m downhill and across the street from ADO.

To reach Santiago's *zócalo*, walk three blocks on Ayuntamiento, away from Route 180 and toward the clock tower. The *zócalo* is laid out with its four corners at the compass points, Ayuntamiento leads into the *zócalo* at its east corner. At the far end of the *zócalo* the largest **Olmec head** ever discovered (40 tons) sits complacently, shaded from the sun by a large cupola. The sculpture is immediately recognizable as Olmec because of its distinctive facial features (heavy lips and slanted eyes), ears, and "helmet." The foosball tables in front of it comprise the town's main source of nightly entertainment. The **Museo Regional Tuxteco,** at the east corner of the *zócalo,* on Ayuntamiento at Zaragoza, displays an interesting collection of Olmec and Totonac artifacts, mostly clay figurines, pottery and small sculptures. On the museum's small, covered lawn sits another enormous Olmec head. (Museum open Mon.-Sat. 9am-6pm, Sun. 9am-3pm. Admission 10 pesos. Free Sun.)

Hotel Castellanos (tel. 7-03-00 or 7-04-00), at the west corner of the *zócalo,* has Santiago's finest rooms. Each chamber of this tall, circular tower yields a magnificent panorama of the town and surrounding countryside, along with the pool out back. The beautiful, pie-shaped, wood-panelled rooms each have TV, A/C, immaculate tiled bathrooms and lots of space. Rooms facing south on the sixth floor are especially high-ceilinged. (Singles 80 pesos. Doubles 100 pesos.**) Restaurant Los Faisanes,** in the lobby offers good food and an especially pleasant atmosphere. (Restaurant open daily 7am-11pm). **Casa de Huéspedes Morelos,** Obregón 15 at Morelos (tel. 7-04-74), has much humbler rooms and tiny bathrooms but is very clean and very friendly. All rooms have fans. (Singles 30 pesos. Doubles 50 pesos.) **Farmacia Central** (tel. 7-00-05) sits on the north corner of the zócalo. (Open daily 8am-2pm and 4-8pm.) **Police** can be found at 2417 in the Palacio Municipal, on the northeast side of the zócalo (tel. 7-00-92). The nearest Red Cross is in San Andrés; for 24-hr. ambulance service, they can be reached at 2-05-00. **Comermex,** at 5 de Mayo 185, on the north corner of the zócalo, will exchange traveler's checks (but not cash) Mon.-Fri. 9am-1pm. In a pinch, the medical clinic on Comonfort (across from Hotel Castellanos) will exchange cash. There is a **larga distancia caseta** on Route 180, just across the bridge (collect calls 10 pesos; fax.).

.   Getting to Tres Zapotes is not as easy as it should be. Autotransportes Dos Tuxtlas buses lumber over from Santiago at 6am, 7am, 8am and noon. The ride takes about half an hour, as the bus stops, oh, say, every few feet. A taxi to the site will cost you at least 20 pesos. As you come into Tres Zapotes, the museum will be on your left, behind a chain link fence. To reach the entrance from the bus stop, walk about 100m back the way you came. If the bus stops in a different place, simply ask for *el museo arqueológico.*

The museum itself is small and simply laid out; very old stones under four covered transepts. A knowledgeable guide is usually running the display. If you have even a cursory knowledge of Spanish, ask questions, since the pieces become fascinating when set in a historical context and with their fading details pointed out. A large (8 ½-ton) Olmec head dating from between 2500 and 2000 BC sits in the west transept and may be the oldest Olmec stela ever discovered. Behind that lie columns (once part of a temple) and a piece of what is thought to have been an altar. The cylindrical green stone lying next to the columns fits into the hole in the altar-piece and was handy for sacrificing birds, the supposed purpose of the altar. In the south transept of the museum, a large figure reclines. This is the partner to another figure in the museum in Santiago. Also in the south transept, behind and to the right of the large figure, is what appears to be a thick stone tablet. This is Stela C, which, together with its more famous other half (now at the Museum of Archaeology in Mexico City; only a fading photograph remains here), is notable for bearing the oldest date in the Americas—31 BC, inscribed in Olmec glyphs similar to those used by the Maya. Stela A, the biggest piece in the museum, lies in the east transcept. The guide will point out (or careful observers will notice) the figure of a man with a jaguar's head lying down on top. On the right side of the stela, a serpent coils upon itself. On the left side, a man holds an axe. Both are discernible with some degree of imagination. Stela D, in the north transept, again resembles a tablet. Within the mouth of a jaguar are renderings of three people whose relative heights symbolize their power and importance. The war god on the far right holds a staff. The woman in the middle is the moon goddess. A character depicting *el pueblo* on the far left is kneeling to both these deities. Opposite Stela D, a large volcanic rock with a jaguar in the center broods unhappily. On one side of this piece, Life is represented by a bloody mouth, while Death, on the other side, takes the form of a skeletal face. Also in the north transept are pieces of large stone arms and a stone disk, part of another altar. (Museum open daily 9am-5pm. Admission 7 pesos. Free Sun.)

To return to Santiago, turn left when leaving the museum, hang a right at the corner (where the bus dropped you off) and walk three blocks to a small *refresco* stand on your left, where a taxi or two may be waiting. Your best bet is to wait here until you are joined by a sufficient number of others (usually four or five) to be ferried back by cab, *colectivo* style. The intimate 20-min. ride costs 4 pesos per passenger.

Southern México

PUEBLA

Although the first part of Mexico to succumb to Hernán Cortés was Veracruz, the Conquest did not really pick up steam until his group ventured inland to Puebla, where many local tribes joined the entourage. Mexico's oldest churches, some built only months after the Spaniards' arrival, demarcate Cortés's trail through Puebla and Tlaxcala. Cholula has served as a religious center for each successive dominant culture in the area since the second century BC.

A glimpse into one of the 16th-century churches which dominate rural towns will inevitably reveal the ways in which the Conquest was incomplete. Images from pre-Hispanic mythology mingle with those of Christianity in church decoration. Pagan mythology shrouds Puebla's two snow-capped volcanoes, **Popocatépetl** (5452m) and **Ixtaccíhuatl** (5282m), respectively the second- and third-largest mountains in the country. In Nahuatl the former means "Smoking Mountain," while the latter means "Sleeping Woman." Legend has it that the warrior Popocatépetl loved Ixtaccíhuatl, the emperor's daughter. Once, when he went off to a battle, Ixtaccíhuatl heard erroneously that he had been killed; she subsequently died of lovesickness and grief. When Popo (as he was known to friends) learned of his lover's death, he built the two great mountains. On the northern one he placed her body, and on the southern one he stood vigil with a torch. *Poblanos* (citizens of Puebla) pay their respects to the supine, death-pale Ixtaccíhuatl on the mountain's snowy summit. Experienced climbers can ascend either or both of these volcanoes, and less audacious backpackers have their pick of extensive trails that connect isolated foothill villages.

■■■ PUEBLA

A 17th-century legend holds that the Bishop of Tlaxcala, Don Julián Garcés, dreamed of a beautiful field next to a sparkling river. In the vision, he saw angels descend from the sky, planting stakes and stretching cords for the streets of a new city. The very next day, on a hike south of Tlaxcala, he recognized the land of his dreams and immediately erected the altar from which Fray Toribio Paredes de Benavente delivered Mexico's first Catholic mass in 1531.

Since then, Puebla has grown to a metropolis of two million, transcended its status as stopover between Veracruz and Mexico City, and yet remained an incredibly liveable residential center. Neither a smog-choked giant crowded with snarled traffic nor a boring historical town intent on reliving an unredeemable past, Puebla has combined its splendid history with a pulsating present in a thoughtful and engaging manner. Gilt churches and trendy clothing stores share the same cobbled streets, and those tired from vying with the youngish shopping crowd can relax with the older generations in the shady *zócalo*.

Much of Puebla's history has been a direct result of its strategic military positioning, which made it a coveted wartime asset. In every war prior to independence, Puebla remained fiercely loyal to the Spanish and proved a formidable fortress of Catholicism, commissioning over 60 baroque churches over the course of colonization. Early in the Mexican-American wars, U.S. troops were lucky enough to have a stronghold in Puebla. In 1847, a pivotal point in the war, Mexican General Santa Ana decided to make a surprise attack against U.S. forces stationed in the city. U.S. troops held up alarmingly well, however, and it wasn't until 15 years later, when the French outpost collapsed, that the Mexican army took the city. Every year

Puebla

TO FORTS

Templo de San Francisco

Blvd Heroes del 5 de Mayo

Av. 20 Oriente
Av. 18 Oriente
Av. 16 Oriente
Av. 12 Oriente
Av. 8 Oriente
Av. 4 Oriente
Av. 2 Oriente
Av. 5 Oriente

Calle 6 Norte

Teatro Principal

Av. 6 Oriente

Museo de Alfeñique

Av. Maximino Ávila Camacho

Av. 7 Oriente

Calle 4 Norte

Av. 16 Oriente
Av. 14 Oriente
Av. 12 Oriente
Av. 10 Oriente
Av. 8 Oriente
Av. 4 Oriente
Av. 2 Oriente

Iglesia de la Compañía

Av. 3 Oriente
Av. 5 Oriente
Av. 9 Oriente

Calle 2 Sur

Casa de Aquiles Serdán

Casa de Cultura and Biblioteca Palafoxiana

Av. 18 Ote.

5 de Mayo

Iglesia de Santo Domingo

La Casa de los Muñecos

Zócalo

Catedral

(i) Tourist Office

16 de Septiembre

Calle 3 Norte

Mercado Victoria

Calle 3 Sur

La Cocina de Santa Rosa

Museo Bello

Calle 5 Norte

Calle 5 Sur

Av. 10 Poniente
Av. 8 Poniente
Av. 6 Poniente

Av. Reforma

Calle 7 Norte

Av. 16 Poniente
Av. 14 Poniente
Av. 12 Poniente

Av. 3 Poniente
Av. 5 Poniente
Av. 7 Poniente
Av. 9 Poniente

Calle 9 Norte

Av. 4 Poniente
Av. 2 Poniente

Calle 11 Norte

Calle 11 Sur

since that victorious battle of 1862, 5 de Mayo has been celebrated as Mexican Independence Day.

Having long suffered relative and undeserved anonymity due to its proximity to Mexico City, Puebla is steadily but unaggressively venturing out on its own. The city's stylish architecture, pleasurable atmosphere, almost perfect climate, and delightfully rich cuisine are enough to make Puebla a destination in itself.

ORIENTATION

Puebla, capital of the state of the same name, lies 125km southeast of Mexico City and 300km west of Veracruz. All **bus** companies operate out of the terminal CAPU (Central de Autobuses Puebla) on Blvd. Norte and Tlaxcala, in the northwest corner of the city. Proximity to Mexico City makes the local **airport** (in Huejotzingo, tel. 32-00-32 or 32-00-38) somewhat redundant. An extensive highway network links Puebla to Mexico City (along Rte. 190, toll 15 pesos for cars and 20 pesos for vans), Oaxaca (along Rte. 190 or 135), Tlaxcala, Veracruz and many other cities. Transportation in and around Puebla is particularly easy in consideration of the many travelers who scuttle back and forth between the coast and the interior.

If your sense of direction still spins from the contorted streets of many Mexican cities, you are in for a treat; the *avenidas* and *calles* of Puebla form a near-perfect grid. The northwest corner of the *zócalo* occupies the center of the grid. The main north-south street is **5 de Mayo** to the north of that point and **16 de Septiembre** south of it. The main east-west thoroughfare is **Avenida Reforma** to the west, becoming **Avenida Máximo ávila Camacho** to the east of the *zócalo*. *Avenidas*, running east-west parallel to Reforma/M. Ávila Camacho, are designated either Pte. or Ote. depending on whether they lie west or east, respectively, of 5 de Mayo/16 de Septiembre. Even-numbered avenues are north of Reforma/M. Avila Camacho, odd-numbered avenues south. *Calles*, running north-south parallel to 5 de Mayo/16 de Septiembre, are denoted as Nte. or Sur with respect to Reforma/M. Avila Camacho. These streets are even-numbered if east of 5 de Mayo/16 de Septiembre and odd-numbered if west.

Yellow **taxis** will take you to the *zócalo* from the bus station for 7 pesos. Ignore the drivers who descend on you as you leave the bus and buy a ticket inside the station to prevent a potential rip-off. The tickets are valid only in the yellow taxis. **Municipal buses** and *micros* or *combis* cost .80 pesos. No maps of the bus routes re available, but anything labeled "CENTRO" should take you close to the *zócalo*. Catch buses to the right of the stations exit. Buses marked "CAPU," running along Calle 9 Nte.-Sur will take you back to the station.

The **train station** is 40 blocks (4.5km) north of the city center. For *combis* or *micros* to the *centro* wait in front of the station. Buses labeled "Estación Nueva Popular" to the station can be hailed along Calle 9 Nte.-Sur (.80 pesos).

PRACTICAL INFORMATION

Tourist Offices: State Office, Av. 5 Ote. 3 (tel. 46-12-85 or 46-20-44), facing the cathedral's southern side. Incredibly friendly employees (all speak a little English; some speak it well). Most of the brochures in Spanish, but some maps have English directions. Open Mon.-Fri. 9:30am-8pm, Sun. 9am-2pm. **Information Booth,** Blvd. Atlixco Nte. at Serdán. Open daily Tues.-Sun. 10am-5pm.

Currency Exchange: Bancomer, On Reforma, within a block west of the *zócalo*. **Bancomer,** Reforma 113 (tel. 22-00-22), **Banco Internacional,** Refroma 120 and **Banamex,** Reforma 135 (tel. 46-98-18). All exchange cash and traveler's checks without commission, and have ATMs for Visa, MC, and Cirrus. All open for exchange: Mon.-Fri. 9am-noon. All **casas de cambio** are in the Zona Esmeralda along Av. Juárez further away from the *zócalo* and offer rates only slightly higher. *Casa de cambio* **Concultoria Internacional,** Calle 23 Sur 506, at Juárez, is open Mon.-Fri. 9am-5:30pm.

American Express: in the Plaza Dorada, on Díaz Ordaz 6A Sur #2914, Suite 301 (tel. 40-30-18, 40-33-08, or 40-32-85). Best for cashing and replacing AmEx Cheques, holds clients' mail for 10 days. Open Mon.-Fri. 9am-6pm.

Post Office: 16 de Septiembre at Av. 5 Ote. (tel. 42-64-48), 1 block south of the cathedral, in the same building as the state tourist office. Open for stamps Mon.-Fri. 8am-7pm, Sat. 9am-1pm; for registered letters Mon.-Fri. 8am-6pm, Sat. 9am-noon. Northern office, Av. 2 Ote. 411 on the 2nd floor. Open Mon.-Fri. 8am-7pm, Sat. 9am-noon. The 2 branches have separate *Listas de Correos*, so make sure you know whither your mail is sent. **Postal code:** 72000.

Telephones: The *casetas de larga distancia* do not place collect calls; you have to pay directly. Place collect calls from **LADATEL** phones along 5 de Mayo and around the *zócalo*. **Telephone Code:** 22.

Telegrams: 16 de Septiembre 504 (tel. 32-17-79), on the south side of the post office. Open Mon.-Fri. 8am-midnight, Sat. 9am-6pm. For money orders: Mon.-Fri. 9am-2pm and 2:30-5:30pm, Sat. 9am-noon.

Train Station: Estación La Unión, known as Estación Nueva, is in the northern part of the city, at Av. 80 Pte. and Calle 9 Nte. (tel. 20-02-79, 20-15-37, or 20-04-07). Buses marked "Estación Nueva Popular" pass along Calle 9 Sur-Nte. A cab shouldn't cost more than 8 pesos to the *zócalo*. The train to Mexico City is insanely slow, but the train to Oaxaca is one of the most popular train routes in Mexico. (2nd class 7:20am, daily, 12 pesos; mixed 1st- and 2nd-class trains: noon, daily, 48 pesos and 12 pesos.) Both take 12-13hrs. Buy ticket 1-1½hrs. before departure.

Bus Station: CAPU (Central de Autobuses Puebla), at the crossroads of Blvd. Norte and Tlaxcala, in the northwest corner of the city itself, you can find a bus to any destination. 1st-class **ADO** (tel. 32-08-68 or 32-73-93) to: Mexico City (every 10min. 7am-8pm; every 20min. 8-10pm; every 30min. 5am-7am; 19 pesos), Veracruz (12 per day; 37 pesos), Cordoba (11 per day, 24 pesos), Orizaba (11 per day, 21 pesos), Zaragoza (8 per day, 13 pesos), Oaxaca (5 per day 41 pesos), Villahermosa (5 per day, 81 pesos) and Jalapa (9 per day, 20 pesos). 1st-class **Cristóbal Colón** (tel. 49-74-39) to: Tuxtla Gutiérrez (92 pesos), San Cristóbal (100 pesos), Tapachula (124 pesos), and Oaxaca (42 pesos). 2nd class **Estrella Roja** (tel. 49-70-99) to: Mexico City (15-23 pesos), Cholula and Huejotzingo (5 pesos). **Autobuses Unidos** (tel. 69-70-71) serves destinations to the north and southwest. Inside, 24-hr. pharmacy, long distance *caseta* (open 7am-11pm), 24-hr. restaurant, luggage storage (6:30am-11pm, 1 peso per hour) and stores.

Taxis: Taxi-Puebla (tel. 35-35-55). **Tari Rápido** (tel. 35-99-66). Dispatcher should tell you the price (at least 6 pesos).

English Bookstores: Sanborn's, Av. 2 Ote. 6 (tel. 42-94-16). Mostly magazines and maps. Open daily 7:30am-11pm. **VIPs,** Av. 2 Ote. and Calle 2 Nte. (tel 32-82-02), mostly English paperbacks, magazines, and newspapers.

Markets: Closest to the city center is **Gigante,** at 4 Nte. and Blvd. Heroes del 5 de Mayo, to the north of the Templo de San Francisco. Also **Superama,** 2 Sur and 17 Ote. and the large shopping complex **Commercial Mexicana,** Calle 5 Sur and Av. 19 Pte. All open daily 9am-9pm.

Laundromats: Lavandería Lucy, Av. 2 Pte. 2503 (tel. 48-54-75), in the distant Comercial Mexicana shopping mall. 12 pesos per load. Self-serve available. Open daily 9am-8pm. Closer to the *zócalo:* **Lavandería Roti,** Calle 7 Nte. 404. Full service 15 pesos per 3kg. Self-service, 4.50 pesos to wash and 4.50 pesos to dry. Open Mon.-Sat. 9am-8pm.

Pharmacies: Farmacia del Carmen, 16 de Septiembre #2107, between Av. 21 and 23 (tel. 40-30-09) and at Reforma #916, between Calles 9 and 11.

Hospital: Hospital Tamaríz (UPAEP) 5 Pte. and 9 Sur (tel. 46-60-99), open 24 hrs. Some English spoken. **Hospital Universitario,** Calle 13 Sur at Av. 25 Pte. (tel. 43-15-42), 10 blocks south and 7 blocks west of the *zócalo.* 24-hr. emergency service. Some doctors speak English.

Red Cross: 21 Ote. and 10 Nte. (tel. 35-80-40), 24-hr. ambulance service.

Police: Dirección de Policía 9 Ote. and 16 Sur (tel. 32-22-23 or 32-22-22), for complaints and walk-in visits. **Policía Auxiliar** (tel. 24-28-35). Open 24 hrs. for emergencies. For all **emergencies,** dial 06.

ACCOMMODATIONS AND CAMPING

The sad truth: budget accommodations in Puebla are more expensive than hotels of comparable quality elsewhere in Mexico. Most of the budget hotels in downtown Puebla sprout up on Av. 3 Pte. Expect to pay at least 60 pesos for a mid-sized comfortable room. Less expensive places do exist downtown, but tend to be gloomy and only moderately clean. Many hotels have hot water only for those awake before the crack of dawn. Ask potential proprietors about their policy.

Hotel Teresita, Av. 3 Pte. 309 (tel. 32-70-72), 2 blocks west of the *zócalo*'s southwest corner. Undoubtedly the best budget option in Puebla. Claustrophobic bare walls, but rooms are clean and well-maintained. Often full; try around 2pm. Hot water in morning and evening, drinking water always. Singles 40 pesos. Doubles 50 pesos, with two separate beds 70 pesos.

Hotel Imperial, Av. 4 Ote. 212 (tel. 42-49-81), just a block north of the northeast corner of the *zócalo*. Inevitably pink large rooms come with imaginative showers and purported 24-hr. hot water supply. Excellent deal for larger groups. Singles 71 pesos. Doubles 87 pesos. Triples 105 pesos. Rooms for 4 (123 pesos) and 5 (138 pesos) usually have 2 big beds and 1 single bed.

Hotel Cabrera, Av. 10 Ote. 6 (tel. 32-85-25). In a modern building above a hardware store, close to a lively market area. Conditions the same as in the Imperial. Overwhelmingly green rooms with phones and empty TV stands. Parking lot. Singles 71 pesos. Doubles 87 pesos. Triples 105 pesos. 4 people 123 pesos. 5 people 138 pesos.

Hotel Ritz, Calle 2 Nte. 207 (tel. 32-44-57). A cheaper and less attractive but very central hotel. Rooms are small and survivably clean. Tiny bathrooms with limited hot water. Beware of fan noise near the first patio. Singles 38 pesos. Doubles 48 pesos. Triples 58 pesos.

Hostal de Halconeros, Reforma 141, ½ block west of the *zócalo*. A hotel, not a hostel. The high-ceilinged rooms, tall creaky doors and stenciled walls are throwbacks to another generation. Beautiful rooms barely illuminated by a single light bulb. Singles 41 pesos. Doubles 52 pesos.

Casa de Huespedes, 5 Pte. 111, almost all at the *zócalo*, ½ block from the cathedral. A very central and very expensive option for travelers that have nothing precious about them. Flimsy locks with beamed ceilings, a few have rooms. Singles 20 pesos, with bathrooms 30 pesos. Doubles 30 pesos, with bathrooms 40 pesos.

FOOD

In Puebla, both visitors and locals alike eat out. Restaurants line the blocks near the *zócalo*. No visitor to Puebla should miss this city's most distinctive culinary delight, *mole poblano*. The dish, in one form or another, is a mainstay on almost every menu in town. *Mole* is a thick, dark sauce of chocolate, chiles, onions and some 20 other ingredients, served over chicken, turkey, or enchiladas. Every animal part including legs, ears, eyes, and brains can be seen in menus, served one way or another. Other typical *poblano* dishes are *chiles en nogada* (nut sauce), *chilaquiles, cemitas* (the rich predecessor of the hamburger), *chalupas* (tortillas with salsa, strips of meat and onions), *molotes* (tortilla, potatoes, cheese, and *huitlacoche* closed and fried), and *tamales.* Most of these dishes were originated by colonial-era nuns.

There's no avoiding Puebla's downtown **markets.** An estimated 8000 people sell goods on the streets. Many stands and street vendors selling sandwiches, fruits and snacks at low prices congregate in the market along 5 de Mayo, starting one block north of the *zócalo*. There is another market along Av. 10 Pte. You can also refuel inexpensively in any of Puebla's numerous bakeries, where a *pastel* (pastry) costs under 1 peso. Particularly memorable is **La Flor de Puebla** on Calle 3 Sur 104. (Open daily 7am-9:30pm.)

Restaurant El Cazadorsa, Av. 3 Pte. 147 (tel. 32-76-26), 1 block southwest of the *zócalo*. Very clean, restaurant with ugly orange chairs, checkered red tablecloths and old photographs of Puebla streets. Those with a hankering for some serious pork products might explore the *manitas rebosadas* (muffled pig hands) or *sesos empanizados* (breaded pig brains). Friendly family members also serve more palatable dishes like *arroz con pollo* (15 pesos) and piping hot chocolate French-, Spanish-, or Mexican-style (3 pesos). 5-course *comida corrida* 12 pesos (1-5pm). Open daily 8am-11pm.

Restaurant Puebla, Av. 3 Pte. 520 (tel. 32-40-82). Almost unnoticeable on the outside, but resplendent with character on the inside. Full of dusty memorabilia and other trinkets that the humble owner has gathered over the centuries. A cheap local favorite. *Pollo con mole poblano* 8 pesos. 3 chicken enchiladas 6 pesos. Nothing costs over 10 pesos. Open daily 10am-10pm.

Super Tortas Puebla, Av. 3 Pte. 317 (tel. 32-69-95). Cheap, wholesome lunchtime snacks. Huge *tortas* stuffed with your choice of ingredients from the counter display. The pink back room is a Marilyn Monroe cult temple. Sandwiches 4 pesos. Open daily 10am-9pm.

Fonda La Esperanza, Calle 5 Sur, between Av. 3 Ote. This *fonda* should not be lost in the crowd. Clean, family-run and family-frequented. Musicians often stop by for a few songs, unheard of in the posh central eateries. An incredible deal with its daily 5-course 7.50 pesos *comida corrida*. Drinks 1.50-3 pesos. Open Sun.-Fri. 8:30am-6pm.

Mercado del Alto Garibalsi, at Av. 14 Ote, between Calles 10 and 12 Nte. The perfect place for lovers of authentic Mexican food and life. Various *puesto* proprietors compete for your business, but all serve the same food at the same prices. No sophistication (i.e. silverware), but plenty of homey authenticity and Mexican cooking lessons. *Antojos, cemitas, tostadas, molotes, chalupas,* and many more Puebla delicacies all cost 5-15 pesos. After 11pm the place starts bursting with life with Mariachis crooning love songs to tweak the heartstrings (and pursestrings) of the lonely. Open daily 8am-3am.

Restaurant Vegetariano, Av. 3 Pte. 525 (tel. 46-54-62). Split-level with wood paneling, pastel watercolors on walls and a non-smoking section downstairs. Surprisingly popular for a city of carnivores. Countless creative veggie concoctions, from creamy spinach crepes (9.50 pesos) to a meatless *comida corrida* (12 pesos) to an *energética* plate for 10 pesos. Most entrees made with soy as a meat substitute. Non-alcoholic beer served. Big portions. Open daily 8am-9pm.

SIGHTS AND ENTERTAINMENT

All of the sights described below, except for those around Las Fuertes de Loreto y Guadalupe, are within walking distance of the *zócalo*. If you have only a short time in Puebla, the **Museo Amparo, Capilla del Rosario,** and **Casa de Aquiles Serdán** should top your list. All museums are open Tues.-Sun. 10am-5pm, unless noted otherwise. Churches usually close between 2 and 4pm and while shorts are acceptable, proper respect is mandatory. Usually all museums give 50% discounts to students with ID.

Generally, the architecture in Puebla has negotiated its way through history intact. Numerous buildings from the 16th, 17th and 18th centuries still stand throughout the city. The oldest buildings in the city, dating from the 16th century, are distinguished by smooth cylindrical columns on square bases that support Romanesque porches. Very few originals are left, but some later buildings on the west and north ends of the *zócalo* consciously imitate their style.

The 17th-century buildings, including many of the nearly 100 churches, are characterized inside and out by classical and Gothic ornamentation. Most of the churches also exhibit a baroque influence; the tourist office and many of the buildings near the *zócalo* exemplify this style, for which Puebla is famous. Red brick and *azulejo de Talavera* (a *mudéjar* tile popular in Puebla during the early colonial period) are the raw materials for this style. Often laid diagonally, the bricks come in a variety of shapes, and each tile is a work of art in itself—intricate paintings on the tile often feature blue or turquoise flowers. Another good example of this style is the 18th-century **Casa de los Muñecos,** just north of the *zócalo's* northeast corner on

Calle 2 Nte. Some of the tiles depict characterizations of the architect's enemies. Inside the *Casa* is the **Museo Universitario,** a museum that chronicles the history of education in Puebla from colonial times to the present. (Open Tues.-Sun. Free.)

Eighty-seven years of *indígena* labor went into building the **Cathedral of the Immaculate Conception,** the tallest cathedral in Mexico (72m) on Av. 3 Ote. at 5 de Mayo, adjacent to the *zócalo*. Construction began in 1562 under the architect Juan de Herrera, and the cathedral was consecrated in 1649. Two organs (one 400-years-old) and a bell tower with 19 bells are occasionally heard, and chandeliers and gold plate sparkle inside. Pedro Muñoz's fine woodwork glamorizes the choir stalls on the pulpit's periphery. English-speaking tour guides will provide their services for a small fee. (Cathedral open daily 10am-2:30pm and 4-6pm.)

From 11am to noon, if the sexton is in the mood, visitors can climb the right tower of the cathedral for a panoramic view of Puebla (5 pesos). If you still have more energy, propel yourself up another 164 steps to see the 8500kg bell, which, according to legend, angels lifted to the top of the tower. The two volcanoes, **Popocatépetl** and **Ixtaccíhuatl,** are visible to the northwest. To the northeast, you can see one other great volcano called **La Malinche,** named in honor of the woman who was Cortés's Aztec lover and interpreter. Be sure to start your climb by 11:30am; the lower door is locked at noon. The stairs are quite dark; bring your own torch.

The **Casa de la Cultura,** Av. 5 Ote. 5, one block south of the *zócalo* in the same building as the tourist office and the post office, houses the impressive **Biblioteca Palafoxiana.** This collection of 43,000 mostly Latin volumes dates from the 16th century. The bishop of Puebla during the second half of the 17th century, Palafox, was perhaps the most powerful man in Mexico. He carried in his pocket a paper signed by the king of Spain empowering him to replace the Mexican viceroy should he deem it necessary. Palafox was also an intellectual force at a time when the Jesuits were isolating the New World politically, intellectually and religiously from Spain. Belonging to no religious order himself, Palafox condemned the Jesuits' aspirations to power, land, and money. Palafox's own 6000-book library, which he donated to the Colegio de San Pedro in 1646, includes a 1493 copy of the Chronicle of Nuremberg, illuminated with 2000 scenes. (Library open Tues.-Sun. 10am-5pm. Admission 3.25 pesos, 1.65 pesos with ISIC card, Tues. free.)

Most of the permanent exhibits in the Casa de la Cultura are uninteresting, but some of the rooms devoted to traveling art shows and in-house work are worth a peek. Folk dances are performed every Saturday and Sunday, and amateur and professional movies are shown during the week. Check the board on the right as you walk in from the street for the latest schedules. (For more information, call 46-53-44, or write: Apdo. 1139, Puebla, Puebla.)

Around the corner and two blocks south of the Casa de la Cultura lies Puebla's newest museum, the **Museo Amparo,** Calle 2 Sur 708, follow the signs from the Casa de la Cultura (tel. 46-42-00 or 46-46-46), one of the very few private museums in Mexico today. This beautifully constructed museum, which opened to the public on March 1, 1991, is devoted to the history of Mesoamerican art. The exhibit begins with a timeline comparing the development of Mesoamerican art with that of Oceania, Asia, Africa and Europe from 2400 BC to 1500 AD. The bottom floor focuses on the production techniques that different indigenous groups used to construct early crafts and tools and on the use of art for ritual, adornment and, of course, the ball game. At the top of the stairs is a gigantic time chart that shows the construction and occupation of each major site in Mexico and the chronological and geographical relationships between different sites. The numerous rooms upstairs divide Mexico into each region, tracing each site through the pre-Classic, Classic and post-Classic periods. The museum contains an incredible number of pieces, all in excellent condition. The explanatory material is in both English and Spanish, and headphones with more information on each piece and its significance, including its relationship to contemporary artifacts from around the globe, are available for rent

(5 pesos). (Museum open Wed.-Mon. 10am-6pm. Admission 10 pesos, 5 pesos for students with ID. Free Mon.)

One block east of the *zócalo*, at M. Avila Camacho and Calle 4 Sur, is the **Iglesia del Espíritu Santo** (or **La Compañía**) dedicated in 1777 as a Jesuit school. Inside the church lies the tomb of the princess Minnha, *La China Poblana*. According to legend, the noblewoman was abducted by pirates from China and brought to New Spain, where her captors sold her into servitude. The princess resigned herself to her fate and adopted the Christian religion but never forgot her blue blood; she distinguished herself from other *poblanos* by wearing elaborate dresses, each bearing an embroidered Mexican eagle on the front. The fashion caught on and remains unique to Puebla. Other versions of the story have her being adopted by a Mexican merchant. In gratitude, she goes on to dedicate her life to the poor. The variability of the legend does not hurt *La China Poblana's* popularity, however, as the multitude of stores and restaurants named after her attest. Open daily 10am-2pm and 4-6pm.

The art collection of the late textile magnate José Luis Bello resides in the **Museo Bello,** Av. 3 Pte. at Calle 3 Sur, one block west of the southeast corner of the *zócalo*. The museum, ornamented with tiles and illuminated by stained-glass windows, contains artifacts from different places and periods in world history. Bello left his collection of ivory, iron, porcelain, earthenware and Talavera objects to his son, José Mariano Bello, who added a gallery of paintings and later donated the entire she-bang to the fine arts academy in Puebla. Highlights of the museum include the collection of Talavera wares in the downstairs rooms and the incredible multiplicity of beautifully wrought ancient keys, locks and spurs in the back room on the upper floor. A staff member will lead you through the exhibit to turn on lights, answer questions. (Open Tues.-Sun. 10am-5pm. Informative guided tours in Spanish. Admission 3.25 pesos, students 1.65 pesos. Some English spoken.)

The extravagant, gold-leafed **Iglesia de Santo Domingo** was constructed between 1571 and 1611 on the foundation of a convent, two blocks north of the *zócalo's* northwest corner along 5 de Mayo, between Av. 4 and 6 Pte. Statues of saints and angels adorn the fantastic altar, but the church's real attraction is to the left of the altar. This marvel of religious architecture, the **Capilla del Rosario,** is a chapel laden with 23½-karat gold. Along each side of the chapel are three doors, each with a mask hung above: an *indígena*, a conquistador in armor and, nearest the altar, a mestizo. On the ceiling, three full statues represent Faith, Hope, and Charity. Both the masks and the statues pull visitors' attention to an altar where 12 pillars represent the apostles (the 6 on the upper level are each made of a single onyx stone). Since there was no room for a real choir, designers painted a chorus of angels with guitars and woodwinds on the wall above the door. Churches in Mexico are usually functioning places of worship, but you can visit when mass isn't being held. Guidebooks in Spanish (15 pesos) and postcards are sold along the left of the main church.

Aquiles Serdán operated a printing press with his wife and his brothers before the Revolution of 1910, reeling off anti-reelectionist posters and other articles for distribution throughout Puebla. He and his sons led the earliest revolt of the Revolution before being gunned down in the **Casa de Aquiles Serdán,** which today serves as the **Museo Regional de la Revolución Mexicana** at Av. 6 Ote. 206. Hundreds of bullet holes, both inside and out, bear witness to the assassination. The most interesting exhibits are those on the top floor of the museum. Some of the photos are of Serdán as the representative of Tlaxcala, Puebla, and Michoacán states at the convention where Madero and Vázquez were elected to run against the dictator Díaz. Be sure not to miss the shots of the Mexican people in the bloody battles of the Revolution, the bedraggled battalions of Reyes and Obregón, and of the dead Zapata and Carranza. The photo of Zapata recently shot is truly stupefying; he lies in the arms of shocked and leaderless *campesinos*. Downstairs, however, is no less thrilling. One room shows Serdán's actual hiding spot below the floorboards as soldiers stormed the house in 1910. Another room is dedicated to Carmen Serdán and other famous female revolutionaries (*las carabineras*), including María Arias, also known as "María Pistolas" (Mary Guns). (Open Tues.-Sun. 10am-5:30pm. Admission 3.25 pesos, children 1.65 pesos.)

At the nearby **Museo del Alfeñique,** Av. 4 Ote. 416 at Calle 6 Nte., a heavily ornamented 18th-century baroque exterior encloses three floors of ceramic works, 16th- and 17th-century documents, paintings and antique furniture that span the history of the city of Puebla. (Open Tues.-Sun. 10am-5pm. Admission 3.25 pesos, students 1.65 pesos.)

Touristique but regional clothing (*sarapes*, blouses and dresses) is sold at the block-long **Mercado El Parián,** a half block east along Av. 4 Ote. (Open daily 9am-7pm.) In front of the market, also along Av. 4 Ote., is the **Barrio del Artista,** where local artists exhibit their work in small cubicles and paint the portraits of passersby. (Open daily dawn-dusk.)

The oldest church in Puebla, begun in 1535 and finished in 1575, is the **Templo de San Francisco,** Av. 14 Ote. and Calle 10 Nte., three blocks east on M. Avila Camacho and four blocks north on 5 de Mayo. The dark bell tower was added in 1672. The church's ceiling is also one of the highest in Puebla, and one of its chapels contains the body of Sebastián de Aparicio, who opened the first highways between Puebla and other cities. Near the church is the **Teatro Principal,** on Av. 10 Ote. at Calle 6 Nte. The *Teatro* was built in 1550 and is a good example of Puebla's 16th-century architecture, with smooth cylindrical columns built on square bases. (Open daily 10am-5pm except when in use.)

One of the biggest celebrations on the Mexican calendar is **5 de Mayo,** commemorating the victory of Ignacio Zaragoza and his 2000 soldiers over 5000 French soldiers in Puebla in 1862. Twenty blocks north and 5 blocks east of Puebla's *zócalo*, a complex of museums and parks surrounds the staunch forts where Mexican armies staved off the French troops. Before the battle, General Elías Federico Forey, having observed the Mexican army at Puebla, assured Louis Napoleon that he could consider the town taken because the French army was superior both in number and quality. The French surrounded the fort, but upon hearing of the siege and learning that the Mexican army was nearly out of ammunition and artillery, the *indígena* inhabitants of the northern part of the state came to the rescue. Arriving barefoot from the fields with only machetes and sticks, the Zacapaaxtlas (descendants of the Totonacs) decimated the French. A monument to Zaragoza marks the battle spot. Six large concrete arms hold replicas of cannon from the battle; that's the general on his horse sitting atop the sixth. The two forts, Loreto and Guadalupe, sit on opposite ends of the hill and complex. (Both open Tues.-Sun. 10am-5pm. Admission 10 pesos, Sun. and holidays free). Fuerte Loreto houses a museum containing uniforms, documents and artifacts from the historic battle.

To the north of the fort is the brick **Museo de Historia Natural,** loaded with artful representations of wildlife habitats. A huge, scary plastic dinosaur guards the entry. (Open Tues.-Sun. 10am-5pm. Admission 3.25 pesos.) In front of the fort, the modern **Museo Regional de Puebla** contains a little of everything, including sculptures, ceramic works, paintings and Aztec art. (Open Tues.-Sun. 10am-5pm. Admission 10 pesos, Sun. and holidays free.) Near the Museo Regional, on 5 de Mayo, lies a silver pyramidal **planetarium,** where the farthest stretches of the universe are brought down to earth in a geodesic dome. (Shows Tues.-Fri. 4 and 6pm, Sat.-Sun. noon, 2, 4, and 6pm. Admission 5 pesos.) The **Parque Rafaela P. Zaragoza,** one block east, unfurls around an amphitheater in which singers, bands and dancers perform (check with the tourist office or the Casa de Cultura for show times). To reach the complex, catch the "Fuertes" bus (.80 pesos) on 5 de Mayo, four blocks north of the *zócalo*; it's at the top of a small hill that affords a panoramic view of Puebla.

The **Museo Nacional de los Ferrocarriles Mexicanos,** the monumental pink building sits alongside a wide stretch of rusted tracks loaded down with freshly painted steam trains. The locomotives are loaded down with kids on Sundays, when families picnic on the grassy plaza to the right of the museum. Some have their own museums aboard, and curious visitors can inspect the giant cranks and gargantuan gearshifts of locomotives that date from 1837. Historical memorabilia and a photo exhibit trace the evolution of the Mexican railways through strikes, *bandidos*, and track-laying on virgin soil. Allow about an hour to explore the museum, located at Av. 11 Nte. 1210 Pte., six blocks north of Paseo Bravo. (Open daily 10am-6pm. Free.)

For evening entertainment, take a stroll along Av. Juárez, starting west of Calle 13 Sur. Called the **Zona Esmeralda,** this neighborhood has scores of movie theaters, shops, ethnic restaurants and bars. Although the best discos kick it in nearby Cholula, Puebla's *Zona Esmeralda* throbs to the beat of **La Boom,** Juárez 1906 (tel. 32-46-85), after Calle 19 Sur. (Cover Fri. 12 pesos, Sat. 15 pesos. Open Fri.-Sat. 9pm-3am.) The **Plaza Dorada** shopping center in the southeast corner of the city, on 5 de Mayo at Calle 4 Sur, offers elegant shopping and *norteamericano*-style dining notable for its preponderance of chewy chocolate-chip cookies.

There is an abundance of movie theaters in Puebla. **Cine Puebla,** on the north side of the *zócalo*, shows North American movies in English with Spanish subtitles for 7 pesos at around 4, 8, and 10pm.

■ Near Puebla

Three side trips beckon from Puebla: the small town of **Tepeaca,** the falls of **Acatzitzimitla,** and the city of **Huejotzingo,** 35km west of Puebla. **Tepeaca** merits a visit because of its large Friday market and a Franciscan monastery that lies just east of the *zócalo*. The **zócalo** is a pleasant place to both sit and explore; there are tiled planters and benches in the center, and some stands from the market are left up all week. Before the Spanish arrived, people brought their carts to Tepeaca from across the countryside to sell their goods in ancient Mexico's largest *tianguis* (*indígena* market). Still the site of the largest *tianguis* in the Republic, Tepeaca carries on this tradition every Friday. On the east end of the *zócalo* stands, still in fairly good shape, one of the 12 Franciscan convents built in Puebla in the early years after the Conquest. The entrance is practically concealed between the shops on the edge of the plaza. On the park's west side is a white octagonal tower built when the Spanish occupied Tepeaca in the second half of the 16th century. This tower is named **El Rollo** and was a whipping stone upon which colonial slaves stood to be physically reprimanded. The small yellow **Parroquia** and the **Palacio de Gobierno** stand on the west side of the plaza.

Since Tepeaca is just one hour away from Puebla by bus, there is little reason to spend the night in the village. If you should need to stay, however, there is one hotel, **Casa de Huéspedes Claudia,** Cuauhtémoc 205, which lies southeast of the *zócalo*. Although the *casa* looks like it hasn't seen a guest in a while, it is a pleasant enough place to spend a night and is run by a very friendly lady. **Restaurant Conchita,** the yellow building on the northeast corner of the *zócalo*, specializes in seafood and *antojitos mexicanos* (around 8 pesos). If you need to change money, **Banco Somex** changes traveler's checks. Long distance **phone service** is available in the Restaurant Conchita.

To reach Tepeaca take (an **Autobuses Unidos**) (tel. 69-70-71) bus destined for Tehuacán from Puebla's central bus station. Buses leave every 30 minutes, 8am-10pm (5 pesos). To catch the bus back to Puebla, walk two blocks east from the plaza's northeast corner. Buses stop at this intersection.

Acatzitzimitla is 30-45 minutes farther south on the same Puebla-Tehuacán line (about 7 pesos). The **bus** to San Juan Ixcaquixtla or to Molcaxac (Sierra Golf bus lines, every 20min., 4:30am-8pm) bypasses a fork in the highway that veers off to the town of Atoyatempan. Five minutes past the fork, a rusty white sign reads,"Cascadas de Acatzitzimitla." Get out and march about 4km west on a narrow dirt road until you reach a garish pink church. It's a steep climb down to the falls from here, and there are many confusing side paths, so you may want to hire a guide from the area if you can find one. To return, walk back to the highway and hail the blue and white bus going east; change to an "AU" bus at the traffic circle where the highway crosses Route 38. Hail one from the east side of the road; you'll recognize the line by the bright orange stripe on the lower front of the bus.

For an alternative excursion, take the Estrella Roja bus to **Huejotzingo,** west of Puebla (every 20min., 4:40am-9pm, 7.50 pesos). This picturesque route follows tree-lined roads past fields of corn and allows you to get off at North America's first Franciscan convent, the **Convento de San Francisco,** founded in 1525. The **bus** stops on Anastasio Roldán, ½ block west of the 16th-century church and convent. At each corner of the convent's high walls is a small house with beautiful stone arches and columns accented by reliefs of thick rope. In the Sala de Profundis, inside just above the entrance, is a mural of the first 12 Franciscans kneeling at the cross. The second floor of the convent holds bedrooms and a small museum, with paintings, drawings, and plaques that explain the rules and rigor of convent life. (Open daily 10am-5pm. Admission 7 pesos.) The **Estrella Roja bus terminal** is across the *placita* from the convent's west wall. Buses to and from Puebla (about 5 pesos) pass by every 20 to 30 minutes.

■■■ CHOLULA

A center of local religious activity since the third century BC, Cholula has been home to the Olmecs, the Zapotecs, the Teotihuacanos, the Toltecs, the Chichimecs, and finally the Cholultecs, a Nahuatl-speaking people related to the Aztecs. In its second-century heyday, Cholula was as influential as Teotihuacán, serving as the powerful center of the region that now comprises the states of Puebla and Tlaxcala. The city developed into a great crossroads for Mesoamerican and Caribbean civilizations, extending its economic and cultural influence south and east. By the time the Spaniards arrived, Cholula had passed its zenith, but as a center for the worship of the much-venerated Quetzalcóatl, the city still presented a major obstacle to the Christianization of the conquered land.

The Spaniards' frustration was only increased when they uncovered Moctezuma's secret plot to murder Cortés while his forces were being put up in Cholula's palaces. Cortés took quick action, ordering his troops to shoot every *indígena* in sight. After most of Cholula's 100,000 inhabitants were killed, the God-fearing Spaniards razed the city's 400 shrines and swore to build a church atop the ruins of every one. To this day most Mexicans contend that there are 365 churches in the area. The state tourist office, however, counts only 45 in the city itself and about 32 more in the general vicinity. Cortés fell short of his mark, but his brutal action has left Cholula with a concentration of religious architecture unsurpassed in Mexico.

Beneath Cholula and buried all around are the remnants of the glorious pre-Conquest past. The area's main attraction is the great **pyramid mound** where seven different civilizations have left their mark. Cholula's pyramid is the world's largest, volumetrically—more than double the size of Egypt's Cheops. Much of what is still hidden will never be uncovered because the intervening layer of colonial buildings is itself treasured today. Cholula's most modern prize, the **University of the Americas** (the only U.S.-accredited college in Mexico), draws many young *norteamericanos* to town.

ORIENTATION

Cholula is on Route 150, 122km west of Mexico City and 20km from Puebla. To reach Cholula from Mexico City by bus take an **Estrella Roja** bus from the Terminal del Oriente (usually called TAPO. Every ½hr, 12.50 pesos). The trip takes just over two hours and crosses through some beautiful countryside, including Liano Grande, a national park. Two snow topped volcanoes, Popocatéptl and Ixtaccíhuatl, dominate the scenery.

The Estrella Roja bus station is at Av. 12 Ote. 4 (tel. 47-19-20). To reach the *zócalo* from here, turn left on Av. 12 Ote and walk 100m, then turn left on to Av. 5 de

Mayo, walk four blocks on Av. 5 de Mayo and you'll be on the north side of the *zócalo*. To leave Cholula, you must get to the bus station in Puebla (usually called CAPU). *Colectivos* running between Cholula's *centro* and Puebla's CAPU cost 1 peso and can be flagged down at the intersection of Av. 6 Ote. and Av. 5 de Mayo, north of the *zócalo*. The *colectivos* run until 8pm, after that, a taxi is your best bet.

The streets in Cholula form a grid with the *zócalo* roughly at the center. But beware: the municipality of Cholula encompasses two towns: Cholula and San Andrés (Hotel Las Américas and the University of the Americas, for example, are actually in San Andrés.) This can be somewhat confusing, as there is no clear boundary between the towns. Cholula's main thoroughfare runs along the south side of the *zócalo*; west of the *zócalo* it is called Av. Morelos. Walking east on Morelos, the town of San Andrés begins just after the pyramid, at which point Av. Morelos becomes Av. 14 Ote.

PRACTICAL INFORMATION

Tourist Office: Cholula has no official office. Your best bet is to ask the people at the base of the pyramid. They can be helpful once they stop offering their services as guides. The expensive **Hotel Calli Quetzalcóatl** (see Accommodations below) is another source of information.

Currency Exchange: Bancomer on the west side of the *zócalo*. Open Mon.-Fri. 9am-1:30pm. Bánamex, on the south side of the *zócalo*. Open Mon.-Fri. 9am-5pm. Changing traveler's checks is easier at **Casa de Cambio Azteca,** Calle 2 Sur 104 (tel. 47-21-90), off the southeast corner of the *zócalo*. Open Mon.-Fri. 9am-5pm, Sat. 9am-1pm. The main desk at **Hotel Calli Quetzalcóatl** will exchange after hours at unfavorable rates.

Post Office: Alemán 702 (tel. 47-01-30), 3 blocks south of the *zócalo*. Open Mon.-Fri. 8am-6:30pm, Sat. 8am-noon. **Postal Code:** 72760.

Telephones: Long-distance *caseta* at the **Farmacia Moderna,** Morelos 12 (tel. 47-11-99), on the *zócalo*. Open Mon.-Sun. 8am-8pm. **Hotel Quetzalcóatl** is always open: local calls cost 1 peso, domestic collect calls 3 pesos and international collect calls 5 pesos. **Telephone Code:** 12.

Telegrams: In the **Telecom** office, Av. 5 Pte. 102A (tel. 47-01-30), 2 blocks south of the *zócalo*. Open Mon.-Fri. 9am-3pm.

Cultural Affairs: Casa de la Cultura, Av. 4 Pte. 103 (tel. 47-19-86), 1 block west of the *zócalo*'s northwest corner. Bulletin board at building entrance advertises special events, local arts programs, new book clubs in the area, and the schedules of local aerobics classes. Public phone inside. There is a bookstore upstairs. Downstairs, the office can be of some help.

General Stores: El Super Hidalgo, Hidalgo 105 (tel. 47-19-12), is conveniently located at the end of the portal, and they speak some English. For your 24-hr. *agua purificada* and snack food needs, run out to **Super Tucan,** Av. 4 Pte. 107A (tel. 47-60-04), 1 block west of Hotel Las Américas. Ring the doorbell after hours.

Laundromat: Lavandería Orion, Hidalgo 305 (tel. 47-44-48). Will wash, dry and fold 3kg of your dirtiest clothes for 10 pesos. Open Mon.-Sat. 9am-8pm. Also, Lavanderia Burbujas (tel. 47-37-66). Open Mon.-Sat. 8:30am-7pm. 3kg for 10 pesos. Home delivery. One block west of Hotel Las Américas on Av. 14 Ote.

Red Cross: Calle 7 Sur at Av. 3 Pte. (tel. 47-03-93). A long walk west from any of the hotels listed below. Walk-in service. Open 24 hrs.

Pharmacy: Farmacia Moderna (see Telephones above).

Hospital General: Av. 2 Pte. 1504 (tel. 47-18-00), 10 blocks west of the *zócalo* on the outskirts of town.

Police: Officially located at the prison, Cárcel Municipal at Hidalgo, Av. 7 Nte. (tel. 47-05-62), across the street from the Red Cross. Officers are more easily found at the Presidencia Municipal, Portal Guerrero 1, on the west side of the *zócalo*.

ACCOMMODATIONS AND FOOD

Cholula is not a budget traveler's haven. One of the more expensive hotels, **Hotel Calli Quetzalcóatl,** Portal Guerrero 11 (tel. 47-15-33), generously provides services for anyone—travel information about surrounding areas, long-distance phone service and currency exchange, plus a gorgeous restaurant. The two inexpensive hotels in Cholula are both located east of the *zócalo*. **Hotel Las Américas,** Av. 14 Ote. 6 (tel. 47-09-91), in San Andres, is worth the hike. Spacious rooms with wall-to-wall carpeting, firm beds and clean bathrooms. Tree-lined courtyard encloses a pool, patio chairs, and, during mating season, nests of madly chirping birds. Cheap restaurant in lobby (open daily 7:30am-10pm) doubles as a TV lounge. More expensive rooms afford a beautiful view of volcanoes. Plumbing and electricity may prove tricky. To reach the hotel from the *zócalo*, walk east on Morelos (which will become 14 Ote.), cross the train tracks and keep going, past the pyramid and the Sanitorio Guadaloupe, 15-20 minutes from the *zócalo*; women may feel uncomfortable walking here alone at night. (Singles 35 pesos, doubles with TV 55 pesos, with view 65 pesos.) Smaller rooms, clean and decorated with photographs of Cholula's church, can be found at **Hotel Reforma,** Calle 4 Sur 101 (tel. 47-01-49). Cheaper than Hotel Las Américas, and only two blocks east of the *zócalo*, but the courtyard and atmosphere can't compare. From the *zócalo*, walk east for two blocks then hang a right. (Singles and doubles 25 pesos, with bath 40 pesos, with two beds 60 pesos.) The **Reforma Bar**, adjacent to the hotel, on Morelos, claims to be the oldest bar in town and boasts a beautiful photograph mural displaying every church in Cholula.

There are two *mercados* in Cholula. The larger, semi-indoor market, west of the *zócalo* at the intersection of Av. 2 Pte. and Calle 3 Nte., sells fruit, vegetables, toys, hardware, shoes, and whole dead animals. The smaller food market sets up on the north side of the *zócalo*. For a good, reasonably priced meal, try **Cafe y Arte Los Portales**, Portal Guerrero 17, on the west side of the *zócalo*. *Comida corridas* 10 pesos and 13 pesos (add 1 peso to each on Sundays and holidays). Prize-winning a la carte fare, as well. Great coffee. Clean bathrooms. Somewhat cheaper, **Super Cocina Conchita** (open Mon.-Sat. 10am-6pm) at Morelos 204 three blocks east of the *zócalo*, serves up *acomida corrida* (soup, main course, dessert) for 10 pesos. Homey atmosphere. Pricey, but with good food and a nice location, is **Restaurant Colonial** (tel. 47-25-08) at Morelos 605, just across the street from the entrance to the pyramid. They proudly accept all credit cards.

SIGHTS

When Cortés destroyed the temple to the rain god and replaced it with the Santuario de Nuestra Señora de los Remedios, he was unaware that buried in the hill below was the **Great Pyramid,** and beneath that, five more pyramids. A tunnel penetrates 1km and 2000 years into the belly of the complex. The entrance to the tunnel is on Morelos, at the base of the pyramid's north side. Walking from the *zócalo* on Morelos, cross the railroad tracks; 50m farther on the right is a ticket booth. The first structure built on this site is known as Tlachihualtépetl (or Handmade Hill), which is at the very bottom of the mound. As each group arrived and came into power, it would bury the structure built by its predecessor. An elaborate drainage system had to be incorporated into each of the pyramids. These drains can be seen from the tunnel and used to facilitate self-guided tours. Along the way, side tunnels permit views of some of the archaeological features off the main tunnel. You cannot lose your way unless you stray from the path open to tourists; the whole tunnel complex is only 8km long. Guides, available at the tunnel's entrance (30 pesos, in Spanish 25 pesos), can illuminate (literally and figuratively) some of the tunnel's more obscure points, including otherwise invisible insect frescoes. Indulge some of your creepy fantasies, but beware: the tunnel is not for the claustrophobic nor the very tall.

Above ground at the end of the tunnel is the base of the exposed portion of the Great Pyramid. Most of the surrounding religious edifices (approx. 400 shrines), demolished as part of Cortés's strategy to convert the Cholultecs, had also been covered over before this final pyramid was built. The Great Pyramid is best appreciated

CHOLULA

from the large square altar on the southwest corner of the pyramid where bleached bones and offerings are displayed. The mass of the mound gives you an idea of the immensity of this structure—it has the largest base of any pyramid in the world (about 450 ft. on each side). The reconstructed area directly in front of the mound, as you gaze out from the altar, is a ceremonial ground dedicated to Quetzalcóatl; just to the west is a fresco of the god.

As you walk beyond the pyramid, you will see various other excavations amidst the green lawn. At the southwest corner of the pyramid, two display-model skeletons grace the altar where adolescents were sacrificed to the gods in times of crisis. Before you leave the grounds, check out the reconstructed pyramid on the west side of the great mound. This appendage to the main pyramid shows the inner workings of the drainage system made to protect the structures.

Upon leaving the site, make a right at the gate (an exit only; tickets must be bought at the tunnel entrance) and head up the mound. The climb up the mound is steep, but worth the effort. To the south, Cholula's many churches are visible, and the two volcanoes, **Popocatépetl** and **Ixtaccíhuatl** (also called *la mujer durmida*, because it is said to resemble a sleeping woman. Squint.), surge skyward to the west. (Tunnel and ruins open daily 10am-5pm. Admission 13 pesos, free Sun. 25 pesos if you want to use a camcorder.)

The admission fee to the pyramid will also gain you entrance to the **Museo Regional de Cholula,** set back from the road. The museum spotlights artifacts found within the mound and in the surrounding area, including several examples of early colonial ceramic painting. The colorful birds of Cholula were a favorite subject. Also displayed is a model of the pyramids in their original configuration, which makes the whole kettle of fish easier to understand. A **bookstore** specializing in the art and culture of the Cholula region adjoins the museum. (Museum and bookstore open Tues.-Sun. 10am-5pm. Free with ticket from pyramid.)

Four churches should round out your itinerary in Cholula. The first of these, interesting only because it squats atop the mound, is the **Santuario de Nuestra Señora de los Remedios.** On the east end of the *zócalo*, the **Capilla Real** occupies the site where Cortés slaughtered Aztecs in their place of worship. Its interior goes unadorned but for its 49 domes, which give it a remarkable structural elegance. To reach the church at Acatepec, catch the Chipilo bus at the intersection of Av. 6 Ote. and Av. 5 de Mayo (1 peso). Most of this church burned down in 1940, but the beautiful facade, more tile than brick, remained intact. Also served by the Chipilo bus is the church at Tonantzintla, famed for having the loveliest interior of any church in Mexico. Every inch is covered with multi-colored, 3-D ornaments; most striking are the hundreds of *indígena* busts among baroque swirls of plaster and tile. The design is a manifestation of the compromises the Catholic church made to ingratiate itself with the *indígenas*.

ENTERTAINMENT

Thanks to its student population, Cholula sprouts distractions. Check the bulletin board at Casa de la Cultura for events around town. **Billares San Pedrito**, a pool hall on Av. 6 Ote 3, rents tables for 6.90 pesos per hr. (open 11am-11pm). **Faces**, the upscale disco in town, charges a cover of 20 pesos and attracts the university crowd on Thursday nights. Just across the street, **Paradise** advertises no cover and is said to attract a less-genteel clientele. Both clubs are open Thurs.-Sat. after 10pm and can be found on Av. 5 de Mayo (from the *zócalo*, walk east on Morelos 14 Ote and turn right ½ block before Hotel Las Américas).

MORELOS

After the Habsburg Emperor Maximilian built his summer residence in Cuernavaca, thousands of Mexicans elected to play follow the leader, making the state of Morelos their vacation spot of choice. Today, Mexicans and foreigners alike march to Morelos to take advantage of Cuernavaca's "eternal spring," Cuautla's many bathing areas, and Tepoztlán's striking landscape. Morelos is a short jaunt from Mexico City; you can easily spend a day in Cuernavaca, Cuautla, or Tepoztlán and return to the capital in the evening.

Morelos' climb to historical significance began when its peasants organized and agitated for land reform; this movement gave rise to Emiliano Zapata's career as a revolutionary leader, as well to the 1911 Plan of Ayala, which called for the expropriation and restoration of the "land, woods, and water that the landlords, *científicos*, and bosses have usurped." Remnants of Morelos's revolutionary past are evident in Cuautla, while vestiges of imperial Mexico remain in Cuernavaca.

■■■ CUERNAVACA

Less than 70km south of the Sierra de Ajusco, a low-lying mountain range cupping Mexico City, sits Cuernavaca, the quintessential colonial city and capital of Morelos state. Home to a considerable number of wealthy Mexicans, Cuernavaca also functions as a somewhat overrated vernal playground for Mexico City residents escaping the hassles of big-city life and as an immersion program for the hundreds of *norteamericanos* who come to participate in the city's numerous language schools. With a median annual temperature of 20°C (68°F), Cuernavaca has long attracted visitors: Emperor Maximilian, Cortés, Gabriel García Márquez, and Muhammed Ali have all, at some point, kicked back in the mansions of Cuernavaca's exclusive *colonias*.

The Tlahuica, an Aztec tribe that first populated the valley, named their city *Cuauhnahuac*, "Place on the Outskirts of the Grove." As the great historian of Mexico William Prescott remarks, "This barbarous Indian name is tortured into all possible variations by the old chronicles." Mexico's *criollo* elite transformed the city into their private summer camp, and the name was corrupted into the more easily pronounced Spanish quasi-homonym *Cuernavaca*.

ORIENTATION

Route 95 from Mexico City intersects many of Cuernavaca's main avenues. To get to the city center, exit onto **Domingo Diez** if coming from Mexico City, or **Emiliano Zapata,** which splits into northbound one-way **José María Morelos** and **Avenida Obregón,** if coming from the north. **Benito Juárez** is the main north-south thoroughfare east of the *zócalo*. Two plazas together make up the Cuernavaca's *zócalo*, which may or may not be marked on the tourist office map. The main one, the **Plaza de la Constitución,** is a few blocks east of Morelos via Hidalgo, at the intersection of Guerrero, Salazar, Juárez, and Hidalgo. Diagonally opposite the *zócalo's* northwest corner sits the smaller **Jardín Juárez.**

Cuernavaca's streets madden with their jumble of irregularities and unexpected turns, especially near the plaza. Alhough even and odd numbers stay on different sides of the street, buildings directly opposite each other may have numbers several hundred apart. Frequent local buses (1 peso) travel Morelos, and from there to the area or *colonia* painted on the windshield. Taxis—small, white Toyotas, Datsuns, or VWs—will go anywhere in the city for 6-7 pesos.

PRACTICAL INFORMATION

Tourist Offices: State Office, Morelos Sur 802 (tel. 14-39-20), a 10-min. walk south from the Ayuntamiento. Elderly staff may attempt English, but consult the

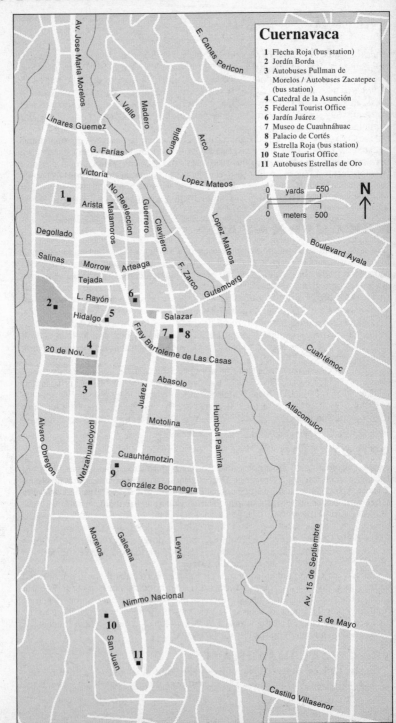

Cuernavaca

1 Flecha Roja (bus station)
2 Jordín Borda
3 Autobuses Pullman de
   Morelos / Autobuses Zacatepec
   (bus station)
4 Catedral de la Asunción
5 Federal Tourist Office
6 Jardín Juárez
7 Museo de Cuauhnáhuac
8 Palacio de Cortés
9 Estrella Roja (bus station)
10 State Tourist Office
11 Autobuses Estrellas de Oro

0   yards   550
0   meters   500

N

brochures and other info instead. Pathetic free maps. Open Mon.-Fri. 9am-8pm, Sat.-Sun. 9am-6pm. **Federal Office:** tel. 12-54-14.

American Express: (tel. 14-22-66) in the Las Plazas Shopping mall on the northern side of the *zócalo*. Holds mail, won't exchange anything. Open Mon.-Fri. 9am-2pm and 4-6pm, Sat. 10am-2pm.

Currency Exchange: Quite a few banks hide in the labyrinth of streets around the *zócalo*, but only a few will be of any use to the traveler. Currency exchange 9am-12:30pm. **Bánamex,** at Matamoros and Arteaga, 1 block north of Jardín Juárez, has ATMs for MC, Visa, Cirrus, and Plus. **Casa de Cambio: Divisas de Cuernavaca,** Morrow 12A and Guerrero 208 (tel. 12-85-68 or 18-35-62), in the *centro* and in the Plaza Los Arcos in the northern part of town. Open Mon.-Fri. 9am-5pm.

Post Office: Pl. de la Constitución 3 (tel. 12-43-79), on the southwest corner of the *zócalo*. Open Mon.-Fri. 8am-7pm, Sat. (stamps only) 9am-3pm; for *Lista de Correos* Mon.-Fri. 8am-7pm. **Postal code:** 62000.

Telephones: Telcom, Salazar 8, on the eastern edge of the *zócalo* behind the market area. Open Mon.-Fri. 8am-8pm, Sat.-Sun. 9am-2pm. **Farmacia Central,** in *Jardín Juárez* at Rayón (tel. 12-78-25). Open daily 7am-10pm. **LADATELs** are easy to find around the *zócalo*. **Telephone code:** 73.

Telegrams: Next to the post office. Open Mon.-Fri. 9am-8pm, Sat. 9am-1pm.

Train Station: Leandro Valle 33 (tel. 12-80-44). Service only to Iguala (10am, 3 pesos, 5hr.).

Bus Stations: 1st- and 2nd-class buses arrive at several small terminals scattered about town. **México-Zacatepec (LASER)/Pullman de Morelos,** Netzahualcóyotl 106 at Abasolo (tel. 14-36-50), 2 blocks south of the *zócalo*. To, among others, Mexico City (every 20 mins., 5-10:40pm, 11.50 pesos), Zacatepec (4 pesos), and Grutas de Cacahuamilpa (8 pesos); many destinations in Morelos state. **Flecha Roja,** Morelos 503, 4 blocks north of *Jardín Borda*. 1st-class service to: Mexico City (16 per day, 15 pesos), Acapulco (7 per day, 60 pesos), Taxco (9 per day, 8 pesos), Grutas de Cacahuamilpa (9 pesos), Iguala (10 pesos), Toluca (every 30 min., 5:30am-9pm, 12 pesos), and Santiago. **Estrella de Oro,** on Morelos Sur at Las Palmas Circle (tel. 12-30-55), 10 blocks south of the intersection of Reforma and Hidalgo. 1st class service to: Mexico City (6 per day, 11.50 pesos), Taxco (4 per day, 8 pesos), Chilpancingo (8pm, 24 pesos), Zihuatanejo (2 per day, 60 pesos), Acapulco (2 per day, 52 pesos), and Lázaro Cárdenas (2 per day, 71 pesos). **Estrella Roja,** Galeana 401 (tel. 12-06-34), 7 blocks south of the *zócalo*. 1st class service to Cuautla (34 per day, 6 pesos), Oaxtepec (28 per day, 6.50 pesos), and Puebla (15 per day, 15 pesos). 2nd-class **Estrella Roja** and **Ometochtli,** on López Mateos at the south end of the Mercado. Buses load in the parking lot across the highway that runs perpendicular to Degollado. Buses to Tepoztlán and Jojutla.

Local Transit Authority: Emiliano Zapata 802 (tel. 16-10-00), in the north part of town, same building as police. Bus schedules as well as highway information.

English Bookstores: Anglo-American Bookstore Las Plazas, in Las Plazas Mall, facing the *zócalo*. Shelves full of best sellers, picture books, and an entire wall dedicated to classics from Dickens to Shaw. Open Mon.-Fri. 10am-6:30pm, Sat. 12:30-3:30pm, but knock if the English-speaking proprietor is inside.

Academic Programs for Foreign Students: A number of centers provide summer- and term-time instruction in Spanish. Weekly tuition includes 6 hrs. of daily language instruction and may also include both group excursions to historic sites and placement in local homes. **Cuauhnahuac** charges US$150 per week for 6 hrs. of classes daily, without lodging. Check with **Cuauhnahuac,** Morelos Sur 1414, Col. Chipitlán (tel. 12-36-73). Open Mon.-Fri. 8am-3pm. **Experiencia,** Leyva 1130, col. Las Palmas (tel. 18-52-09), offers very reliable bilingual programs. Other noted programs are: **Concepto Educativo Bilingüe Cultural,** H. Preciado 171 (tel. 12-23-44); **I.D.E.A.L.,** PO Box 22-B, Cuernavaca, Morelos (tel. 17-04-55); and **Instituto de Lengua y Estudios Latinoamericanos,** Bajada de la Pradera 208 (tel. 17-52-94). **Instituto Cultural Xochilalco,** Nueva Francia 532, col. Reforma Nte. (tel. 13-87-98) and **Centro de Arte y Lenguas "Cale,"** Nueva Tabachín (tel. 13-06-03), may offer more unconventional programs. Check and compare programs in advance.

Markets: Superama, at Morelos, just behind Helados Holanda north of the cathedral. Open Mon.-Sat. 7:30am-9pm, Sun. 8am-8pm. An excellent fruit and vegetable market is located in the triangle formed by Blvd. Alfonso López Mateos.

Laundromat: Nueva Tintoreria Francesa, Juárez 2, next to the Palacio de Cortés. Loads washed, dried, and folded for 9 pesos/kg. Open Mon.-Sat. 9am-7pm.

Red Cross: Ixtaccihuatl at Río Panuco (tel. 15-05-51 or 15-35-55).

24-hr. Pharmacy: Farmacia Blanco, Morelos 710 (tel. 18-23-93), just north of the Flecha Roja bus station.

Medical Assistance: Centro Quirúrgico, Juárez 507-B, has a doctor for every ailment in exchange for a hefty payment. More free help at **ISSSTE** (tel. 14-19-57) and **IMSS** (tel. 12-17-88 or 15-50-00).

Hospital: Hospital Civil, Morelos 197 (tel. 14-14-44 or 14-15-36), directly across the street from the cathedral. 24-hr. emergency treatment free (pay for supplies only). Long lines form at all hours in the waiting room/courtyard. Open 24 hrs.

Police: Emiliano Zapata 802 (tel. 17-11-15, 12-00-36, or 17-10-00). 24 hrs.

Emergency: tel. 06, 24 hrs.

ACCOMMODATIONS

Cuernavaca's hotels suffer the slightly overpriced tendencies that come hand-in-hand with the city's getaway status. The bare rooms may be offset by a swimming pool or the lush courtyard, both useful in fending off the effects of the powerful sun that bakes the entire city. The least expensive conventional lodgings line Matamoros for several blocks north from the *zócalo*. Although a number of the *casas de huéspedes* back-to-back along Aragón y León are cheaper, you'd do best to pass them up—many of the guests have customers of their own.

For an extended stay, it is possible to lodge with a local family through one of the local Spanish-language schools. Students (mostly Europeans and *norteamericanos*) who attend these schools choose from a list of families willing to provide room, board, and language practice. **Cuauhnahuac** is especially willing to lend their family list to backpacking visitors who wish to spend time with *cuernavaquences*. Sharing a room with a student costs US$14 per day for room and board; for a private single, you pay US$20. Contact José Camacho at Cuauhnahuac. Also try the bilingual language school, **Experiencia,** Leyva 1130, Col. Las Palmas (tel. 18-52-09, see Practical Information: Academic Programs for Foreign Students above).

The bulletin boards at the **Instituto Regional de Bellas Artes (IRBAC),** Morelos 405 (tel. 12-13-18), two blocks from the *Jardín Borda*, may display notices from local families with rooms for rent. Most families prefer *señoritas*, and board is optional in many cases. These offers are usually intended for Mexican students, so those who don't speak Spanish may have difficulties. For the most accurate information, contact the schools directly.

Los Canarios Motel, Morelos 713 (tel. 13-44-44), just north of the intersection with Matamoros. This fading semi-resort maintains a weathered pool, as well as an enclosed tennis court (bring your own net). The bungalow-type rooms, complete with miniature front porches, are interspersed with small gardens and little shops. Nice bathrooms separated from rooms by odd, romantic *a la* '60s screens. Friendly staff. Singles 44 pesos. Doubles 88 pesos.

Hotel Colonial, Aragón y León 104 (tel. 18-64-14), in the middle of the block. A nicely renovated colonial building, not much bigger than a private home, centered on a small garden-like courtyard. Rooms are clean but some are stuffy. Hot water available 7-11am and 7-11pm. Singles 55 pesos. Doubles 75 pesos.

Motel Royal, Matamoros 19 (tel. 18-64-80), 2 blocks north of *Jardín Juárez*. Drab pink courtyard rimmed by institutional-blue rooms. The quarters themselves are better, with soft and comfortable beds and small but clean bathrooms. Attractive wooden furniture in the sheltered common area. Hot water in morning and evening only. Singles 46 pesos. Doubles 70 pesos.

Hotel Juárez, Netzahualcóyotl 117 (tel. 14-02-19). Large, bright rooms with homey wooden furniture, glaring bare lightbulbs, firm mattresses, and clean bathrooms.

Some rooms are bright and airy, but others offer only slits for windows. Swimming pool 'round back. Singles 55 pesos. Doubles 77 pesos.

Hotel Roma, Matamoros 405 (tel. 18-87-78), 4 blocks north of the *Jardín Juárez.* Narrow courtyard decorated with palm trees growing out of oil cans. High-altitude stairs with dangerously low railings lead to 2nd floor. Sparse rooms, with sagging beds and functional bathrooms. Singles 45 pesos. Doubles 55 pesos.

FOOD

Cuernavaca provides both better and more expensive food than many Mexican cities of similar size, thanks to the wealth of its residents and the constant influx of domestic and international tourists. Take advantage of the variety of excellent restaurants around the plaza for your main meal; head up the side streets (try Aragón y León or Morelos) for more inexpensive fare. In the market, *comidas corridas* cost about 10 pesos, *con refresco.* Beware of dirty dishes and old, unclean frying oil.

Along Guerrero, north of the plaza, street vendors sell mangos, *piñas* (pineapples), and *elotes* (corn on the cob), along with pocket combs, sunglasses and digital watches. The health drinks sold at the Eiffel Kiosk in the *Jardín Juárez* include everything from the standard fruit and milk *licuados* to a spinach concoction not even Popeye could love. The drinks are cheap (5-9 pesos), delicious and hygienically prepared with pasteurized milk.

Restaurant La Bufa, Comonfort 6-B (tel. 18-66-13). Cheap and plentiful food served in a quiet, cool ambience. Handmade tortillas and personal service. Excellent *comida corrida* 10 pesos. *Café americano* 2 pesos. Open daily 8:30am-6pm.

Marco Polo Pizzería, Hidalgo 26 (tel. 12-34-84), on the 2nd floor. Elegant atmosphere, with a lot of plants and brick and surprisingly low prices. Balconies overlook the street. Meat dishes are expensive (around 27 pesos), but small pizzas can handle 1 or 2 people for 10-30 pesos. Spaghetti with pesto sauce 13 pesos. Open daily 1-10:30pm.

Restaurante Vegetariana, Galeana 110, 1 block down the hill from Hidalgo. May change location in 1994. This completely vegetarian restaurant offers an alternative *comida corrida* (10 pesos) with options like cheese soup and fresh salad. All done with filtered water. Decorated with photos of veggies and healthy-looking folks. Yogurt with fruit and honey 3 pesos. Open daily 9am-8pm.

Restaurant WYM, Aragón y León 7-B (tel. 18-60-53). Recognizable by the orange front. What it lacks in atmosphere it makes up in quality of food and service. Excellent *comida corrida* includes hot fresh tortillas, dessert and coffee or tea (10 pesos). Open daily 8am-7pm.

La Parroquia de Cuernavaca, Guerrero 102 (tel. 12-89-15), on the east side of *Jardín Juárez.* The best of the cheap European cafés. Squeeze in among the tables of executives to snag one of the best people-watching seats in the city. Arabian *kafta* specialties 12-45 pesos, enchiladas 18 pesos, view free. *Menú* 23 pesos. Open daily 7:30am-midnight.

Fonda FIJ, Benito Juárez 500 (tel. 18-96-96). Crosswinds cool the open restaurant while customers enjoy cheap standard fare. 3 tacos go for 9 pesos, *tortas* 4-9 pesos. Open daily 8am-6pm.

Fonda El Recuerdo, Morelos 191 (tel. 12-18-35), on the side of the cathedral. A family-run restaurant in tasteful peach. Coziness that even fake flowers can't ruin. Delightful food: excellent soups 6-9 pesos, including *sopa de enopal* (a kind of cactus) 7 pesos, delicious entrees 9-25 pesos, and great desserts 3-6 pesos. Full breakfasts 5-8 pesos. First drinks always free, any time! Open Sun.-Wed. 8am-9pm, Thurs.-Sat. 8am-midnight.

Nevería La Virginia, Juárez 300 (tel. 12-97-42), across Abasolo from Sauboruis. A standard appearance belies the 40 exotic flavors served. Such titillating delights as cucumber, rice, corn, peanut, *maracuya,* or *jicama.* 1 scoop 3 pesos. *Flotante* (ice cream of your choice served in a *refresco*) 9 pesos. Open daily 8:30am-9pm.

SIGHTS

Cuernavaca's popularity, while well-deserved, is not due to its scintilating sights. The **Plaza de la Constitución,** the larger of the two which comprise the *zócalo*, extends east from the Palacio de Gobierno, home of the Morelos state bureaucracy. Heart and soul of the city, the plaza glows with fiery red *flamboyanes* (royal poinciana) and is shaded by elm and palm trees. Cafés spill into the plaza, and people compete for space on wrought-iron benches while food vendors, balloon-sellers and *mariachis* engage in a Darwinian struggle for pesos.

A wonderful bulbous kiosk designed by Gustave Eiffel and commissioned by Cuernavaca's Viennese colony stands in the **Jardín Juárez,** at the northwest corner of the Pl. de la Constitución, north of the Palacio de Gobierno. At all times of day, the garden is filled with mobile orange shoeshine booths, vendors hawking helium balloons, mobs of *cuernavaquences* and large North American tour groups. Thursdays and Sundays at 6pm, a local band commandeers the kiosk and belts out polkas, classical music and *rancheras* (Mexican country music). The kiosk houses a fruit drink stand which displays a long list of each ingredient's health benefits.

At the southeastern corner of the Pl. de la Constitución, east of Benito Juárez, the **Palacio de Cortés** stand as a stately reminder of the city's grim history. The prolific conqueror Cortés built this fortress with the remains of the buildings he leveled when he set the town on fire in 1521. Like many other legacies of the Conquest, this one rises from the base of a sacred pyramid. A buttressed, two-story stone fortress, the palace has a circular watch tower on the left, a line of spiky parapets running along the roof, and arches marking the entrance. The base of the original pyramid remains visible on the east side. Begun in 1522 and completed in 1524—when Cortés left to destroy Honduras—the building functioned as a prison in the 18th century and as the Palacio de Gobierno during the *Porfiriato* (the dictatorship of Porfirio Díaz).

A grant from the former British ambassador to Mexico (none other than Charles Lindbergh's father-in-law) has transformed the Palacio de Cortés into the **Museo Cuauhnahuac.** On the first floor of the museum, archaeological and anthropological exhibits deal with pre-Hispanic cultures. Timelines highlight the histories of the Toltec, Olmec, Mayan and Aztec peoples; some illustrated parchments enable a closer look at the Xochilimilca, Chalcha, Telpaneca, and Tlahuica cultures. Second-floor exhibits on the Conquest and later Mexican history include the first public clock ever to toll in Mesoamerica and some original clothing and furnishings from the palace. A collection of rare photographs chronicles the Revolution of 1910 and ethnographic exhibits mark the march of "progress" in Tlahuican daily life.

One of Diego Rivera's greatest works awaits on the western balcony on the second floor of the palace. Painted during the building's stint as the Palacio de Gobierno, the mural was commissioned by then-U.S. ambassador to Mexico Dwight D. Morrow as a gift to the people of Cuernavaca. Rivera's mural depicts the history of Mexico from the Conquest until the Revolution of 1910, proceeding chronologically from right to left. A striking statue of Morelos towers over the museum's south patio. (Palacio and museum open Tues.-Sun. 10am-5pm. Admission 13 pesos, free Sun.)

Black soot has darkened the tall walls and towers of the **Catedral de la Asunción,** three blocks down Hidalgo from the *zócalo*, at Morelos. Construction on the three temples of the cathedral began in 1525, and the bulk was finished by 1552, making this one of the earliest churches in the Americas. The high, fortress-like walls and parapets were intended to impress the *indígena* population with clerical power. The stalwart construction retains its impenetrable appearance with thick walls and stark decor. The florid reliefs adorning the cathedral are good examples of the wildly ornamented, post-baroque Churrigueresque style. Removal of the aisle altars 20 years ago disclosed some fabulous Asian frescoes depicting the persecution and martyrdom of Christian missionaries in Sokori, Japan. Historians speculate that these frescoes were created in the early 17th century by a converted Japanese artist who had settled in Cuernavaca. The cross over a skull and bones on the north entrance to the main temple is an emblem of the Franciscan order. (Open daily 7am-7pm.)

Site of glamorous soirees during the French occupation of Mexico, the **Jardín Borda** exists today as the lackluster shell of earlier glory. The stone entrance is on Morelos, across from the cathedral. In 1783, the priest Manuel de la Borda built a garden of magnificent pools and fountains next to the ostentatious residence of his relative, the traveler José de la Borda. The *Jardín Borda*'s grandeur quickly gained fame, and in 1864, Emperor Maximilian and his wife Carlota established a summer residence there. Maximilian's dignitaries rode delicate boats on the giant pool in the park's northern end, which is portrayed in a painting hanging in the city's museum. Today, it takes a vivid imagination to recognize the faded splendor of a past epoch as you stroll down the crumbling, moss-covered sidewalks. In the southern section of the park, circuitous paths radiate from a large, deteriorated stone fountain toward other smaller ones. Unlike the fountains and sidewalks, the mango trees, tropical ferns, ornamental plants, and giant palm trees have flourished through the years. Galleries in the entrance hall display temporary exhibits of contemporary art; and patchwork rowboats are available for rent for those wishing to emulate the emperor's cronies. (Open Tues.-Sun. 10am-5:30pm. Admission 2 pesos.)

The **Pyramid of Teopanzolco** squats on a glistening green lawn at the center of a public park, near the southern end of Teopanzolco, southeast of the market on Guerrero. These Aztec ruins were uncovered during the revolution, when firing tanks loosened the top layer of soil. As is frequently the case in Mexico, the pyramid actually consists of two pyramids, one within the other. The first stairway leads to a ledge, at the bottom of which a second stairway, belonging to the second pyramid, begins. Like other pre-Hispanic peoples, the Tlahuica periodically increased the size of their monuments simply by encasing outdated ones in new construction. An eerie partial staircase suggests that the new pyramid was unfinished when Cortés arrived. To get to the site, walk north (the cathedral will be on your left) on Morelos from downtown, turn right on Pericón, and go right on Río Balsas to Teopanzolco. If this sounds too complicated or exhausting, hop on local bus #9 and ask the driver to let you off at the *pirámide*. (Open Tues.-Sun. 10am-5pm. Admission 10 pesos.)

Once the most glamorous and exclusive hotels in Cuernavaca, the **Casino de la Selva,** Leandro Valle 1001 (tel. 12-47-04), on the northern side of the city center, now ranks second, third, or maybe fourth. Still, the gardens and open-air collection of modern and pre-Hispanic sculpture entice visitors. On the front wall of the hotel, a fantastic image symbolizes the Conquest: an armored centaur wrestles furiously with fiery angels, with the wounded lying scattered on the ground. Opposite, a bland depiction of the new Mexican "race" (symbolized by an *indígena* woman) being shaped by technology and industry contrasts poorly with the other murals. The walls and ceilings of the main dining hall were decorated by young artists, working in conjunction with famous *cuernavaquence* muralist David Alfaro Siqueiros. On the left wall, the myths of pre-Hispanic Mexico are presented in fine detail. On the right is a magnificent rendering of the history of Spanish civilization from the Crusades to the Conquest. The ceiling portrays various historical phenomena of modern Mexico: independence, reform, and events leading to revolution. Take bus #5 or 18 and ask to be shown the inconspicuous stop.

ENTERTAINMENT AND SEASONAL EVENTS

Cuernavaca's age-old popularity as a vacation spot has encouraged the development of a nightlife more glitzy than that in most Mexican cities. Cuernavaca's U.S. expatriate community, which numbers over 20,000, has given many of these activities a northern flair. Bars in Cuernavaca are modern and highly commercialized, and several have live nightly entertainment. Most joints around the *zócalo* cater to tourists; some have no cover charge but expect patrons to buy drinks.

Most discos are open from 8pm to 4am on Friday and Saturday. To deter the fist-fights and *broncas* (brawls) that used to plague Cuernavaca's discos, some now admit only male-female couples and require reservations; most, however, do not enforce these business-diminishing rules. The popular discos are not on the *zócalo* but farther down neighboring side streets. Students from the local language schools get free passes and avoid cover charges. **Ta'izz,** Chapultepec 50 (tel. 15-40-60), emphasizes top-40 over *lambada*. Fog machines and light shows seduce the younger crowd. (Cover 40 pesos. Beer 10 pesos. Open 9pm-4am.) **Shadée,** at the end of Gutenberg, east of the *zócalo*, is a smaller disco. Music and personal attention from the English-speaking manager make this place popular with the city's language students. (Cover Thurs.-Sat. 30 pesos. Drinks 15 pesos. Open Mon.-Sat. 9pm-4am.) **Barba Azul,** Pradera 10 (tel. 13-19-76), hypes up Mexico City's post-college crowd and is also popular with the local language school students. (Cover 30 pesos. Drinks 12 pesos. Open Fri.-Sat. 10am-5am.) Free entertainment is generally available in the main plazas at 6pm on weekends, when local *mariachis* practice for their evening gigs.

Cuernavaca's movie houses charge 6-8 pesos per flick. Downtown, **Cinema Las Plazas,** across from the *Jardín Juárez*, shows imports and high-quality Mexican films. The colonial **Cine Alameda,** Matamoros 1 (tel. 12-10-50), one block north of the *zócalo*, which shows more popular titles on its ultra-wide movie screen, is worth a peek. **Cine Morelos,** on Morelos, about 1½ blocks north of Jardin Borda, shows *excellent* Mexican films (6 pesos, for students with ID 3 pesos). For an alternative source of audio-visual stimulation, feast your eyes and ears at **Las Palmas Video,** (tel. 18-82-86), about a mile down Juárez and at the foot of the hill. Lounge on comfortable couches while watching the latest videos beamed from the U.S. by satellite.

Harry's Grill, Gutenberg 93 (tel. 12-76-39), beside the Las Plazas mall north of the *zócalo*, throbs with top-40 dance hits, old telephone booths, airplane propellers, and U.S. license plates, quirkily approximating a *gringo* bar. Its slogan: "A Sunny Place for Shady People," must entertain the opulent Mexican crowd. The pick-up scene here is no less than frantic; the people are lively, loud, and fun to watch. Free hors d'oeuvres. Drinks ain't cheap: beer 7 pesos, juicy cocktails 10 pesos. In the grill part of the Grill, try the *pollo cerveza* (24 pesos). Open daily 1pm-2am.

On Saturdays and Sundays, the **market** in the *Jardín Juárez* specializes in silver jewelry; don't be afraid to bargain. The famous **Feria de la Primavera** (Festival of Spring) brings parades, costumes, and a splash of color for 10 days a year at the vernal equinox (March 21-22). Ask at the tourist office for information about specific events, or check out the bulletin boards at the museums downtown.

■ Near Cuernavaca

XOCHICALCO

Ceremonial center, fortress and trading post rolled into one, Xochicalco is the most important and beautiful archaeological site in the state of Morelos. Built in the seventh century during the Toltec Classic period, Xochicalco suffered periodic invasions by various tribes, including the Olmecs, Maya, Zapotecs and Mixtecs. By the time of the Conquest, the city had become a tributary of Tenochtitlán, the capital of the Aztec empire.

Although its Nahuatl name means "Place of the Flowers," the hilltops where Xochicalco stands are arid in the summer. Lizards and roadrunners dart away as you pass through the rocky terrain, and more oxen than tourists make the trek to the ruins. Even during the rainy season, when dew sparkles on green hills, an eerie loneliness pervades the site.

Desolation does not diminish the allure of this citadel of debris. The underground observatory is a marvel of engineering and astronomical aptitude. Deep inside the subterranean passageways lie fragments of paved floors and stucco walls. On summer solstices, Aztec sages and star-gazers peered through a shaft in the ceiling to trace the path of the sun and thus verify and adjust the Aztec calendar. The observatory is now locked behind an iron grid, but just say the word and a guard will unlock the bolt to let you play ancient astronomer.

On the first plain, the renowned **Pyramid of Quetzalcóatl,** sloppily reconstructed in 1910, bears carved reliefs of the image of this great feathered serpent, god-hero of the Toltecs. Xochicalco's commercial partnership with southern cultures is reflected in the embrace Quetzalcóatl bestows upon a priest in an elaborate Mayan headdress. Next to the Pyramid of Quetzalcóatl stands the **Temple of the Stela,** where archaeologists found the burial place of a high priest along with ritual offerings. Down the hill on a lower terrace, three pyramids comprise the impressive **Shrine of the Stela,** where the Toltecs worshiped the sun each day at sunrise and sunset. Toltecs also revered the carved obelisk in the center of the park. Its shadow plotted the trajectory of the sun between two identical pyramids that faced each other.

Next to the shrine, two massive rings of rock are attached to the **ballcourt,** of interest because most ballcourts in Mesoamerica have only one ring. Here, some anthropologists claim, teams competed for the privilege of being sacrificed atop the Pyramid of Quetzalcóatl (their strong hearts fed the sun). Below, only the foundations remain of the **Calmecac,** the palace in which Toltec and Aztec priests underwent training and initiation. Next door, 20 circular beds of rock represent the 20-day month of the Aztec and Toltec calendar; nearby rock mounds topped with cacti and shrubs are actually pyramids unexcavated for lack of funding.

Flecha Roja runs buses for about 2 pesos directly to Xochicalco. Or you can take one to Miacatlán for 2.50 pesos from the Autos Pullman station, at Abasolo and Netzahualcóyotl, one block south of the cathedral in Cuernavaca. Ask the driver to drop you off at the Crucero de Xochicalco. **Taxis** pass by this crossroads frequently, and if you have 6 pesos they will take you to the site. Otherwise, the uphill walk to the site (4km) will take about an hour. Ask your taxi driver to pick you up at a specified time, or else hoof it back downhill to the *crucero.* (Site open Tues.-Sun. 9am-5pm. Admission 13 pesos. Free Sun.)

TEPOZTLÁN

In northern Morelos, the quiet *pueblo* of Tepoztlán occupies one of the state's most scenic sites, where towering cliffs form a natural fortress that allows entrance only from the south. Proceeding along Route 95-D toward Tepoztlán, on a clear day you will see the two mammoth volcanoes, **Popocatépetl** and **Ixtaccíhuatl,** jaggedly rising above the land. The cobbled *indígena* village is a bastion of pre-colonial life, with ancient customs still alive and the Nahuatl language still predominant. The archaeological sites for which the town is famous wobble on a peak 1200 ft. above the village. The long walk through thin air may leave you breathless and thirsty, so prepare accordingly.

The valley of Tepoztlán is charged with ages of myth, legend, and magic. It is thought to be the birthplace (about 1200 years ago) of the god-hero of the Toltecs, Quetzalcóatl. Townfolk speak respectfully of a magnetic force present only in Tepoztlán. And Tepoztlán was once the ceremonial ground where pilgrims came to worship Tepoztecatl, god of *pulque* (the sacred liquor of the Nahuas), of fertility, and of the harvest. Celebrations still take place every September 8, when the *pulque* flows and the dance floor fills in honor of Tepoztecatl. *Los chinelos*—colorfully attired folk dancers—may invite you to join their traditional dance, *el salto.*

Travelers also come to visit the **Pyramid of Tepozteco,** perched on the northern ridge of the cliffs that rise above one end of town, about 3km above the valley. Some say the pyramid was a Tlahuica observatory and defense post for the valley, while others swear it served as an Aztec sacrificial temple. The 10m-tall structure has a porch inscribed with both barely discernible Tlahuica glyphs and more modern runic messages like "Juan loves Hortencia." To reach the pyramid, follow Av. 5 de Mayo north out of town (passing the *zócalo* on your right) until its end. The steep and strenuous climb along a narrow path includes such exciting highlights as an old rusty slimy iron ladder situated crucially among the rocks and takes roughly an hour. (Open Tues.-Sun. 9am-4:30pm. Admission 10 pesos, free for students and teachers with ID.)

The **Museo Arqueológico de Tepoztlán,** at the rear of Capilla Asunción (accessible only from the back street), holds a collection that Carlos Pellicer, poet and benefactor, donated to the city. The impressive display includes a wide variety of pottery pieces and clay figures of Olmec, Zapotec, Mayan, Totonac, and Aztec origin, as well as many objects from Teotihuacán. There are also photographs of the main archaeological sites in Mexico, such as Chichén Itzá, Malinalco and Mitla. (Open Tues.-Fri. 10am-2pm and 4-6pm, Sat.-Sun. 10am-6pm. Admission 3 pesos, 1.50 pesos for students and teachers with ID.)

Like Cuernavaca, Tepoztlán has its share of foreigners and *chilangos* (the colloquial term used for residents of Mexico City; it once meant "people who come to spoil things"). Because of its natural beauty, vernal climate, and proximity to Mexico City, Tepoztlán attracts an ever-growing population of *norteamericanos* who establish elaborate weekend homes and summer residences here. Thus it is not surprising that Tepoztlán completely lacks moderately priced accommodations. **La Cabaña,** 5 de Mayo 54, across from the Cristóbal Colón station, rents clean rooms, all with communal baths and *agua purificada*. The proprietor is friendly and helpful. (Singles 25 pesos. Doubles 50 pesos.) The market area offers quite a few inexpensive small restaurants but two more remarkable (and more) expensive ones are **Los Colorines** and **Atlyhuac** along the street (Av. 5 de Mayo) which turns into a path to the pyramid.

Visit Tepoztlán from either Cuernavaca or Mexico City. Ometochtli **buses** to Tepoztlán leave from the Cuernavaca market (1.50 pesos). In Tepoztlán, they arrive and depart from in front of the *zócalo* or a depot outside town. Pullman de Morelos in Mexico City operates buses every ½hr. from Taxqueña for 10 pesos. In Tepoztlán buses arrive and depart from the *zócalo*, close to the market.

MÉXICO

■■■ MALINALCO

Although located in the state of México, the Aztec ruins of Malinalco are most easily reached from Cuernavaca. The bus ride to the ruins is both panoramic and enlightening: *campesinos*, loaded with straw baskets and knitted wools they plan to sell in the big city, chew tobacco, spit on the steel floor, and talk about the crop in Spanish and Nahuatl.

Most important buildings in Malinalco are situated around the *zócalo* and bear their identification (i.e. *farmacia, cantina, hotel*) in the same multi-colored inscriptions. Inside the *zócalo*, vendors display everything from sandals to fried fish. In front of the plaza, the town's huge church, the **Parroquia del Salvador Divino,** is a breathtaking relic built in the 16th century by Augustine monks. Gigantic frescoes from the 17th century, depicting the stations of the cross, reach the church's ceiling. In a spine-chilling adjacent room, at least a dozen Christ figures suffer all sorts of torments and tortures. (Open daily 9am-7pm. Free.)

Getting to Malinalco can be somewhat complicated. The **Flecha Roja station,** Morelos 504 (tel. 12-81-90) in Cuernavaca sends three buses to Chalma, but only on Sundays (7:15am, 8:15am, and 9:15am, 1¾hr., 10 pesos). From Chalma, you'll have to hail a taxi to Malinalco (20min.; 15 pesos special service, 3 pesos *combi* with other people). If you want to go any other day of the week, you can take the Flecha

Roja bus to Santa Marta (every hr. 6am-7:30pm, 1½hr., 6.20 pesos) and then catch another bus (every ½hr., 40min., 1 peso) to Chalma. All in all, if you are lucky enough to make your connections, it will be at least three hours before you gaze upon any ancient splendors at the Malinalco ruins, but the wait compensates with a heart-stopping view.

Though Malinalco has no tourist office, the **Casa de Cultura de Malinalco,** on one corner of the *zócalo*, can help you find the ruins and anything else you might need. (Open Mon.-Sat. 9am-2pm and 4-7pm, Sun. 10am-1pm, ideally.)

The Malinalcs, a small tribe within the ancient Nahua empire, lived in the Valle de Toluca, home of the giant snowy peak of Nevado de Toluca. In addition to building this great city fortress, the Malinalcs left the world fantastic wooden percussion instruments, which are on display at both the Museo Nacional de México and the Museo de Toluca.

Malinalco was the sacred ground for the rituals that officially transformed an Aztec youth into a *caballero tigre* or *caballero águila* (tiger or eagle warrior). On the open circular stone platform—the first structure on the right as you enter—prisoners were bound to a pole with only arms left free and made to wrestle the recently initiated warriors. If the prisoner won consecutive fights with two *águila*, two *tigre* warriors, and the crafty techniques of a left-hander, he was granted life and freedom. If not, the small rectangular basin in front of the entryway to the pyramid to your left used to hold his blood after his ritual sacrifice. Behind the pyramid, the oval bed of rock served as an incinerating grill where the bodies of the sacrificed were turned to ash. To the left of the pyramid facing the Malinalco Valley, the ruins of a temple used for sun worship are now unrecognizable; many stones were taken from the site to build the Santa Mónica church.

The **Temple of Initiation** for eagle and tiger warriors is one of the few truly monolithic structures in the world. All of its statues, rooms, and facades were carved from one giant slab of stone. Two stone jaguars guard the steep steps. To the right of the entrance to the inner chamber, the broken figure of an eagle warrior sits on the head of the feathered serpent, Quetzalcóatl. The frame of the chamber entrance itself is fashioned into the open-mouthed, stylized head of a serpent with fangs bared, its split tongue lapping the floor. Inside the circular chamber, three supine eagles and one jaguar are carved on the floor. In the hole behind the first eagle, the beating hearts of the sacrificed waited to be devoured by the initiates. If you stand directly in front of the door of the temple, with your back towards it, you will see that at this very altitude, the gap in the rocks about 1km beyond is at its widest. It was believed that whenever he was angry at the Malinalcs, the eagle-god would fly out of the temple directly to the south, leaving the tribe without his protection.

Further, to the right from the above temple, stand the remains of *temascál,* an ancient predecessor to the sauna. Behind the *temascál,* you can still make out the small cells in which the elderly *sacerdotes* most likely used to live. Walking to the end of the platform and looking down, you'll see the ruins of the prisoners' cells situated about 15m below the whole complex. The remaining wall-bases suggest very narrow and painful punishing slots/chambers.

Follow the blue pyramid signs along Guerrero from the *zócalo,* along Guerrero to the ruins. (Site open Tues.-Sun. 10am-4:30pm. Admission 13 pesos, free Sun.)

GUERRERO

Tourists slurping down *coco locos* while gawking at Acapulco's Quebrada cliff divers may find it hard to believe that this state was a hotbed of revolution in the early and mid-1970s, when terrorists throughout Mexico attempted to overthrow President Luis Echeverría's administration. Anyone coming to Acapulco over land

GUERRERO

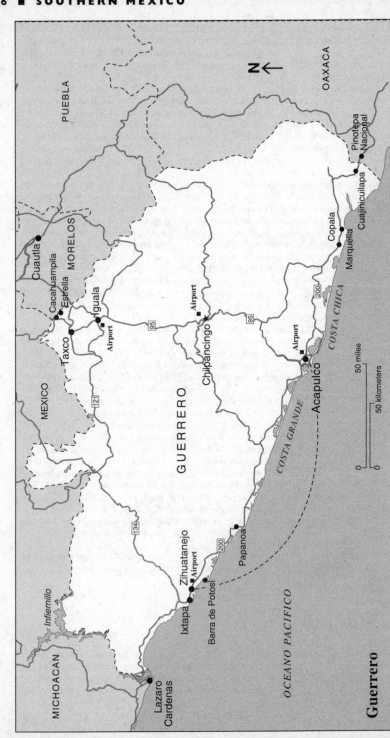

Guerrero

will see evidence of Guerrero's turbulent recent past. Even after so many years, the military still maintains a heavy presence in the state and often stops buses to search baggage at highway checkpoints. Those moving along the coast outside of Acapulco or Ixtapa will encounter intense and widespread xenophobia, in striking contrast to the rest of Mexico's Pacific coast. The threat of violence and the likelihood of theft make camping on the beaches ill-advised. If you must camp, make your way northwest to Playa Azul in Michoacán or southeast to Puerto Angel in Oaxaca state.

There is little of interest in the heart of Guerrero. The major inland magnet for tourists is Taxco, in the northern extreme of the state, just 170km south-southwest of Mexico City. With its 18th-century colonial architecture, stunning hillside topography and gorgeous silver art jewelry, Taxco is a comfortable haven of quiet artisanal bustle.

■■■ TAXCO

After silver was discovered here in 1534, Taxco (pronounced TAHS-co; pop. 150,000) exploded into a tangled confusion of cramped, cobbled *callejones* (alleys) that twist, turn, and slope precipitously through rolling green hills nearly 2000m above sea level. Pedestrians and cars squeeze past each other in the narrow alleys. Tourists, attracted by countless silver shops that sell necklaces, charms, medallions, and bracelets, swarm through town.

Beneath it all lies a dwindling reserve of silver. Tlahuicas, Chichimecs, Olmecs, and Chantales alternately dominated the area until the Aztec empire absorbed it in 1440. Huitamila, the Aztec lord of Tetelcingo, handed over the land and mines to the delighted Spaniards, who changed the city's name to Taxco, a corruption of the Nahuatl term for ball game, *tlachco*. The discovery of silver brought fortune seekers, merchants, artisans, and miners in increasing numbers, and the chaotic city prospered amid the sharp, inhospitable mountains.

In the 18th century, the population stabilized and tranquility reclaimed the town until 1928, when isolated Taxco was connected to the outside world by a paved road stretching from the city gates to Acapulco. Soon after, the Mexican government declared Taxco a national monument and decreed that all new buildings be built in colonial style and all new streets be cobbled. However, little more than lip service was paid to the city's past until 1932, when Professor William Spratling, "Don Guillermo" to locals, gave up teaching and opened a silver workshop in Taxco. He taught the silversmith's craft to locals, and his jewelry quickly gained international repute. Others soon followed suit, and today over 300 silver shops operate in the area, attracting a staggering number of North American tourists. A Mexican comedian once quipped that he couldn't join his friends in Taxco because he didn't speak English.

ORIENTATION

Taxco is at the northern end of Guerrero state, only 185km southwest of Mexico City. **Avenida J. F. Kennedy,** the principal artery, circles the town. From any spot in the city, to get to *el centro* just look for the highly visible **Catedral de Santa Prisca** atop the hill and work your way up to it on any of the many small alleys.

Taxco's most interesting sights and shops center around the cathedral and adjacent **zócalo** (also called the **Plaza Borda** after a philanthropist who made a famous silver fortune in Taxco). *Combis* run along three main routes: from **Los Arcos** (the north entrance to town where Av. Kennedy begins) down Av. Kennedy to the south end of town; from Los Arcos up **La Garita,** through the center and out **Cuauhtémoc-San Nicolás-San Miguel;** and along the **Panorámica,** another avenue bordering Taxco on the west. *Combis* (.50 pesos) run from 7am to 8pm everywhere in town. The white taxis charge 3-8 pesos. However, the reliable feet remain the best mode of transportation in small Taxco. To get to the *zócalo* from the

Flecha Roja bus station, look for the church steeple and head uphill. From **Estrella de Oro,** turn right downhill and you'll come to the Flecha Roja station.

PRACTICAL INFORMATION

Tourist Office: Kennedy 1 (tel. 2-07-98). From the *zócalo*, go down Juárez to Garita, or take the "Garita" *combi*. Information is surprisingly minimal; no regular hours. Generally available daily 9am-7pm.

Currency Exchange: Banca Confía, on the *zócalo*. Open Mon.-Fri. 9am-12:30pm. **Bancomer,** at Cuauhtémoc and Pl. San Juan just off the *zócalo*. ATMs for Visa cash advances. Open for exchange Mon.-Fri. 10-11:30am. **Banamex,** Juárez 17 (tel. 2-44-55), has an ATM: MC, Visa, Cirrus, and Plus. Banks will change traveler's checks, and most silver dealers accept dollars.

Post Office: Kennedy 34 (tel. 2-05-01). Open Mon.-Fri. 8am-7pm, Sat. 9am-1pm. **Postal code:** 40200.

Telephones: Long distance service in **Farmacia de Cristo,** Hidalgo 18 (tel. 2-11-19) down the road from Pl. San Juan. Collect calls about 10 pesos. Open for calls Mon.-Sat. 11am-2pm, Sun. 8am-9pm. Phonecard-operated LADATELs can be found around town; many mini-supermarkets and news agents sell phonecards.

Telegrams: Alarcón 2 (tel. 2-48-85), off the *zócalo*, towards Hotel Los Arcos, to your right. Open Mon.-Fri. 8am-3pm, for money orders Mon.-Fri. 8am-1pm.

Bus Stations: Estrella de Oro, Kennedy 126 (tel. 2-06-48), at the southern end of town. From the *zócalo*, simply head downhill and hang a right on Kennedy. To: Mexico City (3½hrs., 17 pesos); Cuernavaca (1½hrs., 8 pesos); Acapulco (5hrs., 30 pesos). **Flecha Roja,** Kennedy 104 (tel. 2-01-31), straight downhill from the cathedral. To: Mexico City (17 per day, 2½hrs., 14-26 pesos), Cuernavaca (every 30min., 5am-6:30pm, 8 pesos), Acapulco (3 per day, 5hrs., 32 pesos), and more.

Pharmacy: Farmacia de Borda, Celso Muñiz 4 (tel. 2-06-46), in the alley to the left of Santa Prisca. Open daily 9am-3pm and 4-9pm. Also try **Farmacia Oscarín** (see Telephones). Different pharmacies stay on duty every night and at the IMSS hospital you can get an emergency dose of medicine if you need it immediately.

Hospital: IMSS Kennedy 114 (tel. 2-03-36), 24-hr. emergency and ambulance service. Surrounded by 24-hr. emergency clinics.

Police: Kennedy 71-B (tel. 2-06-66). At the **Carcel Municipal.** Open 24 hrs.

ACCOMMODATIONS

Make advanced reservations during *Semana Santa* (Easter week), Día de San Miguel (end of Sept.), or the Feria Nacional de la Plata, a two-week celebration of silver (late Nov.-early Dec.).

Hotel Los Arcos, Alarcón 12 (tel. 2-18-36), just northeast of the Pl. Borda. Handsome whitewashed rooms with every possible luxury: brick floors, original artwork, solid wood furniture, exquisitely tiled bathrooms, etc. Beautiful stairways and outdoor courtyard. Rooftop terrace provides a great view of the town and surrounding hills. Singles 58 pesos. Doubles 85 pesos.

Hotel Los Castillos, Alarcón 7 (tel. 2-13-96), across the street from Los Arcos. Although not quite the palace that Los Arcos is, it comes mighty close. Indoor courtyard comes complete with fountains, murals, and statuettes. Expensive silver shop downstairs. Singles 55 pesos. Doubles 75 pesos.

Hotel Casa Grande, Pl. San Juan 7 (tel. 2-01-23), on the small plaza down Cuauhtémoc from the *zócalo*. Rooms on the upper floor of a closed-in shopping arcade. Generously-sized clean and comfortable rooms. Not exquisite, but nice for the price. Singles 39 pesos. Doubles 55 pesos.

Casa de Huéspedes Arellano, Pajaritos 23 (tel. 2-02-15). From the *zócalo*, walk down the street to the right of the cathedral. Take the stairs almost immediately on the right and descend into the market. The hotel will be on the right, about 3 levels down. Rooms are small and well-worn but clean and cheap. Nice terrace on 2nd floor for sun and conversation with the backpacking clientele. Singles 30 pesos, with bath 35 pesos. Doubles 35 pesos, with bath 40 pesos.

Posada Santa Anita, Kennedy 108 (tel. 2-07-52), 1 block to the left along the avenue as you leave the 2nd-class station. Small, plain rooms are far enough from the highway to be quiet. The furniture is wood; some rooms are bright and cheerful, while others are drearily empty and stuffy. A short hike uphill to the *zócalo*. Singles 44 pesos. Doubles 77 pesos.

FOOD

Prepare to drop your doubloons if you want atmosphere to accompany your meal. The cheaper *taquerías* are outnumbered by Taxco's tourist restaurants, but they multiply as you move away from the Pl. Borda. Cold breakfasts are the specialty of the *neverías*—plentiful in town alleys—which sell coffee, *licuados*, pastries, delicious pieces of *pan de queso* (custard-like Mexican cheesecake) and other goodies. Be sure to choose carefully among *neverías* as some charge inflated prices.

Bora Bora Pizza, Delicias 4 (tel. 2-17-21). Head toward Pl. San Juan from the *zócalo*—you'll soon see the signs on the right. Quite a hopping hangout at night. Low tables with pink cloths; cozy. Pizza 12-48 pesos. Open daily 1pm-midnight.

Restaurant Santa Fe, Hidalgo 2 (tel. 2-11-70), down to the left from the Pl. San Juan. Flower-bedecked, big and cheaper—the most economical of the fancier restaurants. Popular with the Mexican tourists. Soup 6-8 pesos. Daily *menú* 17.50 pesos. Open daily 8am-11pm.

Restaurant Ethel, Pl. de San Juan 14 (tel. 2-07-88). Just a pretty decent restaurant, no real gimmicks—except bunches of fake flowers. Bilingual menu. *Comida corrida* served daily 1-5pm, 19.50 pesos. Most entrees 19-25 pesos. Eggs 7 pesos. Open daily 9am-9pm.

Restaurant Meléndez, Cuauhtémoc 6, inside the Hotel Meléndez. Dining area is beautifully tiled, and the view from the outdoor deck quickens the pulse. Delicious 5-course *comida corrida* costs 17.50 pesos, full breakfast 14 pesos. Open daily 7:30-11am, 1-5pm and 7:30-9:30pm.

Cafetería DIF, just off the *zócalo*, toward Pl. Bernal. Fairly noisy, but the walls are covered with many dozens of beautiful wooden masks. Breakfast 10 pesos. *Quesadillas* 6 pesos. *Comida corrida* 6 pesos. Open 9am-9pm, but irregularly.

SIGHTS

Taxco's main sights sparkle in hundreds of silver shops around town. Though unscrupulus sellers and cheating craftspeople occasionally pass off *alpaca* (fool's silver) or *plateados* (silver-plated metals) as the real McCoy, Taxco's enormous selection of silver and silver-related crafts is its forte. Larger pieces, such as necklaces and bracelets, are consistently striking, and even *alpaca* belt buckles maintain the shine of the serious artisan's careful handiwork. Ceramic crafts and leather products abound, as do fashionable beach clothes and sandals. Many proprietors speak English and accept U.S. currency, but stick with Spanish and talk pesos while bargaining, or risk being charged tourist prices. In general, the farther one walks from the Pl. Borda, the cheaper the sterling products become. Bargain at stores with silver workshops by faking out the clerk and going straight to the artisan. Most shops have two prices: *menudeo* (retail) and *mayoreo* (wholesale), the latter for those profit-oriented people who load their bags with silver in Taxco to resell at lofty prices back home. Remember that only the official ".925" stamp on the object's side guarantees that your shiny new charm is indeed silver; inspect merchandise carefully before purchase.

For an example of original silver craft, stop at **Los Castillos,** at the Pl. Bernal (tel. 2-06-52), one block down from the *zócalo*. Like many Taxco families with great traditions in silverwork, the Castillo family keeps its workshop (right on top of their store) open for tourists to visit. Among their most interesting wares are products of a technique said to be inherited from the Aztecs. (Open Mon.-Fri. 9am-7pm, Sat. 9am-6pm, Sun. 10am-3pm.)

If silver is causing you to spiral into hyper-budget woe, head to the **Market of Artesanías** off Veracruz just behind Santa Prisca to the right for browsing, bargaining, people-watching, and snacking. Merchants sell everything from silver to pomegranates to painted ashtrays. The market is open daily from 10am to 6pm but most crowded during the afternoon siesta, when confused *gringos* hit Taxco's version of a mall instead of sleeping.

A major attraction is the *zócalo's* **Catedral de Santa Prisca,** with its beautiful baroque facade of pink stone. Intense white light illuminates the 40m towers until 9pm in the evenings. On foggy nights, the towering nave and blue-tiled dome are lit up as well. Don José de la Borda hired two Spanish architects, Diego Durán and Juan Caballero, to design and build the church for Borda's son Manuel, a priest. Begun in 1751, the church took only seven years to complete. Among the shapes, designs and figures on the facade, the outstanding features are the Churrigueresque *interestípite*—decorative inverted columns with a Corinthian flourish at the bottom. Inside the church, a canvas by renowned 18th-century Mexican artist Miguel Cabrera depicts the martyrdom of Santa Prisca, who was tortured and killed by Roman guards in the first century for defending Christians. Cabrera also painted the picture on the altar of St. Sebastián, the town's patron. (Open daily 6am-8pm.) For a small *propina* you can conquer yet a further 113-step height and climb the left tower of the cathedral for a spectacular view after 2pm. Inquire inside.

The **Museo de Arqueología Guillermo Spratling,** Delgado 1 (tel. 2-16-60), down the street to the right of Santa Prisca, displays pre-Conquest art, mostly from cultures along Mexico's west coast. William Spratling, a *norteamericano* collector, donated his ceramics and figurines to the museum. On the ground floor is a pictorial mining history consisting of tools, ore, and photographs. (Open Tues.-Sat. 10am-5pm, Sun. 9am-3pm. Admission 10 pesos, students and teachers free with ID.)

The **Museo Arte Virreinal** (also called **Casa Humboldt**), Alarcón 6 (tel. 2-55-01), down the street to the left of the Hotel Los Castillos, is one of the oldest colonial homes in town. With its unusual bas-reliefs in Moorish *mudéjar* style on the front, this was the temporary home of South American explorer Alexander von Humboldt, whose bust still oversees the interior. The beautifully restored house contains artifacts discovered in the basement of the Santa Prisca cathedral. (Open Thurs.-Sat. 10am-5pm, Sun. 9am-3pm. Admission 10 pesos, students and teachers with ID 5 pesos.) The **Convento de San Bernandino,** in the Pl. del Convento, was built in 1592 as a Franciscan monastery. A fire destroyed the building two centuries later, and in 1823 it was reconstructed in Neoclassical style. The struggle for independence officially ended within the walls of this ex-convent when the Plan of Iguala, written by Iturbide, was signed here in 1821. Now a local school convenes under its roof. (Open daily 10am-5pm. Free.)

ENTERTAINMENT

Taxco's already crowded streets somehow manage to accommodate a tsunami of tourists during its two major festivals. The **Feria Nacional de la Plata,** a national contest of silverworkers sponsored by the President to encourage silver artisanship, runs usually in the first week of December. **Semana Santa** festivities are even more popular in Taxco. On Good Friday, hooded *penitentes*—men who volunteer their bodies and spirits—carry huge logs made out of cactus trunks on their shoulders or subject themselves to flagellation in order to expiate their own sins and those of the town.

After silver shops close, most of Taxco's locals and visitors converge on the **Plaza Borda** in front of the illuminated facade of Santa Prisca. Whereas most Mexican discos are open during the week but only crowded on weekends, Taxco's discos don't even bother to open their doors until the weekend. If you are still up for dancing after a day hiking Taxco's relentless hills, two choices exist. In the **Disco Escaparartes,** Pl. Borda 2, great music has plenty of locals jitterbugging and drinking. (Open Thurs.-Sun. 9pm-3am.) **La Lechusa,** Pl. del Torril 3, to the right of Santa

Prisca, plays rock music and serves plenty of Mexican drinks. (Open Fri.-Sun. 8pm-3am; minimum purchase 2 drinks.) At video-bar **Güiri-Güiri,** Cuauhtémoc 2, video games and folk art complement the modern wood-paneled bar, and a large video monitor shows MTV clips and occasionally North American football. The outdoor terrace affords a mind-blowing view of Santa Prisca, the *ex-convento*, and much of eastern Taxco. (Open Fri.-Sun. 7:30pm-1:30am. Occasional live music 9pm-midnight. Minimum purchase 2 drinks.) Boards around the plaza announce the day's movies at Taxco's three theaters. The **Casa de la Cultura** features an excellent art-film series on Saturday and children's matinees on Sunday; check at the tourist office to see if it's open.

■ Near Taxco: Grutas De Cacahuamilpa and Iguala

Natural phenomena and tourism do battle in the caves at **Cacahuamilpa.** Believed to have been a site for religious rites in pre-Conquest times, the 2km-long caverns have lost much of their enchantment due to over-promotion by the tourist office. Nevertheless, their beauty manages to make itself visible in spite of the commercial dominatrix.

According to legend, the cavern was a hiding place for runaway *indígenas*, freedom fighters and revolutionaries. A Tetipac chief is said to have regained his lost throne by having his daughter emerge from the cave disguised as a deity and pronounce the return of the former chief to power. Twenty huge *salones* (halls) consume the visitor with their stalactites, stalagmites, and rock formations of fancy shapes, sizes, and colors. The columns and ceilings—taller than those of any church (some as high as 85m)—are all the work of that great subterranean stream that developed into the Río San Jerónimo.

Tours leave on the hour from the **visitors center** and afford little opportunity for traipsing about on your own. Charter tours bring their own English-speaking guides to the caves. Some guides employed by the caves speak English, but only for a good-sized group of *gringos*. (Caves open daily 10am-5pm. If enough people stay after 5pm, they'll give an extra tour. Admission about 10 pesos, children about 5 pesos.)

Buses run to Grutas de Cacahuamilpa from Taxco's **Flecha Roja** bus station (every ½hr. 8am-5pm, 45min., about 5 pesos), and the last one returns to Taxco at 6pm. The bus will drop you at the crossroads, where you also catch the return bus. Take a right down the street; the cave entrance lies just after the curve. Cacahuamilpa is 30km north of Taxco, 36km south of Ixtapán, 69km southwest of Cuernavaca and 149km from Mexico City.

An hour south of Taxco, on the road between Mexico City and Acapulco, sits a dreary dustbin of a town ringed by high mountains. Ignored by most travelers, **Iguala** lies at the center of Mexican national symbolism. Independence was proclaimed there on February 24, 1821, and the new tri-color Flag of Independence first flew in its central plaza. The tranquil town keeps a low profile most of the year, but beginning eight days before Independence Day and continuing eight days after, Iguala celebrates the **Feria de la Bandera Nacional** (Celebration of the National Flag), the largest non-religious fiesta in the country.

Iguala is served by the first class **Estrella de Oro,** at the intersection of Route 95 and Bandera Nacional, and second class **Flecha Roja,** at Galeana and Salazar. Estrella de Oro departs for Taxco (about 5 pesos), Acapulco (about 20 pesos), and Mexico City (about 18 pesos). Flecha Roja duplicates both routes on the half hour. Both companies run frequently to Iguala from Taxco, Acapulco and Mexico City.

■■■ ZIHUATANEJO AND IXTAPA

Before Zihuatanejo achieved world renown as a quiet nest of idyllic beaches and souvenir shops, it was nothing but a pier on which to unload the day's catch. Centuries before that, its pre-Conquest matriarchal society gave the town its original name—Cihuatlán, from the Nahuatl words *cihuatl* (woman) and *an* (place). When the Spanish arrived, they put men in charge, developed the harbor and mala-propped the name as Zihuatanejo. In the 19th century, larger ports such as Manzanillo and Acapulco assumed Zihuatanejo's trade with Asia, and the city again reverted to a fishing village.

The recent remodeling and development of the area, including the creation of the tourist complex at **Ixtapa,** was masterminded by the Bank of Public Works and Services, contracted by the Mexican government to provide tourists with "a picturesque town on the shore of a small, peaceful bay." Even though the cold hand of urban planning can often be felt in Ixtapa, the development scheme seems to have worked, as witnessed by the planeloads of tourists from around the world that arrive daily. Given the resort's awesome beaches, the developers could hardly have gone wrong.

Although designed by the same people, the beach resorts of Zihuatanejo and Ixtapa have absolutely nothing in common. Ixtapa is little more than a line of expensive hotels along an extremely attractive beach, burst full-grown from the collective mind of its developers. Ixtapa has no public services, no downtown, no residential district and no cheap anything. Zihuatanejo, the area's commercial center and the only base for budget travelers, fills these voids. All of Zihuatanejo's ritzy hotel complexes operate outside town; cheap hotels, open-air restaurants and boutiques cram the small downtown area. In fact, downtown Zihuatanejo looks like a small fishing village in which everyone simultaneously decided to open a souvenir shop. The combination of cheerful informality and frenetic activity makes it one of the Pacific coast's premier vacation spots.

ORIENTATION

Zihuatanejo and Ixtapa rise from the Pacific coast, 115km southeast of Playa Azul and Lázaro Cárdenas and 250km northwest of Acapulco. **Estrella Blanca** and **Estrella de Oro buses** stop in Zihuatanejo, providing the most frequent service to the two towns. There is no significant difference between the two companies, except that the Estrella de Oro station is a 5-min. walk from town, whereas the Estrella Blanca station is a few miles outside the *centro*. To reach Estrella de Oro from the center of town, walk north on Paseo Zihuatanejo to Paseo Palmar and bear right when it forks. **Taxis** from Estrella de Oro to the center of town cost 4 pesos, while those from the Estrella Blanca station cost 6 pesos. A better way of getting from Estrella Blanca to the center of town is to catch one of the buses heading left as you leave the station (.70 pesos). The resort crowd decends from Zihuatanejo's international **airport,** 16km south of the city on the highway to Acapulco. **Mexicana** and **Aeroméxico** provide the most extensive service. Taxis from Zihuatanejo cost 25 pesos.

Downtown Zihuatanejo forms a rectangle of about 25 square blocks bounded by the major streets **Paseo Zihuatanejo (or Morelos)** to the north, **Juárez** (whose signs sometimes say Paseo del Cocotal) to the east, **Paseo del Pescador** (a.k.a. the waterfront) to the south, and **5 de Mayo** to the west.

Ixtapa consists of a single access road, **Boulevard Ixtapa,** which parades past a phalanx of huge luxury hotels and terminates abruptly after the last resort. A smaller road off the boulevard continues to the northwest beaches. Buses shuttling between the two cities leave from the intersection of Juárez and Morelos in Zihuatanejo, and from various bus stops on the boulevard in Ixtapa (every 15min. 6am-11pm, 15min., .70 pesos). Cab fare between the two towns is 15 pesos.

If an address listed here is not on Blvd. Ixtapa, it is in Zihuatanejo.

PRACTICAL INFORMATION

Tourist Office: City Office (tel. 4-22-07), in a booth on Paseo de la Pescador to the left of the small town square as you face the beach. Maps and basic information handed out, but no English spoken. Open Mon.-Fri. 9am-3pm and 5-8pm. **State Office,** in a *caseta* on Blvd. Ixtapa with piles of maps and pamphlets. Officially open Mon.-Fri. 9am-9pm, but it's usually closed 1-4pm.

Currency Exchange: Multibanco Comermex, Ejido at Guerrero. No commission, but occasionally refuses to exchange traveler's checks. Open for exchange Mon.-Fri. 10am-noon. **Money Exchange,** on Galeana (tel. 4-39-91), between Ascencio and Bravo (signs in your face all over town). Rates around .10 pesos less than the banks on the dollar, but no commission. Open daily 8am-8pm.

Post Office: Cuauhtémoc 72 (tel. 4-22-92). Walk inland on Cuauhtémoc, past the small plaza, and follow the pink statues to the right. Open Mon.-Fri. 8am-7pm, Sat. 9am-1pm. **Postal code:** 40880.

Telephones: At **Money Exchange,** on Galeana between Ascencio and Bravo. Collect calls 5 pesos. Open daily 8am-8pm. **Telephone code:** 743.

Telegrams: Edificio Telecomm (tel. 4-33-81). Walking east on Morelos, it's ½ block past Pollo Feliz (a restaurant) on the right, set far back from the road. About a 15-min. walk from the post office. Open Mon.-Fri. 9am-2pm and 3-5pm, Sat. 9am-noon.

Airport: On the coast to the south (tel. 4-21-00). **Aeroméxico,** Álvarez 34 (tel. 4-20-18). Open Mon.-Sat. 9am-7pm, Sun. 9am-6pm. To Mexico City about 250 pesos.

Bus Stations: Estrella de Oro, Paseo Palmar 54 (tel. 4-21-75). To: Acapulco (4hrs., 27 pesos), Mexico City (10hrs., 90 pesos). **Estrella Blanca** (tel. 4-34-77), outside of town. To: Mexico City *Turistar Servicio Plus* (9pm, 10hrs., 95 pesos) or *servicio ordinario* (11hrs., 80 pesos); Acapulco *Turistar Servicio Plus* (4hrs., 35 pesos) or *servicio ordinario* (20 per day, 4hrs., 25 pesos); Cuernavaca (9hrs., 80 pesos).

Laundromat: Disney, Cuauhtémoc 29. 3kg 15 pesos. Same-day service. Open 24 hrs.

Red Cross: On the right side of Av. de las Huertas as you leave town (tel. 4-20-09). 24-hr. emergency and ambulance service.

Pharmacy: La Principal Farmacia, on the corner of Cuauhtémoc and Ejido (tel. 4-42-17). Open daily 8am-9:30pm.

Medical Services: Centro de Salud, Ejido at 5 de Mayo (tel. 4-20-88). Open for consultations Mon.-Fri. 9am-1pm. **English-speaking physician,** Dr. R. Grayeb, at Bravo 18 (tel. 4-26-91), across from the Torito Restaurant. Open 24 hrs. There is also a 24-hr.private hospital with an English-speaking staff on a little side street off the eastern end of Bravo, across from Hotel Casa Bravo (tel. 4-39-91 or 4-30-70).

Police: Álvarez at Cuauhtémoc (tel. 4-21-00 or 4-23-66), in the Palacio Municipal.

ACCOMMODATIONS AND CAMPING

Zihuatanejo supports a youth hostel not too far from the center and a load of reasonably priced hotels smack downtown. Dirtier, cheap hotels cluster along Bravo, the western end of Álvarez, and Morelos. Cleaner, slightly more expensive establishments line the streets that run between Bravo and the waterfront.

The tourist office frantically discourages unofficial camping, possibly because they believe *gringos* can't do without the amenities of a five-star hotel, but most likely because they hate to see tourist dollars slip away. Those who choose not to heed their warnings frequent the point beyond and to the northwest of Playa Las Gatas on the Bahía de Zihuatanejo. Even better, empty sand awaits northwest along Ixtapa's Playa Palmar away from the hotels.

Villa Deportiva Juvenil, on Morelos (tel. 4-46-62). From Playa Municipal, take 5 de Mayo north until you hit Paseo de Zihuatanejo. Turn left and follow the curve—it's on the right (a 10-min. walk). From Estrella de Oro, hike west on the Paseo de Zihuatanejo for 15-20min. Ignore the signs urging you to the center and hang a left at the sewage plant. It's the next building on the right. Basic rooms with 4-6 bunks cooled by a single fan. Sheets, blanket and pillow supplied. Clean bathrooms lack hot water. Check-out 9:30am. Restaurant serves breakfast (7 pesos), lunch (9 pesos) and dinner (9 pesos). Basketball courts. Lobby has TV. 15 pesos per person.

Casa Bravo, Bravo 11 (tel. 4-25-28), west of Juárez. Potted palms in the open-air lobby sway in the breeze as the manager naps in her hammock. Rooms are attractive and clean. Strong ceiling fans and spruce bathrooms with no hot water but huge bars of soap. Balconies in some rooms overlook the street; jugs of *agua purificada* await in every room. Singles 45 pesos. Doubles 65 pesos.

Casa Elvira, on Paseo del Pescador (tel. 4-20-61), 2 blocks west of the basketball courts. Striking plethora of flora and fauna: birds, plants, ducks, etc. Rooms are small but adequate, and the grandmotherly manager is friendly. Small communal porch with 3 chairs, 20 plants and a whole lot of character. Right on the beach. Cheerful restaurant in front. Singles 30 pesos. Doubles 50 pesos.

Hotel Mauer, Cuauhtémoc 5 (tel. 4-25-29), 1 block north of the beach. No lobby to speak of, and the entrance stairs are dark and almost dingy. The rooms themselves are spacious and clean. Rooms facing the front have huge porches but fill first. Singles 30 pesos. Doubles 60 pesos.

Hotel Casa Aurora, Bravo 27 (tel. 4-30-46), between Guerrero and Galeana. Rooms are musty and floors are cement, but the inner courtyard is a welcome respite with comfortable chairs. Singles 25 pesos. Doubles 50 pesos.

FOOD

Most hotels in Ixtapa include meals in the price of a room. For this reason, the resort has failed to spawn the swanky restaurants so common in Acapulco and Puerto Vallarta. In Zihuatanejo, however, you should have little trouble finding a budget meal. In general, restaurants farther inland are cheaper, less polished and more likely to offer something besides seafood.

Los Braceros, Ejido 21 (tel. 4-48-58). Culinary delights you would expect to find only in Ixtapa. The chef prepares all food on a big grill in the front of the restaurant. House specialties are the combination platters, consisting of a huge plate of stir-fried meat, vegetables, or both, with hot tortillas on the side (12-14 pesos). To top off your meal, the "bird of paradise" (crepes with apples and raisins) lives up to its name for 12 pesos. Open daily 4pm-1am.

Pollos Locos, Bravo 15, next to the Casa Bravo. The prototypical beachside chicken joint complete with high tin roof and roaring open barbecue—the only thing missing is the beach. Once the fire cranks up, the inviting smell of barbecued chicken (10 pesos) wafts around the block. All meals come with coleslaw, onions, rice and hot delicious homemade flour tortillas. *Quesadillas* 5.80 pesos. Open daily 1-11pm.

Tamales y Atole Any, Bravo 36, just east of Galeana. Really brightly colored tablecloths cover 2 sizes of tables: adult and kid-size (chairs and tables reach to your knees). *Quesadillas* 10 pesos. Tamales 3 pesos each. Open Mon.-Wed., Fri. and Sun. 5-11pm, Thurs. and Sat. 2-11pm.

Panificadora El Buen Gusto, on Guerrero, ½ block down from Ejido towards the water. Fantastic French pastries and breads. Jelly roll (1.50 pesos) and fruit juice (1 peso) make a perfect snack any time of day. Open daily 7:30am-10pm.

BEACHES

Neither Zihuatanejo's self-conscious charm nor Ixtapa's resort facades could ever eclipse the area's natural beauty. In Zihuatanejo, four stretches of sand line the water. They are, in clockwise order from the municipal pier, **Playa Principal, Playa La Madera, Playa La Ropa** and **Playa Las Gatas.** Ixtapa overlooks the unbroken white stretch of **Playa del Palmar** on the **Bahía del Palmar,** but the most beautiful beaches lie beyond **Laguna de Ixtapa: Playa Quieta, Playa Linda,** and, at the bay's western edge, **Isla Ixtapa.**

Downtown Zihuatanejo's beach, **Playa Principal,** is the most uninteresting of the area's sands. **Playa La Madera,** named after the wood once exported from its shores, is slightly more attractive. To reach it, walk 15 minutes east on one of the trails along the shoreline (some scrambling over rocks is involved), or walk east along the canal on Paseo de la Boquita, cross the canal at the bridge and follow the signs to Playa La Madera.

Zihuatanejo's two best beaches are **Playa La Ropa** and **Playa Las Gatas,** neither of which can be reached by walking along the bay's shores. La Ropa (clothing) takes its name from the silks and other garments that washed ashore following the shipwreck of a trading vessel from Asia. Protected from the rough Pacific by the shape of the bay, La Ropa's crescent of sumptuous white sand attracts tourists from the hotels on the surrounding cliffs. The stretch is quite long and wide, making La Ropa the least crowded of Zihuatanejo's beaches. Several adequate seaside restaurants are close at hand.

To get to La Ropa, follow Paseo la Boquita along the canal, cross over and head toward the airport, as if going to La Madera. Bypass the Madera access road and follow the signs to La Ropa. The 30- to 40-minute walk, which can be uncomfortably hot even at night, affords a view of the bay that makes the drudgery worthwhile. The shortest route to the beach requires an immediate right turn into the drive of Playa Club La Ropa after passing the small park that has benches and flower pots. Hotel Catalina Sotavento's access road also leads to La Ropa. Make your way through the multi-tiered experience of a hotel complex and down the stairs to the bay. The imposing gate at the foot of the stairs (and with a large gap underneath) is often locked at night.

Playa Las Gatas was named for the sharks that once inhabited the waters close to shore. Long before the Spanish conquistadors settled the area, Tarascan King Caltzonzín built an artificial breakwater to create a safe swimming space for himself and his daughters; the sharks had to search elsewhere for sustenance. Since then, a natural reef that supports an abundance of marine life has grown over the original stone barricade.

Because of its reputation as an isolated, exotic spot, Las Gatas is one of the area's most crowded beaches. Actually quite small, the beach fills quickly as boatload after boatload of tourists descend upon it like bees to honey. Thankfully, an army of restaurateurs stands ready to anchor them to wicker chairs away from the water with potent *cocos locos* in hand. Crowds notwithstanding, Las Gatas's white sands and excellent snorkeling make it worth the trip.

To get to Playa Las Gatas, walk along the shoreline from Playa La Ropa. In several spots you will have to use your hands, but the hike isn't terribly difficult. Follow the dirt road as far as Restaurant-Bar Capricho del Rey (look for the pink flags); from there, strike out across the rocks. Ten minutes later you'll be lounging on a beach chair at Las Gatas, *refresco* in hand. A road also accesses Playa Las Gatas, but the strenuous walk takes well over half an hour. A less tiring and more popular way to reach Las Gatas is to pile into one of the *colectivo* boats from Zihuatanejo's municipal pier (every 15min. 9am-5pm, round-trip about 8 pesos). Buy tickets at the base of the pier at the western end of Paseo del Pescador; the boats leave from halfway down the pier. Save your ticket stub for the trip back.

A variety of snorkeling and scuba excursions, from about US$20 and up, are available beachside at **Carlo Scuba, Oliviero's Scuba, Antonio,** or **Zihuatanejo Scuba Center.**

While most of Zihuatanejo's crescent beaches are protected from the waves, three-footers pound Ixtapa's endless stretches of sand. Ixtapa would be beach heaven were it not for the unfortunate fact that it's difficult to purchase any food or drink without selling off the family jewels first. All of Ixtapa's hotels are four- or five-star, and all of its restaurants, beachfront and otherwise, cater to the same clientele. But persevere. Buy some food and drink in cheaper Zihuatanejo and take the bus to paradise. Stride into a glittering hotel lobby as if you owned the place. In a swimsuit—having shed backpack, grimy jeans and your copy of *Let's Go*—you look like any other mundane tourist.

Ixtapa's **Playa del Palmar** measures in as the resort's longest beach and one of the most beautiful stretches of sand in the world. To the southeast, lounges invite loiterers, and parasailers make circuits during daylight hours until gas and demand run out (90 pesos and up). To the northwest, past existing hotels and the foundations for new condominium projects, the beach becomes even more pristine. The beauty of the spot is enhanced by perfectly sloping sands, deep blue water and waves custom-designed for body surfing. In the morning hours particularly, the beach is delightfully deserted. To get to Playa del Palmar, take the bus from Zihuatanejo, get off in front of any hotel, and walk through the lobby. To reach the northwestern end of Del Palmar, drive down Blvd. Ixtapa until it dead-ends by Laguna de Ixtapa, or walk (15min.) along the beach or road.

To the northwest of Ixtapa are **Club Med, Playa Quieta,** and **Playa Linda,** less crowded and more stylish than the beaches at Ixtapa or Zihuatanejo. To drive here from Ixtapa, follow the boulevard northwest beyond most of the hotels and turn right at the sign for Playa Linda. If you're driving from Zihuatanejo, the access road from Route 200 is more convenient; go past the exit for Ixtapa in the direction of Puerto Vallarta and take the next left, marked Playa Linda. The road skirts Laguna de Ixtapa and hits the beach farther northwest. A taxi to Playa Linda or Playa Quieta costs about 15 pesos from Ixtapa, 25 pesos from Zihuatanejo. Crystal clear water and bodysurfing waves await at **Playa Cuatas,** across the street from the tennis courts at Club Med on Playa Linda. Bring a lunch; there are no services here.

Some claim that of all the area's beaches, the most picturesque are those on **Isla Ixtapa,** about 2km offshore from Playa Quieta. Although the view is nice, the beach itself doesn't measure up to Playa del Palmar. Though activity picks up in a few shoreside restaurants by day, the island's 10 acres remain uninhabited at night. Boats to Isla Ixtapa leave from the municipal pier in Zihuatanejo at 11:30am, starting their return journeys between 4 and 4:30pm (round-trip about 20 pesos). A more economical way to get there is to take a bus or taxi to Playa Quieta and then take a boat from there (around 8 pesos). Three stretches of beach ring the island. The two with northeastern exposure sustain crowds, small restaurants (no bargains) and snorkel gear booths. The third is prohibitively rough and therefore generally deserted. Several dealers on the island rent scuba equipment. Prices are higher than at Las Gatas, and snorkeling conditions are worse because of the choppy water.

ENTERTAINMENT

Not surprisingly, Ixtapa also provides the area with its best nighttime entertainment. For dinner, drinks, and beachside dancing, the ever-popular, omnipresent, always-crowded **Carlos 'n' Charlie's,** on Paseo de Palmar (tel. 3-00-85), is the place to visit. Just ask one of the drunken tourists taking swigs from the wandering *sangría* server. Music starts blaring and hips start swinging after 9pm. Huge piña coladas cost 20 pesos. (Restaurant open daily noon-midnight, disco 9pm-3am.)

After Carlos 'n' Charlie's closes, a pack of partiers emigrates to Ixtapa's most popular disco, **Christine's,** Blvd. Ixtapa 429, in the Hotel Kristal. It's one of Mexico's prettiest discos, with tiered seating and hanging vines. *Gringos* swing their hips, getting dangerous on the dance floor. (Open daily 10:30pm-4am.)

■■■ COSTA GRANDE: ZIHUATANEJO/IXTAPA TO ACAPULCO

The Guerrero coast north of Acapulco is often called the Costa Grande to distinguish it from its smaller counterpart (Costa Chica) to the south. Trade with Asia centuries ago left some of the area's inhabitants with Polynesian features. Of specific interest are Barra de Potosí, 20km southeast of Zihuatanejo, and Papanoa, another 60km farther along Route 200.

■ Barra De Potosí

For the *gringo* whose head is spinning from ruins, cathedrals and souvenirs, there is no better tonic than a spell at **Playa Barra de Potosí.** Life here could not get more *tranquila*; both residents and tourists alike have trouble enough lifting themselves from hammocks, let alone exerting their bodies to stroll on the impressively deserted stretch of sand and watch the breaking waves. Now and then, someone stirs for a bit of fishing. The owners of the 20 or so open-air *enramadas* that constitute "town" are proud of Playa Potosí's laid-back friendliness—and its fabulously cheap prices. In keeping with the casual spirit of the place, no restaurant seems to have a menu; they'll whip up whatever you want and then pull an amount out of the air only after you remind them about your *cuenta*. Friendly beyond the call of duty are the folks at **Enramada Bacanora** (the second *enramada* on the beach as you enter the *enramada* area); by the time you finish your breakfast conversation with the proprietor, it may be time to order lunch.

There are no hotels at the tiny village of Barra de Potosí. Visitors are expected to sleep in the hammocks that adorn each *enramada*. The owners don't care if you sack out in their hammocks forever—as long as you buy a meal from them every now and then. *Baños*, too, are free of charge. You can leave your pack in the *enramadas* for as long as you like. The mosquitoes are also free, so bring plenty of repellent.

If you simply *must* exert yourself (which the locals may not understand or appreciate), your only option is to hike the dirt road to the lighthouse on top of **Cerro Guamiule** (2000m), the nearby peak that guards the southern entrance to the bay. After a half-hour walk, you will be rewarded with a view of the bay and its 20km of beaches.

From Playa Potosí, the southernmost beach on the bay, walk north along the shore to aptly named **Playa Blanca** (3km). You will pass **Playa Coacoyul** (8km), **Playa Riscaliyo** (19km), and pebbly **Playa Manzanillo** (24km) before reaching another lighthouse (26km), which overlooks the northern edge of the bay. All beaches are free of tourists.

To reach Playa Potosí, get off a second class bus (from Petatlán about .90 pesos). The microbuses that run between Zihuatanejo and Petatlán also pass by Los Achotes, which is little more than a *crucero* (crossroads). From Zihuatanejo, the microbus costs about .90 pesos and leaves frequently from Juárez. Look for the buses with the purple stripe. From *el crucero*, hop on one of the fairly frequent *camionetas* (flatbed pickup trucks) that travel the dirt road to the *playa* (every hr., ½hr., about 2 pesos). Many hitch with one of the residents. The last *camioneta* returns to *el crucero* at 5pm. From there, try to flag down a second-class bus. Buses won't always stop, though; a better bet is the Zihuatanejo-Petatlán microbus. From *el crucero*, with your back to the beach, Zihuatanejo is to the left and Petatlán to the right.

■ Papanoa

North of Pie de la Cuesta in Acapulco, Route 200 curves inland to skirt Lagunas Coyuco and Mitla before coming in contact with the coast once more at Papanoa. Small-time resorts, with *cabañas* on the beach and fresh seafood in the restaurants, fill this part of the coast.

Club Papanoa caters to those who want to spend a day or two on the less-traveled circuit. The expensive rooms would mess up your budget, but the friendly management may allow camping on the grounds for about 18 pesos per person, particularly during low season or if business is slow. The club sits on a point in the Bahía Papanoa between two often deserted white-sand beaches. An *enramada* on the beach serves excellent seafood; from the hotel, walk toward the ocean and to the right. The seaside site beats the club's in-house restaurant for price and atmosphere. For reservations at the club, write **Hotel Club Papanoa,** Cayaquitos, Guerrero. You can reserve by phone in Mexico City (tel. 753-06-25).

To reach the club, get off the first-class bus in the city of Papanoa (80km southeast of Zihuatanejo), 3km from the club, because the bus won't stop any closer. Most second-class bus drivers will drop you off at the entrance to the hotel, but none will pick up passengers there again. From the first-class station, the club is to the right as you exit; from the second-class station, it's to the left. The walk along the highway isn't strenuous but takes 30 minutes. Taxis are stationed close to both bus stops; collective flat-bed pickups pass frequently, and will drop you off at the club. To catch a *colectivo* from the club back into town, walk left on Route 200 (toward Zihuatanejo) for about 0.5km. On the inland side of the highway, there is a small shaded lot where they stop to make pickups. However, a wildly gesticulating tourist is bound to get the *colectivo* drivers to stop anywhere along the highway. Drivers to Club Papanoa should look for km155 on Route 200.

■■■ ACAPULCO

> *Poor Mexico! So far from God and so near to the United States!*
> —Porfirio Díaz

Acapulco seems farther from God and nearer to the U.S. than any place else in Mexico. The city's cathedral was installed in a cinema intended to show second-rate North American flicks; the most convenient mass in town takes place in the convention room of the five-star El Presidente Hotel and is advertised on the activities board along with bay cruises, fiesta night, shopping trips and such. The city's primary cultural nexus is the Plaza shopping mall.

In the 1530s, shortly after conquering Tenochtitlán, Hernán Cortés discovered Acapulco's natural harbor and committed it to a future of exploration and commerce. For centuries, the port thrived on trade with the Philippines and China. After the Revolution of 1910, Mexico forfeited its economic connections with the European colonies. Acapulco languished in solitude until a highway joined it to Mexico City in 1927. In the 1930s, trade picked up again, and the first luxury hotels appeared. Tourism, however, became an important industry only after World War II.

Today, Acapulco is two things. First, a thin fingernail of a resort that gilds the lily of the Bahía de Acapulco—a glitzy strip with beaches to one side and downtown to the other. Second, a slummish settlement that reaches up into the hills behind the resorts. This second, grimmer Acapulco formed when the heavily monied stopped vacationing on Acapulco's seashore and hotel jobs could no longer keep pace with the waves of immigration rolling seaward from the interior.

ORIENTATION

Acapulco is now the fading grandfather of Mexico's Pacific resorts, 400km south of Mexico City and 239km southeast of Zihuatanejo/Ixtapa. The city's **Estrella de Oro bus station** is on Av. Cuauhtémoc, just northeast of *Parque Papagayo*. To get from here to the *zócalo*, take any bus heading southwest (.70 pesos). To make the walk to the *zócalo* (45min.), follow Cuauhtémoc southwest until it becomes Escudero, which ends at Av. Costera Miguel Alemán. Turn right; the *zócalo* is two blocks ahead. The city's second bus station is **Estrella Blanca** at Av. Ejido 47. Instead of walking, take a bus marked *"zócalo"* (.70 pesos) or hire a taxi (8 pesos).

Taxis charge outlandish rates for passages to the **airport,** 26km east of the city on Route 200. A cheaper option is the door-to-door **collective company;** call 85-29-71 or 85-22-27 one day in advance with flight information. Some English is spoken. They will pick you up 90 minutes before your scheduled departure for domestic flights and 120 minutes before international departures. If you are leaving the country, you will have to pay the US$12 departure tax at the airport gate. If traveling domestically, the departure tax is US$4. (Both can be paid in pesos.)

The crescent-shaped city opens to the south around Acapulco Bay. Route 200 feeds into **Avenida Costera Miguel Alemán** (sometimes labeled Av. Presidente Alemán, but always referred to simply as the Costera). This thoroughfare traces the contour of the bay and connects Acapulco's three main districts: the Peninsula de las Playas, the older city center, and the relatively new strip of luxury hotels that extends from *Parque Papagayo* to the naval base (known as *La Base Naval*). Landmarks along the Costera make easy reference points for locating the city's major sights, most of which lie on or near this divided highway. The **Peninsula de las Playas** forms the southwestern curve of the crescent and shields the bay from Pacific breakers. The Costera begins on the southern (seaward) side of the peninsula at Playa Caleta, and continues past the **zócalo,** the strip and finally to the naval base.

Buses cruise the length of Costera, Av. Cuauhtémoc, and other major streets from 6am to midnight. The old blue and white school buses charge .70 pesos; on the more modern "Paseo Acapulco" buses the fare is 1 peso. Buses marked "Cine Río-La Base" connect the *zócalo* with the naval base via both Cuauhtémoc and the Costera; those marked "Hornos" or "CICI" stick to the Costera.

Taxis await everywhere and charge outrageous fees; a ride from the *zócalo* to either bus terminal costs 8 pesos, to Playa Caleta 7 pesos, to Pie de la Cuesta 25 pesos, to Puerto Marqués or the airport 30 pesos. Always bargain and always set the price before you climb in.

PRACTICAL INFORMATION

Tourist Offices: Acapulco Federal Tourist Office, Costera 187 (tel. 85-10-41). The most helpful. Young and friendly staff speaks English and has maps, brochures and information about Acapulco, Ixtapa and Taxco. Open Mon.-Fri. 8am-8pm, Sat.-Sun. 10am-6pm. In an emergency, contact the state's **Tourist Assistance Bureau** (tel. 84-44-16), Costera 4455, in front of CICI in the Centro Internacional Acapulco. They write up stolen property reports. Although they mean well, this is an office, not an information booth. Open daily 9am-9pm.

Travel Agency: Fantasy Tours, Costera 50 (tel. 84-25-28), in the lobby of the Hotel Embassy, across from the CICI water playground. Tours of the city and its environs as well as cheap stand-by plane tickets, information and brochures. Open Mon.-Sat. 9am-2pm and 4-7pm.

Consulates: U.S., on Costera at the Club del Sol Hotel. Entrance a convenient ½-block inland from the Big Boy restaurant. Mr. Lambert Urbaneck (tel. 83-19-69 or 82-07-57; for messages, 85-66-00 ext. 273), keeps office hours Mon.-Fri. 10am-2pm. **Canada,** Ms. Diana Mclean, in the Club del Sol Hotel (tel. 85-66-21), next to the U.S. Consulate. Office open Mon.-Fri. 9am-1pm. **U.K.,** in the Hotel Las Brisas (tel. 84-16-50). For other consulates, call or stop by the **Casa Consular** in the Centro Internacional Acapulco (tel. 81-25-33). Open Mon.-Fri. 9am-2pm and 4-7pm, Sat. 9am-2pm.

Currency Exchange: Banks lining Costera near the *zócalo* and on the strip have the best rates. All open Mon.-Fri. 9am-1:30pm. On the strip, you won't be able to open your eyes without spotting a *casa de cambio*—usually open until 8pm with rates comparable to banks.

American Express: Costera 709-A (tel. 84-15-79 or 84-68-87), just east of La Diana. Efficient, air-conditioned office. English spoken. Open Mon.-Fri. 9am-2pm and 4-6pm, Sat. 9am-1pm.

Post Office: Costera 215 (tel. 82-20-83), near the *zócalo*. Open for stamps Mon.-Sat. 8am-8pm, Sun. 9am-1pm; for registered mail and *Lista de Correos* Mon.-Fri. 8am-8pm, Sat. 9am-1pm. **Postal code:** 39300.

Telephones: Caseta Carranza, Carranza 9, near the *zócalo*. 15 pesos for collect calls to the U.S. Plenty of payphones in the *zócalo* are the cheaper alternative for collect calls. Open daily 8am-10pm. **Telephone code:** 748.

Telegrams: In the Palacio Federal (tel. 82-26-21), on Costera next to the post office. Open for telegrams Mon.-Sat. 9am-8pm; for money orders Mon.-Fri. 9am-5pm, Sat. 9am-noon.

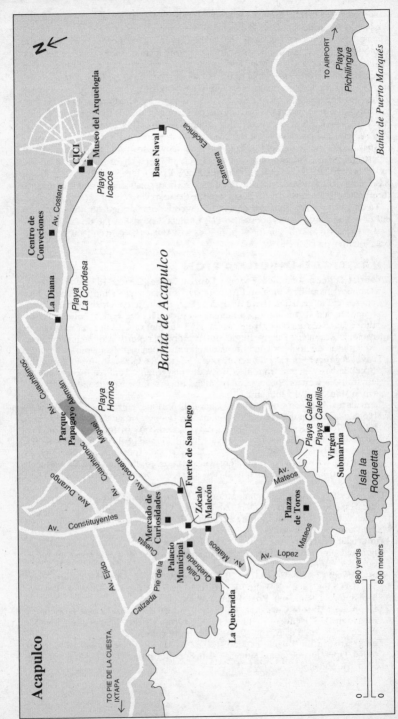

ACAPULCO

Acapulco

TO PIE DE LA CUESTA, IXTAPA

Av. Ejido

Calzada Pie de la Cuesta

Av. Constituyentes

Av. Durango

Av. Cuauhtémoc

Av. Cuauhtémoc

Parque Papagayo

Av. Miguel Alemán

Playa Hornos

Centro de Convenciones

La Diana

Playa La Condesa

Av. Costera

Museo del Arqueologia

CICI

Playa Icacos

Base Naval

Escénica

Carretera

TO AIRPORT

Playa Pichilingue

Bahía de Puerto Marqués

Bahía de Acapulco

Fuerte de San Diego

Zócalo

Malecón

Mercado de Curiosidades

Palacio Municipal

Calle Quebrada

La Quebrada

Av. Mateos

Av. Lopez

Av. Mateos

Av. Mateos

Plaza de Toros

Playa Caleta

Playa Caletilla

Virgén Submarina

Isla la Roquetta

880 yards

800 meters

0

0

Airport: On Rte. 200, 26km south of the city (tel. 84-03-09). **Delta** (tel. 66-94-87), **Continental** (tel. 66-90-63), **Aeroméxico** (tel. 85-16-25), **Mexicana** (tel. 84-92-15), **American** (tel. 66-92-63). Or stop by **Fantasy Tours** (see above). First 2 airlines have their offices at the airport, the others in La Torre de Acapulco (just east of bus stop #18).

Bus Stations: Estrella de Oro, on Cuauhtémoc (tel. 85-93-60), about 10min. east of the northeast corner of the *Parque Papagayo*. To: Mexico City (7hrs., 55 pesos), Chipalcingo (2hrs., 14 pesos), Iguala (4hrs., 30 pesos), Taxco (4½hrs., 35 pesos), Cuernavaca (5½hrs., 32 peso), Zihuatanejo (4hrs., 27 pesos). **Estrella Blanca,** Av. Ejido 47 (tel. 83-33-15). To: Mexico City (7hrs., 55 pesos), Puebla (9hrs., 60 pesos), Puerto Escondido (8hrs., 55 pesos), Pochutla (9hrs., 60 pesos), Zihuatanejo (4hrs., 35 pesos).

Laundromats: Ghost Cleaners, José María Iglesias 9 (tel. 82-70-22), 1 block west of the *zócalo*. Same-day service. 20 pesos for 3 kg. Open Mon.-Fri. 8am-2pm and 4-7pm, Sat. 8:30am-2pm.

Red Cross: On Ruiz Cortínez (tel. 85-41-00), down Madero north of the *zócalo*. 24-hr. emergency service, but no English spoken. 10-peso service fee. Has a doctor on duty at the **Princess Hotel** (tel. 84-31-00).

Pharmacy: ISSTE Farmacias, Quebrada 1 (tel. 82-34-77), at Independencia directly behind the cathedral on the *zócalo*. Open Mon.-Sat. 8am-8pm.

Hospital: Ruiz Cortínez 128 (tel. 85-17-30 or 85-19-96), north of the *zócalo* down Madero. Medical appointments can be made here with English-speaking private doctors. 24-hr. emergency service.

Police: On the ground floor of the Cocos Condominiums (tel. 85-06-50 or 85-04-90), two-thirds of the way to Playa Caleta from the *zócalo* on Costera. **Tourist police** in the *zócalo*, in a white booth just across the Costera from the water.

ACCOMMODATIONS AND CAMPING

Budget accommodations are plentiful and easier to find in Acapulco than anywhere else on Mexico's Pacific coast. Many taxi drivers at the Estrella Blanca bus station will offer to take you to their personal favorite. Given a commission by local hotels, these middlemen charge no fee (but do hang around for a tip) and generally plug reasonably economical places. Before following anyone, clarify the terms of the venture and realize that the final price is determined by the hotel manager. If you have time, however, it's a snap to locate Acapulco's budget neighborhoods and make your own comparisons.

Most of the best deals in the city look out on Calle La Quebrada, which runs from the church behind the *zócalo* to the top of the La Quebrada cliffs. Other cheap hotels squeeze into Teniente José Azuelta and many other cross streets between Quebrada and the Costera. To reach Quebrada from the *zócalo*, walk up the alley to the left of the cathedral and take the first left.

Hotel Asturias, Quebrada 45 (tel. 83-65-48). One of the best deals on Quebrada. Fans. Swimming pool. Brand new springy mattress. Rooms on the bottom level shady and cool. A really nice hotel for the price—that's why it fills so fast. Get there super-early or send money ahead for reservations. Singles 40 pesos. Doubles 60 pesos.

Hotel Angelita, Quebrada 37 (tel. 83-57-34). It doesn't have a swimming pool, but other than that it's as nice as Hotel Asturias. The rooms are large and cool, as are the bathrooms. Angelita herself hangs out watching TV in the lobby downstairs. Worth a visit. 25 pesos per person.

Hotel Mariscal, Quebrada 35 (tel. 82-00-15). Rickety but comfortable and quite cheap. Breezy, colonnaded entry and shared balconies provide plenty of spots to cool down in the evening. TV in the lobby. Clean rooms decorated with peeling but pretty wallpaper. Beware the lumpy beds. Hot water. Singles 20 pesos. Doubles 40 pesos.

Casa de Huéspedes La Tía Conchita, Quebrada 32 (tel. 82-18-82), the blue building a few blocks from the *zócalo* up Quebrada on the right. Simple and rustic but adequate. Small rooms. Only a couple have private bathrooms (others share 2 communal ones), but the price is the same regardless. Terrific front porch. A similar hotel next door. 20 pesos per person.

La Torre Eiffel, Imalámbrica 110 (tel. 82-16-83), all the way up Quebrada and to the left. Worth the climb. Nice pool, and *fabulous* views of La Quebrada and the hills surrounding Acapulco from large breezy patios with ultra-comfortable bright pink furniture. A long way from all but the cliff divers. Singles 60 pesos. Doubles 90 pesos.

Acapulco Trailer Park, office in the "Minisuper," just before Quinta Dora. English spoken. 60 economical sites. Daily laundry service 2 houses away (15 pesos for 3 kg). Site for 1 car and up to 2 people for about 30 pesos.

FOOD

Acapulco restaurants are a god-send for North Americans homesick for Yankee cuisine, fast-food style. Denny's, Pizza Hut and, yes, even McDonald's have invaded the Costera. Unfortunately, along with U.S. food, these restaurants dish up U.S. prices; which might explain the dearth of underpaid local customers.

As usual, *típico* spots serve the cheapest meals; look to the hundreds of *fondas* (food stands) throughout the city as well as in the market, which spans several square blocks and is located inland from Costera between Mendoza and De León. Only slightly more expensive—and generally much better—are the restaurants between Costera and Quebrada south and west of the *zócalo*. Competition here keeps prices low: *desayunos* and huge *comidas corridas* run between 7 and 10 pesos. What's more, these *comidas corridas* (which usually include soup, bread, a choice of several entrees and dessert or coffee) are often available until closing rather than until the typical 5pm.

Near the Zócalo

Prices begin to climb as you inch north and west from the *zócalo* toward the strip.

Angelo's Restaurant and Pizzería, Juárez 2, just off the *zócalo*. Italy is the theme—red, white and green everywhere. Great pizza ranges from 13.50 pesos for small to 33.50 big size. *Comida corrida* 9 pesos. Open daily 8am-10:30pm.

Pizza's Real, Independencia 7, 1 block past the church in the *zócalo*. Less touristy (Italy is absent from the walls and tablecloths) than Angelo's—more of a neighborhood joint, complete with TV and Mexican soap operas—but the pizza is equally good, if not better. From 14 pesos to 22 pesos. Open daily noon-11pm.

Cafetería Astoria, Pl. Álvarez 1 (tel. 82-29-44), tucked into the back corner of the *zócalo*. A shady spot to inconspicuously watch everyone in the *zócalo* watching everybody else. Chicken *a la mexicana* 15 pesos. Chicken tacos 8 pesos. Cappuccino 3.50 pesos. Open daily 8:30am-10pm.

Restaurant Carmon's, Juárez 8. Your basic Mexican restaurant, except that the offerings are slightly more expensive and more varied. *Huevos rancheros* 5.50 pesos. Shrimp consomme 10 pesos. Chicken soup 3 pesos. Open daily 7am-10pm.

Playa Caleta

There are plenty of restaurants in the beach area, but most are low in quality and devoid of ambience. Caleta's cheapest cuisine can be found within the *fondas* across the street from Playa Caletilla, where families set up stalls and sell the same food at the same prices. If you do want to sit by the sea, however, **Restaurant El Costeño,** at the boat launch on Playa Caletilla, off Costera, is one of about 15 look-alike, taste-alike establishments on Caletilla. Like its neighbors, it tends to be a bit expensive, with a fish filet going for 15 pesos and *arroz con mariscos* for 19 pesos. (Open daily noon-10pm.) For a cheaper meal that involves more than seafood, try **Restaurant/Bar Mar Azul,** Gran Vía Trópica 1, above the fountain with the baby-blue railing. It has no charm to speak of. (*Tortas* 4-4.50 pesos, *huevos* 5-7 pesos, *cervezas* 4 pesos. Open daily 7am-11pm.)

LET'S GO® Travel

1994 CATALOG

We give you the world
at a discount!

ORDER
1-800-5-LETS-GO
TOLL FREE!

•Discount Flights •Eurails •Travel Gear

LET'S PACK IT UP

Let's Go Supreme

Innovative hideaway suspension with parallel stay internal frame turns backpack into carry-on suitcase. Includes lumbar support pad, torso and waist adjustment, leather trim, and detachable daypack. Waterproof Cordura nylon, lifetime guarantee, 4400 cu. in. Navy, Green or Black.

A • • • • • • • • • • • • • $175

Let's Go Backpack/Suitcase

Hideaway suspension with internal frame turns backpack into carry-on suitcase. Detachable daypack makes it 3 bags in 1. Waterproof Cordura nylon, lifetime guarantee, 3750 cu. in. Navy, Green or Black.

B • • • • • • • • • • • • • • $130

Let's Go Backcountry

Full size, slim profile expedition pack designed for the serious trekker. New Airflex suspension. X-frame pack with advanced composite tube suspension. Velcro height adjustment, side compression straps. Detachable hood converts into a fanny pack. Waterproof Cordura nylon, lifetime guarantee. Main compartment 6530 cu. in. extends to 7130 cu. in.

C • • • • • • • • $210

Undercover NeckPouch

Ripstop nylon with soft Cambrelle back. 3 pockets. 6 x 7". Lifetime guarantee. Black or Tan.

D • • • • • • • • • • • • • • $9.95

Undercover WaistPouch

Ripstop nylon with soft Cambrelle back. 2 pockets. 12 x 5" with adjustable waistband. Lifetime guarantee. Black or Tan.

E • • • • • • • • • • • • • • $9.95

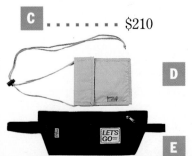

LET'S GO BY TRAIN
Eurail Passes
Convenient way to travel Europe. Save up to 70% over cost of individual tickets.

EURAILPASS
FIRST CLASS

15 days	$498
21 days	$648
1 month	$798
2 months	$1098
3 months	$1398

EURAIL FLEXIPASS
FIRST CLASS

Any 5 days in 2 months	$348
Any 10 days in 2 months	$560
Any 15 days in 2 months	$740

EURAIL SAVERPASS**
FIRST CLASS

15 days	$430
21 days	$550
1 month	$678

**Price per person for 2 or more people travelling together. 3 people required between April 1 - September 3.

EURAIL YOUTHPASS*
SECOND CLASS

15 days	$398
1 month	$578
2 months	$768

*Valid only if passenger is under 26 on first date of travel.

EURAIL YOUTH FLEXIPASS*
SECOND CLASS

Any 5 days in 2 months	$255
Any 10 days in 2 months	$398
Any 15 days in 2 months	$540

*Valid only if passenger is under 26 on first date of travel.

LET'S GO BY PLANE
Discounted Flights
Over 150 destinations including:

LONDON

MADRID

PARIS

ATHENS

ROME

Domestic fares too!
For prices & reservations
call 1-800-5-LETS-GO

EURAIL COUNTRY PASSES

**POLAND   HUNGARY
AUSTRIA   FRANCE
SCANDINAVIA
FINLAND
LUXEMBOURG
GREECE   SPAIN
CZECHOSLOVAKIA
GERMANY   PORTUGAL
NETHERLANDS
BRITAIN   SPAIN**

Call for prices, rail n' drive or rail n' fly options. Flexotel passes too!

WE GIVE YOU THE WORLD...

AT A DISCOUNT!

LET'S GO TRAVEL
53a Church St.
Cambridge, MA 02138
(617) 495-9649 or 1-800-5-LETS-GO
FAX (617) 496-8015

LET'S GO HOSTELING
1994-95 Youth Hostel Card
Required by most international hostels.
Must be a U.S. resident.

F1 Adult (ages 18-55) $25

F2 Youth (under 18) $10

Sleepsack
Required at all hostels. Washable durable
poly/cotton. 18" pillow pocket. Folds into
pouch size.

G $13.95

1993-94 Youth Hostel Guide (IYHG)
Essential information about 4000 hostels in
Europe and the Mediterranean.

H $10.95

LET'S GET STARTED
Please print or type. Incomplete applications will be returned

Last Name	First Name	Date of Birth

Street	We do not ship to P.O. Boxes. U.S. addresses only.	

City	State	Zip Code

Phone	Date Trip Begins	

Item Code	Description, Size & Color	Quantity	Unit Price	Total Price

Shipping & Handling		
If order totals: . . . . . . Add	Total Merchandise Price	
Up to $30.00 . . . . . . $4.00	Shipping & Handling (See box at left)	
30.01-100.00 . . . . . . $6.00	For Rush Handling Add $10 for continental U.S., $12 for AK & HI	
Over 100.00 . . . . . . $7.00	MA Residents (Add 5% sales tax on gear & books)	
	Total	

Mastercard/Visa Order

Cardholder name_____

Card number_____

Expiration date_____

Allow 2-3 weeks for delivery. Rush
orders delivered within one week of
our receipt.

Enclose check or money order
payable to:
Harvard Student Agencies, Inc.
53a Church St. Cambridge, MA 021:

Prices subject to change without notice

On the Main Strip

The many restaurants between La Condesa Beach and *La Base* cater to tourists who apparently don't fret about cost. Still, some have moderate prices and others a certain tawdry chic that calls for a visit.

Some of the best seafood on the strip is dished up at **Pipo's Mariscos,** Costera 105, at the Nao Victoria bus stop just east of CICI. Delicious seafood soup (27 pesos) contains crab, fish, octopus, tuna, clams and other little surprises. Variations on *huachinango* (red snapper) go for 35-40 pesos. (Open daily 1-9:30pm. 2 other locations in Acapulco.) **Mimi's,** Costera 101, a couple of blocks east of La Diana, seems in danger of becoming the U.S. Consulate. *Norteamericana* decorations from every era, the most titillating of which is a huge map of Indianapolis. Atmosphere is fun and relaxed. A sign says "Happy Hour is every hour. You're in Acapulco." (Hamburgers 19 pesos. Taco salad 17 pesos. Open daily 8am-whenever you feel like leaving.)

SIGHTS AND ACTIVITIES

Peninsula de las Playas

World-renowned representatives of Acapulco, the cliffdivers at La Quebrada never fail to impress. These buffed young men judge the speed of the incoming waves as well as the distance between the opposing cliffs on the south side of the peninsula before diving from 25-35m heights into the shallow waters of the inlet below.

The *Unión de Clavadistas La Quebrada* (Divers' Union) adheres to a rigid daily agenda—dives occur at 1pm, 7:30pm, 8:30pm, 9:30pm, and 10:30pm. The last two dives of the day are undertaken by torchlight. The terrace bar of the **Restaurant La Perla** in Pl. Las Glorias provides an excellent view of the death-defying acts and a "complimentary" drink starting at 27.50 pesos, but you can preserve your proletarian consciousness by joining the masses on the platform across from the point where the dives originate (5 pesos, under 12 free). Alternatively, if you pay your pesos and gawk from one of the two higher platforms conveniently located near the divers' dressing room, you might be able to meet the dashing heroes. The cliffs are at the southwestern end of La Quebrada, a 15min. walk up the hill from the *zócalo*.

Many buses marked "Caleta" run down Costera and Cuauhtémoc (.70 pesos) and head for **Playas Caleta** and **Caletilla.** At the westernmost tip of Acapulco Bay, on the seaward side of the peninsula, they lie adjacent to each other and are known as the "morning beaches" because of their eastern exposure. They also tend to be the more local, less touristy beaches. Between them, a short causeway links the mainland to what otherwise would be a tiny island.

A variety of equipment is available for rent on Playa Caleta; canoes, paddle boats and flatboats are available on the beach's eastern side. On its western side, just before Playa Caletilla, is a stand that rents sailboats and bronco motor boats. In addition, innertubes are available all over the beach. For scuba-diving and snorkeling gear/trips, go to **Agua Sport** (tel. 82-53-24) on Caleta. Take a left onto the small street that branches off Costera at the fountain and skirts the waterfront. (Open daily 8am-6pm.)

Perhaps the best attraction at Playa Caleta is the recently-built **aquarium** at the far end of the boat launch. No only are there sea lions, alligators, etc., but the 20-peso entrance fee allows you to spend the whole day lounging by the pool or partaking of the two giant waterslides. The aquarium also has rock platforms from which you can gambol into the ocean. Due to its cleanliness and unique location, the view from the aquarium's pool and rocks probably tops that of any beach in Acapulco. (Open daily 9am-7pm.)

The **Plaza de Toros Caletilla,** Acapulco's main bullring, sits beyond the no-longer-used, yellow jai-alai auditoriums 200m west of the beach area. *Corridas de toros* cease during some parts of the off-season. The best-known *matadores* appear only from December to mid-April. Buy tickets at the Centro Kennedy box office at Costera and Alvaro Saavedra (tel. 85-85-40) or at the ring box office starting at 4:30pm on the day of the fight. Bullfights erupt on Sundays at 5pm.

City Center

Acapulco's *zócalo*, **Plaza Álvarez,** is one of the most pleasant on Mexico's Pacific coast. Huge trees cast shadows over stone benches, children cavort in the fountains, and old men play endless games of chess in the sidewalk cafés and under the bridge at the inland edge of the square. Musicians, dancers, jugglers and clowns strive to amuse along the walkways. The plaza is bounded on one side by Costera and on the other by a cathedral, whose blue-tiled dome is visible from higher points around the bay.

The city's **Palacio Municipal** crowns a hill just inland from the *zócalo*. Go to the top of the white flight of stairs to the right of the cathedral, take a right through the tunnel, and the *palacio's* entrance is around the corner to your left, up another flight of stairs. This circular structure encloses a courtyard, and from its patio most of the old city is visible. Before it became Acapulco's city hall, the building served as a jail; the Mexican painter Sophia Bassi Zolorio did time here. Indicted for murdering her husband, she became a *cause célèbre* before prominent Mexicans secured a pardon for her because of her artistic contributions. During the time of her confinement in the late 1960s, Bassi Zolorio covered a number of the prison walls with paintings. The *palacio's* small auditorium bears one of the most striking works, a surrealistic self-portrait involving a rendition of the artist's imagined trial and execution. Another painting is daubed on the opposite wall. The best-known mural in the building is Roberto Cueva del Río's *Patria es primera*, which covers all four walls of the north stairway. Other works are scattered around the former prison, including a representation of Mexico's presidents hatching from eggs and a chronicle of Acapulco's transformation from small-time fishing village to big-time resort. (Palace open Mon.-Fri. 9am-9pm. No shorts or swimsuits.)

The **Fuerte de San Diego** was built in 1615 to ward off pirates, among them Sir Francis Drake, who hung around the bay, looting ships arriving from Asia. An earthquake in 1776 leveled the entire city of Acapulco, destroying the fort that stood on Costera, a five-minute walk east of the *zócalo*. It was later restored to its original pentagonal shape, and during the revolution the fort proved itself secure enough to hold back Morelos's rebel forces for a full four months. While its strategic importance has vanished, the fort remains a working military compound. Civilian visitors can visit the fort and its attached museum. After hours it becomes a make-out spot for young *acapulqueño* couples who come to pay homage to its glorious history. (Museum open Tues.-Sun. 10:30am-4:40pm. 13 pesos.)

Referred to as a "flea market" by the English-language tourist brochures, the 400-stall **Mercado de Curiosidades** covers several square blocks between Cuauhtémoc and Velázquez de León, north of the *zócalo*. Here you can buy the same *huaraches*, shirts and hammocks sold on the beaches in front of the big hotels for a fraction of the cost. Tourist brochures recommend opening bids on "pre-priced" articles at a quarter of what is asked.

Parque Papagayo

The green grass and cool shade of *Parque Papagayo* can be a relief from too many days of hot sand and bright sun. Sandwiched between Playas Hornos and Hornitos (the "afternoon" beaches), the park, like the beaches it borders, caters largely to a Mexican crowd. Its many diversions include roller skating, boating (on a man-made lake) and go-cart racing. The park also encloses a small but well-equipped amusement park, a *plaza de toros* (but no bullfights), and a concrete toboggan run, whose starting gate at the top of a little hill is accessible by perhaps the only ski lift in Mexico. The summit is also reached by a cable car and a winding road. Of interest, too, is the park's **aviary;** crested cranes, peacocks, buzzcocks, emus, guinea fowl, flamingos, and toucans inhabit the netted sanctuary. For schedules of rodeos and other park activities, call the **park office** (tel. 85-24-90; open Mon.-Fri. 6am-8pm, Sat.-Sun. 6am-9pm). For further information, contact the public relations department (tel. 85-27-56).

East of La Diana

Gatekeeper of the fantasy land of luxury hotels east of her post, a statue of Diana the hunter stands anomalously on a traffic island in the middle of Costera. From her post until the city's easternmost reaches, Acapulco is a conglomeration of resorts, each providing room and board, a swath of sand, built-in entertainment and door-to-door package tours. You could spend your vacation in this part of Acapulco and forget you were in Mexico were it not for the **Instituto Guerrerense de la Cultura,** Costera 4834 (tel. 84-38-14). Part of a state-wide program, the institute was created to develop city spirit and promote regional arts and culture. Paintings by local artists are for sale in the gallery. (Open daily 10am-2pm and 5-8pm.) The **archaeological museum** housed in the Instituto has a small collection of pre-Conquest artifacts. (Open daily 10am-2pm and 5-8pm. Free.) The institute's library invites *guerrerense* writers to give readings, many in English, for an event called "Miércoles Literarios" (Literary Wednesdays), Wednesday at 7:30pm.

The **CICI waterpark** is a state-owned tourist attraction. For about 25 pesos, artificial waves will toss and hurl you headlong down the long, winding water slides. Trained dolphins perform at 12:30pm, 3:30pm and 5:30pm. To reach the park, head east on Costera until you see the walls of bright blue waves and the larger-than-life dolphins, or simply get off the bus labeled "CICI" at the stop labeled "CICI." (Open daily 10am-6pm.) The bus marked "Base" passes the blue wave walls as well; just yell to be let off.

Puerto Marqués

Lacking the pre-packaged polish of the strip only kilometers away, the beach town of **Puerto Marqués** encompasses an unremarkable ribbon of sand lined wall-to-wall by unremarkable restaurants so close to the water that the bay's waves lap at diners' feet. Puerto Marqués would be simply one more seaside village were it not for the magnificent view on the approach from Acapulco. The **bus** ride to this bay (where theiving Sir Francis Drake stalked thieving, bullion-laden Spanish galleons) is the real attraction, thanks to a magnificent vista from the top of the hill before descending into town. Get on the bus at the beginning of the run to ensure yourself a waterside seat (45min., .70 pesos). In Acapulco, buses to Puerto Marqués pass by the post office on the opposite side of the street about every half hour. As the bus rambles along, the Bahía de Puerto Marqués and the pounding surf of Playa Revolcadero fall into full view.

The serenity of the tiny bay makes it an ideal spot for either waterskiing or learning to sail. Rates depend on the season; amiable sailboat owners are generally more than happy to show the novice *gringo* sailor the ropes free of charge. Scuba and snorkeling equipment may also be rented at the beach. A popular afternoon's anchorage for sailboats is **Playa Pichilingue,** a small, often deserted, patch of sand on the Bahía de Puerto Marqués that is inaccessible by land.

Restaurants along the water can be expensive; walk one block inland for the more reasonably priced fare.

Pie de la Cuesta

If you want to swim in the Pacific's calm blue waters, don't go to Pie de la Cuesta; the overpowering surf here sometimes precludes aquatic fun. Just 200m away from the violent waves, however, on the opposite side of the spit of land, spread the placid waters of Laguna de Coyuca, site of the area's best waterskiing. Several clubs devoted to the sport line the lagoon (ski rental 90 pesos per hr.). Pie de la Cuesta is definitely worth at least a day trip, both for its beauty and its serenity.

Most who make the hour-and-a-half trip from Acapulco to Pie de la Cuesta do so to relax as they admire the splendid sunset. Relaxation is all too often interrupted, unfortunately, by aggressive *lancha* agents. Their tours of the lagoon inevitably include the area where the exploding helicopter scene from *Rambo* was filmed. Rates average 8 pesos per person in a *colectivo* boat. The *lancha* agents aside, Pie de la Cuesta provides a great alternative to the hustle and bustle of Acapulco. The air is cleaner here, the water bluer, the surf stronger, the beach less crowded and the scenery more beautiful. Remember, however, that services on the strip are less than minimal (i.e. no phone, post office, etc.). Pie de la Cuesta extends along one main road, beginning at the Oasis snack stand (also the bus stop) and ending at a naval base. **Buses** to Pie de la Cuesta leave from Escudero in Acapulco (90min., .70 pesos) and stop on Costera across the street from the post office near the *zócalo*. Travelers have at least three options for spending a night, or a month. The first option is **Villa Nirvana,** on the ocean side of the road about 100m from the Oasis (look for the blue gate), a utopian fantasy hotel, complete with swimming pool. Rooms are spacious and immaculate, as are the bathrooms. Each is graced by a huge porch with cushioned chairs and a hammock. (Singles 50 pesos. Doubles 70 pesos.) **Hotel Puerta del Sol,** just past Villa Nirvana, off a side street on the ocean side of the road (watch for the sign on the lagoon side), has a restaurant, pool, and tennis court—this place is virtually a luxury resort. (Rooms for 1-2 people 75 pesos. *Cabañas* with kitchen 150 pesos.) Trailer hook-ups at **Trailer Park Quinta Dora,** almost at the base, have 22 lagoon-side sites; 15 sites on the ocean across the street. Hook-ups include water, electricity and sewage. Sparkling bathrooms. (Site for 1-2 people 30 pesos.)

ENTERTAINMENT

Dinner is traditionally served late in Acapulco, and many visitors spend a lot of time and money on the final meal of the day. Those up for shaking some booty at day's end head for either the chic discos on the strip or in the *Zona Rosa*. Remember that loud music is no sure proof of a crowd; try to look inside before paying the cover. Be warned that many of Acapulco's larger, glitzier discos (like **Fantasy** and **Extravaganza,** where cover averages 50 pesos) require reservations on Friday and Saturday nights and, without them, no amount of pleading and name-dropping will get you inside. If you intend to be sexually active with strangers during your stay, keep in mind that Acapulco is one of the cities with the most reported AIDS cases in Mexico; condoms are an especially good idea here.

Baby O (tel. 84-74-74), at the intersection of Costera and Nelson, five minutes from *La Base*, is considered by many to be the best of Acapulco's discotheques. It is also the farthest out along Costera and attracts a younger crowd than the high-tech Fantasy and Extravaganza. In its huge, cave-like interior, videos and the latest dance tunes rock the willing. (Cover 50 pesos. Drinks 10-15 pesos. Open daily 10:30pm-5am.) Also try the **Atrium,** Costera 30 (tel. 84-19-00), for drinks and fake palm trees. (Cover 40 pesos. Open daily 10pm-4am.) These and other discos at the east end of town—such as **Magic,** at Costera and Yucatán (tel. 84-88-16), one block toward the *zócalo* from Boccaccio's (cover 50 pesos, open daily from 10:30pm)—are notorious for picking and choosing their crowd. Bouncers first admit single women, then male-female couples, and finally, if room permits, single men. If you find this practice offensive or prohibitive, you may wish to frequent discos farther west.

Acapulco is still an extremely popular gay and lesbian destination. Although the government has lately taken a harsher stance, tourists mean business and are seldom harassed. **Gallery,** De Los Deportes 11 (tel. 84-34-97), one block inland from the Calinda Quality Inn, is popular for its famous female impersonators, which attract a mixed crowd to both the 11pm and 1am shows. (Cover 40 pesos. Dancing begins daily at 10pm.)

OAXACA

Upon conquering the valley of the Mixtecs, the Aztecs named it *Huaxyacac*, Nahuatl for "in the nose of the *guaje* tree." The Spanish corrupted Huaxyacac to Oajaca, and when the Mexicans gained control, they renamed it Oaxaca (pronounced wa-HA-kah).

Several *indígena* civilizations and more than 200 tribes, including the Mixtec and the Zapotec, have occupied the valley over the past two millennia. Over one million *oaxaqueños* still speak an *indígena* language, and more than a fifth of the state's population speaks no Spanish whatsoever. This language barrier, and the cultural gap behind it, has long exacerbated problems between the Oaxacan government and its indigenous population.

After the Spanish Conquest, in an attempt to eradicate paganism, Catholic missionaries introduced Oaxaca to Catholicism by constructing magnificent baroque cathedrals to symbolically overpower the *indígena* religious architecture. In an attempt to maintain their traditional way of life, the small villages around the city of Oaxaca struggled to perpetuate their artisanal tradition. Take some time to peruse the fruits of their labor: magnificent hand-dyed and hand-stitched *alfombras* (carpets) made on foot-pedaled Spanish looms in Teotitlán del Valle; leather belts woven by hand in Santo Tomás Jalietza; dresses embroidered in San Antonino; inscribed silver hunting knives forged in Ejutla; exquisite black pottery made in San Bartolo Coyotepec. Weavers turn out vibrantly colored *huipiles* (blouses) and other clothing.

Little of this culture is evident once you cross the Sierra Madre del Sur to the coastal resorts of Puerto Escondido and Puerto Angel. The attraction of these two beautiful towns lies not in the opportunity to observe and assimilate ancient and foreign cultures, but rather in the chance to avoid such strenuous thinking. Until recently, these small towns were unknown to all but the most intrepid tourists; lately, however, word of their charm has spread like wildfire among both travelers and developers, and the tourist zone of the Oaxaca coast, which now stretches east of Puerto Angel, is ablaze with expansion. The Bahías de Huatulco—nine magnificent, once isolated bays—are receiving a dose of *desarrollo turístico* (tourist development), including a Club Med, harbinger of the decadent wealthy.

■■■ OAXACA DE JUÁREZ

Deep in the highlands of Sierra Madre del Sur, on a giant plateau that gracefully interrupts the terrain's descent into the Oaxaca Valley, Oaxaca City (pop. 214,000) has gripped Spaniards and visitors ever since Hernán Cortés built a beloved (but unfinished) private estate here in 1535. Nicknamed "City of Jade" after the many buildings inlaid with the emerald gem, Oaxaca chills to a year-round average temperature of 21°C (70°F). Despite its well-deserved popularity among travelers, the state capital maintains a small-town atmosphere. Even locals patronize the colonnaded cafés on the *zócalo*, where prices are high but not stratospheric.

During the last two decades, the city of Oaxaca has expanded from insider's secret to major travel destination. Attractions include Oaxaca's several markets and its unusually large *zócalo*, one of the most amiable in the Republic. Unlike most Mexican *centros*, the entire area is a pedestrian mall punctuated by tall trees and pots of flowers. Just a short distance outside Oaxaca lie many *indígena* villages and, in the hilly environs, a number of outstanding archaeological sites including Mitla, Yagul and Monte Albán—all of which make great daytrips.

Oaxaca has nurtured quite a few Mexican celebrities. Benito Juárez (1806-1872), champion of the reform era, was a poor Zapotec *indígena* born in the nearby town of Guelatao and raised in Oaxaca by a wealthy *ladino* family who lived on Calle García Vigil. His name and image pop up everywhere: on street signs, markets, bus lines, shops and murals. Citizens are less proud of another famous native son, the

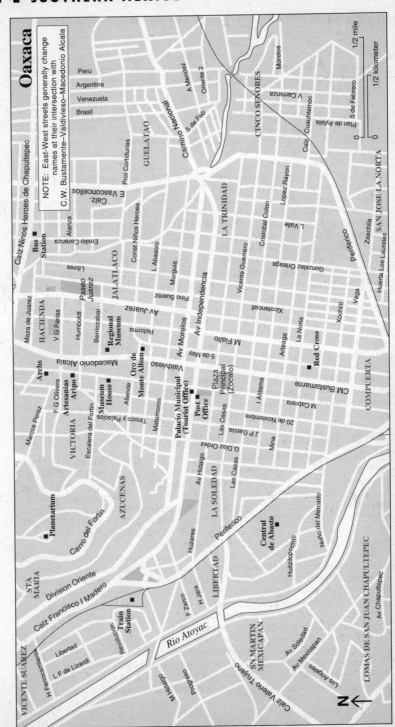

OAXACA DE JUÁREZ

Oaxaca

NOTE: East-West streets generally change names at their intersection with C.W. Bustamente–Valdivieso–Macedonio Alcala

notoriously pesky dictator Porfirio Díaz (1830-1915). His name may be unloved, but it nonetheless designates two major thoroughfares in Oaxaca. *Oaxaqueño* artist Rufino Tamayo is recognized and honored throughout the Republic; the Tamayo museum in Oaxaca houses his impressive collection of pre-Columbian art.

Oaxaca is also full of students; some tearing around on expensive motorcycles, others agitating for labor reform. And while this is a relatively affluent city, expect to see all of Mexico in evidence: merchants, *indígenas*, businesspeople, students, and tourists. Oaxaca has handled the recent upsurge in tourism as well as any city could hope to, and while the sweater vendors in the *zócalo* may depend entirely on visitors's pesos, these merchants are greatly outnumbered by the knife-sharpeners, corn-huskers, and coffee-grinders who go about their business as if Oaxaca were just another mountain town. Oaxaca, like most cities, is at its aesthetic best in the early morning. At first light, Oaxaca's architecture (characterized by high walls, green and aging gracefully) approaches the transcendent. It is an elaborate yet organic source of beauty. Do your best to get lost. When green-sweatered school children begin to hurry past, it's time for breakfast.

ORIENTATION

Oaxaca de Juárez rests in the Oaxaca Valley, between the towering Sierra Madre del Sur and the Puebla-Oaxaca range, 523km southeast of Mexico City, 435km south of Veracruz, and 526km west of Tuxtla Gutiérrez. Principal access to Oaxaca from the north and east is via Route 190.

Oaxaca isn't huge, but orienting yourself can be difficult as many streets change names when they pass the *zócalo*. Most streets are part of a perfect grid, oriented to the four corners of the known world. The large maps posted around the *zócalo* clearly mark all sights in English. The *zócalo*, on Hidalgo (one of the few streets that does not change names), consists of two squares. The main one lies between Hidalgo and Trujano/Guerrero, and the **Plaza Alameda de León** just to the northwest is sandwiched by Hidalgo and Independencia.

Oaxaca's downtown is circumscribed by a busy peripheral expressway called the Periférico in the south before acquiring other names as it loops north. **Avenida Hidalgo** divides *el centro* into two principal areas: the budget district lies south of Hidalgo while the expensive hotels and restaurants cluster around the *zócalo* north of and on Hidalgo. The historic part of town, north of Hidalgo, contains most of Oaxaca's sights and museums between lavish private residences. **Avenida Macedonio Alcalá** splits downtown into east and west sections, serving for a few blocks north of the *zócalo* as a pedestrian walkway, the *corredor turístico*. **Morelos, Independencia,** and **García Vigil** are Oaxaca's other principal streets. Twelve blocks north of the *zócalo*, **Calzada Niños Héroes de Chapultepec** (the Pan-American Highway) runs east-west.

To reach the *zócalo* from the **first class bus station** (home to **ADO, Cristobal Colon,** and **UNO** bus lines), cross the street and catch a bus marked *"Centro,"* heading west on Chapultepec (1 peso). The bus runs south on Juarez. If you get off at Hidalgo, the *zócalo* will be three blocks to the east. To make the 20 minute walk from the station, head west on Chapultepec for six blocks to Alcalá and turn left. Twelve blocks past churches and tourist colonnades will bring you to the main plaza. The **second class bus terminal** lies west of the city center, next to the Central de Abastos: walk east on Trujano for eight long blocks and you'll reach the *zócalo*. A taxi from either station to the *centro* costs 7 pesos.

Hiking from one end of town to the other takes no more than 45 minutes, and walking on the pedestrian mall at night is relatively safe. Though petty crime has surged in Oaxaca with the influx of tourists, it rarely goes beyond pickpocketing. Still, it's a good idea for travelers to take taxis if crossing town late at night. Be aware, however, that cabbies charge extra from 11pm-5am.

OAXACA DE JUÁREZ

PRACTICAL INFORMATION

Tourist Offices: El Secretario de Desarollo Turístico maintains three offices in the city: Independencia 607, at Garcia Vigil on the Pl Alameda de Leon (tel. 6-38-10 or 6-09-84), open daily 9am-3pm, 6-8pm. The office at 5 de Mayo 200 (tel. 6-48-28) contains the **Agencia del Ministerio Público,** which will act as liaison to consulates in case of accident or robbery, open daily 9am-8pm. The third office is at Alcalá 100, and is open daily 9am-8pm. Many of the staff members speak English. Good maps distributed.

Consulates: In an emergency, go first to the Agencio del Ministerio Público (above), whose staff will scare up consular assistance. **U.S.:** Alcalá 201 #204 (tel. 4-30-53). Hidden under an arched doorway. Open Mon.-Fri. 9am-2pm. In an emergency call tel. 4-14-04. **Canada:** Dr. Liceaga 119 #8 (tel. 3-37-77; fax 5-21-47), open Mon.-Fri. 9am-2pm. **Germany** and **Great Britain:** Hidalgo 817 #5 (tel. 6-56-00), open Mon.-Fri. 9am-2pm.

American Express: Valdivieso 2 (tel. 4-62-45 or 6-27-00), in the northeast corner of the *zócalo.* Money wired (2hrs. from the U.S.) for card holders. Travel desk open Mon.-Fri. 9am-2:30pm, 4-7:30pm and Sat. 9am-2:30pm, 4-6:30pm. The financial desk (exchanges cash and traveler's checks at competitive rates) is open Mon.-Fri. 9am-2pm, 4-6pm and Sat. 9am-1pm.

Currency Exchange: Thundering herds of banks encircle the *zócalo;* hours for currency exchange vary. **Bánamex,** Hidalgo 821 (tel. 6-59-00), one block east of the *zócalo.* Open for exchange Mon.-Fri. 9am-5pm. **Bancomer,** García Vigil 120 (tel. 6-33-33), 2 blocks north of the *zócalo* at Morelos. Open for exchange Mon.-Fri. 9am-noon. Also try the many *casas de cambio.* Their rates are lower, but their hours are longer. **La Estrella,** Alcalá 201 (tel. 4-53-65). Open Mon.-Sat. 9am-8pm. On Sun., try the hotels around the *zócalo.*

Post Office: (Tel. 6-26-61), in the Pl. Alameda de León. Lista de Correos. Open Mon.-Fri. 8am-7pm, Sat. 9am-1pm. **Postal Code:** 68000.

Telephones: Long distance collect calls are best made from telephone booths on the street, but lines are long. For some degree of privacy try the *caseta* at **Farmacia Hidalgo,** 20 de Noviembre at Hidalgo (tel. 6-90-60, fax. 6-90-59), 1 block west of the *zócalo.* No collect calls. Open Mon.-Sat. 8:30am-2pm, 4-9:30pm, Sun. 9am-2pm. Open Mon.-Sat. 8am-8pm. **Telephone Code:** 951.

Telegrams: Independencia at 20 de Noviembre (tel. 6-49-02), next to the post office. Open for telegrams Mon.-Fri. 8am-8pm, Sat. 9am-1pm. Open for money orders Mon.-Fri. 9am-6pm, Sat. 9am-noon.

Airport: Aeropuerto Juárez, on Rte. 175, 8km south of the city. Taxis to the airport cost 30 pesos. You can also arrange transportation to the airport through **Transportes Aeropuerto,** Pl. Alameda de León (tel. 4-43-50). Give them advance notice and they'll pick you up at your hotel (*colectivo* 8 pesos, *especial* 13 pesos). Office open Mon.-Sat. 9am-2pm, 5-8pm (for Sun. service reserve on Sat.). **Mexicana:** Independencia at Fiallo (tel. 6-84-14, airport tel. 1-52-29). Five flights daily to Mexico City (50min., 262 pesos). **Aeromexico:** Hidalgo 513 (tel. 6-71-01, airport tel. 1-50-44). Two flights daily to Mexico City. **Aero Caribe:** (call Mexicana, above) to Cancún and Mérida. **Airport information:** tel. 1-50-36.

Train Station: Ferrocarriles Nacionales de México (tel. 6-22-53 or 6-26-26). In a vaguely colonial style building set back from the road on the western end of Madero. To get to the *zócalo,* turn right (south) at exit, walk 5 long blocks, then left (east) on Independencia until you hit the *zócalo.* A 25-min. walk. Or catch a bus directly outside marked "Centro" or "Independencia" (.50 pesos). Open for ticket sales Mon.-Sat. 7-10:30am and 2-6:30pm, Sun. 7-11am and 2:30-6:30pm. Lines are *huge;* get there far in advance. Reservations are recommended 1week in advance. Second class train service from Mexico City to Oaxaca 18 pesos. Leaves Mexico City 1pm arrives Oaxaca 10am. Said to be downright pleasant.

Bus Stations: Only partial listings are given; it is possible to go literally anywhere in the Republic at any time of day or night. **1st class station,** Niños Héroes de Chapultepec 1036, about 10 blocks north and 5 blocks east of the *zócalo.* Clean and well-organized. **ADO** (tel. 5-17-03) runs to Mexico City (9 per evening, 9hrs.,55 pesos), Villahermosa (7pm, 71.50 pesos), Veracruz (6pm, 8:15 pm,

10hrs., 54 pesos), Tuxtla Gutierrez (10pm, 51.50 pesos). **Omnibus Cristóbal Colón** (tel. 5-12-14) to Mexico City (6 per day, 55 pesos), Pochutla (3 per day, 44 pesos), Puerto Escondido (2 per day, 51.50 pesos). To reach Mexico City in true style take the **UNO** bus; it approximates a corporate jet (10pm, 113 pesos). **2nd-class station,** just past the Central de Abastos (big market), across the Periférico from the western end of Trujano or Las Casas. The large number of regional bus lines, many without signs or ticket windows, make the set-up rather confusing. Frequent service to every small town near Oaxaca. In general, each town is served by only 1 line; the staff of each line knows who goes where, so don't be bashful. Most rides cost less than 3 pesos. The **Hotel Mesón del Angel bus stop,** Mina 518, between Mier y Terán and Díaz Ordaz, serves as a 3rd bus station. From here, **Autotransportes Turísticos** (tel. 6-53-27 or 4-31-61) runs buses to Monte Alban (5 per day, roundtrip 8 pesos, with guide 40 pesos). Also to Puerto Escondido (8am, 10:45pm, 29.50 pesos).

Car Rental: Hertz Rent-a-Car, represented by Viajes Caracal, Pl. Alameda de León 1 (tel. 6-29-49). Must be over 25 and hold a driver's license and credit card. Small VWs 200 pesos per day (including insurance and unlimited mileage). Open Mon.-Fri. 8am-8pm, Sat. 8am-2pm, Sun. 8am-2pm.

Bookstore: Librería Universitaria, Guerrero 104 (tel. 6-42-43), off the southeast corner of the *zócalo*. Small selection of used paperbacks in English (about 8 pesos), and a number of English-language books about Mexico. Open Mon.-Sat. 9:30am-2pm and 4-8pm.

Laundromat: Super Lavandería Hidalgo, J.P. García 200 (tel. 4-11-81), at Hidalgo, 1 block west of *zócalo*. 3.5kg washed and dried 15 pesos. Open Mon.-Sat. 8am-8pm.

Red Cross: Armenta y López 700 (tel. 6-44-55 or 6-48-09), between Pardo and Burgoa. Ambulance service. English spoken. Open 24 hrs.

Pharmacies: Farmacia Zarate, Hidalgo 411 (tel. 6-42-80), 2½ blocks west of the *zócalo*; 2nd store around the corner at J.P. García 100 (tel. 6-07-20). Both stores will bring medicine to you at your hotel. Both open daily 7am-midnight.

Hospitals: Hospital Civil, Porfirio Díaz 400 (tel. 5-31-81), 1.5 km out of town, gives free medical service to all. Private hospitals include **Instituto Mexicano de Seguro Social (IMSS),** Chapultepec 621 (tel. 5-20-33), and **Hospital Vasconcelos,** Morelos 500 (tel. 6-36-52), at Padre Angel. Also **ISSST** (tel. 5-31-44).

Police: Aldama 108 (tel. 6-36-18 or 6-26-26), south of the *zócalo* between Miguel Cabrera and Bustamente. Some English spoken. Open 24 hrs.

ACCOMMODATIONS

Oaxaca's accommodations speak very well for the city. There are few pushy advertisements or rip-offs, and even the most expensive hotel in town, the **Hotel Presidente,** occupies a small and unassuming *ex-convento*. Because of Oaxaca's status as a trading center, most of the budget hotels draw their greatest income from the marketeers of nearby villages. High-quality budget lodgings spring from nearly every street corner, especially in the southern part of town.

Several trailer parks lie outside the downtown area. The **Trailer Park Oaxaca,** Violetas 900 (tel. 5-27-96), is near the *Zona Militar* in the northeast part of town. To get there, take the "Colonia Reforma" bus from the stop on García just north of Hidalgo. The **Trailer Park San Francisco,** Madero 705, in the northwest part of town, is accessible on the "Santa Rosa" bus from the same stop as above.

North

The northern part of town is more prosperous, residential, and tranquil than the southern. This does not mean, however, that hotels here are more expensive; rather, these are some of the best deals in town. Cleanliness is universal.

Hotel Virreyes, Morelos 1001 (tel. 6-55-55), 4 blocks from the *zócalo* at Reforma. If you get a room with a balcony, it's the best deal in Oaxaca. Rooms are beautiful: decks, large mirrors, big comfy beds, armchairs and sparkling bathrooms. Hot water in the morning. Soothing indoor courtyard. Some toilets gurgle musically. Singles 35.20 pesos. Doubles 44 pesos.

Casa Arnel, Aldama 404 (tel. 5-28-56), at Colonia Jalatlaco, 2 blocks east and 7 short blocks south of the ADO station, across the street from a greenish colonial church. Feel free to do your laundry in the lush arboreal courtyard; the parrots will keep you company. A good distance from the *zócalo,* but the Juárez bus runs nearby. Staying here means experiencing the quietly residential Oaxaca rather than the busy, hyper-historical one. Singles 25 pesos, with bath 50 pesos. Doubles 40 pesos, with two beds 45 pesos, with bath 65 pesos.

Hotel Reforma, Reforma 102 (tel. 6-71-44), 4 blocks from the *zócalo* above a row of stores. Extremely quiet despite its convenient location. Sixteen clean rooms with jungle-patterned bedspreads. Ask for a room at the top, as these enjoy the tiled roof and afford a great view. Singles 45 pesos. Doubles 55 pesos.

Hotel Pombo, Morelos 601 (tel. 6-26-73), between Vigil and Díaz just around the corner from the *zócalo.* Down-and-out in Oaxaca. This run-down 40-room hotel boasts a great location, small courtyards that encourage international fraternization, and some of the cheapest rooms in town (including a glorified lunchbox for 15 pesos). Ask to see a few rooms, as some of the doubles are downright nice. Singles 25 pesos. Doubles 30 pesos.

South

South of the *zócalo* you'll find a legion of budget hotels; often four or five share the same block, particularly along Díaz Ordaz. Because of the proximity of the market and second class bus terminal, many of these hotels front noisy, dirty streets: if that's not your thing, ask for a room in back. Reservations are necessary during *fiesta* weekends (particularly during the Guelaguetza).

Hotel Aurora, Bustamante 212 (tel. 6-41-45), 2 blocks south of the *zócalo's* southeast corner. Communal baths are clean and equipped with hot water, but dimly lit. Big, spare rooms. Bare bulbs hang amusingly low. Pleasant, sunny courtyard. Run by a nice older man. Singles 30 pesos. Doubles 35 pesos, with two beds 40 pesos.

Hotel Pasaje, Mina 302 (tel. 6-42-13), 3 blocks south of the *zócalo.* Clean, very clean. Snug, green courtyard is home to stark, dim rooms and Guernica-inspired art. Singles 35 pesos. Doubles 45 pesos.

Hotel Chayo, 20 de Noviembre 508 (tel. 6-41-12), 1 block south of Aldama. Skip Monte Alban; stay here and marvel at the cement furniture. Clean rooms around a long, skinny courtyard. Singles 39 pesos. Doubles 45 pesos.

Hotel Típico, 20 Noviembre 612 (tel. 6-41-11). Nice lobby area with comfortable chairs and TV. Enjoy the pretty, flowering tree too big for the narrow courtyard. Rooms are unremarkable save for the cavernous closets. Singles 38 pesos. Doubles 48 pesos.

Hotel Lupita, Díaz Ordaz 3149 (tel. 6-57-33), 3 blocks west of the *zócalo's* southwest corner. Pastel rooms with high ceilings exude a friendly tenement feel. Communal bathrooms are clean. Singles 24 pesos. Doubles 30 pesos, with bath 40 pesos.

Hotel Pacífico, Trujano 420 (tel. 6-57-53), on the corner of Mier y Terán. You can't miss its incredibly noticeable lavender and blue paint job. Fairly close to the second class bus station. Otherwise, clean but unremarkable rooms. Singles 40 pesos. Doubles 45 pesos.

Hotel Guelaguetza, Rayón 215 (tel. 6-56-91), between Fiallo and Armenta y López. Old and well-worn, but functional and friendly. Singles 20 pesos, with bath 40 pesos. Doubles 25 pesos, with bath 45 pesos. Bathroomless rooms are on the roof and are something of a deal, otherwise the prices are steep.

FOOD

Eating well in Oaxaca is as easy as falling off a chair; nearly every side-street café and tourist hot spot serves fresh, well-prepared meals at reasonable prices (most *comidas corridas* cost only 9 pesos). Oaxaca specializes in *mole* (that's MOH-leh, not a groundhog) and also in exotic (but often non-sweet) pastries and ices. When sampling goodies on the streets, exercise caution. Most pastry vendors cover their snacks with glass or plastic, but some don't, and huge flies tend to descend upon unattended delicacies. Most frozen treats (*nieves*) are made from water and are closer to sorbet than to ice cream.

The many mesmerizing cafés around Oaxaca's *zócalo* retain reasonable prices and are especially good for breakfast; *huevos a la oaxaqueña* (scrambled eggs in spicy tomato soup) is a great way to start the day. The best of several large markets, the **Benito Juárez produce market,** occupies the block bounded by 20 de Noviembre, Aldama, Cabrera and Las Casas. Try the large, white, beet-shaped fruit called *jícama* (often seasoned with spicy powder) or a bag of *nísperas* (custard apples).

Restaurant Hippocampo, (tel. 6-41-39), on Hidalgo, 1½ blocks west of the *zócalo*. Wake up and stumble over. Big, fresh-squeezed OJ 3 pesos. Great papaya. *Comida corrida* 8 pesos.

Flor de Loto, (tel. 4-70-93), Morelos 511 at Porfirio Díaz. A vegetarian restaurant specializing in crepes, peculiar and delicious. *Comida corrida* 12 pesos. *Licuados* 3 pesos. Open daily 8:30am-9:30 pm.

Restaurant Lichita, on Fiallo, between Arteaga and Rayón. A family-run kitchen so familiar to locals that there is no menu. A great change from the touristy restaurants north of the *zócalo*. Not much choice, but they're happy to oblige requests. *Comida corrida* 7 pesos. Open daily 8am-10pm.

Café Alex, (tel. 4-07-15), Díaz Ordaz 218. Appealing pink and blue exterior doesn't disappoint: a nice restaurant . Breakfasts 4-9 pesos. *Mole oaxaqueño* 12 pesos. Open Mon.-Sat. 7am-9pm, Sun. 7am-noon.

Restaurant Quickly, (tel. 4-7-76), Alcalá 100. Despite its name and proximity to the zócalo, Quickly caters to a nice mix of people. Big portions. A sense of humor. Open Mon.-Fri. 8am-10:30pm, Sat.-Sun. 2-10:30pm.

Pizzería Alfredo da Roma, Alcalá 400 (tel. 6-50-58), on the *corredor turístico*. Popular student hangout serving good pizza. Often full, perhaps because they accept Visa, MasterCard, and AmEx. Four sizes of pizza: cheese pizzas 14-35 pesos. Try the toppings, as plain pizza may bore. Open daily 1:30pm-11pm.

Restaurant Los Canarios, 20 de Noviembre 502-C (tel. 4-19-37), south of Aldama. Popular with a local crowd. *Comida corrida* 8 pesos. Eggs *al gusto* 4.5 pesos. *Tortas* 3 pesos. Open Mon.-Sat. 7am-10pm, Sun. 8am-6pm.

El Biche Pobre II, Calzada de la República 600, 1 block west of Casa Arnel on Hidalgo (remember, not the main downtown Hidalgo). Popular with local families. Pretty tablecloths and wood-paneled ceilings. Excellent service. *Mariachis* meander between the tables in the mid-afternoon. Order the *botana surtida*—2 big plates (served 1 at a time) juggling bits of *oaxaqueña* cuisine (13.50 pesos). Try **El Biche Pobre I** at Rayón 1133 if II is full. Open daily 1-6pm.

SIGHTS

Oaxaca's **zócalo,** composed of two plazas, is always congested with people. Early in the morning, vendors set up expensive, exotic pastry stalls, women sell fruit from baskets, and toy dealers push huge multi-colored balloons and vend Batman-alia to passersby. Every evening between 7 and 9pm, live concerts shake the square. Local rock groups, *marimba* performers, and the state brass band alternate to keep the people mollified. Often the activity in front of the Palacio de Gobierno is of a political nature. By 10pm, however, foreigners dominate the *zócalo*.

Throughout Oaxaca's streets, vendors push knitted cotton blankets, *sarapes*, jade bookends, *oaxaqueño* guitars, wooden letter openers, masks and straw baskets. Make clear from the beginning whether you intend to buy or not; entrepreneurs become indignant if they think you're just stalling to fetch a better price. A quarter of their asking price for *sarapes* and half for musical instruments is not too low for starting to haggle. Eavesdropping on the final price other tourists pay is usually useless, since most shell out more than twice the bargain rate.

On Saturdays, be sure to visit the *tianguis* setup in Oaxaca's biggest market, the **Central de Abastos** (across the Periférico from the western end of Mina), where virtually every resident of Oaxaca state is either buying or selling food, art or crafts. The market divides into categories, so you'll find immense areas selling only baskets, only peppers, only bread or only rugs, for example. Everyone hawks with vigor. Come in the morning, because pickpockets in Oaxaca seem to rise around lunchtime. During the rest of the week, the market is much more subdued.

The **Catedral de Oaxaca** and the **Palacio de Gobierno** (not to be confused with the Palacio Municipal, which incorporates the tourist office) sit on opposite sides of the *zócalo*. Originally constructed in 1535, the cathedral was damaged and finally destroyed by a series of earthquakes before being rebuilt in the 18th century with *oaxaqueño* green-brown stone and ornamented in filigree. The ornate bishop's seat, in the central altar, provides a structural focus. (Open daily 7am-8pm.)

Inside the **Palacio de Gobierno,** on the south side of the *zócalo*, a mural by García Bustos presents an informative collage of *oaxaqueño* history. The center panel is dominated by Benito Juárez, his wife Margarita Masa, and one of his oft-repeated phrases, "Respect for the rights of others brings peace." Also appearing in this panel are José María Morelos and Ricardo Flores Magón, two other Juárez-era reformers. On the wall to the right (as you ascend the staircase) is a portrait of Sor Juana Inés de la Cruz, the poet, nun, theologian, and astronomer. Often considered Mexico's first feminist, she penned a diatribe against misogynists called *Hombres Necios* (Foolish Men). After impersonating a man for several years in order to attend the university in Mexico City, Sor Juana eventually made her way onto the front of 1-peso bills. The left wall depicts a living *Mitla*. (The Palacio de Gobierno is open 24 hrs.)

Walking north from the *zócalo* on Alcalá—the *corredor turístico*—you will arrive at the **Museo de Arte Contemporáneo de Oaxaca,** Alcalá 202 (tel. 6-84-99). The museum's colonial building is known as the Casa de Cortés, although historians insist that it is not in fact Cortés's Oaxaca estate. The museum contains revolving exhibitions by contemporary artists like Rufino Tamayo. (Open Wed.-Mon. 10:30am-8pm. Donations solicited.)

Farther up Alcalá, six blocks north of the *zócalo*, the **Iglesia de Santo Domingo** has perhaps the most stunning internal decoration of any church in the Republic. Around the arches, on the ceiling vaults and above the altars and chapels, waves of ornamented stucco form elegant arabesques. Time has somewhat eroded the church's facade of rose and green-gray stone. Construction on the church began in 1575, the consecration came in 1611, and improvements and artistic work continued after that. Built 2m thick as protection against earthquakes, the walls served the convent well when it saw service as military barracks for both sides during the reform wars and the revolution. (Open daily 7am-1pm and 4-8pm.)

The ex-convent next door was converted in 1972 into the city's prestigious **Museo Regional de Oaxaca** (tel. 6-29-91). The frescoes, paintings, and especially the stucco work on its walls have withstood a century of military abuse. The museum fastidiously organizes its archaeological and ethnographic exhibits into sections focusing on each of the state's *indígena* peoples. The superb exhibits cover every facet of *indígena* life, even the *teohanacatl* (hallucinogenic mushrooms) used by the Mixtecs. The most outstanding archaeological hall displays Mixtec jewelry found in Tomb 7 at nearby Monte Albán. Elaborately worked gold, silver, and copper artifacts, some set with jewels, demonstrate the sophistication of Mixtec metalworkers. (Open Tues.-Fri. 10am-6pm, Sat.-Sun. 10am-5pm. Admission 13 pesos. Free Sun.)

For a glimpse of the modern, stop in at the **Instituto de Artes Gráficas,** Alcalá 507 (tel. 6-69-80), opposite the Santo Domingo church. Many small rooms display prints and graphic art from around the world. The exhibit changes every three months. Often there is a film series in the evening. (Open Wed.-Mon. 10am-8pm. Free.)

Another renowned museum, the **Museo de Arte Prehispánico de México Rufino Tamayo,** Morelos 503 (tel. 6-47-50), at Díaz three blocks north of the *zócalo,* shows off the *oaxaqueño* artist's personal collection of pre-Conquest objects from all over the Republic. The figurines, ceramics and masks that Tamayo collected were selected for their aesthetic value as well as for anthropological interest. Pieces are arranged in roughly chronological order rather than by culture. (Open Mon. and Wed.-Sat. 10am-2pm and 4-7pm, Sun. 10am-3pm. Admission 10 pesos.)

Five blocks north of the post office on García Vigil is the **Casa de Benito Juárez,** García Vigil 609 (tel. 6-18-60). This may not look like the house of a poor, 19th-century Zapotec *campesino,* and it's not. It all started when Benito's older sister left the Juárez home in Guelatao to come to Oaxaca as the domestic servant of the wealthy Masa family. The Masas were *paisanos* from Spain and good friends with the equally wealthy Salanueva family. The Salanuevas took a keen interest in young Benito, adopted him and brought him to Oaxaca. His subsequent education and upbringing qualified him to marry the Masas' daughter, Margarita, and to embark on a career in law, then politics and finally reform. His memorabilia fill the first room on the right. The rest of the house—living room, bedrooms, kitchen, well and "bookbinding/weaving shop"—is a model of 19th-century upper-middle-class *oaxaqueño* life. (Open Tues.-Sun. 9am-1pm. Admission 5 pesos. Free Sun.) Closed for restoration in the summer of 1993, it is expected to re-open in Jan. 1994.

The **Teatro Macedonio Alcalá,** on 5 de Mayo at Independencia, two blocks east of the *zócalo,* is one of the most beautiful buildings in Oaxaca and an illuminating example of the art and architecture that flourished in Mexico under Porfirio Díaz. Díaz's regime had a serious case of *afrancesamiento,* the taste for French art and French intellectual formulas. Oaxaca, the birthplace of Díaz, remained a favorite of the dictator, and his support was instrumental in this theater's construction, which began in 1904. On the ceiling, scantily clad Muses float above the giant candelabra. (Occasionally open for shows Mon.-Sat. at 8pm, Sun. at 6pm; it is possible to take a peek immediately before shows.)

ENTERTAINMENT

Nightlife in Oaxaca is a bit livelier than in most towns south of Mexico City. Women report feeling relatively safe here, though prefer not to cross the city alone at night. Many **discos** and **bars** are open throughout the week, though usually more crowded on Friday and Saturday nights. Popular and convenient is **Eclipse** disco (tel. 6-42-36) on Porfirio Díaz at the corner of Matamoros. The painted palm trees and mod lights make you feel like you're back in an early-80s music video. (Cover 30 pesos Fri. and Sat., 1 peso on Sun. Open Fri.-Sat. 10pm-3am, Sun. 6-11pm.) In the summer of 1993, one of the hottest clubs was **NBC,** north of town on Calle Heroica Escuela Naval, between Las Rosas and Emiliano Zapata. (Cover 30 pesos. Open Fri.-Sat. 10pm-3am.) Just south of NBC, next to the Hotel Mision de Los Angeles, is **Rojo Caliente,** another hopping disco. (Cover 30 pesos. Open Fri.-Sun.) Both NBC and Rojo Caliente lie 25 minutes north of the zócalo by foot. Taxis charge 8 pesos and know both clubs by name. More conveniently located, **Isis,** at Armenta y Lopez 203B, is said to resemble the clubs listed above in music and clientele. (Cover 25 pesos. Open Fri.-Sat. 9:30pm and onward.) **Candela,** at Allende 211, is a restaurant-bar with live salsa and sometimes reggae. The crowd is older and local. (Cover 15 pesos. Open Tues.-Sat.; music from 10pm-1:30am.) **Los Arcos,** 20 de Noviembre between Hidalgo and Independencia, caters to a younger, local, and slightly rougher crowd. (Cover 15 pesos. Open Fri.-Sun. 9:30pm-2am.)

Oaxacan summer and fall *fiestas* take place with vivid splendor. The biggest summertime festivity is **La Guelaguetza** or **Los Lunes del Cerro** (Mondays of the Hill), when costumed hoofers from different *oaxaqueño* peoples perform fantastic regional dances in Oaxaca City's largest amphitheater. The festival is held on the third and fourth Mondays of July. Front-section tickets cost 200 pesos, mid-section tickets are 150 pesos, and the back section is free (arrive 2-3hrs. early to secure a seat).

■ Near Oaxaca: Zaachila, Cuilapán, San Bartolo Coyotepec, Arrazola, and Guelatao

An interesting **local market** is held each Thursday 18km south of Oaxaca in **Zaachila,** the last political capital of the Zapotecs after they abandoned their ceremonial center at Monte Albán. The Zaachila market vends such treats as preserved bananas, squealing pigs, and stoic turkeys. You can't miss the birthday cake cathedral in the middle of town painted in fuschia pink and bright yellow. Directly right of this church is an archaeological sight that has only partially been uncovered. (Perhaps what lies underground is more interesting than what can be seen.) Until 1962, the locals prohibited excavations, on the grounds that their Zapotec heritage should not be dissected by outsiders. Few potential sites have since been explored, but two Mixtec tombs with well-preserved architecture and jewelry have been uncovered. To the right of the church, across from the market, follow the path uphill to the site. The first tomb's interior is decorated with what were once colorful stucco carvings. The treasure of gold, turquoise, jade, and bone artifacts that distinguished the second tomb has long since been removed to local museums, leaving the uninspired architecture abashedly unadorned. In addition to second-class **buses,** *colectivos* also service these villages, leaving from the Central de Abastos in Oaxaca and from Armenta y López, four and a half blocks south of the *zócalo,* in front of the Red Cross. Prices for most buses are between 1 to 3 pesos; *colectivos* cost about 1 peso more.

Cuilapán is an isolated but lovely ex-convent built by the Domenicos, one of the most powerful and wealthy religious orders of colonial Mexico. (Open daily 10am-6pm, 7 pesos entrance fee.) If you are interested in buying (and lugging around) exquisite ink black pottery at ridiculously low prices, go to **San Bartolo Coyotepec.** A row of humble homes next to the church open their doors to visitors and sometimes give demonstrations. The third house form the main road, dubbed **Alfarena Los Jarrones,** offers a wide variety at low prices. While the entire town of San Bartolo Coyotepec specializes in pottery, **Arrazola** is dedicated to creating fantastically painted wooden creatures. While a meticulously handpainted armadillo may not be cheap, the current vogue for these creations will find you paying triple the price in the U.S. than in Arrazola. Most homes double as studios, so just ask any *nativo* to point out the wooden *animales*.

The *pueblito* of **Guelatao,** 57km north of Oaxaca, became a national monument on March 21, 1967 (the centenary of the victory of Mexican forces over the French occupation) when President Díaz Ordaz ordered the construction of a civic plaza, a museum, statues, and a mausoleum to honor Benito Juárez, Guelatao's native son. Guelatao now seems less a living town than a memorial park, adrift in the Cuenca del Papaluapan mountain range. Should you catch it between national holidays, political campaigns, and TV docudrama filmings, you will find Guelatao empty and peaceful. The grape-sized **Museo Benito Juárez** delineates Juárez's life. The museum balcony commands a view of Guelatao's rugged landscape.

To get from Oaxaca to Guelatao, take a Benito Juárez **bus,** the line farthest to the right as you enter the second-class terminal. Get an early start for this trip; the two-and-a-half-hour ride is rough. The crowded bus back to Oaxaca passes roughly every two hours.

■■■ MONTE ALBÁN

Monte Albán (its original name is unknown), a massive ruin from the great days of the Oaxaca valley, towers atop one of the green mountains surrounding the city.

The separated stone structures, themselves geometrically precise, are widely and evenly spaced apart. This architectural design combined with huge blue horizons creates a space that is both open and expansive. Only 10km southwest of the city, across Río Atoyac, this was the greatest capital left by the Zapotecs, whose descendants now constitute the fourth-largest language group in Mexico. The ancient city, one of 260 Zapotec cities in the Oaxaca Valley, once spread over six square km. Most of its huge complex of tombs, pyramids, platforms, and temples, originally built without the comforts of the wheel or pack animals, have been expertly reconstructed.

The Zapotecs designed and built the city before the Mixtecs appropriated its fields and tombs. Many of the civilizations of the Oaxaca Valley have left a piece of their heritage here. Archaeologists have identified five different stages in Monte Albán's history, which is essentially the story of the Mixtecs' conquest and appropriation of the Zapotec settlement.

Elaborate pottery, hieroglyphic writing, a calendar system, and written numbers date from about 500 BC. Objects from this period, known as **Monte Albán I,** generally show Olmec influence, the Olmecs representing one the first native civilizations of Mexico. By the end of Monte Albán I, the city was the largest and most important community in Southern Mesoamerica. **Monte Albán II** lasted approximately from 1 to 300 AD. During this time, the Zapotecs consolidated their empire and expanded their commercial trading routes. At this point the Maya borrowed the calendar and writing system already in use at Monte Albán. The first of the funerary urns and four-legged vessels, which usually represent gods, also come from this moment in the city's history.

By the period of **Monte Albán III** (300-750 AD), the population of the valley had peaked. Almost all of the extant buildings and tombs as well as several urns and murals of *colanijes* (richly adorned priests) come from this period. Burial arrangements of variable luxury and size among the different tombs show the tripartite social division of the period: priests, clerks, and laborers.

The Zapotec citadel decayed during **Monte Albán IV** (750-1000 AD). Construction ceased, and political control of the Zapotec empire shifted from Monte Albán to other cities such as Zaachila, Eta, and later Mitla. The production of pottery, ceramics, and jewelry all fell. During this period, the Mixtec people invaded from the northwest and took over many of the Zapotec cities.

Late Mixtec culture flourished during **Monte Albán V,** from 1000 AD to the arrival of the Spaniards. By then, Monte Albán functioned as both a fortress and a sacred necropolis. The Mixtec nobility buried its own in the Zapotec elaborate, treasure-filled tombs; when the most noteworthy, **Tomb 7,** was discovered in 1932, the treasure found within more than quadrupled the previously identified number of gold Mixtec objects.

As you enter the **central plaza** the two most prominent buildings are the **Northern Platform** and directly in front lies **Stela 9.**

Bear left as you enter the site, and walk along the eastern boundary of the Central Plaza; you'll pass the ballcourt first, then a series of related substructures, and then two pyramids. The inclined walls that seem like flights of narrow steps were originally flat, covered with stucco and frescoes.

Building P, the first of the two pyramids, fascinates archaeologists because of an inner stairway feeding into a tunnel to the central structures a few meters away. The tunnel apparently allowed priests to pass into the central temples unseen by the public. The second pyramid here, the **Palace,** is a wealthy Zapotec's residence with a patio-courtyard surrounded by several rooms. A cruciform grave was discovered in the center of the garden.

Directly outside are the four central monuments of the plaza. **Buildings G, H, and I** are attached and together constitute what was likely the principal altar of Monte Albán. Directly to the east, between the central Building H and Building P, is the small, sunken **Adoratorio** where archaeologists dug up an intricate jade bat mask.

This is Monte Albán's oldest structure, dating from Monte Albán II. A sacred icon and the most famous piece from this period, the bat mask contains 25 pieces of polished, forest-green jade with slivers of white conch shell forming the teeth and eyes. Unfortunately, the mask has long since flown to a new perch in the Museo Nacional de Antropología in Mexico City.

The fourth of the central structures, **Building J** is formed in the bizarre shape of an arrowhead on a platform and contains a labyrinth of tunnels and passageways. Moreover, unlike any other ancient edifice in Mexico, it is asymmetrical and built at an angle to the other edifices around the plaza—a single anomaly in Monte Albán's gridded perfection. Its broad, carved slabs suggest that the building is one of the oldest on the site. Many of the glyphs have an upside-down head below a stylized hill, thought to represent a place and a name. According to archaeological speculation, this indicates a conquest, the upside-down head representing the defeated tribe and the name identifying the region conquered; others insist that J was an astronomical observatory.

Behind Building J stands the highest of all the structures: the **Southern Pyramid.** On both sides of the staircase on the plaza level, to the right of the platform, are a number of rain-god and tiger stelae. The top of the Southern Pyramid affords a glorious view of the plaza to the north.

Along the western border of the Central Plaza are the foundations of **Building M,** followed by the **Platform of the Dancers** at the foot of Building L. The low platforms in front of Building M were supposedly designed to correct the plaza's asymmetry, caused by the need to build around inconveniently located rock formations. The "dancers" on the platform, among the most interesting examples of pre-Conquest sculpture, date from about the 5th century BC—almost identical to contemporary Olmec sculptures along the Gulf Coast. Many are accompanied by glyphs and number schemes indicating mastery of a system of writing and of calendrical records. The arrangement of the stone dancers is believed to represent historical or mythical events related to the founding of Monte Albán.

Branching off from the road between the Central Plaza and the entrance to the site, a clearly marked path leads down a ravine to the **Northern Cemetery.** Go underground at **Tomb 104** to see a stunning portrait of the handsome noble buried here.

At the entrance to the site, the expensive gift shop and cafeteria attract more visitors than does the small **museum.** The interesting artifacts from the site have been exiled to museums in Oaxaca and Mexico City, but the museum (tel. 6-53-27) at least gives a chronological summary of Monte Albán's history (in Spanish) and displays sculpted stones from the site's earlier periods. (Site open daily 8am-5pm. Admission 13 pesos, free Sun. and holidays.)

Buses to Monte Albán leave from the Hotel Mesón del Angel, Mina 518, between Mier y Terán and Díaz Ordaz in Oaxaca. The site is only 10km away, but the ride through mountainous terrain takes 30 minutes. The normal procedure is to buy a round-trip ticket, with the return fixed two hours (about right for a full perusal) after arrival at the site; if you want to stay longer you can pay an extra 4 pesos to come back on one of the later buses. Buses from the hotel leave daily every hour from 8:30am to 5:30pm during high season, and five times per day during low season (6 times on Sun., 8 pesos round-trip). Travel agencies around the *zócalo* arrange special excursions to the ruins—some with English-speaking guides—at considerably more expense than the do-it-yourself option.

■■■ OAXACA TO MITLA

A number of interesting stops tempt the thoroughgoing traveler on the **Pan American Highway** (Rte. 190) eastward from Oaxaca to Mitla, a distance of 46km. All of the following sights can be reached by buses that leave every 20 minutes from Oaxaca's second-class bus station for a modest sum. If consulted ahead of time, the driver of the bus to Mitla will let you off anywhere. Most people visit these sites on daytrips, but if you'd like to stay overnight, inquire at the Oaxaca tourist office for information about guest houses. Street vendors sell virtually all the food available to non-residents.

Just 9km outside Oaxaca, the arboreal attraction of **Santa María El Tule** awaits. One of the largest, oldest trees on earth stands in the courtyard of the church, just a few meters off the highway. Called **El Tule,** it lays claim to the greatest girth—160 ft. in circumference. To catch a bus back to Oaxaca, hang out on the highway and wave your souvenir.

The walls of the **Iglesia de San Jerónimo Tlacochahuaya** display the application of Zapotec decorative techniques to Catholic motifs. At the end of the 16th century the Dominicans built this church and convent 21km east of Oaxaca in **Tlaco-chahuaya,** far (in those times) from worldly temptations. (Church open daily 7am-noon.)

The **Dainzú** ruins, just off the road branching to Macuilxochitl, 22km east of Oaxaca, date from Monte Albán's final pre-Conquest epoch. At the base of the tallest pyramidal monument, a series of figures magnificently carved in relief represents ballplayers in attitudes similar to the "dancers" at Monte Albán. Two humans and two jaguars, gods of the sport, supervise the contest. Up the hill from the pyramid, another ball game scene is hewn in the living rock. (Open daily 10am-6pm. Free.)

Roughly 20km from Oaxaca, a turn-off leads north to **Teotitlán del Valle,** a community closely resembling an ancient Zapotec city (called Xaguixe). Today the source of most of the beautiful woolen *sarapes* produced in Oaxaca, the town's 200 to 300 families earn their livelihood for the most part by spinning and weaving. Many allow tourists to visit their homes or workshops, and a live demonstration impresses more than any museum exhibit ever could.

About 33km east of Oaxaca, a southerly turn-off leads to **Tlacolula,** an ancient village that hosts a lively **market** every Sunday morning. Merchant action spreads beyond the official roofed market to the rest of the town; nary a street is without temporary stalls. A large influx of tourists flows in every week, but the presence of outsiders has not dimmed the *indígena* nature of the event. Plenty of items might interest travelers—*sarapes* and *tapetes* (rugs), baskets and pottery—but much more fascinating are the things you can't take home. Many vendors sell live pigs and goats as well as a kind of carved wood oxen yoke. The market lasts until 6pm, but the activity starts to wind down by around 2pm.

Yagul, 8 more km east of Oaxaca, was a Mixtec city contemporary to Mitla, built in two distinct sections on the skirt of a large rock outcrop. Most of the buildings and tombs are in the acropolis, the area closest to the parking lot (about 2km north of the highway). Here, the **Court of the Triple Tomb,** the **ballcourt,** the **Palace of the Six Patios** and the **Council Chamber** have all been thoroughly excavated and reconstructed. Farther up, on top of the hill, awaits the second section with the **Great Fortress,** the natural watchtower around to the right and the curious stone bridge built to reach it.

The four temples of the Court of the Triple Tomb include a huge sculpted animal ensconced in the lower section of the eastern temple. You can enter the Triple Tomb itself through an opening near the altar in the center of the plaza. Past the door with glyphs on both sides, the tomb has a facade with two majestic stone heads. The ballcourt here is the largest of all those in the Oaxaca Valley. The only clue to the nature of the game is a stone snake's head that was found attached high on the southern wall of the ballcourt and now nibbles at the glass of a small case in the Museo Regional de Oaxaca.

■■■ MITLA

Tucked away in a mostly Zapotec-speaking village, Mitla is smaller and farther away from Oaxaca than immense Monte Albán. Mitla thus receives less attention, which

MITLA

in itself is a blessing; you will not see hordes of school children or all-too-eager vendors selling pseudo statuettes. When the Spanish arrived in southern Mexico, Mitla, 46km directly east of Oaxaca, reigned as the largest and most important of the Mixtec cities. Earlier Mixtec cultures centered around cities farther north, such as Montenegro, a contemporary of Monte Albán I, and Yucuñudahui, contemporary with Monte Albán II. These, however, have bequeathed relatively few artifacts to the modern world.

Walking about 2km from the bus stop and then through the village, one happens on the doorstep of the Catholic church and the entrance to the official archaeological zone. This fenced-in area encloses the **Group of the Columns,** by far the most interesting of Mitla's several "Groups." After entering, one approaches two small quadrangles joined at one corner.

The tombs of the pyramids form a cross, and for years Spaniards thought this proved that the Mixtecs somehow knew the story of Jesus. Engineers have since discovered that the shape of the tombs, which corresponds to a complex vector formula, enabled the structures to endure the huge earthquakes that were common at the time of their construction. The main temple rises on the north side of the first quadrangle. A raised triple doorway leads into a long gallery whose roof rests on six columns. Beyond a protective passageway is an inner patio with narrow rooms on either side. A mosaic of small stones for which Mitla is famous covers the rooms and patio; they called the designs of repeating geometric forms *xicalcoliuhqui.* Tens of thousands of stones had to be cut to perfect size before being affixed to the stone-and-mud wall.

On the second patio in the Group of the Columns, two tombs in the temples to the east and north of the courtyard are accessible to visitors. In the east temple, fairly large stones feature the characteristic mosaic patterns. The roof of the tomb in the north temple rests on a single huge column, still referred to as the **Column of Life** by local *indígenas.* Some make a pilgrimage here each year to embrace the column; in exchange for the hug, the column tells them how much longer they will live.

A set of three patios comprise the **Group of the Church.** One of the patios is almost completely buried by the Catholic church; only a few of the original palace walls remain visible. Many of the building blocks of the church belonged to nearby Mixtec structures before being reappropriated by the missionaries. Walk to the right around the church to arrive at the central patio to the north. Through a passageway in the northern wall of this patio, you can enter an interior courtyard, at the far end of which you'll find the last surviving band of Mixtec decorative paintings. A few figures barely can be discerned through the dusty red; the accompanying glyphs were calendar references and place names.

Between the Group of the Columns and the Group of the Church is a daily **bazaar** selling mostly *típico* clothing. Although prices are high, bargaining is expected, and the selection is extraordinarily large. On the way back to the village, you can see *sarapes* and *rebozos* (women's scarves) being woven in the shops which line the road.

On the central plaza back in town, the **Frissel Museum** contains thousands of figurines from Mitla and other Mixtec sites. Arranged around a beautiful courtyard, some descriptions are in English. (Open daily 9am-5pm. Donations appreciated.) There's no reason to stay in Mitla overnight, but if circumstances conspire, **Hotel La Zapoteca,** 5 de Febrero 12 (tel. 80-00-26), on the main road to the ruins (a 10-min. walk away), rents rooms around a spacious, sunny courtyard. Bright bedspreads and clean rooms are inviting. (Singles 55 pesos. Doubles 70 pesos.)

Buses to Mitla leave Oaxaca's second-class terminal every 20 minutes all day (2.5 pesos).

■■■ OAXACA TO PUERTO ANGEL

By bus, nine arduous but beautiful hours separate Oaxaca from Puerto Angel. With little more than weekly markets to interest tourists, the tiny villages on the way provide only minimal services.

Ocotlán headlines for exotic cuisine and an eclectic agora second only to Oaxaca's. Metalwork, leather goods, wrap-type traditional clothing, herbal remedies, and fine cattle are to be had for a song. (Market open Fri. 6am-7pm; most active 10am-5pm.) **Buses** heading north to Oaxaca and south to Ejutla and Miahuatlán pass roughly every half hour until 8pm.

The region around **Miahuatlán,** 39km south of Ejutla, is also renowned for its *mezcal*. Market day (Mon.) brings textiles of all types, tall wood *pilones* (for pounding corn or other seeds into tortilla flour) and *huaraches* (sandals) made out of strips of salvaged car tires (steel-belted radials are best). **Buses** head both north to Oaxaca and south to Pochutla about every half hour until around 12:30am. Some of the buses to Pochutla continue to Puerto Escondido, but most of the time you'll have to transfer in Pochutla for either Puerto Angel or Puerto Escondido.

Known for its black coral jewelry, **Pochutla** is important more for its proximity to Puerto Angel than for anything else. There's not much to do here except *pochute* (Nahuatl for "wait for the bus"). Then again, the *tianguis* (*indígena* market) falls on Mondays. Other days, a large market on the northern end of Cárdenas, visible as you enter town from the north, operates until sunset. **Buses** go frequently to Puerto Angel (about 1.50 pesos), Puerto Escondido, Oaxaca and Salina Cruz.

■■■ PUERTO ANGEL

With no bank or newsstand and only a fledgling post office, Puerto Angel's shores are a natural haven for urban escapists. A few beautiful beaches, good food, and some fishing draws a laid-back (and random) assortment of travelers. A decade ago, this secluded fishing village approximated a beachside Eden, but, despite its skimpy facilities, the town has developed considerably since then. Hotels now overshadow palm trees and *palapas* infringe on the Zipolite dunes.

Puerto Angel has evolved into a popular destination for sun-seekers. It is not, as many concerned travelers insist, a dangerous hippie drug town where police wait in ambush to bust the next foreigner who roams unsuspectingly onto its shores. Zipolite Beach, 4km west of town, clings proudly to a counter-culture, however. The drug scene can make the beach somewhat seedy at times, and some degree of caution is always advisable.

ORIENTATION

Puerto Angel caps off a southward bulge in Oaxaca's coastline, 240km south of Oaxaca de Juárez via Route 200, before the shore recedes to form the narrow Istmo de Tehuantepec. Puerto Escondido, 68km to the west on Route 200, is easily reached by **bus** from Pochutla (every hr. 6am-8pm, 1hr., 4 pesos).

Taxis provide a second link between Puerto Angel and nearby towns for about 2 pesos *colectivo* or 10 pesos *especial*. If you must take a taxi, do whatever you can to get the *colectivo* rate and don't let drivers con you into paying extra baggage-carrying fees.

The road from Pochutla becomes Puerto Angel's main drag at the edge of town; **Avenida Principal** curves around Playa Puerto Angel past the municipal pier and military base, becoming **Bulevar Virgilio Uribe.** The thoroughfare then turns inland again to avoid a large hill separating the two halves of town. Soon after leaving the first half of town, the road branches off to the left, leading to private houses and sheer cliffs. The main road crosses a small creek (really a glorified puddle) and forks at a sign for Hotel Ángel del Mar; the upper, right-hand road rambles farther down the coast to Zipolite, and the lower, left-hand road heads for the Playa Panteón. The only significant side street in town climbs the hill directly across the street from the pier on Playa Puerto Angel; it starts out as **Vasconcelos,** then curves to the left, becomes **Teniente Azuela,** and arrives back at Uribe in front of the naval station. Few hotels or restaurants in Puerto Angel have addresses with street names or numbers, and none has phones. In general, no streetlights illuminate Puerto Angel's winding dirt roads and finding your way at night without a flashlight can be a challenge.

Except during high season (Sept.-March), **buses** to Zipolite (1 peso) are few and far between and taxis cost an arm and a leg. Try to bargain the cabbies down from the asking price before embarking, otherwise, hoof it; the walk is an easy (if hot) ½ hr. During high season, *colectivos* make the trip for 2 pesos. All fares increase 2 pesos from sunset until dawn and when roads are muddy.

PRACTICAL INFORMATION

Services in this town are less than minimal; most must be begged, borrowed, or imported from nearby Pochutla. **Change money** in Pochutla or in local restaurants at awful rates. The **post office,** on Uribe at the very beginning of town, sells stamps and provides Lista de Correos service. Open Mon.-Fri. 9am-4pm. **Telegrams** are in the Telecomm office next door to the post office. Open Mon.-Fri. 9am-3pm. The long distance *caseta,* at Vasconcelos 3 (tel. 4-03-98), opposite the pier, is open Mon.-Sat. 7am-10pm, Sun. 2-10pm. Collect calls 5000 pesos Mon.-Fri. 7-9am and 2-4pm. **Telephone Code: 958. Buses** serve to Pochutla every 20min. 8am-7pm (1 peso). **Farmacia Ángel,** up Vasconcelos on the right opposite the Hotel Soraya, is open Mon.-Sat. 7am-2pm and 4-9pm. The owner's husband is a doctor and will consult 24 hrs. in case of medical emergency. Limited **medical services** are available at **Centro de Salud,** at the top of Vasconcelos to the left on a dirt path. Open Mon.-Sat. 8am-2pm and 4-8pm; for emergencies 24 hrs. Some medical services are also available (in emergencies only) at the naval base. There is no **police** station, but naval officers everywhere around the base stand in for them. The **Agency of Public Ministry**, next to the police office, will contact the police in emergencies.

ACCOMMODATIONS

Although many travelers come here only to sleep and sunbathe on the beach in nearby Zipolite, Puerto Angel supports a slew of cheap, charming hotels and *casas de huéspedes*.

Budget lodgings are strung along the hills on the inland side of the town's main road between the two beaches. Hammock spaces are inexpensive and fill up quickly. Only the expensive hotels have hot water, and some have running water only at certain hours.

Pensión Puesta del Sol, past the naval base on the road to Playa Panteón. You'll see the signs on the right; hike up the steep driveway. Newly renovated and perfectly clean. The large, well-kept communal bathrooms are beautifully tiled. Dining room and two comfortable patios often host multilingual conversation. Owned by a hospitable German-Mexican couple. Singles 30 pesos. Doubles 35 pesos, with two beds 45 pesos, with two beds and bath 50 pesos. Terraced triple with private bath 60 pesos.

Posada Rincón Sabroso, on the high hill near the bus station where Uribe curves inland for the first time. Large sign at base of hill points to the steep staircase leading to the inn. Rooms and baths are stellar: clean, cool and lots of windows. Shady flower-strewn terrace adjoins all rooms and overlooks Playa Puerto Angel. Ask for the top corner room. **Restaurant Cha-Cha-Cha,** attached, serves banana pancakes for 8 pesos; the breathtaking view is free. Singles 40 pesos. Doubles 50 pesos.

Casa de Huéspedes Gundi y Tomás, is on Iturbide just before the bridge and across from the naval base. The layout is steep but the prices aren't. Common bathrooms are clean and functional. Singles 20 and 30 pesos. Doubles 25 and 40 pesos. Hammocks 10 pesos.

La Buena Vista, just after the naval base; keep your eyes peeled for the sign on the right. Scenic walk off the main road, with pigs. Charming, family-run establishment. Firm beds, stone walls and tile floors. All rooms have fans and clean bathrooms. Great terrace with chairs and hammocks overlooks the big blue ocean beyond. Probably worth the extra money. Singles 50 pesos, with view and balcony 60 pesos. Doubles 60 pesos, with view and balcony 70 pesos.

Hotel La Cabaña de Puerto Angel, across from the row of restaurants facing Playa Panteón, at the end of the main dirt road. Pretty, clean rooms, each with a hand-woven wall tapestry and spotless tiled bathrooms with hot-water shower. Fans and hanging plants in every room. Singles 45 pesos and 50 pesos. Doubles 70 pesos.

Posada Loxicha, on the road into Playa Panteón, on your right about 150m before the cemetary entrance. Eight big, bare rooms. The screens are hurting, but the fans work. Singles 25 pesos. Doubles 30 pesos.

FOOD

Food in Puerto Angel is usually fresh and filling. Don't spend much time or money in the small shacks along the dirt road; in many, the fare is old and unclean. Reasonable prices and excellent seafood make the beachfront *palapa* restaurants attractive to budget travelers. As in most small Mexican resort towns, closing time is flexible—don't expect to be served if you appear at the last minute, but on the other hand, don't fret about getting kicked out if you feel like sitting around and talking into the night. Many *palapas* on Zipolite will let you cook your own fish.

King Creole, for some of the best international cuisine in the Republic, try this friendly spot on the sand, at the western end of Playa Panteón. Run by a French family and whoever happens to be helping out at the time. Filet Mignon with baked potato, fresh vegetables, and garlic bread 35 pesos. Chocolate sundaes, carrot cake, the incredible list goes on and on. Vegetarian and creole specialties. The owner, John Reilhac, is also in charge of tourism in Puerto Angel and will exchange cash and traveler's checks.

Restaurant Lulu, in town on the landward side of Iturbide, east of the naval station. Good food. Watch the traffic go by; when it does, stand up and dance around. The restaurant and bar are open daily from 7am-midnight. Don't be bothered by the pharmacy in the back; there is no causal relationship. Pharmacy open daily 9am-2pm, 4-8pm.

Restaurant El Capy, downstairs from the *casa de huéspedes* of the same name, on the dirt road between the 2 beaches, to the right as you descend to Panteón. The proprietor-fisherman catches everything El Capy serves. A hangout for international beach bums. Delicious sea fare: shrimp in garlic 15 pesos, breaded filet of fish 18 pesos. Open daily 8am-10pm.

Restaurant Susy, on Playa Panteón next to Brico y Cordelia. Slightly cheaper than its neighbor. Tasty lobster 20 pesos, beer 2 pesos. *Pescado empapelado* (fish stuffed with veggies, 13 pesos) is out-of-the-ordinary. Open daily 7am-10pm.

SIGHTS

Of Puerto Angel's two beaches, the smaller **Playa Panteón,** on the far side of town, is the worthier. Its name derives from a pantheon marking the entrance of a nearby cemetery. The water is calm and warm, the coves great for exploring. To rent a boat at Playa Panteón, inquire at Restaurant El Amigo del Mar, Restaurant Susy, or any of the beachside restaurants. The hourly price will depend on your Spanish, the price of gasoline, and the time of year. You can also rent snorkeling equipment at **Restaurant Susy** (10 pesos per hr). The beach nearer the pier, **Playa Puerto Angel,** has become somewhat polluted and dirty, but people still take the plunge. **Elías Tarias,** the small, white-roofed restaurant on the side of the pier away from Playa Panteón, rents boats as well. Visitors renting boats can pay with part of their catch.

Nightlife in Puerto Angel is comatose, save for a few *fiestas* at the beach cafés along Playa Panteón's moonlit shoreline. Early risers (or perhaps those who never slept) might enjoy heading to the pier between 5-7am to watch the fishermen bring in their catch as the sun rises.

■ Near Puerto Angel

Zipolite, "beach of the dead" in Xenpoaltec, is named more for the visitors who give up their former lives convinced that they have found paradise than for those who have drowned in the unforgiving surf. The long smooth stretch of powdery gold sand is endowed with a row of humble *palapas* and a carefree (if motley) crew, but no hotels and precious few showers. Waves break cataclysmically offshore, slamming the carefree souls who frolic naked in the surf. The beach faces south, while the waves come in from two directions (southeast and southwest) at 45-degree angles to the beach. This creates a series of channels that vacuum unsuspecting swimmers out to sea. Though ferocious, these channels are not very wide: if you find yourself being pulled away from shore, do not attempt to swim directly towards the beach; rather, swim parallel to the beach until you're clear of the seaward current and the waves will allow you back in. Zipolite is also plagued by theft. Keep an eye on everything or leave it locked up. In general, you'll want to keep your wits about you at all times (somewhat at odds with the beach's ethos), and women should not wander the beach alone at night. One final warning: scorpions patronize Zipolite as well: give your cut-offs a good shake before jumping into them.

If you can handle the surf, the scorpions, and the scene, Zipolite can be a beautiful spot. Come here to stroll naked down the long beach, check in with the international vagabond set, and generally partake of the friendly fringe atmosphere. **Shambala,** at the western end of the beach, is a beautiful palapa complex renting rooms, cabañas, and hammocks. Also called Casa de Gloria, it is about as safe a place as you'll find on the beach and the premises are drug free. There is a vegetarian restaurant and meditation center attached. (Singles 10 pesos. Doubles 15 pesos. Cabañas 15 pesos per person. Hammocks 7 pesos.) **El Hongo**, at the western end of the beach behind the first row of palapa huts, serves good food and has the best sound system on the beach. **San Cristóbal,** one of the many restaurants right on the sand, also comes highly recommended.

A few km east of Puerto Angel sprawls **Playa Estacahuites** (a STACK o I WHEATIES is close enough for pronunciation), a nudist beach at least as beautiful as Zipolite. In a small, secluded cove ideal for snorkeling, Estacahuites attracts enough visitors to its shore that thefts are common. To reach Playa Estacahuites from town, head east on Uribe as if you were going to Pochutla. Just outside of town you'll see a huge Corona sign. Turn right at the sign and the beach will be at the end of the dirt path. The spectacular beach is well worth the 20-minute hike to get there.

■■■ PUERTO ESCONDIDO

Puerto Escondido is the heroine of a familiar fairy tale. Less than two decades ago, it was a quiet *indígena* fishing village where visitors had to wheedle overnight lodging from a local family. Today, the Pacific surf rages beneath droves of stocky surfers who break at the crack of dawn for Playa Zikatela. Surf-seekers usually arrive via Acapulco, whose playful pools and mild climate are poor primers for the pounding heat and surf of Puerto Escondido.

Its increased popularity has rendered obsolete Puerto Escondido's reputation as an obscure outpost of wild *norteamericano* and European decadence. Yet this fabulous stretch of beach between two majestic outcroppings of rock still plays host to amiable international company. Where only a handful of scantily clad *extranjeros* used to romp, hotels now outnumber hippies, drug use has dwindled, and nudity is history. Rife with many of the conveniences and exciting nightspots lacking in Puerto Angel, Puerto Escondido is a different kind of escape—a place to get away from inland life, but one that establishes its own fast pace between the peak tanning hours. People strut up and down the main strip here partaking in the thriving consumer culture along the roadside. Excellent food, exotic drink, and kitsch trinkets compete for the pedestrian's pesos and lend the *paseo* an urban air.

ORIENTATION

Like any self-respecting seaside village, Puerto Escondido has its own airport. It is also connected to the outside world by land; a long, treacherous road winds through the Sierra Madres to Oaxaca City, and a beautifully paved coastal road twists through ramshackle fishing towns and coastal forests on its path to Acapulco. The best of Puerto Escondido lies beyond Pérez Gasga, along the grassy dunes.

The **Carretera Costera** (coastal highway), often called Route 200, separates the well-marked perpendicular streets of uptown Puerto Escondido from the maze of walkways to the beach. Route 131, from Oaxaca, crosses Route 200, becomes **Pérez Gasga,** and twists downhill to front the town beach. The intersection of Route 200 and Route 131/Pérez Gasga is usually called *el crucero.* Pérez Gasga meets Route 200 again, 1km east of el crucero, just west of a bridge crossing Laguna Agua Dulce. The **airport** is 3km west, on Route 200, a difficult walk or short cab ride (7 pesos) to the center of town.

Bus stations cluster north of *el crucero,* usually just off of Route 131, and are the only reason for visitors to stray this far from the beach. To get from the stations to the center of town, walk down Route 131 until you hit Route 200. Cross *el crucero* and wind your way down Pérez Gasga, which is closed to traffic at beach level after 2pm, turning the street into a wide pedestrian mall.

Cabs from *el crucero* transport the weary traveler downtown or to the *playas* for about 4 pesos. To leave town, hike the steep hill to *el crucero,* or take a cab from the chained-off entrance to Pérez Gasga. Taxis in Puerto Escondido are outrageously priced for the short distances they cover. Unless your surfboard is weighing you down or it's 105°F (both possible), the walk is easy.

PRACTICAL INFORMATION

Tourist Office: Carretera Costera (tel 201-75), in a modern *palapa* 20 hot min. west of *el crucero,* across from Hotel Las Gaviotas. Staff does not speak English, but is very helpful and provides good maps of Puerto Escondido and Oaxaca. Open Mon.-Fri. 8am-3pm and 6-8pm, Sat. 9am-1pm.

Currency Exchange: Money Exchange, on Pérez Gasga (tel. 2-05-92), across from Farmacia Cortés. Open Mon.-Sat. 9am-2pm and 5-8pm. **Bancomer,** on Pérez Gasga, opposite Rincón del Pacífico. Open for exchange Mon.-Fri. 9am-noon. Lines are long, service is glacial.

Post Office: (tel. 2-09-59), 7 Calle Nte. at Oaxaca, 10 very long blocks north of Hidalgo on Rte. 131 and to the right in a blue bldg. with an antenna. Lista de Correos. Open Mon.-Fri. 8am-7pm, Sat. 9am-1pm. It's a good 45min. uphill walk from the beach. Catch a *combi,* or buy stamps at one of the many vendors on Pérez Gasga. **Postal code:** 71980.

Telephones: On Pérez Gasga across from Farmacia Cortés (tel. 2-04-87). No collect calls. Open Mon.-Sat. 9am-10pm, Sun. 9am-1pm. Collect calls are best made from payphones on Pérez Gasga. **Telephone Code:** 958.

Telegrams: Next door to the post office (tel. 2-09-57). Open for telegrams and **fax** service Mon.-Fri. 9am-1pm and 3-7pm, Sat. 9am-noon. For **money orders** open Mon.-Fri. 9am-1pm and 3-5pm, Sat. 9am-noon.

Airport: 3km west of the *centro* on Route. 200. Taxis to downtown 7 pesos. Both **AeroMorelos** flies to Oaxaca daily (8:30am, 45min., 243 pesos). **Mexicana** flies to Mexico City daily excepting Tues. and Thurs. (12:30pm, 1hr., 328 pesos). Airport open 7:30am-6pm.

Bus Stations: Puerto Escondido has no central bus terminal, but all buses gravitate toward *el crucero.* **Cristóbal Colon** (tel. 2-02-84) is a five-minute walk walk west of el crucero, on the right side of Route 200. It runs first-class buses to Oaxaca (10am, 8:30pm, 50.50 pesos), and to San Cristóbal de Las Casas (9pm, 62.50 pesos), as well as closer destinations. **Estrella Blanca** (tel. 2-04-27) lives on Route 131, 100m north of el crucero, on the right. From here, first-class buses run to

Acapulco (7:30am, 9:30am, 11:30am, 1:30pm, 3:30pm, 11pm, midnight, 46 pesos), and to Mexico City (7:30pm, 95 pesos). **Transportes Oaxaca Istmo,** at Av. Hidalgo Ote., one block east and two blocks north of el crucero, goes to Oaxaca (9:30pm, 30 pesos). From *el crucero,* smaller buses run east on Route 200 to Huatulco, Pochutla, and Salina Cruz.

Taxis: tel. 2-00-26. Rates go up after 11pm.

Car Rental: Budget has an office in Hotel Posada Real (tel. 2-01-33), 3km west of *el crucero* on Route 200.

English Bookstore: El Acuario, on Pérez Gasga downhill from and opposite Casa de Huéspedes Las Dos Costas (tel. 2-01-27). Doubles as a stationery store. A few *norteamericano* best sellers plus a wide selection of *gringo* magazines. Open Mon.-Sat. 8:30am-2pm and 4-7:30pm.

24-hr. Pharmacy: La Moderna, Pérez Gasga 203 (tel. 2-05-49), toward the top of the hill.

Hospital: Seguro Social, 5 de Febrero at 7 Calle Nte. (tel. 2-01-42). Open 24 hrs. **Centro de Salud,** Pérez Gasga 409, below and across from the Hotel Virginia. Small medical clinic open for emergencies 24 hrs. No English spoken.

Police: (tel. 2-07-21), just west of the Agencio Municipio, a five-minute walk west of *el crucero* on Route 200. Open 24 hrs.

Laundromat: Lava-Matic, on Libre, 30m off of Pérez Gasga. Three kilos washed and dried for 18 pesos. Open Mon.-Sat., 9am-6pm.

ACCOMMODATIONS

The beach here is not safe for camping, particularly in the more secluded spots, but a multitude of hotels downtown caters to every budget. The prices given below are for the *temporada alta* (high season), from December through *Semana Santa.* At all other times, prices start much lower; with a little poker-faced negotiation, you can pay less than half the posted rate.

On the Hill

Hotel San Juan, Felipe Merklin 503 (tel. 2-05-18), 1 block down Pérez Gasga from *el crucero* and left, with a big painted sign. Terrace has a stunning view of the beaches and ocean below. Rooms, big and stark with cement floors, are less remarkable but still really nice. Too bad it's such a trek to the beach. Ask for a room at the top. In the lobby: a big strong cage of finches and a frustrated cat. Singles 65 pesos. Doubles 82 pesos.

Hotel Virginia, Camino Alfaro 104 (tel. 2-01-76), off Pérez Gasga. Coming down the hill, take the dirt road to the right after Restaurant Selene. Big sign. Big rooms. Big baths. Terrace has spectacular view, and everything is clean. Singles 50 pesos. Doubles 60 pesos.

Casa de Huéspedes Naxhiely, Pérez Gasga 301. Clean, plain rooms. Very friendly family atmosphere. Singles 44 pesos. Doubles 55 pesos.

On the Beach

Some of the *cabañas* on the beach are quite cheap. This means that neither the prices nor the mosquitoes are open to negotiation. Buy a mosquito incense coil and tough it out.

Cabañas Zihuaraya, on the beach next door to Cabañas Playa Marinero (below). *Cabañas* on the cement roof of a restaurant-bar. *Palapa* huts contain 2 double beds. Communal bathrooms are pretty dodgy. Atmosphere is friendly. Restaurant in front. Singles 15 pesos. Doubles 20 pesos.

Cabañas Playa Marinero, on the beach, 100m past the fleet of fishing boats. *Palapa* huts on cement platforms, each with 2 single beds. Common bathrooms soggy and dirty but functional. Bring a sleepsack and inspect your hut for insects. Nice beachfront restaurant and young international clientele. 15 pesos for 1-2 people.

Restaurant y Cuartos Liza, at the east end of Playa Marinero. Six clean, safe, cool rooms kept by a friendly woman who speaks English. Attached restaurant has great view, good breakfasts, and giant shrimp. Rooms (1 or 2 persons) 60 pesos. Restaurant open 8am-11am.

Casas de Playa Acali, past the rocks close to the beginning of the surfing beach (tel. 2-07-54). In a different league than the other *cabañas*. Each comes with fan, refrigerator, stove, clean bathroom and screened windows. Swimming pool, ping-pong and English movies shown at night. Singles 50 pesos. Doubles 60 pesos. Split-level bungalows with A/C 150 pesos. Pool, ping-pong, occassional movies.

Trailer Park Neptune, at the opposite end of Pérez Gasga from Hertz. Cabañas as well as space for cars, tents, and hammocks. Communal cleaner than those above. Cabañas 20 pesos. Trailer parking. 10 pesos per car and 10 per peson.

FOOD

If dinner is a long time in coming, it's probably because they're having a tough time catching it. Puerto Escondido's fishers net huge amounts of snapper, lobster, shrimp and octopus, and your meal can be served up any way you like it. Remeber: the market is at work here as well; a 15 peso filet of fish will cost you 8 pesos in the off season.

La Gota de Vida, on the beach side of Pérez Gasga, just before it's closed to traffic. A vegetarian restaurant serving cucumber juice, soyburgers, and Olympic-size *licuados*. Great food, healthy portions. Open Wed.-Mon. 8am-10:30pm.

Banana's, the last restaurant on the beach side of Pérez Gasga. Look for the unmistakable jungle entrance en route to the beach. Listen to great music, have an intimate conversation with friends and play ping-pong or backgammon under the palm trees. Upper deck affords a great view. *Quesadillas* 12 pesos. Chicken tacos 15 pesos. Chocolate crepes 9 pesos. Ask nicely and they'll tune the set to CNN. Open daily 7:30am-12:30am.

Restaurant Selene, Pérez Gasga 402, opposite the Centro de Salud. Small, family-run place with a small, reasonably priced menu. Shrimp *al gusto* 16 pesos. *Mole oaxaqueño* 10 pesos. Open daily 7am-11pm.

Restaurant Santa Fe, above the plush hotel Santa Fe, behind the big rock separating the two beaches. Serves great food with a spectacular view. Fettucine alfredo 16 pesos. Cheeseburger 14 pesos. Pasta primavera 17 pesos. Open daily 7:30am-10:30pm.

Perla Flameante, on Pérez Gasga just north of Banana's. Slightly more expensive than its neighbors, but it has a great location and an extensive menu. Any kind of fish (mahi mahi, halibut, etc.) prepared any way (cajun, teriyaki, etc.) 16 pesos. Salads prepared with purified water 8 pesos. Piña coladas 6 pesos. Open Mon.-Sat. 7am-11pm, Sun. 1-11pm.

Cabo Blanco, on Playa Zikatela, just east of Casas Playa Acali. Good food, big portions. Open daily 5-10pm.

SIGHTS AND ACTIVITIES

There isn't much to do here except relax, eat fish and contemplate the tireless erosive efforts of the surf.

A rock outcrop southwest of town divides the main beach at Puerto Escondido into two parts. **Playa Zikatela,** beyond the rocks, is the serious surfing beach; the Mexican pipeline they call it. This is not a swimming beach: the surf injures and kills scores of surfers every year. The long beach is lined with bars, restaurants, and cabañas, frequented by surfers from around the world. **Central Surf,** on Pérez Gasga across from Farmacia Cortés, rents low-quality boards for 5 pesos per hour or 20 pesos per day. (Open daily 9am-2pm and 5-9pm.)

Playa Marinero, the town's quieter beach, harbors the local fishing fleet. An angling trip can be arranged on the sands or with one of the seaside restaurants for 80 pesos per hour, with the average trip lasting three hours. To avoid the dirty work, arrange in advance for your catch to be cleaned and cooked as part of the original fee. A few smaller beaches, suitable for snorkelling, lie west of town. The distance is short enough to hoof it, but you can also take a taxi (5 pesos) or a boat (7 pesos). Walk down Route 200 in the direction of Acapulco (west) and turn left on Hidalgo at the tourist office. At the faded *"Pepsi...es lo de hoy"* sign, turn left and pick a path at the fork. The right branch leads down to Playa Carrizalillo. The left branch leads down and then forks again. The left-hand branch descends steep rocky terrain to **Playa Manzanillo.** Beneath the calm surface of its waters, coral makes wading a bit treacherous but snorkeling very interesting. The path to the right of the Pepsi sign is wider and leads to **Playa Puerto Angelito,** opposite Manzanillo. Both of these beaches are small enough to seem crowded when even a few people are present; their days as secluded coves are irretrievable.

When the sun goes down, the beach crowd becomes the bar crowd at restaurants and pubs along the strip. **Paulin,** a disco in Hotel Fiesta Mexicana (3km west of town on the coastal side of Route 200) was pretty hot in the summer of 1993. Cover 10 pesos. Open Tues.-Sun. 9pm-3am. **Coco,** also on Pérez Gasga, has live salsa as well. No cover.

TABASCO

Occupying pole position as the Gulf coast curves into Yucatán, the state of Tabasco is a lush, flat plain perched on the Isthmus of Tehuantepec. False etymologies flourish in Mexico, but *tabasco* may well descend, as is rumored, from the *indígena* word *tlapalco,* meaning "moist land." Dotted by lakes and swamps, criss-crossed by rivers, and swathed in dense, humid jungle, it could be named—etymology be damned—"sopping land."

The Olmec culture, Mexico's oldest and arguably most influential, flourished in the area now within Tabasco's boundaries. Because few Olmec artifacts exist, their civilization remains draped in mystery, but archaeologists do know that the Olmecs worshipped the jaguar as a divine creature. Manifest reminders of this obsession remain in many of the Olmecs' monumental and grotesque stone carvings, in which man and feline inseparably intertwine. The Olmecs' art, architecture, astronomy and calendar were adopted and refined by the later Mayan and Toltec cultures. To attract tourists, Villahermosa recently underwent a cosmetic makeover, relocating most of the state's archaeological treasures to new museums near downtown Villahermosa.

Tabasco's most important Mayan ruins, **Comalcalco,** lie an hour from the capital, easily reached by bus or car. Many tourists stay in **Villahermosa** to visit the ruins of Palenque in Chiapas state, two hours away. Those bent on seeing Mexico's less accessible ruins fly from Villahermosa or Tenosique into the **Lacandón Rainforest** of Chiapas to explore **Bonampak** and **Yaxchilán.**

■■■ VILLAHERMOSA

Weary of defending the coast against British and Dutch pirate raids, the Spanish colonists of this area migrated inland up the Grijalva River to found Villahermosa (then the fishing village of San Juan Bautista) in 1596. Over the course of the next few centuries, Villahermosa developed slowly into a minor agricultural and commercial center. Transport to and from the capital was fluvial until the late 1940s, when a short connection to Teapa linked Villahermosa by rail to the rest of the nation. Since then, the oil industry has transformed Villahermosa from boondocks to boomtown. Satellite antennae, luxury hotels and PEMEX apartment complexes have sprouted virtually overnight, and what was once a pock-marked swamp has become a cluttered urban metropolis with a population of 1,570,000.

Swimming in oil revenue, the state invested billions of pesos to improve the capital with new museums, monuments, bus stations, libraries and parks. In its archaeological park and anthropological museums, Villahermosa safeguards the remaining artifacts from the region's ancient Olmec culture. A dubious development success, the Tabasco 2000 complex, includes government buildings, a planetarium and a sparkling shopping center. The popular shopping area, however, is still the noisy *Zona Remodelada* with its numerous air-conditioned department stores, and the open-air market Pino Suárez. If you're looking for traditional Mexico, Villahermosa will be a disappointment, for it has been engulfed in the hubbub of fast-paced modern life.

ORIENTATION

Tabasco's state capital lies in the central third of the state, only 20km from the border with Chiapas state. Escárcega, the major crossroads for Yucatán-bound travelers, lies 298km east of Villahermosa via Route 186; Coatzacoalcos, where the Mexican isthmus tapers to its narrowest, lies 169km to the west via Route 180; and Tuxtla Gutiérrez, capital of Chiapas, lies 293km to the south.

Villahermosa has grown in a tangled skein of winding, heavily-trafficked streets. Most areas of interest lie downtown, though the city claims residents in 70 outlying *colonias*. First- and second-class **buses** depart from the city's eastern edge. An international **airport** lies northwest of the city, 14km from the downtown area; taxis shuttle between the airport and downtown (35 pesos *especial*, 10 pesos *colectivo*).

Downtown Villahermosa lies between the Río Carrizal to the west and the Río Grijalva to the east; the large **Laguna de las Ilusiones** winds its way through the northern half of the city. The **zócalo** and city center are on the west bank of the Grijalva, south of the rest of the city. The **27 de Febrero,** which forms the spine of the downtown area, and **Paseo Tabasco,** which winds past Tabasco 2000, see most of the downtown action. Tabasco intersects 27 de Febrero in front of the cathedral. *Saetas* (public buses) and *combis* cost .80 pesos and .50 pesos, respectively, and run from 6am to 10:30pm.

To reach downtown from the first-class **ADO** station, walk two and a half blocks to the right on Mina to Méndez. From there, take a *combi* (.50-.80 pesos) labeled "Tierra Colorada Centro-Juárez" and get off a few minutes later at the **Parque Juárez.** You can find most hotels south of the park on Madero or its parallel cousin Constitución. Walking from the station to the *Parque Juárez* takes 15-20 min; upon exiting the terminal, head straight ahead (east) across Mina and down Fuentes or Merino five blocks to the *Parque de la Paz.* On the far side of the park, turn right (south) on Madero; you will reach the *Parque Juárez* and the hotel zone after six blocks.

To get downtown from the **second-class bus terminal,** cross Grijalva on the pedestrian bridge to the left of the station exit and jump on a bus labeled "Indeco Centro" (.50 pesos). Disembark at the *Parque Juárez* on Madero; the hotels are to the south. To make the 25min. walk from the station, cross the bridge and continue south on Mina until you reach the ADO station three blocks later. Then follow the instructions above. Consider taking a taxi (4 pesos) to avoid the bus hassle or the long walk from the bus station.

PRACTICAL INFORMATION

Because Villahermosa is spread over a large area, always get specific directions to your destination and find out if it is served by public transportation.

Tourist Offices: State Office, Tabasco 1504 (tel. 6-36-33), in the new state office building across from the Palacio Municipal in the Tabasco 2000 complex. Walk halfway into the arcade and go up the staircase to the right. Burgeoning with maps and glossy brochures. Large, kind, English-speaking staff. Open Mon.-Fri. 9am-3pm and 6-8pm. **Federal Tourist Office,** Tabasco 1504 (tel. 6-28-91), in the same office as the state office above. Some English spoken. Open Mon.-Fri. 9am-3pm. **Tourist Information Booths,** in the airport. Open daily 7am-9pm. Also at the Museo La Venta. Open Mon.-Fri. 8:30am-4pm.

Currency Exchange: Bancomer, Juárez at Zaragoza (tel. 2-98-95), 1 block west of Madero. Open for exchange Mon.-Fri. 9am-12:30pm. **Bánamex,** Reforma at Madero 201 (tel. 2-00-11), 3 blocks north of the *zócalo*. Similar rates. Open Mon.-Fri. 9am-noon. Either bank has Kafkaesque lines.

American Express: On Simon Salart 202 at Fedencia (tel. 14-18-88). Some English spoken. Open Mon.-Fri. 9-11:30am and 4-6pm, Sat. 9am-noon.

Post Office: Saenz 101 (tel. 2-10-40), at Lerdo, 3 blocks west of Madero and 1 block south of Zaragoza. Open Mon.-Fri. 8am-7pm, Sat. 9am-noon. **Postal code:** 86000.

Telephones: Long distance calls are best made from pay phones on the street, since many *casetas* do not allow collect calls or don't exist at the locations indicated on the tourist office's map. **Café La Barra,** Lerdo 608 (tel. 2-53-39), up the stairs across from the main telegram office, allows collect calls at no charge, as long as the call is approved by the staff first. Open Mon.-Sat. 7am-2pm and 3-9pm. **Telephone code:** 931.

Telegrams: Lerdo 601 at Saenz (tel. 2-11-90), 3 blocks west of Madero and 1 block south of Zaragoza. Open for money orders Mon.-Fri. 9am-5pm, Sat. 9am-noon; for all other services Mon.-Fri. 9am-8pm, Sat. 9am-1pm.

Airport: On Carretera Rovirosa (tel. 2-43-86). **Aeroméxico,** Periférico Carlos Pellicer 525 (tel. 4-16-75) at CICOM. Open Mon.-Sat. 8am-7pm. To Mérida and Mexico City. **Mexicana,** Av. Los Ríos at Complejo Urbana (tel. 6-31-32), in the Tabasco 2000 complex. Open Mon.-Fri. 9am-6:45pm, Sat. 9am-5:45pm. To Mexico City. **Aerocaribe,** Tabasco 901 at Mina (tel. 4-46-95), serves Cancún via Mérida, Oaxaca via Tuxtla. Open Mon.-Fri. 9am-8pm, Sat. 9am-7pm.

Bus Stations: ADO (tel. 2-14-46), **Cristóbal Colón** (tel. 4-02-86), and **UNO** all at Mina 297, at Merino in the northeast corner of the city. Walk 11 blocks from the center north on Madero to the *Parque de la Paz*, turn left on Merino and walk 6 blocks. Arrive as far in advance as possible to buy tickets; lines at ticket counters will get up to 2-hr. long. 1st-class service, with varying prices and degrees of luxury, to everywhere, including: Coatzacoalcos (3hrs., 14-15 pesos); Mérida (8hrs., 53-118 pesos); Mexico City (13hrs., 82-158 pesos); San Andrés Tuxtla (5hrs., 27 pesos); also Campeche, Oaxaca, Palenque, Tapachula, Chetumal, Cancún, Tuxtla Gutiérrez, Tenosique, and Veracruz. **Central de Autobuses de Tabasco** (tel. 2-41-84), Grijalva/Cortínez, 3 blocks inland from the river in the northeast corner of town. Tickets not usually sold in advance, so arrive at least ½hr. early. 2nd class service to Teapa (1hr., 4.80 pesos). Also serves everywhere, including: Paraíso, Mexico City, Mérida, Puebla, San Andrés Tuxtla, Veracruz, and Campeche.

Taxis: (Tel. 13-69-30.) Almost any trip in Villahermosa costs around 4 pesos, but be sure to settle the price before you get in.

Car Rental: National, Reforma 304 (tel. 12-03-93), at the Miraflores Hotel near the center and at the Villahermosa Hyatt near the Tabasco 2000 complex. Open Mon.-Sat. 8am-2pm and 4-7pm.

Market: Pino Suárez, encompassed by Pino Suárez, Constitución, Hermanos Zozaya and Grijalva, 1 block from the river, in the northeast corner of town. Open daily 6am-6pm.

Supermarket: Bonanza, Madero at Zaragoza (tel. 4-22-80). Open daily 8am-9pm.

Laundromat: Lavandería Automática, Reforma 502 (tel. 4-37-65) at Malecón. 10 pesos per 3kg for next-day service, or 11.50 pesos per 3kg same day service. Open Mon.-Sat. 9am-8pm.

Red Cross: On General Sandino (tel. 13-35-93), in Col. 1 de Mayo. Take the "1 de Mayo" bus from Madero. 24-hr. emergency and ambulance service to any point in the city. No English spoken. A good clinic is **Clínica 39,** Zaragoza 1202 at Carmen Buen Día (tel. 2-51-99). English-speaking staff. Not free. Open daily 7am-8pm.

24-hr. Pharmacy: Farmacia Mediper, Carranza 107 at Sánchez Mármol.

Police: 16 de Septiembre at Periférico (tel. 13-19-00). No English. Open 24 hrs.

ACCOMMODATIONS

Budget hotels in Villahermosa line Madero and Constitución, and quite a few congregate in the nearby *Zona Remodelada*. Madero offers shopping, noise and proximity to the *Zona*, while Constitución is less elegant and a bit farther away from the action. The more decent budget hotels are often full-up, so consider calling a few days in advance to make reservations. **Camping** and trailer parking is allowed in small **La Choca Park** in Tabasco 2000 at no charge and with no facilities to speak of.

Hotel Madero, Madero 301 (tel. 12-05-16), near 27 de Febrero. An old Spanish building that could use some maintenance. Pink staircase leads to small, immaculate rooms. Firm mattresses, bathrooms with hot water, desks, cupboards, and fans make for a comfortable existence. Manager stores packs and gives good directions. Check-out 2pm. Singles 30 pesos. Doubles 40 pesos. Triples 60 pesos. TV 5 pesos extra. Reservations can be made by phone.

Hotel San Miguel, Lerdo 315 (tel. 12-15-00), ½ block from Madero. Centrally located in the pedestrian zone, rooms have all the hallmarks of quality service: hot water, shower curtain, fan, phone and irreproachable bathrooms. Unfortunately, often full. Check-out 1pm. Singles 35 pesos. Doubles 50 pesos. Triples 60 pesos. Call or write for reservations.

Hotel Oriente, Madero 425 (tel. 12-01-21), between shops in the arcade north of 27 de Febrero. Basic rooms have hot water, fans and phones, but are almost devoid of windows and light. Check-out 1pm. Singles 35 pesos. Doubles 35 pesos. Triples 55 pesos. 5 pesos per additional person. Prepay reservations.

Hotel Tabascoob, Constitución 514 (tel. 14-53-22). Rooms are so spacious that they look almost bare. Some have light-flooded windows; all have fans and reasonable bathrooms. No hot water. Check-out 1pm. Singles 30 pesos. Doubles 40 pesos. Triples 50 pesos. Reservations can be made by phone.

Posada Hotel Brondo, Suárez 209 (tel. 12-59-61), near the intersection with Sánchez Mármol. Attractive, pleasantly furnished rooms. Fans and hot water. All doubles have private, wonderfully clean bathrooms; all singles are served by communal facilities which are just a miracle. Prices vary with size. Cheaper rooms are usually taken. Check-out 1pm. Singles 30-35 pesos. Doubles 40 pesos. Triples 45 pesos. MC and Visa accepted. Reservations can be made by phone.

Casa de Huéspedes Teresita, Constitución 224 (tel. 12-34-53). 10 small, moderately maintained rooms off an upstairs lobby where the cheerful manager watches TV round the clock. Tiny bathrooms have no hot water, but rooms do have fans. Check-out 10am. Singles with or without private facilities 25 pesos. Reservations must be paid in advance.

FOOD

Despite booming development and a sincere desire to attract tourism, Villahermosa cooks up paltry few pleasures for the budget traveler's palate. Cafés, *torterías* and frozen yogurt shops permeate the *Zona Remodelada*, and the restaurants that line Madero rarely rise above the ordinary. The main produce market operates off Pino Suárez near Zozaya, a few blocks from Puente Grijalva.

Restaurant Madan, Madero 408 (tel. 2-16-50), diagonally across from Hotel Oriente. A/C, black-and-white photos of old Villahermosa, cheap food and many elderly men passionately discussing politics. Wide selection of Mexican dishes at 4-digit prices. Enchiladas 9 pesos. Tacos 10 pesos. 3-course *menú del día* 18 pesos. Credit cards accepted. Open daily 8am-11:30pm.

El Torito Valenzuela, 27 de Febrero 202 (tel. 4-11-81), at Madero. The friendliest and cleanest of the numerous downtown *taquerías*. Aluminum bars are reminiscent of your sixth-grade cafeteria, and just as shiny. Sandwiches 6 pesos. *Quesadillas* 4 pesos. Open daily 8am-midnight.

Restaurant-Bar Familiar Cheje, Madero 732 (tel. 4-33-25), between Himénez and Sánchez Marino. Bamboo-lined walls, romantic music, and unobtrusive beige light bring intimacy and offset the sting of higher prices. Tortilla soup 10 pesos. *Coctel de camarón* 17 pesos. Fish filets 21 pesos. Excellent cocktails (7 pesos). Credit cards and traveler's checks accepted. Open Mon.-Sat. 11am-midnight.

La Playita Restaurant-Bar, Constitución 212 (tel. 2-27-69), with a riverfront entrance as well. Spruce, casual family restaurant popular with the local crowd.

Sopa de mariscos 22 pesos, 10 varieties of chicken 17 pesos each. Open Mon.-Sat. 9am-1am.

Café Bar Impala, Madero 421 (tel. 2-04-93). Fun hangout serving great *tamalitos de chipilín,* a regional specialty (1.50 pesos). *Panuchos* and tacos only 1 peso each. Colorful tiles surround the interior and loud Mexican pop music fills the air. Great for people-watching. Open daily 9am-8pm.

Ric's, on Mina, in the Las Galas shopping center next to the ADO station. Cushioned booths and simply wonderful muzak. Fruit salad 6 pesos. *Crepas poblanas* stuffed with chicken and coated with salsa 12 pesos. Meats and chicken 19-28 pesos. Open daily 7am-10pm.

Restaurant Mexicanito, Madero 704 (tel. 2-81-49), between Méndez and Magallanes. A busy, popular, local joint permeated by the smell of cooked onions. *Menú para chuparse los dedos* (menu that will make you lick your fingers) offers sandwiches (6 pesos), *tacos de pollo* (8 pesos), chicken and meats (17-21 pesos). Open daily 8am-midnight.

SIGHTS

While exploring a ruin site at La Venta, Tabasco, in the early 1940s, U.S. archaeologist M.W. Sterling discovered six massive sculpted stone heads. Further studies indicated that La Venta—in the middle of a swampy region of contemporary western Tabasco—had been a principal ceremonial center of the Olmecs. In the late 1950s, the monumental pieces were moved to an archaeological park in Villahermosa designed especially for the artifacts, the **Parque-Museo La Venta.**

In 1800 BC, the Olmecs formed the matrix culture of Mesoamerica. At the height of their civilization (between 800 and 200 BC), the Olmecs numbered only 250,000, but their distinctive artistic style influenced groups from the Ríos Sinaloa and Panuco in northern Mexico to the Nicoya Peninsula in Costa Rica. Most nearby cultures adopted their belief in the jaguar as a divine creature and the creator of the peoples of the world. In honor of the cat, sculptors at La Venta produced numerous beautiful jade carvings of the jaguar, but the animal's artistic influence extends much further. The Olmecs even gave their carvings of people what has been called a "jaguar mouth," symbolizing the intermingling of the jaguar and the human, the divine and the mortal. These colossal sculptures range from 2m to 10m in height. Each of the spherical heads wears a war helmet and has the thick eyelids, wide nose and prominent lips of the Olmecs, yet each expression is distinct. The stern, disembodied heads weigh heavily on low mounds of dirt, evoking images of a thick neck, great torso and powerful legs reaching far into the bowels of the earth. Three of the giant heads, along with 30 other stone pieces, are now in the beautiful Parque-Museo La Venta, 3km north of town. The park is enchanting: monkeys sway overhead, deer trot just a few feet away, and armadillos try to stare you down at close range. To complement the Olmec jaguar masks, the park is also equipped with a pair of caged jaguars. A guide will lead you through the park in tours for 45 pesos (English or Spanish, up to 5 people), or you can go follow the hard-to-spot concrete footprints that mark the self-guided tour. There are no signs in the park, and brochures are rarely available at the site; get your free brocure beforehand from the tourist office.

To get to the *parque-museo,* take the "Tabasco 2000," "Circuito #1," or "Parque Linda Vista" **bus** (.50 or .80 pesos) from Madero in the center to the intersection of Tabasco and Grijalva. Walk northeast on Grijalva for five minutes until you reach the "La Venta" entrance. (Site open daily 8:30am-5pm. Admission 5 pesos. 2-hr. tours in Spanish or English 25-45 pesos for 1-35 people, depending on the size of the group.) A complete zoo is only 100m further on Grijalva in the **Parque de Convivencia Infantil,** a play space for local children. (Open Tues.-Sun. 8am-4pm. Admission 1 peso.) Return to Paseo Tabasco through the **Parque Tomás Garrido Canabal,** which also lies on the Laguna de las Ilusiones and surrounds the Parque-Museo La Venta. Landscaped alcoves hide benches and fountains. Climb the 40m *mirador* for an excellent view of Villahermosa and look for the manatees that reside in the *laguna* below. (Main entrance at the corner of Tabasco and Grijalva. Free.)

Northwest on Tabasco, away from the city center and Río Grijalva, lie two more city parks. **Tabasco 2000** is a long strip of sparkling new buildings that includes the city's ultra-modern Palacio Municipal, a convention center, several fountains, a shopping center and a **planetarium** with U.S. Omnimax shows dubbed in Spanish. (Shows Tues.-Fri. at 6:30pm, Sat. and Sun. at 6pm and 7:30pm. Admission 5 pesos.) To reach Tabasco 2000 , take the "Tabasco 2000" bus from the city center.

The great instigator behind the creation of the Parque-Museo La Venta was Carlos Pellicer Cámara, Tabasco's most famous poet. His name graces the **Museo Regional de Antropología Carlos Pellicer Cámara,** the main attraction at Villahermosa's new **Center for the Investigation of Olmec and Mayan Cultures** (CICOM). The museum's well-presented material describes archaeological sites near Villahermosa including Palenque and Comalcalco. The first floor concentrates on the life, times and arts of the two tribes that successfully dominated the region, the Olmecs and the Maya, while the top floor includes representative pieces from all of Mexico's indigenous tribes. Guide books (in English or Spanish) are at the ticket counter. From the *Zona Remodelada*, the museum is best reached by a 20min. walk south along the Grijalva River. The crowded #1 and "CICOM" buses pass frequently. (Open daily 9am-7pm. Admission 5 pesos.)

ENTERTAINMENT

Villahermosa presents two basic nightlife options: the discos in the luxury hotels, and the many cultural activities sponsored by the Instituto de la Cultura.

The enigmatically-named **Snob,** Juárez 106 (tel. 3-44-44), in the Hyatt, contains a sweltering mix of locals and tourists who jam all night long to U.S. rock, *salsa* and tropical music. (Open Tues.-Sat. 8pm-2am. Cover 30 pesos.) **Estudio 8,** Ruiz Cortínez 907 (tel. 2-11-11), at Mina, in the Hotel Maya Tabasco, also packs 'em in (Wed.-Sat. 9pm-2am, Cover 25 pesos), as does **Sheik,** Av. Méndez between Plutarco Elías Calles and Pages Llergo. For mellower diversion, head for **Galeria El Jaguar Despertado,** Saenz 117, near Reforma in the *Zona Remodelada*. The café in back sometimes features live classical music, but even if the tunes are absent, the fountain, the original contemporary Mexican art and the gallery upstairs attract the intellectual crowd in town. (Coffee or tea 1.50 pesos, dessert 2.50-3.50 pesos. Open Tues.-Sat. 3:30-10pm.)

The **Instituto de Cultura Tabasco,** in the Edificio Portal del Agua on Magallanes (tel. 2-90-24), publishes a monthly calendar of musical, theatrical and other cultural events; look for it in museums and major hotels.

■ Near Villahermosa

Two daytrips within Tabasco state are worthy of your attention, and they'll take you out of the heat of the capital. The Mayan ruins at **Comalcalco,** with their unique architecture, make a stimulating prelude to the nearby beach. Or head inland to Teapa to visit the vast the caverns of **Coconá** and spend a lazy afternoon in the sulphurous pools of the nearby **El Azufre** spa. Both sights are accessible by public transport, although you should start early in the day and expect to transfer a number of times.

COMALCALCO

Whereas La Venta documents Tabasco's Olmec past, Comalcalco demonstrates the Maya's dominance over the area in the later Classic period (200-700 AD). One of the northernmost Mayan settlements, Comalcalco grew contemporaneously with Palenque in nearby Chiapas and has yielded evidence of contacts with other Yucatecan Mayan settlements, as well as with the Toltecs, Mexica and Totonacs. The site's most distinctive feature is its architecture; unlike those of other Mayan cities, the pyramids and buildings of Comalcalco were constructed from packed earth and clay and later covered with stuccoed oven-fired bricks, hence its name: "In the house of bricks." Eroded but still imperial, the constructions contrast dramatically with the grass slopes and the jungle backdrop. Do not climb the temples, since Uzi-toting guards are serious about the *"no subir"* signs.

With 10 levels, the hulking 25m-high **pyramid** to the left of the entrance to the site is Comalcalco's best-known landmark. The north face bears traces of the elaborate stucco carvings that once completely covered the structure's sides. Behind the pyramid stretches the north plaza, surrounded by a series of ruined minor temples and mounds, the dilapidated state of which allows a closer look at Comalcalco's brickwork and oyster-shell mortar.

From the plaza, a well-worn path leads up the side of the acropolis area and passes a group of three temples on the way (from right to left, Temples 22, 13 and 12). As with the main pyramid, vestiges of elaborate decorative carvings can be seen on each of these temples.

Farther up the acropolis, turn right to reach the **Tomb of the Nine Knights of the Night,** named after the nine bas-relief figures on the walls of the tomb. Visible from the acropolis, three sides of Comalcalco's ballcourt (to the left) remain unexcavated and covered with tropical vegetation. Several temples and administrative buildings, including one known as **The Palace,** stand in pieces atop the acropolis against a backdrop of tall, square brick columns and several roofless rooms. (Site open daily 10:30am-5pm. Admission 10 pesos.)

The archaeological zone lies 34km northwest of Villahermosa near the town of Comalcalco (2km away) and can be reached by the **bus** that travels to Paraíso via Comalcalco (see Villahermosa: Practical Information). Get off at Comalcalco and walk back a block on Méndez to its major intersection with Route 187. From this corner catch a *combi* (2 pesos) and ask the driver to let you off at the access road to the *ruinas*. From here, the walk to the site is a pleasant 1km. You can also take a taxi (*especial*) directly to the site from the Comalcalco bus station (5 pesos).

TABASCO COAST

In terms of natural beauty, the beaches of the Tabasco Coast pale in comparison to those of the Pacific or those on the other side of the Yucatán Peninsula. Generally speaking, however, Tabasco beaches are clean and good for swimming, although oil drilling has not had a salutary effect on the coastal ecosystem.

Most of the small resort towns offer budget accommodations, and all are adept at preparing delicious seafood. The western most resorts on the coast 70km from Villahermosa, **El Paraíso** and **El Limón,** can be reached by bus. From Villahermosa and El Paraíso, buses also run daily to the resort at **Puerto Ceiba,** where you can rent boats to explore its lagoon. From there, you can reach a number of other small towns on Laguna Mecoacán. These settlements are not beach towns, but rather fishing villages that owe their livelihoods to oysters. Farther to the west and harder to reach, **Pico de Oro** and **Frontera** both bask on the sandy shore and provide possibilities similar to those at the closer El Paraíso and El Limón.

The town of El Paraíso is a brief 20min. drive north on Route 187 from Comalcalco. To catch a **bus** after visiting the ruins, wait where the access road intersects Route 187 and flag down a blue bus or green and white *combi* marked "Paraíso." Many first- and second-class buses leave El Paraíso for Villahermosa. Check out the return times at the corresponding Villahermosa bus stations.

■■■ TEAPA

An hour's drive south of Villahermosa, along roads flanked by banana groves, Teapa (pop. 35,000) attracts visitors to its sulfuric spa and splendiferous caverns. Only 9km apart, the two sites together comprise a full daytrip from Villahermosa. Teapa is a slow-motion town which might just be a welcome rhythm after hectic Villahermosa. A leafy *zócalo* makes for lazy, quiet strolling.

El Azufre Spa, 5km west of Teapa, flaunts two large pools, a picnic area and a modest restaurant. Ignore the dilapidated facilities and the slimy green ooze underfoot; the mountain setting is striking and the waters superb. The first pool is cool and only mildly sulfuric, the second warm, bubbling and loaded with medicinal, malodorous mineral. Should you become addicted to the waters, the site provides huge rustic bungalows (entrance fee is 10 pesos).

Las Grutas Coconá were discovered in the late 1800s by the Calzada brothers during a hunting trip, as several youngsters will recount in unison at the site's entrance. A path winds for ½km into the hillside, passing through truly impressive caverns and underground lagoons. At the entrance you have a choice of picking up a flashlight and exploring the caves on your own or choosing one of a half a dozen eager eight-year-olds as a guide (a generous tip is welcomed). The boys know where all the light-switches for the otherwise dark caves are and can point out (in Spanish) oodles of animal and human likenesses in the rocks. They take you only as far as a bridge over an underground river; afterthat, bats are unpleasantly abundant. If you flash your light up at the bridge, you will see hundreds of them hanging head down. To see the lagoon containing blind fish, on your way back take the left fork when the path splits and watch your head. Twenty meters before the exit the path splits again and the right branch takes you to a natural formation of Noah's Ark and a not-so-natural carving of Jesus Christ above it. To get back to town, catch the *combi* since chances of hitching a ride on a weekday are close to zero. You will need your insect repellent while waiting for the *combi*. (Open daily 9am-6pm. Admission 2 pesos.)

Those journeying by car to El Azufre or Las Grutas can avoid Teapa altogether. To get to the spa, stay on Highway 195 from Villahermosa and do *not* take the "Teapa" exit after the railroad tracks. The spa is 4km farther down the road. To reach the caves, cross the bridge and bear left for the 2.5km ride to the caves.

Teapa has adequate facilities to accommodate an overnight stay. The most expensive and by far the nicest hotel in town is the **Hotel Quintero,** E. Bastar 108 (tel. 2-00-45). Bedspread design overflows into tile design to create a pleasant sense of organic wholeness. Rooms come with snow white bathrooms, fans and hot water. Some have balconies. To get there from the main bus station, turn right and walk up Méndez for about 10 minutes; the hotel is on the right. (Check-out 2pm. Singles 55 pesos, with A/C 69 pesos. Doubles 60 pesos, with A/C 75 pesos. Triples 65 pesos, with A/C 89 pesos. Quads 100 pesos. MC and Visa accepted.) **Casa de Huéspedes Miye,** Méndez 211 (tel. 2-04-20) has dimly-lit but brightly colored rooms and decent bathrooms. Also has floral hallway. All rooms have fans, but only one communal bathroom has hot water. (Check-out 1pm. Singles 25 pesos, with bath 30 pesos. Doubles 25 pesos, with bath 35 pesos.) Across from the church, **Hotel Jardín,** Av. Plaza de la Independencia 123 (tel. 2-00-27), at the end of Méndez, offers immaculate but less attractive dim blue rooms. All rooms have fans and baths, but no hot water. (Check-out noon. Singles 30 pesos. Doubles 40 pesos. Triples 45 pesos. Reservations can be made by phone.)

If you're not sated by the taco stands along Méndez, try **Restaurant Cheje** in Hotel Quintero, an air-conditioned but higher-priced alternative. (Open Mon.-Sat. 7am-noon and 2-9pm.) Better yet, hidden behind big green palms behind the church, is **El Mirador.** Blissful air-conditioning and a beautiful view over the Teapa river and the mountains feed your mind while you dine on chicken or meat (12-21 pesos) or seafood (17-23 pesos). (*Comida corrida* 15 pesos. Traveler's checks and credit cards accepted. Open Tues.-Sun. 8am-1am, Mon. 1pm-1am.)

Getting to Teapa from Villahermosa via public transport is easy: catch a first-class **Cristóbal Colón** bus (5 per day, 1hr., 5.50 pesos), or a more frequent second-class **Transportes Villahermosa-Teapa** bus from the Central Camionera off Grijalva (every 45min., 4am-8pm, 6 pesos). Be sure to arrive a ½hr. early to ensure seating.

The Transportes Villahermosa-Teapa bus lets you off at Teapa's main bus terminal on Méndez, from which local buses whisk you to either the spa or the caves. If you arrive by Cristóbal Colón, walk ½km up Romas toward the town's center; *combis* for the *grutas* leave from Calle Bastar on the right hand side of the church every 20min. They are clearly marked "Grutas" and cost .60 pesos. Taxis charge 8 pesos.

To reach El Azufre from Teapa, take the **Pichucalco** bus (every hr., 1 peso) from the bus terminal at Méndez and ask the driver to let you off at the short access road to the spa. To return to Teapa, walk back to the highway and flag down a returning bus. A taxi costs 15 pesos. Be sure to schedule a return time. Notoriously unreliable and unsafe **trains** connect Teapa to Mexico City (11:17am, 24hrs., 24 pesos) via Coatzalcoalcos (6hrs., 5.50 pesos), and Mérida (6:40pm, 25hrs., 15.50 pesos). The **train station office** (tel. 2-00-03) is open Monday through Friday from 8am to 4pm. To get there, take a taxi from the center.

In Teapa, money can be changed only at **Bancomer,** Av. Méndez 125 (tel. 2-00-38), one block from the church (Mon.-Fri. 9am-noon). The **post office** (tel. 2-02-54) is on Calle Manuel Buelta 212, two blocks down the street which starts across from the church. (Open Mon.-Fri. 9am-4pm and Sat. 9am-1pm.) **Postal code:** 86800 Long distance **telephone** *casetas* do not accept collect calls; you need to go back to Villahermosa. (**Telephone code:** 932.) **Farmacia Espíritu Santo,** Calle Dr. Ramón Medina 106 (tel. 2-00-93) is open daily 8am-10pm, but provides 24-hr. service if you ring the bell in the upper left-hand corner of the doorway. The **police** in the Palacio Municipal on Méndez also have 24-hr. service.

■■■ LA VENTA ARCHAEOLOGICAL SITE

In 600 BC La Venta thrived as the capital of the Olmecs, who were ancestors of the Maya, predecessors of the Aztecs, and founders of modern Mexico. Today, La Venta's glory encompasses one hotel, a few restaurants and two streets. The pole around which these miniscule attractions revolve is the stellar **Museo Arqueológico de La Venta,** paradoxically situated on the edge of the city.

Under a high thatched roof, the museum's single room holds exhibits about Olmec daily life, several large stone artifacts, and a few precision jade pieces. An outdoor trail circles the hill that once was the city's central pyramid, but most of the artifacts that once surrounded the hill have been moved to La Venta Park in Villahermosa. The climb to the top of the hill is arduous in the heat of the day, and the disheartening view from the crest encompasses acres of empty countryside.

To reach the museum, turn right as you leave the ADO station and head down **Benito Juárez,** La Venta's main thoroughfare. The street curves to the right around the Olmec head in the large plaza. Continue until you reach the large thatched roof on your right; two Olmec heads flank the entrance. La Venta makes a daytrip from either Coatzacoalcos or Villahermosa. **ADO** runs first-class buses to La Venta from Villahermosa, as does the second-class station. **Taxis** are at the town's cross street.

CHIAPAS

Chiapas is simply beautiful. Cortés had the Sierra de Chiapas in mind when he answered the question of what Mexico looked like by crumpling a piece of parchment and dropping it on the table. In these rugged green mountains, buses careen around hairpin turns above deep valleys before hurtling down into jungles on rutted roads. One of Mexico's most enchanting cities, San Cristóbal de las Casas, abides high in the mountains. If leaving Mexico City for Oaxaca or the Yucatán, consider a detour to Chiapas. If you planned on striking out for Guatemala and points south via the speedy but boring coastal route, meander instead through the inland mountains.

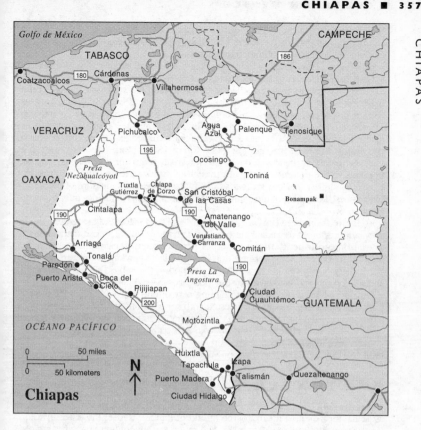

Chiapas

Chiapas is close to the Mayan heartland, the Guatemalan Petén, and the huge Lacandón Rainforest in the eastern part of the state, which hides spectacular ruins, notably Bonampak, Yaxchilán, and Palenque. It took a long while for the descendants of these cultures to mesh peacefully with the invading *ladinos*, and their relationship is still edgy to this day. Throughout Mexico's southernmost state, you're likely to hear diverse languages and find markets and other public places filled with *indígenas*, but mestizo members of the pseudo-aristocracy own most of the land and run businesses in villages where they themselves do not live, a trend sure to worsen with "modernization" and constitutional reform. The descendants of the conquerors are not as brutal as in times past, but they still have the upper hand in *chiapaneco* society.

Chiapas's many different *indígena* cultures were already at war with one another in 1523 when the *conquistador* Luis Marín entered Chiapas. The Spaniards took advantage of this discord by pitting the groups against one another. In 1528, Diego de Mazariego founded present-day San Cristóbal de las Casas as Ciudad Real. The "Royal City" was an administrative center for the *encomiendas*, quasi-feudal allocations which gave Spaniards the "rights" to the labor and tribute of a designated *indígena* community. Each *encomendero* also received a group of slaves to till the land; after being branded, these *indígenas* were worked to an early death. Fray Bartolomé de las Casas was one of the most outspoken advocates of the *indígena* cause long before it was in vogue. A friar of the powerful Dominican order, he permanently abandoned the status quo when he published *La destrucción de las indias* which painted a grim and unglorified portrait of the Spanish conquest. Largely through his efforts, chattel slavery was abolished by royal decree in the 1550s, but exploitation and abuse continued for centuries.

In 1712, a young Tzeltal girl in the village of Cancún had a vision of the Virgin Mary promising relief to the *indígenas* if they would attack the Spanish minority. The ensuing rebellion was quelled at Ocosingo and Huixtán, and the only other major show of resistance occurred a century-and-a-half later. In 1867, Agustina Gómez discovered some *piedras hablantes* in the Tzotzil village of Tzajalhemel. These "talking stones" attracted followers in such villages as San Juan Chamula, Chenalhó, Pantelhó, Tenejapa, and San Andrés. Soon the stones advised the people to rise against the Spaniards, and the Rebellion of 1869 began. The *indígena* forces were no match for the *ladinos*, who quickly crushed the uprising, killing many participants in the process. It was not until 1936, under the guidance of President Lázaro Cárdenas, that the *indígenas* of Chiapas received a measure of autonomy with the establishment of the *ejido*, a system of communal land titles now being dismantled by PRI technocrats.

Today, relations between *indígena* people and the *ladino* and mestizo neighbors they call *kashalán* are steadily improving, as trade in coffee, sugar, cattle and artisanry brings prosperity to the region. A new source of tension, however, is the increase in tourism. Some villagers don't take kindly to gawking foreigners, and they particularly object to photography as a violation of the subject's soul. In *indígena* areas, keep cameras packed away; buy postcards instead.

Outsiders who wear *indígena* clothing may offend natives here, since the patterns and styles of garments are invested with social meaning. If you buy clothing at a *tianguis* (*indígena* market), don't wear it until you've left the region. A second caution regarding clothing: *Chiapanecos*, especially in indigenous areas, are very conservative in dress. Keep shorts and other revealing garments in your backpack until you can feel the ocean spray on your face.

■■■ TUXTLA GUTIÉRREZ

When the Zoque founded a village near the remains of an ancient settlement known as Acala, they dubbed it Coyatocmo ("Land of Rabbits"). After the Aztec invasion, Coyatocmo was renamed Tuchtlán, and when the marauding Spaniards arrived, they "Castilianized" the Aztec name to Tuxtla.

In the 19th century a fresh struggle for power brought about yet another name change. Joaquín Miguel Gutiérrez, son of a Spanish-born merchant, was named governor of Chiapas just when the conservative *centralistas* gained control of Mexico. Liberals took up arms against this new sea of troubles, but by 1838 centralist forces had overwhelmed Gutiérrez and his men, who had holed up in a local church. Some say Gutiérrez was betrayed by one of his own men and dragged through the streets; others have it that he jumped from the church tower, wrapped in the Mexican flag. In any case he died in the fighting, and when the dust cleared 14 years later the city was renamed Tuxtla Gutiérrez in his honor.

Today, Tuxtla Gutiérrez (pop. 350,000) is the capital of Chiapas state and the transportation and commerce center for much of southern Mexico. Though renowned for its gold filigree and carved amber, Tuxtla also supplies the Republic with most of its molded plastics. The city's rapid commercial success has given it a modern gloss, but Tuxtla has endeavored to stem the tide of cinderblock construction with parks, museums and an excellent zoo. A palpable sense of life-enjoyment rules the plazas of Tuxtla; just because it isn't trapped in a 19th-century time warp doesn't mean Tuxtla's cultural muscles have atrophied.

ORIENTATION

Just west of the center of Chiapas state, Tuxtla Gutiérrez lies 289km south of Villa-hermosa via Route 195 and 190, and about 160km east-northeast of the Pacific coast via Route 190. San Cristóbal de las Casas is 84km east on Route 190.

Streets are labeled in Mexico's infamous numeric/geographic system. **Avenida Central** (sometimes called **Avenida 14 de Septiembre**) is the city's east-west axis. Perpendicular to this is **Calle Central** (called Calle Central Nte. above Avenida Central and Calle Central Sur below). Streets on either side of Calle Central are numbered beginning with 1 and increasing away from Calle Central. These north-south streets are designated Ote. or Pte. depending on whether they are east or west, respectively, of Calle Central. Street numbers on streets running east-west increase progressively away from Avenida Central and are designated Nte. or Sur. Occasionally, a street address will include two directions (e.g. 5 Sur Pte.), which locates it in one quadrant of the city. Expect to be confused.

Note that Avenida Central changes its name. To the east of Calle Central it is Avenida Central Ote., to the west Avenida Central Pte; about 15 blocks west of the center of town it becomes Boulevard Dr. Belisario Domínguez, and 11 blocks east Boulevard Ángel Albino Corzo.

The downtown area focuses on the **zócalo** at the intersection of Avenida Central and Calle Central, near most government offices and nightlife. Several bus stations and two airports serve Tuxtla Gutiérrez. To get to the *centro* from the **ADO station,** go left (north) on 9 Pte. for five blocks to Av. Central. Turn right and the *zócalo* is nine blocks ahead. The first-class **Cristóbal Colón bus station** stands at Calles 2 Nte. and 2 Pte. To get to the *zócalo*, go left on 2 Nte. Pte. for two blocks. The *zócalo* is two blocks to the right on Calle Central. The second-class **Autotransportes Tuxtla Gutiérrez station** is in a cul-de-sac near Calles 3 Sur and 7 Ote. From the station, turn right and then right again into the walled-in alley that doubles as a market. Make the first left onto 2 Sur and continue west to Calle Central—the *zócalo* is two blocks to the right. Travelers from Chiapa de Corzo often disembark at a small station on 3 Ote. between 2 and 3 Sur. As you face the street from the bus stop, head left for Av. Central, then left again for the *zócalo*.

If you're heading on to San Cristóbal de Las Casas (often referred to as Las Casas on bus schedules) or Comitán, buy your ticket as early as possible. Both first and second class buses tend to fill up quickly, especially in the afternoon and evening. Cristóbal Colón limits tickets to the number of seats; if they leave you out in the cold, head over to the second-class station.

Municipal buses (.50 pesos) operate from 5am to 11pm. Major lines run west on 2 Sur, east on 1 Sur, north on 11 Ote. and south on 12 Ote. *Colectivos* (.50 pesos) run frequently through the city from 6am to 10pm, but are sometimes difficult to catch. To snag one, stand on one of the corners near a blue *colectivo* sign and hold out fingers to indicate the number of passengers in your party. If the vehicle fails to stop, don't despair—it's probably already full. If it does stop, jump in fast; otherwise someone else will, leaving you to wait despondently on the corner for a taxi (4 pesos).

PRACTICAL INFORMATION

Tourist Offices: Federal and State Office, Blvd. Dr. Belisario Domínguez 950 (tel. and fax 2-45-35), at Edificio Plaza de Las Instituciones, 17 long blocks west of the *zócalo* just past the huge Bancomer building on the north side of the street. Excellent pocket maps of the city and the state, plus useful information on Bonampak and Yaxchilán. Excellent staff speaks English. Open Mon.-Fri. 8am-9pm.

Currency Exchange: Bánamex, 1 Sur Pte. (tel. 2-00-77), at Calle Central. MC and Visa cash advances. Open for exchange Mon.-Fri. 9am-1pm. **Bancomer,** Av. Central Pte. 314 (tel. 2-20-55), at 2 Pte. Open for exchange 9am-noon. Some local businesses may also change currency.

American Express: Pl. Bonampak (tel. 2-43-00), on Blvd. Dr. Belisario Domínguez across from the tourist office. English spoken. Open Mon.-Fri. 9am-2pm and 4-7pm, Sat. 9am-2pm.

Post Office: 1 Nte. and 2 Ote. (tel. 2-04-16), in the large building on the northeast corner of the *zócalo*. Open Mon.-Fri. 8am-7pm, Sat. 9am-1pm. **Postal code:** 29000.

Telegrams: 1 Nte. and 2 Ote. on the northeast corner of the *zócalo* next to the post office. Open daily 9am-8pm.

Telephones: *Casetas* scattered throughout town charge outrageous rates for international collect calls. Use the public phones on the *zócalo* instead. For direct calls, the public phones in Tuxtla take either coins or credit cards; none takes LADATEL phone cards. **Caseta,** 5 Ote. Sur 214 (tel. and fax 2-78-42), between 1 Sur and 2 Sur. 5 pesos for a 10-min. international collect call. 1 peso charge if the call isn't accepted. Open Mon.-Fri. 9am-2pm and 4-9pm, Sat 9am-1pm and 4-8pm. **Telephone code:** 961.

Airports: Aeropuerto Llano San Juan (tel. 2-29-20), about 22km west of the city on the Pan American Hwy. **Aeropuerto Aviacsa,** also called **Aeropuerto Francisco Sarabia** (tel. 5-01-11), 15km southwest of town. 2 groups of *combis* serve the airports (½hr., 11 pesos). One leaves from Hotel Humberto at Av. Central and 19 Pte. The other leaves from Hotel Jas at Calle Central Sur 665. Call 2-15-54 and they will pick you up. Grupo Aviacsa taxis (tel. 1-17-35) charge 15 pesos. **Mexicana,** Av. Central at 2 Pte. (tel. 2-00-20), and at Aeropuerto Llano San Juan (tel. 2-29-20), to Mexico City. **Aerocaribe,** at Blve. Belisario Domínguez 1934 (tel. 2-20-32), at Aeropuerto Aviacsa (tel. 5-15-30). To: Cancún via Villahermosa and Mérida; Mexico City; and Oaxaca. **Aviacsa,** Av. Central Pte. 144 (tel. 2-80-81), and at Aeropuerto Aviasca (tel. 5-07-97). To: Chetumal via Mexico City, and Guatemala City via Tapachula.

Bus Stations: Cristóbal Colón, 2 Nte. Pte. 268 (tel. 2-16-39), near 2 Pte. 1st class to: Comitán (16.50 pesos); San Cristóbal (8.50 pesos); Tapachula (38.50 pesos); Villahermosa (27 pesos); Mexico City (115 pesos). Also serves Salina Cruz and Mérida, among others. *Servicio plus*, with greater comfort and higher prices, is available for a number of destinations. **Autobuses del Oriente (ADO),** 9 Pte. at 5 Sur (tel. 2-87-25). Terminal open 6am-10pm. 1st class to: Puebla (8:45am, 81 pesos); Oaxaca (9pm, 44 pesos); San Andrés (8:45pm, 43 pesos); Acuyucán (9:30pm, 32.50 pesos). **Autotransportes Tuxtla Gutiérrez,** 2 Sur 712 (tel. 2-02-30), between 5 and 6 Ote. Long lines—arrive early. Luggage check available. Terminal open 3:30am-midnight. 1st class to: Ocosingo (12.70 pesos); Palenque (21 pesos) via Agua Azul (17 pesos). 2nd class to a host of destinations, including: San Cristóbal (6.20 pesos); Comitán (11.70 pesos); Comalapa (17.90 pesos); Tapachula (27 pesos); Palenque (4am, 29.60 pesos); Oaxaca (36 pesos); Mérida (1:30pm, 64 pesos); Chetumal (3:15pm, 59 pesos); Villahermosa (20.40 pesos). **Autotransportes Chiapa Tuxtla,** on 3 Ote. between 2 and 3 Sur. To Chiapa de Corzo (½hr., 1.50 pesos).

Taxis: (tel. 3-08-28), but you should have no trouble catching one in the street.

Car Rental: Budget, Blvd. Dr. Belisario Domínguez 2510 (tel. 5-06-72). Cars start at 84 pesos per day plus .65 pesos per km. Open daily 8am-7pm.

Supermarket: Super Aras Bazar, Av. Central Pte. 690 (tel. 2-70-40), at 6 Pte. Credit cards accepted. Open daily 9am-9pm.

Laundromat: Gaily II, 1 Sur Pte. 575 (tel. 2-34-52), at 5 Pte. 3kg for 12.90 pesos. Open Mon-Sat. 9am-2pm and 4-8:30pm.

Red Cross: 5 Nte. Pte. 1480 (tel. 2-00-96), on the west side of town. City-wide ambulance service. Open 24 hrs.

24-hr. Pharmacy: Farmacia 24 Horas, 1 Sur Pte. 716 at 6 Pte (tel. 3-34-20). No English spoken. Delivery service. Open 24 hrs.

Hospital: Hospital Regional Dr. Domingo Chamona, 9 Sur Ote. at 1 Ote. (tel. 2-14-40). 24-hr. emergency service.

Police: In the Palacio Municipal (tel. 2-16-76), at the north end of the *zócalo*. Go to the left upon entering the building. Open 24 hrs. No English.

ACCOMMODATIONS AND CAMPING

Hotel Regional San Marcos, 2 Ote. Sur at 1 Ote (tel. 3-19-40). The best budget hotel. Beautiful and gleeful rooms come with A/C, hot water, phones and irreproachable bathrooms with toilet seats and shower curtains. Check-out 1pm. Singles 50 pesos. Doubles 60 pesos. Triples 70 pesos. Quads 80 pesos. TV 5 pesos extra. AmEx, MC, and Visa accepted. Reservations can be made by phone.

Villas Deportivas Juvenil, Ángel Albino Corzo 1800 (tel. 3-34-05), next to yellow footbridge. A youth hostel. Take a *colectivo* east on Av. Central/Blvd. Corzo. Entrance is on Corzo; the entrance to the hostel proper is to the left of the youth center and café. Bunk beds in well-maintained single-sex dorms. Lockers provided. Communal bathrooms and showers are also clean and well-maintained. Pool available weekends and Mon.-Fri. 7:30am-9:30pm with prior permission. Breakfast (8-9:30am) 6 pesos. Lunch (2-3pm) 8 pesos. Dinner (7-8pm) 8 pesos. Check-out 9:30am. Reception hours 7am-8pm; get previous permission if you plan to arrive after 8pm. 11 pesos per person, plus a 10-peso deposit. Towels, sheets, and pillowcases included.

Hotel Huéspedes La Posada, 1 Sur Ote. 555 (tel. 2-29-32), between 4 and 5 Ote. Big rooms have huge closets for your fabulous new wardrobe. Fan and mosquito netting but no hot water. Bathrooms are large and clean. Check-out noon. Lockout after 11pm. Singles 20 pesos. Doubles 40 pesos. Triples 60 pesos. Reservations can be made by phone.

Posada Aguimar, 5 Pte. Sur 215 at 1 Sur. Run by 3 hospitable women, and centrally located. Rooms with pink walls are inviting and comfy. Decent bathrooms. Fans, but no hot water. Check-out 1pm. Singles 25 pesos. Doubles 32 pesos. Triples 38 pesos. Quads 45 pesos.

Hotel Avenida, Av. Central 244 (tel. 2-08-07), 1½ blocks from the *zócalo*, between 1 and 2 Pte. Clean, therapeutic rooms with lots of nice dark wood furniture, fans, TV in the lobby. Within earshot of the cathedral chimes and traffic jams on Av. Central. A step up from other hotels and more centrally located. Ask for a room off the street. Check-out 2pm. Singles 45 pesos. Doubles 55 pesos. Triples 65 pesos. Quads 75 pesos. For reservations, call and send 50% payment.

Casa de Huéspedes Ofelia, 2 Sur Ote. 643 (tel. 2-73-46), near 5 Ote. An older woman serves home cooking and maintains rooms. Communal facilities are in shape. No fans or hot water. Check-out noon. Singles 10 pesos. Doubles 20 pesos. Triples 30 pesos.

FOOD

Don't expect culinary miracles in Tuxtla. There are, nevertheless, plenty of budget eateries around town, plus a handful of good restaurants. Tuxtla's numerous juice bars serve *licuados* with such delectable ingredients as alfalfa leaves, spinach, soy flour and *taxcalate*. The marketplace *fondas* provide, as always, a penny-pinching alternative. The main market, cleaner and better-lit than most, is two blocks directly south of the *zócalo*. Another market with plenty of foodstands is on 11 Nte. Ote., near *Parque 5 de Mayo*.

Las Pichanchas, Av. Central Ote. 837 (tel. 2-53-51), about 8 blocks east of the *zócalo*, between 7 and 8 Ote. This *palapa* serves outstanding Chiapanecan food in an elegant setting at moderate prices. Live *marimba* band daily 2:30-5:30pm and 8:30-11:30pm; *ballet folklórico* 9-10pm. Chicken and meat dishes 16-22 pesos. Soups 3-7 pesos. *Comida grande de Chiapas* 16 pesos. Open daily noon-midnight.

Restaurante Vianda, 1 Ave. Sur Pte. 126B (tel. 1-25-93), 1 short block from *zócalo*. This airy, peach-colored eatery won't disappoint. *Comida corrida* includes soup, entrée, dessert, and beverage (10 pesos). Breakfast is also generous (6-13 pesos). Open Mon.-Sat. 7am-10pm, Sun. 8am-5pm.

Restaurante Vegetariano Nah-Yaxal, 6 Pte. 124 (tel. 3-36-16), just north of Av. Central. You walk in. It looks like a fast-food joint. You're not happy. But check out the hale and healthful entrees: 3-course *comida corrida* 14 pesos. Large vegetable salads 9 pesos. Huge fruit, yogurt, and nuts combos 7.80 pesos. Open Mon.-Sat. 7am-9:30pm.

Restaurant La Gran Muralla China, 2 Nte. Pte. 334 (tel. 3-08-99). Air conditioning and Chinese decor topped off by excellent service. Most entrees 18-20 pesos; seafood 19-35. Specials for 3 include appetizer, wonton soup, chop suey, chicken special *kong pin* and *kay tian* (23-34.50 pesos per person). Open daily noon-midnight.

Restaurante Los Arcos, Av. Central Pte. 806. Low arched doorways, funky wood chairs and dimness are the atmospherics. 3-course *comida corrida* 12 pesos. Fruit cocktails 5 pesos. The *servicio de abono* offers 3 complete meals per day for 22 pesos (Mon.-Sat. breakfast 7:30-10:30am, lunch 2-4pm, dinner 7-11pm.) Open daily 7:30am-11pm.

Restaurant Tuxtla, Calle Central Nte. 263 (tel. 2-06-48), 1 block from the *zócalo*. Don't let humble appearances discourage you; both food and service are good. Not a *gringo* in sight. *Comida corrida* including soup, rice, and entree 10 pesos. 3 *quesadillas* 7.50 pesos. Open daily 7am-5pm.

Pastelená La Pérgola, 1 Sur Pte. 604 (tel. 2-05-33) on the corner with 5 Pte. French posters add chic and indoor courtyard is a soothing oasis from hustle and bustle outdoors. Triple layer cakes (4 pesos) and coffee (2 pesos) make for a nice break. Open daily 10am-2pm and 4-9pm.

SIGHTS

Downtown Tuxtla is much more hectic than its smaller siblings throughout Chiapas. Unyielding traffic, crowded buses and polluted streets ward off many tourists. There are several escapes within and around the city, however, that preserve one's sanity in the heat and noise. Beautiful specimens of local fauna, feeling less like captives in their native habitats, make the **Miguel Alvarez del Toro Zoo** famous throughout Central America. You could easily spend two to three hours roaming through the cool vegetation and admiring the polecats, tapirs, scorpions, colorful birds and what-have-you. Best to visit in the morning while it's cool. (Open Tues.-Sun. 8:30am-5:30pm. Free.) To get to the zoo, take the "Cerro Hueco" bus, which leaves roughly every half hour from 1 Ote. between 6 and 7 Sur (.50 pesos). The bus traces an indirect and sometimes unbearably slow route to the zoo's front gate. To return to the center, catch a bus at the park's entrance.

The **Parque Madero** unfurls in the northeast part of town, at the intersection of 11 Ote. and 5 Nte. Its focal point is a large and modern theater, the **Teatro de la Ciudad Emilio Rabasa.** Films by Latin American directors and *ballet folklórico* shows dominate the schedule. Films and art shows are often free; prices for theater performances vary. Monthly schedules for city- and state-wide events are available at the tourist information center. Northeast of the theater is the open-air **Teatro Bonampak,** particularly memorable on Sunday evenings when the glamour of Mexican national costumes reveals itself in a three-hour folk dance performance (5-8pm; free).

Between the two theaters is a children's **amusement park** (open Tues.-Sun. 9am-10pm), and across from its parking lot a public swimming pool (open Tues.-Sun. 9am-6pm, 5 pesos). The big hotels will often let you use their pools if you order a drink. A broad concourse, demarcated by fountains and bronze busts of famous Mexicans, leads west of the theater past the **Museo Regional de Chiapas,** which primarily displays regional archaeological finds. (Open Tues.-Sun. 9am-4pm. Admission 10 pesos. Free Sun.) Farther down the concourse, at the **Jardín Botánico Dr. Faustino Miranda,** you can stroll through colorful and curly arrangements of Chiapanecan flora. (Open Tues.-Sun. 6am-6pm. Free.) Near the center, **Cinema Vistarama,** on the corner of 1 Sur and 5 Ote., shows mostly North American films. (At 4pm, 5:30pm, 7:45pm, and 9:30pm, 7 pesos). To work off those tacos and tone the Tecate-belly, hit the **Gimnasio Chiapas** on 1 Ote. Sur 379 (tel. 3-17-70). (Workout machines Mon.-Fri. 6am-10pm, Sat. 6am-8pm. 5 pesos per visit.)

If you're interested in the ruins at Bonampak, visit the **Hotel Bonampak,** Blvd. Dr. Domínguez 180. Its reproductions of the famous murals from Bonampak, the lost Mayan city of the Lacandón jungle, are infinitely clearer and brighter than the originals. In fact, many of the postcard photographs of the murals are actually taken here rather than at the site itself. The hotel is always open; to get there, walk or take a *colectivo* west on Av. Central until it becomes Blvd. Dr. Domínguez past the federal tourist office—the hotel is on the right.

Disco nightlife in Tuxtla centers around the big hotels. Among the most popular discos are **Sheik** in Hotel Flamboyant, Dr. Belisario Domínguez 1081 (open Thurs.-Sat. 9pm-2am, cover 20 pesos); **Colors** in Hotel Arecas, across from Flamboyant (open Thurs.-Sun. 9am-2pm, cover 15 pesos).

■ Near Tuxtla Gutiérrez

Head north on 11 Ote. Nte. toward a string of five lookout points (*miradores*) over **Cañón El Sumidero,** one of the world's most spectacular canyons. The sites are named—in order—**La Ceiba, La Coyota, Los Tepehuajes, El Roblar** and **Los Chiapas** (also called La Atalaya after the restaurant there). La Coyota commands the most awesome view. If you don't have your own car, transportation to the *miradores* is expensive. **Combis Cañón del Sumidero** don't regularly go as far as the lookout points, but will make the trip on request. A dropoff at one of the lookouts costs 10 pesos. However, if you want them to take you to several points, wait and bring you back, the cost is a rather steep 35 pesos per hour. Taxis charge similar rates. To catch a *combi* for the trip, go to the corner of 1 Nte. Ote. and 2 Ote. and wait for one to pass by (there is no office, but they pass frequently).

The excursion from Tuxtla to the **Cascadas de Aguacero** is popular with Mexican tourists. Buses heading west to Cocozocoautla will drop you off at the access road for the waterfalls; a half-hour hike brings you to a stairway, which ascends to the beautiful cataract. Daring visitors to the secluded spot often bathe nude in its cold water.

■■■ CHIAPA DE CORZO

It's said that when the Spaniards came to Chiapa de Corzo in 1528 asking for the town keys, mobs of *chiapanecos* threw themselves into the Cañón El Sumidero to escape slavery under the conquistadors. Nowadays this small town greets the few *extranjeros* who pass through in a calmer fashion; shelter and nourishment are provided by a lone hotel and a few breezy riverside restaurants. The main attraction of the town is the magnificent canyon, El Sumidero, which meanders through town with an audience of playful monkeys, occasional crocodiles, innumerable shades of green and waterfalls dissipating themselves into mist. Return from the sublimity to a town well-endowed with the familiar.

Practical Information Chiapa de Corzo (pop. 50,000) sits on the Río Grijalva, 10km east of Tuxtla Gutiérrez and 74km west of San Cristóbal de las Casas. Most points of interest lie near the sizable **zócalo** (also called **Plaza Ángel Albino Corzo**), which is bounded on the north by 21 de Octubre, on the east by La Mexicanidad, on the south by Julián Grajales and on the west by 5 de Febrero. One block south of the plaza are the city's cathedral and market; a block further flows the river. **Boats** to Cañón El Sumidero leave from the *embarcadero* (dock) at the end of 5 de Febrero, two blocks south of the *zócalo*. The **Cristóbal Colón station** is on 21 de Octubre, one block east of the plaza. **Buses** and *combis* to and from Tuxtla Gutiérrez stop half a block east of the plaza, in an alley on the north side of 21 de Octubre.

Chiapa de Corzo does little to ease the suffering of the lonely tourist. Fortunately, metropolitan Tuxtla Gutiérrez is only a half-hour, 1.50-peso *combi* ride away. Get **tourist info** in Tuxtla Gutiérrez. Practical questions can be answered by the police station (see below). **Bancomer,** on the eastern side of the *zócalo* (tel. 6-03-20), exchanges currency Mon.-Fri. 9-11am. The **post office,** Calle Urbina at Vidal (tel. 6-00-30), is open Mon.-Fri. 9am-6pm. **Postal code:** 29160. **Telephone code:** 968. The **bus station, Cristóbal Colón,** 21 de Octubre 26 (tel. 6-00-20), 1 block east of the *zócalo,* serves San Cristóbal (7:30am-5pm, 7 pesos, buy tickets one day in advance). *Combis* go to Tuxtla Gutiérrez (½hr., 1.50 pesos). **Farmacia San Marcos,** 21 de Octubre 102, on the northeast corner of the *zócalo* among other pharmacies, is open daily 7am-2:30pm and 4-8:30pm.The **police station** is in the Palacio Municipal (tel. 6-02-26), on the northeast side of the *zócalo.* (Open 24 hrs. No English spoken.)

Accommodations and Food Hotel Los Angeles, Julián Grajales 2 (tel. 6-00-48), at La Mexicanidad on the southeast corner of the *zócalo*, is the only game in town. Fortunately, it's also cheap, clean and attractive. Colonial courtyard and arched corridors lead into huge rooms with stained glass and carved dark wood furniture. Bathrooms are respectably clean and include fans. Three rooms don't have windows. (Check-out 1pm. Singles 30 pesos. Doubles 50 pesos. Triples 60 pesos. For reservations, write or call.)

The few stylish restaurants on the eastern side of the *zócalo* are upscale and pricey. A better bet are the more informal and more jovial *palapa* restaurants along the river. **Restaurant Nancy** at the waterfront offers small seafood cocktails (12 pesos) and fish filets (16 pesos) served with a hot live *marimba* band. (Open Mon.-Fri. 8am-8pm. 10% discount for *Let's Go* users.) Score some more *marimba,* along with a view of the river, at the open-air **Restaurant Comitán.** (Pork ribs 10 pesos; an order of 6 tacos 5 pesos. *Comida corrida* with entree, beans, flour tortillas, cheese, and *refresco* 12 pesos. Open daily 8am-8pm.) **Mesón Los Corredores,** on the southwest corner of the *zócalo,* is a recent arrival that serves regional cuisine in a pleasant arched colonial building. (*Cochito horneado* 15 pesos. *Lengua de res guisada* 15 pesos. *Comida corrida* with soup and rice 10 pesos. Open 9am-8:30pm daily.)

Sights Most visitors look blindly past Chiapa de Corzo's colonial comeliness, viewing the town as the departure point for boat tours of the nearby **Cañón El Sumidero.** The two-hour, 47km trip down the Río Grijalva and back provides a dramatic view of the immense cliffs on both sides, as well as of the alligators and exotic birds that teem in the Grijalva's murky green waters and encroaching forest.

Speedboats journey through the canyon along the tranquil waterway formed by the **Netzahualcóyotl Dam,** the biggest electric power station in Latin America. From Chiapa, boats head up the river, passing under the road to Tuxtla Gutiérrez on the way. After the bridge, the banks of the river grow steeper, the cornfields and grazing land disappear, and the Grijalva fills the narrowing chasm, sojourning briefly inside caverns and under waterfalls. The most spectacular waterfall, the **Árbol de Navidad** (Christmas Tree—but why?), plunges over a series of rock terraces and disintegrates into a fine mist that envelops the boat.

Boats leave from Chiapa's *embarcadero* daily 7am-4:30pm. Cruises cost 18-25 pesos per person and boats leave as soon as there are enough people willing to share the cost. Usually at least 10 people pack into each *lancha.* You can also take boats up the canyon from Cahuaré, where the highway to Tuxtla Gutiérrez crosses the river near the island resort of the same name. A *colectivo* boat also runs from Cahuaré with similar prices. The trip is popular year-round, especially during *Semana Santa* and Christmas holidays, but it's best to go at the height of the rainy season in August when all four waterfalls gush their hardest.

Most of Chiapa de Corzo's rich architectural treasures date from the city's colonial period. The **zócalo** contains two colonial structures: a small clock tower and a fountain shaped like the crown of Queen Isabel of Spain. This famous Moorish fountain, often called **La Pila,** brought the town fresh drinking water during an epidemic in

1562. The fountain taps 5km of underground waterways. Inside the fountain, tile plaques recount some of the area's colonial history.

The red and white **Catedral de Santo Domingo** (open daily 6am-2pm and 4-6:30pm) sits one block south of the *zócalo* near Río Grijalva. The most famous of the four bells dangling in its tower, "Teresa de Jesús," is named after a mystic Spanish saint.

Chiapa de Corzo is well known for its lacquerwork and is one of the five places in Mexico where it is still produced. The **Museo de la Laca,** in the ex-convent adjacent to the Catedral de Santo Domingo, celebrates this handicraft. The museum has some interesting festival masks and pottery, and will shelter those unaccustomed to the afternoon *siesta* or the summer rains. (Open Mon. 9am-1pm and 4-7pm, Tues.-Sun. 9am-7pm. Free.) You can join one of the ongoing lacquering lessons (materials and tools included) that run for free Monday through Friday from 4 to 7pm.

On the second floor of the **Palacio Municipal's** main entrance, in the *zócalo*, a map of the city diagrams the Battle of 21 de Octubre, in which the revolutionary Colonel Urdina led local forces against Don Juan Ortega. The mural on the wall of the central stairway gives a fascinating account of the battle.

Used as forts by the revolutionaries, the three churches portrayed in the mural overlook the city and are a hop, skip, and a jump away. **San Gregorio** is visible from the edge of the *zócalo* farthest from the river; take any road uphill from the *zócalo* and bear right toward the white church for the best overview of the town. Facing the river, the ruined **Convento de San Sebastián,** and the dome of another large, colonial church loom to the left. Visit the convent in early morning, before the mob arrives. Because San Gregorio is seldom attended and San Sebastián has been abandoned altogether, both have become popular as late-night partying spots.

Chiapa's **Fiesta de San Sebastián** (Jan. 16-22), is most famous for *Los Parachicos*—men in heavy costumes and stifling masks dancing dawn-to-dusk under the hot Chiapas sun. The fiesta's *gran finale* is the mock **Combate Naval** between "Spaniards" and "*Indios*." More a beauty contest than a battle, the *combate* features elaborately decorated boats, costumed sailors, and fireworks.

■■■ SAN CRISTÓBAL DE LAS CASAS

If San Cristóbal isn't on your list of must-see spots, you're using the wrong list. Swept up into the lush, cloud-bedecked mountains around the Valley of Hueyzacatlán, high in the Sierra de Chiapas, San Cristóbal de las Casas outdoes virtually every other town in the Republic in terms of sheer beauty, and here, *indígena* and European influences merge more successfully than anywhere else. Trendsetters populate the city's elegant cafés, while barefoot Tzotzil women fill downtown streets; local merchants, dressed in the bright patterns of their ancestors, ply their trade at the Sunday market.

The architecture of San Cristóbal is all-out colonial, and those buildings not constructed by the Spanish are artful imitations of the tile-roofed structures that the *conquistadores* wove around courtyards and gardens. Some *indígena* men have switched from their traditional *sarapes* to Western clothing, but most women continue to wear brilliantly embroidered skirts, *huipiles* (blouses) and grand *rebozo* scarves which complement the bright ribbons braided into their long hair. Most of the indigenous people of the *chiapaneco* highlands speak the Mayan tongues of Tzeltal or Tzotzil, although Chol, Tojolabal and sometimes Zoque or Lacandón are also heard.

Founded by the *conquistadores* in 1528, San Cristóbal de las Casas was once the colonial capital of the region. Three-fifths of its name honors the 16th-century bishop Fray Bartolomé de las Casas, the "Protector of the Indians," who opposed the oppression of indigenous peoples. Today, the city is often referred to (especially on bus schedules) simply as San Cristóbal.

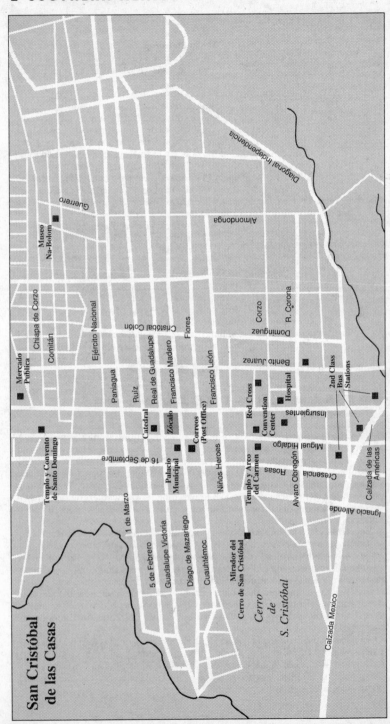

San Cristóbal
de las Casas

ORIENTATION

San Cristóbal de las Casas lies in a valley 2100m above sea level, 85km east of Tuxtla Gutiérrez, 85km northwest of Comitán, 98km west of Ocosingo and 255km west of the ruins of Palenque. **Route 190,** the Pan American Highway, cuts east from Tuxtla Gutiérrez, touches the southern edge of San Cristóbal and then heads southeast to Comitán and Ciudad Cuauhtémoc at the Guatemalan border.

The first- and second-class **bus stations** are on the Pan American Highway at the southern edge of town. The most convenient route to *el centro* is along Av. Insurgentes. From Cristóbal Colón the *zócalo* is seven blocks to the right of the exit. From either of the second-class bus stations, walk east two or three blocks on any cross street and turn left on Insurgentes.

Since San Cristóbal is a popular destination for tourists, most of whom travel by bus, book seats as far in advance as possible during the Christmas season and *Semana Santa*. At other times, reservations one day in advance are sufficient.

Most of San Cristóbal's clearly labeled streets fall into a neat grid. The **zócalo**, also known as **Plaza 31 de Marzo,** is the city center. The four cardinal directions are indicated by prominent landmarks around town: the church and former convent of Santo Domingo to the north, the blue-trimmed Templo de Guadalupe on the hill to the east, the Cristóbal Colón first-class bus station to the south and the Templo de San Cristóbal on the mountaintop to the west.

It is helpful to think of the city as four quadrants, since all streets change names when crossing imaginary north-south and east-west axis centered at the *zócalo*. **Avenida Insurgentes** connects the town center to the Pan American Highway, and becomes **Avenida Utrilla** past the *zócalo*. Municipal buses and *colectivos* criss-cross town with destinations indicated on the window; just wave to catch one (.50 pesos). Taxis (tel. 8-23-53) line up along the north side of the *zócalo* by the cathedral. Standard fare within town is 3.50 pesos; prices to nearby villages are negotiable. In town, you probably won't need a taxi unless you're carrying leaden bags.

PRACTICAL INFORMATION

Tourist Office: On the western edge of the *zócalo* (tel. 8-06-60), under the Palacio Municipal. Well-informed staff speaks English and distributes maps of San Cristóbal. Information available about nearby villages. Two bulletin boards have valuable information on budget accommodations, sight-seeing, horseback tours, cultural events and cycles of the moon and tide. Open Mon.-Sat. 8am-8pm, Sun. 9am-2pm. **Information Booths,** at the Cristóbal Colón 1st class bus terminal on the northeast corner of the *zócalo*, and at the Iglesia Santo Domingo. Maps and brochures and good directions. Some English spoken. All open Mon.-Fri. 9am-2pm and 4-8pm, Sat.-Sun. 9am-2pm.

Travel Agencies: Agencia de Viajes Blanquita, Real de Guadalupe 55b (tel. 8-03-80), offers trips to Palenque (183 pesos), Cañón del Sumidero and Lagos de Montebello (131.50 pesos). Open Mon.-Sat. 9am-2pm and 4-8pm. **Viajes Lacantun,** Francisco I. Madero 16 (tel. 8-25-88), ½ block east of the *zócalo*, offers similar trips and prices. They also have trips on horseback (60 pesos per person, minimum of 4 people). Open Mon.-Fri. 9am-2pm and 4-7pm, Sat. 9am-1pm.

Currency Exchange: Bancomer (tel. 8-01-37), on the south side of the *zócalo* . Changes a maximum of US$600. Visa cash advances 24 hrs. at ATMs. Open for exchange Mon.-Fri. 9-11am. **Banco Internacional,** Mazariegos 6 (tel. 8-30-96), 1 block west of the *zócalo*. Open for exchange 9-12:30am. **Casa de Cambio Lacantun,** Real de Guadalupe 12-A (tel. 8-30-63), 1 block east of the *zócalo*. They also sell LADATEL phone cards. Open Mon.-Sat. 9am-2pm and 4-8pm, Sun. 9am-2pm.

Post Office: Cuauhtémoc at Crescencio Rosas (tel. 8-07-65), 1 block southwest of the *zócalo*. Open Mon.-Fri. 8am-7pm, Sat.-Sun. 9am-1pm. **Postal code:** 29200.

Telephones: Collect calls can be placed from public pay phones at the Palacio Municipal. Some of these phones take LADATEL phone cards, which can be bought at the Casa de Cambio Lacantun (see Currency Exchange above). **Caseta**

at Autotransportes Tuxtla (tel. 8-27-28). 6 pesos for international collect calls. Open Mon.-Sat. 8am-9pm, Sun. 8am-2:30pm. **Telephone code:** 967.

Telegrams: Mazariegos 29 (tel. 8-42-71), 2½ blocks west of the *zócalo*. Open for telegrams Mon.-Fri. 9am-8pm, Sat. 9am-1pm. For money orders Mon.-Fri. 9am-5:30pm, Sat. 9am-noon.

Bus Stations: Cristóbal Colón, Pan American Hwy. at Insurgentes (tel. 8-02-91), seven blocks south of the *zócalo*. Station open daily 6am-9pm. Public toilets. 1st class to: Tuxtla Gutiérrez (8.50 pesos), Comitán (8.50 pesos), Villahermosa (noon, 32 pesos); also Pochutla, Tehuantepec, Juchitan, Puerto Escondido, Tonalá, Pijijiapan, Cuauhtémoc, Chiapa de Corzo, Oaxaca, and many other towns. The only bus to Oaxaca leaves at 5:15pm and is usually packed; buy tickets 1 to 2 days in advance. *Servicio plus* to: Mexico City (4pm, 164 pesos), Mérida (9:15am, 8pm, 87 pesos), Palenque (9:15am and 8pm, 23 pesos). 2nd-class **Autotransportes Lacandonia,** Pino Suárez 11 (tel. 8-14-55), on the Pan American Hwy., 2 blocks southwest of Insurgentes; enter by the sign for "Fonda Chonita." Open daily 4am-8pm. To: Ocosingo (2hrs., 6 pesos), Mérida (14hrs., 61 pesos), Palenque (5hrs., 16 pesos), Chetumal (8pm, 14hrs., 57 pesos). 2nd-class **Autotransportes Tuxtla,** on Ignacio Allende, 1 block north of the hwy., 3 blocks west of Insurgentes. Terminal open 5am-9pm; baggage storage 8am-4pm. To: Tuxtla Gutiérrez (6 pesos), Comitán (5.50 pesos), Tapachula (noon, 21.50 pesos). 2nd-class **Soc. de Autotransportes de Pasaje,** on the Pan American Hwy. (tel. 8-44-03), near the intersection with Insurgentes. Terminal open 4:30am-11pm. Free baggage check. To Motocintla and Comalapa.

Car Rental: Budget, Mazariegos 36 (tel. 8-18-71), 2 blocks west of the *zócalo* between Allende and 12 de Octubre. Prices start at 120 pesos per day, including insurance and unlimited mileage. Open Mon.-Sat. 8am-2pm and 3-8pm, Sun. 8am-noon and 5-7pm.

Bike Rental: Bicitours, Insurgentes 57-D (tel. 8-41-57), at the Centro Bilingüe. 5 pesos per hr., 25 pesos per 8hrs., 30 pesos per 24 hrs., 150 pesos per week. Open daily 9am-1:30pm and 4-9pm.

English Bookstore: Librería Soluna, Real de Guadalupe 13-B, 1 block east of the *zócalo*. English travel guides and guides to archaeological sites. Miniscule selection of other new and used English books. Open Mon.-Sat. 9:30am-8:30pm, Sun. 1:30-8:30pm. Or try **La Pared** at El Puente Cultural Center at Real de Guadalupe #55. New, used, and even rented books bought and sold. Open Mon.-Sat. 10am-7pm.

Laundromat: Orve, Belisario Dominiquez 5 (8-18-02). Wash and dry 4 pesos per kg. Open daily 8am-8pm.

Supermarket: Jovel, Genreal Utrilla 3 (tel. 8-07-74), on the northeast side of the *zócalo*. Open Mon.-Sat. 8:30am-8:30pm, Sun. 9am-2pm.

Markets: Between Utrilla and Domínguez, 7 blocks north of the *zócalo*. Open daily 6am-2pm. Best selection on Sat. Big open-air artisan market forms daily around the Santo Domingo Church, 5 blocks north of the *zócalo* on Utrilla. Open daily 8am-3pm.

Red Cross: Ignacio Allende 57 (tel. 8-07-72), 3 blocks south of the Pan American Hwy. 24-hr. emergency service. No English spoken.

24-hr. Pharmacy: Farmacia Regina, Mazariegos at Crescencio Rosas (tel. 8-02-41). Open 24 hrs.

Hospital: Hospital Regional, Insurgentes 24 (tel. 8-07-70), 4 blocks south of the *zócalo*, by the Church of Santa Lucía in *Parque Fray Bartolomé*. Emergency room open 24 hrs.

Police: In the Palacio Municipal (tel. 8-05-54), on the west side of the *zócalo*. No English spoken.

ACCOMMODATIONS AND CAMPING

Because San Cristóbal has long attracted impecunious Europeans and vacationing Mexican families, inexpensive hotels fill the streets. The best budget hotels are usually some distance from the center of town; more expensive and more convenient ones are clustered on Insurgentes, near the *zócalo*, and on Real de Guadalupe east of the *zócalo*. At this altitude, there are few bugs, but hot water and blankets are necessary as nights can be very cold.

Hotel Villa Betania, Francisco I. Madero 86 (tel. 8-44-67), 4½ blocks east of the *zócalo*. Spacious, comfortable rooms with pink walls, fireplaces, luxurious wooly blankets and immaculate private bathrooms. Hot water that will reaffirm your belief in a higher power available 24 hrs. Check-out noon. 25 pesos per person. U.S. dollars and traveler's checks accepted when there's enough change.

Casa de Huéspedes Margarita, Real de Guadalupe 34 (tel. 8-09-57), 1½ blocks east of the *zócalo*. Pretty blue and white interior and charm galore indoors. Beds come with 2 wool blankets. Spotless communal bathrooms. Hot water 24 hrs. Not all rooms have windows. Check-out 1pm. Singles 20 pesos. Doubles 35 pesos. Triples 48 pesos. Dollars and Visa accepted. Reservations can be made by phone.

Posada Andrianita, 1 de Marzo 29, at the intersection with 5 de Mayo, 2 blocks west and 3 blocks north of the *zócalo*. Welcoming rooms with wood walls and big comfy beds around a lovely, gardeny courtyard. Some rooms have rugs. Miniscule but clean communal bathrooms have hot water 24 hrs. Singles 25 pesos. 1-bed doubles 30 pesos. Triples 40 pesos.

Posada Cerillo, Belisario Domínguez 27 (tel. 8-12-83), 1 block east of the *zócalo* on Real de Guadalupe and 3½ blocks north. Rooms off a quiet courtyard with dozens of green plants have peach walls and clean communal bathrooms. Hot water 24 hrs. Check-out noon-1pm. Singles 20 pesos. 1-bed doubles 30 pesos. 2-bed doubles 35 pesos. Rooms with 2 double beds for up to 4 people 40 pesos. Reservations can be made by phone.

Posada El Candil, Real de Mexicanos 7 (tel. 8-27-55), 2 blocks west of the Iglesia de Santo Domingo. Bright, large rooms surround an uninteresting courtyard, but budget travelers from around the globe provide plenty of company. Communal facilities are decent and have hot water round-the-clock. Curfew 11pm, but knock after hours. Check-out noon. Singles 20 pesos. Doubles 25 pesos. Triples 30 pesos. Dollars accepted. Reservations can be made by phone.

Hospedaje, Madero 83 (tel. 8-04-40). Cheapest decent rooms in town. Rooms are somewhat bare, but are spacious and pleasant. Clean bathrooms. Hot water 24 hrs. Upstairs rooms get a bit more light, and 3 have balconies. Check-out noon. Singles 15 pesos. Doubles 25 pesos. Triples 40 pesos. Mexican breakfast included. Reservations can be made by phone. Kitchen may be used if you ask nicely.

Posada Tepeyac, Real de Guadalupe 40 (tel. 8-01-18), near Cristóbal Colón, a few blocks east of the *zócalo*. 2nd- and 3rd-floor rooms are much brighter and happier than 1st-floor ones, but all have wooly-mammoth blankets. Some much cleaner than others. Hot water 24 hrs. Check-out noon. Singles 20 pesos, with bath 25 pesos. Doubles 25 pesos, with bath 35 pesos. Triples 50 pesos. Reservations can be made by phone.

Rancho San Nicolás, on the extension of Francisco León, 1km east of town (tel. 8-00-57). Rooms, camping and trailer park in a bucolic setting. Often full, especially during the high season (Dec.-March); call in advance. Bathrooms with 24-hr. hot water and trailer sewage hook-ups are tolerably hygienic when working. 1pm check-out is flexible. Motor homes to large trailers 20-25 pesos. Camping with vehicle 10 pesos for 1 person; without vehicle 6 pesos for 1, 10 pesos for 2. Rooms 15 pesos for 1 person. Horse rental 25 pesos per hr.

Na-Bolom, Vicente Guerrero 33 (tel. 8-14-18), at the end of Chiapa de Corzo in the northeast section of town. The private home/museum (see Sights) triples as a hotel. 13 fabulously furnished rooms with fireplaces, each decorated in the style of one of the *indígena*. Enormous, ranch-style meals. Breakfast (10 pesos), lunch (15 pesos) and supper (20 pesos). Singles US$35. Doubles US$45. Triples US$50. Guests get free admission to the museum tour and film. Write or call for reservations.

FOOD

Thousands of villagers flowing in and out of the city every day buoy a street-vendor economy. The street food is cleaner than in most Mexican towns, but proceed with caution nonetheless. Pastries, chili popcorn, fresh mango, coconut slices and all kinds of *pasas* (pickled fruits) are available on the *zócalo* and in the *mercado*. A number of *dulcerías* offer such delicacies as candied orange peel and tiny cookies with raspberry centers. The *fondas* near the Pan American Highway and the bus stations, and in San Cristóbal's *mercado*, serve those with few pesos to spare.

Centro Cultural El Puente, Real de Guadalupe #55 (tel. 8-22-50), 2 blocks from the *zócalo*. It's a cafe! It's a language school! It's a cinema! It's an all-round cultural *centro* that provides fine company in a lovely, high-ceilinged, balustraded courtyard. Cappucino (3 pesos). Breakfast (5-7 pesos). Lunch (6.50-12 pesos). Open Mon.-Sat. 8am-9:30pm. Check for movie schedule.

Casa de las Imágenes, on Domínguez between Flores and Real de Guadalupe (tel. 8-03-70). A small indoor courtyard with a dozen tables and a shelf of discount books. An intellectual refuge for 3 photographers responsible for the black-and-white "Casa de las Imágenes" postcards you have seen throughout México. Accompanying bookstore, photo and art gallery. Coffee 2-3 pesos. Pies 4.50 pesos. Soups 5-7.50 pesos. Pastas 9-12 pesos. Traveler's checks, AmEx, MC, and Visa accepted. Open daily 8:30am-10:30pm.

La Salsa Verde, on 20 de Noviembre 7, one block north of the *zócalo*. Giant open grill cooks up every imaginable type of taco from cactus to cow udder. Tacos *al pastor* for the less adventurous are superb. And besides plenty of *salsa verde* there's also red and yellow hot sauces. Open daily 2-10:30pm.

Restaurante El Teatro, 1 de Marzo 8 (tel. 8-31-49), upstairs, north of the cathedral. Jazz, candles, posters of French plays and a view of the city roofs make for a truly classy and pleasant atmosphere. *Filetes de res* 27-29 pesos. Crêpes with mushrooms 12.50 pesos, chocolate crepes 7.50 pesos. Pastas 8.50-16 pesos. Traveler's checks, AmEx, MC, and Visa accepted. Open daily 11am-10pm.

Restaurant Las Estrellas, Escuadrón 201-2B, across from the Iglesia Santo Domingo. Packed with tourists and more tourists. When the live music begins (8pm) you might have trouble finding a seat. Spinach quiche with salad 7.50 pesos. Enchiladas 7-7.50 pesos. Chicken 12 pesos. Dollars accepted. Open daily 9am-11pm.

Cafetería y Lonchería Palenque, Insurgentes 40, 1½ blocks from the bus station. Relax, sip coffee (1-2.50 pesos) and watch TV; during commercials check out the local goods on display. *Huevos rancheros* 7 pesos. Sandwiches 2.50 pesos. *Pollo en mole* with rice, beans, cheese, and *tortillas* 8.50 pesos. Dollars and traveler's checks accepted in small denominations, when there's change. Open daily 8am-6pm.

Restaurant Tuluc, Insurgentes 5 (tel. 8-20-90), between Cuauhtémoc and Niños Héroes. Pleasant. Cheap. While you wait for your food, check out the *artesanías* on display. *Chiapaneca* breakfast including orange juice, bread, tamales, and coffee 9 pesos. *Menú del día* including *aperitivo*, soup, rice, entree, pastry, and coffee 15 pesos. *Filete Tuluc* 15 pesos. Open daily 6am-10pm.

Restaurante Madre Tierra, on Insurgentes at Domínguez (tel. 8-42-97), 2½ blocks south of the *zócalo*. Much of the clientele is tourists and the "beautiful people." Understandably popular by virtue of the excellent cuisine. Hang in one of the back rooms for more privacy. Great for a meal (6-13 pesos), a sandwich (6.50-7.50 pesos), or just a cup of coffee (2-3 pesos) and a delicious dessert (3-4.50 pesos). Open daily 9am-8pm.

Super Pollo, Domínguez 3 (tel. 8-14-24), 1 block east of the *zócalo*. Eat in or take out. Exceptionally tasty fowl. Roasted ¼ chicken 10 pesos. *Comida corrida* 16 pesos. 4-person plate of *antojitos* 60 pesos. Open daily 7am-10pm.

SIGHTS

Ever since the Spanish built it in the 16th century, the **zócalo** has been the physical and spiritual center of town. Colonial buildings border the plaza on three sides, and the **cathedral,** its patterned wooden roof supported by white Corinthian columns, overlooks the fourth. Consecrated in 1528, the building now tends a bevy of the devout among its pews and a flock of chirping birds in its rafters. The cathedral's baroque façade rises on one side of a small pedestrian park. (Open daily 6am-7pm.)

Utrilla and Real de Guadalupe, the two streets radiating from the northeastern corner of the *zócalo,* contain colorful shops which sell *típico* attire for less than the market stands or neighboring villages. On Saturday mornings, locals do their weekly shopping. Watch, listen, and learn; these experts wrote the book on bargaining.

North on Utrilla, beyond the **Iglesia de la Caridad,** sits the **Iglesia y Ex-convento de Santo Domingo.** Gold leaf covers the interior of the Santo Domingo, running in elaborate patterns up walls, around portraits, and over the exquisite pulpit in the left nave. The church's intricate baroque façade, though faded, stands out from the rest of the unremarkable exterior. A pair of two-headed eagles form the crest of the Spanish empire on the facade. (Open daily 7am-8pm.)

Stashed in Santo Domingo's *ex-convento* is **Sna Jolobil** ("House of Weaving" in Tzeltal), a cooperative of 1500 weavers from 10 Tzotzil and Tzeltal villages in the *chiapaneco* highlands. The members' objective is to preserve and revitalize their ancestral weaving techniques. High-quality woven and embroidered items are sold in Sna Jolobil's showroom. (Tel. and fax 8-26-46. *Huipiles* from 80 pesos, *ponchos* from 250 pesos, ribboned hats 150 pesos. Open Mon.-Sat. 9am-2pm and 4-6pm.)

If Sna Jolobil's prices are too high, you might try another cooperative, **J'pas Jolov-iletic,** Ave. 16 de Septiembre 21A (tel. 8-28-48), on the opposite side of Santo Domingo from Sna Jolobil. Open Mon.-Sat. 9am-1pm and 4-7pm, Sun. 9am-1pm.

Next door to Sna Jolobil, the **Instituto Nacional de Antropología e Historia Centro Cultural de Los Altos de Chiapas** hosts exhibitions on the history of San Cristóbal and the neighboring villages. The fourth room has a collection of Chiapanecan textiles from over 1000 years. (Open Tues.-Sun. 9am-6pm. Admission 8 pesos. Free on Sun. Group tours—in Spanish—are available at no extra charge.)

San Cristóbal's most famous museum is **Na-Bolom,** on Guerrero 33 at the end of Chiapa de Corzo. Located in the northeastern section of the city, Na-Bolom is in fact a private house which moonlights as a museum at exactly 4:30pm. For many decades Trudy and Franz Blom worked and studied among the dwindling communities of the Lacandón Rainforest along the Guatemala border. Since the death of her husband in 1963, Trudy Blom has continued their work and won acclaim as an ecologist, ethnologist and photographer.

Volunteers who live with the 90-year-old Trudy at the home-turned-research-center conduct tours of the library, the gardens and the Bloms' personal museum. The library's manuscripts concentrate on Mayan culture in Mexico and Central America, with numerous periodicals, news clippings, and rare papers dealing with rainforest ecology and the plight of Guatemalan refugees. The building was originally intended as a seminary; a small, ornate chapel now serves as a gallery of post-Conquest *chiapaneco* religious art created by *ladinos* and *indígenas* alike. Other rooms in the main house are devoted to archaeological finds from the nearby site of Moxviquil, religious artifacts from the Lacandón Forest and the work of artists in residence.

The house and museum of Na-Bolom does triple-duty as a guest house (proceeds support the work of the center). Each room is named for a different region from the Bloms' travels and is decorated with textiles, artifacts, and photos from that region. Two rooms in the house are reserved exclusively for visiting *lacandones.* (Museum open by guided tour Tues.-Sun. at 4:30pm. Tours in English and Spanish 10 pesos, followed by a 50-min. film on Bloms' work in the jungle, 3 pesos.) Write or call for information on the volunteer program. (See Accommodations for details.)

Easily visible from Guadalupe, but almost 1km away in the opposite direction, the **Iglesia de San Cristóbal de las Casas** requires an even more arduous ascent broken into 285 easy steps. The church rewards pilgrims with a better view. Behind the church stands a 20-ft. crucifix built of license plates that dares you to feel reverent toward it. To reach the foot of San Cristóbal's steep stairs, walk three blocks west from the *zócalo* on Mazariegos and turn left on Ignacio Allende. Beware of those who haunt the trails surrounding the church; women have been harassed there, especially in the afternoon and evening. (Church open all day Sun. Stairs always open.)

The **Facultad de Derecho** (law school) of the Universidad de Chiapas located on the corner of Miguel Hidalgo and Cuauhtemoc has some wonderfully fanciful **murals** recently painted (1991-92) by Carlos Jurado. Enter the building, turn around, and you'll be greeted by Bosch-like lions, flying zeppelins, and blue devils. Open daily 7am-8pm.

A superb collection of **regional clothes** is displayed in **Sergio Castro's** home at Guadalupe Victoria 47, west of the *zócalo*. In about an hour he'll take you through his collection of gorgeous garments worthy of the title *objet d'art*. Call in advance for an informative and friendly tour given by the same owner (tel. 8-42-89). There is no charge, but a tip would seem to be proper etiquette.

Exceptionally colorful clothing and people jam San Cristóbal's daily morning **market,** at the northern end of Utrilla. Cheap veggies and fruit abound, but the *indígena* clothing on sale can often be had for less elsewhere in the city. Theoretically restricted to one square block, the market splatters onto nearby side streets. It's most interesting on Sunday when *indígenas* from nearby villages turn out in force. (Market open daily 7am-3pm or until the afternoon rain.)

ENTERTAINMENT

The *mariachi* band hanging around with nothing to do at the *zócalo* as early as 10pm should tell you something. Most folks in in San Cristobal turn in early; a few clubs nevertheless provide a lively Latin-music scene for the "oh-so-hip" re-generation of the flower generation passing through San Cristobal. **La Galeria,** Hidalgo 3 (tel. 8-15-47), sometimes stays open until 2am (if business is booming) and has live piano nightly during the high tourist season (cocktails 8 pesos). Fellow merrymakers can be found at **La Taberna,** Guadalupe 73 (tel. 8-16-28), 5 blocks west of the *zócalo*. Dancing to tunes that are mostly Latin and folksy blocks. Open Tues.-Sun. 1:30pm-10:30pm. Another popular hangout is at **Latinos,** Privata del Tivoli 5 (tel. 8-20-83), four blocks north of Santo Domingo, but it's an iffy part of town. Open daily noon-10:30pm. Live music from 8pm on.

If the folk scene isn't lively enough for you, shake your money-maker at **Disco Kristel** or **Disco Palace.** Disco Kristel stomps away in the Hotel Maya Quetzal on the Pan American Highway, 300m toward Comitán from the Cristóbal Colón bus station. (Open Thurs.-Sun. from 9pm. Cover 15 pesos.) Disco Palace rocks into the night at Av. Crescencio Rosas 59 (tel. 8-22-30), two blocks south of the Pan American Highway. (Open Fri.-Sun. 8:30pm-3:30am. Cover 15 pesos.) Also, **El Puente 8** (see Food) sponsors movies and lectures; check at the café. **Cinemas Santa Clara,** on 16 de Septiembre between Escuadrón and 28 de Agosto (tel. 8-23-45), shows North American movies (Mon.-Sat. at 6 and 8pm, Sun. at 4, 6 and 8pm). On Sunday evening, the *zócalo* fills with townspeople who come out for an after-dinner *paseo* (stroll).

An hour or two at **Baños Mercedarios** (tel. 8-10-06) merits consideration. Reach these steam baths, at 1 de Marzo 55, by walking two blocks north of the *zócalo* on Utrilla and then left on 1 de Marzo for four blocks. (Open Mon.-Sat. 6-8pm, Sun. 6am-2pm.) Steam and Turkish (dry heat) baths cost 6 pesos, hot showers 4 pesos.

Horseback riding is extremely popular on the trails around San Cristóbal. The villages of **San Juan Chamula** and **Zinacantán,** both about 10km to the northwest across cornfields and back roads, are good excuses for taking a ride. The route to the villages proceeds along a gravel surface for a stretch before cutting through some beautiful farm country. **El Arcotete,** a natural arch and rock formation 4km east of town, and the **Grutas de San Cristóbal,** 10km to the southeast (see Near San Cristóbal), are also worth a gallop. For rental information, check at the city's travel agencies or drop by the Casa de Huéspedes Margarita. Prices for a several-hour trek are around 50 pesos per person.

Many **hiking** trails twist through the lush hills around San Cristóbal. One of the most convenient hikes leads from the village of Chamula 7km to the village of Zinacantán. The walk winds through rolling *milpas* (cornfields) and typical thatched-roof dwellings, concluding with a stunning view from the ridge above Zinacantán. The journey back is less strenuous; the trail out of Zinacantán starts at the sharp turn in the road, about 0.5km out of town toward San Cristóbal. From Chamula, follow the dirt road that ascends the hill across the *zócalo* from the church. For a longer hike, cover the segment between San Cristóbal and Chamula on foot, which adds another two hours; the route runs uphill the whole way.

Another full-day option is a round-trip trek to a secluded waterfall on a small river east of town. Follow Francisco León east from Insurgentes, past the San Nicolás campground and across a larger highway until you reach the river. Travel four hours upstream through farmland and forest; it's polite to ask permission (almost always granted) before crossing private property. Break out the obligatory picnic and take a well-deserved dip upon arrival. No signs mark the way and tourists frequently get lost; leave early and allow some time for clueless wandering.

Seasonal Events

San Cristóbal's *Semana Santa* is rather *tranquila*. Many business establishments close their doors, and the processions and cultural events that do take place are of a decidedly reverent mood. On Easter Sunday, however, *Semana Santa* gives way to the week-long **Feria de la Primavera y de la Paz.** Before the riotous revelry really gets going, a local beauty queen is selected to preside over the festivities, which include concerts, dances, bullfights, cock fights and baseball games. Hotel rooms for either week must be reserved several months in advance. The fiesta of the city patron, San Cristóbal, takes place July 26-30 with elaborate religious ceremonies and numerous concerts.

One of the most exotic of regional festivals is Chamula's (see Near San Cristobal below) **Carnaval** (Mardi Gras). The celebration begins when about 40,000 *indígenas* pack this small village one week before Miércoles de Ceniza (Ash Wednesday). The event happens to coincide with Lent, but has its origins in an ancient Mayan ritual concerning the five "lost" days at the end of the 360-day agricultural cycle. During the festivities, men don monkey-skin hats to sing and dance while religious leaders run through fires to purify themselves.

In San Cristóbal and the many villages in its vicinity, hardly a week goes by without some kind of religious festival; consult the detailed list at the tourist office.

■ Near San Cristóbal

Sunday morning, when San Cristóbal's market is at its busiest, is the best and often the only time to visit the markets of nearby villages. However, bad roads and infrequent bus service make visiting more than one village in a single morning almost impossible. Buses do not connect the towns directly; all service is via San Cristóbal. Buses and *combis* reach many of the nearby villages and leave from the lot one block past the market at Utrilla and Honduras. Destination signs next to the buses are only occasionally accurate; always ask drivers where they're going. Prepare to rub shoulders with the other passengers.

The exception to this maddening scenario is **Chamula,** 10km from San Cristóbal on a well-paved road. After visiting Zinacantán's morning-only market, you can hike a beautiful 7km nature trail to Chamula, where the **market** lasts into the afternoon (although selection is poorer later in the day). Another option, and probably the best choice, is to take a tour with Mercedes Hernandez Gómez. She is an outstanding and knowledgeable interpreter of culture and an even better storyteller. She meets interested travelers daily at 9am in the *zócalo* and carries an umbrella so tourists can easily spot her. Tours normally go to San Juan Chamula and Zinaxantán and last until 2:30 or 3:30pm. Cost of 30 pesos includes transport, church entrance, and a sip of **posh** inside a Chamula hut.

Many of the town populations are divided between the mestizos, who own and run the businesses, and *indígenas*, who live on the surrounding farmland and show their faces in public only on market day. Each *indígena* group has its own distinctive clothing patterns and colors; this part of Chiapas is one of the few regions in Mexico where people maintain traditional dress codes. On no account should visitors bring a camera to these communities. Many of the people are opposed to photography as a matter of religious belief. Visitors should also pay particular attention to their own dress and conduct—revealing clothing (including shorts) is coldly received in these communities, as are abuses of regional dress. For instance, women should not wear the broad, ribboned hats reserved in most villages for men.

Many *indígena* villages still uphold the *cargo* (charge or burden) tradition. After years of accumulating wealth, prospective *cargo*-holders place their names on a list of political positions ranging from minor village posts to the mayor's office. The election is held on the eve of the new year; new officials must then assume the *cargo*, which means that they foot the bill for the new year's *fiestas*. Tradition places *cargo*-holders under intense pressure to make the year's festivals the biggest and best ever. Major *cargo*-holders spend themselves and their relatives into debt for fireworks, liquor and decorations. In return, they receive unparalleled prestige; the waiting lists for such positions are often filled seven to eight years in advance. Check the tourist office for dates of festivals for each village.

San Juan Chamula

San Juan Chamula is the largest and most touristed of the villages around San Cristóbal. Chamulan men wear white or black wool *sarapes* tied with thick leather belts. Designs decorating the sleeves of their white tunics indicate their *pueblito* or *colonia*. Only village officials or elders drape ribbons over their large sombreros. Chamula is a fascinating place, but the town has seen so many tourists in recent years that it has ceased to be friendly; the 25,000 inhabitants have earned a reputation for hostility to outsiders.

Chamulans resist Mexico's religious and secular authority. Catholic bishops are allowed in the church only for baptisms. The government medical clinic to the north of the *zócalo* goes practically unused.

Before entering the brightly painted **church** (open daily 5am-8pm), you must obtain a permit (2 pesos) from the tourist office on the *zócalo* and show the permit to the guards inside the church. Under no circumstances should you take pictures. Chamulans believe that a part of their soul is captured in every snapshot, and they must go through extensive healing ceremonies to regain it. The Chamulan healing ceremonies, performed inside the church, are permutations of those practiced by the ancient Maya.

In addition to Chamula's *Carnaval* (see Seasonal Events above), the assumption of the *cargo* (Dec. 3-Jan. 1), the **Fiesta de San Sebastián** (Jan. 20), the **Fiesta de San Mateo** (Sept. 21-22), and the **Fiesta de San Juan Bautista** (June 22-24) warrant a trip to the village. **Combis** to Chamula (½hr., 2 pesos) leave when full (every ½hr., 6am-5pm) from Utrilla by the market in San Cristóbal. To reach Chamula by car, drive west from the *zócalo* on Guadalupe Victoria and bear right after crossing the small bridge on Diagonal Ramón Larraínzar. At the fork, bear right for Chamula, which is at the end of an 8km stretch of paved road.

Zinacantán

Close to Chamula is the smaller village of **Zinacantán** (pop. 10,000) whose citizens' short, hot-pink *sarapes* stand out like beautiful sore thumbs. On both men and women, tassels of deep red and purple fly in the breeze, and the men often top their straw hats with Hendrixian colored ribbons as well (long ribbons designate a man's marital status). During fiestas, Zinacantecans maintain ancient Mayan custom by wearing high heel-guards on their *huaraches* (sandals). Their biggest fiestas are **Fiesta de San Sebastián** (Jan. 18-20), **Semana Santa, Fiesta del Patron San Juan** (July 24-29), and the **Fiesta de San Lorenzo** (Aug. 8-11).

Unlike Chamula, this village has accepted the Catholic clergy. The handsome, whitewashed **church** is used exclusively for Catholic worship, while the small, white convent at its side is a separate facility for ritual healing and pre-Conquest forms of worship. To visit the church you must pad the clerical coffers (2 pesos); tickets are available inside, but it's best to report to the Presidencia Municipal (town hall) first. Tourists who step inside the convent are expected to drop a small donation into the *limosna* box. Zinacantán does not tolerate picture-taking here or, for that matter, anywhere else in the village.

Combis to Zinacantán cost 2 pesos and leave San Cristóbal from the lot near the market as they fill up (6am-8pm). To drive to Zinacantán, follow Guadalupe Victoria west from the *zócalo* and turn right after crossing the small bridge on Diagonal Ramón Larraínzar. At the fork, turn left toward the "Bienvenido a Zinacantán" sign.

San Andrés Larraínzar

San Andrés Larraínzar, 26km northwest of San Cristóbal and 16km from Chamula, is more difficult to reach than most other villages, making its 5000 citizens much friendlier toward the outsiders who do make the trip. Mexicans refer to the village as Larraínzar, but local Tzotziles prefer the name San Andrés. Since many of the villagers refuse to carry their produce for an hour and a half over bumpy terrain to San Cristóbal, the **market** (open until 1pm) is better stocked here than at Chamula or Zinacantán; goods are bartered rather than sold. From the main church you can walk up the only hill to **La Iglesiade Guadalupe** and take in the view of beautiful green valleys and patches of corn fields.

Combis make several trips to San Andrés from the small terminal behind the San Crisóbal market. Just continue on the dirt road for about a block and the stop will be on your right, the first bus leaving at 7am (3 pesos). It's best to leave before 2pm, soon after the market begins to shut down and before the *combis* stop running. Hitching is conceivable but difficult. *Let's Go* does not recommend hitchhiking. To reach San Andrés by car, take the road northwest from San Cristóbal to Chamula and continue past the village on the unpaved road. On a curve some 10km later, a prominent sign announcing "S.A. Larraínzar" points left to a road climbing the steep side of the valley; the village lies approximately 6km beyond the fork. The entire journey from Chamula takes roughly half an hour at top speeds of 35-40km per hour.

Chenalhó

Even farther beyond Chamula, Chenalhó (pop. 6000) seems far more remote than its 32km from San Cristóbal would indicate. *Norteamericanos* are rare birds here. In Chenalhó, typical dress for men varies from white or black ponchos worn over pants and bound with heavy belts, to very short, light, white tunics, to Budweiser t-shirts and other such garb. Women who have not adopted more current fashions dress uniformly in dark blue *naglas* (skirts) and white *tocas* (shawls) embroidered with bright orange flowers. One small store behind the enclosed market supplies almost all the clothing for the town. The market spreads out into the plaza in front of the church on Sunday and sells mostly foodstuffs, including *chiche*, a potent drink made from fermented cane. Villagers enthusiastically wave visitors into **San Pedro,** the church in the town's center, which is a secular as well as a religious meeting place; the main aisle often shimmers with the light from candles riding on waves of incense. Chenalhó residents celebrate the **Fiesta de San Sebastián** (June 20), the **Fiesta de San Pedro** (May 27-30), the **Fiesta de Jesús de la Buena Esperanza** (Aug. 6), and **La Purísima Concepción** (Dec. 8).

Autotransportes Fray Bartolomé de las Casas operates **buses** to Chenalhó and the even more remote town of Pantelhó. The San Cristóbal bus leaves from the station on Utrilla north of the market at 2pm. The bus sometimes does not return until

COMITÁN

the next day; be sure to check about the return time before you go. Bus trips take two hours. Driving to Chenalhó can cut transit time in half, but only at a teeth-chattering speed of 35-40 km per hour on the dirt road northwest of Chamula.

Grutas de San Cristóbal

Ten km southeast of San Cristóbal off the Pan American Highway, the Grutas de San Cristóbal, discovered in 1971, is a massive cave penetrating deep into a mountain. A slippery boardwalk descends 295m below sea level and ½km into the illuminated cavern, past some splendid stalactites and stalagmites. The accessible part, however, extends for only 100-150m beyond that (there is a danger sign). To help you uncover some of the natural formations, you can acquire one of the local boys who hang around the cave for a tour (15min., no fee but small tip expected). They will also offer you an hour of horseback riding (no experience necessary) in the lush surrounding forest. To get to the *grutas*, mount a Teopisca-bound *camioneta* from in front of the San Diego Church, a few hundred meters southeast of Cristóbal Colón bus station on the Pan-American Highway (2 pesos), or take a Comitán-bound bus from the second-class bus station (**Autotransportes Tuxtla**) and ask to be dropped off at the *grutas* (2 pesos). (Caves open 9am-5pm. Admission 2 pesos.)

■■■ COMITÁN AND PARQUE NACIONAL LAGUNAS DE MONTEBELLO

South and east 86km from San Cristóbal de las Casas, **Comitán** is the last major town on the Pan American Highway before the Guatemalan border (85km away). Rapid growth has transformed once-tiny Comitán into a dreary maze of tangled streets, but should you find yourself stranded here for a day or two, make the most of this genial, active, mildly historic city, whose very green *zócalo* seems to breed raucous *marimba* bands.

A swell spare hour can be spent at the **Casa Museo Dr. Belisario Domínguez,** Av. Central Sur 29, a ½-block south of the *zócalo*. Domínguez, a native son of Comitán, gained respect throughout Mexico for his medical service to Comitán's poor. Appointed senator in 1913, he protested President Madero's assassination and was instantly martyred by those responsible. The museum contains a fascinating turn-of-the-century pharmacy, doctor's kit, and a slice of the posh aristocratic life of the time.

Practical Information The **tourist office,** on the first floor of the Palacio Municipal, on the north end of the *zócalo*, has maps. (Open Mon.-Sat. 9am-9pm, Sun. 9am-2pm.) **Currency** is exchanged at 1 Ave. Sur Pte. 1 (tel. 2-00-64), on the southwest corner of the *zócalo*, 9-11am only. The **post office,** Central Dr. Belisario Domínguez 45, is exactly two blocks from *zócalo* on right-hand side of street (tel. 2-04-27). (Open Mon.-Sat. 8am-7pm.) All those planning to go to Guatemala by land must obtain a visa beforehand from the **Guatemalan Consulate,** 3a Ave. Pte Nte (tel. 2-26-69). (Open Mon.-Fri. 8am-4:30pm.) The **Cristobal Colón bus station** is quite a distance south of the *zócalo*, but **combis** across the street from the station pass regularly (8 pesos). **Farmacia del Centro** on Calle Central Pte. 1 (tel. 2-00-95), is open daily 8am-11pm. **Red Cross:** Calle Sur Pte. 120 (tel. 2-18-89). **Hospital General:** 9 Sur Pte. 3 (tel. 2-01-35). **Police:** Carretera Internacional 176500 (tel. 2-33-22).

Accommodations and Food Places to stay are boiled down to few alternatives. Fortunately they're all close to the heart of town. **Pensión Delfín,** Central Belisario Domínguez 21a, right on the *zócalo* (tel. 2-00-13) is *número uno* in terms of cleanliness and location. A few healthy plants provide decoration. All rooms have bathroom and hot water. (Singles 45 pesos, doubles 55 pesos, triples 65 pesos.)

Slightly farther but also cheaper is **Hospedaje Montebello**, 1a Calle Norte Pte. 10, One block north from the *zócalo* (tel. 23572). Rooms are on the dark side, but brightly tiled courtyard provides cheer. All listed prices have bathroom and hot water. (Singles 20 pesos, doubles 40 pesos, triples 60 pesos.) Most restaurants cluster around the *zócalo*, but don't expect any surprises.

Sights 15km to the mysterious east, 68 lakes are scattered among pine-covered hills in the national park at **Lagunas de Montebello.** Unfortunately, rather than prevent development, Mexico's park administration seems to encourage it. The marked paths are severely beaten, but the hills above and the river valleys below remain untrammeled. At the lakeside areas where the bus drops off passengers, such as **Laguna Monte Azul** or **Laguna Montebello,** there are picnic tables, assertive restauranteurs, taxis, and public toilets.

Hike a few minutes off the highway that connects Comitán and the lakes to the Mayan ruins at **Chinkultic.** Perhaps more interesting than the sixth- and seventh-century structures themselves are the diminutive *cenote* (natural well) and the striking view of the lake region from the hilltop. Hikers can also venture to **Grutas El Paso del Soldado,** about 1km beyond Laguna Monte Azul (called *Laguna Bosque Azul* by locals).

Popular with locals but more obscure than Montebello is the **Cascada de Chiflón,** a 250m waterfall 45km from Comitán. The lake is safe (albeit cold) for swimming, but don't venture too close to the waterfall, or you may take a once-in-a-lifetime plunge. There are some nice places to camp in this area, but no facilities. To get to Chiflón, take a *combi* from Av. 2 Ote. Nte., directly east of the *zócalo*, to La Mesilla. *Combis* leave every ½ hour, and taxis await your bidding. From La Mesilla, the waterfall is a 5km walk.

■■■ OCOSINGO

Immersed in the greenery of the mountains, Ocosingo (pop. 24,000) leads a mild-mannered life undisturbed by clamoring sightseers. Many of the *indígenas* still wear the traditional long blue skirt and white lace blouse, with richly colored waist and neck. Beyond its charm, the town of Ocosingo has little to interest travelers navigating between San Cristóbal and Palenque. All the same, Ocosingo's poor cousin, the ruined Toniná, is an excellent, rarely visited archaeological site that deserves a slot on every Mayaphile's itinerary.

ORIENTATION

Ocosingo is 100km from San Cristóbal de las Casas and 128km from Palenque. The highway between San Cristóbal and Palenque follows a ridge west of town, and bus lines serving both cities have stations on or near this road. **Avenida I Nte.** runs downhill from Autotransportes Fray Bartolomé de las Casas on the highway, past Autotransportes Tuxtla Gutiérrez and Autotransportes Lacandonia, ending a block north of the *zócalo* at **Calle Central.**

The town is laid out in the customary compass grid, but it's small enough that one can almost ignore street names. From the *zócalo*, cardinal directions are marked by the Hotel Central to the north, the Iglesia de San Jacinto to the east, the Palacio Municipal to the west and nothing much to the south.

Within town, taxis (3 pesos) are unnecessary. To get to the ruins, catch one of the *colectivos* at the market to the *crucero* (crossroads) Toniná (5 pesos). From there, the ruins are only 1km away.

PRACTICAL INFORMATION

Tourist Office: There is no unoffical Tourist Office, but the competent staff at the **Presidente Municipal** on the 2nd floor of the Palacio Municipal on the *zócalo* (tel. 3-00-15) is willing to answer any questions that you might have. Nil English spoken. Open Mon.-Fri. 9am-3pm and 6-8pm.

Currency Exchange: Bánamex on the *zócalo* (tel. 3-00-34) is the only bank in town. They do not change U.S. dollars, but they will give cash advances on major credit cards. Open Mon.-Fri. 9am-1:30pm.

Post Office: 2 Sur Ote. 54. Open Mon.-Fri. 9am-2pm and 3-6pm, Sat. 9am-1pm. **Postal Code:** 29950.

Telephones: Caseta, on 1 Ote. in a white building, one block north of the *zócalo* on the left (tel. 3-00-55). International collect calls 3 pesos. Collect calls daily 8:30am-3:30pm.

Bus Stations: 1st-class **Cristóbal Colón,** 1km down the highway toward Palenque (tel. 3-04-31). Terminal open 7am-9pm; free luggage storage. Once bus per day to: Palenque (12 pesos); Villahermosa (21 pesos); San Cristóbal (7 pesos); Tuxtla Gutiérrez (14 pesos); Puebla (100 pesos); Mexico City (113 pesos). 2nd-class **Autotransportes Tuxtla Gutiérrez,** Av. 1 Nte.,1 block south of the highway. Only buses leaving *de local* and specially-designated *de paso* buses can guarantee a seat in advance; buy tickets for these buses 1 day beforehand. Ticket office open 6am-7pm. To: Tuxtla Gutiérrez (12 pesos) via San Cristóbal (6 pesos); Palenque (8 pesos) via Agua Azul (4 pesos). **Autotransportes Lacandonia** and **Autotransportes Maya,** Av. 1 Nte., uphill from the Tuxtla Gutiérrez station, behind the cinderblock wall with white, hand-lettered sign. Luggage check 1 peso. 2nd class to: San Cristóbal (4 pesos); Villahermosa (18 pesos); Mérida (40 pesos). **Transportes Toniná,** right on the highway across from the end of Av. 1 Nte. Buses leave continuously for San Cristóbal (2am-6pm, 6 pesos).

Market: 2 blocks south and 3 blocks east of the *zócalo*. Open daily 5am-7pm.

Laundromat: Jumar on 1 Ote. 64. Pants, shirts, etc. 1 peso per piece; socks and underwear 3 pairs for 1 peso. Open Mon.-Sat. 8am-2pm and 4-7pm.

Pharmacy: Cruz Blanca, 1 Ote. and 2 Sur (tel. 3-02-33), 1 block south of the *zócalo*. Open 24 hrs.

Medical Emergency: Instituto Mexicano de Seguro Social (IMSS), 800m from the *zócalo* on 1 Ote. Sur (tel. 3-01-52). Open 24 hrs.

Emergency, Lost Property and Police: Policía Judicial (tel. 3-01-13), on Calle Central between 1 Pte. and 2 Pte. No English spoken. 24-hr. service. In an emergency you can also call the **Presidencia Municipal** on the 2nd floor of the Palacio Municipal on the *zócalo* (tel. 3-00-15). See Tourist Office.

ACCOMMODATIONS

Ocosingo's hotel's are cheap, but low in quality. You can **camp** or park a trailer by the town's small airstrip if you obtain permission from the Presidente Municipal (on the 2nd floor of the Palacio Municipal). All the following will take reservations by phone.

Hotel Central, Av. Central 1 (tel. 3-00-24), on the north side of the *zócalo*. This arcaded, colonial-looking building has light, spacious, altogether dreamy rooms with beautiful views of the mountains. TV, hot water and fans. Check-out 1pm. Singles 44 pesos. Doubles 66 pesos. Triples 77 pesos.

Hotel Margarita, Calle Central Nte. 6 (tel. 3-02-80), ½ block north of the *zócalo*. Pleasant spacious rooms with fans, hot water and immaculate bathrooms. Check-out 1:30 pm. Singles 50 pesos. Doubles 60 pesos. Triples 70 pesos. Quads 90 pesos. Traveler's checks and credit cards accepted.

Posada Agua Azul, 1 Ote 127 (tel. 3-03-02). Flowered entrance and courtyard for a graceful welcome. Sunny rooms with fans, hot water and private baths. Check-out 1pm. Singles 30 pesos. 1-bed doubles 30 pesos. 2-bed doubles 35 pesos. 5 pesos per additional person. TV 5 pesos extra.

Hotel San Jacinto, Av. Central 13 (tel. 3-03-79), 1 block east of the *zócalo*. Look for the fabulous blue-tiled exterior. 13 clean, concrete, poorly lit rooms open onto a dreary courtyard. Rooms have fans; baths have hot water. Bathrooms shine as much as cement can. Decent communal facilities. Check-out noon. Singles 15 pesos. Doubles with bath 30 pesos per person. Traveler's checks accepted.

Hospedaje San Jose, 1 Ote. 9 (tel. 3-00-39). 22 rooms in varying shades of blue with desks and tiny windows. Not extremely well-maintained. Baths have hot water, but only rooms with private baths have fans. Bathrooms are a bit musty but acceptable. Check-out noon. Singles 15 pesos. Rooms with double bed and bath 25 pesos for 1-2 people. Rooms with 2 double beds and bath 30 pesos for 1-2 people.

FOOD

Restaurant La Montura, Av. Central 5 (tel. 3-00-24), in the Hotel Central on the north side of the *zócalo*. Somewhat overpriced, but the outdoor tables under the arcade are the most pleasant in town. Entrées around 14-16 pesos. Traveler's checks, MC and Visa accepted. Open daily 7am-11pm.

Restaurante San Cristóbal, Av. Central 22, 1 block west of the *zócalo*. Look for the lime-green exterior. Animal pelts, snake skins, turtle shells and stuffed birds from the Lacandón Rainforest make the place feel crowded even when there isn't a soul around. *Comida corrida* 10 pesos. Open daily 7am-9pm.

Restaurant Los Arcos, Av. Central, on the northeast corner of the *zócalo*, behind the small white arches of the passage. Easy to miss as it lacks any obvious virtues except cheap food. Chicken and meats 10-12 pesos. *Huevos rancheros* 8 pesos. The biggest damn *platano frito* you've ever seen in your life (4 pesos). Open daily 7am-10pm.

■ Near Ocosingo: Toniná Ruins

The ruins of Toniná rarely surface on a list of can't-miss sights in Mexico, but they're larger and more interesting than overbilled Bonampak and as impressive as many better-known sites in the Yucatán. Toniná's glyphs and artwork are well-maintained and relatively unweathered. Located 30 minutes from Ocosingo, the ruins remain difficult to reach and virtually untouristed; travelers without a car can dole out a steep taxi fare, walk for days, or catch a morning *colectivo*.

The Toniná complex, encompassing 15 acres of ruins, was a religious and administrative capital for the Mayan city-state that flourished from 300 to 1000 AD. Unlike the orthodox symmetry of Monte Albán or Chichén Itzá, the structures at Toniná are dispersed and lack an astrological floor plan. Many statues have lost heads and feet to decay and neglect, and the pyramids can never be fully restored since the governor of Ocosingo took stones from the site to build roads around the turn of the century. The entrance path, which leads across the river east of the ruins and up a small gully, emerges on the **Plaza of War,** the first artificially terraced level of the site. Trees and grass have overgrown a pyramidal mound on the left; nearer the river is the grassy depression of the unexcavated **main ballcourt,** beyond which lies a sacrificial altar.

Toniná's chief site is a massive **pyramid** which towers 60m above the plaza. The seven tiers corresponded to the city's different social strata, from the general populace (flush with the plaza) to the high priests, whose four temples rest on the seventh level. Well-preserved panels and sculptures survive from almost all of the levels, but many have been removed to the museum on the premises or to Mexico City.

The ruins of a smaller ballcourt lie forgotten at the back of the plaza, next to chunks of statues and panels scattered near the fence. Extensive glyphs on the back of these figures relate to the scenes on the front, often giving the *fechas fatales* (birth and death dates) of the prominent characters. Three animals— the snake, the bat, and the jaguar—appear together repeatedly. Each was revered for a different kind of natural force: the serpent for the sharp teeth with which it drew blood in self-sacrifice, the bat for its nocturnal perspicacity and the jaguar for its distinction as the most powerful denizen of the jungle. The three stelae at the foot of the first level commemorate the inauguration of new governments.

The fourth level is uninteresting, but in the center of the fifth gapes a royal grave. Here archaeologists found a stone sarcophagus, made of a single piece of limestone, which held a king's body and two unidentified corpses. To the left of the grave on the same level is a shrine to Chac, the Mayan rain god. The stone originally above the figure, carved in 300 AD, now lives in the museum. The **Altar de Monstruo de la Tierra** is on the right on the sixth level.

The seventh level was Toniná's religious focal point, and it supports four large pyramids dedicated to a curious mix of cosmic and civic forces. The lowest and least impressive is the **Temple of Agriculture,** on the far right of the terrace. This crumbling pyramidal building contained private rooms for the ranking priests and governors. Considerably higher, the **Pyramid of Life and Death** rises to the left of the Temple of Agriculture, slightly nearer the pyramid's summit. Archaeologists believe this mound once housed the king and the royal family. Side by side behind the Pyramid of Life and Death loom Toniná's two most important temples. The **Pyramid of War,** on the right, which served as an observatory to scan the countryside for foreign heavies, is higher and clearly the more important of the two, but the **Pyramid of Finances** adds a satisfying touch of symmetry. From the peak of either Finance or War you can enjoy a brilliant view and a cool breeze. Below the Pyramid of War is a newly excavated statue of King Zotz-Choj (the jaguar-bat king), with a giant headdress depicting an eagle, serpents, and the symbols for wind, smoke and fire.

Below, the **museum** contains stature with large, symmetrical holes where precious and semi-precious stones were once set. (Site and museum open daily 9am-4pm. Admission 10 pesos.) A guide is usually available at the entrance for the one- to two-hour free tours; a tip is customary.

Taxis from Ocosingo's *zócalo* charge an outrageous 40 pesos for the one-way trip to Toniná. It will take some perseverance, but try catching a *colectivo* pickup truck from the market or ask for the *cruce*. At this juncture several buses and trucks will go by, and some will take you near the ruins. To get to this *cruce* walk ten minutes right on the dirt road behind the market, or catch a *colectivo* pickup truck from the market. To drive to the ruins, follow 1 Ote. south out of town, past the clinic on the right. Bear right past the radio station on the left. Follow the signs for "Toniná ruins" to the Rancho Toniná, which encompasses the site. The road to the left of the gate leads to the museum and ruins. Inquire at the ranch about camping.

■■■ THE LACANDÓN RAINFOREST

When a mighty tree falls, a star falls from the sky.

—Chan K'in Viejo

La Selva (Forest) **Lacandona** once covered most of the state of Chiapas, but after centuries of incursions by agricultural interests, less than 15% of the original jungle remains. The Lacandón people have always been the most isolated of the country's many indigenous peoples ever since small Mayan clans from different parts of northern Mesoamerica fled deep into the jungle to avoid the Spanish conquistadors. Calling themselves *Hachack-Winick* (The True People), they developed a common dialect and cultural bond, despite their dispersal over a large area. Their isolation continues to this day, and many still live on family *milpas* (cornfields) rather than in villages.

The Lacandón culture has experienced its share of change, however. A single missionary based at Lacanjá began converting *indígenas* in the 19th century, one *milpa* at a time. *Lacandones* have since fused Christianity with their ancient Mayan beliefs, but the ancient rituals and ritual sites are still deeply respected.

Commerce with *ladino* civilization has made the *Lacandones* the wealthiest *indígenas* in Mexico; they sell timber rights to multinational companies that harvest mahogany from the vast tracts of jungle, using these revenues to facilitate their entry into other markets such as chicken-farming. But as the ethic of expedience and fast profit takes hold, the *lacandón* way of life is changing once again. Efforts at reforestation have not been successful on a large scale. The jungle (*Reserva Integral de la Biósfera Montes Azules* in government jargon), once the *Lacandones'* source of security and livelihood, now dwindles toward nothing.

The **Na-Bolom** museum in San Cristóbal (see San Cristóbal: Sights) has the best of the few available maps of the Lacandón jungle. The map is getting on towards thirtysomething, but it marks most settlements. Of primary interest are the ruins at **Bonampak** and **Yaxchilán** and the villages of **Naja** and **Lacanjá.**

Bonampak, Naja and Lacanjá are partially and seasonally variably accessible by road. **Línea de Pasajeros Comitán Lagos de Montebello** runs buses only as far as San Javier, a town 13km from Bonampak. Montebello also provides bus service to such remote locations in the Lacandón Rainforest as Pico de Oro and Benemérito. Naja and Lacanjá are connected to Palenque. For further information about land transit in the area, inquire at the bus stop across the street from the market in Palenque (on Velasco Suárez).

Yaxchilán can be reached only by **airplane** or **boat.** Catch launches down the Río Usumacinta to the site from the town of **Frontera Echeverría** (also called Corozal), 25km farther down a mangled dirt road from San Javier. No public transportation directly serves Frontera Echeverría. You can take a bus to the San Francisco *crucero.* From there, hike to Frontera Echeverría (bring overnight supplies and plenty of water); some hitch rides with the occasional trucks, but *Let's Go* does not reccomend hitching. Locals operate the boats and charge about 17 pesos per person for the two-hour trip. Some private homes in Frontera Echeverría rent beds for the night. You can also arrange trips to Yaxchilán with the *Lacandones* at Bonampak (about 65 pesos per boat). A more exciting, if much pricier, method of transport is by *avioneta* (small airplane).

■■■ PALENQUE

The ruins of Palenque straddle a magnificent 300m-high *palenque* (natural palisade) in the foothills of the Altos de Chiapas. Dozens of thundering waterfalls tumble into the yellow-green savannah, and the vast tropical rainforest blankets the surrounding region in emerald humidity. Most visitors, mesmerized even without the aid of the hallucinogenic herbs and fungi that flourish in the moist shadows of the forest, easily understand why the ruins have been revered as magical for centuries.

Eight km from the ruins lies the sleepy town of Santo Domingo—called simply Palenque after the crumbling temples that put it on the map. Fed on visitors' dollars, the once small, poverty-stricken village has undergone uncontrolled sprawl. Although no one would bother to visit the city just to visit it, Palenque (pop. 25,000) serves as an adequate base for excursions to the nearby ruins. A snazzy European tourist crowd usually makes the scene.

ORIENTATION

Palenque is in the northeastern corner of Chiapas, 315km from Tuxtla Gutiérrez. From the west, it lies at the end of a rough and winding five- to six-hour journey on dirt roads that lead to San Cristóbal via Ocosingo. To the east, the Yucatán awaits, within easy reach by excellent paved roads that pass through Chetumal. If you arrive on the Route 186 bus that connects Chetumal and Villahermosa, get off at Catazajá, from which *combis* and taxis will take you to Palenque. The last *combi* (2.50 pesos) leaves at 7pm. Some traveling after that hitch a ride or find a group to split the 15-peso taxi fare for the 23km trip into town.

Palenque lacks the rational layout of most of Chiapas's settlements, although some semblance of order does exist; streets running east-west are labeled "Avenidas," and those running north-south "Calles." The main avenue, **Avenida Benito Juárez,** links Palenque's *zócalo* to the highway and the ruins. Running north-south, **Calle Independencia** borders the *zócalo* on the west. To get to the *zócalo* from the bus station, walk four blocks uphill on Juárez.

PRACTICAL INFORMATION

Tourist Office: In the Casa de Cultura on the *zócalo* (tel. 5-08-28). Some English spoken and excellent maps of Palenque. Open Mon.-Sat. 8am-2pm and 3-8pm.

Travel Agencies: Palenque's travel agents can arrange some exciting (if expensive) excursions. **Viajes Toniná,** Juárez 105 (tel. and fax 5-02-09), near Allende, organizes trips to Agua Azul and Misol-Ha (20-25 pesos), Bonampak (US$75), Yaxchilán, the Río Usumacinta, Tikal and remote *indígena* villages Lacanjá and Naja. Open daily 8am-1:30pm and 4:30-9pm. **ATC Tours and Travel,** on Allende just north of Juárez (tel. 5-02-10, fax 5-03-56), offers excursions to Bonampak, Yaxchilán, Guatemala's Tikal, ruins, and the ruins of Toniná near Ocosingo and Agua Azul. They also have a 4hr. jungle tour on horseback (no experience necessary). Open daily 8am-2pm and 4-9pm.

Currency Exchange: Bancomer, Juárez 40 (tel. 5-01-98), 2 blocks west of the *zócalo*. Open for exchange Mon.-Fri. 10am-noon. **Bánamex** (tel. 5-01-17), 1 block further on Juárez. Open Mon.-Fri. 9:30am-noon. Equally slow lines. After hours, many hotels and travel agencies will change cash.

Post Office, Independencia at Bravo (tel. 5-01-43), around the left side of the Palacio Municipal, north of the *zócalo*. *Lista de Correos*. Open Mon.-Fri. 9am-1pm and 3-6pm, Sat. 9am-1pm. **Postal code:** 29960.

Telephones: Long-distance *caseta* (tel. 5-00-00) at the ADO station. Collect calls 5 pesos. Open Mon.-Sat. 7am-10pm, Sun. 8am-1pm. **Telephone code:** 934.

Telegrams: Independencia at Bravo (tel. 5-03-68), next-door to the post office. Open Mon.-Fri. 9am-3pm.

Train Station: Just past the Cabeza Maya 6km north of town. Trains to Mexico City, Coatzalcoalcos, and Mérida via Campeche. Trains are notoriously unreliable, unsafe, and slow. Taxis to the station charge 5 pesos.

Bus Stations: ADO, 5 de Mayo at Juárez (tel. 5-00-00), about 4 blocks west of the *zócalo*. **Luggage storage** to the left of the station (fee depends on size, max. 3 pesos), but only if they have space (open daily 8am-10pm). Station open daily 6:30am-10pm. 1st class to: Mexico City (6pm, 14hrs., 110 pesos) via Orizaba (76 pesos); Villahermosa (3½hrs., 15 pesos); Macuspana (noon and 7pm, 2hrs., 5400 pesos); Catazajá (40min., 3 pesos); Mérida (9pm, 55 pesos); Chetumal (10pm, 7hrs., 47 pesos). **Autotransportes Tuxtla Gutiérrez,** Juárez 159 (tel. 5-03-69). Luggage storage costs 2 pesos per piece per day. 1st class to: Tuxtla Gutiérrez (8hrs., 18 pesos); Agua Azul (2½hrs., 4 pesos); Ocosingo (3hrs., 9 pesos); San Cristóbal de las Casas (5hrs., 13 pesos). **Transportes Dag Dug** occupies a hole in the wall a few doors west of Autotransportes Tuxtla Gutiérrez on Juárez. 2nd class buses to: Tuxtla Gutiérrez (8am, 31 pesos) via Villahermosa (2hrs., 10 pesos); Mérida (8hrs., 37 pesos). Also to: Pichucalco, Chiapa de Corzo, Escárcega, and Campeche, among others. The Mérida-bound bus usually sells out by the morning of departure; buy your ticket a day in advance.

Taxis: (tel. 5-01-12), but easier to find on the street.

Laundromats: Lavandería Lavamática, 5 de Mayo across from the ADO station. Wash and dry 10 pesos for 3kg. Same-day service. Open Mon.-Sat. 8am-2pm and 4-7:30pm.

24-hr. Pharmacy: Farmacia Central, Av. Juárez near Independancia. Will also change dollars for slightly lower rates but without the hour wait at nearby banks. Open daily 7am-7pm.

Hospital: Hospital General (tel. 5-07-33), at the end of town nearest the ruins , near the gas station. 24-hr. emergency service. No English spoken.

Police: In the Palacio Municipal on Calle Independencia (tel. 5-01-14). No English spoken. Open 24 hrs.

ACCOMMODATIONS

Hotel prices in Palenque are high and rooms uniform. You can try to bargain, but even Palenque's dives often have their rates clearly posted behind the reception desk, rendering them virtually immutable. The best bet is to cough up the extra pesos and console yourself with the fact that you probably only need to spend a night or two here.

Staying in one of the several hotels en route to the archaeological site makes it easier to get to the site itself, but more difficult to get to a cheap restaurant or to the market. Although most of these roadside hotels are quite expensive, the notorious **Mayabell Trailer Park and Camping** allows guests to string up a hammock or put down a sleeping bag under a *palapa* roof for 5 pesos. Electricity, water, and decent sewage facilities are available for trailers (5 pesos per car, 25-30 pesos per camping vehicle depending on size, plus 5 pesos per person). There are also a few spiffy new rooms, with private baths, hot water, fans, and lovely embroidered decorations on the walls. (Singles 50 pesos. Quads 4 people 80 pesos.) This laid-back hippie hangout is a great place to snag travel tips. Be very wary of tips about popular trails leading to the back entrance of the ruin, however; the paths are very unsafe (see Sights). The campground's **Restaurant Yaxché** serves nothing that costs over 12 pesos. The campground is 6km from town, 2km from the ruins. The best way to get there is by *combi* (1 peso). Or you can gorge on the Sunday buffet (28 pesos) at the more elegant and restful **Restaurant Tucanes**, before the Mayabell Trailer Park.

Another trailer park, **María del Mar,** (tel. 5-05-33, fax 5-05-44) at the Hotel Villas Kin-Ha, lies 3km from town and 5km from the ruins along the same road. You can pitch a tent, but there's no *palapa* on which to hang a hammock. It's considerably less popular, less groomed and more expensive than Mayabell, but it does have a swimming pool. The **restaurant** serves good but expensive regional food (open daily 7am-9pm, entrees 12-35 pesos). (Camping 8 pesos per person. 35 pesos per motor home, including up to 2 people.)

Palenque is not the safest place for wild **camping,** since thieves have figured out that foreigners often carry dollars and other valuable tidbits. Unless indicated otherwise, assume that the rooms described here don't have fans, hot water, or mosquito netting.

Hotel Vaca Vieja, 5 de Mayo 402 (tel. 5-03-77), at Chiapas, 3 blocks east of the *zócalo*, in a quiet part of town. So named when the owner sold his last cow to buy the place. Very spacious, spotless modern rooms and bathrooms. Comfortable beds, dauntless ceiling fans. Check-out 2pm. Singles 40 pesos. Doubles 60 pesos. Triples 70 pesos. Prices rise during the high season to 59 pesos, 69 pesos, and 79 pesos, respectively. Credit cards accepted. For reservations, 50% advance payment is required.

Hotel Santa Elena, on Domínguez off Juárez, 2 blocks west of the Tuxtla and Dag Dug bus stations. Low-ceilinged but large rooms with large, immaculate bathrooms. Hot water and fans create comfort, and proximity to the bus stations creates convenience. Check-out noon-1pm. Singles 40 pesos. Doubles 45 pesos. Call Hotel Avenida (tel. 5-01-16) to make reservations.

Casa de Huéspedes San Antonio, Independencia (tel.5-09-55), a few blocks north of the *zócalo*. Off the beaten path, but cute new rooms, decent bathrooms and an incredible price more than compensate. Fans but no hot water. Check-out noon. Singles 20 pesos. Doubles 25 pesos. Triples or quads 50 pesos. Rooms for 5-6 people 70 pesos. Reservations can be made by phone.

Hotel Avenida, Av. Juárez 173 (tel. 5-01-16), across from the bus station. Green tidy rooms with fans, livened up by curtains with Chinese temples. Very clean. Check-out 1pm. Singles 44 pesos. Doubles 55 pesos. Triples 65 pesos. Quads 75 pesos. Advance payment required for reservations.

Hotel Lacroix, Hidalgo 10 (tel. 5-00-14), just to the left of the church from the *zócalo*. The oldest hotel in Palenque (founded 1956), where many famed archaeologists have stayed through the years. Wild mural complete with giant skull and dancing Mayan decorates the entrance. Semi-clean rooms with ceiling fans. Often full. Check-out noon. Singles 40 pesos. Doubles 50 pesos. Reservations can be made by phone.

FOOD

Palenque has cheap restaurants, but most are completely devoid of atmosphere and appetizing fare. The crowd everywhere is European, or at least "Euro." If you spend

PALENQUE

the day at the ruins, you might want to brown-bag it, since the sole on-site eatery is a glorified snack bar. In town, several small grocery stores line Juárez. For a good selection of cheap fruits and vegetables, try the **market** on Velasco Suárez, four blocks west and four blocks north of the *zócalo*. You can also grab a cheap meal at any of the several marketplace *fondas* (food stands).

Restaurante Las Tinajas, 20 de Noviembre 41, at Abasolo. High-backed chairs, indirect lighting and suave music. Six ways to cook chicken, all for 15 pesos and with excellent service. Try their special *sopa de espárragos* 7 pesos. Credit cards accepted. Open daily 8am-11pm.

Restaurant Girasoles, on Av. Juárez, around the corner from the bus station. White- and red-checkered tablecloths and low-hanging lamps make for a pleasant set on which to stage an inexpensive meal. *Comida corrida* 10 pesos. Enchiladas 7 pesos. Complimentary *agua de fruta* for *Let's Go* users. Open daily 7:30am-11pm.

Restaurant Maya, Independencia at Hidalgo (tel. 5-00-42), on the west side of the *zócalo*. Large and patronized by more *viajeros* (travelers) than locals. Service is less than 5-star, but the food is good. *Pollo a la palenque* (cooked in beer) 16 pesos. Breakfast 8-14 pesos. Open daily 7:30am-11pm.

Restaurant Rocamar, on 5 de Mayo, 1 block west of the *zócalo*. Prices here are higher, but the menu is long and exciting. Squids, snails, octopus, fish and shell-fish prepared in a variety of ways for 10-30 pesos while enjoying a beautiful view of the nearby mountains. Open daily 7am-8pm.

Restaurant Yunuen, 5 de Mayo 42, at Chiapas in the Hotel Vaca Vieja, 3 blocks east of the *zócalo*. Small, friendly place with reasonable prices. Breakfast specials 6-11 pesos. Feast on the *pollo a la palencana*—fried bananas, 2 cheese tacos, rice, beans, salad, and chicken for 17 pesos. Traveler's checks accepted. Open daily 7am-11pm.

SIGHTS

One of Palenque's ancient names means "Place of the Sun's Daily Death"; this was one of the westernmost cities of the Mayan empire. When settlement began in the third century, the Maya had only the slightest notion of other communities; for the most part their jungle civilization flourished in isolation.

Palenque owes much of its spectacular architecture, including the finest examples of stucco bas-relief sculpture anywhere, to the man who ruled it at the apex of its history, the club-footed King Pakal (615-683 AD). One of the inscriptions carved around the time of Pakal's death indicates that he lived into his fifth *katun* (20-year period), when his son Chan-Bahlum succeeded him. Chan-Bahlum, represented by the jaguar and serpent glyphs, celebrated his accession by building his father a crypt (the Temple of Inscriptions). He also ordered the construction of the Sun Plaza group and placed stone tablets inside each of the temples there. After King Chan-Bahlum, Palenque slowly went to wrack and ruin. By the 16th century, Cortés was able to march right by Palenque without marking its existence.

Although the inscriptions in Palenque include self-explanatory pictures of the main characters, props and actions, less than a fifth of the thousands of Mayan glyphs have been deciphered. While experts pore over these tablets, visitors to the ruins marvel at the murals and the stucco sculpture. The "cement" is a concoction of bark, clay and stone, in which intricate details were molded while the mixture was still wet.

Indígena men dressed in all-white gowns sell bows and arrows at the entrance to the ruins. In contrast to most other *indígena* groups, it is the men among the *Lacandón* who continue to wear the traditional garb.

Upon entering the site, you pass the tomb of Alberto Ruz, an archaeologist so devoted to Palenque that he insisted on being buried beside the restored ceremonial plaza. To the right, rises the steep **Temple of Inscriptions,** named for the magnificent tablets inside, although it is actually the tomb of King Pakal. It is the first such burial place found anywhere in the Americas. Originally Ruz found six unimpressive skeletons; intrigued by a mysterious tubular duct, he drilled a hole in the wall of a vestibule and found the perfectly preserved, elaborately carved sarcophagus of the king. (There is a copy in the small museum on the premises.) Inside the five-ton sarcophagus, food, stone sculptures, rings, necklaces, a mask, bracelets, a crown, and a large amount of jade were stored beside the body. The tomb with the six skeletons was that of the tractable young men sacrificed to serve Pakal on his voyage through the afterlife, during which they would carry his dishes, jade and pearl jewelry, red shells, and other personal effects. Visitors can climb down the many slippery stone stairs and peer through a window to see the royal crypt. The hollow duct, which allowed Pakal's spirit to exit the underworld and communicate with Palenque's priests, is visible on the right, after the staircase. (Open daily 8am-4:30pm.)

At the center of the ceremonial plaza, next to the Temple of Inscriptions, is a trapezoidal **palace** complex consisting of four patios on a stepped platform. As you enter the complex from the northern side, you will see a large oval stucco relief, representing the nine gods of the underworld. Detailed stucco reliefs ornament the walls; the northern courtyards conceal scaly monsters. The whole complex is visible from the unique, four-story astronomical tower in the center of the complex. On the inner wall of the eastern patio are several 3m-tall statues standing shoulder-to-shoulder. A steam bath and ancient latrines have also been excavated.

The path between the palace and the Temple of Inscriptions fords the Río Otolum before leading to the **Sun Plaza,** another landscaped platform. The first building here is the **Temple of the Sun,** with the smaller **Temple 14** next to it. The **Temple of the Cross,** so called for a large stucco relief of a cross found inside, is the largest of the temple-pyramids in the Sun Group. This Maya group is the only one known to have worshipped the cross; for them it was the tree of life, with a bird on top and a snake as the horizontal branch. The outer layer of blue-tinted stucco has worn away, but the inner sanctum protects a large sculpted tablet and reliefs on either side of the doors. Needless to say, Palenque's cross inspired a flurry of hopeful religious theories among the conquistadors.

About to be swallowed again by the jealous jungle, the **Temple of the Foliated Cross** lies across the plaza from the Temple of the Sun. Despite the overgrown path, the inner sanctum here, too, contains a surprisingly clear carved tablet with the unusual tree (or cross) with branches remarkably similar to some found in a temple at Angkor-Wat, Kampuchea, but nowhere else in the Americas.

A trail leads up the mountainside to the left of the Temple of Inscriptions. About 100m along this trail, on the right, is the **Temple of Jaguars.** If you descend the stairwell inside the structure, you will come upon the 7-ft. well to the left of the temple, where a few faint traces of paint are slowly surrendering to the green slime of the jungle. The trail continues up the hill before reaching the tiny *indígena* village of Naranjo. The difficult but oddly refreshing hike takes 90 minutes and passes through territory that would make Tarzan homesick.

To the south, through the wall of trees, several more unreconstructed temples surround the uncleared **Plaza Maudslay** (there are over 400 unexcavated structures at Palenque). North from the Temple of the Inscriptions, past the palace, the vestiges of a **ballcourt** persevere on the right, and on the left is the **Temple of Frederick, Count of Waldeck**. The Count lived here for three years while studying the ruins in the 1830s. Beyond and to the right of this temple are the remains of the **North Group.**

The **museum** near the North Group has a few items on display, all from the Palenque archaeological investigations, along with a few cursory plaques in Spanish. Just to the right of the museum a trail leads to the **Queen's Bath,** a beautiful set of waterfalls crashing through a steep, shady ravine; the queens of Palenque bathed here in a bygone age, but even commoners can swim here now. Waterfall enthusiasts should also visit **Cascada Motiepa.** About 600m before the entrance to the ruins, a small sign marks the path to the watery haven.

The archaeological site is open daily from 8am to 5pm. The museum and the crypt are open from 8am to 4:30pm. Visiting the ruins at night is prohibited and extremely unsafe. (Admission to the site 13,000 pesos. Free Sun. Small map available at gate for 2 pesos. 2-hr. guided tours 75 pesos for 1-8 people, 95 pesos for 9-15 people, 120 pesos for 16-24 people.) *Combis* to the site run 6am-6pm and cost 1.50 pesos. Catch them off Juárez on Allende. Do not take popular short-cuts to the back entrance of the ruins from the campgrounds or the road. Many rapes and robberies have occurred on these trails; the denseness of the jungle leaves you isolated even if there are many other tourists nearby. Women should never travel the paths alone, and duos of both sexes have been harassed.

■ Near Palenque: Cascadas Agua Azul and Misol-ha

Both of these large *cascadas* (waterfalls) have overflowed with tourists of late, and for good reason. **Agua Azul,** 62km south of Palenque, breath-taking from the mountain ridge above, is even more so from its rocky shores. The Río Yax jumps down 500 individual falls, then slips into rapids, whirlpools and calmer swimming areas in between. There is a swimming area 1km upstream from the falls, but the whirlpools and tremendous underwater currents have caused more than 100 deaths. Smart swimmers employ the buddy system here.

Since the 4km walk from *el crucero* is tiresome with any baggage, it's best to spend only the day at the falls, returning to Palenque in the afternoon. It's possible, though, to get hammock or sleeping space at the campground here. At Misol-Ha there are both camping spaces and *cabañas* available.

The falls at **Misol-Ha** are 24km from Palenque and only 2km from the highway crossing. There's only one large cataract here, but the swimming area is clean. The small **restaurant** has a few good dishes at reasonable prices. **Buses** between Palenque and Ocosingo or San Cristóbal will stop at the crossroads for either Agua Azul or Misol-Ha (2 pesos from Palenque). Since few buses pass after 4pm, leave the falls in the early afternoon. Steady pickup-truck traffic makes hitching relatively easy. (Entrance to either falls is 2 pesos per person, 5 pesos per carload.)

The most painless way to visit Agua Azul and Misol-Ha is aboard one of Transportes Chambalu's *combis* (25 pesos). Get to the Palenque station at Hidalgo and Allende by 9:30am; *combis* leave daily at 8am, 10am, and noon. After a 30min. photo stop at Misol-Ha, the van continues to Agua Azul (no need to hike—passengers are dropped off right by the falls for a three hr. swimming session). You can be back in Palenque six and a half hours after you left.

■■■ TONALÁ

There are times of year when flocks of screeching *golondrinas* (big-mouthed swallows) invade Tonalá's *zócalo*, nesting on the plaza's incomprehensible bush sculptures and providing free entertainment for the town. The cessation of your amusement at this spectacle should serve as a signal to catch the next bus out of town; you've just had the only fun you'll have in Tonalá.

Tonalá is the major beach bum crossroads in Chiapas, with connections to Paredón, Puerto Arista and Boca de Cielo. On Sundays and holidays, Chiapanecan families arrive en masse at these beaches; during the week, however, the completely deserted expanse of gray sands and crashing surf is conducive only to meditations on futility.

ORIENTATION

Tonalá lies 223km northwest of Tapachula along Route 200, 180km southwest of Tuxtla Gutiérrez on Route 190, and 26km from Arriaga. The town is served by frequent buses and daily trains along the southern Pacific line to the Guatemalan bor-

Centro Mexicano Internacional
14542 Brookhollow, Suite 279
San Antonio, TX 78232

The right Eurail for me is:

Description	Name (Should appear as on passport)	Price

Free Shipping and Handling with this card! | Total | |

Bill my:

☐ Mastercard ☐ Visa ☐ AmEx ☐ Check or Money Order

Card #_____ Name on Card_____

Ship my Eurail to:

Exp. Date:_____

_____
Name   Birthdate   Date trip begin

_____
Street address   City   ST   ZIP   Phone Number

We also offer:
Travel Gear
Discounted Airfares
AYH cards

Mail Order to
Let's Go Travel
53A Church Street
Cambridge, MA 02138

Or Call Toll Free
1-800-5LETS-GO

See our Catalog in
this Guide

der. Both **bus stations** are on Hidalgo, the main drag, which passes the *zócalo*. From the first- and second-class bus stations, walk six blocks left (east) from the entrance to the *zócalo*; all local buses from Tapachula stop on Hidalgo blocks before the *zócalo*. Local *colectivos*, taxis and buses from small neighboring towns may stop near the market (2 blocks southeast of the *zócalo*), on the *zócalo*, or nowhere in particular; ask directions to *el zócalo* when you disembark.

Most of Tonalá's important points hover around **Avenida Hidalgo,** which runs east from the stations, past the post office, the *zócalo*, the Palacio Municipal and a half-dozen hotels and restaurants before continuing to Tapachula and Guatemala as Route 200. **Matamoros** parallels Hidalgo one block south of the *zócalo*, passing several more hotels and restaurants as well as the market.

PRACTICAL INFORMATION

Tourist Office: In the clock-crowned Palacio Municipal (tel. 3-06-04), on the Hidalgo side of the *zócalo*. Map of Chiapas and several informative pamphlets. Some English spoken. Open Mon.-Fri. 9am-2pm and 6-8pm, Sat. 9am-noon.

Currency Exchange: Bancomer, Hidalgo at 21 de Marzo (tel. 3-00-74 or 3-00-48), 1 block east of the *zócalo*, will change dollars but not traveler's checks. Open Mon.-Fri. 9-11am.

Post Office: Zambrano 27 (tel. 3-06-83), 2 blocks west and 1 block north of the *zócalo*. *Lista de Correos*. Open Mon.-Sat. 8am-7pm; for registered mail Mon.-Fri. 8am-7pm, Sat. 8am-1pm. **Postal code:** 30500.

Telephones: Cafetería La Diligencia (tel. 3-20-81), on Independencia off Hidalgo east of the *zócalo*. International collect calls 5 pesos. Open daily 7am-9pm. **Telephone code:** 966.

Telegrams: Dr. Antonio Castro at Av. Aldan (tel. 3-00-40), 2 blockswest and 4 blocks south of the *zócalo*. Open Mon.-Fri. 8am-5pm.

Bus Stations: Cristóbal Colón (tel. 3-05-40) on Hidalgo 6 blocks west of the *zócalo* . Open 24 hrs. Luggage check sometimes, at no charge. 1st class to: Mexico City (95 pesos), via Puebla (80 pesos); Tapachula (31 pesos); Tuxtla Gutiérrez (15 pesos); Oaxaca (9:30pm, 45 pesos); Veracruz (11:30pm, 63 pesos). Also to Córdoba, Villahermosa, Coatzalcoalcos and Salina Cruz. *Servicio plus* to Mexico City, Tuxtla and Tapachula. 2nd-class **Autobuses Fletes y Pasajes** on Hidalgo 73 (tel. 3-25-94) a few blocks east of the *zócalo*. Free **luggage check** if you're planning to travel. To: Tapachula (16.50 pesos); Oaxaca (35 pesos); Mexico City (77 pesos), via Puebla (64 pesos); Tuxtla Gutiérrez (12.50 pesos). Also to Córdoba, Tuxtepec, Huixtla, Escuintla, Mapastepec, Pijijiapan, Juchitan, and Tehuantepec. Buses for Arriaga leave from Hidalgo near the *zócalo*.

Taxis: (Tel. 3-06-20.) Catch 'em at the *zócalo* or near the *mercado*. Taxis run *colectivo* to Arriaga from the east side of the *zócalo*.

Market: On Matamoros, several blocks southeast of the *zócalo*. Walk east on Hidalgo 1 block and right on Independencia to Matamoros. Dirty and dark. Open daily from 4am.

Red-Cross: Av. Joaquín Miguel Gutiérrez (tel. 3-21-21). Ambulance service. Open 24 hrs.

24-hr. Pharmacy: Clínica de Especialidades, Hidalgo 127 (tel. 3-19-90), at Independencia east of the *zócalo*. No English spoken.

Medical Services: Hospital General, Av. 27 de Septiembre (tel. 3-06-87), at Calle Mina, 6 blocks east of the *zócalo* and 3 blocks north. 24-hr. emergency service.

Police: On 12 de Octubre (tel. 301-03), 2 blocks west of the bus station and 1 block to the right at the group of yellow school buildings. Easy to miss the faded sign. No English spoken. Open 24 hrs.

ACCOMMODATIONS AND FOOD

Many of Tonalá's hotels are rather expensive, and the *cucarachas* run wild—a one-two punch that may have you clamoring for a spot on the bus. **Hotel Grajandra,** Ave. Hidalgo 24 (tel. 3-01-44), is on the pricier side but you'll be eternally grateful for its creature comforts and lack of creatures. It's also next to the bus station—

TONALÁ

you can't miss the bubblegum pink awnings. (Singles 77 pesos. Doubles 88 pesos. Triples 105 pesos. Slightly more for air-conditioning.) **Hotel Tonalá,** Av. Hidalgo 172 (tel. 3-04-80) at 15 de Mayo, offers big rooms with balconies, TVs, fans and hot water for a price. Make sure to settle accounts before you stay. (Check-out 1pm. Rooms for 1-3 people 40 pesos, with A/C 70 pesos. Traveler's checks and dollars accepted. Reservations preferably paid in advance.) **Hotel El Farro,** 16 de Septiembre 24 (tel. 3-00-33), offers spacious quarters with high ceilings in an only slightly run-down colonial building. (Check-out noon. Singles 50 pesos. 2-bed doubles 40 pesos. 3-bed triples 50 pesos. Send payment in advance to reserve.)

There are more cheap meals in Tonalá than profanities on an Ice-T album. Inexpensive restaurants cluster around the bus station, a row of taco stands marks the western edge of the *zócalo*, and the *mercado's* fresh produce beckons incessantly. The overweeningly pink **Restaurante Nora,** Independencia 10 (tel. 3-02-43), just north of Hidalgo and 1 block east of the *zócalo*, serves inexpensive Mexican meals. (3-course *comida corrida* 18 pesos. Meat dishes 11-23 pesos. Open Tues.-Sun. 8am-10pm. Traveler's checks and credit cards accepted.) **Cafetería y Restaurant Sanbor's,** Hidalgo 1 at Madero (tel. 3-06-80), on the southwest corner of the *zócalo* under the sign that says "Pizza Zaz," also deals in Mexican standards: the *antojitos* (4-10 pesos) and the *ensalada de camarón* (18 pesos) are good. Juices go for 2 pesos; the *agua de jamaica* is especially scintillating. (Open daily 8am-midnight.) **Restaurante Hotel Galilea,** Hidalgo at Callejón Ote (tel. 3-02-39), on the east side of the *zócalo*, is expensive but original compared to the taco stands; it serves delicious sandwiches with an assortment of vegetables cooked in vinegar. (Sandwiches 5-12 pesos. Chicken 16-20 pesos. Open daily 8am-midnight.)

BEACHES

The coast near Tonalá stretches from El Mar Muerto (a less famous Dead Sea) west of town, along the enormous sandpit extending southeast from Paredón, and past Puerto Arista to its endpoint a peninsula containing a small beach and the village of Boca de Cielo.

Among these settlements, the most popular is **Puerto Arista,** 18km from Tonalá on a paved road served by public transportation. While Puerto Arista cannot compare with the beauty or facilities of Puerto Ángel or Escondido farther north in Oaxaca, it makes a good daytrip for travelers heading south (who won't encounter another decent beach for miles). Along the 16km of dark gray beach at Arista, the undertow is so strong that few swimmers venture more than a few meters from shore. In several spots, *canales* (forceful channels or currents) can take you on a one-way trip far out to sea; ask about dangerous spots before diving in.

There are few palms on Arista's beach to provide shelter at night; a few restaurants on the beach have covered poles on which to hang hammocks, and most eateries rent hammocks; the space is free as long as you order meals at the same establishment. If you don't have a tent, you'll be especially glad you forked over the few extra pesos when it rains (not uncommon in the summer). If you want slightly more privacy and comfort, march left down the beach. There are two or three places toward the end that rent rustic *cabañas* with thatched-roof rooms and sand floors. The privacy is minimal, since pigs and chickens wander through the *cabañas* day and night.

Buses, *colectivos*, minibuses and taxis connect Tonalá with the nearby beaches, running constantly from 7am to 6:30pm. In the early evening, when *colectivos* and buses stop running, taxis become the only means of public transportation. It's best not to travel at this time, since fares go up as cab drivers enjoy their few hours of monopoly. Collective **taxis** (5 pesos) make the half-hour journey to Puerto Arista, leaving from the corner of Av. Juárez and Calle 20 de Marzo. To get to the taxis from the *zócalo*, walk three blocks east on Hidalgo and then two blocks south on 20 de Marzo. *Colectivos* to Boca de Cielo (6 pesos) leave from the same spot. *Colectivos* leave for Paredón (2 pesos) from the corner of Madero and Allende, south of *el cen-*

tro. To reach the intersection from the *zócalo*, walk west on Hidalgo, turn left (south) on Madero and continue three blocks over a white bridge that spans a riverbed full of trash until you reach Allende. Taxis for Paredón (also 2 pesos) leave from Calle Independencia between Matamoros and Juárez. To get there, walk two blocks east on Hidalgo from the *zócalo* and then one and a half blocks south on Independencia.

■■■ TAPACHULA

4000m below the majestic volcano Tacaná, a fertile river basin drains the southernmost part of the Mexican Republic on its run to the Pacific Ocean. Tapachula (pop. 300,000) rises out of a clearing in the jungle which still nurtures jaguars, pumas, packs of *peccaries* (akin to pigs) and *chakalakas* (turkey-like fowl). Topiary trees, their leafy crowns trimmed square and joined to one another, form a green canopy over the *zócalo's* two square blocks. During the rainy season hundreds of mostly Guatemalan emigrants crowd under these trees. Relaxing outdoor cafés provide sanctuary from the rampant *marimba* music that echoes through the city.

Primarily a business center, Tapachula attracts accidental tourists bound for Guatemala or the north. If you must stay for more than a brief layover, you can always escape to the beach at **Puerto Madero,** 27km away, via bus from the second-class station Paulino Navarro on Calle 7 Ote. between Av. Central Nte. and Av. 2 Nte. (45min., 3 pesos). Though not spectacular, it provides ample opportunity to enjoy sand and surf either before or after a long bus journey.

ORIENTATION

Tapachula is 18km from Talismán at the Guatemalan border on Route 200 and 303km west-northwest of Guatemala City. The first-class **Cristóbal Colón bus station** is on 17 Calle Ote./Route 200 at 3 Av. Nte., seven blocks north and six blocks east of the main plaza. From the station, turn left on 17 Calle and left again on Av. Central Nte. Continue six blocks to Calle 5 Pte. and the *zócalo* is four blocks to the right. At night, take a taxi (3 pesos per person). *Colectivos* shuttle travelers to the **airport** (call 5-12-87 to be picked up). The 10-peso fare is much lower than a private taxi's (30 pesos). Tapachula's streets are organized in a logical if complicated manner. *Avenidas* run north-south, and *calles* run east-west. *Calles* north of Calle Central are odd-numbered; those south of the central axis are even-numbered. Similarly, *avenidas* east of Av. Central are odd-numbered, and those west have even numbers. But unlike most *chiapaneco* cities, Tapachula's **main plaza** is not located at the intersection of Calle Central and Av. Central, but at 3 Calle Pte. between 6 and 8 Av. Nte., northwest of the center.

PRACTICAL INFORMATION

Tourist Office: 4 Av. Nte. 35 (tel. 6-54-70, fax 6-55-22), on the third floor next to a bridal shop. Brochures, maps and typically enthusiastic tourist office employees. Open Mon.-Fri. 9am-3pm and 6-9pm.

Consulate: Guatemala, 2 Calle Ote. 33 (tel. 6-12-52), between 7 and 9 Av. Sur. U.S. and Canadian citizens need only a passport to acquire a visa (see Guatemala: Essentials for more information regarding entrance requirements). Visas usually take less than ½hr., but arrive early and be persistent or you may wait all day. Payment accepted only in U.S. dollars. Open Mon.-Fri. 8am-4pm. Ring the bell after hours for emergencies.

Currency Exchange: Banks in Tapachula won't change dollars unless you have an account. **Casa de Cambio,** 4 Av. Nte. and 3 Calle Pte. (tel. 6-51-22), changes U.S. dollars and traveler's checks at good rates. (Open Mon.-Sat. 8am-7:30pm, Sun. 8am-noon.)

Post Office: 1 Calle Ote. 32 (tel. 6-10-28), between 7 and 9 Av. Nte., is open Mon.-Fri. 8am-6pm, Sat.-Sun. 9am-1pm. **Postal code:** 30700.

Telephones: Long-distance *casetas* are located on 17 Calle Ote., 1 block west of the Cristóbal Colón bus station, and also right across from the station (tel. 6-35-77). Collect calls 12 pesos. (Open daily 7am-11pm.) Public LADATELs at the Cristóbal Colón bus station or at the Cine Maya on 2 Av. Nte. at 1 Calle Pte.

Airport: on the road to Puerto Madero, about 17km south of town, is served by **Aeroméxico,** 2 Av. Nte. 6 (tel. 6-20-50). Service to Mexico City daily at 12:25pm (230 pesos). Open Mon.-Fri. 8am-8pm, Sat. 8am-4pm. **Aviacsa,** Av. Central and Calle 1 Ote. (tel. 6-31-47, fax 6-31-59), service to Mexico City (380 pesos), Tuxtla Gutiérrez (190 pesos), and Guatemala City (290 pesos). Open Mon.-Fri. 9am-2pm and 4-7pm, Sat. 9am-2pm.

Train Station: Av. Central Sur 150, at the end of the *avenida* behind a miniature plaza and a small market (tel. 6-21-76), has slow, cheap, unreliable service to, among others, Veracruz (7am, 24hrs., 24 pesos) via Huixtla, Tonalá, and Arriaga. Also to Ciudad Hidalgo (1:15pm, 4hrs., 11 pesos). Tickets go on sale 1 hour before the train is supposed to arrive. Second class only.

Bus Stations: Cristóbal Colón, 17 Calle Ote. (tel. 6-28-81), at 3 Nte. To, among others: Tonalá (22 pesos), Ocozocoautla (35.5 pesos), Tuxtla Gutiérrez (38.5 pesos), Coatzalcoalcos (60 pesos), Veracruz (8:45pm, 79 pesos), Villahermosa (76.5 pesos), Oaxaca (6pm, 64 pesos), Puebla (9:15pm, 103 pesos, *servicio plus* 151 pesos). **ADO** (tel. 6-76-55), in the same terminal. 1st class to Mexico City (2 per day, 110,000 pesos). 1 bus per day each to Acuyucan, Córdoba, Minatitlán, Orizaba and Tierra Blanca. **Luggage check** (2 pesos per day) available across the street at the telephone *caseta*. **Transportes Tuxtla Gutiérrez,** Av. 3 Nte at Calle 9 Ote. (tel. 6-67-75). 2nd class to numerous Chiapanecan destinations, including: Comitán (16 pesos), San Cristóbal (21.50 pesos), Chiapa de Corzo (26.50 pesos), Tuxtla Gutiérrez (26.50 or 27.50 pesos, depending on route). **Fletes y Pasajes,** Av. 3 Nte. (tel. 6-54-83), at Calle 5 Ote. 2nd class buses, 2 per day to: Mexico City (102 pesos), Puebla (91 pesos), Cordoba, Tuxtepec and Matías Romero. 4 per day to Oaxaca (57 pesos), Tehuantepec (35 pesos), Arriaga (22 pesos), Tonalá (19 pesos), Juchitan, Pijijiapan, and Mapastepec.

Guatemala Border Crossing Transportation: Into Guatemala, take a bus to Talismán or Ciudad Hidalgo, cross the border on foot and then catch the **Galgos** bus line to Guatemala City. (See Guatemala: Essentials for more information.) **Autobús Union y Progreso,** 5 Calle Pte. between 12 Av. Nte. and 14 Av. Nte., runs to Talismán (every 5min., 4:30am-7pm, 1.80 pesos). **Cristóbal Colón** also does the route (4 per day *de paso*, 2 pesos). From the 2nd class bus station on Calle 7 Ote. between Av. Central Nte. and Av. 2 Nte., **Paulino Navarro** sends buses to Ciudad Hidalgo (every 15min., 4am-10pm, 3.50 pesos). If need be, take a taxi from the *zócalo* to Talismán (30 pesos).

Red Cross: 9 Av. Nte. at 1 Calle Ote. (tel. 6-29-49), across from the post office. 24 hr. ambulance service. No English spoken.

24-hr. Pharmacy: Originally-named **Farmacia 24 Horas,** 8 Av. Nte. 25 (tel. 6-24-80), at Calle 7 Pte. No English spoken. Delivery to anywhere within the city available 7am-11pm.

Hospital: Hospital Civil Carmen de Acebo: 4 Av. Nte. at 19 Calle Pte. (tel. 6-17-12). Open 24 hrs.

Police: In the Palacio Municipal, at 8 Av. Nte. and 3 Calle Pte. (tel. 5-28-93). Open 24 hrs.

ACCOMMODATIONS

Due to the huge influx of Guatemalan refugees, budget accommodations are a dime a dozen in Tapachula. It's always a good idea to check rooms first, however.

Hospedaje Las Américas, 10 Av. Nte. (tel. 6-27-57), between Calles 3 and 5 Ote. Good value—clean rooms with fans and slightly less clean but tiled bathrooms. No hot water. Sunshiny courtyard. Check-out 1pm. Singles 20 pesos. 1-bed doubles 25 pesos. 2-bed doubles 35 pesos. 2-bed triples 40 pesos. Rooms with 3 beds for up to 5 people 60 pesos. Reservations can be made by phone.

Hotel El Fénix, 4 Av. Nte. 19 (tel. 5-07-55, fax 6-47-47), between 1 and 3 Calles Pte., 1 block west of the *zócalo*. More expensive than the others, but a quantum leap above in quality. Worth the extra pesos if you're recuperating from Guatemala or don't enjoy the Tapachulan heat. Fans and phones in the rooms, hot water in the bathrooms and TV in the lobby. Parking available. Singles 71.5-86 pesos. Doubles 83-98 pesos. Triples 98-116 pesos. (Higher prices are for A/C.) Traveler's checks, MC and Visa accepted.

Hotel Tabasco, Av. Central Nte. 123 (tel. 6-51-33), at 17 Calle Ote.. Near the Colón station. Dingy hotel accompanied by the roar of buses in the night. It does have fans and convenience if you have to catch an early bus. 20 pesos per person for up to 4 people.

FOOD

A moderately priced meal is not hard to come by in Tapachula—but don't expect a feast. The four restaurants on the *zócalo* are pricy; better meals can be had on the streets just off the plaza. The market abounds with fresh fruits, veggies and baked goods, t'he biggest and cleanest is **Mercado San Juan**, Ave. Norte and Calle 17, west of the *zócalo*.

La Parilla, 8 Av. Nte. 20 (tel. 6-40-62), on the west side of the *zócalo*. Fluorescent lights, cafeteria tables and huge birds perched on the wall. Eggs 3-6.5 pesos. Tamales 5 pesos. *Tortas* 4-6.5 pesos. Open 'round the clock.

Restaurante "La Troje," 21 Ote. (tel. 5-35-40) and 11 Nte. Walk through a fancy Tapachulan neighborhood into the limits of local chic. Outdoor grill with white-gloved service. It'll blow your budget, but you won't be sorry. Grilled specialties 18-25.3 pesos. Chicken 17-22 pesos. Seafood 25-30 pesos. Credit cards accepted. Open Mon.-Sat. noon-4pm and 8pm-midnight, Sun. noon-7pm.

La Quinta Carmelita, Central Oriente, 76 (tel. 5-40-07). Go two blocks to Calle Central Pte. then approximately ten blocks east. Tranquil atmosphere and tasty specialties. *Panuchos* are a type of crunchy mini-tortilla topped with beans and pickled veggies; *Queso fundido especial* (11 pesos) is quite decadent. Open daily 7:30am-10pm.

Yucatán Peninsula

Too engrossed in hunting for slaves to watch where he was going, Hernández de Córdoba mistakenly ran aground in 1517. The *indígenas*, when asked the name of the land by the freshly disembarked sailors, replied, *"Tectetán,"* meaning, "We do not understand you." Misinterpreting the Mayan reply, Córdoba dubbed the region Yucatán before shoving off again. This encounter established a paradigm that would hold throughout Yucatán's history; misunderstood and continually molested by outsiders, it would never be fully conquered. Today, the peninsula's culture remains essentially Mayan, but foreign influence fights on. Maya is still the first language of most of the inhabitants, nature worship continues (if with a Catholic veneer), and fishing, farming and hammock-making outproduce big industry and commerce. Burgeoning tourism, however, is threatening the traditional *yucateco* way of life. As international nomads discover the peninsula's fine beaches, beautiful colonial towns and striking Mayan ruins, more workers are drawn by the dubious allure of the tourism industry. Many of those not working in the hotels or restaurants find themselves weaving hammocks for *viajeros* in Mérida, fishing lobster for visitors to Cancún, or driving tour buses to ruin sites.

The peninsula's geography consists mostly of flat limestone scrubland or rainforest dotted with an occasional *cenote* (natural well). Because of the highly porous limestone subsoil, there are no above-ground rivers in Yucatán. Poor soil and the lack of water make farming difficult; corn is still the subsistence crop. The prominence of the rain god Chac at most Mayan ruins testifies to the eternal importance of the seasonal rains, which precipitate from May to early summer.

Since the Maya conquered the peninsula around 500 BC, Yucatán has known several masters. Many of the buildings in the Maya's illustrious city of Chichén Itzá are the creations of Toltecs and were built after the tribe took the peninsula in the 11th century. Spanish imperialists landed first at Quintana Roo but did not attempt to penetrate the region until landing again at Campeche, which was taken and lost several times before being securely fortified during the mid-16th century. The Montejo family orchestrated the Spanish conquest in the Yucatán, establishing Mérida on the site of a Mayan village in 1542 and later installing additional colonial strongholds such as Valladolid. More recently, other European influences have shaped Yucatán's new cities—most notably in Mérida, where the Paseo Montejo imitates the Champs-Elysées of Paris.

Colonialism brought more than just forts and stone cathedrals, however. Spanish settlers received vast land grants and convinced displaced *indígenas* to labor on their estates. Oppressed and humiliated, the *indígenas* rebelled against the white *ladino* overlords repeatedly in 1546, 1585, 1610 and 1624. After gaining independence from Spain, *ladinos* only stepped up their exploitation of Mayan peoples and lands. Thousands of Mayans were conscripted as debt laborers on the expanding *henequén* plantations. In 1847, Mayan discontent exploded in a bloody racial struggle, known as the Caste War, which enveloped the peninsula. At the height of the Mayan advance a year later, only the cities of Mérida and Campeche remained in *ladino* hands. A rebel Mayan community survived in eastern Yucatán as late as 1901, sovereign decades after Mexican troops had retaken most of the peninsula. Yucatán's most recent culture shock resulted from the completion of Route 180, which links the peninsula with mainland Mexico. Desiring to maintain their historical isolation from the rest of the Mexican Republic, proud *yucatecos* originally resisted the federal highway plans. Despite new competition in shipping and transportation from the south and the ongoing invasion of sun- and ruins-seeking foreigners, Yucatán retains its distinctive character: *yucatecos* have held on to their native drawl and continue to brew the dark beers considered to be the nation's finest.

Yucatán Peninsula

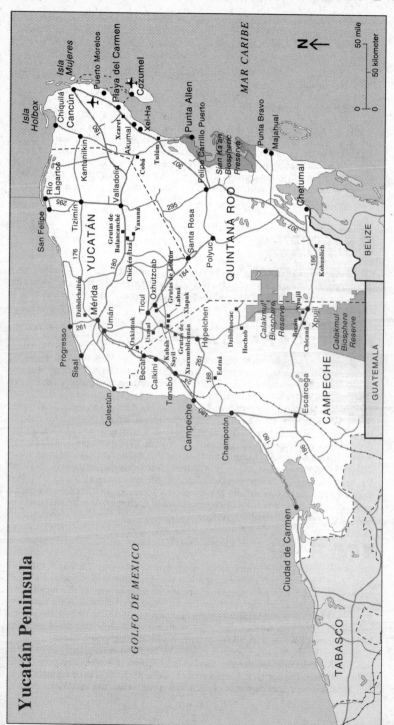

Mayan culture thrives on in the peninsula's small towns, where the only evidence of Western influence arrives weekly in the form of Coca Cola vendors. In the expanses between the touristed archaeological sites, *yucateco* women continue to carry bowls of corn flour on their heads and wear embroidered *huipile* dresses. In large cities like Campeche and Mérida, the stability of Mayan culture manifests itself more subtly in the citizens' unpretentious hospitality.

The Yucatán Peninsula is divided into three states: Campeche, on the Gulf Coast, forms the peninsula's western side; Yucatán constitutes the north; and Quintana Roo, on the eastern side, faces the Caribbean Sea. "The" Yucatán refers to the region, not the state; Yucatán without the article can refer to either entity.

Route 186 connects the Yucatán to mainland Mexico, entering the state Campeche from Tabasco. At the crossroads town of Escárcega, Route 186 heads east past remote ruins en route to Chetumal and Quintana Roo. Route 261 heads north from Escárcega and meets the shorter coastal Route 180 at Champotón shortly before reaching the capital. Several roads encircle Campeche, but all converge on the two routes from Campeche to Mérida.

CAMPECHE

Campeche state languishes in its relaxed colonial ambience but has fewer sights of every type. The state's famous archaeological site, Edzná, is easily reached from the state's eponymous capital city, and more remote Mayan cities may tempt you to wander through other corners of the state.

■■■ ESCÁRCEGA

Escárcega occupies the intersection of Highway 261 and Highway 186. From the first-class ADO station there, numerous **buses** go north to Mérida (330km; 5hrs., 34 pesos), east to Chetumal (264km; 4½ hrs., 26 pesos), southwest to Villahermosa (301km; 5hrs., 30 pesos) and south to Palenque (233km; 2½ hrs., 21 pesos). Service also runs to Mexico City, Veracruz, Coatzalcoalcos, Puebla and Cancún. One km down Av. Hector Pérez Martínex, runs second-class service to similar locations. **Hotel Escárcega,** Av. Justo Sierra #86 (tel. 4-01-87), between the ADO station and the center of town, offers well-equipped, tidy rooms. (Singles 60 pesos,. Doubles 77 pesos. Triples 88 pesos.) **Hotel San Luis,** on the *zócalo* in Escárcega (tel. (982) 4-01-10), provides spotless and comfortable accommodations just three blocks from the second-class bus station. (Singles 45 pesos, doubles 55 pesos, triples 65 pesos. Traveler's checks accepted). The restaurant downstairs serves *típico* entrees for 12-20 pesos. Usually the bus to Palenque arrives full in Escárcega, so expect to stand for most of the ride to the ruins.

■■■ CAMPECHE

Campeche (pop. 170,000) once served as the major port on the Yucatán Peninsula's Gulf Coast. Vicious winds persisting for days at a time drove trade ships to seek shelter in Campeche, and their cargos tempted pirates who sought the wealth that Campeche's inhabitants derived from the logwood dye business. After countless incursions by Dutch and English corsairs between the 16th and 18th centuries, the Spanish decided to construct protective walls around Campeche; the stark stone bulwarks and high fortifications successfully terminated the pirate raids.

After the Bourbons came to power in Spain in the 18th century, Campeche lost its monopoly over peninsular trade. Ciudad del Carmen, a deep-water port on the state's southern coast, quickly replaced Campeche as the center of regional trade. Despite the recent massive influx of petroleum profits that have revitalized flagging

Campeche state, the capital city has changed little. Parts of the fragmented stone wall stand today, as do many of the original bulwarks, houses and sidewalks.

Modern Campeche exerts as much energy attracting *extranjeros* today as it did repelling them some centuries ago. The recent construction of an airport outside town and a highway from Mérida has made Campeche more internationally and domestically accessible; results, in the form of increased tourism, are starting to show. Three gargantuan hotels and a tourism complex have arisen between the old town and the waterfront, and construction is underway on many more.

The effects of these changes, however, are difficult to perceive. The tourists that Campeche does draw don't stay for long because there is little to do in town. Lazy streets begin flooding at the mere forecasts of rain, and *aguadores* with mule-drawn carts sell collected rainwater door-to-door. Adventurous swashbucklers can tackle a few mid-jungle ruin sites in the vicinity, but most modern-day invasions will be brief, staged on the way to or from greater exploits in Yucatán.

ORIENTATION

A convenient 252km southwest of Mérida and 444km northeast of Villahermosa, Campeche is a popular stopover on the trek east and north from mainland Mexico to the northern Yucatán. The city, along the main Yucatán thoroughfare, is served by many bus, train, and air routes.

The most direct link between Mérida and Campeche by car is Route 180. Recent improvements to the pavement have shortened the trip to two hours. From the south, take coastal Route 180 from Ciudad del Carmen, which merges at Champotón with Route 261 from Escárcega. Watch out for speed bumps throughout the area; because of them, the narrow, curving 66km stretch of Route 180 between Champotón and Campeche is excruciatingly slow.

All major routes into the city intersect the peripheral highway that encircles it; a smaller circular road falls within the outer highway, circumscribing the old city. All main roads cross the **Circuito** near the city center. **Avenida Gobernadores** leads in from the Mérida highway northeast of the city, crosses the peripheral highway, and joins the Circuito; it accesses the train station, airport and bus terminal.

To reach the *zócalo* from the first- and second-class **bus terminal**, catch the "Gobernadores" bus (.60 pesos) across the street from the station. There are no fixed stops; ask the bus driver to let you off at Baluarte de San Francisco. Turn right into the old city and walk four blocks on Calle 57 to the *zócalo*. If you'd rather make the 15-minute walk from the station, head left on Gobernadores for a few minutes straight past the large store Baluarte de San Pedro and bear left as it becomes the large divided Circuito Baluartes. Three blocks later, turn right on Calle 57 through the stone arch of Balvarte de San Francisco and walk four blocks to the *zócalo*. Taxis from the airport to the *zócalo* cost 20 pesos; from the train or bus stations, 5 pesos.

Campeche once fit into the 40 square blocks marked off by the still-standing set of seven *baluartes*. Sightseers in Campeche usually find nothing of interest outside this compact area. Most *campecharos* live in large, suburban areas north of the old city.

In the old city, the streets have no names, only numbers. The *zócalo* lies near the sea, bordered by Calles 8, 10, 55, and 57. Excellent city maps are available at the tourist office, at hotels and at a small information stand inside the ADO bus station.

A confusing network of **buses** links Campeche's more distant sectors to the edge of the old city. The fare on regular buses is .60 pesos; minibuses, which do not allow standing passengers, charge .80 pesos. The market, at the point where Gobernadores becomes Circuito Baluartes, serves as the hub for local routes. Buses sometimes stray from their routes and have no established stops; it is possible to flag them down at almost any point on their route. No buses are permitted within the old city; you must disembark at the periphery and enter on foot. Buses run between 6am and 11pm, and crowd to the point of suffocation in early afternoon and evening. Car

CAMPECHE

rentals are fairly worthwhile for groups planning tours of the nearby but hard-to-reach ruins.

PRACTICAL INFORMATION

Tourist Offices: State Office, across the parking lot of Hotel Baluarte (tel. and fax 6-60-68), between Av. 16 de Septiembre and Av. Ruiz Cortínez (the coastal highway). Inside a low, pyramidal building called the Plaza Moch-Cuouh; the obscure entrance faces southwest. Plentiful information provided on tours of the city and the nearby ruins. Students on the staff are friendly and knowledgeable. English spoken. Open Mon.-Sat. 9am-8pm, closed Sun. **Federal Tourist Office:** Circuito Baluartes at Calle 14 (tel. 6-55-93), in the Baluarte de Santa Rosa. Helpful staff hands out maps and brochures. Some English spoken. Open Mon.-Fri. 8am-3pm.

Travel agencies: Agencia de Viajes Jaina, in the Hotel Ramada, Av. Ruiz Cartinez, #55 (tel. 1-16-19). They organize Edzná tours, leaving at 9am, returning at 2pm (50 pesos). Special Ruta Puuc tours on Sat. 7:30am-10pm including Caves at Xtacumbilxumaan and Loltún, Sayil, Xlapak, Labná, Uxmal, and Kabah. **Prof. Augustin Zavala y Lozano** at Calle 16 #348, gives 3-hr. tours of Edzná (45 pesos).

Currency Exchange: Bancomer, Av. 16 de Septiembre 120 (tel. 6-66-22), between Calles 59 and 61. Open for exchange Mon.-Fri. 9am-noon. Another branch is on Circuito Baluartes at Calle 55 (tel. 6-40-52) at the market. Open for exchange Mon.-Fri. 9am-1pm. **Bánamex,** Calle 10 #15 (tel. 6-52-52), at Calle 53. Open for exchange Mon.-Fri. 9am-1:30pm.

American Express: Calle 59 in Edificio Belmar (tel. 1-10-10). Next to Ramada Inn. English spoken. Open Mon.-Fri. 9am-2pm and 5-7pm, Sat. 9am-1pm.

Post Office: 16 de Septiembre (tel. 6-21-34), at Calle 53 in the Edificio Federal. Open for stamps, registered mail and *Lista de Correos* Mon.-Fri. 8am-8pm, Sat. 9am-1pm. **Postal Code:** 24000.

Telephones: Computel, Calle 8 #255 between Calles 57 and 59. International collect calls 5 pesos every 10min. Open 7am-10pm daily.

Telegrams: Edificio Federal, 16 de Septiembre (tel. 6-43-90), at Calle 53 in the Edificio Federal (the post office building) to the right upon entering. Open for money orders Mon.-Fri. 9am-8pm, Sat. 9am-noon; for telegrams Mon.-Fri. 9am-8pm, Sat. 9am-1pm.

Airport: On Porfirio, 10km from the city center (tel. 6-14-38). **Aeroméxico,** at the airport (tel. 6-56-78), to Mexico City, Houston , and Acapulco.

Train Station: Nacozari 26 (tel. 6-51-48), 3km northeast of the city center. Best to arrive 1hr. before departure to reconfirm time and purchase tickets; trains arrive late or never. To Córdoba and Coatzalcoalcos and other destinations on the way (2nd class daily at 10:30pm, *mixto* Mon.-Sat. at 8am.) Price calculated by distance traveled (.05 pesos per km). *Mixtos* are just that; they include passengers, chickens and whatever else happens to be brought on board. Tickets go on sale 1hr. before the train is supposed to arrive. Trains are generally cheaper and much less reliable than buses.

Bus Station: 1st- and 2nd-class buses at terminal on Gobernadores between Calles 47 and Chile, 4 blocks northeast of the city wall. 1st-class ADO terminal, with baggage check (2 pesos per day, 4 pesos overnight), waiting room and so-called restaurant, faces Gobernadores; the 2nd-class terminal lies behind it (access via 1st-class terminal or side street Chile). **ADO,** Gobernadores 289 (tel. 6-28-02). 1st class to: Mérida (17.50 pesos); Mexico City (2 per day, 13 pesos); Puebla (1 per day, 116.50 pesos); Villahermosa (3 per day, 41 pesos); Escárega (3 per day, 14 pesos); Chetumal (2 per day, 38.50 pesos); Ciudad del Carmen (2 per day, 23 pesos); Palenque (2 overnight, 37 pesos); Veracruz (2 overnight, 85 pesos). 2nd-class buses (tel. 6-23-32) run to: Edzná (4.60 pesos); Iturbide, for the Dzibilnocac ruins; Bolonchén, near the Grutas de Xtacumbilxunaan; Kabah ruins; Santa Elena; Uxmal; Becal.

Taxis: (Tel. 6-22-30.) Three stands: at the intersection of Calles 8 and 55, to left of the cathedral; the intersection of Calle 55 and Circuito, near the market; and at the intersection of Gobernadores and Chile, near the bus terminal. Basic rate for intra-city travel 5 pesos; to the airport 20-25 pesos.

Car Rental: Hertz, in the lobby of the Hotel Baluartes at Ruíz Cortínez and Calle 59 (tel. 6-88-48). VW's start at 101 pesos per day plus 78 pesos per km.

Market: At Gobernadores and Circuito, beyond the city wall. Unexceptional handicrafts and cheap food, including many *chiles*. Open daily sunrise-sunset, Sun. until 3pm.

Supermarket: Super Diez (tel. 1-29-59), in the Pl. Comercial A-Kin-Pech on 16 de Septiembre. Large, modern supermarket with a bakery, bookstore, and clothing boutique, next to a small shopping complex. Open daily 8am-9pm. **Super Maz,** on Av. Resurjimiento in the Plaza Universidad, near the university and the hostel. Look for the red *cupola*. Huge, modern, and immaculate supermarket in similar new mall. Open daily 7am-10pm.

Laundromat: Lavandería y Tintorería Campeche, Calle 55 #22 (tel. 6-51-42), between Calles 12 and 8 pesos per kg. Same-day service if dropped off in the morning. Open Mon.-Sat. 8am-4pm.

Red Cross: On Áv. Las Palmas near the market (tel. 6-06-66). Free 24-hr. emergency service.

Pharmacy: Farmacia Gobernadores, next to the ADO station on Gobernadores. Open 24 hrs.

Medical Services: Seguro Social, on López Mateos (tel. 6-52-02), south of the city. Designed and subsidized for affiliates, but legally required to help anyone in an emergency for a small fee. **Hospital General,** Av. Central at Circuito Baluartes, 4 blocks south of market (tel. 6-42-33).

Police: Calle 12 (tel. 6-21-11), between Calles 57 and 59. Open 24 hrs.

ACCOMMODATIONS AND CAMPING

The limited number of budget accommodations in Campeche is due in part to the presence of three waterfront luxury hotels: the Baluartes, Alhambra and Ramada Inn. In a city often overlooked by tourists, few middle-range establishments have survived the competition, and many of the cheaper places have sunk to unusually low levels of cleanliness and maintenance. Even so, cheap accommodations fill up quickly after dark.

Youth Hostel Villa Deportiva Juvenil Campeche, on Agustín Melgar (tel. 6-18-02), several blocks east of the water and the coastal highway. From the *zócalo*, take the "Lerma" bus south along the coastal highway to the intersection with Melgar and walk the remaining few blocks. New, spotless 2-bunk rooms with new spiffy bathrooms. Fans, but no hot water. Lockout 11pm. Dining facilities only for large groups. Curfew 11pm, but you can knock if you arrive later. Fill in July, August, and December. Call to reserve. Check-out 2pm. Bunk rental (includes towel, blanket and pillow) 10 pesos per night plus a 20-peso deposit. Breakfast (7-8:30am) 9 pesos, lunch (1:30-2:30pm) 11.25 pesos, and dinner (11.25pm) 11.25 pesos.

Hospedaje Teresita, Calle 53 #31 (tel. 6-60-56), between Calles 12 and 14 in a quiet residential part of the old city, 3 blocks northeast of the *zócalo*. A welcoming place with bare spartan rooms: a bed and a fan. Communal bathrooms aren't tops and have no hot water. Check-out noon. Singles or doubles 20 pesos, with private bath 30 pesos.

Hotel Campeche, Calle 57 #2 (tel. 6-51-83), on the zócalo. Run-down rooms in back are tight and lack windows, but rooms in front are more spacious and some have a balcony overlooking the zócalo. Bathrooms lack shine and hot water. Check-out 1pm. Single 25 pesos, with private bath 30 pesos. Doubles 40-45 pesos. Triples 55 pesos. Each additional person 10 pesos.

Hotel Colonial, Calle 14 #122 (tel. 6-22-22), between Calles 55 and 57, 2½ blocks from the *zócalo*. Typical colonial building includes quaint courtyard. Freshly painted rooms in pastel blue, green, and pink come with monogrammed sheets. Rooms have fans, phones and hot water. Check-out 2pm. Singles 58.30 pesos.

CAMPECHE

Doubles 60 pesos. Triples 82.50 pesos. Each additional person 16.50 pesos. A/C 16.50 extra. Reservations must be paid in advance for late arrival.

Hotel Castelmar, Calle 61 #2 (tel. 6-28-86), between Calles 8 and 10, 3 blocks south of the *zócalo* under a large sign visible from the coastal highway. Huge, nicely-furnished rooms in a colonial building that collapsed with the Spanish Empire. Fans and hot water. Check-out 2pm. Singles or doubles 44 pesos. Triples 60 pesos. 16.50 pesos per additional person. Reservations must be paid in advance.

Hotel Posada del Angel, Calle 10 #307 (tel. 6-77-18), across from the cathedral. Beautiful balconied establishment with an enthusiastic manager and a panoply of plants. Standard, well-maintained rooms are carpeted and decked out in wood and have A/C, hot water, and fans. Check-out 2pm. Singles 55 pesos, with A/C 71.50 pesos. Doubles 66 pesos, with A/C 82.50 pesos. 11 pesos per additional person.

Hotel Reforma, Calle 8 #255 (tel. 6-44-64), across from the small plaza between Calles 57 and 59. The upper floor rooms (some with balconies) are more spacious and brighter than the dark ones on the lower floor and are the the the best bargain in town. The wall paint is chipping, but bathrooms are decent though lacking in hot water. Check-out 1pm. Singles 30 pesos. Doubles 40 pesos. Triples 50 pesos. 10 pesos per each additional person. Reservations can be made by phone.

FOOD

Campeche's market is amply stocked with sea creatures netted in the tranquil Bahía de Campeche. Sadly, the market places, taco stands and street food don't make up for the dearth of sit-down establishments in a city of this size. A few places dish up excellent seafood, notably shrimp and *pan de cazón* (baby shark wedged between 2 corn tortillas with black beans), but all too often the gourmand must choose between high prices and questionable hygienic conditions. The few budget eateries cluster on Calle 8 south of the *zócalo*, and on Calle 57 in front of the plaza. Mangos and papayas are excellent in Campeche; try the *aguas de frutas* from any of Campeche's snack shops, or pick up some fresh fruit at the city market. Peel the mangos yourself; to avoid Bacteria Bill, stay away from the bags of mango slices sold by street vendors.

Restaurant Del Parque, Calle 57 #8 (tel. 6-02-40), at Calle 8 on the *zócalo*. Friendly service, lots of plants and Mexican rock music. Serves light fare: soups, sandwiches, desserts, giant-sized alcoholic and non-alcoholic drinks, and a number of regional dishes—*filete a la mexicana* (18 pesos) or *a la tampiqueña* (19 pesos). *Antojitos* 8-10 pesos. Freshly-squeezed orange juice 4 pesos. Traveler's checks, MC and Visa accepted. Open 24 hrs.

Restaurant La Parroquia, Calle 55 #9 (tel. 6-80-86), between Calles 10 and 12. A huge cafeteria-like restaurant slings hearty portions of seafood and meats (from 13 pesos). *Comida corrida* 12 pesos. Fruit cocktails 2.60 pesos. Traveler's checks and credit cards accepted. Open 24 hrs.

Restaurant Campeche, Calle 57 #2 (tel. 6-21-28), on the *zócalo*. Plain cafeteria in the birthplace of Justo Sierra, who founded the national university in Mexico City. Diners' eyes usually riveted to big color TV. Fish 15 pesos. Shrimp 18 pesos. Chicken 13-15pesos. Meat dishes 15-20 pesos. Open daily 7am-midnight.

Tortas Colon, Calle 10 between Calles 57 and 59, just around the corner from the zócalo. An 8-stool joint. Delicious fruit, yogurt, and granola cups (4-6.50 pesos), scrumptious tortas from the grill (3.50-5.50 pesos), and a variety of licuados (2 pesos). Open daily 8am-2pm and 6-10pm.

Nutrivida, between Calle 10 and 12. A small health food store stocked with teas, whole-wheat bread, and natural yogurt (2 pesos) that also serves soyburgers (4 pesos). Open daily 8:30am-2pm and 5:30-9pm.

SIGHTS AND ENTERTAINMENT

Campeche was a crucial gateway into Mexico for the first Spanish people in the Yucatán. After the Mayan tribes resisted the advances of Córdoba, Grijalva and Cortés, the Montejos managed to establish a beachhead at Campeche in 1540, building on the site of the Mayan village of A-kin-pech (serpent-tick), which the Spanish bastardized into "Campeche." From here, Montejo began his conquest of the Yucatán as Cortés, having fled west to Veracruz, marched against the Aztecs in the central highlands. During the colonial era, Campeche became an important port city, and until well into the 18th century, Veracruz and Campeche were the only ports in New Spain permitted to conduct international trade. The city attracted British, French and Dutch pirates who resented the Iberian claim to exclusive sovereignty over the Americas. Openly supported by their governments, these buccaneers regularly raided affluent Campeche.

Campeche rewards its visitors with a mildly interesting set of museums and beaches. The city government meticulously maintains a series of museums in the wall fragments as well as at various other points within the old city. You can visit several of the pirate-repelling *baluartes* (bastions) simply by following the Circuito Baluartes around the old walled boundaries. In the **Baluarte de la Soledad,** across from the *zócalo* off Calle 8 near Calle 57, the **Museo de Estelas Maya** has a small but worthwhile collection of Mayan stelae and reliefs taken from sites in Campeche state. Informative texts in Spanish and pictographs reveal details about each piece, and a friendly old caretaker lives to answer questions. Visitors may also climb the walls of the fort, which is surrounded by a park. (Open Tues.-Sat. 8am-8pm, Sun. 8am-1pm. Free.)

The tourist office is rightfully proud of the **Museo Regional de Campeche,** Calle 59 #38 (tel. 6-91-11), between Calles 14 and 16. Downstairs rooms contain well-documented exhibits describing the nearby ruins and displaying the jewelry, pottery and funerary artifacts of the Campeche region Maya. Highlights include an exquisite jade mask and a large phallic sculpture. The history of the city of Campeche is laid out upstairs. A collection of colonial swords, crossbows and cannon transforms images of the tranquil fortresses into scenes of combat, and a large-scale model of colonial Campeche reveals how little the old city has changed in two centuries. The museum inhabits an 18th-century building known as the Casa del Teniente del Rey (House of the King's Lieutenant). (Open Tues.-Sat. 8am-8pm, Sun. 8am-1pm. Admission 10 pesos.)

In the **Fuerte Santiago** at the northern corner of the city, the **Jardín Botánico Xmuch Haltun,** Calles 8 and 51, makes an inviting stop on a hot day or night. Over 250 labeled species of plants thrive amid shade trees and fountains in a pleasant, open-air courtyard, complete with walkways and benches. It takes only 10 minutes to walk through the garden, soothe your mind, and refresh your soul. If more than five people arrive at once, a guide will lead a special tour. (Open Tues.-Fri. 8am-2pm and 5-8pm, Sat. 9am-1pm and 5-8pm, Sun. 9am-1pm. Admission 2 pesos.)

In the heart of the city, on the *zócalo* rises the **cathedral,** site of the first mass conducted on the American continent. Don Francisco de Montejo ordered its construction in 1540, but builders did not finish until 1705. The main attraction is its facade, which includes human figures and obscure carvings. Inside, you'll find the *Santo Entierro* (Holy Burial), a sculpture of Christ in a carved mahogany sarcophagus with silver trim. (Open daily 7am-noon and 5-8pm. Free.)

Removed from the center of town, the **Iglesia de San Román** deserves a visit to see *Cristo Negro,* an object of great veneration among *campechanos.* St. Roman is Campeche's patron, and two weeks of both religious and secular festivities, starting September 15, celebrate his feast. (Open daily 6am-noon and 4-8pm. Free.)

Two high stone forts on the outskirts of town offer panoramas of Campeche that become postcard-perfect at sunset. **Fuerte San José El Alto** is a few km north of the center and near one of the oldest lighthouses in the Americas. If you don't have a car, take the "San José El Alto" bus from the market or make the long walk. Head north on Gobernadores, turn left on Cuauhtémoc, left on Calle 101 and right on Calle 7. A permanent guard has charge of **Fuerte de San Miguel,** a few km south of town near the youth hostel. Walk, or preferably drive, south a few km along the oceanfront road, then turn left on Carretera Escenico just after Melgar. A short jaunt inland will take you to San Miguel. At sunset many *campechanos* turn out in couples to stroll or jog as the sun gradually submerges.

Efforts are currently underway to clean the occasionally dirty **Playa Bonita,** the best beach in the immediate area for swimming. The beach is accessible by the "Lerma-Playa Bonita" bus from the market (.50 pesos). It has lockers and a restaurant and fills with locals on weekends. Another swimming option is 30km away at **Playa Payucán,** 2km from a small town called **Ceiba Playa** (accessible by first- and second- class buses), or **Mar Azul,** near Champotón, also accessible by first- and second class buses. Here the sand is cleaner and more abundant than at Playa Bonita, but the beach lacks basic amenities. **Payucán** also offers good snorkeling and scuba diving areas, but only if you brought your own equipment—rentals are not available.

Campeche's active tourist office and city government sponsor various free outdoor musical events including the *ballet folklórico* in the *zócalo.* Campeche's traditionalism emerges every Friday night at 8pm in the guise of an impressive light and sound show at **Puerta de Tierra** on Calles 59 and 18, which relates dramatically the history of pirate invasions of the city. (In Spanish, 8 pesos.) The **Noche de Trova,** including music and performances by the *ballet folklórico,* is celebrated in the *Parque de Guadalupe* on Wednesdays at 8pm and on Thursdays at 8pm in the *zócalo.* For a complete schedule of events, ask for the *Programa de Actividades* at the tourist information center. Half the city turns out for these shows, which begin around 8pm.

The luxury hotels provide the most modern nightlife, but you must pay for the privilege. **Atlantis,** in the Ramada Inn on Av. Ruiz Cortínez (tel. 6-22-23), hops into the wee hours on weekends. (Cover 20-25 pesos, women free Thursdays. Open Thurs.-Sat. 10pm-4am.) The small **Jet Set** video bar, near the Super Diez supermarket, is the newest rage among local sonic youth. (Open Mon.-Wed. noon-midnight, Thurs.-Sat. noon-3am.)

■ Near Campeche

While in Campeche, a jaunt to the nearby ruins of **Edzná** (House of the Grimaces) is easy and worthwhile. At the site, the huge **Acropolis,** a pyramid of five stories, towers over a large plaza among more than 200 mounds covering approximately six square km. Sixty-five steps lead to the five-room temple that crowns the pyramid. During the Mayan heyday, when the area was called Itzna, the perch atop the monument afforded a view of the network of irrigation canals criss-crossing the valley close to the Río Champotón, more than 20km to the west. Like the huge stone pyramids, the canals were built without the use of wheels, metal tools, or domesticated animals. Nearby, among the many thistle bushes, lie the remains of a ballcourt and several other temples of a central plaza, presently being excavated by Guatemalan refugees and Mexican archaeologists. Also on display are some of the 19 stelae found at Edzná, one crafted as early as 672 AD, others dating closer to the 10th-century evacuation of the ceremonial center. Campeche's state tourist office has further details on the ruins (see Campeche: Practical Information).

The 90-minute **bus** ride to Edzná leaves Campeche at 8am and returns at 3:30pm. Go to the station in advance for details, as schedules change often. Ask the driver to let you off at the access road to the ruins; the site is 500m down this road. Only one bus returns to Campeche; ask at the Campeche station and on the bus en route to Edzná. During *Semana Santa* and July and August the city sponsors cheap guided tours to the ruins every morning at 9am from the Balbvarte San Carlos. In the off-season, tours should run on Sat. and Sun. at 9am (ask for details at the tourist office). A canteen of water is a must. (Site open daily 8am-5pm. Admission 13 pesos. Free Sun.)

■■■ CAMPECHE TO MÉRIDA (LONG ROUTE)

The long route (Rte. 261; 254km) between Campeche and Mérida, sometimes called the **Ruta Maya,** traverses the Puuc Hills, an area that was densely populated in Mayan times, home to about 22,000 people during much of the Classic period (4th-10th centuries). Decimated by Spanish diseases and climatic changes, the Maya eventually surrendered most of their cities and ceremonial centers to the jungle until the 18th century, when the Mayan population began a recovery. Today, most Puuc Maya live in towns with paved roads, but women continue to wear traditional embroidered *huipiles* and Maya remains the dominant language.

Only a few ruin sites have been excavated and opened to the public; of these, **Uxmal** receives the most visitors. **Hochob's** remote location keeps most tourists at bay.

Uxmal, Kabah, the Grutas de Xtacumbilxunaan and Dzibilnocac can be reached by public **bus** (the first 3 from both Campeche and Mérida, the last from Campeche only). Most buses take the "short route," so check to make sure the bus take the "long route." Ask the driver to let you out as close to the sites as possible. The return trip can be tricky. Find out in advance when buses or *combis* will pass the site and wave your arms wildly to flag down a ride; full vehicles will not pick you up.

For a guaranteed ride back, rent a car or go on an organized tour. In Campeche, the state tourist office can refer you to guides who will take you on a private tour to any of these sites. From Mérida, the cheapest way to see the sites is to take the special Autotransportes del Sur "Ruta Puuc" bus that leaves daily at 8am. The bus stops for 45min. to an hour at each of the sites of Uxmal, Kabah, Labná, and Sayil to return to Mérida at 2:30pm. The fare is 31 pesos, a full-blown bargain even though it doesn't include admission to the ruins. Taxis in Mérida charge 350 pesos per carload for the same route. The state tourist office in Mérida also dispenses information on tours organized by travel agencies. Most offer standard daytrips to Uxmal/Kabah and to Chichén Itzá (see Mérida: Practical Information: Travel Agencies). Agencies will also organize private tours to all sites on the peninsula. Poor road conditions can create significant delays, especially when it rains, but inclement weather often means that you will have the site to yourself.

Most sites harbor at least a small gift shop that sells *refrescos,* but hotels and restaurants are scarce. The sole exception is Uxmal; those who cannot afford the sky-high rates there have two options: base yourself in Campeche or Mérida, or take advantage of the cheap accommodations and dining in **Ticul,** just 15km away off Route 261.

Edzná is the closest ruin to Campeche (see Near Campeche). Dzibilnocac and Hochob lie 88km south of the highway at Hopelchén, which in turn is 41km from Campeche. Two-and-a-half km after passing from Campeche into Yucatán state through a 19th-century archway, a road veers east. Sayil (5km from the crossroads), Xlapak (13km), Labná (17km) and three Mayan ruins in the Puuc style lie along the road before it terminates at the Grutas de Loltún (36km). This road is paved, but the ruins themselves are often quite swampy in the rainy season. Continuing north on the highway after the turnoff to Sayil, Kabah is 5km down the road; 22km past Kabah lies Uxmal.

■ Dzibilnocac

Dzibilnocac and Hochob (see below) are unique in the sense that they seldom receive visitors; this alone makes them worth a trip. Dzibilnocac is easier to reach from Campeche, but Hochob is more enticing.

Although many overgrown pyramidal mounds at Dzibilnocac are visible in the forest and *milpas* (cornfields) near the road, the only excavated buildings are a set of three temples in various states of decay. In the worst condition, the first temple has only one wall standing atop a once-symmetrical structure. Roots in the crumbling mortar slowly pull apart the temple's stones. The middle temple looks at first glance like nothing more than a pile of rocks topped by a tuft of trees and bushes; closer examination, however, reveals two corbel-arched, cave-like rooms partially filled with rubble.

The third temple is Dzibilnocac's prize. A tall, narrow building with rounded corners, it has rooms on several stories and still retains part of its stucco facade. Climb to the highest level for a closer view of a gruesome mask of the rain god Chac. At the middle levels, observe simpler and more primitive reliefs executed without perspective or dimensions, in the style of cave paintings. From the top of this temple, larger pyramidal mounds are visible nearby, bulging under the thick underbrush.

The actual site extends for miles—for those who insist on exploring, several roads and paths connect farms and cornfields. Very often, smaller ruins or pyramids rise from the middle of an otherwise cleared corn field. Temples in the area tend to fall to pieces faster than they would at nature's hands alone, since local farmers find the stones from ancient Mayan buildings both cheaper and classier building materials than those available at the local hardware store. Beware of the undergrowth's dangerous thorns and spines, and make sure your legs are completely covered because the poisonous snakes in this area are not always afraid of intruders.

The Dzibilnocac ruins hide some 61km off Route 261, near the small town of **Iturbide.** To reach this village by car, exit Route 261 at Hopelchén and drive south toward Iturbide. You'll soon reach a prominent sign at a fork pointing the way (straight on, *not* to the right) to Iturbide. Well-marked "km" signs are posted all along the road. When you reach the village, bear right around the *zócalo*, passing Iturbide's small, yellow church, and continue out of town on a slightly worse, if less rocky, road (treacherous in rainy season, when it's better to walk). Fifty meters into the forest, the right branch of the fork in the road ends at the ruins. If you don't have a car, take the **bus** from Campeche to Iturbide (5 per day, 3hrs., 8 pesos). The last bus leaves Iturbide for Campeche at 3:30pm. If you miss it, you can attempt to hitch back to Hopelchén on Route 261, where buses run later into the afternoon. The ruins are open daily 8am-5pm. Free admission.

Dzibalchén, between Iturbide and Hopelchén, has no hotels, but stranded travelers can spend the night there in a tent or hammock. Ask at the Palacio Municipal for bathroom facilities and hammock hooks. Small restaurants around the *zócalo* are open during daylight hours. Buses to Campeche leave Dzibalchén early each morning.

■ Hochob

Hochob is the perfect place to experience ruins in silence and solitude, and campers will be hard-pressed to find a more deserted yet equally accessible site. Traveling to Hochob is ill-advised in the rainy season, when access roads do their fantastic quicksand impersonation.

The three temples at Hochob cluster around a central plaza at the area's highest point, which swells modestly from the flat rainforest. Upon entering the plaza, you'll see several small heaps of rubble on the immediate left. Ahead and to the right, deep-relief geometric patterns molded in stucco cover a well-preserved one-room temple. The entire front of the building once resembled an enormous mask of Chac, with the large door serving as mouth for the gaping rain god.

Climb the ruined pyramid immediately to the left of the temple for a good view of the elevated site. To the right of the temple, at the corner of the plaza, a small path leads to a perfect camping spot in a clearing above the otherwise unbroken green rainforest.

At the far end of the plaza from the entrance road, a ruined façade still bears traces of its geometric motifs. Facing this ruined building, you can see Hochob's highest building, a spire-topped temple resting on a steeply sloping pyramid, to the right. The floor plan of the ruined building to the right of the temple is still evident in surviving walls and foundations. Beyond this, a high but decayed pyramid and wall rise to face the temple on the opposite side of the plaza.

Although Hochob, like Dzibilnocac, spreads for miles, the hilltop ceremonial center is the most thoroughly excavated and most interesting area for visitors. Near the site, the right branch of the road has deteriorated to the point where its only value is its view of the highest buildings and the main temple's well-preserved roof comb. Ruins are open daily 8am-5pm. Free admission.

The Hochob ruins lie closer to the town of Dzibalchén than do the ruins of Dzibilnocac, but they are more difficult to reach without a car. Take the road out of Dzibalchén for about 1km toward Campeche, then follow the sign pointing left to the town of **Chencoh**, 9km down a rough but still passable dirt road. In "town," take a left at the second intersection of roads lined with stone walls. After passing a small elevated concrete platform on the right and a barnyard full of pigs and turkeys (1 block or so), turn left again and follow the dirt track some 4km into the jungle. Because of its many potholes, this road becomes especially dangerous in heavy rain. Just after most visitors throw in the towel, the road forks. Bear left, and soon the outline of temples will appear against the sky. Park at the small *palapa* hut below Hochob's hilltop site and continue up the road on foot.

There is no public transportation from Dzibalchén (or anywhere else) to Chencoh, and vehicles pass even less frequently here than on the stretch of road to Iturbide. Those who catch rides ask their driver to let them off at the access road to Chencoh, 1km before Dzibalchén. *Let's Go* does not recommend hitchhiking.

■ Grutas De Xtacumbilxunaan

Along the main highway, 31km past Hopelchén, follow a turn-off to the left to reach the Grutas de Xtacumbilxunaan (Caves of the Sleeping Girl), which sit one km off the highway. A custodian leads a tour past deep *cenotes* (natural wells) that once supplied all of the water for Bolonchén, 3km away, and points out the various barely discernible shapes on the cavern's walls and ceilings. Although these caves compare poorly to the grand ones at Loltún, even novice spelunkers will have a good time poking around. (Open Tues.-Sun. 9am-5pm. Tours in Spanish given only during daylight hours. Free, but guide expects a tip.)

The Grutas lie one km down a well-marked access road that crosses Route 261 2km south of Bolonchén. Drivers of second-class buses usually drop passengers at the access road.

■ Sayil

Sayil, the "Place of Red Ants," offers enough fascinating structures to make the prospect of facing the onslaught of ants worthwhile. The magnificent **Palace of Sayil** contains over 50 rooms on three terraced stories. Eight elegant, second-floor chambers open onto pleasant porticos, each graced by two bulging columns. Walls between porticos are carved with two rows of four slender colonnettes, which together with the open spaces and thick columns create an interesting visual rhythm. From atop the palace, the Puuc Hills form the horizon. Behind the palace sits a *chultún* (plastered catch basin) that ancients used to collect rainwater for the dry season.

After descending the palace stairs, follow a path to the right, which leads to **El Mirador** (lookout), a temple with grandiose columns. Follow the path to the left to find the **Stela of the Phallus,** now protected by a thin thatched roof. A few other temples on the site appear as mounds covered with jungle growth. (Site open daily 8am-5pm. Admission 10 pesos. Free Sun.)

The only **public transportation** to Sayil is the Autotransportes del Sur "Ruta Puuc" bus (31 pesos) that leaves Mérida daily at 8am and stops at several other ruin sites as well. (See Campeche to Mérida: Long Route.) Buses do run, however, from Mérida to Kabah, 10km away on the main highway (see Kabah); hitching from

Kabah to Sayil is not unheard of. Many solicit lifts from enthusiastic four-wheeled travelers at either Uxmal or the Grutas de Loltún (see below).

■ Xlapak

Chac still rules at Xlapak (shla-PAK), where the rain god's image smothers a ruined 20m-long palace that has undergone partial restoration. Of the sites on this road, Xlapak is least important and the most painless to miss if you run short on time or insect repellent.

Entering from the north, give your autograph to the caretaker and walk 200m south to reach the palace. In Puuc style, the lower-floor facade is plain, punctuated only by doorways, but the building is beautifully proportioned. Masks of Chac and various fretted patterns adorn the cornice. The evolution of Mayan architecture over the centuries is evident in the contrasting styles of the western and eastern sides of the buildings. The government will soon open many more structures on the site. There is no public transportaion to Xlapak. Rides may be solicited at any of the nearby sites. Biking from nearby towns is also an option. (Site open daily 8am-5pm. Admission 10 pesos. Free Sun.) See Kabah for information on buses from Mérida to Kabah, 18km northeast of Xlapak.

■ Labná

Labná may have been established as early as the 8th century, when the Puuc cities were connected by a *sacbé* (white road), a trace of which runs nearby. Raised above the surrounding land, this causeway was of great use during times of flooding. Water shortages were a problem, evident by the three dozen huge *chultunes* (catch basins) found at Labná alone. The *chultunes* served the same purpose as *cenotes* (natural wells) did in northern Yucatán in more than one respect. They collected not only water (up to 8000 gallons in each) but also the bodies of the poorest Mayans, who were given simple burials. It seems unlikely, however, that the receptacles were used for both domestic and religious purposes simultaneously.

Labná is famed for its **arch** of stone, a span over 3m wide and 6m high, with an ornate mosaic facade on the west and a geometric design on the east. On either side of its base is a room with a cornice carved in a zigzag design and second-floor stone latticework. Once part of a building that stood between two plazas, the arch stands at the rear of the site by the southern group of buildings, and now more closely resembles a gate. Its structure points out a curious omission in Mayan architecture: their lack of the ordinary keystone arch.

Labná's other well-known attraction, the **palace,** lies on the northern side of the site. The largest edifice in the Puuc region, construction of the palace continued over the course of several centuries but was never actually completed. Labná's palace is similar in design to the one in Sayil, with separate apartments and porticos on the second floor (where there is also a *chultún*). The ornate second-floor cornice culminates at the eastern corner of its façade with the sculpture of a serpent head, its open mouth chomping on a human head. The eastern wall bears an unusually large, stylized mask of Chac in astonishingly good condition. Nearby remains of mosaics depict the palm huts in which most people lived; stone palaces were a privilege of the aristocracy.

East of the arch, on the unrestored base of a pyramid, stands **El Castillo,** also called the Temple-Pyramid and El Mirador (lookout). The "castle's" notable facade rises over the box-like structure and bears sculptures attached by tenons or dowels. The terracing around the temple contained many *chultunes*.

Labná, less restored than nearby sites, is 5km farther east along the road to Xlapak, a total of 17km from the Campeche-Mérida highway. The Autotransportes del Sur "Ruta Puuc" **bus** stops at Labná (see Campeche to Mérida: Long Route, but see Kabah for other transportation information. Site open daily 8am-5pm. Admission 10 pesos. Free Sun.)

■■■ GRUTAS DE LOLTÚN

Below a dense jungle of mahogany, *sapodilla*, *ceiba*, and gumbo-limbo trees, one and a half kilometers of enormous caverns and narrow alleys wind through the rock. Graced by Mayan sculptures, the Caves of Loltún ("flower of rock") are themselves carvings of nature, fashioned long before humans ventured inside. The Maya settled in the area to take advantage of the water and clay in these caves and used the caves as a hide-out as late as the Caste War (1847-1848). Any detailed exploration of Yucatán should include these *grutas* along the Sayil-Labná road, 19km east of Labná and 27km east of the Campeche-Mérida highway.

Major caverns include the **Room of the 37 Inscriptions,** many of which are still visible, and the **Na Cab** (House of the Bees), where you can see the *ka'ob* (grindstones) left by the Maya; the slippery **Gallery of Fallen Rocks,** where the Maya removed the curtains of stalactites at their tips for use as spears and arrows; the **Gallery of the Five Chultunes,** where a sculpted jaguar head drips water into cisterns while a huge warrior and eagle look on; and the **Cathedral,** a palatial room that hosted Mayan feasts, and so named these days for a naturally-formed image of the Virgin of Guadalupe above the entrance. Numerous musical stalagmites and stalactites, a red clay mine, and numerous naturally formed elephants, lions, hearts, torsos and whatever else your imagination discovers.

Technically, entrance to the caves is allowed daily only at 9:30am, 11am, 12:30pm, 2pm and 3:30pm, and then only with a guide. There are often enough tourists, however, to persuade guides to leave as soon as large groups assemble. If you don't understand Spanish, it's worth waiting for an English-speaking group to gather, because the guides relate entertaining anecdotes. (Admission 16.80 pesos, plus a tip of at least 1 peso, 6 pesos on Sun.)

The difficulty in touring the caves is getting to the entrance. If you don't take the ATS "Ruta Puuc" package **bus** from Mérida (see Campeche to Mérida: Long Route), you'll have to catch a bus to Oxkutzcab (at the intersection of Rte. 164 and the road from Labná) and then a *combi* from the market (ask around about the exact location) to the caves (500 pesos). **Cabs** (often pickup trucks) that cluster on the market side of the *zócalo* work in collusion and routinely refuse to travel the quick 7km for anything less than 15 pesos.

The **Restaurant El Huinoc de Loltún,** at the exit for the *grutas* (0.5km from the entrance), has a limited menu of interesting local dishes such as *papadzules* and *poc-chuc* (12-14 pesos). Whether or not you eat here, the restaurant is a place where some solicit rides when they can't bear to wait for the sardine truck back to Oxkutzcab.

■■■ KABAH

Codz Pop Temple, up the grassy slope to the right of the Kabah site, reveals a labor of extraordinary effort. Nearly 300 masks of Chac, each a sculptural mosaic composed of 30 carved pieces, cover its long façade. The site probably served as a judicial court, in which specially appointed justices settled disputes with the help of the gods. The name "Codz Pop," meaning in Mayan "Rolled Mat," is the subject of diverse scholarly speculations.

Codz Pop shows the influence of the Chenes style, a design not often found in the area; two of its neighbors to the east, **El Palacio** (a 25m pyramid) and **Las Columnas,** were designed in the plainer and more common Puuc fashion. Several other monuments in the vicinity remain submerged in jungle growth.

Across the highway from the main site beyond the parking area, a short dirt road leads in three directions: an unrestored group of temples lies to the right, the nearly camouflaged West Group to the left, and a beautifully sculpted arch directly ahead. The arch marks the beginning of the ancient *sacbé* (paved, elevated road), which ended at a similar arch in Uxmal. (Open daily 8am-5pm. Admission 10 pesos. Free Sun.)

Kabah is 153km from Campeche and 101km from Mérida along the Campeche-Mérida highway. Uxmal lies 22km northwest, and the road to Sayil, Xlapak, Labná, and Loltún 5km south. Because of its location on Route 261, Kabah is easily accessible by bus.

In addition to the special ATS "Ruta Puuc" **buses** (see Campeche to Mérida: Long Route), public buses to Kabah leave from Mérida's main bus station, Calle 69 #544 (tel. 24-83-91), and go on to Campeche. Buses from Campeche leave the ADO station, Gobernadores 289 (tel. 6-28-02). Buses will stop at Kabah only if a passenger notifies the driver beforehand or if the driver sees a person wildly gesticulating on the shoulder of the highway. Since almost all the tourists who come here have cars, many hitchers find rides back to Uxmal or to the other ruins and the Grutas de Loltún in the Puuc hills. There are no services at Kabah.

■■■ UXMAL

The most famous archaeological site along the Ruta Puuc, Uxmal (oosh-MAL) emanates both grandness of stature and beauty of detail. Some of the most richly-ornamented facades adorn the ruins here. The finely-sculpted reliefs and immense masks impress even more when one remembers that the Maya didn't have metal tools. Unfortunately, most of the stone sculptures are absent from the site, now sitting in museums (such as the "Governor of Uxmal") or in the hands of thieves (such as the phalli that once ensured the fertility of the ancient city). The *chultunes* and *aguadas*, lime-covered cisterns used to store rain, have been eroded and carried off by the flood of years. All that remains is the monumental shell of the ancient city that the modern Maya call Oxmal (thrice-built), which guides will quickly point out was actually built five times.

Uxmal receives deserved attention from the government, which has provided a tourist center and a good deal of glossy hype. The ruins make for a pleasant daytrip or the anchor of a two-day tour of the many less-accessible ruins in the area.

Orientation and Practical Information Uxmal sits on Route 261, the main highway between the state capitals of Mérida (79km north) and Campeche (175km southwest). The road to the smaller sites at Sayil, Xlapak, and Labná branches east off the main route 27km south of Uxmal near Kabah.

Second-class **buses** connect Uxmal (as with Kabah) with Mérida (1½hrs., 8 pesos) and Campeche (3hrs., 14 pesos). Five buses per day travel in each direction (see Campeche and Mérida listings for details). Ask the driver to stop at the access road to the *ruinas*. To return, catch a passing bus at the *crucero* just outside the ruins entrance. The last buses to Mérida and Campeche pass at 7pm and 6pm respectively.

Try to arrive at Uxmal early in the morning, before the sun is high and the cattle-cars of tourists arrive. The large site is unshaded; wear sunscreen and carry a water bottle.

A stunning **tourist center** containing a small museum, a restaurant, a gift shop and a photographic supply shop greets you at the entrance to the ruins. The **Kit Bolon Tun theater,** also in the tourist center, features melodramatic but informative half-hour video presentations about the Yucatán's archaeological sites and the peninsula's enduring environmental and cultural riches. (6 shows in Spanish and 3 in English daily. Free.)

Accommodations and Food No modern village has arisen at Uxmal; the array of hotels and their clientele constitute the region's population. Prices at these hotels are, as usual, inversely proportional to their distance from the ruins; the only budget accommodations are therefore in the somewhat distant town of **Ticul**, a half-hour drive from Uxmal. Travelers without wheels can either take a series of combis and buses to the site from Ticul (see below) or exchange an arm or a leg to stay at one of the luxurious establishments abutting the ruins.

Cheaper accommodations, camping and trailer facilities are available at **Rancho Uxmal** (tel. 2-02-77), 4km north of Uxmal toward Mérida. It is inconveniently far from everything for those without vehicles. Hitchers find it hopelessly slow; instead, travel on buses passing along the highway (1 peso). Rooms come with tile bathrooms, hot water and strong ceiling fans. Guests and diners at the restaurant are allowed access to the hotel pool. (Singles or doubles 75 pesos, 15 pesos each additional person.) The owner also permits campers to pitch tents or sling hammocks in the large gravel driveway area. (Sites 15 pesos per person, including use of bathrooms and showers. Traveler's checks accepted. Restaurant open 7am-9:30pm daily.)

Restaurant Cana-Nah, right next door to Rancho Uxmal, also allows tent-pitching (6 pesos per group). The extremely friendly staff of this large, well-ventilated restaurant serves regional entrees for 15 pesos. (Soups and salads 10 pesos. Open daily 9am-8pm.)

For food at the site itself there is the air-conditioned **Restaurant Yax Beh,** by the complex entrance. Entrees here are on the expensive side (simple sandwiches go for 15-20 pesos, meals for 25 pesos), but it is substantially cheaper than the pricey, gourmet cuisine in the three nearby hotels. (Open daily 8am-8:45pm.) The budget-conscious should also take advantage of small-town prices in nearby Ticul and brown-bag it to Uxmal.

Sights As with many of the Mayan ruins, the story of the people who once occupied Uxmal is incomplete. Popular legends give entertaining but fictitious explanations of Uxmal's history. Archaeology, however, leaves much unexplained. Most of the structures visible today date from the Classic period (7th century). Uxmal's style, unlike Chichén Itzá's, is Mayan Puuc without Toltec influence.

According to the **Chilam Balam,** a Mayan historical account written in phonetic Spanish, Ah Suytok Xiu invaded with his warriors from the Valley of Mexico around the end of the 10th century. The Xiu dominated until civil warfare toppled the League of Mayapán and ended Uxmal's prosperity in the 12th century. The last ruler of Uxmal was Ah Suytok Tutul Xiu, whose descendants still live in the Puuc region and in the village of Oxkutzcab. Because his priests foretold the coming of the white, bearded men from the ocean, the Xiu put up no resistance against the conquistadors. At Tutul Xiu's baptism as an old man, his godfather was none other than Francisco de Montejo, conqueror of the Yucatán.

The near-pyramid visible upon entering Uxmal is the **Temple of the Sorcerer,** built by a dwarf-magician who supposedly hatched from a witch's egg and grew to maturity in only one year. These events rightfully struck terror in the heart of the governing lord of Uxmal, so he challenged the fledgling dwarf to a contest of building skills. The dwarf's pyramid, built overnight, easily outclassed the governor's Great Pyramid, still visible to the right of the Governor's Palace. Grasping at straws, the spiteful ruler complained that the dwarf's pyramid was actually elliptical at the base instead of square or rectangular. The governor posed a second challenge: to break the small hard-shell fruit *cocoyol* with their heads. This second challenge posed no problem for the dwarf because the witch had incorporated turtle shell into his skull, but it cost the governor his life. He was laid to rest in the Cemetery Group to the east of the Temple of the Sorcerer and the Nunnery Complex.

Archaeologists claim that the 40m-tall pyramid contains at least five superimpositions built at different times. It has four temples, the one on the western side of a particular interest; the structure is a Chac's mask with the entrance as the mouth. To the west of it, the **Nunnery Complex** consists of four buildings around a quadrangle measuring 65m by 45m, abundantly adorned with masks of the rain god Chac, easily recognizable by their long hooked noses.

The **ballcourt,** in contrast to many other ballcourts found in Mesoamerica, is simple and poorly preserved. The two rings, through which the players tried to pass the solid ball of hardened rubber, bear hieroglyphic dates only one day apart.

Emerging from the ballcourt, the path breaks off to the right and runs a few hundred meters to the **Cemetery Group,** which consists of a plaza bounded by a small pyramid to the north, a temple to the west and two other ruined structures. Stones that once formed four small platforms in the plaza bear haunting reliefs of skulls and crossbones. These "gravestones" have given the group its name, although excavations have revealed no human remains.

From the ballcourt, the path branching to the right reaches the **Dovecote,** easily recognizable by the eight triangular sections of cresting pierced by lizard holes. Ahead through the facade of the Dovecote lies the base of the **Chenes Temple.** The pyramid today is a huge mass of jungle-covered rubble, of which only the uppermost crest of the temple that stood atop the pyramid has been excavated. To the northeast lies the **Great Pyramid,** built by the governor in his contest with the dwarf and today one of the better-restored structures at Uxmal. Only the front steps and the first platform can be scaled; guards will not permit you to climb any farther, to prevent erosion.

The **House of Turtles** and the **Palace of the Governor** top an escarpment east of the Great Pyramid. Three buildings comprise the **Palace of the Governor.** Over 100m long and built on three concentric landscaped terraces, the palace is typical of the Puuc style. The eastern frieze is covered by 20,000 pieces of decoration, forming 103 masks of Chac laid out in a line which undulates like a serpent. The Governor's palace is said to be the most beautiful building in Mesoamerica. After the governor's defeat at the hands of the dwarf-magician, laborers filled the many rooms of the palace with stones in preparation for a superimposition that was never completed. The small House of Turtles is on the northwest corner of the escarpment. The House is adorned with an intriguing series of sculpted turtles—symbolizing longevity and still venerated by the Maya—along the upper frieze of the two-story structure.

From the Palace of the Governor, you may be able to spot the overgrown, pyramidal **House of the Old Woman,** which lies to the east. About 400m south of the House of the Old Woman lies the **Temple of the Phalli.** Phallic sculptures hang from the cornices of this ruined building and spurt rain runoff from the roof. Experienced guides are available to give more detaield tours of the site. The normal rate is 65 pesos per group, but pleading poverty and a genuine interest may result in a drastically lowered rate.

Outside the hotels, Uxmal's only nightlife consists of a post-Mayan sound-and-light show that dramatically lauds Mayan history and culture. The Spanish version (6.80 pesos) begins at 7pm and ends after the last of the Mérida or Campeche buses pass Uxmal. The English version (8.40 pesos) begins at 9pm; some have hitched a ride back with other monolingual spectators. (Site open daily 8am-5pm. Admission 18.60 pesos. Free on Sun. Parking 8am-10pm 3 pesos, 5 pesos for buses.) Guidebooks of the ruins are available at the bookstore.

■■■ TICUL, YUCATÁN

A small town (pop. 40,000) off the Campeche-Mérida highway, Ticul is an ideal base for exploring nearby Uxmal, Kabah, Sayil, Xlapak, Labná, and Grutas de Loltún. Although it's extreme proximity to these sights and plethora of budget hotels and restaurants, Ticul draws remarkably few tourists. For those with wheels, Ticul is also a possible base from which to visit a number of nearby attractions, such as *cenotes* and colonial buildings in and near other small towns in the area. There are *cenotes* and *grutas* near Ticul, Teabo (30km southeast of Ticul), Mayapán (45km to the northeast) and Holcá (105km to the northeast). A colonial monastery waits to be explored in Maní (15km east of Ticul). Tekax (35km to the southeast) has a hermitage, and Tipikal boasts an impressive colonial church.

The town's three-wheeled taxis (mostly *huipole* and *rebezo* bedecked *señoras*) place passengers on a bench above the axle, while the driver pedals behind. (Fare .50-1.50 pesos.) Artisans in Ticul, a regional center for red-clay pottery, inflate their prices as much as 100% for tourists; it's cheaper to make purchases in Mérida.

Ticul has several hotels and good restaurants. **Hotel Sierra Sosa,** Calle 26 #199-A (tel. and fax 2-00-08), right off the *zócalo*, has a welcoming, friendly, English-speaking staff who are glad to answer questions, give directions and store packs. Rooms are clean and tidy with hot water and fans but not all have windows. The hotel has long distance telephone service (6.50 pesos per min. to the U.S.) and a package-mailing service. They also rent bicycles (10 pesos per day) and offer a 40 peso tour of nearby ruins (entrance to ruins is not included). Reserve by fax and receive a 5 peso discount. Students may also receive discounts. Check-out noon. (Singles 25 pesos, doubles 35 pesos.) Three blocks from the *zócalo*, the **Hotel San Miguel,** Calle 28 #195 (tel. 2-03-82), is clean, cheap and sunny. Freshly painted rooms are welcoming and have windows, hot water and fans. Reservations can be made by phone. (Check-out 1pm. Traveler's checks accepted. Singles 25 pesos, doubles 35 pesos, triples 55 pesos, each additional person 5 pesos.)

Restaurant Los Delfines, on Calle 27 (tel. 2-04-01) between Calles 28 and 30, serves drinks along with a whole variety of shrimp dishes under a big verdant *palapa* (13 pesos). Meat concoctions cost 12-13 pesos; shrimp omelettes 12 pesos. (Open daily 8am-6pm.) **Loncherias Rubí,** on Calle 25 between Calles 30 and 32, and **Rosita,** on Calle 23 in front of the market, offer cheap antojitos: *salbutes, panuchos, and tostados.* After 7pm on Calle 27 between Calles 34 and 36, a nameless blue-doored Mayan restaurant will fill you (and many locals') belly for 3 pesos. **El Colorín,** Calle 26 (tel. 2-03-14) between Calles 21 and 23, is an informal joint which serve sandwiches, *tortas* and juices for under 6 pesos. (*Menú del día* including entree, *tortillas* and beans 12 pesos. Open 8am-10pm.)

Next to the Sierra Sosa hotel Ticul's well-kept market lies just off of Calle 23 between Calles 28 and 30. (Open daily sunrise -sunset.)

Public transportation in Ticul is not geared for ruin-happy tourists. While the Caves of Loltún , Uxmal, and Kabah are fairly accessible given a modicum of luck with *combi* transfers, the dearth of traffic on the road past the trio of Sayil, Xlapk, and Labná will leave the carless traveler foot-stomping in frustration. While Kabah and Uxmal-bound buses supposedly leave from the station on Calle 24 (tel. 2-01-62), it is actually more expeditious to take a Mérida-bound bus (departing from Ticul approximately every ½hr., 1.70 pesos) and ask to be dropped off in Muna. With luck, southbound buses heading for Uxmal or Campeche can be caught for a ride to Uxmal or Ticul (20min., 1.50 pesos).This option is best for early risers, as buses in Muna thin after morning hours. Another route, also involving the treacherous pueblito transfer, involves taking a *combi* (in this case a covered pick-up) from the corner of Calle 28 and 25 to Santa Elena (30min., 2 pesos). From Santa Elena, Uxmal lies some 16km back up the highway to Mérida or to Kabah which lies on the road to Campeche. Both routes are best traveled in the early morning when workers are busy commuting and thus rides are more plentiful. Reaching Loltún from Ticul also requires changing buses. The first leg of the journey is a *combi* from Ticul to Oxkutzcab that leaves from the intersection of Calles 23 and 26 (15min., 1.50 pesos). In Oxkutzcab, from a lot across from the giant market "20 de Noviembre," *combis* leave for Loltún, 7km southwest. Tell the driver to drop you off at the *grutas* (10min., 1 peso), because everyone else on board is probably bound for the agricultural cooperative 3km further down the road. Traffic to and from the caves at Loltún makes the trip easy compared to the Uxmal-Kabah route. Hitchhikers will find rides on any of these roads infrequent; cars (and shade) are lacking. *Let's Go* does not recommend hitchhiking. Another option is to explore the sites by bike; you can take bikes on *combis* (for an extra fare) to Muna or Santa Elena and pedal from there.

The highway between Ticul and Oxkutzcab, however, should be avoided by bikers; it is very busy and can be dangerous. Women should avoid biking alone in the late evening and at night, especially on weekends. Bikes can be rented at the Hotel Sierra Sosa (10 pesos per day).

Streets in Ticul form a grid, with the main street, **Calle 23,** passing through the center. Even-numbered streets run north-south. Most of the town's commercial activity takes place between **Calles 24** and **30,** a block in either direction from Calle 23.

Ticul's **post office** is in the Palacio Municipal on the *zócalo* (tel. 2-00-40; open Mon.-Fri. 8:30am-3pm). **Postal Code:** 97860. The **telegram office,** Calle 21 #192-C (tel. 2-01-46), in the blue and white building in back of the post office. (Open Mon.-Fri. 9am-3pm.) **Banco del Atlántico,** Calle 23 #195 off the *zócalo*, changes U.S. dollars (traveler's checks or cash) Mon.-Fri. 8am-1pm. The town's **long distance caseta,** Calle 23 #210 (tel. 2-00-00), between Calles 26 and 28, makes international collect calls for a refreshingly cheap 2 pesos. (Open 8:30am-8:30pm.) The **telephone code** is 997. **Lavandería Burbujas,** Calle 28 #197, charges 3 pesos per kg. (Open Mon.-Sat. 8am-1pm and 2-5pm, Sun. 9am-noon.) **Farmacia San Jose,** (tel. 2-03-93) Calle 23 #214-J between Calles 28 and 30, is open 8am-2pm and 4-10pm daily but provides service and access to doctors 24 hrs. **Police** headquarters are just off the *zócalo* on Calle 23 at Calle 24 (tel. 2-00-33; open 24 hrs.). No English spoken.

YUCATÁN

Although the highlights of Yucatán state are the ruins—Chichén Itzá, Uxmal and the triad of Sayil, Kabah and Labná—the colonial cities also deserve a place on your agenda. Mérida and Valladolid are both appealing urban centers, the first bustling with international visitors and one of Mexico's finest markets, the second drowsing amid gorgeous churches and *cenotes* in the eddies of Yucatán's history.

■■■ MÉRIDA

Hub of the Yucatán Peninsula and capital of Yucatán state, Mérida attracts cultural resources centripetally from miles in every direction. Built atop the ruins of the ancient Mayan capital of T'ho, the city is a rich amalgamation of proud *indígena* history, a powerful colonial presence and modern-day international flavor. The stones of the fortress-like cathedral bear traces of the Mayan temples from which they came and the Mayan labor which moved them. The Maya called it the "place of the fifth point," placing it at the center of their universe, bounded by the four points of north, south, east and west.

Mérida (pop. 950,000) is still a fifth point in the new Mexican cosmology of capitalism. It is the region's commercial center; thousands of shops line its narrow streets and flood the sidewalks. Panama hats, made from the leaves of the *jipijapa* plant and the *guano* palm, come from Becal in the neighboring state of Campeche; hammocks arrive from the nearby *pueblito* of Tixcocób; and the raw, stripped *henequén* is trucked to Mérida's industrial zone from all over Yucatán before being exported as hemp.

Diverse cultural influences emanate from the 25 *meridaños* of recent Lebanese and Syrian descent; a small French community is responsible for Mérida's version of the Champs-Elysées, the Paseo Montejo; and increasing numbers of North American expatriates also call Mérida home. A newly discovered focal point for travelers from around the world, Mérida plays host to planeloads of tourists who arrive to spend days museum-hopping and market-shopping, and to pass romantic evenings in music-filled parks. Mérida is the largest city on the Yucatán Peninsula, but it has yet to succumb to big-city indifference. Street cleaners busily maintain its reputation as

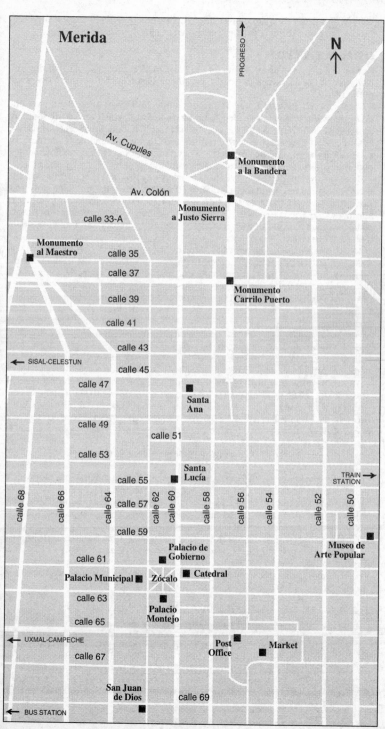

MÉRIDA

"The White City," intimate conversations whisper in *zócalo* loveseats, and every Sunday hordes of strolling families come out to enjoy *Mérida en domingo*.

ORIENTATION

Route 180 rushes over from Cancún (300km) and Valladolid (160km) to the east, becoming **Calle 65,** which passes through the busiest part of town one block south of the *zócalo*.

Those approaching on Route 180 from Campeche 153km to the southwest end up on **Avenida Itzáes** (also called **Avenida de la Paz**), which runs north-south, or on Calle 81, which feeds into the north-south Calle 70. Both intersect Calle 59, the best access to the center of town, running east to a point one block north of the *zócalo*. **Paseo Montejo** begins at Calle 47 and passes some of Mérida's finer homes, continuing north as Route 261 to Progreso and the coast.

Buses arrive and depart from Mérida to every city on the Yucatán Peninsula and the rest of Mexico. To find the *zócalo* from the main terminal, turn right (east) from the entrance, walk three blocks, turn left (north) and the *zócalo* is three blocks ahead; or take a taxi (10 pesos). From the train station, either take a taxi (10 pesos), walk the lonely six blocks west on Calle 55 and three blocks south on Calle 60, or look for a bus called "Seguro Social."

Mérida's international **airport** lies 7km southwest of the city on the highway to Campeche (Rte. 180). Bus #79, called "Airport," runs between the terminals and a midtown bus stop at the corner of Calles 67 and 60 (every 20min. 5am-9pm, ½hr., .80 pesos). A taxi to the airport costs 20 pesos.

Mérida's consistently-gridded one-way streets have numbers instead of names. Using the streets which border the *zócalo* as rough directional axes, numbers greater than 500 usually lie west or south, smaller than 500 north or east. Addresses in Mérida are given using an "x" to separate the main street from the cross streets and "y" (meaning "and" in Spanish) to separate the two cross streets if the address falls in the middle of the block. Thus "54#509 x 61 y 63" reads "Calle 54 #509, between Calles 61 and 63."

Mérida's **municipal buses** (.80 pesos) meander along idiosyncratic routes to arrive at their given neighborhoods. You can go to tourist information booths or the main office for exact information, but the city is small enough that a bus headed in the right direction will usually drop you off within a few blocks of your desired location. Locals and tourists alike tend to catch them at their boarding points, usually in the center, a few blocks from the *zócalo*. City buses run daily 5am-11pm. *Collectivos* or *combis* (1 peso) follow well-traveled routes through the city as well.

Taxis do not roam the streets soliciting business. You must call for one or have your hotel or restaurant call for you. There are stands along the Paseo de Montejo, at the airport and at the *zócalo*. Fares are exorbitant; expect to pay at least 7-8 pesos for a trip of more than a few blocks. Collective taxis, on the other hand, charge only 4 pesos for any destination in the city; dropoffs are on a first-come, first-serve basis.

Car rental agencies in Mérida operate north of the *zócalo* on Calles 60 and 62, near the cross streets of 59 and 57. A few more line Paseo Montejo, and well-established operators have offices at the airport. It is unnecessary to rent a car for trips to Chichén Itzá and Uxmal since day tours of the sites departing from Mérida are numerous and relatively inexpensive, but a car provides the easiest access to the hard-to-reach ruins at Xlapak, Sayil, and Labná.

PRACTICAL INFORMATION

Tourist Information: Central Office, in the Peón Contreras Theater (tel. 24-92-90), on Calle 60 between Calles 57 and 59. Excellent maps and knowledgeable, bilingual staff of students. Disperses large numbers of colorful pamphlets, the most useful of which is *Yucatán Today*, a seasonal guide listing practical information and local events. Open daily 8am-8pm. **Information Booths,** at the airport (tel. 46-13-00; open daily 8am-10pm), on the 1st-class side of the main bus station (open daily 8am-8pm) and on the *zócalo* (open daily 8am-1pm), are as helpful and knowledgeable as the main center. English spoken.

Travel Agents: Yucatán Trails, Calle 62 #482 (tel. 28-25-82, fax 24-49-19), between Calles 57 and 59. Canadian owner Denis LaFoy is a genial source of insider information on Mérida and the Yucatán. Open Mon.-Fri. 8am-2pm and 4-7pm, Sat. 8am-12pm. **Viajes T'Ho,** Calle 59 #508 (tel. 23-66-12, fax 23-66-12), near Calle 62 in the lobby of Hotel Reforma. Organizes daily trips to Uxmal, Chichén Itzá and Kabah (55 pesos not including entrance fee), tours of Mérida, and even weeklong trips to Cuba (US$350). Open Mon.-Fri. 8am-1pm and 5-7:30pm, Sat. 8am-1pm. **Turismo Planeta** (tel. 28-15-60, fax 23-32-58), Calle 59 #501 at Calle 60. Daytrips to the ruins (85 pesos, with meal but not entrance fee) and trips to Guatemala, Cuba, and parts of Mexico. Open Mon.-Fri. 8am-1pm and 5-7:30pm, Sat. 8am-1pm. **Fun Travel,** Calle 60 #459 (tel. 28-57-30, fax 28-31-58), between Calles 51 and 53, offers a 25% discount on local tours for *Let's Go* users. Daytrips to Chichén Itzá and Uxmal are 60-110 pesos, depending on whether food, admission and A/C on the bus are included.

Consulates: U.S., Paseo de Montejo 453 (tel. 25-50-11 or 25-54-09), at Av. Colón. Call first to determine hours for visas. Open for general business Mon.-Wed. noon-3:30pm, Thurs.-Fri. 7:30am-3:30pm. **U.K.** and **Belize** (Honorary Consulate), Calle 53 #498 at the corner with Calle 58 (tel. 28-61-52, fax 28-39-62). Open Mon.-Fri. 9am-1pm.

Currency Exchange: Casa de cambio de Bánamex, in the Casa de Montejo on the *zócalo*. The best rate you're likely to see in the Yucatán. Open Mon.-Fri. 9am-5pm. Banks center on Calle 65 near the *zócalo* between Calles 56 and 62. Open Mon.-Fri. 9am-noon.

American Express: Paseo de Montejo 494, office #106 (tel. 28-42-22, fax. 28-43-73), between Calles 43 and 45. English spoken. Open Mon.-Fri. 9am-2pm and 4-6pm, Sat. 9am-1pm. Money exhange desk closes 1hr. early.

Post Office: On Calle 65 (tel. 24-35-90), between Calles 56 and 56a, 3 blocks southeast of the *zócalo* in the Palacio Federal. Open for *Lista de Correos* and stamps Mon.-Fri. 7am-7pm, Sat. 9am-1pm. *Surcursales* (branches) at Calle 58 between Calles 49 and 51, at the airport and at the main bus station. Open for stamps Mon.-Sat. 8am-7pm. For regulations, call 21-25-61. **Postal Code:** 97000.

Telephones: International collect calls are rarely made from *casetas* in Mérida. Instead, dial "**01" for an AT&T operator or 09 for the international operator from a public phone: the national operator at 02 can transfer the line. Long distance *casetas* at the airport (open daily 8am-9pm) and in the main bus station (5-min. international collect calls 5 pesos, open daily 7am-10pm). **Telephone Code:** 99.

Telegrams: In the same building as the main post office (tel. 28-59-97), but the entrance is around the corner on Calle 56a. 10-word telegram costs 3.25 pesos. Open Mon.-Fri. 8am-11:30pm, Sat. 9am-noon.

Airport: On Rte. 180, 7km southwest of the city. Post office, telegram office, long distance telephone, and car rental available. **Aeroméxico,** Paseo Montejo 460 between Calles 35 and 37 (tel. 24-94-55), and at the airport (tel. 24-85-76). **Mexicana,** Calle 58 #500 (tel. 24-66-33), and at the airport (tel. 23-69-86). **Aerocaribe,** Paseo Montejo 500-B (tel. 23-00-02) at Calle 47, and at the airport (tel. 28-00-99). **Aviateca,** Calle 58 between 45 and 43 (tel. 46-12-96) between Calles 49 and 51, and at the airport (tel.24-36-05). **Continental,** at the airport (tel. 46-13-90). The carriers listed above reach most cities in Mexico and the southern U.S., with limited destinations in Europe.

Train Station: Ferrocarri les Nacionales de México, on Calle 55 (tel. 23-59-44), between Calles 46 and 48, 8½ blocks northeast of the *zócalo*. Open daily 7am-10pm. Double-check train status at the information booth and buy tickets at least 2hrs. before departure (you must buy tickets on the day of departure). To: Progreso, Mexico City, Palenque, Valladolid, and Tizimín.

Taxis: A variety of stands throughout the city. **Palacio Municipal,** (tel. 28-54-84) on the zócalo. **Mercado Municipal,** (tel. 23-11-35) at Calle 56 and 65, **Santa Ana,** (tel. 28-5-13) Calle 47 at Calle 60, just south of the Pasco Montejo.

Bus Stations: Numerous bus lines operate out of the main bus terminal, **Unión de Camioneros,** Calle 69 #544, between Calles 70 and 72, 6 blocks southwest of the *zócalo*. Check departures ahead of time since changes are frequent and complete schedules are often not posted. **Autobuses del Oriente (ADO)** (tel. 24-83-91). 1st class to: Escárcega (38 pesos); Mexico City (200 pesos); Palenque (61 pesos); Puebla (144 pesos); Tenosique (61 pesos); Veracruz (122 pesos); Villahermosa (53 pesos); Campeche (20 pesos). **Autotransportes del Caribe** (tel. 24-42-75). 1st class to: Chetumal (45 pesos). 2nd class: 9 per day to Tulum and Chetumal, among others. **Autotransportes de Oriente** (tel. 23-22-87) also runs 1st and 2nd class to regional destinations, including Chichén Itzá and Tizimín. **Expreso de Oriente** (tel. 24-95-18). 1st class to: Cancún (36 pesos) Tulum (36 pesos); Valladolid (18 pesos). **Autotransportes del Sureste en Yucatán** (tel. 28-28-87). To Palenque (43 pesos), Ocosingo (55 pesos), San Cristóbal de Las Casas (61 pesos), and Tuxtla Gutiérrez. **Autotransportes del Sur,** Calle 50 #531 at Calle 67, 7 blocks southeast of the *zócalo*. To Celestún (13 per day, form 6am-8pm, 9.80 pesos). **Autotransportes del Noroeste,** on Calle 50 (tel. 24-63-55) between Calles 65 and 67. To: Río Lagartos (3 hrs., 24.50 pesos); Las Coloradas (2½hrs., 18 pesos); San Felipe (3hrs., 20 pesos); Tizimin (18 pesos). **Autotransportes de Progreso,** Calle 62 #524 at Calle 64 (tel. 2-4-13-44). To Progreso every 15min., 5am-9pm. **Autotransportes del Sur** (tel. 4-82-43). To Uxmal and Kabah. 5 times daily (1½-2 hrs., 6.50 pesos).

Car Rentals: Mexico Rent-a-Car, Calle 62 #483 (tel. 27-49-16), between Calles 57 and 59. Also Calle 60 #495 between Calles 57 and 59. The cheapest place in Mérida; cars start at 120 pesos per day including mileage. Open daily 8am-12:30 pm and 6-8pm. **Budget,** Paseo Montejo 497 (tel. 46-13-80). 147 pesos per day. Open Mon.-Sat. 7am-1pm and 4-8pm. Branch at the airport (tel. 46-13-80). **Max Rent-a-Car,** Calle 60 #481 (tel. 24-76-06) between Calles 55 and 57. 180 pesos per day. Open daily 7am-8pm.

Market: Covers more than 4 blocks south of Calle 65, behind and on either side of the Palacio Federal on Calle 56. Convenient to the post office for shipping home. Crowded and particularly fun on the weekends. Open daily sunrise-sunset.

Supermarket: San Francisco de Asis, on Calle 65 (tel. 26-34-11), between Calles 50 and 52, across from the market. Open Mon.-Sat. 7am-9pm, Sun. 7am-3pm.

Laundromat: Lavamátic, Calle 69 #541, at Calle 64. They do it for you for 14 pesos per 3kg. Open Mon.-Sat. 8am-6pm. There is no self-serve laundromat in Mérida.

Red Cross: Calle 68 #533 (tel. 24-77-74), between Calles 65 and 67, 4½ blocks southwest of the *zócalo*. 24-hr. emergency and ambulance services. No English spoken.

24-hr. Pharmacy: Farmacia Canto on Calle 60 #513 (tel. 24-24-90) between Calles 63 and 65.

Hospital: Centro Médico de las Américas, Calle 54 #365 at Av. Perez P. (Calle 33-A) (tel. 26-21-1, 26-26-19). 24-hr. service, including ambulance. English spoken. Also **Clínica de Mérida,** on Av. Itzáes between Calles 25 and 27 (tel. 25-41-00, 25-44-22). English spoken.

Police: (Tel. 25-25-55), on Reforma (also called Calle 72) between Calles 39 and 41. Take bus "Reforma." 24-hr. emergency service. Some English spoken.

ACCOMMODATIONS

Behind the old and sometimes non-descript facades of several of Méridas buildings hide 200-yr.-old colonial mansions turned hotels in varying stages of decay. Leaky roofs and faulty plumbing are commonplace in these aging dinosaurs. Nonetheless, they offer unique budget accomodation, often centered around beautiful courtayrds.

North

Hotel Dolores Alba, Calle 63 #464 (tel. 28-56-50, fax 28-31-63), between Calles 52 and 54. Handsome old building in excellent condition. Rocking chairs in the lobby facilitate a pleasant, sociable atmosphere. Pool and restaurant. Spacious, extensively furnished rooms with glistening bathrooms. *Agua al gusto:* cold, purified, or hot. Check-out noon. Singles 50 pesos. Doubles 70 pesos. Triples 90 pesos. A/C 15 pesos more. Traveler's checks accepted.

Hotel Trinidad, Calle 62 #464 (tel. 24-98-06, fax 24-23-19), between Calles 55 and 57. Unique and stylish. Furnishings of the past and paintings of the future (by the owner) decorate this restored colonial mansion. Lobby moonlights as a cafe and art gallery, and the large screen in the bar displays satellite TV and movie videos. Guests have access to the pool at the Hotel Trinidad Galería. Each of the 13 rooms differ in size and decor; prices vary accordingly (30-80 pesos). Aching plumbing. Check-out 1pm. Singles 35-40 pesos. Doubles 40-45 pesos. Rooms with private bath 50-60 pesos. 10 pesos for each extra person. Credit cards accepted.

Trinidad Galeria, Calle 60 #456 (tel. 23-24-63, fax 24-23-19), at Calle 51. Sister of the Hotel Trinidad. Sprawling complex houses 30 rooms, cafe, and two art galleries. Large, leafy swimming pool. Modern art and eclectic antique collection. Some rooms are small and dark, others light and roomy. Check-out 1pm. Singles 35 pesos, with bath 60 pesos. Doubles with bath 70 pesos. 10 pesos per additional person. Credit cards accepted.

Hotel Margarita, Calle 66 #506 (tel. 23-72-36), between Calles 61 and 63, 1½ blocks west of the *zócalo*. A good buy. Rooms are bare and basic with minimal windows, but they do have fans, hot water, and toilet seats. Doubles considerably more spacious than singles. Check-out 1pm. Singles 30 pesos. 2-bed doubles 43 pesos. Rooms with 3 beds 50 pesos. 5 pesos per additional person.

Hotel del Arco, Calle 63 #452 (tel. 28-14-87), between Calles 50 and 52, near the Arcos de Dragones, close to the two secondary bus stations. Small single rooms in brown and yellow, fans and hot water. Long-used but clean bathrooms. Check-out 2pm. Singles or doubles 40 pesos. Triples 50 pesos. Quads 80 pesos. Traveler's checks accepted.

South

Casa Bowen, Calle 66 #521-B (tel. 21-65-77), between Calles 65 and 67, halfway between the main bus station and the *zócalo*. Green, well-tended courtyard surrounded by white, colonial columns. International guests mingle around the arcaded patio. Lobby TV. Some rooms enjoy kitchenettes (1 burner and fridge), but all rooms are hooked up with fans and hot water. Lockout 11pm. Ring the bell or make arrangements with the staff about late returns. Singles 35 pesos. 1-bed doubles 42 pesos. 2-bed doubles 45 pesos. With kitchen 55 pesos. Rooms with A/C 60 pesos. 10 pesos per additional person. Traveler's checks accepted. Send 1 night's cost to reserve.

Posada II, Calle 69 #516, between Calles 62 and 64, 4 blocks south of the zócalo. Unoriginal name for the cheapest thing going. Ancient rooms of municipal building host 3-7 single beds each. Cave-like communal bathroom, lacks hot water, but host-family Alvarez will cook a cheap meal, morning, noon, and night. Tables and TVs in inner courtyard. No locks or lockers, but the family will hold your belongings for you. 18 pesos for a bed.

Casa de Héspedes Peniche, Calle 62 #507 (tel. 28-55-18), between Calles 63 and 65. The least expensive option near the zócalo. Beautiful, disintegrating colonial building with stained glass windows and wooden doors that don't lock. Tolerable communal showers, baths and fans, but no hot water. Best for those with their own locks and towels. Often full. Great place to meet other travelers. Lockout 11pm, but if you knock long enough someone will probably let you in. Check-out noon. Rooms start at 24.20 pesos; with baths start at 35.20 pesos.

Hotel Sevilla, Calle 62 #511 (tel. 23-83-60), at Calle 65, ½ block south of the *zócalo*. Elegant, relatively well-maintained colonial building with marble floors that add a regal air. Handsome lion statues flank the stairs leading out of the courtyard. All rooms have hot water, fans, and *agua purificada*, but little light. Check-out 1 pm. Singles 43 pesos. Doubles 47 pesos. Triples 55 pesos. 5 pesos each additional person. Prices rise by 5 pesos during high season.

Hotel La Paz, Calle 62 #622 (tel. 23-94-46), between Calles 65 and 67, 1½ blocks south of the zócalo. Gaily painted old painting old building in fine shape. Upstairs simple, airy rooms with private bath sectioned off. Fans, hot water, and parking.

MÉRIDA

Check-out 1pm. Singles 30 pesos. Doubles 34 pesos. 10 pesos more per additional person.

Hotel María Teresa, Calle 64 #529 (tel. 28-51-94), between Calles 65 and 67. Plain clean rooms with windows that view the roofs of Mérida; immaculate bathrooms. Nice location goes hand-in-hand with street noise. Hot water and fans. Rooms vary in size, so ask to see several. Sofas for cushion-lovers in front of a lobby TV. Check-out 1pm. Singles 30 pesos. Doubles 40-48 pesos. Triple 54 pesos.

Hotel San Clemente, Calle 58 #586-D (tel. 28-17-95), at Calle 71, in the heart of the hammock shop district, 4 blocks southeast of the zócalo. Comfortably-sized rooms with disappointing bathrooms. Fans and water off of hallway. Check-out 1pm. Singles 30 pesos. Doubles 40 pesos. 5 pesos each additional person.

Hotel Suarez, Calle 69 #563 between Calles 68 and 70, across from main bus station. Run-down but big rooms with clean, new hot-water bathrooms and marble floors off of narrow hallway. Good for taking an early bus, since they'll probably wake you up anyway. Check-out 1pm. Singles 35 pesos. Doubles 40 pesos. Triples 55 pesos.

FOOD

Mérida's diverse population demands a wide variety of food. Look for *yucateco* specialties and international cuisine, as well as the standard selection of *huevos rancheros*, enchiladas and *flan*.

Travelers wary of over-seasoned *chiles* will note that, generally, you can safely explore unknown stews and sauces because the local scorcher, the *chile habanero*, does not lurk within dishes but instead waits patiently in a garnish bowl or in a shaker on the table blended with tomatoes. Mérida's excellent specialties include: *sopa de lima* (frothy lime soup with chicken and tortilla bits); *pollo pibil* (chicken with herbs baked in banana leaves); *poc-chuc* (pork steak with onions doused in sour Seville orange juice); *papadzules* (chopped hard-boiled eggs wrapped in corn tortillas served with pumpkin sauce); *huevos motuleros* (refried beans, fried egg, chopped ham and cheese on a tortilla garnished with tomato sauce, peas, and fried banana); and *horchata* (a Mayan rice drink flavored with vanilla, honey, and almond).

The cheapest food in town fills the **market** that stretches south from Calle 65, two blocks east of the *zócalo*. Stands overflow with fruits, vegetables, and *antojitos*. For more substantial nourishment, head to the market's second level off Calle 56 at Calle 67. Over 20 small *puestos* (restaurants), offering a variety of *yucateco* dishes for 5-10 pesos, cram this cavernous area. (Restaurant complex open Mon.-Sat. 8am-8pm, Sun. 8am-5pm.)

El Louvre, Calle 62 #499 (tel. 25-50-73), between the Palacio Municipal and the Palacio de Gobierno. Big, affordable cafeteria where locals talk politics. Service is prompt but curt. Entrees—including brain, tongue, guts, and satisfying sandwiches—cost 2.75-10.45 pesos. *Comida corrida* 14 pesos. Open 24 hrs.

El Tucho, on Calle 60 #482 (tel. 24-23-23), between Calles 55 and 57. A restaurant/afternoon cabaret popular with both locals and tourists. While singers, musicians and comedians entertain you, troupes of waiters ferry trays of free *botanas* (tacos and hors d'oeuvres) between customers. As long as you keep drinking, the *botanas* keep coming. Real meals 20 pesos. Open daily noon-9pm. Credit cards accepted.

La Prosperidad, Calle 56 #491 at Calle 53. Similar in ambience to El Tucho; live entertainment and plenty of *botanas* with drinks. Meals are 15 pesos. Open daily 10am-8pm.

Restaurant Ananda Maya Gynza, Calle 59 #507 (tel. 28-24-51), between Calles 60 and 62. Offers a variety of vegetarian dishes and pizzas under a thick arboreal shade. Eggplant aubergine curry with cheese and rice 14 pesos. Small pizzas 11 pesos. Open Mon.-Sat. 8am-10pm. Traveler's checks, MC and Visa accepted.

La Jungla, Calle 62 #500, between Calles 59 and 61, on the corner of the *zócalo*. A big papier-mâché zoo ushers you into a long hall overlooking the *zócalo*. An Italian restaurant with murals of the Tower of Pisa and sandwiches. Wafer-thin pizzas (small with topping 9-12 pesos) and spaghetti (6 pesos). Open daily 11:30am-12:30am.

El Patio Español, Calle 60 #496 (tel. 28-37-84), at Calle 59 in the Gran Hotel. Classy, tranquil, hip, and inexpensive. The gorgeous green garden of the hotel doubles as restaurant decor. A great place to sample *yucateco* specialties: *poc chuc* 18 pesos; *pollo pibil* 16 pesos; *postres* 35 pesos; coffee 2.50 pesos. Tortillas or hot bread and butter accompany meals. Breakfast 8-12 pesos. Open daily 7am-10pm. MC and Visa accepted.

Los Almendros and Los Gran Almendros, Calle 50 #493 (tel. 28-54-59), between Calles 57 and 59, by the Pl. de Mejorada. Huge and popular, with 6 branches in Ticul and Cancún. Two nearly identical adjacent restaurants which serve native specialties. The combination (23 pesos) affords a sampling of *yucateco* dishes: *poc-chuc, longaniza* (grilled sausage), *cocherita* (baked pork), and *escabeche* (turkey with black pepper, cloves, garlic and onion). Menus have color pictures, so you can look before you choose. Entrees 15-23 pesos. Open daily 9am-11pm. Live music at Los Gran Almendros between 1-5pm. Traveler's checks and credit cards accepted.

Pancho's, Calle 59 #509 (tel. 23-09-42), between Calles 60 and 62. Paunchless Pancho Villa look-alikes in pseudo-1890 atmosphere show off their incendiary techniques with flaming dishes and wild cocktails. Eats are good but expensive. The outdoor disco in the back is jam-packed with the lonely and the hopeful twisting the night away under *palapas. Sopa de lima* 7 pesos. *Pollo pibil* 19 pesos. Happy hour Mon.-Fri. 6-9pm. Live music Tues.-Sat. 10pm-2am. Open daily 6pm-2:30am. Also serves delicious *jugos* and *aguas* (2-5 pesos). Open daily 7am-11pm. Credit cards accepted.

El Jardín, Calle 59 #496 (tel. 23-15-92), between Calles 60 and 58. Soothing music and vegetarian fare served up by Mexican Hare Krishnas. Comidas corrida 8-10 pesos. Open noon-5pm daily.

SIGHTS

Mérida's salon, the **zócalo,** inspires animated discussions upon *confidenciales* (loveseats with the halves facing in opposite directions). If you speak Spanish, you can easily join or strike up a conversation.

Almost all of Mérida's larger historic buildings are within easy walking distance of the *zócalo,* but don't restrict yourself to the downtown area. Pocket-sized parks and fading colonial arches throughout town reward the ambulatory traveler. The twin spires of the yellow **catedral** loom over the eastern side of the *zócalo.* The three Corinthian doors of solid wood with brass nails and the stark, windowless facade recall, with their fortress-like presence, the bitter centuries of struggle between the Maya and missionaries. The stone blocks were themselves stolen from the Mayan temples of T'ho. Construction began in 1561 and was completed in 1598. The building is an example of the austere Herrerricano architectural style, but the most remarkable is the enormous Blistering Christ inside—the second largest crucifix in the world. (Open daily 6am-6pm. Free.)

As you leave the cathedral, the **Palacio de Gobierno** stands to the right, along the northern edge of the *zócalo.* Built in 1892, it is a combination of two architectural styles: Tuscan (main floor) and Dorian (upper floor). Each of the great walls of this century-old colonial-style palace is graced by a huge painting in a series celebrating the social evolution of the Yucatecan people. Fernando Castro Pacheco, still a Mérida resident, created these works for the city over the course of a quarter-century. The soft colors bleed into one another, lending a timeless quality to the traditional Mayan symbols. Maize dominates the stairwell mural, and the *Popol Vuh*, one of the only books by and about the Maya, reigns over the next layout. The History Chamber upstairs recounts the story of the priest Diego de Landa, who tried to burn every written relic of the Mayan religion and succeeded in destroying all but three of the priceless codices.

Taken together, the murals evoke the protracted, brutal conquest of the Maya by the conquistadors and the peaceful triumph of the elements of Mayan culture that have persisted and influenced modern Yucatecan culture. The History Chamber also contains books on Yucatecan history and Mayan culture. (Open daily 9am-9pm. Free.)

Continue along the *zócalo* until you stand in front of the **Palacio Municipal,** across from the cathedral. A jail until the 18th century, it was rebuilt in colonial style in 1928 in accordance with its new function. Concerts and classes in *jarana,* the Yucatecan colonial dance, now take place here; schoolgirls and grandmothers pass afternoons tapping their sturdy white shoes rhythmically against the tile floor, all the while balancing beer trays on their heads without spilling them. The main floor corridor is adorned with two paintings on the theme of the Conquest by the local artist Manuel Lizama. (Open Mon.-Sat. 8am-8pm. Free.)

On the southern side of the *zócalo,* the **House of Montejo,** the oldest colonial building in Mérida, was completed in 1549 upon the order of city founder Francisco de Montejo. Built with the very stones of the temple of T'ho, the carved façade boasts about the conquest of the Maya. The expressions on the faces of the soldiers have faded, but the anguish of the four Mayan heads on which they stand remains clear. The carving conforms to the Toltec tradition of representing warriors standing on the heads of their conquests. Interjected are the coats of arms of the King of Spain and the Montejo family. The building now houses a bank, but can be explored Mon.-Fri. 9am-5pm.

Celebrating the crafts and craftspeople of Mexico, the **Museo de Arte Popular** lies six blocks east of the *zócalo* on Calle 59, between Calles 48 and 50 behind the Convento de la Mejorada. The ground floor displays a wide array of Yucatecan handiwork, from costumes and masks to pottery, weavings and *huipile* embroidery. Upstairs you'll find a varied collection of handicrafts from all of Mexico's states. The room of sculpted skeletons (you'll see two of them as you climb the stairs) frightens and amuses. (Open Tues.-Sat. 8am-8pm, Sun. 9am-2pm. Free.)

Mérida's most impressive museum, the **Museo de Antropología,** is housed in a gorgeous Italian Renaissance-style building on the corner of Paseo Montejo and Calle 43. Archaeological finds illustrate the *indígena* history of Yucatán, and extensive anthropological information in Spanish accompanies the artifacts. Geology, horticulture, linguistic history, demography, religion and daily life are covered thoroughly. Grimace at the holes drilled in teeth for jewelry stones, stare in awe at the head-flattening devices applied to the craniums of the infants of upper-class families and learn to recognize the *chac-mool* (Mayan for "red fingernails") form of sculpture prevalent in the Yucatán. If you plan to visit any archaeological sites, the shop downstairs sells comprehensive English-language guidebooks for much less than the price charged at the ruins themselves (INAH official guides in English 19.90 pesos). (Museum and shop open Mon.-Sat. 9am-2pm, Sun. 8am-2pm. Admission 3 pesos. Free Sun.)

The **Museo de Historia Natural** lies on Calle 84 near Av. Itzáes. Housed in a beautiful 19th-century *hacienda,* this small but ambitious collection goes about explaining the history of life from the origin of the universe through the emergence of species. (Open Mon.-Sat. 9am-5pm.) Right around the corner on Av. Itzáes is the **Centenary Park and Zoo.** The zoo not only has lions, tigers and bears (Oh, my!), but also peacocks, flamingos, deer, antelope, monkeys, hippos, native Aztec dogs, wolves, and jaguars. A miniature train (.50 pesos) full of shrieking schoolchildren whizzes through periodically, eliciting snarls from the wilder beasts. (Park open daily 6am-7pm. Free.)

French-style mansions and boutiques line **Paseo Montejo,** often called "the Yucatecan Champs-Elysées." In the north it culminates with the **Monumento a la Patria.** In 1956, sculptor Rómulo Rozo imitated Mayan stone carving style in forming major figures from Mexican history. An eternal flame and a filthy waterless fountain stand guard. After the half-hour walk up Paseo Montejo, rest in the **Parque de** las Américas, Calle 20 at Colón, just southwest of the monument, so named for its collection of carved columns from each of the countries of Central and South America.

Mérida takes special pride in the **Theater Peón Contreras** situated on the corner of Calles 60 and 57. The beautiful building in the Italian Renaissance style with internal rococo decor served as a university for nearly two centuries, starting in 1624. The **Universidad de Yucatán** now sits on Calle 57 between Calles 60 and 62. This Hispano-Moorish complex dates from 1938, though the university was founded in 1711. The **Juan Guzmán Gallery** on Calle 59 between Calles 58 and 60 exhibits paintings and sculpture; there is a permanent exhibit of colonial art as well as temporary contemporary art exhibits. (Open Tues.-Sat 9am-4:30pm, Sun. 8am-noon. Admission 5 pesos. Free Sun. and holidays.)

The many parks, churches and statues scattered throughout the center also warrant exploration. Nearby, much of the **Convento de la Mejorada,** on Calle 59 between Calles 48 and 50 and established by Franciscan missionaries, has been converted into apartments, though the church still serves its original purpose. The old gate behind the **Parque** and **Iglesia de San Juan de Dios,** located on Calle 69 between Calles 62 and 64, marks the southern limit of the center, while the **Iglesia de Santa Lucía** (on Calle 60 between Calles 53 and 55) and its park surrounded by colonial arches stand north of the *zócalo*. The **Iglesia Santiago** on Calles 59 and 72 is one of the oldest churches in Mexico and has retained its original altarpiece.

SHOPPING

As the center of the Yucatán shopping universe, Mérida harbors some of Mexico's finest produce, flowers and handicrafts. Its four square blocks of **mercado** (market), which opened in 1909, peddle everything from toothpaste to parakeets. Its streets have been paved with bottle tops pounded in by millions of passersby. The market is a major tourist attraction—expect to receive friendly attention from multi-lingual sandal-sellers and piñata-pushers. In all its richness, however, the market does not offer a huge selection of coral jewelry and other crafted souvenirs, and it tends toward the kitschy and unclean side. It's best to plan a Sunday in Mérida, when the entire *zócalo*, starting at 9am, covers over with vendors.

The main market occupies the block southwest of the Palacio Federal, spreading outward from the corner of Calles 65 and 56. Shops, awnings and tin-roofed shacks ramble for a good many blocks both east and west behind the *palacio*. The only border is busy Calle 65 to the north, but even there stands spill over onto the other side of the street and around the small square formed by Calles 65, 56, and 56a across from the Palacio Federal.

Facing the Palacio Federal, the main building in the market complex lies to the left. Many tourists are directed to the second-story "artisans' market," part of a modern building behind and to the right of the Palacio Federal, but food, *huaraches*, hats and clothing sell at far better prices in the market surrounding the building. Sandal shops face the easternmost edge. Sandal-makers (*fabricadores*) in the market will often custom-make sandals upon request; this service can require a few hours or a day. For the lowest prices on sandals, jewelry and hammocks, ask around to locate the various factories (*fábricas*) hidden within the market.

Mérida's market is the best place in the Yucatán to buy piñatas; a huge selection of shops congregate on Calle 65 between Calles 54 and 56. Piñatas range from 10 to 20 pesos, depending on the size and design, and weigh next to nothing because they are stuffed with newspaper. Neighboring stores sell bags of candy in bulk so that desperate fun-seekers can have a piñata party on the spot. Most hats in the market are imported from Becal, Campeche, where they are woven in underground caverns at precise humidities.

White *huipiles*, with colorful embroidery skirting the neckline and hem, adorn most local women and shop windows. The same is true for the silky, maroon *rebozo*, a shawl. Men wear the *guayabera*, a short-sleeved shirt with four pockets,

MÉRIDA

plentiful buttons and distinctive vertical columns of tiny double-stitching as decoration. **Kary's,** on Calle 64 between Calles 69 and 67, stitches and exhibits a good selection of *guayaberas.* **Jack's,** on Calle 59 between Calles 60 and 62, is a somewhat more expensive factory which also carries women's regional clothing. Be sure to check the fabric content.

Jewelry stores pepper the downtown area, offering excellent buys on silver. Prices are almost always fixed and designs vary little between stores. Bargains can be found at the bazaar on Sundays in front of the Palacio Municipal, although the quality of the silver may not be consistent. Note that most jewelry stores are expensive; the best jewelry prices are usually on the street at random stands. Some of the best *huipiles* are offered in the streets by women who come for one day to Mérida from their villages. Don't bet your head that the larger, more commercial stores offer the best prices or the best selections. Fine *huipiles* should cost 35 pesos and over, *rebozos* 100-150 pesos and up, *guayaberas* 40-60 pesos and up.

Travelers should be wary when approached by Mexican children who want to give a "free" shopping tour. Although you may feel overwhelmed and disoriented in the sprawling market, it's best to go it alone. The kids often receive a commission from the shops, which jack up their prices accordingly. A government craft shop with a wide selection of handicrafts is located on Calle 63 between Calles 64 and 66; prices are reasonable.

And don't forget: Mérida is the hammock mecca of Mexico and the world. All establishments sell hammocks ranging in quality from the finest (good cotton; tight, triple weave) to what locals refer to as *basura* (trash), a flimsy, loosely woven net pawned off on unsuspecting *norteamericanos* as a top-of-the-line hammock. You should not be able to poke your finger through a good quality hammock. Avoid buying from the walking vendors on the *zócalo* and in other city parks, if only because they have a poor selection. Established stores are at the other extreme; most have a wide variety of merchandise in enormous storerooms. While the prices are relatively high, customers can see exactly what they are purchasing, with assurance of quality and size.

Although many stalls such as **La Poblana, El Aguacate, El Campesino,** and **La Bodega** are frequently mentioned by locals, those in the know go to **El Hamaguero,** Calle 58 #572 (tel. 23-21-17), between Calles 69 and 71. They have 30 years of experience, a wide selection and a try-out room; those who ask to test the hammocks are escorted to a back room and treated with more respect than the average *Juan norteamericano.* The owners are pleasant, and since they make the hammocks in-store, prices are reasonable. (Open Mon.-Fri. 9am-6:30pm, Sat. 9am-5pm). Another highly-frequented shop is **El Tixcocób,** Calle 56 #549 facing the market. The sturdy-hearted bargain-hunter may consider a trek to the penitentiary, where all work is is done in-house and prices are 60% less than free-market counterparts. Take the bus labeled *penal directo* at Calle 58 between 67 and 69. Penitentiary shops open 9am-4pm.

ENTERTAINMENT

The municipal government provides a never-ending series of free musical and dance events in the city's parks. On Mondays, the folklore ballet and the police *jaranera* band perform at 9pm in front of the Palacio Municipal. Big band music of the '40s plays on Tuesday nights at 9pm in Santiago Park at Calles 72 and 59. Take your steady to the **Mayab Culture House,** on Calle 63 between Calles 64 and 66, which sponsors concerts of string instruments and piano on Wednesdays at 9pm. Thursday nights feature a 9pm "Yucatecan Serenade," with romantic music and folk dance in Santa Lucía Park, Calle 60 at 55. On Fridays at 9pm, students perform regional dances from all areas of Mexico at the University of the Yucatán, at the corner of Calles 60 and 57. Mérida's *zócalo* enchants on Sundays, when streets are blocked off by 10:30am for the festive **Mérida en domingo** (Mérida on Sunday). A Yucatecan orchestra performs at 11am, followed by a re-enactment of a mestizo wedding at 1pm in front of the Palacio Municipal. The city's other parks feature *marimba* concerts and *jarana* demonstrations throughout the day.

Mérida thrives on constantly rotating nightly activities. Large posters glued to walls about town announce upcoming events. Keep an eye out for the student theater posters near the university. The **Teatro Peón Contreras** (tel. 23-73-54), on Calle 60 near Calle 57, hosts special events and frequent concerts. The *ballet folklórico* performs "Roots of Today's Yucatán" every Tuesday night at 9pm. (Tickets 20 pesos at the door or from travel agencies.) A popular evening activity is to drink beer, munch on *botanas* (which come free with drinks) and enjoy comedians and live *marimba* music at **El Tucho** or **La Prosperidad** (see Food), or, for a bit more, **El Pancho** (see Food). Somewhat further away, but with similar nocturnal diversion, **Tulipanes,** Calle 42 #462-A, between Calles 45 and 47, features non-stop music, *yucateco* dance and a chilling re-enactment of a Mayan sacrifice. The traditional air-conditioned, panchromatic discos in Mérida are far from the center and accessible mostly by taxi (15 pesos one-way). **Bin Bon Bao,** Calle 29 #97, at Calle 18, in Mérida's poshest neighborhood, serves Merida's hip patricians.

■ Near Mérida

Two popular package tours from Mérida are daytrips to **Chichén Itzá** and **Uxmal/ Kabah.** Tours to the ruins cost 60-110 pesos, depending on whether food, admission and air conditioning on the bus are included. All packages include at least transportation and guide. (See Campeche to Mérida: Long Route for other options for seeing the sites.)

DZIBILCHALTÚN

Hidden behind the tiny village of the same name north of Mérida, the ruin site of Dzibilchaltún spreads over more than 25 square miles of barren scrubland. The oldest city continuously used by the Maya as a ceremonial and administrative center, Dzibilchaltún (Place Where There Is Writing on Flat Stones) flourished from approximately 2000 BC until the Conquest. While Dzibilchaltún's importance and continuous influence on Mayan culture is of great interest to archaeologists and historians, the excavated site now open to tourists is neither as impressive nor as accessible as other ruins near Mérida.

The ruins lie some 20km north of Mérida off an access road from Route 273, the extension of Paseo Montejo. You can take a Dzibilchaltún-bound **bus** (1.50 pesos) which will take you all the way to the entrance ruins, or take a Progreso-bound bus and ask to be dropped off at the access road. The access road extends for 4km; some hitch while others hope that a communal taxi (2 pesos) will pass by. To catch a bus, go to *Parque de San Juan* on Calle 69 between Calles 62 and 64 in Mérida. The Progreso buses which leave from the bus station on Calle 62 between Calles 65 and 67 do not make any stops, so you'll have to take the second-class buses that leave from the park if you want to be dropped off. At the entrance to the site is a small museum which exhibits artifacts found during the excavation. The road from the entrance leads past several foundations and partly restored structures to Dzibil-chaltún's *cenote*, **Xlacá,** which served (unsanitarily) as both a source of water and as a sacrificial well similar to those at Chichén Itzá. National Geographic Society divers have recovered ceremonial artifacts and human bones from the depths of the 44m-deep *cenote*. The *cenote* is not as magnificent as those in Chichén Itzá or Valla-dolid, but the water is clear and inviting for a non-sacrificial dip among water lilies and fish.

Intersecting the road to Xlacá, a dirt track to the left passes through an almost unrecognizable plaza. Farther along this road, Dzibilchaltún's showpiece, the fully restored **Temple of the Seven Dolls,** possesses a harmony of proportion and style lacking in other temples. This is also the only known Mayan temple with windows. The seven clay "dolls" discovered here are believed to represent different illnesses or deformities and are now on display in the museum. Less commonly mentioned is another proof of the mathematical and astronomical genius of the Maya; in the early morning (around 6am), while the site is still closed, a huge shadow mask of the rain god Chac is said to appear as the sun's rays pierce the temple. Also, the building is so carefully aligned that it can be used to verify the winter and summer solstices. At 5:30pm on June 21, the sun threads the tiny space between the door jambs on the north side; at 7:30am on December 21 the phenomenon is repeated on the south side.

Mounds and hills marking ancient buildings and temples dot the surrounding countryside, but archaeological excavations have disinterred little of interest to the layperson. (Museum and ruins open daily 8am-5pm. Admission 10 pesos. Free Sun.) The return to Mérida is trickier. Either plan so as to take one of the eight daily **buses** or go out to Route 273 and attempt to persuade a bus from Progreso to stop. If you walk the short road from the ruins to the town of Dzibilchaltún, it is possible to catch a bus or taxi to get out to Route 273; from there you can try to flag down a second class bus. Buses from (and to) Progreso go by about every hour. *Combis* pass even more frequently. Early risers should be able to catch a bus to the site, see the ruins and walk or take a bus back to the highway by noon to catch a bus to Progreso and the beach.

■■■ PROGRESO

During the summer months and holidays, Progreso is a popular retreat for the citizens of Mérida, who make the 33km jaunt northward to enjoy the clean, quiet beachfront, the gulf waters, and the famously surreal greenish sunset; at other times the town is tranquil and tourist-free.

Puerto Progreso was built in the mid-19th century to replace Sisal (40km to the southwest) as Yucatán's major port and *henequén* distribution center. The leaves of the blue-gray *henequén* plant yield strong fibers, used in twine- and rope-making. Progreso-bound buses pass travel out of the city on Paseo Montejo to denuded fields once covered with the sharp, spiky leaves. *Henequén* production peaked with the proliferation of the *hacienda* system under Díaz: prisoners, entire villages from other parts of Mexico—including Yaqui people from faraway Sonora—were imported as *peones* and forced to work on the *haciendas*, often in shackles. The post-WWII discovery of synthetic fibers has strangled world demand for *henequén*, but the century-old mansions built with yesteryear's profits still stand as testimony to Progreso's past. From the bus station, walk east along the Malecón to see the moguls' residences.

In 1985, the federal and state governments decided to market Progreso's natural beauty to North American beach devotees. Yucatán state hopes to lure cruise ships and sun-worshippers to a massive hotel-condominium complex (called Nuevo Yucatán) near Progreso. Covering more than 2.2 square mi., this massive project threatens to become a small city unto itself, with a marina, shopping areas, sports facilities and private residences. To date one can still enjoy the untainted beaches and small-town familiarity of Progreso. Even more isolated and quiet are the beaches of **Chelán,** a quick 8km bus ride from Progreso.

The custodian of the lighthouse **El Faro,** at Calle 80 near Calle 25, welcomes visitors during the day if he is not too busy. A spiral staircase leads to a single 1000-watt bulb and an array of reflectors. The 2km *muelle* (pier), which clings precariously to the sandy beach, facilitates great fishing in the early morning and evening.

Practical Information To reach the port of Sisal, the beaches of Celestún, or the flamingo spectacle in Río Lagartos, you'll have to backtrack to Mérida. Progreso's **bus station** is on Calle 80 between Calles 77 and 79. Buses returning to Mérida (½hr., 3 pesos one-way, 5 pesos round-trip) leave every 15 minutes from 5am to 9:45pm. To reach the quiet *zócalo* from the terminal, turn right and walk two blocks on Calle 80. The *zócalo* lies at the intersection of Calle 80 and Calle 81, the main drag through town. If you want to hit the beach immediately from the bus station, turn left on Calle 80 and walk four blocks to its end. Street numbers in town were recently augmented by 50, but addresses and directions are still given in both the old and the new way. For example, Calle 30 (old) is the same as Calle 80 (new); Calle 27 (old) is the same as Calle 77 (new), etc. The map the tourist office gives out has augmented numbers for even-numbered streets, but old numbers for odd-numbered streets.

Progreso's **tourist office,** Calle 80 #176, near Calle 37 2 blocks away from the beach (tel. 5-01-04), has a friendly and somewhat helpful staff and occasionally small maps of the town. (Open Mon.-Fri. 9am-2pm and 4-8pm, Sat. 9am-1pm, Sun. 10am-1pm.) **Bánamex,** Calle 80 #129 (tel. 5-08-99), between Calles 77 and 79 one block towards the the beach from the *zócalo*, changes currency Monday through Friday from 9am to 1:30pm and from 4 to 5pm, as does **Bancomer,** Calle 80 at Calle 25 (tel. 5-19-18), 4 blocks towards the beach from the *zócalo*. (Open for exchange Mon.-Fri. 9am-2pm.) The **post office,** Calle 81 #150 (tel. 5-05-65), at Calle 78 just off of the *zócalo*, is open Mon.-Fri. 7am-7pm, Saturday 9am-noon (**postal code:** 97320). The **telegram office** (tel. 5-01-28) is in the same building and also features a public fax (open Mon.-Fri. 9am-8pm, Sat. 9am-noon). **Lavandería Progreso,** on Calle 74 #150-A (tel. 5-05-86) between Calles 29 and 31, provides next-day service for 9 pesos per 3kg. (Open Mon.-Sat. 8am-1:30pm and 4-7pm). **Farmacia YZA,** open 24 hrs., sits on Calle 78 at Calle 29 (tel. 5-02-24). Emergency service is provided by the **Health Center** at Calle 25 (5-00-53) between Calles 78 and 76. (Open 8am-3pm, for emergencies 24 hrs.) The **police station** (tel. 5-00-26) is in the Palacio Municipal on the *zócalo* at Calles 80 and 81. (Open 24 hrs.)

Accommodations Cheap accommodations are available close to the town center. **Hotel Miralmar,** Calle 27 #124 (tel. 5-05-52), 3 blocks to the right off of Calle 80 between Calles 74 and 72, offers inexpensive, spacious rooms. Some of these have balconies, but those go hand-in-hand with street noise. All rooms have fan, phone, TV and hot water. (Check-out noon. Singles 35 pesos, doubles 40-45 pesos, 5 pesos each additional person. Traveler's checks accepted. Reservations only during the low season.) **Hotel Progreso,** Calle 78 #142 (tel. 5-00-39), near Calle 29, is more expensive, but well worth the money for wall-to-wall carpeting, furniture in light soft wood and sparkling bathrooms. All rooms have fans, some A/C. (Check-out 1pm. Singles 60 pesos, doubles 60 pesos. A/C 15 pesos extra. Credit cards and traveler's checks accepted. Reservations by phone recommended for weekend visits.) **Posada Juan Carlos,** Calle 74 #148 (tel. 5-10-76), ekes out an existence between Calles 29 and 31. The first and second floors house small unexciting rooms and bathrooms to match, but rooms on the third floor are new, clean, light, and airy. All have fans and hot water. (Check-out 1pm. Singles 25 pesos, doubles 30 pesos, two bed triples 40 pesos, 5 pesos each additional person.)

Food As in most costal towns, the fruits of the sea dominate Progreso's cuisine. **Las Velas Restaurant/Bar,** on Av. Malecón near Calle 66 (tel. 5-02-23), is the raucous newcomer to the Progreso beach scene. This indoor/outdoor restaurant has a splendid view of the beach, live Yucatecan and Cuban music, and a popular dancing platform. Fried fish costs 20 pesos, *filete relleno* 30 pesos. (Open daily noon-whenever.) **Restaurant Pelícanos,** towards the end of Av. Malecón (tel. 507-98), also provides a picturesque ocean view in an informal setting of plastic chairs and plastic tables. (Fish filets 15.50 pesos, chicken 10-16 pesos, meats 17 pesos. Traveler's checks accepted. Open daily 9am-1am.) In town, **El Cordobé's,** Calle 80 #150 at Calle 31 (tel. 5-26-21) on the *zócalo*, has attracted crowds since 1900. Join the fishing folk for breakfast and admire the paintings of Progreso. Sandwiches go for 3.50-9.20 pesos, and a wide variety of fish entrees cost 15-17 pesos. (Open daily 6am-midnight.)

■■■ MÉRIDA TO CHICHÉN ITZÁ

Some travelers hitch or take short bus rides from one Mayan village to another along the busy road between Mérida and Chichén Itzá. Those who hitch should bring water—their waits can be long, and shade is sparse. (*Let's Go* does not recommend hitchhiking.) Second-class **bus** drivers stop anywhere if requested to do so, but a new fare is charged for each trip. After leaving Mérida, the highway passes near the five private *henequén* (hemp) *haciendas* known as San Pedro, Teya, Ticopó, San Bernardino and Holactún. Next come the villages, each dominated by a main plaza and an oversized church. First are **Tahmek** and **Hoctún** (47km from Mérida). From Hoctún, you can turn left for a detour to **Izamal**, 24km north of the highway, although second-class buses do not make the detour. This tiny town contains the largest church plaza in Mexico, ringed with rows of yellow arches around the church and convent, and some of the earliest Spanish buildings, dating from 1533 and built from the boulders of the Mayan pyramid that they replaced. Since almost all the buildings in Izamal are yellow, the city is sometimes referred to as Ciudad Amarilla (Yellow City). Its Mayan name, derived from that of the god Itzamná, means "Dew of Heaven." The ancient *cenote* of **Ixcolasc** is only 1km away.

Upon returning to the Mérida-Chichén-Valladolid highway, you arrive at **Kantunil** (68km from Mérida). **Xocchel,** the "Place Where the Chels Read," is an attractive town along the highway, 17km from Mérida. Next is **Holcá,** then **Libre Unión** (94km from Mérida), with a sizable *cenote*. During squabbles between the territories of Yucatán and Quintana Roo, the town found itself smack on the border. Rather than split in two, the city voted to stick together and become part of the state of Yucatán. Libre Unión means "free union" in Spanish.

■■■ CHICHÉN ITZÁ

For two hours each day, Chichén Itzá suffers under the footfalls of hundreds of tourists running from pyramid to temple and back again. Never fear: with a modicum of planning, Mexico's most extensive, well-preserved, and beguiling remnants of *indígena* culture can be perused in relative peace and leisure.

Chichén Itzá well deserves its status as a tourist magnet. El Castillo is breathtaking from the bottom and harrowing from the top; the ballcourt features elaborate carvings and wholly intact rings left from original games; the sacrificial *cenote* (well) has yielded enough bones and artifacts to reconstruct the fates of hundreds of human victims; and the observatory attests to a level of astronomical understanding far beyond that of Old World contemporaries.

Although nearby Pisté lacks charm, it may be worth it to spend the night near the site in order to enter at 8am and view the ruins at a comfortable pace. Avoid visiting around noon, when the sun scorches and the tourist treads crescendo. Buy a guide booklet or tour-pool, carry a water bottle, and don a hat.

ORIENTATION

There isn't a travel agency on the Yucatán that doesn't hawk Chichén Itzá packages to newly arrived travelers, but these tours usually arrive at midday to crowds and heavy ultra-violets. Budget travelers should have no problem reaching Chichén Itzá early in the day by bus or car for about one-fifth the cost.

Chichén Itzá abuts **Route 180**, the highway that connects Mérida (121km west) to Cancún (213km east) via Valladolid (43km east). The town of **Pisté**, 2.5km west of the ruins, provides travelers with basic services. Ample public transportation to Chichén Itzá makes arriving easy, although few buses travel the 1.5km access road that leads to the gates of the ruins.

One first class **bus** leaves for Chichén Itzá daily from Mérida (11 pesos), and several depart from Cancún (16 pesos). Many second-class buses also connect Chichén Itzá to Mérida and Cancún, but most zip past the access road to the ruins and stop only in Pisté. If you can finagle a ride back to Pisté after seeing the ruins, you will have a better chance of catching the next bus to Mérida or Cancún. Buses stop at the bus station near the Stardust Inn (at the end of town closest to Chichén Itzá) and at the *zócalo*, heading for Mérida every hour (on the hour, in theory) from 6am and continuing long into the late-night (8 pesos, 2½ hrs.); for Valladolid and Cancún also every hour from 7:15am (4 pesos and 15 pesos, respectively; 4½ hrs. to Cancún). As with all second-class buses, a vigorous and supplicatory wave to the driver is a good idea. One first-class bus leaves for Mérida daily at 3pm (11 pesos, 1 hr.¼ min.) and 3 first-class buses depart for Cancún in the afternoon (3 hrs., 19.50 pesos).

Taxis shuttle people between Pisté and Chichén Itzá for 5 pesos. Many hitchhike; walking takes half an hour along the raised sidewalk designed to protect hikers from snakes and other local pests (although harmless giant iguanas have no problem clambering across it). Except during the winter, the jungle quickly turns muggy under the strong sun, so make the hike early in the morning.

PRACTICAL INFORMATION

Most services at Chichén Itzá are located in the large stone edifice at the site's western entrance. Across from the ticket counter is a small **information booth;** if you clear your throat seven times, a Spanish-speaking agent will appear, genie-like, to provide useful information about transportation and lodging; specific questions about the ruins are referred to official guides. The long-distance **telephone** is right around the corner from the ticket counter (tel. 6-27-24), but you can't make international collect calls. (Calls to Cancún, 2 pesos. Free baggage storage at the *caseta*. Open daily 8am-10pm. **Phone code:** 985.) There are also restrooms, a restaurant, an ice-cream parlor that changes money at good rates, a gift shop, a bookstore (which sells guidebooks), a theater showing documentaries about the ruins, and a small museum (see Sights below). Other services are provided in Pisté. Although there is no bank in Pisté, many restaurants, hotels, and shops will accept dollars and traveler's checks for payment, and will often change at only slightly under the going bank rate. The **post office** is in a small gray building near the *zócalo* across from Albarrotes "El Alba" (open Mon.-Fri. 8:30am-3pm). Another telephone *caseta* is **Teléfonos de México** (tel. 6-31-98) at Hotel Xay-beh, at the end of town nearest the ruins. (International collect calls 10 pesos. Open daily 8am-9pm.) **Clínica Promesa,** Calle 14 #50 (tel. 6-31-98, ext. 136), in the blue-green building off Rte. 180 beyond the Cunanchén Hotel 100m back from the road, is open 24 hrs. for medical problems. **Farmacia Isis,** Calle 15 #53, lies a short way past the *zócalo* towards the ruins. (Open Mon.-Sat. 7am-9pm, Sun. 8am-1pm and 5-8pm.) The **police** are right next door, open daily from 5am to 1pm and from 3 to 9pm.

ACCOMMODATIONS

A few luxury hotels snuggle right up to the ruins, but most economical options exist in and around Pisté. If you want to camp or hang a hammock, try the **Pirámide Inn** (tel. 6-26-71, ext. 115), at the end of town closest to the ruins. Tent space rents for 30 pesos for two people, 15 pesos for one person, hammock space 15 pesos; the fee gives you glorious access to the hotel pool. Without exception, Pisté's hotels are lackluster and most endure the booming of trucks barrelling down Rte. 180 day and night. Keep in mind that you can also take advantage of the plentiful budget options in Valladolid and make the 40km commute to the ruins. All listings below are in Pisté unless otherwise indicated.

Posada El Paso, Calle 15 #89, a yellow, L-shaped bldg. in the middle of Pisté. 2nd-floor rooms are big as all outdoors, with windows and beds to match. Fans, hot water, and squeaky bathrooms. Check-out 1pm. Singles or doubles 40 pesos. Triples 49 pesos.

Posada Olalde, to the left of Calle 15 (Rte. 180), 2 blocks down on an unmarked dirt road across the street from the Carrousel Restaurant in Pisté. Friendly family rents 4 huge and gaily colored rooms with arched doorways. Fans and hot water.

Snow-white bathrooms. Singles 40 pesos. Doubles 50 pesos. Triples 60 pesos. 10 pesos to hang your hammock in a room with a *baño.*

Posada Poxil, on Calle 15 (tel. 6-24-62, ext. 123 or 116), slightly past the *zócalo* towards Mérida. Hotel has a restaurant (open daily 7am-9pm, entrees around 15 pesos), a pool, and a disco (Fri.-Sun. nights from 9pm). Standard rooms with white walls, fans, and decent bathrooms with hot water. Windows open on inner courtyard and don't let in much light. Check-out 1pm. Singles 30-35 pesos. Doubles 40-50 pesos. Triples 60 pesos. Quads 70 pesos. Rooms closer to road noise are cheaper.

Posada Carrousel, on Calle 15, in central Pisté at the large *palapa* restaurant with the same name. Standard pink rooms with mismatched orange bedding. Fans, hot water, and *agua purificada.* Singles 35 pesos. Doubles 50 pesos.

FOOD

The Mayan Empire may well rise again on the profits from local restaurants. Once again, stick to Pisté, where the *mercado municipal* across from the *zócalo* allows you to avoid restaurants altogether. All Pisté restaurants listed are located on Calle 15, the main drag. Odd as it sounds, the larger hotel restaurants often provide swimming pools for their diners, even if you just buy a drink.

El Carrousel, in central Pisté. A large thatched *palapa* and tables covered with plastic tablecloths. Regional food at lower prices. *Tacos de pollo* 8 pesos. Meat entrees 13 pesos. Fruit salad 8 pesos. Open daily 7am-10pm.

Restaurant Sayil, Calle 15 #55, near the Stardust Inn. Food inside this plain white restaurant costs half as much as in similar institutions. *Pollo pibil* (chicken cooked in banana leaf) 8 pesos. Open daily 7am-10pm.

El Pollo Mexicano, also in central Pisté; look for the roasting chickens in front. Just what it sounds like: a half or quarter of a chicken, rice, grilled onion, salsa, and tortilla for 7 pesos. Open daily 8am-8pm.

SIGHTS

As the Mayan name Chichén Itzá (Mouth of the Well) implies, the earliest inhabitants chose to settle here because of two nearby freshwater *cenotes* (springs). Pottery shards tell the story of these sedentary people from 2000 BC to the beginning of the current era. The *Chilam Balam,* one of the few pre-Hispanic Mayan texts to survive the early missionaries' book-burnings, describes the construction of the oldest buildings which now constitute the current site. Between the years 500 and 800 AD, construction was purely Mayan. The Maya never developed the true curved arch; because of this, the rooms in these structures are long and narrow beneath lines of corbeled arches.

At its height in the seventh century AD, the Mayan city was abandoned by its rulers, the *itzáes,* who migrated to Chaacanputún, today's Champotón. The *itzáes* did not return for over 300 years, and Chichén was never again a purely Mayan community. Sometime before 1000 AD, the Toltec tribes of Tula, in what is now Hidalgo state, infiltrated the Yucatán and dominated the peaceful Mayan settlements, bringing with them the cult of the plumed serpent Quetzalcóatl, here named Kukulcán. When the Toltecs arrived at Chichén, its second "Maya-Toltec" phase of growth began. Chichén was fortified for the first time and, in the wake of regional imperialism, became the most important city on the peninsula.

The distinctive Toltec architectural influence can be seen in the round building and the pyramid. Their trademark plumed serpents and warrior images grace many pillars and columns, as do jaguars and eagles, the markings of their military order. The Toltec death cult glorified human sacrifice, making the *chac-mool* the predominant altar.

In 1461, Chichén Itzá was abandoned for a second time, this time because of war. But religious pilgrims continued to visit the site until well after the Spanish Conquest. Today, the relentless flow of the curious ensures that Chichén Itzá will never again stand in solitude.

The Ruins

Pause in the **visitors complex** at the entrance to Chichén Itzá for an overview of the site. On the terrace, a scale model artfully shrinks the ruins and lays them at your feet. A small **museum** recaps the history of Chichén Itzá and displays a sampling of sculptures and objects removed from the sacred *cenote*. Notice the board at the entrance for announcements of documentary videos about the ruins in Spanish and in English. (Theater and museum open daily 10am-5pm.)

If you are interested mostly in the architectural significance of the ruins, hiring an official guide at the entrance is unnecessary. If you carry a guidebook (or even just a map) and read the explanatory captions (in Spanish, English, or French) on plaques at each major structure, you can appreciate the ruins inexpensively and at your own pace. Free maps are available around the corner from the ticket counter, at the telephone *caseta* desk. However, to unravel some of the Mayan culture built into the ruins, to decipher some of the symbolism, and to follow the mysterious recurrences of the number seven throughout the structures and images, you will probably need one of the local guides. Save money by hiring one guide and tour-pooling; roaming guides offer their services in and outside the ruins. Before commissioning one, ask to see identification, which should testify to certification and foreign language ability. Private tours (up to 20 people) last two hours and cost 90 pesos. A tour-pool with a minimum of four and a maximum of eight people lasts 1½ hrs. and costs 15 pesos per person for tours in Spanish and English. Tours in French, German, and Italian are 30% more.

From the main parking lot and visitors center, the first group of ruins is up the gravel path and to the left. As the trees give way to the huge cropped lawn, the largest pyramid at Chichén Itzá, El Castillo, appears straight ahead.

El Castillo, Chichén's most famous and intriguing sight, rises in perfect symmetry from the vast green fields, culminating in a temple supported by pillars in the form of serpents. The pyramid's striking appearance, however, is not all that earned it international fame (and a presence on placemats throughout the land). El Castillo testifies to the calendrical obsessions and acumen of the Maya as well: the 91 steps on each of the four faces, plus the upper platform, total 365 (the number of days in the non-leap year); the 52 panels on the nine terraced levels equal the number of years in a Mayan calendar cycle; and each face of the nine terraces is divided by a staircase, yielding 18 sections representing the 18 Mayan months.

El Castillo's axes are so perfectly aligned with the four cardinal directions that during semi-annual equinox, the shadow of the rounded terraces falls on the embankment of the north staircase, and the silhouette of an undulating serpent, whose head is sculpted at the bottom of the staircase, becomes visible. In March, the serpent appears to be sliding down the stairs precisely in the direction of the Sacred Cenote, while in September the motion is reversed. The exact equinox dates and times vary slightly from year to year, but tend to cluster around March 21 and September 21. People from all over the world converge on Chichén to see this man-made phenomenon. Exactly at these times, with similar calendrical precision, all accommodations will be full (keep in mind, however, that the snake can still be seen for a few days before and after the actual equinox). A less well-known but equally stunning feature of El Castillo is the lunar serpent. The light-and-shadow apparition of the god, identical to that of the equinoxes, creeps up and down the pyramid at the dawn of the new moon following each of the equinoxes.

Within El Castillo is nested an early Toltec temple, the inner chamber of which can be entered through a door at the bottom of the north staircase, behind the serpent's ears. (Open daily 11am-3pm and 4-5pm.) A set of narrow, slippery steps ascends to a ceremonial chamber with a grimacing *chac-mool* sculpture (a sculpture on which sacrifices took place) and a rust-red, jaguar-faced sacrificial throne encrusted with jade stones and flint fangs.

As you bust through the gates of Chichén Itzá, just to the left of the entrance (behind you if you're walking toward El Castillo), the **ballcourt** competes for attention with a huge pyramid. The enormous playing field is bounded by two long, high, parallel walls and a temple beyond either end-zone. This is the largest ballcourt in Mesoamerica; amazingly, people speaking at the Temple of the Bearded Man at the north end of the court can be heard clearly 160m away at the southern wall; the ballcourt also has an amazing echo, which repeats exactly seven times. The Maya called the game Pok-Ta-Pok, and the object seems to have been to knock a solid ball made of rubber-like *chicle* through the stone rings still visible high up on the long walls. The game had a religious dimension as well: in the rare event of a goal, members of the winning teams were promptly and gloriously sacrificed to the gods. The famous reliefs at the base of the walls clearly depict freshly beheaded victors, from whose necks issues not blood, but the holy feathered serpent.

The sculptures in the **Temple of the Bearded Man** at the north end of the ballcourt and the paintings inside the **Temple of the Jaguars** on the eastern wall confirm the importance of sacrifice in Mayan fertility rites. On the ground level of the temple facing the plaza, another room with murals also merits a visit. (Inner chambers of both structures unfortunately have sporadic viewing hours. Ask a guard for info.)

A short distance from the ballcourt toward the grassy open area is the **Tzompantli,** Aztec for "Platform of the Skulls." When the Spaniards conquered the Aztecs, they were aghast not just at the ritual of human sacrifice, but also at the racks in Tenochtitlán designed to display the skulls of the sacrificed. This purely Toltec design at Chichén served a similar purpose. Now, eerie rows of skulls in bas-relief decorate the platform's walls.

Just to the side of the long, low Tzompantli is the **Platform of Jaguars and Eagles,** named after the military orders who took the names of these ferocious animals and whose social role was to obtain prisoners for human sacrifice. To either side of the feathered serpent heads on the balustrades of the staircases, reliefs of jaguars and eagles clutch human hearts in their claws. These beliefs and architecture are solely Toltec. Behind (east of) that platform is the so-called **Temple of Venus,** which has representations of the feathered serpent, but this time with a human head inside his mouth. There are also reliefs with symbols of the stars and information on their periods of motion.

The dirt path leading north (away from El Castillo) over the ancient Mayan roadway links the ceremonial plaza with Chichén Itzá's most important religious center, the **Sacred Cenote,** 300m away. The roughly circular well, perhaps 60m across, induced vertigo in the sacrificial victims perched on the reviewing platform before their last plunge into the murky depths. The rain-god Chac supposedly dwelt beneath the water's surface and needed frequent gifts to grant good rains. Young children and occasionally a jewel-bedecked virgin were thrown into the *cenote* at sunrise. If, by some miracle, they could keep afloat until noon, they were then fished out and forced to tell what they had witnessed during the ordeal.

Beyond El Castillo, at the far edge of the central plaza, the **Temple of the Warriors** and **Group of the Thousand Columns** present an impressive army of elaborately carved columns which at one time probably supported a roof of some perishable material. On the temple itself, in front of two great feathered serpents and several sculpted animal gods, reclines one of the best-preserved *chac-mools* at Chichén. The ornamentation of this building is largely Toltec; in Tula, capital of the Toltecs far to the west, stands a nearly identical structure.

The Temple of the Warriors marks the end of Chichén's restored monuments and the beginning of an overgrown area extending behind and to the right of the pyramid. Standing at the walls nearest the pyramid, you can see several rubble walls and smaller, ruined pyramids to the southeast. Dirt paths and roads lead from the columns to these ruins. Paths also run to Chichén Itzá's market complex which consists of several buildings with intact walls and columns.

A red dirt path on the south side of El Castillo leads to the less photogenic **South Group** of ruins, once misnamed Old Chichén. Just beyond the green building and a refreshment stand, the first pyramid on the right is the **Ossuary,** or **High Priest's Grave,** barely recognizable as a pyramid. A natural cave extends from within the pyramid 15m down into the earth. The human bones and votive offerings found in this cavern are postulated to be those of an ancient high priest.

Past the Ossuary, the road forks, presenting two different routes to the second set of ruins in the South Group. The most interesting structure in this group is the **Observatory,** the large circular building to the left of the Ossuary. This ancient planetarium consists of two nested rectangular platforms with large west-facing staircases and two circular towers. Because of the tower's interior spiral staircase (not open to the public), this structure is often called El Caracol (the Great Conch). Back in Mayan times, the slits in the dome of the Observatory could be aligned with the important celestial bodies and cardinal directions. El Caracol was built in several stages by Mayan and Toltec architects; diagrams in front of the ruin explain the plans. Also, notice the small red handprints on the wall of the building just as you come up the stairs; these were supposedly the hands of the sun god Itzamná.

Walking due south from El Caracol, toward the nunnery at the other end of the clearing, you first pass the tiny ruins of a sauna and then the **Temple of the Sculptured Wall Panels** behind it. On the exterior walls of this temple, you can still discern the sculptures for which it is named. Though difficult to decipher, the panels contain emblems of Toltec warriors—jaguars, eagles, and serpents—in three rows.

The largest structure in this part of Chichén is the **"nunnery,"** on the south side of the quadrangle. Although it was probably a royal palace to the Maya who built it, its many stone rooms reminded Spaniards of a European convent. After several superimpositions and some decay, the building is now almost 20m high on a base 65m long and nearly 35m wide. Above the entrance on the eastern side of the building, you can still see Mayan hieroglyphs. On that side you can also see a smaller annex built at an angle. Its many sculpted masks of Chac and its lattice motif are in the Chenes style, usually found only in northeastern Campeche, as at Edzná.

Diagonally across from the nunnery annex is the religious center, its upper walls intricately ornamented with many masks of the hook-nosed Chac. Both to the left and to the right above the door are representations of the four *bacabs*, animal deities who hold up the sky.

A poorly maintained path (which may be closed during rainy months) runs about 130m east from the nunnery group, past the chapel to the long **Akab-Dzib.** The oldest parts of this structure are believed to be Chichén's most ancient constructions. The two central rooms were built around the second or third century; the annexes on either side and to the east were added later. Inside the rooms it is still possible to make out the small rose-red hand prints of Itzamná on the ceiling near the doors.

The **Cenote Xtoloc** lies past the South Group ticket office inside the site and behind the observatory. To reach it, walk 6m past the ticket hut and turn right in the sand driveway—the small path may be obscured, but it's there. This *cenote*, once the source of all Chichén's drinking water, is little more than a deep, muddy pool. The small, ruined temple of Xtoloc, the lizard god, suns itself nearby. The walkway down can be extremely slippery in the rainy season. Swimming is prohibited here because of dangerous underwater currents.

The entire site of Chichén Itzá is open daily from 8am to 5pm. Authorities are diligent about protecting the site, and those who try to sneak in before or after these hours may find themselves paying a hefty fine to get out of the Pisté jail. Admission is 18.60 pesos (free Sun. and holidays, always for kids under 13). There is a free baggage check, but parking (open 8am-10pm) costs 3.40 pesos for cars.

As if the natural spectacle weren't enough, after hours the latter-day priests of illumination prepare the **Sound and Light Spectacular.** The monuments, awash in red, blue, green, and yellow light, fail to look more ancient, but the show makes for an impressive evening. A booming voice details the history of the site (Spanish version daily at 7pm, 4.50 pesos; English version daily at 9pm, 6.20 pesos). To avoid the nighttime walk from Pisté over ruts'n'reptiles, you may want to take a taxi to and from the show (5 pesos each way).

Chichén Viejo

Chichén Viejo, set about 2km apart from the rest of Chichén, is no place for timid or ill-informed travelers; the paths that lead to the site are difficult to follow in the rainy season (May-Oct.). Ask some of the merchants at Chichén if they know someone who would be willing to serve as guide for a fee determined in advance. The unlicensed and mostly young but cheap guides can tell Spanish-speakers nearly as much about these less accessible ruins as their better-paid counterparts can about the main section of Chichén Itzá. Bring food and water. Official guides charge 110 pesos for the tour.

A dirt path lies to the right of the nunnery as you face the great staircase. A 15-min. walk down the path will take you past the intersection of other dirt paths to a couple of huts around a well. Walk through the smaller hut and continue to follow the tracks of the old narrow-gauge *tranvía* (donkey-drawn trolley). Soon the rocky trail enters a clearing with a cluster of ruins called the **Date Group,** dominated by the **House of the Phalli.** The **Date Lintel,** a block upheld by two layered columns, carries the only dated inscription in all of Chichén Itzá. In both classical and hieroglyphic notation the dates "10.2.9.1.9, 9 Muluc 7 Zac" and "10.2.10.0.0, 2 Ahau 13 Chén," both correspond to the year 879 AD. The rest of the temple has been destroyed.

The path continues into the jungle behind and to the right of the House of the Phalli. Another 15- to 20-min. walk leads to the **Principal Group of the Southwest** and to the **Lintel Group.** On the right, the Southwest Group contains a ruined pyramid, **Castillo de Chichén Antigua,** and the **Jaguar Temple,** where only a few Atlantean columns remain to salute the ancient military order of the Jaguars. On the left, the **Temple of the Lintel** is barely recognizable, since the sculptured lintel has long since collapsed.

Turning to the right through the jungle from the Southwest Group, you may stumble upon the **Bird Cornice Group, Temple of the Turtle,** and **Temple of the Sculpted Jambs.** The cornice has a strip of carved birds, the Temple of the Turtle once yielded a turtle-shaped stone, and the jambs of the last temple are molded into human figures.

A cultural center has been slated to open next to the Stardust Inn Hotel in Pisté in November 1993. The center will focus primarily on archaeology, present and past ethnology, and the historical and social identity of the Maya at Chichén Itzá, with a broader focus on Mesoamerica in general. The center will be for use by both tourists and *indígenas* and will have a library, a salon for showing videos, lectures, and displays by local artisans and artists.

■ Near Chichén Itzá

A worthwhile site or two can be squeezed out of the region around Chichén Itzá. To reach the ones on the main highway (Rte. 180), take a second-class bus, and when you get on, tell the driver where you want to be let off.

GRUTAS DE BALANCANCHE

Although the soft limestone of the Yucatán has in many places been carved into subterranean labyrinths by underground streams, the Grutas de Balancanche have always been held in particular regard by the local population. In 1959, a severe storm dislodged the boulder that hid an undiscovered inner cave. An archaeologist who had been working at Chichén Itzá cleared the rubble and began to poke around.

VALLADOLID

Further exploration opened a 300m path which runs past stalactites carved to resemble leaves on the ceiling and a huge tree-like stalactite surrounded by dozens of votive vessels with ghoulish masks. Archaeologists have come to believe that the cave was a center for Mayan-Toltec worship of the gods Chac, Tlaloc (the Toltec rain god), and Kukulcán (Quetzalcóatl) during the 10th and 11th centuries. For unknown reasons, subterranean worship in Balancanche stopped at the end of this period, and the offerings of ceramic vessels and stone sculptures rested undisturbed for eight centuries. Artifacts aside, the impressive stalactites and a strikingly clear underground river make the cave worth a visit.

One more light-and-sound show dramatizes the cave's history and recounts Mayan legends, keeping up with the tour group via a series of hidden speakers. A guide, available for questions, paces the group through the chambers along the 1km path. Self-guided tours are not permitted.

The grottos lie about 6km from Chichén toward Cancún and about 2km from the Dolores Alba Hotel. You may want to take a **taxi** (round-trip plus the wait is 50 pesos). Tours cost 16 pesos (free Sun. and holidays). The small museum and garden complex are open daily from 9am to 4pm. Tours in Spanish begin at 9am, 10am, noon, 2pm, and 4pm; tours in English at 11am, 1pm, and 3pm. No tour leaves with more than 30 or fewer than six people.

YAXUNÁ

Located 30km southeast of Chichén Itzá, Yaxuná is a much less-known site which is well worth visiting but rather difficult to reach. The site has been worked on for the last five years in the hopes that it will one day become another tourist site like Chichén, but, at present, road conditions are poor and few tourists visit. The temple at Yaxuná was built by the Maya of Cobá, who were planning to make war on the people of Chichén. They built their temple in alignment with El Castillo, so as to be able to observe their enemies.

Supposedly, from the top of the temple at Yaxuná, one can see the highest points at the sites of Chichén Itzá and Cobá. In the dry season it is possible, but never easy, to take a road directly from Pisté to Yaxuná. A better combination of roadway involves a trip to Libre Unión, then left to Yaxcabah, a small town 17km down the road. The road from Yaxcabah to Yaxuná is 8km.

There is no public transportation to Yaxuná. For those who lack wheels, however, it is possible to hire a truck in Pisté. The charge is about 40 pesos round-trip with wait and a possible stop at the *cenotes* and caves located between the two sites.

■■■ VALLADOLID

In the middle of the Mérida-Cancún route and only a half hour from Chichén Itzá, Valladolid (pop. 90,000) ought to be jammed with tourists hopping down the *gringo* trail, but in fact most bypass the city, its six churches, and twin Edenic *cenotes*, cavernous natural swimming pools.

A history of struggle, rebellion and suffering has generated a deep sense of community in Valladolid. In 1543, Francisco de Montejo, the nephew of the Spanish conquistador of the same name, was sent to the Mayan town of Zací to convert the population and set up a Spanish enclave. After constructing his home with Mayan stone and labor, he was driven away by their animosity and the sweltering jungle heat. A third Francisco de Montejo (son of the conquistador) came to take his place, succeeded where his cousin had failed and built an array of churches in celebration of his conquest.

Some 250 years later, in 1809, a cabal of Mayan leaders, clergy, and disaffected military personnel devised a revolutionary plot; their scheme was uncovered and the leaders imprisoned, but the rebellious spirit persisted. When Mexico finally resolved itself to independence, a good number of *vallisoletanos* led the fight.

VALLADOLID

Interracial conflict between the elite *ladinos* and oppressed *indígenas* erupted once again in the Caste War (1847-48), during which machete-wielding Mayan rebels besieged Valladolid for two months. The Maya eventually took the city, sending 10,000 *ladinos* fleeing to Mérida. In subsequent years, the caste schism has healed only slowly.

Today, Valladolid is a vigorous metropolitan center. *Indígena* women deal hammocks and colorful *huipiles* in the *zócalo*, eight-year-olds aggressively push chewing gum to passersby and loud trucks crush pedestrians' toes at every corner. Visitors to the city enjoy the commotion of the craft fair and the nearly-free provisions at the food market, then seek out the bat-enhanced tranquility of Valladolid's grand colonial churches and beautiful *cenotes*.

ORIENTATION

Route 180 bifurcates Valladolid on its way from Mérida to Cancún. 150km from each city, Valladolid falls into a grid with streets aligned to the four cardinal directions. Even-numbered streets run north-south, with the city center bordered by 26 on the east and 60 on the west. Odd-numbered streets run east-west and start with 27 in the north, ending with 53 in the south. The *zócalo*, enclosed by Calles 39, 40, 41, and 42, sits literally at the center of Valladolid. Everything of interest is within easy walking distance of it; the Franciscan church lies to the south. To get to the *zócalo* from the bus station either take a taxi (5 pesos) or walk one block to the right to Calle 39, take a left on it and walk straight for six blocks.

PRACTICAL INFORMATION

Tourist Information: Valladolid has no official tourist information center. Try the **Hotel María de la Luz,** on the western side of the *zócalo*. Free map of the city available at arts and crafts shop in El Bazaar.

Currency Exchange: Best rates are offered at **Bancomer** (tel. 6-21-50) on the Calle 40 side of the *zócalo*. 24-hr. ATM. Open for exchange Mon.-Fri. 9:30am-12:45pm.

Post Office: (tel. 6-36-75), on Calle 40 at the *zócalo* . Open Mon.-Fri. 8am-7pm, Sat. 9am-1pm. **Postal code:** 97780.

Telephones: Calle 42 #193-B (tel. 6-20-03), between Calles 37 and 39, ½ block north of the *zócalo*. International collect calls 5 pesos. (Open Mon.-Sat. 8am-9pm, Sun. 8am-3pm.) Also on Calle 42 between Calles 41 and 43. (Open Mon.-Sat. until 10pm, 5 pesos for international collect calls.) International collect calls at the *caseta* at the bus station are also 5 pesos. (Open daily 7am-10pm.) Make a small offering to one of the several non-operational public phones on the *zócalo* by the *palacio* and maybe you'll get a dial tone. **Telephone Code:** 985.

Telegrams: (Tel. 6-21-70), on Calle 40 at the *zócalo*. Open Mon.-Fri. 9am-8pm, Sat. 9am-noon. Fax service Mon.-Fri. 9am-5pm.

Laundromat: Lavanderia Teresita, Calle 42 at Calle 33 (tel. 6-33-93). Self-service 3.50 pesos each for wash and dry, full service 12 pesos. Open daily 7am-7pm.

Bus Station: On Calle 37 at Calle 54 (tel. 6-34-49), luggage check 1 peso per piece per day (open 8am-7pm). Many buses arrive *de paso*; they'll take you only if they have room. Many departures to: Mérida, Cancún/Puerto Juárez, Playa del Carmen, Tizimín. 2nd-class service to Tulum, Cobá, and Chiquilá. 2 additional bus lines operate out of the same terminal. **Autobuses del Norte en Yucatán** goes to Mérida with other destinations on the way and to Tizimín. **Autobuses del Centro del Estado de Yucatán** has 2nd-class service to Mérida (3½hrs., 12 pesos) and **Expresso de Oriente** has 1st-class service (2 hrs., 15 pesos).

Taxis: Available in front of the bus station and on the *zócalo*. 5 pesos through town, 10-15 pesos to *cenote* X-kekén.

Bike Rental: Calle 44 #190, between Calles 39 and 41. The outer *cenote* is reached most easily by bike and so is the San Bernardino de Siena church. 3 pesos per hr. Open daily 7:30am-2pm.

Market: Food market bordered by Calles 35, 37, 30, and 32, 5 blocks northeast of the *zócalo*. Open daily 5am-2pm. Artisans' market occupies the sidewalks near the intersection of Calles 39 and 44. Open Mon.-Sat. 7am-7pm, Sun. 7am-2pm.

Supermarket: Super Economía Vidal, on Calle 46 between Calle 39 and Calle 37 (open Mon.-Sat. 7:30am-9:30pm, Sun. 7:30am-1:30pm), and on Calle 42 on the *zócalo* (open 24 hrs).

Pharmacy: Arco Iris (tel. 6-21-88), on Calle 42 between Calles 43 and 45. Open 24 hrs. More centrally located is **El Descuento** at Calle 42 and Calle 39, just off the *zócalo*. Open 24 hrs.

Medical Services: Clínica Santa Ana, Calle 40 #221 (tel. 6-28-11), between Calles 45 and 47, is open 24 hrs. for emergencies.

Police: Calle 41 at Calle 40 (tel. 6-25-65), around the corner from the *zócalo* in the Palacio Municipal. No English spoken. Open 24 hrs. for emergencies.

ACCOMMODATIONS

Clustered around the zócalo, Valladolid's budget digs are solid and for the most part uninspiring.

Hotel Lily (tel. 6-21-63), on Calle 44 between Calles 37 and 39. Cheapest acceptable accommodations in town. Basic, bare, and occasionally stuffy, but clean rooms at a convenient location. Most rooms have fully equipped private bathrooms, windows, and sometimes even balconies. No hot water. Singles fill up quickly. Check-out 1pm. A few rooms have communal baths. Singles with private bath 25 pesos. 1-bed doubles 30 pesos. 2-bed doubles 40 pesos. 3-bed triples 50 pesos. 10 pesos per additional person per room. No traveler's checks accepted.

Hotel Zací, Calle 44 #191 (tel. 6-21-67), between Calles 37 and 39. Gorgeous manorial courtyard with a pool ushers you into elaborately furnished rooms with low-hanging lamps, huge desks, fan or A/C, TV, and perfect bathrooms. Check-out 1pm. Singles 40 pesos. Doubles 60 pesos. Triples 75 pesos. A/C 15 pesos extra. Traveler's checks not accepted. For reservations, wire 50% payment in advance.

Hotel María Guadalupe, Calle 44 #198 (tel. 6-20-68), between Calles 39 and 41. Undecorated but spotless rooms with miniscule windows. Check-out 1pm. Room for 1-2 people 40 pesos. Triples 50 pesos. 10 pesos per additional person. Traveler's checks not accepted. Reservations can be made by calling and wiring a 50% payment in advance.

Hotel Mendoza, Calle 39 #204 (tel. 6-20-22), between Calles 44 and 46. Tightly-packed beds in dim yellow or tan rooms. Clean bathrooms. Check-out 1pm. Parking available. A few rooms jammed with 3 beds, TV, refrigerator, 2 fans, and A/C (80-100 pesos). Singles 35 pesos. Doubles 40 pesos. Triples 50 pesos. Rooms with communal baths go for 5 pesos less. Traveler's checks not accepted. For reservations send 1 night's payment in advance.

Hotel Maya, Calle 41 #231 (tel. 6-20-69), between Calles 48 and 50. Inconveniently distant from the *zócalo*, but close to the bus station. Plain rooms with very familiar blue linoleum that look like they've been around the track once or twice; they offer fans, hot water, and reasonable bathrooms. Check-out 1pm. Singles and doubles 30 pesos. Triples 35 pesos. During the high season prices rise to 35.60 pesos for singles or doubles and 45.60 pesos for triples. A/C 10 extra. Traveler's checks accepted. For reservations send 50% payment in advance.

FOOD

While in Valldolid, take advantage of a range of regional specialties served in restaurants throughtout the city. Small cuts of pork in tomato sauce go by the name *lomitos de Valladolid*. Hearty and delectable, *escabeche oriental de pavo* is a turkey soup prepared with a compelling combination of onions, whole garlics, and spices. *Panuchos* are (nearly) bite-sized tortillas piled with various combinations of chicken, pork, beans, lettuce, tomato, and the infamous *habanero* chili pepper. Satisfying tamales sold on street corners near the *zócalo* are sometimes accompanied by *pozoles*, served in the half-shell of a coconut-like fruit.

VALLADOLID

El Bazaar, Calle 39 at Calle 40, on the *zócalo*. Not a restaurant, but a pink open-air courtyard supporting cafés and juice bars under shady arcades. Great for a cheap meal and people-watching. At least one café open daily 6am-midnight. **Milo,** closest to the *zócalo*, has the most delicious home-made fruit juices: orange, watermelon, lime, lemon, coco, pineapple, guanabana, mamey, and banana (1 peso). Open daily 8am-2pm and 6-8pm. **La Rancherita** opens earliest to serve all sorts of tacos (1 peso) and *yucateco* entrees (8-10 pesos). **Sergio's** prepares good-sized pizzas: small cheese 6 pesos. Open daily 5-11:30pm.

Casa de los Arcos (tel. 6-24-67), one block east of *zócalo* on Calle 39 between Calles 38 and 40 . Iron arches define this stylish yet reasonably priced restaurant. Scrumptious local specialties (with especially good tortillas) from 12 pesos. Open daily 7am-10pm. MC, Visa accepted.

Restaurant San Bernardino de Siena, Calle 49 #227 (tel. 6-27-20), 3 blocks south and another 3 blocks southwest of the *zócalo* near the church of the same name. Wall murals and a large *palapa* make for a pleasant, relaxing atmosphere. Among excellent regional dishes, try the *poc chuc*, a thin slice of grilled pork (12 pesos). Open daily 7am-10pm.

Cenote (tel. 6-21-07), on Calle 36, between Calles 37 and 39 overlooking Cenote Zací. After dreaming of a quick dip (see Sights below), sit back, relax and ingest in this lovely thatched-roof restaurant. Elegant decor and background music. Excellent liquor selection, including locally produced Xtabentun from rum, anise, and honey (4 pesos per cup, 18 pesos per bottle). Grilled meat entrees 12 pesos. Open daily 8am-7pm.

SIGHTS

Resented by *indígenas* for the imposition of Christianity and despised by laymen for their control of large tracts of land, Franciscan monks in Valladolid built their churches as stout as fortresses for security's sake. Not even these safeguards, however, could hold back the Caste War and the Mexican Revolution, when raiders looted the valuable ornamentation encrusted on the churches.

The most famous of Valladolid's churches is **San Bernardino de Siena,** affiliated with the **Ex-Convento de Sisal,** Calle 41, three blocks southwest from the intersection of Calles 46 and 41 (Cinco Calles). Built in 1552, they are the oldest clerical buildings in the Yucatán and possibly in all of Mexico. The monks abandoned the convent in the 18th century, when the Franciscans and other religious orders in Mexico were obligated to turn their property over to the secular authorities. Interior decoration today is minimal because of theft and vandalism during the Caste War. On the altar at the rear of the church is a large image of the Virgin of Guadalupe, brought from Guatemala. Original frescoes are visible behind two side altars. Although remodeled, the confessionals built into the thick walls have been used for centuries. Outside, an impressive colonial irrigation system and 17th-century horse-drawn well draw water from an underground *cenote*, over which part of the complex was constructed. True to form, the Spaniards bungled the Mayan name for the *cenote*, Sis-Ha (cold water), before bestowing it on the settlement. (Open Tues.-Sun. 8am-noon and 5-8pm. Free.)

The **Catedral de San Gervasio,** on Calle 41 on the *zócalo*, would have been as old as San Bernardino de Siena had the people of Valladolid not violated the sacred right to sanctuary there 250 years ago. According to legend, two alleged criminals who took sanctuary in the church were discovered and brutally murdered by an angry mob. When the bishop learned of the event, he closed up the church and had it destroyed. To atone for the sacrilegious act, he had workers rebuild the church to face south on Calle 41, instead of west on Calle 42, its original orientation. (Open daily 5am-noon and 3-9pm. Free.)

Cenote Zací (pronounced sa-KEY), on Calle 36, three blocks east from the *zócalo* between Calles 37 and 39, draws tourists today just as it fascinated the Maya centuries ago. Walk down the worn stone stairs and the cavernous hollow will half-surround you. Above, bats beat their wings against ghastly stalactites; below, rafts of *chinha* (lake lettuce) float on murky jade-colored water. You can watch Valladolid swans dive from different terrace levels into the awesome pool, although you wouldn't want to join them in the less-than-crystal-clear water. There is also a small museum to the right of the path. (*Cenote*/museum open daily 8am-7pm. Admission 4 pesos, 2 pesos for children. The *cenote* can be viewed from the restaurant for free.)

More spectacular, though farther away, the **Cenote X-kekén** (chay-keh-KEN) plunges into the ground near the town of **Dzitnup**. It can be reached by a half-hour bike ride, a 15-peso taxi trip, or an importunate plea to a Mérida-bound bus driver to drop you at the well-designated access road (a 20-min. walk from the *cenote*). To get to it on foot or by bike, take Calle 41 west out of town, past the Hotel Maya and the Coca-Cola plant. At the highway turn left and then left again at the sign for the *cenote*. Swimming is permitted, and it is a profound experience when alone. Change clothes in the tiny restroom or behind a boulder, and descend the narrow, slick staircase into the cave. If school is out, roving packs of eight-year-old boys will offer to guide you to the natural pool. The luminous turquoise water reflects pendant stalactites and a single brilliant sunbeam emanating from a small hole in the ceiling 40m above the surface of the pool. The best time to swim is between 7-10am, before the whole gang arrives, but the spectacle of ricocheting light climaxes at noon. (Open daily 7am-5pm. Admission 4 pesos adults, 2 pesos children.)

Xtabentun, one of the most popular liquors on the peninsula, was born in Valladolid. Observe the production of this anise- and honey-flavored drink at the **factory** on Calle 42, at the intersection with Calle 47. The Sosa family, who have been making the product for 50 years, sell their entire line here at great discounts (Xtabentun 10 pesos per bottle). You'll get free samples and a tour if you ask politely and they're not too busy watching the Celtics on TV. (Factory open Mon.-Sat. 8am-1pm and 3-6pm.)

ENTERTAINMENT

Valladolid doesn't bend over backwards to entertain visitors. **Cine San Juan** (tel. 624-01), on Calle 51 between Calles 38 and 40 projects double features Mon.-Sat. at 7:15 and 9:30pm. Three shows on Sunday at 5:30, 7:30 and 9:30pm. (Most movies are North American, tickets 4 pesos).

On Friday and Saturday, for 10 pesos you can rock from 10pm-3am at **Color's Disco,** on Calle 39 at Call 38. Across the street, **Casa de Los Arcos** hosts a videobar. If you prefer live entertainment, keep your eyes peeled for occasional functions sponsored by the **Club de Leones** (Lions Club), whose dances, cookouts, and bake sales are announced in the *zócalo*. If you happen to be male, you can converse and tipple freely at the *cantinas*, especially **Barracuda** on Calle 42 near Calle 45. The cheapest and perhaps most rewarding hangouts are the **El Bazaar** café complex (see Food) and the **zócalo** itself, where *vallisoletanos* and visitors alike linger until the witching hour. Women traveling alone should be careful when wandering around the *zócalo* on Saturdays in the late afternoon and evening, however; the overflow from the *cantinas* can become rather unpleasant.

■ Near Valladolid

TIZIMÍN

Although the urban center of a large agricultural area, Tizimín is less cosmopolitan than Valladolid. Trucks burdened with bleating sheep roll past the *zócalo*; in the evening, cowboys lustily down *cervezas* in the *cantinas*. There are no tourists and no souvenir shops. During the heat of the day, the entire local population retreats behind closed doors to observe the afternoon *siesta*. But for all its somnambulant cow-town atmosphere, Tizimín offers enough sights, entertainment, and services to accommodate a lot more tourism than it gets. Tizimín's *zócalo* featurs another colonial church/ex-convent pair; this one still fully operational. The church, **La Venerada Iglesia de los Tres Santos Reyes,** is named after the patron saints of the town. The festival held each year in their honor (Dec. 27-Jan. 12) draws pilgrims from all over the region who come to pay homage to the images of the three kings. The festival is celebrated with processions, dancing, bullfights, and lots of *típico* food. January 6 is the most important day of the festival, when the pilgrims file through the church to touch the patrons with palm branches.

Tizimín also harbors the **Parque Zoológico de la Reina,** established in 1974 to commemorate a visit from Queen Elizabeth II. The zoo houses lions, gray foxes, antelope, and monkeys, among other exotic creatures. Many of the zoo's denizens—including iguanas, pink flamingos, buzzcocks, and peacocks—are native to the Yucatán. To get to the park, go to Calle 51, the street which passes by the *zócalo* in front of Palacio Municipal, and walk straight on it for about 1km. (Open daily 9am-noon and 3-6pm. Admission free.)

The nearby **archaeological site** of **Kulubá,** although largely unrestored, virtually untouristed, and somewhat hard to reach, is well worth a visit, as much for the beauty of the surrounding countryside as for the well-preserved details of the ruins themselves. The ruins date from the Late Classical period (800-1000 AD) and are the easternmost point where influence of the Puuc architectural style has been found. The style here also shows some resemblance to the buildings at Chichén Itzá. Although much of the site remains unexcavated and unrestored, the ruins were partially restored in the late 1970s, when the construction of supports for the two main buildings was begun. Although neither building has survived the years intact (parts of both have long since fallen and the stones have become scattered), the details that remain are still impressive. **El Edificio de Los Ues,** a structure about 40m long, 8m high, and 7m wide, is carved with "U"'s all along its facade. The original red stucco with which the whole building was once painted can still be seen on the carved portions of the stone. The second partially restored building, the more impressive of the two, features two surprisingly well-preserved pairs of masks of the rain god Chac, as well as other carved ornamentation. The building is 50m long, 10m high, and 8m wide, and at one time probably had three pairs of masks of the rain god, all with long curved noses.

The ruins are located on a private ranch 33km northeast of Tizimín. Although the site is not officially open to the public, it can be visited with permission from the owner of the ranch (contact Julio César Espinosa, official promoter of the site). He can be found at his photography studio, Studio Julio César (tel. 3-26-26), in the little square behind the ex-convent in Tizimín. (Open Mon.-Sat. 8am-1pm and 4-8pm, Sun. 9am-1pm.) There is no public transportation to Kulubá; **taxis** from Tizimín charge 100 pesos for round-trip to the ruins with wait. Traveling to the site during the rainy season is possible but can be difficult.

Five km from Tizimín in the tiny town of **Kikil,** the enormous jungle-encroached remains of a colonial church and ex-convent and the fresh waters of a stunning *cenote* are just waiting to be explored. The church, known to locals simply as **Iglesia Kikil,** is just to the right of the highway as you enter Kikil from Tizimín. The church was burned during the Caste War and has been utterly abandoned to the vegetation, but with enormous trees growing atop it, the bulky ruin creates a sublime spectacle. Just inside the gate of the little courtyard to your left as you face the church stands an elaborately carved stone baptismal font which rings like a bell when you strike it with your hand. A beautiful fresh-water *cenote* hides just across the road from the church. (Taxi to Kikil 12-15 pesos.)

Most hotels, restaurants, and other services in Tizimín are near the *zócalo*, which residents call *el parque*. To get there on foot from the bus stations (10 min.), walk two long blocks down the hill on Calle 47, passing the market. Turn left on Calle 50 and walk west one block toward the large stone church.

Practical Information The **Banco del Atlántico,** on the *zócalo* (tel. 3-28-85), is open for exchange Mon.-Fri. 8am-1:30pm. A better rate is offered at **Bancomer** on Calle 51 #394 (tel. 3-23-81), on the little square behind the *ex-convento*. (Open Mon.-Fri. 9am-1:30pm.) The **post office,** Calle 43 #417-A, is open Mon.-Fri. 9am-1pm and 3-6pm, Sat. 9am to 1pm. The **postal code** is 97700. There are two long distance **telephone** *casetas* near the *zócalo*, but neither makes international collect calls. Occasionally operational phones on the *zócalo* may be availed. The **telephone code** is 985. The **police station** (tel. 3-21-13) faces the *zócalo* (open 24 hrs.). There are many pharmacies throughout town, of which the largest, **Farmacia Centro de Drogas** (tel. 3-37-26), is on Calle 51 behind the *ex-convento*, next to Bancomer. (Open Mon.-Sat. 8am-1pm and 5-9pm.) There is a 24-hr. pharmacy at the **Centro Médico de Oriente San Carlos,** Calle 46 #461 (tel. 3-21-57), that has ambulance service and deals with emergencies 24 hrs.

Two bus lines in adjacent terminals serve Tizimín. **ADO** (tel. 3-24-24), at Calle 46 and Calle 47, sends one first-class bus daily to Cancún at 6am. Frequent second-class buses go to Cancún, Valladolid (4.50 pesos), Playa del Carmen (11:30am, 22.50 pesos), and Carrillo Puerto (4:30am, 14.50 pesos). **Autotransportes del Noreste** (tel. 3-20-37), on Calle 47 near Calle 46 , has first-class service to Mérida (regular 14.50 pesos; *ejecutivo* 20 pesos), Río Lagartos (5.50 pesos), San Felipe (6 pesos) and Panabá (3.50 pesos). Second-class buses run to Mérida (10 pesos), Chetumal (25 pesos), Río Lagartos (5.50 pesos), San Felipe (5-5.50 pesos depending on the route), Kantunil Kin (6 pesos), and Chiquilá (10.50 pesos).

Accommodations and Food Three hotels provide accommodation in Tizimín. **Hotel San Carlos,** Calle 54 #407 (tel. 3-20-94), from "Tres Reyes" restaurant on *zócalo* walk one block straight and ½ block right, is the newest and most economical of the three. Plain, spacious rooms with two beds and a fan open on an inner courtyard with a small pool. (Check-out 1pm. Singles 40 pesos, with A/C 60 pesos. Doubles 50 pesos, with A/C 60 pesos. Add 10 pesos for TV. No reservations.) Conveniently located on the *zócalo*, the **Hotel San Jorge** (tel. 3-20-37) provides clean rooms with desks, closets, and fans, some of which have a view of the *zócalo*. (Check-out 1pm. Singles 50 pesos, with A/C 75 pesos. Doubles 60 pesos, with A/C 80 pesos. Reservations can be made by phone.) **Posada María Antonia,** on the *zócalo* (tel. 3-23-84), next to the church, has four clean rooms, each equipped with two beds, a private bathroom, hot water, a fan, and a TV. Some rooms have balconies overlooking the *zócalo*. (Check-out 1pm. Singles 50 pesos. Doubles 60 pesos. A/C 15 pesos extra. 10 pesos per extra person. Reservations can be made by phone.)

The most popular eatery in Tizimín is the air-conditioned **Restaurant Tres Reyes,** on the *zócalo* (tel. 3-21-06). The password is *orange*. (*Pollo frito con papas* 15 pesos. *Camarones al mojo de ajo* 22 pesos. MC and Visa accepted. Open daily 7am-11pm.) **Restaurant Portales** (tel. 3-35-05) provides cheap eats on a pleasant patio on the *zócalo*. (Huge breakfasts 7 pesos. Ham and cheese sandwich 4 pesos. 3 tacos 6 pesos. Open Mon.-Sat. 7am-noon and 5:30-11:30pm, Sun. 5:30-11:30pm.) **Restaurant Las Palmas,** Calle 51 #331-A (tel. 3-24-51), between Calles 38 and 40, is a big, comfortable *palapa* that has regional specialties and occasional live music and dancing. Those who wish to avoid restaurants altogether purchase fruits, vegetables, and bread at the market on Calle 47 and eat in the beautiful *zócalo*.

■ ■ ■ RÍO LAGARTOS

Backed by dense jungle, *Phoenicopteri ruber* cover the acres of beaches and lagoon which surround Río Lagartos. The 5000-odd residents of this small village augment their fishing incomes with the profits from the straggling tourists who trek here to witness the astounding massing of this spectacularly scarlet species of flamingo. Locals claim that the area serves as the breeding ground for the entire flamingo population of the Yucatán Peninsula. Although the birds never disappear, down-time comes in April, May, and June, while the flamingos jealously guard their incubating and newly-hatched eggs. Despite the natural allure, tourism here is unobtrusive, and tranquility reigns over the beautiful lagoon.

Río Lagartos lies 52km north of Tizimín and 103km north of Valladolid, at the end of Route 295. To reach the *zócalo* from the bus station, take a right from the station to the center of the horseshoe of water that defines the town. Behind a stunted obelisk rises the Palacio Municipal, the cream-colored building bordering one side of the *zócalo*. The **municipal president's office** inside (tel. 3-26-68, ext. 29), is open for questions and problems Monday through Friday from 9am to 1pm and 4 to 8pm. The long distance **telephone** *caseta* is in Tienda La Rivera, one block from the *zócalo* in the direction of the lagoon (tel. 3-26-68 or 3-26-69). An international collect call won't cost you anything if the person accepts. The unlucky caller is out a frustrating 10 pesos for an unsuccessful call. (Open daily 8am-noon and 3:30-8pm. **Telephone code:** 986. **Postal code:** 97720.)

The **Hotel Nefertiti,** Calle 14 #123-B (tel. 3-26-68, ext. 14-15), four blocks to the right if you face the Palacio Municipal on the *zócalo*, maintains a monopoly on Río Lagartos's humble tourist trade. The resulting baronial prices for institutional rooms include baths and fans. Rooms are very large and have both beds and hammock hooks. (Singles 40 pesos. Doubles 50 pesos. Triples 60 pesos. 15 pesos each additional room. Discounts for more than 1 night.) Guests receive free admission to adjacent disco **Los Flamingos.** (Cover for non-hotel guests 5 pesos. Open Sat. 10pm-3am.) The colorfully decorated restaurant offers a nice view of the boats sailing through the lagoon.

More economical accommodations can be found in a two-story house of the Sanchez-Maza family on the corner of Calle 10 and Calle 14. Decorated with wagon wheels on the outside and cowboy trappings on the inside, the house has two small, clean rooms with fans, and one communal bath with no hot water. Each room has two beds and space for two hammocks, and both open onto a breezy porch. (Check-out 2pm. Room for 1 person, 30 pesos. For 2-4 people, 40 pesos.) For campers and travelers with hammocks, there are two open-air *palapa* huts donated by the government for free lodging, and advise the municipal president that you will be camping out.

Although viewless, the best eatery in Río Lagartos is the big shack of a place called **Restaurant Los Negritos,** on Calle 10 (tel. ext. 14), two blocks from the bus station away from the *zócalo*. *Langosta al estilo negritos* is 30 pesos, but fish and meats are priced to move at around 15 pesos. (Open daily 8am-6pm. Disco Sat. 10pm-2am; cover 5 pesos for women, 10 pesos for men. *Cerveza* 3.50 pesos.) **Restaurant La Cueva de Macumba,** two blocks to the right of Hotel Nefertit, features kitsch seashell displays, *palapita* tables and meats from 10-12 pesos, and *filete de pescado* from 12 to 14 pesos. (Open in July 9am-4pm, year-round 7pm-midnight.)

Flamingo-watching is not cheap. The only sensible way to catch a glimpse of the birds is by boat. Get in touch with the loveable, genie-like, self-appointed promoter of Rio Lagártos, Adrian Marfil Valdez (call the *caseta* at 3-26-68, stop by his gray cement block house facing the lagoon on Calle 16, #100, or look for him on his miniature bike). Adrian will take two or three people for 80 pesos, four people for 100 pesos, and up to six more people at 20 pesos each in his launch on an extensive, descriptive tour of the area, featuring the dense pink population at Las Coloradas. A fishing trip costs about the same. Another reliable boatman and guide is Daniel, who also runs a small *casa de huéspedes*. Arrangements with other local boatmen can be made on an individual basis. It is possible, but may be disappointing, to travel by car or bus (daily at 1pm from in front of Los Negritos) to Las Coloradas and attempt to see the flamingos on foot. No boats are for hire in Las Coloradas.

If approaching Las Coloradas by car, turn east at the crossroads 1km before the town of Río Lagartos, follow this road for roughly 14km, cross a bridge and continue

2km to Las Coloradas. It is usually not possible to reach El Cuyo by car from this direction; the road is often impassable.

QUINTANA ROO

Decades after much of Mexico came under the thrall of industrialization, Quintana Roo's picturesque coastline and lost ruins were still idylls beneath the Caribbean sun. In fact, the region did not achieve statehood untill the 1970's. Then, with the brutal suddenness of a computer error, Quintana Roo was discovered by government bureaucrats who designed Cancún, on its coast, as Mexico's paradise. After vast sums of money were poured into the construction of resorts as awesome as the beaches themselves, the transformation from tropical idyll to tourist factory was swift. Spendthrift *gringos* realized that Quintana Roo was a mere puddle-jump from the southern U.S., and Cancún became beachhead for what is wryly named "the Second *Conquista*." Isla Cozumel fell next, with Isla Mujers and Tulum close behind.

Small fishing villages along the coast south of Playa del Carmen still possess their *indígena* soul. The "biosphere reserve" of **Sian Ka'an,** a protected jungle and marine habitat for thousands of rare flora and fauna species, comprises a large part of Quintana Roo. The area's natural beauty is more impressive in person than on any of the many promotional packages that the mega-resorts mail out. Untamed landscapes and Caribbean coastline provide the backdrop for many adventures. Small wonder that the region remains one of the most alluring vacation spots in the world.

■■■ CANCÚN

Miles of magnificent white beach sparkle against the steely-blue Caribbean at Cancún. It would make a perfect hamlet of solitude, with its fine sand, rich undersea life, and eternal warm weather. But all tranquility vanished when the Republic of Mexico unleashed the capitalists to cash in on Cancún's beauty.

Now more popular than Acapulco and Puerto Vallarta, Cancún (pop. 300,000) is a frightening success story. The L-shaped island was selected by computer in 1968 to become an international resort, and construction began in 1970. The mainland city of Cancún was given space to grow and plenty of housing for hotel workers, and the *Zona Hotelera* (Hotel Zone) was built with every conceivable tourist need in mind (except wheelchair access). The Mexican government installed a water purification system to provide the Hotel Zone with pure tap water, declared all of its beaches public, and instituted strict zoning laws to prevent a scourge of skyscrapers. Begging was banned on the streets of Cancún to minimize tourists' exposure to the poverty of local workers. While wealthy vacationers cruise in taxis to classy restaurants and spring-breakers flit between the downtown discos, hotel employees are packed like lemmings into lurching diesel buses that ferry them home to humble *colonias* north of the city. Ciudad Cancún grows even more explosively than the *Zona Hotelera*, as thousands arrive looking for work from as far as Mexico City. Meanwhile, "We love the tourists!" signs trim this modern-day St. Petersburg.

Cancún's attractions are obvious. Here, in the middle of *norteamericano* winter, you can parasail and scuba dive, shop in chic boutiques, snack at McDonald's and slam tequila at rowdy Tex-Mex bars ... all the while speakin' English and spendin' greenbacks. But if you have fewer bills to throw around and are searching for the Yucatán of yore, abandon the mega-resort and seek enjoyment at nearby Playa del Carmen or Isla Holbox.

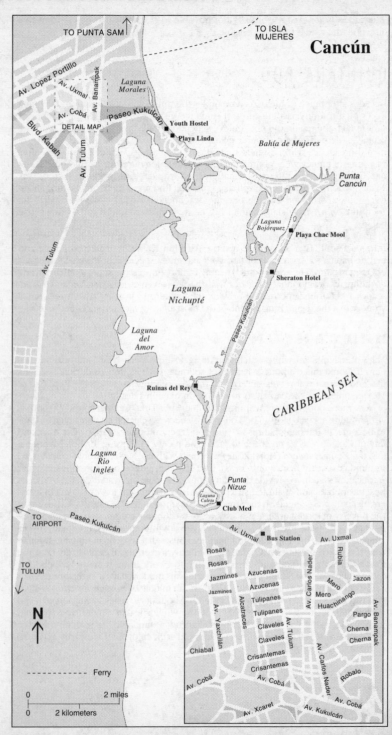

CANCÚN

TO PUNTA SAM

TO ISLA MUJERES

Cancún

Av. Lopez Portillo

Av. Uxmal

Av. Banampak

Blvd. Kabah

Av. Tulum

Av. Cobá

DETAIL MAP

Paseo Kukulcán

Laguna Morales

Youth Hostel

Playa Linda

Bahía de Mujeres

Punta Cancún

Laguna Bojórquez

Playa Chac Mool

Sheraton Hotel

Av. Tulum

Laguna Nichupté

Paseo Kukulcán

Laguna del Amor

Ruinas del Rey

CARIBBEAN SEA

Laguna Rio Inglés

Punta Nizuc

Laguna Caleta

Club Med

TO AIRPORT

Paseo Kukulcán

TO TULUM

N

----------- Ferry

0   2 miles

0   2 kilometers

Av. Uxmal   Bus Station   Av. Uxmal

Rosas

Rosas

Jazmines

Jazmines

Azucenas

Azucenas

Tulipanes

Tulipanes

Claveles

Claveles

Crisantemas

Crisantemas

Av. Cobá

Av. Yaxchilán

Alcatraces

Chiabal

Av. Tulum

Av. Cobá

Av. Carlos Nader

Av. Carlos Nader

Rubia

Mero

Mero

Huachnango

Gazon

Pargo

Cherna

Cherna

Robalo

Av. Banampak

Av. Cobá

Av. Kukulcán

CANCÚN

ORIENTATION

At the easternmost tip of the Yucatán Peninsula, Cancún twinkles 321km east of Mérida via Route 180 and 382km north of Chetumal and the Belizean border via Route 307. The resort has two sections: **Ciudad Cancún,** center of shopping and services, and **Isla Cancún,** home of the **Zona Hotelera** and the pure white beaches. Both are accessible from the airport south of the city by *colectivos* in the form of white and yellow vans (19 pesos). In Ciudad Cancún, main drag Avenida Tulum parallels Yaxchilan, four blocks over. These two streets forma rough parallelogram with Avenidas Coba and Uxmal. From the bus station, Tulum and *el centro* stretch to the right of the large white monument in the center of the traffic circle.

Private green taxis criss-cross Cancún, looking to shuttle tourists from the beaches to the stores and back again in time for sundown (12 pesos and up, depending on how far into the hotel zone you are, around 5 pesos for *intra-ciudad;* settle the price before getting in). Buses marked "Hotels" (2 pesos) run through the hotel strip from 5am to 10pm along **Avenida Tulum,** the city's main street. A signal to the driver may pull a bus over. To get off, follow the example of the locals by pounding hard on the wall: this signals the Evel Knievel drivers to slow down enough that you break only a few bones when jumping off. Many places rent mopeds, which are useful for reaching Club Med at the end of the *Zona Hotelera*.

PRACTICAL INFORMATION

Most services are downtown along Av. Tulum, easily accessible from the *Zona Hotelera* by bus.

Tourist Offices: Several booths all over town. **State Tourist Office** (tel. 84-32-38, fax 84-34-38), at Tulum 26. Open daily 9am-9pm. More helpful is the staff of **Cancún Tips** (tel. 4-40-44), in Pl. Caracol in the Hotel Zone and at the airport . The firm publishes an English-language magazine (*Cancún Tips*) with invaluable maps and practical information. It also provides discounts at various restaurants and clubs. English spoken in all offices.

Travel Offices: (tel. 4-80-73) at Tulum 26; (tel. 4-32-38 or 4-34-38) on Nader, 1 block in back of Tulum as it runs into Loba, right next to Rolandi's.

Consulates: U.S., Nader 40 at Uxmal (tel. 4-13-99 or 4-24-11). Open Mon.-Fri. 9am-2pm and 3-6pm. **Canada,** Av. Tulum 200 in Pl. México (tel. 4-37-16). Open Mon.-Fri. 11am-1pm. For emergencies outside of office hours, call the Canadian Embassy in Mexico City (tel. 915-254-32-88). **Germany,** Club Lagoon, in the Hotel Zone (tel. 3-09-58). Open Mon.-Fri. 10am-2pm. **Spain,** Calle Cielo 17, Depto. 14, S.M. 4 (tel. 4-18-98). Open Mon.-Fri. 9am-2pm.

Currency Exchange: There are many *casas de cambio* along Tulum, but the best rates are given in banks. **Bánamex,** Tulum 19 next to City Hall (tel. 4-32-61), gives cash advances on Visa and MasterCard and has a Cirrus ATM machine. Open for exchange Mon.-Fri. 9am-1:30pm and 3:30-5pm. **Banco Serfín,** Tulum 13 at Cobá (tel. 4-15-13 or 4-10-70), is open for exchange Mon.-Fri. 9:30am-1:30pm.

American Express: On Tulum at Cobá, next to Hotel América (tel. 4-19-99). Personal checks cashed, money wired and mail held (up to 3 months) for cardholders and traveler's check users. Open Mon.-Fri. 9am-6pm, Sat. 9am-1pm.

Post Office: Av. Xel-Ha at Sun Yax Chén (tel. 4-14-18). From Tulum, cut through any side street to Yaxchilán and head up Sun Yax Chén. The post office is 4 blocks farther. Open for stamps and Lista de Correos Mon.-Fri. 8am-7pm, Sat. 9am-1pm. Fax Mon.-Fri. 9am-3pm **Postal Code:** 77500.

Telephones: International collect calls are made in person from *casetas* (6-peso service charge). **Caseta M-28** is in Mercado 28 behind the post office. Open daily 8am-10pm. The public phone in Pl. Mautilus near the youth hostel can be used as well for long distance calls, provided you have a big pile of coins. To make calls within Cancún, prefix the number you are dialing with "8." From LADATEL phones, an AT&T operator can be reached by dialing "**01." Buy phone cards on Av. Tulum and Tulipans at La Surtidora. **Telephone information:** 04. **Telephone Code:** 988.

Telegrams: (tel. 4-15-29), at the **post office** (see above). Open Mon.-Fri. 9am-8:30pm, Sat. 9am-noon. Allow 1 day for the message to arrive.

International Airport: (tel. 6-00-49) on Route 307 just south of the city. Taxis monopolize transport to the airport (35 pesos from Ciudad Cancún, 35-40 pesos from the *Zona Hotelera*). Airlines: **Aerocaribe** (tel. 4-20-00), to Cozumel, Mérida, Chetumal, and Villahermosa; **Mexicana** (tel. 7-44-44 or 7-23-33), to Mexico City, Guadalajara, and major U.S. cities; **Lacsa** (tel. 7-31-01 or 7-51-01), to Central America; **American** (tel. 6-00-55, 6-01-51, and 6-00-86); **Continental** (tel. 6-00-40 or 6-01-69); **Northwest** (tel. 6-00-46); **United** (tel. 6-01-58 or 6-00-25).

Bus Station: On Uxmal, at the corner with Tulum (tel. 4-13-78). You can stow your luggage here for 5 pesos for 24 hrs. There are several different bus lines at this station including **ADO, Caribe, Interplaya,** and **Expresso de Oriente. ADO** provides service to Mérida (5 hrs., 5am-11pm daily, 30 pesos), to Valladolid (2½ hrs., 15 pesos 1st class, 12 pesos 2nd class), to Chichén Itza (3hrs., 18.50 pesos 1st class, 15 pesos 2nd class), and Chetumal (4hrs., 40 pesos). Buses leave from the outside curb for Playa del Carmen, Tulum, and destinations in between. They leave every ½-hr. 5am-10pm daily (13 pesos to Playa del Carmen). Schedules vary— check at the station for details.

Ferries: To Isla Mujeres, take bus #8 or a van with "Pto. Juárez" on the destination display to the 2 ferry depots north of town (Punta Sam for car ferries, Puerto Juárez for passenger ferries). Passenger ferries (45 pesos or 8 pesos, depending on the boat) shuttle across 15 times from 6am-8:30pm. Ferries to Cozumel (15 pesos or 25 pesos, depending on the boat) leave from Playa del Carmen, south of Cancún, accessible by bus from the terminal in town.

Taxis: (Tel. 83-18-40 or 84-12-77.) Taxis along Tulum are abundant but expensive. A ride from Pl. Caracol to downtown costs 18 pesos, and from the CREA Hostel 12 pesos. Within the *centro*, a taxi ride should cost around 5 pesos. Prices are negotiable; settle them before getting in.

Moped Rental: In town and in the Hotel Zone mopeds go for US$5 per hour. US$35-45 per day. Try **Hotel Las Perlas** (tel. 3-20-22) near CREA, **Hotel Flamingo** (tel. 3-15-44) in Pl. Flamingo, or the major hotels.

English Bookstore: Fama, Tulum 105. International newspapers, magazines and trashy beach books in English; also a decent collection of Latin American literature in Spanish. Open daily 8am-10:30pm.

Laundromat: Lavandería Automatica "Alborada," Nader 5 (tel. 4-15-84), in back of the Ayuntamiento Benito Juárez. Self-service 17 pesos. They'll wash your clothes for 22 pesos in about 1½-hrs. Self-service hours Mon.-Sat. 8am-6pm. Laundromat open until 7pm.

Supermarket: Super San Francisco, Tulum next to Bánamex (tel. 4-11-55). Down-home grocery store with a large selection of fresh tropical fruit at affordable prices. AmEx, MC, Visa accepted. Open Mon.-Sat. 8am-10pm, Sun. 8am-9pm. **Super Deli,** a 24-hr. grocery store, is conveniently located near the youth hostel.

Red Cross: Labná 2. Dial 06 in case of emergency. For routine medical services, call 4-16-16.

Medical Services: Seguro Social, at Tulum and Cóba (tel. 84-19-19). Ambulance available at **Total Assist** on Tulum at Claveles (tel. 84-10-58 or 84-10-92). Also **Hospital Americano,** Calle Viento 15 (tel. 84-77-22 or 84-61-33). Off Tulum past Cóba.

Pharmacies: Several along Tulum and Yaxchilán, the largest and most reasonable being **Farmacia Paris,** Yaxchilán 32 (tel. 4-01-64). Open 24 hrs.

Police: Tel. 419-13. Next to to city hall on Tulum.

ACCOMMODATIONS AND CAMPING

If you let it, Cancún will bleed you dry of precious cash in days or even hours. During the high season (July-Aug., Dec.-March), prices rise faster than a skinny parasailer. Budget travelers either stay in the **CREA Youth Hostel** or avoid the *Zona Hotelera* altogether. Even locations in Ciudad Cancún cost at least US$20 for singles or doubles that are less than inspiring. You can pitch a tent at the CREA (see below) or try trailer park **Meco-Loco,** near Punta Sam north of Cancún. Some travelers discreetly sleep on the beach in the *Zona*; be prepared to be woken up by the police eager to check your BAL (blood alcohol level). Participants in **FAMITEL**, a partnership between several local families and the state, built clean, bright additional rooms onto their houses. (45 pesos for 1 person, 50 pesos for two people. Fan, breakfast, and color TV included.) Contact the State Tourist Office (tel. 4-32-38 or 4-80-73). They will call and the family will come pick you up. If you don't mind the distance from *el centro*, the rooms are the nicest in the city for the price. Most hotels accept credit cards and during high season phone reservations are a good idea. With the exception of CREA, all hotels listed are within a 10 to 15 minute walk from Tulum.

CREA Youth Hostel (HI) (tel. 3-13-37), on Kukulkán, 2.5km into the Hotel Zone. Beds available in 100 rooms with 4 bunk beds in single-sex dorms. Reasonable bathrooms. No hot water. Small pool, but the resort hotel beaches are better for swimming. Lock your valuables when showering. Maximum stay is 15 days. Lockers, sheets, towels provided. 30 pesos per person, plus 30 deposit. No ID required, but there is a 25% discount with a *tarjeta plan joven* and ID. No curfew. Check-out 1pm. The **CREA Camping Area** is next to the youth hostel. No facilities provided save those in the hostel. 15 pesos per person, plus 30-peso deposit. Locker not included, but you can place your valuables with hostel security.

Hotel Coral, Sun Yax Chén 30 (tel. 4-20-97). 2 blocks down from intersection with Yaxchilán Ave. Spacious rooms in lively colors. Carved dark wood furniture. Hot water and A/C. Ample lobby with TV. Nice courtyard and pool during high season. Tranquil family atmosphere. Check-out 1pm. Singles 50 pesos. Doubles 60 pesos. Triples 70 pesos. Quads 80 pesos. During the high season, prices rise to 75 pesos for doubles, 100 pesos for triples and 125 pesos for quads. To make reservations, wire 50% payment 10 days in advance.

Hotel Colonial, Tulipanes 22 (tel. 4-15-35), off Tulum. Convenient central location. Inner courtyard with green plants and a bubbling fountain. Spacious rooms, nicely furnished. Hot water and TV. Singles 60 pesos. Doubles 75 pesos. Triples 85 pesos. 15 pesos extra for A/C. 10 pesos more for a 4th person. Check-out 1pm.

Hotel Villa Rossana, Yaxchilán 78 (tel. 4-19-43). Pink building visible from central park. Enormous rooms with sagging beds and big bathrooms. TV and *agua purificada* in lobby. Singles 45 pesos. Doubles 60 pesos. Triples 75 pesos. Bring the whole family and pay just 15 pesos for each additional person. Prices rise by 5 pesos during the high season. Check-out 1pm. You can reserve rooms by mail.

Hotel Canto, Yaxchilán M2#22R5 (tel. 4-12-67). North of the intersection with Yaxchilán, look for the fading pink building. Excellent budget hotel loaded with amenities. Clean rooms have A/C, color TV, hot water, phones and closets. *Agua purificada* in the halls. Check-out 1pm. Singles 70 pesos, 10 pesos for each additional person. Prices fixed year round.

FOOD

In Cancún, the epic battle between Mexican culture and tourism has ended in a glorious triumph for the forces of tourism. As a result, Cancún's food is overpriced and under-spiced. In the *Zona Hotelera*, "cheap" and "restaurant" are mutually exclusive. Don't even think of eating in the *Zona*. Past Mercado 23, at the intersection of Tulum and Lopez Portillo, north of *el centro*, lie several reasonable *roticerias de pollo* and small joints offering *comidas corridas* (9-12 pesos). Head to Ciudad Cancún to dine inexpensively and buy picnic fixings for the beach. The open-air **markets** offer the least expensive comestibles. (For best selection, go between 9am-2pm.) **Mercado 28,** behind the post office and circumscribed by Xel-Ha, is the largest food market. Numerous budget cafés are located in its western courtyard. Try the hearty *comida corrida* at **Restaurant Margely,** at **Acapulco,** or at **La Chaya** (9-10 pesos). La Chaya also offers vegetarian meals. All are open daily 7am-6pm.

If you want to avoid tourists altogether, walk or take a bus north on Tulum, where you'll find the smaller **Mercado 23** nestled between Tulum and Uxmal. Throughout the city, taco shops and *abarrotes* (mini-markets) offer greater convenience and reasonable prices. For tacos, stick to **Avenida Cobá,** between Tulum and Yaxchilán. This stretch of territory boasts two restaurant-style taco joints, **Tacolotes** and **D'Leo's,** as well as several open-air stands.

Except for Carlos 'n Charlie's, all the restaurants listed below are in Ciudad Cancún.

Gory Tacos, Tulipanes 26, off Tulum. Small, friendly, and inexpensive. Popular Mexican music in the background. *Antojitos* 7-12 pesos. Tacos 10 pesos. Hamburgers 7-10 pesos. Open Mon.-Sat. 9am-11pm, Sun. 2-11pm.

100% Natural, Sun Yax Chén 6 at Yaxchilán (tel. 4-36-17). 3 veggie meals a day served on pastel-colored, leafy porch. Artfully displayed tropical fruit and blue and white-tiled floor will soothe sun-dazed spirits. Menus in Spanish/English or French/German. Tropical garden and wall art create the right atmosphere for a mouth-watering tropical shake (9-12 pesos). Open daily 8am-midnight.

Chiffer's, a.k.a. **Café Super San Francisco,** Tulum 18 (tel. 4-11-55), in front of the namesake supermarket . Also at Pl. Quetzal in the Hotel Zone (tel. 3-36-53). Plain but air-conditioned and great for a snack before a difficult day of shopping. Ham and cheese 14.50 pesos. Three chicken tacos 13.60 pesos. Cheesecake 6.50 pesos. AmEx, MC, Visa accepted. Open daily 7am-11pm.

Roticeria del Caribe, on Tulum just before the intersection with Portillo, across from Plaza Dos Mil. A real joint. Walk in past the turning spits and order *pollo rostizado* or *asado.*

Carlos 'n Charlie's, across from the Casa Maya Hotel in the *Zona Hotelera* (tel. 3-08-46). Fun, loud and expensive. "Members and nonmembers only" sign seems clever after a few drinks. Rambunctious waiters will sign autographs with the spirit of celebrities. Leave your shirt tacked to the ceiling of the *palapa* along with many other testaments to Spring Break. Restaurant to the left and outdoor bar/disco to right (cover 10 pesos). Rowdy atmosphere a stronger draw than the food. Entrees US$5-10. AmEx, MC, Visa accepted. Open daily noon-2 or 3am.

SIGHTS

Most visitors do not come to Cancún to see Mexico. Even the powdery sand beaches and glistening blue surf provide only a backdrop for the sight most of the debauched *gringos* have come to see: each other's semi-nude, alcohol soaked, sunburnt bodies. Progress and culture have been summarily executed and buried in a neon tank top. For those seeking a respite from church and ruin overload, Cancún's awesome beaches may be the perfect place to lose yourself among thousands of *norteamericano* rich kids. Don't let your mind wander (fun here requires no more than a credit card and a brainstem), or you run the risk of becoming painfully aware of the reality of poverty and inequality upon which the comfortable fiction of Cancún is built.

Even if you stay inland in Ciudad Cancún, you should still take advantage of the well-groomed beaches in front of the luxury hotels in the *Zona Hotelera.* Remember, all beaches are public (North American?) property, and you can often discreetly use hotel restrooms, fresh water showers and lounge chairs. Deserted strips of shoreline south of the Sheraton Hotel are accessible by city bus (2 pesos).

The beach at the **Sheraton Hotel** is one of the safest and the most mind-dullingly pleasant. The sand is clean, the water transparent, and the waves active. Organized beach activities include volleyball, beer-drinking, egg-tossing, and bikini contests (IQ tests to follow), scuba lessons and Mexican-style painting lessons. To join them, become a visitor of the hotel for the day. Boogie boards rent for 18 pesos per two hours at the small marina on the beach.

To avoid that unsightly tan line, head out to the nude beaches by **Club Med.** Remember that public bus lines don't extend that far, making hitching or a taxi the only options, but *Let's Go* does not recommend hitching. For large waves, try **Playa Chac-Mool** in front of the Miramar Misión Hotel in the *Zona Hotelera.* **Playa Linda,** a five-minute walk east from the CREA Hostel (see Accommodations), affords mellow swimming in calm water.

Cancún offers watersport adventures of all stripes for those with hefty bank accounts. **Marina Agua Ray,** near Pl. Flamingo (tel. 3-17-73), provides water-skiing, wave runners and jet skis, parasailing, scuba diving, snorkeling, and deep-sea fishing, all at obscenely *gringo*-oriented prices. **Scuba Cancún** (tel. 3-10-11), next to Carlos 'n Charlie's offers various dive lessons and services at comparatively reasonable prices. The dock to the right of the CREA hostel supports a dive shop which offers 2½ hrs. of snorkeling for US$20 with equipment and boogie boards for US$5 per hour, US$10 per day.

Consistent with its emaciated conception of culture, Cancún's anthropological museum was closed after the 1988 hurricane, and no one seems to care. Shopping is overpriced and air-conditioned.

To add insult to injury, Cancún's Mayan ruins have been surrounded and overwhelmed by the torrential North Americanization. The Sheraton encompasses some small-scale ruins on the highest point in Cancún, affording vivid views in all directions. Other ruins in the immediate vicinity include **El Rey,** between the Sheraton and Club Med. This site, supposedly a regal burying ground, consisting of a small pyramid and vestiges of Mayan painting, may provide respite from the crispy *gringo* critters who litter the beach. (Open daily 9am-5pm. Admission 5 pesos.) The **Pok-Ta-Pok** golf course (tel. 3-08-71) also contains a small, well-preserved archaeological site near the 12th hole, which was discovered during sand-trap construction. (Open daily 6am-4pm.)

ENTERTAINMENT

At night, Cancún's laid-back decadence is redoubled with frightening drive and endurance, shaming nearby Isla Mujeres and Playa del Carmen. Both in the *Zona* and downtown, discos and bars offer carefree, wallet-emptying nights. Restaurant workers in the *Zona Hotelera* are good at pointing out which spots are hot. Many of the best-loved discos cluster around Pl. Caracol. **Christine** (in Hotel Krystal, tel. 3-11-33) charges a 35-peso cover, but **Tequila Rock** and **Hard Rock Café** do not. The finest of dance-club entertainment on a large scale is yours for US$10 in the terraced, laser-swept halls of **Dady'O** (tel. 31-31-34). Closer to the youth hostel (a 10-min. walk) is a popular modern disco, **La Boom,** and a chic bar with live reggae, **Tequila Boom** (tel. 3-14-58; open bar US$17 on Tues., Thurs., and Sat.; free Wed. nights for women; 2-for-1 specials Sun.). Downtown the more popular discos are **Risky Business** and **María and Mary Juana** along Tulum. Live reggae in **Cat's** on Yaxchilán (free with *Cancún Tips* card). Traditional *salsa* at **Batachá** in Hotel Miramar in the Hotel Zone (cover 15 pesos per person). Wherever you go expect to pay 3-4 pesos for a soft drink and 6-8 pesos for a beer.

A yet more expensive entertainment option is the **Ballet Folklórico** (tel. 3-09-66) at the Hyatt Regency Hotel in the Hotel Zone. (Performances nightly 6:30-9:30pm. Tickets US$40, including dinner, one drink and the show.)

Bullfights are held 'round the calendar, every Wednesday at 3:30pm, in the bullring on Bonampak at Sayil (tel. 4-54-65). Tickets (100 pesos per person, less if you're in a large group) are available at travel agencies on Tulum or at the bullring on a bullfight day. All major credit cards accepted.

■ Near Cancún: Isla Holbox and Chiquilá

Just off the northeastern tip of the Yucatán Peninsula, Isla Holbox (hol-BOSH, "dark hole" in Mayan) remains safely out of reach of Cancún's tour buses. The 1500 *holboxeños* who live in the tiny pueblo have a healthy appreciation for fish and tranquility, both of which they enjoy in abundance. 95% of the men fish the countless variety of creatures in the surrounding waters. For the peace-seeking traveler, Isla Holbox's streets and uninhabited beaches provide ample room for meditative rest and tent-pitching. The *holboxeños* know they have a good thing, however, any visitor should be prepared to take the island on its own terms: relaxed, amiably, and with a graceful composure. Exploring the overgrown, swampy interior can be a blast for the enthusiastic bushwhacker, but in the damp months insects are even fiercer here than on the exposed beach. Aside from meandering walks along the beach, the best way to see Isla Holbox (and the only way to see its lesser neighbors) is by **boat.** Arranging a tour with a local fisherman proves very economically advantageous. Strike up a conversation with a fisherman and see if you might ride along on a daily outing. Even better, strike up a longer conversation and maybe he'll offer you a special tour on the weekend or in his spare time. Zip over to the **Isla de Pájaros,** called **Isla Morena** by locals, where nearly 40 species of birds feed and nest.

Four pleasant hotels subsist off of Holbox's modest but growing tourism. **Hotel Flamingo's,** just to the right of the dock, is far from the beach and has a nice, coconut-shaded view of the mainland. Five straightforward rooms with flaky paint and clean bathrooms, fan, and hot water go for 25 pesos for one person, 30 pesos for two, and 35 pesos for three. During high season prices rise by 10 pesos. Check-out is at noon. To reserve a room (advisable during the high season) send 50% to Hotel Flamingo's, Isla Holbox, Q.R. 77310, or call 7-16-68, 7-14-62, or 7-29-83, ext. 52. Just off the *zócalo,* in a pink house with a small sign, **Posada Amapola** rents spotless, green, and white rooms with good beds, window screens, private bathrooms, and fans. They will also supply a hammock upon request. Singles 20 pesos. Doubles 25 pesos. Triples 30 pesos. Prices remain fixed year around. If you stay for a while, the rate per day drops. Newly built, **Posada Los Areos,** offers a nice view of the beach from under the eponymous arches. Clean white bathrooms, adequate beds, hot water, and fans are easy on the wallet. (Singles 15 pesos, doubles 20 pesos.) Prices rise by 10 pesos during the high season. Inquire at Tienda Dinora across the *zócalo.* They also rent *cabañas* on the beach. Family size, with kitchen, bathroom, and fan 35 pesos. *Cabañas* with bathroom only 20 pesos. If you stay for a while the price goes down significantly. They rent mopeds too (16 pesos per hour, 80 pesos per day). **Posada D'Ingrid,** just off the beach to the left of the *zócalo,* features a neat block of rooms with 2 beds, room for a hammock, clean pink bathrooms, hot water, and ceiling fans 40 pesos each.

Restaurants in Holbox meander through time without a fixed schedule. A good place to try is **Lonchería El Parque,** off the *zócalo,* two doors down from Dinora's. It serves a full-size fried fish for about 6.50 pesos and a variety of *antojitos* for roughly 20 pesos. (Open daily 9am-10pm.) Alternative comestibles are located in the few mini-markets, at fruit stores, and in the town's bakery. They offer food at slightly higher prices than their mainland counterparts.

On the weekends, Holbox's younger crowd amuses itself at **Cariocas Restaurant and Disco,** on Igualdad two blocks east of the *zócalo.* Rock, *salsa,* and lambada shake the covers on the colored lights. (Cover 7 pesos. Beer 2.50 pesos. Open Fri.-Sat. and holidays only.)

Chiquilá is the unfortunate embarkation point for passengers ferrying to the secluded beaches of Isla Holbox. The small settlement will not delay in-transit tourists, but after the last ferry chugs out to sea, late arrivals usually prefer to head back to civilization for a meal and a bed because at dusk mosquitoes strike fear into even the locals' hearts. Sloshing in an incompletely drained swamp, Chiquilá is neither a pleasant nor an inviting place, worthy of no more than the absolute minimum of time required to get to and away from Holbox. The only businesses in this *pueblito* are a **general store** beneath a thatched roof where the bus stops (open daily 6am-8pm), and a modest **food store** diagonally across the street (open daily 6am-9pm). There are neither accommodations nor eateries. For those who miss the last ferry to Holbox and find no Holbox-bound fishermen's boats at the dock, the options are to take a *lancha* for around 80 pesos (up to 5 people) or to return to **Kantunil Kin,** 43km south of Chiquilá, on the Chiquilá access road. In Kantunil Kin beds are available at **Casa de Huepedes "Del Parque"** (tel. 4-68-38, ext.116), whose red-striped roof is just visible from the *zócalo*. Singles 25 pesos. Doubles 30 pesos.

Transportation should be planned in advance, as buses and boats are infrequent. **Buses** leave Tizimín two to three times a day for Chiquilá. From Valladolid they depart roughly twice daily, stopping briefly at Ideal before turning north on the highway to Chiquilá. A bus leaves to Mérida at midnight, stopping at Valladolid at 3am to arrive in Chiquilá in time for the morning ferry. There is one direct bus that leaves from Cancún at 5pm daily, but doesn't arrive in time for the ferry. Ask the driver of a Valladolid-bound bus from Cancún (of which there are many; see Cancún listings) to let you off at Ideal on Route 180, next to the customs office. From there, catch one of the Chiquilá-bound buses from Valladolid. From Chiquilá, buses leave for Tizimín and Mérida roughly twice a day.

You must leave Tizimín before noon in order for the bus to get you to Chiquilá in time to catch the ferries for that day. Cars are neither necessary nor advisable on the island and difficult to transport there in the first place. Returning from Holbox is easier, as both Valladolid and Merída bound buses and Cancún buses (13 pesos) meet the early ferry.

Holbox's **public telephone** *caseta* on Igualdad, is a half block east of the *zócalo* (open Mon.-Sat. 8am-1pm and 4-8pm and 2 pesos to make a call.) The island's **Centro de Salud,** on the right side of Juárez in the blue building, is allegedly open 24 hrs. for emergencies, if you can rouse the sleeping doctor. The one-man **police** force lounges in his office on the *zócalo* at Díaz at Juárez. (Open daily, most of the time between 9am-2pm and 4-8pm.)

■■■ ISLA MUJERES

Some say the men were away on a fishing trip when Francisco Hernandez de Córdoba blew into Isla Mujeres in 1517. Others claim he was blown away by the paintings and statues he found of Ixchel, the Mayan fertility goddess. Either way, he dubbed the small strip of land the "Island of Women."

Present day inhabitants of the island (pop. 13,500) still fish, but now they also sell goods to the boatloads of daytrippers from Cancún. On this tiny isle, everyone seems to be laid-back and amiable—somehow the aura of a small town fishing village persists despite the tourist shops which line the ramshackle streets. For those who choose to linger on Isla, beaches of velvety sand, supreme snorkeling, and postcard-perfect azure water offer more room to breathe than their counterparts in Cancún.

ORIENTATION

The island lies 11km northeast of the northern coast of Quintana Roo. **Passenger ferries** (15 per day, 6am-11pm, 35min., 4.50 pesos) and faster cruisers (10min., 10 pesos) depart from Puerto Juárez, 2km north of Ciudad Cancún, the mainland section of the Cancún resort. Arrive early; ferries are famous for leaving ahead of schedule if full. Puerto Juárez is a 10-15-minute ride from Ciudad Cancún on any bus labeled "Puerto Juárez" (.15 pesos), which can be caught along Tulum behind the station. The bus lets you off at the dock; the modern building to your left holds the amiable **tourist office. Taxis** from Ciudad Cancún to Puerto Juárez cost 9-12 pesos. A **car ferry** (4.50 pesos per person, 26.40 pesos per car) runs to Mujeres from Punta Sam, 5km north of Puerto Juárez.

Isla Mujeres is only 8km long and less than 1km wide, easily accessible to the vigorous walker. The small town on the northern tip of the island can be confusing; the *zócalo* is three blocks straight ahead after exiting the ferry. **Avenida Rueda Medina** runs along the the coastline and is paralleled by **Avenidas Juárez, Hidalgo,** and **Guerrero,** in that order. Turning left on any of them will quickly lead you to **Playa Norte.** Down **Avenida Rueda Medina** several km to the right lie **Playas Paraíso, Lancheros,** and **Indios** (in that order). Finally on the southern tip of the island sits

Garrafón National Park and the nearby Mayan ruins. Rough maps and general information are provided in *Islander*, a local publication available at all travel agency shops and at the ferry dock at Puerto Juárez. Public buses go only as far as Playa Lancheros (2 pesos). Taxis, on the other hand, roam the length of Mujeres; you should have no problem catching one unless you're returning from Garrafón long after the park closes.

PRACTICAL INFORMATION

Tourist Office: Guerrero 8 (tel. 7-03-16), by the *zócalo* basketball court. Casual help with specific questions and a useful list of hotels. A useful map of the town is free when available. More complete maps of the island and tourist information can be found in *Islander, Cancún Tips,* and *Isla Mujeres Tips*. Some English spoken. Open Mon.-Sat. 9am-1pm and 6-8:30pm.

Currency Exchange: Banco del Atlántico, (tel. 7-00-05)on Rueda Medina near the ferry dock . Open Mon.-Fri. 8am-1:30pm; for exchange Mon.-Fri. 9am-noon.

Post Office: Guerrero and López Mateos (tel. 7-00-85), at the northwest corner of town, around the corner from the Poc-Na Hostel. Open Mon.-Fri. 8am-7pm, Sat. 9am-1pm. **Postal Code:** 77400.

Telephones: Long distance *caseta* in the lobby of **Hotel María José** (tel. 7-02-44), on Madero just off Rueda Medina. International collect calls 5 pesos. These phones are card-operated, so for by-the-minute calls you'll have to purchase a card from the tourist office. Also at **Caseta de Larga Distancia,** on Rueda Medina 9-B, between Matamoros and Abasolo, with a fax. Open daily 9am-9pm. **Telephone Code:** 987.

Telegrams: Guerrero 13 (tel. 7-01-13), next to the post office . A/C. Open Mon.-Fri. 9am-3pm.

Taxis: Tel. 2-00-66. Lines form near the docks and at sights and beaches.

Moped Rental: Shop around. Although mopeds rent for 15 pesos per hr. almost everywhere, prices for longer periods vary. At **Arrendadora Cárdenas** (tel. 7-00-79), on Guerrero between Abasolo and Matamoros , the charge is 60 pesos per day (8am-6pm). Credit card required for deposit. MC, Visa accepted. They also rent golf carts for more sophisticated trolling. For 4 people at 120 pesos for the day (30 pesos per hour), this could be the bargain you're looking for. Open daily 8am-6pm.

Bike Rental: Sport Bike, on Morelos and Av. Juárez, a block down from the *zócalo*. 5 pesos per hr.; 12 pesos for 4 hrs.; 15 pesos per day for 8 hrs.; 24 pesos per 24 hrs. Tandems go for double the price of a regular bike. Discounts for large groups. Open Mon.-Sat. 7:30am-6pm, Sun. 7:30am-2:30pm and 5-6pm.

Laundromat: Lavandería Tim Phó, at Juárez and Abasolo. 1 block straight and 2 to the left from the dock. 4kg for 15 pesos. Open Mon.-Sat. 7am -2pm.

Supermarket: Super Betino, Morelos 3, (tel. 7-01-45), on the *zócalo*. Wide selection of dry goods, wine, beer, and *agua purificada* at non-resort prices and a small pharmacy. Open daily 7am-10pm.

Red Cross: Tel. 2-00-46.

Pharmacy: Farmacia Lily, Hidalgo 18 at Madero (tel. 7-01-64). 2 blocks straight from the dock and 1 block left. Open Mon.-Sat. 8am-9:30pm, Sun. 8am-3pm.

Medical Services: Health care is available to tourists at the **Centro de Salud,** Guerrero 5 at Morelos (tel. 7-01-17). Light-blue building at the northwest corner of the *zócalo*. Open 24 hrs. **Dr. Antonio Torres García** (tel. 7-00-50), Matamoros near Guerrero . Speaks a little English. Open 24 hrs.

Police: Hidalgo at Morelos (tel. 2-00-82), off the *zócalo*. Little English spoken. Open 24 hrs.

ACCOMMODATIONS AND CAMPING

Prices rise by as much as 50% during high season (December-March); feel free to negotiate prices during the rest of the year. Camping on the beach is allowed only at Playa Indios, located between Playa Lancheros and Garrafón on the southeastern shore. Ask around for permission before settling in. All hotels listed below are in town, within a stone's throw from the dock.

Poc-Na Youth Hostel, Matamoros 15 (tel. 7-00-90), from the dock walk 3 blocks to the left and then 4 to the right. Popular white-stucco hostel centered around a busy social *palapa*. Cramped rooms are bare and musty, but the atmosphere is friendly and bright. A whitewash on the stucco Tom Sawyer would be proud of. Prices do not change throughout the year. Bunk beds are not automatically segregated by sex, but you can request a single-sex room. 11 pesos per night for room with bunk or hammock hook. Passport or 20-peso deposit required. Check-out 1pm, or 1-6pm for 6.50 pesos more.

Hotel Marcianito, Abasolo 10 between Juárez and Hidalgo (tel. 2-01-11). From the dock walk 2 blocks left, then 1½ blocks right. Firm, new, tasteful color scheme and locks inside the doors of the clean, welcoming rooms of this tranquil, well-run hotel. Check-out noon. Singles 40 pesos. Doubles 50 pesos. Triples 60 pesos. Quads 70 pesos. Prices rise by 5 pesos during the high season.

Hotel Xul-Ha, Hidalgo 23 between Matamoros and López Mateos (tel. 7-00-75 or 2-00-39). From the dock walk 3 blocks left, 2 blocks right, and then ½ block left. Cement box rooms are light, cheery, and nicely furnished with shiny blue bathrooms. A small lobby-like room has a TV and coffee for guests. Pretty courtyard with prominent cement staircase. Quiet location. Check-out 1pm. Singles 40 pesos. Doubles 50 pesos. Triples 60 pesos. Prices rise by 10 pesos during the high season. MC, Visa accepted. 10% discount if you stay for a week or more.

Hotel Carmelina, Guerrero 6 at Madero (tel. 7-00-06). From the dock, walk 3 blocks straight and 1 block left. Rooms in the wing to the right are new and immaculate. Patterned bedspreads decorate the otherwise plain but spacious cement-box rooms. Ongoing construction signals success, but overlooks bare, bright courtyard. Singles 30 pesos. 10 pesos for each additional person (up to 4 people per room). Some 5-person rooms available for 80 pesos. A/C 10 pesos extra. Prices rise by 10 pesos during the high season.

Hotel Las Palmas, Guerrero 20 (tel. 7-04-16), across from the post office . Walk 3 blocks straight off the dock and then 4 blocks left. Ample windows provide plenty of light to rooms decorated in green, pink, and yellow. Naked children decorate the small atrium. All rooms have 2 beds and a fan. Check-out noon. 30 pesos for 1-2 people. 80 pesos for 3-4 people. During the high season singles are 50 pesos and doubles are 57 pesos.

Hotel Osorio, Madero 10 at Juárez (tel. 7-00-18). From the dock walk 1 block left and then 1 block right. Spacious, color-coordinated rooms. Rusty faucets, but otherwise clean bathrooms. Check-out 1pm. Singles 36 pesos. Doubles 40 pesos. Triples 60 pesos. 10 pesos for each additional person (up to 5 per room). As with most places, prices rise by 10 pesos during the high season.

FOOD

The fact that many restaurants on Isla Mujeres aspire to a dash of international chic hasn't completely overpowered the *típico* Mexican atmosphere or the low prices. In addition to the ubiquitous *pescado* (fish) and *camarones* (shrimp), such delicacies as *caracol* (conch) and *pulpo* (octopus) tempt you from the murky depths. Here the *ceviche*, Mexico's famous salad appetizer, made from seafood marinated in lime juice, cilantro and other herbs, is at its most tasty. The food market on Guerrero between Matamoros and López Mateos is small and unexciting, but the four *loncherías* in front of it serve cheap and filling meals. Most meals at the *loncherías* go for around 9 pesos. All open and close in unison daily at 7am and 5pm. The youth hostel cafeteria serves breakfast and dinner (breakfast 7:30am-11am, 5-9 pesos; dinner starts at 5pm, most meals 7-17 pesos, seafood 5-9 pesos).

Café Cito, Matamoros 42, at Juárez. Cool, breezy mix of Mexican, Caribbean and European. Multilingual menu includes breakfast of fruit, bread with scrumptious toppings, and coffee or tea (12 pesos), crepes (6-12 pesos), Caribbean fish filet (20 pesos), and Kahlúa sundaes (from 4 pesos). If this divine fare leaves you thirsting to get in touch with your inner self, or just musing about fate, spiritual consultations, tarot, palm, and face readings, muscle tests, and numerology are also available—ask for Sabina. Open Mon.-Wed. and Fri.-Sat. 8am-noon and 6-10pm, Thurs. and Sun. 8am-noon.

Chen Huaye, on Hidalgo near Matamoros. 6-table *antojitos* joint teeming with locals in the late evening, when tourists are abed. Good *salbutes,* burritos, *quesadillas,* and tamales, all for pocket change (1-5 pesos). Chicken, beef, and pork dishes around 10 pesos. Open daily 6:30-11pm or midnight, depending on how business is going.

El Nopalito, at the corner of Guerrero and Matamoros, just down the street from Poc Na (tel. 7-05-55). Wonderful breakfasts of homemade bread, yogurt, muesli, fruit salad, crepes, and waffles will make you squirm with pleasure in your hand-painted wooden chair. During the high season, a prix fixe dinner will cost 20 pesos. Open Mon.-Sat. 8am-noon and 6-8pm during the high season.

Restaurante La Peña, Guerrero 5 at the *zócalo* (tel. 7-03-09). Just look for the big thatched roof with the flashing light. Favorite among the salty vacationers. Dine on the cool, comfortable terrace and watch the waves break on the rocks below. "*Amigo* time" (Happy Hour) 7-8pm. Menu includes pizza, spaghetti, Mexican food, and seafood. Spaghetti 10 pesos. Seafood from 20 pesos. Site of a popular disco after dinner hours. Open Tues.-Sun. noon-11pm.

Restaurant Miramar, Rueda Medina, just left of the dock as you land. Great ocean view. *Pollo a la yucateca* 17 pesos. Seafood from 17 pesos. Try a delicious papaya-banana milkshake (5 pesos) as you stare at the watery expanse. Open daily 7am-10pm.

SIGHTS AND ENTERTAINMENT

Apparently, even the Maya considered Mujeres's beaches pretty swank; they called it Zacil-Ha, meaning "Sparkling Water." Isla's activity centers around **Playa Norte,** which may well be the best beach in the Yucatán. Two shops spoil the mood by renting water equipment at Scrooge prices. To get to Playa Norte, follow Guerrero, Carlos Lazo, or Hidalgo away from the *zócalo* to their northern end.

Isla Mujeres is a dreamy playground for **scuba** and **snorkel** enthusiasts, with an infinite number of nooks, inlets, and reefs to explore. For information on snorkeling and scuba, go to **Coop. Isla Mujeres,** one block to the left of the dock across from the Hotel Maria José on Rueda Medina (tel. 7-02-74). You'll need a scuba license and mounds of money to rent gear, but the sleeping shark caves and expansive reefs may merit the expenditure. The cooperative runs daily trips (8:30am-4pm) to nearby **Isla Contoy** for US$40; the fee includes snorkeling equipment, lunch, drink, and a chance to spot some of the island's 5000 species of birds. They also have deep-sea fishing trips for US$30 per hour (4hr. minimum). Prices for trips are sometimes negotiable; you may be able to make a deal with the owner of the boat that will be taking you out. The group is a cooperative of several dive shops in town. Ask for Blacki, a.k.a. José Carlos. (Open Mon.-Fri. 7:30am-1pm and 4:30-8pm.) Specific recommended shops are **Bahía Dive Shop,** on Rueda Medina near the car ferry dock (tel. and fax 2-03-40; open daily 8am-8pm) and **Buzos de México,** on Rueda Medina at Madero (tel. 2-01-31, open 8am-5pm). (Both members of the cooperative.) Snorkel gear rentals are fairly cheap in town. The standard rate for mask, snorkel and fin sets is 15 pesos per day, but Bahía Dive shop rents them for 12 pesos. The staff at the dive shops can point you toward alternative snorkeling sites should you want to avoid the tame Garrafón.

At **Garrafón National Park,** you can float around in the champagne waters and hob-nob with huge schools of stunning tropical fishes. The coral reef, best visited early before the influx from Cancún, is only six feet from the beach. Mask, snorkel, and fin sets go for 8 pesos per day, plus a deposit of 90 pesos, or a credit card, driver's license, room key, or close relative. Scuba equipment and instruction is also available. Locker rental 5 pesos (key deposit 10 pesos). (Park and rental open daily 8am-4pm. Admission 5 pesos.) Garrafón is accessible by bike, moped, or taxi (10 pesos from the dock), or a tortuous two-hour walk along the leeward coast to the southern tip of the island. Better yet, hop on the bus (2 pesos) to Playa Lancheros and then take a 20-minute walk up the road.

Playa Lancheros and next door **Playa Paraíso** offer escape from the bustle of town, along with a stunningly surreal view of Cancún. (Open daily 7am-5 or 6pm. Entrance free at the Playa Paraíso entrance, but 2 pesos at the Playa Lancheros entrance 100m further down the road.) Strike up a conversation with the owner of Playa Paraíso, Don Rodríguez, and he might take you for a short, free guided tour across the street to the **Hacienda Mundaca.** In the mid-19th century, Fermín Mundaca de Marechaja, a wealthy pirate and slave trader, built these lovely gardens, archways,and bungalows to woo Prisca Gómez, a Spaniard who vacationed on the island. The more he built, the less interested she became, and she eventually married another Isla gentleman. Mundaca went insane, but not before carving his own gravestone (today in the Isla Mujeres cemetery) which reads, "As you are, I was; as I am, you will be." The last garden at the end of the pathway was built as a sundial, but now the arch that used to stand above the well has fallen and it is no longer possible to tell the time. To see the pirate's monument to his unrequited love, follow the coastal road south for about 3km. Just after you see two signs warning of dangerous curves ahead, the road turns nearly 90° to the right; continue straight on the dirt road for roughly 20m. Watch carefully for a small trail that splits to the right. You can stroll through the open grounds whenever there is enough sunlight to guide you. Playa Paraíso is around the corner at the 90° turn of the road.

Across the Laguna de Makax from the populated tip of Isla Mujeres is **PESCA,** a biological research station where scientists study the conservation of marine species. If you ask you will usually be allowed to see the plethora of tropical fish. The best time to visit is between 9am and 2pm.

On the southern tip of the island, a stone's throw past Garrafón, a **Mayan temple** is falling farther and farther into ruination. Francisco Hernández de Córdoba spotted it in 1519 when a storm blew him in from Cuba. Before the eastern and southern walls collapsed into the waves, this temple to Ixchel, the goddess of fertility, had slits facing the cardinal directions for astronomical observations. The small figurines of deformed women that once decorated the temple have long since been stolen or destroyed, and the ruined remains were almost totally wiped out by Hurricane Gilbert in 1988. But the panoramic view of sea and sky from this windswept, lonely spot is possibly the most beautiful view on the island. Ask permission to climb the lighthouse to view the afternoon sun beams glistening on the sea. You may be charged 2 pesos for the privilege. To reach the ruins, follow the road until you can see the lighthouse, then walk along the track to the right. As you return from the ruins, Garrafón and Playa Paraíso will be to your left, Mundaca's fort to your right.

For a small island, Isla has a big nightlife. **Restaurant La Peña** switches into disco mode at 11pm after the restaurant closes. Colorful crepe paper festoons the lofty *palapa.* Colored lights, reggae, salsa, and rock complete the fun, relaxed scene. (Open Tues.-Sun.) On Playa Norte at Hidalgo you'll find the rowdier **Chimbo's,** a *palapa* which sports a pirate/merman/mermaid-theme Happy Hour(s) 9pm-midnight. (Open till the last Captain Hook stumbles out.) For a beer that's "colder than a penguin's ass," try **Cafe and Bar Los Pinguinos** on Rueda Medina, No. 15A (ask about the story of the penguin). Things usually start up at the bars after 11pm, but their schedules are somewhat erratic, so ask around.

The cheapest and liveliest entertainment is in the **zócalo.** Virtually every night, townspeople flood the plaza to stroll, play tag, chat about the day's catch, or to watch volleyball and basketball games sponsored by local businesses.

■■■ PLAYA DEL CARMEN

Smack dab in the middle of Quintana Roo's proverbial Costa Torqueso ("Turquoise Coast") Playa (as the locals call it) plays the role of a crossroads inn for travelers en route to the ruins at Tulum and Cobá, or the shoreline at Cozumel and Cancún.

PLAYA DEL CARMEN

While its serene beaches are cheaper than most tourist-conquered areas, it is no longer a budget traveler's haven—when the through-traffic to greener *yucateco* pastures heats up, you notice. A favorite among the ever-hip jet-setting European crowd, Playa is a little town with dreams of building better *discotecas* and *palapas*. Moderately expensive seafood restaurants and handicraft happy vendors line the pedestrian walkway which serves as scope-out site, mall, and locale of many pleasant *posadas*.

Playa is centered around the main transportation centers, the ferry dock and the bus stations. The bus drops you off on **Avenida Principal,** the main drag, which drags west from the beach to the Cancún-Chetumal Highway 1.5km away. Most of the services lie along this road. At the bus station/plaza, perpendicular to Avenida Principal, runs **Avenida Quinta,** which encompasses most of the *tiendas* and food places.

PRACTICAL INFORMATION

Tourist Office: Wooden booth in the plaza. Very friendly and helpful English speaking staff. Open daily 6:30am-2pm and 5-10pm.

Currency Exchange: Banco del Atlántico (tel. 3-00-64), on the 1st block west of the plaza on Av. Principal . Don't miss the big blue sign. 1% commission on traveler's checks. Changes US dollars only. Open Mon.-Fri. 8am-1:30pm.

Telephones: Long distance *caseta* in lobby of Hotel Playa del Carmen (tel. 3-02-93), across the street from Banco del Atlántico. 5 pesos for international collect calls. Open Mon.-Sat. 7am-2pm and 3-9pm, Sun. 7am-noon. **Telephone code:** 987.

Post Office, on Av. Principal, 2 blocks west of the plaza (tel. 2-03-00). Lista de Correos. Open Mon.-Fri. 8am-7pm, Sat. 9am-1pm. **Postal Code:** 77710.

Pharmacy: Farmacia Lupita, 3 blocks north of the plaza on Av. Quinta. (tel. 3-03-35). Open Mon.-Sat. 8am-1pm and 5-9pm, Sun. 8am-noon.

Laundromat: Lavandería Yee del Caribe, just past the pharmacy. Do it yourself for 13 pesos wash and dry. They'll wash your clothes, up to 3 kilos, for 22 pesos. Open Mon.-Sat. 7:30am-7pm.

Bus Stations: Autotransportes de Oriente, in the big bus yard on Av. Principal. 1st class service to: Mérida (6hrs., 36 pesos), Valladolid (4hrs., 20 pesos), Tulum (1hr., 6 pesos). Chetumal, (4hrs., 33 pesos). 2nd class to: Mérida (7hrs., 28.50 pesos), Chichén Itzá (5hrs., 19.50 pesos), Valladolid (4hrs., 18 pesos), Tulum (1hr., 5 pesos). ADO also has frequent trips to Cancún throughout the day, as does **Autotransportes del Caribe,** on Av. Principal next to the bus yard. They also go to Tulum and Xel-Ha often. Inquire for details; schedules vary.

Medical Care: Centro de Salud (tel. 3-03-14), across from the post office on Av. Juárez. Doctor speaks English. Open Mon.-Fri. 8am-8pm, Sat.8am-1pm and 5-8pm, Sun. 8am-1pm.

Police: (tel. 3-02-91), on Av. Principal 2 blocks west of the plaza right past the post office. Little English. Open 24 hrs.

ACCOMMODATIONS AND CAMPING

Although Playa's hotels have been bitten by the infectious tourist bug, there are several funky and comfortable *posadas* that may be worth the extra pesos just to hang out in. Be prepared for frighteningly inflated rates during Playa's increasingly popular high season. Prices are at a maximum (except at the hostel), while quality is generally at a minimum.

CREA Youth Hostel (HI), ax 1km a trek from the plaza. Walk 4 blocks on Principal and turn right before Farmacia Lupita. Walk another 4 blocks and turn left after the big concrete IMSS building. The hostel is 100m further to the left. Accommodations available in single-sex rooms with 10 quaking bunk beds. Showers and bathrooms are not in the best shape. 6 *cabañas* with private bathrooms are also available. No hot water. No curfew or maximum stay period. Basketball court. Check-out noon. Cafeteria open during the high season. Dorms 15 pesos per person. 25-peso deposit. *Cabañas* 45 pesos.

Campamento La Ruina, on the beach 200m north of the ferry dock. Offers just about every accommodation option imaginable: *casitas* with private bathrooms, *cabañas*, hammock-space outside or in a *palapa*, camping space and parking and electricity hookups for vehicles of all types and sizes. Communal bathrooms and showers for all but those in the *casitas*. 30 pesos for a 1- or 2-person *cabaña*. 35 pesos for 1-3 people in a *casita* with private bath. Tent space for 1 person 6 pesos, 2 people 12 pesos, 3 people 15 pesos. Hammock-space outside 6 pesos, or under an open-air *palapa* 8 pesos (locker included). Sleeping in a parked car 10 pesos. 12-20 pesos for campers, electricity extra. All accommodations and all vehicles require a 25-50-peso deposit. Hammocks are 2 pesos plus a 50-peso deposit.

Hotel Lilly, (tel. 3-01-16), the bright blue bldg. on Principal, 1 block west of the plaza. Swell bathrooms attached to small, neat rooms. Convenient but noisy location near the bus stop. Often full. Rooms with 1 bed for 1 person 35 pesos, for 2 people 40 pesos. Rooms with 2 beds for 2 people 50 pesos, for 3 people 60 pesos. Traveler's checks not accepted. Check-out 1pm. The hotel fills up most of the time from Dec.-May; for reservations you must pay in advance.

Posada Sian-Ka'an, (tel. 3-02-03)on Quinta, 1 block north of the bus station. Early morning buses disrupt sleep in these clean, comfortable bungalows. Most rooms have a fan, but share common bathrooms. The name means "where the sky is born" in Mayan. Great views of the beach from bright rooms with solid furniture and molding, dubbed with women's names. Call to reserve during high season. Singles 35 pesos. Doubles 45 pesos. Triples 65 pesos. Quads 75 pesos. Prices rise by 25-30 pesos.

Posada Las Floras (tel. 3-00-85), on Quinta 2 blocks north of the plaza. Spotless and airy white rooms with firm beds and alcove bathrooms. Hammock-filled courtyard perfect for taking an afternoon siesta. Check out 11am. Singles 35 pesos. Doubles 40 pesos. Triples 60 pesos. Prices rise 20 pesos during high season.

Posada Marinelly, on Av. Principal, 2½ blocks from the plaza (tel. 3-01-40). Conveniently located. Pleasant, shady courtyard *palapa*. Gray concrete rooms embellished with concrete beds. Check out noon. Singles 35 pesos. Doubles 40 pesos. Triples 45 pesos. Prices rise by 5 pesos during the high season. You can make reservations by phone.

La Rana Cansada (tel. 3-03-89). Bright, well-kept rooms with fan and private bath in semi-circular *palapa*. Central *palapa* with restaurant. Rooms with 1 and 2 beds from 45 to 65 pesos. Prices rise by 15-20 during the high season. Call to reserve.

FOOD

Good restaurants are rare and costly in Playa del Carmen. Questionable hygiene conditions plague the cheaper, less centrally located spots. A better bet is to nibble on fruit and snacks along Av. Principal.

Playa Caribe, on Quinta, 2 blocks north of Principal. Unluxurious, but pleasant and popular. *Ceviche* and *calamari* 12-15 pesos. Open daily 6am-11pm.

Sabor, 2 blocks north on Quinta and ½ block left. Café, cappucino, and espresso served with a variety of pasteries in a small, nice shack. Sandwiches and soyburgers. Try the *chaya* with *limón* and *piña*; they say it's good for your kidneys (2.50 pesos).

La Posadita, on Principal, next to the Autotransportes del Caribe station. Hidden behind the parked buses and choked by gas exhaust, La Posadita offers the cheapest food in town with a marine life mural to get you in the mood. *Tamales* 3.50 pesos. Various *comidas* for 10 pesos. Open daily 6am-4pm.

La Hueva del Coronado, on Quinta, 2 blocks north of the bus station. A pleasant, *típico* restaurant with tablecloths in bright Mexican colors. Chicken 12-18 pesos. *Desayunos* for 6 pesos. Beef and seafood from 12 pesos. Open daily 9am-midnight.

Restaurant Nuestra Señora del Carmen, next door to the Autotransportes del Oriente station. No ambience, but close to the buses. Try the *pulpo en escabeche* (Yucatán-style octopus) for 17 pesos. Most entrees 10 pesos. Open daily 8am-11pm.

SIGHTS AND ENTERTAINMENT

The beach, free of seaweed and coral for 5km along the coast, beams a natural beauty that, for many, blows away its competitors in Cozumel and Cancún. Palm trees line the shore and dense jungle extends inland just beyond the town limits. Windsurfers and other gear can be rented from some of the fancier hotels just south of the pier. One km north of town, the beach goes nude. Although no great reefs for snorkeling grace Playa, 200m past the Shangri-La Caribe Hotel you'll find an acceptable reef.

After sunning and swimming, there is little else to do during the day, in Playa except wander into the shops on **Av. Quinta.** At night, *palapa*-style bar-hopping and disco-grooving satisfies the tan *turistas*. Some discos promise live *salsa*; ask around. The place to find everyone is the **Blue Parrot Inn,** six blocks north of Av. Juárez on the beach. Check out the room upstairs.

■■■ ISLA COZUMEL

Before the Spaniards overran the island, Cuzamil, the "place of the swallows," was a sacred Mayan ceremonial site. Pilgrims often braved the stormy straits in canoes to worship at the shrine of Ixchel, goddess of the moon and of love, or at one of more than 40 carvings of smaller deities. Spanish explorer Juan de Grijalva chanced upon the island in 1518, and a year later Cortés stopped here before going on to loot the mainland.

The first Catholic mass in Mesoamerica was celebrated here by Grijalva, but neither Cortés nor the Montejos could successfully wrest the coveted island from the *indígenas* until 1545. Eventually, conquistador brutality and diseases annihilated the native population. As the Spanish colony on the Yucatán grew, Cozumel became a hideaway for such pirates as Francis Drake and Jean Lafitte. In the late 19th century, it became a safe haven for Mayan refugees fleeing the Caste War.

Attributing strategic significance to the area, the U.S. Air Force built a base here during World War II and in so doing demolished almost all of what remained of the ancient Mayan city now called San Miguel. In the 1950s, Jacques Cousteau's exploration of Palancar Reef drew international attention to Cozumel's marine life, and the military airfield became a welcome mat for a wave of civilian invaders.

Today, direct flights from the U.S. and Mexico land daily, ships cruise into port from around the world, and boatloads of passengers stumble in from nearby Playa del Carmen and Puerto Morelos. The place is crawling with *norteamericano* tourists, elevating the cost of enjoying what remains of Cozumel's authentic life and natural beauty.

ORIENTATION

The island of Cozumel lies 18km east of the northern Quintana Roo coast, and 85km south of Isla Mujeres. Main access is via ferry from Playa del Carmen to the west or from Puerto Morelos to the north. Ferries from Puerto Morelos (tel. 2-09-05) transport cars to and from Cozumel twice daily, docking in the island's only town, San Miguel de Cozumel (nicknamed "Cozumel"), in the middle of its mainland side. (US$30 per car, US$4.50 per person, 2½ hrs.) The **car ferry** is inconvenient and unpredictable; you have to get in line 12 hours in advance to ensure a spot.

Two **ferry** companies shuttle passengers between Playa del Carmen and Cozumel. The "fast" boats, *Waterjet Mexico* and *Mexico II* (tel. 2-15-08), equipped with air conditioning and rock videos, make the trip in 40 minutes. The "slow" boats, *Cozumeleño* and *Xel-Ha* (tel. 2-18-24), lack the glitz but are nearly as efficient. The *Cozumeleño* is also air-conditioned and costs as much as the fast boats (25 pesos), but the open-air *Xel-Ha* is cheaper (15 pesos). If you are coming from Cancún, an alternative to the bus-ferry ordeal is the **air shuttle** operated by Aerocozumel (tel. 2-09-28) for US$42.50.

At 47km long and 15km wide, Cozumel is Mexico's largest Caribbean island. Although public transportation is virtually nonexistent, downtown streets are clearly labeled and numbered with Vulcan logic. If you don't mind occasionally spine-wrenching road conditions, the rest of the island is easily explored by bike or moped.

As you step off the ferry into Cozumel, the dock becomes **Avenida Juárez,** which cuts east-west through town. *Calles* run parallel to Juárez and are labeled *Sur* and *Norte* (Nte.) with respect to Juárez; numbers increase in both directions moving away from Juárez. *Avenidas* run north-south, are numbered in multiples of five, and are designated *Norte* if north of Juárez or *Sur* if south. Juárez becomes the **Carretera Transversal** at the eastern edge of town, extending across the island's midsection to the other shore. The road to the airport forms the city's northern boundary. **Avenida Rafael Melgar** runs along the western edge of town next to the sea and leads to the luxury hotels north of town and the uninhabited northern coast. The national park at Laguna Chankanaab and the popular beach at San Francisco are south of town on the western shore; off the island's southern tip lie the Palancar Reefs. The nearly deserted eastern coast dotted by Mayan ruins supports only a few restaurants.

PRACTICAL INFORMATION

Tourist Office: On the 2nd floor of the "Plaza del Sol," the building to the left of Bancomer (tel. 2-09-72 or 2-02-18). Also 2 open-air booths on the northern and western sides of the plaza which are helpful in providing information on hotels, services, and transportation, but have only sketchy maps. Some English spoken. Open Mon.-Fri. 9am-2pm and 6-8pm. *Cozumel Tips*, available at the boat dock, includes a good map.

Currency Exchange: Ban País (tel. 2-03-18), right off the dock, takes no commission for cashing traveler's checks. Open Mon.-Fri. 9am-1:30pm, for exchange 9am-1pm. **Bancomer** (tel. 2-15-50), on the plaza, charges a flat fee of .50 pesos per check. Cash advances on Visa only. Open Mon.-Fri. 9am-1:30pm, for exchange 9am-noon. **Banco de Atlantico** (tel. 2-09-20), on the SE corner of the plaza, does not give cash advances, but is open for exchange Mon.-Fri. 8am-1:30pm.

Post Office: (Tel. 2-01-06). Off Rafael Melgar along the sea, just south of Calle 7 Sur. Open Mon.-Fri. 9am-6pm, Sat. 9am-noon. **Postal Code:** 77600.

Telephones: Long distance *caseta* next to Hotel López on the south side of the plaza charges 10 pesos per min. for calls to the U.S. No collect calls. Open daily 8am-11pm. *Caseta* (tel. 2-41-98), across from Hotel Yoly on Calle 1 Sur between Av. 5 and Av. 10 charges only 6 pesos. Open daily 7am-10pm. **Telephone Code:** 987. To avoid the charge use any LADATEL phone in town.

Telegrams: At the post office (tel. 2-00-56). 17 pesos per 15 words. Open Mon.-Fri. 9am-6pm, Sat. 9am-noon.

Airport: (Tel. 2-05-03), 2km north of town. Take a taxi (6 pesos covers 1-4 people). **Aerocozumel** (tel. 2-09-28) to Cancún (10 trips per day, US$42.50). Also served by **Mexicana** (tel. 2-01-57), **American** (tel. 2-08-76), and **Continental** (tel. 2-05-76).

Ferries: From the dock at the end of Av. Juárez. Arrive ½ hr. early because ferries often leave before schedule. **Waterjet Mexico** and **Mexico II** to Playa del Carmen (8 per day 4am-6:30pm, 40min., 25 pesos). **Cozumeleño** to Playa del Carmen (5 per day 6:30am-8pm, 40min., 25 pesos) and **Xel-Ha** to Playa del Carmen (4 per day 6:30am-5:30pm, 45min., 15 pesos). Schedules change frequently; check at the dock.

Taxis: Tel. 2-11-67 or 2-02-36. From the plaza to the airport 22 pesos, to Hotel Presidente 30 pesos, to the Chankanaab park 15 pesos. All fares cover up to 4 people.

ISLA COZUMEL

Car Rental: Cars can be rented at nearly every corner in town for over US$60 per day during the high season. For better deals try **Rentadora Cozumel** (tel. 2-15-03) at Av. 10 and Calle 1 Sur, US$50 per day. Open daily 7:30am-7:30pm. **National** (tel. 2-32-63), across from the Catholic church, US$44-79 per day. Open Mon.-Fri. 8am-2pm and 6-8pm, Sat.-Sun. 8am-2pm and 6-7pm.

Moped Rental: On nearly every street and in nearly every hotel. Shop around and bargain during the low season. All mopeds should come with a full tank of gas. US$20 for 24 hrs. with a credit card or US$50 deposit at both **Rentadora Cozumel** (tel. 2-11-20), Av. 10 and Calle 1 Sur (open daily 8am-8pm) and **Rentadora Caribe** (tel. 2-09-61), Av. Adolfo Salas 3 at Av. Melgar (open daily 7am-7pm).

Bike Rental: Best deals are at **Rentadora Cozumel,** Av. 10 and Calle 1 Sur (tel. 2-11-20). Bikes rent for 15 pesos per day (must be returned by 6pm). Open daily 8am-8pm.

Laundromat: Margarita, Av. 20 #285 (tel. 2-28-45), near Calle 3 Sur . 5 pesos per self-service wash, 2 pesos per 10-min. dry. Open Mon.-Sat. 7am-9pm, Sun. 9am-5pm.

Red Cross: Av. Adolfo Salas (tel. 2-10-58), at Av. 20 Sur . 24-hr. emergency service.

Pharmacy: Farmacia Kiosco (tel. 2-24-85), on the *zócalo* near Hotel López. Open Mon.-Fri. 8am-10pm, Sat.-Sun. 5-10pm. 24-hr. pharmacy at the **Medical Center (CEM),** Av. 20 Nte. 425 (tel. 2-29-19). From the dock, walk 4 blocks inland and 4½ blocks left. All major credit cards accepted.

Medical Services: There are several English-speaking private physicians in Cozumel. For consultations, go to **Dr. M. F. Lewis,** Av. 50 (tel. 2-16-16 or 2-09-12), between Calle 11 and 13. 24-hr. tourist medical service. Or go to the **Medical Center (CEM),** Av. 20 Nte. 425 between Calle 10 Nte. and Calle 8 Nte. For an ambulance, call 2-06-39.

Police: Calle 11(tel. 2-00-92), Sur near Rafael Melgar, in the Palacio Municipal . Open 24 hrs.

ACCOMMODATIONS AND CAMPING

Budget rooms in Cozumel are slightly more expensive and significantly less cozy than those in Playa del Carmen, but because of the price of the ferry it makes sense to sleep in Cozumel if you plan to spend more than one day on the island. Hunt down a room before noon, because the few inexpensive lodgings on the island fill quickly. Most of their prices go up during high season.

Campers should encounter no problems with the authorities for short stays, but you might want to consult the tourist office (see Practical Information) about longer stays, as well as to find out where you're allowed to camp. Secluded camping spots in Cozumel are at **Punta Morena** and **Punta Chiqueros,** on the island's Caribbean coast.

Hotel Posada Edem, Calle 2 Nte. 4 (tel. 2-11-66), a block off the plaza, in front of the taxi stop. Very clean rooms with fresh linen, 2 beds, fans, and hot water. Original art on the walls. You can also watch TV in the lobby with the owner. Check-out at noon. Prices remain stable year-round. Room for 1-2 people 40 pesos. Triples 50 pesos. 10 pesos extra for A/C and each additional person. MC, Visa accepted.

Hotel Saolima, Av. Adolfo Salas 268 (tel. 2-08-86), between Av. 10 Sur and 15 Sur. Clean rooms with small bathrooms off a plant-filled hall. Fans and hot water that becomes apparent after you let it run awhile. Check-out noon-1pm. Singles 40 pesos. Doubles 45 pesos. Triples 60 pesos. Quads 75 pesos. Prices rise by 10 pesos during the high season.

Hotel Flores, Av. Adolfo Salas 72 (tel. 2-14-29; fax 2-24-75), at Av. 5 Sur. Clean bedrooms with fans, closets, cement beds, and green bathrooms. Lobby with TV and *agua purificada.* Check-out at noon. Singles 45 pesos. Doubles 50 pesos. Triples 55 pesos. A/C 15 pesos extra. Prices rise by 10 pesos during high season.

Hotel Flamingo, Calle 6 Nte. 81 (tel. 2-12-64), 1 block inland. Offers huge immaculate rooms with matching bright bedspreads, 2 fans, and sparkling bathrooms with flamingo shower curtains. Friendly, English-speaking management. Send deposit to reserve room. Check-out 1pm. Singles 45 pesos. Doubles 60 pesos. Triples 75 pesos. Quads 99 pesos. 15 pesos higher Nov.-Apr.

FOOD

Food in Cozumel is expensive, especially when close to the beach or the plaza. Fortunately, there are several moderately priced restaurants a few blocks from the center, as well as small *típico* cafés hiding on side streets. The market, on Av. Adolfo Salas between Av. 20 Sur and 25 Sur, sells the standard meats, fish, and fruits. The five small restaurants outside the market do minimal damage to your wallet in exchange for generous portions of regional dishes.

Cocina Económica Mi Chabelita (tel. 2-08-96), on Av. 10 Sur near Adolfo Salas . Great budget dining in a bright coral-colored garage. Large fruit salad 6 pesos. Chicken tacos 10 pesos. Try the fried bananas (5 pesos). Open Mon.-Sat. 7am-10pm.

Restaurant El Foco (tel. 2-41-78), Av. 5 Sur 13, 2½ blocks from the plaza . Wooden tables and graffiti-adorned walls give it the nonchalance of a well-loved hangout. A friendly owner serves the hearty "foco special" (a special taco; 15 pesos). *Quesadillas* 7 pesos. Enchiladas 16 pesos. Open daily 4pm-1am.

Restaurant Casa Denis (tel. 2-00-67), across from the flea market on the SE corner of the *zócalo*. Old pictures and a 113-yr.-old Mamey tree glorify this convenient shack. *Comida regional* including *chiles rellenos* (10 pesos), shish kabob (12 pesos), and seafood (10-12 pesos). Open Mon.-Sat. 7am-11pm.

El Abuelo Gerardo (tel. 2-10-12), on Av. 10 between Juárez and Calle 2 Nte. Soothing music and wooden tables and paneling transform this garage into a pleasant dining experience. Grandpa Gerardo dishes up fish filets of every type (16-32 pesos). *Antojitos* 3-9 pesos. Open daily 7:30am-10:30pm.

La Parroquia, on Av. 10 Sur, near Calle 1 Sur next to the church. Cheap eats at 2 tables or standing by counter outside. Tacos 2 pesos. *Tortas* 2.50 pesos. Upstairs a more formal restaurant/bar with nice balcony. Open daily 6am-3am.

The Corner Store and Fruit Bar, Av. Adolfo Salas near Av. 20 Sur, in a building that says "Frutas Selectas" on the roof. Exactly what it sounds like: a produce shop with healthy munchies. Yogurt with fruit, granola, and honey 6 pesos, ham and cheese sandwich 3 pesos, cheesecake 3 pesos. Open Mon.-Sat. 8am-2pm and 5-9pm, Sun. 8am-1pm.

SIGHTS AND ENTERTAINMENT

Cozumel's principal virtue is the coral reefs near the island, which provide excellent opportunities for snorkeling and scuba diving *ad infinitum*.

Fish and coral stir the water near the shore at **Laguna Chankanaab**, the national underwater park. Snorkeling in the enclosed lagoon has been discontinued because the suntan lotion from snorkelers was killing the sea life, and the lagoon is still undergoing rehabilitation. In the open water, snorkeling is its old superb self; the water is clearest and calmest early in the morning (mask, snorkel, and fins US$5 per day). Scuba rentals and lessons are available (lessons US$50). (Dive shops open 9am-4:30pm.) The park has showers and lockers (3 pesos). Chankanaab also has a botanical garden, restaurants, and boutiques. (Open daily 8am-4:30pm. Admission 12 pesos.) The park is 8km south of town along the coastal highway (the extension of Av. Rafael Melgar). The reef at **Dzul-Ha,** 1km north of Chankanaab along the coastal highway, is less touristy. Here the reef is 40m offshore at a depth of only 5m. You can obtain gear and advice from the dive shop in front of the Hotel Club del Sol Cozumel (tel. 2-37-77). They rent snorkel, mask and fins for US$5 per day, and scuba resort courses for US$25. (Courses usually given 8:30am-5pm.) Wave-runners, sailboats and windsurfers are also available. Join the hydrophobic *gringos* on **Fiesta Cozumel's** glass-bottomed boats (at the hotel, tel. 2-03-22).

Most of the larger reefs around Cozumel, like the **Palancar Reef,** are farther offshore and accessible only by boat. Most of the numerous **dive shops** in town are on Calle 3 Sur between Av. Melgar and Av. 10 or on the waterfront. They offer expensive snorkeling trips, scuba trips, instruction, and equipment rentals. One of the most reliable is **Dive Paradise,** Calle 3 Sur 4 (tel. 2-10-07), near the waterfront. Five-hour, two-tank scuba trips are US$45, introduction to scuba and scuba refresher courses are US$60 and US$65 respectively, and full three- to five-day scuba certification courses cost US$350. (Calle 3 Sur office open daily 8am-1pm and 5-9pm; office at Rafael Melgar 601 open daily 8am-9pm.) **Blue Bubble Divers,** Av. 5 and Calle 3 Sur (tel. 2-18-65), has a mellow, English-speaking staff (employees continually murmur "Blue bubble...no trouble") and a choice of 20 reefs to visit. Their two-tank daytrips are expensive (US$50-60), but their package deals are within reason. You can rent snorkeling equipment anywhere on the island, including at Laguna Chankanaab and Playa de San Francisco. The standard rate is US$7-10 plus deposit per 24 hrs.

Between beach stops and reef dives, you may want to explore the jungle interior of Cozumel and locate its several small ruins. From the lighthouse at **Punta Celerain,** Cozumel's southern tip, you can view the entire island and the bobbing fishing boats. The unreconstructed ruins of the **Tumba del Caracol** are near the beginning of the road to Celerain.

The route along the east coast passes many secluded beaches that would make good camping spots. Midway along the coast, Carretera Transversal branches west and loops back through the jungle to town. North of Transversal, the unpaved road winds toward **Punta Molas** and its lighthouse. **Aguade Grade, Janan,** and other small ruins tucked into the jungle on the island's northern tip are difficult to find without a guide, but **Castillo El Real,** just north of the *palapas* of Los Cocos, is hard to miss. This ex-fortress was the largest of the Mayan buildings on the island.

To get to **San Gervasio,** the only extensively excavated and partially reconstructed ruin on the island, take Juárez out of town. After 8km, a dirt road marked by a "San Gervasio" sign branches to the left. Follow this road for another 8km to the ruin site. (Site open daily 8am-4pm. Admission 2 pesos at the dirt road entrance and 8 pesos at the site itself.)

The small, air-conditioned **Museo de la Isla de Cozumel** (tel. 2-14-75 or 2-14-74), on the waterfront between Calles 4 and 6, serves as a sanctuary from the rain, sun, and tourists downtown. Four rooms, filled with colorful photographs and impressive artifacts, politely introduce you to the island's social and geological history. (Open Sun.-Fri. 10am-6pm. Admission US$3.)

For action and romance at the movies, **Cinema Cozumel,** on Av. Rafael Melgar between Calles 2 and 4 and **Cine Cecillo Borques** on Juárez between Av. 30 and 35. Both have showings nightly at 9pm.

Cozumel's nightlife will relieve you of those pesky peso notes which clutter your wallet. Fancy restaurants routinely charge 8.50 pesos per piña colada. **Carlos 'n Charlie's,** on Rafael Melgar just one block north of the dock (tel. 2-01-91), rocks all day long, entertaining *norteamericanos* with crazy drinks, slammer contests and arm-wrestling matches. (*Cerveza* 6 pesos. Open daily 10am-1:30am.) **Scaramouche** (tel. 2-07-99) and **Neptuno** (tel. 2-15-37) are modern and air-conditioned discos on Rafael Melgar, one and five blocks south of the plaza, respectively. Scaramouche docks you a 10-peso cover after 10:30pm. (Opens daily at 9:30pm.) There's no cover at Neptuno. The action everywhere revs up after 11pm and lasts into the wee hours.

■■■ TULUM

On the eastern edge of the age-old Etaib (Black Bees) jungle, halfway down the Caribbean coast of the Yucatán, lies the walled Mayan "City of the Dawn." Although the ruins here are less extensive and less detailed than those at Uxmal and Chichén Itzá, their backdrop is stunning: Tulum's graying temples and nearly intact watchtowers on the city wall rise above palm trees and white sand massaged by the steely-blue Caribbean Sea. Perhaps to unite the city of the rising sun with the god of the setting sun, the Maya endowed Tulum with beautiful representations of a god diving athletically into the water. The diving god appears only on the western walls of buildings, struck by the setting sun's rays.

Unlike the Aztecs, who combined their strength with other societies' to form a federation, the Maya had divided into 15 to 20 warring city-states, including Tulum, on the Yucatán by the late post-Classical period (c. 1200 AD). First settled in the fourth century, Tulum was the Western Hemisphere's oldest continuously inhabited city, when the Spaniards arrived. The Spanish finally defeated Tulum after 50 years of sporadic attacks. It was resettled three decades later by Mayan refugees from the Caste War.

This century's repopulation of the ruins was initiated by the archaeologists who studied here, living in *palapa* huts provided by the Mexican government. In recent times, the former trickle of settlers has become a torrent of camera-toting tourists spilling out of buses for a two-hour visit. Popular tours departing from Cancún and Cozumel stop at Xel-Ha and Tulum, and from about 10am until 3:30pm the ruins teem with sightseers. The archaeological site, often called **Nuevo Tulum,** features a vast parking lot surrounded by souvenir shops and high-priced restaurants. Fortunately, there are some small huts and affordable places to eat on the quiet stretch of sand just to the south. Admire the ruins as the sun rises and try to stick close to the sea, baking in the midday sun, while the tour groups do their thing.

ORIENTATION

The city of Tulum, 42km from Cobá, 63km from Playa del Carmen and 127km from Cancún, is the southernmost link in the chain of tourist attractions on the Caribbean coast of Quintana Roo. Although few people live here, Tulum takes up a good deal of space in three separate venues: **el crucero** (the crossroads), the beach **cabañas,** and **Pueblo Tulum.** Arriving in Tulum from Cancún on Rte. 307, buses first stop at *el crucero*, the intersection with Rte. 180 to Mérida, where restaurants, "mini-supers," and a pair of hotels band together. The parking lot and the entrance to the ruins spread out 200m east on the well-paved access road. More informal food and lodging are provided in the *cabañas* 1km south past the ruins along the same access road. Pueblo Tulum, 4km south of *el crucero* on Rte. 307, offers travelers a handful of roadside *típico* restaurants, more mini-supers, and a few services.

Buses provide cheap transportation from Tulum to nearby cities and to the sights and beaches which lie to the north on Rte. 307. Travelers who have chosen to hitch hike have found it a viable option, especially when hopping from sight to sight along the highway. Drivers may even pull over and offer you a lift if you start walking. Taxis congregate around the ruins, at *el crucero*, and at the bus stop at Pueblo, Tulum's southern end.

PRACTICAL INFORMATION

The few services available in Pueblo Tulum are right along Rte. 307, which serves as the tiny town's main street.

Post Office: A few hundred meters into town on the left side of Rte. 307 as you pass through from the north. Open Mon.-Fri. 9am-1pm and 3-6pm. **Postal code:** 77780.

Telephones: Pueblo Tulum has 2 telephone *casetas*. **Teléfonos de México** (tel. 3-02-30, -31, or -32), on the right side of Rte. 307 just as you enter town from the north. 3 min. to the 47 pesos. The second *caseta* (tel. 216-33) is on the left side of Rte. 307, just past the post office in the same building as the ADO office. 2 pesos for a 5-min. international collect call, 3 pesos for 10 min. Both *casetas* open daily 7am-9pm. Neither *caseta* makes credit card calls. There are no public telephones in Tulum.

Buses: Schedules for all buses are rather variable, so check with locals for updates. **Autotransportes del Caribe,** out of a small *tienda* on the left side of Rte. 307 at the southern end of town. To Cancún (2hrs., 13 pesos for 1st class, 12 pesos for

TULUM

2nd class), Mérida (6hrs., 28.50 pesos), or Chetumal (3½hrs., 18 pesos). North-bound **ADO** buses will also drop you off at Xcacel, Xel-Ha, Chemuyil, or Akumal (3 pesos). These buses pass roughly every couple of hours. Before you buy a ticket, ask when the next bus is supposed to show up. **Playa Express** buses, heading north to Playa del Carmen and Cancún, will also stop at other destinations along the way. Flag them down as they pass and buy your ticket on board (they go by about every 2hrs.). Buses leave Tulum at 6am, 8:30am, 11am, 3:45pm, and 6pm for Cobá (8 pesos), 42km into the dense jungle, before continuing on to Valladolid. These buses are the only public transportation from the south to the Cobá ruins.

Taxis: Available at the ruins, *el crucero*, Pueblo Tulum, and along Rte. 307. Things are spread out in Tulum, so unless you are in a group, taxis are an expensive way to travel. From the ruins to Pueblo Tulum 7 pesos. From Don Armando's Cabañas to Pueblo Tulum 8 pesos. From the ruins to Cabañas Tulum 17 pesos.

Pharmacy: Super Farmacia, on the left of 307 just past the post office. Open Mon.-Sat. 8am-noon and 4-9pm, Sun. 4-9pm. Dr. Arturo Ventre M. is available in an office next door.

Police: (Tel. 2-33-66), on the left side of Rte. 307 as you pass through from the north, just before the post office. Open 24 hrs.

ACCOMMODATIONS AND CAMPING

Tulum offers two kinds of lodging: hotels and *cabañas*. The sterile hotel rooms around *el crucero* cater to wealthier travelers. The beach side *cabañas* (*palapa* huts with hammocks) are a far better choice if you don't mind minimalist conditions. Clustered together on the beach 1km from the ruins, these campgrounds and *cabañas* enable you to meet other travelers, perfect your tan on the spectacular beach, and escape the conventional tourism just a short distance away.

Don Armando Cabañas, follow the access road to the right of the ruins. It's the 3rd one in and the best of the bunch. You can't miss the jocular Don Armando, who once owned Santa Fe but then decided to construct new and better *cabañas*. Cheap restaurant, solid walls, a real bed or a hammock, mosquito netting, candles, real showers, and doors with locks. Good communal bathrooms with flush toilets and electricity. To make a reservation, call. 3-02-27 (the *caseta* in town) and ask for Don Armando's Cabañas, or send a deposit to Aptdo. Postal 41. *Cabaña* with 1 bed and 1 hammock for 1 or 2 people 35 pesos. 2-bed *cabañas* 40 pesos. *Cabañas grandes* 50 pesos. 25 pesos deposit. A plot of land on which to camp or hang a hammock goes for 8 pesos.

Santa Fe Cabañas, next-door neighbor and rival of Don Armando's. Rustic wood construction with hooks to hang a hammock. Rudimentary communal bathrooms and open-air communal showers. Drumming circles on the beach at night. Don't bring the kids. Check-out 1pm. *Cabaña* with bed 30 pesos, with hammock hook 20 pesos. 10-peso deposit per *cabaña*. Space for a hammock under a communal roof 10 pesos. Hammocks rent for 5 pesos with 5-peso deposit. Camping 7 pesos. *Cabaña* prices rise 5 pesos during the high season.

El Mirador. The most Robinson Crusoe-like of the group. The bare essentialist *cabañas* here are more challenging than those of Santa Fe; you might find yourself awakened by a sudden tropical shower. Primitive outdoor bathrooms and no showers. Well water available for washing. Hammocks provided, but have someone experienced help you choose if this is your first time. The management is very friendly. Check-out 24 hrs. after check in. 20 pesos per *cabaña* with 2 hammocks, plus 10-peso deposit. 5 pesos each additional person. 5 pesos per person to camp.

El Crucero, on the highway at the Tulum crossing. Clean, small, and unattractive rooms with big beds. Private showers and bathrooms. Hot water. Fans. Check-out 24 hrs. after you arrive. Singles 30 pesos. Doubles 40 pesos. Triples 50 pesos. Quads 60 pesos. Prices fixed year round.

Cabañas Tulum, near the end of the access road, about 8km south of the ruins. Costly and inconvenient, but tidy and comfortable. Cabins have private bathrooms. Set on the most peaceful and beautiful beach in the area. Restaurant at hotel serves 3 meals a day. Rooms have electricity only from 5:30-10:30pm. Check-out 12:30pm. 80 pesos for 1 or 2 people in rooms with 2 double beds. 10 pesos per additional person.

Hotel Maya (tel. ext. 133), in Pueblo Tulum in the same building as Caribe Interplaya ofice. Noisy but clean rooms with double beds and deodorized bathrooms. Check-out 1pm. Singles 40 pesos. Doubles 60 pesos. Triples 70 pesos. Quads 74 pesos.

A taxi to the farther *cabañas* from Pueblo Tulum is 17 pesos. Hitchhiking is not an option since no cars go that way.

FOOD

Tulum's few restaurants still offer something like the real flavor of Mexican cuisine. For the cheapest and best food, take a hike to the *cabañas*. The parking lot establishments also uphold *típico* menus and atmosphere, at somewhat higher prices. At *el crucero*, restaurants offer more refined and costlier fare. Fruit and groceries can be bought at mini-supers in Tulum Pueblo.

Restaurant Don Armando, at the campground on the beach. The glam international backpacking set crowds this large *palapa*. After the restaurant closes, the gang shuffles over to the disco. Beer 4 pesos. Nachos 6 pesos. *Burritas* and *tortas* 7 pesos. Open daily 7am-9:30pm.

Santa Fe Restaurante, at the campground on the beach. Reggae tunes float interminably through the small *palapa*. Fruit salad 10 pesos. *Menú del día* of chicken tacos 13 pesos. Lentil soup 6 pesos. Open daily 7am-9pm. Bar open all night (*cerveza* 3 pesos).

El Mirador Restaurante, high on a ridge overlooking an enchanted solitary beach and the *cabañas*. Cheapest campground food. They'll prepare a special meal if you ask in advance. Try their nachos (5 pesos). Meat entrees 13 pesos. Open daily 6am-8pm.

El Crucero Restaurante, in the hotel of the same name at the crossroads. Feels like a comfortable local pub. Chicken tacos 15 pesos. Fish filets 25 pesos. Open daily 6am-10pm.

El Faisán y El Venado, across from *el crucero*, at the crossroads. A more modern-looking restaurant and superior in cuisine. The cook is very friendly. Diverse menu offers *norteamericano*, Mexican, and seafood dishes. Meals from 25 pesos. Yummy coconut ice cream with Kahlúa 8 pesos. Open daily 6am-10pm.

SIGHTS

The Ruins

Tulum may well be the ancient city of **Zamá,** Juan de Grijalva's first glimpse of a civilization that impressed him on his voyage from Cuba in 1518. From the parking lot, your first glimpse of Tulum will be of the still-impressive dry-laid **wall** that surrounded the city center's three landlocked sides. Enter to the right through the western gate. The wall, made of small rocks wedged together, was originally 12-ft. thick and 10-ft. high but has deteriorated over the years. It shielded the city from the aggression of neighboring Mayan city-states and prevented all but the 150 or so priests and governors of Tulum from entering the city for most of the year. After Tulum's defeat at the hands of the Spanish in 1544, the wall fended off English, Dutch, and French pirates and in 1847 gave rebel Mayans refuge from government forces during the Caste War.

Just inside and to the left of the west gate stand the remains of dwelling platforms which once supported huts. Behind these are the **House of the Halach Uinik** (the House of the Ruler), endowed with the typical Mayan four-column entrance; the **House of the Columns,** the largest residential building in Tulum; and the **Temple of the Frescoes,** a good example of post-Classical Mayan architecture. Well-preserved 600-700-year-old murals inside the temple depict deities intertwined with serpents,

TULUM

as well as fruit, flower, and corn-cob offerings. Masks of Itazmná, the Mayan creator, occupy the northwest and southwest corners of the building.

As with many Mayan structures, some of Tulum's temples were built along astrological guidelines so that the inner chamber is illuminated naturally at the two equinoxes. In contrast to the remarkably precise architectural planning and execution of such earlier cities as Chichén Itzá and Uxmal, however, Tulum is held together with massive amounts of mortar. The classic Mayan practice of cutting all stones to exactly the right dimensions, fitting them together without mortar, and polishing the surfaces was abandoned here.

El Castillo, the most prominent structure in Tulum, looms behind the smaller buildings and over the rocky seaside cliff. Serving as a pyramid and temple, it commands a view of the entire walled city as well as the Caribbean Sea to the east. Its walls, like those of many buildings in Tulum, slope outward while the doorposts slope inward. Much of the castle's shape arose from its having been built on too many times over the years.

In front of the temple is the sacrificial stone where the Maya held battle ceremonies. Once the stars had been consulted and a propitious day determined, a warrior-prisoner was selected for sacrifice. At the climax of the celebration, attendants painted the warrior's body blue—the sacred color of the Maya—and the chief priest cut his heart out and poured the blood over the idols in the temple. The body was given to the soldiers below, who through cannibalism acquired the strength to conquer their enemies.

To the right of El Castillo on the same plaza is the **Temple of the Initial Series.** Named after a stele found here, the temple bears a date that corresponded to the beginning of the Mayan religious calendar in the year 761 AD. The **Temple of the Descending God,** with a fading relief of a feathered, armed deity diving from the sky, stands on the other side of El Castillo's plaza. Tours in English and Spanish are 50 pesos per person, or 10 pesos per person in a good-sized group. Guides point out the details, like remains of murals and wall reliefs, which you might miss on your own. (Site open daily 8am-5pm. Admission 13 pesos, free Sun.)

The Beach

The beach by the campgrounds makes an attractive conclusion to a day at the ruins. Nude bathing is tolerated here, although it usually takes one uninhibited soul to start things going. The ever-efficient Mexican Navy drops in every once in a while to tell everyone to get back in uniform, but this only lasts until the nudity-patrol is out of sight. Managers of the *cabañas* complain if you walk through the campgrounds in the buff.

Offshore, you can see the waves mysteriously breaking on Tulum's **barrier reef,** the largest in the Americas; it runs the full length of the Yucatán peninsula, including Belize. Although the water here is not as clear as at Xel-Ha or Akumal (see the following section), the fish are just as multifarious. To enjoy them, you can rent scuba and snorkeling equipment from the dive shop (open daily 8am-5pm) at **Santa Fe Cabañas** (see Accommodations). Mask, snorkel, and fins cost 10 pesos per day. Scuba trips to reefs and *cenotes* (natural swimming holes) available (US$10-20). If you snorkel, be sure to get fins, since the 500m swim to the reef sometimes involves a struggle against a north-south current.

For a change from beaches, wave, and salty water, visit one of the *cenotes* punctuating the woods near Pueblo Tulum. Check-out the pulchritudinous **Cenote Kristal,** 5km south of Pueblo Tulum. Watch for the small patch of gravel, large enough for two cars, on the right side of the road as you head toward Chetumal. Follow a rugged path to the *cenote*. For a bigger and more serene *cenote*, go to **Escondito,** 100m back and across the road from Kristal.

Between Playa del Carmen and Tulum are some of the most spectacular beaches on the peninsula. **Xcacel,** the first beach north of Tulum, has the best waves and the fewest humans. Camping 10 pesos per night. Space for vehicles and trailers also available. The **dive shop** offers snorkeling equipment for 15 pesos per day and a scuba resort course with lecture and dive US$35. (4-day PADI open-water certification course US$200.) The beach also has a restaurant (entrees from 22 pesos). **Chemuyil,** 8km north of Xcacel, is billed as "the most beautiful beach in the world;" only a slight exaggeration. This crescent-shaped beach has sparkling, serene waters and warm, fine sand, bordered by a graceful arch of palm trees. As always, beauty has its price, though in this case it's only a 5-peso entrance fee. *Cabañas* for 1-4 people are 50 pesos. Camping costs 10 pesos per person. Meals are 15-25 pesos and up. Nick Williams, the exuberantly friendly young Englishman who runs the dive shop, rents out snorkel and scuba equipment and offers all kinds of trips in the shop's glass-bottom boat. (Snorkeling equipment 15 pesos per day. Scuba trips US$22.50 per 1-tank outing.) Scuba resort courses cost US$60 for a lecture and 35-45 minutes of practice. PADI open-water certification course costs US$250. Snorkeling trips are also available; inquire about prices (better rates for larger groups). The beach is open daily 8am-5pm.

Xcaret, meaning "small cove," lies just south of Playa del Carmen. There you can swim with dolphins or float along an underground river where the Mayans used to purify themselves with water from *cenotes* (open daily 8am-4:30pm; admission 50 pesos).

■ Near Tulum: Xel-ha And Akumal

The clear, semi-fresh waters of the *caletas* (inlets) at Xel-Ha and Akumal, both boasting 75m underwater visibility, were rediscovered only in 1920, when Sylvanus Morley made archaeological finds in the area. The road from Tulum to Puerto Juárez, from which they are easily accessible, was not opened until 1972.

Xel-Ha (clear water), the world's largest natural aquarium, boasts an inlet filled with protected tropical fish. At the entrance, pay the 15-peso fee and abandon all hope for solitary enjoyment of the richness of nature here. The small snorkeling area is packed with busloads of tourists from Cancún and Cozumel. (Open daily 8am-5:30pm.)

Most of the swimmers hover along the edges and near the docks. If you long for peace, search for the altar which was discovered in an underwater cave nearby. It is possible but dangerous to swim into the cave, although the idols have long since been stolen. Mask, snorkel, and fins are available for 25 pesos. Lockers (3 pesos plus 30 peso deposit) and towels (3 pesos) are also available at the changing/showering area. (Open daily 8am-4:30pm.) Xel-Ha also maintains a small archaeological site across the highway from the inlet entrance. **El Templo de Los Pájaros** and **El Palacio,** small Classical and post-Classical ruins, were only recently opened to the public. The former (the ruin farthest into the jungle) overlooks a peaceful, shady *cenote* (swimming permitted). The jungle at Xel-Ha is swarming with mosquitoes, so bring insect repellent. (Site open daily 8:30am-5pm. Admission 8 pesos.)

While visitors to Xel-Ha can observe the fish from above-water walkways, all the action at **Akumal** is below the surface. Two **dive shops** in Akumal offer snorkeling and scuba equipment and trips at identical rates. Snorkeling equipment rents for US$6 per day. Snorkeling boat trips for groups of six or more are US$15 per person. Scuba diving trips are US$21 per one-tank dives. Cavern-diving courses (US$130) and cave-diving courses are also available (inquire for details). Windsurfers rent for US$15 per hour; private instruction is US$60. The **Akumal Dive Shop** is open daily 8am-1pm and 2-5pm; the **Akumal Dive Center** is open 8am-5pm. The inlet at Akumal is smaller than at Xel-Ha and is gradually evolving into a resort area with luxury hotels. Many tour groups visit both sites, but if you only have time for one, choose Xel-Ha.

Xel-Ha lies 15km north of Tulum, and Akumal is 10km past that. Get on any northbound **bus** and ask to be let off at the site of your choice. People who don't feel like waiting for a bus to show up often hitchhike, as the road is well-traveled. Getting back to Tulum at the end of the day can be especially challenging, as buses begin to

COBÁ

thin out. Vigorously wave down a bus if one passes. If you're lucky, a second-class bus will pick you up en route to Tulum or to Cancún. Locals will usually be able to tell you when the next one is coming.

A few kilometers south of Tulum on the coast road lies the 1.3-million acre **Sian Ka'an Biosphere Reserve.** (Entrance free; contact Amigos de Sian Ka'an in Cancún for details, tel. 84-95-83). From within the reserve the tiny fishing towns of Boca Paila and Punta Allen may be reached.

■■■ COBÁ

Deep within the densest part of the Yucatán jungle, 40km northwest of Tulum, Cobá receives fewer tourists and less money than sites like Chichén Itzá and Tulum. As a result, only a few of the estimated 6500 buildings at the site have been excavated. Colorful lizards and butterflies (and the ever-fierce Yucateco mosquito) gambol with a symphony of birds in the jungle which surrounds and covers most of this ancient city which is estimated to have spread over 10 sq. km. Cobá means "wind-ruffled waters" in Maya and the five small lakes which dot the area most likely explain the location of the ancient city. With the right timing at Cobá you may find yourself alone atop a pyramid with a view of the lakes.

Buses leave Tulum at 6am and 11am (6 pesos, 30 min.) to take you to Cobá. Check for first-class Mérida-bound buses that may be able (and willing) to drop you at Cobá on the way. Friendly drivers on the way to Cobá (and also Cobá-bound, possibly cooperative, mega-tour buses) may be intercepted at the Cobá *crucero* north of Tulum Pueblo.

As you enter the ruins, the main path forks. Just to the left, a stele signals the start of one of hundreds of the well-engineered ancient Mayan roads called *sacbe* (white road). The right branch leads to the **Grupo Cobá.** The 25m-high **Temple of the Churches** was built over seven 52-year periods, each associated with a new chief priest. Only the front face of the Temple of the Churches has been excavated to reveal several attached corbel-vaulted passageways as well as a few free-standing ones. From the top you can see some of the lakes that made this region so attractive to the Mayans, and the gray stones of the impressive **Nohoch Múl** pyramid.

As you return to the main trail from the pyramid and continue on farther into the jungle, the remains of a **ballcourt** appear on the sides of the trail. From what is known of the game, neither hands nor feet could be used, and the winning team was sacrificed on the altar of the gods. A right on the road and a left as the path forks will take you to the **Conjunto de las Pinturas** (Assembly of the Paintings). On the way stand several stelae with hieroglyphs placing the Cobá settlement early in the seventh century. Many of the stelae have been badly eroded by the jungle climate, and the murals lining the temple on top of the pyramid have not fared much better, but the imagination-sparking details which remain are exquisite. On the right after 800m the Macanxoc, or Stelae, group offers the chance to ponder a small plaza and eight stelae.

Back on the main path from the Temple of the Paintings, you can bump along 2km to the largest of Cobá's monuments. At the outer limits of the site, the **Nohoch Múl** (Big Hill) pyramid, the highest Mayan structure on the Yucatán Peninsula, soars 40m above the jungle. Just before the pyramid, Stela No. 20 stands in front of a small ruin. The stele depicts a dignitary of high rank (note plumed crest and rich clothing) standing on a board held by two slaves. A deciphered date on the stela reads Nov. 30, 780.

Mayan priests once led processions up the pyramid's 12 stories. All that remains of the carvings on the pyramid are images of the diving god and the honey bee god. (The Mayans gave special value to honey and even used it as money, along with coconuts and jade stones.) A sweeping view of the jungle-camouflaged dead city awaits your weary bones at the top. At dawn and dusk the sun's rays highlight the ruins. The early-bird visitor reaps double rewards, avioding the heat and viewing the site in maximum relief. In any case, bring a water bottle, a hat, and mosquito repellent. During the high season, 11am-2pm are peak tourist hours. (Ruins open daily 8am-5pm. Admission 13 pesos, free Sun. Tours US$25 per person in Spanish, US$33 per person in English, French, or Italian.)

The **Hotel Bocadito** (next to the restaurant) offers budget accommodations for overnight visitors. Small but decent rooms with private showers and bathrooms, but no hot water. (Room for 1-2 people 30 pesos. AmEx, MC, Visa accepted. To make reservations call 87-16-65.) Another option is **Hotel Isabel,** but the rooms are stuffy and bathrooms are communal. (Check-out noon. Singles 15 pesos. No charge for additional people in the room.) The restaurant adjacent to the hotel serves *típico* dishes; *pollo a la yucateca* goes for 15 pesos. (Restaurant open daily 6am-9pm.) Swimming is sometimes possible in **Hotel Villa Arqueológica's** pool for the steep price of a drink or a meal. Inquire politely at the restaurant or bar. Hotel Villa Arqueológica also rents pool tables (10 pesos per hour). Tennis rackets are available to restaurant customers as well (US$20 deposit). While you hope and pray for a bus to arrive, you can eat at **Restaurant Bocadito,** 200m before the bus stop, on the right when entering town. The four-course *menú del día* costs 25 pesos (open daily 6:30am-9pm). Avoid the overpriced stands in the parking lot of the site advertising "real" Mayan food. If you must, **Los Flamingos** is the cheapest of the lot.

Swimming in the lagoon near the ruins is free. The shore nearest the ruins is a bit weedy and mucky, but the far shore is reputedly much nicer. Ask a kid to show you the best place to swim.

The only **bus** that can take you back to Tulum leaves Cobá at 3pm, but buses occasionally steer clear of the Cobá area entirely. For at least a crack at public transportation, walk the 3km to the highway, where buses have no choice but to pass. The bus stops on the highway about 150m south of the Cobá access road. Buses appear without warning, so arrive early; check at the intersection for up-to-date information. **Taxis** leave from the Tulum parking lot (50 pesos, 100 pesos round-trip with 2hrs. at the ruins and a stop at a *cenote* on the way back). Buses leave Cobá for Valladolid at noon and 6:30pm (2 hrs., 10 pesos). If you want to visit the ruins from Cancún or Puerto Juárez, you'll have to take a bus to **X-Can,** an unpleasant truck-stop of a town, on the Yucatán-Quintana Roo border, and then connect with the bus from Valladolid. At Cobá, those not on a set schedule often arrange rides with other Cobá visitors or friendly guests at the Hotel Villa Arqueológica by Lake Cobá, at the opposite end of the road from the ruins. *Let's Go* does not recommend hitching.

■■■ CHETUMAL

Chetumal (pop. 190,000), the capital of the state of Quintana Roo, basks on the Caribbean's western shore just minutes north of the Belizean border. No beaches or hidden ruins here, just deteriorating brick streets and hip teenagers perusing the numerous duty-free shops. Mexican and Belizean tourists come to Chetumal to snap up appliances, electronics, and clothes. Since statehood was granted in 1975, customs procedures between Quintana Roo and its neighbors Campeche and Yucatán have become more stringent, but officials continue to wink at domestic tourists smuggling cheap imports back to their home states. For foreigners arriving from Cancún or Cozumel, Chetumal's cheap goods will come as a welcome relief. Otherwise the town serves mainly as a rest stop between the Yucatán and Tikal or Belize.

ORIENTATION

Tucked into the Yucatán's southeastern corner, Chetumal is just north of the Río Hondo, the natural border between Mexico and Belize. There are three principal approaches: Route 186 from Escárcega (273km); along the Caribbean coast from Cancún (379km); and from Mérida via Peto (414km) or Valladolid (458km).

The spiffy new **bus station** at Av. de los Insurgentes and Av. Belize is Chetumal's ground transportation hub. **Autotransportes del Caribe** serves the terminal, as does **Batty Brothers** with connections to Belize City. It is also possible to wind up at the **Autotransportes Peninsulares** station, two km further out of the city, also on Av. de los Insurgentes at Av. Palermo. This station serves Mérida exclusively with mostly first-class buses.

Travelers passing through Chetumal may wish to check luggage (1 peso per hr.) at the bus station. Next to the bus station, **Super San Francisco de Assisi,** a fully stocked **supermarket,** sells everything from sodas to swimsuits in air-conditioned comfort.

Take a taxi (3 pesos) into town. Campeche's thriving shopping district lines Av. de los Héroes, starting at Av. Efrain Aguilar at the city's market and extending one km south to the bay. Along the way, between Aguilar and the bay, Héroes crosses Héroes de Chapultepec, Lázaro Cárdenas, Plutarco Elías Calles, Ignacio Zaragoza, Obregón, O. Blanco, Carmen Ochoa and 22 de Enero, in that order. This compact commercial area encompasses most of Chetumal's hotels and restaurants. At the southern terminus of Héroes lies **Bulevar Bahía,** a wide avenue flanked by statues and small plazas that follows the bay for several kilometers. From here you can see part of Belize: it's the long spit of land stretching out to the right as you face the sea.

PRACTICAL INFORMATION

Tourist Office: On the 2nd floor in the Palacio de Gobierno (tel. 2-02-66), at Héroes and Carmen Ochoa. A/C alone makes a visit worthwhile. Best to drop by in the morning to pick up a map of the city. Open Mon.-Fri. 9am-1:30pm and 6:30-8:30pm. The office's **information booth,** on Héroes near Aguilar, also has maps of the city and is equally helpful but not as cool. Open Mon.-Sat. 8am-1pm and 5-8pm.

Consulate: Guatemala, Obregón at Av. Rafael Melgar (tel. 2-85-85). Will happily help you with your Guatemalan jaunt; for a 90-day tourist visa you'll need your passport and a photocopy, of your passport (fee US$5). For a 30-day free tourist visa, you'll need your passport plus photocopy and you'll also have to prove you have sufficient funds for your trip. Open Mon.-Fri. 9am-3pm.

Currency Exchange: Bánamex, Juárez 51 (tel. 2-11-98), at Obregón, 8 blocks south and 1 block west of the Mercado. Open Mon.-Fri. 9am-5pm. Cirrus ATM open 24 hrs. Open Mon.-Fri. 9:30am-1pm.

Post Office: Plutarco Elías Calles 2A (tel. 2-25-78), 6 blocks south and 1 block east of the Mercado. Open for stamps and *Lista de Correos* Mon.-Fri. 9am-6pm, Sat. 9am-1pm. **Fax** service available.

Telephones: Long distance *caseta* on Héroes at the Mercado near Aguilar (tel. 2-12-51). International collect calls 5 pesos. Open Mon.-Sat. 8am-2pm and 4-9pm. Public phones in Chetumal take either the rare 1 peso coins, credit cards, or LADATEL phone cards, which can be purchased at Hotel Tulum on Héroes at Aguilar. **Telephone code:** 983.

Telegrams: In the same building as the post office (tel. 2-06-51). A 10-word telegram to the U.S. costs 3.30 pesos. Open Mon.-Fri. 9am-9pm, Sat. 9am-5pm.

Airport: (tel. 2-04-65), 5km south of the city on Aguilar. **Aerocaribe** (tel. 2-66-75) serves Cancún (235 pesos). Also served by **Aerocozumel** (tel. 2-28-71), **Aviacsa** (tel. 2-77-65) to Mexico City, and **Bonanza** (tel. 2-83-06) to Mérida, Cancún, and Isla Cozumel.

Bus Stations: At Insurgentes and Belize (tel. 2-78-86). Lockers available for 1 peso per hr. **ADO** offers 1st-class service to Palenque (7 hrs., 47.50 pesos), Veracruz (16 hrs., 103 pesos), Mexico City (22 hrs., 151 pesos), Villahermosa (8 hrs. 55 pesos), Campeche (1 per day, 6 pesos), and Escárcega (5 hrs., 26 pesos). **Autotransportes del Caribe** and **Caribe Inter** (tel. 2-78-86) offer 2nd-class service to Valladolid (5 hrs., 25 pesos), Cancún (5 hrs., 42 pesos) via Tulum (3½ hrs., 21 pesos) and Playa del Carmen (4 hrs., 35 pesos), San Cristóbal de las Casas (14 hrs., 57 pesos). **Bally Brothers** offers 4 trips daily to Belize City at 11am, 2pm, 4pm, and 6:30pm (4 hrs., 15 pesos). Buses to the border (3 pesos) and Belize City

(15 pesos) leave every hour from the Mercado Lazaro Cardenas (also called Mercado Nuevo) at Calzada Veracruz and Segundo Circuito. Take a taxi (3 pesos) or a bus going to Mercado Nuevo (50 pesos). **Autotransportes Peninsulares,** Av. Insurgentes at Av. Palermo. Service exclusivelyto Mérida with **Linea Dorada** (7-13-57) and **Bus Peninsular** (7-13-58), 1st and 2nd class service 43 and 38 pesos respectively.

Luggage storage: At the bus station (1 peso per hr.).

Market: City market is located on the corner of Aguilar and Héroes. Open daily 6am-3pm daily.

Laundromat: There is no self-service laundromat in Chetumal, and nearly all full-service laundries charge by the piece rather than by the kg. **Lavafácil,** Segundo Circuito 203 (tel. 2-04-95) at Héroes, charges by the kg, but the price is steep: 12 pesos per kg. Open Mon.-Sat. 8am-6pm.

Red Cross: Chapultepec at Independencia (tel. 2-05-71), 1 block south and 2 blocks west of the main bus station, in the back of Hospital Civil Morelos. Open 24 hrs.

Pharmacies: Farmacias Canto are scattered throughout the city. One is conveniently located at the northern end of the market on Héroes (tel. 2-04-83). Open daily 7am-10pm.

Hospital: Hospital Civil Morelos, Aguilar at Juárez (tel. 2-45-98).

Police: Insurgentes at Belize (tel. 2-15-00), at the northern end of town next to the bus station. Open 24 hrs.

ACCOMMODATIONS

Chetumal caters to travelers just off the bus who would willingly sacrifice their grandmothers to Chac for a bed and a shower. Most hotels resemble motor lodges out of the late ' 70s.

CREA Youth Hostel (HI), Obregón and Calzada Veracruz (tel. 2-34-65), 5 blocks east of Héroes. Pretty far out of town, but reward is clean, modern, single-sex rooms with 2 bunks each. Student ID not required; no maximum age. Check-out noon. Palmy lawn for camping (6 pesos). Bed with sheets, towel, and locker 12.50 pesos. 20-peso deposit for sheets. Breakfast (6.50 pesos), lunch and dinner (8 pesos). Fills during July and Aug.; call to reserve.

Hotel Brasilia, Aguilar 186 (tel. 2-09-64), at Héroes, across from the market, has lobby rooms which are a bit musty, but the spacious rooms upstairs enjoy a strong breeze. Antiseptic lobby is as clean as it gets for the price in Chetumal. Private baths with hot water. Check-out noon. Singles 27 pesos. Doubles 40 pesos. Triples 52 pesos. No traveler's checks. To make reservations, wire money in advance.

Hotel Jacaranda, Obregón 201 (tel. 2-03-20), just off Héroes 5 blocks south of the market. Nicely furnished rooms are clean; bathrooms come with hot water and multi-legged creatures. Friendly management a plus. Check-out 1pm. Singles 35 pesos. Doubles 40 pesos. Any room with A/C 50 pesos. 10 pesos per additional person. Send 50% in cash to reserve.

Hotel Doris, Héroes 49, between Obregón and O. Blanco, 5½ blocks south of the market. Uninspired rooms with cement beds and surprisingly clean bathrooms (with hot water). Check-out noon. 1 bed 30 pesos. 2 beds 35 pesos. 3 beds 50 pesos. 10 pesos per additional person.

Hotel María Dolores, Obregón 206 (tel. 2-05-08), near Héroes, has clean and friendly service. Although the mattresses are lumpy, rooms have fans—plus there's a restaurant. Check-out 1pm. Singles 33 pesos. 1-bed doubles 38 pesos. 2-bed doubles 44 pesos. Triples (2 or 3 beds) 55 pesos. No traveler's checks accepted.

Trailer Park, in Calderitas 9km northeast of Chetumal, overlooks Chetumal Bay. Well-kept with thin grassy lawn and large coconut palms. Electricity, water hookups and clean bathrooms. Vehicles 28-35 pesos. Tents or hammock spaces 10 pesos per person. Spacious bungalows with kitchen 70 pesos for 1-2 people.

Security guard at night. Discounts for long stays. Local buses to Chetumal pass park gate every ½ hr. (20 min., .70 pesos).

FOOD

The café-restaurants at the end of Héroes, on 22 de Enero near the bay, are small on atmosphere but even smaller on price. Although somewhat out of the way, they're well worth the trek.

Restaurante Pantoja, M. Gandhi 181, next to Hotel Ucum just north of market, is an extremely popular family restaurant. Wash down large servings of enchiladas (8 pesos) with gigantic lemonades (2 pesos). Open Mon.-Sat. 7am-9pm.

Arcada Super and Restaurant (tel. 2-08-84), at the corner of Av. Héroes and Zaragoza is an open-air café and bar, and has a supermarket in back. "Aztec soup" 6.70 pesos. Specials 14-21 pesos. Open 24 hrs.

El Taquito, Plutarco Elías Calles 220, near Juárez 1 block west of Héroes, is the only place that makes an attempt at atmosphere. Enjoy a meal of 4 or 50 tacos (1.70 pesos each) under a huge thatched roof. *Bistec grande con verduras* 15 pesos. Open Mon.-Sat. 9am-midnight.

SIGHTS

Mexicans and Belizeans converge on **El Mercado.** Nothing else in town is of much interest to strangers, although a new **Museo de la Cultura Maya** featuring replicas of ruin sites and the history of Chetumal is scheduled to open soon at Héroes and Mahatma Gandhi, just north of the market. (Scheduled to be open daily 9am-8pm.) The nearest beach is the *balneario* at **Calderitas,** a 20-minute bus ride from Chetumal. Buses (.70 pesos) leave every ½hr. between 5am and 10pm from Av. Belize between Colón and M. Gandhi. Although the water is turbid and the shores rocky, the beach looks like a *Where's Waldo* puzzle during summer and school holidays.

Much nicer, both for atmosphere and for swimming, are the three watering holes near the town of **Bacalar,** 34km away. The local **bus** to Bacalar (3.50 pesos) leaves every hour between 5:30am and 10:30pm from Chetumal's bus station; *combis* leave every hour from the corner of Hidalgo and Primo de Verdad in front of the public library (30min., 3 pesos). The route passes **Laguna Milagros** and **Cenote Azul** before reaching Bacalar. Quieter than the popular Bacalar, especially during the week, both have bathing areas, dressing rooms, and lakeside restaurants. The huge dining room by Cenote Azul, though expensive, is right on the water.

Past the uninteresting Fuerte de San Felipe in Bacalar lie the docks of the **Laguna de Siete Colores,** named for the colors reflected in its depths. The fresh water is warm, perfectly clear, devoid of plant or animal life, and carpeted by powdery limestone, making it excellent for swimming. Best of all, it's not yet a tourist attraction; schools of bathing *niños* and novice snorkelers populate the waters. Nearby are bathrooms, dressing rooms, fruit vendors, and expensive dockside restaurants.

Much further afield from Chetumal, the small seaside town of **Xcalac** (200km, 3hrs. from Chetumal), the southernmost center of population on the spit of land extending south from the Sain Ka'an reserve, provides mellow-time bungalows, restaurants, snorkeling, and boat rentals. Nearby off the coast lies the enticing **Banco Chinchorro,** the second-largest shipwreck site in the world, making for a gnarly deep-sea treasure-hunting dive. Buses to Xcalac and the closer, less service-laden **Mahahval** (150km from Chetumal) depart daily at 7am from Av. 16 de Septiembre at M. Gandhi, 20m from the Restaurant Pantoja (18-21 pesos). For information on special tours, call 2-77-01.

■■■ CHETUMAL TO ESCÁRCEGA

The 276km road between Escárcega and Chetumal, rarely traveled by tourists, passes several Mayan ruins that cluster on the Campeche-Quintana Roo border. Largely unexcavated, undeveloped, and unrestored, these sites are mosquito-infested piles of rubble, yet awe-inspiring nonetheless. Bus service is poor and hitching difficult—this trip is not for those who need spoon-feeding, but for those who wish to see ruins before their cosmetic surgery.

Though there may be a scheduled stop at Xpujil, the numerous **buses** that travel the highway daily in each direction often refuse to stop at the ruins. From Chetumal, most drivers are going only to Bacalar (a few km west of the city); those continuing to Escarcega will have to be sold on ruins-hopping. A ride only part of the way to either main city will leave you without services along most of the route. If you gather a large group, a **taxi** will make the trip for approximately 40 pesos. Bring water and snacks in case you get stranded.

KOHUNLICH

The ruins of Kohunlich (66km west of Chetumal) consist of some 180 mounds, the vast majority of which have yet to be excavated, though plans to turn it into another Chichén Itzá are underway. Ignacio Ek and his son, both local farmers, discovered the site when they unearthed several large clay masks and jars. Nobley, they reported their findings to authorities instead of observing precedent and selling them to foreigners for a quick peso. In recognition of his scruples, Ignacio was named custodian of the site and still serves in that capacity.

The ruins' earlier Mayan name, Kohunrich, which means "Place Where the Date Trees Fruit Richly," was reportedly changed to Kohunlich because a Mexican archaeologist thought the old name sounded more Germanic than Mayan. The Eks have begun planting date palms again to re-create the oasis described in Mayan texts. Aside from this beautiful new growth, take note of the **Pyramid of the Masks.** Of the eight original larger-than-life masks flanking the central stairway, six suffered near-destruction at the hands of looters. The two that remain in good condition represent the sun god. Traces of color related to the east (red) and the west (black) remain on the masks which have thick features reminiscent of the Olmecs. The Eks sometimes give tours of the site.

The road to Kohunlich branches south off the main highway 58km west of Chetumal; the ruins lie 9km from the highway. To get there take a **bus** from the station at Av. de los Insurgentes in the direction of Escárcega and get off at Francisco Villa. Some people hitch from there, but we recommend taking a taxi to the ruins. No public transport connects the highway with the site; pray for a taxi.

XPUJIL, BECÁN, AND CHICANNÁ

The ruins of Xpujil, Becán and Chicanná lie in Campeche state, near the midpoint of the Chetumal-Escárcega highway. All are open daily 9am-5pm.

Xpujil presents a face more martial than regal. The three towers of its largest structure, visible from the highway, are topped by lattice-work rims. Very little else has been excavated. Xpujil ruins are 3km east of Becán and 34km west of the Quintana Roo border. Many buses stop in Xpujil for gas. Wait here for the next bus to the ruins, or take your chances hitching. *Let's Go* does not recommend hitching.

Becán's name, "Path of the Snake," refers to the moat (nearly 2km long) that encircles the site. Seven bridges once crossed the 16m-wide moat into the walled city's center. Built between 650 and 1000 AD, Becán's temples, visible from the highway, once towered 19-35m above the ground.

Chicanná ("House of the Snake's Mouth") was probably named after the many Chenes-style buildings still being excavated here. Their portals are dominated by huge animal figures, most with ornamentally carved, wide-open mouths. Some of these represent the earthly and celestial incarnations of the god Itzamná. Building 2, with foundations for two façade towers, is a superb example of the Río Bec style of Mayan architecture (named after the undeveloped site at Río Bec, about 40km east of Chicanná). Chicanná is on the north side of the highway.

■ Belize

Still in late post-colonial development, peopled with a wildly heterogeneous population and graced with a nearly untouched natural beauty, the tiny nation of Belize fills a unique role in Central America.

First settled in 1638 by shipwrecked English sailors, Belize gave up large quantities of precious mahogany and logwood (used for dyes) to buccaneering. After the 1655 capture of Jamaica from Spain, British soldiers and their families joined the growing settlement. The white settlers imported slaves from Jamaica and other English territories to log the wood. After 200 years of uncertain legal status and frequent skirmishes with Spain, England won decisive control over Belize at the Battle of St. Georges Cage in 1798. British Honduras became an official colony in 1862.

Belize did not achieve full independence from Great Britain until September 21, 1981. Since the 1950s, a two-party system has gradually developed in the country with the domination of the centrist People's Unity Party (PUP), headed by the cautious liberal George Price. On June 30, 1993, in an early election called by the PUP, the United Democratic Party (UDP), headed by Manuél Esquivel, broke the PUP rule for the second time in nearly 30 years in a fantastically close election. The 2000-man British garrison which has long guarded Belize against Guatemala's one-time onerous claims of sovereignty over the area is scheduled to withdraw by September 1994 amidst considerable controversy and debate.

Although the official language of Belize is English, Belizeans more commonly speak an lyrical, difficult Creole. Refugees from the Caste war of 1847-48 and from more recent fighting in Guatemala, Nicaragua, Honduras, and Salvador add a heavy infusion of Spanish, especially in the Cayo, Orange Walk, and Corozal districts. A Maya people flourished here between 300 and 1000 AD, and then, for reasons unknown, abandoned their homesteads and migrated elsewhere. Their Ketchi and Mopan-Maya speaking descendants still live in Belize. In the Stann Creek and Toledo districts to the south live Garifunas, descendants of a race created when survivors of an African slave shipwreck intermixed with so-called Red Caribe natives, forming a new culture called Garifuna or Black Caribe, unique in Belize and the Bay Islands of Honduras. East Indian and Chinese laborers who came looking for work in the beginning of the century even out the cultural melange, along with a few expatriate Americans and several thousand Mennonite farmers. Just off the coast, snorkelers and scuba divers gawk at the largest barrier reef in the hemisphere. Even jaded veterans of the Yucatán peninsula will be delighted by the beach life of Belize's 175 tiny cayes. The fishing, for anything from triggerfish to tarpon, is some of the best in the world. Some 70% of Belize's land area is covered by forest that has been only selectively or thinly logged. In addition, Belize's population of just 200,000 leaves it the most sparsely populated country in Central America. The serendipitous result is the preservation of misty jungles of the massive private and public wildlife sanctuaries, including the world's first jaguar preserve. Over 600 Mayan ruins – mostly unexcavated and unrestored—will keep archaeologists and ruin-stalkers busy for years to come.

Belizeans proudly enjoy one of the best pirated cable TV systems in the world and keep themselves well abreast of international news and national news through several weekly papers (*The Amandala* is the best). National pride runs high: nearly everyone wears Belizean t-shirts and the phrase "Belize da fu we" ("I am a Belizean too") resounds. A growing body of Belizean literature includes Zee Edgell's most recent book *In Times Like These* which explores one woman's struggle for self-definition and Zoila Elli's bright collection of short stories, *On Heroes, Lizards, and Passion*.

PLANNING YOUR TRIP

■■■ CLIMATE

A brisk prevailing wind from the Caribbean cools this sub-tropical climate. Hot and humid summer rarely sizzles at more than 95°F; winter cools dip rarely below 60°F. The rainy season extends from June through August.

■■■ USEFUL ADDRESSES

For publications and travel organizations of general interest, see Planning Your Trip in the Mexico General Introduction.

Embassy of Belize: 2535 Massachusetts Ave. NW, Washington, DC 20008 (tel. (202) 332-9636, fax (202) 332-6741).

Belize High Commission to Canada, 112 Kent St., #2005, Place de Ville, Ont. K1P 5P2 (tel. (613) 232-7389 or (613) 232-7453).

Belize Consulate: Germany, Honorary Consul, D7120 Bietigheim-Bissingen, Lindenstrasse 46-48 (tel. (+49 71) 42-39-25, fax 42-332-25).

Belize Tourist Board: In **U.S.** and **Canada,** 415 Seventh Ave., New York, NY 10001 (tel. (800) 624-0686 or (212) 268-8798, fax (212) 695-3018). Exhaustive information sheet available. In **Belize,** 83 N. Front St., P.O. Box 325, Belize City (tel. 02-772-13 or 732-55, fax 774-90). Detailed maps of Belize (BZ$5 or BZ$6) and loads of information.

Belize Tourism Industry Association, 99 Albert St., Belize City (tel. 02-757-17).

Belize Audubon Society, 12 Fort Street, Belize City (tel. 02-350-04, fax 02-349-85). Information about all national parks and wildlife, as well as where to find the birds of Belize. Sells guide to Belize's wildlife (BZ$10).

■■■ DOCUMENTS AND FORMALITIES

Passports are required of all visitors to Belize. Visits are limited to one month and travelers must demonstrate that they have sufficient funds for their visit (US$50 per day) and a ticket to their next destination. Extensions beyond 30 days cost BZ$25 and are granted by the Immigration Office, 115 Barrack Rd., Belize City.

Visas are not required for travelers from the U.S., Canada, the U.K. and Commonwealth countries, Australia, Ireland, New Zealand, France, Germany, or European Community countries. Other citizens may need visitor permits; inquire at the embassy in the U.S. (see Useful Addresses).

You will be charged a US$10 **airport departure tax** and a US$1.25 **security tax** upon leaving Belize. **Liability insurance,** required of everyone driving into Belize, can be purchased at the border from the Belize International Insurance Company (Belinsco) for around BZ$25. Be aware of potential limits on goods brought into and out of the country; for **customs** information, contact the Embassy of Belize in Washington, DC (see Useful Addresses). Carrying certain goods will keep you out of the country; Belize will not let you in if an immigration officer suspects you of drug use.

■■■ MONEY

US$1 = BZ$1.82	BZ$1 = US$0.55
CDN$1 = BZ$1.53	BZ$1 = CDN$0.65
UK£1 = BZ$3.50	BZ$1 = UK£0.29
AUS$1 = BZ$1.35	BZ$1 = AUS$0.74
NZ$1 = BZ$0.99	BZ$1 = NZ$1.01

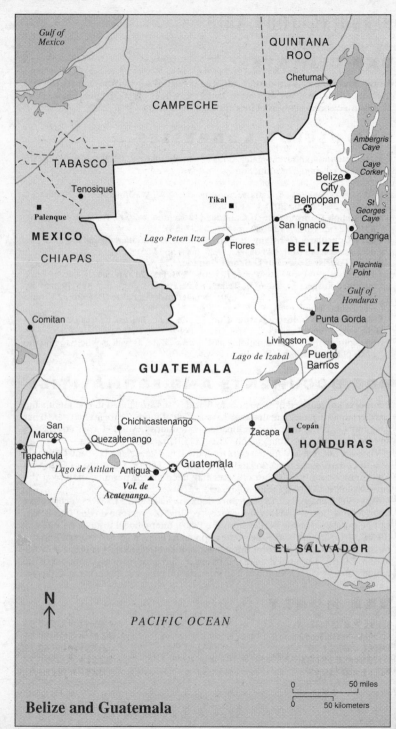

Belize and Guatemala

The Belizean dollar is tied directly to the U.S. dollar, so exchange rates are guaranteed for Americans. The official rate is fixed at US$1=BZ$2 but actual currency exchange rates at banks are slightly below two for one. U.S. dollars and traveler's checks are widely accepted. One must show a passport and a ticket out of Belize to change traveler's checks for more than US$250, or obtain a permit from the **Central Bank of Belize,** 2 Bishop St. (tel. 772-16), in Belize City. (Open Mon.-Thurs. 8am-3pm, Fri. 8am-6pm.)

If you are coming from Mexico, it's best to exchange all your pesos for Belizean dollars at the border.

■■■ HEALTH AND SAFETY

Belize hosts no endemic diseases, and there are no required inoculations. Anti-malaria tablets are recommended for extended stays in jungle areas. Water is potable in towns and resort areas.

The non-medical hazards of Belize come in three categories: the inebriated rowdy, the on-the-make male, and the anxious-to-sell-drugs heavy; a few Belizeans manage to wear many hats. Public drunkenness is not infrequent in Belize, and women should be very careful when entering a bar unescorted. Members of the British garrison stationed in Belize are somewhat notorious in this regard. Women can expect to hear various catcalls and propositions.

The intensified drug trade (some say half again as much of Belize's official GNP of 190 million is earned through illicit trafficking) has resulted in an infusion of U.S.-style gang violence into Belize. Crips and Bloods graffiti à la LA shows up on the streets of Belize City. Visitors are often approached by dealers. To avoid a confrontation, try explaining that you already got yours elsewhere, thanks. In general the South is safer than the North. Visitors to Belize City, Orange Walk and Corozal should be especially cautious.

■■■ KEEPING IN TOUCH

The **mail** system is fairly reliable. It costs BZ$0.60 to mail a letter from Belize to the U.S., BZ$0.30 for a postcard. To Europe, letters are BZ$0.75 and postcards are BZ$0.40. Have mail sent to you in Belize through general delivery. Address letters: [name]; Poste Restante; [city], Belize; CENTRAL AMERICA. First class airmail takes about 10-15 days to travel between the U.S. and Belize. Pharmacies sell stamps and have mailboxes. Belizean telephone offices generally provide cheap and reliable service.

Direct dial service is available between Belize and the U.S. and Canada. To dial Belize from either country, dial 011-501, drop the first zero from the local number, then dial the remaining numbers. For example, to reach 02-12345, dial 011-501-2-12345. **Collect calls** and **AT&T credit card calls** can be made to the U.S. through an operator in Belize (dial 115).

ONCE THERE

■■■ TRANSPORTATION

The **international airport** is located 16km northwest of Belize City on the northern highway. U.S. cash is accepted in Belize, so you need not change money at the airport. Try to share a cab, as the fare will run you BZ$30. There is also a shuttle bus that runs regularly into town (BZ$2). It heads to town on Freetown Rd., passing Barrick Rd. and Hydes Ln., crossing the river over the Swing Bridge and down Albert St. (25 min.). The **municipal airport** in Belize City offers flights to points within Belize, including Ambergris Caye and Caye Chapel (US$35). (See Getting There: Documents and Formalities for information on departure taxes.)

Travel is often over water rather than land—you'll find yourself hopping on launches and ferries instead of buses or trains. Water routes connect Belize City to Caye Caulker and Ambergris Caye; from Punta Gorda you can catch a ferry to Puerto Barrios, Guatemala. (For details, see the Practical Information sections of the corresponding areas.) Traditional overland routes are extensive, too, and Belizean buses are cheap (US$20 to cross the country the long way, north to south).

■■■ BELIZE CITY

Young Creole day-laborers wearing Chicago Bulls baseball caps over their dreadlocks blast reggae music from shiny boom boxes while smoking joints the size of large cigars. The gospel yells of a Seventh-day Adventist revival meeting mingle with the roar of buses arriving at the station. Hustlers wander through Chinese restaurants, hawking dope and faux-Mayan artifacts. Unlike the rest of the country, Belize City (pop. 60,000) lives up to Aldous Huxley's bleak commentary: "If the world had any ends, British Honduras would surely be one of them." Streams of sewage flow in the canals that line the streets. Buildings wobble on weak foundations, and the entire city needs a paint job. Poverty is endemic, and police seem to be conspicuously absent as dealers ply drugs openly in doorways across the city. The introduction of crack has sent red-eyed hustlers to tourist spots in search of easy cash. Don't even think about giving large sums of money to anyone who claims that the drug deal of the century is waiting to be made. Be careful not to show money on the street in Belize City, and remove all jewelry; you'll look fine without it. Common sense and a quick step should keep most visitors out of alleyways (at any hour) and most trouble during the daytime. In this lazy town, you should be wary of anyone who moves too quickly. Belize City is especially unsafe after dark; walk with friends along a busy main street or take a taxi in the evening. Never park your car on the street in Belize City; it almost certainly will be broken into if not spirited away altogether. Find a private, guarded lot instead, or avoid driving your car into the country in the first place.

Most visitors to Belize City are just passing through, out toward the Cayes or in toward the interior. Those dead-set on passing the day in the city can enjoy a leisurely seafood fest in one of the several fine budget restaurants and marvel at the heterogeneous street life outside.

ORIENTATION

Belize City is 154km south of Belize's northern border with Mexico and 134km east of the western border with Guatemala. The Caribbean Sea virtually surrounds the city, lapping upon the (essentially beachless) eastern, northern and southern shores. **Haulover Creek**, which runs southeast to the sea, splitting the city into northern and southern sections, is spanned by the **Swing Bridge;** most services are within a short walk of the bridge. **Queen Street** runs northeast from the Swing Bridge, and **Albert Street** forms the major thoroughfare south of the bridge. **Town Park,** at Church and Albert St., occupies the center of town and is two blocks south of the Swing Bridge.

Taxis, usually monstrous station wagons identifiable by their green license plates, can be flagged down on the street or at the stand in Town Park. The standard fare is BZ$5 per stop within Belize City, plus BZ$1 for each extra person. *Always* ask the fare before getting in.

Batty Brother and **Venus** buses serve northern routes, **Novelo's** buses go west to Benque Viejo, and the **Z-line** takes the southern route to Dangriga and Punta Gorda. Bus stations are clustered around the pound yard on Orange St., six long blocks from the center of the city (it's probably best to take a cab where you're going, especially if you have a lot of gear).

PRACTICAL INFORMATION

Belize Tourist Board: 83 N. Front St., 2nd Floor (tel. 772-13, fax 774-90). New and improved office, 3 buildings from the Swing Bridge. Offers cutting-edge maps of Belize (BZ$15) and large spoonfuls of information. (Open Mon.-Fri. 8am-noon and 1-5pm. Closes ½hr. early on Fri.).

Embassies: U.S., 20 Gabourel Ln. (tel. 771-61), at Hutson St. Take Queen st. northeast until it meets Gabourel and turn right—the embassy is the old white house on your left. Open Mon.-Fri. 8am-noon and 1-5pm. **Mexico,** 20 N. Park St. (tel. 301-93), on the waterfront. Pass the U.S. Embassy on Hutson St. and turn right—it's at the end of the block. Don't make the trip from Belize to Chetumal twice in the same day—get a Mexican tourist card in the embassy's consular division before leaving. Travelers without cards have been turned back at the border. Open Mon.-Fri. 9am-1pm. **Canadian Consulate,** 83 N. Front St. above the Tourist Bureau. Open Mon-Fri. 8am-1pm. The **British High Commission** is in Belmopan. **Guatemala** has no diplomatic corps in Belize. Obtain your visa at the border (US$5).

Currency Exchange: Any of the commercial banks clustered around Town Park change money. **Banca Serfin,** corner of Eyre and Hudson (tel. 78-25), changes dollars or Mexican pesos.

American Express: Global Travel Services, 41 Albert St. (tel. 771-85). Full-service office (including mail). Open Mon.-Fri. 8am-noon and 1-4:30pm, Sat. 8am-noon.

Post Office: Queen and N. Front St. (tel. 722-01, fax 309-36), near the Swing Bridge. Beautifully decorated stamps. Poste Restante. Open Mon.-Thurs. 8am-5pm, Fri. 8am-4:30pm; for registered mail Mon.-Thurs. 8am-noon, Fri. 1-4:30pm.

Telephones: There are public phones on both sides of the Swing Bridge. **Belize Telecommunications Limited,** 1 Church St. (tel. 1-13), off Albert St., has A/C and private booths. Direct and collect calls (no surcharge). To the U.S. or Canada, BZ$0.32 per minute, to Europe BZ$0.60 per minute. BZ$30 deposit required. Open Mon.-Sat. 8am-9pm (until 10pm for collect calls), Sun. 8am-6pm (collect calls only). **Faxes** sent at same rate as international calls. **Telephone code:** 02.

Telegrams: In the same office as the phones (tel. 1-13). To the U.S. and Canada BZ$0.32 per word, to Europe BZ$0.60 per word. Open Mon.-Sat. 8am-5pm.

Airports: Belize International Airport, 16km northwest of Belize City. Regularly scheduled flights to Houston on **Continental,** 32 Albert St. (tel. 778-27), departing daily at 12:40pm. Miami, New Orleans, San Francisco and central Mexico are serviced by **Taca Airlines,** 41 Albert St. (tel. 771-85). In addition to servicing these cities, **Tan Sanasa,** at Queen and New St. (tel. 720-57) in the Valencia Bldg., flies to all of the Central American countries. Panama Mon. and Thurs. **Aerovías,** 55 Regent St. (tel. 733-56), flies to Guatemala City (Tues.-Wed., Fri.-Sun. at 3pm, BZ$221.75) via Flores. There is an airport shuttle six times daily with pick-up points around the city. (BZ$2, call 739-77 or 778-11) Cheaper flights to the Cayes and the interior depart daily from the international airport and from the **Belize Municipal Airstrip,** on the waterfront north of town (BZ$4 for a cab ride). **Maya Airways,** 6 Fort St. (tel. 440-32), flies to San Pedro (every 2hrs., ½hr., BZ$39), Punta Gorda (½hr., BZ$120) via Dangriga (20min., BZ$50) and Placencia (1hr., BZ$90).

Bus Stations: Batty Brothers Bus Service, 15 Mosul St. (tel. 720-25), is the most comfortable. To Chetumal (every hr. 4-11am, 5hrs., 6am express 3hrs., BZ$9). To Belmopan (4 departures before 10am, 1½hrs., BZ$3) continuing on to San Ignacio (3hrs., BZ$4). Only the 6, 6:45, and 10:15am buses go to Melchor de Mencos, Guatemala (BZ$4.50)—there is a pick-up service for the express if you buy your ticket in advance. **Venus Bus Lines,** 2371 Magazine Rd. (tel. 733-54). Take Orange St. 3 blocks west of Collet Canal, then make a right onto Magazine Rd. Afternoon trips to Chetumal (BZ$10), Orange Walk (BZ$4.50), Corozal (BZ$7.50), and Sarteneja (BZ$9.50). **Z-line,** same building as Venus (tel. 739-37). To Dangriga (BZ$10) and Punta Gorda (BZ$20; both 2-5 per day). **Escalante** sends 3 yellow school buses from the pound yard across the bridge from Batty

Bros. to Orange Walk (1-3 per day, 1½ hrs., BZ$3.50). **Novelo's,** 19 W. Canal (tel. 773-72). Take Orange St. west, turn left immediately after the bridge and walk 1 block. Service to Benque Viejo (every hr. 11am-7pm, 3hrs., BZ$9) via San Ignacio (BZ$4) and Belmopan (BZ$4). Call the bus stations or contact the tourist bureau as schedules change often.

Supermarket: Brodie's, on Albert St. (tel. 770-70 ext. 266), off Town Park . Everything from groceries to mail-order abdominizers. Open Mon.-Thurs. 8:30am-7pm, Fri. 8:30am-9pm, Sat. 8:30am-5pm, Sun. 9am-12:30pm.

Laundromat: Larry's Laundry, 33 Barracle Rd. (tel. 330-83). BZ$8 self-service or BZ$10 full-service. But you don't want to be in Belize City long enough to have to do laundry. Open Mon.-Sat. 8am-5:30pm.

Pharmacy: Central Pharmacy, 1 Market Square (tel. 738-42), just south of Swing Bridge. Amply stocked. Open Mon.-Sat. 8am-9:30pm.

Hospital: Belize City Hospital (tel. 772-51), on Eve St. Outpatient entrance on the corner of Eve and Craig St. Open Mon.-Fri. 8am-4pm. On weekends, go to the casualties entrance, 1 gate to the right. Open 24 hrs. Pray against sickness.

Emergency: Call the **police emergency** number at tel. 722-43.

Police: 9 Queen St. (tel. 722-22), at New Rd. Open 24 hrs.

ACCOMMODATIONS

The best that budget hotels in the area can offer is information and a retreat from the dirt of the city. At the very least they should be safe. Door locks should be solid, with at least one extra chain lock on the inside. Because hustlers swarm to popular hotels, managers lock their main entrances at regular hours each night. Be aware of the type of neighborhood in which a hotel is located. If it feels shady, it is. Most places serve a breakfast of toast, eggs and coffee for around BZ$5. There is a 5% room tax at all hotels.

Sea Side Guest House, 3 Prince St. (tel. 783-39). 5 blocks south of Town Park on Albert St., then left on Prince St. Breezy rooms overlooking the sea, breakfast, maps and a wealth of information. A good deal in this quiet neighborhood. Frequented by businessmen and backpackers alike. Usually full, so call ahead. Beds in a 7-bed dorm BZ$15. Singles BZ$25. Doubles BZ$35. Breakfast BZ$3.

North Front Street Guest House, 124 N. Front St. (tel. 775-95), just past A&R's Service Station. Newly renovated hotel, but dungeon-like baths in the basement. Breakfast room and balcony catch a nice breeze. A bar across the street caters to vocal locals; back rooms are less noisy. Singles BZ$15. Doubles BZ$25. Triples or quads BZ$10 per person including hotel tax.

Eyre Street Guest House, 7 Eyre St. (tel. 777-24). Turn right on N. Front St. over the Swing Bridge, past Texaco station, left on Eyre St. 1 block from U.S. Embassy. Colonial-style house with a nice porch, but no breeze and no view. Rooms have fans, but ask for a room with a window. Shared bathrooms with hot water. Owner will store backpacks. Singles BZ$40. Doubles BZ$60. Breakfast BZ$7-9.

Freddie's Guest House, 86 Eve St. (tel. 443-96), near the hospital. Walk away from the Swing Bridge on Queen St. 4 blocks to Eve St. Simple, well-kept rooms in a nice home. Room with two fans, double bed and mysterious insects BZ$35 for 1 person or BZ$40 for 2 people. Double with 2 beds and bath BZ$40. Tax included..

Marin's Travel Lodge, 6 Craig St. (tel. 451-66). Walk north from Swing Bridge on Queen St. to Barrack, 2 blocks on Barrack, then right on Craig. Antiseptic, dark basement rooms off of labyrinthine hallway. Shared bath with hot water. BZ$16 for 1-2 people.

FOOD

Lunch is the queen of meals in Belize, with dinner referred to as "tea." Good rice and beans can be had at **Babb's** (Queen and Eve St.) or **Gon's** (Barrick Rd. and Hyde's Ln.). To cool off, fresh lime juice and the domestic Beliken brew (BZ$2 per bottle) are the drinks of choice. Meat pies and fruit tarts are Creole specialties that make a good snack. In addition, the multi-ethnic community supports some high-quality Chinese and Indian restaurants. Lobster is available in season (July 15-March 15). Beware: open sewers indicate a low standard of sanitation.

Macy's Restaurant, 18 Bishop St. (tel. 734-19), 1 block southwest of Town Park, between Albert and S. Side Canal St. Outstanding Belizean food cooked with coconut milk and fresh ingredients. Menu changes daily but whole fish, rice and beans are ever at hand with huge glasses of lime juice to rinse it all down (with coleslaw and fried plantain, BZ$7). Open Mon.-Sat. 11:30am-9:30pm.

Dit's Restaurant, 50 King St. (tel. 733-30), between Albert and S. Side Canal St. A café/bakery, fanned by fancy saloon-style fans. Standard rice and bean dishes. Try the *garnaches*, tortillas fried with beans and topped with hot sauce and cheese (BZ$0.35 each). Known locally for great pastries, including coconut, custard and lemon pies. Open Mon.-Sat. 7am-9pm, Sun. 8am-4pm.

Ark Restaurant and Community Center, 109 N. Front St., just past the Texaco Station. A shining jewel in the moral morass of Belize City. Bernard, the chef and owner, is a retired nutritionist from the U.S. Army who returned to his native Belize and found God on a late-night evangelical TV show. The community center helps teens stay off the street. Bernard serves a great cowfoot soup (BZ$5), plus other regional specialties, and loves to talk politics and religion. Open Mon.-Sat. 7am-midnight, Sun. 2pm-midnight.

Picadilly, 35 Queen St., below the Hard Rock Café. Eat on the balcony and observe local behaviors, or enjoy the air-conditioned bar. A variety of dishes at a variety of prices. Specialties include *tandoor* chicken (BZ$8) and curried shish-kebob. Open Mon.-Thurs. 11am-3pm and 6-10pm, Fri.-Sat. 11am-midnight, Sun 1-11pm.

GiGi's Café and Patio, 2-B King St. (tel. 743-78), 2 blocks from Broodies. A red and yellow arcade ushers you inside. Outside patio dining is avilable. Selections include burgers (BZ$6.50) and stewed chicken (BZ$6). Rum and raisin ice cream BZ$3.50. Open Mon.-Sat. 11:30am-2pm and 5:30-9pm, Fri.-Sat. 11:30am-2pm and 5:30-10pm.

SIGHTS AND ENTERTAINMENT

Belize City unfortunately lacks tourist attractions. For entertainment try heading to the Swing Bridge to watch muscular Belizeans hand-crank the bridge to let tall boats pass (5:30am and 5:30pm, when there's a boat). The one building worth going out of your way to see is **St. John's Cathedral,** on Albert St. at the southern end of town. Dating from 1826, the building was built with bricks used as ballast on English ships and stands as the oldest Anglican cathedral in Central America. The lavish kings of the Mosquito Coast were crowned here.

Go for a breezy waterfront stride along **Marine Parade** or **Southern Fore Shore** road, where the city's poshest homes are isolated from the squalor. A few beaches outside of town offer some relief, but the walk back is quite a workout in the heat. It's best to stifle your urge to swim until you make the Cayes. Belizeans head to **Gillett Beach,** 7km out on Western Highway, to picnic. Check local newspapers for sporadic outdoor concerts at **Bird's Eye,** located at the southern end of Albert St. A visit to the **Belize Zoo,** 45 minutes west of the city by bus, makes a good day-trip, but leave your pack at the hotel to ease the pain of the mile-long hike into the zoo. (For directions see Belize City to Guatemala.)

The recent increase in LA-style gang-related violence threatens nighttime entertainment. As our researcher says, for now, "nightlife is abundant for the stupid white tourist with a death wish." If the situation improves: reggae bands draw large crowds to the **Lumba Yaad Bar and Grill,** 1½ miles out on Northern Highway. Locals and tourists dance under thatched roofs on decks overlooking Haulover Creek. **The Pub,** 921 N. Front St., caters to a younger crowd. **The Big Apple,** 67 N. Front St., is open on weekends. A tougher, local crowd dances here alongside neon statuettes of liberty and multi-colored Christmas lights. The **Upstairs Café,** a hang-out for British soldiers and locals in the know, has live music on Thursdays (cover BZ$4).

■ Near Belize City

So loud is the lion-like scream of the black howler monkey (called "baboon" in the local Creole) that it can be heard for over a mile and a half. The unique **Community Baboon Sanctuary** was established in 1985 when local farmers signed a voluntary pledge to abide by certain conservation plans in order to protect the playful, vocal humanoids. Centered on the tiny village of Bermudian Landing, eight villages and entirely privately held land make up the 20 square miles of sanctuary which protect approximately 1600 black howler monkeys. Visitors to the sanctuary will be certain to hear the endangered monkey's loud, respiring howl and most probably will also catch sight of the dark vegetarians hanging out in troops in the tree canopy.

A small natural history museum (Belize's only one), a number of local guides knowledgeable not only about the monkeys but about local flora as well (tours BZ$10) and basic bed and breakfast accommodations (BZ$15) welcome the visitor to friendly **Bermudian Landing.** One bus leaves Belize City for Bermudian Landing (25mi.) daily at 12:30pm from Mosul St. just down from Batty Brothers terminal (1hr., BZ$4.50). Another bus leaves from Euphrates Ave. at 5:15pm. Industrious travelers have taken the early bus and caught rides back into Belize City by nightfall. If you stay the night, a bus returns to Belize City at 5:30am daily. Call Bermudian Landing (tel. 444-05) for more information.

Thirty-one miles north of Belize City near Rock Stone Pond Village, off of the old Northern Highway, the ruins of **Alton Ha** once functioned as a major ceremonial center in the Classic Period (250-900 AD) and through trade linked Caribbean shores with inland Maya centers. Two main plazas and 13 temples and residential structures complete the site. Two trucks make the 1½-hr. trip daily, leaving Belize City Sun.-Thurs. at 11am, Fri.-Sat. at 3:30pm. It is possible to hitch a ride back in the afternoon, although accommodations are available at the site. (Site open daily 8am-4:30pm; BZ$3.)

THE CAYES

The Cayes (more than rhymes with "keys"), Belize's 175 coastal mini-islands, are this age's service-enhanced answer to the perennial quest for the perfect tropical isle. Like pennies from heaven, world-class diving, snorkeling, and fishing opportunities await both experienced lovers of the deep and the newly converted. Investors have become increasingly hip to the isles' built-in tourist appeal, however, and both the town of San Pedro on Ambergris Caye and Caye Chapel boast landing strips and posh hotels. For the time being, activity remains concentrated on Ambergris Caye and, to a lesser extent, nearby Caye Caulker; most of the islands remain uninhabited mangrove swamps.

The cayes right off the Belize City shoreline are the most accessible. Flights from the municipal airport take vacationers to Ambergris Caye and Caye Chapel, and regularly scheduled launches zip travelers from Belize City to Caye Caulker, the less commercialized favorite of budget travelers. Charter a launch to reach the other cayes (ask at the Shell Station by the Swing Bridge in Belize City). Goff's Caye and English Caye are popular daytrips.

■■■ CAYE CAULKER

Caye Caulker cools and calms the spirit after the dingy crowdedness of Belize City. Gekkos sun themselves, coconut trees sway in the afternoon breeze, and the pace of life is slow, slow, slow. Five Mestizo families from the Yucatán settled here in 1850 to fish. Their descendants now run modest seaside hotels where you can feast on lobster tails (in season July 15-March 15) and beer. There is a seductive impulse to just sit back, nurse another rum punch, and forget what day it is.

The local community is quiet, laid-back, and uniformly friendly, but they aren't receptive to loud North American tourists on their island. Guest house signs warn against raucous late-night behavior. This is the perfect sleepy town if Jimmy Buffet is one of your personal heroes, but it isn't the place to party hard. Wind down and enjoy yourself.

Snorkeling and scuba trips to the reef offer an escape from the heat, the pesky mosquitoes and the raging lassitude of the shore. True, there's no sandy beach, but you won't find jet-skis, T-shirt boutiques, or tequila-crazed teen vacationers on the rampage, either.

ORIENTATION

Zoom from Belize City to Caye Caulker by **high-speed launch** (45 min., BZ$15). Several islanders make daily round trips leaving the caye promptly at 6:45am and heading back between 10:30 and 11am from **A&R's Service Station** (a.k.a. the Texaco station), 73 N. Front St., two blocks from the Swing Bridge. Skippers circle like sharks outside the station, trying to recruit passengers. Ask inside for a reliable boatman named Chocolate, who runs a mahogany skiff called *Soledad* and is the first to leave in the morning. The other boats leave whenever a group gathers. Generally boats leave every half-hour between 9am and 4pm, so don't fret if you get into town after noon.

Inspect all crafts before boarding; a charter ride on an overcrowded boat with a puny motor can become a three-hour tour. Any boat going to San Pedro will stop at Caye Caulker on request. To avoid the clamor of Belize City harbor, fly to Caye Caulker from the municipal (or the more expensive international) airport (15min., BZ$39 one-way, BZ$70 round-trip).

In 1961, Hurricane Hattie split the elongated Caye Caulker into two pieces. The town of Caye Caulker lies on the northern tip of the southern portion. There are no street signs in Caye Caulker—indeed, there are no street names and no addresses. Two parallel dirt roads, known informally as "the front street" and "the back street," run north-south through town. A leisurely walk from end to end takes 15 minutes. A hand-drawn map, on display at most restaurants and guest houses, will help you get your bearings. Landmarks include the police station, on the front street at the center of town, and the two largest piers, which jut out on the east and west sides of the island, a bit south of the police station.

PRACTICAL INFORMATION

Tourist Information: Dolphin Bay Enterprise (tel. 22-14), on Front St., is a good source of information about flights, scuba, and snorkeling trips, as well as daytrips to the outlying cayes. (Open Mon.-Fri. 9:30am-noon and 2-5pm, Sat. 9:30am-noon.)

Currency Exchange: The spiffy new **Atlantic Bank** on Back St. near the middle of town offers cash advances on MC and Visa, and money exchange. (Open Mon.-Fri. 8am-noon and 1-2pm, Sat. 9am-noon.) **Celi's Mini-Supermarket** (see below) will also change cash and traveler's checks during store hours.

Post Office: Celi's Mini-Supermarket (tel. 21-01), at the southern end. Mail picked up on Tues. and Fri. Poste Restante available. Open for postal services Mon.-Fri. 8am-noon and 3-6pm, Sat. 9am-noon. Mini-supermarket open until 7pm.

Telephones: Belize Telecommunications Limited (tel. 21-68 or 21-69), on the 2nd floor of a green and tan building near the middle on Front St. Free international collect calls. Open Mon.-Fri. 8am-noon and 1-4pm, Sat. 8am-noon. Deposit required. **Telephone code: 022.**

Telegrams: Same office and hours as telephones.

Boats: Boats returning to Belize City leave at 6:30am, 7am, 8am, and 3pm (BZ$10). At 9:45am a boat leaves Caye Caulker for San Pedro (BZ$15, ½hr.)

Airstrip: In easy walking distance from town. Any San Pedro-Belize City flight will stop on request at Caye Caulker. (See San Pedro listing.)

Market: Jan's Deli, between Chocolate's and Cabana's at the north end of Front St. Buy batteries, tampons, film, and other necessities. Open Mon.-Sat. 7am-1pm and 3-7pm, Sun. 8am-noon. **Chan's,** on Back St., is open Mon.-Sat. 7am-9pm, Sun. 7am-1pm.

Medical Services: Caye Caulker Health Center (tel. 21-66), 2 blocks from the police station. Open Mon.-Thurs. 8am-noon and 1-5pm, Fri. 8am-noon and 1-4:30pm. Emergency only after hours.

Police: (Tel. 21-20), in a green- and cream-colored house by the basketball half-court on the front road. 1-man squadron available 24 hrs. inside or out on the court.

Laundromat: Just in front of Pinx on Front St. BZ$10 a load, wash and dry. No self-service. Open daily 9am-9pm.

ACCOMMODATIONS

Simple hotels, communal showers, cold water and fans keep the Cancún jet set away. Look for a place on the Caribbean side, right on the water; a steady breeze keeps you cool here while giving the cold shoulder to voracious mosquitoes and sand flies. Campers can wander to a desolate part of the isle or pitch tents at Ignacio's for BZ$3.50 (see below). To minimize attacks by kamikaze mosquitoes, burn mosquito coil (BZ$1.50) and keep the lights off. Many places have few rooms and fill up between Nov. and April; a reservation isn't a bad idea.

Tom's Hotel (tel. 21-02). Arriving at the island, it's on the far left overlooking the Caribbean. Cut through the cemetery at Tropical Paradise and walk up the beach a bit. Unassuming, cozy rooms with feeble ceiling fans. Spiffy, communal bathrooms. Young travelers read, rap, and drink rum on the breezy veranda. Check-out 10am. Singles BZ$15. Doubles BZ$21. Triples BZ$34. Cabañas for 3 people with private bath and hot water BZ$53.50.

Hotel Miramar (tel. 21-57), to the right of the main pier in the center of town, offers clean rooms on the cheap side, although its location isn't so cozy. Check-out 10am. Still, it's hard to beat singles for BZ$12, 1-bed doubles for BZ$18, 2-bed doubles for BZ$21, and triples for BZ$25. Special 3-person room with hot-water private bath BZ$45.

Riva's Guest House (tel. 21-38), at the north end of town, above one-time Aberdeen's Chinese Restaurant. 8 turquoise fan-bedecked rooms off a yellow hall. Pleasant veranda. Check-out 10am. Singles BZ$11. Doubles BZ$16.

Vegas' Far Inn (tel. 21-42), on Front St. across from BTL, the telephone office. Tony, the proprietor, had a bit part in the film *Mosquito Coast.* Summer camp-like lodge with hammocks by the sea for all the lounging you can stand. Shared bathrooms with hot water and strong fans. Check-out noon. Singles BZ$35. Doubles BZ$45. Camping BZ$12.60 per person. Send 50% deposit to reserve. Visa, MC, and traveler's checks accepted.

Daisy's Hotel (tel. 21-50), very close to Celi's, but disadvantageously set back from the water. A symphony in bright tropical blue. Spacious big blue rooms in excellent shape, if set back from breeze. Cold-water bathrooms in blue. Strong fans. Genuinely friendly management lives next door, past the contingent of canines. Check-out 10am. Send 50% deposit to reserve. Downstairs singles and doubles BZ$20 (BZ$15 if you stay a week), with private bath BZ$30. Upstairs 2-3 person room BZ$25. Add BZ$10 during high season.

FOOD

Caye Caulker's restaurants are legendary for cheap seafood and laid-back (i.e. slow) service. Lobster and eggs for breakfast cost just BZ$5.50, but your food may not arrive until lunchtime. To some, the wait is annoying; to others, it's simply an excuse to down a few more beers. Several homes post signs advertising daily specials, including some of the best pastries and conch fritters on the island. A few restaurants close in the off-season.

Sandbox (tel. 22-00), past the police station on the way to the cut. Under the cozy light shed by low-hanging lamps, eat mounded platefuls of local specialites prepared with a dash of international style. Homemade pasta and vegetarian dishes also served. Fish filet with sweet pepper and onions, rice, and salad (BZ$10), conch fritters (BZ$4), and not-to-be-missed coconut ice cream for dessert (BZ$3). Open daily noon-3pm and 5-10pm. Kitchen closes at 9pm.

Marin's Restaurant and Bar (tel. 21-04), on the back path behind the church. An old favorite. Inside, lights pulse to a reggae beat, while cooler and quieter dining takes place on the back patio. Conch soup for BZ$5.50 and Marin's outrageous special, including lobster, fish, shrimp, and conch for BZ$17. Rocky, the bartender, will deny that there is any rum punch left, but it's worth the plea (BZ$3). Open daily 8am-2pm and 5:30-10pm.

Glenda's, behind Syd's (below). The place for breakfast. Icy, fresh orange juice (BZ$4 per bottle). Coffee, eggs, bacon, and delicious newly baked bread and cinnamon rolls (BZ$5). 5 small tables upstairs. Lobster burritos (BZ$1). Open Mon.-Sat. 7am-10pm for breakfast, noon-3pm lunch.

Pinx Restaurant and Bar, Front St. next to the police station. Friendly atmosphere and homestyle cooking. Spanish and Creole specialties; try the delicious conch fritters. *Tostadas* BZ$1, waffles and coffee BZ$5. Open Mon.-Sat. 7am-10pm.

Syd's, on the back path by Glenda's. If open, best bet on the Caye for lunch. Tacos BZ$0.25, 3 *garnaches* BZ$1, burritos BZ$1.50. On Saturday night, catch the island-renowned BBQ. Open daily noon-3pm and 6-9pm.

SIGHTS AND ENTERTAINMENT

Faintly visible to the east of Caye Caulker lies a stretch of the 250km **Barrier Reef,** the largest reef in this hemisphere and just 10min. away by launch. Half-day snorkeling trips to the reef's shallow coral gardens and deeper channels are the most popular and economical diving options. Boats leave between 9-10:30am, stop at three snorkeling sites, and return by early afternoon. A competitive alternative to hallucinogens, both in price and sensory stimulation (BZ$25 plus gear rental, no flashbacks). Rent fins, a mask, and a snorkel from the snorkel/pastry shop in the center of town. (Rentals BZ$5 plus credit card deposit. Open daily 8am-5pm.)

Captains hang out at the docks soliciting passengers. Before arriving at the docks, ask around for the name of a reliable operator. Be sure to leave your valuables ashore. Chocolate is a reliable informant: ask for him between November and August at **Chocolate's Gift Shop** (tel. 21-51). Other local fishermen offer spearfishing trips to the reef (BZ$15-20 per person). Ask for Harrison and his boat, the Rice & Beans, to take you on a relaxing, day-long cruise to **San Pedro** and the **Hol Chan Marine Reserve** at the Barrier Reef, including two snorkel stops, for BZ$25. Most hotels can also arrange trips.

Frenchie's, past Chocolate's, caters to the scuba enthusiast. 2-tank dives cost BZ$80, with gear BZ$105. They also offer night diving for BZ$55. **Belize Diving Services** (tel. 21-43), behind the soccer field, offers a 2-tank dive for BZ$70, with gear BZ$100. A 4-day NAVI or PADI certification course costs US$300. (Open Mon.-Sat. 8:30am-5pm, Sun. 10am-4:30pm.) Ambergris Caye offers more extensive diving opportunities.

For sailing trips to the surrounding cayes and to San Pedro, find Gamuza at Pinx Restaurant or at the dock. Bring rum, and he'll supply coconut milk and the sailboat *Tina* for snorkeling on the high seas (BZ$20, snacks included). In the near future camping trips to nearby, deserted Goff's Caye may be available. Ask for Harrison.

Caye Caulker's only strip of sandy beach lies north of town at what locals refer to as the "split" or the "cut," where Hurricane Hattie split the island. Although this is a good area for snorkeling, would-be tanners beware: insects are especially fierce here because of the heavy vegetation nearby. Opt instead for the piers on the Caribbean side of the island.

For entertainment, islanders and oven-toasted travelers tend to follow a two-stop circuit. **Pinx Restaurant and Bar** serves rum and lime around the bar to locals and *gringos* alike, and you'll get a good dose of Caye Caulker humor and outrageous fish stories. Pinx often shuts down before the official midnight closing time. Afterwards, islanders drift down to the **Reef Bar** for rum and Coke and reggae.

While you're on Caye Caulker, find Ellen McCrae, a resident marine biologist and conservationist who wisely changed her research from the Bering Sea to the Caribbean and moved to Belize for good. She conducts marine biology tours of the reef, as well as bird-watching expeditions. She can tell you everything you could possibly want to know about coral reefs and marine life.

■■■ AMBERGRIS CAYE AND SAN PEDRO

A paltry 36 miles north of Belize City lies Belize's leading tourist destination, Ambergris Caye. Although fishing remains a vigorous industry for many of the town's 2500 permanent residents, tourists are fast becoming the island's most lucrative catch. The main attraction—the Barrier Reef—brings in hordes of scuba enthusiasts, although **San Pedro,** the main town on the isle, also attracts travelers seeking a tropical respite with a little more to keep busy than Caye Caulker.

Ambergris Caye does have a good beach, and because the Barrier Reef runs right along the isle's eastern shores, diving is easier here than at Caye Caulker. The **Hol Chan Marine Reserve,** just south of Ambergris, attracts an assortment of pampered fishies who expect stale bread from divers. (Admission BZ$3.)

Several flights depart daily for Ambergris Caye from the international and municipal airports in Belize City (BZ$78 round-trip; see below Practical Information). Several boats link the island with the mainland. The Hustler leaves from the Bellevue Hotel Mon.-Fri. at 4pm, Sun. at 1pm, 1¼hrs., BZ$40 round-trip. Triple J (tel. 02-443-75) leaves at 9am daily from the foot of the Swing Bridge, to return to Belize City at 3pm.

ORIENTATION

Boats from Belize City arrive at the Texaco dock on the eastern shore of the island. The first sandy road you will hit is Front St. The three streets of San Pedro that run from north to south have official names, but few locals know them by anything other than **Front, Middle,** and **Back Streets.** The center of town is on Front St. at the Children's Park and the Barrier Reef Hotel. The northern and southern ends of the island cater to the jet set while the rest of the town offers attractions for every budget. Most hotels, shops, and restaurants are located along Front St. To avoid the heat of midday, don't wander far from there; the other streets have no breeze and are home to many happy mosquitoes and sand flies.

PRACTICAL INFORMATION

Tourist Information: Gift shops have maps of the island and the Cayes. Any number of travel agencies have information about diving, mainland excursions, and flights to various destinations in Belize, Guatemala, and abroad. **Travel and Tour Belize** (tel. 20-31), on Front St. across from the Atlantic Bank, is reliable. Open Mon.-Sat. 8am-8pm.

Currency Exchange: Atlantic Bank Ltd. (tel. 21-95), located just south of town center on Front St., will change dollars and traveler's checks, and give cash advances on Visa and MC. Open Mon., Tues., and Thurs. 8am-noon and 1-3pm, Wed. 8am-1pm, Fri. 8am-3pm, Sat. 8:30am-noon. **Belize Bank** (tel. 24-82), across the street, offers the same services but fewer hours. Open Mon.-Thurs. 8am-1pm, Fri. 8am-1pm and 3-6pm.

Post Office: (Tel. 22-50), just off of Front St. near the banks. Poste Restante. Open Mon.-Thurs. 8am-noon and 1-5pm, Fri. 8am-noon and 1-4:30pm.

Telephones: Belize Telecommunications Ltd. (tel. 21-99), located at the north end of Middle St. next to the bellowing electric generator. Free collect and AT&T credit card calls to the U.S. Open Mon.-Fri. 8am-noon and 1-4pm, Sat. 8am-noon. **Telephone code** for San Pedro: 026.

Airstrip: The **San Pedro airstrip** is located at the southwest end of town and can be reached by taxi or on foot. Several airlines have offices clustered around strip. **Island Air** (tel. 24-35), sends hourly flights to Belize City Municipal Airport daily from 7am-5pm (BZ$39 one-way, 15min.). **Tropic Air** (tel. 20-12) also sends hourly flights to Belize City 7am-5pm. (BZ$70 round-trip to municipal airport. BZ$140 round-trip to international airport.) Any flight will stop on request on Caye Caulker. Reserve several days in advance during the high season (Nov.-May).

Market: Rock's Store, on Middle St. (tel. 20-44), stocks everything from suntan lotion to fresh bread. Open Mon.-Sat. 6:30am-10pm, Sun. 7am-1pm and 5-9pm. Also try the market below Milo's Hotel.

Laundry: J's Laundromat (tel. 23-73), on Middle St. near the center of town. Look for the dancing frog sign. Self-service BZ$6 wash and dry. They do it for you for BZ$8. Open Mon.-Sat. 8am-8pm (except Wed. closed at 6pm), Sun., 8am-2pm.

Pharmacy: San Carlos Pharmacy (tel. 29-28), in the "shopping center" on Front St. Open Mon.-Thurs. 8am-noon and 1-9pm, Fri.-Sat. 1-10pm, Sun. 8am-noon and 6-9pm. 24-hr. emergency service.

Medical Services: San Pedro Lion's Clinic (tel. 20-73), located behind the airstrip. Open Sun.-Fri. 8am-4pm.; Sat. 9am-noon. Emergencies 24 hrs.

Police: (tel. 20-22), located in the center of town in the San Pedro Town Hall. Open 24 hrs.

ACCOMMODATIONS

Inexpensive rooms are more scarce here than on Caye Caulker, especially during high season, but during low season many proprietors will negotiate their prices.

Milo's, north end of Front St. (tel. 20-33). Best deal in town. Simple rooms with shared bath. Try to get a room facing the water. Singles BZ$15. Doubles BZ$20. Triples BZ$25.

Rubie's Hotel, across from the school on Front St.'s south end (tel. 20-63; fax 24-34). Best bet for a sea view. Check-out noon. Doubles BZ$26, with bath (hot water) on 2nd floor BZ$52, on 3rd floor BZ$73. Triples with bath BZ$72.50. To reserve send 1 nights' deposit. Personal checks and traveler's checks accepted.

Thomas Hotel, north side of Front St. (tel. 20-61). Thomas, the endearing proprietor makes all feel welcome. Clean rooms with newly tiled bathrooms. Strong ceiling fans, but lumpy beds. Singles BZ$40. Doubles BZ$50, with A/C BZ$70.

Martha's Hotel, Middle St. near the center of town (tel. 20-53; fax 25-89). You choose: the 2nd floor has newly renovated rooms, but the 3rd floor has the breeze and the verandas. The prices are the same. All rooms have private bath with hot and cold water. High season: singles BZ$46, doubles BZ$69, triples BZ$92, quads BZ$115. Low season: rooms are BZ$15-20 less.

Hotel San Pedrano, next to Thomas Hotel on Front St. (tel. 20-54; fax 20-93). The white walls with sea-colored trim make up for the lack of ocean view. All rooms have private bath. Low season: singles BZ$40, doubles BZ$50, triples BZ$60. Add BZ$10 in high season, and BZ$20 for A/C. Send 1st night deposit to reserve.

FOOD

Most restaurants in San Pedro offer continental cuisine with some local dishes and a lot of fresh seafood to spice things up. Great rice and beans with potato salad (BZ$5) is served nightly on Front St. in front of the **Barrier Reef Hotel.** The **deli** in the center of town serves cool drinks and delicious bread pudding (BZ$1, open daily 6am-6pm).

Elvi's Kitchen (tel. 21-76; fax 21-85), on Middle St. near the center of town. Famous old favorite. Built around a tree with sand on the floor. Will make you feel like you never left the beach. "Di place for seafood," a mix of Creole, continental, and seafood from BZ$8-12. Open Mon.-Sat. 11:30am-2pm and 6-10pm.

Leny's Restaurant (tel. 20-41), near the airstrip. Known locally for its Mexican food. Try the chilemole, an *escabeche*-like chicken soup prepared with lots of black *recado* (pepper), BZ$10. Enchiladas, BZ$12. Open daily 7am-2pm, 5-10pm.

Fido's and the San Pedro Grill, at the north side of Front St. Located on the water, this thatched-roof bar-and-grill is a local favorite. Live music on weekend nights. TV with CNN most of the time. The grill is open daily 7am-3pm, the bar 9am-midnight. The pizza joint is closed Wed.

Coconut's Cajun Café and Bar-B-Que House (tel. 25-05), on Middle St. near the center. Bright palmy murals on the walls and sand on the floor. Just what it sounds like. BBQ conch with veggies (BZ$15), southern fried chicken (BZ$10), bread pudding (BZ$3). Open daily 6am-10pm.

SIGHTS AND ENTERTAINMENT

Dive-a-rama. Dives-R-Us. Diver-roni. *Ad nauseam*. This is some of the best diving in the world. Even experienced divers will be amazed by the colorful array of fish and coral around Ambergris Caye, as well as the variety of diving experiences available. For non-certified scuba divers, snorkeling at the nearby **Hol Chan Marine Reserve** (BZ$3) affords an opportunity to swim amid barracudas, eels, lobsters and even an occasional benevolent shark.

A glass-bottomed boat leaves twice daily from the **Tackle Box Bar** dock near the center of town, escorting snorkelers and anyone else to the Marine Reserve. The *Southern Beauty* leaves daily at 9am and 2pm for half-day excursions (BZ$20, with snorkel gear BZ$26).

Many dive shops on the island offer similar trips and similar rates to local dive sites along the reef. The **Bottom Time Diveshop** (tel. 23-48; fax 27-66) at the Sun Breeze Resort on the south end of the isle offers a free introductory scuba lesson. Divers can go by motorboat twice daily (9am and 2pm) with certified diving instructors to various dive sites around Ambergris. (1-tank dive BZ$50, with all rental equipment BZ$70.) Bottom Time also offers PADI certification (5-day course US$350). **Tortuga Dive Centre** (tel. 24-26; fax 28-06) offers two back-to-back dives in the morning for US$40, a single dive for US$28, and a night dive for US$30. US$15 for diving equipment, US$6 for snorkeling equipment.

Stop at the **Tackle Box Bar** at the end of the pier on the southern side of town to see the sharks they keep out back. (Live music Fri.-Sat. Open Mon.-Thurs. 9am-midnight, Fri.-Sat. 9am-2am.) **Tarzan's Nite Club** (tel. 29-47), right in the middle of town. The big dance floor is complete with flashing lights, videos (Fri. and Sat.), Jane look-alike barmaids, and a waterfall. (Open Tues.-Thurs. and Sun. 9pm-midnight, Fri.-Sat. 9pm-3am. BZ$5 cover for men, BZ$5 cover for women on Sat.) **Big Daddy's** is just across the way. Dancing and live music on weekends with cover charge (varies but usually BZ$15). And it's easy to meet people any night at **Fido's Bar** (see Food).

WESTERN BELIZE

Belize's **Western Highway** runs 124km from Belize City to the frontier, spanning grassy savannas before winding into the Maya Mountains. Although you can power from Belize City to Tikal in one exhausting day, a few hours of sightseeing in western Belize will make the trip far more pleasant.

According to Belizean archaeologist Jaime Awe, there are more unexcavated Mayan sites in Belize than there are modern houses. Many of the small, grass-covered mounds visible from the roadside are, in fact, Mayan platforms, temples and plazas that will remain untouched until the money can be found to begin excavating new sites. You can visit the Belize Zoo and tickle a jaguar, spend the night in **San Ignacio,** trek through the nearby ruins of **Xunantunich** or the **Mountain Pine Ridge** national forest, or float down the nearby Macal River. From San Ignacio, the great ruins of **Tikal** in the Guatemalan Petén are a hop, skip and a bumpy three-hour bus ride away.

■■■ THE BELIZE ZOO

U.S. naturalist Sharon Matola opened a zoo when the British nature film company she worked for failed in 1983. 46km west of Belize City on the Western Highway, the menagerie has expanded to house 70 species native to Belize. Tapir, jaguar, ocelot, monkey—the sublime, the bizarre and the ugly—coexist side by side for your pleasure and bewilderment.

The zoo is refreshingly unorthodox, lacking moats, concrete platforms and cotton candy. The watchword here is symbiosis. Young guides lead you among the enclosures, pointing out elusive denizens and patiently answering questions. They may even allow you to pet Gregory and Victoria, a couple of bristly peccaries (small boars). Hand-painted signs drum home a conservationist theme, e.g. "We Macaw parrots are as scarce in this region as rice and beans on the North Pole."

Well worth a stop on the Tikal-Belize City trail, the zoo is easily accessible by car or bus. East and westbound **buses** on the Western Highway pass the 1.5km dirt access road about every hour. The fare from Belize City is BZ$2 (45 min.). (Zoo open daily 10am-4:30pm. Admission with ½hr.-tour BZ$10. Buy a distinctive zoo T-shirt for BZ$20 and help support the underfunded park.)

■■■ SAN IGNACIO

San Ignacio's (pop. 7100) tightly packed throughfare and the rough-and-tumble attitude of its inhabitants give it a spunkiness beyond its size. The village really boomed between 1920 and 1950 as a center for the vigorous exploitation of local mahogany and *chicle.* Eventually the trees dwindled, and Mr. Wrigley found cheap synthetic substances to placate gum chewers. Although livestock and agriculture account for much present-day revenue, the Cayo district—of which San Ignacio is the capital—attracts increasing numbers of so-called "eco-tourists," who come to hike, canoe, and ride on horseback through the area's stunning and varied parks and archaeological sites. San Ignacio's inexpensive food and lodging, as well as its bank and telephone office, make it a good base for exploring the bountiful **Mountain Pine Ridge** forest reserve or the Mayan ruins of **Xunantunich** (see below) before moving on to Tikal or Belize City. The San Ignacio region is also home to two Mennonite communities. Originally German farmers, the Mennonites have made Belize their home for over 50 years and grow much of the nation's fruits and vegetables on their large plantations north of the Western Highway at Spanish Lookout. They are an old-fashioned, self-sufficient community and may often be spotted trotting through San Ignacio in traditional horse and buggy.

Entering San Ignacio after passing through unexceptional next-door neighbor Santa Elena, you'll pass over the Macal River on Belize's only suspension bridge (built in 1949). The bridge entrance requires stopping at Belize's only traffic light, but don't worry about congestion in this backwoods outpost. To continue toward Benque Viejo del Carmen and Guatemala, make the first left on Old Benque Viejo Rd. and head uphill out of town. To reach the town center, take the first right onto Burns Av. and walk two blocks to Belize Bank. **Buses** stop near here. **Burns Avenue,** running north-south, is San Ignacio's commercial strip. Fast becoming legend, **Eva's Restaurant,** 22 Burns Av., serves as-official-as-it-gets **tourist information** to nearly every traveler who sets foot in San Ignacio. (Open daily 6am-midnight.) **Belize Bank,** 16 Burns Av. (tel. 20-31), changes money (open Mon.-Thurs. 8am-1pm,

Fri. 8am-1pm and 3-6pm). After hours, Bob, the owner of Eva's Restaurant, will exchange U.S. dollars or traveler's checks for Belizean dollars or Guatemalan quetzales. The town **post office** (tel. 20-49) is located above the police station near the bridge. (Open Mon.-Thurs. 8:30am-noon and 1-4:30pm; Fri. 8:30am-noon and 1-4pm; Sat. 8:30-10:30am and 1-4pm.) Across from the Venus Hotel on Burns Av., the **telephone/telegram office** (tel. 220-52), permits free international collect calls. (Open Mon.-Fri. 8am-noon and 1-4pm, Sat. 8am-noon.) If the office is closed, there are public phones in the small park in front of the police station, or try phoning from Eva's Restaurant. The **telephone code** for San Ignacio is 09. The **pharmacy** on Burns Av. under the Venus Hotel stocks many North American toiletries and stomach aids. (Open Mon.-Sat. 8am-noon, 1-5pm and 7-9pm; Sun. 9:30-11am.) **Buses** make the 75-mi. trip to Belize City daily almost every hour on the hour. Before 11am the **Novelós** bus line makes the run, after noon it's **Batty Bus Service** (BZ$5, 2½ hrs.). The **Z-Line** also goes to Belmopan (BZ$2, 1½ hrs.) and changes to Dangriga (BZ$10, 4 hrs.). **Taxis** take passengers from San Ignacio to Ciudad Melchor de Mencos at the Guatemalan border for BZ$4.

Several hotels in San Ignacio provide comfortable **accommodations** at comfortable rates. The stately **Hi-Et Hotel**, 12 West St. at Waight St. (tel. 28-28), lacks Hyatt splendor but does have tight, clean rooms with balconies, and the owner may lend you his canoe. (Check-out 11am. Singles BZ$10. Doubles BZ$20.) Just across the way, **Martha's Guest House** (tel. 22-76) offers three new lofty rooms in white, use of an airy kitchen, and a spiffy shared bath with hot water. Martha will cook breakfast for BZ$4.70. (Singles BZ$26. Doubles BZ$28.) The **Venus Hotel**, 29 Burns Av. (tel. 32-03), with its large rooms and immaculate lounge, is the Ritz-of-the-village and worth the few extra dollars. Rooms with private bath and cable TV. (Check-out noon. Visa and traveler's checks accepted. Singles BZ$22, with bath BZ$38.50. Doubles BZ$27.50, with bath BZ$44. Each additional person BZ$5.50.) **Central Hotel** (tel. 22-53), located on Burns Av. next to and upstairs from Eva's, offers simple rooms with minimal fans and hot water for those who need a hot shower in the tropics. The balcony has two hammocks for siesta. (Check-out 10am. Singles BZ$19. Doubles BZ$22. Triples BZ$28. Weekly rates available.) If it comes to it, Bob at **Eva's** may be able to put you up.

The jungle around San Ignacio hides an increasing number of retreats and lodges ranging from back-to-basics affairs to full-blown resorts. Three miles out of San Ignacio, in Bullet Tree Falls, **Parrot Nest** (tel. 237-02) cozies right up to the Mopan River. Listen to the overwhelming sounds of the jungle from your treehouse or cabin. Horseback riding (BZ$35 for a full day) and canoeing available. If you can find one, a *colectivo* from San Ignacio costs BZ$2, otherwise a cab costs BZ$6-10. (BZ$35 for a cabin. Breakfast BZ$4.50, dinner BZ$9.) Even farther away from civilization is the **Rancho de Los Amigos** (tel. 322-61), a strenuous 2km hike from the turnoff into San José Succotz directly across from the Xunantunich ferry. An acupuncturist and nutritionist have cleared only enough trees to build two immaculately clean huts and a dining area where all the cooking is done over fires. (Two meals are included for US$18 per person. Camping available.)

Low-cost **food** abounds in San Ignacio's dining establishments. At **Eva's Restaurant**, 22 Burns Av. (tel. 22-67), you'll find locals downing brews with their eggs and beans (BZ$4.75) first thing in the morning. Eva's also stocks a large collection of international postcards and Chicago Cubs posters. (Open daily 6:30am-11:30pm.) The sparsely populated **Serendib Restaurant**, 27 Burns Av., is famed for its spicy Sri Lankan curry but also offers a wide variety of steaks (BZ$10) and curry dishes. (Open Mon.-Sat. 9:30am-3pm and 6:30-11pm.) The **Paradise Café**, at the corner of Burns Av. and Waight St., serves ice cream in air-conditioned comfort. (Open daily 10am-2pm and 4-10pm.)

Only ½ mile from San Ignacio lie the lazy traveler's Mayan ruins; it's no trek at all to **Cahal Pech** (Place of the Ticks). Although Cahal Pech is only considered a medium-sized Mayan center, it has produced some of the earliest evidence of occupation in the area (from 1000 BC until 900 AD). Excavation at the site began only in 1988, and part of its attraction is the chance to see archaeologists performing the delicate excavation and restoration necessary to make a tourist site. Visiting archaeologists grumble about the overly imaginative restoration of the site. Make the call yourself, but take a cab from San Ignacio to avoid the uphill climb in the midday sun (BZ$5). Be sure to clarify that you're going to the Cahal Pech ruins. (Admission BZ$3.) On the way down, stop for a drink mixed with local bitters at the **Cahal Pech Bar and Grill** and enjoy a great view with the best breeze in San Ignacio.

To enjoy the local rivers without getting wet, "Remo Dan" at **Float Belize, 28** Benque Rd. (tel. 32-13), rents fully-outfitted, three-person **canoes** for full-day trips (BZ$30). Canoe tours are the best way to visit the **Panti Nature Trail** at Ix Chel Farm, 6 miles west of San Ignacio near Chaa Creek where you can take a self-guided tour to learn about the astounding medicinal uses of the area's flora. (Self-guided tour BZ$5, guided tour BZ$30. Call 08-231-80 for more info.) Ask for Tony at Eva's.

Dance and sweat at the **Blue Angel** night club on Hudson St. Ugly rumor has it that the fence on the second-floor balcony was constructed after rambunctious British soldiers nearly threw someone over. (Cover charge on weekends for live bands. Open Tues.-Thurs., Sun. 7pm-midnight, Fri.-Sat. 7pm-3am.)

■ Near San Ignacio: San Antonio, Mountain Pine Ridge, Xunantunich, and Caracol

Half an hour from San Ignacio by taxi (BZ$5) is the Mayan village of **San Antonio** (not to be confused with the San Antonio near Punta Gorda). Three Mayan families settled here in 1890. Since then, the population has grown to 1000 and San Antonio has become a celebration of Mayan culture. The five García sisters, Mayan sculptors and artists, run a **museum** of Mayan art (admission BZ$6). The sisters have devoted their lives to the preservation of Mayan sculpture, and they make slate carvings of figures and glyphs from Mayan mythology. Their work has been exhibited in Japan, England and Germany. You can stay overnight in San Antonio at the **Chichan Ka Lodge,** a traditional Mayan building. (Singles BZ$25, doubles BZ$30.) From there, Mountain Pine Ridge is a short drive.

Mountain Pine Ridge, just south of San Ignacio, is a great daytrip for civilization's discontented, especially if they have a car. Tall conifers, mountains surpassing 1000m, ancient caves and clear streams grace the large forest reserve, accessible by a road branching off the Western Highway just east of San Ignacio at Georgeville. Don't miss the **Hidden Valley Falls** in the park's northwest corner, where a stream plunges 300m into a misty valley. Other attractions include the cave at the Río Frío and the naturally formed pools of the Río On which make for great swimming and sliding. To camp in the reserve, obtain a permit (BZ$15) from the Ministry of Agriculture in Belmopan. Contact Mr. Rosado (tel. (22) 10-21-06), Director of the Forestry Department. If you're stuck without one and you believe in miracles, try arguing. Remember to bring food, since there are no facilities in the park. If you do not have a car but want to visit the reserve, you and up to five other people may wish to hire a taxi in San Ignacio. Ask for Chris and his Mercedes-Benz Unimog at Eva's (BZ$35 per person with a 5-person minimum for a full-day tour).

Past San Ignacio on the road to Guatemala, **El Castillo,** the main temple of **Xunantunich,** towers in the distance to the right. Xunantunich (Maiden of the Rock) was an important city in the late Classic period (700-900 AD) and either a rival or a satellite settlement of Tikal. Only partially excavated and studied, the ruins at Xunantunich include an impressive pyramid and a view of the Belize-Guatemala border.

Xunantunich rests atop a hill, across the Mopan River and 1.5km up a dirt road from the hamlet of **San José Succotz.** About 9km from San Ignacio, Succotz is accessible by *colectivo*, several of which shuttle between the Esso station in San Ignacio and the town of Benque Viejo del Carmen on the border (BZ$1). **Batty Bus Service** heads to Benque Viejo from San Ignacio at 9am (BZ$0.50). At Succotz take the small cable-drawn **ferry** across the Mopan. (Operates daily 7:30am-noon and 1-4:30pm. Mon.-Fri. free, Sat.-Sun. BZ$1.) The dirt road leading up to the ruins is rough and steep, making for a vigorous hike or a jangly drive. Because of theft in the past, if you are walking, there should be guards at the ferry with ID cards to escort you to the ruins.

El Castillo dwarfs the other temples and unexcavated mounds. Scamper up the lower portion of the pyramid, which is still engulfed by vegetation, to the partially restored stucco frieze on the eastern corner. Here a mask is devoted to Kinich Ahau, the sun deity, and Ixchel, the moon god. From El Castillo's reconstructed roof, the settlements of Succotz, Benque Viejo del Carmen and Melchor de Mencos (in Guatemala) are visible from left to right, tucked into the green hills. (Site open daily 8am-5pm. Admission BZ$3.)

The recently excavated remains of **Caracol,** south of the Mountain Pine Ridge, have recently opened up stony doors to tourists. Canaa (Sky Place), one of the pyramids, hits the 42m mark, making it the tallest edifice in Belize. Carved monuments found at the site indicate that a war with Tikal, the major Mayan site in Guatemala, may have occurred. The road to Caracol requires a sturdy vehicle and is only passable from December through June. Trips can be arranged at Eva's in San Ignacio for about US$50 per person.

BELIZE/GUATEMALA BORDER

Unless you're toting ancient Mayan vases or the guards suspect you of drug use, the border crossing should be quick and easy. (Border open daily 6am-9:30pm.) Money changers will approach you on the Belize side, claiming to offer the best rates outside of Guatemala City on U.S. dollars for Guatemalan quetzales. They lie. The **Bank of Guatemala** branches, on the other side of the border in Ciudad Melchor de Mencos and in Flores, both convert at substantially better rates. (Open Mon.-Fri. 8:30am-6pm.) If you are going directly to Tikal and are unable to change money in a bank, the money changers at the border offer a slightly better rate than the hotels in Tikal.

In theory, all passport-carrying citizens of non-communist countries can obtain Guatemalan visas at the border, although citizens of the U.K. should attempt to confirm this beforehand. The length of the visa ranges, in apparently random fashion, from 30 days to several years. Even if you have obtained a visa beforehand, you may be asked to pay a visa fee, ranging from Q5 to US$10, at the border. Groups of tourists seem to be hit up for this fee more often than individual travelers. There is an official departure tax of Q5 when leaving Guatemala.

From the Rosita Station in Melchor, **buses** leave twice daily to Guatemala City (Q45-55, 12 hrs.), three times daily to Flores (Q10, 3½ hrs.), and four times daily to Santa Elena.

SOUTHERN COAST

■■■ DANGRIGA

Crack the bus or car window on the way down **Hummingbird Highway** to catch the scent of fresh blossoms and fruit trees. The tropical, rolling hills give way to the town of Dangriga (pop. 8100). Once known as Stann Creek, this ocean-front community is a cultural microcosm of Belize. Dangriga is home to the Garifunas-Black Caribs of mixed African and native Caribbean descent as well as mestizos, a few *gringos* and *indígenas*, and people whose families moved (or fled) here from all over Central America.

Practical Information One main road runs parallel to the ocean and crosses the **Stann Creek River,** which flows into the sea. The road is called **St. Vincent St.** south of the bridge and **Commerce St.** north of it. The **tourist information** center is located near P.J.'s Gift Shop down Commerce St. Staff takes healthy siestas. Free-lance tour guides roaming about town will arrange boat trips. **Belize Bank** on St. Vincent St. changes money and traveler's checks. (Open Mon.-Thurs. 8am-1pm, Fri. 8am-1pm and 3-6pm.) **Post office** awaits at 16 Caney St., on the south side of the bridge. Turn left off St. Vincent St. at the Belize Election Board onto Mahogany St. (Open Mon.-Fri. 8am-noon and 1-2:30pm.) Make collect and credit card calls for free at **Belize Telecommunications Ltd.,** across the street from the police (below). (Open Mon.-Fri. 8am-noon and 1-4pm, Sat. 8am-noon. **Telephone code:** 05.) **Z-line buses** (tel. 221-60), next to the river on the south side, serve Punta Gorda (Mon.-Sat. at noon, Sun. at 3pm, 5 hrs., BZ$8), and Placencia (Mon., Wed., Fri. and Sat. at 2pm, 2½ hrs., BZ$7). If you miss the connection to Placencia, catch a bus over the bumpy road through the banana fields to Mango Creek. From Mango Creek, Placencia is just a short boat ride away. Expect to pay at least BZ$5 per person, BZ$35 to charter a boat. Also to Belmopan and Belize City (3am runs and one in the late afternoon, 3½ and 5 hrs.). The **laundromat** on Commerce St., across from the statue of Christ, charges BZ$7 per load. (Open Mon.-Sat. 9am-noon and 2-8pm.) **Young's Drug Store,** on Commerce St. Alberto Paquiul, chemist and druggist, is "licensed to sell drugs and poison" as well as fresh popcorn. (Open daily 8am-noon, 2-4pm and 7-9pm.) **Clinic** (tel. 226-07) on St. Vincent St., run by Dr. Sankaar, is open Mon.-Fri. 8am-noon and 2:30-8pm, Sat. 8am-noon. The **police** are at 107 Commerce St., north of the river, 24 hrs.

Accommodations and Food Lodging in Dangriga is nothing to write home about. Where the river meets the sea, **Río Mar Hotel** (tel. 22-01) has clean rooms with flowered curtains and a view of the Caribbean. Check-out noon. All rooms have private bath. (Singles downstairs BZ$25, upstairs BZ$35. Doubles downstairs BZ$30, upstairs with TV BZ$50.) Ralph, a native Canadian, and his Belizean wife run a café and bar on the ground floor. **Pal's Guest House,** 868 Magoon St. (tel. 220-95), on the north side of the canal south of town, has simple concrete rooms with fans. (Singles with bath BZ$15, doubles with bath BZ$25.) **The Hub Guest House,** 573 S. Riverside (tel. 33-89), conveniently located across from the Z-line bus station, features eight second-story rooms off a lounge with TV. Check-out 10am. (Singles BZ$10, with bath BZ$20. Doubles BZ$20, with bath BZ$30.)

While you're in Dangriga, take some time to sample Garifuna and Creole dishes, which combine seafood with cassava, plantain, coconut and green bananas, as well as a healthy dash of the ubiquitous Melinda's hot sauce. Many women sell baked goods right out of their homes. **Ritchie's Dinette Creole and Spanish Food** (tel. 21-12), dishes out the fryjacks and johnnycakes with eggs for breakfast (BZ$5); *Panades* (4 for BZ$1), *salbutes* (BZ$0.75) and *garnaches* (BZ$0.35) for lunch. (Open Mon.-Sat. 7am-3pm and 5-11pm.) **Starlight Restaurant,** on Commerce St., serves Chinese food, curry and special cowfoot soup (BZ$6). CNN on TV, in case you care what's happening outside Belize. (Open daily 7am-3pm and 7-11pm.) **Hub Restaurant,** downstairs from the Hub Guest House, serves breakfast (BZ$5) and rice and beans (BZ$6). A good place to find information about boat trips. (Open Mon.-Sat. 7am-9pm, Sun. 7am-3pm.)

Sights and Entertainment may be synonymous in Dangriga, where there's a bar for every language and dialect. While in Dangringa, try to find some *punta* rock. On the northern end of town, the second-floor **Kennedy Club** jams on Thursday through Sunday.

Ten miles south of Dangriga (as the crow flies), the inhabitants of the friendly fishing community of **Hopkins Village** still pull wooden dugout canoes (called "dories") up onto the beach. Chickens, dogs, and children outnumber everything but coconuts in this old Garifuna village. Electricity came to Hopkins last year but the village remains unscathed. For those who are interested in nearly untouched Garifuna culture, Hopkins's relative accessibility and basic services (not to mention its beautiful beaches) make it an ideal stop. The **Sandy Beach Resort** (tel. 220-33) is a thatch-roof establishment located at the south end of the village and run by a local women's cooperative. (Check-out 11am. Singles BZ$15, with bath BZ$23. Doubles BZ$23, with bath BZ$32. Bed in a 6-bed dorm BZ$15.) The new **Caribbean View Hotel** (same tel. as above), located at the north end of town, delivers the view from two ocean-facing rooms; simple rooms with fans flesh out the hotel. (Check-out 1pm. Singles BZ$18.90, BZ$5 per additional person.) To drink with the fishermen, check out **Isabahari** or **Larubeya** ("by the beach"), both open pretty much all day. There is bus service to Hopkins leaving from the Hub in Dangriga Monday, Wednesday, Friday, and Saturday at noon (2 hrs.).

The **Cockscomb Basin Wildlife Sanctuary,** in the Maya Mountains about 20 miles south of Dangriga, 7 miles past the village of Maya, was established as a reserve in 1984 to protect the jaguar population. Although jaguars and pumas are rarely seen along the scenic trails, deer, lizards and to-die-for tropical birds abound. **Victoria Peak,** Belize's highest point (3675 ft.), rises from within the sanctuary, and a two-day hike will take prepared hikers to the summit. A visitors center, basic bunkhouse (BZ$12 for a bed), and campsites are available. Contact the **Belize Audobon Society** in Belize City (see Belize Essentials: Planning Your Trip: Useful Addresses) for more information, or write Cockscomb Basin Wildlife Sanctuary, P.O. Box 90, Dangriga. Day trips can be arranged.

Set squarely atop the reef, **Tobacco Caye** is a most excellent overnight or weekend adventure for wanna-be castaways. Ask around the bridge in Dangriga for the unmistakeable Captain Buck to charter a boat (BZ$30) out to the caye and stay overnight at **Baxter's** (BZ$25 per person) on the five-acre island. Meals are BZ$9 each, but the coconuts are free and fresh off the tree. Ask Foxy to make some coconut ginger candy, gratis.

■■■ PLACENCIA

With only a small strip of land separating the Placencia lagoon and the ocean, it almost seems as if this small peninsula could be swallowed by the sea at any moment. Not so. This resilient, (pen)insular community of old sea salts has a staying power that attracts. Main Street is a path that winds through town, just wide enough for two to walk hand-in-hand. Even for the most industrious, a day in Placencia creates a relaxed I-am-a-palm-tree-and-will-take-root-in-the-sand feeling. You'll find the best beaches in Belize here, and there is no off-season.

Practical Information Boats and buses arrive near the gas dock at the southern tip of Placencia at the very end of the 16-mile peninsula and more than 100 miles south of Belize City. The main **sidewalk,** barely wide enough for a wheelbarrow, heads north along the beach, serving as the only artery through town. Left from the dock, the **Paradise Vacation Hotel, Tentacles Restaurant and Bar,** and **Brenda's Restaurant** sit 100m down the sandy path. Otherwise, most of the activity in Placencia is located along the north-south sidewalk.

The inimitable Janice Leslie, alumna of Baruch College in New York City, lords over Placencia's service industry. Everyone who visits this village will have to reckon with her at one time or another. She holds court at the small hut next to the gas dock. This is the only beer-serving **post office** in Belize, and it also serves as an office for **Belize Telecommunications Ltd.,** a travel agency and booking agent for **Maya Airways** (to Punta Gorda, BZ$60; to Dangriga BZ$50; to Belize City BZ$93), a bus stop, a **tourist information office,** and a bar. Make free collect calls home while dangling your toes in the water. The **phone code** is 06. (Tel. 231-01. Open Mon.-Fri. 8am-noon and 1-4pm, BTL open Sat. 8am-noon.) Change money or stock up for a camping trip at **Wallen's Market,** located down the dirt road from the post office. Everything from mosquito coils to Snickers bars. Fresh produce arrives on Sundays. (Open Mon.-Wed., Fri.-Sat. 8am-noon and 4-7pm, Sun. 8am-noon.)

One **bus** leaves Placencia for Dangriga (Mon., Wed., and Sat. at 6am, BZ$7) where connections can be made on **Z-line** to Belize City. For a southern connection, catch any boat to Mango Creek or nearby Big Creek (schedule a ride at the post office; BZ$5 if the boat is full, BZ$35 for the whole boat) to make the 2pm daily bus to Punta Gorda (BZ$5, 2½ hrs.). Placencia has its own **airstrip** two miles from town with flights six times daily to points within Belize. Flights can be booked from the post office in Placencia or by calling Maya Airways directly (tel. 027-23-12).

Accommodations and Food There are a few budget hotels in Placencia, and some locals turn their homes into guest houses during busy times of year. Keep your eyes open for "Room for Rent" signs in windows of private houses along the main walkway. The well-run **Sea Spray Hotel** (tel. 231-48), on the north end of the main sidewalk across from Flamboyant's, has a spot on the beach, if you don't mind hearing the neighbors snoring. Cozy *palapa* out back on the beach is paradisiacal. Rooms with private bath are quieter. (Singles BZ$20, with bath BZ$40. Doubles BZ$30, with bath BZ$50. Nicer rooms with refrigerator, hot water, and coffee pot, BZ$50 for one, BZ$70 for two. Reserve several days in advance.) **Jamie's** (tel. 231-38), midway through town, is also on the beach. Two of the four rooms face the sea for the best deal in town. Simple clean cold-water bathroom. (Check-out noon. Singles BZ$12. Doubles BZ$24.) Although not exactly prelapsarian, the **Paradise Vacation Hotel** (tel. 231-18), next to Tentacles Restaurant and Bar, is a common rest stop for backpackers. British officers based in Placencia fill some of the simple rooms. (Singles and doubles BZ$25.) For a no-frills, budget, single room try **Lydia's** (tel. 231-77), past the Sea Spray at the north end of the sidewalk. Lydia has five tight rooms (with fans) on the ground floor of her home. Even if you don't stay, sample some of Lydia's aromatic baked goods, fresh daily. (Breakfast BZ$2-10. Check-out noon. Singles BZ$14.50. Doubles BZ$21.) If you're nostalgic for summer camp, **Lucille's Traveler's Inn** (tel. 231-90) offers rustic rooms with wood floors, fans and private bathrooms. (Singles BZ$12, doubles BZ$21.)

While the cuisine on the peninsula lacks variety, it's generally fresh and tasty. Besides the local restaurants, some women serve rice and beans with chicken out of their homes (watch for signs along the sidewalk or ask around, BZ$5). Try **Brenda's,** halfway between Tentacles and the post office, for whopping multi-course home-cooked meals for BZ$15-25. For devotees of grouper, conch steak, lobster (in season) and snapper, Placencia is, well, ecstasy. **Flamboyant's** in back of the Sea Spray serves a fish dinner for BZ$12, along with conch (BZ$10), shrimp (BZ$18), and lobster (BZ$20). (Open Tues.-Sun. 8am-11pm.) In back of the soccer field, the **Galley Restaurant and Bar** (tel. 231-33) has great fruit shakes and seaweed punch (BZ$3) in addition to conch fried rice (BZ$12) and Galley special burger (BZ$5). (Open daily 7:30am-10pm.) **Daisy's Homemade Pastries and Ice Cream** serves up a frosty dish of homemade ice cream for BZ$2. Go for rum raisin if they have it. (Open Mon.-Sat. 11am-5pm and 7-9pm.) The deck of the **Tentacles Bar and Restaurant** (tel. 231-56) is the best spot from which to view the setting sun and meet local fishermen or migratory yacht owners who might take you for a ride on their boats. Also a good spot to ask about nearby cayes. Happy Hour on Saturday evenings. (Open Thurs.-Tues. 7:30am-10pm.)

Sights and Entertainment Placencia is a good place to end the quest for a deserted island getaway. The local cayes are the tropical dream of every red-blooded Northerner. Boaters will take tourists to many of the small, uninhabited cayes around Placencia to fish, snorkel and camp in the protective environment of these isolated mini-islands. The cayes are all privately owned, but no one seems to mind if people visit them.

Ask at Tentacles for a reliable driver to take you to **Laughing Bird Caye** or **Ranguana Caye**—there are others, but these are the closest and among the nicest. Expect to pay a whopping BZ$250 for the round-trip escort, but boats can usually take up to six people, making the cost slightly more bearable. Daily sailboat excursions are also available for about BZ$50 per person. A beautiful trimaran called *Adios* runs to some of the more obscure islets. (Free soda and sandwiches. US$25 per person, 3 person minimum, 6 maximum.) Eight miles northeast of Placencia, camping (BZ$10 a night) and cabañas (BZ$30 a night) are available on **Wippari Caye.** A sailboat leaves early Monday, Wednesday, Friday, and Saturday (US$25 per person). Ask David Dial at Tentacles for more info. **Kitty's Place,** on the beach 1½ mi. north of town, has the most extensive dive shop for those interested in scuba trips to the cayes. For a one-day excursion, including lunch and two dives, Kitty's charges US$65 per person. They also arrange trips to the Jaguar Preserve for US$40 per person.

For evening entertainment, imbibe at **Tentacles Dockside Bar.** Afterwards, head to the **Cozy Corner,** behind the police station, for dancing to reggae and funk. Place bets on the "chicken drop" on Wednesdays. (See Ambergris Caye, Entertainment for the nasty details. Open Tues.-Thurs. and Sun. 8pm-midnight, Fri.-Sat. 8pm-2am.)

■■■ PUNTA GORDA

Pristine, multi-cultural, and definitely soggy, the rainforested **Toledo District** is nirvana for the dashing adventure traveler (*machete* optional). Punta Gorda, the seaside capital (pop. 3100), was founded by Puritan traders in the 17th century. Formerly an outpost for both English pirates and Spanish soldiers, Punta Gorda is now home to a British army contingent and Voice of America. After the U.S. Civil War, a group of Confederate veterans tried to establish plantations here like the ones they had left behind in the Deep South. Although their settlement failed, the descendants of their imported laborers add to Punta Gorda's ethnic and cultural mix of Garifuna, Mayan, Creole, and East Asian peoples. This town's proximity to Mayan villages and tracts of rainforest makes it a good base for both cultural and natural history explorations.

ORIENTATION AND PRACTICAL INFORMATION

Punta Gorda hugs the coastline. **Front Street** runs along the sea, and **Main Street** runs parallel to it. Most town activity is on these two streets.

Tourist Information Center, on Front St. next to the customs office. Information on tours, flights and attractions in Punta Gorda and the Toledo District. Chet Schmidt at Nature's Way Guest House (below) can tell you about jungle tours and can arrange for you to stay in a Mayan village for a day.

Post Office, on Front and King St., across from the customs office. Open Mon.-Fri. 8:30am-noon and 1-5pm.

Telephones: Belize Telecommunications Ltd. (tel. 20-48), in the same building as the post office. Free international collect calls. Open Mon.-Fri. 8am-noon and 1-5pm, Sat. 8am-noon. **Telephone code:** 07.

Buses: Z-line, on Back St. south of town, goes to Dangriga (BZ$10) and Belize City (7½hrs., BZ$20) at 5am and 11am daily.

Flights: Maya Airlines and **Tropic Air** go to Belize City from the airstrip on the west side of town (5 per day, BZ$120). Buy tickets at **Penill & Penill's Hardware Store** on Front St. (tel. 22-014). Open daily 8am-noon and 1-5pm.

Ferry: To Puerto Barrios, Guatemala, Tues. and Fri at 2pm. (BZ$10.70, 4 hrs.). Definitely get tickets ahead of time at **Maya de Indita Tienda,** 24 Main Middle St.

(tel. 22-265). Open Tues. and Fri. after 7am. Be sure to get your **visa** stamped at the police station by 1pm. If you can't bear to wait for the ferry, Paco, up the block from Honeycomb Club, runs charters to Livingston or Puerto Barrios for BZ$20.

Market: Vernon's Store, on Front St. by Sylvia's, has a wide selection of snacks and dry goods. Open Mon.-Wed. and Sat. 8am-noon and 2-5pm, Thurs. 8am-noon.

Pharmacy: Genus Pharmacy (tel. 223-18), on Main St. near the bank. Stomach aids and headache relief. Open Mon.-Sat. 8:30am-noon, 2-5pm, and 7:30-9pm.

Medical Services: Punta Gorda Hospital (tel. 20-26), at the end of Main St. near the bus station and the cemetery. Outpatient clinic and emergency room.

Police: (tel. 20-22), next to the post office. Open 24 hrs.

ACCOMMODATIONS

Guest houses in Punta Gorda are of exceptional value for the dollar. Both the less expensive and the mid-scale hotels provide clean and rather spacious rooms and renovate constantly without raising prices. In addition, proprietors don't inflate prices during the high season, so you don't find the Jekyll-and-Hyde seasonal rates common in other parts of the country.

Nature's Way Guest House and Restaurant, at the south end of Front St. (tel. 221-19). The best deal in town, with airy rooms and wooden floors. Proprietor Chet Schmidt is an endless source of information and can arrange trips to the jungle, nearby cayes and Mayan villages. Singles BZ$16. Doubles BZ$25.50. Triples BZ$35.

The St. Charles, 23 King St. (tel. 22-149). Slightly more expensive but worth it. Spacious rooms with flowered curtains, big wooden beds and vintage televisions. Check-out 1pm. Singles BZ$25, with bath BZ$32. Doubles BZ$35, with bath BZ$50.

Pallavi's Hotel, 19 Main St. (tel. 224-14). Freshly painted white and gray wooden rooms. Singles BZ$16. Doubles BZ$21.

Goyo's Inn, 49 Main Middle St. (tel. 22-086; fax 224-69), conveniently located at the center of town by the clock tower. Serves breakfast, lunch and dinner for BZ$7 per meal. Check-out noon. Singles with bath BZ$31.50. Doubles with bath BZ$35.

FOOD

Punta Gorda is a hotbed of Creole kitchens, and a hungry traveler is seldom more than 20 paces from a heaping plate of seafood, rice and fried plantain. Generally, prices are low and restaurant proprietors are talkative. Like it or not, they will often throw a lecture into the bargain. **Shaiba Tropical Restaurant and Bar** is on Front St. near the Texaco station. Owner Lida Vernon is an artist, songwriter and cook, and the godmother of Creole culture in Punta Gorda. She'll serve you a plateful of rice and beans with fish for BZ$7, along with an earful of Creole history and culture. Her famous potato pudding is BZ$2. If you only have one meal in Punta Gorda, eat it here. (Open daily 7am-2pm and 6:30pm-2am.) Visit **Man Man's 5-Star Restaurant,** on Far West St. at the northwest corner of town. When a vacationing employee of Duncan Hines said the food was "5-star," Man Man was so proud that he put a sign out front. Dining here is an unforgettable experience. Drop by in person to give Man Man a few hours' notice and he will cook you a 3-course Creole feast for BZ$9. **Miramar Restaurant,** on Front St. near the post office, has a juke box, pool tables and a malt-shop atmosphere. Shrimp sandwiches (BZ$5), slightly pricey Chinese food and papaya milkshakes (BZ$2). (Open daily 8am-4pm and 7pm-midnight.) Some people consider the newest addition to Punta Gorda's cuisine, **Punta Caliente,** 108 José Maria St. (tel. 225-61), to be its best. Located on the southern end of town, the liberally festooned thatched-roof establishment serves a variety of fresh fish filets and burgers. (Open Mon.-Sat. 7am-11pm, Sun. 7am-4pm.)

SIGHTS AND ENTERTAINMENT

When the school bell rings in Punta Gorda, flocks of children rush to the green and white striped tent that houses the **Ice Cream Parlour,** 57 Main St. From here, you have a view of Creole dancers and drummers as they parade through the streets. Chocolate-covered bananas are BZ$1 and the Black Angel ice cream is a specialty of Punta Gorda. (Open daily 4-10pm.) Older locals, farmers and fishermen frequent the **Honeycomb Club,** on Front St. Just a mile west of Punta Gorda, the **Habia Barra Garinago Cerro** is a 19-station botanical trail with an educational center and examples of self-sufficient and sustainable farming practices among the Garifuna. Ask at Nature's Way for more info. Sixteen miles outside of Punta Gorda lies the Dem Dat's Doing farm (tel. 224-70), an appropriate technology farm. For BZ$10 you can tour the farm and check out the solar lighting system, biogas, and organic perfume production. This could be the future.

An hour away from Punta Gorda is the largest Mayan village in the area, **San Antonio.** It is relatively inaccessible unless you can find a ride in town (some have had success at the Texaco station) or charter a van (BZ$75). Once there, **Bol's Hilltop Hotel** is pretty much the only place to stay, but the rates are reasonable (doubles BZ$20), and the proprietor will cook meals. About two miles down the road from Bol's is a **waterfall** and **swimming hole,** a good place to cool off and escape from insects. San Antonio is good for a day-long off-the-beaten-track excursion.

■ Mayan Village Guest House Program

Ten miles northwest of Punta Gorda is **Laguna Village,** a Ketchi-speaking Maya community. Farmers here raise corn, rice, cacao and citrus using traditional farming methods. This village, along with the other Maya villages of Santa Cruz, San Miguel, San Jose, San Pedro and the Garifuna village Barranio, has recently acquired another source of income: an eight-bed guest house, part of a pilot program to help Mayan and Garifuna villages benefit from and control the impact of tourism upon their communities. The **Mayan Village Guest House Program,** run under the auspices of the Toledo Ecotourism Association, is a 24-hr. cultural experience suited to anthropological-minded travelers who yearn for immersion.

Only eight visitors are permitted in the village at a time and are accommodated at the guest house, a rustic but cozy thatched building with bunk beds and mosquito nets. A kerosene lamp provides light in the absence of electricity. (BZ$15.50 per person.) At meal times, visitors are split into groups of two or three to eat with Mayan families in their homes (BZ$6 per meal). While you dine on tortillas and whatever was recently harvested, caught or slaughtered that day, the head of household will introduce you to his family and tell you about village life. A special drink made out of ground cacao beans accompanies each meal, and the discussion is open-ended. If there's anything you ever wanted to know about life in a Mayan village, this is your chance to find out.

In the afternoon, one of the villagers will take visitors on a nature hike on trails surrounding the village (BZ$5 per hour). After dinner and an evening of folk music, most travelers sleep soundly. In the morning, there is a hot breakfast of eggs and tamales. Participants are then required to fill out an evaluation of their experience which the villagers use to modify and monitor the program. If you are interested, the best time to arrive in Punta Gorda is Tuesady or Friday evening. Market trucks leave for the villages early Wednesday and Saturday (BZ$3). To get back to Punta Gorda, you can charter a van in advance (BZ$75), try to catch the 5am 2-line bus as it meanders through or walk out to the main highway where some travelers have caught rides (see Mexico Essentials: Once There: By Thumb).

If San Pedro is the summer blockbuster movie with no redeeming social value, then Laguna is the seldom-viewed, thought-provoking masterpiece that wins all the awards. To make arrangements, contact Chet at **Nature's Way Guest House** in Punta Gorda (see Accommodations above).

Guatemala

In May, 1993, as our researchers were preparing to depart, President Serrano of Guatemala suspended the constitution. After weeks of nervous tension, Serrano lost the backing of the military and was forced to resign. Though civilian democratic rule has been restored to the country, *Let's Go* was unable to research and update Guatemala for this edition. All the information and prices listed may have changed since the summer of 1992, when Guatemala was last researched.

All of the violent and beautiful contrasts of a post-colonial American nation coexist in Guatemala, but without the vast spaces and economic resources that have worked to diffuse tensions in the U.S. and Mexico. Guatemala struggles to withstand all of the strains that plague the ex-colonial world as a whole—the cultural, political and economic divisions between the native and the imported. This Greece-sized country contains a modern metropolis, a Mayan necropolis, misty mountain farming villages and a land-that-time-forgot landscape of volcanoes, rivers and lush, intensely green jungle. Guatemalans write the annals of their difficult history in 23 *indígena* languages and dialects, as well as in Spanish.

About half of Guatemala's nine million citizens are descended from the Quiché, who KO'd the Guatemalan arm of the Mayan Empire in 1000 AD and became the dominant force in the area. In 1524 one of Cortés's lieutenants, Pedro de Alvarado, claimed the whole country with that strange ease characteristic of Spanish explorers—his army of 635 men and four cannon sustained six casualties.

Like many other Central American countries, Guatemala first gained independence from Spain (on September 15, 1821) as a part of the Mexican Empire and then as a member of the American Federation of States, which eventually collapsed in 1840. Guatemala was then governed by a succession of military and civilian dictators, all members of the quasi-ethnic, quasi-socio-economic group Guatemalans call *ladinos*, people of European culture. In 1944 the reformist October Revolutionaries overthrew the dictatorship of General Jorge Ubico. Guatemala experimented with a socialist government, under President Juan José Arévalo Bermejo, and then a communist one, under Jacobo Arbenz, who in 1952 tried in vain to effect limited land reform. Arbenz's attempt unnerved many groups, including the U.S., which controlled a monopoly on the banana crop through the United Fruit Company. The U.S. government helped instigate a successful military coup in order to safeguard its economic interests. A procession of military dictators followed, each opposed by various semi-powerful guerrilla rebel forces.

Recently, the government has made a nominal transition to democracy. The constitution of 1986 established the election of a civilian, democratic government. The Guatemalan government has implemented economic reforms according to World Bank austerity policies in return for financial assistance, often at the expense of the more precarious sectors of the economy such as the small farmer. Despite rhetoric throughout Guatemalan history preaching for land reform, today approximately 20 extended families own more than eighty percent of the land in Guatemala in the form of plantations called *fincas*.

However, Guatemalan political leaders have remained ever-faithful to the sanguine quip of the French Revolution: "Terror is the order of the day." In the past three decades it is estimated that the army has carried out 100,000 political *extrajudicia* killings. Guatemala has one of the worst human rights records in Latin America. The country became more stable after 1985, when civilian president Vinicio Cerezo was elected, but the situation has improved in only some respects. New and powerful civil rights groups formed, and the Marxist rebel forces were politically weakened to the extent that a sane process for selecting Cerezo's successor was possible.

The private watch-dog organization Americas Watch announced in 1990 that human rights abuses had returned to the levels of the old military regimes, and "Vinicio's" government acquired a reputation for corruption and indifference. Eighty percent of Guatemalan children under five is malnourished, and half the population is either unemployed or underemployed. Guatemala is posted on the U.S. State Department's "drug problem" list in honor of its work in the transportation of cocaine and the manufacture of opium.

Discrimination against the large *indígena* population has been widespread historically and continues today. Because of this troublesome history, Guatemala hosted the international conference of indigenous peoples: *Majawil Q'ij*: 500 Years of Indigenous and Popular Resistance." *Indígenas* gathered in October 1991 to commemorate the tragic significance of Columbus's mistake and to proclaim the "New Dawn" of an era to claim the social, economic and political respect they deserve. Perhaps as a sign of change, exiled activist for indigenous peoples in Guatemala and Nobel Peace Prize laureate, Rigoberta Menchú, was allowed to return to participate in the conference. Her autobiography, *I, Rigoberta Menchú*, is a horrifying account of life on the *fincas*.

Even through adversity, Guatemala manages to maintain a veneer of normalcy, and the country is, in fact, a pleasant place to visit. Tourism is the second-largest source of foreign exchange behind coffee, so foreign visitors are eagerly courted. Guatemala City is decked out with theaters, a symphony orchestra and ritzy *salsa* discos. The massive ruins of the Mayan city Tikal is the most compelling archaeological site in the Americas, and the surrounding jungle can be parted to reveal peacocks, wild parrots, lizards and the occasional sacred jaguar. Mayan-descended Guatemalans carry out their village life on the volcanic shores of Lake Atitlán much as they did 500 years ago.

Life in Guatemala is far easier for the tourist than the native. Guatemala provides many excellent places to shop and live in high comfort on a microscopic budget. The markets are filled with dashing local clothing, leather, pottery, and woven blankets and rugs which cost a ridiculous fraction of what they would elsewhere. The budget *viajero* can find excellent meals for, believe it or not,the equivalent of about US$2.50.

PLANNING YOUR TRIP

■■■ CLIMATE

Temperature averages about 75°F. In the coastal regions it can get as hot as 100°F, while in the highlands it can get down to freezing. Nights can be cool anytime of the year. The rainy season lasts from May to October and is characterized by clear skies and afternoon or evening showers.

■■■ USEFUL ADDRESSES

The **Embassy of Guatemala** is located at 2220 R St. NW, Washington, DC 20008 (tel. (202) 745-4952). Guatemala has **consulates** in New York, Miami, Chicago, New Orleans, Houston, Los Angeles and San Francisco. For publications and travel organizations of general interest, see Planning Your Trip in the Mexico General Introduction.

■■■ DOCUMENTS AND FORMALITIES

U.S., Canadian, U.K. and New Zealand citizens need a **visa** or **tourist card** to enter Guatemala. A tourist card can be obtained upon entering Guatemala for US$5. Visas are free at Guatemalan consulates outside Guatemala. Obtain one before leaving home or at consulates in Comitán, Tapachula, or Chetumal, Mexico.

Citizens of most western European nations need only a valid passport to enter the country. Citizens of the U.K.—and often also New Zealand and Australia—may have difficulty obtaining the necessary visa, due to the ongoing dispute over the sovereignty of Belize.

■■■ MONEY

US$1 = 4.28 quetzales	
CDN$1 = Q3.61	Q1 = US$0.23
UK£1 = Q8.19	Q1 = CDN$0.28
AUS$1 = Q3.16	Q1 = UK£0.12
NZ$1 = Q2.33	Q1 = AUS$0.32
	Q1 = NZ$0.43

U.S. dollars is the only directly exchangeable currency. For other currencies use **Banco de Guatemala** or **BanQuetzal,** which has a branch at the airport in Guatemala City. They will first change your currency into U.S. dollars. All banks offer the same exchange rate and charge no commission for exchanging traveler's checks.

Bargaining is expected in markets and handicrafts shops, but not in urban shopping centers. A 10 to 15% **tip** is customary as most restaurant bills do not include gratuities.

■■■ HEALTH, SAFETY, AND SECURITY

As in Mexico, one has to be very watchful of one's health while in Guatemala. **Diarrhea** strikes most foreigners traveling here, and local amoebas love to induce cases of amoebic dysentery, generally transmitted by water, improperly cleaned foods or the handling of currency. Some travelers have found that food from road-side stands has disastrous effects on their digestive systems.

The **water** in Guatemala City and Antigua has been chemically treated and is theoretically safe to drink. Nonetheless, bottled water is a smart idea in the cities and absolutely necessary in the smaller villages. Also, avoid vegetables and fruits that absorb a lot of water that can't be peeled.

Cholera was still a presence in Guatemala as of the summer of 1992. To guard against this nasty disease, make sure your food—especially vegetables and shellfish—is well-cooked, and try to devour it before it gets cold. Always, always wash your hands before eating. For an update call the up-to-the-minute advisory recording of the U.S. State Department Emergency Hotline (tel. (202) 647-5225), or the Centers for Disease Control International Travelers' Hotline (tel. (404) 332-4559).

As of the summer of 1992, **violent crime** in Guatemala had become a serious problem. Clashes have taken place between government forces and guerrillas. Bus loads of passengers both within the city and en route to major tourist destinations have been robbed. The U.S. State Department advises tourists not to climb Guatemala's volcanoes because of the high incidence of armed robberies and violence there. To minimize danger, avoid bringing anything to Guatemala that you don't need, like jewelry. Travel only during daylight hours (before 6pm) and avoid travel on secondary roads, where assaults and rapes have occurred.

Don't go to Guatemala without familiarizing yourself with the current travel advisory through the State Department Emergency Hotline (see above). For more details, consult the U.S. embassy in Guatemala City, which provides print-outs of the travel advisory (Mon.-Fri. 8am-noon and 1-3pm). U.S. citizens can contact the embassy guard there in after-hours emergencies (see Guatemala City: Practical Information).

■■■ ALTERNATIVES TO TOURISM: LANGUAGE STUDY

Guatemala, and Antigua in particular, is full of **language institutes** where you can pick up or polish Spanish-speaking skills. Most schools offer individual instruction at flexible times (usually 4-7 hrs., 5 days per week). In a one-on-one situation, the skill of the individual teacher is the crucial factor. Weekly payment plans make it easy to switch instructors. Schools encourage potential students to make written reservations well in advance, but it is often possible and even advisable to arrive without arrangements and then shop around. Tuition averages US$40 for five days of four-hour daily instruction, five days per week. Some students have had success bargaining higher tuition down to this level. You can avoid commissions by not arranging study through a second party.

All schools can arrange homestays with Guatemalan families. Room and board goes for about US$30 per week. Many schools will also help students find apartments for extended stays.

Antigua is the center of the language study universe; at present, nearly 30 schools teach Spanish to foreigners from around the orb. The following are but a few of the schools in Antigua and elsewhere:

Proyecto Lingüístico Francisco Marroquín, Apdo. 237, Antigua. The oldest and largest school in Antigua. A non-profit foundation whose money goes back into preserving Mayan languages. Also organizes excursions to many parts of Guatemala and regular fiestas for their students. 7 hrs. per day of 1-on-1 instruction US$100 per week.

Centro de Español Don Pedro de Alvarado, 4 Calle Pte.27D, Antigua. Rates as low as US$35 per week for 4 hrs. per day.

El Centro de Estudios de Español Pop Wuj, Apdo. 68, Quetzaltenango, Guatemala (tel. 618-286). A cooperative program which donates its profits to university scholarships and educational and health programs for Guatemala's poor. US$100 per week includes homestay and all activities. In the U.S. write to P.O. Box 43685-9685, Washington, DC 20011-9685.

GETTING THERE

La Aurora International Airport in Guatemala City is served by many major **airlines** of the world. In the summer of 1992, a round-trip ticket based on a four week stay was US$580-654 from New York, US$474-710 from Los Angeles and US$520-570 from Mexico City. **American Airlines, Aviateca** (the Guatemalan national airline), **British Airways, Continental Airlines** and **Mexicana** are among the carriers serving the city.

When entering Guatemala **by land,** it is advisable to arrive at the border as early in the day as possible, both to facilitate transportation connections and to avoid delay if the border closes at an unofficially early hour (as has been known to happen). You will also want to make sure you have enough time to reach a town from the border before sunset.

Overland **bus** service connects Guatemala City and the interior to all major border crossings from Mexico, El Salvador and Honduras. (See Guatemala City: Orientation: Transportation, below, for details.) You can drive your own **car** into Guatemala. Coming from Mexico, two points of entry are recommended: at Tecún Umán on Highway CA-2 on the Pacific Coast or at La Mesilla on Highway CA-1 in the highlands. From El Salvador, use the border crossing at Las Chinamas, El Salvador/Valle Nuevo, Guatemala. From Honduras, El Florido and Agua Caliente are the crossings of choice. The Mexico/Guatemala border crossings at Ciudad Cuauhtémoc and Ciudad Hidalgo/Tecún Umán are officially open from 6am-9pm, but have service 24 hrs. The crossing at Talismán is officially open 24 hrs.

ONCE THERE

■■■ USEFUL ORGANIZATIONS

The government tourist bureau is the **Instituto Guatemalteco de Turismo (INGUAT)**, and its offices are generally widespread and helpful. Another good source of information is *Así es Guatemala*, a small newspaper-like publication put out roughly monthly detailing festival days and other tourist attractions. For the most current information on 24-hr. pharmacies, consult a local paper and look for the *Farmacias, servicio 24 horas* listing.

■■■ TRANSPORTATION

Travel **by air** within Guatemala is not particularly cheap, but it may be worth a premium to skip the hassles of bus travel during the rainy season. (See Guatemala City: Practical Information below for details on flights.) **Common buses,** cursed by some as "mobile chicken coops," are converted school buses that sit three to a bench. The long and winding road between Flores and Guatemala City will dominate your nightmares in years to come if you make the passage in one of these. **Driving** your own vehicle in Guatemala can be a hazardous experience. Road conditions are generally poor; those involved in accidents can be put in jail regardless of who is at fault; and armed car thefts are common. The safest strategy if cornered by armed bandits on the road is to surrender your car without resistance.

■■■ ADDRESSES

Many streets in Guatemalan cities are not named but numbered. This can be confusing because addresses also include the number of the building. The name or number of the *avenida* or *calle* always comes first. For example, *6 Av. 25* refers to #25 on Sixth Avenue. You will also see *6a Av. 25*, which means the same thing (*6a* short for *sexta*). We will use *6 Av. 25*. In cities that are divided into zones, we designate the zone with *z. #*, e.g. *6 Av. 25 z. 1*. A building with the address *12 Calle 6-14*, is on 12 Calle between 6 and 7 Avs. at #14.

Buildings can also be specified without any number; the two closest cross streets are used instead. For example, an address could be *6 Av., 1 Calle*, meaning at the intersection of Sixth Avenue and First Street. In a further permutation, addresses can specify the street and the *two* cross streets. For example, *6 Av., 1/2 Calles*, meaning on Sixth Avenue between First and Second Streets.

■■■ KEEPING IN TOUCH: MAIL AND TELEPHONES

Guatemala's **postal service** is plagued by strikes and poor management. If necessary, packages can be sent to the U.S. using the United Parcel Service (UPS), which has an office in Guatemala City. **First-class air mail** takes roughly 10-14 days to reach the U.S. You can receive mail general delivery at most post offices through the *Lista de Correos* (see Mexico General Introduction: Planning Your Trip: Keeping in Touch for details). Mail should be addressed: Dov WAISMAN, a/c Lista de Correos, [city], Guatemala, CENTRAL AMERICA.

Telephones are handled by **Guatel,** the national communications network. Phoning is incredibly difficult here, even from Guatel *cabinas*; try the more expensive hotels when placing international or domestic calls. Collect calls and AT&T credit card calls can be made from pay phones free of charge by dialing 190 for AT&T, 189 for MCI or 171 for an international operator. Some cities (like Antigua, for example) have limited direct dial and international operator service. Guatemala's **country code is 502**. Listen for the amazing Guatemalan feedback effect. Within the country, there are no area codes; when dialing outside of the immediate urban area it may be necessary to dial 0 first.

■■■ GUATEMALA CITY

Guatemala is not a backwater capital, with a population of two and a half million people, several universities and large European and North American cliques. The city is characterized by a particularly Central American brand of cosmopolitanism, a mingling of Guatemalans who essentially come from different planets. It plays home to both poor *indígena* ex-farmers and *ladino* high financiers. There is no middle class. It's a short, mind-blowing walk from the market on the border of Zones 4 and 9 to the shopping malls in Zone 10, but a walk that will transport you between worlds. The market is an ankle-deep bog of rotten fish and vegetables where dirty children play, kneeling women offer you huge bags of bananas for Q1, and buses spew poison into the air. In Zone 10, the streets are wide, full of shining private cars, and lined with fancy boutiques and big white mansions with manicured gardens; the mostly white population dresses in the latest European fashions.

Tourists tend to keep their sojourns here brief, and they have their reasons: grave pollution and perilous streets come nightfall. Still, the museums are quite interesting, the food fabulous and cheaper than in Mexico or Belize, the club scene intense, and people-watching on the Plaza Mayor as much a microcosmic tour of the Republic as the giant *Mapa en Relieve*.

ORIENTATION

The enormous capital divides into 21 *zonas*, but nearly all sights and services of interest to the budget traveler are in *Zonas* 1, 4, 9, 10 and 13. Walking around at night is not recommended anywhere in the city. Taxi cabs should be hired only from stands in the airport, at major hotels or at major intersections.

Zona 1, Guatemala City's **"downtown,"** is its oldest section. It houses all the budget hotels and restaurants. It has a solid reputation for muggings and robberies and is unsafe for walking after dark. Be on guard with your belongings in the daytime as well. *Calles* run east-west, with street numbers increasing as one moves southward. *Avenidas* run north-south, with numbers increasing as one moves eastward. The major thoroughfare is **6 Avenida,** which passes the **Plaza Mayor** (the city's main plaza) in the northern part of *Zona* 1 and continues south through *Zonas* 4 and 9.

Zona 4 lies immediately south of *Zona* 1. More industrial, it is full of car and tool shops and relatively free of tourist attractions. A series of northeast-to-southwest *vías* and northwest-to-southeast *rutas* (with numbers increasing north to south) complicate the established street pattern of *Zona* 1. Fortunately, *Zona* 4 is too small for you to lose your bearings.

Zonas 9 and **10** are Guatemala City's *Zonas Rosas*, realms of exclusive boutiques, fancy restaurants, five-star hotels and elite homes. The southern portion of *Zona* 10 is the *Zona Viva* (Lively Zone), where the bulk of the city's most happening (and expensive!) nightclubs and discos provide entertainment late into the night. These two *zonas* are generally pickpocket-free and relatively safe. They are divided by north-south **Avenida de la Reforma;** *Zona* 9 is to the west and *Zona* 10 to the east. *Avenidas* run parallel to La Reforma and increase eastward, starting at 1 Av. in each *zona*. *Calles* run perpendicular and increase southward. **Zona 13** lies south of *Zona* 9 and consists of several museums, parks and the international airport. It is generally safe and pleasantly remote from the hubbub of the metropolis.

Dilapidated, crowded *camionetas* (buses) go almost anywhere in the city for Q0.40. Bus #82 follows perhaps the most useful route, from 10 Av. in *Zona* 1, through *Zona* 4, and down Av. Reforma between *Zonas* 9 and 10. Returning, it travels north on Av. Reforma, through *Zona* 4, and up 9 Av. in *Zona* 1. Bus #83 goes from 10 Av. in *Zona* 1 to the airport and the *Zona* 13 attractions and returns to 9 Av. in *Zona* 1.

Micros (vans or smaller buses) observe the same routes as *camionetas*, plus many additional routes, charging Q0.40 as well. Destinations are posted on the windshields. Wave to the driver to indicate you'd like to get on, for otherwise buses might just puff by. If the one you wish to take arrives already brimming over with passengers, don't fret; there's usually room for one more.

Guatemala City has no central **bus terminal**; dozens of bus companies maintain separate offices across the city. Many buses leave from 19 Calle between 7 and 10 Avs. (near the train station in z. 1). Several others leave from the huge combined terminal/market in *Zona* 4, between 1 and 4 Avs. and 1 and 7 Calles. Few companies have offices here; buses simply idle in one of the two enormous parking lots while crews call out their destinations.

PRACTICAL INFORMATION

Tourist Office: Instituto Guatemalteco de Turismo (INGUAT), 7 Av. 1-17 z. 4 (tel. 311-333), in the Centro Cívico just south of the *Zona* 1 border. Staff helpful, knowledgeable and fluent in English. Maps (Q3) of the city and surrounding areas and invaluable free lists of bus destinations, terminals and schedules. Open Mon.-Fri. 8am-4:30pm, Sat. 8am-1pm. **Airport branch,** before passport control as you exit the plane (tel. 314-256). Open daily 6am-9pm.

Embassies: U.S., Av. Reforma 7-01 z. 10 (tel. 311-541). Open Mon.-Fri. 8am-noon and 1-3pm. Emergency assistance after hours at embassy Marine Guard, tel. 323-347. **Canada,** 7 Av. 11-59 z. 9 (tel. 321-419 or 321-413), 6th floor of Edificio Galerías España. Open Mon.-Fri. 8-11am. **U.K.,** 7 Av. 5-10 z. 4 (tel. 321-601), 7th floor of the Centro Financiero Torre II. Open Mon.-Thurs. 9am-noon and 2-4pm, Fri. 2-4pm. Consult the blue section of the phone book for other embassies (**New Zealand** and **Australia** have no embassies in Guatemala).

Consulates: Mexico, 13 Calle 7-30 z. 9 (tel. 363-573), ½ block from Av. Reforma. Get your Mexican tourist card (FMT) here. Open Mon.-Fri. 8:30am-2:30pm, Sat. 9:15-11am. Arrive as early as possible. For points farther south, inquire about visa requirements, etc., at the following Central American consulates: **Belize** is represented by the U.K. embassy. **Costa Rica,** Av. Reforma 8-60 z. 9 (tel. 319-604), #320 in Edificio Galerías Reforma. Open Mon.-Fri. 9am-3pm. **Honduras,** 16 Calle 8-27 z. 10 (tel. 373-921). Open Mon.-Fri. 8:30am-1:30pm. **Nicaragua,** 10 Av. 14-72 z. 10 (tel. 374-264). Open Mon.-Fri. 9am-1pm. **Panama,** 5 Vía 4-50 z. 4 (tel. 320-763), on the 7th floor of the Edificio Maya. **El Salvador,** 12 Calle 5-43 z. 9 (tel. 325-848). Open Mon.-Fri 8am-2pm.

Immigration Office: 41 Calle and 18 Av. z. 8 (tel. 714-670). Open Mon.-Fri. 8am-3pm. Catch bus #71 from 10 Av. z. 4. (Q0.40).

Currency Exchange: BanQuetzal at the airport keeps longest hours: Mon.-Fri. 7am-8pm, Sat.-Sun. 8am-6pm. **Banco Agro,** 9 Calle 5-39 z. 1 (tel. 514-026) is open

GUATEMALA CITY

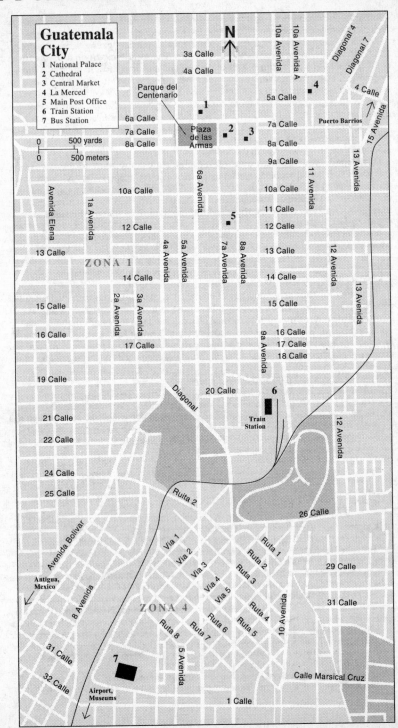

Guatemala City
1 National Palace
2 Cathedral
3 Central Market
4 La Merced
5 Main Post Office
6 Train Station
7 Bus Station

N

3a Calle
4a Calle

10a Avenida
10a Avenida A

Diagonal 4
Diagonal 7

Parque del
Centenario

5a Calle

4 Calle

1

Puerto Barrios

6a Calle
7a Calle
8a Calle

Plaza
de las
Armas

2   3

7a Calle

8a Calle

9a Calle

15 Avenida

13 Avenida

0   500 yards
0   500 meters

10a Calle

6a Avenida

10a Calle

11 Calle

11 Avenida

12 Calle

12 Avenida

5

12 Calle

ZONA 1

13 Calle

4a Avenida
5a Avenida
7a Avenida
8a Avenida

13 Calle

14 Calle

13 Avenida

Avenida Elena

1a Avenida

14 Calle

15 Calle
16 Calle

2a Avenida
3a Avenida

15 Calle

17 Calle

16 Calle
17 Calle
18 Calle

9a Avenida

19 Calle

Diagonal

20 Calle

6

21 Calle

Train
Station

22 Calle

12 Avenida

24 Calle
25 Calle

Ruta 2

26 Calle

Antigua,
Mexico

Avenida Bolivar

8 Avenida

Via 1
Via 2
Via 3
Via 4
Via 5

Ruta 1
Ruta 2
Ruta 3
Ruta 4
Ruta 5

29 Calle

10 Avenida

31 Calle

ZONA 4

Ruta 8
Ruta 7
Ruta 6

31 Calle

7

5 Avenida

Calle Marsical Cruz

32 Calle

Airport,
Museums

1 Calle

Mon.-Fri. 9am-7pm, Sat. 10am-2pm. **Banco Metropolitano,** 5 Av. 8-24 z. 1 (tel. 25-360), **Lloyds Bank International,** 11 Calle 8-20 z. 1 (tel. 532-250) and 6 Av. 9-51 z. 9 (tel. 327-580) and **Banco Internacional,** 7 Av. 11-20 z. 1 (tel. 518-066) are all open Mon.-Fri. 9am-3pm.

Central Post Office: 7 Av. 11-67 z. 1 (tel. 29-101), in the enormous pink building. Open Mon.-Fri. 7am-7pm, Sat. 8am-6pm. Lista de Correos in Room 110 (ext. 106); open Mon.-Fri. 8am-4:30pm.**Postal Code:** 01001. **United Parcel Service,** 2 Calle 6-40 z. 9 (tel. 343-794), open Mon.-Sat. 8am-8pm.

American Express, Av. La Reforma 9-00 z. 9 (tel. 311-311 or 340-040), in the Banco del Café bldg. Will hold mail for card holders or traveler's check holders. Also, will issue traveler's checks in exchange for personal checks to card holders. Open Mon.-Fri. 8:30am-4:30pm.

Telephones: Guatel main office, 12 Calle 8-42 z. 1 (tel. 531-399). Open 24 hrs. Phone, fax and radiogram service. Long distance calls may also be placed from any of the Guatel branches located throughout the city, including 7 Av. 3-34 z. 4 and 8 Av., 12 Calle z. 1. Open 7am-2pm daily. **Telephone Code:** 2.

Telegrams: At any Guatel office. Open 24 hrs.

Airport: La Aurora International Airport (tel. 318-392), about 7km south of downtown, in z. 13. Served by **American** (tel. 311-361), **British Airways** (tel. 312-555), **Continental** (tel. 353-208) and **Mexicana** (tel. 518-824) as well as several other local and international airlines. **Aeroquetzal** (tel. 347-693), **Aerovías** (tel. 325-686), **Tapsa** (tel. 319-180) and **Aviateca** (tel. 318-222) all fly to Flores (close to Tikal) for about US$130 round-trip. Bus #83 shuttles passengers between *el centro* and the airport for Q0.40. A taxi from downtown costs Q35.

Train Station: 9 Av. 18-03 z. 1 (tel. 83-031). Slow, uncomfortable, unreliable, but cheap. To Puerto Barrios Tues., Thurs. and Sat. at 7am (12 hrs., Q7). To Tecún Umán Tues., Thurs. and Sat. at 7:30am (10 hrs., Q6.30).

Buses: A morass of different terminals and lines. Consult the tourist office for their free list. Regular service to all over the country. **Border/international transport: El Condor,** 19 Calle 2-01 z. 1 (tel. 28-504), to La Mesilla, Mexican border (4 per day, 8hrs., Q20). **Transportes Galgos,** 7 Av. 19-44 z. 1 (tel. 23-661), **Rutas Lima,** 8 Calle 3-63 z. 1 (tel. 515-627), **Fortaleza,** 19 Calle 8-70 z. 1 (tel 517-994) and **Rápidos del Sur,** 20 Calle 8-55 z. 1 (tel. 51-66-78), to Talismán, Mexican border (2-24 per day, 5hrs., Q22). Rápidos del Sur also goes to Tecún Umán, Mexican border (22 per day, 6hrs., Q20) and Anguiatú, Honduras border (1:30pm, 4½hrs., Q17). **Melva International,** 3 Av. 1-38 z. 9 (tel. 310-874) and **Transportes Centroamérica,** 7 Av. 10-59 z. 1 (tel. 84-985), to San Salvador, El Salvador.

Taxis: Many companies operate taxis, but always be sure that the car is marked as a taxi and has a number. 24-hr. service: **Elma,** z. 1 (tel. 201-556), **Camino Real y Biltmore,** z. 10 (tel. 374-019), **El Corado,** z. 9 (tel. 323-052), **Sheraton,** z. 4 (tel. 316-258). From *Zona* 1 to *Zona Viva* Q35, from the airport to *Zona* 1 Q35, to *Zona* 9 or 10 Q30.

Car Rental: Tally, 7 Av. 14-60 z. 1 (tel. 51-41-13), open Mon.-Sat. 7am-8pm, Sun. 8am-6pm; at the airport (tel. 326-063), open daily 6am-9pm. Cars Q155 per day (including insurance and 100 free km, Q0.30 per additional km). **Dollar,** 6 Av. "A" 10-13 z. 1 (tel. 21-177), open Mon.-Fri. 8am-5pm; Av. Reforma 6-14 z. 9 (tel. 341-541), open daily 6am-9pm; and at the airport (tel. 317-185), open daily 6am-9pm. Cars US$37 per day, including insurance and free mileage.

English Bookstores: Arnel, 9 Calle, 7 Av. (tel. 24-631), Edificio el Centro 108. Large selection of books, but hours unreliable. Try your luck Mon.-Fri. 11am-12:30pm and 3:30-7pm, Sat. 11am-12:30pm. Best selection of U.S. magazines is at the **Book Nook** in the Camino Real Hotel, Av. Reforma 14-30 z. 9 (tel. 334-633). The latest best sellers (Q10) and U.S. newspapers (Q11-15) also on sale. Open daily 7am-9pm.

Market: Central Market, 6/8 Calles, 8/9 Avs. Open Mon.-Sat. 6am-6pm, Sun. 7am-noon. There is also a big **food market** around the bus terminal in *Zona* 4, open daily 7am-6pm. **Supermarket: Facilitos,** 7 Av. 5-34 z. 4 (tel. 341-264), open daily 7:30am-10pm.

Laundry: El Siglo, 4 Av. 13-09, (tel. 21-469). Q6 per wash, Q6 per dry. Other locations around the city. Open Mon.-Sat. 8am-6pm.

Crisis Hotline: INGUAT, the tourist office, has a 24-hr. information and crisis hotline (tel. 333-075). English spoken.

Red Cross: 3 Calle 8-40 z. 1 (tel. 125). 24-hr. emergency service.

24 hr. Pharmacies: Farmacia Sinai Centro, 4 Av. 12-74 z. 1 (tel. 515-276). **Farmacia de Urgencia,** 7 Av. 3-20A z. 9 (tel. 343-059).

Ambulance: (Tel. 128.) 24-hr. service.

Police: 6 Av. 13-71 z. 1 (tel. 120).

ACCOMMODATIONS

Zona 1 is hardly hurting for cheap hotels, but one must be willing to tolerate the noises and stench of the unmuffled, fire-breathing behemoths that traverse the streets. Even the upscale hotels in this area will only set you back about US$10. Caution: muggings are on the rise in *Zona* 1. It is not advisable to venture out alone at night.

Hoteles Centroamérica, 9 Av. 16-38 z. 1 (tel. 26-917). All you ever wanted from a hotel: peaceful lobby adorned with hanging flowers and beautifully wrought metal grates, irreproachable rooms with mirrors, closets, cupboards, TVs, hot water and free local phone calls. Singles Q24, with bath Q35. Doubles Q41, with bath Q62. Triples Q61, with bath Q90.

Pensión Meza, 10 Calle 10-17 z. 1 (tel. 23-177). The best place to overhear travel tips. Major hangout for the hippie crowd. Play ping-pong in the game room, lounge in the courtyard, or sip a beer in the attached café. Helpful bulletin board. Singles Q25. Doubles Q30. Bed in dormitory Q12.

Hotel Chalet Suizo, 14 Calle 6-82 z. 1 (tel. 513-786). "Ambiente Internacional," declares the sign out front, and it is no idle boast: the hotel's luxurious rooms attract all sorts of global nomads. Very popular and often full; get here early in the day. Tiles sparkle and water's hot. Singles Q46.80, with bath Q70.20. Doubles Q50.50, with bath Q93.60. Triples Q70.20, with bath Q117.

Hotel Colonial, 7 Av. 14-19 z. 1 (tel. 26-722). Relive the grandeur of the colonial past in crimson-colored rooms with exquisitely polished furniture, brass sinks, night tables and mirrors. Add hot water and immaculate cleanliness to get a pictureof this hotel. Singles Q58.50, with bath Q81.90. Doubles Q89.90, with bath Q105.30. Triples Q105.30, with bath Q128.70.

Hogar del Turista, 11 Calle 10-43 z. 1 (tel. 25-522), literally "home of the tourist" and aptly named. Cozily decorated with Guatemalan tapestries and rugs. Rooms have private baths, hot water and a comforting feel. Singles Q60. Doubles Q80. Triples Q100.

Hotel Tikal, 16 Calle 9-47 z. 1 (tel. 28-489). Big, bright rooms with rippling curtains and bedspreads. You can trade peace and quiet for a terrace over a busy street. Alas! Cold water only. Singles Q14.50. Doubles Q22. Singles or doubles downstairs Q20.

Hotel Villa Christ, 15 Av. 11-63 z. 1 (tel. 511-722). Large beds nearly fill up the rooms. Spotless and friendly. Enjoy complimentary toothpaste, shaving cream and morning coffee. Singles Q20, with bath Q30. Doubles Q30, with bath Q35.

Hotel Las Vegas, 16 Calle 9-49 z. 1 (tel. 276-778). In an area of a dozen budget accommodations, slightly above average. Big bare rooms with big bare beds and acceptable communal facilities. Cold water only. Singles Q15. Doubles Q20. Triples Q30, with TV Q35.

FOOD

Living solely for the sake of eating is encouraged in Guatemala City. The capital is home to various ethnic cuisines, *típico guatemalteco*, irresistible *pastelerías*, rustic and market outdoor *fondas* and luxurious five-star establishments. At many moderately priced restaurants, you can enjoy a good-sized, savory meal for little more than *tres dólares*.

Zona I

Productos Integrales, 8 Calle 5-36 z. 1 on the south side of *Parque Central*. Whole grain breads and cakes (Q3, Q2), fruit salads (Q4) and vegetarian cuisine at lunchtime in an airy and popular atmosphere. Open Mon.-Sat. 9am-7pm.

El Mesón de Don Quijote, 11 Calle 5-27. z. 1. Dine in the quaint atmosphere of Spanish bullfights and Picasso faces. *Tortilla española* Q10. *Pavesa* Q10. *Paella* for 4 Q80.

Restaurant Fu Lu Sho, 6 Av. 12-09 z. 1, or "Happiness, Prosperity, Longevity." Informal setting and huge menu popular with both tourists and locals. Chicken in curry or pineapple Q9. Meat dishes with a variety of spicy vegetables Q8.50. Open daily 10am-midnight.

Restaurant Los Tecomates, 6 Av., 15 Calle. Walk gently over the pine needles covering the floor and let the many flowers remind you of *indígena* churches. *Violín,* specialty of the house, Q18. Sirloin with salad, *aguacate* (avocado) and fries Q20. Tacos Q2.50. Open daily noon-10pm.

Piccadilly, 6 Av. 11-01 z. 1. Centrally located, cheap and spacious, it is a budget travelers' favorite. Choose from the full spectrum of Italian cuisine: tortellini, macaroni, ravioli,spaghetti (Q6-7), minestrone (Q4.50) or pizza (Q11-15). Open Mon.-Sat. 6am-midnight.

A Guy From Italy, 12 Calle 6-23 and various locations throughout the city. Laid-back, pleasant setting to have the lunch of the day (soup, bread and lasagna, canelloni, or ravioli Q4.70) or the specialty of the house, pizza de spaghetti Q12.05-17.10. Open daily 11am-10:30pm. Zonas 9 and 10

Las Tertulias, Av. Reforma 10-31 z. 10. Fancy, with a large menu, but its main attraction is the *Super Lunch Ejecutivo*: a huge multi-course meal—soup or fresh fruit, excellent bread, 2 vegetables, entree, dessert and coffee or tea—all for Q10.50. Similar *Super Cena* Q11.50. Open daily 7am-10pm.

La Spaghetteria, Av. Reforma, 11 Calle, across from the American Express office in *Zona* 10. Popular outdoor café reminiscent of Italy. Great cappuccino, pizza (Q18) and ravioli (Q18). Extensive menu includes many toothsome desserts. Open Mon.-Thurs. noon-1am, Fri.-Sat. noon-2am, Sun. noon-midnight.

La Crepe, 14a Calle 7-49 z. 9. Skip 3 meals before coming here. 36 varieties of crepes with asparagus, mushrooms, tuna, beans, chicken, meat, spinach, fruits, ice cream and just about anything else (Q9-19) will be your absolutely delicious and memorable reward. Open daily 8:30am-11pm.

The Book Exchange Café, Av. Reforma 14-32 z. 9, is the place to have a sandwich (Q7.50) or a cup of coffee (Q3) surrounded by hundreds of English books. Open Mon.-Sat. 10am-7pm.

Yogurt's Shop, 3 Av. 16-51 z. 10. Somewhat remote, but the homemade Bulgarian yogurt is well worth the trek. Yogurt comes with fruit (Q2-8), frozen (Q3.55) or in pies and cakes (Q3.40). Open Mon.-Sat. 8am-7pm.

SIGHTS

Zona I

La Plaza Mayor (also called *Parque Central*) consists of two large plazas—**Parque de Centenario** and **Plaza de las Armas,** bounded on the west and east by 6 and 7 Avenidas and on the north and south by 6 and 8 Calles. Permanently animated by persistent *limpiabotas* (boys who shine your shoes for Q1) and often besieged by political demonstrators, Plaza Mayor never bores the wanderer. It's been called "the center of all Guatemala," and it is easiest to understand why on Sundays, when *indígenas* from all groups and regions come to sell their textiles or simply go for their afternoon strolls. The color is truly spectacular.

To the east of the plaza rises the beautiful, neoclassical **Catedral Metropolitana,** constructed between 1782 and 1868. (Open Mon.-Sat.7am-6pm, Sun. 7am-8pm.) To the north, guarded by dozens of camouflaged and gun-toting soldiers, is the **Palacio Nacional,** uncomfortable seat of the Republic's troubled government. It was built between 1938 and 1943 under the orders of president Jorge Ubico. The public is allowed in the two most impressive of the 350 rooms in the palace—**La Sala de Recepción** and **La Sala de Banquetes,** decorated with real 18-karat gold and Bohemian crystal. (Free tours in Spanish or English Mon.-Fri. 8am-4:30pm.)

Right behind the cathedral, between 8 and 9 Avenidas and 6 and 8 Calles, is the **Central Market,** with a fantastic selection of food, crafts and flowers. With great deals offered in every stall, this market caters primarily to locals. (Open Mon.-Sat. 8am-6pm, Sun. 8am-noon.)

The **Miguel Angel Asturias Cultural Center** is at the south end of *Zona* 1, located in the Civic Center. It houses the National Theater, a chamber theater and an open-air theater. The oldest church in the Ermita Valley, **Cerrito del Carmen** (finished in 1620), rests peacefully at 12 Av., 2 Calle z. 1. The first public clock in the city is to be found in one of the two towers of the **Santo Domingo Church,** 12 Av., 10 Calle z. 1. But the church most often praised for its elaborate paintings, sculptures, woodcarvings and mosaics is **La Merced,** 11 Av., 5 Calle z. 1.

While in *Zona* 1, you can also visit the small **Museo de Artes e Industrias Populares,** 10 Av. 10-71 z. 1, which has a collection of Indian musical instruments, ceramics and drawings. (Open Tues.-Fri. 9am-4pm and Sat.-Sun. 9am-noon and 2-4pm. Admission Q0.25, free with student ID.)

Zona 2

The Mapa en Relieve, an enormous horizontal relief map of Guatemala, fascinates and puzzles tourists and Guatemalans alike. The vertical scale of the map is twice that of the horizontal, which contributes to the overwhelming impression it creates. Viewers mount towers on either side of the map, designed and built in the early 1900s, to look down upon a precise representation of the mountainous country. If you bring a microscope you can watch a tiny replica of yourself looking at the map.... The *mapa* is at the end of 6 Av., about 2km north of the plaza (take bus #1 from 5 Av. in *Zona* 1 or the #45 or 46 from 5 Av.).

Zonas 4, 9 and 10

The most architecturally playful chapel, **Iglesia Yurrita,** is in *Zona* 4, on 6 Ruta 8-54; unfortunately it is closed most of the time. The border between *Zonas* 4 and 9 is marked by a smaller Guatemalan version of the Eiffel Tower, known as **El Torre del Reformador.** Just a block west of it is the **Botanical Garden.** (Open Mon.-Fri. 8am-3:30pm, Sat.-Sun. 8am-noon and any other time that the entrance of the CECON building is open.) Eight blocks down on Av. Reforma is Guatemala's most famous museum, **Popol-Vuh,** Av. Reforma 8-60 z. 9 (tel. 347-121) on the sixth floor of Edificio Galerías Reforma. Named after the sacred Mayan book, a great cyclical cosmological epic, the museum contains a large collection of pre-Columbian Mayan pottery. There are no signs in the museum, so you might consider buying a guide book (Q5 in English, Q2.50 in Spanish). (Open Mon.-Sat. 9am-5pm. Admission Q5,with student ID Q3.) The other interesting museum in the area is the **Ixchel Museum of Indigenous Costumes,** 4 Av. 16-27 z. 10 (tel. 680-713), which exhibits the largest collection of Guatemalan textiles and traditional clothing with detailed historical explanations. (Open Mon.-Fri. 8:30am-5pm, Sat. 9am-1pm. Admission Q5.)

Zona 13

Only a 20-minute walk from the airport, this zone is full of tourist attractions and provides a great way to wile away the hours till your flight. The **Mercado de Artesanías,** Bl. Aeropuerto, 6 Calle z. 13, is a good opportunity for last-minute shopping for traditional textiles, ceramics and jewelry from each region of the country, but it is clearly meant for tourists and so are the prices. (Open Mon.-Sat. 8am-6pm, Sun. 8am-noon.) Right next door the zoo, also called **Parque Aurora,** gives you a chance to stare at all those animals and birds of which you caught only fleeting glimpses in the jungle of Tikal or down the Río Dulce. If small cement cells make your stomach turn, spare yourself the visit. (Open Tues.-Fri. 9am-5pm, Sat.-Sun. 8am-5pm. Admission Q1.) Behind the market and the zoo is **Museo de Arte Moderno** (tel. 720-467), featuring contemporary Guatemalan artists such as Carlos Mérida and Humberto Garavito and well worth a trip to the area even if you are not on your way to the airport. (Open Tues.-Fri. 9am-4pm, Sat.-Sun. 9am-noon and 2-4pm. Free.) **Museo Nacional de Arqueología y Etnología** has hundreds of Mayan artifacts from all over Guatemala, an excellent scale model of the ancient city at Tikal, an exhibit of regional *típico* apparel and a large collection of ceremonial masks, both pre-Columbian and modern. (Open Tues.-Fri. 9am-4pm, Sat.-Sun. 9am-noon and 2-4pm. Admission Q1.) **Museo de Historia Natural** (tel. 720-468) is home to a stuffed effigy of the sacred bird of the Mayas, the *quetzal*. (Open Tues.-Fri. 9am-4pm, Sat.-Sun. 9am-noon and 2-4pm. Free.) To get to any of these places catch bus #83 from 10 Av. or #63 and #85 (red) from 4 Av. (Q0.40).

ENTERTAINMENT

For a current listing of cultural events and movies, check **La Prensa Libre** (Q0.75) or any other of the local newspapers. Theater and opera performances in both English and Spanish are staged by **Teatro IGA,** 1 Ruta 4-05 z. 4 (tel. 310-022), on Friday and Saturday nights at 8pm (tickets Q10). Sometimes there are free showings of movies. For information call the office Mon.-Fri. 8am-5pm. Theater performances in Spanish are also presented in the **Teatro Nacional,** 24 Calle 3-81 z. 1 (tel. 531-743), in **Teatro La Universidad Popular,** 10 Calle 10-32 z. 1 (tel. 25-181), and in several other theaters throughout the city. (Universidad Popular performances Fri. 8:30pm, Sat. 4:30pm and 8:30pm, and Sun. 4pm and 6:30 pm. Tickets Q10.) The **Conservatorio Nacional de Música,** 5 Calle, 3 Av. z. 1 (tel. 28-726), organizes performances every other Thursday at 8pm (tickets Q25). **Alianza Francesa,** 4 Av. 12-39 z. 1 (tel. 531-129), has free movie showings (in Spanish or French) Mondays at 6pm and Saturdays at 4pm.

Guatemala City's nightlife gets pretty active, particularly in the newly developed **Zona Viva** (*Zona* 9). Outside this area it's unsafe to walk alone at night. The pace picks up at 11 pm and winds down around 3am. The **Tropical Room** (between the Sheraton and a strip joint on 6 Av. z. 1) is the best place to practice your *salsa*, but there is no pressure to dance. All age groups hang out harmoniously. (Open Mon.-Sat. 6:30pm-12:45am, cover Q8, beer Q6.) The grown-up wanna-bes swarm down the street two blocks to **Dash,** in the Geminis commercial complex on 10 Calle z. 10. It's a modern disco; Thursday nights feature *música en vivo*. (Open Mon.-Sat. 8pm-1am. Cover Thurs.-Sat. Q15. Beer Q12, vodka Q5.) Next on the city's "hot spot" list come **Le Pont,** 13 Calle 0-48 z. 10 (open Thurs.-Sat. 7pm-1am; cover Q12; beer Q8), **Baco's Discotheque,** 16 Calle 0-55 z. 10 (open Thurs.-Sat. 6pm-1am; cover Q15; Thurs. Q20; beer Q7), and **Manhattan,** 7 Av., 14-44 z. 9 (open Tues.-Sun. 7pm-1am; no cover; beer Q8). They all have a fairly modern setting and play rock, disco, salsa and *un poco de todo*. If you are staying in *Zona* 1, you should add in Q35 each way for a taxi since buses stop running at 8pm.

■ Near Guatemala City

Volcán Pacaya

Robberies, rapes and murders plague **Pacaya Volcano;** as of the summer of 1992 a visit was out of the question. Hikers lucky enough to have visited in safer times rate Pacaya as the most beautiful summit in Guatemala. Check with the INGUAT office in Guatemala City or Antigua and the U.S. embassy in Guatemala City for updated safety information about travel to any of the volcanoes (see Practical Information). Buses leave Guatemala City from the terminal in Zona 4 to San Viciente Pacaya, El Cedro and San Francisco de Salle. If "risk" is your middle name, it's best to stay the night at any of these villages and start the two-hour ascent early the next morning in order to catch the early afternoon bus back to Guatemala City.

ANTIGUA

San Juan de Comalapa

Comalapa is a small Cakchiquel village famed for some of the best indigenous "primitivist" art in Guatemala. It is 40km from the capital, in the province of Chimaltenango.

Most of the works of indigenous art in the Museum of Modern Art in Guatemala City come from Comalapa, but many more can be seen in a trip to the village. Seven art galleries line up on **Calle Principal** and some excellent pieces of art sell at poster prices (US$20-30). Most of the works depict traditional folk rituals and customs, which are still lived and performed in Comalapa. To experience the real thing, plan your visit in the week of June 20-26, when the local *feria* in honor of the patron saint of the village, San Juan, takes place. Daily processions, *marimba* orchestras, dances with masks, hot air balloons and a dancing, fireworks-spewing *torre* make the experience unforgettable and create the right perspective to appreciate the art. **Buses** to Comalapa leave Guatemala City from the Panajachel terminal at 20 Calle, 1 Av. z. 1 (every hr. 7am-5:30pm, 2hrs., Q2.50). The last bus returns to Guatemala City at 4:30pm.

■■■ ANTIGUA

In 1527, the second capital of Guatemala was improvidently built at the base of the magnificent Volcán de Agua. Twenty years later, thevolcano paid belated tribute to the city by spewing forth enough lava to erase it from memory. By 1543, the Spaniards had laid out another town in the Valley of Panchoz; originally named Santiago de los Caballeros de Guatemala, Antigua reigned as the southern capital of Spanish Central America for 200 years before being destroyed by a gargantuan earthquake in 1776.

The quake jostled Antigua from its position as a political, social and spiritual center for the Spanish holdings in the New World, but the city remains a major tourist epicenter to this day. Rugged green mountains encroach upon *colonias* of majestic colonial architecture, providing a beautiful backdrop for the thousands of students who come to the city to learn Spanish (see Guatemala: General Introduction: Alternatives to Tourism for details).

Antigua will, no doubt, remind travelers coming from Mexico of San Cristóbal de las Casas. Both are colonial outposts sequestered high in the mountains, deep within *indígena* territory. Yet the Guatemalan city enjoys several advantages over its near-twin: Antigua is warmer, the nearby *indígenas* are friendlier to outsiders, and the roving vendors are less pesky with their sales pitches. On top of all this, Antigua is less expensive.

ORIENTATION

Antigua is only 45km west-southwest of Guatemala City, but the trip over winding mountain roads can consume an hour and a half.

Frequent second-class school buses connect the capitals of past and present. **Transportes Unidos, América Preciosa,** and several other lines leave Guatemala City every half-hour (see Guatemala City: Practical Information: Buses) and arrive in Antigua at **el mercado** on Alameda Santa Lucía, 3 blocks west of the central plaza. Fare is Q2.35.

Though compact, Antigua can prove tricky to navigate. Very few *calles* and *avenidas* are marked, street numbers follow no obvious plan, and many streets look alike. *Avenidas* run north-south and are numbered 1 to 7 beginning in the east. North of 5 Calle, *avenidas* are designated *Norte* (Nte.); south of it, *Sur*. *Calles* run east-west and are numbered 1 to 9 starting in the north. East of 4 Av., *calles* are named *Oriente* (Ote.); west of it, *Poniente* (Pte.). The **Parque Central** is bounded by 4 and 5 Calles on the north and south, respectively, and, happily enough, 4 and 5 Av. on the east and west.

PRACTICAL INFORMATION

Tourist Office: 4 Av. Sur, in the Palacio de los Capitanes (tel. 320-763), on the southeast corner of the *Parque Central*. Friendly employees are knowledgeable about Antigua and environs, but be prepared to spend a long time listening. Staff speaks English, as does almost everyone else in Antigua. City map Q0.25. Open daily 8:30am-6pm.

Currency Exchange: Banco Industrial, 5 Av. Sur 4 (tel. 320-958), 1 block south of *Parque Central*, provides Visa cash advance service. Open Mon.-Fri. 8:30am-2pm. **Banco del Agro,** 4 Calle Pte. 8 (tel. 320-793), on the north side of *Parque Central*. Open Mon.-Sat. 9am-6pm. If the bank is closed, look for their special window next door.

Post Office: Alameda de Santa Lucía at 4 Calle Pte.(tel. 320-485), across the street from the market and the bus stop. Packages going abroad must be under 2kg. Open Mon.-Fri. 8pm-4:30pm. **Postal code:** 6.

Telephones: Guatel, on 5 Av. Sur 2 (tel. 322-498), just south of the southwest corner of the park. Often crowded. Open daily 7am-midnight. **Telephone code:** 0.

Telegrams: Alameda de Santa Lucía at 4 Calle Pte. (tel. 320-875), next door to the post office. Open daily 8am-7pm.

Bus Station: Behind the market on 5 Calle Pte. To: Guatemala City (every 20min. 3am-7pm, 45min., Q2.35), Chimaltenango (every ½hr. 5am-6pm, 40min., Q1), San Antonio Aguas Calientes (every hr. 9am-6pm, ½hr., Q0.50) via Ciudad Vieja (15Min., Q0.35), Sta. María de Jesús (13 per day 7am-6:30pm, ½hr., Q0.80), Esquintla (4 per day, 2hrs., Q3).

Taxis: (Tel. 320-479), lined up along the east side of *Parque Central*. To Ciudad Vieja Q20.

Car Rental: Avis, 5 Av. Norte 25 (tel. 322-692). Open Mon.-Fri. 8am-noon and 2-6pm, Sat. 8am-noon. Cars Q270 per day, including insurance and free mileage.

Moto Rental: Moto Rent Antigua, 4 Calle Pte. 30 rents *motos* for Q95 per day (insurance and free mileage) and requires only a Q100-deposit. Open daily 8am-noon and 2-7pm, Tue. and Fri. until 6pm.

Bike Rental: In **Posada de Don Pedro de Alvarado,** 4 Calle Pte. 27-D for Q15 per 8hrs. (passport required). Open daily 8am-6pm. **Villa San Francisco,** 1 Av. Sur 15 (tel. 323-383) for Q5 per hour or Q25 per day. Inquire any time in the hotel.

Camping Equipment Rental: Casa Andinista, 4 Calle Ote. 5, next to Mistral. Rents an assortment of novels (Q2.50 per week) and camping gear (tents Q10 per day). Open Mon.-Fri. 9am-6:50pm and Sat.-Sun. 9am-8pm.

Travel Agency: Turansa, 5 Av. Norte 17 (tel. 322-664), ½ block north of *Parque Central*. Makes ticket reservations, organizes tours to Panajachel (US$9) and Chichicastenango (2 days, US$40) and operates a shuttle service to Guatemala City (US$6) and to Copán (Honduras), Quiriguá and Esquipulas (US$50, round-trip US$80). Open Mon.-Fri. 8am-1pm and 2-6pm, Sat. 8:30am-1pm.

Market: On the west side of Alameda de Sta. Lucía, 1/5 Calles Pte. Food and craft goods. Open daily 7am-6pm.

Laundromat: Lavandería Antigua, 6 Calle Pte. 6 E-10, 1 block south of the *Parque*. Wash and dry small load with cold water Q10, with hot Q12. Same-day service. Open Mon.-Sat. 7:30am-6:30pm.

Pharmacy: Farmacia Santa Ana, 5 Av. Norte (tel. 320-572) on the west side of *Parque Central*. Open daily 8am-10pm. Rotating schedule for 24-hr. pharmacies; consult a local paper.

Hospital: Hospital Pedro de Betancur, 6 Calle Ote. 20, ¾ Avs. (tel. 320-883). English spoken. Open daily 7am-8pm.

Emergency: Los Bomberos, on the north side of the bus station (tel. 320-234).

Police: Policía Nacional (tel. 320-251), on the south side of the *Parque Central* in the Palacio de los Capitanes Generales. 24-hr. emergency service.

ACCOMMODATIONS

The spigots deliver hot water, the floors are clean, and the company good. In general, Antigua is a city of great budget accommodations. Many families rent out rooms on a weekly basis (around Q125), all meals included. Ask at the tourist office or in the local Spanish schools for details.

Hospedaje El Pasaje, Santa Lucía Sur 3, south of the bus stop. Enormous immaculate rooms and well-maintained bathrooms with hot water. One of the best values in town. If they're full, let them direct you to their annex. Curfew 1am. Singles Q15. Doubles Q20.

Posada San Francisco, 3 Calle Ote. 19 (tel. 320-266), 1 door past Alianza Francesa. Quiet end of town, but a social lobby inside. Great owners and great foreign crowd. Q20 per person, with bath Q25.

Posada Landívar, 5 Calle Pte. 23 (tel. 322-962), ½ block southeast of the *mercado*. Modern and clean with extra perks: soap, towels, hot water, big beds and water jugs in the halls. Doubles Q32, with bath Q42. Triples with bath Q63.

Posada de Don Pedro de Alvarado, 4 Calle Pte 27-D. Rooms are small, but irreproachable, and service is motherly, kind and comforting. Singles Q23, with bath Q30. Doubles Q30, with bath Q36. Triples Q45. Ask about rooms at their Spanish school (you don't have to be a student), which rent for Q15.

Posada la Quinta, 5 Calle Pte. 19. Fairly standard rooms at one of the lowest prices, Q15 per person. No singles.

Hotel La Plaza Real, 5 Av. Sur 8 (tel. 320-581), ½ block from the *Parque Central*. Central location and a scenic view of the mountains and rooftops from the upstairs rooms. All rooms have private bath and *agua caliente* (let it run a while first). Back rooms are quieter. Singles Q35. Doubles Q64. Triples Q96.

Villa San Francisco, 1 Av. Sur 15 (tel. 323-383). Big inviting beds and exemplary cleanliness. Rent bikes at their doorstep (Q5 per hour) and cut all distances short. Singles Q23, with bath Q29. Doubles Q35, with bath Q41. Triples with semi-private bath Q57.

FOOD

Some only half-jokingly call Antigua "the capital of international budget cuisine;" restaurants here cater to *gringo* taste and the backpacker's budget. Vegetarians can finally feel at home. Ten percent seems to be the customary tip.

Quesos y Vino, 5 Av. Nte. 31A, just past the arch. Small, two-burner café that serves homemade pasta and wine from Chile, Argentina, France and Italy. *Pasta con ricotta y romate* Q13.25. Individual pizza Q14. Open Wed.-Mon. 9am-10pm.

Sueños del Quetzal, 5 Av. Nte. 3. An 8-page menu of vegetarian cuisine, including vegi-dogs, burgers, tofu dishes ... give yourself some time to choose. Bagel with cream cheese Q8.50. A serving of tabouli Q5.95. Delicious baklava Q3.25. Open daily 7am-10pm.

Restaurant Zen, 3 Av. Nte. 3, 1 block east of the park. Look for the small wooden sign outside. Huge portions of excellent Japanese food. Vegetarian dishes with eggs and rice Q9, with shrimp Q11.50. Fried ginger chicken Q13.50. Open Thurs.-Tues. noon-10pm.

La Cenicienta, 5 Av. Nte. 7. The most popular pastry shop and café, with tortuously delicious-looking cakes. Try the brownies (Q1.50), banana split cake (Q2.25), or other local specialties. Everything goes well with Peter's papaya and milk *licuado* (like a milkshake, Q2). Open daily 8:30am-8pm.

Café El Jardín, 5 Av. Nte., on the west side of *Parque Central*. A budget traveler's favorite, and understandably so with strawberries and cream for Q3.25, waffles or pancakes with honey for Q8.25 and *integral* sandwiches for Q7. Open daily 8:30am-7:30pm.

SIGHTS

Antigua boasts what may be the most elaborate Semana Santa in Guatemala, but Antigua is by no means ordinary the rest of the year. The broad peaceful streets, the lace of beautiful colonial buildings and church ruins, and the green of the mountains rippling into the city make for a place that is best described as a jewel. Its centerpiece is **Parque Central,** where frenetic foreigners practice their *español* with patient locals. The central fountain, **Llamada de las Sirenas** (The Sirens' Call), built in 1739, and the park's stone benches are prime places for people-watching and *amigo*-bonding. On the north side of the plaza is the **Palacio del Noble Ayuntamiento;** to the south is the **Palacio de los Capitanes Generales;** to the east, Antigua's **cathedral.** The **Palacio del Ayuntamiento,** unlike most of Antigua's other buildings, survived both the 1773 and 1776 earthquakes and preserves its original 1743 form. Once a prison, it is now home of the municipal authorities and two museums—**Museo de Santiago,** which exhibits colonial furniture, tools, coins, clothing, paintings and weapons(open Tues.-Fri. 9am-4pm, Sat.-Sun. 9am-noon and 2-4pm; admission Q0.25, students with ID free) and **Museo del Libro Antiguo** (Old Book Museum), which muses on the mysteries of New World printing and bookmaking and displays some lustrous 17th-century books and manuscripts (open Tues.-Fri. 9am-4pm, Sat.-Sun. 9am-noon and 2-4pm; admission Q0.25).

The **cathedral** was provisionally built in 1545, demolished in 1668 and finally completed in 1669. The 1773 earthquake turned it back into dust, leaving a few broken arches, which still can be appreciated behind the present day cathedral. A small crypt at the east end of the ruin site houses a much venerated, completely charred 313-year-old Black Christ. (Site open daily 9am-4:30pm. Admission Q0.50.) Half a block east of Plaza Mayor is the old building of the **University of San Carlos de Borromeo.** Founded in 1676, it was the third university in Hispanic America. Today it houses the permanent exposition of the **Museo de Arte Colonial** and temporary exhibits of contemporary Guatemalan art. (Open Tue.-Fri. 9am-4pm, Sat.-Sun. 9am-noon and 2-4pm. Admission Q0.25, students with ID free.) **Casa K'ojom,** Recoletos 55 (tel. 323-087), behind the bus station, is a museum and center for indigenous music. Buy tapes (Q25) or ask for a guided tour (signs and tours in Spanish only). (Open Mon.-Sat. 9:30am-12:30pm and 2-5pm. Admission Q2. Audio/visual shows at 11am and 3pm, Q5.) Among Antigua's many remnant and full-bodied churches, a few are particularly worth a visit. One of the most interesting colonial earthquake casualties is **Las Capuchinas,** at 2 Calle Ote. and 2 Av. Nte., constructed in 1736 and destroyed only 37 years later. It was a convent for cloistered nuns. Of special interest is the **Torre de Retiro** (Tower of Retreat) on the north side, where nuns used to close themselves for weeks and months of meditation. To compensate for the complete deprivation, they had one (unheard of at the time) luxury—private baths with running water. As you wander through the complex you can still see their kitchen, chimneys, food-storage areas and chambers with dripping water used for corporal and psychological punishment. (Open daily 9am-5pm. Admission Q0.50.) Another fabulous ruin site is **Iglesia y Convento Santa Clara,** 2 Av. Sur 27, 6a Calle Ote. As with many structures, its beauty only grew with its ruination. The stunning semi-restored grassy courtyard and the vistas framed by crumbling archways make it gorgeously photogenic. (Open Tue.-Sun. 9am-5pm. Admission Q0.25.)

Don't miss the church **La Merced,** 1 Calle Ote., at the northern end of 51 Av., whose façade is the best example of the baroque style which dominates most of Antigua's buildings. At **Iglesia de San Francisco,** 7 Calle Ote., 1 Av. Sur, one wall is covered with letters of gratitude to "Hermano Pedro" (Pedro de San José Betancur), a Catholic believed to have healing and miraculous power and interred in a sepulchre there. On Sundays, a local **market** takes place in the courtyard. (Both open daily 6am-6pm.) Also of interest is **Casa Popenoe,** 1 Av. Sur 2. This 17th-century house, including its first bathroom and kitchen, has been restored to its original condition. (Open to the public for guided tours Mon.-Sat. 2-4pm. Admission Q2.)

El Cerro de la Cruz (The Hill of the Cross) affords a beautiful view of Antigua, the Volcán de Agua and the Volcán del Fuego. Take 1 Av. Nte. to the hill and follow the sign marked "Al Cerro" to the top (30 min. walk from downtown). This area is not wholly safe and the tourist office does *not* recommend the hike; if you insist, best to try it in the morning and not solo.

ENTERTAINMENT

Antigua has one of the best selections of movies you'll ever find, both high quality and latest hits. Toss a coin to choose among 15 films shown daily in **Cine-Café Oscar,** 3 Av. Nte. 2, one block south of Café Doña Luisa; the **Fisco Video-Bar,** 1 Av. Sur 15, in Hotel San Francisco; **Cinemala,** 3 Av. Nte. 9, next to Café Doña Luisa; **Elektra Video-Café,** 7 Av. Nte. 2; or **Café Flor,** 4 Av. Sur 1, half a block south of Plaza Mayor. (Admission for each Q5.)

If you get a craving for good old CNN news or a basketball game on TV, head to the **Mistral Bar and Lounge,** 4 Calle Ote. 7, open daily 11:30am-11pm. A snug joint with jazz or tasteful European music is **", y ."** (*Coma y Punto*), on 6 Av. Nte. 19. (Open Mon.-Sat. 8am-10pm and Sun. 10am-10pm.) Pub-crawlers will find their haven on 7 Av. Nte. near 3 Calle where the action picks up around 10pm. Don't miss **Latinos Bar's,** 7 Av. Nte. 16. Happy hour is 6-9pm, when rum and vodka pour for Q1, and there is live reggae nightly at 10pm. (Open Mon.-Sat. 6pm-1am). **Picasso's,** 7 Av. Nte. 3, is always packed with travelers and students (open Sun.-Fri. 7:30pm-midnight), while **La Chimenia,** 7 Av. Nte., 4 Calle Pte., is more spacious, with comfortable sofas and 70s rock and roll. (Open daily 7:30pm-1am.) Beer in most places is Q4.

■ Near Antigua

Ciudad Vieja, an even earlier former capital of Guatemala, is only 5km from Antigua, but even so, it is hardly worth the trip for the few ruined colonial buildings. Buses for Ciudad Vieja leave from Antigua's market every half hour from 9am to 5pm and charge Q0.35.

Several of the *pueblitos indígenas* near Antigua make excellent day trips. **San Antonio Aguas Calientes,** a weaving center 9km from Antigua and 4km from Ciudad Vieja, has a colorful craft market and a wonderful traditional celebration of the *pueblo's* patron saint day, June 13. Buses leave Antigua from the main bus station every hour from 9am to 6pm (½hr., Q0.50). The last bus returns at 5:30pm. Another village reached by frequent buses from Antigua (13 per day 7am-6:30pm, ½hr., Q0.80), **Santa María de Jesús,** marks the origin of the trail leading to the summit of **Volcán de Agua** (3766m). Check U.S. State Department warnings before climbing any volcanoes. Ask locals for directions to the trail; once out of Santa María, it's easy to follow and takes about five hours to hike. The last bus back to Antigua leaves at 5pm, but there is a *pensión* in the village in case you have to spend the night.

Other nearby volcanoes, more arduous climbs than Agua, are **Acatenango** (3975m) and **Fuego** (3763m). Most climbers tackle these two peaks from **Finca de Soledad.** (Buses from Antigua to Acatenango will drop you off at the Finca intersection.) For best results, climb Acatenango first, spend the night at the hut in the saddle that connects the two volcanoes, and scamper to Fuego's summit in the morning. One bit of useful information: Fuego is an active volcano which emits sulfur fumes and occasionally spews out a large quantity of molten lava, giving the climb an added dash of danger. It is not advisable that beginners start their climbing career here.

CAUTION: Guerrillas have robbed and harassed tourists climbing the volcanoes. In the summer of 1993, the U.S. State Department warned tourists not to climb any volcanoes in Guatemala. Consult the U.S. State Department, the U.S. Consulate in Guatemala City and/or the local tourist office (see Guatemala: General Introduction) for the latest advisories. Any warnings they give should be taken with the utmost seriousness.

LAGO ATITLÁN

Whether you are in search of Guatemala's rich indigenous culture, its rare bird species, or its stunning natural beauty, your travels will take you to the shores of Lake Atitlán. The descendants of the Mayas arrived in the area long before the Spanish. *Los conquistadores* found themselves especially unwelcome, and European colonization of the region was not fully enforced until late in the 17th century. Even after that, the firmly rooted indigenous culture continued its vibrant existence as it still does today. The majority of people living in the twelve villages surrounding the lake still wear their traditional costumes (some of the most colorful you'll find in Guatemala) and speak their native tongues. Backdrops to this array of color are three magnificent volcanoes (one still smoking) reflected in the crystal-clear waters of the lake.

■■■ PANAJACHEL

Thanks to a highway linking it to Guatemala City, Panajachel plays host to swarms of tourists. In recent years, it has even seen the development of a community of drop-out expatriate North Americans. The *pueblo's* streets, snuggled up next to Lake Atitlán, are filled with *típico* vendors purveying bananas, bracelets and peanuts to charmed visitors. If watching the moon rise and the sun set over the surrounding crags isn't enough nighttime entertainment for you, bars and fine restaurants line Calle Principal. Panajachel is also a place of departure for destinations around Lake Atitlán and throughout western Guatemala.

ORIENTATION AND PRACTICAL INFORMATION

Panajachel has yet to be introduced to the high-tech concept of street signs, but a 20-minute walk covers the entire town. Most everything (with the exception of the beachfront luxury hotels) lies along **Calle Principal,** which connects Panajachel with Sololá, or **Calle Santander,** which branches off to the south or right (coming from Sololá) at Banco Agrícola Mercantil. The **public beach** is to the left at the end of this street. **Calle Los Árboles** branches off to the left from Calle Principal just after Banco Agrícola. Most establishments in town are full of tourists and thus safer for women, and in general the streets in the center are more secure at night.

Tourist Office: (Tel. 62-1392), on C. Principal before Banco Agrícola. Free maps of Panajachel and the lake and useful updates on safety on and around the volcanoes. Bus and launch schedule posted on the door after-hours. Open Mon. 8am-noon, Wed.-Sat. 8am-noon and 2-6pm.

Currency Exchange: Banco Agrícola Mercantil (tel. 621-386), on C. Principal. Open Mon.-Sat. 9am-2:45pm. **Banco Inmobilario** (tel. 621-056), on C. Los Árboles, about 2 blocks from C. Principal. Open Mon.-Fri. 9am-8pm, Sat.-Sun. 10am-2pm.

Post Office and Telegrams: Up C. Principal and behind the Catholic church. Post office open Mon.-Fri. 8am-4:30pm, telegram office open 24 hrs.

Phones: Guatel, halfway down C. Santander. Long distance calls. Open daily 7am-midnight.

Buses: All buses depart from and arrive at the **tourist office** (see above). To: Guatemala City (hourly 5:30am-3:30pm, 3½hrs., Q8), Chichicastenango (7 per day 7am-6pm, 1½hrs., Q5), Quetzaltenango/Xela (6 per day 5:30am-2:30pm, 2½hrs., Q6), Cocales and the Pacific Highway (4 per day, 2½hrs., Q5), Santa Catarina and San Antonio (2 per day plus many unscheduled vans, ½hr., Q2.50) and San Lucas Tolimán (2 per day plus many unscheduled vans, 1½hrs., Q5). To get to Huehuetenango, take a Quetzaltenango-bound bus and get off at Cuatro Caminos, where you can make a Huehuetenango connection. To Antigua, take a Guatemala City bus and change at Chimaltenango. All buses pass through Los Encuentros and connections can be made there to all points. For other locations and connections, consult the bus schedule posted at the tourist office.

Launches: From the docks in front of Hotel del Lago, to Santiago (6 per day, 1hr., Q7.50) and San Pedro (13 per day 8:20am-7:30pm, 1¼hrs., Q6). From Santiago to San Pedro (10 per day 7am-5pm, 45min., Q5). **Santa Fe Boat Co.** organizes day-long lake tours (9am-3:30pm, Q30), with 1-hr. stops in Santiago, San Pedro and San Antonio.

Taxis: (Tel. 622-028), or look for one in front of Grapevine on C. Santander.

Car Rental: Daiton Rent-a-Car, represented by BIGSA Moto Rent, on C. Los árboles (tel. 621-253), between Circus Bar and Restaurant Al Chisme. Cars US$40 per day including insurance and free mileage. Mopeds Q25 per hr., Q85 per 8 hrs.

Bike/Moped Rental: Moto Servicio Queché, at the corner of C. Los árboles and C. Principal (tel. 622-089). Bikes Q5 per hr., Q30 per 8 hrs. Mopeds Q25 per hr., Q65 per 8 hrs. Q200 deposit required. Open daily 7:30am-7pm. **Taller Gaby,** next to the Lavandería (below). Bikes Q2.50 per hr., Q20 per 10 hrs. Open daily 8am-6pm. **Daiton Rent-a-Car** (see above) also rents mopeds.

Boat Rental: Diversiones Balam, on the beach. Individual (Q8 per hr.) or double (Q15 per hr.) kayaks, canoes (Q15 per hr.),water bicycles (Q15 per hr.) and 8-person *lonchas* (Q200 to Santiago, Q225 to San Pedro). Open daily 8am-5pm.

Market: At the end of C. Principal. Open daily 7am-6pm.

Laundry: Lavandería, 1½ blocks from C. Santander, down the street which branches off to the left (facing the lake) after Guatel. Washes for you, Q2 per large piece, Q1 per small piece. No same-day service. Open daily 7am-6pm.

Pharmacy: Farmacia Priscy, on C. Principal (tel. 621-537), 1 block past Banco Agrícola. Open daily 7am-11pm.

Medical Emergency: Call Dr. Bracamonte (tel. 621-008) 24 hrs.

Emergency/Police: In the municipal bldg. (tel. 621-120), at the end of C. Principal.

ACCOMMODATIONS

Pana, as locals affectionately dub it (they also call it *Gringotenango*, not so affectionately), is more expensive than Antigua, Guatemala City and the surrounding villages. None of the budget rooms available has much personality. If you're planning on an extended stay in town, consider renting a house for about US$50 per week, or better yet, stay in San Pedro across the lake for US$1.20 per night. **Camping** on the public beach (at the end and to the left of C. Santander) is supposedly legal, but there are no facilities, and you should be watchful of your belongings.

Hospedaje Pana Rooms, walk up C. Los árboles and turn left (west) at the dirt road just past Galería a Mano. Best of the low-budget basic. Beautifully set at the foot of the mountain with passable general bathrooms. Hot water all day and attached workout room. Singles Q17. Doubles Q23. Triples Q28.

Hospedaje Ramos, on lake shore on a drive behind Bungalows El Rosario. Tidy, barracks-like rooms with private bath and hot shower, rare luxuries in this town. Singles Q25. Doubles Q42. Triples Q55

Hospedaje El Tikalito, ½ way down C. Santander (tel. 622-042), shortly after Guatel. Spacious rooms a good value with decent communal facilities and hot water (pressure reliably high in the daytime). Singles Q17.75. Doubles Q21.10. Triples Q28.60.

Mario's Rooms, on C. Santander past Guatel. Incredibly comfortable beds, coal-stuffed pillows and hot water (8am-6pm, Q1). Rooms of varying vintages. Restaurant in front serves the cheapest breakfast in town (Q5). Singles Q18.75. Doubles or triples Q24.60.

Hospedaje Eli Rooms, next to Hospedaje Pana Rooms. Basic but bright and clean rooms at lower than average prices. Hot water. Singles Q14.05. Doubles Q20.

Hospedaje Casa Linda, 1 block from C. Santander, down a small street marked by huge signs indicating the way. Tiny rooms, big comfy beds, shining communal bathrooms and hot water. Singles Q17.60. Doubles Q23.10.

Bungalows El Rosario, just off the lake behind the line of restaurants (tel. 621-491). Stand on your threshold and gasp at the vista of Lake Atitlán and its surrounding volcanoes. Comfortable courtyard, spacious rooms and private baths with hot water. Singles Q35.50. Doubles Q46.80. Triples Q70.20. Quads Q93.60.

FOOD

If *plátanos* and peanuts don't tempt your tastebuds, fear not: Panajachel's gourmet restaurants are sure to pacify the palate. The large tourist population has had its creeping influence, and most establishments serve granola, yogurt, corn flakes, pancakes and other hallmarks of northern cuisine. Also, most restaurants have vegetarian listings, and many have dishes prepared with tofu—a real rarity for Central America.

La Única Deli, on C. Principal, 2 blocks past the bank; the restaurant is peacefully hidden behind a few trees on the right. The best breakfast in town, hands down. 3 whole-wheat pancakes with fruit Q7.50. Quiche Q7. Amazing chocolate-peanut butter ice cream pie Q3. Bagel sandwiches Q8-11. Open Thurs.-Tues. 8am-6:45pm.

Restaurant Vegetariano Hsieh, C. Los árboles, just after the intersection with C. Principal. *Típico* atmosphere, international health-conscious menu: crepes (Q6), granola (Q6), steamed vegetables (Q8) or the special of the day (lasagna, pizza, pasta or *chile relleno* with soup, salad and whole-wheat bread Q10). Open Tues.-Sun. 9am-10pm.

Los Amigos, on C. Santander, halfway to the lake. You can't walk away without new friends. At the least, you'll know Coquí, the flamboyant owner. Enjoy delicious *chile rellenos* (Q15), enchiladas (Q17) or burritos (Q14). Open daily 6am-10pm.

El Dragón, on C. Santander. Candles, low-key music and top of the line service guarantee a good meal. Choose from Indonesian, German, Chinese and Guatemalan dishes. Chow mein Q12.75, beef skewers with pineapple, rice and plum sauce Q20. Open Wed.-Mon. 1-10:30pm.

Ranchón Típico, on C. Santander. Well laid-out, central and inexpensive. Check out the *churrasco ranchón típico,* which brings soup of the day, roasted meat, fried bananas with cream, beans with cheese, guacamole, fries, mixed vegetables and tortillas for only Q8. Open daily 9am-7:30pm.

ENTERTAINMENT

If you've missed any of the big hits in movies, Panajachel is the place to catch up. Three video salons—the **Grapevine** and **El VideoClub** on C. Santander and **El Cine** on C. Los árboles—show a total of 10 movies a day, changing their listings daily (Q5).

The after-dinner bar crowd heads first to **The Circus Bar and Pizzeria** on C. Los árboles, where circus posters decorate the walls and the nights with live blues are entertaining even for the non-aficionado. (Beer Q5.50. Open daily 2pm-1am.)

Dancers will cap off the night at **Chapitol** across the street, where the beat's live and the floor's crowded. (Open daily 6pm-1am, no cover but you must purchase your first drink at the door.) Down the street is **Pache's Discotheque,** whose less-crowded floor leaves more space for your artistic expression. (Open Tues.-Sun. 7pm-1am. No cover. Gin and tonic Q6.)

■ Near Panajachel: Villages

There are three volcanoes and 12 villages around the lake, some accessible only by bus, boat or foot from Panajachel. The biggest and most colorful of the *pueblos* is **Santiago-Atitlán,** directly across from Panajachel. The population, almost entirely *indígena*, is of Tzutuhil origin, and both men and women still don traditional attire. You will see many women wearing the *xocop*, an incredibly long woven strip, wrapped around their heads. The people of Santiago are said to have a great talent for art, and the streets of the village are lined with art galleries that sell true master-pieces. The tourist industry here is growing and little children take advantage of it by chasing visitors and offering to be photo-models in exchange for a *quetzal.* But don't let this deter you from a beautiful **boat ride** across the lake or a visit to Santiago, especially during Semana Santa or the Fiesta of Santiago (the week of July 25). Santiago is perhaps most famous for its worship of **Maximón,** a wooden idol dressed in *típico* clothes, a cigar drooping from his pursed lips. On Wednesday of Semana Santa, Maximón is paraded through the village, and worshipers pay their respects by chomping on unlit stogies as the icon passes.

An overnight visit gives a more genuine impression of the community. An immaculate hotel, **Chi Nim Ya's,** lies up the hill and left of the dock. Two spacious floors of shelter are frequented by laid-back travelers. (Q7 per person, Q10 with bath and a view of the lake.) Another option is **Pensión Rosita,** to the right of the Catholic church, which is equally basic but more desolate. Balcony rooms watch the Volcano San Pedro bide its time. (Q8 per person.) Your best bet for food is **Santa Rita,** near the market. Omelettes with cheese (Q6) or meat and beans (Q9), as well as a variety of chicken and fish dishes (Q15) are served daily 7am-9pm.

The **post office** is in front of the market, near the municipal building (open Mon.-Sat. 8am-2pm) and **Guatel** for phones is on the main street, behind the church (open 24 hrs.). Buses leave from one end of the market for Guatemala City every hour 7:30-11:30am and for Esquintla via San Lucas at 1:30pm.

Launches run from Santiago to Panajachel (7 per day, 1hr., Q7.50) and to San Pedro (7am and hourly 9am-5pm, 45min., Q5).

Another oft-visited village is **San Pedro La Laguna.** It is slightly less rustic than the others, but it is at the foot of the **San Pedro Volcano** and is the starting point for those interested in climbing it. **Pensión Chausinahi,** also called **Hotel Villa Sol,** in the big cement complex to the right of the docks, has clean, comfortable rooms and houses almost the entire backpacker crowd. (Doubles Q11. Triples Q16.50, with bath Q22.) Right next door, **Hospedaje Ti-Kaaj** feels more like a cement box, but it is the best alternative when Chausinahi fills up. (Singles Q6. Doubles Q11. Triples Q16.) Most food establishments in San Pedro have nothing that costs more than Q8, but **Comedor Ranchón,** attached to Villa Sol, beats them and serves nothing for over Q7. Choose from pasta, fish, chicken, pancakes and yogurt. (Open daily 6am-7pm.) **Café Arte,** on the main street from the dock, offers fish, chicken or meat (Q8), omelettes (Q4.50) and pancakes with fruit (Q4.50). They will also be glad to make you sandwiches for your volcano hike. (Open daily 7am-9pm.)

The **post office** is tucked behind the church (open Mon.-Fri. 8am-4pm and Sat. 8am-noon) and **Guatel** phones are on the main street from the dock (open daily 7am-10pm). There are no bus lines from San Pedro. **Launches** leave for Panajachel (15 per day 4:15am-5pm, 1¼hrs., Q6) and for Santiago (8 per day 6am-3pm, 45min., Q5). Be aware that the last boat to Panajachel does not leave from the main dock in front of Villa Sol, but from the one in front of Restaurant Johana, about 1km away. The trail between the two docks winds through the village and branches several times, but one of the local boys can lead you through for a small tip.

If you decide you want to do more than just climb the volcano, you can rent a **kayak** (Q2 per person per hr., Q3 per duo per hr.) or a **horse** (Q10 per hr.) at Hospedaje Ti Kaaj.

Many other villages of Cakchiquel origin in the area make interesting destinations on horse or *moto.*

On Thursdays and Sundays, **Chichicastenango** (37km north of Panajachel) becomes a blur of pigments, looms and textiles as indigenous artisans swoop down from the hills to sell their goods in a colorful and extensive **market.** You can spend hours browsing through the *típico* clothing; deal-making is best on Saturday. The market closes around 4 or 5pm, or later on market day. The last bus back to Panajachel or Antigua leaves at 3:30pm. Although Chichicastenango used to be the best place for deals, prices wing their way up 50% when busloads of tourists arrive.

Be warned that the south side of Lake Atitlán is unsafe for tourists at night, according to the U.S. State Department's advisory. Don't visit without an up-to-date report.

■ Near Panajachel: Volcanoes

Volcán Atitlán, at 3535m (11,604 ft.), is the tallest of the three volcanoes in this region, and **Volcán Tolimán** (3158m, 10,360 ft.) is the only active one. The ascent of both starts at the village of **San Lucas Tolimán** and requires spending a night at the top. In the summer of 1992, however, climbing the volcanoes was strongly discouraged and very dangerous due to the high incidence of armed robbery and violence. Be sure to consult an INGUAT office or the latest U.S. State Department advisory for the status of thevolcanoes before you even consider climbing them. **Volcán San Pedro** (3020m, 9908 ft.) is easier to climb. The ascent starts in the village of San Pedro and takes five hours, so a round-trip will fit in one day. The reward is a spectacular view of the lake from the top. The trail, however, is poorly marked, so it is wise to hire a guide in San Pedro. You can get one at **Hospedaje Ti-Kaaj** (see Near Panajachel: Villages) for Q10 per person, or ask around in the village and you may be able to find a boy who will do it for Q5 per person.

■■■ IXIMCHÉ

Iximché is the ancient capital of the Cakchiquel people and the first capital of Guatemala. The city was founded in 1470 under the governors Juntoh and Vukubatz. The Cakchiquels eventually achieved independence from the Quichés only to fall in 1524 under the rule of the Spaniards. The city surrendered peacefully to Pedro de Alvarado, but abuses and the cruel extraction of tribute (in gold and services) caused two bloody rebellions in 1526 and 1532. The conquest was concluded in 1535 with the death of the Cakchiquel governors of the city.

Iximché is a naturally fortified city, surrounded on all sides by deep ravines. The present **archaeological site** encompasses the palaces and temples of the governors. The majority of the people lived in the surrounding countryside, their houses and lifestyle much like that which can be observed today. (Site open daily 8am-5pm. Admission Q0.50, free Sun.) There is a **museum** exhibiting pictures and objects from the excavation project. (Open daily 8am-noon and 1-4pm.) There are no guides, but a small brochure (free, in Spanish) summarizes the information in the museum.

Iximché is located about 5km from the small village of **Tecpán.** To get to Tecpán, catch a **bus** from the Panajachel bus terminal in Guatemala City on Calle 20 z. 1 (every ½hr., 2hrs., Q4). If coming from elsewhere, take a Guatemala City-bound bus to Los Encuentros and there change to Tecpán (1hr., Q2). From Tecpán to Iximché either walk the 5km or hire a taxi (Q20). If you plan to take a taxi, do so at the road where the bus drops you off, because it is hard to find one in town.

The site is small and easy to do in a day trip, but if you decide to spend the night in Tecpán, you can do so in **Gran Hotel Iximché,** which rents rooms for Q7.50 per person.

■■■ SANTA CRUZ DEL QUICHÉ

The village of Santa Cruz del Quiché is located about 30km north of Panajachel. Though small, the undeveloped ruins of Utatlán are the only reason enthusiasts make the trip here.

ORIENTATION AND PRACTICAL INFORMATION

Santa Cruz del Quiché is built in the familiar grid of north-south *avenidas* and east-west *calles*. There are five *zonas*, but they do not affect the regularity of the grid. **Parque Central** is framed by 1 Avenida to the east, 2 Avenida to the west, 4

Calle to the north and 5 Calle to the south. The church is on the east side of the park.

Change checks at **Banco de Guatemala,** 3 Calle, 2 Av. z. 1 (tel. 551-395), at the northwest corner of the park (open Mon.-Thurs. 8:30am-2pm, Fri. 8:30am-2:30pm). The **post office** is hidden in abuilding with no sign on 3 Calle, 0/1 Avs. z. 5 (tel. 551-085), and is open Mon.-Fri. 8am-4:30pm. The **postal code** is 14501. The **telegraph office** is next door to the post office and is open 24 hrs. Knock on the door if it appears locked. **Guatel,** 1 Av., 2 Calle z. 5, will make calls for you daily 7am-midnight. The **bus station,** 1 Av., 10 Calle, has service to: Guatemala City (every ½hr. 2am-5:30pm, 4hrs., Q8.50), Panajachel (every 2hrs. 4am-2pm, 2hrs., Q6.50), Quetzaltenango (6 per day 4am-2:45pm, 3hrs., Q6.50), Tecún Umán (via Quetzaltenango at noon) and Navaj (3 per day, 4½hrs., Q6).

For medical **emergencies** contact the *bomberos* (tel. 551-122) on 2 Calle 0-11 z. 1. **Farmacia Santa Cruz,** 7 Calle 0-15 z. 1 (tel. 551-383), is regularly open 8am-10pm daily, but will answer emergencies 24 hrs. The owner is a doctor, should you need one. For other emergencies, call the **police,** 0 Av., 3 Calle z. 1 (tel. 120), open 24 hrs.

ACCOMMODATIONS AND FOOD

Since visitors are rare, there is almost no well-oiled machinery to cater to their needs. The best place to spend the night is **Hotel San Pascual,** 7 Calle, ½ Avs. Rooms are large and pleasant and communal baths well-kept. Hot water 6:30-8am only. (Singles Q12, with bath Q23.40. Doubles Q20, with bath Q30. Triples Q23.40, with bath Q40.) Somewhat darker, but comfortable and immaculately clean are the rooms in **Posada Calle Real,** 2 Av. 7-36 z. 1 (tel. 551-438). Hot water. (Q11.70 per person.)

Food alternatives are even more limited. The best atmosphere is in **Restaurante Maya Quiché,** 2 Av. 5-30 z. 1, on the west side of the central park, where you can choose among chicken *a la española*, with curry, *a la crema* or *chimichurry* (Q11-13). (Open daily 8am-9pm.) Entertainment is free with meals at **VideoBar 2000,** 4 Calle, 3 Av. z. 5, not to be confused with a restaurant with the same name in z. 1 near *Parque Central*. Reproduced, untranslated U.S. action hits. Pizzas are Q9 and *queso fundido* Q4.50, but they are usually not available, so be content with a hamburger for Q4. (Open Sun.-Fri. 8:30am-8:30pm.)

SIGHTS

K'umarkaaj, also known as Utatlán, was the capital of the Quiché Kingdom, which formed during the Post-Classic period (1000-1523) of Maya civilization and under the ruler Q'uk'ab extended from the Pacific almost to the Atlantic, encompassing nine different nations. Two of these, the Tzutuhil and Cakchiquel, are the two major indigenous groups around Lago Atitlán today. The name *K'umarkaaj* has been translated as "Houses of Old Reeds," but local Quiché people insist that this is a Cakchiquel interpretation and that the name in fact means "Houses of False Sky" and refers to the step-shaped and flat roofs of the buildings in the city.

There is little left of the glorious capital of Quiché today. The **archaeological site** covers an area of 8 square km, but the few discernible structures are located around a single plaza. Most everything else is mounds of grass, the regular shapes of which suggest underlying buildings. Perhaps the most interesting element of all is a **small cave,** 100m from the plaza along an indicated trail, where the past and the present come together in the livingtradition of the *indígenas*. The cave is still used by local people for religious and healing ceremonies much as it was 500 years ago. If you smell incense and see smoke coming out of its entrance, don't hesitate to enter; just be considerate and keep your camera in your bag. You need a flashlight to enter the cave and if you have not brought your own, you can rent one at the museum for Q2. The **museum** itself has posters explaining the social and political structure of the Quiché Kingdom and the chronology of its history and its rulers. (All signs are in Spanish.) If interested in the history and legends of the Quiché people, ask for Sr.

Morales, who will gladly and proudly retell you what he heard from his father, who heard it from his father before him. (Site open daily 8am-4:30pm. Admission Q0.25, students free.)

To get to K'umarkaaj, either walk the 5km or hire a taxi from the bus station at 1 Av., 10 Calle z. 5, which will take you there, wait and bring you back for Q40.

■■■ QUETZALTENANGO/XELA

Quetzaltenango—ancient capital of the Quiché kingdom, one of the first settlements of the Spanish *conquistadores*, and Guatemala's second largest modern city—encompasses the dipolarity of Guatemalan society. A beautiful ex-colonial city, its surrounding hillsides are quilted with the small farms of the Quiché people.

The name Quetzaltenango (literally "the land of the *quetzal*," Guatemala's national bird) was given to the city by the Aztec warriors who arrived with Pedro de Alvarado, but local people still use almost exclusively the Quiché name: Xela (SHEH-la) or Xelajú. ("Xelajú" refers to the ten gods worshipped by the Quiché people.) Although Quetzaltenango attracts many students who prefer to study Spanish outside tourist capital Antigua, most travelers make the pilgrimage to the Guatemalan highlands to commune with the surrounding countryside, bargain at some of the best markets in the country, experience the Maya culture and enjoy the therapeutic effects of the hot sulfuric springs in nearby Zunil and Fuentes Georgina.

ORIENTATION

Quetzaltenango is 200km west-northwest of Guatemala City and has a population of 500,000 people. As is often the case in Guatemala, Quetzaltenango's *avenidas* run north-south and the *calles* run east-west. *Avenidas* increase to the west and *calles* to the south. The **Parque Centroamérica** is at the center of town in *Zona* 1 and is bordered by 11 Avenida on the east, 12 Avenida on the west, 4 Calle to the north, and 7 Calle to the south. Most of the city's services are located in *Zone* 1.

PRACTICAL INFORMATION

Tourist Office: INGUAT, 7 Calle, 12 Av. (tel. 614-931), at the south side of the park. Free city maps and some English spoken. Open Mon.-Fri. 8am-noon and 2-5pm, Sat. 8am-noon.

Currency Exchange: Banco de Guatemala, 12 Av. 5-12 z. 1 (tel. 612-421), on the west side of the park. Open Mon.-Thurs. 8:30am-2pm, Fri. 8:30am-2:30pm. **Banco Agrícola Mercantil,** 11 Av. 4-43 z. 1 (tel. 612-573), on the east side of the park. (Open Mon.-Fri. 9am-4pm.)

Post Office: 4 Calle 15-07 z. 1 (tel. 612-651). OpenMon.-Fri. 8am-4:30pm.

Telephones: Guatel, 12 Av., 7 Calle z. 1 (tel. 612-200), at the southwest corner of the park. Phone, fax and radiogram service. Open daily 7am-midnight. **Telephone code:** 0.

Buses: Most buses leave from **Terminal La Minerva** at the northwest end of *Zona* 3. To get to the terminal, take bus #6 from 8 Calle, 12 Av. z. 1 (Q0.25). Most buses from La Minerva pass through La Rotonda on Calzada Independencia in *Zona* 2, which is a 15 min. walk from *Zona* 1 or a Q6 taxi ride. To: Talismán, southern Mexican border (every 20 min. 5am-4:30pm, 5hrs., Q12) via Tecún Umán (3½hrs., Q8); La Mesilla, Mexican border (hourly 5am-3pm, 6hrs., Q8) via Huehuetenango (2hrs., Q5); Guatemala City (every 15 min. 5am-5:30pm and 8pm, 4hrs., Q12-16); Huehuetenango (every ½hr. 5am-5pm, 2hrs., Q5); Panajachel (6am and noon, 2½hrs., Q9). Frequent service to Chichicastenango, Momostenango, San Francisco El Alto, Santa Cruz del Quiché. **Rutas Lima,** Calzada Independencia, 3 Calle z. 2 (tel. 614-134), and **Lineas América,** Calzada Independencia, 5 Calle z. 2 (tel. 612-063), have first class service to Guatemala City.

Public Transportation: City buses begin running at 6:30am.

Taxis: (tel. 614-085), lined up along the east side of the park. To Terminal La Minerva Q10. To La Rotonda Q6. Round-trip to Georgina thermal springs Q75 per vehicle.

Library: In the Casa de la Cultura, 7 Calle 11-27, z. 1. Open Mon.-Fri. 8am-noon and 2-6pm.

Market: At Terminal La Minerva, *Zona* 3. Open Mon.-Sat. 6am-5pm. To get there, catch bus #6 from 8 Calle, 12 Av. z. 1.

Supermarket: La Selecta, 4 Calle 13-16 z. 1 (tel. 612-004). Open Mon.-Sat. 9am-1pm and 3-7pm, Sun. 9am-1pm.

Laundromat: Lavandería Mini-max, 14 Calle C-47 z. 1 (tel. 612-952). Wash and dry for Q8.60 per load. Open Mon.-Sat. 7:30am-7:30pm.

Pharmacy: Farmacia Nueva, 11 Av. 4-29 z. 1 (tel. 616-277). Open Mon.-Fri. 9am-8pm, Sat. 9am-6pm. There is a rotating schedule for 24-hr. pharmacies.

Red Cross: (Tel. 125), 8 Av. 6-62 z. 1. 24 hrs.

Medical Services: Hospital San Rafael, 9 Calle 10-41 z. 1 (tel. 614-414). Open 24 hrs. Private institution. English spoken.

Police: (Tel. 630-202), 10 Calle 12-21 z. 1. Open 24 hrs.

ACCOMMODATIONS

Pensión Altense, 9 Calle 8-48, z. 1 (tel. 612-811). Tidy rooms circumscribe a courtyard and a small restaurant. One of the best values in town. Diurnal hot water. Friendly proprietor. Q8 per person, with bath Q15.

Hotel Horiami, 2 Calle, 12 Av. z. 1. Ask for room #1, which has a three-wall window. Otherwise, rooms are basic, but pleasant and communal baths are irreproachable. Water moderately hot. Q10 per person.

Pensión Radar 99, 13 Av. 3-27 z. 1. Most popular with budget travelers, though not the cheapest option. Rooms are small and dark, but reasonable, clean communal baths have hot water.Singles Q17.50. Doubles Q23.40. Triples Q29.25.

Pensión Andiana, 8 Av. 6-07 z. 1 (tel. 614-012). Really pleasant, clean and bright rooms, but in a somewhat beat-up area of town. Hot water from 6:30-9am. Singles Q11, with bath Q16.50. Doubles Q23.40, with bath Q30.80.

Hotel Río Azul, 2 Calle 12-15 z. 1. Spacious, secure, sparkling and super-friendly. Private baths with hot water. Singles Q34. Doubles Q45. Triples Q55.

Hospedaje San Nicolás, 12 Av. 3-16 z. 1. Small and suspiciously yellow general bathrooms. Rooms are losing color. Cold water only. Then again, it is the cheapest in town. Q5 per person.

FOOD

Quetzaltenango offers the full spectrum of nourishment environments—from European-style intellectual cafés to bohemian *cantinas*, from fancy restaurants to unpretentious eateries. Most of them cloister on and around 14 Avenida.

Café Baviera, 5 Calle, 12-50 z. 1. Come and practice your Spanish by reading the worldly wisdom inscribed on the walls, or relax and chat with the predominantly English-speaking crowd. Excellent coffee Q2. Banana bread Q1.95. Pecan pie Q4.25. Open daily 8am-8pm.

Pizza Ricca, 14 Av. 2-42. An open brick-oven fills the air with an irresistible smell of delicious and cheap food. 1-person pizza Q9. Lasagna, ravioli or spaghetti Q10. *Queso fundido* Q7. Open daily 11am-9:30pm.

La Polonesa, 14 Av. "A" 4-45 z. 1. Variety of choice, and never more than Q8. Pancakes or cereal with honey Q3.50. Better yet, *económico del día* (including soup, salad, rice or pasta, tortillas and a soda) for Q5. Open Mon.-Sat. 7:30am-9pm.

Restaurante Deli-Crepe, 14 Av. 3-11. Steer clear if you are on a diet, but do not think twice if you are out to enjoy a meal. Just imagine crepes with peaches, bananas, chocolate, cream *de chantilly*, strawberries, ice-cream or any combination thereof (Q7.25). Open daily 9am-9pm.

SIGHTS

More people travel to Quetzaltenango to visit the surrounding countryside, but while in town amuse yourself at the **Casa de Cultura,** 7 Calle 11-27 z. 1 (tel. 616-427), next to the tourist office on the south side of *Parque Centroamericano*. The museum there is a swirl of Mayan artifacts, taxidermy, old manuscripts and local herbology. (Open Mon.-Fri. 8am-noon and 2-6pm, Sat. 8am-4pm. Free.) The Casa de Cultura is also the source for information on current cultural events.

The **Municipal Theater,** 14 Av., 1 Calle z. 1 (tel. 612-218), houses ballet, *marimba*, orchestra and theater performances (every other Fri. and Sat., Q3-25). And of course, there's always the movie option at **Cine Cadore,** 13 Av. 6-92 z. 1, or **Cine Roma,** 14 Av., ½ Calle z. 1. (Tickets Q2.50-5.)

■ Near Quetzaltenango

Visit the hot springs of **Zunil** and **Fuentes Georgina** to purge the cool, wet weather of Quetzaltenango (average temp. 65°F) from your system. Men and women in Zunil shed their traditional colorful dress on Sundays to relax in the local baths. Hike scenic mountain trails and listen to the gurgling volcanoes; you may get lucky and spot a *quetzal* or its ilk. Cabins are available for overnight stays, which include fireplaces and hot tubs. (Singles around Q35. Doubles around Q55.) To get there catch a bus to Zunil, get off at the intersection and walk the remaining 9km, or go all the way to Zunil and from there hire a pick-up truck for Q20. Taxis from Quetzaltenango charge Q75 round-trip plus waiting time.

There is another set of thermal baths, **El Recreo,** about 4km from Quetzaltenango near Almolonga, which is accessible by public transportation. Take the Almolonga bus from Terminal La Minerva or from 9 Calle, 10 Av. z. 1 (every 20 min., 15min. Q0.50). Group baths cost Q3 but there are also private tubs.

Other popular destinations include **San Francisco el Alto** on Friday market day and **Momostenango** where hand-woven wool blankets are made. Both can be reached by bus from Quetzaltenango.

■■■ TECÚN UMÁN

The small town of Tecún Umán, situated 250km west of Guatemala City, is the main stopover before (or after) crossing the Mexican border to the south. As soon as you set foot in town, you'll be overwhelmed by two things: the oppressive heat and the effusive crowd of men offering to help you do anything, be it change money or take care of irregular papers and passports. There is nothing memorable in Tecún Umán, but it is a convenient place to spend the night if you arrive late or would like to depart at the break of dawn.

CROSSING THE BORDER

There are two options: either cross the border in Tecún Umán, which takes you into Ciudad Hidalgo in Mexico, from which there are frequent connections to Tapachula, or cross at the border station **Talismán** (also called El Carmen), which is 18km from Tapachula. **La Aduana** (customs) in Tecún Umán is located at the end of 7 Calle z. 2 (tel. 768-132) and is regularly open daily 8am-9pm, though there is someone on duty 24 hrs.

To get to Talismán, catch a *camioneta* (van) to Malacatán from 3 Calle z. 1, in front of the central park and the church (every 15 min. 5:45am-7pm and randomly until midnight, 1hr., Q2). Get off either in Malacatán or at the intersection 5km earlier and catch another bus or *camioneta* to Talismán (every 15 min. until 7pm and then larger intervals until midnight, 20min., Q1.50). Taxi fare is Q10. **La Aduana** at Talismán is open 24 hrs. There is no village, however, so if you are arriving from Mexico through Talismán, you can either catch a direct bus to Guatemala City (every hr. until 5pm) or take one of the buses/*camionetas* to Malacatán and there

TECÚN UMÁN

change to a bus heading to Tecún Umán, Castepeque, Quetzaltenango or Guatemala City. The last buses to Quetzaltenango and Guatemala City leave by 5pm, but service to Tecún Umán and from there to Castepeque is available every 15minutes until 9pm and at longer intervals until midnight. If you arrive late, consider spending the night in Tecún Umán. Connections from Castepeque are few and unreliable after 7pm.

ORIENTATION AND PRACTICAL INFORMATION

In imitation of larger cities, the town is nominally divided into three zones. The zones are arbitrary and do not affect the layout and numbering of *calles* and *avenidas*. The **central park** is bounded by 2 and 3 Avs. and 3 and 4 Calles z. 1. **La Aduana** is three blocks west and one north of the park, at the end of 7 Calle z. 2. Bicycle taxis will take you anywhere in town for Q2.

For Mexican **visas** and **tourist cards (FMT),** visit the **Mexican Consulate,** 2 Calle 3-32 z. 1 (tel. 768-114), which is open Mon.-Fri. 8am-2pm. If you make your way through the packs of *cambistas* awaiting your arrival, you can change money at **Banco del Occidente,** (tel. 768-159), on the corner of 2 Av. and 6 Calle z. 2. (Open Mon.-Fri. 9am-6pm, Sat. 9am-7pm.) The **post office** (open Mon.-Fri. 8am-4:30pm) and the **telegraph office** (open daily 8am-9pm) are located at the intersection of 5 Av. and 9 Calle z. 3. **Guatel,** 3 Calle, 4 Av. z. 1 (tel. 76-821) offers phone and fax services daily 7am-midnight. The **Red Cross,** 5 Calle, 2 Av., is open 24 hrs., as is the **police** station, 3 Av., 4 Calle.

There are no bus terminals, only young boys hawking their favorite destination; take care to double-check where you're going, since these young salesmen are more eager to get you on board than to answer questions. **Camionetas** leave frequently from 3 Calle in front of the central park for Malacatán (1hr., Q2) and for Castepeque (½hr., Q2.50). Most connections for the interior are made from Castepeque. Direct **buses** leave from the corner of 2 Calle and 3 Av. for Quetzaltenango/Xela (3hrs., Q7.50), Guatemala City (4hrs., Q19) and Talismán (1hr., Q5). To get to Panajachel, take a Guatemala City-bound bus and get off at Los Encuentros. The last bus from Los Encuentros to Panajachel passes at 5pm.

ACCOMMODATIONS AND FOOD

The best value is at **Hotel Don José,** 3 Av. 2-14 z. 1 (tel. 768-164). The excellent rooms are equipped with private baths, crucial fans and TVs. (Singles Q30. Doubles with 1 bed Q40, with 2 beds Q45. Triples Q60.) The cheapest place is **Hospedaje Mariela,** 3 Av. 5-25, two blocks from *La Aduana*. Rooms are tiny, but acceptably clean, and communal facilities are decent when functioning. (Q6 per person.) **Hotel Central,** 5 Calle near 2 Av., has tidy, basic doubles for Q20. At the same price but a step down in aesthetics are the rooms at **Hospedaje Bienvenidos,** 6 Calle 2-33, next to Banco del Occidente, which provide only cold water, which should suffice in simmering Tecún Umán.

Inexpensive *comedores* and food stands abound in the streets of Tecún Umán, but one would be hard-pressed to find an upscale place. Approaching scale-ness is **Restaurante Bamby,** 3 Av. 3-59, in front of the central park, but even here the menu ends after *chile relleno* (Q10) and *carne asada* (Q10). Perhaps the rest disappeared with the mother in a big fire. (Open daily 8:30am-10pm.)

ALTA Y BAJA VERAPAZ

For years the Kikché Indians of the area successfully resisted the Spanish conquest, which gave rise to the Kikché name of the region:*Tuzuntohil,* or "Land of War." Meanwhile Fray Bartolomé de las Casas and the Franciscan friars organized a powerful campaign in defense of the *indígenas*. The result was something the world had never seen before or after: the most powerful empire in the world at the time halted its military conquest to discuss questions of its morality and justifiability. Las Casas was granted five military-free years for the peaceful and "humane" conversion of the Kikché. His success was spectacular. He and the friars learned Kikché and composed songs with the gospel in it. They had a few merchants who frequently visited the warring areas sing these songs, while showing mirrors, knives and other objects of European civilization. The chiefs, assured that the friars were not interested in their gold and their land, finally let them in and conversion followed peacefully shortly after. Thus the region obtained its present name, *Verapaz* or "true peace."

■■■ COBÁN

Cobán, the capital of the Alta Verapaz, is situated 213km northwest of Guatemala City. Enjoy this sleepy towns balenarios and its surrounding natural beauty.

ORIENTATION AND PRACTICAL INFORMATION

I **Avenida** (north-south) and I **Calle** (east-west) divide the city in four quadrants. The northwest is labelled *Zona* 1, southwest is *Zona* 2, southeast *Zona* 3 and northeast *Zona* 4. The central park is framed by 1 and 2 Avs. and 1 and 2 Calles in z. 2.

Tourist Office: Información Turística, 1 Calle 1-11 z. 1 (tel. 511-305). Helpful information on sights in the region and city maps for Q1. English spoken. Open Tues.-Sat. 8am-noon and 1-5pm.
Currency Exchange: Cobán may be your only chance to change money in this part of the country. **Banco del Café,** 1 Av. 2-66, z. 2 (tel. 511-011), changes traveler's checks Mon.-Fri. 8am-5pm.
Post and Telegraph Office: 3 Calle 2-00, z. 3 (tel. 511-140). Post office open Mon.-Fri. 8am-4pm. Telegraphs 24 hrs. Prices double after 4pm.
Phones: Guatel, 1 Calle, 2 Av. z. 1 (tel. 511-498). Open daily 7am-midnight.
Buses: Transportes Escobar y Monja Blanca, 2 Calle 3-77 z. 4 (tel. 511-952) has 1st- (Q16) and 2nd-class (Q11.25) service to Guatemala City (4hrs.). All other buses leave from the bus terminal at the end of 2 Calle z. 4. To San Cristóbal (4min., Q1.25). To Lanquín (2½hrs., Q5). The 6am bus leaves from 1 Calle and 3 Av. z. 4, in front of Cine Norte; be there ½hr. early.
Taxis: (Tel. 511-897), lined up on the north side of the central park.
Laundromat: Lavandería La Providencia, Diagonal 4, 2-43 z. 2, on the south side of the central park. 7 lb. wash (Q2.50) and dry (Q3.50). Open Mon.-Sat. 8am-noon and 2-5pm.
Red Cross: Cruz Roja (tel. 125).**Pharmacy: Farmacia Carvi,** 1 Calle 4-53 z. 3 (tel. 513-094). Open 24 hrs.
Medical Emergency: Los Bomberos (tel. 511-212), 3 Calle, 3 Av. z. 4. This fire department is open 24 hrs.
Police: 1 Calle 5-12 z.1 (tel. 511-225). Open 24 hrs.

ACCOMMODATIONS AND FOOD

Hospedaje Maya, 1 Calle 2-33 z. 4 (tel. 512-380), has basic but big rooms and comfy beds. Often full. Q5.85 per person, with bath Q6.50 per person. For bright rooms with private bath go to **Hotel La Providencia,** Diagonal 4, 2-43 z. 2 (tel. 511-209), on the southwest corner of the central park. Singles Q11.70. Doubles Q20.55. **Pensión Familiar,** Diagonal 4, 2-49 z. 2, is next door to Hotel La Providencia. Rooms for more people have more light and smell nicer. Q10 per person. **Hotel Nuevo Monterrey,** 6 Av., 1 Calle z. 1 (tel. 511-131), is connected to Hotel Cobán Imperial and has well-maintained rooms and decent communal baths with hot water. Singles Q10.75, with bath Q14. Doubles Q22.25, with bath Q30.40. Triples Q33.35, with bath Q38.60.

Schwarzenegger videos provide a distraction for both clients and waiters at **Restaurant El Refugio,** 2 Calle 1-34 z. 4., where prices are smashingly low. Executive lunch (noon-3pm) Q5.50. *Chile relleno* Q7.50. Lasagna Q10. Open daily 11am-11pm. **Cafetería Ticos Pancakes,** 1 Calle, 4/5 Avs. z. 3, hits all 3 Bs: *bueno, bonito* and *barrato* (good, nice and cheap). Pancakes with banana, apple, strawberries, blueberries, or cream Q6. Cereal with fruit Q5. Sandwiches Q6. Open 24 hrs. **Restaurant Kam-mun,** 1 Calle 8-12 z. 1, serves the traditional Chinese fare of fried rice with shrimp and eggs for Q12 or chicken chow mein for Q10. Open daily noon-10pm.

ENTERTAINMENT AND SIGHTS (NEAR COBÁN)

Cobán's mellow atmosphere gets movin' on Thursday, Friday and Saturday nights in **Le' Bon,** 3 Calle, 3 Av. z. 3 (open 8:30pm-3am, cover Q5) and **El Oasis,** 6 Av.,1 Calle z. 1 (open 8pm-2am, cover Q3). Otherwise be content with action movies in **Cine Norte,** 1 Calle, 3 Av. z. 3 (Q2.50-4).

During the day, take refreshing walks through **Parque Las Victorias,** seven blocks west and two blocks north of the central park, or go swimming in Cobán's two *balnearios,* **Hermanas del Leon,** 20 min. down Diagonal 4 (free camping), and **La Colonia.** To get to La Colonia take a Carchá bus from the terminal (every 15 min.), get off at the bridge and walk for about 30 min. east. **Carchá,** 7km north of Cobán, also has a picturesque *balneario,* **Las Islas,** reachable from Cobán by bus (every 15 min., 10 min., Q0.40). And if you haven't had it with swimming, **Balneario de Camché,** near Tactic, 31km north of Cobán, is yet another local favorite. Three daily buses (6am, 1pm and 3pm, 1hr.) pass through Tactic on their way to Lanquín.

■■■ LANQUÍN

"Picturesque" fits just about any part of Guatemala, but you really haven't seen it until you've been to Lanquín. Far from Cobán, at 70km north, the little village possesses two jewels—the natural bridge and cascades **Samuc Champey** and the enormous cave, **Grutas de Lanquín,** said to be Guatemala's most beautiful. The cave is 2km before the village, but first go to the village and look for the policeman in the big municipal building in the center, who can turn the electricity on for you (Q10 per person). The police are open until 5pm, but the cave is open 24 hrs.; the flocks of bats at dusk are a specialexperience in themselves.

Visiting Samuc Champey is more of a challenge. It is a long 10km (2½-hr.) walk from Lanquín. Hotel El Recreo organizes tours for Q150, but it is much cheaper to ask around in the village and find out if there is a pick-up which can take you in that direction for a small fee (Q2.50-5).

Only three **buses** get to Lanquín (6am, 1pm and 3pm buses from Cobán; 3hrs.; Q5) and only three go out (5am, 7am and 2pm buses to Cobán). Times are not exact, so be there at least half an hour early and be ready to wait as much as an hour. Limited transportation makes Lanquín difficult as a daytrip, so spend the night at **Pensión La Providencia,** on the main street, which has basic rooms and decent general baths with hot water for Q5.50 per person. Or try **Hotel El Recreo,** 1.5km after the cave and 0.5km before town, which has immaculate but basic rooms for Q15 per person, and carpeted ones for more (singles Q25, doubles Q55, triples Q66, quads Q88). Both places have attached **restaurants** where beans and eggs go for Q7 and beefsteak with potatoes for Q8.

■ Biotopo Quetzal Mario Dary

The last remaining *quetzals,* the bright green and red bird which is the national emblem, hang out at this reserve 160km north of Guatemala City on the highway to Cobán. The reserve is in a cloud-strewn highland forest with trails twisting throughout. The free park is open from 6am to 4pm, but these regal and rare, long-plumed ornithoids (whose tail feathers can reach a yard and were used to adorn the head-dresses of Mayan royalty) only deign to appear between 5:30 and 7am. Bizarrely, the best place to view them is not the *biotopo*, but rather the **Hospedaje Ranchito del Quetzal** about 50m farther down the road to Cobán. Viewing them in a zoo is not an option as these proud birds cannot live in captivity. Be sure to bring binoculars or the super zoom for your camera if you want to get an in-your-face view of these *pájaros*. The Hospedaje has basic dorms for Q8.80 per person and private rooms for Q20 per person. Tumble out of bed and see the birdies right outside your door. The attached restaurant serves eggs and beans for Q7 and coffee for Q2. (Open 7am-8pm.)

THE EASTERN ROUTE

Want to lose the crowds in *Gringotenango* (Panajachel) and the highlands? Head east, my friend. The eastern *biotopos* (wildlife preserves), ruins, and *aguas bonitas* offer diversions unparalleled in the west, and served in the sauce of a hang-loose atmosphere. The well-maintained and leafy Atlantic Highway accesses the eastern hot spots. A car, though ever-so-convenient, may be too luxurious, but never fear— **Litegua** is here. Litegua, (tel. 275-78) at 15 Calle 10-40 z. 1 in Guatemala City is unre-servedly the best bus line in all of Guatemala. Spacious modern pullmans trip gaily along the Atlantic Highway from Guatemala City to Puerto Barrios (7 per day, 5½hrs., Q30. 2nd class buses every hr.) Advance reservations over the phone make the whole bus-catching ordeal even more of a joy.

■■■ QUIRIGUÁ

The Quiriguá ruins, 67km from Río Hondo on the Atlantic Highway, are known for their enormous and intricate stelae, carved stone monuments of the Maya. **Stela E,** a strapping 35 ft., is the tallest in Mesoamerica and is featured on the 10-centavo Guatemalan coin. All the stelae were found in and around Quiriguá, which flour-ished during the Early Classic (250-400 AD) and collapsed by the Late Classic period (600-900 AD). The site consists of the **Plaza Central,** where the stelae are located, the **stadium** for the Mayan ball game at the southwest end of the plaza and the **Acropolis,** the residence quarters of the elite, south of the plaza. The surrounding forest provides a beautiful green backdrop, but try to go early in the day to avoid the heat and humidity and lather up with mosquito repellent. (Open daily 8am-5:30pm. Admission Q1.) To get there, take one of the buses, which run from the highway down a dirt road and through 3.5km of banana plantation to the ruins (every 20 min., 15min., Q1).

Pickin's are slim for **food** and **hotels;** Quiriguá is better as a day trip from Río Hondo or a stop en route to somewhere else on the Atlantic Highway. If you *must* stay overnight, Los Amates, km200 Carretera al Atlántico, 4km west of the turnoff to the ruins, does have the **Hotel/Restaurant Santa Monica,** at the Texaco station on the Atlantic Highway. The yellow brick building has balconies, wrought iron and fans. (Singles Q16.50. Doubles Q33.)

There is a **public phone** at the Texaco station and an administered phone half a block farther (open daily 7:30am-9pm). Along the single main street of Los Amates you'll also find a **post** and **telegram office** (open Mon.-Fri. 7am-6pm) and a phar-macy, **Farmacia Salud** (open daily 7am-7pm). From Los Amates there are **bus** con-nections to Guatemala, Puerto Barrios and Chiquimula.

LAGO IZABAL

Lake Izabal, the largest lake in Guatemala, empties through Río Dulce into the Caribbean. These three bodies of water together make one of the most picturesque and richest in wildlife parts of the country. The lake is still home to the nearly extinct manatee (or sea cow). Some of the best swimming in the country, the enormous variety of colorful birds and the idyllic harmony of peasant life are all promises that Izabal faithfully keeps.

■■■ MARISCOS

Mariscos is situated on the southern shore of **Lago Izabal,** 14km from **Cruzero Trincheras** (km230 on the Atlantic Highway). The mountains around Mariscos are truly gorgeous, and as they smooth out into the lake they turn into beautiful green lawns with cattle and horses grazing in the expanse. You don't have to travel faster than light to see time slow down here. In Mariscos this happens naturally. The quiet beat of Lago Izabal's waves has given life a rhythm that is as yet untouched by the frantic high-tech neuroticism of modern civilization. Bamboo shacks with thatched roofs, uninhibitated mountains and a 14km rarely-traveled winding dirt road set the scene of untamed beauty and complete oblivion.

Everything is located on its one street. The **post office** is immediately north of Distribuidora Marinela (open Mon.-Fri. 7:30am-noon and 2-6pm), the **police** are on a small lane which startsopposite Comedor Los Pilotos (open 24 hrs.) and the medical center, **Puesto de Salud,** is right next door (open Mon.-Fri. 8am-4pm). For all other services (phones, banks, etc.), go back to civilization.

One **bus** leaves daily at 8am for Guatemala City (5hrs., Q14) and one for Puerto Barrios (8am, 3hrs., Q6). Other than that, Mariscos's only connection with the outside world is one truck which shuttles at random intervals between the village and Cruzero Trincheras on the highway (1hr., Q3). The earliest bus out of Mariscos is at 8am and the last into the village is at 5pm. There is a **ferry** which runs to El Estor daily at 1pm (2hrs., Q7) and returns the following day at 8am.

Three nearly identical **hotels** house the rare tourist. Rooms in all three are minimalist and communal facilities reasonably clean. The cheapest is **Hospedaje Los Almendros** on the curve of the road. (Q10 per person; some rooms have fans.) But if you wish the lake to wash your feet while you sleep, go a little further down the street, to **Hotel Karinlinda** (singles Q15, doubles Q27.50, triples Q38.50, quads Q55, quints Q66; a couple of rooms with fans) or **Hotel Marinita** (Q12 per person; no fans at all). These two have attached **restaurants** with gorgeous views of the lake (open daily 6am-9:30pm), where pancakes go for Q10, vegetable soup for Q15 and fried fresh fish served with salad and fries for Q20.

For daytime entertainment—if swimming and contemplating the surrounding beauty aren't quite enough—hike to **Playa Dorada,** a beautiful beach 4km west along the shoreline, or rent a boat (Q60 per hour per boat, 10 person maximum) from what looks like a parking lot at the curve of the road. Nighttime is a challenge for your imagination, but if you are completely stuck, try the U.S. action movie shown daily at 7:30pm on the video in **Cantina El Corazal** (Q1, films change daily).

■■■ EL ESTOR

Some of that relaxed Caribbean feel must have swum upstream to El Estor; the mellow atmosphere alone is worth the trip. In addition, El Estor is within a boat ride from the ravishing beauty of the **Boquerón Canyon** and a dive away from the calm swimming waters. El Estor is located on the north side of Lago Izabal, at a distance of 262km from the capital and 128km from Puerto Barrios. The village is much larger than it may seem at first, and its broad streets form a regular grid of north-south avenidas and east-west *calles. Calles* start with 1 along the lake shore and increase north. *Avenidas* start at 1, also at the waterfront, and increase east. The street that starts at the main dock is 5 Av.

The **post office,** 5 Av. 3-53, on the east side of the park, is open Mon.-Fri. 8am-4pm. **Guatel,** 8 Av., 5 Calle, has the only telephone in town (Open Mon.-Fri. 7am-9pm, Sat.-Sun. 7am-7pm.) The **market,** 7 Av., 3 Calle, is open daily 6am-6pm. **Farmacia Providencia,** 5 Av. 3-04, at the southeast corner of the park, is open daily 6am-10pm. **Clínica Médica,** 4 Calle 4-80, a half block west of the park, responds to emergencies 24 hrs., and so do the **police,** 5 Av., 1 Calle, across from the dock.

The only land connection from El Estor is to Cobán, served by two companies: **Brenda Mercedes** (1:30am and 4am, 6hrs., Q11; catch the bus from 3 Calle at *Parque Central* or east of it) and **Valenciana**(5am, 8am and 10am, 7hrs., Q12; buses leave from 7 Av. 2-77). By water, the connection is to Mariscos at 6am (2hrs., Q7), from whence buses take passengers on to Guatemala City or Puerto Barrios (see Mariscos).

All accommodations in El Estor are budget, but some more than others. The best value is **Hotel Villela,** 6 Av. 2-06, which has immaculate rooms with private baths and fans with the added bonus of a marvelous inner courtyard. (Q12 per person.) The cheapest is **Pensión El Milagro,** 2 Calle 4-63, where use of a bed and a remote general bathroom/shower go for Q5.

The best place to make travel connections, overhear tips, or just have a good meal is **Hugo's Restaurant,** 5 Av., 3 Calle. While conquering the steak (Q14) or chicken (Q14), see if Señor Hugo can take you on a boat ride up the Boquerón River the next day. (Open daily 9am-9pm). For good music and welcoming ambience, take refuge in the bamboo hut of **Ranchón y Disco Bambú,** 4 Av., 2 Calle. A variety of sandwiches go for Q3.50, and fresh fish for Q13.50. (Open daily 11am-11pm.)

At night, choose between **Disco Bambú** and the daily 7:30pm showing of action movies in **Salón Alan,** 11 Calle, 7/8 Avs. (Q0.50, films change daily.) In the daytime, an alternative to the fine swimming in Lago Izabal is to take the exceptionally scenic boat ride to the **canyon** of the Boquerón River. The trip lasts 3 hours and includes a visit to a set of small caves and time for swimming up- and downstream (US$10 per person, 2 person minimum). Make arrangements with Hugo at his restaurant (see above).

RÍO DULCE

A conduit between Lago Izabal and Amatique Bay on the Caribbean, the Río Dulce offers some of the most scenic boat rides in the country, occasional manatee sightings, and the unique Caribbean culture of Livingston at its mouth. It is also a marvelous diversion of a few hours from the formidable capital-to-Tikal trek.

A bridge spans the Río Dulce where it begins at the northeastern end of Lago Izabal. To the south of the bridge is the town **El Relleno;** to the north is **Fronteras,** where you can spend the night if you must. Just south is fortress/town **Castillo San Felipe. Fuente del Norte** buses from Guatemala City to Flores pass through the area. Alternately, take the **Litegua** bus to Puerto Barrios and get off at **La Ruidosa,** the highway junction nearest the Río Dulce bridge. From there, take one of the infrequent local buses the 34km to the Río Dulce bridge. Launches beneath the bridge will shuttle passengers to and from nearby sights (see Livingston for details).

■■■ CASTILLO SAN FELIPE

A 17th-century Spanish fortress built to stave off plundering pirates, the **Castillo de San Felipe** roosts in all its cannon-entrenched splendor at the mouth of the Río Dulce at the end of Lake Izabal. Bring a flashlight if you've got one—it'll help when spelunking the maze of tunnels leading through the dungeons. A cartoon history of the oft-plundered castle (in Spanish or in English) is free with the Q5 entrance fee. The Castillo grounds also include a creature-from-the-deep-colored pool (Q2), bathrooms, clocks, picnic facilities and a **restaurant.** (Fried chicken Q15.Burger Q5.50. Open daily 7am-6pm). Hordes of Guatemalan weekenders flock to the castle for family outings. (Open daily 8am-5pm.) An alternative to swimming in the pool is swimming in the lake at **Playa La Cabaña,** 300m west.

The budget option of the area is the **Hotel Don Humberto,** 300m west of the Castillo San Felipe. Small rooms have royal beds and private baths. The reign of tranquility is regularly shattered here by an early-morning radio show. (Q21 for 1, 2, or 3 people.) RV parking is available at the **Tienda Glendy** next to Don Humberto. **Restaurant La Cabaña,** near Playa La Cabaña, serves *mojarra* (Q20) and sandwiches (Q4.50) daily 9am to 10pm.

San Felipe can be reached with the mail boat, which leaves Livingston Tuesday and Friday at 9am (Q30) or by private *lancha* (from Livingston one-way Q40 per person, round-trip Q50; from the Río Dulce bridge one way Q15 per *lancha*, round-trip Q25). To leave San Felipe, catch the mail boat to Livingston (Tues. and Fri. 6am), or hire a private *lancha*. There is also a 4km-long road between Fronteras and San Felipe, but there is no regular transport, so either walk the distance, or hire a pickup from Fronteras' main street (Q25).

■■■ LIVINGSTON

Livingston may very well be your long-sought paradise. Here the people hang out in hammocks, wear colorful dresses, bake coco bread, shake to a reggae beat, laze under palm trees, and fish for a living. They work to live, not live to work; they don't have much, but there is no sense of poverty. Unlike elsewhere in Guatemala, there is no sense that this is only a man's idyllic world—women hang out in the streets and socialize on equal terms.

Kicking back at the mouth of the Río Dulce, Livingston was once the largest port in Central America. Now an isolated enclave of Caribbean culture, its population is primarily *gariganu*, descendants of Africans brought to the Caribbean in the 16th century. Their language, *Garifuna*, is a blend of Spanish, English and Dutch.

ORIENTATION AND PRACTICAL INFORMATION

Livingston really only has two main streets perpendicular to each other. Each is parallel to a different beach, however, because the town is on a promontory. The largest street leads directly up a hill from the main dock; the secondary one branches left at the public school. There are no banks in Livingston, so try the stores for **changing money. Guatel** is on the hill leading up from the dock. (Open daily 7am-7pm). The **post office** is right behind it. (Open Mon.-Fri. 8am-4:30pm. **Postal code:** 18002.) **Farmacia Livingston** (open daily 8am-8:30pm) is also on the main drag. The **Centro de Salud** is above Playa la Capitanilla about 200m to the left of the Guatel sign on the main street (open 24 hrs.). The **police** are on the main street, right after the Guatel sign. (Open 24 hrs.; knock if door is closed.)

There is no transportation by land. Public **boats** leave for Puerto Barrios daily at 5am and 2pm (1½hrs., Q2.40-3.50). Private *lanchas* leave from the same dock every hour or as soon as there are five to six people (Q15 per person, 25min.). *Expresos* leave as soon as you want them for Q150 per trip (6 person maximum). To the RíoDulce bridge and Fronteras (to connect with the road to Flores, Tikal or Guatemala), there is a direct service with the mail boat (Tues. and Fri. at 9am, Q30). Otherwise private *lanchas* make the trip for Q300 (Q50 per person minimum), stopping on the way at the hot springs, the *biotopo* and Castillo San Felipe (4hrs). Add Q10 per person for the return trip. With a *cayuco*, a smaller and less stable boat, the same trip is Q40 per person, plus Q10 for the return. You can also hire boats to less common destinations, but then prices are per trip, and it is up to you to find people to share the cost; six to eight people fit in a boat. Crafts go to Punta del Pirata, the Siete Altares waterfalls, the *biotopo* and the *aguas calientes* for Q100-250 round-trip. You can also hire a *lancha* to Punta Gorda, Belize, for Q500 per *lancha* (6-8 people). **NB:** Get your exit stamp at the Immigration Office in Livingston, located 100m to the right of the main street at the Guatel sign (open daily 8am-6pm).

ACCOMMODATIONS

El Chiringuito, a 1-hr. walk (or hire a launch) from Livingston on the beach, and 15 min. from the cascades. Beauty of a deserted beach, comfort of cane bungalow suites with sitting room and bedroom, and unparalleled friendliness of Spanish owner make this ideal for longer vacations. Q14 per night. Q12 per night for 3 nights. Q8 per night for a week. Q200 per month. Attached restaurant serves amazing food (vegetarian spaghetti Q17, fresh fish Q20).

African Place, at the end of the secondary street. Looks more like an African Palace. The white castle with breezy rooms even has a drawbridge. Spanish owner trades English books daily 5-6pm. Singles with fans Q20. Doubles Q25, with bath Q35. Triples Q30, with bath Q40. 5-occupant rooms Q75, with bath Q100.

Hotel Caribe, 50m left from dock, the 1st hotel you come to. Most travelers never go farther. Simple but spacious rooms with immaculate bathrooms. Singles Q9. Doubles Q18, with bath Q23. Triples Q35. Fans Q5 per night.

FOOD

If the Caribbean street specialties par excellence—*pan de coco* and *pie de piña* (coco bread and pineapple pie)—haven't filled you all up, Livingston's two main streets are lined up with cafeterias and inexpensive eateries. For more sophisticated ambience, options are limited.

African Place, (see Accommodations). The spot to corner in town. Some tables overlook the jungle. Chicken *a la nigeriana* Q15. Crab soup Q10. Pancakes with honey Q6. Open daily 8am-3pm and 6-10pm.

Restaurant El Tiburón, behind Hotel Tucan Dugú. The classiest in town, with a gorgeous view of Río Dulce's surrender to the Caribbean. A whole fish Q20. Conch or shrimp Q33-35. Lobster Q50. Open daily 7am-10pm.

Cafetería Christy, 50m down the secondary street. A popular cheapo. An entire fish goes for Q9, vegetable soup for Q8 and sandwiches for Q4. Open daily 8:30am-2pm and 6pm-2am.

SIGHTS AND ENTERTAINMENT

Another half hour down the Río Dulce through the looming escarpments lie the **aguas calientes** (hot springs). Your boat driver can take you to them, but those with decent nasal skills may be able to sniff out these sulfur springs on their own. The piping-hot waters form a natural hot tub beneath the encroaching jungle. The Río Dulce boat ride is well worth the time and money, even just for the last half hour, when the river winds through a towering chasm.

Another half hour up the river is the **Biotopo Chocon Machacas,** which supposedly protects manatees. (Open daily 7am-4pm). Your 15-minute jaunt along the jungle path in the *biotopo* will only rarely flush out a jaguar or a tapir, and the shy "sea cows" do a great job of hiding in the river. Still, the *biotopo* is worthwhile—if not for the giant tree ferns and butterflies on the walk, then for the eclectic collection (from a manatee skeleton to "white tail deer legs donated by a hunter") in the "museum." (Donations accepted.) The resident flat-footed monkey named Pancha does passable Fred Astaire imitations on your luggage. The aquatic part of the *biotopo* includes several scenic lagoons; negotiate with your boat driver to take you through them. The *biotopo* has a free camping area with bathrooms, kitchen facilities and well-trained mosquito squadrons.

On the Caribbean side of Livingston are the cascades, **Siete Altares,** an hour-and-a-half walk from town along the beach (or hire a launch). Crisp clear pools dappled by sunlight are light years better than Livingston's beaches. You can stop for refreshments or a stay at **El Chiringuito Hotel** on the way.

Two-thirds of the way to Siete Altares, you will cross the **Vuelve Mujer River** and you can hire a motor boat or paddle with a small *cayuco* (ask one of the local people living nearby) up the river to where it disappears in the stones. Small but refreshingly cool pools will reward your efforts. The best place to play in the water in Livingston is **Playa La Capitanilla,** at the end of the Guatel street. The water is sweet, but unfortunately never gets more than waist-deep.

Livingston makes up for its sleepy-village atmosphere on weekend nights. **Bars** and beachside **discos** (like **Luguti Barana**) open whenever a client shows up. Beachside discos, however, have a bad reputation for drug and alcohol problems, robberies and fights. Popular in town is **Raymundo,** near the dock (open Sat.-Sun. only). Keep your eyes peeled for crowds and your ears open for the thumpin' reggae to find a given night's happenin' spot. Alternatively, catch the nightly 7:30pm showing of action movies at the **Video Centro,** immediately left of Almacén Xelajn on the secondary street (Q1).

■■■ PUERTO BARRIOS

Puerto Barrios is at the end of the highway from Guatemala to the Caribbean. Once Guatemala's most important port, the city lost significance with the development of Pacific ports, but it never lost the trappings of bustling trade. Dens of ill repute and lusty-eyed men still fill the unbearably hot and dusty streets. Truly unpleasant to visit, Puerto Barrios is just a stepping stone to Livingston or Punta Gorda in Belize.

If you decide to stay, you'll feel safest at **Caribbean Hotel and Restaurant Calypso,** 7 Calle, 6/7 Avs. (tel. 480-494). They have live music nightly (7-11pm) in the attached restaurant, cable TV and powerful fans. (Singles Q35, with A/C Q48. Doubles Q70, with A/C Q96. Triples Q88, with A/C Q105.) The restaurant serves conch with coconut milk (Q25) and seafood sheesh kebab (Q25). (Open 24 hrs.)

Litegua buses, 6 Av., 9/10 Calles (tel. 481-172), go to Guatemala City (14 per day, 5-6hrs., Q22-30). Other buses leave from 6 Av., 9 Calle, to Chiquimula, Zacapa, Bananera and San Cristóbal at the El Salvador border. **Ferries** dock at 1 Av., 12 Calle, and go to Livingston (2 per day, 1½hrs., Q2.60-3.50) and Punta Gorda, Belize (Tue. and Fri. 8am, 2½hrs., Q21.40). Buy tickets to Belize at least one day in advance from **Agencia Lineas Marítimas Empornac,** 1 Av., 11/12 Calles. (Open Mon.-Sat. 7am-noon and 2-5pm.)

Change currency at **Banco del Café,** 13 Calle, 7 Av. (Open Mon.-Thurs. 8:30am-8pm, Fri. 8am-8pm.) The **post office,** 6 Av., 6 Calle (tel. 480-748), is open Mon.-Fri. 8am-4:30pm. The **postal code** is 18001. Phones are at **Guatel,** 8 Av., 10 Calle (tel. 480-121), open daily 7am-midnight. The **24-hr. pharmacy** rotates, but for extended hours go to **Farmacia Americana,** 9 Calle, 6/7 Avs. (tel. 480-842); open Mon.-Sat. 7am-9pm, Sun. 7am-noon. In a **medical emergency,** call the *bomberos* 24 hrs., 5 Av., 5/6 Calles (tel. 122). The **police** are available 24 hrs. at 6 Av., 5 Calle (tel. 480-730).

■■■ POPTÚN

Though considerably less spectacular and popular than Tikal, southern Petén is a vital part of Guatemala's archaeological record. Unfortunately, the numerous sites remain largely undeveloped and would hardly attract anyone besides certified archaeology fiends. The real reason to visit Poptún, the largest town in South Petén, is **Finca Ixobel,** a garden of Eden within daytrip distance of fascinating caves and gorgeous rainforest.

ORIENTATION AND PRACTICAL INFORMATION

Poptún's muddy streets want for names and numbers. **Buses** arrive at and depart from the gas station on the main streets, but services are dispersed throughout town.

The only bank, **Bandesa** (tel. 507-312), is located three blocks west and four-and-a-half blocks south of the gas station. (Open for exchange Mon.-Fri. 8:30am-2:30pm.) The **post** and **telegraph office** is in front of Salón de Usos Múltiples, 300m north of the gas station. (Open Mon.-Fri. 8am-4:30pm and 24 hrs. respectively). **Guatel** (tel. 507-298) is three blocks west and half-a-block south of the gas station and will make your calls daily 7am-9pm. The **market,** a block west of the gas station, is busy daily from 6am to 6pm. **Farmacia Hermano Pedro** (tel. 507-218), on the main drag and behind the gas station, is open daily 7am to 9pm. The **Centro de Salud** (tel.507-303), 150m north of the gas station, is open 24 hrs. for medical emergencies. For other emergencies, the **police** (tel. 507-315), next to the municipal building two block west of the gas station, is also open 24 hrs.

Maya Express (tel. 507-483), one block south of the gas station, has first class buses to Guatemala City (2 per day, 9 hrs., Q45) and to Flores (2 per day, 3hrs., Q15). **Fuente del Norte** (tel. 507-290), just north of the gas station, operates first-class buses to Guatemala City (4 per day, Q40) and to Flores (4 per day, Q10). A second-class bus goes to Guatemala City at 5am (Q25).

ACCOMMODATIONS AND FOOD

Consider spending the night (and a couple of days) at **Finca Ixobel,** 3km south of Poptún, but if you are set on sleeping in town, there are several good places to do so. **Hospedaje Fonda Ixobel,** right where the bus drops you off, is run by the same people as the Finca and has big clean rooms and big, but not-so-clean communal baths. (Cold water only. Singles Q6. Doubles Q10, with bath Q15. Triple with bath Q20.) For more comfort, try **Posada de los Castellanos** (tel. 507-222), in front of the market, one block west and half-a-block south of the bus drop off. Spotless rooms have neither hot water nor fans, but always private baths. (Singles Q11. Doubles Q16.50. Triples Q22.)

The best food is at **Restaurante La Fonda Ixobel,** in front of the gas station. Also run by the same people as the Finca, it gives you a chance to find out what the Finca is all about and make plans to visit the next day. All food (including bread, granola, yogurt, etc.) is deliciously home-made. *Chimichangas* (big tortilla with meat, beans, cheese and onions) go for Q8.50, granola with fruit for Q7. The banana bread of your dreams is Q1.25. (Open daily 7am-midnight.)

SIGHTS AND ENTERTAINMENT

Finca Ixobel, 3km south of Poptún, has become notorious for the spell it casts upon travelers, who come for a day, but end up staying for several days, several weeks, or even several months. The Finca offers thrilling one-day cave excursions—you'll swim parts, dive in deep dark pools and do a bit of rock-climbing, all the while balancing candles and flashlights (Q12, bring flashlight and sturdy shoes in which you could swim). Also available are four-day jungle trips (Q350, 2 days on horseback), inner-tubing on the Machiquila River (Q50), horseback riding (Q30 for 2 hrs.), self-guided tours to two nearby (25min. and 45min. walk) caves, swimming in a pond with an exceptionally scenic background, soccer, volleyball, ping-pong, frisbee and the super-friendly company of other travelers. At night sleep in a hammock or a sleeping bag (Q2, bag rental is free), a dorm bed (Q13), or an adult-size tree houses. You can also camp (Q7) or take a comfortable private room (singles Q25, doubles Q32). And watch your weight, for the cook is a virtuoso and everything is homemade—from the bread and the granola to the unforgettable family-style buffet dinners (Q18), enormous sandwiches (Q9.50) and five-star banana, apple, or carrot bread (Q1.50). To get there, ask the bus driver to drop you off at the big sign for

Finca Ixobel and walk the remaining 1.5km, or borrow a bike from Fonda Ixobel in Poptún and bike the 3km south.

At least partially developed, though still very small, are the archaeological sights of **Poxté** (40km), **Ixtupu** (30km) and **Dolores** (28km), all north of Poptún. Dolores has the most to offer to enthusiasts. The person to look for is Sr. Dacio Castellanos, an inspector of national monuments. (Ask local people for his whereabouts.) He will gladly take you for free to and through the ruins of **Ixcun,** 8km north of Dolores, or **Ixtonton,** 1.5km northeast. Both have stelae and small temples and are accessible only on foot or horse (rented horses Q10 per day). The tour and entrances are free. If you have a hammock or a sleeping bag, you can also stay at the guardians' house for free. All Flores-bound buses pass through Dolores (45min., Q3) from Poptún.

■■■ SANTA ELENA AND FLORES

Connected by a causeway, Santa Elena and the island city Flores are the staging grounds for trips to Tikal. Regular **buses** only go as far as Santa Elena; to get to Tikal you must catch a minibus there or in Flores (at 6am and 8am). If you miss these early morning vans or if you find Tikal's lodgings prohibitively expensive, don't despair. Santa Elena and Flores make it cheap and painless to stay.

To kill time in Flores, local fisherfolk often take visitors on tours of the lake. Boats stop at a small zoo, a waterslide and a humdrum Mayan ruin (Q15 per person). Swimming in the lake is not recommended because of pollution. Instead, visit the **Actun Can Cave,** 2km south of Santa Elena. The cave has 300m (½hr.) of well-illuminated paths with signs pointing to imaginative natural shapes, and several km of unilluminated pathways, which have outlets as far north as Santa Elena and on the southern side of the mountain (the adventurous should bring their own flashlights). To get to the cave follow the street which is a continuation of the causeway; at its end bear left and then turn right at the red arrow marked "Actun Can." (Open daily 8am-6pm. Admission Q7.)

ORIENTATION AND PRACTICAL INFORMATION

Buses stop in **Santa Elena**'s dusty market, just a few hundred meters across the causeway. Stock up for long hauls here, then head across the lake to Flores. An **INGUAT office** is located at Santa Elena's airport, but tourist information is available in town at **Información Turística El Tucan,** on Av. Central America (tel. 501-380), near the intersection with Calle 30 de Junio (open Mon.-Sat. 8am-noon and 2-6pm). The **Banco de Guatemala,** at the end of Calle 30 de Junio in Flores (tel. 501-363), is open Monday through Thursday from 8:30am to 2pm and Friday for an extra half hour. In Santa Elena, **Bandesa,** 0 Av. and 2 Calle is open Monday through Friday 8am to 4pm. If you need cash after hours, several luxury hotels change money. Beyond the causeway, walk left on Central America and bear right at the end of the street. **Hotel Petén,** on the left, changes traveler's checks until 9pm at a fair rate. The **post office** is in the center of Flores on Pasaje Progreso, just east of the central park (open Mon.-Fri. 8am-4:30pm). **Guatel** is on the corner of 6 Av. and 5 Calle in SantaElena (tel. 501-299) and is open daily 7am to 9pm. Hotel Petén in Flores makes international calls before 9pm. There is a Q5 fee on collect calls for non-guests.

Second-class **Fuente del Norte** buses (tel. 500-517) leave Santa Elena from a yellow building on the right three blocks through the market. Buy tickets in advance to Guatemala City (2 per day, 14hr.s, Q35) via Río Dulce (Q25). First-class buses leave thrice daily (12hrs., Q50) via Río Dulce (Q40). One bus a day goes to Malchor on the Belizean border, at 7am (3hrs., Q10). The office will store your luggage for the day (7am-10pm) for Q1 per piece. **Maya Express** (tel. 500-127) has a direct bus from San Benito to Guatemala City leaving at 5pm and 8pm (12hr., Q50). **Pinita** buses go to Melchor, Belizean border (3hrs., Q10); El Naranjo (5hrs., Q12); and Sayaxché (2hrs. Q5), departing from the Santa Elena market. **Rosita** serves Melchor and **Del Rocío** serves Sayaxché. Both leave from Santa Elena's market. To Tikal, there are regular

Pinita buses at 6:30am and 1pm (2½hrs., Q10) and numerous express vans (1hr., Q20 one-way, Q30 round-trip). You can sign up for a **van** at any of the travel agencies and at most hotels in Flores and Santa Elena. To Poptún (3hrs., Q6) and to Río Dulce (7½hrs., Q50), take any of the Guatemala City-bound buses. **Taxis** shuttle between Flores and Santa Elena for Q10 and to the airport for Q15. To order one in Flores call 500-034 or walk to the corner of Central America and 30 de Junio. In Santa Elena, catch one around the bus station. **Travel Agency San Juan** in Hotel San Juan just off the causeway in Santa Elena (tel. 500-042) has special bus services to Belize, Chetumal and Ceibal. Airplanes leave Santa Elena's **airport** for Guatemala City (3 per day, US$53.50); Belize City (1 per day, 5 days per week; US$46.80); Chetumal, Mexico (1 per day, 3 days per week; US$81.90); and Cancún (1-2 per day, 4 days per week; US$111.15). Make reservations at any travel agency. For best deals contact **Agencia de Viajes Arco Iris,** on Central American in Flores (tel. 501-266). He will drive you to the airport for half the price of other hotels and taxis, and if you buy the tickets from him, for free. (Open Mon.-Sat. 8am-noon and 2-6pm, Sun. 8am-noon.)

ACCOMMODATIONS AND FOOD

Both cities have an array of budget accommodations. Flores is the more expensive of the two, but it's also cleaner and nicer. **El Tucan,** Central America (tel. 500-577), at the far end of the avenue on the water, has a gorgeous lake view, several overly garrulous parrots and spotless bathrooms. (Doubles Q33. Triples Q49.50. Bungalow for five Q15 per bed.) **Hotel Itzá,** on C. Principal along the lake shore, has unattractive decor but private baths and fans. (Singles Q20. Doubles Q30. Triples Q35.) **Hotel Leo Fu Lo,** 6 Av., ½ Calles, on the lake's shore, has spacious well-fanned rooms and all-helpful staff. (Singles Q15. doubles Q25. Triples Q35.) Two dorrs away, the **Mesón de Don Quijote** has high ceilings and low beds. (Singles Q14, with bath and fan Q35. Doubles Q23, with bath and fan Q35. Triples Q30.) **Hotel San Juan,** on 2 Calle, one block from the causeway, is where the 5am bus to Naranjo departs. (Singles Q20, with bath Q50. Doubles Q25, with bath Q50. Triples Q60.)

The only alternative to the pricy restaurants in Flores are thenumerous *comedores* that line the street. They offer standard fare of eggs and beans for Q8. Beans and chicken or meat go for Q12. If you're craving unauthentic nachos (Q17) and burritos (Q18), join other travelers for a modest serving at **El Tucan.** (Open daily 8am-10pm.) **La Mesa de los Mayas,** on El Crucero off Central America, serves atypical typical fare: grilled deer (Q25), armadillo (Q25), wild turkey (Q25) and tongue (Q12). (Open daily 8am-11pm.)

In Santa Elena, **Restaurante Leo Fu Lo,** at the end of the causeway, has a gorgeous view of the lake and authentic Chinese cuisine. (Fried rice with chicken and eggs Q15. Chinese style fish or duck Q30. Open daily 10am-midnight.) Serving a few vegetarian dishes is **Restaurant Lago Azul,** 2 Calle and 4 Av. (Small portions of vegetable soup Q5, spaghetti Q7, chicken with fries and salad Q15.)

■■■ TIKAL

Tikal is probably the most fascinating archaeological site in the Americas. Situated in northern region of Petén 670km north of Guatemala City, the ruins encompass over 3000 different Mayan stone constructions, including six towers, of which two are entirely excavated. You'll need at least two days to do Tikal, both the complex center and the surrounding **Parque Nacional Tikal** (222 square mi.). Those fortunate enough to witness a full moon rising over Temple IV and the encroaching jungle often cite it as one of the most memorable sights of their life. The jungle is as intriguing as are the ruins themselves. Falling fruit is a tell-tale sign of spider monkeys overhead; remote paths hide wild parrots, peacocks, lizards, iguanas and buzzcocks; and lucky early risers may spot a sacred jaguar slinking through the undergrowth.

ORIENTATION

Not all roads lead to Tikal; in fact, it's hard to get there. Most **bus** connections are made through Flores, one hour outside Tikal. Overland routes connect Tikal with Tenosique (Mexico), Guatemala City and Belize City. The Belize route is the most comfortable and popular of the three. Buses from Belize City run daily to the Guatemalan border (see Belize City to Guatemala above); buses to Flores leave the border between 5am and 4pm (3hrs., Q10). Get off at the intersection two-thirds of the way to Flores at El Cruce (**Ixlu crossing**) and catch the Pinita bus which runs to Tikal at 6:30am and 1pm (2½hrs., Q10). Microbuses (45min., Q20) run at 6am and 8am. Few cars go to Tikal, making hitching virtually impossible and not recommended. Consult either the U.S. State Department or the U.S. Consulate in Guatemala City about the safety of overland routes to Tikal (see Health, Safety and Security in the General Introduction).

Buses from Flores directly to Tikal (2½hrs., Q10) leave at 6:30am and 1pm from Hotel San Juan near the causeway. Tikal-bound microbuses leave from most hotels at 6am and 8am (45min., Q20) returning at 2pm and 4pm.

Four **airlines** shuttle daily between Guatemala City and **Santa Elena,** which is just across the lake from Flores and is served by the same buses and microbuses. Buy your ticket in the capital or Santa Elena and book at least one day in advance. The planes leave Guatemala City at 7am and 4pm, returning at 8am, 4pm and 5pm (1hr., US$55). Charter flights from Mexico and Belize also serve Santa Elena.

Not surprisingly, buses from Guatemala City are cheaper than planes, but by land you'll suffer through 280km of jarring dirt roads in the leg between Morales and Santa Elena. Should you decide to brave the bus, take the first-class Pullman, which has shock absorbers and doesn't make rest stops to relieve the chickens (12hrs., Q50). The regular bus takes at least 15 hours on a good day (Q35). The recommended bus to take is the 5pm Maya Express which leaves the capital from 17 Calle 9-36 z. 1 and arrives in Santa Elena at 6am, in time for the microbuses to Tikal.

To keep up with the Indiana Joneses, take the wildest and most cinematic alternative: a boat and bus odyssey from Tenosique, Mexico. This involves a four-hour cruise up the Río San Pedro to El Naranjo, Guatemala (expensive at Q75, but fun). From El Naranjo you'll bounce five hours east over dirt roads to Santa Elena (Q12).

Passing into **Tikal National Park,** officials will relieve you of Q30 at a checkpoint 17km from the site itself. Save the ticket; you'll need it to enter the ruins. If you plan to stay in the ruins past 5pm for the sunset, have an inspector stamp it (good until 8pm; the stamp is free).

Because of its remoteness and its high price, Tikal requires no special safety precautions. Camping, solo walks in the jungle and sleeping in the ruins (though illegal) pose no unusual dangers.

PRACTICAL INFORMATION

As befits a small jungle outpost, Tikal offers minimal services. There is a small **visitors center** which has a scale model of the site and sells maps (Q2) and guidebooks (Q45). It is located in the large building on the left next to the Café Restaurant del Parque. The **post office** (open Mon.-Fri. 8am-noon and 2-4pm, till 6pm for the **telegraph**) is on the right as you enter the complex. For **medical emergencies** go to Flores; the clinic in Tikal has minimal resources. (Open Mon.-Fri. 7am-noon and 2-5pm.) There are public bathrooms in the visitors center and throughout the archaeological site. Change money before you get here, because the exchange rate in hotels here is 10% lower than banks and even Flores hotels.

ACCOMMODATIONS AND FOOD

Tikal has one good campground and three moderately priced hotels. Single rooms are expensive, and travelers would be wise to travel in groups of two or three to Tikal to cut costs. The popular **camping complex,** set in a vast grassy field, consists of large concrete platforms with thatched roofs. Less amiable than your fellow backpackers are the mosquito squads and occasional scorpions or tarantulas. Communal bathrooms have showers, but lockers are not available. Camping costs Q30 per person. To rent a hammock add Q10, and for a mosquito net another Q5. (2-person tents Q20.)

Hotel Jaguar Inn offers well-furnished bungalows and three meals a day. Electricity only runs 6-10pm. (Singles Q150. Doubles Q200. Triples Q275. Tent Q40 per person.) **The Jungle Lodge** has basic bungalows and no meal plan. (Electricity 5-7:30am and 5:30-11pm. Singles US$15, with bath US$30. Doubles US$20, with bath US$40.) **Tikal Inn,** after Jaguar Inn, has attractive rooms around an even more attractive garden, but is lit only 6-9:30pm. Breakfast and dinner meal plan is optional. (Singles US$20, with meals US$30. Doubles US$30, with meals US$50. Triples US$45, with meals US$75.)

A couple fly-infested *comedores* and a **mini-mart** face the visitors center. They have identical menus and prices: eggs and beans for Q8, chicken and beans for Q12, beef and beans for Q12 (open daily 6am-9pm). **Comedor Tikal** offers the best selection for budget travelers. (Sandwiches for Q6, vegetarian dishes or spaghetti Q10. Open daily 7am-9pm.) The **Restaurant Jaguar Inn** caters to the millionaire-at-eighteen crowd, with bean prices set accordingly. A full breakfast (pancake, eggs, fried bananas, homemade bread and coffee) costs Q12.50. Complete lunches are Q20, dinners Q25. (Open daily 7am-8:30pm.)

SIGHTS

Ceramic shards prove that ancient Maya settled the site at least as early as 600 BC, and seashells from the Pacific Coast and jade from the highlands testify to Tikal's extensive role in the Mesoamerican trade network. Architectural details and artifacts from several tombs suggest that Tikal was influenced by distant Teotihuacán, near modern Mexico City. Most of the temples and other constructions at Tikal date from the late Classic period (550-900 AD), when Tikal may have had anywhere from 20,000 to 70,000 inhabitants. It thrived longer than any other ancient metropolis, but like Palenque and other important Mayan lowland centers, Tikal collapsed mysteriously at the end of the Classic era. Theories of its downfall include war with the Aztecs, a fast-spreading plague, or a catastrophic rebellion. While post-Classic descendants of the original population continued to live and worship at Tikal, they did little of significance but pillage the tombs. By 1000 AD, the jungle was the final usurper of Tikal's civilization. The modern world did not rediscover Tikal until 1848, when Guatemalans Modesto Méndez and Ambrosio Tut stumbled upon the site. It was left undisturbed for another 58 years, when excavation exposed layer upon layer of platforms and monuments.

Begin your tour at the **Great Plaza,** Tikal's geographic and ceremonial heart, 2km west of the site entrance. Facing north in the plaza, the terraced **North Acropolis** lies ahead. To the right and left are the symmetrical **Temples I** and **II.** The **Central Acropolis** is behind, designed to exhibit the spiritual importance of the number nine—Mayans believed in a world beneath the earth ruled by the Nine Lords of the Night.

Temple I, or the Temple of the Great Jaguar, towers 45m (145 ft.) above the Grand Plaza. Built around 700 AD, this structure, the modern-day symbol of Tikal, has nine sharply ascending terraces supporting a three-chambered temple on top. The first seven steps have been restored to their original state, but the stairs to the top are well-worn, making them slippery when wet. Its westward orientation (toward the setting sun) and the fact that the other temples face it emphasize its importance among Tikal's constructions. Only a few carved lintels remain in the upper chambers, but the view is fantastic. Many of Tikal's artifacts have been snatched by museums in Europe and the U.S.

Across the plaza, **Temple II,** or the Temple of the Masks, is shorter and easy to scale. Excavations at the **North Acropolis,** a partiallyrestored complex of temples, have revealed at least 10 levels of construction dating from progressively earlier eras, as well as several stelae and rich burial tombs. Descendants of the Mayans now leave their mark on the acropolis in brightly colored spray paint. The **ballcourt,** just south of Temple I, used to host a *pok-ta-pok* game akin to soccer but played with a hard rubber ball. Sacrificial decapitation awaited the winners. Rulers occupied the Great Plaza, burying their dead in large pyramids, while commoners lived in thatched huts outside the area, laying their dead to rest under the kitchen floor.

One kilometer west of the Great Plaza, on Tozzer Causeway, is **Temple IV,** or the Temple of the Two-Headed Serpent (dating from 741 A.D.), the tallest construction in pre-Columbian America. 70m (212 ft.) from base to roof, the pyramid is almost completely shrouded in jungle growth. Clamber up the tangle of roots and ladders at the structure's northeast corner to the summit, where a satisfying view awaits. It takes walls 40-ft. thick to support the massive ornamental roof comb.

Temple V faces east, 500m south of the Great Plaza. The 57m (190-ft.) temple has a small chamber at the top, accessible only by a daring ascent up metal scaffolding. At the subterranean **Palace of the Masks,** 0.5km southwest of Temple V, bas-relief carvings depict a number of gods; one is a pregnant woman. Ornate hieroglyphs cover the towering roof comb of the **Temple of the Inscriptions,** 2km southeast of the Great Plaza. Most visible at dawn, the monumental symbols record the Mayan date 9.16.15.0.0 (766 AD). Ancient graffiti at **Maler's Place** tells of the Mayan practice of squeezing the head of a ruling class infant between two boards to create the high-status flattened skull. At **Group G,** the walls depict a human sacrifice with the victim spread over an altar to facilitate the removal of his heart. The walls are channeled, to allow orderly outflow of freshly liberated blood. Unfortunately, the tunnel with the drawings has been closed to the public. Southwest of the Great Plaza is **Mundo Perdido** (Lost World). Rumor has it that the name derives from a depiction of two men making love, found in one of the tunnels in the complex.

The small **Museum of Tikal,** at the entrance to the site, displays a collection of ceramics, stelae, jade offerings, and carved and painted bones. Richly detailed Stela 31 depicts "Stormy Sky," a 5th-century AD governor of Tikal. Peer down at the reconstruction of Tomb 116, which contains a full skeleton accompanied by shells and ceramics, as well as 16 pounds of jade. (Admission Q10.) The **Litico Museum of Stelae** at the visitors center is free. (Both open Mon.-Fri. 9am-5pm, Sat.-Sun. 9am-4pm.)

Visit the ruins at dawn or dusk, when the air is cool and the animals most active. Climb **Temple IV** at sunrise for a breath-taking view of the ruins and the jungle coming alive. Leave from the camping or the hotels by 5:30am to arrive on time. The Mundo Perdido pyramid is great for viewing the sunset. Bring mosquito repellent and a flashlight (for exploring dark corners and finding your way out at nightfall). The site is officially open daily from 6am to 6pm (admission Q30), but you can stay until 8pm if you get the back of your ticket stamped in advance at the administration building (left up a small slope at the site entrance). The ticket must be renewed each day. No food is available at the site.

To sightsee intelligently, invest in a handbook to the ruins or hire a guide; a quick study of the scale model by the museum provides a good introduction to Tikal but won't suffice. Tikal's major attractions are dispersed over a four square-km area, and few signs point the way. A useful map of the site (Q2) is available at the visitors center and hotels (see Practical Information, Accommodations). Better yet, pick up William Coe's *Tikal,* the classic guide to the ruins (at the visitors center) with a large pull-out map, beautiful illustrations and a tiresome text (Q45). Tour guides are available at the hotels and site entrance (some of the "most studied" guides have merely memorized Coe's handbook). Tours that include the ruins, the flora and the fauna last three hours and cost Q100.

Costa Rica

This is nature at its sexiest. Well-endowed by dripping cloud forests, red-hot volcanoes, and lush flora, Costa Rica easily seduces even the most fanatic of urbanites. Even childhood fantasies of storybook jungles filled with wild beasts are realized. Getting to many of these idyllic settings, however, may mean risking bodily integrity over potholed roads in torrential tropical rains. (The entire resort towns of Quepos and Manuel Antonio were shut down in the summer of 1993, preventing tourists from leaving.) More worrisome still is the temptation to wealthy investors and less wealthy locals who stand to benefit economically from the nation's natural resources. Yet Costa Rica steadfastedly pursues the most enlightened preservation policies in Central America. Visitors will soon find themselves frolicking in the magnificent surroundings of talking parrots and voluptuous orchids.

Christopher Columbus surely hoped to find more tangible signs of wealth when he skimmed the Central American coast during his fourth voyage in 1502. The wealth and power of the Costa Rican *indígenas* did not compare to the mega-empires of the Aztecs of Incas.

The arrival of the Spaniards (and of their European diseases) wiped out many of the various small indigenous populations. Most *ticos*, as Costa Ricans call themselves, are of European descent, rather than of mestizo or indigenous heritage. *Indígenas* comprise less than one percent of the country's population of three million and currently live on reservations, and Black Caribs concentrated in and around Puerto Limón comprise only about three percent of the population. Because of the homogeneity of the population, the established socio-economic structures common in the rest of Latin America—poor *indígenas*, middle-class mestizos and rich *criollos*—never developed in Costa Rica. The small number and territorial concentration of minorities have hidden the class disparities that do exist.

Since its independence in 1848, Costa Rican society has managed to be more egalitarian and democratic than any other in the region. The adoption of a republican form of government and the abolition of the army under the Constitution of 1949 have spared Costa Rica the political instability which has plagued other Central and South American countries. In fact, Costa Rica has been at the head of the movement for peace and stability in the region. Two prominent Costa Ricans have been nominated for the Nobel Peace Prize, and former President Oscar Arias Sánchez received the award in 1987. The current president, Rafael Ángel Calderón Fournier, of the PUSC (United Christian Socialists), succeeded Arias in 1990.

The political and judicial systems closely parallel those of the U.S., but presidents and vice-presidents cannot run for two consecutive terms. *Ticos* are justifiably proud of their strong democratic tradition and their excellent social security system. Medical insurance here is universal and elementary education is free and compulsory, achieving a literacy rate of more than 90 percent. Roman Catholics make up an overwhelming 95 percent of the population, and society is based around the family. There is no characteristic more common to *ticos* than their friendliness; to *hacer amistades* (make friends) is always a *tico*'s top priority, so get in the spirit and enjoy.

Three mountain ranges run north-south through the country, bounded by extensive Pacific coastline on the west and the Caribbean to the east. The province of Guanacaste in the northwest is the only relatively dry region, characterized by a subtropical ecosystem. The rest of the country has been richly endowed with lush tropical flora and fauna. The country has 24 national parks and biological reserves, comprising a total of 15 percent of the country's territory. Most reserves are open to the public and are directly accessible from San José.

The official language is Spanish, though a sizable minority descended from former slaves speaks a Jamaican dialect of English in and around Puerto Limón.

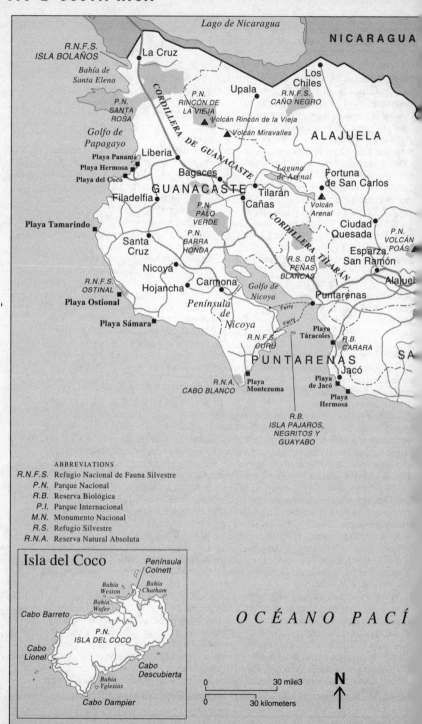

Lago de Nicaragua

NICARAGUA

R.N.F.S. ISLA BOLAÑOS

Bahía de Santa Elena

La Cruz

Los Chiles

P.N. RINCÓN DE LA VIEJA

Upala

R.N.F.S. CAÑO NEGRO

P.N. SANTA ROSA

Volcán Rincón de la Vieja

Volcán Miravalles

ALAJUELA

Golfo de Papagayo

CORDILLERA DE GUANACASTE

Playa Panamá

Liberia

Playa Hermosa

Bagaces

Laguna de Arenal

Fortuna de San Carlos

Playa del Coco

GUANACASTE

Tilarán

Filadelfia

Cañas

Volcán Arenal

Playa Tamarindo

P.N. PALO VERDE

Ciudad Quesada

P.N. VOLCÁN POÁS

Santa Cruz

P.N. BARRA HONDA

CORDILLERA TILARÁN

Esparza

San Ramón

Nicoya

Carmona

R.S. DE PEÑAS BLANCAS

R.N.F.S. OSTINAL

Hojancha

Golfo de Nicoya

Alajuel

Playa Ostional

Península de Nicoya

Puntarenas

Ferry

Playa Sámara

Ferry

R.N.F.S. CURÚ

Playa Táracoles

R.B. CARARA

PUNTARENAS

SA

R.N.A. CABO BLANCO

Playa Montezuma

Playa de Jacó

Jacó

Playa Hermosa

R.B. ISLA PAJAROS, NEGRITOS Y GUAYABO

ABBREVIATIONS

R.N.F.S. Refugio Nacional de Fauna Silvestre

P.N. Parque Nacional

R.B. Reserva Biológica

P.I. Parque Internacional

M.N. Monumento Nacional

R.S. Refugio Silvestre

R.N.A. Reserva Natural Absoluta

Isla del Coco

Península Colnett

Bahía Weston

Bahía Chatham

Bahía Wafer

Cabo Barreto

P.N. ISLA DEL COCO

Cabo Lionel

Cabo Descubierta

Bahía Yglesias

OCÉANO PACÍ

Cabo Dampier

0   30 mile3

0   30 kilometers

N

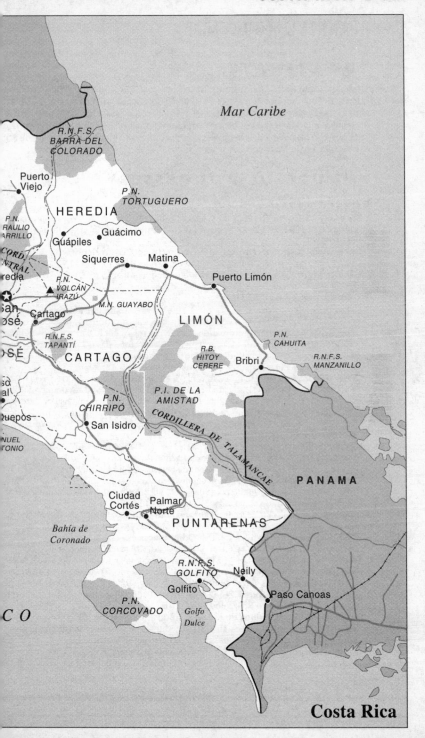

Mar Caribe

R.N.F.S. BARRA DEL COLORADO

Puerto Viejo

HEREDIA

P.N. TORTUGUERO

P.N. BRAULIO CARRILLO

Guápiles

Guácimo

Siquerres

Matina

Puerto Limón

CORD. CENTRAL

edia

P.N. VOLCÁN IRAZÚ

San José

Cartago

M.N. GUAYABO

LIMÓN

P.N. CAHUITA

R.N.F.S. TAPANTÍ

CARTAGO

R.B. HITOY CERERE

Bribri

R.N.F.S. MANZANILLO

P.I. DE LA AMISTAD

P.N. CHIRRIPÓ

San Isidro

CORDILLERA DE TALAMANCA

PANAMA

NUEL TONIO

uepos

Ciudad Cortés

Palmar Norte

PUNTARENAS

Bahía de Coronado

R.N.F.S. GOLFITO

Neily

Golfito

Paso Canoas

P.N. CORCOVADO

Golfo Dulce

C O

Costa Rica

PLANNING YOUR TRIP

■■■ CLIMATE

There are three types of climate in Costa Rica: wet and tropical on the Caribbean side (with high temperatures—24-32°C or 75-90°F—and torrential rains); tropical with a dry season on the Nicoya Peninsula and the Central Valley; and temperate in the higher regions of the country (with temperatures of 18-22°C or 65-72°F). The rainy season (*invierno*) lasts from May to December, and chances are that if you are in Costa Rica, you *will* need rain gear.

■■■ USEFUL ADDRESSES

Government Agencies

Embassy of Costa Rica, 1825 Connecticut Ave. NW, #213, Washington, DC 20009 (tel. (202) 234-2945). Contact them for the address of the consulate nearest you.

Costa Rica National Tourist Bureau/Instituto Costarricense de Turismo (ICT), 1101 Brickel Ave., BIV Tower #801, Miami, FL 33131 (tel. (305) 358-2150). To have general information mailed to you, call (800) 372-7033.

Travel Organizations

Costa Rica Expeditions, Apdo. 6941-1000, Av. 3, Calle Central, San José (tel. (506) 57-0766 or 22-0332, fax 57-1665), 1 block east of the San José post office (see San José: Practical Information). They organize jungle tours to Tortuguero National Park (US$199 for 1 day and night; US$299 for 3 days, 2 nights), as well as 1-day tropical forest adventures (US$65), white-water rafting (US$65), and volcano tours (US$45). Fluent English spoken. Open daily 7am-9pm.

Costa Rica Sun Tours, P.O. Box 1195-1250, Escazú (tel. (506) 55-3418 or 55-3518, fax 55-4410). Dedicated to responsible tourism and recommended by the Audubon Society of Costa Rica. Custom itineraries for natural history, birding, and educational and adventure tours, including cycling and rafting trips. 2-4 day packages US$165-495, including transportation, lodgings, meals, bilingual guides and park fees.

Geotur, Apdo. 469, Y Griega 1011, San José (tel. (506) 34-1867, fax 53-6338). Operates daily natural history tours to national parks for individuals or groups. Custom itineraries; senior and student discounts. All guides are bilingual.

Gonzalez Travel Service, 4508 Academy Dr., Metairie, LA 70003-2835 (tel. (800) 688-4058 or (504) 885-4058, fax (504) 469-7500). Summer and Christmas student airfares for stays of up to 90 days. Group rates offered all year.

Interviajes, Apdo. 296, Heredia 3000 (tel. and fax (506) 38-1212). Offers "super saver" 5-hr. natural history tours to Poás Volcano National Park and other sights. US$25 includes fees, guides and car. Other tour packages start at US$40 per day.

Journey Latin America, 14-16 Devonshire Road, Chiswick, London W4 2HD, U.K. (tel. (+44 81) 747 8315, fax 742 1312). Extensive 14-day tours hit almost all major points: white-water rafting, Poás Volcano, Monteverde, Tortuguero, and Limón. £1022 includes meals and accommodations (with airfare to and from U.K. about £1550). 1-day excursions £25-65. Also offers "Economy Journeys" and "Environmental Expeditions" to Belize and Guatemala.

Jungle Trails/Los Caminos de la Selva, Apdo. 2413, San José (tel. (506) 55-3486, fax 55-2782). Specializes in nature tours and conservation programs. Bird-watching and botany trips, as well as custom itineraries. Invites visitors to meet with subsistence farmers to understand the motivations and circumstances behind deforestation. Tours 1-9 days. Portion of fee is donated to reforestation groups.

Preferred Adventures Ltd., 1 W. Water St., #300, St. Paul, MN 55107 (tel. (612) 222-8131, fax 222-4221). The Upper Midwest's pioneer in Costa Rica travel, with natural history and soft adventure tours. Birding, wildlife study, rainforest tours, photography, rafting and language/culture programs for US$100-125 per person per day (including accommodations, most meals, transport, guides and park fees). Student prices US$75-100.

Publications

South American Explorers Club, U.S. Headquarters, 126 Indian Creek Rd., Ithaca, NY 14850 (tel. (607) 277-0488). A great information resource for travel in Central and South America. Sells books, maps and tapes, but their best tools are the trip reports written by club members who describe the practical details of their travels. Their catalog lists and reviews travel guides to the region. Also publishes quarterly *South American Explorer*. Membership (US$30, couples US$40) entitles you to the magazine, access to their club houses (in Ithaca; Lima, Peru; and Quito, Ecuador), use of their extensive archive of maps and trip reports, and trip planning assistance.

■■■ DOCUMENTS AND FORMALITIES

Tourist Cards, Passports and Visas

All visitors entering Costa Rica must obtain a *tarjeta de turismo* (**tourist card**), available from Costa Rican consulates or from airlines serving the country. You'll need your plane ticket and US$2. In general, tourist cards are valid for 30 days and must be presented along with a valid **passport** to enter the country. Cards may be renewed for up to three months by going to the Dirección de Migración in San José (see Once There: Useful Organizations, below) with your return plane ticket, two photographs, and a passport. Be sure to carry your tourist card and passport at all times.

U.S. citizens do not need a passport to enter Costa Rica; proof of U.S. citizenship will suffice (usually a birth certificate or voter registration card, along with a valid photo ID). You will not be able to renew your tourist card without a passport, however, and some U.S. travelers have had trouble cashing traveler's checks without the document.

U.S. citizens may remain in the country for 90 days on a single tourist card, as can nationals of **Canada,** the **U.K.,** and most other European countries. Tourist cards for travelers from **Australia, New Zealand,** and the **Republic of Ireland** are valid for 30 days. If you stay even a day beyond your allotment, leaving Costa Rica becomes a serious problem. You will have to obtain an exit visa (US$12) and pay a fine (US$3). If you overstay for longer than 30 days, you will be charged an additional US$3 for each subsequent month. To get the exit visa you will have to provide a court certificate, which will cost you about US$0.50 and a lot of hassle.

Customs

Duties on goods entering and leaving Costa Rica can be extremely high. In addition to your personal effects, you are allowed to bring in 500g of tobacco products, three liters of alcohol and a mere 2kg of candy duty-free. If you exit Costa Rica temporarily and can prove absence from the country for a period of three consecutive days, you may bring back an additional US$100 or its equivalent in Costa Rican currency duty-free. There is an **airport departure tax** of US$5.

Driving Permits

The **Dirección de Transporte Automotor,** Av. 18, Calle 5, San José (tel. (506) 27-2188 or 23-4626), grants temporary driving permits to visitors. If you plan to drive in Costa Rica longer than three months, you must qualify to stay beyond the expiration of your tourist card, have a valid passport and apply for a Costa Rican driver's license. Applicants must have a valid foreign license, a medical certificate of good health, and a valid passport.

■■■ MONEY

US$ = 105.97 colones (¢)
CDN$ = ¢89.41
UK£ = ¢203.52
AUS$ = ¢78.79
NZ$ = ¢57.71

¢100 = US$0.94
¢100 = CDN$1.12
¢100 = UK£0.49
¢100 = AUS$1.27
¢100 = NZ$1.73

The Costa Rican currency is the **colón** (¢). Printed prices may use two periods where other countries use a comma and a period (e.g., ¢1.234.56 means one thousand two hundred thirty-four *colones* and fifty-six hundredths).

All hotels are required by law to include 10% **general tax** and a 3% **tourism tax.** In restaurants, a 10% **gratuity** is added to the check, but it is customary to leave an extra tip for particularly good service (perhaps an additional 5%).

■■■ HEALTH AND SAFETY

Life expectancy in Costa Rica is an impressive 74-plus years, a testimony to the quality of the universal medical care provided to all citizens. Serious health hazards are limited to **cholera, diarrhea, amoebic dysentery, malaria** and **typhoid;** these are most frequent away from San José. Drinking water in major hotels and restaurants in the capital is purified. Outside San José, water should be boiled before drinking.

The 1991 earthquake greatly damaged the infrastructure of the Puerto Limón area, and the slow pace of reconstruction has resulted in poor sanitary conditions and a heightened risk of associated diseases. Insect repellent should be bought before departing for Costa Rica, as available brands do little to thwart the hefty appetites of swarming mosquitoes.

As in many parts of Latin America, the relation between the sexes is undeniably different than in North America. Basically, women are subject to more attention than might be expected or desired. Inappropriate overtures can normally be avoided by a firm negative or *lo siento, no me interesa* (I'm sorry but I'm not interested). *Mi amor* is frequently used by both women and men as a term of endearment, much like the British "love."

■■■ ALTERNATIVES TO TOURISM

Costa Rica's extensive nature reserves and high level of environmental consciousness allow visitors to combine sight-seeing with ecological education and activism. **Volunteer** and **internship** positions exist at many conservation groups.
Spanish language study is a well-developed sector of the Costa Rican educational system; numerous schools operate in or near San José. The **Universidad de Costa Rica** offers language and culture programs as well as direct enrollment through several U.S. universities. **WorldTeach Costa Rica/Enseñanza Mundial** turns the tables, recruiting volunteers to serve for one year of teaching English in Costa Rican primary schools, high schools and language institutes. Contact them in the U.S. at the Harvard Institute for International Development, 1 Eliot St., Cambridge, MA 02138-5705 (tel. (617) 495-5527); in Costa Rica at Apdo. 181-2350, San Francisco (tel. (506) 23-7464). Participation fees are about US$3150.

Ecotourism/Environmental Activism

Asociación Preservacionista de Flora y Fauna Silvestre (APREFLOFAS), Apdo. 917-2150, Moravia, San José (tel. (506) 40-6087). A non-profit, volunteer organization that works to guard Costa Rica's natural resources from illegal and destructive exploitation. Promotes reforestation projects. Supported by the World Wildlife Fund. They have a wealth of information on ecotourism in Costa Rica's national parks.

Centro de Derecho Ambiental y de los Recursos Naturales (CEDARENA), Apdo. 134-2050, San Pedro, Costa Rica (tel. (506) 24-8239 or 25-1019, fax 25-5111). A non-profit, apolitical association specializing in environmental law research. Their mission is to incorporate environmental concerns into legislation. Projects include land tenure/use reform, forest conservation, and coastal zone management.

Fundación Neotrópica, Apdo. 236-1002, Paseo de los Estudiantes, San José (tel. (506) 53-2130, fax 53-4210). Promotes sustainable development projects in communities bordering protected areas. Publishes a guide to ecotourism on the Osa Peninsula.

Study

Costa Rican Language Academy, Apdo. 336-2070, Av. Central, Calles 25/27, San José (tel. (506) 21-1624 or 33-8914, fax 33-8670). Language and cultural study custom tailored for the individual. Homestays and weekend excursions plus lessons in Latin dance, Costa Rican cooking, Spanish music and drama. Monthly programs US$750-1100.

Institute for Central American Studies (ICAS), Apdo. 300-1002, San José (tel. (506) 24-9810 or 33-7710, fax 33-7221 or 33-7710). Hosts journalism and Latin American studies internships (min. of 6 months). Arranges paid English instruction positions for interns. Publishes monthly magazine *Mesoamerica*.

Instituto Centroamericano de Asuntos Internacionales (ICAI), in San José. Offers 2-4 week total immersion language programs. 4 hrs. of instruction per day, 5 days per week, plus excursions. 4 weeks with accommodations, 2 meals per day and all activities US$800-2100. For information contact Language Studies Enrollment Center, P.O. Box 5095, Anaheim, CA 92814 (tel. (714) 527-2918, fax 826-8752).

Institute for Central American Development Studies (ICADS), Dept. 826, P.O. Box 025216, Miami, FL 33102-5216 or **Instituto de Estudios de Desarrollo Centroamericano,** Apdo. 3-2070, San José, Costa Rica (tel. (506) 25-0508, fax 34-1337). Offers semester abroad programs in Costa Rica, Belize, and Nicaragua aimed at students who wish to work for social justice in Central America. Areas of study include women's studies, environmental/ecological studies, public health, journalism, and agriculture. 30-day intensive Spanish program US$900, including classes, homestay, meals, field trip, and afternoon volunteer opportunities.

Mesoamerica Language Institute, (tel. and fax 24-9810), the language study arm of ICAS. Survival Spanish for Tourists, 1-day, 6-hr. crash course with tips on travel and local customs (US$60 includes lunch). Conversationally-oriented regular program gives 20 hrs. of instruction per week. Classes average 3-4 students. Instruction US$95 per week. Homestays US$110 per week. Contact ICAS (above).

Monteverde Institute, Apdo. 10165-1000, San José (tel. and fax (506) 61-1253). A non-profit group offering courses in tropical ecology and biology for students from abroad. Field trips, lectures, and Spanish language study. Longer 8-10 week programs accredited by CIEE and the University of California Education Abroad Program. Also runs workshops, supports local women's groups, and directs a volunteer coordinating center.

Universidad de Costa Rica, Oficina de Asuntos Internacionales, San Pedro M. de Oca., San José (tel. (506) 24-3660, fax 25-5822). The Spanish Language and Culture Institute (SPLACI) offers 1-month intensive and regular semester language programs to students and professionals. In the U.S. contact Dr. Celestino Ruiz, 1031 North Wheeles, Griffith, IN 46319 (tel. and fax (219) 972-3366). Students proficient in Spanish may enroll in regular university programs. Many U.S. universities coordinate direct enrollment; see the listings here.

University at Albany—SUNY, Office of International Programs, Library 84, Albany, NY 12222 (tel. (518) 442-3525, fax 442-3338). Arranges direct enrollment in the Universidad de Costa Rica. Must have completed 5 semesters of college-level Spanish or equivalent. Courses in natural sciences, social sciences, Spanish linguistics, and Spanish literature, among others. Semester about US$4800 (US$4600 for SUNY students). Full year about US$8800 (US$8300 for SUNY students). Price includes documents, airfare, room and board, books and tuition.

University of Kansas, Office of Study Abroad, 203-F Lippincott Hall, Lawrence, KS 66045-1731 (tel. (913) 864-3742, fax 864-4555). Has arranged direct enrollment in the Universidad de Costa Rica since 1960. Initial 3-4-week language and cultural orientation, plus excursions. For sophomores and higher; 16 hrs. college-level Spanish with B average required. Semester about US$3900 (US$3600 for KU students). Full year about US$6000 (US$5500 for KU students). Price includes orientation, room and board, tuition, activities, insurance, and documents.

■■■ KEEPING IN TOUCH: MAIL AND TELEPHONES

Mail service to and from Costa Rica is quite reliable. Airmail letters to the U.S. take about seven to 10 days each way (¢40 for postcards, ¢45 for airmail). Steep customs duties (up to 100% of value) can be charged for anything larger than a letter, so bulky mailings can be expensive. If you do plan to receive packages, remind the sender to mark the contents and value clearly on the outside. Mail can be received general delivery through the *Lista de Correos;* address envelopes: Alexis AVERBUCK, a/c Lista de Correos, [postal code] [city], Costa Rica, CENTRAL AMERICA. The use of postal codes is not essential.

Costa Rica has one of the best and most extensive **telephone** systems in Latin America and the Caribbean area. Phones function with coins of ¢5, ¢10 and ¢20. There are no long distance area codes; for any call made within Costa Rica you need only dial the six-digit phone number. This will change next year, however, as one digit will be added according to region. **International collect** and **credit card** calls are made by dialing 116 first, or dialing the USA Direct operator at 114. Phone information is available by dialing 113 or 124. The **country code** for Costa Rica is **506.** Costa Rican time is two hours behind U.S. Eastern Standard Time.

GETTING THERE

Costa Rica's national airline is **LACSA,** 630 5th Ave., #244, New York, NY 10111-0334 (tel. (212) 245-6370). Other carriers serving San José's **Juan Santamaría Airport** include **American, British Airways, Mexicana, TWA, Continental,** and **United.** In the summer of 1993, round-trip airfares from the U.S. for stays between one and four weeks were reasonably cheap: from Chicago US$579; Houston US$299-461; Los Angeles US$349-694; Miami US$199-329; New Orleans US$300-449; New York or Washington, DC US$299-749; and San Francisco US$349-790. Fares from Mexico City ranged from US$316 to $367. There were virtually no charter flights from the U.S. in 1993, and only a few from Canadian cities like Calgary and Toronto.

ONCE THERE

■■■ USEFUL ORGANIZATIONS AND PUBLICATIONS

For a list of **embassies** and **consulates,** see San José: Practical Information.

Dirección de Migración, (tel. 20-0355), on the road to the airport in San José. Take the red bus to Alajuela from Av. 2, Calles 12/14 and tell the driver to drop you off at *La Oficina de Migración*. The place to go for permission to stay beyond the 30- or 90-day limit or to obtain costly exit visas if you overstay (see Planning Your Trip: Documents and Formalities: Tourist Cards, Passports and Visas).

InfoTur, Av. 10, Calle 3, San José (tel. 23-4481). A government information agency; can answer most tourist concerns and make reservations for all national and international tours, flights, hotels, etc. English spoken. Open Mon.-Fri. 8am-6pm, Sat. 9am-2pm.

Instituto Costarricense de Turismo (ICT), Apdo. 777-1000, Located on the Pl. de la Cultura, Calle 5, Avs. Central/2, San José (tel. (506) 23-1733, fax 23-5107). The national tourist bureau, with additional offices at the San José airport and at the northern and southern border crossings.

OTEC Tours, Calle 3, Avs. 1/3, San José (tel. 55-0554). Budget travel office. See San José: Practical Information for details.

Newspapers: In Spanish, *La Nación* and *La República* each represent the alternative views of the two main political parties in Costa Rica. In English, the *Tico Times* is an extensive summary of cultural events, hotels, restaurants, and current events. All 3 readily available on street corners and in candy shops.

■■■ TRANSPORTATION

The national airline **LACSA,** Apdo. 1531-1000, Calle 1, Av. 5, San José (tel. (506) 21-7315 or 32-3555, fax 32-3372), makes reservations for round-trip tickets to Panama (US$230), Guatemala City (US$166), Managua (US$196) and San Juan, Puerto Rico (US$309). (Open Mon.-Fri. 9am-5pm, Sat.-Sun. 9am-noon.) **SANSA,** Calle 24, Av. Central/1 (tel. 21-94-14), handles domestic flights from San José to tourist areas, including Tamarindo and Quepos.

The national rail line, **INCOFER,** runs **trains** from San José to Puerto Limón and to Puntarenas. Most transportation in Costa Rica, however, is over land. The **bus** system is appropriately complex. In most large cities, each destination is served by a different company, and each company has its own bus terminal in a different part of town.

If you're traveling by **car,** you'll have a good network of highways at your disposal. Watch out, however, for the aptly named **Cerro de la Muerte** (Hill of Death) section of the **Cartago-San Isidro** highway, plagued by frequent sink holes and thick fog. The road from San José to Puntarenas—narrow, twisty, and full of heavy trucks—is dangerous also. A seat belt must be used by the driver and any front seat passenger, and a safety helmet is required when driving a motorcycle. The speed limit is 80km per hour on toll roads and highways, 40 to 60km per hour on other roads. The national service station chain is RECOPE (open 6am-6pm, 24 hrs. in large cities and provincial capitals).

Tourists report that hitchhiking is generally safe, but *Let's Go* does not recommend it. In accordance with the *tico* creed of friendliness, most Costa Ricans would pick up a hitcher, but few outside San José own cars. Between some smaller villages in the rural provinces, it is not uncommon to wait for a couple of hours before a single car passes. (See Mexico: General Introduction for more details on hitching.)

■■■ ADDRESSES

Even medium-sized cities in Costa Rica often have no formal system of street addresses. To the dismay of new arrivals, a tourist's orientation is gained by dead reckoning from landmarks well-known only to locals. Buildings have no numbers. Sometimes their locations are specified by a certain number of *metros* north, south, east, or west from a particular point. *Metros* here refers to city blocks, not meters; *100 metros al norte del Parque Rey Eduardo* indicates a building one block north of *Parque Rey Eduardo*. *Let's Go* uses blocks in its directions. Other times, they are referred to by the closest intersection: *Av. 1, Calle 2* indicates the building at or near the corner of Avenida 1 and Calle 2. In still another variation, addresses list the street the building is on and the *two* closest cross streets: *Av. 1, Calles 2/3* indicates the building on Avenida 1 between Calles 2 and 3.

■■■ ACCOMMODATIONS

Rooms in Costa Rica are a budget dream; you can spend less than US$5 a night at some places. Amenities are few in the sub-US$6 range (rooms are often merely cardboard partitions and hot water is not guaranteed), but a relatively painless step up to the US$9-15 zone can get you a furnished room with private bath and access to a laundry service and cable TV.

■■■ SAN JOSÉ

Roaring buses, Burger Kings, and sportswear stores mark San José as an unwelcome interruption to the lush tropical landscape which crowds Costa Rica's capital city. Though it houses well over a third of the nation's population, urbanization and commercialization have yet to mask the traditional *tico* friendliness. Resting in the Central Valley at 3800 ft. (1162m) above sea level amidst a ring of mountain ranges, the city is blessed with glorious blue skies and drenched in tropical showers every afternoon.

ORIENTATION

The city's streets form a regular grid. *Calles* run north-south and *avenidas* east-west. Odd-numbered *calles* are east of **Calle Central,** while even-numbered ones are to its west. Odd-numbered *avenidas* are to the north of **Avenida Central,** while even-numbered ones are to the south. The address "Calle 3, Av. 3" is in the northeast part of town. The grid system should make navigation through the city easy, but unfortunately most addresses and directions you will receive are given with respect to major landmarks and many streets are not marked. For example, if an address says *"200 metros al sur del Teatro Nacional"* (200 meters from the National Theater), you will have to first find the National Theater and then walk two blocks south of it. *Metros* refers to city blocks, *not* to actual meters; *100 metros* is one block, *150 metros* is one-and-a-half blocks, etc. If the address is given as Calle 2, Avs. 3/5, it means the building is on Calle 2 between Avenidas 3 and 5. The **public transportation system** within the city is also pegged to the landmark system and is practically unusable by those spending just a few days in San José. Luckily, most places you will ever need to reach are within walking distance. For more information, see the Addresses section of the Costa Rica General Introduction.

PRACTICAL INFORMATION

Tourist Office: Instituto Costarricense de Turismo (ICT), Calle 5, Avs. Central/2 on the Plaza de la Cultura (tel. 22-1090), down the wide staircase and to the left of the Gold Museum. Provides extremely helpful information on sights, bus schedules, hotels, and gives out excellent country and city maps for free. English spoken. Open Mon.-Fri. 9am-5pm, Sat. 9am-1pm. **Airport branch** (tel. 42-1820), right behind customs before the exit of the building. Provides similar services as the other branch. Open daily 8am-9pm.

Embassies and Consulates: U.S., Rohmuser, Carretera Pavas (tel. 20-3939), in front of Centro Comercial. Open Mon.-Fri. 8am-4:30pm. **Canada,** Calle 3, Avs. Central/1 (tel. 55-3522). Open Mon.-Fri. 8am-noon and 1-4:30pm. **U.K.,** Po. Colón, Calles 38/40, Edificio Colón, 11th floor (tel. 21-5566). Open Mon.-Fri. 8:30am-noon and 1-2:30pm. **Australia** has no embassy, but has official representatives at Calle 33, Avs. 5/7 (tel. 24-1152), in Barrio Escalante. Open Mon.-Fri. 8am-noon and 1-5pm. **Guatemala,** Carretera Pavas (tel. 31-6654), ½ block east from Semaco. Open Mon.-Fri. 9am-noon. **Mexico,** Av. 7, Calles 11/13 (tel. 22-5528). Open Mon.-Fri. 8:30am-noon and 3-4pm. **Panama,** San Pedro (tel. 25-0667), 6 blocks south from Más Por Menos supermarket. Open Mon.-Fri. 8am-noon. **France,** Indoor Club, 200m south, 25m west, Curridabat (tel. 25-0733). Open Mon.-Fri. 8am-4:30pm. **Germany,** Rohmuser, 200m north, 50m west from Residencia España (tel. 32-5533). Open Mon.-Fri. 9am-noon.

Currency Exchange: Banco Anglo Costarricense and **Banco de Costa Rica** (directly behind the post office) generally have long lines and charge commissions on traveler's checks. **Casa de Cambio GAB-International,** Av. Central, Calles 1/3 (tel. 21-9480) has long hours and good rates. Open. Mon.-Fri. 8am-6pm, Sat. 8:30am-4pm.

American Express: Av. Central, Calles Central/1, Edificio Alde, 4th floor (tel. 33-0044). Look for a big sign for TAM tours with a giant leopard hanging in front of the building. English spoken. Open Mon.-Fri. 8am-5:30pm.

Post Office: Calle 2, Avs. 1/3 (tel. 23-9766), in the enormous white building. There are no street mailboxes in San José, so all mail has to be dropped off here. *Lista de Correos.* Open Mon.-Fri. 7am-9pm, Sat. 8am-noon. **Postal code:** 1000 (not vital for delivery).

Telephones: Calle 1, Av. 5 (tel. 87-0515). Free collect calls. Calls to U.S. and Europe approximately US$4 per minute with a 3-min. minimum. Open Mon.-Fri. 8am-10pm, Sat.-Sun. 8am-8pm.

Telegrams: Radiográfica, Av. 5, Calles Central/2 (tel. 87-0087). **Fax** and **telex** also. Open Mon.-Fri. 8am-10pm, Sat.-Sun. 8am-8pm.

Airport: Juan Santa María International Airport (tel. 41-0744), about 15km northwest of San José, near Alajuela. Departure tax ¢517 or US$4.25. **Taxis** to and from airport charge ¢1300 (tel. 54-6667). Red buses from Alajuela (¢50) run every 5 min. to and from airport and San José Station at Av. 2, Calles 12/14.

Trains: Atlantic Train Station, Av. 3, Calles 19/21. Actual building closed, but train leaves daily at 5:45am for Heredia ½hr., ¢50). 2 more leave for Heredia from the suburb of San Pedro (noon and 5:15pm, ½ hr., ¢50). Tickets and information at the Pollo Panchico bar (tel. 23-3753), across the street from the station. **Pacific Train Station,** Av. 20, Calles 2/4 (tel. 26-0011). Service to Puntarenas (2 per day, 4hrs.).

Buses: No central terminal; each destination served by a different carrier. Consult tourist office for list of companies and destinations. Frequent service to Alajuela, Ciudad Quesada (San Carlos), Fortuna and Volcano Arenal, Quepos, Jaco, Liberia, Nicoya, Puntarenas, Heredia, Limón (hard to reach because of 1991 earthquake damage), and Cartago.

Public Transportation: Unless you learn all the major sights in San José, you'll have difficulty figuring out intra-city buses. Your best bet is to ask directions and rely on help from *ticos.*

Taxis: (tel. 54-6667 and 54-6768). Most routes within San José cost about ¢100-150. The fare to the airport is ¢1300. Surcharge of 20% after 10pm.

Car Rental: Complete list of rental offices available at the tourist office. **Budget,** Po. Colón, Calle 30 (tel. 23-3284). Open Mon.-Fri. 7:30am-6pm, Sat. 7:30am-4pm, Sun. 7:30am-2pm. Also at airport (tel. 41-4444). Open daily 6am-10pm. US$40 per day, including insurance and free mileage. Those under 25 pay extra US$8 for insurance. **Santos Rent-a-Car,** Av. 3, Calles 26/28 (tel. 57-0035). Open Mon.-Fri. 8am-6pm. At the airport (tel. 41-3044). Open daily 6am-9pm. US$33.50 per day includes insurance; US$.23 per km. Must be 21.

English Bookstore: The Bookshop, Av. 1, Calles 1/3 (tel. 21-6847). Books, travel guides and maps. Also *Business Week, Time, The New Yorker, The Economist* and current issues of other major periodicals. Open Mon.-Sat. 9am-7pm, Sun. 9am-2pm.

Market: Central Market is framed by Avs. Central and 1 and Calles 6 and 8. Open daily until 4pm. This is a fascinating but dangerous neighborhood, so be on the lookout here. **AM-AutoMercado,** Av. 3, Calle 3 (tel. 33-5511). Supermarket. Open Mon.-Sat. 8:15am-7:30pm.

Laundromat: Laundromats are in a galaxy far, far away from central San José. If you must wash, you're better off using the laundry service at your hotel.

Red Cross: Tel. 128 or tel. 21-5818.

24 hr./Late Night Pharmacies: Fischel, Calle 2, Av. 3 (tel. 23-0909), near the center of town. Open daily 8am-midnight. **Clínica Bíblica,** far enough from downtown that locals give only "very far" as an address; consider taking a taxi. Open 24 hrs.

Hospital: Hospital San José, Po. Colón, Calles 14/18 (tel. 22-0166, ext. 386 or ext. 387 for emergencies), in the big white bldg. just where Av. Central turns into Po. Colón after Calle 14. Emergency services open 24 hrs. Doctor consultations free, but no English spoken.

Police: Tel. 117, 22-1365 or 21-5337.

ACCOMMODATIONS

Budget accommodations in San José are evenly dispersed throughout the city. The east and northeast sections of town, home to most of the bus stations and the market, are filthier and more dangerous. Since these are not necessarily cheaper, it is worth the little time and effort it takes to find accomodations in safer parts of town. Rooms in many budget hotels are formed simply by partitioning a large space with cardboard walls, so privacy and seclusion are minimal.

Toruma Youth Hostel (HI), Av. Central, Calles 29/31 (tel. 24-4085). To get there catch the San Pedro bus (¢18) from Teatro Nacional. Single-sex rooms with tightly packed bunks. Adjacent *soda* open 7:45am-8pm. Ping-pong and conversation tables in spacious lobby. Communal facilities shine and hot water available 24 hrs. No curfew. ¢1299 per bed, HI members ¢1054 per bed, ISIC holders ¢1169 per bed. Storage facilities available; laundry ¢350 per 5 pieces.

Pensión Otoya, Calle Central, Avs. 5/7 (tel. 21-3925). Probably the best value for your *colón*: Tiled entrance way and indoor garden should endear weary travelers to this *pensión*. Large rooms, wood floors, and furniture beyond bare essentials. Communal facilities include fridge and TV room. Desk attendants are extremely efficient. Singles ¢952, with bath ¢1266. Doubles ¢1586, with bath ¢1903. Triples ¢1903, with bath ¢2203.

Casa Ridgeway, Calle 15, Av. 6 bis (tel. 33-6168), in the little half-street between Avs. 6 and 8. This sunny yellow *Casa* serves as both a hostel and hotel. Wood floors and lush indoor garden. Use of kitchen, fridge, laundry, and immaculate communal bathrooms and showers make this place well worth the search. Singles ¢1100. Private single ¢1400. Double ¢2500.

Hotel Boston, Av. 8, Calle Central/2 (tel. 21-05-63) next to Hotel Berlin. Family-run, clean, and safe. All rooms have TV and private bathroom, but ask for hot water. Laundy ¢200. Singles ¢1486. Doubles ¢1945. Triples ¢2400.

Hotel Rialito, Calles 2, Av. 5, 3rd floor (tel.21-7456). Newly painted beige walls and central location rescue small rooms from ultra-budget category. Clean and safe. Respectable communal bathrooms, but hot water 6am-noon only. Singles ¢700. Doubles ¢1000, ¢1100 with private bath. Triples ¢1500.

Hotel Boruca, Calle 14, Avs. 1/3 (tel. 23-0016). If cleanliness is your priority, this is your place. Rooms and facilities in immaculate order. Safe feel despite proximity to bus station and unpleasant, smoky bar. Singles ¢506. Doubles ¢1012.

Hotel Marilyn, Calle 4, Avs. 7/9 (tel. 33-3212). Dingy but decent rooms and bathrooms in the gray region of the spectrum. Running hot water. Cheap and secure. Singles ¢500. Doubles with 1 bed and bath ¢1000. Triples ¢1500.

Tica Linda, Av. 2, Calles 5/7 (tel. 33-0528). Marked only by a tiny door sign, it is the last door before the broad entrance of Bar Esmeralda. A backpackers' favorite—the best place to get travel hints from veterans. Rooms are of the cardboard box variety and conditions are primitive, but the common plight builds strong camaraderie among guests. Hot water runs 24 hrs. Reception closes at 11pm, so night revelers should get a key (deposit ¢150). Singles ¢600, shared with 2 or more strangers ¢460. Doubles ¢1200. Triples ¢1380.

FOOD

As in many countries in and around the Caribbean seafood dishes, black beans, and rice abound. Most Costa Ricans eat in the ubiquitous *sodas* (diners), which offer inexpensive *empanadas* and tropical fruit shakes. Costa Rica also grows some of the best coffee in the world; have a pleasant and inexpensive coffeebreak at one of the numerous *panderías* (bakeries) around the city. Food is reasonably priced nearly everywhere, but the cheapest is to be found in the eateries of the **central market**.

Soda La Perla, Av. 2, Calle Central, (tel. 22-7492), across from Parque Nacional. Cross paths with local soccer fans, German backpackers, and 50s-style waitresses at this centrally located soda. Serviche (¢475) is freshly prepared with diced red peppers and lemon juice. Likewise, the paella Valencianca (¢700) teems with every imaginable sea creature and can easily feed two. Open 24 hrs.

Restaurant Vishnu, Av. 1, Calles 1/3 (tel. 22-25-49). Two other locations as well: Calle 1, Av. 4 and Calle 14, Avs. Central/1. Fresh fruits and big jungle posters make for lively and amenable atmosphere. Vegetarian menu especially popular among budget travelers as well as locals. *Integral* sandwiches (¢125), fruit with yogurt and granola (¢150) and salads (¢225). Fruit *jugos* (juices, ¢75) are simply divine. Open Mon.-Sat. 9am-6pm, Sun. 8am-9pm.

Cuartel de la Boca del Monte, Av. 1, Calles 2/3 (tel. 21-03-27). Elegant in a très chic, bohemian kind of way. Live music every Monday and Wednesday from 9:30pm on, but good food is served all the time. Specialties include *lomito cuartel* (ham, cheese and tomato, ¢590). Open Mon.-Fri. 11:30am-2:30pm and 6pm-2am, Sun. 6pm-2am.

Restaurant Shakti, Calle 13, Av. 8 (tel. 22-09-96). Vegetables everywhere, even growing under the glass table-tops. Completely vegetarian menu includes *chalupa* (beans, cheese, and soya, ¢225), spaghetti with mushrooms, raisins, and cheese (¢350). Open Mon.-Fri. 11am-6pm, Sat. 11am-3pm.

Spoon, Av. Central, Calles 5/7 (tel. 21-67-02). Red brick paneling, woven grass chairs, quiet Latin American pop music, and delicious desserts make this café irresistible. Featured pastries (¢166) include exotic flavors *Kahlúa con nuez* (with nuts), *chocofresa* (chocolate strawberry), and *caramelo con crema Chantilly* (caramel with Chantilly cream). Coffee or tea ¢54-65. Lunch also served. Open Mon.-Fri. 9am-9pm, Sat. 10am-5:30pm.

Soda Nini, Av. 3, Calles 4/2 (tel. 33-77-71), across from the post office. Inexpensive, self-serve *soda*. Watch locals watch "Dallas" clumsily dubbed into Spanish. *Ensalada mixta* ¢95, meat in salsa ¢110, mixed vegetables ¢65. Open daily 10:30am-11pm.

SIGHTS AND ENTERTAINMENT

Of the myriad museums in San José, four are particularly worth seeing. The **Museo del Oro** (Gold Museum), in the Pl. de la Cultura across from the tourist office, has a magnificent collection of pre-Columbian artifacts. There are 2300 pieces of jewelry and figures used for religious devotion and spiritual healing. Check the miniature gold animals in exhibit 42 and the lip rings in the adjacent case. (Open Fri.-Sun. 10am-5pm. Free.) The same building houses the **Numismatic Museum** and several art and sculpture exhibits. Not surprisingly, a large collection of jade, along with ceramic and gold exhibits, inhabits the **Museo de Jade,** Av. 7, Calles 9/13, on the 11th floor of the INS building on the north side of Pl. de España. (Open Mon.-Fri.

9am-3pm. Free.) The **Museo Nacional,** Calle 17, Avs. Central/2, is housed in a fortress that looks fantastically dilapidated from the outside but is meticulously preserved inside. Huge indoor garden and view of San José will soothe your nerves. It displays pre-Columbian art and objects of historical significance. There are various exhibit halls of Costa Rican history, archaeology, geology, and colonial life. (Open Tues.-Sat. 8:30am-4:30pm, Sun. 9am-4:30pm. Admission ¢100, students with ID free.) The **Museo de Arte Costarricense,** Calle 42, Po. Colón, in the Sabana Metropolitan Park, exhibits the works of native Costa Rican artists from 1950 to the present. On the second floor is the Gold Room, famous for its four gold bas-reliefs by French artist Louis Feron depicting the history of Costa Rica. (Open Tues.-Sun. 10am-5pm. Admission ¢20, students with ID free.) A complete list of museums can be obtained from the tourist office (see Practical Information above).

The **Teatro Nacional** (National Theater), Av. 2, Calles 3/5, built with the money of 19th-century coffee barons who levied a tax on all coffee exports to finance its construction, is considered an artwork in and of itself. Visit just to look or catch one of the numerous performances held there. For information on current shows check the *Tico Times*. Performances often cost no more than a movie (¢300).

One unusual but very interesting exhibit is the **Serpentarium,** Av. 1, Calles 9/11, a collection of native serpents, other reptiles and amphibians. Amidst the other creepers and slitherers you'll find the legendary red or green poison arrow frogs that appear on all cards and books on Costa Rica. Signs are in English and Spanish. (Open daily 10am-7pm. Admission ¢200, students with ID ¢100.) By comparison, the **Simón Bolívar Zoo,** Av. 11 past Calle 7 in the northeast part of town, is a bit past its prime. (Open Mon.-Fri. 8am-3:30pm, Sat.-Sun. 9am-4:30pm. Admission ¢50, students with ID ¢20.)

Parque de España is a beautiful and lush park enclosed by Avs. 3 and 4 and Calles 9 and 11. This little refuge from busy city life is full of happy couples holding hands. To the west of the park is the **Escuela Metálica,** so called because it was constructed completely out of iron.

El ritmo tropical pulses in San José after sundown. **Salsa 54,** Calle 3, Avs. 1/3, is a veritable dance emporium. Separate dance floors play love songs, U.S. 60s music and—by far the most popular—salsa. Monday nights feature live music. (Open Mon.-Thurs. 8pm-2am, Fri.-Sat. 8pm-3:30am, Sun. 7pm-1am. Cover charge ¢0-400 depending on day of the week and featured performers.) Other nighttime options downtown include the *mariachi* bar **La Esmeralda,** Av. 2, Calles 5/7, next door to Tica Linda. After 7pm, Latin American favorites fill the air into the wee hours. For ¢1000 they will sing your favorite. Beer only ¢152, but ¢500 minimum per person after 11pm. Open Mon.-Sat. 11am-5am. However, most of San José's nightlife is concentrated in the *centros comerciales* in the suburbs. The most popular and diverse bars are to be found in **Centro Comercial El Pueblo.** Among them is **El Tango Bar,** a retro-style joint where the pianist revives the Argentinian tangos of his heyday. (Open Mon.-Sat. 9pm-3am. No cover. Drinks start at ¢180). Those in love should seek out a secluded nook at **El Rincón Romántico** (the Romantic Corner), which features live romantic—some might say sappy—music and candlelight. (Open Mon.-Sat. 6pm-2am, music after 8pm.) For a fairly standard modern disco, there's the expensive and busy **Plaza Disco Club.** (Open Fri.-Sat. 7pm-6am, Sun.-Thurs. 7pm-4am. Cover Fri.-Sat. ¢400, Sun.-Thurs. no cover but ¢300 minimum consumption.) Nearby **Coco Loco** and **El Infinito** are also popular. Covers range from ¢300 to ¢700, depending on the day. Disco action usually picks up after 10:30pm. Taxis will shuttle you back and forth to the *centros comerciales* for ¢100-150, but on the way back try to catch one from the main road because those waiting at the *centros* charge double or triple.

■ Near San José: Poás Volcano National Park, Irazú, and Sarchí

Twenty-two miles north of San José is the steam-belching crater of **Poás Volcano**. Bright green **fumaroles**—the bubbling vents in the earth's crust—glare from the bottom of the 1.5km-wide, 300m-deep hole. In a 1910 eruption, the volcano produced a cloud of ash 8km high, and it still occasionally emits a geyser-like plume. The surrounding national park also includes a lake and *indígena* trails through the vast cloud forest. Unfortunately, it is the most developed and most visited park in the country and thus increasingly difficult to see the allegedly numerous birds and mammals living there. It is best to visit the park in the early morning before clouds and tourists impede your enjoyment.

The **Visitors Center** is equipped with a museum, souvenir shop, bathrooms, and a small restaurant. Museum is free; signs are mostly in Spanish. (Entire complex open daily 8am-3:30pm. Admission ¢100.)

On Sundays, **buses** run directly but slowly to the park from San José, leaving from Calle 2, Avs. 2/4, at 8:30am and returning at 3:30pm (round-trip ¢350). During the week there is no direct transportation to the park. The closest town reached by bus is the small village of **Poasito**, a 10km trek away. A taxi from **Poás**, 25km from the park, costs ¢900 each way.

Another alternative is **Volcán Irazú**, which erupted only 30 years ago during John F. Kennedy's visit to Costa Rica. It spewed "cold" lava (mud) and caused 200 villages in the nearby town of Fatima to evacuate. Today the 100m deep crater is filled with a greenish boiling water that changes colors according to the gases that are emitted. The 1963 explosion dramatically altered the green forests into a grey moonscape. The funerary stillness and eerie mists encircling the crater continue to command respect. Dress warmly, as the high altitudes make for low temperatures. To get there catch the yellow school bus in front of the **Gran Hotel de Costa Rica** next to the Pl. de Cultura at 8am on Saturdays, Sundays, and holidays. Bus returns at 12:15pm. Round trip costs ¢600 and park rangers charge another ¢200 to enter the park.

The small village of **Sarchí**, about 30km from San José, is famous for its beautifully painted ox carts. To see how this arwork on wheels is born, visit the **Fábrica de Carretas Joaquín Chaverrí** at the entrance to the village. Ask for 65 year-old Carlos Chaverrí, who has dedicated himself to the art since he was seven years old and loves to tell the story of the carts. Every several years there is a parade of ox carts, from which the best among hundreds is chosen. The factory is open daily 7am-5pm, as is the large souvenir shop attached to it. To get to Sarchí, catch a bus from Alejuela (roughly every hour, 1½hrs., ¢58). To get back to San José, go first to Grecia (every ½hr. until 8:30pm, ½hr.) and then catch a bus back to San José.

■■■ VOLCÁN ARENAL AND LAGUNA DE ARENAL

Volcán Arenal inspires jaw-dropping awe by virtue of its still-threatening power. This perfectly conical structure roars by day with the din of falling rocks and under the cover of billowing smoke. The evening show is more spectacular when the red-hot lava bursts from the top and trickles down the sides of the gigantic black mass. Unfortunately, the summit is often obscured by thick cloud cover. However, only then can you observe clouds lit with an eerie red glow. The volcano has been active since 1968, when an earthquake triggered an enormous eruption which killed several dozen people. Since then it explodes several times daily, going through sometimes more and sometimes less active phases. Climbing the volcano is dangerous and strongly discouraged. Ambitious but naïve tourists have been injured or killed. There are several safe ways to enjoy this awesome display of nature's power. Budget travelers usually choose to spend the night in nearby **Fortuna** or to camp near the **Tabacón** thermal springs just outside that village.

Dams built for hydroelectric power have created the resevoir **Laguna de Arenal** whence irrigation water is tapped. The lake also serves as excellent fishing, boating and windsurfing grounds. For information on **fishing tours** in Laguna de Arenal contact the tourist office or **Agencia Aventuras Arenal** in Fortuna (tel. 47-9133). Tours with all equipment provided cost US$23 per hour, with a minimum of four hours.

■■■ FORTUNA

As its name suggests, you may find your luck changing for the better in this ideally situated village. With a population of 5500, Fortuna is blessed with proximity to a mystical volcano, a scenic waterfall, and wonderfully relaxing hot springs. Small-town hospitality is alive as locals will go out of their way to help you.

Orientation and Practical Information Fortuna lies 33km northwest of Ciudad Quesada (San Carlos) and can be reached by bus from San José (4½ hrs., ¢300) or from Arenal (2hrs., ¢150). The road which leads into Fortuna and runs east-west serves as the main and only street. Most businesses line the big soccer field, which serves as the town's center.

The **tourist office** is on the south side of the soccer field, in front of the bus stop. (Open daily 7am-noon and 1:30-7pm.) Exchange currency or traveler's checks at the **Banco Nacional de Costa Rica** (tel. 47-9022) in the northeast corner of the soccer field.(Open Mon.-Fri. 9am-3pm.) The **post office** (tel. 47-9178) is three blocks east of the soccer field in the white building on the main drag. (Open Mon.-Fri. 7:30-11:30am and 1:30-5:30pm, Sat. 7:30-11:30am.) The **postal code** is 4417. Make **phone calls** at **Cabinas Amistad,** 1 block west from the soccer field; look for the yellow sign.(Open daily 7am-10pm.) All **buses** leave from in front of Restaurant El Jardín, 1 block east of the soccer field. To: Tilarán (2 per day, 3 hrs., ¢260), Ciudad Quesada/San Carlos (all buses say only "San Carlos"; 5 per day, 1½ hrs., ¢135), Guatuso (3 per day, 1½ hrs., ¢200) and San José (1 per day, 4½ hrs., ¢400). Rent **bikes** from **Repuestos y Accesorios Fortuna,** facing the gas station 1 block east of soccer field. (¢150 per hour. Open Mon.-Sat. 7am-5pm.) The **pharmacy** is in the general store across from Restaurant La Central. (Open Mon.-Sat. 7am-8pm, Sun. 9-11am.) For emergency **medical assistance,** contact the **Clinica del Seguro** (tel. 47-9055), 2 blocks north from the gas station. (Open Mon.-Fri. 7am-4pm. Some English spoken.) The **police** (tel. 47-9178, ext. 117), are in the same building as the post office, and open 24 hrs.

Accommodations and Food Almost all accommodations in Fortuna are geared to budget travelers. **Hotel La Central** (tel. 47-9004), on the south side of the soccer field, is the best deal in town. Rooms are basic, but some have large windows. Communal facilities are in good shape. Rooms ¢500 per person. Laundry service available (¢50 per large piece, ¢30 per 2 small ones). **Cabinas Don Bosco** (tel. 47-9050), 2 blocks north of the gas station. Newly renovated, this is one of the sunniest and cleanest buys in town. All rooms have hot water and a private bath. Student discount (10%) with ISIC card. Singles ¢1400. Doubles ¢2400. Triples ¢2800. **Cabinas Grijalba,** (tel. 47-9129), is next door to Cabinas Amistad. Clean but lacking in character (unless you count the giant cartoon posters of rolly-polly children). Hot water 24 hrs. Singles ¢1000. Doubles ¢1500, with bath ¢2000. Triples ¢2000. **Cabinas Amistad** (tel. 47-9035), one block west of La Central. Fans and friendly smooth colors make for welcoming rooms. Singles ¢1000. Doubles ¢2000. More for ¢2500.

It is not difficult to find a homecooked meal in this sleepy village. **La Choza de Laurel,** in front Cabinas Grijalba and Armistad, serves Costa Rican specialities under a giant thatched roof. Fellow customers include a highly social green parrot. Try the *casado* with *picadillo arracache* or *papas y zanahorias* (¢350-400). Open daily 6:30am-8pm.

ARENAL

Sights Every night at 7pm a yellow van leaves for a 3-hour tour (¢1000) of the **volcano**. On the way back it stops for half an hour at the Tabacón hot springs. Hop on in front of Hotel La Central and buy your tickets on board or make arrangements with the management at Cabinas Don Bosco. Taxis charge roughly the same price to go to the volcano; they charge more for small parties.

To visit the **waterfall**, popularly known as *La Catarata*, either walk the 5.5km (coming from Fortuna), turn left on the road behind the church and follow the signs leading to the waterfall, or take a taxi (¢400), which will drop you off where the road becomes too steep. Tours on horseback are also available for ¢2000. Check the tourist office or Cabinas Don Bosco for more information. As you climb the remaining 2km, the views of the surrounding countryside in unfathomably sublime shades of green become more and more magnificent. The waterfall will appear on the left. You can hike the steep and narrow trail that starts at the bottom of the falls. The pool right under the falls is dangerous for swimming, but farther to the left there are a few calmer spots where you can cool off.

■ Near Fortuna: Tabacón

The **hot springs** of Tabacón lie 10km west of Fortuna on the road to the volcano. The only way there by bus is to catch one headed for Tilarán (2 per day). although the recently opened **Tabacón Resort** (tel. 506-33-07-80) promises to soon offer a shuttle for its customers. Shuttle or no shuttle, for US$10 (US$5.50 with ISIC card or after 6pm) you can submerge your troubles and sore muscles in a veritable labyrinth of hot springs, pools, waterfalls, and watch the Volcano Arenal ooze its orange juices at the same time. If you're really in a decadent mood get a full-hour massage (¢2500). Open daily 10am-10pm. Some travelers resort to hitchhiking, but *Let's Go* does not recommend hitching. The **campground** near Tabacón provides a beautiful view of the volcano and easy access to the springs. There are bathrooms at the springs but no food, so bring your own. (Springs open daily 6am-10pm. Admission ¢200.) You can skip the entrance fee by using any of the several unattended springs along the road. The bus driver can drop you off at one if you ask.

■■■ ARENAL

This tiny village lies on the scenic route between Fortuna and Tilarán, which follows the north shore of the lake. The scorching sun and slow-paced life may make you think you've stumbled into Dalí's *Persistence of Memory*. If you're feeling particularly surreal, take a boat ride on the lake or a cave expedition to **Cavernas El Venado,** 10km to the north. It also offers some of the best views of the erupting Volcano Arenal.

Should you have to spend the night, the best place is **Cabinas Rodríguez,** which has bright, well-ordered rooms and hot water (¢400 per person). Rudimentary but sufficient, **Cabinas Mama-Lina** will house you for the night for ¢200 per person, but has no hot water. Have a bite to eat at **Restaurant Mirador Típico Arenal,** next door to Cabinas Rodríguez. The outdoor terrace provides a beautiful view of the lake. *Gallo pinto* (national traditional dish of fried rice and beans) ¢150, minced vegetables with meat ¢100, tortilla with cheese ¢50, full meals ¢300-400. (Open daily 9am-9pm.)

The entire village is centered around the loop formed by the road, and all phones are extensions of a single telephone line, tel. 69-5266. The **tourist office** (tel. ext. 134) can provide information on the tours of Cavernas El Venado (US$20 per person for 2-4 persons) and of the lake (sightseeing US$15 per couple; fishing US$23 per hour, 4 person max.). Office open Mon.-Fri. 8am-4pm. **El Banco Nacional** (tel. ext. 122) changes traveler's checks. (Open Mon.-Fri. 9am-3pm.) **Buses** leave for Fortuna (2 per day, 2hrs., ¢150), for Tilarán (5 per day, 1hr., ¢90), and for Guatuso (1 per day, 2hrs., ¢100).

The **post office** (tel. ext. 117) serves also as a **telegraph** post. (Open Mon.-Fri. 8am-4pm.) The **police** (tel. ext. 117) answer calls daily from 6am to midnight.

■■■ TILARÁN

Tilarán is a sleepy town which serves as a second choice to Fortuna for exploring Lake Arenal and the surrounding sights. It does not particularly cater to tourists, but it is a convenient stopover in the complex web of bus connections from Fortuna to the Pacific coast.

Despite the fact that it has more than one street and a population over 10,000, Tilarán's streets have no names and its buildings have no numbers. You'll be forced to grope around using the sun, the stars, or a compass. If you accidentally dropped your astrolabe into the bright green *fumaroles* of Arenal Volcano, the Catholic church serves as a crude but effective substitute—Tilarán's church is positioned east-west, with the entrance to the west and the altar to the east.

The town of Tilarán itself holds nothing of great interest. Most visitors who spend more than a couple of hours here do so in order to join one of the tours from **Travel Tours Arenal** (tel. 69-5008), which also offers rafting on Río Corobicí (US$40 per person) and horseback riding in Chirripa (US$30 per person).

Hotel choices in Tilarán are few, but so are tourists, so you shouldn't have a problem finding a place. **Cabinas Mary** (tel. 69-5479), in the southeast corner of the plaza, is the best buy. Rooms are spacious, windows big, water hot and bathrooms private—all offered with a smile to boot. (Singles with bath ¢750. Each additional person ¢600.) **Hotel Lago Lindo** (tel. 69-5977), located under its more prominent and expensive neighbor, Hotel El Sueño, is tidy, sunny, and conveniently located one block from the bus stop. (Singles ¢798 with communal facilities. Doubles ¢1368 with communal facilties. Single or double with private bath and hot water ¢2166.) **Hotel La Central,** (tel. 69-5363), 1½ blocks south of Banco de Costa Rica, is a last alternative. Walls are paper-thin, security is lax, and communal facilties leave much to be desired. (Singles ¢550. Doubles ¢900, with hot water and bath ¢1050. Triples ¢1500.)

Cheap nourishment is abundant in the *sodas* around the bus station and the plaza. **Soda Familiar,** conveniently located one block from bus station, offers *huevos a caballo* (¢140) or *sandwich de caballo* (¢125). Open daily 6am-5pm. The restaurants listed here take a step up in atmosphere by using tablecloths. **Restaurant Mary,** in Cabinas Mary, has the longest and most varied menu in Tilarán. Serves tongue in salsa (¢380), spaghetti (¢300), *gallo pinto* with eggs (¢200), and chop suey in salsa(!) (¢300). Open daily 7am-10pm. For the least expensive food you can get with a table cloth, try **El Parque,** ½ block north of the plaza. *Comida atípica* (Chinese food) can be had for ¢325, or simple *típica* plates for ¢150. Open daily 6am-10pm.

For tourist information, ask at **Travel Tours Arenal** (tel. 69-5008), 1 block east and 2 blocks north of the plaza. (Open Mon.-Fri. 9am-12:30pm and 1-6pm). **Banco Nacional** (tel. 69-5028), in the southwest corner of the plaza, changes traveler's checks. (Open Mon.-Fri. 8am-3pm.) Tilarán's **post office** (tel. 69-5387), 1 block east of the plaza, serves as the telegram office, too. (Open Mon.-Fri. 7:30am-5:30pm, Sat. 8am-noon.) For free collect phone calls, try **Agencia ICE** (tel. 69-5023), 2nd floor of the Edificio Municipal, ½ block west of the plaza. (Open Mon.-Fri. 8am-12:30pm.) The **bus station,** located 1 block west of the plaza, serves San José (4 per day, 3½ hrs., ¢330), Puntarenas (2 per day, 2hrs., ¢165), Ciudad Quesada/San Carlos (2 per day, 4hrs., ¢200), Guatuso (1 per day, 2½ hrs., ¢200), Arenal (5 per day, 1hr., ¢90) and Cañas for connections to Liberia (6 per day, 1hr., ¢60). There is no public laundromat, but **Señora María Siriez,** 4 blocks north and ¾ blocks east from the Red Cross station, will wash your clothes for ¢300 per dozen pieces.

For medical assistance, call the **Red Cross** (tel. 69-5256), 1 block east of Banco de Costa Rica. (No English spoken. Open 24 hrs.) **Farmacia Tilarán** (tel. 69-5064), is on the south side of the plaza. (Open Mon.-Sat. 7am-8:30pm, Sun. 7am-noon.) Though they speak no English, the **police** (tel. 69-5001), ½ block west of the bus station will answer the phone 24hrs. (Office open daily 6am-midnight.)

■■■ LIBERIA, GUANACASTE

Guanacaste, Costa Rica's driest region, roughly resembles the African savannah minus the cheetahs. Liberia is Guanacaste's capital and is mainly a working-class town. The oppressive heat and humidity make nearby beaches all too tempting. The **Rincón de la Vieja** and **Santa Rosa National Parks** contain thermal springs, waterfalls, beautiful nature walks, and volcanoes. The Pacific beaches are no less attractive to windsurfers and beach bums. Liberia is only one-and-a-half hours away from the Nicaraguan border, making it a convenient stop for those heading north.

ORIENTATION AND PRACTICAL INFORMATION

The city is built as a regular grid, but the well-organized streets have no names and all addresses are given with respect to major landmarks at the **Parque Central.** The most important of these are the church on the east side of the Parque Central, **La Gobernación** government palace on its southeast corner, and **Banco de Costa Rica** on its northeast corner.

Tourist Office: (Tel. 66-1606), 3 blocks south and 1 block east of the church; follow the signs from the south side of the plaza. Competent, English-speaking staff will be able to answer most questions. Open Mon.-Sat. 9am-6pm, Sun. 9am-1pm.

Currency Exchange: Banco Anglo-Costarricense (tel. 66-0355), 4 blocks west of La Gobernación. Open for exchange Mon.-Fri. 8:30am-1pm. **Banco de Costa Rica,** (tel. 66-0148), at the north end of the Parque Central. Open Mon.-Fri. 9am-3pm.

Post Office: (Tel. 66-1649), 3 blocks west of the Parque Central. Telegraph, fax and Lista de Correos. Open Mon.-Fri. 7:30am-8pm, Sat. 8am-4pm. **Postal Code:** 5000.

Telephones: ICE Office (tel. 66-2255), ½ block south of Banco Anglo-Costarricense. Open Mon.-Fri. 7:30am-5pm, Sat. 8-11:30am.

Buses: Bus station, approximately 5 blocks to the northeast of the Parque Central, opposite the market. To Playa del Coco (6 per day, 40min., ¢100), Playa Hermosa and Panama (2 per day, 1½ hrs., ¢100), Puntarenas (5 per day, 3hrs., ¢200), San José (5 per day, 4hrs., ¢360), La Cruz, Frontera Norte (8 per day, 1½hrs., ¢125), Santa Cruz, Nicoya (hourly 5am-8:30pm, 3hrs., ¢140), and Cañas (3 per day, 50min., ¢100).

Car Rental: Aventura Rent-a-Car (tel. 39-4821), in Hotel Bramadero, rents cars for US$37 per day, US$.21 per km. 3 day minimum. Open Mon.-Fri. 8am-5pm, Sat. 8am-3pm.

Market: Municipal market, 5 blocks diagonally to the northeast from the Parque Central across from the bus station. Open daily 8am-noon.

Laundry: No laundromats, but Doña Socorro Serrano (tel. 66-2147), on the same block as the tourist office, might wash clothes for ¢25 per piece if you ask kindly.

Luggage Storage: No official storage area, but the tourist office (above) will keep your bags for you during its working hours.

Pharmacy: Farmacia Liberia (tel. 66-07-47), 3 blocks east from the church. Open Mon.-Sat. 8am-8pm, Sun 8am-noon, or **Farmacia Margarita** (tel. 66-16-65), 1 block from church. Open Mon.-Sat. 8am-8pm, Sun

Emergency: Contact the **Red Cross** (tel. 66-09-94), 2 blocks east of La Escuela Enseñanza Especial .

Police: tel. 117 or 127. Big white building in the northwest corner of Parque Central.

LIBERIA

ACCOMMODATIONS AND FOOD

The general quality of budget accommodations in Liberia is low, so scale down your expectations and keep an open mind. Most hotels have only cold water, though perhaps not cold enough to provide relief from the smothering heat. **Hotel Liberia** (tel. 66-0161), ½ block south of the church, is the most amicable option; the cabins in the back are the best of the lot. The beds are large and comfortable, and communal facilities are well-maintained. (¢650 per person.) **Hotel Guanacaste** (tel. 66-0085), is one block west of the Court of Justice on the main road which leads into the city. All rooms have private bathrooms, but are otherwise basic and seem to have been in use for a long time. (Singles ¢1368. Doubles ¢2052. Triples ¢2736.) **Pensión Margarita** (tel. 66-0468), is 2 blocks east of the church. Huge gaps between walls, ceiling and floor suggest the use of non-Euclidean geometry in the construction of the building. Rooms are clean, but irregularly bulging mattresses eschew comfort. (¢600 per person.)

There are numerous little restaurants and *sodas* in Liberia, but few are major attractions. **Restaurant-Taberna Do,** one block north of the church, is the least lackluster. A random collection of art, tapestries and photos of Billie Holiday creates a pleasant, comfortable setting to enjoy a *plato del día* (¢200). (Open 24 hrs.) A beer in the *taberna* will set you back ¢100, but will earn you a free *boca* (bite-sized snack). (Taberna open Mon.-Fri. 3pm-midnight, Sat.-Sun. 11am-midnight.) **Los Cuatro Mares** and **Hong Kong**, 1½ blocks east of the church, receive local praise.

SIGHTS AND ENTERTAINMENT

Traditional sightseeing in Liberia is limited to two museums. **Museo del Sabanero,** joined to the tourist office, is a single hallway with an exhibit depicting daily peasant life. (Open Tues.-Sat. 9am-noon and 1-6pm, Sun. 9am-1pm. Free.) The **Museo de Arte Religioso** is located in Iglesia Hermita, 5 blocks east of the church. (Open Sat.-Thurs. 2-4pm, Fri. 7-10pm. Free.)

The real attractions, however, are some distance away. The I**Rincón de la Vieja** National Park, with its *cataratas* (waterfalls), *azufrales* (hot springs), *pailas* (mineral rich mud holes) and volcano, lies 26km north of the city (admission ¢100). The beautiful **Santa Rosa** national park lies 43km to the north (admission ¢100), and the Pacific beaches **Playa del Coco, Playa Hermosa** and **Playa Panamá** are only 45 minutes to the west. There is public transportation to the beaches (see Practical Information: Buses), but the national parks are accessible only by car, taxi or private tour. **Rincón de la Vieja Mountain Lodge** (tel. 66-2369) organizes tours to *las pailas* (US$74 per person), *los azufrales* (US$74 per person), *las cataratas* (US$80), or a four-day and three-night excursion to all three, including horses, food and accommodations (US$252). Lodge open daily 7:30am-7:30pm. **Buena Vista Lodge,** (tel. 69-5147), also organizes tours to the hot springs (US$15 per person), to the volcano (on horseback US$15 per person) and to some butterfly gardens (US$10 per person). Lodge open daily 6am-8pm.

Nighttime diversion is limited to **Discoteque Kuru,** across from the gas station. (Open Thurs.-Sat. 9pm-4am. Admission Thurs. ¢200, students free; Fri. ¢300, women free; Sat. ¢300.)

PENÍNSULA NICOYA

The Nicoya Peninsula offers the rare combination of beaches and solitude, its natural beauty unexploited by the tourism industry. Every silver lining, however, has a cloud, and lack of development makes transportation very difficult in this region. Travel down the Pacific coast is impossible; getting between two beaches often requires backtracking to Liberia. Allow a day for each beach, even if it they seem close by. Few buses run between beaches, and those to and from Santa Cruz or

Nicoya run at best twice a day; cars are scarce. To further deter the determined, the beaches generally lie several kilometers down dirt roads from the main road. These obstacles, however, may only increase the satisfaction of meditative solitude and soothing swims in the gently caressing waters.

■■■ PLAYA DEL COCO

Playa del Coco, only 37km west of **Liberia,** is the most easily accessible and, not surprisingly, the most developed and touristed beach on the peninsula. Many Costa Rican families choose to spend their vacations here. If you are looking for an idyllic solitary place, Playa del Coco will be a disappointment with its several busy restaurants and numerous anchored boats. If you are looking for nightlife, on the other hand, you'll find plenty at **Discoteque CocoMar,** on the beach, right next to Cabinas Coco. The big dancing platform plays all kinds of music nightly from 7pm to 1am. (There is a ¢200 cover on Saturday nights.)

Accommodations in Playa del Coco are expensive, with few budget alternatives. Well-maintained rooms with fans, mirrors and private baths suffice at **Cabinas Tica Luna,** one block to the left (facing the ocean) of Hotel Tica Luna Anexo (tel. 67-0127). Breakfast is included. (Singles ¢1300. Doubles ¢2200. Triples ¢3100. Quads ¢3900.) **Cabinas Coco** offers similar rooms at similar prices, but no breakfast. (Singles ¢1331. Doubles ¢1667. Triples ¢2021, with an ocean view ¢2425. Quads ¢2828.) Both places are a short walk from the splashing waves. **Guardaropa y Camper Afor,** (follow the big signs from the main street) provides camping facilities (tent and trailer space, electric outlets, bathrooms and showers) for ¢200 per person, but is open only during high season (Dec.-Feb.). During that time it also provides luggage storage space, shower privileges and bathrooms for ¢150 per person.

Several inexpensive eateries cluster on the block northeast of the bus drop-off. To enjoy a meal with the sight and sound of the ocean, however, you should try **Restaurant El Coco.** An entire fish costs ¢350 or ¢500, depending on size. Chicken and rice is ¢300, *camarones jumbo al gusto* are ¢1400. (Open daily 6am-10pm.)

A direct **bus** leaves San José for Playa del Coco at 10am. The return bus leaves Playa del Coco at 9:15am (5hrs., ¢390). From Liberia, six buses head to the beach throughout the day, and four go the opposite way (40 min., ¢100). There are also buses to Filadelfia at 11:30am and 4:30pm (1hr., ¢90). There is a **post office,** a **public phone** and a **supermarket,** all visible from where the bus stops, but for all other services you need to go back to Liberia.

■■■ PLAYA HERMOSA

Well deserving of its name, Playa Hermosa has shown immense fortitude in resisting the pressure from wealthy foreign investors to develop. Its blissful sands remain secluded; during the low season, you may have the beach completely to yourself.

The only diversion from tranquil lounging is provided by **Aqua Sports,** (tel. 67-0758), which rent snorkeling equipment (US$10 per day), windsurfers (US$12 per hour), and boats with guides for cruises (¢4500 per hour, 6-person maximum) or fishing (¢4000 per hour, 6-person maximum). The boats and windsurfers are rented out only from June to November when the winds are low. (Office open daily 9am-9pm.)

The area has not been developed with the budget traveler in mind. The cheapest decent accommodations are in **Cabinas Playa Hermosa,** where rooms are spacious, irreproachably clean, and equipped with closets, mirrors, fans, and—though you probably won't need it—hot water. (Singles ¢2342. Doubles ¢3990. Triples ¢4939. Quads ¢5888.) There is a ¢500 per person option: the owner of **Restaurant El Rancho,** right next door to Cabinas Playa Hermosa, unofficially rents some of the rooms in her house, but cleanliness is not a priority. Some people choose to camp on the

PUNTARENAS

beach. Finally, you can call Agua Sports (tel. 67-0450) and ask if any locals rent rooms.

Restaurant El Rancho, the cheapest in the area, serves *gallo pinto* with an egg and coffee for ¢300. A whole fish runs ¢250-¢500, depending on size. More expensive is the restaurant at Cabinas Playa Hermosa. Dr. Doolittle or Darwin would have loved this place: monkeys, iguanas, and parrots freely roam this lush garden restaurant. Offerings include spaghetti (¢600), fish filets (¢800), and sandwiches (¢400). (Open daily 6:15am-9:30pm.) The most inexpensive alternative is to buy food beforehand and cook right on the beach. Some stale goods and a few vegetables can be found at **Derby Market** heading north 15 minutes on the beach from Cabinas Hermosa.

Playa Hermosa lies 10km north of Playa del Coco on the same paved road, and then a kilometer's walk west down a dirt road for those using public transportation. A **bus** makes the five-hour trip from San José at 3:30 pm and returns at 5am (¢460). From Liberia the buses leave at 11:30am and 7pm and return at 4pm (1hr., ¢110). Buses leave Playa Hermosa for Liberia at 5am and 4pm. **Post office** and **phone service** at Aqua Sports (tel. 67-0450; see above).

■■■ PUNTARENAS

Puntarenas, the fading capital of the province which shares its name, provides access to the beaches closest to San José, only 1½hrs. away. Once the busiest Costa Rican port on the Pacific coast, much of Puntarenas's economic prowess has been sapped by the newly constructed port of **Caldera,** 16 miles to the south. Half abandoned, the city has descended into a tragic decrepitude. Despite the sad state of the city, the nearby beaches and plentiful seafood easily compensate for the surroundings. From the market to upscale restaurants, marine dishes dominate the fare. The most popular specialty is *la chucheca,* a type of shellfish whose culinary quality threatened its existence. Reserves have now been set up for its protection, but it is still readily available in *puntarenense* restaurants. Other shellfish specialties include *la almeja* and *el mejillón.*

Puntarenas, literally "sand point," is a peninsula only 6km long and 1km wide. Ferries arrive on the north side, where Avenida 3 is packed with services, shops and cheap restaurants. **Paseo de los Turistas** encompasses the southern side of the peninsula and holds most of the good hotels, restaurants, and discos.

Practical Information Get tourist information from the **Cámara de Turismo** (tel. 61-1985), the first of a series of offices of the Casa de la Cultura, in front of the INS. The office has phone and fax services, too. (Open Mon.-Fri. 9am-6pm and Sat. 9am-5pm.) More tourist information in fluent English and free maps are also provided by **Pacific Adventures** (tel. 61-0328), 2 offices down from the Cámara de Turismo. (Open Mon.-Sat. 8am-6pm.) **Banco de Costa Rica** (tel. 61-0444), at the corner of Av. 3 and Calle Central, will **exchange currency** Mon.-Fri. 9am-3pm. The **post office** (tel. 61-04-40), ½ block north of the church or ¼ block north of Surtidor la Lapa, has a Lista de Correos, telegrams and fax. (Open Mon.-Fri. 7:30am-6pm, Sat. 7:30-11:30am.) **Postal Code:** 5400. **Taxis** (tel. 63-0250) cruise the peninsula for ¢100-150.

The **train station** (tel. 26-0011) on the southeast side of the peninsula, five blocks from Calle Central, serves San José only. **Buses** leave from several different locations. From Calle 2, **Paseo de los Turistas,** (tel. 61-21-58), to San José, (Mon.-Sat. every hr. 6am-7pm, Sun. every 15min. 7am-7pm, 2hrs., ¢290). From **Paseo de los Turistas,** Calles 2/4, to Liberia (5 per day, 3hrs., ¢200), Tilarán (2 per day, 3hrs.), Santa Elena (1 per day, 3hrs.), Quepos (3 per day, 3hrs., ¢330) via Jacó (1½ hrs., ¢170), San Ramón (8 per day, 1¼ hrs., ¢90), and Barranca (hourly, 20min., ¢40). From **Super Mercado Palí,** to Orotina (6 per day, 1hr., ¢99). **Ferries** serve the Península de Nicoya from the Puntarenas peninsula. **Playa Naranjo Ferry,** in the northwest end of the peninsula (tel. 61-2830). Ferries leave daily at 7am and 4:30pm and Thurs., Sat. and Sun. at 11am (45min., ¢110, ¢800 per car). Take the bus to Barrio Carmen from Av. 1, Calle 2, in front of the Chung Wah Restaurant (¢15) and get off at the last stop. **Paquera Ferry,** in the northeast, behind the market and Hotel Río, ships passengers only. Departures are daily at 6:15am and 3pm (1½hrs., ¢190).

In a medical emergency, contact the **Red Cross,** 2½ blocks west of the church (tel. 61-0184), open 24 hrs. **Botica Central,** Calle Central, Avs. Central/1 (tel. 61-0361), 1½ blocks south of Banco de Costa Rica, takes care of **pharmacy** needs. (Open Mon.-Sat. 7:30am-10pm, Sun. 8am-7pm.) The **police** (tel. 61-2399 or 117), 1 block north and ½ block west of Banco de Costa Rica are open 24 hrs.

Accommodations

Though budget hotels and *pensiones* abound on almost every block in the center of town, the maintenance and quality have dwindled along with the city's prosperity. Fans are of the essence. Camping on the beach is not recommended. **Hotel Verano,** (tel. 61-01-59), in front of Casa de la Cultura and next to the INS, is somewhat dark but reasonably clean. Comfy beds, fans and private bathrooms cost only ¢700 for singles and ¢1400 for doubles. Though everthing is dark and rectangular in the **Hotel Ayi Con,** Calle 2, Avs. 1/3 (in front of the market, tel. 61-01-64), fans and private bathrooms rescue it from complete anonymity. (Singles ¢600, ¢825 with bath; doubles ¢1650, ¢1755 with bath; triples ¢1730, ¢2475 with bath.) **Hotel Helen,** Calle 2, Paseo de los Turistas/Av. 2 (tel. 61-2159),½ block from where buses leave for San José, has basic but OK rooms and decent communal facilities. Fans provided upon request. (¢600 per person.) For that much-desired hospital feel (including rickety fans) try the **Hotel Río,** Av. 3, Calle Central (tel. 61-0331), ½ block from Banco de Costa Rica. The rooms lack the whiteness that would complete the illusion, but plants at entrance give welcoming appearance. (Singles ¢500, with bath ¢900; doubles ¢800, with bath ¢1600.)

Food

Try the area in and around the market for cheap *sodas,* a welcome relief from the pricey establishments along the Paseo de los Turistas. In the market, the **Soda Adita** is one of the nicer *sodas,* fully equipped with tablecloths. Tongue, ribs, steak and most everything else is ¢135-160. (Open daily 6am-4pm.) **Restaurant As de Oros,** Av. 2, Calle 2, 1 block from where buses leave for San José, is a cute fast-food joint specializing in chicken (2 pieces plus tortilla ¢240); open 24 hrs. **Restaurant Club de Playa San Isidro** is on the beach behind Cabinas San Isidro, 7km inland. Ocean breeze, big *palapa* and tropical music make a meal on the beach seem especially attractive. Fish filet in garlic sauce ¢450, rice with octopus or *calamari* ¢450, pasta ¢300. (Open Wed.-Mon. 9am-10pm.)

Sights and Entertainment

If you have a choice, come to Puntarenas during **La Feria del Marisco** (Nov. 29-Dec. 1) or **La Fiesta a la Virgen del Mar** (July 16). During those times the city comes alive with concerts and dances on the beach. La Feria del Marisco is the best time to try the very best of the local culinary art. La Fiesta a la Virgen del Mar commemorates the miraculous rescue of Don Meregildo in 1913. The Don and his crew sailed out every January and returned for Semana Santa with pearls, shells, and a lot of money, with which they organized big celebrations in town. In 1913, however, there was a big storm and the crew lost control of the boat. Don Meregildo kneeled down and prayed to the Virgin, promising her a big celebration in her honor, if only they could get back safely. Just when they had lost all hope, a clever maneuver allowed them to save themselves. Don Meregildo kept his promise and organized an enormous fiesta, which is now an annual tradition in Puntarenas.

At any other time of the year, however, there is little to do in Puntarenas. The night time "hot spots" are **Bar Oasis** and **DiscoMar,** across from each other on Paseo de los Turistas. DiscoMar has a beautiful open-air terrace over the ocean waves, big dancing platforms and loud, diverse music. (Open daily 8pm-2am.

Admission ¢100.) Bar Oasis is an open-air discotheque, where fresh breezes and lovely music feel as good as a few trees in the desert. (Open Tues.-Sun. 8pm-1am. Admission about ¢50, women sometimes let in free.) **Cine Central** on the northeast-ern corner behind the church shows mostly US films at 7pm (tickets ¢100). There are no daytime sights of interest to the tourist. "Sightseeing" here involves boat cruises to nearby islands, fishing, or visiting national parks in the province. Your list can include any or all of the **islands** Chira, Sombrero, Aballo, San Lucas (an old prison), Los Negritos, Tortuga, Piedra Amarilla, Pan de Azúcar, and Guayabos and Pájaros. **Tortuga Island,** a protected forest, and **Los Negritos** and **Guayabos and Pájaros,** biological reserves, are among the most popular destinations.

Taximar, in Hotel Río (tel. 61-0331), and **Aventuras Pacíficas,** in the Casa de la Cultura (tel. 61-0328), offer expensive island tours and fishing trips. Spend a day at the beach instead; **Playas de Doña Ana,** 14km from Puntarenas and 2km from Caldera, is a well-maintained beach with swimmable waters. (Open daily 8am-4pm. Admission ¢50.) Another option is the beach behind Cabinas de San Isidro, 7km from Puntarenas. Take any of the buses to Esparza, Miramar, Barranca or El Roble (¢20). The beaches in Puntarenas are said to be too polluted and are not recom-mended for swimming. There is a **municipal pool** in town at the western tip of the peninsula (take a Barrio Carmen bus, ¢15). It has clean water, showers, bathrooms and a small refreshments kiosk. (Open Tues.-Sun 9am-4:30pm. Admission ¢100.)

■ Near Puntarenas: Carara Biological Reserve

The province of Puntarenas has many national parks and wildlife refuges, but many of them are more easily accessible from San José than from Puntarenas. Aventuras Pacíficas (see Puntarenas: Sights and Entertainment) offers tours to any of the reserves.

Carara Biological Reserve, 57km southeast of Puntarenas on the road to Quepos, is the park most easily reached from the city. A lush, green tropical forest, it is home to *pizotes, mapachos,* white-faced monkeys and numerous other birds and animals. It is also the best place to spot the bright red macaw. The park is situated on an estu-ary of the **Tárcoles River.** Coming from Puntarenas, you'll find the entrance of the reserve 4km after you cross the river (look for the huge alligators lazing on the river bank). From this entrance, however, there is only one short 1km trail. A longer (5km) and more interesting trail straight into the heart of the forest starts 2km before the official entrance. Look for a gate with a small black sign in yellow letter-ing. Both trails are well marked once you find them and not especially strenuous, so you can engross yourself in the sights and sounds of the jungle. (Park open daily 7am-4pm. Admission ¢100.)

Other national parks accessible from Puntarenas are **Curú Wildlife Refuge,** 4km north of Paquera, and **Cabo Blanco Strict Nature Reserve,** 11km southwest of Montezuma. For both, take the ferry to Paquera and then the appropriate buses.

■ Manuel Antonio National Park

At **Manuel Antonio National Park,** jade green waters meet lush, tropical forests. Popular with both nationals and foreigners, Manuel Antonio does not provide abso-lute seclusion, but if you search the right places at the right times, you can easily have a generous stretch of sand all to yourself.

The entrance to the park (and the most beautiful beaches) is just past Cabinas Manuel Antonio and a short stretch of sand. Cross the stream, enter the forest, and you'll see the park ranger's booth (admission ¢200). For another ¢50 you can get a photocopied map (open daily from 7am-4pm). The walk to the **Mirador** is only about an hour hike through jungle paths adorned by lazy blue butterflies, hanging vines, and many acrobatic white-faced monkeys.

Direct buses leave San José to Quepos at 6am, noon, and 6pm (¢625) and return at 6am, noon, and 5pm. Makes sure to arrive early and buy a ticket at the market place near the "Coca-Cola" building, as seats fill up extremely quickly. From Quepos buses leave for Manuel Antonio on the hour (¢60). Buy your return ticket to San José behind the bus station at the window before leaving Quepos as you can catch your return right at Manuel Antonio.

Accomodations at Manuel Antonio are on the pricey side, and for some bizarre reason do not cater to the solo traveller. If you can, double up for the best buys. Rooms are available at **Albergue Costa Linda,** (tel. 77-0304). Go up the hill from the main street at Soda Marlin. Flimsy locks don't inspire security, sheets are threadbare, and bathrooms are communal, but this is still one of the cheapest buys in town. (Singles ¢800, doubles ¢1600, triples ¢2300.) Another option is **Cabinas Irarosa.** Turn at Soda Marlin and walk almost to the end of the road, just past Coca-Cola sign on the left side and across from the ANEP building. Basic bed and bath combo for between ¢1000-¢1300 per person depending on the season. Satisfactory rooms can also be found at **Cabinas Espadilla,** where spic-and-span quarters include fridge, fan, and private bath; some have kitchen facilities. (Singles or doubles ¢3000, triples ¢4000.)

Most restaurants in Manuel Antonio offer authentic dishes in a realtively simple setting. Three or four little *sodas* past Soda Marlin offer inexpensive, authentic cuisine. Most of them are quiet, family-run establishments. **Vela Bar Hotel** (tel. 77-0413) is a little pricey, but the soothing atmosphere makes up for the cost. Sandwiches ¢400, fruit drinks ¢200. **Bar Restaurante del Mar,** features a gorgeous view, five minutes from Soda Marlin as you enter Manuel Antonio. Specialties include rice with shrimp, squid, or mussels (¢650).

■■■ MONTEZUMA

Most budget travelers in Costa Rica either have been or are going to Montezuma, and you should be no exception. A marvelous spot on the southern tip of the Nicoya Peninsula, Montezuma's rocky coast is interspersed with choice swimming beaches. The incredible aesthetic display of foaming surf cascading over black rock easily compensates for the lack of endless sand. Montezuma's appeal does not cower along the shore, as the town sits a scant 11km from the original Costa Rican nature reserve, **Cabo Blanco.** Strict regulation protects the park's expansive green forest filled with monkeys, pumas, armadillos, and numerous colorful birds. As if this weren't enough, **Río Lajas,** a short kilometer hike from town, features three playful waterfalls, each with a pool suitable for swimming, diving, or sedate appreciation.

Montezuma lies 41km west of Paquera and 7km south of Cóbano and consists almost entirely of *pensiones* and *cabinas*. Local people and tourists alike are very ecologically conscious and development has been unobtrusive. Only two **buses** can get you into Montezuma—the 7:30am and 7:30pm buses from **Paquera.** If you are coming from the mainland, get to Puntarenas in time for the 6am or 3pm **ferry** to Paquera. Be sure to take the ferry to Paquera, *not* Playa Naranjo, because there is *no* way of getting from Playa Naranjo to Paquera except by back-tracking to Puntarenas. The buses in Paquera leave for Montezuma as soon as the ferry arrives.

If you are coming from other beaches on the Nicoya Peninsula, take one of the buses headed for San José, get off at Barranca and change there to Puntarenas, where you can catch the 6am or 3pm ferry to Paquera. It may seem longer on the map, but it is infinitely faster that any route down the Nicoya Peninsula—even with the best of planning and the best of luck, one could still get only to Playa Naranjo (the only buses into Playa Naranjo are the 5:30am and 1pm buses from Nicoya, and there are virtually no cars offering rides). The road between Playa Naranjo and Paquera is extremely tough and there are no buses or cars that attempt it. If you are hopelessly masochistic and just *must* go overland, you'll have to rely on one or more of the 15-ton trucks, which will take you across the 27km stretch in 2½-3hrs.

Practical Information Tourist information can found at **Monte Aventures** (tel. 61-2320), located on a little hill above Cabrinas Karen, diagonally from Cabinas el Tucán. In keeping with Montezuma's hip reputation, this office also provides information on yoga classes and has a shelf of novels in English you may borrow. (Open daily 8am-8pm; 8am-noon and 4-8pm during the low season.) Alternatively try the tourist shop next to Hotel Montezuma, **El Fondo Ecológico,** where some English is spoken (open Mon.-Sat. 8am-8pm), or simply ask local *ticos*. Stamps are sold at **El Fondo Ecológico,** which impersonates a post office. (Open Mon.-Sat. 8am-8pm.) **Chico's Tienda,** 1 block east of Hotel Montezuma, has a **public phone** and is open daily 8am-8pm (with a brief intermission during lunchtime). **Buses** to Paquera depart at 5:30am and 8pm (1¾hr., ¢300) via Cóbano (20min., ¢100). **Taxis** to Cóbano ¢600, to Paquera ¢400, to Cabo Blanco ¢700. The **market** is a small and slightly overpriced *pulpería*, **Abastecedor Montezuma,** 1½ blocks east of Hotel Montezuma. (Open daily 6am-9pm.) The **police** are located in the little white house between Hotel Montezuma and Pensión Arenas with Guardia Rural sign, but speak no English. (Open daily 6am-midnight.)

All other services are located in the village of **Cóbano,** 7km north. In Cóbano, **Banco Nacional** in the center (tel. 61-1122, ext. 210) changes traveler's checks Mon.-Fri. 9am-3pm. The **post office,** 3 blocks from the center on the road to Paquera, has a Lista de Correos and can send **telegrams** Mon.-Fri. 7:30-11:30am and 1:30-5:30pm, Sat. 7:30-11:30am. The **public phone,** ½ block toward Paquera (tel. 61-0566), is open daily 7am-noon and 1-8pm. Dr. Duncan Frerich speaks Engilsh and gives **medical assistance** in **Clínica de Cóbano** Mon.-Thurs. 7am-4pm (¢1632 per consultation). For emergencies, he can be found in Hotel Los Rodríguez. The **police** station (tel. 61-1122, ext. 117), next door to the post office, answers emergencies 24hrs. No English.

Accommodations The supply of accommodations in Montezuma is homogeneous in both price and quality, so it probably matters little where exactly one spends the night. Hot water is unavailable and unnecessary, and the strong ocean breeze makes fans redundant (though the latter do help to keep mosquitoes away). **Camping** on the beach is common, but no communal facilities are available. **Hotel Moctezuma,** (tel. 61-1122 ext. 258) has the most central location and offers some of the tidiest rooms in towns. Rooms include fans and private baths and back rooms have an ocean view. (Singles ¢1000, doubles ¢1800, triples ¢2500.) **Pensión Lucy,** 300m up the road to Cabo Blanco, couldn't be closer to the water if it were on a boat. Views are great and fans work. Communal facilities, if you can fit yourself in, are well-maintained. (1-bed singles or doubles ¢1100, triples ¢1700; 2-bed doubles or triples ¢1500.) **Pensión Arenas** is on the beach slightly past Hotel Moctezuma. When tired of lying in the hammocks or sitting in the chairs out front, crawl into a comfy bed in a well-fanned room. (Singles ¢600. Doubles ¢1000. Triples ¢1500. No private baths.) **Cabinas Karen,** halfway up the hillside, was named after the wife of the man who set up Cabo Blanco, the first nature reserve in Costa Rica. Rooms are small, one block from the beach and have no fans. Communal bathrooms are respectably clean. Singles between ¢800-¢900 depending on season. **Casa el Tucán** (tel. 61-11-22, ext. 284), right behind Cabinas Karen and across from the tourist information booth, has a Robinson Crusoe feel with shiny wood paneling and floors. Fans and communal bath facilities. (Single ¢1100, doubles ¢2200, triples ¢3300.)

Food Food choices in Montezuma are extremely limited—if you stay longer than a day, you will probably exhaust them all. Find vegetarian and health-conscious cuisine at **El Sano Banano,** halfway up the hill, just under Cabinas Karen. Prices are hiked, but your purchase helps support the Montezuma Ecological Fund. Here you can find much-missed homemade muffins (¢180), hummus on pita bread (¢275), carrot cake and banana bread (¢80). (Open daily 7am-10pm.) **Restaurante El Pargo**

Feliz, ½ block east from Hotel Moctezuma, has the best ambiance, but is on the expensive side. Palm trees, *palapas*, dry wood shapes and ocean breeze come with chicken in coco milk (¢580), fish filet (¢580), or a vegetarian dish (¢325). (Open daily 6-9:30pm.) **Chico's Bar,** underneath Hotel Moctezuma, is where, in the evening, you'll find everyone you wanted or did not want to find in Montezuma. They serve omelets (¢300), *gallo pinto con natilla* (with curds, ¢250), and delicious fruit shakes (¢100). Open daily for meals 7-10:30am, noon-3pm, and 6-8:30pm. Bar closes at 11pm. **Restaurante El Parque,** in front of Pensión Arenas, has a one-plate menu of rice, beans and eggs, but is the cheapest in the area at ¢200 a plate. Look for the cook in the house directly across.

Sights And Entertainment

The **beaches** of Montezuma are ideal for relaxed contemplation. If you walk east you'll find sand stretches and a few clear spots where you can jump in the water and race enormous waves, but always beware of the rocky bottom. If you walk west toward Cabo Blanco, you will pass a *palapa* and a small bridge, immediately after which starts the trail to the **cataratas** (waterfalls). (Don't go past Cabinas Amor de Mar or you'll miss the entrance.) Simply follow the riverbed and in less than 15 minutes the largest waterfall of the three will loom before you. The water looks brownish, but is good for swimming and the basin is deep and safe for diving from the surrounding rocks. Also watch for the brilliant purple, red, and yellow crabs (*tajarines*) that scuttle away as you approach. Across from the waterfall, a steep and slippery trail leads up to the other two, but it is probably best to find a *tico* who can show you the way. The person to look for is Orlando Calderón, often more of an attraction than the *cataratas* themselves. It is likely you'll find him at the falls, but check first around Chico's Bar (see Food) the night before you go. Orlando can climb the waterfall, stop the water from flowing, perform spectacular diving, and do acrobatics on swinging ropes. He can also take you on a 5hr. horse tour of the waterfalls for ¢2500.

A dirt road runs 11km from Montezuma to the nature reserve **Cabo Blanco.** The reserve covers 1172 hectares at the southernmost tip of the peninsula. Founded in 1963 through the efforts of the Swiss pioneer Niel Olof Wessberg, the reserve became the cornerstone of the extensive system of natural reserves in Costa Rica today. Toucans, parakeets, pelicans, howler and white-faced monkeys, armadillos, pumas, boas, iguanas and legions of marine life and insects have all been observed within its bounds. A beautiful, 4½km nature trail leads through the heart of the forest to several miles of rocky coastline and sandy beaches. Shortly before its end, the trail splits, with the right branch (Balsitas) going to a group of small waterfalls. For the return trip, you can either take the same trail through the forest (the other two have been closed off for biological research) or walk around on the beach. The **ranger station** provides maps for ¢20. If you plan to walk on the beach, be sure to check tidal schedules with the ranger, because you will not be able to complete the walk during high tide. Bug repellent and drinking water are absolutely essential for the 5hr. round trip hike through the hot and humid forest. The ranger station has a small museum, bathrooms, and drinking water. (Open daily 8am-7pm. Admission ¢100.) To get there, catch the 7am or 9am taxi-vans from in front of the Moctezuma Hotel in Montezuma. Return is at 3pm (round-trip ¢600).

If you are interested in spending more time at the reserve, there are beds at the ranger station rented out in return for some trail maintenance work (¢500 per night). Another option is to spend the nights in **Ancla de Oro** in **Cabuya,** a tiny village 2km from the reserve. There one can sleep in thatched-roof cabins hoisted 10ft above ground for ¢500, and eat under a *palapa* for ¢600.

Montezuma is not nocturnal. The only nighttime alternative to drinking beers in **Chico's Bar** is the 8pm movie at the **Tucan Movie House.** Find out the movie of the day at **El Sano Banano** (movies ¢250, or included with a ¢675 *plato del día* dinner at El Sano Banano).

Nicaragua

There is something about Nicaragua—the scale of it, the people, their history, or some combination thereof—that has rendered cause and effect somehow accessible. In Nicaragua, you can get a handle on a whole nation: its triumphs and failures, its problems and its prospects. You can come to know an idealistic people always aspiring but sometimes weary. And you can draw your own conclusions about what went on here recently and what may yet come to pass.

Nicaragua is not a country that is going to embrace the tourism industry in the near future. Much of the country simply isn't ready, and while many cities have tourism offices (Inturismo is the government tourism agency), the staff is often so surprised to see a real, live tourist walk through the door that they don't know quite what to do. Many Nicaraguans see tourism as a sell-out, they want a future economy based on something more substantive. Eco-tourism is in its infancy here. In terms of environmental policy, Nicaragua is far behind a country like Costa Rica. But Nicaragua is also the largest country in Central America. Its unprotected virgin forests, saved only by an economy that can't build roads, dwarf the ecologically progressive Costa Rican park system. The fate of these lands is sure to become a controversial and important issue in the future.

The advantages to traveling in a relatively untouristed country are obvious. While few travel experiences can put you in the shoes of a native, in Nicaragua, a traveler has the opportunity to gain a very real appreciation of the land. Awaiting each visitor are beautiful places, interesting people, and at least one once-in-a-lifetime experience. You can also observe or take part in the process of an idealistic country dealing with its turbulent past, and searching for a viable future.

PLANNING YOUR TRIP

■■■ CLIMATE

Nicaragua has three climatic zones: Atlantic, Central, and Pacific. All three have two seasons, rainy *(invierno)*, and dry *(verano)*. In the Pacific zone, nine months of the year is *invierno*. February-April is *verano*. Most of Nicaragua remains dry from March to May, but even then intermittent rain is not unheard of. In Managua temperatures tend to range from 30°-38°C for most of the year. Masaya And Granada are comparable to Managua. In Granada, the lake has a moderating effect. Isla de Ometepe is perfect, a bit wet, but very pleasant. The east coast remains cooler than the west, but wetter. Nicaragua is one of the most humid nations in Central America.

■■■ USEFUL ADDRESSES

Embassy of Nicaragua, (tel.(202) 939-6570), 1627 New Hampshire Ave. NW, Washington DC 20009.

South American Explorers Club, (tel. (607) 277-0488), U.S. Headquarters, 126 Indian Creek Rd., Ithaca, NY 14850 . An excellent resource for information on travel in Central and South America. Publishes the quarterly *South American Explorer* and provides an extensive archive of maps and trip-planning assistance.

Nicaragua

■■■ DOCUMENTS AND FORMALITIES

Passports and Visas

All visitors entering Nicaragua must have a passport, valid for at least the next six months. **U.S. and U.K. citizens** do not need visas and are permitted to stay 30 days in the country after arriving. Nationals of other countries will need visas, good for a 30-day stay, which can be obtained from a Nicaraguan embassy or consulate prior to arrival in Nicaragua. After 30 days, visitors may renew their visa at the immigration office in Managua (Carreterr Sur, tel. 65-00-14 or 65-00-20). There you can get a 30 day extension twice. After that you must leave the country and re-enter. To drive a car you need only what is called a *"Provisional"* to be carried at all times and produced on demand. This can be obtained in Managua, at the Oficina de Transito, in front of the Mercado Roberto Huembes. Insurance is optional in Nicaragua.

■■■ MONEY

US$1=6 córdobas
CDN$1=4.50 córdobas
UK£1=8.82 córdobas
AUS$1=4.14 córdobas
NZ$1=3.29 córdobas

1 córdoba=US$0.17
1 córdoba=CDN$0.22
1 córdoba=UK£0.11
1 córdoba=AUS$0.24
1 córdoba=NZ$0.30

The Nicaraguan unit of currency is the **córdoba** (C$). There are 100 centavos to the córdoba. Colloquially, córdobas are sometimes referred to as pesos. 10 centavos may also be called a *real*. Córdoba notes appear in denominations up to 100 córdobas; large bills are hard to break. There are no coins in Nicaragua and instead centavo notes come in denominations down to .50 centavos.

Dollars are widely accepted, especially by large hotels, airlines, and especially on the east coast. Changing dollars to córdobas is never a problem and most banks will exhange at the official rate. **Banco Nacional de Desarollo (BND)** and **Banco Nicaraguense de Industria y Comercios** are the two large banks with branches all over the country. Nicaragua's *coyotes*, found on streetcorners, will also safely change U.S. dollars at competitive rates. Make a sure all the bills are genuine; counterfeit currency is rampant in Nicaragua. Also, avoid changing currency at night.

Changing traveler's checks is more difficult. Many *casas de cambio* in Managua will do this, and León also has a *casa de cambio*. Most banks will not change traveler's checks, and those that do will usually make you pay a service charge. Try the *coyotes;* many will change traveler's checks at competitive rates. The big supermarkets often change traveler's checks and the lines are often shorter. All foreign currency other than U.S. dollars should be changed into dollars or *córdobas* in Managua. There is no American Express office in Nicaragua nor are there ATMs that accept North American bank cards. The best way to receive money abroad is through Western Union, sent to their office in Managua.

■■■ HEALTH

Health concerns in Nicaragua are the same as in much of Central America. All visitors should take chloroquine prophylaxis for malaria prevention. The only other major concerns are cholera and hepatitis. For reliable and current public health information contact the **Ministerio de Salud Publica** in Managua (tel. 971-64 or 971-18), located at Complejo Concepción Palacio, in Barrio Rubenia. Water in Managua is considered quite safe, but to be extra careful, purified water is readily available.

■■■ SAFETY AND SECURITY

Because some impressions are slow to change, Nicaragua is often thought of as a dangerous country. For the most part, this is a misconception and should not keep you away. Managua, like any large Central American city, demands a certain degree of caution and common sense. But this, truth be told, is part of the experience.

For women travelers, Nicaragua's extensive network of AMNLAE offices provide information and assistance to both nationals and foreigners. Offices are located in most cities and listed under Practical Information.

U.S. citizens planning to travel in Nicaragua may feel apprehensive about how they will be received. This concern turns out to be relatively unfounded; despite the mined harbors, most Nicaraguans carry no perceptible grudge. What you may notice is the absense of emulation of the U.S. which often occurs in other Central American countries. Call the State Department's Travel Advisories Hotline for recorded information at (202) 647-5225.

The most dangerous areas in Nicaragua are in the north of the country. Land ownership remains a major issue here, and violence is not uncommon; the Centro Nicaraguense de Derechos Humanos (CENIDH) counts 213 "politically-motivated deaths" between Jan. 1 and July 15, 1993. Foreign visitors will almost never come into physical contact with these issues (unless they choose to do so), and the most that Nicaragua asks of its visitors is a sene of diplomacy. All visitors should notify their respective embassies in Managua upon arrival in the county.

The recurrance of violence in Estelí during July 1993 serves as a visible reminder that tensions remain high in Nicaragua. Though the incident, involving disgruntled former Sandanistas and Contras, seems to be isolated, it shows the volatility of a highly militarized country accustomed to (though weary of) violence.

■■■ ALTERNATIVES TO TOURISM

STUDY

Short-term study opportunities for foreigners are somewhat more limited in Nicaragua than in other parts of Central America. You could always try to make informal arrangements on your own. The **Universidad CentroAmericana (UCA),** in Managua, offers 8-week intensive programs in Spanish language. **The Centro Nicaraguense de Aprendizaje Cultural (CENAC),** in Estelí teaches Spanish for US$120 per week. The price includes 4 hours of class per day, room and board with a local family, and weekend excursions. Or you can skip the classroom part; CENAC will place you with a local family for US$40 per week. The **University of Mobile** (that's Mobile, AL) has just opened a branch campus in San Marcos, a small town 20min. outside of Masaya. Intensive Spanish and English will be taught to an international student body. The University is primarily designed for full-time undergraduates, but may also be a good place to find out about other educational opportunities within Nicaragua (tel. (043) 336, 331, or 314).

GETTING INVOLVED: Activism and Public Service

Perhaps more than in any other Latin American country, public service in Nicaragua is needed, ethically warranted, and hassle-free. Volunteer opportunities in Nicaragua include reforestation, land management, public health, community organization, human rights, and education. Many organizations in the United States and elsewhere can provide information and direct individual initative. There are hundreds of reasons to get involved in Nicaragua, and if you'll be there anyway, very few excuses not to.

In Managua, the **Fundacion Nicaraguense de Desarollo Communitario Integral (FUNDECI)** functions as an informal clearing house of volunteer opportunities within Nicaragua. They are headquartered in the Casa Benjamin Linder, in Barrio Monsenor Lezcano (tel. 66-43-73, fax 66-33-81). One of the best ways to network is to attend the Thursday morning meetings held at Casa Ben Linder (see Managua; Community Activities). FUNDECI's U.S. contact, and your best bet for researching volunteer opportunities from the States, is Rita Clark, at the U.S.-Nicaragua Friendship Office, 225 Pennsylvania Ave. SE, 3rd floor, Washington, DC, 20003 (tel. (202) 546-0935).

In Nicaragua, you could also try **AMNLAE** offices. AMNLAE (Associación de Mujeres Nicaraguensas Luiza Amanda Espinoza) is a high-profile national women's organization, working with women and their families in health care, legal services, job training and education. There is an AMNLAE office in most major Nicaraguan cities, check for a listing in Practical Information.

Centro Nicaraguense de Derechos Humanos (CENIDH) will take on qualified, committed volunteers. Make arrangements in advance (tel. 66-84-05, fax 66-89-40). **The National Union of Farmers and Ranchers (UNAG)** does work in land management, agricultural advocacy, and countryside reconciliation. They are headquartered in Matagalpa (tel. 2355 or 2449). U.S. contact: Circles Robinson, 1150 Flower St., Los Angeles, CA 90015. **The Nicaraguan Center for Community Action (NICCA)** sends work brigades to Nicaragua twice a year, they can be reached at 2140 Shattuck Ave. #2063, Berkeley, CA, 94704. Witness for Peace is another organization that sends brigades to Nicaragua. In Managua, contact Sharon Hostetler (tel. 51-9-33 or 50-3-17); in the U.S., contact Judith Weir, 2201 P Street, NW, Washington, DC (tel. (202) 797-1160). **Witness for Peace** is a non-denominational, faith based movement dedicated to changing U.S. policies towards Central America and fostering peace and justice. For information contact Judith Weir, 2201 P St., Rm 109, Washington DC 20037 (tel. (202) 797-1160, fax (202) 797-1164). **CEPAD** is a coalition of churches doing work in Nicaragua; their U.S. contact is Robert Buescher, 32867 SE Highway 211, Eagle Creek, OR, 97022. The Presbyterian Church also has its own U.S. contact for those wishing to work in Nicaragua: Julia Ann Moffett, 100 Witherspoon St., #3221, Louisville, KY, 40202-1399 (tel. (502) 569-5325).

GETTING THERE

Traveling **by air** to Nicaragua is relatively inexpensive when compared to other Central American countries. Carriers such as **Continental, American,** and **Aeroflot** airlines fly to Managua from points in the U.S. and Europe. In the summer of 1993 roundtrip fares were reasonably cheap: from New York US$712; from Chicago US$658; from Los Angeles US$676; from Miami US$345; from London US$2826. There is US$10 **airport tax** upon entry.

By land there are two international **bus** lines that run between Managua and nearby captials (San José, San Salvador, Guatemala City, and Tegucigalpa). **Tica Bus** (tel. 26-06-94), is headquartered in the Barrio Marta Quezada, two blocks west of the Cine Dorada (or, rather, *donde fue el Cine Dorado*). Times and prices are as follows: to San José, Costa Rica from Managua (daily 7:30am, 8½hrs., US$15); to Managua from San José (daily 7:30am, 8½hrs., US$15); to Tegucigalpa, Honduras from Managua (daily 6am, 9½hrs., US$20); to Managua from Tegucigalpa (daily 9am, 10hrs., US$20); to San Salvador from Managua (daily 6am, 12hrs., US$35); to Managua from San Salvador (daily 6am, 12hrs., US$35); to Guatemala City from Managua (same bus as to San Salvador) (daily 6am, 1-night layover in San Salvador, US$43); to Managua from Guatemala City (daily noon, 1-night layover in San Salvador, US$43). **Sirca Bus** (tel. 73-8-33 or 75-2-26) is located behind the Plaza de Compras. The fares and timetable are comparable to those at Tica.

All visitors must pay the overland entry and exit tax of US$3 (US$6 on the weekends). Both Sirca and Tica buses actually cross the border and take passengers's passports inside to be stamped. Should you cross the border at any point other than a designated border crossing, find an immigration office immediately.

ONCE THERE

■■■ USEFUL ORGANIZATIONS

The government tourist office is the **Instituto Nicaragüense de Tursimo (Inturismo)** (tel. (505-2) 26-719 or 26-790, fax (505-2) 25-314), one block south, then one block west of the Intercontinental Hotel. Maps and information are available with a helpful staff. (Open Mon.-Fri. 8am-noon and 1:30-5pm.) Another excellent source of information are the newpapers **La Prensa, El Nuevo Diario,** and **La Tribuna.** They list festivals and provide useful information on other upcoming events. **AMNLAE** offices, listed in the Practical Information for most cities, provides information and assistance for women, both national and travelers.

■■■ TRANSPORTATION

Tranportation within Nicaragua is quite easy with **buses** as the primary mode of transport. Most of Nicaragua's bus fleet is composed of sturdy-but-cramped yellow school buses retired from North America. Whenever possible, take an express bus to your destination; the few extra córdobas (usually) assure you of a seat and increase the likelihood of arriving before your passport expires. The Nicaraguan bus network leaves little danger of being stranded, and you can get to Managua quite easily from almost anywhere. If necessary, however, you can always take a taxi, as many trips involve short distances. The roads, if paved, are usually in decent condition (see Documents and Formalities for information on driving in Nicaragua). **Trains,** slow but cheap, run between León, Managua, Masaya, and Granada. **Planes** fly to Bluefields and Isla de Maiz Grande, among others. Flying to these destinations will save you a day of travel, and the fares are still quite cheap. In the summer of 1993 the fare roundtrip from Managua to Bluefields was 552 córdobas (US$92). Roundtrip from Managua to Isla de Maiz Grande was 734 córdobas (US$123).

■■■ ADDRESSES

Nicaragua is funny this way. Addresses are almost always given in terms of their relation to a nebulous canon of landmarks within a given city: a museum is three blocks west and two blocks south of a gas station, a pharmacy is 1½ blocks north of a playground. The plot thickens, however, with the occasional subsitution of *arriba* and *abajo* for east and west, respectively. Then again, if you happen to be in a city set on a hill, *arriba* and *abajo* may only refer to relative elevation. In Mangua, north becomes *al lago* and some of the cardinal landmarks haven't existed for years. Another directional device is *al salida* or *al entrada*, as in *"al salida a Jinotega."* Look for this address where the road for Jinotega leaves town. Many streets are named, but the names are almost never used.

■■■ KEEPING IN TOUCH

While in Nicaragua, your link with the rest of the world is through TELCOR (Instituto Nicaraguense de Telecommunicaciones y Correos). Most every city, town or hamlet in Nicaragua has a TELCOR, home to the postal and telephone office, and usually identifiable by a tall mircrowave tower. TELCOR staffers will place your international call and direct you to a booth to take the call. If you're calling with

AT&T USADirect, they will still ask you for the two names and a number; if you want to place a call with a credit card or phone card, simply explain that you must speak with the AT&T operator in person. Collect calls through the Nicaraguan phone system are harder (sometimes impossible) to make. To reach a U.S. AT&T operator, dial 164 (in Managua) or 02-164 (outside of Managua). If these don't work try dropping the 1, that sometimes helps. The Nicaragua country code is 505.

Nicaraguan mail is comparable to other Central American postal systems, perhaps a bit slower. Allow a good 15 days for addresses withing the U.S., 20 days for Europe. TELCOR also has its own courier service, E.M.S., slightly cheaper than private couriers, at C$92 to Miami, C$103.50 to the rest of the U.S., for up to 100 grams. You can receive *poste restante* mail at any TELCOR office in Nicaragua, in most cases, mail will be held for one month, though some offices will hold mail for only 2 weeks. Mail should be addressed as follows: Jonathan Taylor; Lista de Correos; TELCOR Estelí (town name); Estelí (department name); Nicaragua.

Perhaps just to be difficult, Nicaragua sets its clocks one hour ahead of every other country in Central America. This puts the country six hours behind Greenwich Mean time, one hour behind the East Coast of the United States. This was Violeta Chamorro's idea, and for this reason, many Sandanista *campesinos* in the North still live on the old time, a potentially confusing political gesture.

LIFE AND TIMES

In 1519, a Spanish expedition under Gil González de Avila encountered an indigenous settlement on the southern shores of what would later be known as Lago de Nicaragua. They would name the new country Nicaragua, after Nicarao, the *indigena* chief who welcomed them. León was founded in 1524, only to be destroyed by an earthquake 86 years later. The city moved west, became the colonial capital, and went on to become the liberal and intellectual center of Nicaragua. Granada, on the northwest shore of Lago de Nicaragua, capitalized on its commercially and militarily strategic location to become a powerful, affluent and conservative city. León and Granada remained ideological rivals, often feuding violently, until 1846, when Managua was declared the compromise capital. Nicaragua gained its independence from Spain in 1821. For a while, the country was part of Mexico, and then part of the Central American Federation, before becoming completely independent in 1835. But with the withdrawal of the Spanish, British and North American influence grew, creeping east from the Carribean. Cornelius Vanderbilt started the Accessory Transit Company, which transported thousands of forty-niners (among others) from the Caribbean, across Nicaragua by boat and stagecoach, to the Pacific, and from there to California.

William Walker, a renegade North American, with liberal León support, attacked Granada in 1855 with 56 men, captured the city and had himself elected president. After drawing Vanderbilt's ire by seizing his company, Walker was expelled from Nicaragua by the U.S. Navy in 1857, only to make two subsequent attempts to recapture the country; he was finally captured by the British and executed in Honduras in 1860.

During the latter half of the nineteenth century, Nicaragua's conservatives gained power, until 1893, José Santos Zelaya overthrew the conservative government and became dictator. In 1889, the U.S. government, portending future foreign policy in Latin America, orchestrated Zelaya's overthrow and sent in the Marines, controlling the country through puppet governments for the next 16 years. The Marines left their replacements, the brutal Gardia Nacional, under the command of Anastasio Somoza García, who used the hated unit to support the Somoza family dictatorship for 50 years. In 1934, Somoza assassinated Augusto Cesar Sandino, national hero and anti-American inspirational leader.

The Somozas and their cronies plundered the country, amassing huge fortunes and vast land holdings while Nicaragua wallowed in terrible poverty. Vicious repression, torture and disappearances were commonplace. U.S. support for the regime was unfaltering. FDR once said of Anastasio Somoza, "He may be a sonofabitch, but he's ours." On September 21, 1956, Rigoberto Lopez Perez shot and killedAnastasio Somoza in León. Perez, a poet, was immediately killed himself, and became an instant martyr. He was succeeded by his son, Luis Somoza Debayle, who ruled until his death 11 years later. Anastasio Somoza Debayle assumed the presidency in 1967.

Opposition grew as the Somoza dynasty endured. Carlos Fonseca Amador, born in Matagalpa in 1936 was a radical student leader and prominent Somoza opponent. In 1961, he and other radicals formed the Frente Sandinista de Liberación Nacional (FSLN). The name was meant to invoke the memory of Cesar Augusto Sandino. They were called *Sandinistas* and their movement was *Sandinismo*.

When international relief money, intended for the victims of the 1972 earthquake that leveled Managua and killed 6,000, went straight to President Somoza's personal piggybank, opposition to his regime solidified. By 1974, both the Union Democratica de Liberación (UDEL), and the FSLN were gaining ground. As opposition to the government increased, so did brutal repression by the Gardia Nacional. In the January of 1978, Pedro Joaquín Chamorro, leader of the UDEL and publisher of the poular and respected newspaper La Prensa, was assassinated by the Gardia Nacional. The Revolution began in earnest. For a year and a half, the country was beset with general strikes and armed standoffs, with firefights and pitched battles. On July 17, 1979, President Somoza fled the country (he was assassinated a year later in Paraguay). Two days later, the Sandinistas marched victorious into Managua.

But that, of course, is not the end of the story. After the masses had toppled all the Somoza statues they could find, after the euphoria of popular victory had subsided, the victors set about resuscitating a country in sorry shape. Murals, no matter how uplifting or Revolutionary, cannot feed children or clean streets or plant crops. But the Sandinistas, like any opposition movement turned Revolutionary government, immediately faced a new opposition movement, in this case, the Contras. Some Contras were ex-Gardia Nacional, others ordinary Nicaraguans ideologically opposed to the Sandinistas, mercenaries, or scared teenagers pressed into service by thuggish Contra units. Whoever they were, they and the guerrilla war they fought were bankrolled by the U.S. government.

The Sandinistas had the gross misfortune of coinciding with the rise of Ronald Reagan. Only a year after they marched into Managua, he marched into Washington. The movie-star cowboy turned cowboy President was determined, he said, to halt the spread of Communism in Central America. The Sandinistas, after all, were backed by the USSR, and Nicaragua looked like a classic cold war arena. On the other hand, Reagan may have simply been afraid of what came to be called the Threat of a Good Example. The downtrodden citizenry of a third world country had united behind a Socialist Revolution to throw of a US-backed government. Whatever its reasons, the Reagan Administration provided the Contras with massive support. The President was so adamant in his support for more aid to the Contras, the operation continued covertly, in flagrant violation of U.S. and international law. The resulting "Iran-Contra" scandal caused a ruckus, but, incredibly, left the President politically viable, even unscathed.

The Sandinistas have never been infallible. They, too, forced unwilling teenagers to fight. Their mandatory military service policy (jail was the only other option) was enough in itself to turn many against them. Their tactics could be heavy-handed. On the East Coast, especially, the Sandinistas showed very little tolerance or appreciation for Nicaragua's ethnic and cultural diversity.

Throughout the 1980s, the war ravaged Nicaragua. In 1984, Daniel Ortega of the FSLN won a popular presidential election neurtrally monitored and generally accepted as honest. The U.S. mined Nicaraguan harbors and spearheaded an economic embargo of the country. Food and supplies ran short. Inflation spiraled to a staggering 30,000%. Revolutionary idealism began to wane, and as the war became a war of attrition, it became clear that if the Nicaraguans chose a new ruling party in the 1990 elections (something more amenable to U.S. interests), conditions would improve. Sure enough, under economic siege, the electorate went to the polls in 1990, and replaced the Sandinistas with Violeta Chamorro of the Unión Nacional Opposición (UNO), a coalition of fourteen smaller parties. Mrs. Chamorro, who gained credibility as widow of Pedro Joaquín Chamorro, carried 55% of the vote. When Chamorro took office, the Contras disarmed. Though some violence continues to this day, the war, for all intents and purposes, was over.

Today, Nicaragua is peaceful. Travel is safe. It often seems hard to believe that violence reigned here for ten recent years. Much of the country's infrastructure is in understandable disrepair. Nicaragua is a very poor country, and a few families control what little wealth there is. The official unemployment figures hover at around 70%. No longer burdened with an econmic embargo, however, Nicaragua suffers no serious shortages. On the contrary, the UNO government is doing its best to promote market-driven capitalism, a trend opposed by the socialist Sandinistas. The result is a country in a kind of extended limbo: Nicaragua's elite (many wealthy Nicaraguans fled the country during the 1980s and returned only recently, encouraged by Violeta's victory) whisk themselves around in tint-windowed Land Cruisers, sporting a wealth only slightly subdued. Hundreds of striking Revolutionary murals all over the country remind passerby of the enormous popular victory that took place here, and of the angry idealism that still today makes its ominous or inspiring (depending on where you stand and how much you own) presence felt. Sandino's image is everywhere. As an outsized silhouette, a blurry, black and white poster, a stylized portrait, or stenciled vandalism, he is always surveying the country from beneath his wide-brimmed sombrero.

There is, about the country, an atmosphere of the could've been, the might've been, and happily, the might-still-be. It is a wonderful place to travel, offering a cerebral as well as sensual adventure. One of the country's greatest treasures is its conversation; Nicaraguans will talk with you about what they've lived through. If you remain open-minded, you can easily hear all sides. Like an ornithologist trying to sight as many bird species as possible, you can collect points of view, keeping an ear out for rare strains like those waxing nostalgic for the Somoza years. Language may be an initial barrier to conversation, however. Nicaraguan Spanish is delicious, and that is why its native speakers swallow half of every word. The letter "s," perhaps because of its association with the Somoza family, has fled the country, and makes only occasional appearances in Nicaraguan Spanish.

■■■ MANAGUA

Upon arrival, Managua may strike you as a confusing city, scarred and guarded. After you've spent a few days exploring and conversing, Managua will still be those things, but also exciting and noble and even, sometimes, uplifting. It takes some getting used to because this is not a city made for tourism; it is much too real, far too gritty.

"Managua" comes from the Nahuatl, meaning "where there is an extension of water." Ten thousand years ago, those who were living here ran from an erupting volcano; the lava that pursued them preserved their fleeing footsteps. Since then, Managuans haven't run from anything. Situated midway between liberal Leon and conservative Granada, Managua was declared the capital of Nicaragua in 1857 in an attempt to quell the feuding between rival cities. Some cities have greatness thrust upon them.

In December of 1972, Managua was levelled by an earthquake that killed 6,000 people. The city center has never been rebuilt, and Managua remains today a sprawling, almost suburban city, characterized by distinct *barrios*, or neighborhoods. This earthquake-induced demography has created a city of many communi-

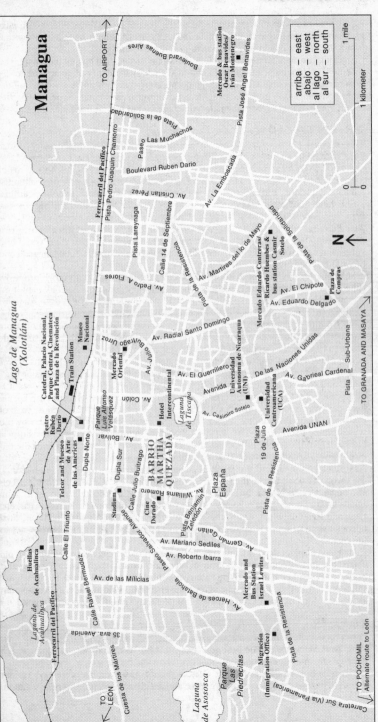

Managua

MANAGUA

N

TO AIRPORT

Boulevard Buenos Aires

Mercado & bus station Oscar Benavides/ Iván Montenegro

Pista José Ángel Benavides

Pista de la Solidaridad

Paseo Las Muchachos

Boulevard Ruben Dario

Pista Pedro Joaquin Chamorro

Ferrocarril del Pacífico

Av. La Emboscada

Av. Cristian Pérez

arriba — east
abajo — west
al lago — north
al sur — south

1 mile

1 kilometer

Pista Lareynaga

Calle 14 de Septiembre

Av. Martires del 1o de Mayo

Mercado Eduardo Contreras/ Ricardo Huembes & bus station Casmir Sotelo

Pista de la Solidaridad

Av. El Chipote

Plaza de Compras

Av. Pedro A. Flores

Pista de la Resistencia

Av. Eduardo Delgado

TO GRANADA AND MASAYA

Av. Radial Santo Domingo

Lago de Managua (Xolotlán)

Catedral, Palacio Nacional, Parque Central, Cinemateca and Plaza de la Revolución

Museo Nacional

Train Station

Mercado Oriental

Av. Julio Buitrago Urroz

Av. El Guerrillero

Universidad Autónoma de Nicaragua (UNI)

De las Naciones Unidas

Av. Gabrieal Cardenal

Pista Sub-Urbana

Avenida

Hotel Intercontinental

Laguna de Tiscapa

Av. Casimiro Sotelo

Universidad Centroamericana (UCA)

Plaza 19 de Julio

Avenida UNAN

Teatro Rubén Dario

Telcor and Mueseo de Arte de las Americas

Parque Luis Alfonso Velásquez

Av. Colón

Av. Bolívar

Dupla Norte

BARRIO MARTHA QUEZADA

Plaza España

Pista de la Resistencia

Calle El Triunfo

Dupla Sur

Calle Julio Buitrago

Stadium

Cine Dorado

Av. Williams Romero

Pista Benjamín Zeledón

Av. Germán Gattán

Plaza España

Huellas de Acahualinca

Laguna de Acahualinca

Ferrocarril del Pacífico

Calle Rafael Bermúdez

Paseo Salvador Allende

Av. Mariano Sediles

Av. Roberto Ibarra

Av. Heroes de Batahola

Mercado and Bus Station Israel Levites

35 ava. Avenida

Av. de las Milicias

Cuesta de los Mártires

TO LEÓN

Parque Las Piedrecitas

Migración (Immigration Office)

Pista de la Resistencia

Laguna de Asososca

Carretera Sur (Vía Panamerica)

TO POCHOMIL Alternate route to León

ties spread out over a large area. Add to the equation ten years of revolutionary idealism, and you arrive at Managua today, a city full of neighborhood initiative and *barrio* identity, a city in which navigation can prove tricky.

Strolling through Managua, you will cross busy streets and empty meadows, you will pass busy markets and gutted buildings. The city is full of public art sure to disturb capitalist imperialists: revolutionary murals and radical graffiti, a huge silhouette of Sandino and, perhaps most striking, an outsized, wrought-iron *campesino* triumphantly lifting a (Russian made?) machine gun in his left hand.

ORIENTATION

This is tough. Managua has dispensed almost entirely with the unnecessary formality of naming its streets. A precious few *Avenidas* and most of the *carreterras* have names (though these may be disputed), but most addresses are given in terms of their relation to recognized landmarks. These landmarks include a Texaco station, a university, a statue, and where a cinema used to be. What's more, even the cardinal points have Managuan pseudonyms: south remains *al sur*, but north becomes *al lago*, east is *arriba* and west is *abajo*. Thus when told that your destination is *"De Tica Bus una cuadra abajo y media cuadra al lago,"* you must first find the Tica Bus Station, then walk one block west and ½ block north. (In that case, you'd find yourself at Comedor Doña Pilar, one of Managua's best *fritingas*. See Managua Food below.) It is not unlike chess.

Managua lies on the south shore of Lake Managua (locally, and more properly, called Lago Xolotlan), which sits 39m above sea level. From the old city center on the lake shore, Managua expands in all available directions. The **Cesar Augusto Sandino International Airport** is 12km east of the city on the Carreterra Norte. Taxis from the airport to Marta Quezada (see Accommodations) cost an unreasonable US$10-12. But walk 100m out front to the Carreterra and the price suddenly drops to US$4-5. It's the easiest five bucks you'll ever save.

The plush **Inter-Continental Hotel,** an attempt at neo-Mayan architecture, was one of the few structures in Managua to survive the earthquake. It is a major landmark, and can be considered the effective center of the city. The "Inter," as it is often called, sits just below the crest of a hill; when you can see its distinctive façade head-on, you are north of the hotel, facing south. On the same hillside, just west of the Inter-Continental, looms a giant silhouette, easily identified as Sandino by the wide-brimmed sombrero. The north-south avenue running just west of the hotel is Bolivar. From the Inter-Continental, it descends ¾km to the lake shore and the old city center, arriving at the Teatro Ruben Dario. Along the way it passes the **Asamblea Nacional** and the **Bank of America skyscraper,** the **Palacio Nacional,** the **tomb of Ruben Darío,** the ruined **Santo Domingo Cathedral,** and the main **Telcor office. Barrio Marta Quezada,** west of the Inter-Continental, is home to Managua's budget hotels and *hospedajes*. From here, one of Managua's major markets, **Mercado Israel Lewites,** lies to the southwest, as does the highway to Leon. Two other markets of note, **Mercado Oriental** and **Mercado Roberto Huembes,** are to the east.

Managua's **universities** occupy the southern part of the city. After cresting the hill above the Inter-Continental, Bolivar curves east around the Laguna Tiscapa and becomes Paseo Tiscapa. From the Paseo, Av. Universitaria leads south to the universities. A few hundred meters east of Av. Universitaria, Av. Ruben Darío heads south as well. It soon becomes Carreterra Masaya, to Masaya and Granada and beyond.

SAFETY

Concerned friends and well-meaning Managuans will tell you a great deal about how dangerous Managua is. The best advice is probably to take those warnings with a grain of salt, and then watch that grain like a hawk lest it be stolen.

Managua is not a dangerous city. Visitors should, however, keep their wits about them, as well as exercise common sense and an urban, Central American caution.

The greatest risk is probably that of being pick-pocketed. Managuan buses are notorious for their pick-pockets; some routes, the locals will tell you, are *puro ladrones*. For this reason, many visitors avoid the buses altogether, which is unnecessary and impractical, as Managua is a big city, tiring on foot and expensive by cab. The truth is, the buses are reasonably safe. If you can, get a seat, and stay alert. Most of the time, though, you will be standing; use one hand to steady yourself and keep the other one down around your pockets. When push comes to shove (literally), hold tight to your córdobas; they'll emerge a sweaty wad, but they'll emerge. The *camiones* (truck buses, boarded from the rear) are said to be safer, as they have a conductor and only one door. Buses can take you most everywhere in Managua, and mastering public transportation is sure to make the traveler feel proudly local.

It is also possible that someone may try to simply grab your bag and run. For this reason, bags should always be carried in front of you, and held firmly in crowded situations. Finally, there is the possibility of being mugged. This is relatively easy to avoid, however: simply be well clear of the markets by dark. Another area to be avoided at night is the cathedral and shacktown east of it. (The train station is in this area, but the last train of the day leaves at 6pm. If uneasy, spring for a cab.) If you find yourself lost at night, stick to well-lit streets and ask for directions. In general, try to look like you know where you're going at all times.

Again, Managua is not unsafe, it simply requires a certain degree of caution. Contrary to travel habit, your documents and money (all but the córdobas you need for the day) are probably best left back at your *hospedaje* (distributed in two or three places throughout your luggage). The *hospedajes* are usually more secure than the streets.

Barrio Marta Quezada is relatively safe to walk around throughout the night, though you may feel somewhat uncomfortable doing this by yourself. Women traveling alone should probably avoid walking through the city at night.

PRACTICAL INFORMATION

Tourist Office: Inturismo (tel. 22-4-98). 1 block south and 1 block west of the Hotel Inter-Continental. Friendly, helpful staff. Office sells a bi-monthly, quasi-helpful guide to Managua (7 córdobas) and an invaluable, if cumbersome, map (25 córdobas). When you run out of questions, stall for time in the air-conditioning. Open Mon.-Fri. 8am-1pm and 2-5pm. Airport office (tel. 3-12-97) open Mon., Wed., and Fri.-Sun. 8am-noon and 1-7pm.

Embassies: U.S.: km 4½, Carreterra Sur (tel. 66-60-1, 66-60-12 or 66-60-13). In Barrio Botahola Norte, southwest of Barrio Marta Quezada. Open for consultation Mon.-Fri. 9am-1pm. **Canada:** Costado norte TELCOR (tel. 62-75-74 or 62-48-21), across from the big TELCOR, next door to the Museo de Arte Contemporanea Julio Cortazar. Open for consultation Mon.-Thurs. 9am-noon. **U.K.:** Reparto Los Robles (tel. 66-86-77 or 66-86-78), south of Av. Ruben Darío. Open for consultation Mon.-Fri. 8am-noon and 2-4pm. **Germany:** from the Plaza España, 1½ block north, Bolonia (tel. 66-39-17 or 66-39-18), seven long blocks south of the Cine Dorado. Open for consultation Mon.-Fri. 9am-1pm. **Honduras:** Planes de Altamira #29 (tel. 67-01-82 or 67-01-83), south of Av. Ruben Darío. Open for consultation Mon.-Fri. 8am-1pm. **Guatemala:** km 11½ Carreterra Masaya (tel. 79-6-97), south of town. Open for consultation Mon.-Fri. 9am-1pm. **Costa Rica:** segundo piso antiguo edificio IBM (3rd floor of the old IBM building, tel. 62-55-73). In Barrio Batahola Norte. Open for consultation Mon.-Fri. 9am-3pm.

Currency Exchange: If you have US dollars, this is a cinch: on many streetcorners (on Bolivar, outside the Inter, and in the Mercado Roberto Huembes, most reliably) *coyotes* wait to change your dollars. Some wear picture ID, this means that they are authorized by the Bank of Nicaragua, most don't. No one seems to mind. Despite the name, changing money with *coyotes* is safe, just make sure you know the current rate of exchange, and don't exchage money after dark, or when you're going to have to carry it around the city. **The Buro Internacional de Cambio** (tel. 66-32-96) in Plaza España, 7 long blocks south of the Cine Dorado, is one of the few places in the city that will change other Central American currencies. They also change US dollars and traveler's checks. If you change more than US$100 in traveler's checks, you will get half the amount in US dollars and the other half in córdobas. If you change less than US$100, you must take it all in córdobas. Remember, most hotels require payment in US dollars. Another *casa de cambio,* **Cambiocentro**, km 4 Carreterra Masaya, 20 yards south of the Gimnasio Coliseo (tel. 78-26-37 or 78-26-40), open Mon.-Sat. 8:30am-4:30pm. Many banks change US dollars as well. When the *casas de cambio* are out of dollars, as is often the case, try the big supermarkets (La Colonia in Plaza España, for example). They, too, will exchange traveler's checks, at the same (or sometimes better) rates.

Post Office and Telephones: Each TELCOR office keeps its own hours, but the big TELCOR in the old downtown is often your best bet. Look for the antennae on the roof, 1 block west of the tomb of Carlos Fonseca. Open Mon.-Sat. 7am-7pm.

Courier Services: You probably don't want to trust anything very important to the Nicaraguan post. **DHL** (tel. 23-3-12 or 22-3-25), 1 block north of the Inter-Continental Hotel, starts sending to the US at US$44 (2 day service). **Trans-Express** (tel 26-3-52 or 22-2-70), 20 yards west of the Inter, is just up the street, just as reliable, and certainly more reasonable; they'll send up to 1 pound to the US for US$30. Open Mon-Fri. 8:30am-5:30pm.

Pharmacy: Super Farmacia Xolotlan (tel. 66-55-55). 3 blocks south (uphill) of the Inter-Continental, on Bolivar. Open Mon.-Fri. 8am-7pm., Sat. 8am-1pm.

Supermarket: La Colonia, in Plaza España. Open Mon.-Fri. 8am-8pm. Impressive collection of North American paperbacks. Animal crackers 2 córdobas.

Car Rental: Hertz, in the Hotel Inter-Continental (tel. 62-35-34 or 62-35-39 ext. 1140). Rents cars from US$35 per day, including unlimited mileage, to those over 25. Insurance an extra US$10, but, remember, optional in Nicaragua.

Bicycle Rental: Casa Shannon y Candy (tel. 49-50-01). Semaforos Rubenia, 200m southwest. 1 km east of Mercado Roberto Huembes. Sells and repairs, but will also rent good quality bikes for US$3 per day, US$15 per week. This may be the best way to get around Managua. Open Mon.-Sat. 9am-7pm.

Travel Agency: Senderos (tel. 24-3-26 or 24-2-08), ½ block east of Inturismo. Open Mon.-Fri- 8am-noon.

City Buses: Read "Safety in Managua," shove your córdobas way down in your pocket, and take the plunge. The #119 may prove quite useful: its stops include the Mercado Roberto Huembes, Carreterra Masaya, Universidad Centroamericana, Plaza España, and Iglesia Noseñor Lezcano. The #118 serves the Mercado Ivan Montenegro, the Red Cross, the Hotel Inter-Continental, Cine Dorado, and the Centro Civico. The #110 makes slow progress between three markets: Israel Lewites, Roberto Huembes, and Ivan Montenegro. The big Managua map sold at Inturismo has a helpful key to the bus routes.

Regional Buses: In **Roberto Huembes,** buses leave from the west end of the market. To Masaya, "every five minutes," (more like every 20, 2 córdobas, 40min.), to Granada (every 20min., 3 córdobas, 1½hrs.), to Rivas (every ½hr., 8 córdobas, 4hrs.), to Matagalpa (every ½hr., 12 córdobas, 3hrs.), to Estelí (3:15pm, 12 córdobas). From **Israel Lewites**: to Chinandega (every ½hr., 13 córdobas), to Leon (every ½hr., 9.50 córdobas), to Jinotepe (every ½hr, 4 córdobas), to Pochomil (every 40min., 7 córdobas). From **Ivan Montenegro**: to Tititapa (every 10min., 1.50 córdobas), to Rama (at 4am, 5am, 6am, 7:30am, 8:45am and 11:30am daily).

Train Station: 6 blocks east and one block north of the Palacio Nacional (tel. 24-3-37). Served by buses #112 and #123. Trains depart for Masaya (2 córdobas, 1hr.) and Granada (3.50 córdobas, 1½hrs) at 8am, 1pm, and (less reliably) at 6pm. Trains depart for Leon (2hrs.) at 8am (5 córdobas), "express" at 1pm (6 córdobas) and 6pm (5 córdobas). Buy tickets 10 minutes before departure.

AMNLAE: Casa Nora Astorga (tel. 71-6-61 or 73-5-98). Provides services and information for women. 2½ blocks south of the Entrada Principal San Juan, #582. Behind the UCA.

Police: tel. 71-2-95 or 71-1-30.

Red Cross: tel. 65-11-97 or 51-7-61. 24 hr. ambulance service.

ACCOMMODATIONS

All the hotels and *hospedajes* listed below are in the Barrio Marta Quezada, an amiable neighborhood of comfortable homes, bohemian lodgings, and the occasional wandering pig. The barrio is about ten blocks north of Plaza España and lies between the Inter-Continental to the east and the stadium to the west. If you're planning to be in Managua around July 19 (the anniversary of the Revolution), book ahead, as even revolutionaries must sleep and all the hotels are packed. Most of the *hospedajes* in the barrio have scrub tubs, but many have little clothesline space, a real concern as Managua has no laundromats. Marta Quezada receives no water on Monday or Thursday. Most *hospedajes,* however, have holding tanks that (usually) manage to carry the day.

Guest House Santos, 3 blocks north and ½ block west of the Cine Dorado (tel. 23-7-13). Another earthquake could only improve the overall aesthetic effect, but probably wouldn't detract from the Guest House's popularity. International clientele spends the evening in the eclectic collection of lawn furniture, comparing notes and running up Victoria tabs. The Big Bad Wolf wouldn't dignify the cardboard walls with his huffing and puffing, and the padlocks are of diary caliber, but security is a function of the conscientious management and the comradely atmosphere. Rooms are thoroughly basic, but are rendered habitable by a fleet of gasping fans. Probably the best deal in town. 18 córdobas per person.

Casa de Huespedes Molinito, two doors north of Hotel Jardin D'Italia (see below) (tel. 66-44-31). 28 gloomy rooms. Sheets are cleaner than at Santos, but the atmosphere can't compare. Clean, close-quartered bathrooms make for introspective showers (but not Mon. or Thurs., as the place is not tank-equipped). 20 córdobas per person.

Hotel Jardin D'Italia: 3 blocks east and ½ block north of Cine Dorado (tel. 27-9-67). Look for the lime-green facade. Seven relatively luxurious rooms with private bathrooms. Safe and quiet. 36 córdobas per person, 60 córdobas with A/C.

Hospedaje El Dorado, ½ block east of Cine Dorado (tel. 26-0-12). *Hospedaje* or top-secret NASA bunker? The number of keys needed to gain access would seem to indicate the latter. Rooms vary, so don't be afraid to be choosy. Artwork is the Bob Ross school. 30 córdobas per person.

Hospedaje Norma, 1 block south and 75m east of Cine Dorado (tel. 2-34-98). Friendly. Rooms perhaps maintained by the shaggy, yawning dog. Still, the bathrooms are cleaner than you might expect. 15 córdobas per person.

Hotel Sultana, (tel. 26-0-94). Connected to the Tica Bus office, and hence somewhat of a trap. But a comfortable trap, with big clean rooms, private bathrooms and gleaming fans. 36 córdobas per person.

Hospedaje Carlos, ½ block north of the Tica bus station (tel. 22-5-54). Homey atmosphere would work better if the courtyard were bigger; somewhat oppressive as it stands. Clean, comfortable and safe. 42 córdobas per person.

Hospedaje Quintana, 1 block west of Guest House Santos. No tanks means no water Mon. or Thurs. No such explanation for the lack of windows. 25 córdobas per person.

FOOD

Good food is not hard to find in Managua; there is no reason to have Gallo Pinto coming out your ears. Perhaps Managua's greatest culinary asset is its *fritangas*: sidewalk *comedors* offering a sort of deep-fried buffet. You point to it, they throw it into a pan of boiling oil (be careful what you point to). Bananas and cheese go especially well together. You can easily eat meatless for under US$10. The food in the markets is good, too, and cheap. There, though, it's best to eat only what you've seen fried up, and stick to bottled drinks.

Comedor Sara, one door east of Tica bus station. Corrugated roof lends the place an airplane hangar feel, but a clean airplane hangar with excellent curries. The shrimp curry is the hottest; try to look tough when you order it. Fried rice with chicken 25 córdobas. *Tortilla Españolade papa* 10 córdobas. Vegetarian curry with rice 22 córdobas. Open daily noon-11pm.

Comedor Popular Los Chilamates, 1 block north and 2 blocks west from Montoya. Fantastic *típico* lunches served buffet style; heap your plate for 13 córdobas. The intense atmosphere is free. Open Mon.-Fri. 11am-2pm.

Pancakes Myrna, 1 block east and 1 block south from Cine Dorado (tel. 27-9-13). For best results, stick to the title dish. Open daily 7am-3pm.

Re-Cafe La India, On Bolivar, 2 blocks north of Inter-Continental (tel. 27-4-72). Breakfast and lunch both cost 15 córdobas. Lunch has an Indian slant. Gaze longingly at the Inter. Open daily 8-10am and noon-10pm.

Tacos, 3 blocks south of Cine Dorado (tel. 27-2-28). Select from a wide (chicken or cheese) variety of tacos. Try to contain your joy at seeing the Ché Guevara posters. Quite a political hangout; sells hard-to-find leftist journals. Open Mon.-Fri. 11am-3pm and 5:30-10pm, Sat.-Sun. 5:30-10pm.

Tonali, 2½ blocks south of Cine Cabrera in the heart of Martha Quezada. A collective bakery run by Nicaraguan women. Black bread, whole wheat bread, granola, yogurt, natural pastas. Open Mon.-Fri. 8am-6pm.

When down and out has got you down, dig your nattiest duds from the frame pack and try these places near the Inter. You'll pay for the swank, but it may just be worth it.

Antojitos, On Bolivar, 1 block south of the Inter-Continental. Posh Mexican restaurant with great food and beautiful parrots (well clear of the menu). Open daily noon-midnight.

Ristorante Magica Roma, ½ block west of Inter-Continental (tel. 27-5-60). Pizzas start at 55 córdobas, but the subdued decor, air-conditioning and wine list may justify the price. Open Mon.-Sat. noon-3pm and 6pm-midnight, Sun. noon-midnight.

Hotel Inter-Continental, (tel. 23-5-31). No longer do battle-scarred journalists nurse stiff drinks and swap war stories at the bar, but you may still want to partake of the atmosphere. The restaurant offers a breakfast buffet for 50 córdobas, a lunch buffet for 60 córdobas, and on Sundays from noon-4pm, a poolside grill buffet for 75 córdobas (towels and pool use included). Add a 15% gratuity to all prices. The bar has just as much history and longer hours. Dress sharp.

SIGHTS & ENTERTAINMENT

For a city of its size, Managua offers surprisingly little in the way of standard sights and entertainment. In the summer of 1993, the city contained a whopping three museums. Two others, **El Museo de la Revolución** and **El Museo de Alfabetazación** (telling the story of the highly successful Sandanista literacy campaign), have both been closed, political victims of budget cutbacks. But ask around; they are both said to have been great museums and rumors abound that they will eventually reopen. **El Museo Nacional**, seven blocks due east of the Palacio Nacional and the ruined cathedral (tel. 25-2-91) is a small museum illustrating Nicaragua's natural history. (Open Mon.-Fri. 8:30am-noon and 1-5pm. Admission for foreigners 10 córdobas, with camera (no flash) 15 córdobas, with camcorder 50 córdobas.) **El Museo de Arte Contemporanea** (tel. 22-4-40) across from TELCOR, next to the Canadian Embassy, is a wonderful museum displaying contemporary artwork from all over Latin America. The museum also has a small collection of cultural and historical books for sale. (Open Tues.-Fri. 9am-5pm. Donations solicited). The third museum, **El Museo Huellas de Acahualinca**, displays Managua's 10,000-year-old, lava-preserved footprints. Take bus #102, the museum lies on the western edge of the old city center. (Open Mon-Fri. 8am-noon and 1-4pm).

Most of Managua's sights, such as they are, can be taken in by strolling down Bolivar. Walking north (downhill) from the Inter-Continental, you will first pass, on your right, the **Casa Presidencial** and the **Asamblea Nacional.** The Bank of America skyscraper rises behind both. When the Assembly is not in session, you can walk in and have a look around. On the other side of Bolívar from the Asamblea Nacional is a scrubby park that often harbors a tent village, home to whatever group of workers or *campesinos* is agitating for reform at the time. Continuing north, you will arrive in the **Plaza de la Revolución,** arranged around the tomb of Sandinista leader Carlos Fonseca and a monument to poet Rubén Darío, the "Prince of Spanish-American literature." In the southeast corner of the Plaza, find the Palacio Nacional, a colonial building that survived the earthquake and now houses government offices. The front door is flanked by two huge portraits: Carlos Fonseca on the right and Augusto Sandino on the left. The murals inside are worth a look. On the east side of the plaza, next to the Palacio Nacional, stands the ruined Cathedral Santo Domingo: a beautiful and eerie convertible cathedral. You can go inside, but exercise caution; visitors have been robbed. Also on the Plaza, near the lake, is the large, boxy **Teatro Rubén Darío,** which also houses the **Teatro Experimental.** Both theatres have quality programs; check the schedule of events posted by the ticket booth.

Managua's *mercados* are a must-see. **Mercado Roberto Huembes,** east of the universities, features a good selection of Nicaraguan *artesanía*s, including hammocks from Masaya. **Mercado Israel Lewites** has quite a few sizzling, busy *comedors.* **Mercado Oriental,** a sprawling labyrinth, sells some quality wooden products, but is somewhat sordid. It is said that, at the height of the US embargo, it was possible to walk in here and, if you had the money, buy a new Mercedes Benz. **Mercado Ivan Montenegro** is notable primarily for its buses to Rama.

When they are in session, Managua's universities ebulently display the nation's dynamism; here are Nicaragua's best and brightest. To get to the **Universidad Centroamérica (UCA)** catch buses #103, #105, #110 or #119. Alternately, you could walk the pleasant half hour south down Av. Universitaria from the Inter-Contintental. To your left, you will see the **UNI (Universidad Nicaraguense Ingenieria)** are right next to each other, and the surrounding area is full of happening sidewalk sandwich joints. Managua's AMNLAE office, Casa Nora Astorga, lies behind the UCA. Managua's more radical university, **Universidad Nacional Autonoma Nicaraguense (UNAN)**, lies south of the other two, at the end of Pista La UNAN, and can be reached on the #117 bus.

Managua has a few discos. **Lobo Jack,** near the intersection of Pista Portezuelo and Carreterra Masaya (tel. 67-01-23), is said to be the biggest disco in Central America. Cover 30 córdobas for men, with expensive drinks. (Open Wed.-Sun. 8pm-4am.) **Mansion Reggae,** km 6 Carreterra Norte (tel. 94-8-04), plays West Indian music from the Atlantic coast. (Open daily 7pm-3am.)

The VCR has decimated Managua's cinemas; the few that remain show mostly porn. Between October and April, you can often catch a free baseball game in the big stadium in Marta Quezada. There are also quite a few pool halls in Managua, though some are pretty tough.

COMMUNITY ACTIVITIES

The North American community in Managua holds a weekly seminar/discussion on Thursday mornings at 8:30 in the **Casa Benjamin Linder** (see Nicaragua Introduction Getting Involved above for more information). Guest speakers discuss social and political issues current in Nicaragua. Interested guests are welcome (be sure to arrive on time). It's a great way to find out what's going on in Managua and the rest of the country, and about current volunteer opportunities. Named after a North American *internacionalista* who was killed by the Contras in 1987, the house itself contains FUNDECI and functions as a community center. The murals tell the story of Linder's life.

Managua's celebrations all have a common radical (or at least progressive) element. International Women's Day (March 8) is supposed to be quite an event here, thanks in part to the work of AMNLAE. On June 26, 1979, the Sandinistas, unable to hang on to the large chunk of Managua they held, marched to Masaya. Every year since, thousands of Nicaraguans repeat this march after a rally in Managua. The mood is festive and revolutionary. Managua is also one of the few places in Central America where International Gay and Lesbian Day (June 28) is celebrated. But the real fireworks are saved for June 19: the anniversary of the Revolution.

■ Near Managua

Xiloa (hel-WA) lies about 10km west of Managua. A volcanic lake with a lush backdrop of mountains, Xiloa has become quite developed; picnic tables and *refresco* stands line its swimming shore. But the lake is still clean, and very popular with the family crowd, especially on weekends and during *el verano* (Feb.-April). It costs two córdobas to use the lake facilities, 10 if you're driving. During Semana Santa, buses run frequently from Mercado Israel Lewites to the *centro turistico* at Xiloa. These buses also run, though less frequently, on the weekends. At all other times (when the lake will probably be yours for the swimming), your best bet is to board any bus plying the Carreterra a León (Highway to Leon) and ask to be let out at the *entrada principal a Xiloa*. Most of these buses leave from Israel Lewites bound for Mateare, Nagorote and León. Once in Xiloa, people wait at the *entrada* (usually with others), across from the 24-hr. Texaco, until a pickup happens by. Still, caution should be exercised, especially by women and solo travelers. Xiloa is a windy five minutes up the road. Alternately, you could walk the 5km through fantasic scenery. To return, get back to the *carreterra* and jump on a bus headed back to Managua. The **Hotel Xiloa** has rooms starting at 76 córdobas, and accepts Visa and MC.

El Trapiche is another nearby swimming spot, not nearly as nice as Xiloa, is only crowded on the weekends and during *el verano*. The park charges 2 córdobas (10 if you're driving). To reach El Trapiche, catch a bus to Titpitapa at the Mercado Ivan Montenegro (served by the #110 bus) and ask to get off at El Trapiche. This bus also serves the airport, but braving it with your bags is ill-advised. Buses return to Managua frequently.

Volcán Momotombo, west of the city, on the lake shore, can be climbed. Because of a geothermal plant, however, you'll need permission from the Instituto Nicaragüense de Energía (INE) to climb the volcano.

León Viejo (founded in 1524) lies at the foot of Volcán Momotombo, a location the city came to regret in 1610, when it was destroyed by a volcano-induced earthquake. León, the Spanish capital of Nicaragua, simply up and moved 30km west (where you can still find it), leaving its old self to be slowly buried by volcanic ash. Now partially excavated, León Viejo makes an interesting day trip. You can see the cathedral, in front of which Hernández de Córdoba was beheaded. There are also a few private homes, as well as the church and convent of La Merced.

To get to León Viejo, head first to La Paz Centro, 40km from Managua along the Managua-León highway. Buses run hourly to La Paz Centro from Mercado Israel Lewites, but it would be just as easy to take a bus bound for León and ask to be let off at La Paz Centro. From La Paz Centro, León Viejo is another 16km. An occasional bus covers this distance; otherwise, it probably wouldn't be too hard to hitchhike.

Pochomil is a popular Pacific beach 60km from Managua, a long, beautiful beach offering many good restaurants and a few good hotels. There is also horseback riding on the beach for 20 córdobas per hour. **Hotel Altamar** has rooms for 50 córdobas per night (1 or 2 people) and serves good food. **Bar Piragua** sits right on the beach and serves good shrimp.

Masachapa is another nearby beach, somewhat less popular (and therefore less crowded) than Pochomil. Both beaches are about two hours from Managua, and are served by hourly buses from Mercado Israel Lewites.

L
E
Ó
N

WEST OF MANAGUA

■■■ LEÓN

In León, the voices of schoolchildren echo over high adobe walls, crumbling colonial grandeur competes with plain old disrepair, the sun beats down and the murals cry out to all who care to listen.

León is Nicaragua's second-largest city, and was the capital of the country for over 300 years, until Managua assumed that title in 1807. The first León, now known as León Viejo, was founded in 1524 on the shore of Lake Xolotlán by Hernández de Cordoba. This city was destroyed by an earthquake in 1610, and León was rebuilt 32km to the west; though poorer than Granada, it soon became a cultural and intellectual stronghold. León's cathedral, begun in 1746, is the largest in Central America. The Universidad Nacional Autónoma de Nicaragua (UNAN), the country's first university, was founded here in 1812. Rubén Darío (1867-1916), Nicaragua's beloved poet-statesman, was born and died in León.

Historically, León is Nicaragua's most liberal city. Today, it proudly retains that title; it was one of only two cities to carry the FSLN in the elections of 1990 (the other was Estelí). The university is in session March-December, and the student population here gives the city a radical edge. The murals and graffitti (some of the best in Nicaragua) complete this picture.

ORIENTATION

If you've spent any time in Managua, León is a cakewalk. The bus terminal lies just east of town, three long blocks past the train tracks. Express buses from Managua, however, will sometimes drop you off at a gas station a few blocks southeast of the terminal. Either way, you can walk to the center of town (often hot and dusty, but very doable), or take a taxi for about 5 córdobas. The train station, and the *mercado* that surrounds it, are on the eastern edge of town, five blocks north and three blocks east of the cathedral. At both the train station and bus terminal, you can find León's carriage taxis, still in use, pulled by mangy, high-relief horses.

León's center is the **Parque Jerez**. In the middle of the plaza stands an amusingly diminutive statue of General Jerez, a 19th-century liberal figure. The plaza, however, is usally referred to as *el parque central*. On its west side is the TELCOR office; the high microwave tower can be seen from much of León. Opposite the TELCOR office, on the east side of the plaza, sits the cathedral.

León's streets *are* named, though this would probably come as a surprise to most of the locals. East-west streets are *calles;* Calle Central Rubén Darío fronts the north side of *el parque central*. From here, numbered streets ascend north (1a Calle Norte, 2a Calle Norte, etc.) and south. This won't help all that much, though; most *Leones,* when asked for directions or addresses, will stick to the standard Nicaraguan method. (You may begin to feel as though you've landed in a BASIC program.) Thus, the Museo Archivo Rubén Darío is *cuatro cuadras abajo del* TELCOR (four blocks down from the TELCOR office). Hotel America lies three blocks east of the Cathedral; the four other hotels listed are all northeast of *el parque central*.

PRACTICAL INFORMATION

Tourist Office: Inturismo, 120 yards up from the Colegio Mercantil (tel. 36-82). They'll be pretty excited to see a real live tourist. Handy local guide (with less handy map) distributed. Open Mon.-Fri. 8am-1pm.

Currency Exchange: Banco Nicaraguense de Industria y Comercios (tel. 50-51). A flimsy looking building across the street from La Iglesia de la Recollección. Cash, but not traveler's checks, exchanged Mon.-Fri. 8:30am-12:30pm and 1:30-4pm. **SuperCambios** (tel. 67-11 or 57-44), 20 yards up from the Esquina de los Bancos (Corner of the Banks). Exchanges cash and traveler's checks. Open Mon.-

Fri. 8am-12:30pm and 2-5:30pm. Sat. 8:30-11:30am. Also try the coyotes (easily found on the esquina de los bancos) and the supermarkets.

Post Office and Telephones: TELCOR (tel. 66-55). On the west side of *el parque central*. Building opens at 9am. **Fax** service closes at 5pm, post office at 7pm and phone service at 9pm. **Telephone code:** 0311.

Train Station: From the northeast corner of the *zócalo,* 5 blocks north and 3 blocks east. 3 trains daily to Managua: 5am, 6:30am (express), and 11am, 7 córdobas. Buy tickets 10 minutes before departure.

Bus Terminal: One block north of and three blocks east of the train station. Express buses to Managua (10 córdobas) at 5am, 6am, 7am, 8am, 9am, 10am, 11am, noon, and 4pm. There is an express to Estelí at 5:30am and one to Matagalpa at 4:30am. There is direct service to both of these cities again in the early afternoon, but this is quite unreliable. If you're not a morning person, your best bet is to catch a bus to San Isidro (every hr., 2½hrs., 9 córdobas). From San Isidro, buses pass for Estelí to the northwest (every ½hr., 1 hr., 3 córdobas) and for Matagalpa to the east (every ½hr., 1 hr., 3 córdobas). Buses also run from San Isidro to Managua, Chinandega, and Somotillo.

City Buses: A few *rutas* ply León's streets. There is an east-west bus that runs between El Terminal (bus terminal) and El Mercadito, west of town, where buses depart for the beach (see **Near León**). These are often *camionetas*, and usually cost 1 córdoba. Another bus runs from Guadalupe, north of León, to San Geronimo, south of León. These buses are sometimes newer, and also cost 1 córdoba.

Library: Biblioteca Publica Maria Eugenia (tel. 56-09). Above Capilla La Asunción, a soothing place to work or read. Open Mon.-Fri. 8-11:45am and 2-4:45pm.

Pharmacy: Farmacia Meg-24, across from the fire station, off the northeast corner of *el parque central.* Open Mon.-Sat. 7:30am-10pm.

Supermarket: El Extra (tel. 22-08), in Plaza Metropolitana, 25 yards up from the Esquina de los Bancos. Open daily 8am-8pm.

AMNLAE: (tel. 45-25) 2 blocks west, ½ block south of the Estatua de la Madre (Statue of the Mother). Offices include a library for women's health and issues, a clinic, classrooms and legal services. A photo mural commemorates those women who died during the revolution. Open Mon.-Fri. 8am-noon and 2-5pm.

Police: tel. 115.

Red Cross: tel. 26-27. 24 hr. ambulance service.

ACCOMMODATIONS

Leon's hotels may disappoint, and the selection is not astounding.

Hotel America (tel. 55-33), 2 blocks east of the southeast corner of *el parque central.* 10 big, comfy, run-down rooms around an overgrown, orange-porticoed courtyard. Wheezy fans and private bathrooms. Ceilings sag, but beds don't. Singles 57 córdobas. Doubles 70 córdobas.

Hotel Telica (tel. 21-36), by the railroad tracks, 2½ blocks north of the street leading to the bus terminal. Simple, gloomy rooms may depress, but price, water pressure, and number of sheets per bed (2) sure to please. Singles 18 córdobas. Doubles 36 córdobas.

Hotel Europa (tel. 25-96 or 60-40), 4 blocks north of *el parque central,* and then just across the train tracks. The classiest place in León. With private bath and A/C, singles 130 córdobas, doubles 150 córdobas. With private bath, singles 70 córdobas, doubles 90 córdobas. With shared bath, singles 40 córdobas, doubles 50 córdobas.

Restaurant Pilar (tel. 65-16), 1 block south of Hotel Telica, rents big bare rooms with fans. Very secure. Good breakfasts. Singles 40 córdobas. Doubles 60 córdobas.

Hotel Primavera, 10 blocks north of el parque central, 1½ blocks west of the train tracks. For those counting córdobas. 15 córdoba singles are hot; the conspicuous lack of fans creates a sweathouse atmosphere. More expensive rooms have fans and private bathrooms. Note also, this hotel was once squarely in the red-light district. This and its distance from the center may concern women traveling alone.

Singles 15 córdobas, doubles 30 córdobas. With private bath, singles 30 córdobas, doubles 60 córdobas.

FOOD

Casa Vieja, across from the front door of the Casa de Cultura. 2 blocks west, 1½ blocks north of *el parque central.* A hip local spot with good food and cool art. Fries 5 córdobas. Licuados 6 córdobas. Cheese sandwich 6 córdobas. Hamburger 10 córdobas.

El Barcito (tel. 69-29). From the northwest corner of *el parque central,* 3 blocks north, 2½ west. Cheap food (tacos 5 córdobas, steak sandwich 5.50 córdobas) and great *refrescoes naturales,* small 2.50 córdobas, large 4.50 córdobas.

Antojitos Solmar, on Avenida Central, 2 blocks north of *el parque central.* A good lunch for 10 córdobas. At night, fare is finer and more expensive (lobster, steak, chef salad).

Restaurant Las Ruinas (tel. 47-67), on Calle Central Rubén Darío, one block west of el parque central. Once inside the pleasant, open courtyard, the name expands to "Las Ruinas de Bagdad 17/12/90," making this restaurant a comment on a certain world superpower. The food is good and apolitical. Shrimp shishkabob 37 córdobas. *Gallo Pinto* 8 córdobas. *Comida corriente* 10 córdobas. Open daily for lunch and then from 9pm-midnight.

Cafetin Intimo (tel. 21-18), in the Casa de la Cultura (see Sights and Entertainment). *Intimo* or not, this is a nice place with a friendly crowd. *Comida corriente* a steal at 8 córdobas. Open Mon.-Sat. 10am-10pm.

El Rincon Azul, on Calle Central Rubén Darío, west of *el parque central,* kitty-corner from Parque Rubén Darío. The art on the walls may be fingerpainting or photographs, but there are cigarettes on the menu in case you want to tuck into a big plate of smokes. Great *refrescoes naturales.* Open mid-afternoon to midnight.

Comedor Doña Enma (tel. 57-58) may be the best dining experience in León. Walking east on the same block as Hotel Europa, on your left about halfway between the Shell station and the train tracks, a small white sign on a wooden door says: *"¿Vos Estudias? Doña Enma se encarga de tu comida."* Stop by in the morning, tell her what you'd like for lunch or dinner, and return at the appointed time. Great food. Great bargain. You can even watch Nicaraguan soaps.

SIGHTS

The **Museo Archivo Rubén Darío** (tel. 23-88) is a super-shrine to the country's favoite poet. It is on Calle Central Rubén Darío, two blocks west of Parque Rubén Darío. (Get the picture?) Some of the creepier exhibits include the poet's death mask and photographs of him on his death-bed. The museum also has a collection of his manuscripts and first editions. Especially interesting is a series of caricatures done of Darío by various political cartoonists of the day. With permission, you can read the books in the archive. (Open Tues.-Sat. 8am-noon and 2-5pm, Sun. 8am-noon. Admission 5 córdobas.)

One block east and 1½ blocks south of the museum, find the **Centro Popular de Cultura** (tel. 21-16). This was once the plush home of a Somoza crony; when he fled the country, the Sandanistas turned the house into a community center displaying local (often political) art. So it goes. The center also holds classes in music, painting, woodworking, Spanish, and English. Ask about upcoming performances, presentations, and *noches festivos.* Or just walk around digging the paintings and sculpture, the clack of typewriters, and the strains of radical guitar. (Open daily 9am-7pm.)

León's **cathedral,** on *el parque central,* is the largest in Central America. Rubén Darío is buried beside the altar, and the paintings of the Stations of the Cross are quite famous. The cathedral has recently undergone a restoration, and though some locals complain about the poor quality of the paint used on the exterior, the inside of the cathedral is quite a sight. (Open Fri.-Wed. 7am-noon and 4-7pm, Thurs. 7am-7pm.)

Also on *el parque central,* at its northeast corner, is the **Mausaleo de Héroes y Mártires,** commemorating the victims of the Revolución. (The ones on the winning side, anyway.) While you're in *el parque central*, check out the murals by the basketball court, ½ block north of the northwest corner of the plaza. In the summer of 1993, there were three very interesting political murals here: two were expansive, pro-Sandanista works showing socialists building schools and tearing down regimes. Another, a somewhat more impressionistic effort, depicted UNO as a many-tentacled monster, and accused it of (among other things) being "Made in America."

From the basketball court, walk ½ block north, one block west, and ½ block north again to see the house where, on the 21st of September, 1956, Rigoberto Lopez Perez shot Anastasio Somoza Debayle. You cannot go inside the house, but it is marked outside designating the event as the beginning of the end of the Somoza dictatorship. The **university (UNAN)** is in a yellow building, two blocks north of the northeast corner of *el parque central*. It is a nice place to read or relax as you absorb the academic vibes. The **Old Jail**, which is now a garden, lies four blocks south of *el parque central*, on Avenida Central. Political prisoners were once incarcerated here, until the Sandanistas defeated Somoza's Guardia Nacional's last stand in León.

León also has an impressive number of churches; some are quite interesting. These include: **La Iglesia de la Recollección**, three blocks north of the cathedral. Four blocks east of the cathedral near the train tracks, find **Iglesia El Calvario. Iglesia La Merced** is one block north of *el parque central*.

At the **Collectivo Faribundo Marti y Sandino**, you can see blankets being dexterously woven on traditional looms. To reach the collective, first find the Iglesia Hermita Dolores, about 10 blocks north of *el parque central*. From the church, walk one long block north and turn left. Walking west, look for a dirt track on your right about mid-block. The cooperative is down this track about 50m, on the right. They sell blankets for US$20-25; that's somewhat pricey, but the quality is very high and the cause worthy. (Open Mon.-Fri. 8am-5pm.)

ENTERTAINMENT

El Tunel del Tiempo is a bar/restaurant/disco outside of town at the salida a Chinandega, in a big white building. The crowd is young and rather affluent. When in disco mode, they do charge a cover, but the amount varies. A taxi there will cost you 5 córdobas, but coming back at night, expect that to inflate. **Las Ruinas** (see **Food**) often has live music Fri.-Sun. The cover is usually less than 10 córdobas, and the dancing is cooler thanks to the club's open-air design. Students from the University often hold parties at the **Club Universitaria**, ½ block east of La Iglesia de la Recollección. Look for these parties when UNAN is in session (March-December); they're usually announced by raucous crowds of students circumnavigating *el parque central* in the back of blaring pick-ups.

The basketball court (see **Sights**) also serves as an informal center of nightlife. There is a pool hall across the street, and, on the corner, a nice bar called **El Alamo.**

■ Near León

Two pleasant Pacific beaches, **Poneloya** and **Las Peñitas,** lie within easy reach of León. Expect crowds only during *el verano*, and especially during Semana Santa. Otherwise, the beach should be relatively empty, especially on weekdays. Catch a bus to these beaches at El Mercadito, on the western outskirts of León. The ride to Poneloya takes about 45 minutes. Las Peñitas, slightly smaller, is another 10 minutes. The fare to either beach is 2.65 córdobas.

NORTH OF MANAGUA

■■■ ESTELÍ

Estelí, a city of 100,000 and capital of the department of the same name, lies 150km north of Managua, halfway between the Capital and the Honduran border. It is a pleasant town to pass through, and has a number of interesting sights to take in. The city is also a liberal stronghold, and saw extremely heavy fighting during the Revolution; Estelí's recent history is a proud and painful one. During the 1980s, there were many collective farms in the region, and the international volunteer presence was strong. Today, Estelí is still an important agricultural center and work remains to be done. INPRHU works with street children here. CENAC offers intensive Spanish classes, as well as placement with a Nicaraguan family. (For information on these programs, see **Alternatives to Tourism** in the Nicaragua introduction.)

Tensions remain high in Estelí. In July, 1993, violence broke out in a skirmish involving a group made up of former Sandanistas and former Contras which rebeled in frustration with the government. The outbreak, heavily imbued with political maneuverings and power posturing, clearly demonstrated the volatility of post-Revolution Nicaragua and the continued threat to peace.

ORIENTATION

There is only one main street in Estelí, and navigation consists primarily of going up and down it. Even if you had a big Cadillac convertible, you would soon tire of this. Avenida Bolivar runs north-south, the whole length of Estelí's blocks. The bus terminal lies at the south end of town, one block west of Bolivar and 13 blocks south of the plaza. Six blocks north of the plaza, the city ends at the river. The only other street of note is Calle Peru, which runs east-west one block south of the plaza. The Pan-American Highway runs along the eastern edge of town, six blocks east of Bolivar.

PRACTICAL INFORMATION

Tourist Office: Inturismo (tel. 26-51), ½ block west of Bolivar, north of the hospital. A Coke/Inturismo sign points the way. Staff distributes a faded brochure that makes a handy drink coaster. Open Mon.-Fri. 8am-noon and 2-5pm.

Currency Exchange: Banc Nicaraguense de Industria y Comercios, on the southeast corner of the Esquina de Bancos. Changes cash Mon.-Fri. 9am-4:30pm.

Post Office and Telephones: TELCOR (tel. 27-09), 1 block south, 1 block east of the plaza. **Mail:** open daily 7am-10pm. **Phone and fax service:** open daily 7am-9:30pm.

Buses: From the terminal at the south end of town buses to León (every hr., 3hrs.), to Matagalpa (every hr., 2hrs.), to Ocotal (every hr., 1hr.), to Managua (every hr., 3hrs.). In the afternoon, buses run much less frequently. León can also be reached via San Isidro. Buses also run to Somoto.

City Buses: One route runs north-south 1 street west of Bolivar from Barrio Rosario to el Instituto Nacional. It serves the bus terminal (.75 córdobas).

Library: Biblioteca Publica Dr. Samuel Meza, 1 block south of the *esquina de bancos.*

Bookstore: Librería Rufo Marín, ½ block west of the northwest corner of the plaza.

Pharmacy: Farmacia Estelí (tel. 25-31) on Bolivar at Calle Peru. Open Mon.-Sat. 8am-1:30pm and 3-6:30pm. There is also a natural pharmacy in town, **La Farmacia Popular,** which grows its herbs organically on a *finca* outside of town. They are also located on Bolivar, across from the *mercadito verde.* Open Mon.-Fri. 8am-noon and 2-5:30pm, Sat. 8am-noon.

AMNLAE: Casa de la Mujer Mercedes Rosales (tel. 26-96), on the Pan-American Highway, opposite the Shell station. Open Mon.-Sat. 8am-noon.

ESTELÍ

Red Cross: Tel. 23-30.
Police: Tel. 26-15.

ACCOMMODATIONS

Hotel Mariela, just behind the bus station, good for late arrivals and early departurs. Very clean. Front door locks at 10pm. 20 córdobas per person.

Hospedaje San Francisco, on Bolivar, a few blocks north of the bus station. Tall rooms, period bunk-beds. Front door locks at 11pm. 15 córdobas per person.

Hospedaje Chepito, on Bolivar, ½ block south of the *parque infantil* (children's park). 9 clean, plain rooms around a very small courtyard. Resist the urge to swing Tarzan-like from the bare, pendulous bulbs. Front door locks at 11pm. Singles 15 córdobas. Doubles 25 córdobas.

Hotel Nicarao (tel. 24-90), on Bolivar, near the plaza across from the Librería Argenial. Big rooms around a modest jungle. 25 córdobas per person. With private bathroom 35 córdobas per person.

Hotel Meson (tel. 26-55), one block north of the northeast corner of the plaza. Classy. 17 rooms with ceiling fans and precious hot water. Restaurant and travel agency attached. Parking. 80.50 córdobas per room (1, 2, or 3 people).

FOOD

Doña Pizza, just west of the northwest corner of the plaza. 15 varieties of pizza. The masks on the walls were made by children from Estelí. Open Mon.-Fri. 6-11pm. Sat.-Sun. noon-11pm.

El Porchecito, on Bolivar, opposite the *parque enfantil* (children's park). Good, basic food. Cheery restaurant affords a view of the main drag. Chicken sandwich 8 córdobas. Licuados 4 córdobas. Open daily noon-10pm.

Cafetin el Mirage, on Bolivar, just south of Ferreteria Briones. A good *comida corriente* for 12 córdobas. Open Mon.-Fri. 8am-10pm. Sat.-Sun. 8am-midnight.

Restaurante Nahuali, (tel. 23-60), kitty-cornered from the Hotel Meson. Swank. Polish up your Tevas. Shrimp salad 55 córdobas. Stuffed shrimp 65 córdobas. Fried chicken 35 córdobas. Open daily noon-10pm.

Restaurante Moderna, (tel. 23-78), 3 blocks south of the plaza, 1 block east of Bolivar. Cool, dark, and pricey. Good soups for 15 córdobas. If you've always wanted to pay 7.50 córdobas for toast, you can do it here. Open daily 7-9:30am and 11am-10pm.

SIGHTS

Estelí's **cathedral** is on the east side of the plaza. It is a very modern (1962), rather pleasing structure. The **Galería de Héroes y Mártires** is ½ block south of the cathedral; it commemorates Estelí's revolutionary *callidos* (fallen). The abstract mural along the outside wall is amazing. There are many of these galleries in Nicaragua; this one is especially effective. For another graphic reminder of the violence that transpired here, visit the large bomb fragment and accompanying monument. From the red Firestone outlet on Bolivar, walk three blocks west. The **Casa de la Cultura Leonel Rugama Rugama, Poeto y Revolucionario** is just down the block from the Gallery of Heroes and Martyrs. A variety of classes are held here, and Saturday nights the Casa holds Las Peñas Culturales, performances, and exhibitions by local artists. There is also a pool here, but in the summer of 1993, it was closed indefinitely, in need of serious repair. On the south side of the plaza, find the boulders from Las Pintadas, which bear pre-historic carvings.

■ Near Estelí

Las Cascadas de Salta Estanzuela can be found seven km south of Estelí. During the rainly season, the falls are said to be quite spectacular; you can even swim in the pool below them. To reach the *cascadas,* catch a *camioneta* (buses can't handle the road) at the Salida Sur, south of the bus station.

Ducuale Grande is a community near Estelí where fine ceramics are made. There are said to be some fabulous bargains. To get there, take a bus to Condega, ask to get off at Guanacaste de Ducuale Grande, then walk three km west to the town of Ducuale Grande; ask for the Taller Comunal.

■■■ MATAGALPA

High mountains and low clouds surround Matagalpa, a small, drowsy city on the eastern slopes of Nicaragua's central mountain range. This is coffee country. Matagalpa's favorite son is the Revolutionary leader Carlos Fonseca. *"Carlos vive,"* assures a sign on the *parque catedral, "porque su obra es inmortal"* ("Carlos lives because his work is immortal.") His house is now a museum. There is also good hiking nearby. You will quickly exhaust this city's reserve of legitimate sights, but you may find yourself sticking around, wooed by the cool green climate and the lazy pace.

ORIENTATION

Matagalpa sits on the east bank of the Río Grande Matagalpa, which eventually empties into the Caribbean. Parque Rubén Darío lies at the south end of town, four blocks east and three blocks north of the bus terminal. Avenida José Benito Escobar fronts the west side of the Parque Rubén Darío and then runs north to meet the *parque catedral* in another seven blocks. Avenida Central comes off the southeast corner of the *parque catedral* and runs roughly parallel with Benito Escobar.

PRACTICAL INFORMATION

Tourist Office: Inturismo, in the Centro Comercial Catalina, on Avenida Central, 3 blocks south of the cathedral. Open Mon.-Fri.

Currency Exchange: Banco Nacional de Desarollo, on Avenida Central, 4 blocks south of the cathedral. They will exchange cash. Open Mon.-Fri. 8:30am-12:30pm and 1:30-4pm.

TELCOR: 1 block east of the cathedral. Post office open Mon.-Fri. 8am-noon and 1:30-5pm, Sat. 8am-noon. Telephone office open Mon.-Sat. 7am-10pm.

Buses: To Managua (every hour, 3hrs., 9 córdobas), Estelí (every hour, 2hrs., 5 córdobas), Jinotega (every 2hrs., 45min., 3 córdobas). For León, go first to San Isidro (every hr., 1hr., 3 córdobas). Buses also go to Boaco and from there to Juigalpa. As always, the frequency of buses to all points decreases in the afternoon.

Library: 1 block west of Benito Escobar, 4½ blocks south of the cathedral.

Pharmacy: Farmacia Blandon (tel. 30-80), on Benito Escobar, 1½ blocks north of the Parque Rubén Darío. Dr. Armando J. Parajóa speaks English and will consult 24 hrs. in case of emergency. Knock on the door after hours.

Supermarket: La Fe (tel. 24-68), 1 block north, 1 block west of the Parque Rubén Darío. Well-stocked, but you'll have to check your bags and guns at the door (seriously). Open daily 8am-8pm.

Police: tel. 35-11, on the south side of the *parque catedral*.

Red Cross: tel. 20-59.

ACCOMMODATIONS

Matagalpa offers up a nice batch of hotels and *hospedajes*. Know, though, that running water is rather sporadic; most places keep tanks and a bucket on hand.

Hospedaje Plaza, (tel. 23-80), on the south side of the Parque Rubén Darío. Eight spotless rooms above a friendly home. A bargain. 17 córdobas per person.

Hotel Bermudez, (tel. 34-39), 2 blocks east of the Parque Darío. Big rooms all with *agua purificada*. Nice courtyard. Restaurant attached. 25 per person.

Hotel Ideal, (tel. 24-83), 2 blocks north, 1 block west of the cathedral. The riziest digs in Matagalpa. Rooms are big and comfortable, with ceiling fans, *agua pura*, and wicker lamps. Try to ignore the sad little tank of turtles in the lobby. The hotel also has a disco (open Fri.-Sun. 7pm-1am, 20 córdobas drink min.). Singles 100 córdobas. Doubles 132 córdobas.

Casa Communal, (tel. 26-95). Very run-down and very friendly. If you can fix roofs you can stay for free. Black and white photographs on the wall tell an interesting (though absolutely inscrutable) story. 10 córdobas per person.

FOOD

Comedor San Martin, on Benito Escobar, a few steps north of the Parque Rubén Darío. Step in and pretend you're a regular. Great simple fare, but order your coffee *sin azucar,* or it will arrive as syrup. Open Mon.-Sat. 6am-9pm, Sun. 9am-9pm.

Cafeteria Fili, (tel. 29-01), 2 blocks east of the Parque Darío, or ½ block south of Hotel Bermudez. Cheese pizzas from 12 córdobas, vegetarian pizzas from 29 córdobas. They also have playing cards and Monopoly. Open Mon.-Wed. 11am-3pm and 5-11pm, Thurs. 5-11pm, Fri. 1-3pm and 5pm-midnight, Sat. 11am-3pm and 5pm-1am, Sun. 11am-3pm and 3-10pm.

Jin-Shan Jaspe, (tel. 30-24), ½ block west of Benito Escobar. You've had better Chinese food, but all things considered, this is a very impressive effort. Chicken chop suey 25 córdobas. House chow mein 35 córdobas. Open daily 11am-10pm.

El Bamba, on Benito Escobar, midway between the two parks. A popular place which strives for a tropical ambience. *Comida corriente* 10 córdobas. Great *refrescoes naturales.* Open Mon.-Sat. 9am-9pm.

Restaurant Ideal, in the Hotel. Pleasant outdoor dining. Sneak here to watch satellite TV from the States. Filet mignon 55 córdobas. Chicken salad 30 córdobas. Lobster soup 45 córdobas. Open Mon.-Thurs. 7am-11pm. Fri.-Sun. 6am-10pm. (After 10, the "action" shifts to the disco.)

SIGHTS

The **Museo y Casa Carlos Fonseca** is a must-see. Grainy black and white photographs trace the making of a Revolutionary. The few artifacts on display (his typewriter, his eyeglasses, his gun) would seem to have been carefully selected to convey his socialist fervor. The museum also sells a slim biography of Fonseca for 10 córdobas. Open Mon.-Fri. 8am-1pm. The local FSLN headquarters also has a small memorial to fallen Revolutionaries. The office is on Avenida Central, a few blocks south of the *parque catedral.* (Open Mon.-Sat. 8am-5pm.) The **Casa de Cultura** is located next to the library.

■ Near Matagalpa

The **Selva Negra** (Black Forest), north of Matagalpa, has a fair amount of hiking trails. The forest is full of wildlife (including monkeys) and is good for bird-watching in the early morning. To reach the forest, board any bus heading north from Matagalpa and ask to be let out at the Hotel Selva Negra, which is quite expensive, but is said to have a good restaurant.

Jinotega lies 34km north of Matagalpa, and probably warrants a day-trip. The ride there (through mountainous farmland) is supposed to be spectacular. The church at Jinotega is said to be one of the most beautiful in all of Central America. The plaza has some interesting murals.

SOUTH OF MANAGUA

■■■ MASAYA

A small city known for its *artesanías,* Masaya lies 26km southeast of Managua. While the city itself would probably not warrant a stay of any great length, Masaya boasts a considerable number of attractions, a few nearby points of interest, and at

MASAYA

least one quality *hospedaje*. Stickball (and innumerable variations thereon) is another draw; in the late afternoon many streetcorners double as playing fields.

Practical Information Buses from Managua arrive at and depart from an empty lot next to the closed and crumbling **Mercado Viejo** (peek inside; there are some neat paintings along the walls). The **Church of la Asunción**, in the Parque 17 de Octubre, is one block to the west. Calle Ernesto Fernandez fronts the park on its south side and runs east, over a small bridge and to the Mercado Nuevo. Calle Real San Jerónimo comes off the north side of the park and runs north to **La Iglesia San Jerónimo. CECAPI,** the Malecón and Hospedaje Masayita, lie to the west of the park.

Inturismo (tel. 29-36) at the *entrada a* Masaya, a 15-minute walk north of the Parque 17 de Octubre, claims to have information on Masaya, but that remains to be seen. (Open Mon.-Fri. 8am-noon and 2-5pm.) **Banco Nicaragüense de Industria y Comercios** (BANIC, tel. 20-21), 1 block east of the southeast corner of the Parque 17 de Octubre, changes cash Mon.-Fri. 8:30am-12:30pm and 1:30-4pm, Sat. 8:30am-noon. The **supermarket, Lorreto,** on the west side of the park, accepts Visa and MasterCard. (Open daily 8am-8pm.) **Farmacia Masaya** (tel. 27-80), is ½ block east of the southeast corner of the park on Ernesto Fernandez. (Open Mon.-Sat. 8am-1pm and 2-5pm.) Women's services are provided by **AMNLAE: Casa de la Mujer Sylvia Marlene Ramirez** (tel. 21-38), ½ block north of the park (across from Pizza Jazz). (Open Mon.-Fri. 9am-noon and 2-6pm, Sat. 9am-noon.) **Buses** depart for Managua every 20min. (less frequently in the afternoon) from beside the Mercado Viejo. From the east side of the Mercado Nuevo, buses leave for Granada (½hr., 2 córdobas) about every ½hr. Catarina, Niquinohomo and San Marcos are all served by the same bus (which leave every ½-hr and usually end up in Jinotepe). The **train** station is a few blocks north of La Iglesia San Jerónimo, across from the Shell station, with 3 trains daily to Granada and 3 to Managua. The **police** can be reached at 25-21, the **Red Cross** at 21-31 or 25-56.

Accommodations and Food Hospedaje Masayita, 4 blocks west of the park (from the supermarket), is very homey and very friendly. If you lose your ring down the shower drain, they will tear up the bathroom floor to get it back. (20 córdobas per person.) **Hospedaje Rex,** on the southwest corner of Parque San Jerónimo, sports clean, gloomy attic rooms without fans. Named after the annoying dog. (15 córdobas per person.) **CECAPI** (Centro de Capacitación de la Pequeña Industria y Artesanias) is housed in a big, low building at the western edge of town, near the Malecón. Their impressive (but bargain) facilities are reserved for large groups of volunteers, seminars, or other good-will travelers.

The restaurant scene in Masaya leaves something to be desired (like, say, good restaurants). Conspicuously absent is a place for breakfast. There is, however, a bakery off of the southwest corner of the park that's open from 6:30am. **Pizza Jazz** (tel. 43-59), also called Chupi's, on San Jerónimo ½-block north of the park, serves variations on a theme from vegetable (39 córdobas) to Hawaiian (50 córdobas). Ice cream parlor and soda fountain as well. (Open Mon.-Fri. noon-9:30pm, Sat.-Sun. 11am-9:30pm.) The waiters at **Alegria,** 1 block north of the park, on Jerónimo, would win no track events, but the chicken in wine sauce (30 córdobas) is pretty good. (Open until 10pm, later on weekends.) To get to **La Confianza** (tel. 41-42), begin at the northwest corner of the park, and head 1 block north, 1 block west, and ½ block north again. Tables huddle around an open air dance floor. Fish dishes are a good bet. (Open Mon.-Thurs. until midnight, Fri.-Sun. until the wee hours.) In the same style, **Discotheque Restaurant Bahia Tropical** (tel. 20-97), ½ block south of southwest corner of the park, serves roast chicken (27 córdobas), conch cocktail (33 córdobas), and other delights. The disco is a sight: a neon tropical night graces one wall, deflated monkeys cling to dusty palm trees, and the requisite mirrored disco ball completes the scene.

Sights You may very well be in Masaya for the sole purpose of visiting its market. In the **Mercado** you can buy woven mats, small stone sculptures and handpainted ceramics, as well as Masaya's famous hammocks and hammock chairs. As always, the quality varies; look around first, and when you do decide to buy, bargain. The western end of the market has the highest concentration of *artesanías*.

Another source for handicrafts is the showroom at **CECAPI** (see Accommodations). The prices tend to be higher, but the mood is lower-key, and it's a good way to see what's out there.

Volcán Masaya (actually 3 smoking craters; Volcán Santiago is the biggest) is easily accessible from either Masaya or Managua. There is a perhaps apocryphal story about how Somoza would drop undesirables into the volcano from a helicopter. The entrance to the volcano is along the *carreterra*, about 4km northwest of Masaya (towards Managua). There is a small museum 2km from the entrance gate, and from there, it's another (steep) 5km to the top. The walk, though tough, is very doable. It is also possible to catch a ride. Taxis to the top are expensive. However you get there, enjoy the view; Laguna Masaya lies below you, with the city beyond. There is a 2-córdoba admission fee at the gate, which is open Tues.-Sun. 8am-5pm.

If you're itching to take a lakeside stroll, you've come to the right place. The **Malecón,** at the western edge of town, is a pleasant walkway looking down on the Laguna de Masaya and across to Volcán Santiago. For your RDA of creepy, visit **Coyotepe,** the large fortress that looms over Masaya from the top of a nearby hill. A colonial structure, the fortress has a somewhat mysterious (though certainly gruesome) history. What is clear is that many were tortured and killed in the dungeons here. Local children are usually on hand to guide you through the most macabre bits. Bring a flashlight if you have one.

Masaya's **Alcaldía** houses the city's **Gallery of Heroes and Martyrs.** Many interesting photographs are displayed, as well as masks worn by some of the first Sandanista guerillas. The Alcaldía is a two-story building on the west side of Calle Real San Jerónimo, 2½ blocks south of La Iglesia San Jerónimo. The gallery is open Mon.-Fri. 8:30-11:30am and 1-4pm.

La Iglesia de la Asunción, in the Parque 17 de Octubre, was built in 1833, and has a painted wooden ceiling that's worth a look. On the southern side of the park, a small plaque commemorates the defeat of the *filibustero* (pirate) William Walker in Oct.-Nov. 1856.

■ Near Masaya

One bus (from the Mercado Nuevo) serves four towns of note near Masaya. **Catarina** is a small town with an absolutely spectacular lookout. Walk right up through the town, about 1.5km, to a windy bluff that overlooks a beautiful lagoon and a magnificent sweep of countryside (and Lake Nicaragua) beyond. A 10-minute walk from here lies the town of **San Juan del Oriente,** know for its **ceramics.** Numerous cooperatives sell local wares. From San Juan de Oriente, you must walk back up the highway a few hundred meters to catch a bus to **Niquinohomo** ("valley of the warriors"), birthplace and boyhood home to Augusto Cesar Sandino. His home is now a library-museum (open Mon.-Sat. until 5pm). Catch the same bus again to go on to **San Marcos,** where you may stumble upon a branch campus of the University of Mobile, as in Alabama. (For more information, see Alternatives to Tourism: Study in the Nicaragua Essentials). San Marcos also has an **AMNLAE** office.

■■■ GRANADA

Granada's strategic location on the western shore of Lake Nicaragua has shaped much of its history. Francisco Hernández de Córdoba founded the city in 1524, and though the Spanish soon exhausted the region's supply of gold, Granada continued to prosper as a trading center, taking advantage of its proximity to the Pacific coast and its access to the Caribbean via the Río San Juan. Granada soon became the country's conservative stronghold, and a rivalry with liberal León ensued. Granada remains today as colonial a city as you'll find in Nicaragua: big, two-story homes line wide boulevards; tall palm trees shade the *parque central*.

A breeze from the lake takes the edge off the toaster-oven heat, and the most enjoyable pastime is simply walking, either within the city itself, or along the lake shore. There's not that much else to do, really. Granada's historic value is more atmospheric than tangible; it has to do with all those who've kicked its cobblestones. Most were just passing through, others came to stay; there are few museums or sights per se.

Practical Information Buses from Managua wind up in the western part of town, six blocks west and two blocks north of the *parque central*. Buses from Masaya pull into a small lot two blocks west and two blocks south of the *parque central*. The park is bordered on its west side by Calle Vega. **La Calzada** comes off the eastern side of the park, by the cathedral, and runs 1.5km to the lake and pier. All four hotels listed are on La Calzada. Also, if you're coming from Managua, remember: *al lago* is no longer north, it is now east.

As always, tourist information, or at least the Nicaraguan imitation, is provided by **Inturismo** (tel. 33-13), on the western side of the park, next to the plush Hotel Alhambra. (Open Mon.-Fri. 8am-noon and 2-5pm.) **Banco Nacional de Desarollo** (tel. 28-11), west of the park on Atravesada, changes cash Mon.-Fri. 8:30am-12:30pm and 1:30-4pm. **Banco Nicaragüense de Industria y Commercios** (tel. 27-22), west of the park in front of the Teatro Gonzalez, changes cash Mon.-Fri. 8:30am-12:30pm and 1:30-4pm, Sat. 8:30am-noon. The *coyotes* in Granada will change traveler's checks as well. **TELCOR,** in a relatively unmarked light blue building (you can only just see the top of the microwave tower) on the northeast corner of the park, has **telephone service** from Mon.-Sat. 7am-10pm, and **mail** 8am-noon and 1-5pm. **Supermercado Lacaya** is two blocks west of the park. (Open Mon.-Sat. 8:15am-12:30pm and 2-10:30pm, Sun. 8am-1pm.)

Buses to Managua (6 córdobas) run every ½-hr., from a station 6 blocks west and 2 blocks north of the park. Buses to Masaya (2 córdobas) leave every 20 minutes or so from a small lot 2 blocks west and 2 blocks south of the park. Buses to Rivas leave from a gas station 1 block west and 4 blocks south of the park (5 per day). From the same stop a bus leaves for the Costa Rican border at Peñas Blancas daily at 7:15am. If you miss this bus, go to Rivas, and from there, 12 buses daily run to Peñas Blancas. The **train** station lies north of town, at the end of Calle Atravesada, beyond the playground. Three trains daily (5am, 10am and 4pm) run north to Masaya (2 córdobas), Managua (4 córdobas), and León (7 córdobas). On Mondays and Thursdays two **boats** leave from the pier at the end of La Calzada. Usually, both of these boats are bound for San Carlos, but only one of them via Isla de Ometepe. The first boat leaves at 3pm and the other at 4:30pm, but you'll want to buy your ticket (at the pier) at 9am, anyway, so find out then which boat is yours and when it leaves. The trip to Isla de Ometepe takes 4 hrs. and costs 5.50 córdobas. **Farmacia el Rosario** (tel. 29-44), on Calle Atravesada 1 block west of the park. (Open Mon.-Sat. 8am-8pm, Sun. 8am-1pm.) **AMNLAE: Casa de la Mujer Claudia Chamorro** (tel. 20-96), on La Calzada 1 block east of the cathedral, provides women's services Mon.-Fri. 8am-noon and 2-6pm. Contact the **police** at 29-29, the **Red Cross** at 27-11.

Accommodations and Food Find 13 spotless rooms around a pleasant, scraggly garden at **Hospedaje Cabrera** (tel. 27-81), on La Calzada, 2½ blocks east of the park. The huge bathrooms have toilet seats and paper. Family atmosphere and playful menagerie put this place over the top. (Singles 25 córdobas. Doubles 40 córdobas.) **Hospedaje Vargas** (tel. 28-97), across the street from Hospedaje Cabrera, has the same idea, but a smaller garden, less atmosphere, and no animals.

(Singles 20 córdobas. Doubles 40 córdobas.) **Hospedaje China-Nica** (tel. 21-44), on La Calzada, 1½ blocks east of the park, contains four big rooms behind a restaurant of the same name. Clean and bare rooms, with green brick walls are a bargain at 15 córdobas per person. **Hotel Granada** (tel. 29-74), on La Calzada across from La Iglesia Guadaloupe, a few blocks west of the lake, is a sprawling, white-tiled hotel with two restaurants, scores of wicker rockers and a few dusty pool tables. Most rooms are quite expensive, but some larger air-conditioned rooms sleep many and are charged per person. (1 person US$10, 6 people US$44.)

The restaurants along the lake shore have some very good fish. All of them are a bit pricey, but the view is nice. **Restaurant La Calzada,** on the north side of La Calzada, just east of the primary school (look for the shark sign), has a pleasing atmosphere and plenty of oscillating fans. Excellent *comida corriente* (with *refresco naturale*) goes for 13 córdobas. (Open daily until 10pm.) **Café Astoria,** is one block west of the southwest corner of the park. Flags of the world give the place a General Assembly feel. Hamburgers 8 córdobas, pizza 7 córdobas. (Open daily 8am-10pm.) The plainly-named **Coffee Shop,** 1 door west of Hospedaje Cabrera, serves good breakfasts. Pancakes may be worth the 10 córdobas. (Open daily 8am-6pm.) **Restaurant China-Nica** on Calzada fronts the restaurant and has the best Chinese food for meters around. The *comida corriente* is good and cheap. (Open daily until 10pm.)

Sights On the park there is the **cathedral,** an interesting obelisk monument to Rubén Dario, and various municipal buldings. These include the **Alcaldía** and the **Palacio de la Cultura,** with a few murals, colonial architecture worth a stroll, and a great-smelling library. Even if you have no cause to visit the train station, you may want to walk north on Calle Atravesada, just to take in the big houses.

La Calzada also makes a very nice walk. Locals fish (and dive) off the pier in the late afternoon, and you can do your best to see a shark. Walking south of the pier along the lake shore, you will come to a tourist park lined with restaurants, and beyond this (about ½ hour from the pier) lies **Puerto Asese,** where you can hire a *lancha* to see Granada's **Isletas,** a number of small, populated lake islands. A basic tour of the near islands may cost you as little as 40 córdobas. To go to the larger, more distant islands (and perhaps stay for dinner) will cost you upwards of 70 córdobas.

■■■ RIVAS

Rivas lies two hours south of Granada and only 45km north of the Costa Rican border at Peñas Blancas. Twelve **buses** per day run from Rivas to Peñas Blancas. Buses also leave every ½ hour for San Juan del Sur on the Pacific coast (1hr., 3.50 córdobas). The lake port of San Jorge is four km to the east (buses from Rivas 1.50 córdobas). From here, **boats** leave for Moyogalpa on Isla de Ometepe at 11am, noon, and 4:30pm daily (1 hr., 4.50 córdobas).

Should the need arise, you could easily spend the night in Rivas. **Pensión Primavera** has basic, clean rooms. There is also a **bank** to change cash and a **TELCOR** office.

■■■ SAN JUAN DEL SUR

This is the kind of place to which you might escape to write a novel, or to hide from a powerful crime syndicate. It is a popular spot with Nicaraguans during *semana santa,* and with the frame-pack set year-round. Despite its popularity, however, San Juan del Sur remains a decidedly sleepy beach town, downright comatose in the off-season, in fact.

Practical Information San Juan del Sur is set on a hill and is only a few blocks deep. The town sits in a sheltered cove, along a pretty comma of easy beach. At the southern end of the beach, a "river" (your toenails will get thoroughly soaked while crossing) meets the Pacific. At the northern end of the beach, a long pier tends to the light boat traffic. **TELCOR** lives in a disarmingly pastel-colored building on the boulevard that fronts the beach, a few blocks south of the pier. Medical attention can be had at **Servicios Médicos Communales**, north of the TELCOR. There is no **police** station in San Juan del Sur, but, in a pinch, try the **Alcaldía,** one block west of TELCOR.

Accommodations and Food A note on accommodations: the mosquitoes discovered San Juan del Sur long ago. Bring or buy repellent and/or mosquito coils. If you're packing a mosquito net, feel self-satisfied. At **Casa 28,** 1 block west of the beach, a very friendly management rents big, bare rooms in barn-like buildings. Upstairs rooms get something of a breeze. Extra arthropods. (20 córdobas per person.) A few extra cords buy a prime location and ace second story balconies, but little else at **Hotel Estrella,** on the boulevard that faces the beach, just south of the TELCOR. (35 córdobas per person.) For distinctly *norteamericano* prices, try the **Hotel Berlovento** (worth visiting for the magnificent view) or the **Casa Internacional Joxi,** west of Hotel Estrella, which also rents sailboards and charters a sailboat.

For good, cheap, basic food, head to **Restaurant Soy,** across the street from Casa 28, run by AMNLAE. They also have a good buy/trade/lend library. **Bar/Restaurant Timon** is one of many such places along the beach; the fish here is very good. At the southern end of the beach, beyond the "river," **Restaurant Lago Azul** is said to have especially fine fare. Directly behind the TELCOR tower, find **El Lugo,** with pleasant outdoor (though inland) dining. Lobster in garlic 40 córdobas and a plethora of squid dishes. You probably want to at least have a drink at **Restaurant Barlovento,** in the hotel. The view more than makes up for the climb.

Sights You can swim right off the town beach; the northern end is the nicest. For more unspoiled beaches, head north along the road to Ostional; Playa del Coco, Playa del Tamarindo, La Flor, and nearest, Playa Sucia (what's in a name?) all offer good swimming and decent snorkelling. Five km south of town, within walking distance, Playa Marselles is also a nice swimming spot.

The only "sight" in town would have to be **La Escuela Integral Cultural,** north of the TELCOR. An ex-Somoza home, the school is architecturally interesting and contains a few murals, as well as a small café. For those experiencing hoops withdrawal, there is pickup basketball on the school's courts.

■■■ EL CASTILLO

El Castillo de la Inmaculada Concepción, a Spanish fort built in 1675, is eight hours down the Río San Juan. The fort has been restored, and is said to be very interesting. Both banks of the river are heavily forested, and the trip is spectacular. At El Castillo, there is a hotel with rooms for US$15 and an *hospedaje* with rooms for 15 córdobas. Boats leave twice a week.

■■■ SAN JUAN DEL NORTE

San Juan del Norte lies at the end of Río San Juan, on the Caribbean coast. The river here constitutes the border between Nicaragua and Costa Rica, as it flows through dense, virgin jungle. Getting to San Juan del Norte might prove difficult. Your best bet is probably to head to El Castillo, and from there, try to secure onward passage, perhaps on cargo boats making the trip. Alternately and more expensively, you could try to hire a boat. Once you tire of San Juan del Norte, you'll have to either return to San Carlos or try your luck with the boat traffic along the Atlantic coast.

LAGO DE NICARAGUA

Lago de Nicaragua, fed by over 40 rivers, is the largest lake in Central America and the 10th-largest freshwater lake in the world. The navigable Río San Juan, at the southern end of the lake, flows all the way to the Caribbean, and was once a heavily traveled waterway. The lake's most famous inhabitants are its sharks. There is a popular belief that these sharks constitute an aquatic vestige of a time when Lake Nicaragua was part of the Pacific Ocean. In fact, the sharks are Caribbean bowl sharks that arrive via the Río San Juan, and are seldom seen. Along with its much-touted sharks, the lake also contains numerous islands. There are 300 *isletas* just offshore from Granada. Easily accessible by *lancha,* some of the *isletas* are populated, and all are notable for their abundant birdlife and important archaeological finds, mainly petroglyphs done by pre-Conquest *indígenas.* On one *isleta,* **San Pablo,** a Spanish fort from the 1700s, is still standing. The **Isla de Ometepe,** four hours by boat from Granada, is a large volcanic island well worth a visit. In the south of the lake, off of San Carlos, another series of small islands makes up the **Archipiélago de Solentináme,** now well-known as a Nicaraguan artists' community.

Boat travel on Lago de Nicaragua is easy and cheap, and, like most boat travel, sort of fun. Twice a week, two boats make the Granada to San Carlos roundtrip. One of these boats goes via Isla de Ometepe, while the other puts in at a few ports along the lakeshore. The quickest crossing to Isla de Ometepe (1hr.) is between San Jorge, 4km from Rivas, and Moyogalpa, on the western side fo the island (3 times per day, 6 days per week). La Señora del Lago makes this trip.

■■■ ISLA DE OMETEPE

Islands are, of course, something else entirely. Some people are drawn to them. If you are one of these people, do not leave Nicaragua without seeing Isla de Ometepe. Ancient petroglyphs, friendly people and great fish dinners aside, the sheer natural beauty of the island is cause enough for a visit. Isla de Ometepe is formed by two volcanoes, **Volcán Concepción** (1610m above sea level), which is still active, and **Volcán Madera** (1394m above sea level), which is quite inactive, having last erupted 2600 years ago.

A relatively well-maintained road circumnavigates the Concepción side of the island, while a much poorer road makes it halfway around the Madera side. The wide green belt surrounding both volcanoes is extensively farmed, and there are countless walks just waiting to be taken. If your walks require a purpose, visit some of the many petroglyphs on the island (some of the best and most easily accessible examples lie between Balgue and Magdalena, on the Madera side of the island), which were carved by island inhabitants approximately 800 years before the arrival of the Spanish. It is not clear exactly how they were made.

Then, of course, there are the volcanoes. During the rainy season, the peak of Volcán Concepción is usually shrouded in clouds. Often, these clouds take the shape of a perfectly domed, quietly rolling mantel. The effect is, at times, actually awe-inspiring. With an early start, you can climb to the crater-lake peak of Volcán Madera. The best ascent begins in Balgue, and from there, it is a difficult (but very rewarding) all-day hike. Volcán Concepción can also be climbed, though you may have to stop short of the peak. It is a long trip, made quite difficult at the top by sulphur springs and treacherous footing. Much of the island is protected as a natural preserve, though this would come as a surprise to most of the locals.

■ Moyogalpa

Sitting on the island's western coast, Moyogalpa is the second largest town on Isla de Ometepe. The **boat** from San Jorge arrives and departs three time daily (except on Sunday, when it makes the trip only once, sometimes twice). The *carreterra* that circumnavigates the Concepción side of the island is a few blocks east (uphill) of the pier. **Buses** run to Altagracia every 1½ hours. If you miss these, you could try to find a ride, or simply relish your stranded state until Monday morning. **TELCOR** is in a humble wooden building three blocks east, 1½ blocks south of the pier. **Mail** and **telephone** services are open Mon.-Sat. The surprisingly modern **hospital** can be found on the *carreterra*, a five-minute walk south of the church. **Banco Nacional de Desarollo,** four blocks east of the pier, will change cash Mon.-Sat. The **police** are located in an unmarked white building 2½ blocks east of the pier.

On your right as you walk off the pier is **Hospedaje Moyogalpa.** They offer clean, wallpapered (?!) rooms for 15 córdobas per person, with fan for 20 córdobas per person. Three blocks east (uphill), on the other side of the street, is **Hospedaje Aly.** They have big, clean rooms with concave beds as well as a pleasant arboreal dining area (20 córdobas per person). **Hospedaje El Pirata,** the nicest place in town ("nicest" as in "has the best collection of rock star posters," including Julio Iglesias and Dee-Lite) is one block east of the TELCOR. Hospedaje El Pirata also rents vehicles: a Yamaha motor bike (150 córdobas per day), a Suzuki Samurai (286 córdobas per day), or, if you must keep up appearances, a Toyota Land Cruiser (345 córdobas per day). All three *hospedajes* serve excellent food.

Volcán Concepción is best ascended from its Altagracia side, but from here you can enjoy a long beautiful walk through farmland as it approaces and begins to ascend the volcano. Walk up (east) through town to the church, one block east of the *carreterra*. Turn right and walk a few hundred meters until a dirt road leads off to the left. Wander.

■ Altagracia

With 6000 inhabitants, Altagracia, on the northeast coast of the Concepción side, is the island's biggest town. It sits about a mile inland. If the hustle and bustle of the place gets to you, you've gone insane; there's very little to do here, but Altagracia serves as an excellent base from which to explore the island or climb its volcanoes.

TELCOR lives in the Alcaldía, a white building on the southwest corner of the park (open Mon.-Sat. 8am-noon and 2-5pm). The **Centro de Salud** is one door west of Hospedaje Castillo (open Mon.-Fri.), and the **pharmacy** sits in the middle of the park (open Mon.-Fri. 8am-noon and 1-5pm). Island **buses** leave from the park, bound for Moyogalpa once every hour (last bus at 5:30pm). Five buses run daily to Balgue. **Boats** leave from the dock: to Granada, Tues. and Fri. at 11pm and Sun. at 10am; to San Carlos, Mon. and Thurs at 7pm.

If there is a center of eco-toursim in Nicaragua, it may just be **Hospedaje Castillo.** Señor Castillo is the island authority on the petroglyphs, and with luck, you may share his *hospedaje* with knowledgeable grad students collecting data for heavy theses in tropical ecology. The rooms are spare and clean; the food is good. (20 córdobas per person.) Whether or not you're staying here, feel free to drop by for a meal and/or to speak with Señor Castillo, who can arrange for you a guide to the petroglyphs (25 córdobas for four hours). **Bar Restaurant Central,** on the *carreterra*, one block south of Hospedaje Castillo, is another good place to eat. In the summer of 1993, the restaurant also had a *hospedaje* in the planning stages. The only "sight" in town is the **church,** on the east side of the park. The rough-hewn statues in front were made by the island's ancient *indígenas*.

■ Climbing the Volcanoes

VOLCÁN MADERA

If you plan on making it to the top of Volcán Madera, you'll need boots and a full water bottle, and you'll want to be on the first bus to Balgue (5am from Altagracia). The bus terminates beside a scruffy baseball field. Cross the field, then make your way through the derelict banana plantation. After a few minutes in the plantation, the path will lead you across a small stream and then through a few cow pastures. This is Magdalena. In another 10-15 minutes, you'll reach a large farm; try to walk around either side of it; after all, it's not your farm. Another 10 mintues beyond the farm, look for a small house: the trail begins behind this house. For the first 5-10 minutes, the climb is quite steep and it will probably be muddy as well, so watch your step. The trail becomes more manageable quite soon, ascending through the lush forest. At the volcano's lower altitutdes, the vegetation qualifies as tropical dry forest (do not, however, take this to mean that you will stay dry). As you ascend higher, you'll enter tropical moist forest; here the trail is densely vegetated. For most of the climb, you're following the west side of a ridge. After a few hours, however, the trail turns east (left) and wraps around the volcano, approaching the crater lake (*el cerro*) from the south. The last kilometer is tough going, and will require balance and both hands. The descent is a bit quicker, but can be quite difficult if the trail is extra muddy.

While climbing, keep an eye out for petroglyphs; there are a number of them scattered throughout the forest, also many birds. The rare turquoise-brown Mot-Mot, Nicaragua's national bird, is colorful, with a turquoise crown and a long rocket tail. Much more common, but still fun to spot, is the Uracca (white-throated magpie-jay), a large, blue jay-like bird with black crown feathers. You may also have the rare pleasure of seeing an Agouti. These animals, the size of a small dog, are the world's largest species of rodent.

VOLCÁN CONCEPCIÓN

Climbing Concepción is a more serious undertaking. While the climb is not a technical one, it is long and very difficult. Rock slides are a danger. Unless you're a volcanologist, you'd do best to hire a local guide, or at least speak to Señor Castillo before you begin.

■■■ SAN CARLOS

San Carlos, at the southern end of Lake Nicaragua, sits on the north bank of the Río San Juan. It is a crossroads: people move quickly through this place, and it feels rather like a boom town from the Old West. All that's missing are hitching posts, wooden sidewalks, and burlesque music from behind saloon doors. From San Carlos you can head west, back toward Granada and Managua, by bus or boat. You can float down the Río San Juan to El Castillo, and, with some luck, to San Juan del Norte on the Caribbean coast. You can also get to the Atlantic coast by bus, via Juigalpa and Rama to the north.

San Carlos is on Nicaragua's southern border; the Costa Rican town of Los Chiles is just down the river. The border, however, is not open to foreigners. Only Nicaraguans from San Carlos and Costa Ricans from Los Chiles may cross here, and they only for 24 hours. This may change in the future, however. One hears of foreigners who've managed to talk their way across, but there is probably some money involved.

Practical Information The big boats from Granada and Isla de Ometepe dock at one end of the lakeshore avenue. Just beside them, smaller boats depart for El Castillo, down the Río San Juan. Walking along the water, away from the dock, you'll pass the immigration office (where you can check on the status of the border), then the **Banco Nacional de Desarollo** (open Mon.-Fri. 8:30am-12:30pm and 2-5pm) to exchange U.S. dollars. After the bank is the muddy lot that serves as a **bus terminal,** and beyond that, a crowded **market street.** The **park** is two blocks back from the water, uphill. The **police** station is on the park. The **TELCOR** is ½ block off of the park. The **Red Cross** is four blocks beyond the park, on your left. **Boats** to Granada via Isla de Ometepe leave Tues. and Fri. at 4pm; to Granada via San Miguelito, Tues. at 3pm; to Granada via San Miguelito and Morito, Fri. at 3pm; to El Castillo (6 hrs.), Tues. and Thurs. at 9am; to El Archipiélago de Solentináme, *lanchas* from beyond the market (10 córdobas).

Except on Tues. and Fri., **bus** service is quite limited. The road from San Carlos to Juigalpa is 139km and unpaved but is, however, a beautiful ride. The road from Juigalpa to Rama is only partially paved, and gets progressively worse as it proceeds east. To Granada via Juigalpa and Managua, leaves Tues. and Fri. 2am (and sometimes 3am). This is a very long haul, so consider the lake route to Granada and Managua. Buses to Rama leave Tues. and Fri. at 6am. The other 5 days, buses to Juigalpa leave twice daily, and from there, head east or west.

Accommodations and Food If you're arriving by boat from Granada or Isla de Ometepe, it will be early morning (late night) when you put into San Carlos, and you may very well find the *hospedajes* full and/or shut up for the night. Both of the *hospedajes* listed below will accept reservations, and they will also answer the door in the wee hours if you knock loudly enough (though they may then try to overcharge you; stick to your guns and try not to look desperate). You can also just stay on the boat until morning. It's not the most comfortable place to sleep, but you'll have lots of company. **Hospedaje El Madroño** (tel. 102), on the water above the market, has 14 plain, wooden rooms (18 córdobas per person). **Hospedaje Peña** (tel. 25), a two-story maroon building, one block above the market across from a pool hall, has 13 more plain, wooden rooms.

THE ATLANTIC COAST

Nicaragua's Atlantic coast is very unlike the rest of the country. The region is part of a larger geographical area known as La Mosquitia, a vast and sparsely populated expanse of rainforest, plain, and coast, extending the length of Nicaragua, and on to the northern coast of Honduras. In the north, especially along the Río Coco (which serves as the border between Honduras and Nicaragua), live some 70,000 Miskitos, an indigenous population. Other *indígenas*, in lesser numbers, include the Sumos,-Ramas and the Garifunas. In the south, most of the inhabitants are of West Indian descent, and speak English.

The politics here are different as well. Sandinista policies meant to unify and develop the country included mandatory military service and the declaration of Spanish as Nicaragua's national language. To many, it smacked of forced cultural assimilation. Some even preferred the Somoza years because under his regime they had been, for the most part, left alone. For this reason, the Atlantic coast is sometimes called the failure of the 1980s.

Today, Nicaragua's Atlantic coast remains distinct from the rest of the country. Politically, it is semi-autonomous. Culturally, it is almost a spearate entity. Most Atlantic coasters identify more strongly with their West Indian heritage or their indigenous community than they do with Managua.

The Atlantic coast has a great deal to offer the traveler: a colorful Caribbean atmosphere; beautiful, remote communities; and a number of do-nothing beaches. Here is also the opportunity to simply and truly explore. Travel, though, is tricky as there are almost no roads. Unless you fly (small planes serve Bluefields, Puerto Cabezas, Islas de Maíz, and a few towns in Honduras) getting from one place to another will involve a great deal of waiting around for a boat that may or may not show up, and when it does, may or may not agree to take you where you want to go. You'll have to remain very flexible; still, therein lies much of the adventure.

■■■ RAMA

Rama sits at the confluence of the Río Síquia and the Río Rama. These two rivers become the wide, brown Río Escondido, which flows east to the Caribbean. Rama is a drowsy little town, and a fine layover point between western Nicaragua and the Atlantic coast. If you're running late, another option is Juigalpa, halfway between Managua and Rama.

Buses come into Rama from the north and drop off beside the market. 2½ blocks south of the market is the park, where you'll find the tall modern **church,** which is very appealing in a concrete sort of way. The **dock** (and Hotel Amy) is 1½ blocks south and one block west of the bus stop. **TELCOR,** which has no long-distance telephone service, is one block east of the bus stop. **Banco Nacional de Desarollo,** two blocks east of the church, will exchange U.S. dollars Mon.-Fri. 8am-1pm and 1:30-5pm. The **Red Cross** is two blocks east and ½ block north of the bus stop. Four buses daily leave for Managua; the first is an express and leaves quite early.

The best place to crash in Rama is **Hotel Amy,** next to the dock. Plain, clean rooms with colored rice-paper windows cost 15 córdobas per person. No fans, though. **The Ramada Inn,** three blocks east of the church, bears no resemblance to its namesake. Rather, it is a worn wooden building with 10 rooms and friendly family management. Pin-up posters may offend (20 córdobas per person). **Hotel Johanna** is two blocks east and one block south of the church. If you stay here, ask for a room on the south side of the hotel to avoid the bar music from below at night (20 córdobas per person, 25 córdobas per person with fan). Hotel Amy also serves pretty good food.

■■■ BLUEFIELDS

Bluefields is a breezy and colorful Caribbean town. A *paella* of a city. Languages spoken are English (with a sonorous West Indian lilt), Spanish, Miskito, and maybe a few other indigenous languages. Or any combination thereof. The theme music is reggae and soca from every doorway. Once you've finished dancing, there isn't all that much to do in Bluefields, but it's an excellent place from which to explore the Atlantic Coast.

Getting There The "Expresso" (the name is probably an attempt at humor) chugs between Rama and Bluefields on Tues., Thurs., Sat., and Sun. It is supposed to leave the town dock at 10am, but usually runs late. The crowded, friendly trip takes five hours and costs 25 córdobas. The other option is to take a *panga,* the big outboard launches. With eight or more passengers, the ride shouldn't cost any more than 60 córdobas per passenger. At two hours, the *panga* trip is much faster than the Expresso, a very nice way to see the river (unless it rains), and also allows you to arrive in Bluefields ahead of the crowd. If you need to make the trip on a day when the Expresso is not running, a *panga* is your only option. Every now and then, a *panga* and its passengers are robbed at gunpoint. Rarely, however, does the banditry escalate to violence.

The ride along the Río Escondido is an enjoyable one. The thick forest along the banks is interrupted every now and then by small wooden huts. You'll also see a few small banana plantations; they were hurt badly by Hurrican Joan in 1988, but most have recovered. Further downriver, Joan's damage is still evident; the forest here is low, only a few spindly trunks rise where once there was a high canopy. Many ships, quietly dying a rusty death, also line the river's banks. Some were victims of the hurricane, others of bankruptcy. Note, especially, the rusty irony of the once-gleaming, now rotting Hope, named after Somoza's wife.

Practical Information In Bluefields, the Caribbean Sea is always to the east. A long avenue runs north-south along the water; at the northern end of this avenue, just north of the tall, red-roofed Moravian church, is the town pier. One block south and three blocks west of the pier is the big, scruffy park. About halfway between the water and the park, rises the spire and clock tower of the Catholic church.

The **TELCOR** office is three blocks west of the red-roofed Moravian church, on the park. (Telephones open daily 8am-9pm. *Correo* open Mon.-Fri. 8am-noon and 1-5pm, Sat.-Sun. 8am-1pm.) **Banco Nacional de Desarollo,** across from the Moravian church, will exchange U.S. dollars Mon.-Sat. and will also exchange traveler's checks, but at a service charge of 20 córdobas per check. *Coyotes* hang out outside. The **hospital** is 2km southwest of town.

The **Expresso boat** leaves for Rama at 5am on Sat., Sun., Tues., and Thurs. You can buy your ticket the night before, but you'll still want to be on the pier by 4:30am. (30 córdobas.) The **Lynx,** another big passenger boat, sometimes makes this trip as well; inquire at the Lynx office or the pier. The Lynx also sails to Corn Island every Wed. at 9am. The only other direct service to Corn Island is on Sun. morning. Three boats daily leave for Laguna de Perlas, and there is also daily service to Rama Cay.

All the big boat traffic goes through **El Bluff,** Bluefields' off-shore port. From Bluefields, a *panga* to El Bluff costs 10 córdobas. In El Bluff, you can try to catch a ride to Corn Island with a passing *pescadero* or *langostero.* This is usually not too hard, but then again, you may end up spending the day on the dock, watching metal rust, only to return to Bluefields in the evening. There's just no way to know. In El Bluff, it is also possible to get to other, more distant points along the Atlantic coast, though this would almost certainly require superhuman patience. In general, boat travel from either Bluefields or El Bluff is tinged with a certain chimerical quality. Sailings to Rama are extremely reliable, but beyond these, no one seems to know just when a boat is likely to happen by.

The airport (airstrip, really) lies about 2km south of town. **Nica** flies a 22-seat plane round-trip from Managua to Corn Island (stopping twice in Bluefields) on Sun., Mon., Wed., and Fri. The flight leaves Managua at 10:30am, leaves Bluefields at noon, leaves Corn Island at 12:30pm, leaves Bluefields once again at 1:30pm, and arrives back in Managua at 2:30pm. From Managua to Bluefields, the fare is US$46, from Bluefields to Corn Island it's US$16, and from Managua to Corn Island it's US$60. (Nica tel. in Bluefields 500, in Managua 66-31-36.) **La Costeña** makes the same flights. The fares are about the same, but the plane is smaller, and at least one of their pilots wears trifocals.

Accommodations and Food If you're on the Expresso from Rama, waste no time in finding a place to stay in Bluefields. There is often a rush on the town's hotels. **Hotel Hollywood** (tel. 282), overlooking the water 2½ blocks south of the Moravian church, has 12 green and white, clean and breezy rooms, a wide, wooden veranda and a good, expensive restaurant. (Singles 35 córdobas, doubles 50 córdobas, with 2 beds 60 córdobas.) Rooms are somewhat shabbier at the **Hotel Cueto,** across from the Hollywood, but allow you to get chummy with Bluefields' arthropod population. Private bathrooms. (Singles 30 córdobas, doubles 50 córdobas.) **Hotel Marda Maus** (tel. 492), around the corner from Hotel Hollywood, has clean rooms, fans, and nifty key rings. (Singles 30 córdobas, doubles 40 córdobas, with 2 beds 50 córdobas.)

Cafet'ín y Mini Hotel Central, 1½ blocks north, and ½ block west of Hotel Hollywood, serves cheap grub all day long. **Galaxy Restaurant,** ½ block west and ½ block north of the Cafetín (above), in a blue house set back from the street, has good local fare, but the service could be speedier. **Restaurant Hollywood,**

beneath the hotel, is close-quartered and expensive, but the sea-bass (30 córdobas) transends it all. **Restaurant Tropical,** across from the Cafetín, is al place with inexpensive food. **Chez Marcel,** up near the park, is the ritzy place; meals start around 60 córdobas. **Los Pepitos,** one block west of Hotel Marda Maus, has good ice cream.

Entertainment Bluefields is a hopping place. The music from the clubs at night may loosen your teeth, but it'll keep you dancing. On the other hand, women may feel unsafe walking home alone at night. There is a raging, unmarked **reggae club** in a tumbledown building on the north side of the park. When they charge a cover, it's 5 córdobas. **Lego-Lego** is a bigger club, a winding 10-minute walk north of town. Follow the music. Cover 5 córdobas) **Bacchus,** around the corner from Chez Marcel, is more upscale and plays salsa, merengue, and disco for a hefty cover. You can often get into a basketball game in the gymnasium of the **Colegio Morava,** across from the Moravian church.

■■■ OTHER ATLANTIC COAST DESTINATIONS

Rama Cay, an island community of Ramas two hours by boat from Bluefields, might make a very nice day trip. The beaches are said to be good for swimming. The **Laguna de Perlas** ("Pearl Lagoon") is 80km north of Bluefields. A stay here would allow you a closer look at indigenous and coast culture. **Miss Ingrid's** in the village offers rooms and food. **Puerto Cabezas,** farther north, sits at the mouth of the Río Wawa. It is a fishing village, and so would probably be a good place to catch a ride with a passing boat. Travel to these and other more remote points along the coast would most likely be a difficult and rewarding experience.

A stay on **Corn Island,** on the other hand, would not be difficult at all. The Islas de Maíz are said to have a demotivational effect on visitors. Isla de Maíz Grande (usually called Corn Island) lies 75km northeast of Bluefields. Fishing, snorkeling, hiking, and Caribbean degeneration are the big draws here. There are four hotels and a few restaurants. There is also a bank. The smaller island, though inhabited and accessible by boat, has no facilities for visitors.

Appendices

■■■ GLOSSARY

abarrote: a corner grocery store
abanico: fan
abono de ahorro de transporte: money-saving transit pass available in some cities
aduana: customs
aire acondicionado: A/C
albergue (juvenil): youth hostel
almuerzo: lunch, midday meal
amigo/a: friend
antojitos: literally "little cravings," appetizers
avenida: avenue
azufral: mineral spring
bahía: bay
balneario: spa or resort on the water
baño: bathroom
barato/a: cheap
borracho: drunk
cabina: a class of transportation ticket, with which you get your own room and bed
calle: street
cambio: change
camino: path or track
camioneta: small, pickup sized truck
campamento: campground
campesino/a: person from a rural area
cantera: water-holding vessel
cantina: a drinking establishment, usually male dominated
caro/a: expensive
carretera: highway
carro: car, or sometimes a train car
casa de cambio: currency exchange establishment
casado/a: married
caseta de larga distancia: long distance phone booth
catarata: waterfall
cena: dinner, a light meal usually served after 8pm.
cenote: natural well
centro: city center
cerca: close by
cerveza: beer
ceviche: fish marinated in lemon juice, herbs and vegetables
coche: car
colectivo: a municipal transit bus
colonia: a neighborhood in a large city
combi: a municipal transit bus
comida corrida or **comida corriente:** a multi-course *á la carte* meal
consulado: consulate
correspondencia: in Mexico City this refers to points where you can change between subway lines
cruda: hangover
cruz roja: Red Cross
cuadra: street block
cuarto con dos camas: a room with two beds; **con una cama:** with one bed

de paso: refers to buses that pass through to pick up passengers in a city, as opposed to originating in that city

desayuno: breakfast

descompuesto: broken, out of order

embajada: embassy

eje: axis, the name for main arteries leading into Mexico City's center

emergencia: emergency

farmacia: pharmacy

feria: a fair

ferrocarriles: trains

finca: in Guatemala, a plantation-like agricultural enterprise

ganga: bargain

guarache: sandal

herbido/a: boiled

hospicio: hospice

kilo: kilogram

ladrón: thief

larga distancia: long distance

lavandería: laundromat

lejos: far

Lista de Correos: the general delivery system in Mexico, Guatemala and Costa Rica

litera: bunkbed

malecón: pier or seaside thoroughfare

maneje despacio: drive slowly

mariachis: Mexican folk musicians

menú del día: fixed daily meal often offered for a bargain price

mercado: market

micro: a municipal transit bus

mordida: literally "little bite," bribe

oficina de turismo: office of tourism

panadería: bakery

parque de trailer: trailer and RV park

parroquia: parish

peligroso/a: dangerous

pesero: a municipal transit bus

Quitos: diminutive of Marcos

ranchera: a popular song genre

reloj: watch, clock

remolque: RV or camper

ropa: clothes

sala: room

salida: exit

seguro/a: a lock, the adj. safe

semana: week; **Semana Santa:** Holy Week

SIDA: the Spanish acronym for AIDS

soda: a small food establishment in Costa Rica

solo carril: one-lane road or bridge

taquería/taquetería: a taco stand or vendor

tienda: store

tipo de cambio: exchange rate

torre: tower

torta: in Mexican Spanish, a sandwich

virrey/virreina: viceroy

■■ NOTES ABOUT LANGUAGE

n the many and varied regions of Mexico, certain geographical and civic features
re constants: *palapas*—open restaurants—are ubiquitous, particularly in the
Yucatán and on the Pacific Coast. These breezy, thatched bistros lease hammock
1ooks to weary travelers. Every city has its *zócalo*, or town square, a useful orienta-
ion point for *viajeros* (travelers) landed upon alien soil. The seeds of the term
zócalo were planted in 1843, when the dictator Santa Ana (see Life in Mexico: His-
ory) ordered the construction of a monument to independence in the city's Pl. de
a Constitución. With only the *zócalo* (pedestal) in place, the project was aban-
1oned. Soon everyone began to refer to the square as *El Zócalo*, which was soon
absorbed as the generic term for town square.

Even if you speak no Spanish, a few basics will help you along. Any attempts at
Spanish are appreciated and encouraged, and you'll find that many people in larger
rites understand some English. You are likely to hear *indígena* languages as well as
Spanish in Oaxaca, Chiapas and the Yucatán. Those who already know peninsular
Spanish will find that many common nouns and expressions are different in Mexico.

Pronunciation is straightforward. Vowels are always pronounced the same way:
a ("ah" in father); e ("eh" in escapade); i ("ee" in eat); o ("oh" oat); u ("oo" in boot);
y, by itself, is pronounced like i. Most consonants are the same as English. Important
exceptions are: j, pronounced like the English "h" in "hello"; ll, pronounced like the
English "y" in "yes"; ñ, which is pronounced like the "gn" in "cognac"; rr, the trilled
"r"; h is always silent; x, uniquely Mexican, has a bewildering variety of pronuncia-
ions

Let's Go provides approximations for particularly tough town names. Stress in
Spanish words falls on the second to last syllable, except for words ending in "r," "l"
and "z," in which it falls on the last syllable. All exceptions to these rules require a
written accent on the stressed syllable.

■■■ USEFUL PHRASES

No hablo español
(no AHB-loh eh-spahn-YOHL) is "I don't speak Spanish."

¿Habla Usted inglés?
(AHB-la oo-STED een-GLEHS?) is "Do you speak English?"

¿Puede Usted ayudarme?
(POOEH-deh oos-TED a-yoo-DAR-meh?) is "Can you help me?"

¿Cuánto cuesta un cuarto para x personas?
(KWAHN-toh KWEH-sta oon KWAHR-toh PAH-rah *x* PEHR-soh-nahs) is "How much
does a room for x person(s) cost?"

¿Dónde hay un hotel, restaurant?
(DOHN-deh aie oon oh-TEL, res-taw-RAN?) is "Where is there a hotel, restaurant?"

¿Dónde está el hotel x?
(DOHN-deh es-TAH el oh-TEL x?) is "Where is the hotel x?"
¿Puedo ver un cuarto? is "May I see a room?"

¿El cuarto tiene agua caliente, baño privado, un abanico? is "Does the room have
hot water, a private bathroom, a fan?"

¿A qué hora es el tren a Guadalajara? is "At what time is the train to Guadalajara?"

Hola is "Hello."

Yo me llamo ... is "My name is ..."

¿Cómo se llama Usted? is "What is your name?"

Mucho gusto conocerlo/la. is "Pleased to meet you."

¿Qué hora es? is "What time is it?"

Learn the vocabulary of courtesy as well; you'll be treated more kindly if you can be polite to those around you:

Por favor (pohr fah-VOHR) is "please"

Gracias (GRAH-seeahs) is "thank you."

De nada (deh NAH-dah) means "You're welcome" (literally "It's nothing").

Con permiso (con pehr-MEE-so, "excuse me") is "Excuse me", an important phrase used more frequently than its English counterpart, whether on a crowded bus or to excuse yourself from someone's company.

¿Qué pasa? (keh PAH-sah) means "What's up?"

Learn the numbers, if only to bargain and to reassure yourself that you're on the right bus. 1: *uno;* 2: *dos;* 3: *tres;* 4: *cuatro;* 5: *cinco;* 6: *seis;* 7: *siete;* 8: *ocho;* 9: *nueve;* 10: *diez;* 11: *once;* 12: *doce;* 13: *trece;* 14: *catorce;* 15: *quince;* 16: *dieciséis;* 17-19: *dieci*-plus the units; 20: *veinte;* 21: *veintiuno;* 30: *treinta;* 31, 32, etc.: *treinta y*-plus the units; 40: *cuarenta;* 50: *cincuenta;* 60: *sesenta;* 70: *setenta;* 80: *ochenta;* 90: *noventa;* 100: *cien;* 101, 102, etc: *ciento*- plus units; 1000: *mil;* 2000, 3000, etc.: units plus *mil.*

No offense is meant if you are called a *gringo/a* (GREEN goh/gah). You may offend, however, if you call yourself an *americano/a*; as part of the Americas, Central and South Americans resent monopolization of the term by the U.S. Instead, refer to yourself as a *norteamericano/a. Güero/a* (GWEH-roh/rah, light-haired or light-skinned person) and *moreno/a* (moor-REH-noh/nah, dark-skinned person) are common forms of address among strangers in the streets. The most appropriate term for the descendants of the Aztecs, Olmecs, Maya and other groups—Native Americans, indigenous peoples, aboriginal peoples, *indígenas*—varies from country to country and person to person. *Let's Go* uses *indígena* (in DEE heh nah) or indigenous; the only term that is guaranteed to be universally *offensive* is *indio.*

To protect yourself, learn some basic self-defense phrases:

¡Déjame (en paz)! (DEH ha may) is "Leave me (alone)!"

¡Ayúdame! (ah-YOO-dah-meh!) is "Help me!".

Index

A

Acapulco 318
Acatzitzimitla 290
Actun Can Cave 532
Agua Azul 386
Agua Caliente hot springs 124
Agua Caliente, Colima 217
Aguascalientes state 217
Aguascalientes, city 217
AIDS (SIDA), Information 73
Ajijic 198
Akumal 463
Alameda 89
Altagracia 595
Ambergis Caye 482
AAA 6
AMNLAE 569
Angahuan 253
Angeles Verdes (Green Angels) 45
Anthropology Museum 93
Antigua 508
Arch Rock 137
Arenal 553
Arenal Volcano 551
Arias Sánchez, Oscar, president of Costa Rica 537
Armería 212
Arrazola 336
AMA 6
ANA 6
Atenquique 216
Avenida Revolución 113
Aztec calendar 83
Aztecs 49

B

Baboon Sanctuary 478
Bahía Chamela 205
Bahía de la Concepción 128
Bahía de la Paz 130
Bahía de Navidad 206
Bahía Manzanillo 211
Bahía Santiago 211
Bahía Tenacatita 205

Baja California ferry service 113
Ballenas Grises National Park 124
Ballet Folklórico de México 90
Barra de Navidad 208
Barra de Potosí 317
Barrancas del Cobre (Copper Canyon) 155
Barrier Reef, Belize 481
Basílica de Guadalupe 97
Becán 469
Belize 470
   Currency 471
   Documents and Formalities 471
   Health, safety, security 473
   Transportation 473
Belize City 474
Belize Zoo 485
Belize/Guatemala Border 488
Big Fun, see Tampico
Biotopo Chocon Machacas 529
Biotopo Quetzal Mario Dary 524
Bluefields 598
Boca de Tomatlán 204
Bosque de Chapultepec 93
Brownsville, Texas 181
La Bufadora, geyser 124
Buses, Mexico 41

C

Cabo Blanco 561
Cabo San Lucas 136
Cahal Pech 486
Campeche 394
Campeche state 394
Camping, Mexico 48
Cancún 439
Cañón El Sumidero 363, 364
Caracol 488

Carara Biological Reserve 560
Carranza, Venustiano, revolutionary leader 52
Casa K'ojom 511
Casas Grandes 148
Cascadas de Aguacero 363
Caste War 454, 461
Castillo San Felipe 527
Catarina 590
Catedral Metropolitana 85
Catemaco 274
Catholic church 50
Caye Caulker 478
Cempoala 273
Cenote X-kekén 435
Center for the Investigation of Olmec and Mayan Cultures (CICOM) 353
Chacala 186
Chamula 373
Chapala 198
Chelán 422
Chenalhó 375
Chencoh 403
Chetumal 465
Chetumal to Escárcega 468
Chiapa de Corzo 363
Chicanná 469
Chichén Itzá 424
Chichén Viejo 430
Chichicastenango 516
Chico's Paradise 204
Chihuahua state 143
Chihuahua 149
Chilam Balam 426
Chiquilá 445
Cholula 291
Churrigueresque 55
Cinco de Mayo 289
Circuito Interior 64
Ciudad Juárez 145
Ciudad Universitaria 101
Class Struggle 83
Coahuila state 170
Cobá 464
Cobán 523

Cockscomb Basin Wildlife Sanctuary 490
Colima 213
Colima state 210
Colimilla 209
Columbus, Christopher, accidental tourist 48
Comala 217
Comalcalco 353
Comitán 376
Concepción Volcano 594, 596
Copper Canyon 155
Corn Islands 600
Cortés, Hernan 50
Costa Azul 135
Costa Careyes 205
Costa Rica 537
   Accommodations 546
   Climate 540
   Currency 542
   Health 542
   Safety 542
Coyoacán 98
Cardenas, Lazaro, president of México 52
Creel 152
Criollos 50
Cuernavaca 295
Cuevas de San Borjita 127
Cuilapán 336
Currency
   Costa Rica 542
   Guatemala 497
   Mexico 13
   Nicaragua 566
Cuyutlán 212

D

D.F., Mexico City 58
Dainzú 339
Dangriga 488
Darío, Rubén 579
Díaz, Gen. Porfirio, military dictator 52
Diego Rivera 224, 227
Diet restrictions, travelers with 37
Disabilities, travelers with 36
Dolores 532

Dolores Hidalgo 230
Dr. Atl 55
Driving,Mexico 44
Durango 163
Durango state 163
Dzibalchén 402
Dzibilchaltún 421
Dzibilnocac 401
Dzitnup 435
Dzul-Ha reef 457

E

Edzná ruins 400
Ejes Viales 64
El Castillo 488, 593
El Estor 526
El Hervidero 217
El Limón 354
El Paraíso 354
El Paso, Texas 144
El Pinacate volcanic
    area 139
El Real 276
El Relleno 527
El Tajín 263
Ensenada 122
Escárcega 394
Escárcega to
    Chetumal 468
Estelí 585

F

ferry service
    Baja to mainland
    127
    Baja 113
Film, Mexican 56
Fonseca, Carlos 579
    museum 587
Fortuna 552
FREE BEER!!! 177
Fronteras 527

G

Gay, Lesbian, and
    Bisexual travlers:
    Colectivo Sol 73
    publications 104
Glossary 601
Gogorrón 223
Granada 590
Gray Whales
    National Park 124
Grito de Dolores 50,
    232
Grutas de
    Balancanche 430
Grutas de
    Cacahuamilpa 311
Grutas de Lanquín
    524
Grutas de Lotún 405
Grutas de San
    Cristóbal 376

Grutas de
    Xtacumbilxunaan
    403
Guadalajara 187
Guadalupe 169
Guanajuato state 224
Guanajuato, city 224
Guatemala 495
Guatemala City 500
Guatemala/Belize
    Border 488
Guaymas 142
Guelatao 336
Guerrero 305
Guerrero Negro 124
Guzmán 216

H

Health 497
    Costa Rica 542
    Mexico 19
    Nicaragua 566
Hermosillo 140
Hidalgo, Miguel 50
Hidden Valley Falls
    487
History of Mexico 48
Hitchhiking 45
Hoctún 424
Hol Chan Marine
    Reserve 484
Holcá 424
Hopkins Village 490
Huejotzingo 290
Huitzilopochtli 49
Hummingbird
    Highway 488

I

Ice-T 388
Iguala 311
International
    Student Identity
    Card (ISIC) 10
International Youth
    Card 10
Isla Cozumel 454
Isla de la Piedra 163
Isla de Ometepe 594
Isla Holbox 445
Isla Ixtapa 316
Isla Mujeres 447
Islas Venados 163
Iturbide, Agustín de,
    Spanish general 51
Ixcolasc 424
Ixcun 532
Iximché 517
Ixtaccíhuatl volcano
    281, 303
Ixtapa/Zihuatanejo
    311
Ixtlán 186
Ixtonton 532

Ixtupu 532
Izamal 424

J

Jalapa (Xalapa) 264
Jalisco Coast 205
Jalisco state 187
Jocotepec 198
José Cardel 273
Juárez, Benito 51,
    84, 336, 335

K

K'umarkaaj 518
Kabah 405
Kahlo, Frida 56, 99
Kantunil 424
Kohunlich 469
Kurisu, Koichi, see
    High Priest 429

L

La Avedencía 212
La Barra 276
La Laguna Encantada
    278
La Manzanilla 205
La Paz 130
La Playa del Amor
    137
La Venta 356
Labná 404
Lacandón Rainforest
    380
Lago Atitlán 513
Lago de Chapala 198
Lago de Nicaragua
    594
Lago de Pátzcuaro
    247
Lago Izabal 526
Laguna Carrizalillo
    216
Laguna Catemaco
    275
Laguna Chankanaab
    457
Laguna de Arenal
    551
Laguna de Santa
    María del Oro 186
Laguna La María 217
Laguna Ojo de
    Liebre 124
Lagunas de
    Montebello
    National Park 376
Lake Ararreco 155
Lake Arenal 551
Lanquín 524
Las Ánimas 204
Laughing Bird Caye
    492
León 581

León Viejo 580
Liberia, Guanacaste
    555
Libre Unión 424
Livingston 528
Los Arcos 203
Los Mochis 156

M

Madera Volcano
    594, 596
mail 28
Majawil Q'ij 496
Maler's Place 536
Malinalco 304
Malinche 50
Managua 572
Manuel Antonio
    National Park 560
Manzanillo 210
Marine Reserve Hol
    Chan 484
Mariscos 526
Marta Quezada 574
Masaya 588
Masaya Volcano 590
Matagalpa 587
Matamoros 177
Maximilian von
    Habsburg,
    emperor 51
Maximón 516
Mazatlán 157
Melaque 206
Menchú, Rigoberta
    496
La Merced 84, 107
Mérida 410
Mexica 49
Mexicali 119
Mexican-American
    War 51, 238
Mexico
    Accommodations
    46
    Climate 1
    Currency 13
    Essentials 1
    Government
    Agencies 1
    History 48
    Literature 54
    Mail 28
    Vehicle Permits 11
México City, D.F. 58
México state 304
Mezcal 57
Miahuatlán 341
Michoacán de
    Ocampo state 241
Misol-Ha 386
Mismaloya 202, 204
Mitla 339
Moctezuma II 49

Momostenango 521
Momotombo
  Volcano 580
Monte Albán 336
Monterrey 173
Montezuma 561
Monumento a la
  Revolución 93
Morelia 242
Morelos state 295
Morelos, José María
  50
Mot-Mot bird 596
Mountain Pine Ridge
  487
Moyogalpa 595
Mulegé 126
Mundo Perdido 536
Museo Nacional de
  Antropología 93
Museo Nacional de
  Arte 90
Museo Nacional de
  Costa Rica 550
Museo Nacional de
  Historia 94

N

Na-Bolom museum
  371
NAFTA 54
Nayarit 185
Netzahualcóyotl
  Dam 364
Nevado de Colima
  volcano 216
Nicaragua 564
Nicaragua, Atlantic
  coast 600
Nicaraguan
  Embassy 564
Niquinohomo 590
Nogales 138
Nogales, Arizona
  138
Nohoch Múl 464
Northeast México
  170
Nueva España 50
Nuevo León state
  173
Núñex de Guzmán
  247

O

Oaxaca de Juárez
  (Oaxaca City) 327
Ocosingo 377
Ocotlán 341
Ojo Caliente 223
Older Travelers 35
Olmecs 49

Orozco, José
  Clemente, muralist
  56, 90

P

Palace of the Masks
  536
Palacio de Bellas
  Artes 89
Palacio Nacional 83
Palancar Reef 457
Palenque 381
Pallavi's Hotel 493
PAN (National
  Action Party),
  opposition party 53
Panajachel 513
Papanoa 317
Papantla, Veracruz
  260
Paquimé 148
Paraíso 212
Paricutín Volcano
  253
Parque Papagayo
  324
Passports 8
Pátzcuaro 246
Paz, Octavio 55
Peewee 201
Peninsula de las
  Playas 323
Península Nicoya
  556
Pérula 205
PESCA biological
  research station
  451
Pie de la Cuesta 325
Piedra del Sol 83
Placencia 490
Playa Azul 254
Playa Bruja 162
Playa Caleta 323
Playa Caletilla 323
Playa Chac-Mool 444
Playa Chamela 205
Playa Cuatas 316
Playa de los Cocos
  209
Playa de los Muertos
  202
Playa de Médano
  137
Playa de Olas Altas
  202
Playa de Pichilingue
  133
Playa del Carmen
  451
Playa del Coco 556
Playa del Palmar 316
Playa El Coronel 133
Playa El Coyote 128

Playa Escondido 128
Playa Estacahuites
  344
Playa Estero 124
Playa Hermosa 556,
  557
Playa La Fortuna 205
Playa La Ropa 315
Playa Las Brisas 212
Playa Las Gatas 315
Playa Las Gaviotas
  162
Playa Linda 316, 444
Playa Los Cocos 128
Playa Manzanillo 348
Playa Marinero 347
Playa Norte 121,
  162, 450
Playa Panamá 556
Playa Panteón 343
Playa Pérula 205
Playa Pichilingue
  325
Playa Puerto Angel
  343
Playa Puerto
  Angelito 348
Playa Punta Arena
  128
Playa Punta Estrella
  121
Playa Quieta 316
Playa Resquesón 128
Playa Sábalo 162
Playa San Miguel 124
Playa San Quintín
  124
Playa Santa María
  124
Playa Santispac 128
Playa Tecolote 132
Playa Zikatela 347
Playas Burro 128
Poás Volcano
  National Park 551
Pochomil 580
Pochutla 341
Popocatépetl
  volcano 281, 303
Popol Vuh 417
Poptún 530
Porfiriato 52
Poxté 532
PRI 53
Progreso 422
Puebla 281
Puebla state 281
Puerto Angel 341
Puerto Barrios 530
Puerto Ceiba 354
Puerto de Anzar 217
Puerto Escondido
  344

Puerto Marqués 325
Puerto Peñasco 139
Puerto Vallarta 199
Punta Gorda 492
Puntarenas 558
Purépeche 241
Pyramid of
  Quetzalcóatl 303
Pyramid of
  Tepozteco 303
Pyramid of
  Tlatelolco 97

Q

Querétaro state 237
Querétaro, city 237
Quetzalcóatl 49
Quetzaltenango/
  Xela 519
Quimixto 204
Quiriguá 525
Quiroga 251

R

Rama 598
Ranguana Caye 492
Rape Crisis, Mexico
  City 73
Reed, W. C. S., victor
  428
Rincón de la Vieja
  National Park 555
Río Cuale 202
Río Dulce 527
Río Lagartos 437
Río Lajas 561
Rivas 592
Rivera, Diego,
  muralist 56, 83
Rocky Point (Puerto
  Peñasco) 139
Rosarito 118
Rubén 579
Rubén Darío 581,
  583
Ruta Maya 401

S

Safety
  Costa Rica 542
  Guatemala 497
  Mexico City 70
  Nicaragua 567
Salinas de Gortari,
  Carlos 53
Saltillo 170
Salto de Eyipantla
  278
Samuc Champey
  524
SAN 485
San Andrés
  Larraínzar 375

San Andrés Tuxtla
276
San Angel 100
San Antonio 487
San Antonio Aguas
Calientes 512
San Bartolo
Coyotepec 336
San Carlos 596
San Carlos hot
springs 124
San Cristóbal de las
Casas 365
San Felipe 120
San Francisco el Alto
521
San Ignacio 125, 485
San José 546
San José del Cabo
134
San José Succotz 487
San Juan Chamula
374
San Juan de
Comalapa 508
San Juan del Norte
593
San Juan del Oriente
590
San Juan del Sur 592
San Lucas Tolimán
517
San Luis Potosí 218
San Marcos 590
San Mateo 206
San Miguel de
Allende 232
San Pedro 482
San Pedro La Laguna
516
San Pedro Volcano
516
Santa Ana, General
Antonio López de
51
Santa Clara del
Cobre 251
Santa Cruz del
Quiché 517
Santa Elena and
Flores 532
Santa María de Jesús
512
Santa María del Río
223
Santa María El Tule
339
Santa Rosa National
Park 555
Santa Rosalía 127
Santiago Tuxtla 279
Santiago-Atitlán 515
Sarachí 551

Sayil 403
Schardt, J. Steven,
see Temple of the
Bearded Man 428
Selva Negra 588
Senior Citizens 35
Servicio Educativo
de Turismo de los
Estudiantes y la
Juventud (SETEJ) 6
Sexually
Transmitted
Disease
Information 73
Siqueiros, David
Alfaro 56, 90, 95, 97
Sonoita 139
Sor Juana Inés de la
Cruz 54
Spota, Luis 55
Stann Creek 488

T

Tabacón 553
Tabasco Coast 354
Tahmek 424
Tamayo 94
Tampico 183
Tapachula 389
Taxco 307
Teapa 354
Tecpán 517
Tecún Umán 521
Telephones 32
Temple of
Quetzalcóatl 110
Templo Mayor
(Teocalli) 85
Tenacatita 205
Tenochca 49
Tenochtitlán 49, 85
Teocalli (Templo
Mayor) 85
Teotihuacán 55, 109
Teotitlán del Valle
339
Tepeaca 290
Tepic 185
Tepotzotlán 111
Tepoztlán 303
Tequila Sauza 196
Thuraisingham, The
Krush, see
ferocious animal
428
Ticul 408
Tijuana 113
Tikal 533
Tilarán 554
Tizimín 435
Tlacochahuaya 339
Tlacolula 339
Tlaquepaque 197
Tlatelolco 96

Tlatelolco Plaza
massacre 53
Tlaxcala 295
Tobacco Caye 490
Tócuaro 251
Todos Santos 133
Toledo District 492
Toltecs 49
Tomatlán falls 204
Tonalá 198, 386
Toniná ruins 379
Totonacs 260
Tourist Card (FMT) 7
Traveler's Checks 15
Tres Zapotes Ruins
279
Trotsky, Leon 99
Trumbull, Sam, see
celestial bodies 429
Tula 255
Tule 339
Tulum 458
Tuxpan (Tuxpam),
Veracruz 257
Tuxtla Gutiérrez 358
Tzaráracua 253
Tzarárecuita 253
Tzintzuntzán 251
Tzompantli 256

U

UCA 579
Universidad de
Costa Rica 543
UNAM 26, 101
UNAN 579
UNI 579
University of the
Americas 291
Utatlán 518
Uxmal 406

V

Valladolid 431
Valley of Mushroom
Rocks 154
Vasco de Quiroga,
bishop 246
Vehicle Permits 11
Villahermosa 348
Volcán Arenal 551
Volcán Atitlán 517
Volcán Concepción
596
Volcán Concepción
594
Volcán de
Acatenango 512
Volcán de Agua 512
Volcán de Fuego
216, 512
Volcán Finca de
Soledad 512
Volcán Irazú 551

Volcán Madera 594,
596
Volcán Masaya 590
Volcán Momotombo
580
Volcán Pacaya 507
Volcán Poás 551
Volcán Tolimán 517
volcano Nevado de
Colima 216
Vucic, Ante, see
Siesta
Vuelve Mujer River
530

W

Waisman, Dov 500
Western Highway,
Belize 484
WHEATIES, a
STACK o 344
Women And Travel
34, 70

X

Xalapa(Jalapa) 264
Xel-Ha 463
Xiloa 580
Xlapak 404
Xocchel 424
Xochicalco 302
Xochimilco 103
Xpujil 469
Xtabentun 435
Xunantunich 487

Y

Yácatas 251
Yagul 339
Yaxuná 431
Yelapa 204

Z

Zaachila 336
Zacatecas, city 166
Zamá 461
Zapata, Emiliano,
revolutionary
leader 52
Zapopan 197
Zempoala 273
Zihuatanejo/Ixtapa
311
Zinacantán 374
Zipolite 344
Zirahuén 251
Zócalo, Mexico City
82
Zona Libre (Free
Zone) 39
Zoo, Belize 485
Zunil 521